YALE UNIVERSITY PRESS
PELICAN HISTORY OF ART

FOUNDING EDITOR: NIKOLAUS PEVSNER

PAUL FRANKL

GOTHIC ARCHITECTURE

REVISED BY PAUL CROSSLEY

Paul Frankl
Revised by Paul Crossley

Gothic Architecture

Yale University Press
New Haven and London

First published 1962 by Penguin Books Ltd
Revised edition by Paul Crossley
first published 2000 by Yale University Press

Library of Congress Cataloging-in-Publication Data
Frankl, Paul, 1878–1962.
   Gothic Architecture / Paul Frankl, revised by Paul Crossley
      p.   cm. – (Pelican history of art)
   Includes bibliographical references and index.
   ISBN 0-300-08798 5, ISBN 0-300-08799 3 (paper: alk. paper)
                            00-13153
                            CIP

Set in Monophoto Ehrhardt by Best-set Typesetter
Printed in Singapore
Designed by Sally Salvesen

TITLE PAGE ILLUSTRATION: Reims Cathedral. West front

Acknowledgements

In editing this book I have been encouraged, helped and corrected by many colleagues and friends. Without the energy and
quick understanding of Alexandra Gajewski-Kennedy, who
cheerfully stepped in at the later stages of the work to help as my
research assistant, this edition would probably have never seen
the light of day. Over the years, Christopher Wilson has put his
learning and judgement at my disposal and saved me from many
a faux pas. Peter Kidson has let me ransack his library and profit
from his wisdom, and Peter Lasko deserves my thanks because he
asked me to write the new edition, and then showed a super-
human patience at its intermittent progress. The work of bringing Frankl up-to-date began in the History of Art Department of
Manchester University and ended at the Courtauld Institute in
London, so I can look back with gratitude on two great art historical institutions and on friends and colleagues who inspired
and supported me there. In Manchester I would single out Reg
Dodwell (much-missed), Sue and Andrew Causey, Suzy and
Humfrey Butters, David O'Connor, Christa Grössinger and
the constant inspiration of Jonathan Alexander. Diane Sanderson
engendered, and endured, my enthusiasms. I have also had
the privilege of teaching and working at the Courtauld, where I
have found encouragement and generosity of spirit. Eric Fernie
kindly but firmly rescued the project from impending stagna-
tion. I look back with pleasure and profit on conversations with
him and with Ron Baxter, Georgia Clarke, Jas Elsner, Michael
Kauffmann, John Newman and Rose Walker. Lindy Grant generously shared with me her knowledge of French Gothic, and, as
Curator of the incomparable Conway Library, has always been
willing to help in more practical ways. I have also enlarged my
understanding of medieval art history in the civilized ambience
of her Courtauld medieval work-in-progress seminars. I owe a
particular debt to Joanna Cannon and John Lowden for their
inimitable mixture of good humour and humane intelligence. As
well as colleagues and friends, my students at the Courtauld
deserve my thanks. They may have delayed the completion of
this book, but it would be a poor thing without them. I can think
of many who have given more than they have got, as their names
in the text will show: Tim Ayers, Steffani Becker-Hounslow,
Giovanni Freni, John Goodall, Alexandra Kennedy, Zoe Opacic,
Lucy Ormerod, Richard Plant, Andreas Puth, Achim
Timmermann.

Without the help of a wider community of scholars and friends a
book of this scope would have been a thin offering. Corrections, off-
prints, books, unpublished manuscripts, insights, suggestions and
general messages of good will, came, in various forms, from the fol-
lowing: Klara Benešovská, Paul Binski, Yves Bottineau-Fuchs,
Christoph Brachmann, Louisa Connor, Peter Diemer, Peter Draper,
Peter Fergusson, Roza Godula, Reiner Haussherr, Sandy Heslop,
Lech Kalinowski, Terryl Kinder, Marian Kutzner, the late Larry
Hoey, Dobroslav Libal, John Maddison, Adam Milobedzki,
Phillip Lindley, Richard Morris, Norbert Nussbaum, Anne Prache,
Mayra Rodriguez, Willibald Sauerländer, Wolfgang Schenkluhn,
Ulrike Seeger, Veronica Sekules, Robert Suckale, Krysia and
Wojtek Sztaba, Marvin Trachtenberg, Tomasz Torbus, Tomasz
Weclawowicz, Christopher Welander, Jeroen Westerman, Evelin
Wetter, Mary Whiteley, George Zarnecki and Marlene Zykan. To all
these friends and colleagues I extend my warmest thanks.

A project as bibliographical as this one depends wholly on good
libraries. The John Rylands Library in Manchester and the British
Library in London have proved essential on many occasions. My
greatest debts, however, are to Sue Price and Michael Doran and
the staff of the Courtauld Institute Library, and to the librarians of
the Warburg Institute. Without their courtesy and helpfulness,
without the remarkable resources in their care, and without free
access to both libraries, this edition would have been unthinkable.

In the end every book depends on the good will and efforts of
the publisher, and among those many individuals at Yale
University Press (and those connected with it) whose ability and
enthusiasm contributed to this volume, I would like to thank Ruth
Applin, Beatrix McIntyre, John Nicoll, Sally Nicholls, Susan
Rose-Smith (the most sympathetic of picture researchers), and the
dedicated and discerning editor, Sally Salvesen, who had every
reason to lose faith in the project, but never did so. Without her
perceptive encouragement this edition would simply not exist.

During the fifteen years this edition has taken to complete (it
was meant to be five) 'Frankl' has distracted me more than it ought
from my long-suffering children, Nicholas and Katy, and from my
wife, Joany. Despite all that, they have tolerated and supported me
in every way. It is to Joany that I and the readers of this edition owe
their greatest debt.

Paul Crossley
Courtauld Institute

Contents

Introduction
by Paul Crossley

FRANKL'S TEXT: ITS ACHIEVEMENT AND SIGNIFICANCE

THE NEW EDITION

In its breadth of outlook, its command of detail and its theoretical enterprise, Frankl's *Gothic Architecture* has few equals in the ambitious Pelican History of Art series. As a comprehensive study of the Gothic style and its roots in the spirituality of the Middle Ages it is still unsurpassed. But its very qualities have always made it something of an outsider. Published in 1962, a few months after the author's death at the age of eighty-three, it seemed to belong to a foreign intellectual world – not the England and America of the 1960s but the academic Germany of the 1920s and 30s. One American reviewer summed up the book as 'curious';[1] another found it 'difficult to review because of Frankl's highly personal combination . . . of theory and fact'.[2] No volume in the Pelican series depends so heavily on a theoretical matrix, no comparable study pursues so intently the general principles which inform all aspects of Gothic architecture and its surrounding culture. To explain Frankl's theory critically is one of the main purposes of this edition, and particularly of this Introduction.

Our second aim is to bring Frankl's text up to date in the light of recent literature on Gothic architecture. This has proved to be a daunting task. Geographically, Frankl's subject stretches from Poland to Portugal, from Sicily to Scotland; chronologically it ranges from Durham in 1093 to Halle an der Saale in 1530. While it might just have been conceivable that Frankl (who was prodigiously learned on the literature of Gothic) could have read everything of importance on medieval architecture within those vast limits, it is now clear that any pretence to inclusiveness would be futile. The proliferation of literature on Gothic architecture in the last forty years – books, reviews, exhibition catalogues and periodicals – in a variety of languages, has made it technically impossible for any editor to be an authority on the whole period. Indeed, it is doubtful if anyone today could write a book of such scope. Worse still, Frankl's text is not as advanced as its 1962 date might suggest. Effectively, it was written between 1947, when Nikolaus Pevsner, the general editor of the series, commissioned it, and 1956; it then took six years to translate the finished text from German into English and prepare it for publication. In those six years there appeared a number of works which decisively altered our understanding of Early and High Gothic in Europe.[3] The editor of this edition was therefore faced with the task of mastering almost half a century of scholarship on every aspect of European Gothic architecture. Complete coverage of this colossal body of information and commentary is inevitably a futile quest, but the challenge cannot be avoided. If Frankl's text is to be of real use it has to be re-presented in terms of what we now know and think. I have therefore included as much recent literature as I can master, though some readers will no doubt spot the gaps left unplugged, and find my treatment selective, even arbitrary.

The new edition is intended to make Frankl's book, which has long been out of print, once again usable as an introduction to the study of Gothic architecture. With that in mind, I have added to, or altered, the text in four ways. Firstly, the Introduction explains Frankl's theoretical method and tries to clarify those areas of his argument where the student might find him obscure or misleading. It also assesses Frankl's influence in the historiography of the Middle Ages, and sketches out general trends in the more recent study of Gothic architecture. Secondly, I have been forced to alter Frankl's text on points of fact rather than opinion (though the distinction is not always clear), sometimes quite radically, but without, I hope, disturbing the unique tone of his writing. Where he was wrong or misleading I have either omitted the material or re-written it, as I believe he would have done himself. The third, and most extensive revision concerns the footnotes. Here I have had the space to correct, supplement and discuss Frankl's text, and to update his treatment of individual buildings in the light of the latest research. The footnotes are therefore pointers to a more recent literature and at the same time commentaries – some of them extensive – on matters of style, chronology, patronage and meaning. They sometimes amount to resumés of the latest thinking on the subject in hand. They are best read in parallel with Frankl's text. The fourth component of the revision is the bibliography. It is bound to be incomplete, but its aim is to be reasonably comprehensive for a synoptic survey of this kind and to point readers to a secondary literature that they might otherwise have missed.

PAUL FRANKL (1878–1962)

Paul Frankl was born in Prague on 22 April 1878, into an old Jewish family of writers and scholars. He first studied architecture, but then took his doctoral degree at Munich University under Berthold Riehl, submitting his dissertation on south German stained glass in 1910.[4] To the end of his life, medieval stained glass remained one of his special interests. A second, equally long-term, fascination was the theory of art and its relationship to art history. His period at Munich brought him under the spell of one of the founding fathers of German and European art history, Heinrich Wölfflin, Professor of the History of Art at the university from 1912 to 1924. Wölfflin became his teacher, mentor and life-long inspiration. In 1914 Frankl published his *Habilitationsschrift* on Renaissance and post-Renaissance architecture, entitled *Die Entwicklungsphasen der neuren Baukunst*,[5] which he respectfully dedicated to Wölfflin (it was translated into English in 1968 under the title *Principles of Architectural History*).[6] *Die Entwicklungsphasen* was a response to Wölfflin's *Renaissance und Barock*, and an application of Wölfflin's theoretical principles from the history of Renaissance painting to that of architecture, but it was also a radical criticism of his master's formalism, and its method anticipated the character and scope of Frankl's theoretical ambitions to the end of his life. Appointed to the chair of art history at Halle-Wittenberg University in 1921 Frankl began to apply these theoretical concerns to the third area of major interest in his scholarly career – medieval architecture. In 1924, in Wölfflin's *Festschrift*,[7] and in his seminal study on Romanesque architecture, *Die frühmittelalterliche und romanische Baukunst* (Wildpark–Potsdam), published in 1926, Frankl grappled with defining the general stylistic laws governing Gothic and Romanesque architecture. The exercise led to an increasing immersion in basic theoretical principles, in particular, the mystery of artistic style and its categorization. Frankl's ambition to create a 'systematic' art history, in which all art forms, from all periods, could be presented within a framework of explicitly stated general principles, led to what he hoped would be the crowning work of his career, *Das System der Kunstwissenschaft* (Brn0, Leipzig, 1938). This ponderous treatise, 1063 pages long, firmly identified Frankl as one of the last representatives of an heroic period of German philosophical art history. What Alois Riegl and Heinrich Wölfflin had begun at the turn of the new century Frankl hoped to complete and extend in his own encyclopedic project: to uncover those general conceptions of art which give meaning to the variety of its styles and purposes. *Das System*, with its organization of all artistic data into broad categories such as 'things', 'persons', 'places' and 'time', and then into increasingly complex subcategories such as 'membrism', 'akyrism', 'regularism', 'limitism' and 'harmonism', constitutes probably the most ambitious morphological and phenomenological study of the visual arts ever undertaken. But its length, its language and its armature of abstractions (it makes little reference to specific works of art) condemned it to a very limited readership. Published in 1938 with a limited print run in Brno (Moravia) between the Munich crisis and the outbreak of the Second World War, much of the first edition was destroyed by fire. Frankl's Jewishness ruled out any circulation in Germany; while in the English-speaking world, particularly in America, where Frankl was soon to make his home, it found few sympathizers. The demise of *Das System* was one of the great disappointments of Frankl's career, and right up to the last days of his life he was preparing a shorter and more accessible version, which was eventually published in 1988.[8]

In 1933/4 the Nazis expelled him from his chair in Halle, and in 1938 he came to the United States, where in 1940 he was accepted as a member of the Institute for Advanced Study at Princeton, a position he held until his death. At Princeton he worked on what is considered his greatest book, *The Gothic. Literary Sources and Interpretations through Eight Centuries*, which appeared in 1960 – a vast and erudite commentary on almost everything that had been written about Gothic architecture from Abbot Suger to the 1950s. And while he was finishing this *summa* he was writing *Gothic Architecture*, a book which was to become his memorial. On 29 January 1962 he closed the envelope which contained detailed comments on the plate proofs of the book, and left his desk in the Marquand Library in Princeton. On 30 January he died.

FRANKL'S ART-HISTORICAL 'PROGRAMME'

To cite these major studies gives a one-sided impression of Frankl, as the grand theorist and historiographer. A glance at his bibliography[9] will show that less than a quarter of his published work was devoted exclusively to general art-historical problems; the rest – a massive sixty-two articles, books or reviews – dealt with 'practical' art history, most of it on medieval subjects, and the majority on architecture.[10] Frankl's qualities as a conventional, what he called 'a philological', art historian – his erudition, his visual acuity, his intellectual finesse and rigour – injected new life into Anglo-American scholarship in the years after the Second World War. It was Frankl who first untangled the geometric 'secrets' of the medieval mason in the controversy over the building of Milan Cathedral, and laid the foundations for a proper appreciation of constructive geometry in the medieval mason's craft.[11] It was Frankl who first truly appreciated the 'eccentric' Gothic of St Hugh's choir at Lincoln and recognized its kinship with the styles of a much later period, particularly German Late Gothic.[12] And it was Frankl's recognition of the 'classic' qualities of French High Gothic which introduced English-speaking scholars to the visual refinements of Amiens Cathedral and the chronological complexities of Chartres.[13] Equally impressive was the scope of Frankl's interests. They speak of his desire to subsume all art into his 'system': church architecture from the Early Christian period to the Baroque; stained glass from Chartres to Peter Hemmel; Rubens and Rembrandt. One of his last articles was a study of Boucher's *Girl on the Couch*,[14] where he moves effortlessly from the erotic gossip of Louis XV's court to the theoretical notion of 'akyrism', a term he coined to describe the changing contexts and meanings of artistic forms and images (see below).

Indeed, the breadth of Frankl's art historical interests grew out of the principal strength of his work – its constant need to organize historical facts into theoretical systems. It was this interaction of history and theory which gave coherence and purpose to Frankl's achievement.[15] Although Frankl's work 'develops' over his long life, and shows an impressive range of interest, its stages seem less like radical departures into new fields than variations on one underlying theme, one single, central vision. The Greek poet darkly suggested that 'the fox knows many things, but the hedgehog knows one big thing'.[16] Frankl was a hedgehog. His first publication was on German Late Gothic stained glass, as were three in the last year of his life.[17] There is a sense in which his theoretical arguments were present *in toto* right from the beginning, and merely worked themselves out –

achieved greater clarity and self-realization – in the course of his long career. *Die Entwicklungsphasen* of 1914, for example, established the general theoretical method which, with progressively greater refinements, was to inform *Das System* of the 1930s and *Gothic Architecture* of the 1950s. Frankl was known to friends and colleagues as one of the 'soldiers of science' (*Soldaten der Wissenschaft*),[18] and there is a whiff of the military commander in the strategic pattern of his career, as if he had carefully mapped it out from the start, arranging all his projects consistently, often simultaneously, towards a pre-determined end. In the 1940s and 50s particularly, his creative concerns with theory and with Gothic overlapped with the publication of a number of articles on individual buildings, with preparing the new edition of *Das System*, with the completion of *The Gothic* and with the writing of *Gothic Architecture*. *The Gothic* opens with the claim that 'in this book have been assembled comments and commentaries on Gothic which have to do with its basic principles',[19] while *Gothic Architecture* sets out to 'clarify by examples' the 'few basic principles' of the Gothic style, to chart 'the logical process' by which . . . the Gothic style . . . developed from one basic principle'.[20] *The Gothic* was to uncover those principles via written testimony, *Gothic Architecture* via the buildings themselves. Both were the double prongs of a single enterprise – to lay bare, via the definition of theoretical principles of style, the forces which shaped the Gothic church and, beyond them, the 'root' of those forces themselves, the common source which informed all aspects of medieval art, architecture and culture. In both books this final 'essence' is identified as 'the personality of Jesus Christ'.[21]

Gothic Architecture is therefore no ordinary synoptic survey; its direction and energy is informed by a metaphysical quest, whose religious and intellectual credentials are remote from our own. Its narrative is conventionally chronological, beginning with 'Transitional' and ending with 'Late Gothic', but unlike the great French surveys of the nineteenth and early twentieth centuries, it does not split the building into its main constructional features and discuss their development separately.[22] Whereas the usual text books, including Frankl's own exemplary general history of pre-Romanesque and Romanesque architecture,[23] deal with the subject in terms of 'regional schools' and country by country, Frankl's Gothic is not a national but a European phenomenon, where buildings from France, Spain and Germany share the same sections, even the same paragraphs. This internationalism we now take for granted, but for Frankl it was a hard-won article of faith. By temperament an individualist and a liberal internationalist, Frankl had been a victim of the worst excesses of xenophobia and racism, and he shied away from all national categories in the history of art. Gothic, he argued, is 'a spiritual problem common to Normans, Frenchmen and Englishmen', not a physiological one (p. 124). Although Nikolaus Pevsner, the general editor of the Pelican History of Art, favoured separate volumes on British art, and had commissioned Geoffrey Webb to write a study of medieval architecture in the British Isles,[24] Frankl insisted on including English architecture in his book.[25] And while Pevsner postulated the existence of permanent national traits in his popular *Englishness of*

English Art, written in the same years as Frankl's text, Frankl strongly rejected the influence of biology in artistic creation and refused to admit that Gothic architecture showed 'any common national denominators', though he recognized national versions of the style.[26] Frankl's book is also distinguished from most other surveys of its period, and indeed from his own survey on Romanesque, by its emphasis on theory and its long discussions on the general problems of style, which take up as much as the last third of the book.[27] Here the usual proprieties of the text book – 'balance' and 'objectivity' – are replaced by a passionate, at times poetic, immersion in what the author felt to be the secrets of the Gothic.

FRANKL'S ARGUMENT

Gothic Architecture begins with a statement which tells us what the book is about, and what it is *not* about: 'the subject of this volume is the meaning and the development of the Gothic style in medieval church architecture' (p. 33). The book therefore concentrates on *church* architecture; secular building is touched on only as far as it is dependent on religious building. And while the 'meaning' of Gothic is discussed in the second section, the real meat of the book, its first 260 pages, is an account of the development of the Gothic style as a history of forms. But that formal history is underpinned by a half-hidden theoretical structure, which has to be understood if Frankl's narrative is to have any sense and direction. The structure is a refined mental scaffolding built up around Frankl's conception of style. 'By style is meant a unity of *form* governed by a few basic principles. In this book these principles will be clarified by examples' (p. 33).

The Physiognomy of Style

Before he begins his analysis of the stylistic principles of Gothic Frankl mentally fits his observations into four broad categories peculiar to the medium of architecture, categories which he had already set up in *Die Entwicklungsphasen* as early as 1914, and which reappear in *Gothic Architecture* (especially pp. 48–50) in more implicit form, and with slight changes in nomenclature. Architecture, firstly, involves a quality peculiar to it and it alone: 'spatial form' (in *Die Entwicklungsphasen* he called it 'spatial composition') – the organization of the space we move in, the space that extends around us. Secondly, architecture treats mass and surface in certain ways. Under a heading which Frankl calls 'mechanical forces' (*Die Entwicklungsphasen* describes this category as 'corporeal form'), he describes how architecture supports and transmits physical force (weight and support) and, more importantly, how those forces are expressed (or, in the case of Gothic, denied) by pillars, walls, capitals or buttresses.[28] Frankl's third category, 'optical form' ('visible form' in *Die Entwicklungsphasen*) touches on the observer's perception of the building, and deals with the mental images which the purely optical qualities of the architecture imprint on the viewer's memory, 'the abstractions', as he put it, 'corresponding to that on which the science of optics depends' (p. 48). We are here dealing with the superficial qualities of architecture – light, colour, and surface effects – and with the 'articulation' of its members – plinths, jambs, mouldings, arches, responds etc. But 'optical form' also includes the kinetic experience of the building as we move round it, and the memory of those impressions compressed into a single, synthetic mental 'image'. Although we see a building as a continuous series of different and isolated views, its members have a dominant shape or disposition, so that the various partial images will, according to Frankl, cohere into a single mental image of the whole. 'Optical form' presupposes a unifying and syn-thesizing act of perception.[29] Frankl's fourth category of analysis, 'purposive intention' (*Zweckgesinnung*) is concerned with the function of architecture in terms of social or religious intention, and is discussed in Part Two of the book, quite separately from the evolution of forms in Part One.

Into the first three general categories of all architecture – spatial, mechanical and optical form – Frankl inserts the 'basic principles' which (he believes) underlie the Gothic style. For most art historians, 'style' is a conventional term used to classify periods, movements or the individual characteristics of artists; it is a descriptive framework for a common set of forms. But it does not correspond to any 'thing' or 'essence' in reality. To Frankl and his teachers, trained in the Hegelian *Kunstwissenschaft* of late nineteenth-century Germany, style was something quite different; not a conventional label used as a convenient way of organising similar particulars into general categories, but a real, active entity – a powerful and objectively existing fact. 'To regard stylistic classification as conventional', Frankl warns us, 'leads to superficiality. We are not trying to find comfortable divisions, but to find the essence of each individual work and its position on the ladder of development' (p. 90). 'Style', in *Gothic Architecture*, and in all the outstanding works of German critical art history in the first half of the twentieth century, is an actual phenomenon, a mysterious force or pressure, working within artistic forms and shaping them in conformity with a series of fundamental 'principles'. 'Style', says Frankl, 'is a unity of *form* governed by a few basic principles' (p. 33); and by 'principles' Frankl means a deep stratum of abstract concepts that distinguish all forms of art within a given style. These concepts, deduced from the particular characteristics of individual works of art in a specific period, shape the forms of art in much the same way as the laws of the natural sciences determine physical behaviour. To clarify these concepts still further, Frankl pairs them with their 'polar opposites' – those concepts which determine the very different qualities of the previous, or succeeding, artistic styles. Both sets of concepts can then act as coordinates, as theoretical constructions and imaginary pure cases, against which the actual historical works of art can be judged to incline to one pole or another. 'Polar opposites', Frankl reminds us, 'are necessary if history, which is *per se* a continuous chain of networks, is to be meaningfully organized.'[30]

Frankl's 'principles', expressed as 'polar opposites' can be demonstrated quite simply within his three broad categories – spatial, mechanical and optical – of architectural experi-

ence. Spatially, Romanesque buildings work by 'addition', Gothic by 'division'. Where Romanesque builds up its compositions from a series of independent spaces, Gothic conceives its interiors as wholes, which are then divided and subdivided. The Romanesque chevet (e.g. Saint-Benoît-sur-Loire) consists of sharply isolated elements – apse, half-dome, aisles, radiating chapels and ambulatory, joined in juxtaposition and superposition; the Gothic east end of Amiens Cathedral allows the chapels to merge with each other and with the ambulatory, suggesting that all the individual spaces are (descriptively, not genetically) the subsequent *divisions* of a pre-existing whole.[31] Mechanically, the Romanesque is a style of 'structure'; the Gothic – at least the Late Gothic – a style of 'texture'. In Romanesque, and in much of Early and High Gothic, architectural elements behave, or seem to behave, structurally: load and support are clearly distinguished, the structural parts keep, or seem to keep, each other in balance under pressure and counterpressure. The forms of Gothic architecture – at least in its later phases, from *c.*1300 onwards – are 'textural' rather than 'structural'. 'Texture' is a noun used by Frankl to describe all things which cover (Latin *tegere*) some structure or are stuck to it, or held up by it (like mosaic). Unlike structure, they are not, or do not seem to be, self-supporting (p. 49). In later Gothic 'textural' architecture, capitals are omitted from arches and piers to replace the impression of weight and support with that of continuous flow, as if the building was a vertically rising stream of force, an organism growing like a plant. Ribs (which may never have had any real structural function) lose their structural appearance and emboss the surface of the vault, or hang from it, as decorative meshes or pendants.

The polar opposites within Frankl's third category of architectural experience, 'optical form', elicit some of his most penetrating analyses. Optically, Romanesque forms are 'frontal', Gothic are 'diagonal'. The elements of Romanesque architecture – piers, shafts, arches – are placed with their axes parallel to the main axes of the church – north–south for the bay divisions and east–west for the aisles. Their axes therefore form angles of 90 degrees, and they demand to be seen frontally. Although the main axes of aisles and bays in the Gothic church run the same way, the pier axes are set in a diagonal position (turned 45 degrees), and this diagonality is applied everywhere, in the ribs, the flying buttresses, the profiles, the pier bases. With this diagonality goes an increasing multiplicity of images, so that a Gothic building demands to be seen from a variety of viewpoints, where a Romanesque one (and a Renaissance one) are best seen from a single position. 'Frontality versus diagonality' thus generates another polar contrast – 'unity versus multiplicity'.

These fundamental visual distinctions allow Frankl to draw useful comparisons between the sculptural effects of walls, shafts, arches and mouldings in the interior elevations of Romanesque and Gothic churches – what he calls Romanesque and Gothic 'relief'. 'Romanesque relief' – for example a wall shaft and its backing dosseret at the bay divisions of the nave at Vézelay – is conceived as one layer lying *behind* another; it is read through from the plane nearest to the spectator (the shaft) to the most distant (the wall against which the dosseret is placed), creating a recession through steps, each step arranged frontally to the viewer. 'Aesthetically this type of relief keeps the visitor at a distance from the final plane of the wall-surface itself. He feels that there is a boundary holding him at a respectful distance' (p. 70). 'Gothic relief', on the other hand (for example the choir elevation of Noyon Cathedral(conceives its layers as projecting *in front* of each other, and – in a way which completely reverses the visual procedure of 'Romanesque relief' – is read first from the plane furthest from the spectator: from the outermost plane of the wall (sometimes this is the window) to the innermost. Unlike Romanesque recessions, these planes – often in the form of clusters of vault responds or orders of arches – are not arranged frontally but diagonally to the viewer, and are read as a series of continuous projections and recessions. Whereas 'Romanesque relief' establishes boundaries, 'Gothic relief' seems to abolish them, to 'embrace' the viewer by coming forward from the core of the wall. In a corresponding projection outwards, also beginning at the plane of the clerestorey windows, 'Gothic relief' proceeds from window jambs, to wall buttresses, to flying buttresses, to the outer buttress uprights which project as they descend (pp. 70–2, 86–7). This identical process of 'relief', taking place either side of the window plane, suggests the seamless expansion of the interior space onto the exterior. No frontal steps or boundaries prevent this smooth, recessive fusion of inside and outside. The windows and walls between the projections seem no more than screens, optically removable. All forms are potentially 'open' to the viewer. In that sense, the suggestive concept of 'Gothic relief' moves from the category of optical form to that of spatial form. The relief 'draws us into this spatial unity, which is ours as well as theirs. The Gothic choir embraces us; it unites us with the building, and by opening both inwards and outwards it also unites the interior with the exterior' (p. 72).

In the wake of these main polarities, Frankl developed further sets of polar opposites, not in order to distinguish Romanesque and Gothic, but to contrast buildings, or stylistic tendencies, within the Gothic style itself. One set, borrowed from Wölfflin, was the contrast between a style of 'being' and a style of 'becoming'. Romanesque was judged to be a 'style of being', and Early and High Gothic seen as retaining some aspects of that style – namely, a concentration on separate and self-contained forms that express the static and immutable. But other aspects of earlier Gothic betray a change towards a style of 'becoming', in which forms appear organic and incomplete. The result was an aesthetic tension, or 'balance', which was broken only with the emergence of Late Gothic. Late Gothic architecture shook off all remnants of the style of 'being' and emerged as a style of pure 'becoming' of 'growing and flowing' of 'passion' and 'yearning' (pp. 227, 258).[32] Another, less strict, polarity within the Gothic style Frankl identified as the contrast – or the 'alternatives' – between 'akyrism' and 'the norm' (p. 65). 'Akyrism' (from the Greek *akyros*, meaning 'improper') was developed by Frankl out of the related and rather diffuse idea of Mannerism, a label popular in the years either side of the Second World War. Frankl gave 'akyrism' a more specific meaning than Mannerism; it refers

to the translation of a form which had a certain position, structure or meaning into a similar form but with a new position, structure and meaning.[33] Thus, at Lincoln Cathedral, Gothic ribs which in earlier Gothic vaults suggested a structural purpose (strengthening the four edges of a groin vault) are transformed into purely decorative arches called tiercerons (ribs which run across the flat surfaces of the vault, not its edges) (p. 101). Thus, in the ambulatory at Coutances Cathedral the staircases are re-shaped to look like oriels (p. 165). The 'attractive' akyrisms of Coutances are contrasted (p. 161) with the choir of Cologne Cathedral, which, for Frankl, is the consummate expression of 'the norm' – a notion which goes beyond the idea of 'the average' or 'the standard' to evoke uniqueness, perfection, the realization of an absolute 'Gothic-ness' to which other cathedrals seem mere approximations. Just as the square is the absolute image of the regular quadrilateral to which all rectangles and trapeziums approximate, so Cologne, claims Frankl, 'is *the* Gothic choir, *the* final solution' (p. 164).

All these polar concepts, particularly the principles of 'division', 'diagonality' and 'texture', are seen as descriptions of the essential governing forces of the Gothic style. If one polar contrast could include them all it would – for Frankl – be the opposition between 'totality' and 'partiality'. Romanesque, he argues, is a style of 'totality', where parts appear 'as wholes within a whole'; Gothic is a style of 'partiality', where the parts are no longer sub-wholes but dependent fragments of a larger whole ('*partes* not *tota*') (p. 49). The purpose of Part One of *Gothic Architecture* was to submit the whole history of Gothic, from the 'Transitional style' of the early twelfth century to the latest Gothic of the early sixteenth, to the concept of partiality; to assess how specific Gothic buildings exemplified ever more clearly the 'essential principles' of Gothic by integrating hitherto separate forms into the open and interdependent parts of an all-encompassing whole. 'The central thread of this book is the logical process by which changes from the Romanesque to the Gothic style, and those within the Gothic style until its fulfillment in the late Gothic phase, developed from one basic principle' (p. 33–4).[34]

Critical in this long process of stylistic refinement is the rib vault. The first sentence of *Gothic Architecture* lays down categorically that 'the Gothic style evolved from within Romanesque church architecture when diagonal ribs were added to the groin-vault' (p. 41). Throughout the text, the rib is identified as *the* key element in Gothic architecture, and for that reason Frankl's Introduction (pp. 41–50) devotes a long discussion to the construction, behaviour and shape of various types of rib vault. Its technical tone conceals a concerted attack on a technical theory – a theory which counts among the most influential in the historiography of Gothic. It revolved around the belief, current since the middle of the nineteenth century among the French 'Rationalists', that the rib was the progenitor of Gothic, the key element of the style. For Viollet-le-Duc and his followers Gothic developed according to the laws of structure and statics by making its structural parts – shafts, arches, flying buttresses and ribs – one and the same as its visual 'skeleton'. More than any other feature of the Gothic church, the rib, by carrying and strengthening the vault cells, demonstrated to the Rationalists the truth of the dictum that form followed structure.[35] For Frankl, and for many of his German contemporaries, the idea that styles developed from technical or structural – that is material – procedures was anathema. To reduce the formal and theological complexities of the Gothic cathedral to matters of structural development ignored the aesthetic and psychological urges underlying artistic creativity; it constrained the free exercise of the mind with materialist notions of craft, technique and function. Frankl's *Gothic Architecture* is a raid on the Rationalist camp to steal its most precious asset, the rib, and transform it from a structural into an aesthetic principle. Whatever the statical properties of a given vault actually are (sometimes they support the vault cells, sometimes they do not) the importance of the rib, for Frankl, is primarily aesthetic. If the Rationalists saw the groined rib vault as the generator of the Gothic *structural* system, Frankl saw it as the driving force behind the *aesthetic* character of all Gothic buildings. The four-part rib vault, he argued, was the first element in the church to embody the three fundamental principles of Gothic: spatially it *divided* the whole vault compartment into four interdependent fragmentary spatial parts (it therefore also obeyed the principle of 'partiality'); optically, the diagonal direction of its ribs disturbed the frontality of the Romanesque and required the viewer to stand *diagonally* in relation to all forms and to experience the space in recession, not in the flat; and mechanically, it had, by the beginning of the fourteenth century, lost any sense of weight or support and become *texture* – a continuous stream of decorative lines embellishing the vault cells. And all three principles then spread from the vault to the rest of the structure, making the whole elevation skeletal, slender, diagonally organized and spatially open. This process did not proceed at an equal pace throughout the building. The interiors of churches became 'Gothic' quicker than the exteriors, which had to wait for the advent of the flying buttress to transform them, like the interiors, into open, skeletal ensembles. But the essential lines of development all sprang from the single source of the rib vault. Gothic architecture developed from the top downwards. Successive generations of architects, going right back to the first rib vault at Durham 'had organically developed the principles that seemed to be inherent in the original introduction of the rib' (p. 259). Part One of *Gothic Architecture* is an exercise in charting 'the logical process' by which the inherent principles of the rib vault transformed the Romanesque into the Gothic, and the Gothic into the Late Gothic.

But what drove this 'logical process'? What mechanisms allowed the law of partiality to permeate the whole structure with increasing conviction? Are there theoretical principles which account for changes of style, and if so, what are they? Frankl's answer is twofold: stylistic change is both 'immanent' and 'transcendent'; each sphere of human activity develops autonomously by following its own demands and solving its own problems, but each discipline also responds to a 'common root' at the centre of a civilization, a generating force which determines the evolution of the separate strands of a culture. Like 'the double root of style' – the purely visual tradition and the mood and social attitudes of the age – which Wölfflin identified as the joint conditions of High Renaissance art, Frankl's mechanisms of change are both intrinsic and extrinsic.[36]

Intrinsic Mechanisms of Stylistic Development

It comes as no surprise that technical and material factors play no part in Frankl's theory of stylistic transformation, though his rejection of the Rationalist explanation of Gothic style left him exposed to the charge of 'aestheticizing' a style which, by any account, is remarkable for its structural achievements. We will not find, in *Gothic Architecture*, long disquisitions on the structural behaviour of the flying buttress. In fact, the structure of the flyer is given only eleven lines in the whole book, before its aesthetic qualities are once again emphasized (p. 56). Nor can we expect a consideration of the part played by the use of brick in the Late Gothic of the German lowlands or the Lombardy plain, either in facilitating the construction of complex vaults, or in simplifying Rayonnant tracery or pier forms. Function, too, hardly comes into the reckoning as a constituent of style. By placing a section on the purposes of church architecture in Part Two (pp. 274–300), Frankl effectively cordons off his discussion of medieval liturgy – of screens, crypts, choirs, altars and processions – from the history of the buildings in Part One. The whole remarkable process of building a Gothic church – the logistics, the workforce, the financing – clearly touched Frankl's interests, for he devoted long sections of *The Gothic* to these problems.[37] But his avowed hatred of 'materialism' and his aversion to any kind of Marxism left him convinced that questions of economics and production were irrelevant to the mystery of architectural creativity. There is nothing in this book on the financing of the cathedrals, on the growth of architectural drawing, on professional specialization in the lodges, on quarries and cut stonework. Frankl was passionately *parti pris* about the style he loved.

If material phenomena, and all problems surrounding productivity, can be denied as agents of change, what factors really drive stylistic evolution? Disentangled from Frankl's text, they might be described as 'dialectic' and 'directional'. Frankl believed that all styles or artistic genres, including the Gothic, develop dialectically, by way of conflict and resolution, towards greater integration and order. Developments are set in motion by opposing elements within the style (e.g. between interiors and exteriors, or between two-dimensional and three-dimensional forms) which demand reciprocal adaptation. Gradually, by a process of adjustment, these are reconciled and integrated into a temporary balance, out of which new tensions arise, requiring new efforts of integration. In this pursuit of order and synthesis the style develops its inherent principles with ever greater clarity and conviction, almost like a process of self-realization. Frankl sees the increasing sophistications of Gothic relief, for example, as an indication of how 'the Gothic style, so to speak, discovers its own true nature' (p. 70). And he traces the evolution of the High Gothic cathedral in France as a problem-solving exercise, with each cathedral a 'correction' of the last, until 'the final solution' is reached in the choir of Cologne. Frankl's step-by-step self-realization of the Gothic, culminating in the normative perfection of Cologne, and later in the Late Gothic, recalls the deterministic drive of Hegel's Divine Spirit, impelled by the need to resolve contradictions, moving in dialectical steps to a higher and higher plane of articulation. But its more immediate sources lie in the teleological evolutionary schemes of Riegl's study of the Dutch group portrait, and in Wölfflin's history of the Roman triumphal arch.[38]

If Frankl's 'dialectical' process is presented as overcoming a difficulty, his 'directional' model looks more like seizing an opportunity,[39] or submitting to a set of demands. Here the style itself, at first largely through the rib vault, pointed the way forward to a clearer articulation of its latent principles. Evolution came not from conflict and adjustment but from 'listening' to the implicit requirements of the forms and seeing their potential for new types of partiality. 'The problem facing Gothic architects was . . . of strengthening the tendency towards partiality and of widening its scope until it embraced every part of the building' (p. 268).

What was the role of the architect in this evolution towards the 'essential Gothic'? In Part Two of *Gothic Architecture* Frankl is at great pains to deny the deterministic and super-personal overtones of his model of evolution. He emphasizes the imaginative energy of the medieval architect, 'which demanded these changes, devised them, and finally realized them' (p. 266). He proclaims his disbelief in the idea that 'the final solution' of the Gothic style, in the last Late Gothic buildings, 'existed in some other sphere outside our world since 1093, waiting for [its] own realization'. Historical development, he argues, is not goal-oriented, but is 'immanent' within the process of history itself:

> Immanence, on the contrary, operates the other way round. The introduction of the rib-vault proposed a general sense of direction, leading to a goal which could not be foretold, but could only be realized through a strict adherence to this direction. This is not like a search for the North Pole, which already exists, but is a chain of creations, providing a chain of surprises, which culminates in the final surprise of the ultimate Late Gothic style (p. 268).

But Frankl's system is far too teleological to resemble a chain of surprises, and his appeal to the individual creativity of the architect as a counterweight to determinism looks patently disingenuous. As so often in the book, the theoretical pronouncements of Part Two do not integrate logically or historically with the visual analysis of Gothic buildings in Part One. Nothing in Part One suggests that Gothic develops through the surprising accidents of human choice. On the contrary, it is styles – or forms themselves – which change, demand, require. 'The side views of Romanesque churches are wonderfully closed; those of Gothic churches are wonderfully open. This is what the two styles demanded' (p. 87). The 'demands' of the pointed arch sharpen the oculus into the spheric triangle (p. 146). 'The Gothic style adapted itself to the demands of the rib so successfully that patrons and architects must have thought the Romanesque completely superseded'. Frankl's language suggests that individuals were mere spectators, at best

enablers, of processes beyond their control. Even Peter Parler, the most individualistic of Gothic architects, acts as the executor, not the maker, of style. He may have displayed a genius for novelty in building polygonal apses with even numbers of sides (conventional apses have odd numbers), but Frankl reminds us that 'the important fact for the historian is that, by building an even number of sides, architects were demonstrating yet another consequence of the diagonal emphasis first established in a rib design' (p. 205). Architects may *demonstrate* stylistic principles, but it is the principles themselves, via the rib, which impel change. As early as 1914, in *Die Entwicklungsphasen*, Frankl had described the development of style as 'an intellectual process overriding national characteristics and individual artists.'[40] Like his mentors Riegl and Wölfflin, Frankl never shook off the notion that style (and its 'principles') is a force inherent in the forms themselves; it is, to borrow Riegl's famous formulation, a *Kunstwollen* ('that which wills art'), a kind of 'aesthetic will', with requirements of its own at particular historical moments. Just as, in Riegl's *Stilfragen*, the later Greek Corinthian capital brought the Greek palmette to the end towards which it had been consistently striving for centuries, so Frankl's Late Gothic church brought the rib vault to the culminating point towards which Gothic had been working since Durham.[41] The task of artists is perfectly to adjust their own intentions to the purposes of the *Kunstwollen*. Architects, 'these men of genius' as Frankl calls them, 'were firmly bound by the whole process of development' (p. 268).

Frankl's quest for the mainsprings of Gothic evolution did not end, however, in the forces of style working through form. His theory of historical change was too Hegelian to ignore the development of Gothic as the concrete manifestation of a Gothic 'spirit' at work at the centre of medieval civilization. While each sphere of human activity, including Gothic architecture, developed 'immanently', solving its own artistic problems within its own separate traditions, it was also plain to Frankl that every aspect of medieval culture was, in turn, subject to a higher and all-embracing generating force at the centre of medieval civilization as a whole. The rib (and its ramifications) as the 'root' of Gothic history was no longer adequate. 'We are seeking,' he says, 'a secret force which provided every sphere of human activity with the spiritual factor, the spiritual aim, and the spiritual sense of direction by which all immanent processes converged, by which all spheres remained related to one another, and which created a style common to all cultural spheres' (pp. 298–9). The final, generating point of the Gothic style lies outside the history of forms altogether, in the history of culture.

Extrinsic Mechanisms: Frankl and Cultural History

In the final section of *Die Entwicklungsphasen* Frankl introduced to his theoretical structure a fourth element of architectural analysis, logically different from the three formal elements of 'spatial', 'corporeal' and 'visible' forms. Frankl called it 'purposive intention' (*Zweckgesinnung*), a variation of the Vitruvian category of *commoditas*. Although it includes relations between form and function, the category goes well beyond 'commodity' (in the sense of the accommodation of design to use) and embraces the 'content' of architecture – its relations to ideology, culture and social behaviour.[42] In the same way, *Gothic Architecture*, having dealt with the formal attributes of the style in Part One, devotes a lengthy Part Two (called misleadingly 'the general problems of the Gothic style') to the non-formal categories of Gothic, that is, to the 'creative wealth of the spirit of the Middle Ages', and its possible relations with architecture. In both books, the clear-cut division between the visual tradition and its surrounding culture poses serious problems for Frankl's contextual analysis of style.

Frankl's paradigm of cultural history is clearly Hegelian. It resembles Gombrich's celebrated diagram of the 'Hegelian wheel' – in which the various manifestations of a culture, visible on the circumference, lead back, via their own spokes, to the hub which gives them meaning and shape, the *Zeitgeist* or *Volksgeist*.[43] For Frankl the spokes represent the immanent developments of each sphere of human activity, controlled from the centre not by Hegel's 'Mind', but by a force equally transcendent – the essential, spiritual, character of the society in question: 'The ring that forces the diverging lines towards each other until they converge – here, as in the case of architecture and the fine arts – is Man, or Society, which strives after unity, after a harmonious civilization, after a style common to every cultural sphere' (p. 297). The crowning realization of *Gothic Architecture*, indeed of all Frankl's publications on Gothic, is the conviction that the root of Gothic, of 'Gothic Man' and 'Gothic Society', was the personality and teaching of Jesus Christ. Taking his cue from Dvořák's *Idealismus und Naturalismus in der gotischen Skulptur und Malerei*,[44] with its emphasis on Christianity as the dominant ideal of the medieval 'world view' (*Weltanschauung*), Frankl identified the root of Gothic in terms of his all-important concept of 'partiality', now transferred from a description of forms to a description of mental and spiritual attitudes. All aspects of high and late medieval culture can, he states, be traced back to an interdependent relationship between man, God and society, expressed in terms of 'partiality'. The principle conviction of 'Gothic civilization', and its Christian values, 'is that man is a fragment of creation, who can find his totality only by taking his place within the kingdom of God'(p. 300). Personally, therefore, men saw themselves not as isolated individuals, but as dependents. Institutionally, the Gothic period coincided with the moment when the Christian church, under Innocent III, Saint Dominic and Saint Francis, saw itself for the first time as a fully unified entity, in which every individual was a part. All barriers, all isolations and individualities, were dissolved into a superior whole. Spiritually, the same 'partiality' was at work. Where Romanesque art and architecture present a God who is 'unapproachable, *tremendum*', Gothic forms 'symbolize the disappearance of the boundary between Man and God', the reconciliation of man to God through Christ's suffering, and the 'absolute dependence' of mankind on divine grace. This world and the next were in no real sense divided. 'Out of this fundamental meaning of partiality . . . the style of partiality appears' (p. 277).

How this spiritual energy from the centre of the Hegelian wheel invigorated the 'spoke' of Gothic architecture, and what influence other spokes of Gothic art and culture had on the architectural one, are the essential issues of Part Two. Two points in Frankl's discussion are worth noting. In the first place, he sees the relationship between Gothic architecture and other cultural phenomena as radial and not concentric. The characteristics which the spokes share derive largely from the common, unifying hub, not from cross-connexions between spokes. Frankl is convinced that the immanent development of various spheres of activity, the closed nature of their traditions, immunizes each from the other. What Gothic architecture and scholasticism had in common is the shared 'form of thought' (p. 295) which informed the *Weltanschauung* of architect and cleric; their similarities did not come about in an architectural–theological dialogue between the masons's lodge and the schoolroom. Faced with long sections on 'Gothic Painting' and 'Gothic Sculpture' in Part Two the reader should not expect a disquisition on the relationships of meaning and liturgical use between the architecture of the great cathedrals and their sculptural and stained glass ensembles, critical though this might seem in any attempt to relate the building to the culture of its day. Frankl treats Gothic sculpture and painting not as common bearers of meaning for the public they address, but as separate problems, of a largely stylistic nature. He discusses the different tempi at which the Gothic style developed in various media, and the rare moments – at Late-Gothic Blutenberg, or the choir of St Lawrence in Nuremberg – where all art forms, created simultaneously, obey the same *Kunstwollen* (p. 294). Once again, it is the autonomous responses of each medium to the demands of the Gothic *Kunstwollen* at the centre of medieval culture that fascinates Frankl. 'The internal, immanent process of the Gothic style is not guided step by step by connexions with other spheres, even where such connexions exist; its direction of development simply springs from the same common root' (p. 277).[45]

The second important point about Frankl's model of cultural history is its concentration on style. The influence of separate cultural spheres on Gothic architecture is largely seen in terms of their power to shape the stylistic features of the church. Thus the section on 'function' and 'purpose' contains only a cursory consideration of crypts, altars, screens, processions, because these same activities can co-exist with many different architectural styles. And it is not surprising that Frankl is keen to underplay the influence of utilitarian motives, including economic and financial constraints, on the final shape of the church by invoking the power of the architect's 'margin of freedom' in creative design (p. 270). For the same reason, Frankl underplays the influence of theological doctrine, literary symbols or poetic concepts on 'the understanding of the Gothic style' (p. 274). Their presence in the church – often evoking the idea of the Heavenly Jerusalem, or the Twelve Apostles, or the Trinity – Frankl calls 'the symbolism of meaning' (pp. 271–4), though nowadays we would place this category of sign under the umbrella of 'architectural iconography'. Frankl has many interesting things to say about the status of these architectural signs as metaphors and representations and not as literal images, but he is reluctant to promote them as symbols of a specifically Gothic *Weltanschauung*. For one thing, they do not determine style, since similar literary symbols or theological concepts had found, over the centuries, very different formal expressions. Christian churches from the very beginning had symbolized, in their different ways, the Kingdom of God on earth. Besides, the symbolism of meaning is allegorical and conventional – what he calls, pejoratively, 'intellectual'. As a conventional sign system it has no necessary, visual, relationship with what it symbolizes (Durandus called the tiles on the church the warriors that defend it against the heathens); and as embodiments of literal meaning these symbols belong as much to the 'separate' spheres of theology, literature, painting or sculpture. As such, they can have only a limited influence on the equally 'autonomous' world of architecture. Frankl's reservations on the influence of function, economics and mental concepts on the shape of the church severely underplayed the role of patrons in Gothic architecture.

The real bridge between Gothic architecture and contemporary patterns of life was provided by what Frankl called the 'form symbol'. The concept refers to the expressive and emotional power of architecture as form or style (pp. 274–6). If symbols of meaning require knowledge and intellect to decode their messages, form symbols appeal simply and immediately to an aesthetic sense – an 'artistic sense', which 'enables a man to apply his aesthetic feelings to the meaning of a building and deduce the meaning from its form, even if he has read no learned books on the subject of this meaning' (pp. 277–8). The spectators' 'aesthetic feelings' are, for Frankl, exercises in empathy, in the projection of their own emotions, at times their own bodily states, onto the building. We endow every part of a Gothic church, from its spaces to its tracery, with moods and postures which are our own, just as we respond to its own silent language of bodily forms. 'In the symbolism of form, we can see splendour or asceticism, oppression or verve, sterility or elastic vitality, a cheerful enjoyment of life or sombre depression. One says of space that it spreads, it rises, that it is quick or slow in tempo, that it circles, it spirals, or it concentrates'. 'Perfectly to understand the symbolism of form is like understanding the mime of a great actor' (p. 276). In the rare moments when Frankl allows himself emotive description – for example on the nave of Amiens (p. 122), or the choir of Cologne (p. 164) – empathy offers an emotional entrée into the elusive and overwhelming power of a great cathedral. More importantly, empathy also suggests a link to its surrounding culture. For the architect, as well as the viewer, projects his emotional and bodily states, in ideal form, into his creation. 'The architect lives perpetually in this realm of empathy in which forms are felt' (p. 276). And the architect, as the executant of the deepest feelings of a culture, tacitly communicates, through his building, the cultural temper, the *Lebensgefühl*, of his age. 'A man who feels in a Gothic way, and who stylizes himself accordingly, requires, for divine services, not only a building which fulfills its utilitarian purposes . . . but also a building which, through its Gothic form, symbolizes what that particular man feels' (p. 275). Empathy theory, therefore, makes the temper of the age immanent in the style. Architectural style takes on the

psychology of its maker and the mentality of its period, until 'style' and 'man' merge to create that strange hybrid – 'Gothic Man': 'Gothic man reflects God in a Gothic way, and Gothic church architecture is art because Gothic forms symbolize the conception of God that was valid in the Gothic age' (p. 277). Frankl genuinely believed that it was directly through this anthropomorphic psychological construct of 'Gothic Man' that the Gothic 'spirit' – its 'partiality' in the deepest sense – entered the anatomy of Gothic architecture, and propelled the style towards its ultimate formal and spiritual partiality in the Late Gothic. The shape of the church, as a form symbol, is the transparent indicator of the mood of the age. Thus the exterior of Romanesque Tournai cathedral is 'warlike, proud and unapproachable' (p. 91), presumably because Frankl believed that 'Romanesque Man' came from a society dominated, like its style, by the concept of 'totality' – it was a world both individualistic and aggressive. 'The leading men of the Romanesque period stood side by side, socially and politically, as autonomous individuals, as barons – whether in friendship or enmity'.[46] The exterior of Laon, by contrast, is 'so much more friendly', presumably because 'Gothic Man' felt himself to be a humble and dependent part of a greater whole. Collective psychology replaces Hegel's *Zeitgeist* at the centre of the cultural wheel.

FRANKL'S ACHIEVEMENT

Frankl's theoretical structures need such lengthy explanation because in no other volume in the Pelican History of Art is theory so obviously the motor of art historical narrative. When Frankl began writing *Gothic Architecture* in 1947 he had published very little 'empirical' art history on the subject.[47] His real investigations into Gothic began in the domain of theory, with two articles published in the mid-1920s on the origins of the Gothic system. Not surprisingly, they anticipate all the antithetical principles which he was to use a quarter of a century later: 'diagonality and frontality', 'structure' and 'texture', 'addition' and 'division', 'partiality' and 'totality'. Even the rib vault was here recognized as the primary formal agent of stylistic change.[48] When he came to write the Pelican volume just after the war the theoretical structure was therefore in place, waiting for a new and extensive mass of empirical evidence to demonstrate its truth. The rich, detailed history of Gothic in this book was to show the 'law' of partiality inexorably unfolding in individual buildings.

By now it is quite clear that Frankl was, to borrow Karl Popper's pejorative term, an 'historicist' – a believer in 'spirits', 'rhythms', 'patterns' or 'laws' which determine the evolution of history.[49] 'Historicism', in Popper's sense of the word, means much more than the imposition of general patterns on the detailed stuff of history in order to make it intelligible and coherent; it contends that history is driven by superhuman 'forces' and 'principles' towards a pre-ordained end, and that all historical experience and thought can be synthesized by some sort of general Mind or Spirit. When *Gothic Architecture* appeared in 1962 historicism – particularly in the Hegelian variant beloved by Frankl – was profoundly unfashionable in a world dominated by post-war analytical philosophy. It lacked scientific rigour. It was blamed for sloppy, 'continental' thinking, for bombast and obfuscation, and – worse still – for the political evils of total-itarianism, whether of a Marxist or a fascist kind. The critique of historicism launched in the post-war years by Popper and his allies, notably Ernst Gombrich,[50] now looks almost as problematic and doctrinaire as the deterministic assumptions of historicism itself.[51] Looking back on those controversies of over a half century ago, it is now a little easier to appreciate the merits of the historicist cast of mind and to disentangle from its schematic generalities the lasting achievements of its practitioners. Historicist systems, particularly in the hands of the founding fathers of stylistic art history, Riegl and Wölfflin, have always depended on the deft combination of apparently opposite skills: on the one hand, a grasp of empirical detail and a talent for visual analysis, and on the other, a capacity to offer the broadest explanations of stylistic change. Not surprisingly, Frankl was a master of both, and in that mastery lay, paradoxically, the justification for Frankl's claim to be a 'scientific' art historian. The breadth of his vision remains unsurpassed in any single-author survey of Gothic architecture. His building types range from chapels and monasteries to parish churches and cathedrals; his chronology encompasses nearly half a millenium; his Gothic Europe extends from Naples to Durham. Frankl's narrative proceeds on a colossal front, throwing up insights and juxtapositions which nation-based surveys would have missed: the tracery of the choir of Sees in Normandy and of the nave of Minden in Westphalia (p. 168); the slender columns of Saint-Serge at Angers, and those in the contemporary Lady Chapel of Salisbury (p. 124); the 'autonomous' (or 'harp-strong') tracery of the west front of Strasbourg and the undercroft windows of St Stephen's Chapel in Westminster (p. 173). This synoptic sweep, with its command of detail and its sharp eye for nuances of form and physiognomy, comes straight from Wölfflin, the acknowledged master of twentieth-century 'formalism'.[52] Frankl rightly senses a new conception of the Gothic exterior in the lavishly decorated clerestorey and flyers of Reims Cathedral; and his description of their crockets as 'reminiscent of pointillism' (p. 116) exactly conveys their 'painterly' denial of mass. West façades inspired some of his most telling observations, perhaps because their structural similarities provided the neat framework within which to observe subtle changes of detail (pp. 138–46). He senses (what later scholars went on fully to articulate) the transitional nature of the west façade of Laon, between Early and High Gothic (p. 90). His analysis of the west façade of Cologne Cathedral (pp. 178–9) – the conformity of its details subtly extended across its layered and tapering storeys – remains unsurpassed.[53] He is particularly sensitive to Rayonnant architecture (though he calls it 'High Gothic'), probably because its metallic delicacy suggests to him an 'unworldliness and spirituality' which he identifies as the essence of Gothic (p. 298). His analysis of the general character of the style – its sharpening of profiles, its piers without capitals, its desire 'to use pure light as the only building material' (p. 176) – is consistently accurate. At Saint-Urbain at Troyes, or Saint-Nazaire at Carcassonne, he

conveys the linearity and brittleness of Rayonnant (pp. 166–8); at Saint-Ouen at Rouen he captures its ethereal elegance: 'Some of the shafts are so slender that they look almost like mere lines; they are so delicate that their third dimension almost disappears, and the whole elevation amounts to almost nothing more than a surface crossed by lines of varying thickness, pointing upwards – floating dreamily in space, elegant yet ascetic' (p. 176). Often dismissed as an 'academic' and 'doctrinaire' style by writers of Frankl's generation, this sympathetic analysis of Rayonnant prepared the way for its rehabilitation in the 1960s.[54]

Descriptions of this quality are not random insights; they are closely allied to Frankl's theoretical inclinations, or to his personal taste. Where buildings, or elements of buildings, conform to his polarities, or come close to his sense of the spirituality of the Middle Ages, then he is capable of deep understanding. The polarity of 'diagonality versus frontality' shapes an impressive separate section on the development of capitals and bases (pp. 84–6); the polarity of 'structure versus texture' allows a similarly useful exercise for the evolution of the rose window (pp. 266–7). The 'addition versus division' polarity neatly corresponds to the 'still Romanesque' or 'Transitional' narthex of Saint-Denis, and the 'unity and grace' of the fully Gothic choir (p. 67). Especially versatile as an analytical and descriptive tool was Frankl's principle of 'Gothic relief' (see above), which belongs to 'optical form' in that it dominates the surface effects of interior elevations or façades, but also shares characteristics of 'spatial form' since the relief divides the total space into a skeleton of interdependent parts. 'Gothic relief' gives him an immediate purchase in the analysis of the west façade of Saint-Denis, and is particularly helpful in defining the spatial fluidity and sculptural subtlety of Noyon Cathedral (pp. 70–2) and of the early Gothic in the Aisne valley and the Laonnois in the 1160s–80s. The concept also defines what he calls 'the Gothic profile' of early Rayonnant window tracery at Amiens and Saint-Denis, although here with a subtler and more wiry relief. The principle of repetition by division in the clerestorey tracery of both buildings results in ultra-fine projections and recessions of the tracery mullions and the wall and vault shafts, creating a flowing connexion between one bay and the next – the whole effect described with Frankl's customary clarity and patience (pp. 119–21, 126–7). Frankl's most surprising application of the principle of 'Gothic relief' is to the exteriors of the great High Gothic cathedrals. The 'Gothic relief' that had hitherto dominated the interior now extended to a half-open, half-closed composition of flying buttresses, pinnacles and pyramid roofs. The result was an 'organic unification' of the whole church (pp. 106–14, 116). At Chartres, Le Mans, Reims and elsewhere vaults, piers, shafts and buttresses are united into a single visual, as well as constructional, system – they form (following the 'law' of partiality) the fragments of a whole, a whole which is the church itself. Frankl's descriptions of this phenomenon, and of the most spectacular of these exterior ensembles, the choir of Le Mans (p. 118), rank among the most searching in the literature of Gothic.

Frankl's polarities of 'akyrism' and 'the norm' offered positive insights into buildings hitherto labelled as 'eccentric' or 'academic'. *Akyros*, the mutability of the functions and meanings of forms, was Frankl's key to rescuing a whole category of architecture dismissed by the general surveys as 'provincial' or eccentric because it refused to obey the norms of the mainstream, that is, the Gothic of the Ile-de-France. Inventive and unorthodox types of vault, especially those where ribs acquired new aesthetic purposes, fascinated him. The triangular vaults of the ambulatory at Notre-Dame in Paris, the spider-like vaults of Saint-Quiriace in Provins, and the decorative nets and liernes of early thirteenth-century Anjou, were, for the first time in a general survey, given as much prominence as the conventional elements of Gothic. Frankl's most influential application of 'akyrism' came in his analysis of St Hugh's choir in Lincoln Cathedral. He was the first to appreciate that the oddities of this building, particularly what he called its 'crazy' vaults, were not the product of changes of plan, still less of the 'madness' of the architect, but reflected a consistent aesthetic intention, at odds, certainly, with mainstream French Gothic, but curiously prophetic of the dissonances and richness of the Late Gothic style, especially in Germany (pp. 101–2).[55] Frankl's 'akyrism' helped to undermine conventional Franco-centric histories of Gothic and to open up new, pluralistic approaches to the development of Early and Late Gothic in Europe.

'The norm' – what Frankl defines as 'a unique case' (p. 164) – poses problems of definition and application. At times it may mean nothing more than the sense of a single blueprint connecting a set of very similar buildings, such as the southern French cathedrals of Toulouse, Narbonne and Rodez (p. 169). Or it may refer to the very real tendency in thirteenth-century great churches in northern France to conform to increasingly refined standards of regularity and consistency, as each cathedral competed with, and 'improved on' its immediate predecessors. Thus, for Frankl, 'Reims was a correction of Chartres: Le Mans is a correction of Bourges' (p. 116). But in some passages of Frankl's writing there is a clear implication that the 'norm' means something close to a metaphysical entity – the transcendent existence of a single, perfect mental model of the Gothic cathedral to which all actual cathedrals aspired. At Reims and Amiens, he admits, 'one can feel the tendency towards the norm', but it is the absolute clarity and regularity of Cologne Cathedral which makes it '*the* Gothic choir, *the* final solution' (p. 164). Frankl's Platonic language may not command agreement, but the idea of French cathedral Gothic as the search for a paradigm is not wide of the mark, for we know that the cathedral builders had a competitive and corrective view of precedents, and entertained definite ideas about what a great Gothic church should look like. Certainly, Frankl's emphasis on the aesthetic perfection of Cologne was timely. Just as his idea of akyrism rescued 'odd' buildings from undeserved obscurity, so the idea of the norm undermined the widespread prejudice that later thirteenth-century great churches, particularly Cologne, were 'doctrinaire'. Frankl was the first to locate Cologne Cathedral in its proper place as the supreme achievement of French Rayonnant.

Allied to the idea of the norm is Frankl's concept of 'the classic', which touches no less profoundly on our sense of *quality* in architecture. Like akyrism, 'the classic' can describe a work of any period, not necessarily from Classical or Neoclassical art. It refers to 'summits of achievement' at which 'the highest degree of the particular harmony inherent in the premises of any style are reached' (p. 122). 'Classic' buildings are the fruits of what we defined earlier as Frankl's dialectic model of architectural evolution, where the inherent tensions in the components of a style are integrated step by step into a final and ideal solution. Classic solutions, such as the nave of Amiens Cathedral, embody that short-lived moment of equilibrium. Here a host of polar opposites are reconciled: a sense of the infinite within finite bounds, of flowing movement in repose, of the supernatural within the natural, of 'solid matter overcoming its own mass', of unity in multiplicity. 'The formal conditions imposed by the rib vault organically permeate the whole structural system' (p. 122). No other description of Amiens approaches so closely the paradoxical sense of harmony and 'perfection' latent in this most exhilarating of Gothic cathedrals. But the virtues of the 'classic' are not confined to High Gothic. They also infuse the German hall churches of the later fifteenth century, the acknowledged masterpieces of German *Sondergotik* – Nördlingen, Dinkelsbühl, Amberg and Annaberg. If the ultimate balance of High Gothic lay in the reconciliation of the Gothic style of 'becoming' with vestiges of the Romanesque style of 'being', the 'classic' in German Late Gothic is found in a seamless flow of vaults, pillars and spaces in perpetual equilibrium: 'the harmony of movement within itself, a living vibration from within, a current which always returns to its own beginning'. Frankl had a profound feeling for the spatial poise and controlled dynamism of the German Late Gothic, a style of 'soft contrasts' and 'poised tension' (p. 227), its best works, 'tranquil and reassuring, noble and unhurried, in spite of the agitation within them' (p. 225).

The eloquence of Frankl's response to these 'classic' works, his masterly characterization of form and feeling, is personal without being sentimental. There is a strongly empathetic quality in his writing, but an empathy disciplined by a sharp eye and a rigorous intellectual system, so that the architecture, as a 'form symbol', is convincingly translated into his own experience of harmony and well-being. Classical antiquities, he says, may produce in us a *serene* belief in ourselves, 'but it could be metaphorically said that Gothic, in its own classic phase, shows a *passionate* belief in itself . . . we can surrender to being lifted far above ourselves by it and translated into a sphere in which we can taste the highest, all-embracing harmony of existence' (pp. 122–3, my italics). In Master Gerhard's choir in Cologne, 'the spirit of God embraces what is cold and what is warm, what is German and what is French, what is dead and what is living. But the cathedral is not dead; it is solemn, festive and sublime, *fascinans* and *tremendum* at the same time, as clear as mathematics and as irrational as life itself' (p. 164). Few writers on Gothic architecture have evoked the transcendent power of a great cathedral with such directness and conviction.

Frankl's sensitivity to German *Sondergotik* is bound up with his eccentric belief that Late Gothic represents the culminating point of the Gothic style as a whole, and that only after 1300 did Gothic attain 'its ultimate perfection' (p. 33). By the second half of the fifteenth century, he argues, Gothic architects had 'drawn every possible conclusion from the premises which had been laid down when the first rib-vault was built at Durham' (p. 258). Spatially, especially in hall churches, the Late Gothic interior became increasingly unified, indeterminate and penetrable – a 'whole' which could be freely divided and subdivided. Optically, its diagonality was so insistent that the increased continuity between forms – the fluent interpenetrations of flowing tracery, spiral piers, or double-curved ribs – led Frankl to coin the term 'continuous recession' as the hall-mark of the style (p. 242). Above all, it was the transformation of Early and High Gothic 'structure' into Late Gothic 'texture', from a sense of counter-pressure to a sense of continuous flow, which signalled the culmination of the principles of Gothic. The aim of the Late Gothic architect was, Frankl asserts, 'to correct the High Gothic style with the unbelievably complicated forms of his own geometrical fantasy, to turn his work into pure texture, and thus to make it completely Gothic' (p. 244).

Few would agree with Frankl that Late Gothic is more 'Gothic' than earlier stages of the style, and even fewer would subscribe to his notion that Late Gothic was a 'correction' of High Gothic, implying as this does that there was something missing or wrong with twelfth- or thirteenth-century architecture.[56] But his concentration on Late Gothic happily denies the prejudice (still evident in the cursory attention given to Late Gothic in modern surveys and text books) that the late phase of the style was in some way 'decadent' and therefore undeserving of serious study. And many of Frankl's most original insights come in the long Late Gothic chapter. He had the advantage over most other scholars in combining a life-long familiarity with German Late Gothic with a lively interest in English architecture. He was one of the first scholars to see the importance of St Stephen's Chapel in Westminster as the fountainhead for both the Perpendicular and the Decorated styles (pp. 193–4). He properly isolates curvilinearity and decorative vaulting as the key elements of the Decorated style (pp. 187ff). And the similarities he notes between English decorative vaulting and the vaults of Peter Parler in Prague Cathedral (pp. 202–4) prepared the way for investigations into English influence in the genesis of the German *Sondergotik*. His sections on German Late Gothic still remain the best account in English of this complex and inventive style, and his appreciation of the mixture of genres in the fifteenth century, particularly the stylistic importance of the small-scale decorative architecture of fonts, screens and sacrament houses (pp. 243–7) prefigures the explosion of interest in 'micro-architecture' in the last twenty years. Frankl's refined perceptions of architectural space must have attuned him to the spatial intricacies of Late Gothic, but so did his modernist sensitivity to the pervasiveness of style. Like the *Jugendstil* which surrounded his early life in Prague and Munich, Late Gothic forms, from vaults to thuribles, have a universality and a formal coherence which is almost obtrusive. Frankl's theoretical principles – 'the premises of the first rib vault' – were as evident in the 'geometrical fantasies' of the north spire of Chartres as they were in the choir screen of St Pantaleon in Cologne, or sanctuary vaults of Pirna (pp. 246, 248).

THE PROBLEMS OF FRANKL'S SYSTEM

The wealth of insights which Frankl's system throws up is a tribute to the resilience of historicism after a century of art-historical application. In the hands of a master like Frankl it can still offer a profound understanding of architectural style. But if theory underwrites the strengths of *Gothic Architecture* it also generates its weaknesses. Frankl's polarities as descriptive categories, his mechanisms for stylistic change, and his model for the relations between architecture and culture leave us with a one-sided history of Gothic – impersonal, abstract and 'spiritual'.

The descriptive categories

By raising mere descriptive tools to the status of 'stylistic laws' Frankl exposes his 'polarities' as what they are – not forces but labels: generalizations which stand or fall by the insights they throw on particular cases. When submitted to the sheer diversity of Gothic architecture, his Gothic 'principles' simply do not apply to certain buildings or classes of building. The transformation of structure into texture only occurs in the later Gothic period. The notion that Gothic tends towards spatial 'division' fails to explain the continued popularity of the basilica (with its more 'additive' and 'separate' spaces) over and against the relative rarity of the Gothic hall church (a far more unified and 'divisive' space). The concept of division may underlie the interpenetrating spaces of French cathedral chevets, but how does it explain the equally 'Gothic' character of contemporary English cathedrals, with their separate, box-like compartments of space? Are we to believe that English Gothic is 'Gothic' only because of its 'horizontal fusions' (pp. 123–4), while its ground plans and massing are still 'Romanesque'? Frankl's concept of spatial continuity should be at its strongest in the later Middle Ages, yet how does it explain the Late Gothic tendency to festoon the core of the church with semi-independent burial and chantry chapels? The privatizing and individualistic tendencies of later medieval piety run counter to his 'law' of 'partiality' and 'division', at a time when those 'laws' are, he argues, at their most forceful and explicit.

The most problematic of Frankl's 'laws' is the optical category of 'diagonality', since it is a law which fails to cover a number of critically important cases. It cannot, for example, account for the special qualities of Parisian architecture from the Early Gothic to the Rayonnant, since the thin murality of this architecture, and its spectacular development of bar tracery, are best appreciated frontally, not diagonally. As an indicator of medieval perceptions of architecture, Frankl's 'diagonality' proposes an argument which is both circular and anachronistic. Medieval spectators were expected 'to stand diagonally, and visually to experience the space in recession, not in the flat' (p. 49), but the only verification for this diagonal act of perception are the diagonal forms of Gothic. No evidence of medieval standing or seating arrangements in churches, or of processional directions, is brought to bear from outside this circle. Not only does 'diagonality' fail to include important categories of Gothic, it rests on a dubious conception of optical form which grew out of late nineteenth-century theories of perception, theories long since discredited. Frankl's belief that memory sifted out the characteristic features of objects and presented them to the spectator in their most distinctive shape (the diagonal) may owe something to Gestalt psychology; it was certainly indebted to the work of Adolf von Hildebrand, Wölfflin's mentor in matters of perceptual psychology. Hildebrand postulated the existence of dominant or typical shapes in the mind as the residue of many sense impressions deposited in the memory, shapes which then determined the artist's schematic representation of the world.[57] But it is now clear, after a century of psychological investigation, that Hildebrand's schematic systems, and even Gestalt's desire to integrate discrete perceptions into an intelligible whole, simply fail to take into account the immense complexities involved in the reading of forms and images, particularly images as intricate as the cathedral's. Is 'diagonality' or any other concept – 'verticality' or 'spatial enclosure' – the 'dominant' visual impression left by the Gothic great church? In fact, is there a dominant impression at all? The elusive welter of competing sensations transmitted by the Gothic cathedral makes the prospect of reconstructing the real perceptions of medieval viewers a daunting task. A first step might be to move away from theories of perception altogether and examine the more mundane evidence of medieval seating plans, processional routes and the placement of altars.

Frankl's 'diagonality' is, of course, particularly evident in the Gothic rib vault, and it is in his discussion of early rib vaults that the concept of 'diagonality' is most obviously elevated from a descriptive term to a stylistic force, with misleading consequences. As we have seen, the rib vault, as the quintessentially 'diagonal' element in the Early Gothic system, must, for Frankl, be the motor of the style; all aspects of Gothic, he argues, grow out of the aesthetic character of the rib. To demonstrate this he has to prove, of course, that no Gothic element was present in a building before the rib. Yet this is patently not the case. As early as 1925 Ernst Gall (and later Jean Bony) had clearly demonstrated that the skeletal qualities of the Gothic elevation – qualities of partiality and spatial openness which Frankl derived from the rib – first appeared as a structural system in Anglo-Norman Romanesque architecture, usually in the context of wooden-roofed buildings, and therefore quite independently of the rib vault. It was the conjunction of the two systems – Anglo-Norman elevation and north French rib – not the priority of the rib, which forged the Gothic structure.[58] Frankl went to great pains to reject Gall's position, on the grounds that this Anglo-Norman wall relief was 'frontal' and typically Romanesque, and not 'diagonal', and therefore not strictly 'Gothic';[59] but there can be little doubt that Gothic architects were profoundly influenced by Anglo-Norman elevations. The niceties of 'optical form' and late nineteenth-century theories of perception had, at least in this case, nothing to do with the stylistic intentions of medieval masons. Indeed, the 'partiality' of Frankl's Gothic rib is a prime example of confusing descriptive tools with historical forces: the Gothic rib is certainly 'diagonal' and 'partial', but it is not the single engine which drives the creation of Early Gothic in France. Frankl's confusion meant that Anglo-Norman Romanesque, a critical source of inspiration for much Early Gothic architecture in the Ile-de-France, was left out of the account.

Frankl's reluctance to acknowledge Anglo-Norman architecture points to a wider issue in the text – its limited appreciation of artistic tradition. For Frankl, the real agents of stylistic evolution are the 'basic principles' of the style, and the history of Gothic is the increasingly refined conformity of each building to them. 'Style' he reminds us, 'is a unity of *forms* governed by a few basic principles. In this book these principles will be clarified by examples' (p. 33). It follows that tracing changes in the stylistic physiognomy of Gothic over its long history is not, for Frankl, an account of architects and patrons drawing on previous works, it is only tracing changes in the look, to us, of the finished products, and how those products show more and more accurate pointer readings to the 'principles' of Gothic. Frankl is, of course, aware of the sources of particular buildings (Canterbury looked to Sens Cathedral, Bourges to Notre-Dame in Paris), but these borrowings are not the real factors in stylistic change. What propels the style is its attentiveness to Gothic 'principles'. Thus, St George in Limburg an der Lahn is not discussed in terms of its transformation of the advanced Gothic vocabulary of Laon Cathedral into the language of the Rhenish Romanesque, but how 'Gothic' it is, and how diagonal its shafts are (p. 150). High Gothic Soissons is not assessed in terms of its relationship to Chartres Cathedral, or of its borrowings from its own, earlier south transept, but in terms of its diagonality, its merging of spaces, its 'complexity versus serenity' (p. 112). Frankl's buildings are fundamentally progressive – they all look towards the laws of Gothic, laws which unfold step by step, and with ever greater clarity, towards their ultimate fulfilment in the Late Gothic. There is less sense of where the architecture comes from than of where it leads to. For Frankl, Gothic proceeded like the demonstration of a mathematical theorem. 'There are few periods in the history of art in which the logical sequence of successive steps is so patent and so convincing. In this sense, therefore, the historian can adopt a forward-looking position' (p. 33). The 'essence' of each building is revealed only when its position is clarified 'on the ladder of development' (p. 90).

In this abstract and forward-pointing account of Gothic, there is little sense of the real diversity of forces inherent in tradition: varieties of inspiration, conflicting choices and possibilities, local and regional 'schools' of Gothic, and their interaction with more mainstream centres. Curiously, in his Romanesque survey Frankl had shown real sensitivity to regional 'schools', but in *Gothic Architecture* they hardly figure. 'Akyrism', for all its stress on the eccentric, is too narrow a concept to register such diversity. The choir of Coutances may transform its staircases into oriel-like projections (p. 165), but it is the debts to Bourges and Le Mans, and their transformation into Norman ways of thinking, that define the creativity of the building and its place in a

Norman Gothic style. Similarly the 'akyristic' vaults of Airvault and Saint-Serge at Angers are not considered in the wider context of Angevin Gothic c.1200, and its other defining characteristics (domed rib vaults, hall churches, etc.). Nor does Frankl convey any sense of the variety of styles – Parisian, Laonnois, Sénonais – that enliven early Gothic in the Ile-de-France. The choir of Saint-Remi in Reims belongs to the Laonnois version of Gothic; it is not 'in its arcades, its shafts, its gallery, a faithful reproduction of Notre-Dame [in Paris]' (p. 48, first edtn). Not surprisingly, High Gothic in France (c.1190–c.1240), a period of remarkable stylistic diversity, emerges as a one-dimensional episode. Frankl's progressive theory of evolution, where each building is placed 'on the ladder of development', restricts his interest to the mainstream cathedrals of Chartres, Reims and Amiens, while the thriving regional 'schools' of Normandy and Burgundy, or the 'para-Chartrain' movements of High Gothic identified by Bony in the north-east and east of France, get little attention.[60] The reception of Gothic into England is treated, not as a series of creative compromises between new French impulses and older Anglo-Norman traditions, but as a process of 'horizontal fusion' – a concept which ignores all the vertically-divided elevations of the Early English style (Worcester west bays, Glastonbury, Rochester and Southwark). Such diversities can find no place in a system where conformity to the general 'laws' of Gothic constitutes the 'essence' of each building, and its position on a developmental ladder. A horticultural metaphor might not be too far-fetched: Frankl's 'Gothic garden' is not teeming with different species; it is populated only with sunflowers, all in different stages of development, but all turning, as one, to the 'sun' of Gothic partiality. Formal variety, individual intention and agency, as well as material and technical imperatives, are all casualties of this teleological model of stylistic history.

Stylistic change: intentionality and material history

Because the *Kunstwollen* of partiality is the real motor of stylistic change, architects rarely figure in this book as agents with choices and intentions. Even Frankl's notion of 'correction', the modifications and amendments which successive High Gothic architects made to their designs in the light of 'mistakes' in immediately preceding buildings, implies a quasi-deterministic drive towards a perfect 'end cause'. The reader of *Gothic Architecture* will find nothing on the changing social status of the architect, or on the uses of drawing and its implications for work practices. A short discussion on craft training in the lodge only serves to emphasize the limitations of the architect's creativity (pp. 223–5). Frankl, of course, was deeply familiar with these aspects of the mason's profession, and had devoted many illuminating pages to them in *The Gothic*,[61] but they had no place in the evolution of style. He was even more dismissive of economic, functional and structural factors as agents of stylistic change. How were the Gothic cathedrals funded? How did changing liturgical practices influence the dispositions of interior space? What technological principles, if any, determined the use of the flying buttress? These issues are hardly touched on – economic questions are not even raised – and when they do make a brief appearance they are seen, not as forces that interact with individual choice, but as phenomena which restrict and even oppose creativity. They are the utilitarian or 'materialist' pressures which help, negatively, to define the architect's creative 'margin of freedom' (which, of course, is not a 'freedom' at all). When Frankl does (rarely) deal with questions of liturgical function, his unfamiliarity with the subject is apparent. There is no evidence that the galleries at Laon are for pilgrims (p. 76) or that the cathedral of Poitiers 'is a church for nuptial Masses' (p. 61, first edtn).

Questions touching on the mason's lodge and on purpose and function are relegated largely to Part Two, as if they were theoretical or 'general' problems having little bearing on the 'immanent' development of style described in Part One. Frankl's confidence in drawing such a clear division between the visual tradition and its surrounding culture stems directly from Wölfflin's 'double root of style' – the idea, advanced most clearly in his *Classic Art*, that changes in the visual tradition and changes in other manifestations of a culture proceed autonomously ('immanently') within each of their spheres, but also interact in such a way that the social and religious ethos becomes the background condition, in some cases the determinant, of stylistic evolution. Wölfflin constantly revised his position on the influence of social and religious factors on visual style, and that ambiguity is reflected in Frankl's separation of the visual and the cultural history of Gothic in the two halves of his book.[62] While he looks for 'profounder' meanings for stylistic change in the 'metaphysical idea of the men who commissioned [the buildings]' (p. 298), he feels it unnecessary to examine how that interaction of mind and style took place within the history of particular buildings. In fact, Frankl's post-Hegelian model of cultural history is ill-equipped to uncover the connexions between motif and milieu.

The Limitations of Cultural History

Frankl's holistic picture of medieval culture proceeds on two typically Hegelian assumptions. Firstly, it suggests that the various 'spokes' on the cultural wheel – religion, art, architecture, politics, economics, social history – derive their vitality radially, that is, not through direct contact with each other, but through their common root at the hub; and secondly, it assumes that cultures tend towards order and unity, that each 'spoke' proclaims, in its separate language, the meaning of the centre: 'the ring that forces the diverging lines towards each other until they converge . . . is Man, or Society, which strives after unity, after a harmonious civilization, after a style common to every cultural sphere' (p. 297). Both models erase and distort historical connexions between architecture and its surrounding culture.

One obvious casualty of this Hegelian model is medieval secular architecture. On the face of it, secular and religious architecture seem to fit neatly into the Hegelian mould, since they give the impression of clearly distinct 'spokes'. Castles show no inclination to look like churches, or to obey Gothic stylistic principles, and they convey values diametrically opposed to the Christian humility and 'partiality' which Frankl isolates as the central driving force of medieval culture. 'Secular architecture shows man as he was: church architecture shows him as he would have liked to be' (p. 299). But the Hegelian system demands the existence of some common factor between these two architectures at the hub of the wheel, and so Frankl is forced to read them both as aspects of the fragmentary nature of 'partiality', sacred buildings symbolizing Man 'as a fragment of the kingdom of God', secular 'as a fragment of Society' (p. 290). But *how* precisely the 'form symbols' of Gothic secular architecture express this notion of 'secular partiality' is never discussed, and the whole device comes close to tautology: secular architecture embodies secular society. In fact, the relationship between secular and ecclesiastical architecture runs directly counter to the Hegelian paradigm; it consists, not of mysterious connexions at the centre, but of contacts across the 'spokes' – between each field. For in the later Middle Ages, particularly from the late fourteenth century, important exchanges – ideological and stylistic – between castle-palaces and churches radically altered the development of late Gothic in France, England and Germany. Frankl glances against this problem (pp. 245ff), but his Hegelian theory of culture artificially separates the two genres – to such an extent that secular architecture is banished from Part One and leads a separate existence in Part Two under 'The General Problems of the Gothic Style'.

Another victim of the Hegelian model is the patron, who finds himself – like secular architecture – artificially separated from a history of actual Gothic buildings by being sidelined into Part Two. (Patrons rarely trespass as named individuals into Part One.) Under the section 'Symbols of Meaning' Frankl shows how little he is prepared to concede to the patron and benefactor in the shaping of the medieval church. Their financial contributions to building do not interest him. Their liturgical concerns have no bearing on style, and are therefore irrelevant to the shaping of Gothic. Patrons have no more control over the character of the church than an overseer (p. 228). Their scholastic, theological and literary interests – what he calls 'symbols of meaning' – belong to a cultural 'spoke' that has, he contends, little or no direct connexion to architecture. For Frankl, 'symbols of meaning' are not only logically separate from the visual history of forms, but their 'intellectual' properties tell us far less about the 'spiritual' meanings of Gothic architecture than the empathetic and intuitive revelations of the building as a 'form symbol' (p. 236). All this amounts to a narrow and misleading view of the relations between Gothic architecture and patronage. As we shall see, it privileges empathetic deduction (and all its subjective pitfalls) over an historical understanding of the patron's interests. It also ignores classes of architecture with a strong ideological content, and it distorts our understanding of buildings where we know that the patron's concerns were formative. We cannot explain the skeletal quality of the new Gothic choir at Saint-Denis without its windows, yet these depended for their inclusion on Abbot Suger's famous fascination with neo-platonic theologies of light. The retrospective oddities of the Wenceslas Chapel in Prague Cathedral can only be ascribed to the exotic tastes of the Emperor Charles IV; they have lit-

tle to do with Peter Parler's avant-garde treatment of German Rayonnant. And what of patrons who took such a keen interest in their buildings that they helped to decide on their spatial organization, on their decoration and even on the specific stylistic precedents which they required their architect to copy? Richard Krautheimer's notion of the medieval architectural 'copy', demanded by the patron as a way of associating his building, liturgically or formally, with a venerable archetype, seems to have passed Frankl by.[63] Yet it would have explained why Archbishop Albrecht of Magdeburg (one of the few patrons mentioned by Frankl) inserted the marble columns of the old Ottonian church into his new Gothic choir. Frankl the modernist is not interested in this clear example of the client intervening in the cause of tradition; for him, Albrecht is an importer of a new style he scarcely understands.

Behind Frankl's denigration of the patron lies his suspicion that patronal interests, in so far as they embody concepts, ideas and literary and theological systems, are too 'intellectual' to be of any relevance to the style of Gothic. 'Symbols of meaning' are logically separate from the visual history of forms. 'Form symbols' on the other hand – the way Gothic forms express the 'spirit of Gothic partiality' – are central to Frankl's notion of cultural history. The principle of partiality is somehow infused by the architect and (more mysteriously) by his society, into the building and then re-lived, intuitively and empathetically, by the modern spectator. But when we examine more closely this 'spirit of partiality' in later medieval society we encounter little more than a vague collective psychology, usually expressed in the form of two polar constructs: 'Romanesque Man' and 'Gothic Man'. 'Romanesque Man' and 'Romanesque Society', for example, are as 'additive', 'independent' and 'total' as Romanesque architecture. They are worldly, war-like and autonomous; they posit a clear separation between this world and the next; and their behaviour, even at its most pious, is impervious to a genuine sense of the spiritual ('not a really permanent religious feeling') (p. 241). This Romanesque *Weltanschauung* is clearly a travesty of the real social and religious history of the Romanesque period. It ignores, for example, the deep spirituality of the monasteries of the eleventh and twelfth centuries, monasteries which were largely responsible for much of Romanesque art and architecture. But the construct, unhistorical as it is, is obviously invented as a pseudo-historical equivalent to the visual characteristics of Romanesque. It is also set up as the simple polar opposite to 'Gothic Man' and 'Gothic Society', concepts equally detached from the complexities of real history. In contrast to the 'divisiveness' and duality of the Romanesque world view the Gothic psyche embraces partiality and unity in all aspects of its culture. Its supreme moment was represented by the all-embracing unity of the Church at the time of the Fourth Lateran council, and by the humble self-abnegation and world-embracing spirituality of St Francis and St Dominic (p. 241). As a characterization of later medieval history this notion of 'cultural partiality' is as inadequate as Frankl's caricature of Romanesque society. If the Gothic cathedral finds its closest equivalent in the absolute 'partiality' of the friars, why did mendicant architecture radically reject the partiality of High

Gothic and Rayonnant in favour of a mural simplicity closer to Cistercian Romanesque, and even Early Christian models?[64] And if the idea of the superior unity of the Christian Church in the early thirteenth century lay at the centre of Gothic partiality, why did the Late Gothic style, which supposedly carried that partiality to its perfect fulfillment, coincide with the fragmentation of Christian Europe into rival nationalities and the decline in the authority of the universal Church? The connexions between the hub and the spokes do not work, because history does not proceed from an 'essential' centre and cannot be reduced to unitary psychological constructs. Even where centre and periphery seem historically to coincide Frankl's cultural connexions are too vague to define the real character of the building. Florence Cathedral and Dante's *Divine Comedy* belong to the same period and the same milieu, but in what sense is the cathedral (like the poem) a 'symbol of the progress of the human spirit towards the absolute' (p. 214)? Is it *more* of a symbol than any other Gothic great church of its day?

Perhaps the most problematic aspect of Frankl's cultural history is his reluctance to use 'symbols of meaning' – ideas, concepts, programmes – as the links between motif and milieu, and instead to rely on 'form symbols' – the 'eloquence' of architectural form experienced empathetically by the viewer – as the signifiers of Gothic culture. The weakness of this position comes out clearly in his discussion of the links between Cistercian architecture and its monastic milieu. Instead of assessing the 'symbols of meaning' – the contemporary literary evidence for the Cistercian aesthetic of art (St Bernard's letters, the order's building statutes etc.) – he relies solely on the architecture as a 'form symbol', as a language of expressive forms. 'A visitor', he claims, 'who understands the language of stone will be aware of this background [Cistercian culture] without literary proof' (p. 96). But will he? What Frankl thinks Cistercian churches reveal, in their murality and simplicity, and in their 'aristocratic' and 'proud' demeanour, is a typically 'Romanesque' spirituality, and in this (he argues) they reflect the 'aristocratic' and 'princely' character of St Bernard himself. It was here, he suggests, that Cistercian architecture differed from the openness and humility of the 'Gothic friars' (p. 68). But many would argue that the humility of the friars' architecture is not dissimilar to that of the Cistercians – indeed is directly indebted to it – and that the mural and 'proud' qualities of Cistercian churches are shared by other classes of Romanesque architecture. What makes Cistercian architecture distinct is its espousal of poverty and asceticism, an economic and spiritual ideal which belongs, as much, if not more, to the conceptual world of 'symbols of meaning' as to the empathetic domain of 'form symbols'. Bernard's famous *Apologia*, Stephen Harding's *Carta Caritatis*, Ailred of Rievaulx's description of the ideal Cistercian monastic life, the *Statuta* of the General Chapters, the ideological clashes with Cluny – all these 'symbols of meaning' fail to reach Frankl's text. By ignoring the more 'intellectual' aspects of the Cistercian programme Frankl misses the essential links between architectural form and spiritual policy. In fact, 'form symbols', as Frankl's favoured link between the centre and the 'spoke', turn out to be vague and subjective guides to historical reality. They also rest on a huge tautology:

Gothic architecture is the symbol of Gothic Man, and Gothic Man, or Gothic Society, infuses his architecture with Gothic principles. In effect, Gothic is Gothic. Frankl himself says so: 'Gothic Man reflects God in a Gothic way, and Gothic church architecture is art because Gothic forms symbolize the conception of God that was valid in a Gothic age' (p. 277).

High Gothic and Rayonnant

For all Frankl's sensitivity to the visual qualities of Rayonnant, it is the architecture of thirteenth-century France which reflects most clearly the weaknesses of his idealist method. High Gothic embodies the virtues that Frankl's theoretical armature has little room for. It was a period of rapid technical and productive change. Architectural drawing emerged as a new tool for design and an indispensable medium for communicating ideas and fixing them as models for the future. More refined methods for the production of standardized carved masonry were introduced to the lodges. The mastery of practical geometry, a traditional skill of the master mason, took on – at least to those outside the lodges – a more intellectual character. These productive changes led to a new appreciation of the architect as designer and creator, and an inevitable rise in his social status. Nothing of this reaches Frankl's text. High Gothic is also an architecture of spatial splendour, but this is hardly registered in *Gothic Architecture*. The complexities of its tiered elevations at Bourges, Le Mans and Beauvais, the expansiveness of the transepts at Reims and Amiens, the fascination with the five-aisled church as a re-incarnation of Romanesque and Early Christian antecedents – all this diversity of spatial experiment escapes Frankl's generalized spatial concepts of 'partiality' and 'verticalism'. Such adventures in the handling of interior space depended, of course, on phenomenal progress in techniques of abutment and the coordination of structural forces. High Gothic architecture in northern France is, as Bony reminds us, 'the architecture of the flying buttress'.[65] The ingenuity with which Gothic engineers refined their structures, their failures and their experiments, constitutes one of the most heroic chapters in the history of architectural engineering, but it passes Frankl by. Instead, the sections on this most structural and spatial style are organized around small-scale decorative elements such as 'finials and balustrades' and 'the High Gothic pier, tracery and gargoyles'. These forms may, indeed, demonstrate Frankl's stylistic principles as well, if not better, than space and abutment; but here the principles simply do not marry with the realities of the style.

Frankl's treatment of thirteenth-century France was not helped by his failure to distinguish between High Gothic and Rayonnant styles, and his merging of all buildings of the thirteenth- and early fourteenth-century under the blanket title of 'High Gothic'. It would be unfair to blame Frankl for this confusion, even though an earlier generation of French commentators had already made the distinction.[66] It was not until Robert Branner published his study on the 'court style' of Saint Louis in 1965 that the implications of what Rayonnant meant became fully clear.[67] But the modern student may still find Frankl's undifferentiated 'High Gothic' confusing, since it distorts the history of European Gothic. The Rayonnant style (*c.*1230–*c.*1360?), as Branner and Jean Bony underlined, represented a radical change in the appearance and structure of the Gothic church as well as its sources of patronage.[68] Originating in Paris in the middle of the thirteenth century, the style quickly spread to the 'provinces' of the expanding kingdom of France as well as to Spain, England and the Rhineland. Royal as well as ecclesiastical patrons became the propagators of the style, and their secular concerns gave new inflections of meaning to an architecture hitherto associated with the higher clergy. Paris, and not the scattered sees of the French bishops, emerged as the dominant centre of stylistic invention. A concentration on window tracery and increasingly refined moulded surfaces replaced the grand experiments with space and structure which characterized High Gothic. At every level – stylistic, structural, patronal and ideological – Rayonnant represented a real break with the values of High Gothic.

For all his sensitivity to the visual qualities of Rayonnant, Frankl was unaware of these deep stylistic changes, and of the new interests which they presupposed. He had no historical or ideological structure within which to place his 'High Gothic' buildings. His sections on the second half of the thirteenth century may therefore be confusing for the student (pp. 126–71). Under detailed headings such as 'glazed triforia', 'the spheric triangle', 'cusps in tracery', 'elimination of capitals' and 'piers with grooves', his churches float in and out of our view like untethered vessels. Buildings that really belong to High Gothic (Bayeux, Naumburg and Coutances) appear in no meaningful context. Westminster Abbey is discussed without reference to one of its key sources, the Sainte-Chapelle, and without acknowledging Henry III's admiration of the French monarchy (p. 136). And while minute details are examined for their obedience to the laws of 'diagonality' or 'penetration', Frankl loses sight of the larger picture, particularly the dominant influence of the new Saint-Denis on the elevation design of most front-rank great churches in Europe for the next half century. To submerge his analyses of Clermont-Ferrand, Strasbourg, Leon and particularly Cologne Cathedrals in disconnected details is to miss the creative twists which each of these designs gave to the Dionysian archetype. It may be significant that Frankl's insights into the formal qualities of Rayonnant were completely at variance with his ignorance of its historical structures. Only with the Late Gothic, when stylistic diffusion depended less on centralized institutions and more on local conventions and the architect's own ingenuity, did Frankl's system of formal analysis based on stylistic 'principles' come more into its own.

FRANKL'S LEGACY: OPEN QUESTIONS AND NEW DEVELOPMENTS

To submit Frankl's text to such detailed criticism is itself a back-handed tribute to the greatness of *Gothic Architecture*. Frankl's Hegelianism may by-pass the contradictions of real history, but it is still, with all its insights, the only concerted attempt at a cultural history of Gothic. Frankl's 'principles' may turn out to be little more than descriptive devices, but no scholar has come closer to isolating the essential visual characteristics of Gothic architecture. All great works attract, with time, criticism and revision; but when the blemishes to Frankl's edifice have been scraped away a colossal achievement still remains. It is therefore ironic that we have had to wait until this new edition of *Gothic Architecture* for a proper appreciation of Frankl's extraordinary contribution to the historiography of Gothic. The neglect may be attributed to the vagaries of intellectual fashion and the misfortunes of timing. When *Gothic Architecture* appeared in 1962 it could hardly have encountered a less sympathetic audience. In the mid-1960s its Anglo-American readership, traditionally sceptical of theory and grand explanatory systems, was in the grip of a new post-war positivism, and found Frankl's intellectual structures opaque and old-fashioned. One American reviewer was amazed that 'it contained so much more theory than most of the volumes in the Pelican History of Art series'.[69] Robert Branner thought that the book should 'bear the imprint date not of 1962 but 1920', a shot which provoked a sharp response from Nikolaus Pevsner.[70] Despite (perhaps *because of*) its intellectual demands and its outstanding command of evidence, *Gothic Architecture* did not, therefore, initiate a new approach to the study of medieval architecture. The distinguished exception was Jean Bony, who in 1976 adopted Frankl's concept of diagonality as the starting point for his analysis of Early Gothic rib vaults.[71] Frankl's scholarship had, of course, made its mark in Germany long before the publication of *Gothic Architecture*. His emphasis on interior space as a category of analysis was reflected in the work of Pevsner and Giedion;[72] and the first book of his most distinguished pupil, Richard Krautheimer, on the architecture of the friars in Germany, explicitly acknowledged the influence of Frankl's theoretical principles.[73] But Krautheimer's interests soon turned from Frankl's historicism to a more empirical history which emphasized precisely those approaches which Frankl sidelined. Krautheimer's 'architectural iconography' centred on liturgy and function, on the concerns of the patron, on the specific associations of meaning surrounding specific – archetypal – buildings.[74] Here Frankl's 'symbols of meaning' bore much richer fruit than his 'form symbols'.

The direction of Krautheimer's research is symptomatic of Frankl's impact on the historiography of Gothic architecture since the last war. Paradoxically, the territory Frankl staked out as his own has been the *terra incognita* of most recent scholarship. In the last thirty years the starting point for research has been precisely in those areas ignored by Frankl.

The Monograph

Frankl never wrote a major monograph on a Gothic building, yet the architectural monograph, 'the biography' of a church, remains one of the most flourishing categories of medieval architectural history. Based ultimately on the forensic techniques pioneered by Robert Willis in his classic accounts of the English cathedrals, and on the deductive methods of analysis laid out by the French *archéologists* of the Ecole de Chartes, modern masters of archeological analysis, among them Arnold Wolff and Richard Hamman-Mac Lean, as well as John James and Jan van der Meulen, have found the monograph a congenial vehicle for exercises in the most precise and detailed examination of a great church's fabric. From moulding profiles, stonecoursing, building breaks and the smallest Morellian details, the single Gothic church can be dismembered into complex phases and 'campaigns' of construction.[75] The dangers of fragmentation posed by this method are obvious, but the monograph has proved to be a versatile instrument for exploring broader questions of style and meaning. Robert Branner's study of Bourges Cathedral, Stephen Murray's monographs on Troyes, Beauvais and Amiens, and, most recently, Christoph Brachmann's study of Metz and its churches, have used the conventional monograph as a platform for addressing a range of issues – on meaning, imagery, urbanism, function and broad stylistic contexts.[76] Indeed, there is no sign that the analysis of Gothic around a single major monument is on the decline. Quite the contrary, multi-author publications, in England led by the British Archaeological Association's *Conference Transactions*, have allowed single buildings to be scrutinized from a variety of critical angles. The explosion of interest in archaeology in the last twenty years has served even further to focus attention on the material analysis of architecture, and to encourage autopsies on the fabric of single, complex structures.[77] Combined with new investigative techniques, such as dendrochronology and photogrammetry, the modern monograph offers the most empirical and 'scientific' insights into the making of individual buildings and their often complicated histories.[78]

The Gothic church as a Gesamtkunstwerk *and the notion of 'artistic integration' in Gothic architecture*

Paradoxically, the monograph's concentration on a single building opened it up to new synthetic approaches which have broken out of the traditional limits of the monograph and extended the perspectives of specialized research. These developments have come from an unlikely quarter. In the years immediately after the Second World War, when the brutalities of recent history had made the notion of the spiritual cathedral especially attractive, Hans Sedlmayr and Otto von Simson put forward the idea of the Gothic cathedral as a mystical *Gesamtkunstwerk*, as a totality of all artistic media, whose meanings resided in the experience of the building as a *whole*.[79] This theological presentation of the cathedral as an integrated statement of figural art and architecture found little favour with contemporary scholarship, partly because the specialized disciplines ('architectural history', 'sculptural history') were still happily exploring their own territories, and partly because the 'integrated' approach of Sedlmayr and von Simson was too generalized to stand up to specific historical criticism. Sedlmayr's enterprise, in particular, foundered on its heroic, but flawed, attempt to draw every aspect of medieval culture – from furnishing to

liturgy, from literature to stained glass – into the mystical embrace of the cathedral. Nor has von Simson's understanding of French Gothic as the manifestation of a neo-platonic cosmology stood the test of time. But to the present generation of art historians, intent on rescuing the cathedral from its archeological and stylistic isolation, the idea of the Gothic church as 'artistic integration' seems to offer a way back to the original cathedral in all its multiplicity.[80] It is equally plain that the monograph, and not the synoptic format of Sedlmayr and von Simson, offers a more manageable framework for this kind of 'synthetic' history. And when this inclusive method is refined by developments in recent critical theory, coming largely from the neighbouring fields of literature and history, then the combination of 'integrated' method and monographic focus seems to represent a real breakthrough in the historical analysis of architecture. In Madeline Caviness's history of Saint-Remi at Reims and Saint-Yved at Braine, and in Paul Binski's monograph on Westminster Abbey, the modern scholarly boundaries between various media – architecture, sculpture, painting and stained glass – boundaries which reflect nothing more than the artificial requirements of academic specialization, have been dissolved, and with illuminating results. The building is now seen as a totality of art forms and activities, all connected to a web of institutional motives and pressures, and all developing – sometimes together, sometimes as an unplanned accumulation – in response to the cultural habits and political intentions of their users.[81] This history, diachronic in its response to changes in artistic fashion, synchronic in its interconnexions between many forms of cultural expression, is usually concentrated within the narrow compass of a single building. But it can also shed light on a much wider range of issues: on the relations of style to local traditions, on the uses of architecture for liturgical performance and varieties of devotion, and on the social and ideological context which shaped the great church. Andreas Köstler's recent monograph on the church of St Elizabeth at Marburg addresses a similar set of integrated problems but with the more specific aim of highlighting a widespread phenomenon in later medieval liturgy and 'cult management': the tendency to 'aestheticize' the church interior.[82] According to Köstler, High and later medieval churches show opposing but related tendencies – on the one hand denying the laity close access to liturgical and para-liturgical performances, and to relics and reliquaries, but, on the other hand, and by way of compensation, giving these devotional focuses an increasingly visual emphasis through decorative splendour and theatrical forms of exhibition. The 'real' withdraws behind an aesthetic carapace which conceals the increasing remoteness and privacy of later medieval habits of devotion.

There are, of course, dangers in this new 'holism', not least in reconstructing a coherence that did not exist, or in reading a set of conscious intentions and 'programmes' into what were, in reality, the chance accumulations of history.[83] But the merits of an 'integrated' conception hardly need underlining. Besides rescuing scholarship from the fragmentation of media-based specialization, it reminds us that churches were settings for diversified rituals with social, political and religious dimensions, and that the art forms which the church brought together celebrate the variety and complexity of medieval creativity, not its obedience to some uniform principle. One recent study applies this holistic technique beyond a single building to a whole class of architecture: Johannes Tripps's examination of the 'theatrical imagery' (*handelnde Bildwerk*) of Gothic churches – those moveable Palm Sunday Christs, or sculptures of angels or the Virgin of the Assumption, that were wheeled through the late Gothic church, or dropped from its vaults, in a liturgical re-enactment of biblical narrative that transformed the whole church into a living theatre.[84]

Regional and National Studies

Frankl's pan-European vision depended on the mastery of a body of regional and national studies of Gothic architecture, but his internationalist approach quite properly pointed to the persistent dangers of post- nineteenth-century nationalism, with its search for ethnic identity and its tendency to identify artistic 'schools' around modern political boundaries. Gothic architecture raises special problems for the sub-discipline of 'artistic geography'. A pan-European phenomenon, its identity was defined as much by ideals of family, estate, class, city and religion as by ethnic or national boundaries. It often served a multi-ethnic population, and benefited from a patronage that was international, or at least para-regional, in its outlook. The dissonances between modern political boundaries and real *Kunstlandschaften* are especially sharp in the territories of 'Central Europe'. A recent study of towns in 'medieval Hungary' ignores the thriving settlements of Transylvania, presumably because that Hungarian province is now part of Romania.[85] The latest general survey of Gothic architecture in Austria confines its consideration of Hapsburg patronage to the modern boundaries of the Austrian Republic, yet many of the most important Gothic buildings begun in the fourteenth century under Hapsburg initiative are to be found in modern-day Switzerland and south-west Germany, buildings whose connexions with their 'Austrian' counterparts would repay close examination.[85A] The problem is particularly acute for the 'artistic geography' of medieval Poland. The recent magisterial survey of Gothic architecture in Poland, *Architektura Gotycka w Polsce*, has to accept the modern Oder–Neisse line as the western boundary of the nation state, at the same time admitting that it has nothing to do with the real cultural situation along the Oder in the later Middle Ages, where Germans and Poles shared their churches and freely moved across modern boundaries.[86] This is not to insist that modern regions, especially when loosely defined, can not correspond to distinct cultural entities in the Middle Ages. Thus Recht's important book on the Gothic of the Upper Rhine neatly unfolds around the dominating influence of the cathedral of Strasbourg, while Branner's pioneering study of Burgundian Gothic architecture examines a constellation of art-historical influences – from the counts of Nevers and the abbots of Cluny to the counts of Burgundy and Champagne – which happen to coincide in and around the modern territory of Burgundy.[87] Even those regional inventories which have no pretensions to relate to medieval polit-

ical entities, such as the ongoing series of *Les Monuments de la France gothique* (under the direction of Anne Prache), or the long-standing *Congrès Archéologiques*, provide an invaluable record of the monuments, and reveal distinctly 'local' styles of architecture. Particularly informative are those studies which trace the transformations of style from one region to another, and the creation of a new *Kunstlandschaft*, in a context foreign to the ambience of the parent style. In this respect, Christian Freigang's monumental study of the fortunes of Parisian Rayonnant in the south of France in the second half of the thirteenth century is a model for any student wishing to understand, not only the migration of forms, but the multiple factors – financial, ideological, personal – which shaped their reception.[88] At a time when the idea of the marginal is enjoying exceptional critical attention, Freigang's study, and Binski's examination of Parisian influence at Westminster Abbey,[89] have been important in questioning an older, Parisian-centred conception of thirteenth-century Gothic, advanced in the post-war years by Branner and Bony.[90] Instead of a centralized Parisian patronage, often called a 'court style', imposing its architectural and political value system on the 'courts' of western Europe, Freigang and Binski paint a more fragmented picture, where local imperatives guarentee a rich, sometimes ambiguous, diversity of forms and meanings.

As far as national surveys are concerned, there is no question that the rise of Gothic in the thirteenth and fourteenth centuries – especially in England and France – did coincide with the emergence of nation states and their centralized apparatuses of government. Indeed, centralized and permanent architectural institutions – 'offices of works' – grew directly out of centralized organs of government, and both worked hand in hand. Jean Bony's analysis of the English Decorated style, and John Harvey's studies of the English Perpendicular, both in terms of 'court' styles developed first in metropolitan circles and then imposed on the country at large, point, therefore, to real parallels between national institutions and stylistic diffusion, despite the problems implicit in the unitary notion of a 'court' and the tendency to oversimplify the exchanges with the 'provinces'.[91] It is obvious that the correspondences between 'court style' and 'national style' cannot be pressed too far, especially when – as Bony showed – the English Decorated, with its roots in a London court milieu, emerged later in the fourteenth century as a major inspiration for continental Late Gothic. By elevating the Decorated to the status of fountainhead for the Late Gothic of France and Germany, Bony transferred the paradigm of French thirteenth-century cultural hegemony to fourteenth-century England, and re-arranged the conceptual boundaries of national and Late Gothic styles. 'German' Gothic, corresponding as it does to no single political entity, presents a more delicate problem of definition, but Nussbaum's exemplary study of Gothic architecture in the Empire sensibly sets his subject in the context, not of a fictitious medieval 'Germany', nor even of the Holy Roman Empire, but of the integrating forces of Christian culture.[92] Medieval 'France' is also an anachronism needing careful definition. Bony's magisterial vision of French Gothic in the twelfth and thirteenth centuries by-passed the problem of historical geography by ignoring the political, the institutional and even the theological; it centred around the 'accidents' of the masons' choice and invention, and the exhilarating demands of modernity. French Gothic, for Bony (as it was for Frankl), was a progressive style, a style of the avant-garde, but it was also a laboratory of diverse ideas, all of which Bony lucidly organized into trends and movements. Here precisely was that sense of experiment, of the unexpected mutation of the eccentric into the orthodox, and *vice versa*, which Frankl's unitary system had levelled away. In its eloquent analysis of architectural style as a set of aesthetically expressive forms, Bony's book has never been surpassed.[93]

The 'Material Picture': Techniques, Production and Structure

The material hinterland of the Gothic cathedral, the substructure rather than the superstructure of the Gothic style, has been the object of intense research for over a quarter of a century. The growth of neo-Marxism in Germany in the 1970s found the material culture of the lodge and the social conflicts of the building site a welcome antidote to the idealist *Kunstwissenschaft* of the pre-war period and the positivist monographs of the 1950s and 1960s. Martin Warnke reconstructed a 'sociology' of medieval architecture from the primary sources – in which the great church and its liturgies were seen not, as Frankl envisaged them, as the realization of an inner unity, but as the result of a hard-won consensus between conflicting social groups, joining forces to create a building which aesthetically transcended the interests of any one faction.[94] The mechanics of this cooperation, as revealed in the organization of the building site, the financing of the structure, the responsibilities of clerical patron and lay architect, and the logistics of the workforce, is the subject of Wolfgang Schöller's formidable study on the legal organization of cathedral building, with special reference to Germany and France.[95] Schöller's argument had no ideological thrust, but Barbara Abou-el-Haj applied Warnke's dialectical sociology to the building history of Reims cathedral and concluded that the process of cathedral building may have created a temporary consensus, but it also broke it. The higher clergy of some of the High Gothic cathedrals of northern France provoked revolt from their citizens by their exorbitant taxation for building funds and their ruthless suppression of urban liberties.[96] In the particular case of Chartres, Jane Welch Williams argued that the cathedral, contrary to all appearances and assumptions, was not the product of social harmony between burgher and bishop; it took shape against a background of anti-clericalism and intense urban strife. Its famous 'trade windows', supposedly donated by the guilds of Chartres, most probably owe their existence to the cathedral chapter, who manipulated their subject matter in order to stress the duty of the new commercial classes to make offerings in money and kind to the cathedral. In portraying an ideal Christian society uniting cleric and citizen, and at the same time concealing real social antagonisms, the windows of Chartres are, in the literally Marxist sense, 'ideological' (promoting false consciousness).[97] The financial infrastructure of Gothic architecture was also the subject of Henry Kraus's vivid study of European cathedrals, though here he laboured under the old illusion that the bourgeoisie were principal contributors to cathedral construction. In fact, the vast agricultural wealth of northern France, which he rightly saw as the motor for the upsurge of cathedral building, was controlled largely by an ecclesiastical aristocracy of bishops and their chapters. The cathedrals were, in most senses, the children of the clergy.[98]

These Marxist re-evaluations of the 'spiritual cathedral' went hand in hand with a Marxist examination of the methods of cathedral production. Dieter Kimpel, in a series of important articles on the building of Amiens cathedral, saw a radical change taking place in the cathedral workshops of the early thirteenth century in techniques of stone-cutting and assemblage – productive changes which altered the actual appearance of the finished building. New methods of mass-producing cut stone in the quarry and lodge, and of storing it in the lodge over the winter months, not only made construction cheaper and quicker, but changed the appearance of the interior. By separating the production and the installation of the cut stone (that is the stone 'skeleton' of the cathedral – its shafts, responds, ribs and arches) from the cutting and assembling of the 'filler' walls, the 'skeletal' quality of Gothic, particularly in the early Rayonnant style, became a factor that was built into its making. The increasingly delicate armatures of thirteenth-century French Gothic proceeded, therefore, not just from the aesthetic preferences of the architect and patron, but from new techniques of production.[99] Kimpel also pointed to Amiens as the earliest instance of the extensive use of stones of standardized size and shape. Bony, however, demonstrated that such procedures have (an admittedly rare) precedent in the late eleventh century, in the standardized stone blocks making up the incised cylindrical piers at Durham.[100]

The role of the architect in Gothic design is a field less prone to ideological argument. The patient archival researches of such scholars (for the British Isles) as John Harvey and Howard Colvin have revealed a wealth of information about the careers of architects and the high value put on their skill and expertise.[101] In the light of that massive evidence, few would now follow John James's eccentric claim that Chartres, and other High Gothic cathedrals, were not designed by architects, – i.e., a single controlling intelligence – but by bands of wandering 'contractors'. Nor would they subscribe to his view that the church was an *ad hoc* amalgam of 'campaigns', in which the 'contractors' periodically returned to the same site and added their contributions, without regard to an overall design.[102] In his demotion of the architect, James may have (unintentionally) added colour to the notion of the 'death of the artist' fashionable in post-structuralist circles in the 1970s and 80s, but no serious scholar of the masons' lodge doubted the importance of the master mason as the guiding intelligence of the work. What interested them was *how* the architect conceived and executed the building: his tools, his training, his uses of geometry. At the High Gothic end of the picture the creative talents of Villard de Honnecourt and his famous portfolio were examined in minute detail and found wanting. Villard, it is now recognised, was not an architect but a mysterious amateur (perhaps a metalworker?), an admirer of the mechanics of architecture and its sister arts.[103] At the other end of our period, the various 'treatises' by German Late Gothic architects, such as Lorenz Lechler and Matthäus Roritzer, provide rich insights into the mason's craft, explored first by Paul Booz, and then, more fully, by Ulrich Coenen and Lon Shelby.[104] Shelby's familiarity with the German manuals allowed him to draw a crucial distinction between the Euclidean geometry of the schoolroom and the 'constructive' and purely practical geometry of the mason's lodge, and thus to undermine ambitious attempts to promote the architect to the status of intellectual.[105] In the absence of the forthcoming publication of Peter Kidson's monumental study of medieval masonic geometry, the most ambitious account of geometry and numbers in medieval architecture still remains the extensive articles by Hecht.[106] Primary evidence for the master masons' geometrical skill comes from drawings, some deriving from the Reims workshop in the thirteenth century, published by Branner and Murray,[107] but most connected to the German lodges of Strasbourg, Ulm and Vienna. The two latter collections have been published by Koepf,[108] and much of the Strasbourg material by Recht.[109] Meanwhile, Pause has devoted a long study to architectural drawing in Germany[110] and Bucher published drawings by Hans Böblinger, though his projected volumes on all the German manuals have not so far materialized.[111] In Italy, the architectural drawing showed more 'painterly' characteristics, and Middeldorf-Kosegarten has assessed the possible uses of such drawings as those at Siena and Orvieto in the peculiarly Italian mode of architectural competition, as well as pointing to their status as visual documents having a semi-legal force.[112] If the architect stamped his personal qualities on the drawing he may also have revealed himself in the templates for moulded stonework that he gave to his masons. To this Morellian world of obscure but significant detail Richard Morris has devoted a lifetime of study, assembling at Warwick University an archive of continental and English profiles, and building up a database of evidence vital for the identification, if not of individual architects, then of groups or 'schools' of masons.[113]

The architect's skill depended on the reliability of his tools and the quality of his materials. Shelby contributed an important paper on masons' instruments,[114] and Chapelet and Benoit's collection of studies on the use of stone and metal in medieval building indicates the recent strength of interest in a subject that attracts a variety of disciplines, from ethnography to metallurgy.[115] The vital importance of quarries, not just for good building stone, but as training grounds for masons and masonic factions, is the subject of much of Evelyn Welch's recent analysis of Milan cathedral.[116] Many of these issues, from building organization to planning and construction, are discussed in detail in Binding's authoritative compendium on the building trade in the Middle Ages.[117] None of these works, however, discuss the structural behaviour of medieval buildings and its impact on design. The statics of the great cathedrals has been a bone of contention between 'rationalists' and 'anti-rationalists' for over a century, and the subject of a long-standing scholarly cooperation between art historians, architects and structural engineers. Fitchen's classic study

of vault construction, which appeared in 1961, remains unsuperseded,[118] but there was still much work to be done on the actual statics of the Gothic structure. Most of the running in this field has been made by two scholars, both of whom are structural engineers: Jacques Heyman, who developed a theory of 'hinging' in relation to Gothic structures, and who plotted their stress patterns mathematically, and Robert Mark, who used photo-elastic model analysis to reveal strain patterns in models of cross-sections of cathedrals under simulated loading.[119] Intriguing though their conclusions are, especially in their vindication of nineteenth-century intuitions about the structural behaviour of the cathedrals, their precise analysis of force patterns in no way corresponds to the rough-and-ready knowledge of statics possessed even by the best Gothic engineers; and their mistaken diagnoses of the causes of structural collapse in certain medieval buildings, such as Beauvais, shows that a close examination of cracks and repairs in the building itself is sometimes more revealing than a 'scientific' reconstruction of stress patterns.[120]

The sheer diversity of these 'technical' and 'material' problems, and their interdisciplinary overlaps, pose serious challenges to any attempt at synthesis. One solution is a multi-author volume, such as the stimulating and well-illustrated collection of essays assembled by Roland Recht.[121] Another, less likely, option is to find a scholar with an equal familiarity with art history, mathematics, physics and chemistry. In Werner Müller's formidable study of Gothic building technology, many of the issues raised in this section – the uses of geometry and of drawing, the manufacture of the building parts and the technical problems of structure – are discussed with the insight of a scientist (a chemist) and the knowledge of an architectural historian.[122]

Meaning and Milieu

The *Gesamtkunstwerk* of the cathedral has made it particularly susceptible to symbolic reading, especially of a theological kind. Erwin Panofsky's correlation between the guiding principles of High Gothic and the 'mental habits' of the scholastic theologian, represents, with Frankl's *Gothic Architecture*, one of the last attempts of Hegelian cultural history to translate 'style' into 'mind' and to trace the theological implications of the cathedral back to a single unifying force at the centre of medieval culture.[123] Hans Sedlmayr's sensational book on the Gothic cathedral, published in 1950, came from the same intellectual milieu – the *Geistesgeschichte* of Max Dvořák and the *Strukturforschung* school in Vienna, with its belief in the power of 'form symbols', of style and composition, to convey the essence of a culture.[124] One of Sedlmayr's more influential insights was his suggestion that the Gothic cathedral was a literal copy of the image of the Heavenly Jerusalem as described in the Book of Revelations, largely because of the dominant luminosity of its stained glass. This focused his attention on Suger's choir at Saint-Denis, where Panofsky had advanced his persuasive theory that the final form of the choir was indebted to Abbot Suger's infatuation with the 'light metaphysics' of Dionysius the Pseudo-Areopagite.[124A] Here, instead of the vague parallels of Hegelian *Geistesgeschichte*, was a convincing literary and theological source for what was seen as the essence of the Gothic style – its luminosity and (springing from it) its lightness of structure. At a stroke, neo-platonism replaced the rib vault in the genesis of Gothic architecture; the driving force of Gothic could now be found, not in triumphs of structural engineering, but in the direct translation of theology into architecture. Not surprisingly, much of the iconography of Gothic architecture in the aftermath of Sedlmayr's and Panofsky's work concentrated on Saint-Denis. Otto von Simson's erudite study used Suger's choir as the foundation for his conception of Gothic as a marriage of 'Pseudo-Dionysian light metaphysics' and the harmonic ratios of musical cosmology.[125] And Saint-Denis continues to be a magnet for explanations of Gothic as the embodiment of neo-platonic mysteries, in both American[126] and German[127] research. Recent contributions by a number of German scholars have pointed to Suger's liturgy of the consecration as critical evidence for the abbot's overriding concerns for neo-platonic resonance and biblical symbolism in his new choir.[128] But this equation of Gothic light with Dionysian light has not gone unchallenged. Martin Gosebruch questioned it in his review of Sedlmayr's book in 1950,[129] and in the 1980s it came under sustained attack. Martin Büchsel proposed a more comprehensive reading of the Gothic church as *Ecclesia universalis* rather than as the Heavenly Jerusalem and pointed to the traditional, non-Dionysian, sources for Suger's symbolism.[130] Peter Kidson denied the influence of the Pseudo-Dionysius in any specific sense on Suger or on his choir, and stressed the pragmatic and propagandist nature of the abbot's patronage,[131] as well as the craftsmanlike contribution of the architect to the design. His 'despiritualized' and anti-intellectual picture of Suger is vividly accentuated in Grant's recent biography.[132]

The concentration on Saint-Denis and neo-platonic light symbolism, begun by Panofsky and reinforced by Sedlmayr and von Simson, set a narrow agenda for the 'iconography' of Gothic in the post-war years. An escape from its theological straightjacket was provided by Marxist and Marxist-influenced historians in Germany in the 1970s and 80s, who revived Richard Krautheimer's and Günter Bandmann's suggestive notion of the architectural 'copy'. In his classic article of 1942, Krautheimer offered iconographers of architecture the idea of the 'copy' as a vital method for unlocking meaning within form.[133] By copying certain venerable archetypal structures, patrons could surround their own buildings with the associations and prestige of the original. The 'copy' need not be exact; just enough of the original – its general shape or its liturgical disposition – would trigger the appropriate response. By linking symbolism with the perceptions of the medieval onlooker, Krautheimer found a way of understanding the loose associations between form and meaning in the Middle Ages, and relating meaning to tradition and patronal intention. Though Krautheimer confined himself to early medieval architecture, his notion was rich in possible applications to later periods. It struck at the whole idea of Gothic as an avant-garde achievement shaped largely by architects, and presented instead a potential view of Gothic as a patron's style, dependent on tradition, locality

and history. Hans-Joachim Kunst adapted it to Marxist social history via his theory of 'architectural quotation'. Kunst posited a dialectical relationship between a building's use of novel (modern) forms and its reliance on meaningful 'quoted' forms, and he interpreted those quoted forms in terms of political rivalries and institutional power struggles, particularly in the High Gothic cathedral of Reims.[134] In his stimulating study of friars' architecture, Wolfgang Schenkluhn used this method to correlate the rivalries between Dominicans and Franciscans, with their self-consciously different modes of architectural design.[135] In Kimpel and Suckale's magisterial history of French Gothic architecture the idea of architecture as a socio-political language becomes a vital tool in embedding Gothic in its historical milieu – thus rescuing the whole subject from Jean Bony's beguiling formalism. The contrast in method between the two books, appearing within two years of each other, is instructive. Where Bony sees his buildings as autonomous forms, freed from the trivial constraints of politics, economics, and function, subject only to the creative and progressive genius of their architects, Kimpel and Suckale present a more traditional Gothic, responding to the needs of its patrons and anchored in its specific political, economic and social conditions.[136] This historical reading is largely dependent on the authors' 'iconographic' conception of Gothic as a language. By copying the idioms of a significant model, patrons, through their buildings, can signal an affiliation with a church province, or a religious order, or symbolically 'appropriate' and supersede the earlier forms of churches belonging to rival institutions. There was nothing intrinsically new in this method, though it tallied with the popularity of semiotics in the 1970s and 1980s and the belief that written and spoken language offered an explanatory model for all systems of communication, including the non-mimetic arts of music and architecture.[137] What gave it such resonance was its intelligent application to a style at once familiar and historically complex.

Particularly susceptible to these semiotic approaches are the strongly 'ideological' architectures of the reforming orders: the Cistercians and the friars. Here the classical notion of architectural 'decorum', the suitability of forms to the aims and ideals of the institution, is critical. Peter Draper has applied it to good effect, not primarily to monastic architecture, but to the diversity of styles employed by the English cathedrals of the early thirteenth century. The diversity, he argues, does not derive solely from the free invention of the architect and the variety of his models; it is the result of the patron's conscious choice of a style or 'manner' for ideological reasons.[138] Peter Kurmann and Dethard von Winterfeld argued for similar restrictions on the architect's range of choice in their analysis of the thirteenth-century master mason, Gautier de Varinfroy. His ability to alter his style to fit the occasion of the commission suggests that medieval architects were able to marry 'modes of design' to the demands of the building type or the patron.[139] I argue for a similar use of decorum in Charles IV's interventions in Prague Cathedral.[140] But it is in the controlling architectural policies of the reforming orders that programmatic meanings are most obviously allied to architectural form. Peter Fergusson has used Krautheimer's model of 'the copy' to illuminate the Italian, specifically Roman, connexions in early Cistercian architecture in England.[141] Schenkluhn's iconographical analysis of the friars' architecture in Europe uncovers the programmatic debt to the Cistercians, but also, and more surprisingly, reveals a conscious alliance with Parisian Rayonnant, an alliance which underlines the character of the new orders as theological as well as demotic.[142] The interest in womens' studies in the last twenty years – an interest which has transformed our conception of late medieval devotional art – has rarely penetrated into the largely 'masculine' world of the masons' yard and the schoolroom. But Caroline Bruzelius's investigations of womens' monastic architecture, particularly of the Clarissan order in Naples, raise intriguing questions about the relationship between architecture and specifically female religious practice. What were the economic circumstances of the convents, and how did these effect the environments in which the nuns lived? How did their devotional practices differ from their male counterparts, and are these differences reflected in architectural form? Most importantly, how did the strict demands for female enclosure effect the decoration of their churches, and their spatial divisions?[143] Many of these questions have been answered in Hamburger's perceptive study of art, architecture and devotional life in nunneries in the Empire.[144]

The functional and ideological imperatives of the reformed orders underline how easily an 'iconographical' analysis of medieval architecture moves between 'principles' and 'programmes' on the one hand, and liturgy and function on the other. Banished for over a century to the remoter fringes of ecclesiology, liturgy – meaning, in the broadest sense, the ritual of the church's services and any other form of corporate or public worship – is now coming into its own as a critical link between precept and performance, ideology and form. Recent developments in the analysis of medieval imagery and its relationship to changes in the nature of the Mass, especially around the doctrine of transubstantiation, have focused attention on the architectural setting of the Mass and its audiences;[145] and architectural historians are beginning to locate that public-orientated imagery in the whole liturgical topography of the church. In England, Draper's liturgical analyses of Durham, Ely, Wells and Salisbury have thrown new light on spatial enclosure and applied decoration, as well as bringing the empty shell of the architecture alive as the liturgical theatre for Masses, processions and relic cults.[146] In Germany, Renate Kroos has reconstructed the liturgies of Bamberg, Cologne and Magdeburg Cathedrals, while Tripps's analysis of theatrical imagery in a different class of church, the Late Gothic German parish and collegiate church, connects popular liturgies and late medieval lay devotion with a wealth of surviving architectural imagery.[147] Sturgis's unpublished work on the liturgy of the Early and High Gothic cathedrals in France serves, however, as a warning to the liturgical enthusiasts not to claim too much for function in the shaping of the great church. There is little evidence, he argues, that liturgical rites influenced the forms of architecture, and where ordinals survive it is clear that the liturgy adapted itself to the demands of the architecture and not vice versa.[148] Sturgis's reservations are timely, but to deny that liturgy played a role in the shaping of architectural space, or in architectural decoration, or, finally, in the authentic experience of the medieval building as a symbolic and aesthetic whole, would be to take a very narrow view of architecture. The real impediments to liturgical research are not these methodological reservations, but an ignorance brought on by a lack of sources. We cannot always reconstruct liturgical rites, nor situate them in the surviving buildings. Medieval churches, now denuded of their original altars, screens and fittings, give few clues as to their real day-to-day functions.

The Problem of Secular Architecture

Frankl was not alone in dismissing secular architecture from a developmental history of Gothic. The Middle Ages itself quite clearly placed church architecture at a higher level than all other kinds of building, and as if in obedience to that ruling, the historiography of Gothic has kept the genres separate ever since. Most surveys on Gothic architecture include a perfunctory section at the end of the text on secular buildings; while scholars who specialize in the history of castles or palaces hardly mention churches at all. Indeed, each field has its own academic journals and its own conference structures. But there is a growing disquiet at the artificiality of this division. On all sides, from historians of vernacular architecture to specialists in the history of urbanism and chivalry, it is becoming clear that secular and sacred overlapped at almost every level of medieval art and architecture.[149] How else can we explain a building as bizarre as Karlstein Castle in Bohemia, except in terms of sacro-political meanings?[150] How can we assess the 'spiritual' importance of Florence, Orvieto or Siena Cathedrals without recognizing their centrality in the celebration of republican virtue and civic independence? It is, significantly, in the city-states of Trecento Italy that some of the most important advances have been made in the dissolution of the sacred–secular barrier. Building on Braunfels's classic exposition of the Florentine city as a *Gesamtkunstwerk*,[151] a number of recent studies have examined the overlaps of personal piety, group identity and communal patronage in Florence,[152] Siena[153] and Milan.[154] Chiara Frugoni's classic work on images of urban experience, though not touching directly on architectural history, has given art historians an invaluable insight into the changing concepts of the city in Italy from Antiquity to the Renaissance, concepts which might help to re-define the cultural history of its architecture.[155] And in a series of distinguished publications, Marvin Trachtenberg has examined the urban planning of Florence as if it were a theatre of memory. Florence emerges as a totality – a theatrical ensemble, a kind of urban *mise-en-scène* – in which civic virtues and local pieties reinforce each other in a controlled kinetic experience.[156]

While the history of towns and 'urbanism' flourishes in France and Germany, no such ambitious attempts at interdisciplinary analysis have so far materialized for cities north of the Alps. But in a pioneering article, André Mussat examined the financial and physical relations between the French cathedrals and their growing cities,[157] and many of the approaches sketched there were fleshed out in

Erlande-Brandenburg's book on the social 'dynamics' of the cathedral.[158] Erlande-Brandenburg collects a wealth of miscellaneous material on the secular and sacred topography of the (largely French) city from the early to the late Middle Ages, with special insights into the relations between the city as a whole and what he calls the 'sacred city' – the semi-independent enclave of the cathedral.

The castle and its late medieval transformation into the 'castle-palace' has fared no better than the city in terms of inclusive art history. The military aspects of castles seem always to have kept them separate from churches in the minds of the historian. Some bizarre hybrids, such as Charles IV's Karlstein Castle[159] or the great headquarters of the Teutonic Knights at Marienburg,[160] have attracted the kind of 'symbolic' and aesthetic reading usually given to cathedrals. But even the papal palace at Avignon, ostensibly the most 'ecclesiastical' of these giant fourteenth-century enterprises, has resisted any systematic discussion of its sacred character. In this reluctance to cross the boundaries of architectural genres, Uwe Albrecht's work is a welcome exception. His broad syntheses of French palace architecture in the later Middle Ages, and his more recent examination of the whole history of the castle-as-residence in northern Europe, promise much, since they examine palace architecture as an economic, legal and social phenomenon, and they submit the elaborate late fourteenth-century palaces of the French royal family to the same kind of symbolic analysis as we would a great church. There is every justification for this trespass of method, for not only did the architects of Charles V and his brothers apply ecclesiastical Rayonnant to secular architecture with a skill and latitude never seen before; their patrons gave to palace building a numinous authority hitherto associated only with churches. In these fourteenth-century palaces, Albrecht reminds us, the 'religion of kingship' found its finest secular expression.[161]

CONCLUSION

Each age builds its own Gothic cathedral. Frankl's was appropriately 'architectural' – it structured its material around a carefully contrived theoretical armature, refined over many years, and offering – at least to him and other systematizers – an exhilarating glimpse of total history. Krautheimer remembers Frankl as a visionary, telling his pupils, only half in jest, that he wanted to find out 'how the Good Lord made all this'.[162] As a true Hegelian, Frankl needed to survey the apparently God-given aspects of a culture from one privileged centre. Such dreams of omniscience now seem almost touchingly over confident in a 'post-modern' world of relative values and uncertain identities. They convey something of the panoptic sensibility of the nineteenth-century museum or the library. In his espousal of theory Frankl has found no successor, at least in the field of medieval architecture. Architectural historians of the 1950s and 60s, schooled in the positivist optimism of the post-war years, were suspicious of the generalities of theory; they even shied away from the demands of the great synoptic survey. 'One good monograph' a Berlin professor assured

me in the 1970s, 'is worth a dozen general stylistic histories'. More recently, postmodernist relativism and the notion of intellectual pluralism have called into question the whole idea of an 'objective' and 'scientific' truth as the aim of historical inquiry. In this uncertain climate, where any theoretical system clamours to be considered just as valid as any other, it is hardly surprising that historians have retreated into the rich, pluralistic particularities of the cathedral. Where art history in the last twenty years has been particularly fertile in advancing broader explanations of 'meaning and mind' – post-structuralist critical theory, feminism, visual semiotics, notions of audience and reception, the central and the marginal – the beneficiary has been medieval imagery, with all its semiotic implications, not the nonmimetic language of architecture.

But art history is more than a science of singularities, particularly when it confronts a phenomenon as culturally resonant as Gothic architecture. Gothic, like any other style, may be understood as a number of specific conjunctures and processes; but it also presents us with large scale problems of historical interpretation. Only two kinds of broad explanatory system have come anywhere near posing a theoretical alternative to Frankl's idea of Gothic. The first was the Frankfurt- and Marburg-based Marxist social history of the 1970s, with its critique of the 'spiritual' cathedral and its stress on social conflict and political authority. The failure of this approach to come to terms with the *primary* concerns of medieval religion, and its reluctance to acknowledge the proper relations between religious practice and social regulation, has left this Marxist position looking one-sided and doctrinaire.

The second, more pragmatic standpoint – one passionately advocated by Popper and Gombrich – entails shifting our gaze from holistic 'laws' and general processes to questions of individual artistic choice. Behind this strategy lies the belief in the artist or architect as a stable individual self, consciously acting as an independent agent. This assumption of the validity of artistic intention was seriously questioned in literary circles in the 1970s and 80s, and met with a sympathetic response from art historians eager to demolish the myth of the artist/architect-as-hero.[163] But to deny some irreducible core of individual purposeful rationality in artistic creation, to disregard areas of choice for which the artist/architect is solely responsible, now seems like pretentious artifice. Historical and common sense recognize a functional relation between makers and their making.[164] What was needed was a more searching definition of artistic intention, one which avoided the pitfalls of romantic individualism and speculative psychology. For Michael Baxandall, the process of rationality and reflection which we call artistic intention can be inferred by re-enacting, not so much the narrative of how the architect came to his design (that will remain opaque) but the circumstances out of which the design grew and the factors which were causally involved in its final shape.[165] How well this more refined idea of artistic intention can work for a general understanding of Gothic is demonstrated by Christopher Wilson's recent study of the Gothic cathedral. Wilson's masterly narrative unfolds according to at least one general rule: to retrieve 'some of the creative processes [of cathedral architects] through reconstructing the situations of constraint and choice in which they worked'. Each major design is seen as 'an exercise in aesthetic and practical problem-solving'.[166] This form of explanation understands a finished piece of work by reconstructing a purposiveness or intention in it, and as such it deals – often illuminatingly – with its *causal* registers; it reconstructs 'reflective consciousness' – processes of thought. But Baxandall and Wilson would be the first to insist that such a way of thinking about objects is not *the* single proper way to look at works of art; there are many proper ways which in normal perception we combine.[167] The manifest diversities of the Gothic appeal to a whole range of perceptive concepts which go beyond reflective consciousness: to a comparative register of objects that may have no causal connexion with the work in hand (parallel or contrasting solutions); to an audience who were not involved in its making; to a set of functions or purposes which were irrelevant to the aesthetic solution, and to a string of consequences unseen in the original act of creativity.

It is here, in this extended list of approaches to the phenomenon of Gothic, that the sheer comprehensiveness and subtlety of Frankl's system comes into its own. Pevsner, in his forward to the first edition, praised him as 'one of the giants of German *Kunstwissenschaft* (literally, the 'science of art'), and the emphasis here on 'science' unlocks much of Frankl's achievement. In his long section in *The Gothic* on 'The Study of Art as a Scientific Discipline', he identifies his intellectual mentors – Burckhardt, Riegl and especially Wölfflin – as the first to take the critical step towards an 'objective', 'scientific' and value-free art history. It was the stated direction of Frankl's own rigorous *Kunstwissenschaft*. He recognized, of course, that there is no such thing as a totally disinterested enquirer, and that no enquiry can be wholly bias-free. But he held firmly to the scientific assumption that some things are verifiably true and others are not, and that the aim of the scientific historian is to arrive at conclusions that are verifiable and justified. In the concluding pages of *The Gothic* he recognized Gothic architecture as just such an objective fact which would, with proper scientific investigation, gradually yield up its secrets. It is 'an objective phenomenon' which 'remains what it was and is, while our attempts to reach its core from one side after another gradually leads us closer and closer to the truth'.[168] Much of Frankl's life was devoted to the patient search for the 'core' of Gothic. It was a quest disciplined by scientific method: the accumulation over many years of empirical data, the classification of that information, and the wealth of inference drawn from it to establish unrestricted general statements of a law-like character, statements which throw light on Gothic as a whole. With the benefit of hindsight, it is easy to see the holes in Frankl's edifice; to test, against the facts of the architecture itself, and against more recent developments in art theory, the 'verifiability' of Frankl's laws. What we cannot do is to deny the rigour of Frankl's 'science', the transparency and single-mindedness of his method, and the colossal achievement that it represents.

When *Gothic Architecture* appeared in 1962 no one knew more than Frankl about the characteristics and idiosyncracies of actual Gothic buildings, taken across the whole of Europe (and this may still be true). His grasp of the raw material of the style was prodigious. Despite his deep emotional commitment to the aesthetic and spiritual qualities of Gothic, he could describe the most complex, and the most overwhelming buildings with the precision and clarity of a scientific report. Like a good scientist, Frankl also left himself open to scrutiny. There is nothing coy or obscure in the clarity with which, in the Introduction to *Gothic Architecture*, he lays out his theoretical categories, or, in Part Two of the book, the purposeful way in which he pursues those insights into the cultural history of the Gothic. Theory, for Frankl, was not private conjecture or loose prescriptive generalization, still less was it a 'metadiscipline' dedicated to philosophical abstraction. Theory offered him, in the strictly scientific and practical sense, a set of hypotheses at the service of a system of verification, a system which presumes a reciprocity between theory and fact.

The subtlety of Frankl's system lies precisely in that 'empirical reality' and its relations to our general inferences about style. When Frankl began his systematic study of the Gothic in the early 1940s he started, not with the buildings but with opinions about the buildings, and the result, twenty years later, was *The Gothic*, a monumental assemblage of comments and commentaries on Gothic from Suger to the middle of the last century. As we have seen, the project was part of his strategic quest for the general principles of Gothic, a search for the secret 'essence' of the style, embedded in its historiography. But in another sense Frankl's strategy implies a deep insight: that understanding architecture, and conveying what we think about architecture, are part of a single operation. Gothic does not come to us directly, as a 'pure' object of scrutiny, but through the filter of description, interpretation and emotional response. We do not explain architecture, we explain remarks about architecture – and every explanation of a thing includes or implies an elaborate description of it.[169] And it is the relationship between that description and the object itself, and of both to our inferences about its making, that constitutes a 'scientific' and 'verifiable' art history. Much of the value of *Gothic Architecture*, written while Frankl was finishing *The Gothic*, lies in its genesis in this rich and lively territory between architecture and concepts. For Frankl is constantly testing the reciprocal relationship between description, generalization and meaning on the one hand, and the actual buildings on the other. Description and concept can only work if they sharpen our insight in the presence of the building. Frankl handles all these areas of investigation, and their interrelations, with an authority and knowledge unmatched by any scholar of Gothic architecture before or since. The result is a heightened sense of the visual cogency of Gothic architecture and a profound understanding of its cultural context. No other synoptic survey of Gothic can match the wisdom of this indefatigable 'soldier of science'.

Editor's note to the first edition

PAUL FRANKL died in his 84th year on 30 January 1962. On 29 January he had closed the envelope which contained detailed comments on the sheets of plate proofs of this book. It is sad that a book in the progress of which he took so fanatic an interest should now have to come out as a memorial to him. He was – this can be said without hesitation – one of the giants of German *Kunstwissenschaft*. Never did he write a book or a paper without wanting to get at something more than facts. The essence of a style was what fascinated him from the beginning to the end. Five books stand out in his *œuvre* and they show the variety and yet the consistency of his work. He had been a pupil of Wölfflin at the time when Wölfflin published his *Die klassische Kunst* and worked on his *Grundbegriffe*, i.e. when he was engaged on definitions of the High Renaissance and then of Baroque in contrast to Renaissance. This is where Paul Frankl started from. In 1914, nearly fifty years ago and before the publication of Wölfflin's *Grundbegriffe*, he brought out his *Entwicklungsphasen der neueren Baukunst*, taking up, modifying, and further elucidating the contrasts between the Renaissance and the periods that followed and confining the investigation to architecture. Then in the years from the end of the First World War to 1926 he worked on the volume of Burger and Brinckmann's *Handbuch* dealing with the Romanesque style under comparable categories. The book is still the boldest synopsis of the style in existence. After this he felt ready to put on paper his categories, not only those so far demonstrated in his two masterly volumes. The result is the *System der Kunstwissenschaft*, published inauspiciously at Brno (outside Nazi Germany) in 1938 and little read. When he had left Germany and settled down at Princeton he went on working on a fourth *magnum opus: The Gothic; Literary Sources and Interpretations through Eight Centuries*. This nine-hundred-page history of what the Gothic style has meant to many writers in many countries came out very belatedly in 1960. Meanwhile I knew that he had intended to continue his Romanesque volume by a Gothic one and so, in 1947, I asked him to write the present book. It will, I hope, speak for itself as the work of a man of great scholarship, energy, and courage. That he was a perfectionist I can assure readers, and I want to place on record my gratitude to Mrs Jane B. Greene and Dr Weitzmann-Fiedler, who helped him (and me) through the perilous stages of interpretation and production. That he was also a most lovable man, the last chapters of this book at least will convey an inkling of.

THE subject of this volume is the meaning and the development of the Gothic style in medieval church architecture. Secular architecture will be touched on only in so far as it is dependent upon religious architecture. An account of the ways in which secular architecture created its own independent style would require a separate volume.

By style is meant a unity of *form* that is governed by a few basic principles. In this book these principles will be clarified by examples. The term style is applicable also where in a civilization meaning follows the same principles as architectural form. When we speak of art, we mean the particular interrelationship of form and meaning in which form becomes the symbol of meaning. So, in our particular case, the form of Gothic church architecture symbolizes the meaning of the civilization of the time.[1] In the second part of the book, something will be said about this, but the main subject of the first part is the history of the Gothic style, its birth, its development, and its ultimate perfection in the Late Gothic.

The consequence of this limitation in subject matter is that the choice of buildings to be discussed is largely restricted to those which represent the first appearance of each of the decisive forms and changes in form. No history of the Gothic style could analyse, or even enumerate, the many thousand buildings which exist or could be reconstructed. The selection that has been made here is designed as a guide. The literature that is quoted will lead the reader to buildings which are not mentioned, and to the controversies that surround them.

This book contains no discussion of the different interpretations of the Gothic style which have in the past supplanted each other, nor of those which, today, stand side by side, each with its own claim to indisputable truth. These are considered in another book, where the theories which are the basis of the present work are also more fully expounded.[2]

In planning this book I have tried to break away from the principles which characterize earlier books on the Gothic style. I have avoided setting up a standard for the style as a whole, such as Amiens Cathedral, so as not to give the idea that the value of every Gothic building is to be measured against this standard and that it is regrettable that this cathedral was not created simultaneously with the Gothic style, to be followed only by copies.

I have also tried not to overdo classifications. Since Thomas Rickman (1776–1841) analysed the structure of churches according to their significant members, and discussed each separately, this has been regarded as the only really scholarly method, because it is analytical and systematic. Indeed it is irreproachable. If, in historical research, we want a swift overall view of the development of porches alone, or buttresses, or plinths, or pinnacles alone – in short of any single member – then books based on clarification are very useful. However they do not give the history of the whole. They remain preliminary studies of the parts. An analysis of totalities leads to a grouping based on principles other than that of the classification of porches, windows, towers, etc. These members will appear in the chapter headings, but in their chronological sequence.

Thirdly, this book has avoided a division into chapters or groups of chapters, each dealing with a single country. This is another way of destroying the conception of a whole. When the reader has followed the history of the Gothic style in France right through to the last stages of the Flamboyant, he is expected, in a second group of chapters, to make a mental jump back to the earliest period, this time in England, and so on with each succeeding country. The Gothic style is a European phenomenon, and must be understood in its full breadth. An attempt to make a simultaneous survey of all the buildings erected at the same time leads to an advance by short steps in time over the entire field. This does not mean that national differences need be levelled out; on the contrary, in this way they may perhaps be more clearly visible.

In such an attempt it is natural that the emphasis should fall on those countries which proved themselves creative within the development of the Gothic style. There will be complaints of neglect from champions of various regions, but there are already enough monographs dealing with these. The present book cannot cover the entire field. I hope that, though it cannot offer *multa*, it may offer *multum*. The reason why the Gothic style in England is so briefly treated is that a separate volume is devoted to it within the Pelican History of Art.[3]

Fourthly, I have avoided threading together a series of monographs. In their own right, these make useful preliminary studies for a comprehensive history. In shortened form, in guide books, they are welcome to the traveller who requires a survey of the entire history of a building on the spot. But they are out of place in a history of style. The historian does not move in space: his aim is to move along the passage of time.

One of the tasks which particularly preoccupy the historian of art is to demonstrate the dependence of works of art on those that went before, and the influence of different regions or schools on one another. This approach to the problem is important and is a specifically historical one. What it must avoid, however, is giving the negative impression that there is nothing new under the sun. It has been rightly stressed that there is no such thing as passive influence; for those who are influenced always accept only what is in harmony with their nature, and out of it create something new. In this book the emphasis is laid on the ability to draw from the old a creative stimulus for the new. There are few periods in the history of art in which the logical sequence of the successive steps is so patent and so convincing. In this case, therefore, the historian can legitimately adopt a forward-looking position.

The central thread of this book is the logical process by which the changes from the Romanesque to the Gothic style, and those within the Gothic style until its fulfilment in the Late Gothic phase, developed from one basic principle. But this central thread acquires substance and value only when it is the core round which a rope is wound. By this I mean that it must be shown in conjunction with the creative wealth of the spirit of the Middle Ages.

The nature of the reader's response to the wonders of the Gothic style will depend entirely on his own aesthetic susceptibility. Whether he happens to love the Gothic style as a whole, to hate it, or to be indifferent to it; whether he happens to prefer one building, one national variation in style, or one phase, to another; all this is his own personal affair, as it is also in the case of the author. Historians often believe that they must educate their readers, and so they leaven their work with their own highly personal judgements. It betrays a lack of understanding on the part of an eminent historian when he cannot refrain from making disparaging remarks about flying buttresses, or from expressing a preference for churches designed on the basilican principle (i.e. with aisles and a clerestory) over hall-churches (i.e. with aisles of approximately the same height as the nave); or when he expresses the opinion that a certain aisle should have been wider or narrower. It betrays a lack of understanding of the development of the style also when he persists in regarding the Late Gothic as decadent, or when, even if he does not set up a single building as the absolute standard, he clings to the belief that a single school or a single nation is unsurpassable. Every nation has always striven for, and often reached, perfection in the purely *aesthetic* sense. But perfection in the all-round *artistic* sense – that is, the perfect symbolization of the spirit of an age in its style – is different. To the artist or architect these things are indispensable: from the historian they require the ability to judge, not according to his own tastes, but through the spirit of the generation for which a building or a part of a building was created.

Gothic buildings were created through the combined work of many men. In addition to the architects, stone-carvers with their sculpture and painters, especially glass-painters, contributed to them. Villard de Honnecourt's illustrated sketch book for the use of the members of his lodge gives the impression that he was capable of directing and possibly of executing both sculpture and painting. We know of other masters who designed buildings and themselves carved figures for them. On the other hand the glass-painters seem to have specialized exclusively in their own field. Without their sculpture and painting, the great cathe-drals, especially Chartres and Reims, are inconceivable. It is not the task of this book to discuss them: they will be dealt with in other volumes of the Pelican History of Art. Nor can decorative sculpture within the building, such as capitals and cornices, be fully treated here, though specialists like to use it in elucidating and demonstrating the history of any one building. Its development is closely linked with that of architecture. How far this is true of figure sculpture and stained glass as well will be touched on in the second part.

A period as long as that between Durham and Halle an der Saale, that is 1093–1530, requires division, not only into many small sections, but also into a few larger ones. I have followed the traditional divisions: Transitional, Early Gothic, High Gothic, and Late Gothic. Many positivists preach that a classification should be judged by the value of what it realizes in actual usefulness. It would be more proper to demand, not only that it be useful, but also that it correspond to the nature of the matter in question.

Many readers may demand a justification of the choice of the illustrations. One would of course like to show, in the illustrations, everything that is discussed in the text, but this is ruled out by restrictions of cost. One would like to take advantage of the opportunity to print as much as possible that has never yet been illustrated, but the reader will also expect to find things that have been published countless times elsewhere. So the selection remains a compromise, and the reader will ultimately have to turn to other illustrated books, because the fullest description cannot achieve what an illustration can convey at a glance, although of course everybody realizes that the finest illustration is no substitute for the impression produced by the original.

Finally, I should like to record my gratitude to the late Dr Aydelotte, who in admitted me to membership of the Institute for Advanced Study at Princeton, and to Dr Robert Oppenheimer, who has continued that membership; without them, after leaving Germany, I should not have had the opportunity to write this book. I also want to thank the editor, Professor Nikolaus Pevsner, for much assistance, particularly concerning English architecture, and Mr Dieter Pevsner for his translation of the German manuscript, a task which presented many difficulties.

To state once again the aim of this book: it is not a substitute for travel and the wealth of personal experience. It is a history – a view of things created, and more than that, an analysis of the essence of the Gothic style and of the ideas which inspired its development.

FRANCE & THE LOW COUNTRIES

Inset

- Bellefontaine
- Beauvais
- St Germer
- Clermont
- Soissons
- Cambronne-les- Bury Pierrefonds
- St Leu-d'Esserent Rhuis Morienval
- Royaumont Longpont
- Senlis Berzy-le-Sec
- Chars
- Pontoise Chaalis
- Mantes
- St Denis
- Poissy Meaux
- Paris
- Vaux-de-Cernay Voulton
- Provins
- Chartres
- Étampes

Map by András Bereznay

NORTH SEA

THE NETHERLANDS

Utrecht

s'Hertogenbosch

Antwerp

BELGIUM

Ypres Brussels Louvain
Tienen
Tournai Villers-la-Ville Liège
Aulne Orval
Avioth

Lucheux Solesmes
Abbeville Cambrai
Airaines
Amiens
Noyon Coucy Laon
St Martin-de-Boscherville Beauvais Braisne Reims
Verdun Metz
Senlis Pont-à-Mousson
Pontoise Chaalis L'Epine
Orbais Châlons-sur-Marne
Meaux Toul
Voulton Strasbourg
Provins St Nicolas-de-Port

Fécamp
Montivilliers Caudebec
Bernières-sur-Mer Rouen
Pont-Audemer
Bayeux Jumièges Louviers
Lessay Ouistreham
Creuilly Caen Evreux
Coutances Lisieux

Sées
Alençon Chartres
Étampes
Sens Troyes Clairvaux

Brou
Laval Le Mans Cléry Pontigny R. Seine Longuay
Auxerre Fontenay Morimond
Vendôme Vézelay
Mouliherne St Thibaut Dijon
Angers Tours Amboise Citeaux
Nantes Cormery Loches Bourges Meursault
St Jouin-de-Marne Nevers La Ferté
Airvault Noirlac
Poitiers

F R A N C E Cluny

Celles-sur-Belle
Ambierle
Aigueperse Lyons
Limoges Riom
Angoulême Clermont-Ferrand

B a y   o f □
B i s c a y

Brantôme La Chaise-Dieu
Périgueux

Bordeaux

Rodez
Moissac Villeneuve-lès-Avignon
Mézin R. Garonne Avignon
Albi St-Gilles Tarascon
Aigues-Mortes Arles Silvacone Le Thoronet
Bayonne Toulouse Lérins Is.
Marseilles

Carcassonne Narbonne
Fontfroide
Perpignan

M E D I T E R R A N E A N   S E A

R. Rhône

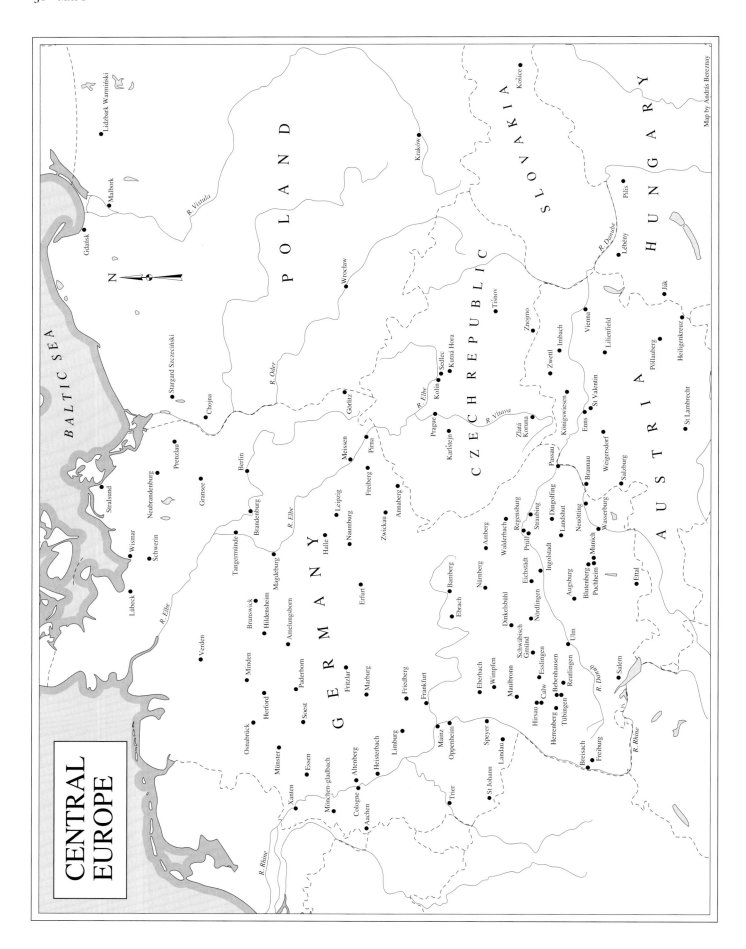

CENTRAL
EUROPE

Map by András Bereznay

BALTIC SEA

POLAND

GERMANY

CZECH REPUBLIC

SLOVAKIA

HUNGARY

AUSTRIA

R. Vistula

R. Oder

R. Elbe

R. Elbe

R. Rhine

R. Rhine

R. Danube

R. Vltava

R. Danube

N

Lidzbark Warmiński

Malbork

Gdańsk

Kraków

Wrocław

Tišnov

Košice

Pilis

Znojmo

Lébény

Ják

Vienna

Imbach

Lilienfield

Pöllauberg

Heiligenkreuz

Zwettl

St Valentin

St Lambrecht

Königswiesen

Enns

Stargard Szczeciński

Chojna

Görlitz

Kolín
Sedlec
Kutná Hora

Prague
Karlštejn

Zlatá
Koruna

Passau

Braunau

Weigersdorf

Salzburg

Wasserburg

Neuötting

Prenzlau

Berlin

Meissen

Pirna

Neubrandenburg

Gransee

Stralsund

Wismar
Schwerin

Brandenburg

Leipzig

Freiberg

Annaberg

Naumburg

Zwickau

Tangermünde

Magdeburg

Halle

Erfurt

Bamberg

Nürnberg

Amberg

Walderbach
Regensburg

Prüll
Straubing

Dingolfing

Landshut

Ingolstadt

Eichstädt

Nördlingen

Augsburg

Blutenberg
Puchheim

Munich

Ettal

Lübeck

Verden

Brunswick
Hildensheim

Amelungsborn

Minden

Paderborn

Fritzlar

Marburg

Friedberg

Frankfurt

Ebrach

Dinkelsbühl

Schwäbisch
Gmünd

Esslingen

Ulm

Salem

Osnabrück

Herford

Soest

Limburg

Heisterbach

Mainz

Oppenheim

Eberbach

Wimpfen

Maulbronn

Hirsau
Calw
Herrenberg
Bebenhausen
Tübingen Reutlingen

Breisach
Freiburg

Münster

Essen

Mönchen-
gladbach

Altenberg

Cologne

Aachen

Xanten

Trier

St Johann

Speyer

Landau

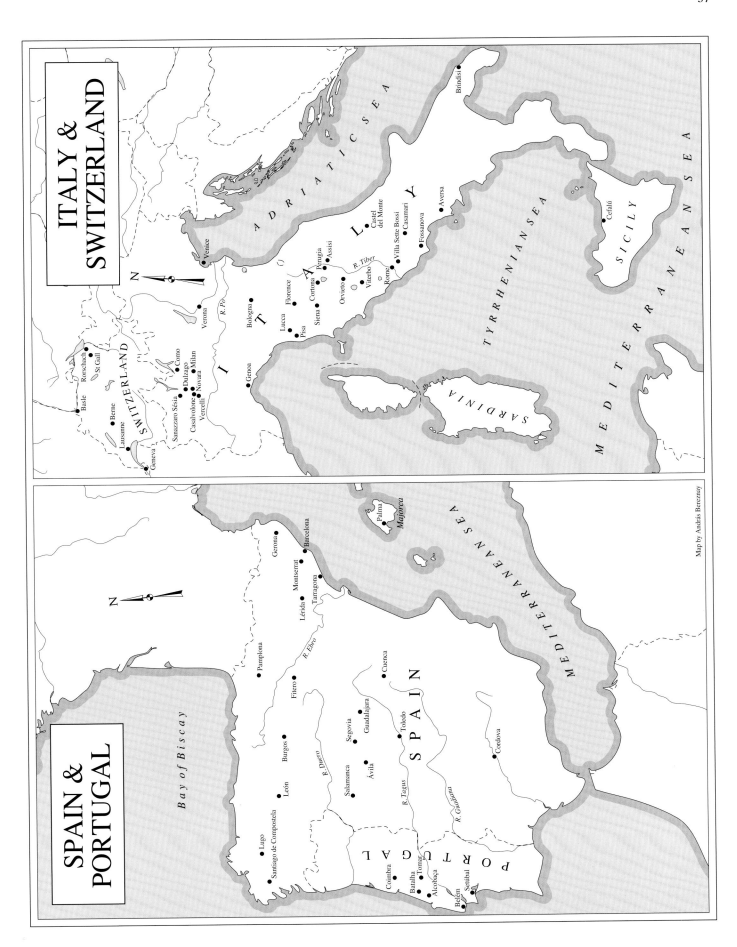

ITALY & SWITZERLAND

N

SWITZERLAND

Rorschach
St Gall
Basle
Berne
Lausanne
Geneva
Sanazzaro Sésia
Casalvolone
Vercelli
Dulzago
Novara
Milan
Como

I T A L Y

Venice
Verona
R. Po
Bologna
Lucca
Florence
Siena
Cortona
Pisa
Genoa
Perugia
Assisi
Orvieto
Viterbo
Rome
R. Tiber
Villa Sette Bossi
Castel
del Monte
Casamari
Fossanova
Aversa
Brindisi

A D R I A T I C   S E A

T Y R R H E N I A N   S E A

SARDINIA

SICILY
Cefalù

M E D I T E R R A N E A N   S E A

SPAIN &
PORTUGAL

N

Bay of Biscay

Lugo
Santiago de Compostela
León
Burgos
Pamplona
Fitero
R. Ebro
Tarragona
Lérida
Montserrat
Barcelona
Gerona

Palma
Majorca

S P A I N

Salamanca
Ávila
Segovia
Guadalajara
Cuenca
Toledo
Cordova
R. Duero
R. Tagus
R. Guadiana

P O R T U G A L
Coimbra
Batalha
Tomar
Alcobaça
Belém
Setúbal

M E D I T E R R A N E A N   S E A

Map by András Bereznay

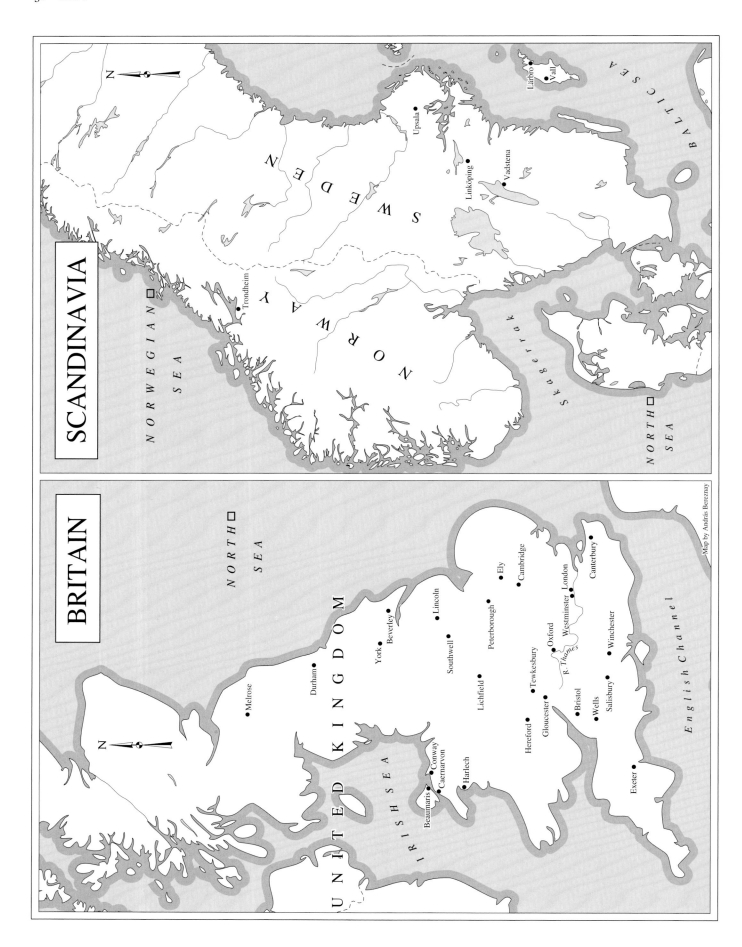

SCANDINAVIA

N

NORWEGIAN SEA

SWEDEN

NORWAY

Trondheim

Upsala

Linköping

Vadstena

Lärbro
Vall

BALTIC SEA

Skagerrak

NORTH SEA

BRITAIN

N

NORTH SEA

UNITED KINGDOM

Melrose

Durham

York
Beverley

Lincoln

Southwell

Peterborough

Ely

Cambridge

Lichfield

Tewkesbury

Oxford

Westminster London

Canterbury

Winchester

Hereford
Gloucester
Bristol
Wells
Salisbury

R. Thames

Conway
Caernarvon
Harlech
Beaumaris

Exeter

IRISH SEA

English Channel

Map by András Bereznay

PART ONE

The History of Gothic Architecture

Introduction

I. THE AESTHETIC FUNCTION OF THE RIB

THE Gothic style evolved from within Romanesque church architecture when diagonal ribs were added to the groin-vault.

In common usage, any kind of arch which lies within the surfaces of a vault is called a rib. So, also, is the ridge-rib, which appears later, and is not in fact an arch at all. In our consideration of the beginnings of the Gothic style, we need for the moment concern ourselves only with those ribs which are arches.

Suger, abbot of St Denis, who in about 1144 was the first man to write about the Gothic style, called the rib *arcus*, the same term which was used for any other arch.[1] Gervase of Canterbury, about 1188, used the expression *fornices arcuatae*, or arched vaults.[1A] About 1230 Villard de Honnecourt was the first to use the word *ogive*, which, after being incorrectly used for several decades during the nineteenth century to mean the pointed arch as well, has remained the French term for a Gothic rib to our own day.[1B] The word *ogive* is generally derived from the Latin verb *augere* (to strengthen), and this derivation corresponds to the belief that the purpose of these arches was to reinforce the vault. Some philologists say that the word originates from *algibe*, the Arabic word for cistern, and that it did not, therefore, apply to buildings with rib-vaults, but to those with groin-vaults, and more particularly to Spanish cisterns.[2] It is unlikely that Villard borrowed the word from Spanish. In English, arches within the surfaces of a vault are called ribs, in German *Rippen*, in Italian *costoloni*: all these words suggest a similarity to the human and the animal skeleton, which also has a function in terms of statics. In English literature on the Gothic style, the words rib and groin were sometimes used synonymously, which makes for unnecessary confusion. The word groin in this book means only the *one*-dimensional or linear edge where the curved surfaces of a vault penetrate one another, while rib means only the *three*-dimensional arch within the surfaces of a vault.

After 1835, when Johannes Wetter declared the rib to be one of the integrating members of the Gothic style, it became more and more the centre of discussion. The question of the date of the earliest ribs appeared so significant because it seemed that the correct answer to it must surely lead to the discovery of the birth date of the Gothic style. Instead it was found that ribs had already been used in Roman buildings. These ribs have never been fully studied. Two or three examples will here be sufficient. A cellar in the Villa *Sette Bassi* near Rome, built in *c.* 140–160 A.D., has projecting ribs. It was probably a tepidarium.[3] A careful examination of these segmental arches shows that they project

only because the facing-stone and the plaster, of which there are some remains, have fallen away. These arches can be described as crypto-ribs, a term which can be extended to include all known Roman ribs. A second example occurs in the arches in the substructure of the forum at *Arles*, which were added to the Augustan building about 310, in the time of Constantine.[4] Here too the plaster has been partially preserved, but the greater part of it has fallen. The 'ribs' in the so-called Trouille, the palace of Constantine at Arles, were also originally invisible. They lie within the surfaces of the vault of a large niche.[4A]

It is wrong in this context to mention the series of arches in the Early Christian churches and houses of *Syria* (Haûran), as they are not connected with vaults. They are transverse arches carrying a flat ceiling, and each one of them is so wide that it can be called a short tunnel-vault.[5] The forty ribs in the dome of St Sophia in *Constantinople* are projecting three-dimensional forms, but quite understandably they are never given as the source of the Gothic style. It would be more tempting to point to the Islamic ribvaults in *Toledo* and *Cordova*, and in *Egypt* and *Persia*, but all these are different in character from Gothic vaults.

In the search for examples, buildings were found much nearer home, such as the tower of *Saint-Hilaire* at *Poitiers*, of the mid or late eleventh century,[5A] or the porches in the towers of *Bayeux* in Normandy, which may have been finished by 1077. The architects who designed churches in England must have been in contact with Bishop Odo of Bayeux, who was a brother of William the Conqueror. The first architect of *Durham*, begun in 1093, was clearly English, but trained in Normandy. He may have known the ribs at Bayeux; and the Norman conquest of Sicily and the recent capture of Toledo may have made Islamic architecture more accessible to him and his patrons.[5B] It is more likely that the master of Bayeux was familiar with Roman vaults, but the strange thing is that the two vaults at Bayeux have no analogy with the crypto-ribs of Roman vaults. The vault in the south tower is a tunnel-vault with a transverse arch in the middle, which should not be called a rib. The vault in the north tower has two intersecting transverse arches which spring from the centre of the four sides, and lie within a domical vault [2].[5C] The master of Durham was the first to connect the arches with a groin-vault and lead them diagonally out of the corners.[5D] If the master of Bayeux was acquainted with classical crypto-ribs that had become visible through dilapidation, one may ask whether he had not been in *Lombardy* and found other examples there. Circumstantial evidence suggests that north Italian rib vaults did have a decisive influence on the earliest ribs north of the Alps, but the question is fraught with problems, not least because the dates of the earliest Lombard ribs are not at all clear.[6]

So we return to the first of our premises: the Gothic style begins with the combination of diagonal ribs with a groin-vault. It is useless to trace the ancestry of these two members

1. Lincoln Cathedral. Nave vault, *c.* 1220–35

2. Bayeux Cathedral. North tower vault, *c.* 1070

3. Durham Cathedral. Choir aisle vault, begun 1093

4. Lärbro. Tower, original centering, *c.* 1330

Durham, begun in 1093 and finished about 1095 [3]. The high vault of the choir was executed in the same way, and finished in 1104, but had to be replaced from 1242 when there was a danger of its collapse.[7] The third element of Wetter's formula for the Gothic style, the buttress, appears already in these first Gothic vaults: it was inherited without essential change from the Romanesque. The fourth element of the formula, the pointed arch, was combined with the rib at a much later date.

The purpose of crypto-ribs in Roman vaults was a purely technical one. The word technique is here used to mean only what contributes to the execution of a building. The erection of a brick skeleton of arches made the technical process easier. It is difficult to say whether the first Roman ribs were also an improvement in terms of statics. After drying, the mortar keeps the individual stones together so firmly that, in terms of statics, these vaults behave as though they were made of a single block of stone.[8] As the crypto-ribs were invisible, they had no aesthetic function.

The Byzantine and Islamic ribs which were left uncovered, and the Romanesque transverse arches, had, in addition to their technical function, an aesthetic one, but this was not the same in every instance. In some cases one can say that they have been exploited for a decorative purpose. The meaning of decoration is that one art serves some of the others: as sculpture, painting, and ornament may serve architecture, or small-scale architecture (altar canopies, tombs in the form of small buildings, etc.) may serve large-scale architecture. To call ribs decoration leads to the question as to which other members of a building, within architecture on both its smaller and its larger scales, can be called decoration. It is often debatable whether a part of a building is exclusively decorative or belongs exclusively to architecture proper. If architecture is reduced to include only what is functional, it ceases to be 'architecture'. The

separately. It is only their combination that produced Gothic ribs and Gothic vaults: in other words, it is only within the groin-vault that the rib becomes Gothic. Johannes Wetter already had some inkling of this, for he spoke specifically not merely of ribs, but of their union with the groin-vault. In his time research had not reached the stage where it could name the earliest vaults with diagonal ribs, and, as Wetter's point of departure was later buildings, he also stipulated pointed arches and buttresses as essential factors of what he called the Gothic style. The date of the combination of rib and groin-vault has since been established. It is the date of the vaults in the choir aisles at

5. System of Groin vault centering (after Fitchen)

6. A cerce

7. Ely Cathedral. Groin-vault in south aisle of nave, *c.* 1120

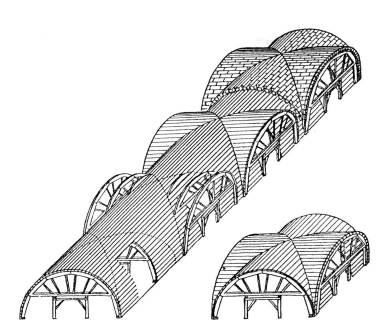

symbolic forms in architecture, such as bases, shafts, capitals, arches, mouldings, which aesthetically reveal beginnings and ends, movement upward and downward, supports and loads, are all adornment of the basic functional form of a building. The Islamic rib-vaults are decorative because they form a pattern of intrinsic aesthetic value. The question is whether the first Gothic ribs were similarly intended as a decorative addition.

To give an objective answer one must go back to the construction and building technique of the Romanesque groin-vault. By construction I mean the geometrical construction of a particular form of vault. The master mason must understand this clearly before he can approach the question of technique, especially the erection of centering. The way in which experiments were actually made can only be surmised, partly because in many cases a vault cannot be accurately dated. It is quite certain that the experiments were not aesthetically satisfying, that gradual corrections were also disappointing, and that the solution at Durham was only a provisional one.

To judge what was the function of the first Gothic ribs, a knowledge of this hypothetical series of experiments must be presumed. The problem reduces itself to the geometrical construction of the arches and the technique of building the centering; for the problems of statics were the same in every case, and financial questions played no appreciable part. Considerations of economy in the use of wood are insignificant beside the technical problem of cutting the wood for centering. In the Romanesque period, there were practically no saws available. Planks and posts had to be cut with an adze, and each trunk provided a single board. The only medieval centering which has been preserved – in the tower at *Lärbro* in Gotland[9] [4] – consists of small, short planks, supported by thin curved rods, to the shape of the cells, with other thin posts bracing the wooden arches from the

ground. Although this centering dates only from the fourteenth century, one can assume that the technique was not different in the eleventh century, where the successive centering frames supported continuous planking on which the stone vault webs were laid [5]. It is reminiscent of the method still used today for building boats and, as the Normans were sea-going people, shipbuilders were presumably entrusted with the work of constructing centering. Changes in the construction of vaults continually demanded new forms of centering, but the aim was not so much economy as an aesthetically satisfying vault.[10] The purpose behind the later use of the cerce [6], which is an extending

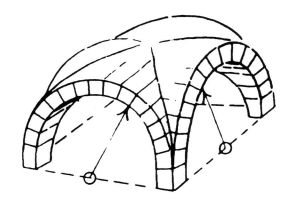

8A

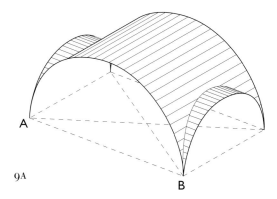

9A

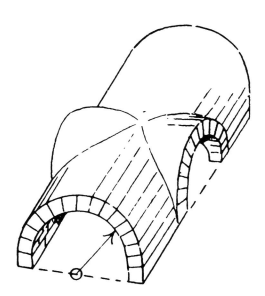

8B

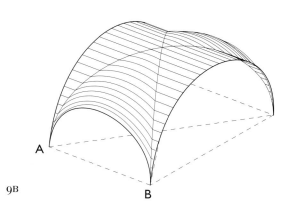

9B

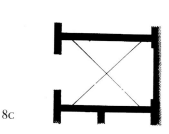

8C

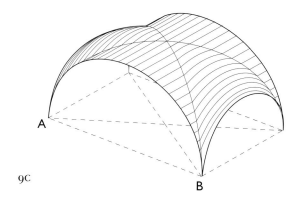

9C

8. A: Roman groin-vaults over a square bay with elliptical groins
   B: Roman groin-vaults over a rectangular bay with tunnel vault
      continuing either side of it
   C: Rome. Baths of Diocletian, vault, *c.* 305–6

9. A: Type 1. A tunnel vault with lower lateral penetrations
   B: Type 2. A tunnel vault with the shorter sides as its diameter (A–B)
      This system is sometimes built over side aisles, but never over
      main aisles, where tunnel vaults always use the longer side as the
      diameter
   C: Type 2. The same system as 9B, but with the main tunnel on the
      longer side (A–B)
   D: Type 3. Rectangular groin vault with raised lateral tunnels
      Note the stilting of the smaller, lateral, arches

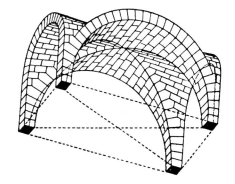

9D

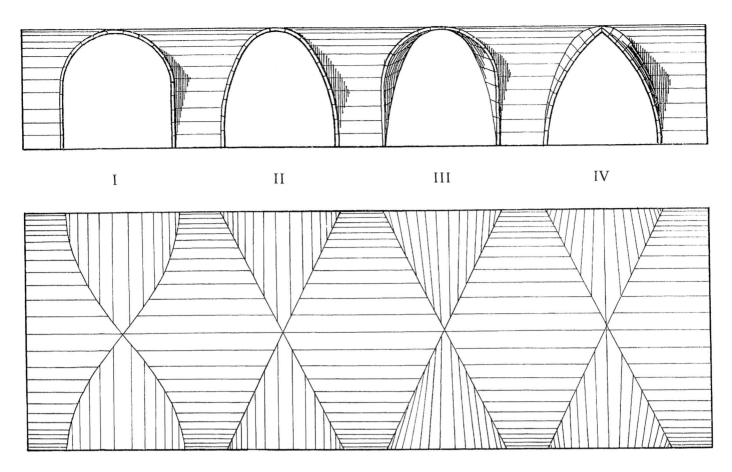

10. Construction of varieties of groin-vault centering, according to Ungewitter-Mohrmann

strip of curved centering wide enough to carry one course of stones for a cell, was to make the work easier rather than to make it more economical. In saying this, the fact that the shaping of the stones further increased costs is an additional consideration.[10A]

Roman groin-vaults were generally built on a perfectly square plan; the four supporting arches were semicircular; the surfaces of the vault were semi-cylindrical. The groins were therefore elliptical [8A]. In the case of a rectangular plan, the Romans used the expedient of building a semi-cylindrical surface over the shorter sides of the bay, and a semi-cylindrical centering and vault of the same shape and size over the longer sides. The groin vault does not, therefore, occupy the whole length of the longer sides: the longitudinal tunnel continues symmetrically on either side of it. The groins, consequently, do not spring from the four corners of the bay, but from intermediate points along the longer sides [8B]. In Roman building this technique was developed to the stage where separate centering frames were built over the longer sides, the shorter sides, and the diagonals of a bay, and the cells were then filled in with domed surfaces. No continuous wooden planking between the frames was deemed necessary. The Romans thus had already mastered this highly developed structural system, which the

medieval masons only gradually rediscovered. An example of this technique exists in the Baths of Diocletian in *Rome* [8C].[11]

In older medieval buildings, the technique for constructing the centering of the vaults consisted of building a wooden tunnel in one direction and two partial tunnels in the other [8]. The drawings of centering in Choisy's otherwise excellent book are questionable in their treatment of the boarding. His centering is drawn as it is built today, a method which can certainly not be considered to date from before the Renaissance. It is possible that the Roman technique was inherited by the Byzantines, but the masters of the Romanesque style had to rediscover it.

In cases where medieval buildings with flat ceilings were later vaulted, the builders must nearly always have been faced with the problem of building a groin-vault over a rectangular bay, however near it might be to a perfect square. In cases where a vault was planned from the outset, square bays could be arranged; yet rectangular bays were often chosen, because the builders apparently wanted one direction to predominate for aesthetic reasons. In addition, new conditions were produced in ambulatories.

The construction of centering in the form of a wooden tunnel with the longer side as its diameter, and of two semi-

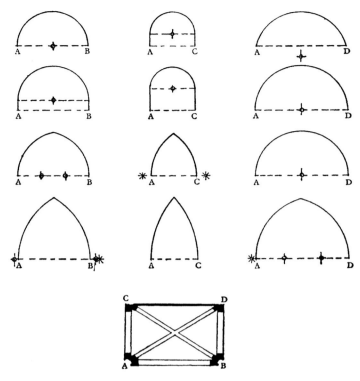

11. Construction of the rib-vault, with all apexes at the same level. Top three lines after Bilson; the fourth line shows the High Gothic solution, with pointed arches in all three pairs of arches

circular tunnels on the shorter sides, produced a tunnel-vault with lateral penetrations, not a true groin-vault. That is to say that if the lateral tunnels had a horizontal ridge, they did not reach the height of the main tunnel (Type 1) [9A]. The opposite procedure, that of constructing a tunnel with the shorter side of the bay as its diameter, produced downward-sloping ridges, from the higher lateral cells (Type 2) [9B]. The fact that in both cases the lines where the cells penetrated one another produced curves which were really beyond the scope of the geometrical knowledge of the time has little significance, since these curves simply appeared as the centering was erected, so that the boarding could then be cut to shape by eye [8, 10].

Were one to go back to the choice of building a continuous tunnel over the longer side of the rectangle, and to make the lateral cells rise, as in Type 2, then the level of the ridge of the main tunnel would still not be reached by the lateral arches [9C]. The solution to this problem was to begin these smaller lateral tunnels at a higher level, and to join their bases to the springing of the arches with vertical pieces of masonry (Type 3) [9D].[12] This stilting was used as an expedient until well into the High Gothic, for example on the closely spaced piers of apses [11]. In using this method (Type 3) the groins were neither semi-circular nor elliptical, as in the Roman examples: they were not entirely on the same vertical plane. In fact, they were sinuous lines, curved in plan as well as in elevation and moreover distorted, because the weight of the rubble distorted the centering.

These double-curved groins, of which there are countless examples in Romanesque vaults,[13] do not disturb most visitors to a church [7]. Sometimes one needs to stand in one corner of a bay and look straight across at the corner diagonally opposite to notice the deviation from the vertical diagonal plane at all. All architects, however, must have noticed it, and, as they always tried to produce precise lines, these unintended curves may have been offensive to them.

Mohrmann therefore presumed that, to regularize geometrical construction, the architects tried to construct the centering by starting out from the arc of the diagonal groin, rather than from the two intersecting tunnels. They decided to make the groin straight and single-curved [10.II].[14] This, he says, was easy, as it was only necessary to build a horizontal wooden semi-cylinder over the longer sides of a bay and then to stretch two ropes over it diagonally from the corners and project the line of those ropes on to the top of the tunnel at intervals, joining the points with painted lines. But there is no evidence that this ingenious method was ever actually used.[14A] If, however, it was, then it would have been possible to lay boards back from the painted straight lines to the lateral, clerestory, walls. If constructed in this way, the cross-section of the groin-vault, particularly on its short, lateral, sides, is semi-elliptical, since the groins are not the result of the horizontal projection of points around the curves of the transverse or lateral arches of the bay. There is indeed evidence of such elliptical contours along the clerestory walls of churches; but they are very unsatisfactory, as they most certainly resulted in irregular lines [10.II].[15]

According to Morhmann's hypothetical reconstruction, the next step was to straighten out the potentially irregular and semi-elliptical curvature of the lateral vaults at the points where they met the clerestory walls. The solution was to reinstate a clerestory of stilted semi-circular openings, which had then to be connected by boards to the straight diagonals of the groin arcs. The result, however, was conical webs in the form of 'ploughshares' between the wall arches and the groins [10.III]. In their own way, 'ploughshares' were as unsatisfactory as curvilinear groins (and more difficult to construct), so the practice of making a longitudinal wooden centering tunnel was at last given up. Instead three pairs of wooden arches, one pair diagonally and two pairs at the four sides, were built with apexes of equal height, and these were joined by boards. The choice of the curves of the arches was now free, and the surfaces produced themselves. If it was found that the apexes of the arches were higher than those of the diagonals, a segmental arch could be used instead of a semicircular one.[15A]

Exactitude in the curves had been reached, and the problem appeared to have been solved; but actually what had been reached was only exactitude in the centering. The laying of stones on the centering was also a part of the building technique. Small rubble was used and embedded in mortar, and so a kind of concrete was produced which, on hardening, took on the character of a homogeneous mass. This method was known in Roman times, as well as that of laying regular surfaces of bricks. The latter method may also have been generally used in Byzantine vaults.

The Roman groin-vaults with crypto-ribs brought regularity to the surfaces of the cells, because the ribs prevented any warping. Such weak wooden centering as that at Lärbro cannot always have fulfilled the builders' expectations that the vault would be as exact as was the centering. This is the moment at which, in our reconstruction of events, we can presume the idea to have arisen that flexible wooden centering must be replaced by firm centering, made of stone ribs – a 'cintre permanent' as Viollet-le-Duc called it. Once again economy in wood or wages played no part in causing this development, because a wooden scaffolding still had to be erected to build the stone centering.[15B]

A clear idea of this technique leads to the realization that the boarding that was laid on the wooden arches for a groin-vault filled a gap between the surface of the vault and the wooden arches. It was therefore essential to cut the boards at the point of contact in such a way as to make a sharp and regular curve, and this was not easy. If, however, a stone arch was built for the boards to lie on, they could then be pulled out when the surface of the vault had dried, and the irregular edge where the cells met would be concealed.[15C] Later, when the spur, a narrow projection on the upper side of the rib, actually penetrated the cells, the stone surface could be laid smoothly against the spur, but in early rib-vaults the cells often do not rest on the ribs, and one can slip one's hand into the gap in which the boarding had lain to support the stones. After the last two wars there were cases where one could see overhanging fragments in a vault whose ribs had collapsed, and in these cases one saw not one, but two parallel groins, corresponding to the width of the rib. These double groins also appeared in Roman vaults as a consequence of the building of crypto-ribs, and Choisy has drawn examples from the Palatine illustrating this phenomenon. No Romanesque vaults with parallel double groins have yet been discovered. This can be explained by assuming either that these particular vaults happen to have disappeared, or that they were never built, because the builders, foreseeing their appearance while making their plans, immediately took the mental leap to the conception of the rib.

Ribless vaults had produced groins which were double-curved and also distorted because of the displacement of the stone masses. The rib eliminated both these faults. The original purpose of the rib was, therefore, not a financial one; nor was it to improve the statics of a vault, nor had it a specifically technical purpose, since it did not make the actual erection appreciably easier. The purpose was *aesthetic*.[15D] In the presence of a completed vault, few people ask themselves how much it cost, or whether it could have been built more economically. Similarly, few people ask themselves what the centering looked like. They take it for granted that the vault will not collapse, and they can see for themselves that the geometrical layout was physically realizable. Their questions refer almost exclusively to the aesthetic result. The architect must overcome all the technical and financial problems in order to achieve a satisfactory aesthetic result.

Although the theory that has just been formulated may be correct, one must also consider the possibility that, in introducing the rib in 1093, the architect of Durham was influenced by the belief that it was an improvement in terms of statics. The statical and the aesthetic factors do not exclude one another. As early as about 1800, the decisive characteristic of the Gothic style was said to be the tendency to make the actual distribution of forces among the parts of the building the keynote of the aesthetic effect. The theory of functionalism developed more and more clearly, and was long the generally accepted one – until doubts grew as to whether the rib really bears any weight at all. Research into the actual distribution of forces in Gothic vaults, especially among the ruins left by the two world wars, has given us no universally valid answer. Some ribs bear weight; others do not. The testimonials of the experts assembled at Chartres in 1316 show that they were convinced that the rib does bear weight.[16] In other cases, such as the choir aisles at Durham, the vaults seem to have sufficient intrinsic equilibrium not to have to rely on the ribs; and yet, in the same cathedral, in 1235, the high vault of the chancel either collapsed or almost did so, and nobody knows whether this was because the ribs did not bear any weight, or in spite of the fact that they did.

Since it must be admitted that ribs do at least sometimes serve a statical function, there seems to be some truth in the old belief that they carry the weight of the vault on to the four corners, and so on to the piers, and that they therefore invite the architect to eliminate the walls. That they carry the weight on to the corners there can be no doubt; but it has rightly been said that this principle applies equally to Romanesque groin-vaults. The partisans of the old school of thought must therefore fall back on the argument that, in a Romanesque vault, the weight of the cells is concentrated on the groins, that these are the weakest points, and that it is precisely these points which were re-inforced by ribs. According to this reasoning, the real aim of the rib, therefore, was this reinforcement.

Saunders seems, in 1810, to have been the first to claim that the groins are the weakest points.[17] His theory has never been disputed, although it is untenable. If groins are taken to be one-dimensional lines, it is correct, because a line cannot bear any weight. What can and does bear weight is the three-dimensional mass behind this line. At this point, where there is oblique penetration between two cells, these cells are in fact thicker than at the ridge or anywhere else. Groin-vaults never develop cracks along the groins, but always approximately at right angles to them. Saunders's theory should be corrected by saying that the rib strengthens the strongest areas in a vault. Consequently vaults could be thinner: which, in turn, allowed the building of slenderer piers. But the aim of the earliest ribs was not to allow the building of thinner cells and piers, because at first these remained as heavy as those in other Romanesque churches. This theory was deduced from later stages of the Gothic style and was erroneously applied to its earliest stages.[17A]

Nevertheless the statement remains valid that the statical and aesthetic factors do not exclude one another. One must only add that statics do not in this case mean physical reality, but aesthetic appearance. Even though ribs do not actually bear any weight, they appear to do so. Even though the cells are heavy, they appear to be light. The same is true of the statement that, although the forces seem to tend exclusively upwards, they actually correspond to a downward pressure. Even in Romanesque buildings in Normandy, shafts reaching to the ceiling appear to be bearing weight, when it is really the core of the pier or the wall behind them that actually bears the weight. From about 1040, the date of the abbey church at Jumièges, Norman building shows a differentiation among its members into those that bear weight and those that are borne. The architects were trying to achieve an impression of pure structure, and because the rib gives the effect of being a structural member, the theory arose that the rib was the logical continuation of the articulation of the wall. Both shafts and ribs, the arguments goes, are structural factors; the articulation of the wall is older; 'therefore' the rib is a logical continuation of the articulated wall on to the groin-vault. This theory would be valid if both these structural members were stylistically the same at the inception of the Gothic style. Certainly both are structural, but the articulated wall is Romanesque structure, while the rib is Gothic structure. In the later stages of the development of the Gothic style they are both Gothic. The problem is therefore to distinguish the two *styles*.

We can now return to the term decoration and say that in discussing this problem it is not essential to agree on the meaning of decoration. What is essential is to understand that there is Romanesque as well as Gothic decoration. The theory of functionalism claimed that structural and decorative elements excluded one another. It aimed to differentiate between the shaft and the rib, which it held to be structural members in that they really carried weight, on the one hand, and, on the other, everything that is superfluous in terms of statics, and therefore 'pure decoration'. If we understand the terms structural and decorative clearly we realize that they are not opposites on the same conceptual level. It is not these two terms that are here under discussion, but the concepts Romanesque and Gothic. Why, when they appear within the surface of a dome, or in the diagonals of a domical vault, are ribs not Gothic; and why are they Gothic when they appear in a groin-vault?

2. THE STYLISTIC SIGNIFICANCE OF THE RIB-VAULT

Any single arch, for example a Roman triumphal arch, has a front and a rear surface. Each of these two sides is a one-dimensional arch which lies on a (two-dimensional) plane. In a construction such as a triumphal arch this plane is clearly visible. The whole arch, with the rectangle underneath it, is cut out of the vertical plane. If we walk through the arch we see and experience three clear spatial units: the space in front of the arch, the space beyond it, and the space inside, that is in the passage between the two.

In a Romanesque building with transverse arches the same is true, except that what, in the case of the triumphal arch, was the space in front of the arch and the space beyond it is now the first and second bays of the building, while the passage between them, corresponding to the transverse arch, is very narrow. If the building has aisles, then the arches of the arcade represent the passage and the nave and the aisles the spaces in front and beyond. We count bays, because the separation between one and the next is marked by the passage between them, which is formed by the transverse arch on its piers. In a Romanesque building the sharply marked interval between the bays produces the impression that the bays are separate units of space which form a whole only by their *addition*. The whole does not seem to exist before the parts. This aesthetic impression of genesis by addition has nothing to do with actual genesis. We are in this instance describing the finished building, and we find that the decisive geometrical factor is the frontal projection of the transverse arch and its supports, i.e. shafts or flat responds.

In the Romanesque period the vaults were set between the transverse arches. In the case of groin-vaults with a horizontal crown, the four cells, set opposite one another in pairs, appear as two continuous surfaces. They give the effect of horizontally placed half-tunnels, and in spite of their penetration of one another they appear to form a whole, resting horizontally on the structures beneath them. Thus the space within the vault is separated from the space underneath it, and the two form a whole by addition, exactly as in the case of the bays. If these two spatial sections were separated only by the mathematically thin plane of the springing of the vault, they would merge into one another; but in the Romanesque style the zone of the capitals and abaci is inserted, and this creates a separate horizontal layer of space between the two. Mentally we continue these horizontal planes as we did the vertical ones. The principle of addition of spatial sections is the basis of the composition of the Romanesque style. The geometrical characteristic of this principle is re-entrant angles on responds, plinths, arches, window jambs, doors, etc. Since, however, the Romanesque style demanded, apart from this principle of addition, also that of strict regularity (e.g. in the distances between piers, windows, etc.), it was not angles of 30 degrees, 60 degrees, or 125 degrees that were chosen, but angles of 90 degrees. These decisions made by the mason on his piece of parchment resulted, after execution, in the impression of *frontality*. Just as the members of the building are placed frontally in relation to its main axes, so we place ourselves frontally to these members. Even if we take a diagonal position we still recognize that the building consists of frontal images. The spatial form of a building is an abstraction corresponding to the abstraction on which the science of geometry depends. Similarly the *optical* form of a building is an abstraction corresponding to that on which the science of optics depends. But in order fully to understand architecture the building must also be considered from the point of view of the science of mechanics, that is of the form of the *mechanical forces*. The Romanesque style stresses the solidity of stone and its capacity to preserve its spatial form under pressure. The term structure is used to denote any system of building where members keep each other in balance under pressure and counter-pressure. In structures every member is a whole and within the wholeness of the building it is (to borrow a term from Gestalt theory) a sub-whole.

This analysis according to the three factors – of spatial form, optical form, and mechanical form – gives us the three principles of addition, frontality, and structure. All three in their interplay make the individual naves, bays, apses, etc., and also the individual visual impressions and the individual parts of a pier, an arch, etc., appear as wholes within a whole. It can therefore be said that the Romanesque style is a *style of totality*, and for this reason it was disturbed by the introduction of the rib.

Wherever we see an arch, our psychological reaction is the same as in the case of the triumphal arch. We have a mental image of a vertical continuation of the planes of the front and rear elevations over the opening – that is why we speak of an opening. The same is true wherever we meet arches, even in the case of the diagonal arches which we call ribs. Ribs are not one-dimensional lines but broad solid arches, and they form two intersecting archways within the vault. They are not merely fixed to the vault surface, but divide the whole space contained in the vault, from the springing of the arches up to the crown. The four parts that are produced, even though they can be precisely separated from one another, are incomplete in themselves. They are parts in a different sense from that of addition. They are not independent entities, but the result of a *division* within a pre-existent whole. They are fragments – *partes*, not *tota*. Here the case is not one of addition of single spaces, but of a sub-division of one space.

The diagonal direction of the rib brings new life into the composition. The main axes, from west to east, and from north to south, are still the determining lines; they are the permanent co-ordinates. The Romanesque style set out to build every angle and the axis of every member parallel to these co-ordinating lines. Ribs disturbed this principle of frontality, and led to the new principle of *diagonality*. This is an objective spatial factor and at the same time, from the point of view of the visitor, a subjective visual one. The images that he saw before were designed to be viewed frontally. Now he is expected to stand diagonally, and visually to experience space in recession, not in the flat.

The cathedral of *Durham* is a Romanesque building because it represents the principles of addition, frontality, and structure. But the introduction of ribs was in contradiction to the first two of these principles; for the ribs created the effect of division in the spatial form of the vaults and of diagonality in the optical form. The principle of structure on the other hand was not disturbed. As long as the ribs were arches keeping in balance by means of pressure and counter-pressure, the Gothic style had not reached its ultimate conclusion. This analysis reveals the paradox that the rib in terms of spatial form and optical form converts Romanesque totality into Gothic partiality, but as a structural member still opposes partiality. The masons of the Gothic style were for a long time satisfied with this contradiction, and only much later made the decision to convert structure into its contrary: into *texture*.

In the science of mechanics the distinction is made between pressure and pull. Nature offers us materials which (within limits) keep their spatial form under pressure. The most familiar example is the rope. However, if one wants to suspend on object from a rope, the rope must be fixed to a structure which can stand up on its own. Textiles made of threads, whether they be carpets or curtains or blankets or clothes, fall down without a supporting structure. The term *texture* (from Latin *tegere*, to cover) can be used and will here be used in opposition to structure, as a cumulative noun for all such things which cover some structure. In addition the term also applies to all things which hang held by a structure, or which are stuck to a structure (e.g. plaster, tarsia, mosaic, wallpaper, etc.).

For an understanding of the Gothic style in its consecutive phases it is necessary to use the term texture in this sense as a contrast to structure. Late Gothic masons used systems of rib-vaulting with detached or flying ribs or suspended pendants or even with 'net' patterns. They also omitted capitals between shafts and arches or ribs in order to replace the impression of counter-pressure by that of continuous flow, and in order to create the effect of growth as in plants.

The problem which posed itself in the earliest phase of rib-vaulting was as follows. The introduction of the rib had disturbed the unity of the Romanesque style by creating division of space and establishing diagonality. It opened the way towards a style of full *partiality* in which parts would no longer be sub-wholes but *fragments*. This being so, one of two decisions could be taken: one could renounce the rib to save the purity of the Romanesque style; or one could keep the rib because of the precision of its curvature and, in obedience to its divisional character, transform all Romanesque members until they conformed to the character of the rib. Which of the two decisions was taken is shown by the subsequent development. The rib was not rejected; for it seemed to be the only means of smoothing out the ugly irregular curves of the groin. However the deeper reason why the rib and its tendency to division brought about such radical changes was that men no longer regarded themselves as totalities, but realized that they were parts of a higher, or even an infinite, whole. This factor is more significant than regularity of curves, or unity of style in its formal sense. It bears on the artistic unity of form and meaning, or style and culture. However, our primary consideration must be the history of form.[17A]

There remains the question of why ribs are Gothic when they appear in a groin-vault, whereas in a tunnel-vault, a dome, or a domical vault they are not. In the case of transverse arches in a tunnel-vault, it is obvious that, because of their frontal position, they give the impression of the addition of smaller independent sub-units. Therefore the transverse arch in the south tower at *Bayeux* is Romanesque and cannot even be called a rib. In the north tower there are two intersecting frontal transverse arches which spring from the centre of the four sides of a domical vault [5]. They divide the domical vault into four parts. So this is an example of division of space. The four quarters cannot be said to exist independently of one another. The arrangement of transverse arches in the diagonals of domical vaults, such as that in the tower of *Saint-Hilaire* at *Poitiers*, at *Mouliherne*, at *Cormery*, etc.,[18] and in apsidal vaults, such as at *Saint-Martin-de-Boscherville* (*c.* 1120) and in S. Abbondio at *Como*, come under the same heading. In all these cases, however, the embracing shape of the whole vault outweighs its division into quarters or fifths, etc. The individual spatial unit, i.e. the area under the tower or within the apse, remains isolated from adjoining spatial units or from space outside the building. Though mentally we continue the vertical surfaces of each of the intersecting arches, we also continue this flat curved surface, so that the strongest impression is that the arch lies within the surface of the dome or domical vault and belongs to it. The arches do not appear to subdivide three-dimensional space, but to subdivide only the two-dimensional surface of the vault.

To speak of Romanesque ribs in these cases is not entirely wrong, but is better avoided. They are transverse arches, mostly in a rectangular section of the Romanesque type, transplanted from their normal position between the bays to the diagonals, and are incapable of destroying the inward concentration of a Romanesque vault.

The combination of diagonal arches with a groin-vault, however, does destroy this inward concentration, and opens each bay on all four sides – to the adjacent bays, or to the space outside the building. The ribbed dome in the church of St Sophia has the same character, because cells have been set between the ribs. This is the reason for the opening statement of the introduction, which is that the Gothic style evolved from within the Romanesque. The Gothic style is a historical phenomenon. Even when all traces of the Romanesque had disappeared, the Gothic style was still a descendant of the Romanesque. It is the transformation of the historical style of totality into a style of partiality.

Each of these two terms comprises the interaction of spatial, optical, and mechanical forms. In the Romanesque we find spatial addition, opposition of forces, and a predominance of frontal views. In the Gothic style we are faced with spatial division, the smooth flow of forces, and a predominance of diagonal views.

The terms addition and division are not here used in their arithmetical sense. The area of the plan and the volume of the enclosed space are unimportant. The fact that a spatial division makes one part two-thirds, or any other calculable fraction, of the whole is equally unimportant. Both terms must be taken in a geometrical sense. That is why the opposite of addition is not, in this case, subtraction. Nothing is subtracted: the whole remains, even after it has been subdivided. The terms are only distantly related to mathematics. They are really terms which have meaning only within the 'geometry of aesthetics'.

CHAPTER I

The Transition

I. THE GOTHIC RIB-VAULTS OF THE FIRST GENERATION (1093–1120)

No existing groin-vault with ribs can, according to Bilson, be dated before the choir aisles of *Durham* Cathedral, which were begun in 1093.[1] This statement by Bilson is partially supported by the buildings in *Caen*. Had there been rib-vaults in the Anglo-Norman world before 1093, the architects of the churches in Caen would probably have used them, as Caen was the political capital of Normandy. It was from Caen that William set out to conquer England. Here, the later 1060s to 1081, William built the nave of *Saint-Etienne*, at that time with a flat ceiling. The choir, which has not survived, can hardly have looked different from the choir of *Saint-Nicholas*, which is in the same town, close to Saint-Etienne, and was built only a few years later, the last years of the eleventh century.[1A] In Saint-Nicholas the choir has a groin-vault and an apse with a half-dome. From this we can conclude that before 1093 there were no rib-vaults in Caen, and probably none anywhere else.[1B]

In *c.* 1059–60, William's wife Matilda had founded a nunnery in Caen called L'Abbaye aux Dames, with the church of *La Trinité* attached to it. The original form of this building can be partly reconstructed. The nave had a flat ceiling, and the aisles had groin-vaults with no transverse arches. The original appearance of the east end is not so clear, but the vault of the choir certainly had no ribs, since even the present building has none, though it was built after the death of Matilda [12]. She was buried in the existing choir in 1083, and left legacies of great value to the nunnery.

La Trinité [13] is a veritable museum of vaults. The groin-vault in the choir wa s planned in the 1090s and executed in the 1120s.[1C] It has a horizontal ridge, which can be seen better from the loft above the vault than from below. The shape of the centering that was used can be deduced from the curve where the surface of the vault meets the wall,

and from the curves of the groins. It was built at the stage when centering was constructed with a continuous wooden tunnel and elliptical groins, from which the boarding was laid horizontally to the wall. Both these vaults, then, date from before the time when it was decided that the point of departure should be the centering of the groins, and not of the wooden tunnel.

While the alterations to the choir of the Trinité were in progress, the abbey church at *Lessay* was begun *c.* 1090 [14].[2] The ribs here are not forerunners of those at Durham, because at the east end, where the building was begun, there is no member corresponding to them on the springing-line. The ribs were not, therefore, planned until the building had reached the height of the springing of the vault. The shafts are set frontally on the walls, and contradict the diagonal direction of the ribs springing from them. The thought which occupied the mind of the architect can be seen in the crossing. The master of Durham had overcome the failures of groins. The criticism of the master of Lessay was that they had been overcome by the introduction of a segmental arch, lacking uniformity with the shape of the longitudinal and transverse arches. However, since semicircular diagonals would have led to a very high ridge, he began his diagonals below the level of the springing of the arches in the crossing. The piers of the crossing were already finished, so the ribs begin in a re-entrant angle between two responds on the piers. We can see that, initially, every improvement brought in its wake a concomitant disadvantage. One of these was the crescent-shaped piece of wall left over the transverse and longitudinal arches of the crossing. The discrepancy between the two curves was due to the fact that the crossing arches were semicircular, while the construction of a wooden tunnel by laying boarding horizontally from the diagonals produced an elliptical curve where the surface of the vault met the wall. This was nothing new, and can be seen in many Romanesque vaults, especially in crypts. The

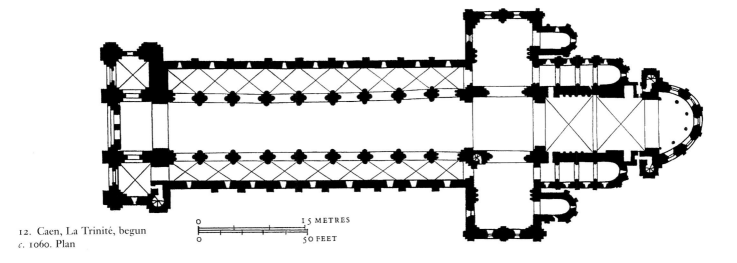

12. Caen, La Trinité, begun *c.* 1060. Plan

0   15 METRES

0   50 FEET

13. Caen, La Trinité, begun *c.* 1059. Nave vault *c.* 1130, renewed in the mid nineteenth century

14. Lessay Abbey Church, begun *c.* 1090. Interior of nave

ribs at Lessay have no spurs, and can only have carried weight while the building was actually in progress. This was clearly shown after the serious damage that was caused to the church in 1945. Although the ribs were not intended in the original design of the choir or transept, they were integral to the construction of the upper part, and date a few years before 1098, when a burial is recorded in the choir.

One would like to be able to put exact dates to all the early rib-vaults; but this is impossible. It is sufficient that the dates which we have, should support one another. The rib-vaults at *Winchester* give us additional information. They were built immediately after the collapse of the crossing tower, in 1107.[3] The Norman transepts had east and west aisles, with galleries above. As these aisles extend right round the transept ends as well, they were vaulted in sixteen bays. Two of these collapsed. They were replaced with rib-vaults, and four other bays had ribs added to them. In the two new bays, the ribs are segmental arches, as they are at Durham. They are segmental arches also in the other four bays, without any consideration being given to the shape of the surviving vaults. The space between the surface and the ribs was filled with masonry. The purpose of these diagonal arches was not to carry the weight of the vault, but to transfer the lateral thrust of the new crossing tower on to the

outer buttresses, and to provide a strengthening link between the piers. The Romanesque shafts had been set frontally on the piers, and were preserved throughout the church, except that one corbel was added in the south-east corner of the south transept to correspond to the diagonal direction of the rib which it supports. This detail, and the detail in the springing of the ribs in the crossing at Lessay, strengthens the argument in favour of a conception of the rib as having been introduced independently of the articulation of wall and piers. The Gothic style originated in vaults and developed downwards, but at Winchester this principle appears only in the addition of one corbel set diagonally in place of a shaft.

A decade or so after the Winchester vaults, ribs were used in the chapter house at *Jumièges*, a small, now ruinous, rectangular building with a semicircular apse [15]. The wall-arches are not stilted, and the lateral cells therefore rise sharply to the ridge. If Lanfry's reconstruction is accurate, this is the first time that a Romanesque vault, which closes inwards towards its centre, was replaced by a Gothic vault, that is, a vault which opens outwards through its funnel-shaped cells. The principle of division was thus applied to the apse; for in this apse, too, the cells rest on ribs. The chapter house was in all probability constructed *c.* 1100–20.[4]

Perhaps the church of *Saint-Lucien*, near Beauvais, begun between 1089 and 1095, completed *c.* 1130, damaged by English troops in 1346, restored later, and finally pulled down in the French Revolution, had the same kind of rib-vault in the choir and transepts. Gall has reconstructed the building after old drawings and shows groin-vaults in the aisles and galleries, but ribs in the high vaults.[5]

At this stage English architecture did not develop beyond the segmental rib. Examples are in the aisles at *Peterborough*, begun soon after 1107, and at *Southwell*, built from *c.* 1120.[5A]

In the cathedral at *Evreux* the former existence of ribs throughout has been deduced from the shape of piers that have been excavated, and from those dating from 1119 that have been preserved. This theory has, however, not been definitely proved; what we know is that all the shafts at Evreux were still set frontally.[6]

In the second and third decades of the twelfth century the flat ceilings of the churches of La Trinité and Saint-Etienne at *Caen* were replaced by vaults, and these vaults embody definite innovations.

2. DIAGONALITY OF SHAFTS, MULTIPARTITE VAULTS, POINTED ARCHES, KEYSTONES

In the transepts of *La Trinité* at *Caen*, the original vaults have been preserved. The ribs are elliptical arches,[7] and the shafts were designed and built to correspond with them. The capitals and shafts supporting the transverse arches are frontal; those supporting the ribs are diagonal. The plinths and bases are all frontal and probably date from the time when the church had a flat ceiling. The outermost bay of each transept has a quinquepartite vault, with one rib rising from the centre of the end wall up to the ridge. The chronology of the vaults in the two churches is uncertain. The

16. Caen, Saint-Etienne. Nave, early 1070s–81. Vault rebuilt in 1616, presumably like the original of *c.* 1120

15. Jumièges, Notre Dame, chapter house, main structure *c.* 1100, vault 1120s. Plan

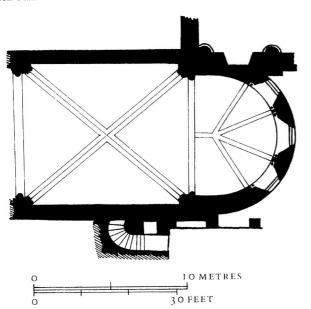

0   10 METRES

0   30 FEET

crossing vault of La Trinité is original. It must have been designed at the same time as the vaults of the transepts and the choir, because the shafts in the corners of the crossing also have diagonally set capitals; but is seems to be later than the easternmost bay of the nave which adjoins it.[7A]

The vault of the nave collapsed in the eighteenth century, and was replaced with a light plaster replica. Pugin's drawing is evidence that this replica had a horizontal ridge.[8] It presumably repeated the original form, with quadripartite rib-vaults cut by transverse arches in the centres of the bays. These transverse arches were surmounted by a thin stone wall reaching up to the surface of the vault. This form was preserved by Ruprich-Robert in his nineteenth-century restoration, except that he gave the ridges of the cells an ascending shape [13]. Such vaults are called pseudo-sexpartite. The intermediate transverse arches seem to show that, at the time when the building had a flat ceiling, there were diaphragms at these points, as there were in many Romanesque churches. But since the whole superstructure of the walls of the nave was rebuilt *c.* 1125–30, and is partly supported by the vaults of the aisles, these transverse arches cannot have been part of the original building of the 1060s and 1070s, or date from the stage before the imitations of the eighteenth and nineteenth centuries.[9] It is questionable whether the shafts originally continued above the level of the springing of the arcade, as at this point the fact that the mouldings have been hacked off suggests that there were originally abaci on the ends of the lower part of the shafts, presumably resting on capitals like those that support the arches of the arcade.[9A] The lengthened shafts rise to the transverse arches or diaphragms. Only when they reach the foot of the blind triforium are two diagonally-set shafts joined to them to support the diagonal ribs. The capitals of these shafts, too, are set diagonally.

In *Saint-Etienne* at *Caen* [16] the vault of the nave was rebuilt in 1616.[10] It is sexpartite, not pseudo-sexpartite. The sexpartite vault proper can theoretically be called a development of the pseudo-sexpartite. Instead of having one cell continuing on either side of the intermediate transverse arch, it has two cells on either side which meet on the transverse arch. It is not known whether this theoretical development corresponds to the actual chronology.[10A] Both buildings appear to have been vaulted at about the same time, possibly by two different architects. In Saint-Etienne, as in the Trinité, the short shafts which are set on the older frontal responds to support the ribs are turned diagonally. The central transverse arches rise steeply and then bend in on a different curvature. Judging by other sexpartite vaults preserved in their original form, the construction was fairly correctly copied in 1616.

In Saint-Etienne the original alternation in the eleventh-century supports explains why the twelfth-century vault is sexpartite [17]. It has been asked whether the pseudo-sexpartite vaults of the Trinité are later than the sexpartite vaults of Saint-Etienne and are an adaptation of pre-existing diaphragm arches. The Trinité never had alternating supports. The pseudo-sexpartite vaults of the Trinité can therefore be interpreted as a translation of the quadripartite vaults of Durham into a nave with diaphragm arches. Thus both vaults at Caen could be contemporaneous essays, adapted to different situations.[10B]

The sexpartite vault at Saint-Etienne was designed to correspond to alternating supports. In that sense the process of its creation moved upward from the arcade, not downward. But since the Romanesque supports had no diagonal shafts, as they were needed for ribs, they were added a little below the springing of the vault. The diagonal shafts, therefore, were suggested by the ribs above and not by the frontal Romanesque responds. Both are undeniably structural members, but the point to be emphasized is that the frontal responds are Romanesque structure, the short diagonal shafts and the ribs Gothic structure. The ugliness of the curves in the intermediate transverse arches (as rebuilt in the Baroque) is no argument against the theory that the rib was created to correct three-dimensionally double-curved groins; for the first ribs at Durham are earlier than the original ribs at Caen. The western bay of the sacristy vault at Saint-Etienne is an example of particularly misshapen groins. In view of such a failure as this, the rib must indeed have been a welcome innovation.

According to Gall the crossing vault of *La Trinité* was built last of all, when the adjacent parts of the building were capable of taking the thrust.[11] Where the nave meets the crossing the beginnings of a round arch have been preserved, standing at the same level as the three original semi-circular arches of the crossing. The central part of this round arch was pulled down, flat responds were added to the piers, and then a pointed arch was built – possibly the first ever to have been built in connexion with a rib-vault; yet the apex of this pointed arch is considerably lower than the ridge of the vault.[11A]

In the south chapel of the ambulatory in the cathedral at *Gloucester*, the line where the vault meets the wall is elliptical. Below this line there is a wall-arch, and this is pointed. One notices the pointed shape only on the lower edge of the arch, but one hardly notices at all that the point of the upper edge is cut into by the elliptical surface of the vault. It is as obvious here as in the case of early ribs that the aim is purely aesthetic. Bilson, basing his judgement on the history of the

17. Caen, Saint-Etienne, begun in the 1060s. Plan

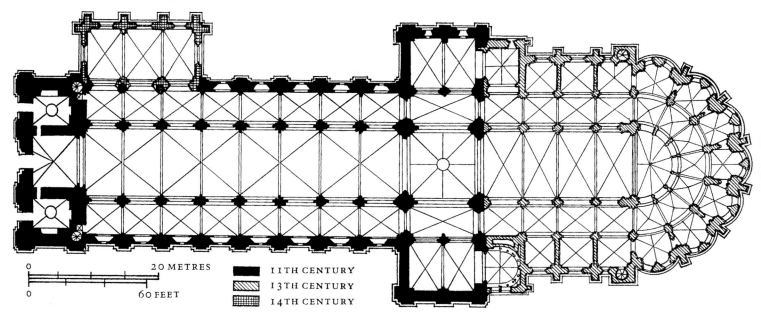

0   20 METRES
0   60 FEET

■ 11TH CENTURY
▨ 13TH CENTURY
▦ 14TH CENTURY

18. Moissac. Interior of porch,
c. 1110–15

whole cathedral, dated this detail 'about 1100'.[12] If this is correct, then the pointed arch here is earlier than the one in the Trinité, but it is not connected with the vault itself. The crypt at Gloucester, which was reinforced with rib-vaults in the early twelfth century, has ribs in the form of segmental arches surmounted by masonry, as at Winchester, designed to stabilize the piers. As this crypt is very low, the builders were forced to use segmental arches, and there was no reason to beautify the structure by adding wall-arches.

Pointed arches as such were not new. Even in prehistoric ornament they appear automatically as the product of intersecting circles. The Treasury of Atreus has a dome whose section is a pointed arch. Greek mathematicians and Roman architects must have known the form. The important factor, however, was not the knowledge of the form, but the decision to use it in architecture. The Egyptians made use of it in the section of canals, but they, and after them the Romans and the Byzantines, would not have thought of using it in an exposed position. Islamic architects were the first to recognize its aesthetic and stylistic value.

The architects and theoreticians of the Renaissance hated the pointed arch, claiming that it was capable of carrying less weight than the round arch, and that it was ugly.[13] They created the legend that the wicked Teutons, who lived in forests and could not even cut down trees, used to tie the branches of two trees together as a shelter, and so discovered the pointed arch. Later they had destroyed the good architecture of the Romans, and developed their bad 'Gothic' manner instead.[14] Christopher Wren, on the contrary, knew that Islamic architects used the pointed arch as a decisive form, and he evolved the theory of the Saracenic origin of the Gothic style. It remained the rival of the theory of the origin of Gothic in the trees of the forest until Schopenhauer, and after him Spengler, declared that the

Gothic style had its roots both in the German forests and in the Arabian desert. After the Renaissance, the tendency was to identify the whole Gothic style with the pointed arch. It was therefore generally thought that if the first pointed arch were discovered, the sources and the beginning of the Gothic style would be discovered with it. As early as about 1760 the English architect Essex seems to have known that the pointed arch took on a constructional role in the Gothic style, and in 1810 Saunders published an article in which he explained that the significance of the pointed arch in the Gothic vault was to permit all three pairs of arches in a bay to reach the level of the ridge.[15] If the two main pairs of arches were pointed, then they needed no stilting, and the diagonals could be semicircular. In Johannes Wetter's formula of 1835 the pointed arch was not meant to be taken as an incidental factor in the Gothic style, but as one of the integrating elements. Neither in the crossing arch in the Trinité nor in the south chapel at Gloucester had this integration really been reached. One of the first rib-vaults built entirely on pointed arches is at *Moissac* [18]. The west porch there, including a part of its famous sculpture, was carried out in the time of Abbot Roger, after 1115, the year when he succeeded to office, and probably between 1120 and 1125.[16]

At Moissac all three pairs of arches are pointed, and all three are segmental arches; the points are not very distinct. The vault is a strange mixture of progressiveness and conservatism. Its position in the south of France tempts one to draw the conclusion that the architect knew classical cryptoribs, exposed by dilapidation (such as those at Arles, not far away); one is reminded also of Lombard examples. Moreover, the mouldings of the ribs and the wall arches in the porch at Moissac are not Gothic. Ever since Durham, architects had tried to replace the rectangular mouldings of the ribs by less isolating forms [19]. The rib is meant to sep-

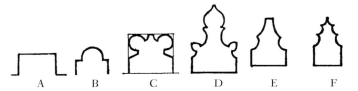

19. Profiles of ribs in the Early, High, and Late Gothic periods

arate the cells, but this separation should not be too strong. By placing a roll-moulding on a rib of rectangular section with the corners of the rectangle gouged out to form hollows, the architect of Durham had already progressed towards making the triangle the enveloping form of the rib-profile. This enveloping form is exactly what the mason carves as a preparation for the chiselling out of the final form. The emphasis on the centre line of the rib acts as a division of the vertical layer of space created by the rib. Each of the two halves of the vertical layer belongs to its neighbouring cell. We therefore feel the existence of the whole of the single compartment as strongly as its division into fragmentary parts.

The entire nave of *Gloucester* was rib-vaulted in the early twelfth century. Only the north aisle preserves its original vaults. The ribs have two rolls with a member between which is triangular in section and thus accentuates the centre.[16A]

In the porch at *Moissac* the ribs had no weight-bearing function, even during the actual construction, for there is a crescent-shaped gap between them and the cells, which are differently curved. This gap was then filled with blocks of stone, placed radially. At the intersection of the two diagonals there is no genuine keystone. One arch carries through with no break, and the other consists of two separate parts lying up against the first, and widening slightly at the joint. There are also examples of this continuation of one arch through another among Roman crypto–ribs. At Moissac evidence exists of the mental process which led to the development of the keystone as an independent architectural member.

The upper storey over the porch, which forms a unity with the porch, and was certainly built by the same architect, also has a rib-vault, but one of a different type. The

square chamber has diagonally set shafts in the corners and two frontal shafts between them on each wall. These twelve shafts support twelve ribs with a rectangular section, which touch one another on the circumference of a ring, but without intersecting. This apex ring is probably the oldest keystone within the Gothic style, although it still has a Romanesque profile.[16B]

The abbey church at *Morienval* plays a different historical role [20]. It was entirely roofed with a flat ceiling, except for the choir, which had a tunnel-vault, and the apse, roofed with a half-dome.[17] To the east of the apse there is a sharp drop in the ground, and this fact probably caused a subsidence of the foundations, as a result of which the east end had to be restored. About 1125 the tunnel-vault in the choir was replaced with a rib-vault with pointed transverse arches.[18] This date is supported by the section of the ribs, which is similar in type to that of the aisles at Gloucester (*c.* 1120). The pointed transverse arches in the 'ambulatory' have the same section. One hesitates to use the word ambulatory, because the passage between the piers and the wall is only 26 inches wide; not an ideal passage, it would seem, round which to lead crowds of pilgrims. The whole ambulatory seems to have been designed primarily as a series of inner buttresses for the apse, the upper part of which was restored later.[18A] The vault of the ambulatory is primitive: it has four bays around the semicircular apse, and thus one pier stands on the central axis of the apse (as it does in some Late Gothic buildings). To have had five bays would have involved even greater difficulties. The semicircular transverse arches are excessively stilted. In each bay one of the ribs is semicircular in one vertical plane, while the other is three-dimensional double-curved. The lines where the cells meet the transverse arches are asymmetrical, the ridges are horizontal, and the lines where the vault meets the walls are three-centred arches.[19] It is not necessary to consider what the centering must have been like, because this vault, with its small span, seems to have been largely constructed freehand. The ribs have a common keystone which is not emphasized. The result of this arrangement is that they form a very acute angle at their intersection. With only three bays this angle would have been even more acute. Everything points to the supposition that this is one of the first rib-vaults in an ambulatory.[20] Another innovation is the cutting back of the section of the rib at its rear so as to form a vertical spur against which the cells are laid. This helped to make centering almost dispensable.

The crypt of *Saint-Gilles* [22] also has rib-vaults [21]. These vaults are important in connexion with the study of the sculpture on the west front. Within the history of the Gothic style they are less significant, being no more than variants of the vaults in the crypt at Gloucester and in the porch at Moissac, in so far as the curve of their ribs does not coincide with that of the cells. This again made it necessary to fill in the entire space between the ribs and the surface of the vault with masonry. Inscriptions show some at Saint-Gilles began in 1116, but this date cannot be definitely assigned to the ribs, as building may have been delayed by

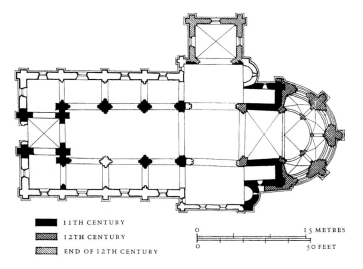

■ 11TH CENTURY
▨ 12TH CENTURY
▧ END OF 12TH CENTURY

0   15 METRES
0   50 FEET

20. Morienval Abbey Church, east end *c.* 1125. Plan

21. Saint-Gilles. Interior of crypt, after 1116

22. Saint-Gilles, crypt. Plan begun soon after 1096, vaults after 1116.

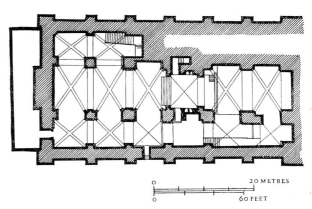

political unrest from 1117 to 1125.[21] The ribs are segmental arches and their ornamentation clearly connects them with the Norman school. It seems that most controversies over Saint-Gilles have not taken into account the groin-vaults in the bays lying further east. They are built of ashlar and have such miraculously sharp and exact groins that one would be inclined to regard them as contemporary with the master-pieces of French stereotomy of the seventeenth or eighteenth centuries. Hamann, however, after long study, concludes that the groin-vaults and the rib-vaults of the crypt were built by the same master and belong to the same period, having been begun in 1116. If it is true that the original aesthetic function of the rib was to avoid the ugly curves of the groins, it must have been introduced here for other reasons. Hamann has given a few;[22] he has also stated that the two western rib-vaults of the south aisle were rebuilt possibly in the thirteenth century. Originally a tunnel-vault may have been planned for the nave of the crypt. Groin-vaults would hardly have been feasible in view of the oblong shape of the bays and also of the fact that the nave is so low. Ribs therefore facilitated the construction in this case, quite apart from their original aesthetic function. If, as Hamann suggests, the rib-vaults were begun soon after 1116, they cannot be regarded as early essays, for they are later than the rib-vaults of Durham, Lessay, Winchester, Speyer and perhaps the early north Italian examples.[22A] Vaulting was difficult, and every compartment posed different problems. But, while the achievement is worthy of recognition, the rib-vaults of Saint-Gilles do not represent an advance in the development of construction.

The choir of the church is in ruins. The ambulatory had groin-vaults. In the rectangular north chapel the springing of a rib is preserved. It carries decoration of Norman design similar to that of the third bay of the 'nave' of the crypt. Chronologically it probably follows the latter immediately.[22B]

In this case too the diagonal position of the corbel above the frontal corner of the pier proves that the decision to introduce ribs was made only when the springing-line of the vault had been reached.[22C] If the choir was started while work was still in progress in the western part of the crypt, the transition from groin-vaults to rib-vaults took place in both choir and crypt in the midst of building operations.

Recent research has convincingly shown that the rib-vaults over the transepts at *Speyer* cathedral, usually dated after a fiRe in 1159, are in fact part of Henry IV's rebuilding of the cathedral ('Speyer II') undertaken between *c.* 1082 and 1106.[22D] They thus belong, with Durham, to the earliest rib-vaults in western medieval architecture. But, unlike Durham, their origins seem to point to northern Italy, since the ribs at Speyer are 'band ribs', with simple rectangular profiles, and were built in two stages (like those at Bayeux): the first diagonal was constructed as a single continuous arch, and the second was built as two separate arches rising to meet the first near its centre.[22E] The Speyer ribs were soon followed by those in the eastern choir of *Worms* cathedral, also recently re-dated much earlier than hitherto supposed:

23. Durham Cathedral. Nave *c.* 1115–33

the choir was begun *c.* 1125–30 with the intention to rib-vault, and was finished in *c.* 1140.[22F]

In the third decade of the twelfth century rib-vaults spread to Lower Saxony, Alsace, and Swabia. The earliest of these may have been the band ribs built in the western porch of SS Peter and Paul in *Hirsau* (1120–30). It may be significant that Hirsau belonged to the diocese of Speyer. Some time between its beginning in 1122 and its consecration in 1134 the choir of the abbey of *Murbach* received band ribs. Band ribs also appeared in the west porch of the Hirsau-controlled monastery of SS Peter and Paul on the *Petersberg* at *Erfurt*, built some time between 1127 and 1147. The band ribs in the western porch of the *Frauenkirche* in *Magdeburg* were constructed soon after 1129, and the ribs used throughout the high vaults of *St Johann bei Zabern* in Alsace date from *c.* 1140–50.[23]

The most important question is where and when the pointed arch was connected more systematically with the rib-vault. Once again *Durham* Cathedral took the lead [23]. The vault of the nave has segmental pointed transverse arches. The porch at *Moissac* is an exactly contemporary example of this form, and there the ribs are also pointed, with their centre below the line of the springing. When the nave of Durham was begun there was no intention to cover it with a high vault, so when the present vaults were actually

incorporated into the structure between 1128 and 1133 the ribs had to be supported on corbels inserted into the gallery wall. The system of alternating supports had led to the building of frontal responds on the piers and shafts rising to the line of the springing. Instead of a sexpartite vault, as at Caen, two quadripartite vaults were built across each bay of the arcade, with their ribs supported on corbels. These pairs of bays are not separated by a transverse arch. This was a new attempt at uniting the rib-vault and the alternating supports, and, at the same time, at superimposing the form similar to that at Moissac on to a completely Romanesque nave at Durham. The Gothic vault does not make the substructure Gothic, and the vault itself shows that here, as in Saint-Etienne at Caen, the ribs did not develop upwards from the structure below. The vault is a compromise, forced upon the architect by the situation which faced him when he began. A logical solution could only be reached in a completely new building.[23A]

It was this opportunity that the architect of *Saint-Etienne* at *Beauvais* found when he began work in *c.* 1120. Building started at the east end with the now-destroyed choir, the earliest surviving parts of the twelfth-century church being the transepts and the first, eastern bay of the nave [24]. The vaults are more primitive than those at Durham: the transverse arches are semicircular and highly stilted in order to reach the level of the apexes of the semicircular ribs. All that remains of the period when the building was planned has the heaviness of the Romanesque style, together with its isolating qualities, produced by the broad transverse and arcade arches. Excavations have shown that the choir was probably vaulted with quadripartite ribs. Vaults may not have been originally intended in the transepts, but inserted *c.* 1150 with the construction of the north rose. The choir, transepts and the first bay of the nave were part of the same building campaign. A subsequent campaign was responsible for the following three bays of the nave aisles (where the ribs change from chamfered profiles to torus mouldings), and a final campaign completed the two westernmost bays of the nave, the west façade, and the high vaults of the nave by *c.* 1220–35.[23B]

The aisles, which have been preserved, are among the earliest attempts to attain a unity between the new architectural members. The supports for the ribs with their *bases* and *capitals* are set *diagonally*; they stand in the re-entrants of the cruciform piers, and so, in spite of the feeling of isolation of nave and aisles, they bind the structure of the wall and the vault in the aisles together. This solution, too, seems to be heralded at Moissac, but at Beauvais the effect is more fluid, because the round arches continue the movement without interruption, while at Moissac the pointed arches beginning as segmental arches have a hampering effect. In addition, the ribs are slenderer at Beauvais. At the east end this is achieved by bevelling their corners; in the west bay by adding a roll-moulding as at Morienval. The shape of the *capitals* also emphasizes the upward tendency. The capitals at Durham [23] are, in principle, still like Romanesque block-capitals – convex in their lower part, so as to produce re-entrant angles of less than 180 degrees; whereas in Saint-Etienne at Beauvais the surfaces are concave, continuing the line of the shaft, and making an angle of 180 degrees, and in this we can see a decisive criterion for distinguishing between the Romanesque principle of addition and the Gothic principle of division in relation to the form of the corporeal members of the building as well as the form of the empty spaces between them.

The shafts that support the arches of the arcade are keeled, that is, pointed in section. It is surprising to find this form appearing here; for all the arches themselves are round, and the use of a sharp edge to emphasize the centre-line of a member is a characteristic of a far later stage of development.[23C]

The choir of Saint-Etienne was completely rebuilt from *c.* 1500 to *c.* 1545, at the end of the Late Gothic period.[24] The original twelfth-century choir had a straight-ended plan with a rectangular ambulatory similar to English precedents, in particular the choir of Romsey Abbey. In this it differed from the choir at *Saint-Germer* [25]. This church near Beauvais was begun sometime after the acquisition of relics of Saint-Germer in 1132, probably in *c.* 1135. The six western bays of the nave, which belonged to a second phase of construction, were in building 1172–80, but the west façade was probably not finished until just before *c.* 1206 (the date of a consecration). The single choir bay is rectangular; its aisles have square bays; the semicircular apse has five chapels, set close together. Most Romanesque churches with

24. Beauvais, Saint-Etienne, begun *c.* 1120. Interior of the nave looking west. In the south aisle the nearest (earliest) vault has bevelled ribs, those further west have roll mouldings

an ambulatory have the chapels standing apart from each other, so that there is room for a window to light the ambulatory between one chapel and the next. When the chapels stand immediately adjacent to one another, the ambulatory is invisible from outside the church.[25] In Saint-Germer a gallery rises above the ambulatory and preserves the stepped-up elevation which demonstrates so clearly the idea of building by the addition of one spatial unit to another. This gallery has groin-vaults. All the other parts of the church have, or once had, rib-vaults. In their geometrical construction the rib-vaults are similar to those in the nave at Durham. The ribs are semicircular, and the transverse arches are pointed. But here the trans-verse arches do not begin as segmental arches, as they do at Durham, but are a smooth continuation of the vertical shafts. Another sign of progress is that the wall arches have the form of ribs, thereby defining precisely the joint of the vault with the wall; they also have their own shafts, beginning at the level of the springing of the vault. Pointed arches are used in the arcade, too, as they had been in Romanesque churches in Burgundy; but the arches of the gallery and the clerestory windows are semicircular. Between the gallery and the clerestory, rectangular openings are let into the roof-space of the gallery. The stunted wall passage below the windows of the apse harks back to Norman works, as does most of the

25. Saint-Germer, begun *c.* 1135. Interior of choir

26. Cluny Abbey Church. Lallemand's drawing of the narthex, begun *c.* 1130, two eastern bays vaulted *c.* 1130–40

ornamentation.[25A] But the keystone in the choir, with its rich decoration, is one of the earliest to be emphasized by sculpture.

The piers of the crossing, with their thickly clustered shafts rising uninterruptedly, form a powerful frame of simple grandeur, beyond which the choir gives an effect of rich complexity. The wealth of invention gives the building great freshness, but also unevenness. Some parts, such as the three-dimensionally double-curved ribs in the ambulatory, seem as primitive as those of the church of Morienval.

The nave of Saint-Germer continues the system of the chancel. The shafts rise uniformly, without alternation in the supports. The aisles are very similar to those in Saint-Etienne at Beauvais, but the stilted semicircular transverse arches are replaced by pointed arches. On the outside horizontal lines predominate, and the exterior of the whole building is still purely Romanesque, with buttresses ending below the eaves of the roof. The Gothic windows in the south transept and the single flying buttress against the old stair-turret are later additions.

Pointed arches in the arcade like those in Saint-Germer can be found earlier in Burgundy.[25B] Before Saint-Germer was begun, the Benedictine church at *Cluny* had been completed. Cluny was the most magnificent church of the Romanesque age in France, and all the architects of the time must have known it. The foundation stone was laid in 1088; three altars in the choir were consecrated in 1095; the eastern part of the church, including the western transepts, was almost certainly complete by 1109; the nave was substantially finished by 1120; and the whole church dedicated in 1130.[25C] The narthex was probably begun in the early 1130s, and completed some time before 1200. If Lallemand's drawing of the narthex [26] can be trusted, the transverse arches and ribs of its vault were segmental or semicircular and the wall arches were pointed. The two bays at the east end of the narthex had four storeys: arcade, triforium, clerestory and second clerestory. The triforium forms a continuation of the blind gallery in the main body of the church. The next three bays of the narthex towards the west had a three-storey elevation of arcade, triforium and single large clerestory.[26] When the narthex received its eastern rib-vaults, in about 1130–40, Germany already knew the use of the rib. The German rib-vault cannot, therefore, be an off-shoot of the vaults in Burgundy. Its ancestry must be traced to Speyer and Worms and the early examples in Saxony and the Upper Rhine of the 1130s and 1140s.[26A] The development of the Gothic style did not proceed along a single line. It would be more correct to speak of a field of forces.

The Parisian region also lay within this field of forces. *Bury*, between Paris and Beauvais, and the choirs at *Poissy* and *Pontoise*, built in the fourth decade of the twelfth cen-

27. Saint-Denis Abbey Church. Interior of narthex, c. 1135–40

Mertens, and independently, at the same time, by Kugler and Schnaase.[28] However, one must differentiate between the choir and the two western bays, which must have been designed by different architects.[28A] It is in the chancel that the beginning of the Early Gothic style is to be found [28]. The west porch cannot claim this distinction. This must be stressed in justice to the second master. It is not merely a question of setting up a more or less useful dividing-line of the conventional kind. On the contrary, to draw this line firmly leads to the recognition of what it is that raises the Early Gothic style above the level of the style of the experimental period. This need not diminish our respect for the master of the west porch. Within the limits imposed by the Transitional style, he created an important work [27].

As a young monk, Suger had seen the congestion that resulted on feast days when the faithful came to admire and worship the precious relics. The entrance to the Carolingian building, still standing at the time, was far too narrow. So his first aim was to build a façade with three wide doorways. It was to have two towers, and between them and over the central doorway was to be a chamber, the *camera*, serving as a chapel, with two further chapels to the left and right of it, at a slightly lower level. The central chapel was dedicated to the Virgin Mary, St Michael the Archangel and St Romanus, and contained the relics of the latter. The inaccessibility of the chapel suggests that it may also have served as a strongroom for the safe keeping of treasures, though Suger never mentions this function.[29]

The architect pulled down the west part of the Carolingian basilica, and replaced it with two bays. The westernmost bay contains the approaches to the three doorways. The central portal is higher than the portals on either side, because the floor of the *camera* lies on a higher level. A spiral staircase goes up inside each tower to the level above the vaults of the aisles. From this level a flight of steps leads up to the *camera*. The *camera* extends over both bays, and has two rib-vaults. The circular west window gives the chamber a bright and magnificent appearance. In the side aisles, in the lower storey, the second bay is as high as the

tury, all have some importance as designs executed before Saint-Denis, or at the same time.[27]

The significance of *Saint-Denis* as the first building of the Early Gothic style was first recognized in 1806 by Dallaway and in 1809 by Whittington, then again in 1843 by Franz

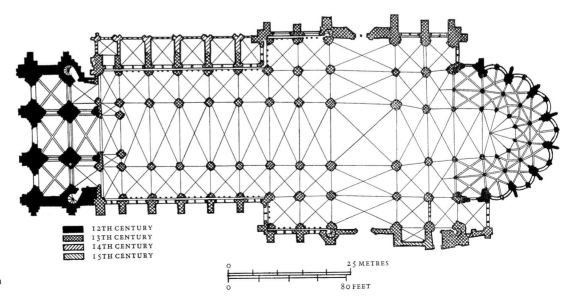

■	12TH CENTURY
▨	13TH CENTURY
▨	14TH CENTURY
▨	15TH CENTURY

0   25 METRES

0   80 FEET

28. Saint-Denis Abbey Church, begun *c.* 1135. Plan

first. So the second bay of the *camera* rises above the level of the aisles, giving this part behind the towers the cross-section of a basilica. The ribs on the upper and lower levels are slightly pointed. The introduction of the pointed arch in the diagonals must be recognized as the completion of the first phase in the development of the rib-vault. The earliest example is, once again, to be found in the porch at Moissac, built about 1120. However, in the west bays of Saint-Denis some of the ribs have Gothic mouldings, the same as those in the aisles at Gloucester – two rolls, and a member between which is triangular in section.[30] At Saint-Denis there is no gap between the ribs and the cells. To give ribs the form of the pointed arch was an innovation significant in several ways. It made the construction of a vault completely independent of the shape of the bay in plan. It also brought complete conformity to the arches of a building. Previously it had to be accepted that a building might contain segmental, semicircular, stilted, and pointed arches, according to the chosen construction. Thirdly it united the vault and the lower structure vertically. As long as the rib was segmental (and Moissac, in spite of its pointed arches, is therefore included), a clear horizontal division remained between the vault and the structure below it. It has been recognized since Schnaase that the round arch and the pointed arch are aesthetic opposites. One's glance moves in a semicircle from the lowest point on the left of the arch, over the apex, and down again to the lowest point on the right, or vice versa. The round arch is always a whole, rising over the horizontal lines of its diameter. In a pointed arch the movement starts from both sides of the base at once, and proceeds upwards to the apex. The two halves of the arch unite, as they are seen in relation to the vertical axis. In a building with round arches standing on any type of supports, whether they be piers or the jambs of a doorway or a window, an effect of addition is always produced between the upper and the lower parts of the structure. Where there are pointed arches, although capitals are still kept as a legacy of the principle of addition, the vertical unity of each arm of the arch with its support predominates, especially where the capitals are concave and not convex in outline. The pointed arch enhances the verticality of the thin layers of space produced by the ribs.

However, the master of the west bays of Saint-Denis was not altogether aware of the constructional advantages of building ribs in the form of pointed arches; for the various compartments are differently constructed. In some bays the springers are on more than one level; in others the springing of the ribs lies below the level of the springing of the transverse arches (as it did in the crossing at Lessay). It is impossible to say whether or not ribs in the form of pointed arches existed in earlier buildings, because many small churches cannot be accurately dated, and even the date when Saint-Denis was begun, usually given as 1137, is not certain. It may have been some years earlier.[30A]

It is the façade of Saint-Denis that marks the beginning of a new epoch [29]. The west façade of Saint-Lucien at Beauvais (*c.* 1130), reconstructable from lithographs and drawings, consisted of a large single west portal flanked by two stair-towers. It had a considerable following in the Oise valley *c.* 1130–50, but it represented a very different type of design form the two-towered 'harmonic façade' of Saint-

Denis.[30B] In the façade of Saint-Denis the three doorways are fused into a unity by the slight predominance of the central one, and by the uniform use of all-round figures in the jambs.[31] There are forerunners of this in Lombardy, and Languedoc. In Saint-Denis, however, the three doorways are incorporated into the vertical system of the façade with its towers; we see the horizontal unity of the lower part simultaneously with the unity of the whole façade. The different levels within the *camera* led to different levels for the windows. The small windows above the two flanking doorways light the lower storeys of the bases of the towers, while the long windows above them light their upper storey. Some parts of the façade are not original, especially the little blind arcade with its figures which lies above the longer windows. The battlements were restored in the fourteenth century and had round projections added over the rectangular buttresses. The upper storeys of the south tower have been preserved: those of the north tower have not.[31A]

The oculus was taken over by the façades that followed. About 1150 an oculus was built in the north transept of Saint-Etienne at Beauvais. In the case of Saint-Etienne the character of the exterior is pure Romanesque. The circular window in Saint-Denis was probably in the same style, with a hub in the form of a ring, and the spokes connected by trefoil arches.[31B] In Saint-Denis the style is no longer Romanesque. This is not just a matter of the appearance of a few pointed arches – in the two flanking doorways, and in the blind arcades and glazed windows[32] – nor of the force of the projecting buttresses and their predominantly vertical emphasis. In Saint-Denis a change has taken place, affecting the relief of the building as a whole. The west façade of Saint-Lucien at Beauvais and the 'harmonic' façades of Saint-Etienne and La Trinité at Caen seem flat compared with Saint-Denis.

The iconography of the sculpture of Saint-Denis can also be called Gothic. In Romanesque buildings the subjects of sculpture are loosely strung together, and chosen quite haphazardly. In Saint-Denis they are based on a coherent theological plan, and each piece of sculpture is part of that plan. The figures around the doorways, of which only drawings and several heads remain,[33] portrayed the ancestry of Christ. They could also be taken to be the ancestry of the kings of France, who were held to continue, in spirit, the royal line of the Old Testament. This ambiguity would be in place at Saint-Denis, where the French kings were buried.[33A] The church is truly regal in character, combining an impressive aloofness with a gracious condescension.

Suger was preoccupied with speculations on the metaphysics of light. Everything that shone stimulated him. He immersed himself in this atmosphere of mysticism. As he had seen mosaics in Italy, at least in Rome, he ordered a mosaic to be set in the tympanum of one of the smaller doorways. The architect and the sculptors must have been surprised, because mosaics could not fit in with the high relief of the architectural detail and the sculpture; they contradicted its emphasis on the third dimension. The combina-

29. Saint-Denis Abbey Church. West front, *c.* 1135–40, restored 1833–44

30. Airaines, Notre-Dame, *c*. 1140. Vault of westernmost bay of nave

31. Montivilliers. Vault of north transept, *c*. 1140–50

tion was never repeated in France, and appeared only rarely in other countries. In Saint-Denis the mosaic is not preserved.[33B]

3. THE RIDGE-RIB

The first innovation to enrich the rib-vault was the ridge-rib. Tripartite, quadripartite, quinquepartite, sexpartite vaults on rectangular bays, and tripartite and multipartite vaults on semicircular apses all had arched ribs. With the introduction of the ridge-rib into the crown of a vault, and by calling it a rib, the concept of the rib was extended to include a straight horizontal member. It had the three-dimensional projection from the surface of the vault in common with the arched rib, and it seems always to have been considered closely akin to the genuine rib. The ridge-rib divides only a surface, not three-dimensional space. The theory that its purpose was to cover the joints along a line where the stones lie parallel to the ridge may be correct in certain cases, but ridge-ribs were also used in cases where the stones do not lie parallel to the ridge, and they can therefore not have been intended as a 'couvre joint'.

One of the earliest existing ridge-ribs are generally taken to be those in the westernmost bay at *Airaines*[34] [30]. Here they run along both the longitudinal and the transverse ridges. They have a cylindrical section like the diagonal ribs, but they are considerably thinner, and this suggests that we may indeed have here the earliest experiment in a form which was to have such a rich future. The point where the diagonal ribs cross is decorated with a very small rosette. From his study of the building history Aubert suggested that this relatively small abbey church dates from about 1140.

The date is corroborated by the equally hypothetical date – between 1140 and 1150 – that has been applied to *Montivilliers*, near Le Havre.[35] Here the ridge-rib looks later than that at Airaines, because its section, similar again to

that of the diagonal ribs, is richer. In the north transept a ridge-rib connects the keystones of the two bays. Quadrant arches rise to these keystones from the north wall as well as the wall of the crossing. Both carry vertical walling just like the diaphragm arches at the Trinité at Caen [31].[36] In the south transept, which also has two rib-vaults, a ridge-rib runs only from the keystone of the south bay to the apex of the south wall, and there merges with a moulded member which starts only at the height of the springing of the ribs in the middle of the end wall of the transept. These experiments, which are based on Norman tradition, may date from even before 1140. The southern aisle of the chancel still has groin-vaults with double-curved groins, and these are only slightly older than the rib-vaults in the transepts. It is impossible to determine whether the half-diaphragms in the north transept were designed first and led to the joining of the north transept bay by a ridge-rib or vice versa. In any case, one can see that, as they were given a section similar to that of the rib, both the diaphragm-arch and the ridge-rib were regarded as members of the same kind as the diagonal rib. In the Romanesque period the stylistic purpose of the diaphragm-arch had been to separate the bays by addition into compartments each of which made up a totality – a purpose achieved by the use of a rectangular profile. As soon as the diaphragm-arch was given the same section as the rib and was set in the middle of a quadripartite vault, its character changed. It now divided space in the particular sense of division which has been defined earlier (p. 54). In contrast to this, the ridge-rib remains an inseparable part of the surface of the vault. The simultaneous use of both forms at Montivilliers produces a combination of two spatial divisions with a rib running along the ridge. Whether one chooses to interpret the two forms aesthetically, either singly or in conjunction with one another, or, in a more restricted sense, stylistically, these 'ribs' look like genuine ribs, but they no longer have the function of concealing ugly groins. Their meaning is entirely new, and is far from being merely decorative. When it is used as it is in the north transept at Montivilliers, the ridge-rib serves to melt one bay into another. At Airaines, where its use is restricted to a single bay, it divides the surface of the severies, and could almost be described as an elongated keystone.

The transference or transplantation of an architectural member from the position for which it was originally intended to another, where it takes on a new meaning, is a phenomenon that recurs often in the history of style. It was first recognized by Jakob Burckhardt: in 1843 he described it as an element of 'Rococo' which appears at the end of the development of any style. Later this use of forms in a sense other than their original and inherent one was called Mannerism. Nowadays it would be as confusing to call the vaults at Airaines and Montivilliers Rococo as it would be to describe them as works of Mannerism, a word which would be reserved for the style of the sixteenth century. In ancient Greek there were two words that expressed this shift in meaning – 'akyros', and the word that has come into English as 'metaphor'. The latter cannot be used in this context because it has acquired a different shade of meaning. The word 'akyros', however, has not been invested with any special meaning by traditional usage, and may therefore be used to describe stylistic formations such as the ridge-rib.

At first the ridge-rib remained rare. At *Lucheux* there is one which joins the second bay of the choir to the vault of the apse; and the other five cells of the apse here also have ridge-ribs. Their torus moulding is similar to the vaults at nearby Airaines, and to those of the western bays of Saint-Etienne at Beauvais, and they should be dated *c.* 1130–50, probably before 1152.[37]

4 · VAULTS WITH ARCHED RIDGES

The Norman rib-vault inherited from the groin-vault the tendency to bring all three pairs of arches on to the same level. This still left the choice of making the ridge of the cells a straight line or a curve [32]. Where the latter occurs, the resulting vault is called domical. Domical vaults appear very early. Their purpose was to reinforce the statics of the ridge in the cells. Curved ridges resulted in cells whose surfaces were neither cylindrical nor absolutely spherical in the process of building as soon as cut stone and a cerce were used. According to whether the curve replaces a horizontal or a sloping ridge, the surfaces differ mathematically – and, of course, visually too. Where the ridge rises sharply, the impression is almost one of a dome with ribs.

The domical vault, in its tendency to focus upon the centre, is similar to the dome. There are domical vaults, reinforced with intersecting transverse arches, in France, most of them in towers. The north tower of *Bayeux* [2] is not the only one: there are others at *Cormery*, *Loches*, and *Tours*.[38] The members in these vaults are definitely transverse arches, and not ribs in the Gothic sense of the word. This is true also of genuine spherical vaults supported by arches with a section like that of a rib. The number of variations is surprisingly large in terms of mathematics, and attempts at stylistic analysis and evaluation are faced with ever new difficulties. It is easy to sense that a domical vault closes inwards on to its centre, while a groin-vault opens outward. However, if the cells of a groin-vault rise beyond a certain degree, a geometrical form is reached which begins as a cross-vault, and becomes in its upper part a domical vault. A horizontal cross-section across the bottom shows re-entrant angles. As cross-sections are taken higher, the angles widen until a point is reached at which they are 180 degrees, after which they steadily decrease. In the basic form of the ribless cross-vault, the groin becomes a channel, and in practice the upper part of the vault is often spherical, or approximately in the form of a sphere. This form of vault was often chosen in regions where a dome over each bay was the norm, for instance in Anjou. The series of domes in the cathedral of *Angoulême*, begun in about 1105, and the cruciform arrangement of the five domes over *Saint-Front* at *Périgueux*, built some time after 1120, are extreme examples of the application of the principle of addition within the Romanesque style.[38A] The earliest continuation of ribs with a dome is considered to be the first storey of the tower of *Saint-Aubin* at *Angers*, begun in 1130.[38B] When cross-vaults began to be built in the school of Anjou, the architects preserved their native steeply-rising cells, and reached a mixture of groin-vault and domical vault terminating in a spherical surface at the top of the bay. The choice of the pointed form for the transverse arch and the wall-arches made the geometrical form even more complicated. This form can be seen in the cathedral of *Le Mans* [33], where following the fires of 1134 and 1137 the nave was rebuilt with the use of older parts. The reconstruction began some time after 1145 under Bishop Guillaume de Passavant, and the vault was completed before the consecration of 1158.[38C] The aesthetic function of the ribs in such cases is to clarify the lines which begin as groins, turn into channels, become indistinct near the ridge of the vault, or finally disappear. The result of the sharp rise in the ridge is that, seen from the west entrance, the nearer bays overlap the further ones. This is the converse of the effect achieved by vaults with a horizontal ridge and a ridge-rib, where the aim was to produce a smooth flow from one bay to the next. At Le Mans the

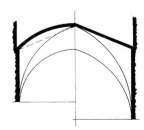

32. Vaults with rising and with arched ridges

33. Le Mans Cathedral. Interior of nave, c. 1145–58

transverse arches are broad in the Romanesque way, as are the profiles of the wall-arches. The outer member of these profiles is supported on piers that begin in the recess in the wall at the level of the triforium. These upper piers are the continuation of the arcade piers. The frontal shafts, the adaptation of the lower part of the church by the reinforcement of every other pier, the eccentric insertion of pointed arches below the old round ones, the row of round arches in the triforium, and the form of the coupled windows – all these factors are Romanesque, and even the pointed arches of the arcade have the broad Romanesque profile which makes the thickness of the walls so intensely felt. The final result of this combination of a Romanesque elevation with a rib-vault which by the rising and falling line of its ridges isolates each bay from the next, is closely related to that of other Transitional buildings. It is hard to say whether this church is a case of 'active transition', that is, whether it is a conscious perseverance in the stylistic effort to achieve a unity between the rib-vault and the wall, or whether it is a case of 'passive transition', that is merely the admission of the rib-vault into the formal heritage of the Romanesque school. The eclectic process is all the more striking as this is one of the first buildings after the porch of Moissac in which ribs are deliberately built in the form of pointed arches.

This uncertainty as to whether one ought in some cases to speak of active or passive transition does not affect the validity of the term Transitional. The opposition of some scholars to the use of the term has never been justified. There was never a sudden break with tradition: there was never a moment when a totally Romanesque building was followed by a totally Gothic one. No better term than Transitional has yet been applied to the gradual wane of the Romanesque and the gradual appearance of the Gothic style.[38D]

Saint-Martin near *Etampes* (Seine-et-Oise) is a building which belongs to the transition.[39] The three chapels of the ambulatory stand far apart, leaving space for two windows with round arches between one chapel and the next. The transverse arches are pointed, while the ribs are distorted. The shafts and all the other forms are heavy. Except for the flying buttresses, the exterior is completely Romanesque in style. The choir was begun partly in 1142, just after the choir of Saint-Denis. Even in terms of statics, Etampes was far from perfect; many parts of the church are out of true. None the less, this church, standing back from the busy streets, is exceptionally attractive – and not merely because of its willingness to advance with the times.

CHAPTER 2

The Early Gothic Period

1. THE BEGINNINGS OF THE GOTHIC STRUCTURAL SYSTEM

According to Suger, the Carolingian church at Saint-Denis had two faults: the entrance was too narrow for the crowds of pilgrims, and the space round the main altar was not large enough on feast days when the relics were being shown. The first of these faults was eliminated in 1140, when the new west part was finished. When the building at the west had reached the level of the horizontal above the *camera* and the original battlements were finished, Suger turned to the reconstruction of the east end.[1] Suger describes how the old crypt and the chapel to the east of it were used to put the new choir on a higher level so that the relics might be more easily viewed. He praises his architect for making the measurements of the new choir so exact that, after the removal of the old choir, the new axis continued that of the nave. Considered in the light of the primitive means of measuring available in the Middle Ages, this skill certainly merits recognition.[1A] Nowadays we are less interested in the achievement in terms of geodesy than of style. Though he speaks indirectly of this, Suger does not make any direct remarks about it.[2] Presumably the abbot and his architect decided together not to have only one ambulatory with seven chapels round the main apse, but to dispense with the walls separating the chapels, and in this way create a second ambulatory round the first [34]. This was the solution to the problem of how to facilitate the circulation of the pilgrims. On feast days one could climb the flight of steps on one side, obtain an excellent view of the relics, and walk round the choir and down the steps on the other side. If people wanted to take part in a service held in one of the chapels, they could interrupt their walk round the choir and step into the chapel. We do not know whether the chapels, too, were used to display relics.[2A]

The double ambulatory gives the effect of a 'hall-church'. The main choir rises above them as it would in a church of basilican type. This central section was replaced from 1231 by a High Gothic structure.[3] Suger's choir presumably had a three-storey elevation supported on slender columns with a small clerestory of paired windows and a middle storey consisting of a series of subdivided arches opening into the spaces over the ambulatory vaults beneath a lean-to roof very like the elevation of the choir of Vézelay [50] or at Sens [35].[4] Suger mentions the rib-vault in the choir.[5] It must have been similar in its geometrical construction to the vault in the ambulatories.[5A]

The most obvious difference between the two western bays and what is preserved of the east end is that the latter is extremely light, whereas the former is much heavier. The massive piers of the west narthex were built because high towers were to rise above them. There was no such necessity at the east end. It has been debated whether both plans were drawn by the same architect, who merely suited his design to the exigencies of the case in point. However, the details contradict this theory, and so, even more strongly, does the complete mastery of the construction of the rib-vaults that is displayed in the choir.[5B] Perhaps the second architect carried his tendency to lightness too far, making the piers of the chancel too slender. The superstructure was perhaps not stable enough, for it was pulled down in the years following 1231.[5C] Since the publication of Crosby's research we know that Suger left the Carolingian nave standing, so that, after finishing the new Rayonnant choir and transepts, an unknown architect, from c. 1237[5D] replaced the Carolingian nave. In this one building, then, the Transitional, Early Gothic, and High Gothic stand side by side.

After the diversity of the heavy vaults of the two west bays, those in the double ambulatory seem endowed with great unity and grace. In the choir aisles the ribs are semi-circular, and all the other arches are pointed. In the trapeze-shaped bays of the ambulatories the keystone does not lie at the intersection of the diagonals, as this would create an asymmetrical crossing of two vertical semicircular arches. The point chosen for the keystone is the intersection of the radial axis with the centre-line of the ambulatory, and it is to this apex that the ribs rise in four separate arms. Because of this abrupt change in direction, they look like pointed arches. In the outer ambulatory there is a similar construction which sets the apexes in the centres of the chapels. The chapels themselves stand one beside another and form a wall in the shape of a series of segmental niches, each chapel lit by two windows. On each axis of each chapel, therefore, one pier stands between the pair of windows, from which a fifth rib rises to the ridge of the vault. The two sets of nine vaults are supported between the two ambulatories on ten slender columns, which realize the desired impression of lightness in the vaults without interrupting the views. The result is a complexity of overlapping forms which, however, in no way diminishes the clarity and simplicity of the whole. The concave, chalice capitals are decorated with acanthus leaveswhich cling closely to the core of the capitals themselves. The relief is delicate throughout, and hardly differs from that of the west part. The difference lies in the greater elegance of the details at the east end.

It is the combination of all these qualities that is important in the stylistic evaluation of the interior of Saint-Denis as the first work of the Early Gothic style. In addition, the windows are furnished with stained glass. By insisting on having a mosaic in the façade, Suger put his mystical leanings before unity of form. Stained glass, however, achieved both purposes. It produces the unreal and mystical Gothic light which softens the alternation of dark and light in the mouldings and also unites the space of a church by its atmosphere of mystery. Suger says of it that 'it transfuses the interior with wonderful and uninterrupted light.' From Saint-Denis on, stained glass became one of the integrating elements of the Gothic style, influencing even the form of

34. Saint-Denis Abbey Church.
Ambulatory, 1140–3

the windows – their shape and their size. At first the design of the glass was still purely Romanesque, an example of how two arts can develop at a different tempo. But, by collaborating with Gothic architects, the painters were gradually stimulated into making their figures and compositions Gothic. In Saint-Denis, the rows of windows were one of the means of creating continuity of space, and their subdued, coloured light contributed to this impression.[5E]

To understand the development of style it is essential to rid oneself not only of the preconceived idea that progress in style takes place at the same rate in every one of the arts, but equally of the conception that, within architecture itself, the interior and the exterior always develop simultaneously. Naturally the architect tried to find a form for his exterior that would correspond to that of the interior. This stylistic intention is evident in Saint-Denis, but it was not sufficient. The task itself proved very difficult. During the period of transition, exteriors remained completely Romanesque. This is true of Saint-Etienne at *Beauvais*, *Saint-Germer*, and Saint-Martin near *Etampes*. In churches in which the new type of vault was an afterthought, the exterior naturally remained the same – for example, in the two main churches at *Caen*. At *Saint-Denis* the exterior of the chapels is divided by the horizontal line at the base of the windows [96]. Below this the round Romanesque-looking windows of the crypt have no imposts and are set on an axis different from that of the relieving wall-arches. On the main storey the pointed arches of the windows correspond to the relieving arches, but the latter are at a higher level, their springing lying at about the same level as the inner apex of the window arches. This shift, which reminds one of the adjustable tubes of a telescope, was the result of the fact that the cells of the vaults in the chapels rise. The only other examples of this loose relationship between two arches are to be found in the inte-

35. Sens Cathedral, begun *c.* 1140.
Interior

riors of the collegiate church at *Mantes*, and the parish church at *Chars*. Considered separately, the exterior of the bottom storey can only be called Romanesque, or even Roman. However, the pointed arches and the slender shafts continuing on the outer frame make the main storey Gothic. The buttresses with a section in the form of half an octagon could be called Gothic too, but would be more accurately described as Transitional. The slender columns at the sides of the windows repeat the form of the interior; they are a rhythmic echo of the columns that carry the vaults of the ambulatories. The translation of the appearance of the exterior into the idiom of the Gothic style lagged far behind the development of the interior. The Gothic style developed downwards from the vault, and this explains the slower development of the exterior.[5F]

If we are right in dating it its beginning to about 1140, then the choir of *Sens* was built at the same times as that of

Saint-Denis. It is possible that preparations for the building were made before 1140, perhaps before 1137.[6] For reasons of statics the choir aisles and ambulatories were always built first, and these were designed as part of the first campaign, begun a little before the choir of Saint-Denis.[6A] The rib-vaults here rise from corbels which have been squeezed in over the capitals of round transverse arches, confirming that groin and not rib-vaults were originally planned.[6B] The ambulatory windows with their round arches, and the dado of round arches below them, look pure Romanesque. However, the internal elevation of the choir itself is comparatively Gothic [35]. The alternation of supports, so rich in contrast, resulted in a sexpartite vault. The intermediate supports consist of two round piers which stand, not one beside the other, but one behind the other, as they do in the church of Saint-Martin near Etampes, going up from about 1142, just after the beginning of Sens, and under its influence.[6c] From the strongly-projecting abacus a very slender shaft rises, between the pointed arches, to the level of the window-sill, which is also the level of the springing of the vault. Between the arcade and the windows lie the false gallery openings, each consisting of two pointed arches which in turn are divided into two sub-arches. The original clerestory was also divided into two sections, with two windows in each, but it was replaced after 1268 in the Rayonnant style.[7] The wall-arches are supported by shafts which stand on a horizontal moulding at the springing of the vault. Each group of two bays lies within a frame composed of groups of uninterrupted vertical shafts. The extensive wall-surfaces in the region of the triforium are a remnant of the Romanesque, but the pointed arches with their openings, together with the arcade and the former windows, form a convincing unity. We can recognize only by going to later works of the Gothic style that at Sens there is already a beginning of the Gothic type of relief. The main triforium arches are given the same profile as is given to the archivolts of the arcade below. They still form a receding layer of space (which is a Romanesque feature), but the narrow shaft of the intermediate transverse arch projects, and the elevation seems to be conceived as a system pri-marily concerned with the whole and only secondarily with the parts, and in this, to some extent, it goes beyond the Romanesque. Whether to call this Transitional or Early Gothic must remain the decision of each individual observer. There is a soothing tranquillity in the building, which is largely due to the proportions of its cross-section. The measurements are $49\frac{1}{2}$ by $78\frac{1}{2}$ ft (15.25 by 24.40 m.), which is almost exactly the *sectio aurea*, so beloved of the High Renaissance. The rectangle between the main piers, extending upwards to the line of the springing of the arches, has almost the same proportions. However, it must not be overlooked that the secondary proportions of the individual members also play their part. Though at Sens the *sectio aurea* governs two important sets of dimensions, it cannot be claimed that these proportions are characteristic of the Gothic style.[7A]

The choir at *Noyon* [36] is far more characteristically Gothic. While the choir of Sens can give us clues to the appearance of the lost choir of Saint-Denis, the choir of Noyon represents a more advanced stage of development. In the ambulatory at Saint-Denis the creations of a 'hall' of two aisles was specifically Gothic. At Noyon the chancel rises – as at Saint-Denis and Sens – above the gallery, but the elevation at Sens leads to the conclusion that at Saint-Denis also Gothic features did not appear very clearly. At Noyon we see the earliest extant building in which all parts of the system – the rib-vault, the pointed longitudinal and transverse arches, the piers and shafts – form a single skeleton which, in order to establish itself as the dominating factor, both allows and demands the dissolution of the wall. Structure prevails, and the loads therefore appear light.

The choir at Noyon was begun about 1148. Work started on the two choir towers and the western bays of the choir and worked eastwards, with the exterior walls at aisle and gallery levels preceding, respectively, the choir arcades and gallery openings. The whole choir was finished probably by *c.* 1165, though it probably remained faithful to the general plan laid down in about 1148.[7B] This date, then, is a decisive

one in the history of the style, although no influence was visible in other buildings until the work at Noyon had made at least some progress.[7c]

Ever since 1835, when Johannes Wetter explained that the dissolution of the wall was the product of four main factors – the cross-vault, the rib, the pointed arch, and the buttress – this principle has always been emphasized as one of the main characteristics of the Gothic style. However, the piercing of the wall is a phenomenon that also exists in other styles. Within the Gothic style it is not the size or the quantity of the openings in the wall which is decisive; it is what can only be called the specific Gothic relief.

In the fine arts – sculpture and painting – the word relief is applied to the degree of curvature and projection in the finished work, by comparison with that in the actual model. When depth is reproduced in the same proportions as height and breadth, we speak of high relief. If we diminish depth without diminishing the other dimensions, we have bas-relief in its various degrees. Finally the dimension of depth can reach zero, when it is either omitted entirely, as in a line drawing or a silhouette, or suggested through light and shade or different tones of colour. However, the word relief can also be used in architecture, e.g. in relation to a Romanesque wall with pilasters and a frieze of small round arches on corbels, a motif which for no very good reasons is known in England as a Lombard frieze. Here one sees more than one layer, as the surfaces of the pilasters and the round arches lie in one plane, while the wall itself lies in a second plane further back. Even where there are more than two planes, for instance in a portal with a series of receding arches on a corresponding series of receding columns, or in a window, the Romanesque principle always produces an effect of recession by steps. Aesthetically, this type of relief keeps the visitor at a distance from the final plane of the wall-surface itself. He feels that there is a boundary holding him at a respectful distance. It can be said of Romanesque relief that one reads through it from the nearest plane to the most distant.[8]

The relief at Noyon is quite different. Mathematically speaking, it makes no difference whether the planes of the relief stand one in front of the other or one behind the other. Aesthetically speaking, however, the only valid statement in considering Gothic buildings is to say that the planes stand one in front of the other. This can be most clearly seen in the gallery at Noyon. Halfway through the thickness of the wall stands a column which supports the inner arch. In front of it stands another, supporting the archivolt. Close to it, and allowing none of the wall and only a small section of the pier to show, are the shafts supporting the diagonal ribs. They stand on either side of the still further projecting shaft which carries the transverse arch.

A comparison with the choir at Saint-Germer shows that the main planes there still stand behind one another, but that already the new inversion can be felt. This inversion increases in intensity as the Gothic style, so to speak, discovers its own true nature.

36. Noyon Cathedral, begun *c.* 1148. Interior

The cathedral of Noyon is rich in forms. The architect obviously took pleasure in modifying the elevation of the choir in the north and south ends of the transept, although they have no ambulatory and no gallery [37, 41]. So he put the triforium directly above the arcade, and above this built a series of windows to correspond to the gallery in the choir. Then, above, a clerestory lies within the vault. There is a wall-passage along the triforium, a second one along the inside of the lower windows, and a third at the outside of the upper ones. Convincing proof exists that the models for these wall-passages are to be found in Normandy, for example in the apse of La Trinité at Caen.[9] In such structures in Normandy, the wall, as seen from the interior, appears to consist of two layers; as seen from the exterior, this was already the case in Romanesque buildings in the Rhineland and in Italy because of the dwarf galleries.[9A] The sources of the Gothic style lie in the Romanesque, and especially in that of Normandy. The Gothic style is a transformation of this Norman style, and because this is so, it is legitimate to look for the adoption of Norman forms in the Gothic style itself.[9B] But this is not enough. The question is: why can the division of the wall into two layers at Noyon no longer be called Romanesque? The answer is that, in La Trinité at Caen, the surface of the wall, in spite of the increased size of perforations, remains a unit. The piers look as if they were joining hands. They are a row of frontal members. Every part of the building faces us. We feel that we could run our hand over these surfaces as we could over that of the semi-dome above. At Noyon, however, the columns in the gallery seem to face one another, with their flanks towards us. If we were to stretch out our hand now, we would find no surface, but we could insert it into the gap between each column and the next. This impression is produced by the relief treatment. The forms come towards us from the core of the wall. No longer do they stand aloof, holding us at a distance. Now they draw us into this spatial unity, which is ours as well as theirs. The Gothic choir embraces us; it unites us with the building, and by opening both inwards and outwards it also unites the interior with the exterior.

The projection of the planes of the wall into the interior finds its necessary complement in the equal projection of the members towards the outside, which produces the characteristically Gothic exterior. This is hardly noticeable at Noyon, but, since the windows of the apse lie close to the buttresses, and these in turn (in as far as they are original) are changed into flat projecting members which could not be called a plane in the sense of Romanesque pilasters, one can say that the glass in the windows is a visible part of the central layer of the wall, from which the other layers of the relief project towards us. Because the principle of the internal and the external relief is the same, it makes the whole wall appear a unity.

At Noyon the small flying buttresses supporting the chevet gallery may reflect the original twelfth-century system. The clerestory flyers are eighteenth-century, and those in the nave belong to the original construction of c. 1185.[9C] The transepts have the original buttresses with steeply pitched tops, in contrast to the capitals at the top of the buttresses of the choir at Saint-Denis. Buttresses with this sort of slope were known in the Romanesque period. In the Gothic period they become the general rule. At Noyon the buttresses already form a deeper projection at the bottom, or conversely project less at the top, which, in mathematical terms, is the same thing. The rational explanation for this is that the line of forces set up by the vault permits economy of materials at the upper levels. However, this possibility was exploited because the resultant form fitted in, stylistically, with the Gothic form of relief. It made it more difficult to see the exterior as a surface determined by the points that project to the very outside layer, and, conversely, made it easier to consider the wall as determined by the innermost layer, that is, the glass in the windows. Aesthetically, the buttresses project towards us, and, at the bottom, where they are nearest to us, they project furthest. In terms of mathematics this difference is unimportant; in terms of aesthetics, however, it has a decisive significance.

The analysis of the increasing tendency to partiality is only one of the stylistic factors of this building. The design of Noyon is characterized as much by its wealth of forms as by its lack of preoccupation with economy of materials or labour. The form of the semicircular ends of the transepts area case in point. They are built in five storeys, if one counts the lower, rather Romanesque blind gallery. Another example of richness of form is the multitude of shaft-rings. Here again there exists a rational explanation. These stones bond into the wall itself, and serve as a support for the monolithic sections of the shafts. Thus they facilitate the actual building, and to some extent increase the stability of the shaft. All this must be conceded. However, to our eyes, these stones do not penetrate the wall; they look like rings that have been added, and where they appear at the same levels as a horizontal ledge, they look like continuations of the ledge, bent and moulded round the shafts. Their ring-like character is emphasized by their section, which has identical, symmetrically receding curves above and below the horizontal centreline. Corbels, which penetrate the wall and reach deep into it, have a very different profile. These rings add life to groups of shafts; they form an aesthetic bond between them, and indicate a horizontal layer when they appear on the same level on each group of shafts. At Sens shaft-rings are still used in moderation. At Noyon, they are the product of a deep-felt need for wealth and vivacity. In the nave they appear only in the two easternmost double bays (and only at arcade level in the western of those two bays). As is to be expected from the alternation of its supports, the eastern double bay of the nave was projected with sexpartite vaults. It was laid out c. 1165–80, as part of the campaign on the transepts. But the sexpartite system was abandoned in favour of quadripartite vaults when work reached the upper parts in c. 1180.[10]

The cathedral of *Senlis*, begun in 1151/2, vaulted throughout by about 1185 and consecrated in 1191, also had sexpartite vaults. After a fire in 1504, the transepts were lengthened in the latest Late Gothic style. The plan and details of the chevet owe something to Saint-Denis, Saint-Germer and Noyon, while the lack of a transept in the original church, together with the strong alternating system, show the inspiration of Sens.[11] The interior elevation combined the three-storey scheme of Sens and Saint-Denis with the large vaulted tribunes of Noyon, and, with its expanses

37. Noyon Cathedral. Interior of transept, designed *c.* 1165/70

of flat wall, anticipated that of Notre-Dame in Paris. But it was simpler than these in every way, and its charm was of a more intimate kind. The Late Gothic clerestorey has robbed the interior of all its harmony. The exterior of the choir clearly shows the contrast between the 'Romanesque' style, in the emphasis on the closed wall in the chapels, and the Gothic dissolution of the wall, in the flying buttresses and the windows of the upper storey. In the Middle Ages the modern principle that restoration should follow the style of what could be preserved was seldom recognized. Each generation held that its own style was the only permissible one.

If we deplore the particularly sharp and disturbing discrepancies in style at Senlis, we must not base our judgement on the purist ideals which did so much damage in the nineteenth century. In many cases architects succeeded in producing a unity out of the work of various periods. Some did not succeed, and others did not even attempt to do so, thinking that such a unity was impossible to achieve.

Saint-Germain-des-Prés in *Paris* is an example of a successful blend. The west tower was built by Abbot Morard (990–1014), the nave and crossing later, in the course of the eleventh century. The segregated crossing is therefore several decades later than that of St Michael at Hildesheim (from *c.* 1100). Saint-Germain-des-Prés is thus Early French Romanesque, not, as Franz Mertens believed in 1845, the start of the Gothic style. The Romanesque choir was altered at the same time as the choir of Saint-Denis was being erected, or when it had just been completed [38]. In

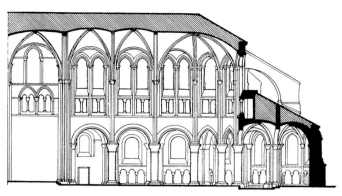

38. Paris, Saint-Germain-des-Prés, choir, consecrated 1163.
Longitudinal section

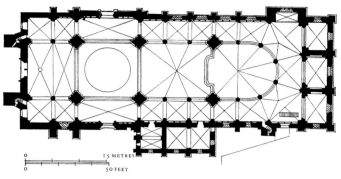

39. Provins, Saint-Quiriace, begun c. 1157. Plan

plan and elevation the two are closely related, but in Saint-Germain there is only a single ambulatory. The choir was built with a false gallery which in the straight bays opened into the choir with four coupled openings per bay, or at Sens and probably Saint-Denis. The original elevation is preserved in the two towers that flank the entrance to the choir. In the seventeenth century the windows were extended downwards to the level of the springing of the arches of the original gallery, and this gallery then became a triforium. The Early Gothic choir, consecrated in 1163, must have made a fine combination with the Romanesque nave and transepts, whose rib-vaults are seventeenth-century work – an early example of the care of ancient monuments according to modern principles. We also see some not very pleasing wall-paintings of 1810, some even less pleasing modern stained glass in the windows, and some restored capitals. Yet, in spite of all this, the church is homely and attractive, and extends a powerful invitation to quiet meditation.

The date at which this Early Gothic choir was consecrated makes it probable that it was begun after Noyon and at the same time as Senlis.[11A] Compared with the almost frighteningly slender columns in the apse at Senlis, those in Saint-Germain look robust, probably a conscious effort to make them match the Romanesque piers in the nave.[12] The heavy capitals, too, hardly differ in style from the Romanesque ones in the nave (or rather from the originals of these at the Cluny Museum in Paris).

The church of Saint-Quiriace at *Provins* [39], begun soon after 1157, also has these short, stocky columns.[12A] The broad archivolts of the arcade rest on the abaci leaving between them only just room for a very slender shaft with rings round it, reminiscent of the shafts at Sens. This shaft rises past the great double openings of the triforium to support a multipartite vault with a highly developed keystone. The architect does not seem to have seen any contradiction between the round arches of the triforium and the windows, and the pointed arches of the arcade. The bay adjoining the apse has an octopartite vault. Two intersecting ribs form normal diagonals, and between them two more ribs spring from the side walls, which they divide into three parts, and also intersect at the apex of the vault. These ribs, which look rather like a spider, were repeated, probably by the same architect, at *Voulton*,[13] and there is a later, similar vault in the east chapel of the cathedral at *Auxerre*. The capriciousness

of the designer of Provins is further shown in the form of the ambulatory. The straight eastern wall of the ambulatory opens into three rectangular chapels. The rectangular form, unusual for an ambulatory, resulted in unusual forms of vaults, which, however, could be easily constructed by using the pointed arch. However, the originality of this architect did not prove fertile. The Gothic style developed from Noyon, and not from Saint-Quiriace. It is in the cathedral at Laon that the forms of Noyon are taken up and developed.

In trying to date *Laon*,[14] we know that the cathedral was begun by Bishop Gautier de Mortagne, who held office from 1155 to 1174 [40, 42] The Carolingian church was renovated 997–1030 and damaged by fire in 1112 in a rising of the populace against the bishop. It was repaired, but by 1155 it was either considered unsuitable or unsafe. Gautier also built the little two-storeyed *private chapel* in the bishop's palace. This is designed on a central plan. Both storeys are built round a square central space; the lower floor has piers with shafts, the upper one round piers. The plan thus forms a Greek cross with four supplementary square spaces in the corners. The transverse arches are pointed, while the windows have round arches. The lower storey has groin-vaults throughout: the upper floor has tunnel-vaults in the four arms, groin-vaults in the corner squares, and a rib-vault, supported on corbels, over the central square. This plan is reminiscent of Byzantine churches built round a main central space, and the polygonal apse also reminds one of churches of this kind. However, the east choir of the cathedral at Verdun, consecrated in 1147, may be a nearer model for the polygonal apse.[14A]

There are two reasons why this private chapel was considered important to the study of the *cathedral* at *Laon*. First, it seemed older in style, and was therefore considered to have been built before the cathedral. If the chapel had been begun in 1155, immediately after Bishop Gautier's taking office, then the cathedral must have been begun some years *after* 1155. Second, the polygonal apse of the chapel was thought to be the precursor of the original choir of the cathedral, which was reconstructed by some scholars as having a polygonal apse. On both counts, the chapel cannot now be considered significant for the cathedral. First, it may have been begun at any time during the construction of the cathedral.[14B] Secondly, the cathedral's original choir termination, which was pulled down some time after 1205 and replaced by the present square-ended choir, was almost certainly semicircular and not polygonal.[14C] However, the two apses on the east side of the transepts have been preserved in their original state, and are polygonal from the level of the lowest lancet windows.

Polygonal apses existed in Byzantine, Roman, and Early Christian times, but those at Laon are the earliest in a completely Gothic building. The advantage of departing from the circular plan at the level of the sill of the windows or yet lower down was to alleviate the discrepancy between the curved window surrounds and the flat surface of the glass. This contrast can be seen very distinctly in the windows of the choir at Saint-Denis. The demand that all windows should be filled with stained glass became increasingly strong. The new principle of the dissolution of the wall increased actual window-space, and so made the contradiction between the curve of the wall and the flat surface of the stained glass even more obvious. At the same time a similar aesthetic conflict had sprung up between the rib-vault in the apse and its semicylindrical form. The polygonal plan would have resolved all these problems, and, moreover, it fitted in admirably with the new emphasis on the diagonals which the rib had brought to bear on the two main axes which had earlier marked the only decisive directions of every church. Even seen at an angle, a semicylindrical apse will always appear frontal, whereas in a polygonal apse, though one may stand frontally to one side, one will always see slanting sides at the same time. Several images are seen simultaneously, and all are included in the optical impression of the whole. The polygonal plan is a manifestation of the Gothic desire for the 'multiple image',[14D] and, at the same time, it is the result of the extension of the use of stained glass.

This multiplicity of images is one of the main factors in the charm of the interior and the exterior of Laon. On the exterior it is achieved, above all, by the towers. These have rightly been connected with the towers of the cathedral at *Tournai*, where the heavy crossing tower, together with the two slenderer towers over the ends of the transepts, form a group of monumental prodigality [57]. Its silhouette changes with the angle from which it is seen. So the result here is a multiple image also. The tendency towards what, since the writings of Gilpin in the eighteenth century, has been called 'picturesque' is a feature of the later stages of many styles, and it is also one of the integrating factors of the Late Romanesque, to which the transepts of Tournai, built *c.* 1130–60, certainly belong.[15] The Gothic style, considered as an offshoot of the Romanesque which developed at the same time as the Late Romanesque style, also shows this tendency towards the picturesque, but used totally new architectural members to achieve its effect. Moreover, on the exterior it used the new Gothic concept of relief. One must assume that the decision to build a crossing tower, four towers over the transepts, and two at the west façade of Laon was made about 1170–75, but the west towers were not complete until *c.* 1200, and the two transept towers were built later in the thirteenth century.[15A] A comparison with Tournai shows that a complete change in style had taken place. The relief of the church at Tournai is still Romanesque throughout.

40. Laon Cathedral, begun after 1155. The choir is shown in its original form

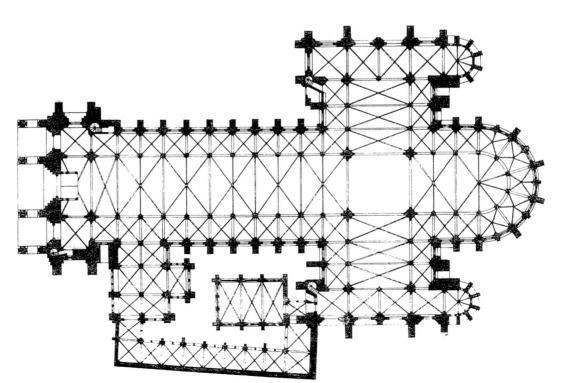

41. Noyon Cathedral, longditudinal section

It appears that the first architect at Laon began with the east bays of the transepts, starting on the south side, and then moved into the choir. The elevation is four-storeyed, is similar to the choir at Noyon, although it still has some round arches. The triforium is a genuine passage, as it was in the later parts of Noyon.[15B] The relationship between Laon and Noyon can be traced chronologically, almost bay for bay. One has the impression that the two architects visited one another and discussed each successive step. In the transepts at Laon each bay received a quadripartite vault, and in the choir and the nave each double bay a sexpartite one. Conversely, at Noyon, the choir has quadripartite vaults, built sometime between about 1170 and about 1185, while the easternmost bay of the nave was planned to be covered with a sexpartite vault, like those at Laon, but when in about 1180–85 the masons reached the level of the vault springers on the south side of that bay it was decided to adopt the present quadripartite vaults.[16] At that time the double bay in the choir at Laon, with its sexpartite vault, was already finished [40]. This double bay at Laon is preserved in its original state. The systematic arrangement of the shafts to correspond to their respective ribs is common to both churches. At the corners of each sexpartite bay, where a transverse arch, two diagonals, and two wall-arches had to be considered, there are five shafts, standing side by side, while in the middle of the bays there are only three [42]. This is usually called logical. However, the premise for this logic is that every arch should have its own support; so it is surprising that this logic is nullified by the arrangement of the arcade piers, which are round in every case. At Noyon in the easternmost bay of the nave the groups of shafts at the corners of what was intended originally to be a sexpartite bay rise uninterrupted. This produces a powerful alternation and distribution of accents. The same had been done at Sens [35]. At Laon, the regular row of round piers partly

does away with the Romanesque emphasis on square superordinate bays. This regular row of identical piers later became a specifically Gothic motif. At Laon, the combination of the identical piers with the alternating groups of shafts above them, while it possessed richness and charm, certainly made architects wonder about its illogicality. This problem remained, and, in about 1180, the third architect tried to solve it in the nave by setting four shafts round each of the piers at the corner of the two double bays next to the crossing. These four shafts stand on the same plinth as the round pier and help to carry the abacus, but are joined to the pier only by rings. These piers are similar to some piers in the presbytery of Canterbury cathedral, dated precisely to 1177 and 1178, which show various combinations of thin shafts grouped around the core of the pillar.[16A] This arrangement was, however, not continued at Laon.[16B] The transepts at Laon have aisles, and, above them, the gallery continues round the two ends, as it does in some older Norman churches.[16C] The reason for this preoccupation with continuous circulation at Laon was that many pilgrims visited the church. The effect of a multiplicity of images is created by the aisles of the transept, together with their chapels below and above. The interior is Gothic also by reason of the relief and the close connexion of the vaulting-shafts with the columns of the gallery and those of the triforium. As at Noyon, the members project, beginning from the innermost layer of the walls. As at Noyon also, the openings of the gallery create by the mouldings of their members the effect of division. The whole always strikes one as existing aesthetically (not genetically) before the parts. Groups of openings were prefigured in Romanesque times. However, in the Gothic style they were transformed by the new kind of relief.

In common with Noyon, Laon has a multitude of shaft-rings, and also the tendency to a wealth of different architectural members. This characterizes both the interior and the exterior.[17] The monumental character of Noyon is reproduced and enhanced. Each of the great Gothic cathedrals has its own special atmosphere, which can hardly be expressed in words. Laon, with its light yellow stone and its abundance of unbroken light, is as joyful and festive in feeling as Noyon, but even more powerful. The cathedral of Notre-Dame in Paris can be clearly distinguished from both of them by its gloom.

The cathedrals of *Paris* and Laon were under construction at the same time, though they seemed to have exercised no architectural influence on each other.[17A] The foundation of the choir of Notre-Dame in Paris is supposed to have been laid in 1163 by Pope Alexander III, but it is likely that the building was begun a few years earlier in *c.* 1160. Laon may have been started *c.* 1155–60.[17B] In Paris there are sexpartite vaults [44], and the way in which the shafts rise above the abaci of the round piers is also the same as at Laon [43].[17C] There is one simplification. In the choir, at the main bay divisions, and in the nave throughout, the shafts supporting the wall arches only begin at the springing of the vault. The main impression, therefore, is of a series of

42. Laon Cathedral, begun after 1155. Interior looking east

43. Paris, Notre-Dame. Interior of choir and north transept, begun *c.* 1160

44. Paris, Notre-Dame, ground plan. *c.* 1160–*c.* 1220

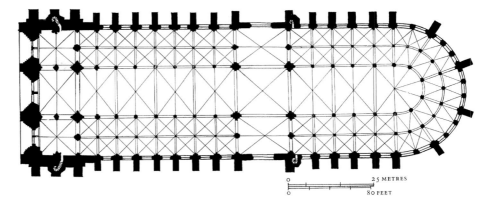

groups of three shafts, as in the apses of Noyon and Laon, where there is no alternation of ribs with transverse arches. This has led to the hypothesis that the simplified form in Paris is later, as does the fact that in Paris there are exclusively pointed arches, and that the shaft-rings have been omitted. The original semicylindrical form of the apse, before its remodelling into the present radiating chapels in the early fourteenth century, had much smaller windows, which probably minimized the discrepancy between the curved wall and the flat surface of the glass. In any case the original apse in Paris may not have been smooth but – like the later Bourges – had niche-like radiating chapels.[17D] It is extremely noticeable today, however, as the large windows of about 1300, with their tracery, made it necessary for the two sides of each of the stained-glass windows (which are modern) to meet at an obtuse angle on the centre mullion. The glass in the rose-window above them lies on a plane that cuts across the angle below. In this discrepancy the connexion between the polygonal apse and the stained glass can be seen more clearly than anywhere else. Bar tracery was not easily combined with rounded choirs, and bar tracery originated at Reims cathedral, which was only begun in 1211, long after the polygonal plan had appeared in the 1170s in the Soissonais and at Laon. (The original stained glass at Laon has not been preserved, except that in the east wall dating from *c.* 1210, and some original medallions from the north transept rose.[17E])

The cathedral in Paris is double-aisled, with a gallery over the inner aisles. This means that it has the basilican system of elevation twice repeated. This is true also of the choir, where building began. It has a double ambulatory, like Saint-Denis. This type of interior creates special lighting problems. The sloping roof of the outer aisles makes it necessary to put the gallery windows relatively high. The light they give is sufficient for the gallery, but too little to affect the nave or the chancel. The sloping roof of the gallery, in turn, forces the clerestory windows up above the springing of the vault. The space inside this sloping roof corresponds to what is normally an unlit triforium, but here the architect pierced it with an oculus in every bay. Their tracery is different from that of the wheel-windows of Saint-Etienne at Beauvais and Saint-Denis. Before their restoration by Viollet-le-Duc, they consisted of vertically arranged crosses, with straight or curved sides and decorated with chevron or bead ornament. Originally the small gallery windows were such oculi.[18] The smaller dimensions of the windows are a consequence of the double aisles. The thrust of the gallery vault [54] could only be carried by a buttress which could not project far, because it stood over the transverse arch of the vault of the outer aisle. Similarly, the buttresses bearing the thrust of the main vault stood over the transverse arches of the gallery vault. The architect apparently believed that the vault also exercised a thrust on the wall between the transverse arches, and therefore did not dare to build wider windows. The improvements in the lighting which followed the introduction of new flying buttresses in the 1220s were partly offset by the addition of chapels along the outer aisles and round the outer ambulatory, begun in *c.* 1225–30.[18A] Notre-Dame remains one of the dark churches of a 'dark age'. To us it is the darkness of this cathedral which gives it its mystery and solemnity. Every time the windows were enlarged, the possible increase in light was eliminated by the obscurity of the stained glass. Most of this glass dates from the nineteenth century, but even in the twelfth and thirteenth centuries all the glass in the windows was coloured.

The choir and transepts were completed in about twenty-five years. The transepts did not project further than the outer wall of the outer aisles. We do not know whether the windows in the north and south walls of the transepts were large or small.[18B] Certainly the degree of dissolution of the wall was much less than that achieved in the lengthened transepts that were added by Jean de Chelles from about 1245 (north transept) and by Pierre de Montreil from about 1258 (south transept).[18C]

The cathedral in Paris made relatively rapid progress. In following this chronological development, we need, for the moment, consider only the choir of Notre-Dame and conceive it in its original state – without its surrounding chapels [44]. The plan for the whole church, perhaps with a shorter nave and without transepts, must have been made *c.* 1160. In contrast to Laon, and to the choir of Notre-Dame itself, the transepts have no aisles. Each of the double choir aisles, cut off from the choir by the high screens, now gives the impression of a hall-church of two naves, and this must have been the impression even before the screen was erected.

The vaults in the double ambulatory in Notre-Dame are unusual. The apse has five sides, while the inner ambulatory has ten. Thus one of the piers stands on the central axis. The effect of the larger number of piers in the ambulatory is to make all the arches look almost the same width [44]. The best way to describe the vaults is to number off the piers of

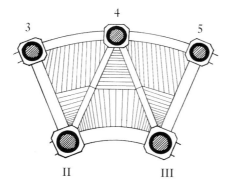

45. (*above, left*) Reims, Saint-Remi, *c.* 1170–80. Interior of ambulatory

46. (*left*) Paris, Notre-Dame, begun *c.* 1160. Vault of ambulatory (after Viollet-le-Duc) with Frankl's numbering

47. (*above*) Mantes, Collegiate church of Notre-Dame, begun *c.* 1160. Interior looking east

the apse from the beginning of the semicircle on each side with Roman numbers – I left, II left, III left, I right, II right, III right – and the free-standing piers between the two ambulatories with Arabic numbers – 1 left, 2 left, 3 left, 4 left, 5 left, 1 right, 2 right, 3 right, 4 right, 5 right, 6, being the pier standing on the central axis. I and 1 , II and 3, and III and 5 are connected on each side by pointed transverse arches; and two pointed ribs (with a slenderer profile than that of the transverse arches) run from each of the piers in the ambulatory to the piers in the apse – that is two from 2 to I and II, two from 4 to II and III, and two from 6 (the central pier) to III left and III right. This gives a total of fifteen bays. The vault of each triangular bay consists of two cells

which meet on the horizontal groin joining the apexes of the ribs. Thus in plan half of each triangular bay forms another triangle, the other half a trapezium. In the triangular bays the stone courses lie parallel to the horizontal ridge of the penetration; the others have purely empirical surfaces in which the stone courses rise more or less vertically to the horizontal ridge (or groin) that connects the apexes of the ribs. The outer ambulatory has similar vaults, but with the difference that the first two bays are triangular and have cells like those in the inner ambulatory. Viollet-le-Duc described the vaults, and a simplified version of his sketch can be seen in Plate 46.[19]

While the choir of Notre-Dame was being built, in about

48. Reims, Saint-Remi, *c.* 1170–80.
Interior of choir

1170, the abbot Pierre de Celle began to build a new choir in the church of *Saint-Remi* at *Reims* [48]. This was to be a simplified version of the spatial plan of Notre-Dame. In the three bays towards the apse the choir has double aisles, but there is only a single ambulatory, and in vaulting it the architect found a new solution to the problem. He set two free-standing columns in the opening of each chapel, so that the ambulatory vault consists of a series of almost square bays, each flanked by two triangular ones [45].[20] The result is uncommonly rich in effect, as the columns standing in front of the shafts of the chapels and the entrances to them create a free rhythm and a great wealth of changing views.[20A]

In its arcade, and its gallery, the choir follows the general disposition of Notre-Dame, and the small windows must give an approximate notion of what the Paris church originally looked like. Otherwise the upper part of the choir is very different. The windows are arranged in groups of three, and the shafts that frame them rise from the level of the triforium – an early attempt to achieve some kind of unity between these two storeys.[20B]

While the circular windows which were used in Paris were rejected by the architect of Saint-Remi at Reims, they were repeated at *Mantes* [47]. However, here they are used in the gallery over the ambulatory. At Mantes the triforium is omitted. Instead the architect set the arches in the apse high above the openings of the gallery, similarly to the method that was adopted on the exterior of the choir of Saint-Denis. The church at Mantes was begun probably around 1160,[21] and, in spite of its smaller proportions and its simpler plan, it is, in many ways, closely related to Notre-Dame; it is, however, far more intimate. As there are no transepts, the impression is of a hall with aisles and a gallery. The three sexpartite vaults, connected by the alternating supports, allow a comprehensive view of the whole church. The main piers have shafts rising from the ground, as at Sens; the secondary piers between them are round, with groups of shafts rising from the capitals, as at Noyon, Laon, and Paris. This combination is especially striking as the shafts on the round apse rise from the abaci of the circular piers. The openings of the gallery in the apse are not divided. In the nave, however, they are divided into three arches on two columns, as in the nave of Notre-Dame, which was not begun until c. 1170.

The gallery has a series of pointed transverse tunnel-vaults, which shows how undecided architects could still be at this time. These vaults are supported on transverse architraves standing on columns. A cross-section through the choir[22] shows that these vaults explain the raised pointed arches and the large round windows in the gallery. The tunnel-vaults were probably intended to strengthen the main vault.[22A] In the fourteenth century, many of these vaults were replaced by quadripartite rib-vaults. The original bays in the gallery, particularly those at the round end of the choir, form a series of separate spatial unities which make up a whole by addition, and are rich in picturesque views between the columns. The exterior of the choir as we know it today has been altered by the addition of thirteenth-century chapels.[23]

The choir of the priory church at *Saint-Leu-d'Esserent* was built at the same time as that of Mantes. It still has a round apse, and, as at Mantes, the absence of transepts gives the whole building the appearance of a hall. The shafts supporting the wall-arches rise together with the shafts for the main ribs, beginning on the abaci of the round piers. Five chapels which, in plan, form a series of segmental arches stand round the ambulatory, as at Saint-Denis, but here the vaults in these niches are separated from those of the main ambulatory. Its proportions and profiles give the building a restrained elegance. The specifically Gothic profile is strong enough to decrease the aesthetic value of the large remaining expanses of wall. Only the upper windows have no framework and leave large, bare surfaces around them. The relatively small span of the vaults allowed the use of thin walls and slender supports.[24]

The choirs of Notre-Dame in Paris and of Laon Cathedral (in its original form) were complete by c. 1190 and c. 1170 respectively. They were no doubt known to William of Sens, the master who was called to *Canterbury* in 1174 after the fire which had destroyed the choir there. At Canterbury, soon after the conquest of England in 1066, Archbishop Lanfranc had erected a new building. Having been Prior of Saint-Etienne in Caen, he followed the Norman scheme of that time.[24A] Prior Ernulf replaced Lanfranc's choir and Prior Conrad, who succeeded him, finished it. The choir received a second transept, a new chancel with an ambulatory, and three isolated chapels, the first of them on the left and right placed in an oblique direction

adapted to the curve of the apse.[24B] This choir was burned down in 1174. William used the old foundations but lengthened the choir beyond the Norman ambulatory. William's activity ceased after his fall from the scaffolding in 1178 and he was replaced by a second William, called William the Englishman, who extended William of Sens' sanctuary eastwards by building the Trinity Chapel and, opening eastwards from it, a circular chapel called the *Corona*. Canterbury choir brought English architecture into line with the most progressive achievements of French early Gothic. Durham and the rib-vaults following Durham were Norman. Even if one regards as Englishmen the Normans of the first generations after the Conquest, they were more Norman than English. Between the time of the nave vaults of Durham (1128) and the appearance of William the Englishman half a century had passed. But for the development of style this interval had not been eventful in England, however one may appreciate the individual buildings.[24C] The plan with two sets of transepts comes from Cluny and is neither particularly Gothic nor particularly English in this first copy. However the English took Canterbury as their model, accepted the uncommon length of the twice-lengthened cathedral, and found it more magnificent than the harmonious relation of length to width in French architecture.

At Sens (as at Mantes) space is grouped into twin bays by alternating supports and sexpartite vaults. In the liturgical choir at Canterbury this conception is contained in the vaults, but the alternation of supports is reduced to alternation of circular with octagonal piers. In the sanctuary William of Sens used twin columns, taking Sens as his model, and William the Englishman continued this solution for all the main supports of the Trinity Chapel.[24D]

When William of Sens designed his new choir, the nave at Laon had just been begun. So the circular piers with detached shafts in the eastern bays of the nave at Laon (c. 1170–75) are contemporary with Canterbury. England knew such grouped piers at an earlier date (in the crypt of York Minster soon after 1154)[25] and specially liked to use them, often in conjunction with the use of dark stone for the detached shafts and light stone for the central round pier. At Canterbury much is made of this motif. French buildings of this period are on the whole monochrome, and colour appears only in the stained glass of the windows and perhaps in some capitals.[26] From the physical standpoint the colour of the Purbeck shafts belongs to the same range of optical means as stained glass, but the function is diametrically opposed. Stained glass spreads out, where the innermost layer of a wall becomes visible, the plane which in the Gothic style is meant to appear as the real spatial boundary. Coloured shafts however are structural parts in front of this plane. Their free projection in space strengthens the Gothic tendency to dissolve the wall. The shafts stand free in space, however much they may be part of the load-bearing framework.

The exterior is little affected by the new principle. The north and south walls of the main transept are essentially still Romanesque. Gervase, who compares the new with the old choir, points out the differences clearly – the earliest known analysis of style and an invaluable document for checking the rightness of our aesthetic interpretation.[27]

What he described and stylistically understood is the essentially French system of interior elevation.

At the same time as Canterbury the much more English cathedral of *Wells* was built. It was begun probably sometime between 1175 and 1180.[26A] Chancel, transepts, and the nave were complete early in the thirteenth century. The piers have twenty-four shafts, set so closely that the cross-shaped core is completely hidden. The rolls of the pointed arches correspond to the shafts. The hollows between the rolls create a rich general form. The Gothic diagonal flow has to a very marked degree replaced even the slightest memory of the sharp rectangular moulding of the Romanesque. Above the arcade is a false gallery with narrow openings and above that the clerestory with a Norman wall-passage.

The decisive non-French feature is the manner in which three horizontal zones stand almost unconnected above each other. Whereas in France shafts rise from the abaci and the general tendency is to link bays vertically, the shafts in the spandrels of the arcade are missing at Wells. In the nave they only appear in the zone of the false gallery, and not even at its sill, but between the arches, which do not have capitals. The effect is a horizontal fusion of space instead of the French vertical fusion. A French counter-example is the abbey of *Fécamp*, begun before Wells, after the fire of 1168. From that period date parts of the choir and the whole of the transept. Transverse and wall-arches are pointed, the ribs still semicircular.[28]

A somewhat later counterpart in Normandy is the nave of the cathedral of *Lisieux*, designed probably around 1165.[29] All three pairs of arches in the quadripartite rib-vaults are pointed, as at Wells. The upward movement that the pointed arches of the ribs so unmistakably impart to the vault is conducted along shafts that stand on the abaci of the round piers.

This principle of vertical movement, therefore, develops from the rib, and, although the aesthetic effect is of upward movement, historically it grew downwards from the apex.[29A] The development from the rib is so obvious that partisans of the principle of vertical movement claim that the English architects had misunderstood it, and that their application of a principle of horizontal movement was not truly Gothic. However, the English deduction of horizontalism from the rib-vault is as legitimate as French verticalism. A series of bays where the transverse arch has the same profile as the ribs produces a smooth continuity from bay to bay in the cells that meet at the transverse arch, and this continuous flow draws the whole nave into a horizontal unity. The later development of the Gothic style shows that this was the intention of these architects. After many attempts they achieved in Late Gothic a unifying fusion of space, both horizontally and vertically. The full consequences of the introduction of the rib-vault were only attained by this spatial fusion in both directions – and in the diagonals as well. The two main directions were first developed separately, one in England and the other in France.

The choir of *Notre-Dame-en-Vaux* at *Châlons-sur-Marne* [49] is so similar to that of Saint-Remi at Reims that it could be omitted from this book. However, the juxtaposition of the choir and the transepts is exceptionally instructive

49. Châlons-sur-Marne, Notre-Dame-en-Vaux. Interior. Transept begun *c.* 1140; choir rebuilt 1187–1217

in differentiating between the new Gothic style and the old Romanesque. In the transepts, built *c.* 1140–1157, the profile of the piers recedes step by step in right angles, and the same is true of the openings of the gallery above. Both storeys of the choir are similar to those of the transept, in their basic form as well as in their proportions. The impression they make, however, is quite different, owing to the softness of the profiles, which, in the arcade, seem to project into the church from the innermost core of the round piers. The openings of the gallery have the same character. Above this level also the choir is very different from the transepts, with their solid wall surfaces and their broad, massive piers. However it is not the quantitative degree in which the wall has been dissolved that makes the piers, the arches, and the other members Gothic; for the same degree has been achieved in the lower structure of the transepts. The difference lies in the way in which this dissolution has been achieved. The rebuilding of the choir was begun *c.* 1187.[30]

50. Vézelay, La Madeleine. Interior of choir, begun after 1165, under construction in 1170s

51. Development of capitals: Romanesque cushion capital and Gothic chalice capitals. The two capitals on the right are crocket capitals

2. CHANGES IN CAPITALS AND BASES

The early phase of the Romanesque style found in the cushion capital the small-scale representation of the principle of addition that it needed [23]. The cushion capital was superseded by a mixture of the cubic and the chalice forms, beginning at the bottom in the shape of a chalice, and broadening into a square section. The Gothic style preferred the pure chalice shape [51].

Around this core, sculptors carved ornament, foliage, branches, animals, human figures, figures drawn from their own fantasy, scenes from religious history, symbolic forms, and combinations of all these subjects. Thousands of variations have been preserved, standing mid-way between sculpture and ornament. In the history of architectural style, their most important feature is the way in which the diagonals are emphasized, and the specific kinds of relief which they embody.

The cushion capitals of the Early Romanesque presented the sculptor with frontal surfaces which he decorated according to the principle of recession in parallel planes. The main ornamental forms are flat patterned bands, palmettes, and acanthus leaves which spread out symmetrically and look as if they had been compressed between the front and the back plane of the thickness of the relief. Even where figure sculpture is combined with ornament or foliage, and the depth is increased, the principle that the planes are parallel to one another is upheld. This is gradually broken down, and in chalice-shaped capitals, like some of those at Vézelay,[33] the surface surrounding the figures no longer follows the same curve as that behind the figures, the actual surface of the chalice, which can hardly be traced in its entirety. The sculptor is trying to make the background an indeterminate shadow.

Figure sculpture does not disappear entirely in the Gothic period, but it occurs only rarely. Sculptured foliage clings to the surface of the cube or chalice, as it does at Saint-Denis, and gives an illusion of actual growth [52]. The outside corners become as important as the central axis, and, even before the time when the whole capital is set diagonally, the diagonals begin to predominate. As the capitals were usually put in position in the form of rough-hewn blocks, and only carved après la pose, their chronology within a building is not always the same as that of the surrounding members. The individuality of each architect and sculptor increases the infinite degree of variation in these works. The dating of capitals to determine the chronology of the surrounding building must often confine itself to naming the nearest decade, and, in actual fact, one is usually forced into

The choir of *Vézelay* [50], which, in elevation, was perhaps inspired by the original design of Saint-Denis, was set out sometime after a fire of 1165, and was under construction in the 1170s. Here the upper part of the walls between the chapels is left open, and the closely set shafts show an unusually advanced form of Gothic relief.[31]

The cathedral of *Meaux* was begun around 1175, and the choir completed by c. 1215. Villard de Honnecourt, the architectural commentator of the High Gothic period, was interested in this Early Gothic church, and, in the 1220s or 1230s, drew its plan in his 'sketchbook'. The three chapels of the ambulatory stood separately, as in Romanesque plans, leaving space between them for direct lighting of the ambulatory. The choir and ambulatory are built on a semicircular plan, while the chapels are polygonal (7/10). This polygonal plan was probably a copy of the chapels at Laon or other early polygonal terminations in north eastern France, e.g. the transepts of Valenciennes. At the beginning of the fourteenth century, two more chapels were built in the spaces between the three original ones, making a continuous series, as at Saint-Denis. The building history of the rest of the cathedral at Meaux is extremely complicated: its present state is the result of gradual construction and extension in which each successive architect built in the most advanced style of his own generation. The styles which are represented range from Early Gothic to Late Gothic.[32]

52. Saint-Denis Abbey Church. Capitals, *c.* 1137–40

53. Development of bases: High Gothic (*above*) and late Gothic (*below*)

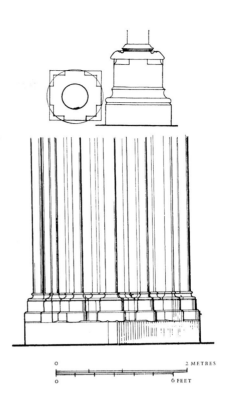

dating the capitals according to the architecture around them. The sculptor was always either behind his time or drastically in advance of it. The effect of different schools must also be taken into consideration. Capitals carved in the same year, but in different places, may belong to different stages of five or even ten years in the progress of style.[34] By and large, however, the development is directed towards an emphasis on the interaction of front and back plane of the relief. The purest form of this interaction was achieved in the crocket capital.

When it became increasingly usual for the leaves in the corners to bend forward and end at the top in a scroll turned inwards, the shorter leaves in the middle of the capital also began to bend forward. Whether the capital was carved in a workshop *avant la pose*, or after it had been put in position, its original stage was always in the shape of a block with convex sides which embraced the outermost points of the finished capital. In crocket capitals this outer surface has strong projections, and, from their highest point, the chisel is driven into the stone. The crockets at the corners emphasize the diagonals. Whereas the block capital of the Romanesque, with its even relief, blends with the direction of the wall, the Gothic crocketed capital launches out diagonally into the space of the interior. The whole support seems to penetrate into the interior space, and at the same time, *vice versa* the interior space seems to penetrate the surface of the capital [51].

Abaci were almost always added to capitals. In principle, their profile is a heritage of the form and the symbolic value of the Romanesque ledge, which, in turn, can be traced back to Roman architecture. The abacus sometimes widens step by step, and usually finishes with a projecting ledge at the top. As long as the abacus is square, it lends frontality to the chalice capital. In England, circular abaci were used. In fact they here became almost the norm, though they remained an exception in France and Germany (Marburg). Square abaci form re-entrant angles, and thus preserve something of the demarcation lines and the sense of addition between bays, or, in triforia and porches, between layers, whereas round abaci spring from intermediate points on the wall and the interior space continues in its smooth flow round them [42, 89].

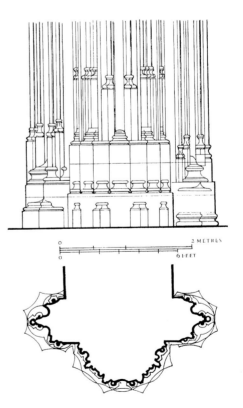

Bases and plinths remained much the same in the Early Gothic period as they had been in the time of the Romanesque [53], though there were slight changes in height, in slope, and in the degree of projection of the mouldings. Here again, the English began to avoid right angles at a very early date. The east crypt at Canterbury, built from 1180, where the bases and the abaci are round, is perhaps the earliest case. Here the thick, short, round piers have no real capitals and the whole crowning member can be regarded as an abacus. The slenderer piers in the middle of the crypt also have round abaci, and there is more justification for speaking of capitals. In the choir at Canterbury there are also round bases to the shafts which rise from the rectangular abaci of the circular piers.[35]

It would appear that the first capitals with genuine crockets date to around the same period (*c*. 1180) as the round bases and abaci in England. There are early attempts at crockets in the galleries at Laon and Paris, but it is impossible to say exactly when they were carved; for even if they were carved *après la pose*, it would have been necessary to make provision for their shape *avant la pose*. Even so, the mature form may have been created before 1180.[35A]

3 · THE EXPOSED FLYING BUTTRESS

In its leading buildings, in Noyon, Laon, Paris, and Canterbury, the Gothic style had succeeded to such an extent in adapting itself to the demands of the rib-vault that by 1180 architects and their patrons must have regarded the Romanesque style as completely superseded. This was true of interiors, but not to the same degree of exteriors. Here the innovations which had been introduced were pointed arches on windows and doors, buttresses rising in steps, and the disappearance of the round-arched friezes and other similar details which established the recession by layers in Romanesque relief. The emergence of the nave and choir above the aisles and the separation of the attics remained operative, because the line of the eaves was not cut by any vertical member.

Another change, not so obvious, but still noticeable, was a general reduction in weight and mass. This was partly the result of enlarging the area of the windows, and partly of introducing the new relief into the jambs, which made the surface of the glass actually seem to be the real wall. Such stained glass of this period as has been preserved has a silver-grey patina on it which makes it look like stone. But the walls themselves became thinner too. This was the logical consequence of the use of the rib, which, since the building of the choir of Saint-Denis, had led to the construction of thinner vaulting-cells. In the building of these cells out of blocks of stone small enough to be laid by hand, the ribs were certainly used as a support, at least during the period of building. Thinner cells permitted thinner supports and thinner walls.[36] Nevertheless, the piers still had to be sufficiently thick to bear the thrust of one vaulted bay or two neighbouring vaulted bays. In churches of basilican type with aisles, and especially in those with two aisles on each side, the maximum thickness of the piers was limited by the fact that they could not be allowed to reduce the width of the aisles. A way out of these difficulties, which had their root in the statics of the vault, was found by leading the lateral thrust over the aisles to the outside wall from the corners of the bays, that is, from the springing of the transverse arches. This was done by adding galleries, and in some cases by building thin walls over the transverse arches of these galleries. Many different methods existed which had already

been developed in the Romanesque period. They were employed until almost the end of the Early Gothic period, and always in such a way as to conceal the fact that they contributed to the stability of the building.[37]

These methods solved the problems in churches with only one aisle on each side. However, where there were double aisles both of these had to be bridged, for if only the inner aisles had galleries added, the supports between the two aisles would have to have been considerably stronger.

In the nave of *Notre-Dame* in *Paris*, the piers between the two aisles corresponding to the corners of the sexpartite bays of the nave were actually reinforced with shafts [54]. So the change in the supports, which had been avoided in the central vessel of the nave, was permitted here. However, this expedient did not remove the basic evil, the darkness of the interior; for the architect did not dare to pierce the walls with large windows because of the lateral thrust of the vault. One could claim that the gloom created a mysterious atmosphere and could be brightened by candlelight on festive occasions, but it is obvious that this atmosphere was not really created from choice. It is not known precisely when and where an architect first dared to build exposed flying buttresses, but Lefèvre-Pontalis, Aubert and the many authorities who have followed them, have argued that the first examples supported the nave of Notre-Dame in Paris, in building in the 1180s.[37A] In recent years this axiom has been persuasively challenged. Evidence has been found for the use of exposed flying buttresses in a number of first-generation Gothic buildings: the choirs of Sens cathedral (*c*. 1150), Saint-Germain-des-Prés in Paris (1150s), Saint-Martin at Etampes (*c*. 1150), Laon cathedral (*c*. 1160) Notre-Dame in Paris, and even Suger's Choir at Saint-Denis.[38]

The exposed flying buttresses were immediately adaptable to churches with one aisle on each side. Their static qualities might be improved, but the main question was whether or not they were admissible on aesthetic and stylistic grounds. Their general use in succeeding churches, both large and small, shows that they were hailed not only as an improvement in the statics and the lighting of the churches, but also as a welcome addition to the store of specifically Gothic forms.

The stylistic significance of the exposed flying buttress has not always been understood. Dehio called it 'artistic crudity'. He should have called it boldness. What is more, it is the basic premise underlying the whole form of the cathedral at Chartres, and the entire High Gothic style. Even in Notre-Dame in Paris, where the four-storeyed elevation of the interior could no longer be altered, it served the stylistic purpose of so altering the exterior elevation that it no longer looked Romanesque. Just as the Romanesque triforium and capitals in the interior seem to invite one to pass one's hand over their flat surfaces, so on the exterior, and, in spite of their depth, the dwarf arched galleries too form large, flat surfaces. But, just as the Gothic constructional system of the interior with its reduction of solid bodies to a skeleton invites one to thrust one's hand between the members, so the flying buttresses transform the character of the exterior into that of a series of arches, rising diagonally, and substituting for the continuity of the clerestory wall a direction

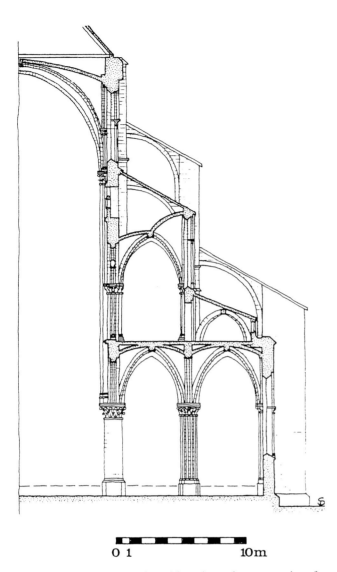

54. Paris, Notre-Dame, nave section with conjectural reconstruction of original buttress system, *c.* 1180 (reconstruction by Clark, drawn by Donald Sanders)

terms of statics.[38A] Viewed aesthetically, forces here rise from the ground, bend over in a continuous flow, and finally press themselves against the clerestory wall. The physical truth of the matter, however, is the exact opposite. The thrust of the vault is led down obliquely by the flying buttress, which acts as a bridge or a channel of forces, on to the outer buttress, which must project sufficiently at its base not to fall outwards. The aesthetic impression is powerful enough to make one imagine that, if the vault were to collapse, the flying buttresses would force the clerestory walls inwards. However, Francis Bond has demonstrated from ruins such as those at Melrose that, where vaults did collapse, the flying buttresses remained standing.[39] Any man of wide interests will wonder about the actual distribution of forces in a Gothic building; but if he has any aesthetic sense, an understanding of the actual mechanics of vaulting will not make him underrate the stylistic value of the flying buttress. The Gothic style has been decried surprisingly often because it is impossible to see, if one stands outside, 'what can be the purpose of such a gigantic expenditure of force', and if one stands inside, 'how such fragile supports can carry the vaults'.[40] It is true that flying buttresses allow much slenderer supports in the interior, but concealed supporting walls in the roofs of galleries had allowed the same much earlier. On the other hand it is also true that to understand the expenditure of force on the exterior, one must know the interior. No one should regard the flying buttress as a piece of superfluous decoration. Every man in the Middle Ages was a churchgoer, and knew the churches not only from the outside. The criticism that the interior, as one stands outside, is a world beyond conceiving, as is also the exterior from within, may be justified for a child or someone seeing a Gothic church for the first time. This, however, was not the intention of the creators of these structures. The conclusion which the master of Chartres drew from the flying buttresses of early Gothic was that they made it possible to unite the interior and the exterior into an organic whole. For this reason it is wrong to claim that Gothic cathedrals have a mystic interior and a scholastic exterior.

4. FAÇADES, TOWERS, GABLES, TABERNACLES

Flying buttresses had made lateral elevations Gothic; very soon they brought about the same change in east ends. However, they were quite unsuited to adapt to the new style the façades of naves and transepts. Here, too, the immediately available means were pointed arches for windows and doorways, Gothic relief, the elimination of Romanesque friezes of round arches, and the building of buttresses in set-offs. The continuation of a buttress over the entire height of a wall, as at Saint-Denis and Senlis, draws the storeys into a unity and overcomes the Romanesque principle of considering each storey as a separate entity. This is especially true in the case of towers, whether they are seen separately or as integral members of a façade.

In this sense, the north tower of the cathedral at *Chartres*, begun as a free-standing structure between 1134 and 1138, counts among the first Gothic towers, built at exactly the same time as the west façade of Saint-Denis [55]. Its

into depth. The flying buttresses turn their flanks towards us and create an intermediate zone of uncertain boundaries which is not exclusively a part of the exterior, but rather a continuation of the interior. Whether the sun or the moon shines, and casts the shadows of the buttresses on to the roofs and the walls; or whether there is snow or mist moving between them and the walls; or whether the weather is gloomy or the light fails, the exact outline of the building can never be traced. The side views of Romanesque churches are wonderfully closed: those of Gothic churches are wonderfully open. This is what the two styles demanded. The twentieth-century historian may personally favour one or the other of these principles, but, as an historian, he has no business to favour either, but only to understand both and to interpret both as symbols of human attitudes.

This understanding of the Gothic style must be applied not only to the stylistic function of the flying buttress, its character of extreme partiality, but also to its function in

55. Chartres Cathedral. West front; north tower soon after 1134 (spire 1507), south tower before 1145, portals *c.* 1145, rose window designed after 1194

interior is Gothic in its rib-vault. The diagonal shafts at the corners are flanked on either side by a shaft for the wall-arches. The next storey has a domical vault, and the one above that had a flat ceiling. The wooden spire probably had the shape of a simple pyramid. The vault in the lower storey necessitated the building of buttresses at the corners of the exterior. The buttresses in the middle of the sides serve to strengthen the aesthetic unity of the storeys.

Sometime before 1145 a second tower was begun, on the south side, together with a triple portal which was planned to lie between the two towers.[41] The supports at the corners of the rib-vault on the ground floor are different from those in the north tower. In each corner one shaft supports the rib and the wall-arches. The exterior treatment is also different, but there are, as on the north tower, buttresses at the centres of the sides. Above the octagonal top storey there rises a very slender stone pyramid. The base-line of this pyramid is not clearly defined; for its lower section is steeper than its upper parts, and the gables of the windows on the main sides, as well as those of the smaller dormer-windows in the diagonals, overlap the horizontal (decorated with a round-arched corbel-frieze), which marks the start of the pyramid proper. The gables on the main sides cover three openings, set one above the other, and the whole group forms a single opening resting on the central buttress. The gables on the diagonal sides cover two openings, one above the other, and stand astride the two frontal buttresses at the corners. They face the solid diagonally-placed tabernacles of the octagon with their pyramidal stone roofs.[42] This arrangement is a successful attempt to produce a smooth transition from a square to an octagon. It is surprising that this first solution should stand so well beside the addition that was made to the north tower in 1507, at the end of the Late Gothic period, and equally surprising that the north tower should preserve such harmony with this early work of the Early Gothic style. However, the south tower does suffer from the proximity of the new rose-window, added after 1194. The balustrade and the Gallery of the Kings cut into the tower.

The gables round the base of the pyramid, which look like the points of a crown, are Gothic because the points of the arches below them penetrate their base-line. Here this penetration is still tentative. Similar compositions existed even in some Romanesque buildings.[43] The tower at *Brantôme* (Périgord), built sometime in the first half of the twelfth century, seems to be a little earlier than the south tower at Chartres, while that at *Berzy-le-Sec* (near Soissons), built about 1150, seems to be a little later. Both have arches piercing the baseline of the gables.[43A]

The towers at *Chartres*, the Portail Royal which was begun about 1145 and was inserted between the towers, and the façade of Saint-Denis, substantially finished in 1140, still belong to the Transitional style. The same is true of the west façade at *Senlis*, in so far as it dates back to sometime after 1153,[44] and of the parts of the façade at *Sens* which belong to the original building.[44A] Certainly these works were not as predominantly Gothic as, for instance, the interior of the choir of Noyon. Even the architect of *Noyon* was not so progressive in the exterior of his choir as in the interior. If names given to styles are to have any significance, and not be a mere empty convention, a classification into Transitional and Early Gothic must base itself on a consideration of the essence of the average design of the period in question. The fact that the date of the choir of Saint-Denis is 1140 does not prove that anything built by any architect after that date must be Early Gothic. The Transitional style continued in every case where the unity of the choir of Saint-Denis was not achieved. Even the architect of Saint-Denis, like the

56. Laon Cathedral. West front, begun *c.* 1180

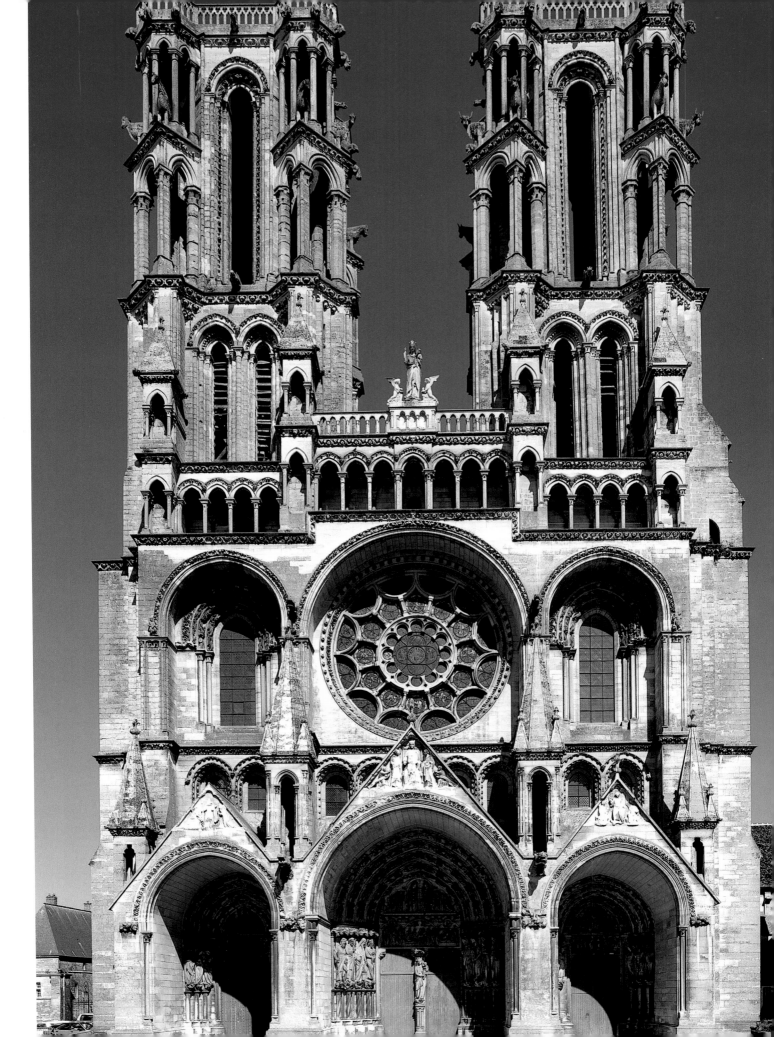

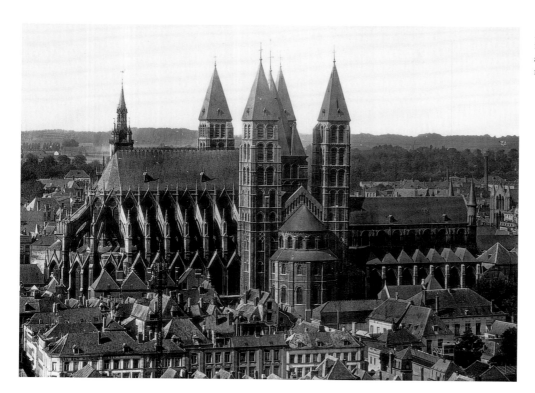

57. Tournai Cathedral. Exterior from north. Choir 1243–55; transept and transept towers begun *c.* 1130; nave *c.* 1110–*c.*1130

architect of Noyon, did not reach such an advanced stage of development in the exterior as in the interior. The reason for this time-lag is that, while the diagonal rib produced immediate changes in the interior, its effects on the exterior were only secondary. To regard stylistic classifications as conventional leads to superficiality. We are not trying to find comfortable divisions, but to find the essence of each individual work, and its position on the ladder of development. This applies to the study of all styles, and therefore equally to the differentiation between Early Gothic and High Gothic. The façade of Laon stands on the border-line between these two styles.

Beginning about 1180–85, the fourth campaign at Laon saw the completion of the four western bays of the nave and the west façade [56]. If the first master, who was building a generation earlier, left a plan for this part of the church, the younger man must have altered it radically; for this is the first façade that breaks absolutely with the Romanesque principle of the flat surface. Here all remnants of the Romanesque are outweighed by the new emphasis on depth.[44B]

The façade has three layers. In front of the two towers rises the main wall of the façade with its windows, and the dwarf gallery, which is also part of this second layer. In front of this lies the third layer, with the three porches, pierced in depth by the three doorways. It is hard to tell whether the doorways lie on the same level as the little windows that appear above the gables which break slightly into their base. These gables are the first monumental example of the penetration of arch and gable. The higher apex of the central gable, and its close connexion with the two flanking it, led to the asymmetrical form of the side gables. In a Romanesque porch the basic idea of the architect was that a gable is only

the frontal aspect of a saddleback roof and, as such, stands on a horizontal beam which is the level of the floor over the vault or the arch below. So the triangle of the gable, in accordance with the stylistic principle of addition, stands as a unity of its own, and is separated from the arch by a horizontal member. The Gothic gable, however, is pressed so close to the arch that its sides actually touch the arch. Here the vault penetrates the space enclosed by the roof, which has now lost its floor and is reduced to a fragmentary existence. The architect of Laon provided an early model for this development in the pinnacles which he built between the three gables of his façade and at its corners. (These pinnacles are miniature turrets and can equally well be called tabernacles, since they actually enclose a space.)[44C] He did not yet dare to draw the conclusion and connect their spirelets with the narrow openings below them. They are separated by a horizontal ledge, as they were in Romanesque gables. In the pinnacles at the corners, however, the openings penetrate into the spirelet in the truly Gothic way.[44D]

In the next storey the Romanesque principles have not been fully overcome either. This is shown most clearly in the continuity of a flat surface without separating the three main axes by buttresses. Romanesque also is the large round window – a heritage preserved by the High Gothic generation – but the inner divisions of its opening are Gothic. The term tracery is generally used to refer to the divisions in the upper parts of long windows, which appear for the first time in a pure form after 1210 at Reims, but radiating spokes in round windows are one of the preliminary forms of tracery. Here there is a large inner ring in the middle, and a circular frieze of twelve round arches rising from the circumference and turned inwards. The two rings are joined by short radial spokes, which meet the apexes of the round arches. There is a clear relationship with the present oculi in the nave of Notre-Dame in Paris. However, it is not known whether Viollet-le-Duc's restoration of these oculi reproduced the original tracery.[44E]

Because the top of the round window is higher than that of the windows on either side, the dwarf gallery rises by one step. Buttresses within the gallery separate the central section and mark the ends of the outer sections. Over the buttresses there are tabernacles, the two central ones raised because of the stepping-up of the gallery. The roofs of the tabernacles again remain independent entities above a horizontal course.

The two upper storeys of the towers are octagonal. Early Romanesque towers were square, and their roofs were pyramids on a square plan. The increasing tendency to the diagonal, which began in the Late Romanesque period, produced octagonal pyramids, and added pinnacles at the corners, or it led also to the building of an octagonal top storey, and in this case the pinnacles were relegated to the storey below. Both the Transitional and the Early Gothic style took over these forms.[45] From the point of view of the architect, this led to designing downwards from the top. The north tower of *Saint-Denis* (designed at the same time as the façade, built some time after 1145, pulled down in the nineteenth century, but preserved in an engraving)[46] was square up to the octagonal roof and had a pinnacle at each corner and in the middle of each side. In the stylistic development of towers in general, the south tower at Chartres marks the beginning of the Early Gothic style, in spite of its little frieze of round arches. The towers at *Laon* surpass it considerably. The transformation of the buttresses to form rectangular, diagonally placed tabernacles is logically prepared on the storey below in the tapering of the tower. On top of these rectangular tabernacles stand octagonal ones, out of which peer figures of oxen, a weird and unique monument of gratitude to the beasts who had dragged the building-materials up the long hill. Besides this emphasis on the diagonal, the continuation of the long bell-openings through two storeys is a bold effort to draw all the storeys into a unity.[46A]

Each transept was also intended to be flanked by two towers, but for a variety of reasons only one was built on each transept. The rose-window in the north façade is slightly different from that in the west façade. Instead of spokes, eight small circles fill the space between the inner ring and the circumference. Including the crossing tower, the cathedral at Laon was designed to have seven towers. Standing on the top of a hill in the middle of a plain, and visible from a great distance, it was intended to look like a crown. So it does – even in its incomplete form.

Tournai Cathedral is the most likely pattern from which Laon was developed [57].[46B] But a comparison between the two shows, besides what is common, the extremely Romanesque characteristics of the towers at Tournai on the one hand, and the Gothic characteristics of those at Laon on the other. An analysis of the relief of the two churches helps one to understand why Tournai looks so warlike, so proud, and so unapproachable, and why Laon looks so much more friendly. The synthesis that was achieved at Laon gives a happy impression of monumental massiveness enduring to eternity, combined with noble vigour.

58. Poitiers Cathedral. Interior; choir *c.* 1150–1215, nave finished in the second half of the thirteenth century

5 · HALL-CHURCHES

The first monumental example of a Gothic hall-church is the cathedral of Saint-Pierre at *Poitiers* [58]. Henry II of England and his queen, Eleanor, founded a new ring of town walls here in and around the year 1162. Building on the cathedral may have begun earlier. Certainly the church is contemporary with Laon and Paris. The two eastern bays of the choir were vaulted by *c.* 1175, the transepts were finished by *c.* 1215, but the final, western, vaults of the nave and the west façade (excluding the portal gables and the upper storeys of the towers) were not built until the last quarter of the thirteenth century. The hall-form of the choir decided the form of the later parts, in spite of the fact that the vaults of the six westernmost bays have ridge-ribs, whereas the two bays at the east end have only diagonal ribs.[47]

It is not difficult to find earlier examples of churches in which the aisles are the same height as the nave. Saint-Hilaire, also at Poitiers, can hardly be considered as a model, since it was altered in the first half of the twelfth century, and the resultant form is most unusual. Still at Poitiers, Notre-Dame-la-Grande may well have had some influence, although the tunnel-vault in the nave gives a very different impression from that which is created in the cathedral.

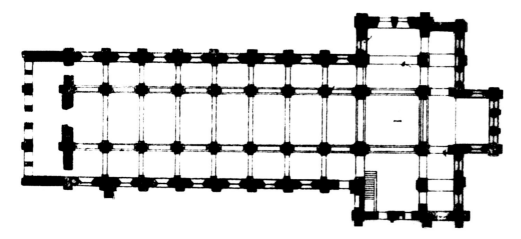

59. Fontenay Cistercian Church,
1139–47. Plan

Under the heading 'churches without galleries', Dehio has grouped a considerable number of French Romanesque churches, such as *Lérins*, Saint-Martin-d'Ainay at *Lyons*, and the nave of Saint-Nazaire at *Carcassonne* [161].[48] All these have tunnel-vaults in all three parts, or tunnel-vaults in the central vessel and half tunnel-vaults in the aisles. The master of Poitiers certainly knew churches of this type. It is unlikely that he had seen the group of hall-churches in Bavaria, which includes *Prüll*,[48A] built between from *c.* 1100, and several other churches modelled on it. The form of the hall-church could be found in many crypts with one or more aisles on each side of a central area of equal width, and in monastic dormitories and refectories with just two naves side by side. In common with these, Saint-Pierre at Poitiers gives the aisles the same width as the nave. Where the widths of a nave and its aisles are set in the ratio two to one, the aisles have the character of subsidiary space. If they are narrower, they become mere passages. Conversely, if the aisles are the same width as the nave, they no longer give the impression of subordinate spaces accompanying the central area, and the outer wall of the aisles becomes the primary boundary, within which all three parts are on a par. Thus the new partiality is achieved.

The vaults at Poitiers Cathedral have diagonal ribs, but the ridges rise sharply, as at Le Mans, so that each bay is concentrated inwards. The piers are frontal, and these two factors characterize a transitional stage, still firmly rooted in the Romanesque.

The cathedral has stained glass in most of the windows. That in the three segmental east chapels is of the highest quality. It softens the light without obscuring the interior. Visually, the lighting of the church at Poitiers is the opposite of that in Paris. In spite of its solemn atmosphere, the general effect is cheerful. 'How lovely is thy dwelling place, O Lord of Hosts!'

The wall-passage at the very high level of the sills of the windows is the horizontal complement to the vertical character of the nave and aisles. This contrast, in which each factor reinforces the other, reappears in the Late Gothic style. All the wall-passages in churches in Normandy, and later in Champagne, aim at this antagonistic contrast, though in most cases the emphasis has been heightened by the later addition of parapets.

We have become wary of applying the word beautiful, but the visitor to Saint-Pierre who accepts his impressions without allowing preconceived ideas to affect them will find the word on the tip of his tongue. There are, of course, people who are not of the same opinion. The great problem of the Gothic style was the vaulting of basilican churches. Where nave and aisles, however, are of the same height, the problem of leading the thrust of the central vault outwards does not arise, as this thrust is carried by the vaults of the aisles, whose thrust, in turn, is carried on the buttresses on the exterior, which can project as far as necessary. This is true; but the question then arises why, if the problems of statics were so much less complicated, all architects did not build hall-churches. Were they deliberately creating difficulties for themselves? If not, is the basilica a better form because its problems were a spur to the development of the Gothic style?

These questions miss the real impulse of the Gothic style. The rib divided each bay into spatial fragments and necessitated a complete change in the other forms of the whole building. It led to a reconsideration of the basilican form because this form is characterized by the emergence and thereby the self-sufficiency of one particular part. Re-entrant angles in the plan produce the isolation of parts (such as the transepts) within the contour of the exterior, and they have the same effect in the cross-section of a basilica. The essence of the hall-church lies in its flowing contour, in its lack of re-entrant angles on the exterior, and, in the interior, in the inclusion of all the individual compartments in one overall three-dimensional contour.[48B]

The history of Gothic architecture shows that this aesthetic or, more narrowly, stylistic function of the hall-church was only gradually recognized, and that the preservation of the basilican form led to the creation of certain specifically Gothic forms, especially the flying buttress. The architects of Late Gothic hall-churches were ready to deny themselves flying buttresses because by then the style had infused every architectural member with new life. The Early Gothic hall-church at Poitiers is a conservative first attempt to achieve Gothic partiality in this spatial type. But this partiality could really be reached only when the piers were altered in the way that was to be discovered by the masters of the fourteenth century. Those who look round in Poitiers Cathedral without knowing or being able to picture the subsequent developments in the forms of the piers and all the other later advances will ask themselves what ought to be the solution to the problem. If they do not find it, they will understand the position of the great master of Poitiers who was gifted enough to take the first step, but could not leap straight to the end of the train of development which he had begun. One man cannot achieve what is properly the task of many generations.

6. THE EARLY GOTHIC STYLE IN THE CISTERCIAN ORDER

The interaction of progress and hesitation which can be seen in the cathedral at Poitiers is to be observed in the development of every style. Advancing ideas are slow to overcome the difficulties in their path. In some cases these difficulties lie in the limitations of the individual, even where he is as gifted as the master of Poitiers, in others they are of a quite different nature. In Cistercian architecture they lay in the special religious convictions of the order. Within it the Early Gothic style, which began about 1154 in the new choir at Clairvaux, and about twenty years later in the new choir at Pontigny, can only be understood through a knowledge of the earlier stages in the development of Cistercian architecture. The development began with modest Romanesque churches built at the time of the building of the choir at Durham. There followed a short transitional stage, and the end was the specifically Cistercian Early Gothic style.

Robert, abbot of Molesme, left his monastery with a small group of men who shared his beliefs to put the rules of Saint-Benedict into strict practice. In 1098, with the consent of Gautier, Bishop of Châlons, he founded a new monastery called *Cîteaux*, in a wilderness fourteen miles south of Dijon. On the instructions of the pope, Robert returned to Molesme in the following year and installed Alberic as first abbot of Cîteaux. Alberic continued to work out the rules of the new community and brought it to a modest fruition. After his death in 1109, an Englishman, Stephen Harding, who was one of Robert's companions, was chosen to be the second abbot. His exaggerated interpretation of the principle of asceticism weakened the monks and seriously reduced their number, and it seemed that the monastery was doomed to extinction, when, in 1113, Bernard of Fontaines and thirty companions, mostly noblemen, entered the order.[48C]

After this, Cîteaux made a rapid recovery. After a year the available land was insufficient and a second monastery was founded in 1113 at *La Ferté*. In 1114 this was followed by the foundation of *Pontigny*; *Clairvaux* and *Morimond* followed in 1115. The other monasteries were off-shoots of these first five, Cîteaux and its first four daughter foundations. When, in 1153, Bernard died at Clairvaux, the order had 343 communities, and by the year 1200 this number had risen to 525. By 1500 it reached 738, to which must be added about 645 nunneries which were, to a greater or lesser degree, attached to the rules of Cîteaux.[48D] The buildings of most of these monasteries, including their churches, have disappeared. As early as the fourteenth century, during the Hundred Years War (1339–1453), monasteries in lonely French valleys were plundered by English and French soldiers and bandits.

Most of the rest were destroyed in the French Revolution. In England, too, only ruins remain. So, in spite of buildings that have been well preserved in Germany, Italy, Spain, and a few other countries, our knowledge of Cistercian architecture is extremely fragmentary. Nevertheless, the close relationship between the forms of so many of these monasteries gives us a fairly clear overall picture of the architecture of the order. It has often been stressed that what is common to many of these buildings is mostly of a negative nature. Decoration with sculpture, painting, and carved or painted ornament was not allowed, and its absence produced the characteristic cool emptiness of the churches, and the exclusive emphasis on the purely architectural.[48E] A very characteristic trait is the absence of stone towers, which were not allowed, and which were replaced by small wooden bell-cotes, designed to hold only two small bells.[48F]

Many of the first settlements, and also the first oratory at *Cîteaux*, must have been modest wooden structures.[48G] The oratory, however, was soon replaced by a stone building. The nave, which had no aisles, was about 15 feet wide and was vaulted, presumably, with a tunnel-vault. The choir was about 30 feet long. This building, consecrated in 1106, was still standing in 1708. If we call this chapel Cîteaux I, then the church of about 1130 was Cîteaux II, and that begun *c.* 1180 and consecrated in 1193 Cîteaux III.[49]

Little is known about Cîteaux II, for it was systematically demolished in the French Revolution. No views survive of its interior. Seventeenth- and eighteenth-century drawings show a large church with projecting four-bay transepts and a nine-bay nave with a west porch. The aisled choir, with its low ambulatory and straight-ended eastern chapels returned behind the sanctuary, was the result of an extension, begun *c.* 1180 and consecrated in 1193. The original sanctuary was probably single-aisled and straight-ended, like Fontenay and Pontigny II. If the regular crossing and nave and choir clerestories shown in the drawings belong to the original church, then the building may either have had a timber roof over the central vessel, or, more plausibly, it may have been groin-vaulted.[50]

Clairvaux II, demolished in the early nineteenth century, was built at the same time as Cîteaux II. Bernard, who was born in 1090, was twenty-five when, in 1115, he arrived at Clairvaux with a group of monks to found a new monastery. Here he became abbot, and from here his religious and political ideas went out into the Catholic world, and governed it. The wooden oratory of 1116 was a square building with aisles on all four sides, and a taller central space crowned with a stepped roof.[51] It was replaced from *c.* 1135 onwards,[51A] and this new building (Clairvaux II), because of the esteem in which Bernard was held, became the model for many later Cistercian churches. In particular, it is generally believed (until recently) that the church at Fontenay, begun in 1139, is a reproduction of Clairvaux II.[51B]

Fontenay (1139–47) has a nave of eight bays with one aisle on each side [59, 60].[51C] To the east of the transepts there are two chapels on each side which are shorter and narrower than the choir. Whereas the east chapels of most Romanesque churches ended in apses, those at Fontenay have straight ends, and this elimination of semicircular forms at the east end became a feature of the characteristic

60. Fontenay Cistercian Church. Interior, 1139–1147

the aisles, but each bay gives the effect of a separate enclosed space. The regular use of pointed arches for the vaults, the arcades, the transverse arches, and the windows is Burgundian, and is suggestive of the Gothic style. The architect's model for the pointed arches and barrel vaults at Fontenay may have been the then recently built third church at Cluny, begun in 1088 and finished at the west about 1120. But it was also the splendour of this church and of Cluniac Romanesque art in general that stirred Bernard's opposition. Such expenditure, he felt, may have been justifiable in a cathedral, which was built for laymen, but not in a monastic building. In his famous *Apologia* to William of Saint-Thierry, written in 1124–25, in which he castigated the distractions and excesses of Cluniac sculpture and architecture, Bernard showed an exceptionally sharp eye for vivid detail and a highly developed sensitivity to visual form. But the primary intention of his critique was to show just how unsuitable Cluniac Romanesque was as a setting for monastic life. He was not directly concerned with the stylistic character of Romanesque. He did not take an interest in the form of the arches at Cluny, nor in the stylistic significance of Cluny as a whole, or if he did, he did not formulate any clear ideas on the subject.[51D] At that time Saint-Denis was in course of construction, and, if he regarded this church too as needlessly expensive, he did not share our view of the Gothic style as a formal and spiritual contrast to the Romanesque. Many historians, such as Dehio and Bilson, have rightly refused to speak of a specifically Cistercian style. The Cistercian spirit in architecture is equally effective in the Romanesque and Gothic styles. The west façade at Fontenay[52] has round arches on the doorway and the seven windows and is purely Romanesque in every aspect; the interior has pointed arches but is still Romanesque rather than Gothic. Both are Cistercian in their characteristic asceticism.

At Fontenay this tendency to asceticism led to a reduction in height. The springing of the tunnel-vault lies so low that the nave has no upper windows, and the result of this is a pseudo-basilican type. The choir is even lower than the nave, and there are windows in the east wall of the crossing, above the eastern crossing arch, which light the nave. There

simplicity of many Cistercian churches. The nave is vaulted with a typical Burgundian pointed tunnel-vault; its transverse arches are supported on shafts. Each bay of the aisles is vaulted with a transverse pointed tunnel-vault, running from north to south, springing from above the apexes of the transverse arches which separate the bays of the aisles from each other. One can pass down the length of

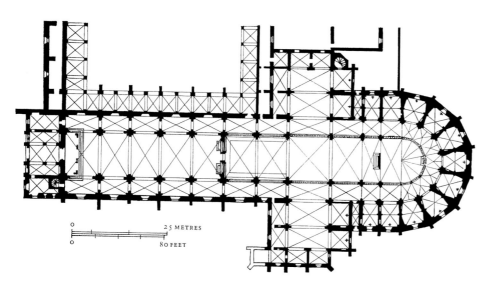

0   25 METRES
0   80 FEET

61. Pontigny Abbey Church, plan of second church, begun *c.* 1140, with choir of third church, *c.* 1180–1206

was probably considerable variety within the Cistercian Romanesque, but its essentially modest character remained a common factor.

This judgement of the Cistercian churches of the second generation is confirmed by those which have been preserved in England and Germany. England is discussed in another volume of this series;[52A] in Germany it is characteristic that *Amelungsborn*, begun soon after 1135, has typically Saxon alternating supports and a flat ceiling, and is quite unaffected by problems of vaulting.[53] Vaulting among German Cistercians was clearly intended as early as *c.* 1145 in the planned (but never built) barrel vaults over the choir and transept chapels at *Eberbach*. Around 1160, under the influence of the eastern choir at Worms, band ribs were built over the north transept chapels and choir of *Maulbronn*.[53A] However, the abbey at *Heisterbach*, which is actually in the Rhineland, has no ribs, although it was begun as late as *c.* 1202.[53B] Buildings like the narthex at *Maulbronn*,[54] begun about 1210, are still Transitional, and in them we see a struggle with constructional problems going on at a time when, in France, the cathedral of Reims was already being begun.

In France the Cistercians first used the rib at Fontenay (chapter house, *c.* 1155), in the transepts and nave at Ourscamp II (after 1154), in the nave of Pontigny II (*c.* 1140) and possibly in the high vaults of Clairvaux III (before 1153).[54A]

A new church was begun at *Clairvaux* before 1153. The relaxation of the principle of modesty and simplicity in the years after Bernard's death (1153) are clearly anticipated in the new plan. The 'Bernardine' choir was replaced with a round apse surrounded by an ambulatory with nine chapels. These chapels were trapezoid, set one against the next, so that their outside walls formed a continuous polygon. The whole choir can be seen as one of the first chevets built on a polygonal plan. This form of choir – and it was always the choir which interested the Cistercians most – compared with the straight east ends of earlier buildings, was a simplified version of the choir of Cluny III, and possibly borrowed its continuous chapel wall from early Gothic choirs in northern France (Saint-Denis, Saint-Martin-des-Champs in Paris). It may even have looked to early Christian architecture in Rome. Dehio has said that the chapels opening from the transepts are almost a divided aisle and that, because of the pent-roof that covers them all, they give this effect from outside. Similarly the east chapels look like an ambulatory, in spite of their polygonal form. Another concession to the style of northern French early Gothic may have been the use of rib vaults in the church, perhaps over the central vessel of the nave and transepts, perhaps also in the aisles.[55]

Since the destruction of Clairvaux III, *Pontigny* II remains as a representative of this stage of development. The first monastery at Pontigny, which dated from 1114, had a rectangular oratory.[55A] The plan of the east end of the second has been discovered by excavation.[56] It had a 'Bernardine' arrangement, like Fontenay, with a straight-ended sanctuary but with additional chapels flanking the transepts on all three sides.[56A] This second church at Pontigny was begun in the 1130s, and finished by about

62. Pontigny, Cistercian church. Interior. Nave *c.* 1140, choir rebuilt *c.* 1180–1206

1150–60 [61, 62]. The aisles have groin-vaults and transverse arches, and although these are pointed and even the groins are pointed (that is executed on pointed centering), the general impression is Romanesque, chiefly because of the rectangularly stepped mouldings of the transverse arches. Some historians presume that the nave was also intended to have groin-vaults, giving two reasons for their supposition. First, since the building progressed from east to west, the transepts are earlier than the nave. They have groin-vaults, and so it is probable that the nave, which has bays of the same width, but slightly longer, was intended to be covered with groin-vaults too. The second reason is that the projecting supports in the nave are frontal; only the capitals are diagonal [62]. To have turned the capitals so that their centres lie on the corners of the supports is so contrary to all geometrical and architectural logic that one may well believe that they were intended to be frontal and were turned through 45 degrees only after they had been carved. This seems to be confirmed by the fact that in some places the wall has been cut away to allow room for the corner of the capital. In opposition to this opinion others have argued that the same phenomenon appears elsewhere, at *Silvacane*

(Bouches-du-Rhône), at *Fitero* in Spain, and *Alcobaça* in Portugal.[57] For this reason, both Aubert and Rose say that at Pontigny this strange combination of diagonal capitals with frontal supports was part of the original design, and that, if groin-vaults had been intended, the supports would have been round, as they are in the transepts. In addition, the square rib-vault in the crossing also has its capitals diagonally set over the edges of the frontal supports. Since this vault was being built at the same time as the groin vaults in the adjoining transepts, there can be no reason to assume that the idea of rib vaulting the central vessel was an afterthought, conceived only subsequent to the vaulting of the transepts and the laying out of the nave.[57A]

The nave and crossing at Pontigny are an extant testimony of the transition to the Gothic within the Cistercian order. The difference between the elevation of these parts and that of the east end of the choir of Saint-Denis or Sens, which date from the same time, lies in the refusal at Pontigny to dissolve the wall. This, too, is a negative characteristic inspired by motives of economy, and even more by the desire to produce an aesthetic expression of economy. Of course, a positive factor can be expressed in negative terms, and vice versa. The refusal to accept the gallery, the triforium, and the wall-passage at Pontigny is, in positive terms, a recognition of the wall. Here it seems a remnant or a heritage of the Romanesque. In principle, taken independently of individual periods and styles, the wall is as much a basic architectural form as the free-standing support. The wall is a continuous spatial boundary; the free-standing support is a discontinuous one, which gains continuity only by the formation of a regular series along straight lines or along curves to form together one layer of a relief. The main theme of the Gothic style is the interplay of wall and supports in the layers of the relief of the three directions, longitudinal, lateral, and diagonal. In the transepts at Pontigny, the round shafts which support the transverse arches, with their frontal bases and capitals, form part of the boundary between the bays. In combination with the groin-vaults they are Romanesque. However, if we consider the shafts in combination with the wall, then they form one layer along the wall, and it is the continuity of the wall which now predominates. The narrow windows are merely cut into the wall, without producing the specifically Gothic relief. The wall therefore remains a firm boundary between the interior and the exterior, without connecting the two. The window openings remain separate spatial entities within the thickness of the wall.

At Pontigny II, then, the Gothic rib-vault is combined with a Romanesque wall. The term 'style' can be limited to mean only an absolute unity of principles, and this definition is valid for theoretical considerations. Historically, however, 'style' is often found to include disparate features which can yet offer a specific aesthetic charm and give positive expression to a spiritual movement. To judge Cistercian architecture fairly, one must understand that, from its principle of asceticism, its surrender to the rib-vault could be justified by the constructional and technical advantages which accompanied it, but that a surrender to the principles of the dissolution of the wall and of strict partiality, which were the logical consequences of the acceptance of the rib-vault, could not have been justified.

There is hardly another example in which the fact that the introduction of the rib required some spiritual authorization is proved so convincingly. Only the absolute immersion of the individual in the congregation of Christ and the humble abandonment of any *hubris* could give blessing to the division of the interior into spatial fragments and allow the architect to work out its full logical consequences. St Bernard was a reformer of the monastic world, and he was a man who, with admirable earnestness, accepted the teachings of Christ and of St Benedict, demonstrating their significance in a life of great self-denial. But there was, as Dehio has pointed out, a powerful contradiction at the root of his doctrine. As a monk his aim was to shun the world, and yet he incessantly entangled himself with the world in his tireless political work, especially in his sermons of 1147–9, in which he urged the world to undertake a crusade which became the great failure of his life. The responsibility, which should rather have fallen on the shoulders of the complacent, intriguing, and credulous princes, fell on him. Our aim here is, however, not to apportion the blame, but to recognize that St Bernard in his behaviour always remained the great nobleman that he was by his birthright, an ascetic prince. Following the principles of Abbot Harding, he set out to develop even the architecture of the Cistercian order in opposition to Cluny, and yet to uphold the mastery of the client, the Romanesque nobleman. So his order could accept the Gothic rib-vault for practical reasons, but found that it could be combined with the Romanesque wall which expressed the monks' ideal of isolation from 'the world'. The Cistercians were always noblemen, who, in spite of their asceticism and their labours, had many servants, extensive estates, and great wealth. Only small parts of their churches were accessible to laymen – *odi profanum vulgus* – and none to women. To understand the Cistercians and their architecture one need only compare them with the mendicant orders and their churches. St Francis was a monk like St Bernard. But he was not a prince, he was a beggar.

This consideration illuminates the purely artistic aspects of all church architecture. If a visitor to a Cistercian church whose approach is chiefly literary is told that St Bernard always remained an aristocrat and that he considered that any monk stood on a higher level than a layman, it will assist him in his understanding of the architecture. A visitor who understands the language of stone will be aware of this background without literary proof. The personality of St Bernard belongs to the Transition – that of St Francis is Gothic. These translations of notions of style to personalities, which may seem hazardous, represent exactly what the architects of the Cistercians and of the Friars expressed. Those who understand the language of stone need no literary sources to understand either from the architecture of the cathedrals that the bishops, too, remained aristocrats, or that they gave their architects free rein. The architects used this liberty to express in their art the desire that the social superiority of the governing forces of the Church should give way to the more Christian idea of a humble unity of the Church with the laity. The history of the Gothic style is a formal process which accompanies developments of religious thought.

63. Angers, Saint-Maurice. Interior
of nave, after 1149

At *Pontigny* there are still many remnants of the Romanesque. Amongst these are the cruciform piers with shafts on all four sides, those of the inside of the nave beginning only at a height of about ten feet, and also the rectangular section of the arcade arches and the transverse arches. The general effect of the exterior is extremely Romanesque, especially in the uninterrupted horizontal line of the roof, which joins the choir and the nave into a unity unbroken by the much lower transepts. However, until 1793 there was a wooden bellcote over the crossing.

The choir at Pontigny was replaced by the present choir (in building in the 1180s), so that the building as it now stands is a combination of the work of Pontigny II and III [61].[57B] The plan is modelled on that of Clairvaux III, except that the choir was lengthened to allow eleven chapels to lie around the ambulatory instead of the nine at Clairvaux. In principle the spatial forms of the Gothic cathedral have been adopted, and in the details, too, this new choir comes much nearer to the Gothic type of composition. In the apse of the

choir there are monolithic piers, and above them, supported on corbels, shafts rise to the ribs. The shafts supporting the wall-arches of the vault and those supporting the round arches of the windows produce a Gothic relief above the line of the springing of the vault. However, between the capitals of the round piers and the springing of the vault, the flat surface of the wall reigns. On the exterior, the sloping roof of the ambulatory rises only slightly above the chapels. The chapels are set adjacent to one another so that, on the outside, they form a single cylindrical surface, and while this is a protest against the liveliness of east ends such as that at Noyon, it is equally a protest against the projecting volumes of a Romanesque east end such as the one at Cluny. In the Late Gothic period chapels round ambulatories were also joined to one another in this way, so that there were no projections, but the simplicity of Pontigny is not a precursor of the Late Gothic. It is rather a remnant of Romanesque flatness. The flying buttresses are an original part of the choir, but one can feel the undisturbed Romanesque grandeur of

64. Santiago de Compostela
Cathedral. Crypt, *c.* 1170

the roofs as they rise step by step. All the original buttresses on the choir and the nave end below the horizontal line of the guttering.

The upper part of the west front is Gothic in its effect because of the three pointed arches on it. The central one of these surmounts the great west window; the other two are blind. The double shafts with rings round them are Gothic too. The lower part of the façade is covered by the narthex, a feature which appears in many Cistercian churches. Rose thought that it dated from about 1140, and Fontaine agreed with him.[58] It was probably built around 1150–60.

When *Cîteaux* also required a wider choir, it was not built on the system of those at Pontigny III and Clairvaux III, but was made rectangular and given a similarly rectangular ambulatory with rectangular chapels on each of its three sides. An engraving of 1674[59] shows how the composition of the east end was stepped up. The choir had simple buttresses, but the nave had flying buttresses. The choir is presumed to be contemporary with that at Pontigny. The return to the rectangular east end became the rule for most, though not all, later Cistercian churches.[59A]

7. THE SPREAD OF THE EARLY GOTHIC STYLE AND THE PASSIVE TRANSITION

In the 1150s, when the Cistercians had accepted the Early Gothic style at Clairvaux and Pontigny, the order spread the style wherever it had communities and built new monasteries or churches. Before about 1150, they had spread the Transitional style, or rather a specifically Cistercian Transitional style. In speaking of Transition as a general phenomenon, one has to differentiate between its very different forms; for wherever people came to know and accept the Gothic style, a compromise had to be reached with local traditions. The differences between the Romanesque

schools of architecture resulted in more and more new combinations.

In *France* itself, there appeared in Anjou a group of buildings whose style can be called Angevin Transitional. In the same decade as the vaulting of Le Mans (1145/50–58) the nave of *Saint-Maurice at Angers* received new rib-vaults (after 1149 and well advanced by 1160) [63].[59B] The transverse arches have thin roll-mouldings added at the edges, and the profile is softened also where the cells meet it. Otherwise the vault is similar to that at Le Mans: even the frontal shafts supporting the ribs are repeated. The vault can therefore still be called Transitional. The aisleless nave of Saint-Maurice was created out of a Romanesque nave which had also been aisleless. The new vaulting entailed the insertion into the old nave of compound wall responds to support each transverse arch, and massive new exterior projecting buttresses to carry the lateral thrust of the vault: none of the mechanical problems of the church of basilican type arose. Angers presents a variant of the type of vaulted church of which *Angoulême* is the main example – the vaulting consisting of a series of domes. The introduction of steeply domed cross-vaults with ribs produced a totally new mood. In Angoulême it was serene, festive, and light; in Angers it became majestic, imposing humility on the visitor. These differences, however, lie in details which are hardly traceable. About thirty years later a replica of Angers was built at La Trinité (now cathedral) at *Laval*.[59C] But it entirely lacked grandeur.

Outside France, in Germany, Italy, and Spain, variations grew up so different from one another that it is only their common effort to imitate and exploit the rib-vault which brings them together under the heading of the Transitional style.

Knowledge of the rib had been brought to *Germany* before 1106, some years before its acceptance by the Cistercians. It had been used in High Romanesque churches, such as the cathedrals at *Speyer* and *Worms*, and from the second quarter of the twelfth century, in Late Romanesque churches.[60] These preserved all the other Romanesque architectural members, but began to merge members with each other, used a higher relief with deeper shadows, and introduced diagonal views and other means of creating partiality. The result thus produced was a style parallel to the Gothic. The development of the Transitional style in Germany from about 1150 must be understood not as a union of a general Romanesque character with Gothic ribs, but as a union of a specifically Late Romanesque character with the Early Gothic style. In Normandy, and within the Norman school in England, the rib was introduced into High Romanesque forms. Dehio called this spontaneous development which reached the Gothic style without a preceding Late Romanesque phase, *Active* Transition, as against the development outside the Norman and French schools, which either proceeded from the High Romanesque forms customary in other schools, or, as in Germany, from Late Romanesque forms, which he called *Passive* Transition. A discussion of the results of these combinations, with their wealth of fantasy and imagination, belongs to the history of the Romanesque style.[61]

The active Transition in *Italy* does not require detailed discussion in a history of the Gothic style. Of course, the very early dates which have been ascribed to Italian rib-vaults by Kingsley Porter are not easily defended.[62] But the earliest rib-vaults in northern Italy appear at about the same time as the earliest English and Norman examples. The Italian series begins with a group of churches in and around Milan, under construction in the first decades of the twelfth century. Krautheimer's sagacious study of the building history of the Milanese churches suggested that no rib-vault can have existed in this city before 1120 since, if it were not so, there would not have been such uncertainty and so many changes in the form of vaults during the building of these churches.[63] But more recent research has established conclusively that the rib-vaults in the nave and transepts of *S. Nazaro in Milan* can be dated to around 1112.[64] The much-discussed rib-vaults over the nave of *S. Ambrogio in Milan* have been recently dated to *c.* 1128–30.[65] In his longitudinal section of S. Ambrogio, Dartein drew walls over the transverse arches of the nave.[66] These, he suggested, were intended to isolate the vault from the vertical thrust of the roof. There can hardly have been a flat ceiling originally, as the system of alternating supports was clearly designed for a vault. But the lower parts of these supports, built together with the lower storey of the narthex and western half of the church form *c.* 1110, suggest the intention to cover the central vessel with groin-vaults. Only in around 1128, just after the first rib-vaults at S. Ambrogio had been built in the lower storey of the narthex, was it decided to use ribs in the high vaults. Since the north tower of the church, the Torre dei Canonici, was well advanced by 1128, and since it was built together with the outer walls, aisles, piers and galleries of the church, these rib-vaults must have been under construction *c.* 1128–30. Contemporary, or perhaps even a little earlier than the S. Ambrogio vaults, are the rib-vaults over the central vessel of the church of *S. Sigismondo at Rivolta d'Adda*, begun *c.* 1120.[67]

65. Ávila Cathedral choir, finished in the 1180s. Interior of choir and transept

A slightly later series of early rib-vaults appear in churches in Novara, probably under Milanese influence.[68] The rib-vault of *S. Pietro di Casalvalone* belongs to the church dedicated in 1118 or 1119. At *S. Guilio di Dulzago*, one bay (the western) is groin-vaulted, two bays are rib-vaulted, and the rest have tunnel-vaults. It is not certain if a consecration of 1133 included the rib-vaults,[69] but they can be dated between 1118 and 1148. According to Kingsley Porter, the cathedral of *Novara*, which no longer exists, was completed in 1125 with a rib-vault. He mentions that one vault of the sacristy and half of the second vault in the adjoining passage have been preserved. In their geometrical construction and in the rectangular section of their ribs, they are similar to the vaults in *S. Ambrogio in Milan*. The rib-vaults must date to some time before the dedication of the cathedral in 1132. The vaults at *Sannazaro Sesia*, near Novara, which Porter claimed to date from 1040, can be put between 1130–40.[69A]

All the early Italian rib-vaults are domed, and have ribs with characteristic rectangular sections. Both features clearly separate them from the contemporary English and Norman rib-vaults, and suggest that the Italian and northern series developed as parallel and independent experiments, although perhaps derived from a lost common source. The closest contacts with north Italian vaulting occured in the Rhineland (e.g. Speyer II), where Romanesque architecture shows many points of similarity

66. Lincoln Cathedral. Vault of St Hugh's Choir, probably designed *c.*
1200

with Italian Romanesque, and in southern France, where the rib-vaults of *Moissac* and Saint-Victor at *Marseilles* have the rectangular profiles of the Italian examples.[69B] There were, however, connections between northern Italy and Normandy in the late eleventh and early twelfth centuries, *S. Fermo* and *S. Lorenzo* in Verona show that there were architects in Italy who knew Norman churches.[70] In turn, certain domed rib-vaults in Normandy from *c.* 1120 onwards, notably the chapter house at *Jumièges* and the remains of the choir at *Evreux* cathedral, suggest Lombard influence.[70A] The north Italian vaults are also similar to Angevin domes vaults, as in *Angers* (after 1149) or *Le Mans* (*c.* 1145/50–58) cathedrals. The difference between these two French vaults and those in S. Ambrogio is that in the latter the transverse arches are round and the ridges of the cells domed, while in the former the transverse arches are pointed and the ridges of the cells straight.[70B]

If it is accepted that there are no ribs in *Spain* earlier than those in the narthex of *Santiago de Compostela*, then the Spaniards were the last people in Western Europe to adopt the rib. This Romanesque church, an impressive replica of Saint-Sernin at Toulouse, had a narthex added by the architect Mateo. The falling ground on which it stood made it necessary to build a crypt underneath it. Both the crypt and the narthex have heavy ribs [64]. The name of the architect, Mateo, is inscribed on the Portico de la Gloria, which was built sometime before 1188. He took over the direction of the building in 1168, so the ribs in the crypt probably date

from about 1170, and those in the narthex from the following decade. Their Norman profile and ornamentation shows a close relationship with the North. (The western bays of the crypt still have distorted groins).[70C]

The choir of the cathedral at *Ávila* was finished the 1180s. It was influenced by that at Vézelay [50], but the piers at Ávila are heavier and the triforium and clerestory are far more massive in form [65]. The double ambulatory is reminiscent of Saint-Denis and Notre-Dame in Paris, but again the proportions are so different that the resemblance is far from obvious.[71] Since the architect of the choir, Eruchel or Fruchel, died in 1192, and since, according to Lozoya, the choir was in use as early as 1181, this gives a *terminus ante quem* for the choir at Vézelay. The ribs at Ávila form pointed arches and are relatively light; the transverse arches in the ambulatory are also pointed and have a rectangular section. The windows, however, still have round arches. Because the church is built into the city wall, the exterior looks more like a piece of military architecture than a church. The exposed flying buttresses behind the sentries' walk at the top of the wall are probably the first to have been built in Spain. They appear to have been added after the completion of the wall.[71A]

The cathedral at *Tarragona*, begun some time after 1171, gives an impression of even greater heaviness than that at Ávila. It is a work of almost pure Romanesque. The decision to introduce rib-vaults was made only when the building was already in progress, probably during the episcopacy of

THE SPREAD OF THE EARLY GOTHIC STYLE AND THE PASSIVE TRANSITION 101

Archbishop Ramón de Rocabertí (1199–1215). Characteristically the main apse and the south apse are semicircular, while the north apse ends in five sides of an octagon. This shows the indecision of the architect. The grey stone and the very limited lighting with no stained glass create an atmosphere of almost overwhelming gravity, although the brighter light from the crossing tower shines down like a ray of hope. In this church there is evidence of a hesitant concession to the Gothic style, but, as a whole, it is a Transitional work, in which the general atmosphere is predominantly Romanesque. It is an unforgettable expression of the spirit of Good Friday.[71B] The same is true of *Fitero*, with its massive walls, piers, transverse arches, and ribs. The capitals stand on frontal responds, but are turned through an angle of 45 degrees to face diagonally, as at Pontigny.[71C] In the 'Old Cathedral' at *Salamanca*, a building easy to take in and to appreciate, there are diagonally set figures mounted on frontal responds to carry the ribs. The exact date of this clearly conceived church is not known. The design for the east end is said to date back to about 1150, and the transepts and the tower above the crossing were finished about 1180. The tower is purely Romanesque, stylistically perfect, and of outstanding quality. Lambert gives the date of the nave as the end of the twelfth century, which is probably correct. This church is more progressive than those at Ávila and Fitero. Yet, in spite of its positive qualities, historically it can only be described as conservative.[72]

The cathedral at *Lérida*, begun in 1203, reproduces the plan of Tarragona, but with a nave of only three bays. The architect followed his model closely and felt no ambition to advance in step with the architect of Chartres. Here again, a historical judgement must not be confused with an individual evaluation.[73]

8. THE TIERCERON

In the century following the building of Durham Cathedral, the rib-vault had been improved in many ways. Once the pointed arch had been incorporated into the geometrical construction of vaults, all its technical and mechanical advantages were recognized, and architects worked to exploit to the full its consequences in interiors and exteriors. The rib-vault itself was built over rectangular and trapezoid plans; it was enriched with the ridge-rib, and its keystones were emphasized. The rib was introduced into vaults with steeply rising ridges, where it made the transition from groin to groove inoffensive to the eye. With the achievement of all these improvements and expedients, the development of the rib-vault seemed to have reached its end.

However, a new vista of possibilities was opened by the rib-vaults in *Lincoln* Cathedral.[74] Bishop Hugh of Avalon and his mason began a new choir, an eastern transept, and an apse with chapels in 1192. The crossing tower collapsed in 1237 or 1239. This necessitated a renewal of the first bay east of the crossing, which was restored with a sexpartite vault. The rest of the vaults in the choir survive from the campaign beginning in 1192. They are of an uncommon form [66, 67]. A ridge-rib connects them from west to east. In each bay this rib is divided into three sections by two

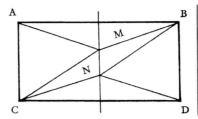

67. Lincoln Cathedral, vault of St Hugh's choir, designed *c*. 1200. Plan

68. Lincoln Cathedral. Crocket pier in St Hugh's Choir

bosses. The ribs AM and BM rise to the point M, the ribs CN and DN to the point N. The two cells ABM and CDN do not meet at the ridge-rib; they avoid each other. To M and N a third rib rises from the corners B and C. These ribs do not form the boundary of a cell; they lie on the cylindrical surfaces of the cells. Some critics have found this 'senseless', others have called the third rib 'decorative', using the word to indicate that the ribs have no static function. The name of such ribs, tierceron, means 'third rib', and it may have originated with reference to Lincoln. St Hugh was a Frenchman, but his architect was English.[74A]

The architect used below the windows of the choir aisles and also in other parts blank arcades, a traditional motif, but their form is again unusual. They are two arcades behind each other, or two tiers of colonnettes and arches, arranged in a syncopated rhythm. Each column of the front tier stands in front of the apex of a back arch. In as much as this motif also has a merely decorative and not a static meaning, it has a stylistic affinity to the vaults. That the front row was built at the same time as the rear row is proved by their common plinths.

The Lincoln architect must have known French crocket capitals in 1192. Several of the capitals in the choir executed after 1200 are more progressive. The crockets here show twisted leaves. But the strangest motif is the use of crockets up the shafts of the piers at the corner of transept and aisles [68]. In capitals it is easy to interpret crockets; they sprout out where the shaft seems to open into a blossom. At Lincoln, where they grow up a shaft, they are again 'decorative' and 'senseless' to any critic who sticks to his own

69. Angers, Saint-Serge. Interior of choir, 1215–25

norms. These transplanted or even displaced crockets belong to shafts partly hidden by free-standing Purbeck shafts. Again the architect plays with the conceit of the Gothic type of relief readable from back to front. In some of the piers he hollowed out grooves in front of which shafts rise. Some of the shafts themselves have such grooves, reminiscent of Late Gothic sections of mouldings. The purpose in the Late Gothic style is to allow space to penetrate into the pier, whereas before the aim had been to make the pier penetrate into the surrounding space.

All the motifs at Lincoln which have been commented on here have an affinity with one another: the mouldings of the ribs, the rich contrasts of light and shade, the displacement of the crockets, the increased difficulty of seeing the syncopated blank arches, the grooves of the shafts. They all express the wilful character of their inventor, a man who made a boldly personal use of the forms of the Gothic style and instilled a new sense into them. Those who call them senseless have not grasped their stylistic sense.

Now that the phase between High Renaissance and Early Baroque is no longer called Late Renaissance but Mannerism and that Mannerism is being understood and defined as a style *sui generis*, it has become possible to recog-

nize related phenomena also in other periods. They have consequently been labelled 'Mannerist' too, and in that sense the architect of St Hugh's choir can be called a 'Mannerist'. If the original apse had survived at Lincoln, there would be one more 'Mannerist' motif to discuss. According to what excavations indicate it must have been different from any apse ever added to a choir.

Out of the architect's asymmetrical vaults his successor evolved the earliest regular star-vaults of Europe. His 'Mannerism' remained at first an isolated intermezzo, though it had its consequences in the further development of the High Gothic style. It is not merely a matter of utility or convention to refuse to establish the phase of the choir of Lincoln as one of 'Mannerism'. For the essence of the contrast between Romanesque and Gothic remains. Lincoln in its choir (and the western transept, probably completed by a successor) is Early Gothic or 'Early English'. Hugh's architect's Mannerism is both English Early Gothic and a subspecies of normal Early Gothic. The way in which he departed from the latter was to use a form in a new sense. Thus first and foremost there is the rib which is not placed in front of the groins of a groin-vault, either according to its original function (to replace the groins by a regular curve) or according to its later function (to facilitate construction, technique, and statics), but which runs on the surface of a cell just like the ridge-rib, only not straight but curved and with its curve following that of the cell.[75] The tierceron rib is not a rib in the original sense of the term. Much is decorative that is not 'Mannerist'.

The term 'Mannerism' was introduced to describe the style of the years from about 1520 to about 1580. If its principle can be found also in the styles of other generations, then there is a need for a name to embrace all such stages in the history of style, including the particular example known as sixteenth-century Mannerism, and also for separate names for each one of these stages. The example at Lincoln, which depends almost entirely on the individual creativity of the architect, might be named after him, if we knew his name.[76] As the principles of Mannerism appear at various stages in the development of the Gothic style, it will be necessary to find a suitable term for each such appearance.

Historians have never agreed on a term to embrace all manifestations of the principles of Mannerism, or indeed of many other principles in the history of style. Some of them claim that such terms are unnecessary. However, those who are sensitive to such expressions as 'manneristic Gothic' or 'baroque Gothic', and regard them as intellectual and linguistic monsters, will always try to find terms unencumbered by preconceived ideas. Inspired by Jakob Burckhardt, I suggested earlier in this book (p. 65) the word 'akyrism', as, in this phenomenon, forms are used in a sense which is not properly their own. The Greek work 'akyros' means 'improper'. Each reader is free to translate the terms 'akyrism' and 'akyristic' back into his own terminology.

Lincoln's akyrism is not an isolated phenomenon. The transplantation of the rib on to vaults of the domical type in Anjou is related to it from the moment the profile of the rib becomes truly Gothic. As long as the surface of the vault is part of a sphere, the ribs seem to attach themselves to it, but in domical groin-vaults such as those in the nave of the

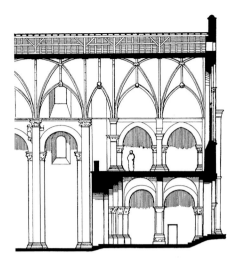

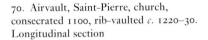

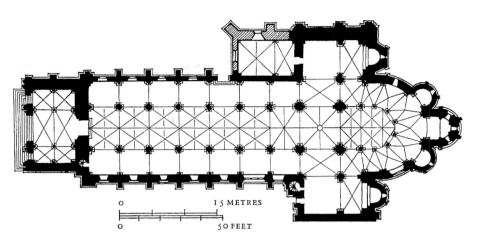

70. Airvault, Saint-Pierre, church, consecrated 1100, rib-vaulted *c.* 1220–30. Longitudinal section

71. Airvault, church. Plan

cathedral at *Angers* they form spatial divisions. When ridge-ribs are added, as they are in the choir and transepts at Angers, the result is an aesthetic effect based on both these principles. As the ridge-ribs and the diagonal ribs, and even the transverse arches and the wall-arches, have the same profile, they are generally accepted as co-ordinate forms. The most fascinating work in this style is *Saint-Serge* at *Angers*[77] [69]. The choir, a smaller and more intimate version of the cathedral at Poitiers, is that of a hall-church. The slender round piers and the octagonal bases and abaci make it more Gothic than the cathedral. In the corner bays and in the rectangular sanctuary, the number of ribs is increased. The ridge-ribs over the windows and the blind arches of the walls meet the diagonal ribs in the middle of their upward course. The lower sections of these ridge-ribs are really part of the cells. This complicated system gives an effect of vitality and wealth which stimulates both the intellect and the senses. Mussat dates the church to between 1215 and 1225. It is therefore later than the vaults of St Hugh's choir at Lincoln.

Cells with their own ridge-ribs were also used in conjunction with the traditional tunnel-vaults of Poitou. These are even more difficult to grasp at first sight. In the nave at *Airvault* [70, 71], one gradually realizes that two adjacent bays, *a* and *b*, are joined by one pair of diagonal ribs; *b* and the next bay, *c*, are similarly joined so that the two identical systems intersect, or, as the French put it, ride one on the other.[78] The actual bays are separated by pointed transverse arches with the same profile as the ribs. A ridge-rib connects with the semi-overlapping bays of the rib-vault; and the cells which end on the diagonal ribs also have ridge-ribs. The intersections are emphasized with bosses, but this emphasis confuses rather than elucidates the system, even though the main intersections, where the diagonals cross, have larger bosses than the secondary ones, which correspond to the intermediate points of the cells. The plan helps one to understand the system, but it must not be overlooked that the cross-line of each bay cannot be regarded as a simple transverse arch. It must rather be considered in terms of

four separate arcs, each of which shows a different curve and a different direction. The ridge-rib of the cells rises and curves to the boss on the diagonal rib, from where it moves through an obtuse angle to follow the flat segmental curve of the tunnel-vault to the intermediate keystone on the main ridge-rib, and from here it repeats these two curves symmetrically on the other side of the vault. The spaces between the meshes of this net do not make up a continuous surface, and therefore to call this a pointed tunnel-vault is to describe its overall effect, not its actual geometry.

When one has understood the form of this vault, one wonders what induced the architect to set the visitor such a complicated problem. When the church at Airvault was consecrated in 1100, it had a simple tunnel-vault. The piers and arches that supported it have been preserved. If this vault was dilapidated, it could easily have been replaced with an identical one. However, what was desired was not this simple form of vault with its strong additive quality, but an expression of Gothic partiality, which the architect transferred to a tunnel-vault. In this way, he retained the original unity of the nave, yet also achieved a rich and complex quality of division. The means to this end was the transplantation of the rib on to a tunnel-vault. The result is a work of the same akyrism as that of St Hugh's Choir at Lincoln. The vaults at Lincoln are certainly earlier than the Angevin examples, but the net vaults at Airvault, *Saint-Jouin-de-Marnes*, and others of the same type were certainly not imitations of those at Lincoln.[78A] The only factor common to both the French churches and the English cathedral is the transplantation of the rib on to the surface of a kind of tunnel-vault.[79]

The name 'Plantagenet style' which has been given to these French churches leads to the idea that they represent a combination of French and English ideas, grafted on the forms of the Romanesque schools of Anjou and Poitou.[79A] According to Berthelée, this style ceased about 1250. It remains to be seen whether it changed completely, or survived in the High Gothic period as an akyristic variant.

CHAPTER 3

The High Gothic Style, 1194–1300[1]

I. THE ORGANIC UNIFICATION OF INTERIOR AND EXTERIOR. FINIALS AND BALUSTRADES

The exposed flying buttresses at Notre-Dame in Paris did not influence the structure of the interior. Galleries, with quadrant arches or buttress walls concealed below their roofs, continued to be used, and the same was done wherever this new member was added to earlier buildings in order to improve their stability.[1A]

The master who rebuilt the cathedral at *Chartres* after the fire of 10 June 1194 was the first man to draw the logical consequences from the construction of flying buttresses [72, 73].[1B] He eliminated the galleries, which were no longer required to bear the thrust of the vaults.[1C] Once this was done, the roofs over the aisles could stand immediately above the vaults of the aisles and the sills of the clerestory windows could be lowered far below the level of the springing of the main vault.[2] These windows could also be enlarged upwards and sideways, as the clerestory walls seemed to be relieved of their load.

The desire to enlarge the windows sprang not only from the wish to improve the lighting but also from the enjoyment of stained glass and its softening of the light in the interior. This diminution of light necessitated larger windows, and these again needed more stained glass: the two factors mutually stimulate one another. At the same time the surface of the stained glass, seen from inside, took on the character of actual wall – a result of the acceptance of the Gothic relief. Seen from outside this effect is even more striking, because the glass is covered with a silver-grey patina.[3]

Since the buttresses of the nave are broader at the bottom than at the top, the windows in the aisles are relatively narrow. The upper windows are so wide that each had to be divided into a pair of lights surmounted by an oculus, and these oculi were the reason for making the wall-arches for the vault round. In conjunction with the spacing of the flying buttresses, the round wall-arches led to the decision to give up sexpartite vaults and make all vaults quadripartite on an oblong plan. This so-called 'Gothic *travée*' is a departure from the traditional plan of the Romanesque style with its square bays corresponding each to two square bays in the aisles.[3A] Rows have replaced groups. However, it almost appears that the architect lacked the courage to make a clean break with tradition, since he stuck to the use of alternating supports, which had been the source of the sexpartite vault. Although all the piers are of equal mass, they are alternately octagonal with round shafts and round with octagonal shafts on the four frontal faces. It must not be supposed that this alternation arose because the architect had originally planned a sexpartite vault, since the piers nearest the crossing in the nave are round, whilst the corresponding ones in the transepts are octagonal. This alternation continues in the ambulatory, and outside even in the short shafts which support the flying buttresses, but these shafts strike the eye only if one climbs on to the roofs of the aisles.

The regularity of the rows of flying buttresses, vaulted bays, and windows justified regularity in the groups of shafts

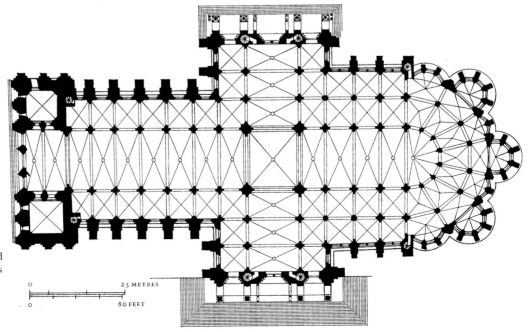

72. Chartres Cathedral, begun 1194. Interior of nave, photographed after the removal of the stained glass during the Second World War

73. Chartres Cathedral, begun 1194. Plan

0   25 METRES

0   80 FEET

74. Chartres Cathedral, begun 1194.
Exterior of south aisle of nave. The
Vendôme chapel of 1417 occupies the
aisle bay on the right

75. (*facing page*) Chartres Cathedral.
Upper part of choir, begun *c.* 1210

above the abaci more than at Notre-Dame. At Chartres each group comprises five shafts, as those supporting the wall-arches also spring from the abaci of the piers. The shafts have their own bases on plinths and, as the shafts supporting the transverse arches are octagonal above octagonal shafts and round above round ones, the plinths also alternate in form. Beside them stands the archivolt of the arcade, its profile set back in plan to correspond to the width of its own shafts on the inner side of the arcade. The horizontal mouldings above and below the quadripartite triforium form rings round the group of shafts, shafts which rise half-way up the jambs of the paired windows. These windows, lengthened downwards, make the area of the vaulting cells seem to reach further into the space below. In working out on the drawing board the relations between all the members, such as the flying buttresses, the windows with their stained glass, the vaults, and the piers, the architect sought to achieve the same interplay as that existing between windows and vaulting cells. They have all been united into an organic whole. In the choir, the increase in the area of stained glass demanded polygonal instead of rounded apses. The exterior and the interior, governed by a few principles, form a unity. To say that exterior and interior are incompatible is to mis-understand the ideal which the architect strove for and achieved. The exterior must be understood as a function of the interior, and vice versa; the building demands that we first walk round the outside, then go inside, and finally look at the outside again, so that we can, in our minds, build up the sense of a unity out of the fragments. Because of all this, the church is specifically Gothic, specifically 'partial', and at the same time a unity in which the principles which were inherent in the first rib-vaults have been transferred to the whole.

It is the achievement of this organic blending of the

interior and exterior which gives the cathedral at Chartres its position of historical significance as the birthplace of the High Gothic style;[38] in some details, the architects were even astonishingly progressive – for instance, in turning the abaci of the shafts in the chapels of the ambulatory diagonally, so that they deny the Romanesque frontality. This also appears in the radiating chapels at Soissons cathedral, and afterwards became a preference for High Gothic architects.[3C]

Chartres represents a first step beyond the Early Gothic style, but not the last. There remained much in the church for later architects with a constructive critical sense to correct. The architect of the nave of Chartres had for instance not fully understood the statics of the flying buttresses, so that he had to supplement them by a third slender flying buttress above the two lower ones, which stand one over the other.[4] The two lower flying buttresses of the nave are connected by radially set columns supporting small round arches, so that the flying buttresses look like parts of a spoked wheel [74]. The flying buttresses on the choir are similar, also with radial spokes [75]. Yet a few details are different: the small arches on the diagonally set spokes which have a square section and no capitals are pointed. The double ambulatory made it necessary to divide the flying buttresses into two parts. The inner series of flying buttresses carries the thrust of the vault on to piers standing over the middle row of piers of the ambulatory, and a second series leads the thrust from there on to the buttresses between the chapels. As in the nave, a third arch mounts up to the eaves of the roof, and is unadorned, like the outer one of the lower pair. The tabernacles at the bottom of the flying buttresses have the form of small square pavilions, each consisting of four columns at the corners and one central one, supporting a flat ceiling on which stands a saddleback roof. The gable is separated from the lower part of the structure by a horizontal ledge, as at Laon, and ends in a finial. In front of these tabernacles, the buttresses form a step which is part of the gallery running along the gutter-level of the roof. For safety there is a balustrade which is led round the front of the buttresses, and this balustrade is repeated at the eaves of the upper roofs of the choir, the transepts, and the nave. It is a new Gothic structural member, though it still consists of trefoils with round central arches.

The flat niches in the sides of the buttresses on the nave are surmounted by similar trefoiled arches and contain statues of bishops (those on the south side dating from 1865). The niches penetrate into the little gables, as they do on the south tower which the architect saw every day. However, the gables on the upper section of these buttresses are separated by horizontal cornices, as they are on the tabernacles on the east side.

As the west façade was spared by the fire, it was only on the transept that the architect had the opportunity fully to express his ideas. Both these façades are almost square in proportion and have flanking towers which were never completed; a door leads into each tower, so that, including the central door, each transept has three entrances, like Saint-Denis and Laon [117].[5]

Above the level of the doors there is a row of five narrow,

76. Bourges Cathedral, begun before 1195. Exterior of the choir from the east

closely spaced windows between the towers, and above them an oculus with tracery which still shows hints of the interpretation of the round window as a wheel. Though both façades follow the same general scheme, they differ in their details. On the north side the two middle buttresses form octagonal turrets, while on the south side they are rectangular. On the rougher north side there are tabernacles in front of the buttresses, while on the south side the surfaces are decorated with delicate blind arcades of extremely slender proportions.

The vaults of the church, including those of the transepts, were finished by about 1217. The big rose-windows in the transepts were probably built later, the first being that at the south. Their style, as well as that of many details of both porches, betrays the hand of a new architect, whereas the wheel-window of the west façade is still the work of the main master, who here used the forms of the flying buttresses on the nave. The chronological sequence of the main parts of the cathedral is still controversial.[6]

As in so many other medieval buildings, part of the organic effect of Chartres Cathedral lies in the interplay between the forms of different medieval periods, but it also lies partly in the fact that the cathedral has remained unfinished. Besides the pairs of towers on the west, north, and south façades, a

further tower was begun on each side of the choir. The church is a fragment, not in the sense that follows from the Gothic principle of partiality, but because it is only a fragment of what had been visualized by its architect and his patron. One is tempted to imagine how it was intended to complete the church, and to wonder whether the total effect would have been improved. But when one considers the whole church, from the Romanesque crypt to the Late Gothic spire on the north-west tower, one is so filled with admiration that one hesitates to answer this question. The church is undoubtedly not as mature as, for instance, Amiens, and it undoubtedly contains details which are not harmonious, but, paradoxically, because it contains so much irregularity and tension, the general effect is one of harmony; for harmony is the concordance of essentially different factors.

The cathedral at *Bourges* is only a little later than Chartres. In 1195, the archbishop Henri de Sully, brother of Eudes de Sully, archbishop of Paris, donated a large sum of money for the repair of the collapsing cathedral. Henri's charter may imply a decision to rebuild the whole cathedral, and work seems to have started at least by 1195. Building progressed from east to west. By 1214 the choir (that is the turning bays and the first two double bays immediately following it) was complete. In 1218 the body of Sully's succes-

77. Bourges cathedral, begun before
1195. Plan

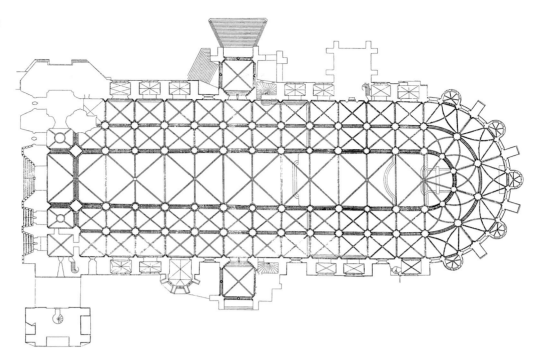

sor, Bishop Guillame (1199–1210) canonized in that year, was translated into the new choir. The relationship between the first patron of Bourges and the patron of Notre-Dame in Paris explains why the cathedral in Paris, rather than that at Chartres, was the model on which Bourges was built. Like Notre-Dame, it has two aisles on each side of the nave and choir, and a double ambulatory [77].[6A]

As it was decided to build the choir of the new church farther east than that of the older building, it had to extend over the town ramparts, and it therefore became necessary to build a crypt, or rather a substructure, with a double ambulatory [76]. The outer ambulatory of this substructure is divided into triangular bays, similarly to that of Notre-Dame, while the inner ambulatory consists of trapezoid bays in which the intersection of the ribs coincides with that of the two main axes of the trapezium. In plan, the ribs form segmental arches, and are therefore curved in three dimensions, both in plan and in elevation. However, they must be regarded as something different from the much earlier three-dimensional groins of the Romanesque. It required all the experience of masons, accumulated since the time of the Romanesque, to make their construction possible, and their execution at Bourges is the performance of a past master.

Above, in the church itself, the inner ambulatory has ribs like that in the crypt, while in the outer ambulatory the large bays, broadening towards the outside, are divided. A triangular cell is cut off from each side, leaving a trapezium which tapers outwards, and here, too, the ribs form three-dimensional curves [77]. Branner thought that this complicated solution was caused by the late addition, while work was already in progress, of five 'limpet' chapels in the form of small oriels, each attached to a section of the ambulatory, and taking up the central third of the periphery of each curving bay [76]. It is now, however, considered that these chapels were intended and built from the start.[6B]

The whole ambulatory and the choir within it end in a semicircle, again derived from Notre-Dame in Paris. By comparison with the polygonal choir at Chartres, it is definitely conservative.

Equally conservative is the use of the sexpartite vault, but there is at Bourges a new solution to the demand for combining uniform piers with sexpartite vaults [78]. Around each of the round piers, which are so surprisingly high because the double aisles on either side of the nave force the triforium upwards, there are eight shafts at equal intervals [76]. Above the abaci, the shafts supporting the ribs can therefore go up between those supporting the transverse arches and those supporting the wall-arches. This is certainly more intelligent than any other similar attempt to solve the problem. The shafts pierce the capitals; only the abaci go round them. The profile of the arcade is divided, as at Chartres, its central member being supported on the frontal abacus which stands on the stronger shaft in the archway between the nave and the inner aisle, while its outer member rests on the abacus of the pier itself. The form of the piers in the aisles derives from this admirably clear arrangement.

In section, Bourges is identical with Notre-Dame, except that it has no galleries.[7] The piers between the aisles have a vertical continuation outside, above the roof, as at Chartres, forming a support like the pier of a bridge between the first arch of each flying buttress, which leads the thrust down from the main vault, and the second one, which leads it down on to the outside piers.[7A]

The two steps of the cross-section suggested the introduction of a triforium in the nave and in the tall inner aisles. At the east end, each bay of the triforium has six narrow openings with pointed arches, framed by a single, larger one. The four central openings are of the same height and are slightly higher than the two outside ones – a form that can

78. (*facing page*) Bourges Cathedral, begun before 1195. Interior, looking east

79. Rouen Cathedral, begun soon after 1200. Interior of north aisle of nave

also be seen on the east towers at Chartres, with blind arches instead of openings.

The upper windows consist of three openings with pointed arches, embraced by a single, larger pointed arch, and their form is typical of plate tracery in northern France around the year 1200. In the nave, from the third bay westward, plate tracery is replaced by bar tracery in the windows of the intermediate aisles. Bourges has no transepts, and only two towers on the west façade; therefore, by comparison with Laon and Chartres, it appears closed in spite of the degree of dissolution achieved by the flying buttresses. (The strange pairs of pinnacles date only from 1835.) Not all the windows have stained glass, so that the interior is largely flooded with bright daylight. Although the work of con-

struction was not completed until 1255, the interior has great unity and is one of the most beautiful of the entire High Gothic period – rich in overlapping vistas, a masterpiece of the combination of multiple images with perfect clarity in the whole. The freshness of the details is still very reminiscent of the Laon period.[7B]

Some time after 1205, the old apse at *Laon* was pulled down and the choir lengthened to form five double bays, ending on the Cistercian model in a flat east wall [42]. The choir is designed on the Romanesque system of square bays in nave and aisles. The reason for pulling down the main apse may have been its imminent collapse, owing to the absence or inadequacy of the flying buttresses, while the unusual length of the new choir may have been the need for

80. Soissons Cathedral. Interior of choir, c. 1200

greater liturgical space, and the desire to balance the long nave and extensive transepts with a correspondingly long choir.[7C] As the flat east end includes elements to be found also in the west façade, it is probable that the architect of the new choir also built the westernmost bays of the nave and the west façade. Because the first three bays of the old choir were to be preserved, it was advisable to build the new bays according to the same system, in order to achieve unity. This is why the architect declined to be influenced by the tempting new models at Chartres and Bourges.[7D]

The first major response in Normandy to High Gothic architecture was the nave of the cathedral of *Rouen*. Here, in 1200, a great fire destroyed most of the Romanesque cathedral. Of the old church only the north-west tower (the Tour Saint-Romain) and the jambs and archivolts of the side doorways have been preserved. Contrary to normal practice the building of the new church was begun, soon after 1200, at the west. Jean d'Andeli, probably the first architect since he is mentioned as master of the works in 1206, began with the piers, an arcade of pointed arches, and a 'false' gallery above it – that is, he constructed large gallery openings on to the central vessel but with no gallery floors over the aisles [79]. The tendency to follow the example of Chartres and leave out the gallery led to akyrism, for in this case we are

really faced with pseudo-galleries. Strangely enough, the architect did not completely eliminate the possibility of walking along the nave at the level of the intended gallery, at least for those people with a head for heights, for the sill-line of the pseudo-gallery is made to project round each pier, inside the aisle, like a kind of balcony, each projection being supported on a central column surrounded by five free-standing columns. The central columns stand on the abaci of the piers and the surrounding ones are supported on corbels. In its transparency, the whole group is specifically Gothic, and, as in most examples of akyrism, it is the expression of an uninhibited imagination working within the tendencies of the style of its time.

The choir was under construction by the early 1220s and probably complete by 1237; its plan followed the foundations of the previous church, with three separated chapels round a semicircular ambulatory. The main apse, however, is polygonal, forming five sides of a decagon, and in elevation it is High Gothic, with slender round piers and a triforium above, similar in principle to that at Soissons cathedral.[8]

The cathedral at *Soissons*[9] is a High Gothic unity, except for the south transept and the chapel which was added diagonally to it. A comparison between this south transept, an imaginative masterpiece of Early Gothic architecture, built about 1180, and the remainder of the cathedral is most illuminating, since it shows that the new generation of about 1200[9A] rejected the charm of complexity in favour of an emphasis on necessity and severity. The architect tried to connect the group of shafts above each pier with the pier itself by adding a single shaft below, but this was not wide enough to form a logical sequence with the three shafts above [80].

Around the ambulatory there are five chapels, set close to one another, which are round in plan at ground-level but become polygonal at the level of the window-sills.[10] The ribs inside them have a pointed, almond-shaped section; they join those of the corresponding bay of the ambulatory at a common keystone which lies in the transverse arch at the entrance to the chapel. In this way the corresponding sectors of the ambulatory become parts of the chapels, and vice versa. At Soissons the shafts are turned through 45 degrees, as had been done in the eastern chapels of Chartres, so that the corner of the abacus lies in the same vertical plane as the edge of the almond-shaped shaft. The small spatial layer marked by the ribs and shafts is thus divided down the middle, making each half appear to belong to the spatial area beneath which it lies. In this way the transverse arches seem to lose their separating force: the separation is still present, but the spaces which the transverse arch is supposed to separate from each other pour through it, merging almost completely.[10A]

The north transept was built soon after 1240. It follows closely the design of the choir and nave, even to the use of (by then outdated) plate tracery windows.[10B] The general impression of the exterior is determined by these windows, the double flying buttresses, and the limitation of the num-

81. Reims Cathedral, begun 1211. Interior of nave

ber of towers to the two at the west façade. Of these, the south tower was completed in the fourteenth century, while the other remains incomplete today, showing how wise the architect had been to keep his original design within the realm of possibility.[10C]

2. THE HIGH GOTHIC PIER. TRACERY. GARGOYLES

Chartres, Bourges, Rouen, and Soissons were all being built at the same time, and in each of these cathedrals there is a personal attempt in an individual fashion to draw the logical conclusions from the introduction of exposed flying buttresses. The tendency to let the whole interior of a church merge into a single unity had been born at Saint-Denis and seemed to allow of many variations, but in this variety there are traces of a norm, and the younger architects of the time seem to have been mainly preoccupied with finding this norm. The architect of the new choir at *Reims* – whether he be Jean d'Orbais or Gaucher of Reims[10D] – was the leader of this new generation. We know the names of the four architects of Reims, but not the order in which they succeeded one another. Several different orders have been suggested, but the most convincing is Gaucher of Reims, Jean le Loup, Jean d'Orbais, and Bernard of Soissons, in that order.[11]

It was once thought that the choir of the church at Orbais was designed by Jean d'Orbais, and was a prototype for Reims cathedral. It is now widely recognized that the choir, dating from after 1165, and completed in the early years of the thirteenth century, is an eclectic derivation from Laon and Soissons cathedrals, and from the choir of S. Remi at Reims. It has little or no direct connection with Jean d'Orbais's designs at Reims. However, the bar tracery in the eastern bay of the nave clerestory at Orbais may pre-date the bar tracery in the radiating chapels at Reims, and some scholars have attributed this part of the church to Jean d'Orbais.[12]

In 1210, when the cathedral at *Reims* was designed, the building of Chartres had reached a stage where the architect of Reims could criticize its effect and make his own design accordingly. The spatial form of Reims is of the same type as that of Chartres, but the nave is three bays longer; each transept, with its two flanking aisles, is one bay shorter, and the chapels round the choir do not alternate as at Chartres,

where older foundations were used. At Reims the chapels are identical, except for the central chapel, which projects further to the east [82, 83]. The criticisms of the architect of Reims were directed less at the proportions of Chartres than at the forms of the piers and the windows.

The grouping of shafts in naves always tended to force the shaft supporting the transverse arch far forward. The rule had been to make the round piers roughly the same thickness as the walls, as it probably was believed that they would otherwise look stocky. The architect of Bourges did not worry about this rule; he made his round piers much thicker than the walls, but he continued them upwards to the springing of the vault, giving the impression that each bay of the wall consists of a single stone slab, set between the piers. If, on the other hand, an architect preferred to follow the old rule and build the shaft supporting the transverse arch on a base standing on the abacus of the pier, it then projected beyond the line of the round pier and did not seem to follow logically from what stood below.

The architect of Chartres corrected this defect by making the lower shaft so large that it supported the base of the upper one, thus avoiding the impression that the upper one overhangs [72]. The architect of Reims accepted this solution, but added capitals to the lower shafts, so that the piers now had a clear connexion with the arcade and the thickness of the wall [81]. At Noyon, Laon, and Paris, no answer had yet been found to the problem of making the groups of the upper shafts flush with the piers. At Reims, on the other hand, the architect devised the pier as a whole, making it symmetrical on all four sides to carry the weight both of the walls and of the vaults of the nave and aisle in a logical way.

At the same time as the shafts, the abacus itself is also corrected. At Chartres, the important junction in the zone of the capitals is still confused. In plan, the abaci are bevelled off at an angle of 45 degrees, partly because of the form of the piers. The abaci of the shafts supporting the arcade arches are rectangular, while those facing the central aisle are alternately round and polygonal. Furthermore, the capitals of the shafts supporting the arcade are only half as high as those of the piers. Compared with this multiplicity, the solution at Reims is simple and clear. The abaci of the core of the piers are set diagonally; those of the shafts supporting the arcade arches and the transverse arches of the side aisles are polygonal, so that the plan of the whole pier at this

83. Reims Cathedral, begun 1210.
Exterior of choir

height gives on the whole, the effect of a diagonally set square with slight differentiations. The capitals on the shafts are cleverly corrected to reach the same height as those of the piers, thus making a unit of the zone of the capitals. The plinths of the shafts supporting the transverse arches lie in the same plane as the shafts below, so that, at this point on the piers, the diagonal direction of the Gothic profile has achieved its perfect form.

The plinths and bases are similar to those at Chartres, the main octagonal plinth supporting the pier, while the projecting rectangular ones, which are a legacy of the Romanesque principle of addition, carry the shafts. Except for this feature, the piers have been entirely merged into the diagonal relief, and the space flows smoothly from the central to the side aisles and from one bay into the next.

In the evaluation of these piers, it is important to remember that Gaucher of Reims, like the other architects of his school, used round piers. If he knew the cathedral at Rouen at the stage it had reached by 1210, he must have realized that the solution arrived at there was an improvement on all those that had preceded it. On the frontal side of the piers at Rouen there are five shafts, rising from ground-level and only interrupted by rings at the level of the abaci on the corresponding five shafts within the arcade opening. Here, too, the line from the central shaft within the arcade to the shaft supporting the transverse arch is a diagonal, but the abaci of the five shafts within the arcade and the profile of the arches themselves are still governed by the frontal principle of the Romanesque style, and the general effect of the piers is determined by the frontality of their core. Round piers seemed to be more favourable to the principles of the Gothic style, and although in The Rayonnant period the

84. Reims Cathedral. Capital, after 1210

style reverted to the use of the type of pier found at Rouen, the architect of Reims was more convinced by the solution reached at Chartres.

The new window-forms at Reims were also developed from those at Chartres and Soissons cathedrals, but, although at Chartres each group of two lights and an oculus was intended as a unity, it nevertheless remained a juxtaposition of three separate openings, while at Reims the architect – in accordance with the development which the Gothic style had already undergone – used the whole as his starting-point, made a single opening, and then divided it into three with a central shaft, two pointed arches, and a circle on top [83]. The architect of Chartres had made the arch over each group concentric with the curve of the oculus, but at Reims the architect insisted on pointed arches even here, so that there is a spandrel between the arch and the oculus, and similar spandrels between the oculus and the lower lights. The whole group is therefore actually divided into three main parts and four small spandrels. Inside, the oculus is sexfoiled by six round arches along its periphery. The profiles of the oculus and the two pointed arches below merge into one another where their central members meet.

Tracery is structure within structure. It makes it possible to divide by safe supports large openings to be filled with stained glass, but it presupposes the use of straight walls and the building of polygonal choirs and chapels.[12A]

The architect of the cathedral at Reims also incorporated all the other features of Chartres: inside oblong bays in the high vault, and outside buttresses and flying buttresses, tabernacles and balustrades.

Another innovation is the treatment of the gargoyles. These had existed earlier, for instance on the west towers at Laon, but at Reims the architect included them among those members which appear in series at certain points within the structural system.[13] Compared with Chartres all parts are more elegant, and the lightness and the buoyancy of the flying buttresses is surprising. The design of the tabernacles is so free and sumptuous that it makes those at Chartres look comparatively modest and clumsy. Instead of central columns in the tabernacles, there are angels standing guard round the church. The main, steeply-pitched spires on the tabernacles are separated from the structure below by horizontal ledges, and each is accompanied by four smaller

spires like those on the façade porches at Laon. The balustrade is increased in height and has a more important function than that of a mere parapet; its purpose is to veil the roofs over the chapels and to counteract by a broad band of vertical members the emphasis on the horizontal caused by the effect of the gutters of the main roofs [83].

The first architect's successors completed the transepts, and the three eastern bays of the nave (the liturgical choir) by 1241,[13A] but the features of the cathedral which have always been admired are the work of the first architect.

The exterior of the choir has remained essentially unaltered [83]. A photograph of 1855, however, shows the high openwork balustrade in front of the chapel roofs without the animal figures and without the lion gargoyles which Viollet-le-Duc added to the south chapels after 1860. Much of the balustrade has been restored, but it was already in existence when the photograph was taken in 1855.[14] Originally there may have been battlements intended at the gutter line of the chapel roofs, which Villard de Honnecourt mentions and shows in a drawing.[15] The upper balustrade at the gutter-line of the roof of the chancel and the apse was different in 1855 from what it is today. It owes its present form to Viollet-le-Duc; its original form seems to be unknown.[15A]

Outside the choir the sculptural decoration is a row of large angels on the tabernacles, a row of smaller ones on the buttresses of the chapels, the caryatids below the main cornice, and the gargoyles. The position and size of the figures were certainly decided in the original design, but the sculpture itself cannot be attributed to the architect. The direction of the construction would hardly have left him time for sculpture, for, as the building progressed, more and more detailed drawings were needed. The style of the figures must have depended on the degree to which the chief sculptor and his apprentices were able to conform with the style of the architect.[15B]

To a lesser degree this is also true of the decorative sculpture which forms an intrinsic part of some of the structural members, especially of the capitals. All the bays of the choir are built in the same architectural style, which is later repeated in the nave, but there the sculpture of the capitals is different. Crockets become rarer and are replaced by foliage which is naturalistic in detail though not in the way in which it grows [84]. On the other hand crockets appear in hundreds and even thousands outside – on the straight upper surfaces of the flying buttresses, on the edges of the spires on the tabernacles, and also on cornices. They accompany the main lines, and, in their transplantation, as at Lincoln, they take on a new sense, creating an optical effect of rows of dots which gives all sharp edges and some of the hollows a sparkling outline, reminiscent of pointillism.

Reims was a correction of Chartres: *Le Mans* is a correction of Bourges.[15C] In cross-section the gradation of a nave with lower double aisles is the same as at Bourges, but since the apse has seven sides, the piers at the east end stand closer together [85, 86]. The inner ambulatory consists of seven trapezoid bays in which the ribs rise to the central axis of each bay, and are straight in plan. Each rib, therefore, consists of two arms which, in plan, meet at an angle. The outer ambulatory has alternate rectangular and narrow triangular bays, of which the latter are directly lit by windows. The

85. Le Mans Cathedral. Interior of choir, begun 1217

86. Le Mans Cathedral. Plan of the choir

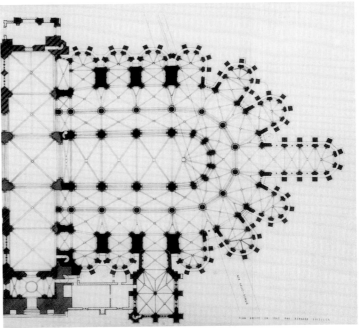

rectangular bays are joined by seven strongly-projecting chapels; each of the six lateral chapels has one bay and an apse consisting of five sides of an octagon, while the central one has three bays and a similar apse. The choir itself consists of a polygonal apse and three bays of almost identical elevation.

Building was begun in 1217, but not completed until 1254. The architect could thus make use of the progress in other places.[16] Most of the windows have no tracery, but those on the north side of the outer ambulatory, in the bays between the chapels, have simple tracery, and the triforium above the inner ambulatory, which corresponds to the space behind the roofs of the chapels, also contains tracery, similar to the triforium of the choir of Bayeux cathedral, under construction at the same time (1230s). The windows above, with their pointed lights without capitals, rising towards the centre, also derive from Normandy. There is a low-pitched saddleback roof over the inner ambulatory, sloping just sufficiently to allow for drainage. The form of this roof allows the clerestory windows of the main apse to continue down to the level of the apexes of the arcade, so that there are only

87. Le Mans Cathedral. Exterior of choir, begun 1217

two storeys – the tall piers with stilted pointed arches and, on the string course directly above them, the narrow windows with tracery. The tracery in the apse clerestory copies that in the Sainte-Chapelle in Paris, while the clerestory straight bays resemble the clerestories of the transepts and choir at Amiens in that each window is divided into two groups of three lights each. These observations and a knowledge of the dates of the Sainte-Chapelle, Amiens and Saint-Denis (1231 ff.) give a clear picture of the stages in the history of the building of Le Mans.[16A] In the differences between the forms and details one can also recognize relationships to different schools and, through them, the work of different architects. The first came from the Domaine Royale from the region around Laon and Soissons, the second from Bayeux in Normandy, and the third, from Paris. The first architect's design is, of course, the decisive factor, but the position of the clerestory windows directly above the arcade is equally important in determining the impression of the interior of the choir. There is hardly any other French

Gothic choir which can compare with Le Mans in joyfulness and soaring buoyancy, and the effect is emphasized by the contrast with the Romanesque nave, whose rib-vault dates from about 1150.

The exterior, too, presents one of the most magnificent views of French Gothic [87]. The large square to the east which now allows the church to be viewed from some distance, and the terrace on which the choir now stands, are both modern creations. The town wall which originally hid part of the choir was an expression of the desire to emphasize layers one in front of the other. The men of the nineteenth century, on the other hand, liked to clear a space round cathedrals, and, in doing so, destroyed one of their charming effects. But here at Le Mans, one must admit that the result enhances the impression of monumentality.[17]

The buttresses and flying buttresses of the choir are similar to those at Bourges, but at the polygonal east end they split up in two, because the buttresses follow the radial direction of each chapel. This disposition forms intersections which confuse some people, but which must have seemed clear and splendid to the medieval beholder. It forms huge empty spaces and transparent passages like theatrical wings out of which the chapels protrude at the bottom, first standing within the solid parts, then projecting into the space outside it, and always pointing back into the centre of the choir. This choir has rightly been called half a central building. Today the slender finials on the balustrade on the roof, and elsewhere, and the gargoyles which project far into space, are strongly accentuated, but it is debatable whether or not these details formed part of the original plan.

A year after the beginning of the choir at Le Mans, the old cathedral at *Amiens* was burnt down (1218). It was a Romanesque church, consecrated in 1152, possibly including Transitional elements. The church of Saint-Firmin, which stood to the east of it, was preserved, and in 1220 the new cathedral was therefore begun with the nave. The whole new church must have been designed at this time, and the two later architects, who worked on the upper parts of the choir from *c.* 1245 onwards, only altered details to conform with the style of their own generation.[17A]

For his plan, the architect of Amiens, Robert de Luzarches, took Reims as his model [88].[17B] Both churches are about the same length, but the crossing at Amiens lies further to the west. At Reims there is a nave of ten bays, then the crossing, and then a choir of two bays and an apse: at Amiens the nave has seven bays, followed by the crossing and a choir with four bays and an apse. Both churches have transepts with aisles, though, unlike Reims, Amiens never intended to add towers flanking the transept façades. At Amiens the number of chapels round the choir was increased to seven, as at Le Mans, and the general measurements are more regular than at Reims or Chartres. The thickness of the walls was reduced, partly because the wall-passages, which are such an important feature at Reims, were eliminated.

At Amiens, too, the decisive problems in the elevations were the piers and the tracery. The round piers are given a diagonal direction by their socles, as at Reims [89]. The socle of each of the four shafts in the main directions forms part of an octagon, set frontally, so that its oblique sides are parallel to those of the main socle. The abaci of the shafts within the arcade, however, are rectangular and therefore purely frontal, while at Reims they are octagonal, a form which contains both the frontal and the diagonal directions. The shafts of the piers at Amiens have no capitals; the upper ledge of the abaci merely bends round them like a ring and the shafts rise on unbroken. This problem had almost been solved at Reims, but not quite, for the continuations of the shafts still have round bases and plinths, which express the idea than an upper shaft had to be set above the lower one. At Amiens, however, these members are eliminated. The architect at Reims had already done the same thing on his crossing piers, where the ledges of the abaci run round the shafts in the form of rings, so that the progress made at Amiens consists of the transfer of the scheme devised for the crossing piers at Reims to the piers of the nave. The shafts on the crossing piers at Amiens rise without interruption to the vault in the way practised since the building of Saint-Germer. The capitals of the central shafts in the nave are turned through 45 degrees, so that one corner projects into the nave, clearly defining the division between one bay and the next, as at Soissons. On the other hand, the shafts supporting the ribs and the wall-arches are frontal; the former stand on small bases and plinths over the abaci of the piers, while the latter begin only at the level of the triforium.

The choice of a hexagonal form for the abaci of the columns in the triforium shows the preoccupation of the architects of Amiens, Robert de Luzarches and Thomas de Cormont, with the differences between frontality and diagonality. Just as the upper octagonal capitals in the nave define the limits between the bays and reduce them to thin mathematical planes, so these hexagons, with one corner on each side standing in the centre of the thickness of the wall, create the main mathematical plane of the Gothic relief, exactly as does the glass of the windows.

This triforium is treated almost as though it were tracery. Each pair of pointed arches is divided into three lights, and the surface between each large arch and the three smaller ones below it, which are all the same size, is pierced by a trefoil. Each group of two large arches is flanked by the shafts supporting the wall-arches, and a similar shaft, standing in front of the central pier, divides the group down the centre.

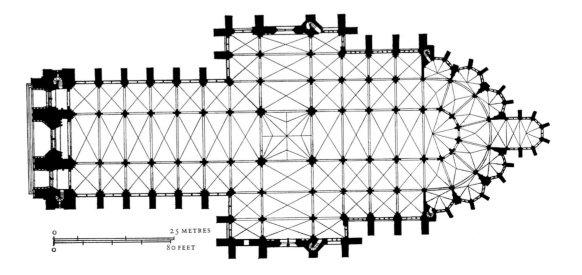

88. Amiens Cathedral, begun 1220. Plan

0 ⊢⊢⊢⊢⊢⊢ 25 METRES
0 ⊢⊢⊢⊢⊢⊢ 80 FEET

This central shaft is continued in the tracery of the window above, where it serves as the central mullion, supporting the two pointed arches below the oculus. It therefore has to have the same profile as the shafts of the wall-arch on either side. Each half of the window has a secondary mullion in the middle, supporting small pointed arches. The quadripartite window repeats in its interior the form of the whole. Since all the members have the same section, complete fusion is achieved between the arches, because they do not touch each other with their extrados, but with their central lines. The draughtsman's setting-out must therefore start from these central lines and the thickness of the mouldings must be added on both sides. The shafts on either side, and the wall-arch over them, embrace each bay of the triforium and the window above it, binding them into a unit, and the uninterrupted central shaft joins each half of the bay in the triforium with the corresponding half of the window above. The whole group is clear, rational, and simple. The first step

89. (*facing page*) Amiens Cathedral, begun 1220. Interior of nave

90. Amiens Cathedral. Exterior of choir, *c.* 1240–69

towards this fusion was made at Reims, where the windows have only two lights and are still quite separate from the triforium; the changes which were made in the system at Amiens led to a train of development which could not have been foreseen at that time.

The system at Amiens is richer in detail than that at Reims, but it is equally compelling and as immediately effective. After the fire of 1218, and before building actually began, the first architect, Robert de Luzarches, must have made a design for the whole church, including the façade. By 1236 the nave and the aisles of the transepts had been completed, and it is possible that the same architect may have begun the choir aisles, the ambulatory, and the chapels [90]. Above the choir and transept arcades the style changes; these upper parts may therefore be the work of Robert's successor Thomas de Cormont, and the latter's son Regnault de Cormont.[17c] To visualize the original form of the nave aisles, one must mentally eliminate the chapels, which were added between the far-projecting buttresses after 1292 and also radically alter the appearance of the church from out-

side. The original windows in the aisles had simple tracery.[18] Without the chapels the aisles, seen from inside, must have conveyed a sense of complete enclosure. The central aisle must have been more dominating than it is now, especially when seen from the side aisles. On entering the nave, one's first impression is one of height and length, and of piers each half overlapping the next, like a series of theatrical wings, only hinting at the existence of the aisles.

The shafts which rise uninterruptedly from the floor to the vault and those which unite the triforium with the windows combine with the heightened emphasis on verticalism to produce fusion between arcade, triforium, windows, and the space in the vault – while the Gothic relief creates a flowing connexion between one bay and the next, and between the nave and the aisles. Standing at the entrance, one is aware of the existence of the aisles, owing to the profile of the row of piers, in the same way as one feels that the space within the cathedral continues smoothly through the triforium and the windows into the space outside. These are the *formal* themes of the Gothic style.

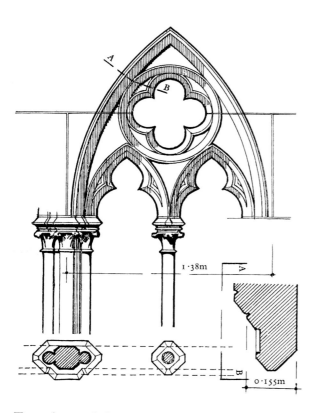

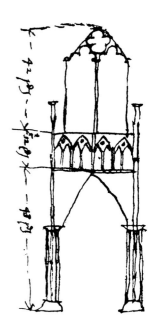

91. Reims, St Nicaise, begun 1231. Triforium

92. Reims, St Nicaise, nave elevation, begun 1231. Seventeenth-century drawing, Paris Archives National N III Marne 46r

To understand the *artistic* result of this form, one must recognize its meaning. St Bernard did not like churches to be too high; to his mind the decisive factor was the monk in his humility and devotion. In a cathedral he was prepared to allow a greater display of luxury, because here the purpose was to impress the simple minds of laymen, but even here he would have set a limit, and would no doubt have preached withering sermons in condemnation of the cathedrals of the thirteenth century. To the minds of Robert de Luzarches and of his bishop, Evrard de Fouilloy, however, the decisive factor was God. Their aim was to present every possible expression of the combination of sublimity, majesty, and might, with lucidity, harmonious wealth, and a sense of the infinite, and to create a formal symbol worthy of God. Their church was to look as if it did not belong to this world.[18A]

The height of the nave and choir, the slenderness of the piers, the airiness of the aisles, and the elegance and firmness of all the forms are immediately obvious; but there are also less obvious characteristics. Among these are the mouldings of the ribs, which here have an increased significance. To emphasize their central line, a narrow fillet was added to the roll, producing a pear-shaped section. In the high vaults of the nave at Amiens, the transverse arches have the same section as the ribs, the only difference being that the transverse arches are considerably stronger. In the aisles the transverse arches are broad, because of the load that they have to carry,[19] and the ribs again have a pear-shaped section [cf. 19D]. The exact chronology of the profiles is not known. The triforium arches also have a pear-shaped moulding, but with a keeled edge instead of a fillet, so that even here there are nuances. The double curve in which the roll merges into the hollows on each side is common to all these profiles; it is the curve which was later, as the ogee arch, to reign supreme as a two-dimensional figure in tracery.

Today the nave at Amiens is praised as the purest work of the classic Gothic style. It has not yet been established when this judgement was first made, but it has certainly not always been considered a valid one. Already in the next generation the stage of development reached in the nave was surpassed in the upper parts of the choir. The works of the later periods tended to depart more and more from the special classicity of Amiens. With the Renaissance, the phrase 'classic Gothic' became meaningless, as classic was considered to apply only to classical antiquities, while the Gothic style was regarded only as a barbaric opposition against all true classicity. Since then there has been a change, not only in this verdict on the Gothic, but also in the conception of the classic. If classic is used only for Greek and Roman antiquities, then no Gothic building can be classic; but if one interprets classic as referring to certain summits of achievement within classical antiquity, measured by the degree of harmony attained, then it is legitimate to note similar climaxes at which the highest degree of the particular harmony inherent in the premises of any style are reached and to call them classic. Amiens was singled out as the representative of classic Gothic because the formal conditions imposed by the rib-vault organically permeate the whole structural system, and this new 'unity in multiplicity' fulfils the paradoxical ideal of presenting a sense of the infinite within finite bounds, of flowing movement in repose and the supernatural in natural reality, and of allowing solid matter to overcome its own mass. Here opposites are resolved because they achieve a state of rest inherent in themselves. It has been said that classical antiquities produce in us a serene belief in ourselves. It could be metaphorically said that Gothic, in its own classic phase, shows a passionate belief in itself. Unlike antiquity, the Gothic style has a separate, individual existence; we can surrender to being lifted far above ourselves by it and translated into a sphere in which we can taste the highest, all-embracing harmony of existence.

Amiens was an especially successful attempt to find the balance of the Gothic style in a majestic, aristocratic, and completely elegant form; but, in their own way, other works of this generation also came near to reaching the same summit of achievement.

In 1229 the architect Hugues Libergier was contracted to build the new church of *Saint-Nicaise* at *Reims* and, in 1231, under the patronage of Abbot Simon de Dampierre, work on construction began.[19A] The architect borrowed some features from the cathedral of the same town, but also adopted a number of forms from Robert de Luzarches' work at Amiens.[19B] Work began at the west façade, and, when Libergier died in 1263, Robert de Coucy finished the choir and the south transept by his death in 1311. He seems to have adhered to his predecessor's plan, but introduced a glazed triforium such as had meanwhile been built at Saint-Denis.[19C]

Saint-Nicaise was one of the masterpieces of the classic Gothic,[19D] but in 1798 it was sold for 45,000 fr. and pulled down; the materials were subsequently sold for 600,000 fr. Poterlet, a French architect of that time, described this transaction as 'un nouvel acte de vandalisme, qui déshonore le département de la Marne et le nom français'.[19E] Every nation produces men who work only for gain and who only understand material values. The French Revolution had its own high ideals of democracy and saw the traditions of the Church as an obstacle to achieving them. The destruction of Gothic buildings was also connected with the general discredit in which the Gothic style had stood since the concept of 'le bon goût' had been accepted as applicable only to the buildings of Greece and Rome. The self-seeking acts of vandalism of the 'bandes noires', however, called forth active protest from the Romantics, who not only prevented any further destruction of works of art, but also organized the study of the Gothic style in the way in which it is continued to this day.

In plan, Saint-Nicaise was a considerably smaller version of the cathedral at Reims. In the triforium, Libergier replaced the cathedral's groups of four arches to each bay with groups of four subdivided arches – a correction probably made under the influence of Amiens. The central mullion of the clerestory window ran down into the triforium [92].[20] The other details are known to us from fragments which were built into private houses and came to light in the bombardments of 1916. From these we know that Libergier added cusps inside the superordinate triforium arches [91]. These lobe-like forms first appeared decorating the oculi of rose windows with plate tracery (north transept Laon, or west façade Chartres), but one of the earliest applications of the form to pointed arches was made by Robert de Luzarches in the lower buttresses of the west façade at Amiens [120]. In this detail, as in others, Amiens was probably the model for Saint-Nicaise. From the fragments found in 1916 we also know that the sections of the transverse arches and ribs were pear-shaped or almond-shaped, in both cases accompanied by rolls. The transition from the roll to the hollow on either side is again a continuous undulating line, or rather an undulating surface, and this is a detail

which was to become important; for it, too, helps to blend forms which were originally clearly separated.

Compared with the cathedral at Reims, the most important simplification on the exterior of Saint-Nicaise is the absence of tabernacles on the buttresses. The little gables which appear on the buttresses where they step forward at the level of the eaves are reminiscent of Chartres. Here the reconstruction may well be correct, for it corresponds to the form of the gables on the west façade, of which we have definite knowledge from an etching of 1625 [121].

Within the periods of antiquity, the term classic has been stretched to include a considerable number of works, and different stages of classicity have been noted. Within the Gothic style, too, this epithet of praise should not be limited to a single church; for, side by side with the classic Gothic in France, there stands also the totally different classic Gothic of England.

3. HORIZONTAL FUSION IN ENGLAND AND SPAIN

In the same year as Amiens, 1220, the cathedral of *Salisbury* was begun. Amiens represents Gothic verticalism, Salisbury Gothic horizontalism. At Amiens the bay is a whole in its total height, at Salisbury the nave and choir are a whole in their total length.

The length is of eighteen bays: nave ten, main crossing, choir three, east crossing, presbytery three. Except for the crossings the system is the same from east to west: arcade, triforium, clerestory. Low, unlit galleries, with flying buttresses concealed under their sloping roofs, abut the high vault in a manner borrowed from the nave at Wells. (Exposed flying buttresses were introduced in the 1320s to stabilize the crossing steeple). So the section is kept relatively low. Later the abutment has been improved by strainer-arches in the crossing. The purpose was to secure the crossing tower, but the effect is increased emphasis on length.[21]

The three storeys are kept, as at Wells, as horizontal bands [93]. There are no verticals to divide arcade bay from arcade bay or gallery bay from gallery bay. The circular piers carry the richly moulded arches, and the frontal shaft carries no more than the archivolts of these arches. The gallery bays correspond to those of the arcade, but since the proportion of the gallery arches is very different (wide pointed arches, starting segmentally) the gallery band seems independent and not tied much to the vertical of the bay. Above the gallery cornice the quadripartite vaults start. Their corners are carried by narrow clusters of shafts which rise in the spandrels of the galley, here and only here dividing the bays from each other. The galley cornice is at the same time the line of the springing of the vaults. The master thus renounced the innovations of Chartres and consequently also renounced exposed flying buttresses (which were added later). Conservative also are the groups of stepped lancet windows in the clerestory and the wall-passage. These groups of windows separated by shallow pilaster-strips dominate the side views of the cathedral. Only the aisles have more strongly projecting buttresses crowned by frontally placed gables. Here also the composition of two slender lancets for each bay, without an oculus above, must be considered conservative. The view of the gallery from the nave with its two parts, again subdivided into two subparts, the piercing of the spandrels with quatrefoils or octofoils in circles, and in addition the Gothic relief in the diagonal placing of the colonnettes give an impression close to that of tracery. Closer still to tracery are the windows which in the main transept correspond to the triforium. But by their proportions these groups stress breadth, not height.

In accordance with the principle of horizontal fusion of the bays all bases and all abaci are circular. The absence of all re-entrant angles renders the boundaries of the bays soft and fluid. The Early English style had tried this motif already at Canterbury. It was then made a principle and used in a genuinely Gothic sense to create spatial continuity.

Building at Salisbury started from the east. The Lady Chapel (delicated to the Trinity), the rectangular ambulatory, and the aisles of the presbytery were complete by 1225. The Lady Chapel is designed as a hall-church of three bays, with narrow aisles. The westernmost bay is at the same time part of the ambulatory. The piers are as thin as shafts. Everybody is amazed that such slender stalks can carry a vault. Despite general similarities, one cannot assume any connection with Saint-Serge at Angers, and the difference is that Salisbury had level crowns to the vaults and all arches pointed. We are today spoilt by modern achievements of technique and statics. We know what can be done, but the Lady Chapel of Salisbury remains to strike one as a miracle.[21A]

The building as a whole has this tendency everywhere. The thin shafts standing free of the aisle walls are intended to look as if they were carrying the vaults. Everything is elegant yet vigorous. The exterior is favoured by being placed in isolation on a lawn. The silvery-grey stone is covered with lichens varying in colour from green to violet. So, although there is nothing but right angles, there is no impression of hardness. The building blends optically with nature around. At the time of the dedication of 1258 a low crossing tower may have existed; for it can hardly be assumed that no vertical motif was provided at all. But it remains very doubtful, in spite of the enthusiasm of all modern critics since Wren, that the original master who believed in horizontalism would have appreciated the tall spire of c. 1310.[21B]

Slightly earlier than Salisbury is the nave of *Wells*, c. 1200–30.[21C] In comparison with Salisbury certain features are even more conservative.

To the same generation belongs *Beverley* Minster, begun about 1230. Choir and transepts were complete by c. 1260. The system is as horizontal as at Salisbury, though the vaulting-shafts here start as low down as the spandrels of the arcade. They are detached from the piers. The piers must be considered circular; but they disappear completely behind eight shafts. The shafts differ in section: those in the diagonals (which carry ribs only towards the aisles, whereas towards the nave they support part of the arch of the arcade) are keeled, those inside the arcade round, those towards the nave have fillets. There is a good reason for every one of these three shapes.

The triforium is a variation on the theme of the syncopated two-tier arcades in the choir-aisle of Lincoln. The piquancy is made yet more attractive by the placing of the pointed trefoil arches of the front tier on clustered Purbeck colonnettes. The short colonnettes at the back carrying plain pointed arches are also black.[21D]

In the wall-passage of the clerestory the arches of each group rise towards the centre, similar to the arrangement made at the same time in the choir of *Toledo*. Direct connexions are all but impossible. Such similarities simply prove a community of roots, however distant the ramifications.

The great differences between Salisbury and Amiens have tempted many critics into speculations on the relations between national characters and art. But it is not permissible to attribute to nations immutable characters or to judge conditions in 1220 from those of 1174 (Canterbury) or those of the twentieth century. Both nations changed, and the Gothic style changed. How these changes are interconnected is obscure, and obscurity only becomes deeper if one tries to name the unknown root race. The Gothic style is a spiritual problem, common to Normans, Frenchmen, and Englishmen. To reconstruct what happened physiologically in the bodies of Robert de Luzarches when he designed Amiens, of Nicolas of Ely (or Elias de Dereham?) when he designed Salisbury, is a job for materialists and positivists.[21E] Their best explanations would not help us; for we are not concerned with chemical processes but with an understanding of art through its meaning. That can only be achieved by remaining in the field of the spirit, and that means in our case of the 'school'. There is spiritual inbreeding in spite of the exchange of ideas, and so an English tradition developed in the lodges of Canterbury and after, as a French tradition had existed ever since Saint-Denis.

Every architect is the product of physiological factors, but his education and his work are the product of a spiritual tradition growing within his personality and influenced by patrons and their advisers. The permanent physiological basis is obvious, and it is as true of the French water-carrier at Amiens and the English one at Salisbury as it is of the respective architects. The fact that two such completely different buildings were created, however, is not due to the national characteristics of the two water-carriers, but to those of two architects who were also the spiritual functionaries of their two spiritual employers. Not that I wish to prevent people from drawing conclusions from the style of the two churches as to the characters of water-carriers, ploughmen, carters, or merchants; but to reverse the process is fruitless and has hitherto produced only superficial theories from over-emotional nationalists. For our purposes it is best to look only at the character of the buildings themselves, and not to try to conclude that Salisbury is the product of a nation of conquerors and Amiens that of a nation of rationalists, or to develop any other theories of national character.[21F]

93. Salisbury Cathedral, begun 1220. Interior of nave c. 1245–60

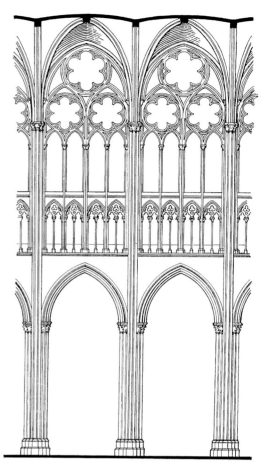

94. Saint-Denis Abbey Church. Interior of transept and choir, begun 1231. Ambulatory 1140–44

95. Saint-Denis Abbey Church, elevation of nave, begun after 1231

4. GLAZED TRIFORIA. WINDOWS AND THEIR GABLES. THE SPHERICAL TRIANGLE. CUSPS IN TRACERY

The fusion between the triforium and the windows of the nave at Amiens led to the idea of turning the triforium itself into windows. From 1231 the whole upper part of the choir of Suger's Saint-Denis was pulled down and rebuilt by the so-called Saint-Denis Master.[216] He was not the first architect to open the triforium to the outside, but Saint-Denis is the earliest building where a glazed triforium was planned as an integral part of large-scale church.[21H] Until this time, triforia had been the zone which corresponded to the sloping roofs of aisles. With the increasing verticalism in the interior and in the bays of the exterior, main roofs were made higher; the pitch of the roofs over aisles was made correspondingly

steeper, and triforia became correspondingly higher. The Saint-Denis Master broke with this tradition; he detached the roofs over the aisles from the wall underneath the clerestorey and placed them at the base of the triforium, giving them a slight slope downwards. He was thus free to choose any height for his triforium, which he opened to the outside with four windows in each bay.

Work began simultaneously on the north transept, the north choir aisle, and the polygonal apse, and it is here that the new kind of elevation is developed [94].[211] Suger's semicircular apse was replaced by a polygonal one. As at Reims, the windows are divided into two lights with an oculus above, and each bay of the triforium therefore also has two lights. In each bay of the transepts and the nave there are two of these pairs of windows with a third oculus above them [95]. The three frames of these openings, which are of

96. Saint-Denis Abbey Church. Exterior of choir, 1140–3 (radiating chapels) and 1231 onwards

the same basic kind, are set one inside the other in a masterly way; the outer frame is formed by the shafts and the wall-arches. Within this outer frame stand the bays of the arcade and, above each of them, the four lights of the triforium. The shafts for the two main pairs of lights in each bay, each of which is further divided by a central shaft beginning between the secondary pairs of triforium lights, stand within the outer frame, and over the middle of each bay of the arcade. The upper oculus repeats the form of the two smaller ones below, and all three are sexfoiled. This whole group is a manifestation of structure by division, rigidly regular and very simple; the profile projects from the innermost plane, the surface of the glass. This close connexion between all the members, from the innermost one right to the final projection of the shafts supporting the transverse arches, is a full realization of the Gothic profile, its structural rationalism and its characteristic formation of a framework round the stained glass. The whole church is not a work of compilation like those built in the regions of Europe to which the Gothic style now spread, but a synthesis.[21J]

Outside, the back wall of the triforium projects beyond the surface of the window above, forming an open passage [96]. On the piers in the wall of the triforium there are free-standing columns which appear to support the flying buttresses where they join the wall. The balustrade of the passage above the triforium is repeated higher up at the level of the eaves of the main roof, and again on the outside of the choir, lower down, above Suger's apses, where it helps to lessen the stress on the most sensitive joint, marking the transition from the old lower storey to the new upper one.

Of all the depredations and restorations which the church suffered, that which damaged it most was the destruction of the thirteenth-century stained glass and the substitution of the present modern glass.[22] These windows are painful in their composition and colouring; even their subjects are out

of place – certainly the one which portrays Napoleon is a terrible mistake. The gaudy, obtrusive stained glass makes it difficult to appreciate the real quality of the architecture.

The core of the piers is cruciform, and the shafts supporting the arches of the arcade are set frontally; only the capitals of the shafts supporting the transverse arches are turned through 45 degrees. The walls are thin, and the gradations of the profile of the arcade make them seem even thinner. To those factors which have already been mentioned as contributing to the synthesis achieved in this church must be added its lightness and elegance, which combine with its austerity to give an impression of perfection. The façades of the transepts, with their great round windows with spokes of tracery, and the glazed triforium completely dissolve the upper parts of the walls. The great round window in the south transept at Reims had probably been designed, if not executed, by 1233, and the west rose of Notre-Dame in Paris was under construction in the 1220s.[22A] The Saint-Denis master copied them and improved upon them by increasing their size, and by making some of the details more delicate.

The cathedral at *Beauvais* was begun after a fire in 1225. Work started in the transepts and western parts of the choir aisles [99]. It was interrupted in 1232/33, and restarted in c. 1238 when the rest of the choir aisles, the pillars of the central aisle, and the chevet were begun. Soon after the accession of Bishop William of Grez in 1249 the triforium and clerestory were started according to a more delicate design, and some five metres were added to the total height of the central vessel. The whole choir was complete by 1272.[22B] The projection of the shafts to the edge of the abaci on the piers is a retrograde step. But the architect was among the first to accept the glazed triforium [97–8]. The gradation of the cross-section is the same as at Le Mans, so that the inner choir aisles and the ambulatory have windows above the

97. Beauvais Cathedral. Interior, begun *c.* 1225

98. Beauvais Cathedral choir, reconstruction of the original choir elevation before the collapse of the high vault in 1284 (after Branner)

99. Beauvais Cathedral, begun in 1225. Plan of choir

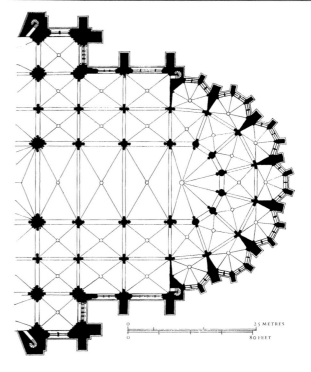

roofs of the outer choir aisles and its chapels. Instead of a division into five lights, as at Le Mans, the aisle windows at Beauvais have tracery, and as they are quite short, each is framed only by a pointed arch, with no rectangular space below, similarly to those in the Liebfrauenkirche at Trier, begun probably in 1227.

The polygonal apse at Beauvais still stands in its original form, but the straight bays of the choir were rebuilt after the collapse of the vault in 1284. New piers were inserted between each pair of the old ones, and the original quadripartite vault changed to sexpartite. One should not draw from this collapse the moral conclusion that it was a punishment for *hubris*. Gervase said of the fall of the architect William from the scaffolding at Canterbury that he did not know whether it was a punishment from God or the envy of the Devil. The collapse at Beauvais was caused by the thin-

100. Beauvais Cathedral. Exterior
of choir, begun *c.* 1238

ness of the choir aisle pillars and walls, by the excessive
overhang of the intermediate buttress piers above their supports in the aisles, by the over-wide bays (the largest then
built in Gothic architecture), and by the last-minute heightening of the superstructure to a vertiginous 158 feet.[22c] It
was not the architect as an artist who was at fault, but the
architect as an engineer. Nor did the fault lie in the style
itself; for buildings in other styles and with less daring proportions have also been known to collapse. Nevertheless,
verticalism, measured in actual figures, reached its ultimate
limit at Beauvais. This preoccupation was, for a time, a characteristic of French Gothic, but it was never fundamentally
bound up with the Gothic style as a whole, as can be seen
from a study of the Sainte-Chapelle.

The nave at *Amiens* was completed in around the year
1236, and work was begun on the choir and transepts probably before the church of Saint-Firmin, which is supposed
to have stood where we now see the north transept of the
cathedral, had been pulled down.[22d] The first stage included
the building of the whole lower part up to the vaults of the
choir aisles, and including the chapels round the ambulatory. Durand has observed subtle differences between some
of the profiles in the choir and those in the nave, which make
it probable that the first architect, Robert de Luzarches,
died about 1236, and not as early as 1232, as had been previously supposed. The differences must therefore spring
from the work of the second architect, Thomas de Cormont.
However, Kimpel and Suckale see the lower parts of the
choir and chevet as a natural extension of the style of the
nave, and therefore attribute these parts to Robert de
Luzarches (while Murray sees the hand of Robert in the
lower parts of the nave and the choir aisles, and attributes to

Thomas de Cormont, working in the 1230s, the upper parts of the nave, the radiating chapels, and the choirs and ambulatory vaults.[22E] The building of these parts went on until the 1240s, and the central chapel was presumably begun in the 1230s and finished about 1240 or a little later; for it is a prototype of the Sainte-Chapelle in Paris.

The *Sainte-Chapelle* in *Paris* was begun sometime before 1244, and as it was consecrated in 1248, the date of its beginning is probably 1241 [101–4].[22F] The reason for its construction was the acquisition of the crown of thorns, part of the cross, the iron of the lance, the sponge, and other relics of martyrdom of Christ, which were brought to France from Syria and Constantinople in 1241. Louis IX went to meet them, and himself carried them into the city bare-footed, placing them in the chapel of Saint-Nicholas in his palace in the Cité until such time as a chapel more worthy of them should be built and dedicated to the holy crown of thorns. Being the chapel of a palace, it lies on the level of the residential suite, as did the chapels of every castle and even those of some bishops' palaces at that time. It has, therefore, an undercroft, and this was dedicated to Notre-Dame and intended for the servants. At the west there is a projecting structure, housing porches for both the lower and the upper chapel. Adjoining the north side was a sacristy which looked like a separate little church and can be seen on an engraving by Boisseau;[23] this was pulled down after 1776 to allow for the enlargement of the Cour d'Honneur of the new Palais de Justice. The whole north side of the chapel is now hidden by the south wing of this building.

In other ways, too, the chapel has not been perfectly preserved. In 1630 the roof and its original turret were burnt down, and the interior was damaged during the Revolution. The restoration by Lassus, Viollet-le-Duc, and Boeswillwald established the chapel in its present condition; it was certainly done with laudable accuracy, but some arbitrary features inevitably occurred, particularly the ornamental painting of all the architectural members, the replacement of the sculpture on the doorways, and the restorations of some of the figures of the apostles on the piers.[24] The architecture itself, however, has been almost entirely preserved in its original condition, the main alteration, the new tracery of the rose-window on the west façade, dating still from the Middle Ages, from about 1490–95. The original form of the tracery in this window can be seen in the illustration of the month of June in the Book of Hours of the Duc de Berry.[25] Instead of spokes, giving the window the form of a wheel, it had eight fields of tracery joined radially. Each of these fields was rather similar to the windows in the choir at Reims, with the difference that the sides converge instead of running parallel to one another. This transplantation of tracery into an oculus was to be used in the rose windows of the north transept façade of Notre-Dame in Paris, and in the west façade of Reims cathedral, but there the tracery is divided into sixteen and twelve fields respectively.

The lower chapel is of the hall type, with two side aisles, for it is so low that there was no possibility of building a single, vaulted nave. The slenderness of the short columns makes the relatively heavy vault appear quite light. In the narrow side aisles the transverse arches are stilted, and

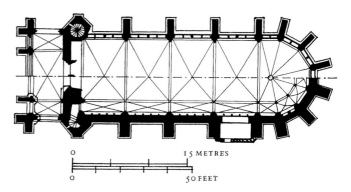

101. Paris, Sainte-Chapelle, *c.* 1241–8. Plan (*above*: upper chapel; *below*: lower chapel)

102. Paris, Sainte-Chapelle, *c.* 1241–8. Exterior; rose window *c.* 1490–95

below them flying buttresses run horizontally from the vault of the nave to the buttresses on the walls, a constructional form which was never to appear anywhere else.[26] At the polygonal east end the aisles form an ambulatory. On a small scale, this lower chapel is a prototype of the hall choirs of later churches – not, of course, that the architects of these hall choirs regarded the Sainte-Chapelle as a model, for their conditions and stylistic tendencies were quite different.

Along the walls there is a blind arcade of pointed arches framing pointed trefoil arches. The close contact between the two kinds of arches produces the form of cusps, as it had in Saint-Nicaise at Reims and in the very similar dado arcades in the radiating chapels at Amiens cathedral. This form is related to the earlier insertion of round or pointed trefoil arches into larger pointed arches, or directly into gables. Cusps are not, however, secondary arches which may be isolated; they grow out of the main arches or gables which contain them and form an integral part of their profile. Each of the inner flying buttresses in the lower chapel also has one cusp. The height of the blind arcading on the wall in the undercroft is determined by the size of the isolated columns, and there is therefore little space for the windows, which are pointed arches standing directly on the line of their springing, similarly to those at Bourges and Trier. They contradict the general emphasis on verticals, as would also have been the case with oculus windows. The architect decided to give the base-lines of the windows the form of inverted segmental arches, into which could be fitted sexfoiled oculi. These windows, together with those lighting the western walls of the side aisles of the Amiens nave, are the earliest examples of the so-called spherical triangle.[27]

In the upper chapel the articulation of the walls is governed by the vault [104]. The windows in the side walls have very similar tracery to that in the north easternmost nave chapel of Notre-Dame in Paris. The form of the tracery, with its members projecting logically in front of the surface of the glass, closely connects it with the shafts supporting the vault. The walls have been entirely replaced by the windows; the stained glass, which has been completely pre-

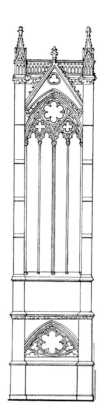

103. Paris, Sainte-Chapelle, c. 1241–8. Elevations and section

104. (*facing page*) Paris, Sainte-Chapelle, c. 1241–8. Interior of upper chapel

served or expertly restored, really forms the substance of the walls. All the members are structural, except for the lowest band of the walls, which is a traceried blind arcade.

Statues of the twelve apostles (three of them still original) stand on corbels on the shafts supporting the transverse arches, and their position is such that they cut across the sill-line of the windows, thus weakening the horizontal division between the area of the lowest band of the walls and that of the windows. Their canopies are progressive in form; their pointed arches have cusps and the gables are pushed down to them.

On the side walls there are special seats for the king and his family; they are emphasized by architectural means, but without any show of splendour. Above the altar, in the apse, a platform was built for the shrine of the relics. Of the two spiral staircases leading to this platform the northern one has been preserved in its original state, and the whole of this extremely delicate ciborium has been correctly restored; only the six angels which have been stuck on to the lower pointed arch are modern additions. This piece of miniature architecture had the advantage that it could go further in the direction of lightness and imagination than could the chapel itself.[27A] The character of the whole chapel is one of intimacy and privacy, combined with splendour and the particular quality of the fantastical which, in the more highly developed Gothic style, was held to be the most suited to a place of miracles. Nevertheless, the proportions are free of any exaggeration. The ratio of its breadth to the height of the ridge of its vault is one to two – and this at the time when the choir of Beauvais was already under construction. The proportions of the windows, too, are comfortable.

The Sainte-Chapelle has always called forth unanimous admiration. Gothic forms have here been reduced to their simplest structural factors. The system devised in the lower parts of the choir at Amiens[27B] is here adapted for a chapel without aisles. The decoration of the corbels, capitals, and other members is full of charm and variety. This wonderful building is covered in plant-forms reminiscent of actual nature, but stylized into Gothic Nature. Every detail seems to exist only to enhance the effect of the stained glass, which wraps the little interior in unreality. In these windows there are some Gothic details, and, with the illuminated manuscripts of about 1250, they can be of considerable assistance in solving the problem of when, in the realm of painting, the Gothic style began, and when it prevailed.[28] The nineteenth-century painting of the whole interior of the chapel gives a fairly reliable idea of its original, richly coloured finish, reminiscent of metalwork.[28A] The polychromy of the lower chapel took no account of the original traces of colour, but in the upper chapel (apart from the west wall, which is wholly nineteenth-century) the restorers are supposed to have followed accurately the original colour scheme.[29] It is questionable whether its colours harmonize with those of the stained glass.

Outside, the intrusion of the windows into their gables is only the transference of a combination which had already appeared frequently in other architectural positions. Here it is, however, used to penetrate the eaves-line of the roof and even the balustrade, and it combines with the buttresses and their pinnacles to create a new system. From then on this system became a formula which, although derived from the rib-vault, is a free creation of the architectural imagination.[30]

In 1245, soon after the Sainte-Chapelle, *Westminster Abbey* in London was begun. The choir and transepts were complete by 1259, and by 1272 the first five bays of the nave

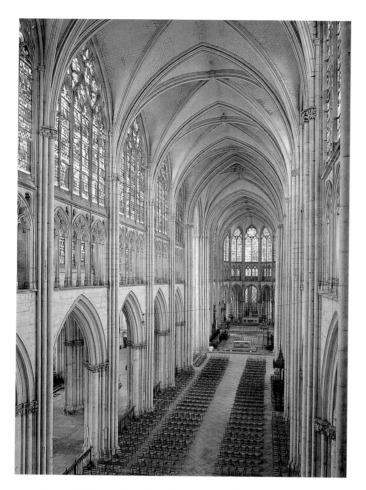

105. Troyes Cathedral. Interior of nave and choir; choir triforium late 1230s

106. Tours Cathedral. Choir begun *c*. 1210. Triforium and clerestorey *c*. 1240–*c*. 1244

had been constructed.[31] Henry III's personal admiration for the French Gothic explains its French character, while the English education of its architect, Henry of Reynes, is supposed to excuse the many elements which cannot stand up to French criticism. However, it is debatable whether everything that is wrong, as seen from the viewpoint of, say, Pierre de Montereau, is therefore necessarily English. Certainly the ridge-rib and the round base mouldings and abaci are English. Instead of a triforium, there are galleries with flat ceilings and windows in the outer walls. After those of the Sainte-Chapelle, which Henry of Reynes had apparently seen, these windows are the earliest copies of its spherical triangles. Only in the apse the gallery openings are made into normal windows, and there, in accordance with English horizontalism, they are not bound into a unity with the clerestory windows.

Glazed triforia were introduced into several French churches, even into some which had already been begun, as, for example, the cathedral at *Troyes*.[32] Here the triforium had been reached in 1228 when a storm destroyed the old church, which had been preserved for the holding of services, and stopped work on the new cathedral. When work began again probably in the late 1230s, a glazed triforium was introduced [105].[32A] In combination with the west walls of the transepts, which date from the end of the thirteenth

century, and the even later nave, the moderate proportions of the choir express the ideals of this generation without showing that stress which characterizes Beauvais, or the extreme verticalism of Reims and Amiens.

A second noble building with a glazed triforium is the choir of the cathedral at *Tours*, begun in *c*. 1210. The windows in the chapels round the choir received no tracery as yet; this first appears in the glazed triforium and in the windows above [106]. The tracery of these windows is similar to that in the Sainte-Chapelle, and, as the triforium and clerestory of the choir at Tours were built about *c*. 1240–44, it has been attributed to the anonymous architect of the Sainte-Chapelle.[33] The arguments for this attribution, however, are not very convincing.

The architect of the nave at *Strasbourg* must also be counted among the followers of the Saint-Denis Master and of the latest Parisian Rayonnant of the 1250s. The only certain date of the nave is that of its completion in 1275. It was begun probably *c*. 1235.[34] The emphatic diagonal position of the bases of the piers shows the influence of Amiens, where the bases corresponded to the round piers [107]. The architect began with the diagonal form at the bottom, but made the shafts frontal, as at Saint-Denis and Troyes cathedral. As the ridge of the vault in the nave is only 105 feet high – the height of Amiens is over 130 feet – only one arch was

107. Strasbourg Cathedral. Interior of nave, begun after 1235

108. Strasbourg Cathedral. Flying buttresses of nave, begun after 1240

needed for each flying buttress [108]. Each of these is pierced with only a single circle containing a quatrefoil, but otherwise presents a smooth surface – very similar to the flying buttresses added to the nave and choir of Notre-Dame in Paris soon after 1220. A further argument in favour of a beginning in the late 1230s and early 1240s is the frontality of the tabernacles on the buttresses – so far as they are of the first phase of building activity – and the pinnacles above the eaves-line of the roof.

Although the system and nearly all the details of Strasbourg are French, this cathedral is always described as specifically German. This is probably a result of Goethe's famous and thrilling eulogy of it: however, he spoke only of the façade, and was not yet acquainted with the development of French Gothic architecture. The factor which is still described as specifically German is the choice of the proportions. The nave at Strasbourg is about $53\frac{1}{2}$ feet wide and 105 feet high, but these proportions were dictated by those of the transepts, which had already been completed, and by the width of the Romanesque nave which the present one replaced. It is legitimate to call this nave German as long as one does not base this judgement on proportions which were common in Early Christian building in Italy and in Romanesque churches all over Europe, but rather on the combination, at Strasbourg, of wide proportions with

Gothic style. Even Saint-Denis is not as high as might be expected in a church built at this period of the Gothic age. Unquestionably the proportions of the nave at Amiens, one to three, were not those to which the architect(s) and his patrons, the bishops and chapter of Strasbourg, were accustomed, but it must not be forgotten that there are French buildings with almost equally low proportions, for instance the Sainte-Chapelle, where the ratio is one to two, and that there are also German works, such as the nave at Speyer and the aisles of the church of St Elizabeth at Marburg, the latter dating from about the late 1240s, with very steep proportions. German writers criticize these aisles but nevertheless proudly call them German.

Similarly comfortable, moderate proportions were also chosen for the western choir of the cathedral at *Naumburg*, begun under Bishop Dietrich II around 1250, and this again was the work of a German architect trained in France. In his opinion, it was right not to dissolve the wall completely, but to leave a solid wall between the shafts supporting the vault, and the windows. He decorated the wall-passage, which is similar to those in the Champagne, with canopies. The present choir stalls were not envisaged in the original plan, and the eastern bay of the choir was planned to have direct access to the tall spaces between it and the western towers. But during the construction the choir stalls were inserted

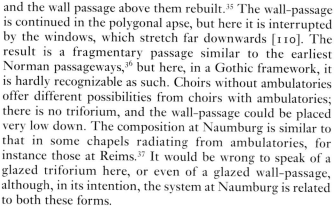

109. Naumburg Cathedral. Exterior of western choir, *c.* 1250, lower, Romanesque, parts of towers begun *c.* 1230–40. First Gothic storey of north west tower *c.* 1250–60

110. Naumburg Cathedral. Interior of western choir, *c.* 1250

and the wall passage above them rebuilt.[35] The wall-passage is continued in the polygonal apse, but here it is interrupted by the windows, which stretch far downwards [110]. The result is a fragmentary passage similar to the earliest Norman passageways,[36] but here, in a Gothic framework, it is hardly recognizable as such. Choirs without ambulatories offer different possibilities from choirs with ambulatories; there is no triforium, and the wall-passage could be placed very low down. The composition at Naumburg is similar to that in some chapels radiating from ambulatories, for instance those at Reims.[37] It would be wrong to speak of a glazed triforium here, or even of a glazed wall-passage, although, in its intention, the system at Naumburg is related to both these forms.

There is no way of knowing whether the nameless sculptor, 'The Master of Naumburg', who carved the figures of the donors, was also the architect of the choir. It is more probable that there were two artists, for there was certainly enough work for both, especially if it is agreed that the architect of the western choir was also the man who began building the western towers [109].[37A] As the towers of the cathedral at *Bamberg* were only completed before 1237, a repetition of their form, which depended on the earlier ones at Laon, could not, at that time, be called out of date.[37B]

Not every architect accepted the glazed triforium. The cathedral at *Clermont-Ferrand*, begun in around 1248, at the same time as the cathedral at Cologne, follows the system of Saint-Denis and Beauvais, but keeps the dark triforium [111]. This has rightly been interpreted as an act of opposition to the tendency to dissolve the entire height and width of the walls.[38] The glazed triforium also changed the usual distribution of light, and patrons may have had preferences, either for areas of darkness, or for increased light. It can hardly be argued that the purpose of not lighting the triforium here was to rest the eyes in darkness, after the hard, brilliant light in the streets of a southern town, for Clermont-Ferrand is not really a southern town. *León*, in Spain, lies much further south, and yet the cathedral there, begun soon after 1254, has a glazed triforium [112, 113],[38A] while in the north the cathedral at *Bayeux* has an unlit triforium, and even lancet windows without tracery.[39] Here Norman details were preponderant and Norman traditions prevented even French innovations. Bayeux is influenced by the choir of Saint-Etienne at Caen and the cathedral at Lisieux.[39A] Also indirectly dependent on the choir of Saint-Etienne at Caen for some of its Norman Gothic vocabulary is the choir of *Coutances* cathedral, begun in the 1220s and complete by 1238 [114].[40]

112. León Cathedral, begun soon after 1254. Interior of choir and north transept

111. Clermont-Ferrand Cathedral, begun *c.* 1248. Interior of choir

113. León Cathedral, after 1254.
Exterior of choir

114. Coutances Cathedral. Interior of choir, c. 1220–38

115. Noyon Cathedral. West front, begun c. 1205

5. FAÇADES. DOORS. BLIND ARCADES AND TRACERY. THE ELIMINATION OF CAPITALS

The west façade of the cathedral at *Noyon* was begun about 1205 [115]. It has in front of it a porch in the form of a horizontally projecting block. Behind the porch, the four buttresses rise to the roofs of the towers, but the bands of the galleries make the horizontals as strong as the verticals. There is the springing of an arch on the south tower, which proves that the two towers were meant to be connected by a gallery, as was later done in Paris. In the south tower each of the storeys has three long belfry openings. Their axes do not coincide with the six of the blind gallery below. When the north tower was rebuilt after the fire of 1293 the blind gallery was given four axes which coincide with the four axes of the belfry openings above, making the vertical unity of the whole tower much clearer.[41]

It is not clear whether the façade at Noyon was intended as a protest against the tendencies of the façade at Laon. In its own way it is an attempt to match the style of the rest of the church and to correct the irregularities of Saint-Denis and the gradations of the dwarf gallery at Laon.

In the west façade of *Notre-Dame* in *Paris*, too, one of the decisive factors is the balance between the horizontal and vertical lines [116]. A comparison with illustrations of earlier façades shows that the architect here was critical of the multiplicity of forms which they displayed and aimed at a more economical harmony by using a smaller number of accents. The double aisles helped his own sense of the majestic and allowed him to build each of the two towers as wide as its corresponding pairs of aisles. The central posts dividing the two flanking doorways and the windows above correspond to the piers between the pairs of aisles, and the façade is thus reduced to two storeys with three openings each (with a slight emphasis on the middle axes). A third storey above consists of the isolated parts of the square towers. The two lower storeys are separated, and at the same time joined, by a gallery of kings, while the much more slender and loosely placed gallery which conceals the gable and encircles the beginnings of the towers like cuffs serves the same purpose between the two towers.

There is no porch; the façade is flat, and only its details are unobtrusively governed by the principle of Gothic relief.

116. Paris, Notre-Dame. West front; lower storey c. 1200–20, windowed storey c. 1215/20, towers and gallery c. 1235–50

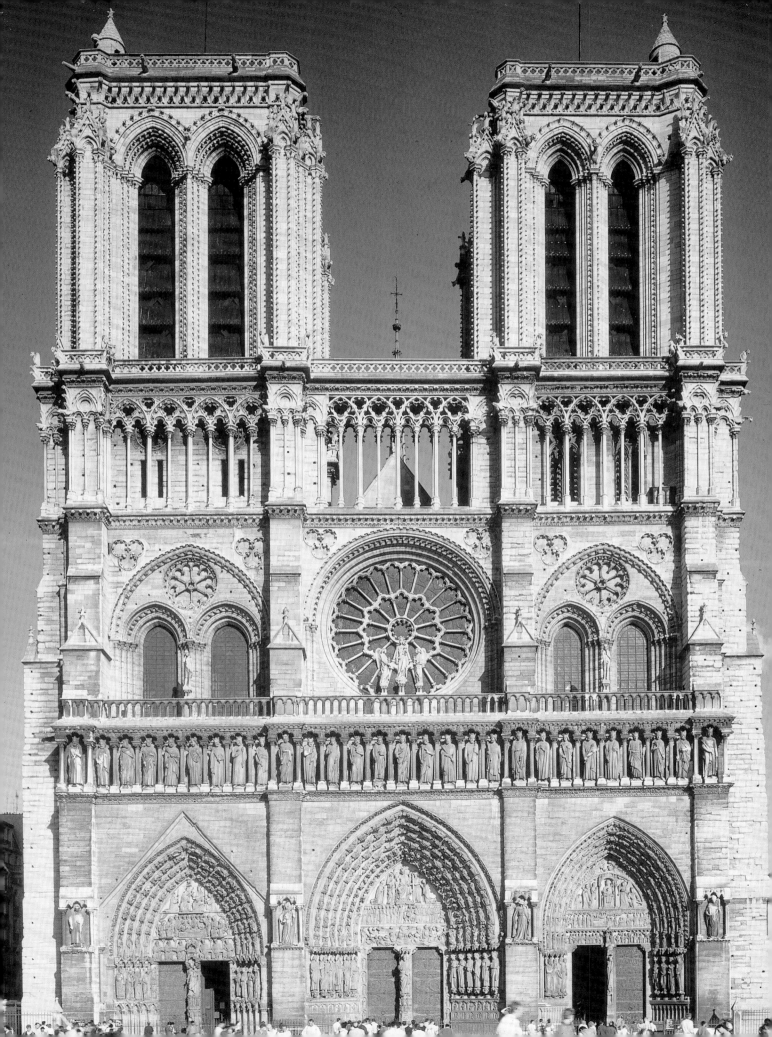

It is almost square in shape, but originally it was a little more slender, as eleven steps led up to the doors. The proportions of the doors themselves, 1 : 2.2, recur in other parts of the façade.[42]

The lower storey was begun on the north side, perhaps as early as *c.* 1190, but the earliest sculpture dates from about 1200. The rose storey was begun about 1215–20, and completed by *c.* 1225. The gallery above that was started in *c.* 1235, and the towers followed in 1240–45, both containing some of the new forms of their own generation. In the gallery of kings and in the storey in which the windows stand there are still trefoil arches, and inside the pointed arches in the windows the oculi in the form of wheels are similar to those which appeared inside the church (in the original triforium). In the upper gallery the tracery is progressive, and on the towers there are little gables penetrated by pointed arches. Another irregularity is a slight asymmetry which appears, not only in the roof-line of a gable over the left-hand door, but also in the greater breadth of the north tower, which therefore has room for one more figure of a king than does the south tower. Harmony is dependent on slight irregularities; it breathes an atmosphere of warmth and vitality. Complete regularity is cold as crystal.

117. Chartres Cathedral. South porch, *c.* 1210–40

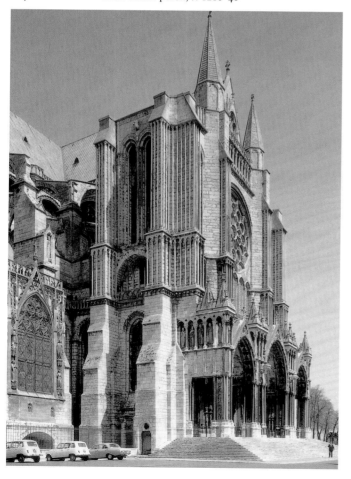

118. Fritzlar. Crypt, begun 1171, capital

119. Naumburg Cathedral. Capital, thirteenth century

In these doors, and in the figures surrounding them, the stepped jambs of Romanesque doorways with columns are replaced, by diagonal jambs which open the wall to the outside in a single sweep.[42A]

Thenceforth, the diagonal fusion of the plinths of the doorways and of the jambs themselves became the general rule. This had not yet been achieved in the transept portals of Chartres cathedral, whose porches and general design are obviously dependent on the west façade of Laon.[43] Quite apart from the sculpture, the south porch, with the tabernacles between its gables and the finials at their apexes, is the richer of the two [117]. The trefoil arches and spiral fluting of columns are Late Romanesque in style, while the vertical fluting is High Romanesque. In the north porch the foremost piers stand on octagonal plinths, have guttered bases with foliage at the corners and, directly above them, capitals which form the feet of full-bellied columns decorated with little figures under trefoils with pointed arches. The upper parts of the columns are visible only above these, where they have spiral rings like Iron Age jewellery. Above all this there are crocketed capitals. Each pier offers a different variation on this theme. This overwhelming display of imagination is in direct contrast to the reserve and the emphasis on the larger features of the façade in Paris. The placing of capitals directly on bases is a striking case of akyrism.[43A]

The west façade of Laon also influenced the lower part of the façade at *Amiens*, begun in around 1225, a few years after the beginning of the nave, and was substantially complete, at the level of the rose window, by the 1240s [120].[43B] However, at Amiens the gables are steeper, their edges are decorated with crocketed foliage, and the pointed arches contain a frieze of hanging, round arches in the archivolts. The portals are like those in Paris: they increase the depth, and the diagonal line of their jambs begins only with the front plane of the wall, as the buttresses project at right angles, although they give the aesthetic impression of forming part of the framework of the doorways. As at Laon, and on the south façade at Chartres, there are pinnacles between the gables, their front surfaces decorated with blind tracery. The spirelets of the pinnacles are more complicated than at Laon and on the choir at Reims, but they still stand on a horizontal cornice, and the two flanking gables partially conceal the windows of the aisles behind them.

The form of the upper storeys is determined by that of

120. Amiens Cathedral. West front, begun *c.* 1225

the cross-section through the interior. The rose-window, whose tracery was replaced by Flamboyant work about 1500, lies high on the façade, between the upper storeys of the two towers. The expanse between the lower storey with the doorways and the rose-window is filled with two horizontal bands. The lower of these is a gallery with open tracery like that in the triforium in the nave, while the upper is a gallery of kings, similar to the one in Paris which had been completed by about 1220. The lower gallery, with its outer layer of tracery, continues along the front of the towers. Inside, this arrangement resulted in the building of a passage behind the royal gallery and, above its flat ceiling, of yet another passage.[44] The relationship between the two surfaces is similar to that in the façade of Laon, but the individual forms at Amiens are already much more Gothic.

The inside surfaces of west walls were usually left very simple and plain, as though it was intended that the churchgoer should not be held up by any display of grandeur on his way out of church. Reims is an exception to this general rule. At Amiens there is no more than a blank arcade, corresponding to those in the aisles.

To trace the development of blind arcades would require a lengthy discussion.[45] However, although the development of architecture as a whole can be seen very clearly in these details, the separate stages are secondary and are merely the consequence of those principles in the field of architecture in its entirety which were the preoccupation of successive generations of architects. There are changes in the forms of arches, in the forms of their supports, in overall proportions, and in the relief and the decoration of capitals [118, 119]; but all these are matters of decoration – architecture on a small scale, whose function is the service and support of architecture on the larger scale.

The impressive west façade at *Lincoln* clearly shows how decisive the principle of Gothic relief is to the Gothic style. Here the older parts have blank Romanesque arcades lying within the wall, and the newer parts have Gothic ones pro-

jecting in front of the wall, with their most forward pointed arches projecting on corbels. The exact date of the Gothic part is not known,[45A] and these arches should be judged only by the purpose which they serve in this particular case; they do not serve as models in the general chain of development of the composition of façades.

The façade of *Saint-Nicaise* at *Reims*, however, which must have been begun in or soon after 1231, since Libergier started building from the west, is of historical importance [121].[45B] Basically it follows the system of the façades on the transepts at Chartres, but the porch, with its three gables, is more closely fused with the façade itself, and, in addition to these three, has two more gables on either side, one for each of the two flanking doors, and another, with blind tracery, decorating the outer buttresses. Between the gables there are tabernacles turned diagonally through 45 degrees. In the centre, Libergier drew the rose-window and the windows below into a stronger unity than had been achieved at Chartres by giving the lower windows tracery. The rose-window is drawn into the group in the same way as had been done in the nave windows at Saint-Denis. In an etching of 1625 the church can be seen in its original state, except for the tracery in the great rose-window, which was replaced in the Flamboyant style about 1550.[46] This whole group of windows with the lower windows in the towers forms a triangle. Above the windows in the towers there is a high parapet in front of the belfry openings, which are divided into two by tracery, and above these lie the upper ends of the four main buttresses. Both the smaller and the larger gables are complete triangles based on a common horizontal line, which is an old-fashioned motif. As at Laon, the octagonal upper parts of the towers are accompanied by octagonal turrets in two storeys which correspond to the slender single openings on the four sides of the towers. At the lower level of the rose-window the outer corners of the main towers are bevelled off – a smooth preparation for the diagonal position of the secondary turrets above. The towers are connected by a free-standing gallery which is overlapped by the central gable.

This façade was the immediate forerunner of that of the cathedral of *Reims*, which, according to Demaison, was built by Jean le Loup after he had taken over the direction of the work in 1231. The façade itself, however, may not have been begun until after the choir had been completed in 1241 [122], and Ravaux's recent discovery of two documents, of 1230 and 1252, refering to the future westward extension of the cathedral, suggests that by as late as 1252 the west façade of the old twelfth-century cathedral was still standing, and that no work had yet been begun on a new façade. However, soon after 1252, probably in 1254 or 1255, the foundations of the present west façade were laid.[46A]

The appearance of the lower storey, which projects sharply, is determined by five gables, which increase progressively in height and width towards the centre. The outer, blind gables are filled with tracery, and the same form

121. Reims, Saint-Nicaise, begun soon after 1231. Façade (drawing based on De Son's etching of 1625)

122. Reims Cathedral. West front, begun 1211–18? or 1252–6

is repeated on the north and south faces of the corners, as though outer gables, like those at Saint-Nicaise, had been folded round at right angles.[46B] The basic dimensions are dictated by those of the choir, but the line at the foot of the rose-window lies lower than was at first intended, also forming the base-line of the tabernacles, which would have had to lie at the same level as that of the tabernacles along the north and south sides of the nave if the design had followed regular lines.[47] The rose-window is set so low that it was impossible to put – as at Saint-Nicaise at Reims – traceried windows below it. At both sides of the rose-window the towers have pairs of narrow openings under very steeply pitched gables with extremely slender pinnacles. For the spires on the tabernacles the architect used the same form as had been used for those on the nave – probably in order to maintain a sense of unity. The upper gallery is a gallery of kings; it stands in front of the main gable and continues round the main towers and the octagonal plinths of their smaller accompanying turrets. In the free-standing storeys above there is no division into two storeys, as there is in the smaller turrets; this division, which exists at Laon, must have seemed petty to the architect of Reims. The Gothic principle of fusion is, in this façade, a determining factor of the whole design and of every detail, but at the same time there is also fusion here in another sense of the word. The determination to exercise and to master the full range of imaginative design shown here is similar to what was much later termed the *maniera grande*, or 'seeing in the large'. At Reims the gallery of kings again runs round the towers like a pair of cuffs, and the towers themselves, for all their many parts, give the impression of being a single unity in their combination of strength and transparency, and in spite of the fact that they are composed of a number of parts. The central openings with their tracery correspond to the open twin windows in the storey in which lies the rose-window. The band formed by the gallery of kings terminates the two lower storeys, whereas the dwarf gallery at Laon had still been proportioned to form part of the storey occupied by the windows. From the diagonal jambs of the doorways right up to the towers one feels a strong tendency to recession; for in many places there exists not only the projection of one layer of the façade in front of another, but also a contrary movement towards the inner core of the wall and the interior of the church itself. There is hardly another façade as rich and, at the same time, as easily comprehensible as that at Reims. The interrelationship between the heights of the doorways, the windows, the galleries, and the towers forms a harmonious rhythm, as do the measurements of breadth, of the north tower in relation to the central section and the south tower, and of the piers in relation to the different openings. The bevelled outside corners, with their panels of blind tracery, help to make the gradual narrowing towards the top unobtrusive.

Within this organic system the rose-window forms a point of rest and stability in the upward stream of gables and spires.[48] Within the chain of development of rose-windows, which began with the Wheel of Fortune of Saint-Etienne at Beauvais, the design at Reims marks the transformation of the idea of spokes in a wheel into pure tracery. The idea of incorporating a circular window in the framework of a pointed arch was taken from Saint-Nicaise, and shows that, in the new vocabulary of the Gothic style, the circle was beginning to be viewed as a form too closely connected with the traditions of the Romanesque. The architect also let an oculus into the space within the arch over the central doorway, but here the tracery springs from the circumference instead of from the hub. The quatrefoils in the two flanking doorways are an imitation of those at Saint-Nicaise.[49]

Between the gables over the doorways there are delicate tabernacles, turned diagonally through 45 degrees; they are reminiscent of the diagonal pinnacles separating the portal gables of the west façade of Saint-Nicaise at Reims, or those of the north and south transept façades of Notre-Dame in Paris.[49A]

The inexhaustible wealth of the carved figures takes its place within the simple architectural composition of the façade. It abounds in ideas and symbols and is truly vibrant in form, expressive of the spirit of this cathedral where the kings of France were crowned – where secular might stood to receive its authority and the blessing of Heaven.[49B]

The chronology of the building of the façade was clarified by Ravaux and Kurmann. Work began soon after 1252 and before 1256. The six prophet figures on the right hand portal, carved about 1220 with the likely intention of decorating and modernising the old mid-twelfth century façade, suggest that at that point no new west façade was planned.[49C] However, full-scale tracings of the arches of a central and side portal found on the back wall of the south transept triforium and dated *c.* 1225 show that planning for a west façade was by then under way, a fact confirmed by a charter of 1230 which looked forward to an eventual extension of the cathedral westwards.[49D] Some of the jamb figures carved for this unrealised west façade were later incorporated into the present façade. They include the famous Visitation Group, which must have been carved well before 1237, since sculpture influenced by these and related Reims figures appears in the Prince's portal at Bamberg cathedral, dated as much as ten years before the consecration of that cathedral in 1237.[50] Other pre-cut sculptures at Reims assembled on the later west portals include a group of Amiens-influenced figures such as the Marys of the Annunciation and Adoration of the Magi, Simeon and Saint-Dionysius.[50A] The rest of the sculpture, however, belongs with the architecture of the façade. A *Magister Walterius*, identified by Ravaux as the putative third architect Gaucher of Reims, is cited in a document of 1256.[51] According to an inscription on the now-lost labyrinth, once in the nave floor of the cathedral, Gaucher of Reims 'worked on the voussoirs and the portals', so Ravaux argues that Gaucher was working on the lower storey of the façade in the later 1250s and early 1260s.[51A] Since the labyrinth showed the fourth architect, Bernard of Soissons, drawing a rose window, it is likely that he designed the rose and its storey. This was constructed probably in the early to mid 1260s because his rose is indebted to Pierre de Montreuil's rose in the south transept façade of Notre-Dame in Paris, designed at the earliest in 1258, and under construction in the early 1260s.[51B] The portals were certainly complete by 1274, when a chapter ordinal regulated the entrance of Palm Sunday processions through the west doors.[52] The rest of the façade went up gradually, largely under the direction of Bernard of Soissons (in charge up to 1289–90), in the last quarter of the thirteenth century, and was completed in the early fourteenth century.[52A] Ravaux's and Kurmann's conclusions have, however, been radically questioned by Hamann-Mac Lean and Schüssler, who argue that the lower parts of the west front were laid down by Gaucher of Reims (whom they considered the *first* architect), between 1211 and 1218. The portals were continued by Jean le Loup (1219–34), and finished by Jean d'Orbais (1236–*c.* 1251). Bernand of Soissons (*c.* 1252–*c.* 1287) completed the façade from the triforium zone upwards. No reconciliation between these two fundamentally opposed views of the chronology of the façade, and its architecture, has been proposed. Nor is one likely.[52B]

In the case of the *Sainte-Chapelle* there was no opportunity for the architect to take part in the task of solving the problems of façades, since the two-storeyed porch conceals the façade right up to the level of the oculus. This opportunity did, however, present itself to another architect of the same generation, when, beginning in around 1225, chapels were added between the buttresses of *Notre Dame* in *Paris*,[52C] and it was decided to lengthen the transepts accordingly. It is not known what the old façades of the transepts looked like, but they cannot have been designed later than 1180, and must certainly have been earlier in style than the façade at Laon. The citizens of Paris of about 1250 must, in any case, have welcomed the opportunity to replace them with something more modern. Jean de Chelles began the north transept façade in *c.* 1245 and completed it by 1258. In that year he died, having started the foundations and the lowest courses of the south transept façade [123]. His place was taken by Pierre de Montreuil who, as a tribute to his dead colleague, had the inscription carved which has given us this exact date of 1258. The inscription itself contains no words of praise, but it is a monument to both architects. The system adopted for these façades goes back to the Saint-Denis Master's two transept façades at Saint-Denis, here enriched in many ways, especially by the incorporation of the five gables of the doorways – a device borrowed from the screen of gables in front of the west façade of Saint-Nicaise at Reims. As the transepts have no aisles, and only one doorway is therefore required, the lateral pairs of gables stand over blank bays. The two outer bays are filled with blind tracery, and each of the two inner ones divided into three parts to contain three figures each. The three pointed arches in each of these two inner bays are supported on vertical members which continue *without capitals* to form the arches, and this innovation is repeated in the framework of the main doorway. (There are forerunners at Chartres, especially in the eastern flyers.)

Here, for the first time, then, an architect achieved the unity between jambs and arches which the pointed arch seemed to have demanded ever since its introduction. The piercing of the tympana, or rather the filling of them with blind foils, was the first stage in the development which led in the end to the dissolution of these surfaces. The pinnacles turned through 45 degrees which stand between the gables are modelled on those at Saint-Nicaise at Reims. The balustrade of the gallery runs in front of the base of the triforium which is decorated with blind arches, again without

123. Paris, Notre-Dame. Façade of south transept, begun 1258

capitals. On the south transept every second vertical member of this blind storey continues upwards to form the row of eight windows, which are divided by tracery. The gallery above these windows, the square frame round the rose-window, and the piercing of its lower spandrels are all copied from the forms used at Saint-Denis, though the tracery in the rose-window at Notre-Dame is more refined. The decoration of the spaces enclosed by the gables, and the octagonal tops of the buttresses, too, follow Saint-Denis, though in Paris the tops of the buttresses are opened to form tabernacles. The niches for statues on the buttresses, like those in the nave of Chartres, are an enrichment of the system, and on the south façade there are also figures at the level of the row of windows.

On the south façade there are spherical triangles filling

124. Lincoln Cathedral. Nave looking east, c. 1220–35

the spandrels round the oculus, but they seem to be the natural product of the design of the rose-window rather than a reproduction of the lower windows in the Sainte-Chapelle; for here, in the rose-window of the south façade, there are twenty-four pointed arches, pointing inwards, each of which, with the section of the circumference on which it stands, forms a spherical triangle.[53]

The introduction of the spherical triangle into the realm of tracery must be interpreted as another act of opposition to the form of the circle; for this new form, which could be called a self-contained series of three pointed arches, is better suited to a style from which the semicircle had already been eliminated. However, it was not easy for architects to deprive themselves of the splendour of rose-windows, and it remained the task of future generations to achieve a logical solution to this dilemma. The moderate criticism of the circular form which appears here is related to the elimination of the capitals in the doorway, in that, in both cases, the

architect has understood the demands of the pointed arch. In the former case this is true only of the demands of the point itself, whereas in the latter case the architect has understood the pointed arch in terms of the upward stream of forces which begins in its two supports.

6. THE TIERCERON STAR-VAULT

Out of the tierceron-vaults in St Hugh's Choir at *Lincoln* the successor of the master who had designed them developed for the Lincoln nave the first tierceron star-vaults. What he did was to carry through the diagonals which his predecessor had cut short, to carry through also the ridge-ribs from west to east, and to add short north-south ridge-ribs so that the severies from north and south stop about half-way between the clerestory wall and the centre of the bay [124]. Ribs connect the bosses at the end of the north–south ridge-ribs with the springers of the vaults. These ribs are genuine ribs in so far as they form the boundaries of cells, and at the same time tiercerons in so far as they rise on the severies of transverse tunnel-vaults. The term star-vault is derived from the figure which vaults such as those of the nave at Lincoln form in plan. In perspective the seven ribs issuing from the same springer form one bunch. As there is not enough space for them, the tiercerons start only at the level of the windows. This makes one wonder whether the form of the vault was determined only when in the course of building the springers had been reached. However, the English in this respect were less logical than the French, who demanded a separate shaft for each arch of a vault.[53A]

At *Ely* in c. 1234 a choir of six bays was begun to replace the old apse. The vault, completed by 1252, when the consecration took place, seems to be the earliest copy of the tierceron star-vault of Lincoln. (I believe that the vault of the Lincoln nave was designed a short time after 1220.)[53B] At Ely the ribs have more space on the abaci of the shafts, but in spite of that they are not separate at their start.[53C]

Star-vaults look more central in plan than in perspective. In rows and over oblong bays they close up and make the bays merge with each other in a typically English way.

In contrast to the English stars, the one tierceron star-vault over the crossing at *Amiens*, built shortly before 1269,[53D] possesses the full power of concentration. It is in keeping with French verticalism, as are the English tierceron star-vaults with English horizontalism.

7. THE SPREAD OF THE GOTHIC STYLE, 1200–50

The great French cathedrals are the work of lodges in which the most gifted masons, under the guidance of masters, gradually became architects. They began their education on the site, and, through their journeys, became familiar with the work of other lodges. The buildings themselves are evidence of the interchange of ideas between a master and his apprentices, and the schools which they formed can be clearly recognized in their works.[53E]

The architectural ideas of neighbouring countries came

into contact with those of the French school, especially through the clergy, who travelled widely, came to know French cathedrals, and wanted to build similar churches in their own dioceses. They then had either to invite French master masons to their own country, or to send their own master masons to study in France, and such recommendations from one bishop to another gave a foreigner an introduction to any lodge.

Even within the frontiers of modern France, however, there was already, at this time, a school of architecture which was separate from the establishments of the master-masons of the cathedrals, and, indeed, had its own establishments propagating the Gothic style: this was the school of the Cistercian order. A concrete example of what this society meant by the Gothic style a few years before the building of Chartres can be seen at *Fossanova*, near Rome. Begun just before 1173, and under construction at about the same time as the new rib-vaulted choir at Pontigny.[54] This church still has groin-vaults in the nave and choir [125]. The rib-vault in the crossing was probably built shortly before the consecration of the church in 1208, and is related to that at *Casamari*, not far from Fossanova, which was built between 1203 and 1217 by masons from Fossanova. At Casamari, however, ribs were used in every compartment. These ribs do not stand on separate springers but merge with the transverse arches and the wall-arches. Both churches have that cool beauty which was achieved in all the works of the Cistercian order. At the time at which they were built these churches must have caused a sensation in Italy, and even now, visited from Rome, they give the impression of being foreign to their surroundings. Measured by French standards, Fossanova is still a work of the Cistercian Transitional style, whereas Casamari is Early Gothic.[54A]

In France itself, the style of the Cistercian church at *Longpont*, built between *c.* 1205–10 and 1227, closely follows that of Soissons, and, with this church, the Cistercian Transitional style comes to an end and changes directly into the High Gothic.[55] The Cistercians did not build towers, but they now transformed the 'oratorium', the 'prayer hall', as St Bernard wished monastery churches to be called, into a mundane and festive place. This is equally true of the Cistercian church at *Châalis*, built between about 1201 and 1219, which has sexpartite vaults [126]. Already at Pontigny, the architect had built quadripartite vaults with bays shorter than they were broad, a form native to Burgundy, and at Châalis the sexpartite vaults over the hexagonal radiating chapels are direct quotations from the radiating chapels of the choir of Pontigny. The Châalis use of sexpartite vaults in the main vessel of the nave, combined with an alternating system, probably derives from early Gothic buildings in the Yonne valley, especially Sens cathedral. Châalis's polygonal transept ends may owe something to Noyon and Cambrai cathedrals, but the source may be the slightly earlier

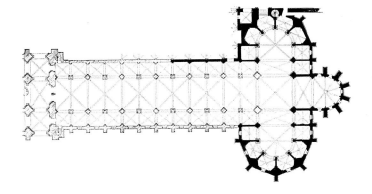

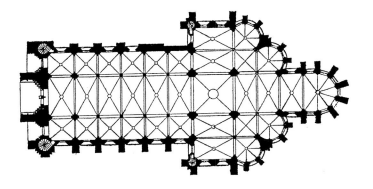

125. Fossanova, Cistercian church, begun 1187. Interior

126. Châalis, Cistercian church. Ground plan. *c.* 1201–19

127. Braine, Saint-Yved, ground plan. *c.* 1176–1208

128. Magdeburg Cathedral. Interior of choir, begun 1209

129. Limburg on the Lahn, St George. Interior of choir and transepts
c. 1215–20

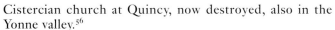

130. Auxerre Cathedral. Interior of choir, begun just before 1217

Cistercian church at Quincy, now destroyed, also in the Yonne valley.[56]

The church of Saint-Yved at *Braine*, built probably between *c*. 1176 and 1208,[56A] belonged to the order of the Premonstratensians. These canons did not show such highly developed individuality in their architecture as did the Cistercian monks. The architect at Braine was trained in the Laon school, and adopted the three-storey elevation (with triforium passage but no gallery) used earlier at Saint-Vincent at Laon (1174–1205). The round pier on each side, east of the crossing, is also reminiscent of both Saint-Vincent and the cathedral at Laon, and may have been inspired by the desire not to obstruct the chancel chapels. These pairs of chapels stand diagonally – a daring introduction of the principle of the diagonal into the realm of whole spatial unities [127]. Diagonally placed chapels like these were built in the Liebfrauenkirche at Trier perhaps begun in 1227, to the west and to the east of the transepts, and thus produced a central plan (see below, pp. 159–61). Others appeared in the church of St Victor in Xanten begun in 1263[56B] and in Košiče in Hungary, begun in the last decade of the fourteenth century, and

in a large number of smaller churches in France[57] and other countries.

The cathedral at *Magdeburg* is an example of the introduction of the Gothic style at the express wish of a patron [128]. Archbishop Albrecht had studied in Paris and therefore knew Notre-Dame and probably several other cathedrals of the time of about 1200. Shortly after he took office in Magdeburg, in 1207, a fire destroyed part of the town, including the old cathedral which dated from about 955. The architect to whose design the choir was begun in 1209 decided to build a polygonal apse and ambulatory, for which, at this time, besides those at Laon, there were already models at Chartres and Soissons.[57A] He built the arches of the apse, the transverse arches, and the openings to the chapels in the form of pointed arches, but vaulted the ambulatory with Romanesque groin-vaults in which the groins, halfway to the ridge, disappear into its spherical surface. The vaults are matched by their massive Romanesque supports with their frontal bases and capitals. The church is the work of a German architect with slight knowledge of the Gothic style. The fact that it has often been called the first really Gothic building in Germany is due to the incorrect suppo-

131. Auxerre Cathedral. Ambulatory and eastern chapel, begun just
before 1217

132. Vercelli, S. Andrea. Interior of nave, c. 1219

sition that its later parts may date from the same time as the
lower parts of the ambulatory. This cathedral, with its special history, is evidence of the gradual infiltration of the
Gothic style. As such it is very interesting to the historian of
local style, but it plays no leading part in the history of the
Gothic style. In its earliest parts the church is, at best, a
work of passive transition, and this is even true of the higher
stage of development reached in the gallery round the choir,
the so-called Bishop's Gallery, of 1230.[58]

The collegiate church of St George at *Limburg on the
Lahn* occupies the same kind of position in the history of
the Gothic style. In the interior, begun *c.* 1190, there are
Gothic elements – rib-vaults supported on shafts, some of
which even have crocketed capitals turned through 45
degrees [129] – but the exterior is Late Romanesque. The
dominant position of the church on a rock above the river
makes it unforgettable. Within the German Late
Romanesque it is a masterpiece, but, seen in the larger perspective of European architecture, that is as contemporary
with the choir at Le Mans, it is, even in the forms of its
Gothic elements, out of date.[59]

The cathedral at *Auxerre*, too [130, 131], belongs to these
buildings which demand a dual appreciation, a historical

one and a timeless one. Since the parts of the cathedral were
built at different times, a timeless judgement must be based
on its rich harmony and on the high intrinsic quality of each
part. Stylistically the choir, begun in a little before 1217, was
not yet influenced by Reims; for the alternating supports
suggest that it was intended to build sexpartite vaults. The
triforium is derived from that at Chartres, but it is much
higher and its slender columns and small capitals make it
much lighter. The upper windows of the choir, which have
plate tracery, also show the same stage of stylistic development as those at Chartres, though here each oculus is
enriched by a circle of eight trefoils along its circumference.
In the ambulatory the different levels of the capitals are a
means to achieve vivaciousness, but it is achieved at the
expense of classic tranquillity. However, one need only compare this ambulatory with the Bishop's Gallery at
Magdeburg to see that, with the building at Auxerre, the
High Gothic had attained ascendancy in Burgundy. On the
other hand, a comparison with the ambulatory and the
chapels at Reims leads to the opposite conclusion. At
Auxerre the presence of two extremely slender columns at
the entrance to the east chapel produced something of the
charm and fascination of Early Gothic imaginative exploits,
such as those in Saint-Remi at Reims [45] and in Notre-
Dame at Châlons. The architect was not prepared to eliminate these vistas, whereas the masters of the mature High
Gothic style reckoned in terms of a larger unity and
regarded details of this kind as diversions leading the eye on
to things of secondary importance.[60]

The difficulty of blending the French Gothic style with

133. Sées Cathedral. Nave begun soon after 1240

134. Burgos Cathedral. Interior of choir, begun 1221

135. Burgos Cathedral. Reconstruction of the original chevet plan 1221–30 (after Karge)

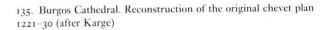

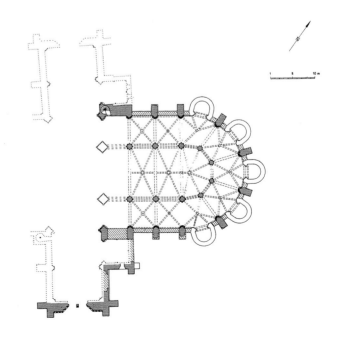

Italian traditions can be seen in the church of S. Andrea at *Vercelli* [132]. The groups of uninterrupted shafts, the diagonal position of the shafts supporting the ribs, the pointed transverse arches, and the crocketed capitals are French; the blank surface of the wall above the arcade with its pointed arches and the small dimensions of the upper windows, which still have round arches, are Cistercian; and the details on the inside of the dome over the crossing – squinches supporting a drum with a gallery of round arches and an octopartite groin-vault – are more Romanesque than Gothic. Finally, the whole exterior is a typical work of the North Italian Romanesque. The French influence has been explained by the transference of the church, in 1219, to Victorine canons from Paris, as well as by the generous patronage of the church's founder, Cardinal Gualo, bishop of Vercelli, and sometime papal legate in England. The fact that members of the workshop of Benedetto Antelami worked on some of the details, such as the capitals, has led to the assumption that this sculptor may have designed the church.[61] In this connexion the formal similarities with the baptistery at Parma and the cathedral at Fidenza (Borgo San Donnino) are extremely illuminating. Part of the Italian character of the church lies

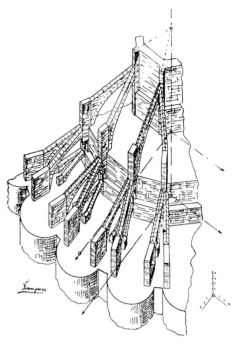

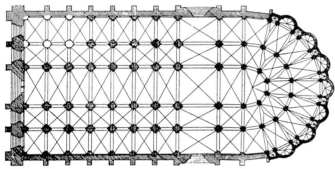

136. Toledo Cathedral, begun , *c.* 1220. Interior of ambulatory

137. Toledo Cathedral. Ground plan. Begun *c.* 1220

138. Toledo Cathedral. Diagram of flying buttresses of chevet, begun *c.* 1220 (after V. Lampérez y Romea)

in the materials used. A brick flying buttress is a simplification which can almost make one forget that, even in this heavy form, the flying buttress remains a Gothic element. It is hardly justifiable to call Vercelli the earliest really Gothic building in Italy.

The cathedral at *Coutances*[62] contains some traditionally Norman characteristics, such as the wall-passage at the sill level of the windows, and the octagonal crossing tower which lights the interior [114]. The rebuilding of the Romanesque nave began in about 1200, and was finished by *c.* 1220. Groups of triple shafts, like those in the earlier nave at *Fécamp*, rise from the floor to the vault. There is a typically Norman interior wall passage in the clerestory and rectangular bays with four-part vaults, again like Fécamp. These features, and some characteristics that look English, combine to produce a Norman High Gothic church.[63]

Parts of the cathedral at *Bayeux* also belong to the Norman High Gothic. Here, about *c.* 1240, the nave was continued, above a Romanesque arcade, in the Gothic style; only the transepts and the east end are Gothic throughout.[63A]

At *Sées*, where the nave was begun about probably soon

after 1240, the shafts rise separately in front of the round piers, pass through capitals, and continue as complete cylinders, crossing the recessed sexfoils in the spandrels between the arches of the arcade [133]. As in England, the round abaci serve to produce a fusion between the spatial parts of the church. The division of the wall into two layers is a Norman legacy, but its relief is adapted to the Gothic style.[63B]

The choir of the new Gothic cathedral at Burgos in Spain was founded in 1221 and was already in use in 1230 [134, 135]. Before the construction of the present radiating chapels in the 1270s the original choir plan consisted of an ambulatory with six-part vaulted bays and a semicircular chevet with small apsidal chapels alternating with single buttresses in a manner clearly indebted to Bourges cathedral and its follower, the lost choir of Saint-Martin at Tours. Burgos's debts to Bourges extend to the proportions of its elevation (a low arcade and a tall triforium, prefigured in the inner aisle elevations at Bourges), to the oculi in the webs of the apse vault, and to the shape of its piers (circular cores with eight engaged shafts) and the prolongation of their inner curved surfaces as wall responds up to the vault departures. It is obvious that the Gothic style in Spain, at the

139. Toledo Cathedral, begun *c.* 1220. Interior of transept and choir

140. Dijon, Notre-Dame, begun *c.* 1220. Interior of north transept and choir

stage which it had reached in 1221, was entirely imported from France.[64] Burgos must be regarded as the beginning of the Spanish High Gothic, for it shows a higher degree of development than *Tarragona*, begun some time after 1171, and changed to receive rib-vaults in around 1200,[65] and *Cuenca*,[66] and it also adopts the tracery of Reims. Compared with German works of the same period, Burgos is less original in its ideas, but completely up-to-date. It is difficult to determine how Spanish it was in its original state, from 1221 to its consecration in 1260; for its Spanish character grew gradually stronger through the additions of later generations, among them the *coro* of 1497. The practice of shutting off part of the nave with high screens, for the use of the clergy, completely obstructing the view from west to east, and partially obstructing that from north to south, did not become general in Spain until the fifteenth century.

The cathedral of Burgos has one aisle on each side of the nave; the architect of the cathedral at *Toledo*, however, was more ambitious and built his church with two aisles on each side, and a double ambulatory [136–8]. The stepped cross section, with a taller inner ambulatory and inner choir aisles with their own clerestories and triforia, is modelled on Bourges, as are the pillar forms and many of the mouldings. The choir was begun probably in *c.* 1220, long before the official foundation in 1226. Master Martin, the first architect, mentioned in chapter documents in 1227 and 1234, had clearly worked (perhaps trained?) at Bourges, but he also knew Notre-Dame in Paris, Saint-Denis, and the newly begun choir of Le Mans, whose tri-radial vaults in the outer ambulatory and bifurcating system of Y-shaped flying buttresses around the chevet are repeated at Toledo.[67] Unlike his French models, however, Martin introduced low, wide proportions in all his aisles, creating a horizontal and lateral conception of space that was to dominate Spanish basilican churches to the end of the Middle Ages. Street has described Toledo as 'thoroughly French in its ground-plan and equally French in all its details' but he clearly overlooked the very Mudejar-looking multi-cusped arches in the triforia of both the inner aisles and central vessel of the choir [139].[68] What makes the exterior look different from that of French churches is the very flat pitch of the roofs, which, though it is to some extent the product of the southerly climate, is even more a proof of the preservation of a classical tradition.[69]

The Gothic style in Spain is not really a Spanish Gothic

141. Ypres, Saint-Martin. Exterior of choir, begun in 1221

style but rather the French Gothic style in Spanish territory. The Gothic style in Burgundy is, however, Burgundian, and it can be seen in the cathedral at *Nevers*, which was begun after a fire had destroyed the old cathedral in 1211, that is, soon after the beginning of the building of the cathedral at Reims. However, in evaluating this church, one must exclude the choir, begun in the 1230 or 1240s, and complete by 1331, and all that was added in the fifteenth century, especially the tracery.[70]

In the cathedral at *Toul*, begun in 1221, only the choir and the transepts are the work of this generation. The choir has no ambulatory, which was normal in small churches, but is an exception in churches of the size of Toul Cathedral. Having reached a logical solution which was to be a model for many later architects, the master of Toul built windows which rise uninterrupted from above the altar to the vault.[70A]

Notre-Dame at *Dijon*, a church described by Soufflot in the eighteenth century and Viollet-le-Duc in the nineteenth, both of whom admired it, has a polygonal choir with no ambulatory.[71] If this church was really not begun until *c.* 1220, then its architect was far behind his time, for it still has sexpartite vaults and shafts projecting to the very edge of the abaci on which they stand [140].[72] The apse does not have long, uninterrupted windows like that at Toul, but two rows of windows, one above the other, separated by a delicate triforium.

The Swiss cathedrals at *Lausanne*, begun in *c.* 1170, but fully underway from *c.* 1192, and at *Geneva,* showing the influence of Lausanne from *c.* 1215, should be considered as part of the Burgundian group. Both are older and much heavier and more massive than the church at Dijon.[73]

The interest of the Gothic style in Belgium at this time, too, is mainly a local one. At *Orval* (begun *c.* 1180), *Aulne* (1214/21–45), and *Villers* (begun a little before 1208), the Cistercians turned increasingly to Gothic forms,[74] and, of these churches, Villers also has the classic tripartite elevation and crocket capitals.[74A] Saint-Martin at *Ypres*, begun in 1221, is, however, the first really Gothic Belgian church [141].[74B] The nine sides of the polygonal choir are extremely narrow and slender; for the more sides choirs have, the more compressed and slender is their effect. The chapels in the angles between the transepts and the choir stand diagonally, as at Braine and Trier.[74C]

The choir of Ste Gudule in *Brussels*, the first French chevet (with ambulatory and radiating chapter) in Brabant, was begun under champenois influence in 1226, and completed towards the middle of the thirteenth century. Its details are extremely French in character, but here, too, there are many conservative elements compared with the nave of Amiens.[75]

The number of churches which play a part in the spread of the Gothic style is very large, and it is difficult to achieve an overall view of them, for each one really demands individual consideration. Richard Hamann presented the development of European architecture of the generation of 1210 to 1240 by explaining the appearance of similar architectural details in buildings far apart as a sign that groups of masons travelled from place to place.[76] It was mainly forms from the early Gothic of Laon and the Soissonais which were exported in this way; for they seemed extremely modern to people in the east, and, with the granting of certain concessions, could readily be assimilated with local traditions.[76A] The most impressive products of this trend are the cathedral at *Bamberg*, where the nave was built in the 1220s,[77] the Cistercian church at *Tišnov* (*Tischnowitz*) in Moravia, and in Hungary the churches at *Ják* and *Lébény*.[77A]

In all these churches the exterior is still almost purely Romanesque in character; for they have not only almost

142. Assisi, S. Francesco, 1228–53.
Exterior from the south-east

143. Assisi, S. Francesco, 1228–53.
Interior of lower church

unbroken and very massive walls, but also the Romanesque
relief in which the walls recede from their outside surface to
their innermost core, and the predominant emphasis is on
frontality. In the interior of the cathedral at *Bamberg*, the
shafts supporting the ribs stand on either side of a broad
lesene, which looks almost like a pilaster. The lesenes carry
the broad transverse arches. The piers present the same
form in all four directions, and the arches of the arcade are
correspondingly flat and broad, giving a Romanesque effect
of being cut into the wall. Thus the whole thickness of the
wall separates the nave from the aisles, forming a deep spatial layer between the two. The treatment of the windows,
too, is the same. The vaults join the almost unbroken wall
similarly to those in the lower storeys of the towers at
Chartres, and this is largely true of all the many churches
which Richard Hamann correlated in his book.

In the exterior of Bamberg Cathedral, even in the west
choir, where the interior is relatively Gothic in style, the for-
bidding, Romanesque character of the walls, with their
friezes of round arches, predominates. Only in the upper
storeys of the towers, built in the 1230s and substantially
complete by 1237 under the influence of the towers at
Laon, does the Gothic style assert itself. The west towers at
Naumburg, follow Bamberg as their model, but the three
very transparent storeys rise abruptly over the compact
lower storey [109].[78]

The common factor among all the European schools of
architecture at this stage is the fusion of their local styles
with Gothic forms. The early churches of the mendicant
orders exhibit a third principle, in addition to these two –
the principle of simplicity as a visual representation of the
asceticism demanded by St Bernard.

Dominicus Guzmán, born about 1170 in Caleruega in
Old Castille, studied in Palencia and personally experienced
the struggle with the Albigensians at Albi, Toulouse, and
other places. This sect fulfilled the demand for asceticism to
an exaggerated degree, equating the desire for salvation with
suicide after the achievement of complete purification from
sin, and it fought the Catholic Church, regarding it as a
creation of the devil. As the sect spread from Bulgaria
throughout southern Europe and as far as southern France
and Spain, the struggle that followed was, for the church, a
fight for survival, and it ended with the liquidation of the
Albigensians about 1244. To ensure that there could be no
revival of the sect, the Church founded the Inquisition. St
Dominic evolved his methods for fighting heresies in Spain

144. Assisi, S. Francesco, 1228–53. Interior of upper church, looking west

and Southern France, and subsequently in 1215, in Italy, founded the order of the Dominicans.[78A]

Giovanni Bernadone, born in 1181 in Assisi, was the son of a rich cloth merchant. He was nicknamed Franciscus, the little Frenchman, because his mother, Pica, came from Provence, and from her he learnt not only French, but also a desire for an ascetic life. As a young man he became a soldier, and in 1202 was taken prisoner-of-war in Perugia. After seeing visions he decided to embrace radical poverty, and, together with a few men who shared his ideas, he founded the Franciscan order, which was recognized by the pope in 1209.[78B]

Both Dominic and Francis taught as wandering preachers, in the open air, and in barns, but both also had the privilege of preaching in parish churches and cathedrals. After the death of Francis in 1226, the jealousy and protests of parish priests forced the Franciscans to abandon the idea of absolute poverty, and so, in 1228, they built a monastery with a church at Assisi.

In the church of *S. Francesco* at *Assisi* [142], which stands on the side of a hill, on ground given to the order, the sloping site necessitated the building of a crypt, which is mysterious and dark, with massive walls and a Romanesque apse.

The broad ribs form segmental arches and the transverse arches are semicircular, while the transepts have tunnel-vaults [143]. The general layout is usually considered to be 'Lombardo-Umbrian'. But the upper church shows the influence of northern French Gothic, especially the broad nave of Angers cathedral and the Remois passages derived from Champagne [144]. It was decided to build the church at Assisi as a worthy expression of the honour in which St Francis was held by the members of his order, although some of the monks regarded this as a denial of St Francis's ideal of poverty. The first design, begun in 1228, envisaged the present double-storeyed church, but with the nave of the upper church consisting of only three bays, and with no campanile or circular nave buttresses. This was rapidly followed by the present solution, including an extra nave bay, a new entrance bay and portal opening off the south flank of the lower church, circular nave buttresses, and the large campanile. All this, which was at least decided upon by 1239, and probably substantially complete by 1243 (there are mentions of bells in both years), emphasized the south-eastern (principal) approach to the church and monastery. In 1253 Innocent IV consecrated the church.[79] The exterior has more of the characteristics of the traditional Italian

145. Bologna, S. Francesco, begun 1236. Interior looking east

146. Toulouse, Church of the Jacobins. Interior

Romanesque than of the French Gothic style, and the free-standing tower is purely Romanesque in style. The façade of the upper church has a Gothic doorway, a rose-window, and an oculus in the gable, but the simplicity of the horizontal lines is not Gothic, not even in the English sense of the Gothic style, for the lesenes give the façade an essentially Romanesque relief.

At Assisi the wall-surfaces and the frescoes are the predominant factors, and it was found acceptable to combine these with stained glass in the windows [144]. The windows in the apse contain some of the oldest surviving stained glass in Italy, executed by a German atelier probably working in Assisi.[79A]

Among the Franciscan churches which show the influence of the mother church are *S. Chiara* at *Assisi* (built between *c.* 1254 and 1265), S. Francesco at *Perugia* (begun *c.* 1251), and perhaps also S. Francesco at *Viterbo*.[79B]

The Dominicans began a new shrine church for their founder in Bologna from *c.* 1228 onwards, and substantially completed it by 1233. In building at exactly the same time as the earliest work on S. Francesco at Assisi, it was intended to rival the Assisi church, and promote the cult of St Dominic. Built in brick, its plan and elevation followed the precedent of Lombard Cistercian architecture, with a "Bernardine" east end, and round columns supporting domical four-part rib-vaults.[80]

With S. Francesco at Assisi, one of the first churches of a mendicant order to be planned as a Gothic building was that of *S. Francesco* at *Bologna*, begun in 1236 [145]. In the very year in which the nave of Amiens was near completion, this church was designed with sexpartite vaults and no tracery. Admittedly it has pointed arches and flying buttresses, but it also has a predominantly Romanesque façade. All these early churches must not, however, be judged in comparison with Amiens, for, to the citizens of Bologna at this time, their church must have seemed both very modern and very Gothic.[80A]

The church of S. Francesco at *Cortona*, built between 1245 and 1253, represents one of the simplest types of the churches of the mendicant orders. It consists of a long, rectangular hall with a choir flanked by two chapels at the east end. The choir and chapels have rib-vaults, and pointed arches opening on to the nave and the nave has an open timber roof.[81] As one comes into the church through the Gothic doorway, one's eyes move immediately to the Gothic choir; what lies between is purely utilitarian.

147. Florence, S. Maria Novella, begun after 1246. Interior looking east

148. Marburg, St Elizabeth, 1235–83. Exterior from the south-east

149. Marburg, St Elizabeth. Interior of choir, 1235–c. 1243

From the 1220s, the mendicant orders started to build churches in Germany. Of these, that at *Schwäbisch Gmünd* is generally considered to be one of the oldest surviving buildings. The Franciscan church at *Ulm* dates from about 1250.[82]

One of the earliest Dominican churches in France was the one in which Bonaventura taught in *Paris*. It followed the normal design for refectories[83] in that it had a row of piers along its middle axis, i.e. two naves, a choice which can possibly be explained by the fact that it was supposed to be a kind of lecture-hall for students. The Dominican church at *Toulouse*, the Jacobins church, is of the same type [146]. The first church, begun directly after the foundation of the university in 1229, and finished in *c.* 1235, consisted of a simple wooden-roofed rectangular building divided into two unequal aisles by five pillars. Parts of its west wall are retained in the present west façade. Between *c.* 1245 and 1252 this hall was extended eastwards in the form of a large chevet with a crown of eleven chapels separated by interior buttresses. This chevet stood at the same height as the older church, and was covered by a wooden roof, probably supported on diaphragm arches. Between *c.* 1275 and 1292 the eastern bay was given its present "palm" vault, the walls of the choir were raised, and the space divided into two aisles

150. Trier, Liebfrauenkirche, begun *c.* 1227. Exterior from the east

151. Trier, Liebfrauenkirche, begun *c.* 1227. Interior of choir and transepts

by tall centrally placed columns. Under Cardinal Guillaume de Peyre Godin, between 1323 and 1335, the old nave was demolished and replaced by the present structure, its columns matching those in the choir. The colossal building, reminiscent of an enlarged chapter house or monastic refectory, served as the mausoleum of St Thomas Aquinas, as a preaching hall, and as a choir for the friars, (positioned in the north aisle of the nave).[84]

The mendicant orders were free to choose any type of design, and they sometimes adopted that of Cistercian churches, as for instance in *S. Maria Novella* at *Florence*, begun after 1246, where the straight-ended main choir is adjoined by two almost square chapels, half as high as the main choir.[85] The use of pilasters on the piers between the chapels adds a note of classical antiquity to the effect of this otherwise Gothic church, but the pilasters on the piers in the crossing, while they are also classical in form, are Gothic in their proportions [147].

Through the consideration of all these buildings which were touched by the influence of the Gothic style, but which, at the same time, were permeated with local tradition, one can reach an historical judgement of the churches at Marburg and Trier.

The church of St Elizabeth at *Marburg* on the Lahn in

Hesse is known to have been begun in 1235 [148, 149]. The east end is trefoiled in plan, as at Noyon, and the nave has the form of a hall-church with two west towers [181]. The church, except for the upper parts of the towers and of the façade, was finally finished in 1283. It is not known whether the nave was originally intended to be built in the form of a hall church, but this was done soon after the completion of the choir and transepts, by *c.* 1244.[85A] The architect drew his inspiration for certain details from Reims and Soissons[86] – not, however, from the cathedral at Soissons, but from the church of Saint-Léger there, now no longer used as a church – and the disposition of the two rows of windows, one over the other, is also taken from this same building.[87] The triforium and the lower row of niches along the walls have been omitted, and tracery like that at Reims has been added. The double row of windows has been explained as a reminiscence of the chapels round French Gothic choirs. The same motif was repeated from about 1244 in the nave. It should probably be interpreted, however, as the expression of the architect's unwillingness to build very high windows, a form that architects did not dare to put into execution until much later.[87A]

The other Gothic church of this generation in Germany,

the *Liebfrauenkirche* at *Trier*, was probably begun around 1227, much was completed by 1253, and it was finished some time before 1283.[88] It is built on a central plan, even more emphatically so than the east part of Marburg; for not only the chancel and the transepts but also the west front is polygonal. Here, too, the windows are in two tiers; in the corners of the transepts, those of the lower tier form the entrances to the pairs of chapels which stand diagonally, as at Braine [127, 150, 151]. The tracery throughout the church is again similar to that at Reims, with sexfoils in the oculi, while at Marburg tracery appears only in the central windows of the choir and of the transepts. In both churches the abaci on the piers and the bases are round, but at Trier the ledge at the sill-line of the windows runs round the shafts, and the free-standing piers have rings round them at the same level, so that the interior seems to be divided by a horizontal plane, and the same feature is repeated at the sill-line of the upper windows. The lower parts of some of these upper windows are covered by the sloping roofs over the chapels, but instead of forming a triforium, they are treated as blind forms. The architect of Trier either was not acquainted with the new parts of Saint-Denis, which had been begun in 1231, or he preferred his own solution.[88A]

Both at Trier and at Marburg, the articulation of the exterior is a clear and logical product of the form of the interior. In both churches flying buttresses were unnecessary, and the combination of the buttresses and the windows between is treated according to the principle of Gothic relief. Both churches employ French Gothic elements, but they are used in the service of completely different types of building. The decisive characteristic of both is their originality; the freshness of their details and the beauty of their whole form are evidence that their architects had been deeply imbued with the spirit of the Gothic style. The fact that when they were built they were not in line with the style reached at Amiens and in the new parts of Saint-Denis must, of course, influ-ence one's judgement of them in terms of the history of style, but an architect can be old-fashioned and still create something of eternal value.

Although the Gothic style was transported beyond France by travelling French architects (e.g. William of Sens) there are few surviving records which name such architects. The 'lodge-book' of Villard de Honnecourt, dating to the 1220s or 1230s, has survived; and we know that Villard, besides visiting Reims, Laon and Lausanne, also went to Hungary.[89] But it is not certain if he was an architect or simply a gifted amateur with a keen interest in architecture.[89A]

8. REGULARITY OF STRUCTURE. PIERS WITH GROOVES. TRIRADIALS

Whereas originality distinguishes the architects of Marburg and Trier, it was to the credit of Gerhard, the architect of the cathedral at Cologne, that he continued the French trend of stylistic development with genuine understanding [152–4].

The Carolingian cathedral at *Cologne*, which was in a state of collapse, was burnt down on 26 April 1248, and, as soon as 15 August of the same year, the foundation-stone of the new cathedral was laid. The new plans can hardly have been finished in three and a half months, but Gerhard must have collected enough material in his notes made at Amiens, Notre-Dame in Paris, Beauvais, and Saint-Denis to be able to give his first instructions by the time that the foundation-stone was laid.[89B] The choir was consecrated in 1322, and, although some of the details of the original plan were altered during the construction of the later parts, it remained basically unchanged until the building of the west façade, when it was radically altered.[90]

Gerhard was familiar with the design for the choir at Amiens, where Thomas de Cormont had completed the nave clerestory, the choir aisle vaults and windows and the

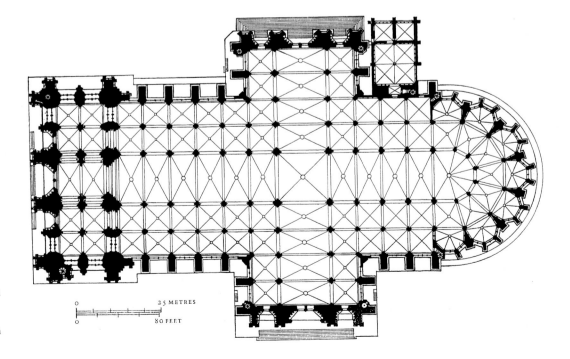

152. Cologne Cathedral, begun 1248. Interior of choir

153. Cologne Cathedral, begun 1248. Plan

0   25 METRES

0   80 FEET

154. Cologne Cathedral, begun 1248. Exterior of choir

ambulatory and the radiating chapels, probably by *c.* 1240. Sometime before 1258 (probably in the mid-1240s) work had begun on the upper parts of the transepts and choir, which were completed by 1269.[90A] The earliest phases of work on the Cologne choir overlap with the Amiens construction, and are dependent for many of their details on it. At Gerhard's death in *c.* 1260 the ambulatory and radiating chapels were substantially complete; two of them were finished by 1261. Under Gerhard's successor Master Arnold (active *c.* 1261–*c.* 1299) the sacristy was built, and the whole lower storey of the choir completed by *c.* 1265. By *c.* 1300 the upper choir and buttressing was finished, and the choir clerestory glazed in 1310. Arnold's son and successor, Master Johannes, worked under his father in the lodge, and replaced him *c.* 1300, at the level of the choir clerestory. The complexity of the blind tracery over the buttresses, and particularly in the gables over the exterior of the choir clerestory, is a new departure. The gable tracery consists of

triradial figures[91] in the form of an inverted letter Y with all the arms the same length. This motif in particular, and the complexity of the tracery in general, reflects a new influence from the west front of Strasbourg.[92]

Just as the introduction of this motif made exteriors more Gothic, because through it tracery conquered new fields, so in interiors the introduction of hollows between shafts is an extension of the Gothic principle of fusion to include the form of piers. At Amiens the addition of the four main shafts leaves the round piers fully visible, but at Cologne the architect has taken the step of dissimulating the form of the piers by cutting channels into them. These give a visual effect of shadowy grooves and soft transitions. Here the space within the church seems to enter the solids of the piers, whereas previously these solids had protruded into the space within the church, in accordance with the principle of the Romanesque. Now the fluidity of the upward movement seems due to the shafts only.[92A] At Amiens

155. Altenberg, Cistercian church, begun 1259. Exterior from the south-east

156. Altenberg, Cistercian church, begun 1259. Interior

Regnault de Cormont built gables over the windows of the glazed triforium; at Cologne the stream of forces rises from the floor to the vault without these interruptions, as it does also at Beauvais. The arrangement of statues on corbels in the choir at Cologne is modelled on that in the Sainte-Chapelle, but this horizontal belt of figures standing against the spatial limits of the interior does not inhibit the upward stream.[92B] At Amiens, the architect had begun to pierce even the spandrels in the triforium,[93] and at Cologne this innovation is adopted and also repeated in the interior.

The question as to how many of the forms in the upper storeys, especially those outside, were re-designed by Gerhard's successors has been dealt with in monographs. The addition of blind tracery to the buttresses serves to increase the sense of upward movement and of lightness, although the buttresses are relatively heavy.[93A] Even on the chapels, the tabernacles reduce the strength of the horizontal eaves-line and they, and the upper ends of the piers, combine to produce a rich stream of forces, reminding one of plants being drawn upwards by the sun. This impression is confusing to eyes unaccustomed to Gothic architecture, and may lead one to use the time-worn simile of the forest.

Forests, however, do not grow in the inexorably regular forms of the cathedral at Cologne. Gerhard outdid the architect of Amiens in regularity – a fact that should be verified by all who are not satisfied with mere impressions. The regularity and the normative quality of the cathedral at Cologne lie not only in the perfect mutual compatibility of the axes of all the spatial parts and of the thicknesses of the piers and their members, but even in the convincing clarity of every single one of the spatial parts. Gerhard is supposed to have designed the choir at *Mönchen-Gladbach*, built

157. Coutances Cathedral. Capital in ambulatory, c. 1220–38

ness, and the cathedral at Cologne has been criticized as being monotonous, cold, and too academic. The rational Frenchmen criticized it for its excessive rationalism, while it was this very rationalism which the irrational Germans praised in it. Was Gerhard a German? The fact that his wife was called Guda perhaps proves that she was German, but tells us nothing of the nationality of her husband. It would, of course, suit the nationalists to say that his mother was French. However, the most understanding appreciation of his work is that of Jakob Burckhardt, who said of the cathedral that it is 'the peerless manifestation of a great and heavenly genius'.[95A] In his work, the spirit of God embraces what is cold and what is warm, what is German and what is French, what is dead and what is living. But this cathedral is not dead; it is solemn, festive, and sublime, *fascinans* and *tremendum* at the same time, as clear as mathematics and as irrational as life itself.[95B]

158. Utrecht Cathedral. Interior of choir, begun after 1253

between 1256 and 1275. It is similar in type to the chapels at the east end of the cathedral at Cologne, but two bays longer, and it has shafts and a rib-vault inside, and buttresses, frontal pinnacles, and large expanses of wall outside: in other words it uses a greatly reduced number of individual members, but those which are used are slender and noble, achieving the ultimate degree of poise.[94]

The design for the Cistercian church at *Altenberg* has also been attributed to Gerhard [155, 156]. In spite of the fact that the building of this church took from 1259 to 1379, the original plan was followed throughout. As in some places in the cathedral at Cologne, the bases are round, but here the piers, too, are round, with thin, octagonal abaci, standing diagonally, so that one corner lies on the division between the bays. If this design has been rightly attributed to Gerhard, one must conclude that he never felt himself bound to any absolute architectural types, but certainly to norms.[95]

The concept of the norm can be defined as a unique case. One can quote the square, which represents a unique phenomenon among quadrangles, to explain this definition. A square can be of various sizes, and can occupy various positions within the universe, but its shape represents the only possible absolutely regular quadrangle. In dealing with an organism as complicated as the Gothic choir with ambulatories, one can only understand the concept of the norm by analogy with an example such as the square. At Reims and at Amiens one can feel the tendency towards a norm; but, viewed theoretically, they are single cases among many possible variants, just as every rectangle or every trazpezium is a single case among the many variants of its geometrical type: *Cologne* however gives the impression of being *the* Gothic choir, *the* final solution.

Aesthetically, regularity always creates a feeling of cool-

Although it is impossible to deduce the biological ancestors of an architect from his work, it is quite possible to recognize his spiritual ancestors from it. The relationship of the cathedral at Cologne with French works can be seen very clearly if one compares it with the cathedral of *León* in Spain, begun soon after 1254, and with the Angel Choir at *Lincoln*, built between 1256 and 1280. The Lincoln choir is truly English in its horizontalism, in the Norman gallery and the Norman wall-passage along the windows, in the splendour of its capitals and corbels, and in its star-vaults. León, on the other hand, is not specifically Spanish; it stands about as close to the French High Gothic as Cologne. Even the Angel Choir at Lincoln contains certain French elements, for instance the tracery in the east window, but the overall English character predominates, whereas one can see little that is specifically Spanish or German in character at León and Cologne respectively, because, in these two countries, the Gothic style had not yet created any tradition of its own. One can, of course, turn back to the national characteristics of Spanish and German Romanesque churches, but this nationalist search leads into uncharted territory; for national characteristics change, and, because of the unpredictability of individual personalities, a common denominator can rarely be found.

In Normandy, from *c.* 1220 to *c.* 1238 the choir of *Coutances* was built. It is an instructive contrast to the 'normative' qualitites of Cologne.[96] Compared with Cologne, many, or perhaps even all, of the details in this choir are old-fashioned, but its unusual and imaginative features, such as the staircases which have been inserted in the upper part of the inner ambulatory like oriels and the corbels sticking to the shafts of slender columns which support the ribs, make it uncommonly attractive [157]. It can be said that, if corbels on shafts can be allowed to support figures, as in the Sainte-Chapelle and at Cologne, they can also support ribs, but there is a subtle difference. Both this form and the staircases in their oriels at Coutances are extremely imaginative examples of akyrism. One can best appreciate this choir, with its double ambulatory, if one sees it as a foil to the strict spirituality of the choir at Cologne. Both are the fulfilment of certain human desires, and both widen the range of our sympathetic emotions, for akyrism and the norm are two equally valid alternatives.

The choir of the cathedral at *Utrecht* in Holland, too, is dependent on Cologne, though both the exterior with its simpler flying buttresses[97] and the interior with its unglazed triforium are less ambitious [158]. Only the ambulatory and radiating chapels date perhaps from 1254 (the year the construction is supposed to have begun) to *c.* 1300. The lower storey of the main choir, and its aisles and chapels, was probably begun in the first decade of the fourteenth century, and was complete by *c.* 1360. It has an arcade with no capitals but otherwise remains fairly faithful to what was begun in 1254 – fairly close to the norm. Compared with the choir at Cologne, the proportions have less élan. The absence of a choir-screen, while it stresses the Gothic idea of the interrelationship between the chancel and the choir aisles, at the same time makes the choir itself more sober, which suggests that originally such a screen may have been intended.[97A]

9. THE SHARPENING OF PROFILES. PIERS WITHOUT CAPITALS. THE OGEE CURVE

Work was begun on the upper parts of the choir and east transept walls at *Amiens* in the mid- to later 1240s [90], but the new generation of architects accepted the original design only where this was necessary to maintain a unity with the nave. The most noticeable changes are the introduction of a glazed triforium with gables (which could be called akyristic) in the interior, and the form of the flying buttresses, which have rows of tracery standing between their lower arches and their straight upper slopes. The other differences demand careful study. Durand has made such a study, and adds the criticism that the principles of the Gothic style had here been carried to the point of exaggeration and that the development of technical knowledge ('*science*') had stifled artistic sensibility. He writes: 'C'est presque le commencement de la décadence.'[98] Many critics have repeated this

159. Troyes, Saint-Urbain. Interior of choir and transept, begun 1262

judgement, and continue to do so, even to the extent of omitting his careful 'presque', but if this were true, then it would have been better had all the Gothic architects who worked from 1260 until well into the sixteenth century never lived at all.

These architects did not exaggerate the expression of the principles of the Gothic style: they merely developed it. They criticized the excessive volume of supports; they made profiles finer; they allowed concave channels to penetrate more successfully into solid masses; and they made pear-shaped members form sharp dividing lines among the soft transitions of light and shade. The dissolution of the wall had finally been achieved; the aim was now also to dissolve the solidity of piers, tracery, arches, arcades, and vaults. In this connexion it is characteristic that the mullions of the tracery in the choir at Amiens have, in their section, the double curve which had already appeared at Saint-Nicaise at Reims.[99]

This task of making the members sharper and more slender was taken up most energetically by the architect who in 1262 began building the choir of *Saint-Urbain* at *Troyes* [159, 160].[100] Although it has no ambulatory, and the windows could therefore be extended downwards, rather like those at Toul, their lower part is treated as a glazed triforium, forming a real spatial layer which, outside, projects beyond the surface of the windows. Outside, this triforium, treated like a grille, has steeply pitched gables which end at the line of the parapet of the upper gallery. From inside, the tracery of the glazed outside triforium openings can be seen through the open tracery of the inner ones. The spandrels of the tracery inside are pierced, and the surfaces beside the gables, like those beside the gables of the upper windows, are dissolved into tracery. The slenderness of all the members makes them appear to be made of metal. In the single bay of the choir which is half open to the choir aisles, the eastern half of

160. Troyes, Saint-Urbain. Exterior
of choir and transept, begun 1262

161. Carcassonne, St Nazaire.
Interior; nave begun *c.* 1096, choir
begun *c.* 1280

162. Carcassonne, St Nazaire, nave
begun *c.* 1096, choir begun
c. 1280. Plan

each of the two arches is lightened by blind tracery and the
western half by open tracery.[101]

On the piers of the arcades between the chancel and the
aisles, the shafts in the first bay beyond the crossing have
capitals, while the piers have none, rising uninterrupted and
penetrating the concave channel in the profile of the arcade.
This is repeated in the eastern transverse arch of the
crossing and in the other three arches of the crossing.
Although the line of the springing of the arches, in spite of
the partial deletion, remains quite clear here, its force has
been devalued.

Each of the transept façades contains two windows, and a
porch stands in front of them [160]. The buttresses supporting the vaults of the porches stand several yards clear of
the walls – a feature reminiscent of the flying buttresses
which were added to the chapter house at Lincoln. At
Troyes, however, they were part of the original plan. A
'Johannes Anglicus' is referred to in 1267 as 'magister fab-

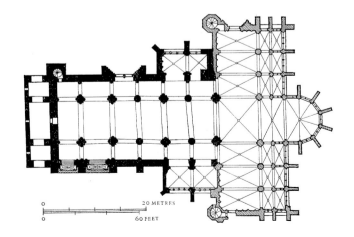

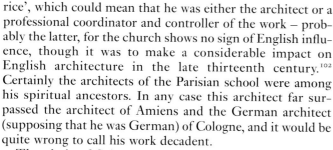

163. Carcassonne, Saint-Nazaire. North transept and choir, c. 1280–c. 1310

164. Sées Cathedral. Interior of choir, begun in the 1270s

rice', which could mean that he was either the architect or a professional coordinator and controller of the work – probably the latter, for the church shows no sign of English influence, though it was to make a considerable impact on English architecture in the late thirteenth century.[102] Certainly the architects of the Parisian school were among his spiritual ancestors. In any case this architect far surpassed the architect of Amiens and the German architect (supposing that he was German) of Cologne, and it would be quite wrong to call his work decadent.

The choir of Saint-Nazaire at *Carcassonne* [162, 163], begun around 1300, is in some ways similar to Saint-Urbain, but some of its details and profiles are both later and more highly developed than those at Troyes.[103] The connexion between the short choir and the adjoining chapels, and the similar openings between the other chapels, are variations of the form used at Troyes, producing an aisle to the transepts. Since the transepts are the same height as the chapels, the result is an almost transparent hall in which every spatial part is a fragment of the whole,[104] and this tendency to join all the spatial parts can be seen also in the fact that even the vertical parts of the cells are pierced. The piers continue above the abaci as at Troyes. The transepts and the choir at Saint-Nazaire form a surprising contrast to the dark nave with its tunnel-vault, begun about 1096, and the splendid tracery of the rose-windows in the transepts, too, is amaz-

ingly progressive [163]. Here the spandrels between the rose-windows and the pointed arches framing them already contain the Late Gothic form of the 'mouchette'. In several places the spherical triangle also plays an important role in the tracery. Outside, the almost flat roof seems to be a negation of the completely vertical stress of the windows and the buttresses, and there are no gables.

The desire to make the structural members more slender was also a main preoccupation of the architect of *Sées* about 1270 [164]. Here the arches of the arcade are crowned by gables. From their apexes shafts rise into the triforium and on into the windows of the clerestory, where the central mullions pass through the oculi of the tracery. This detail is similar to that of the shafts in the older nave which cross the sunken oculi, thereby assigning the two halves of each oculus to two different bays.[105] In the windows there are two strata, one in front of the other, as in the triforium of Saint-Urbain at Troyes. In the choir the inner one is glazed and the outer one open, while in the nave this is reversed.

This enthusiasm for tracery was taken up in the nave at *Minden* in Westphalia, in building in the 1250s and 1260s [165, 166]. The extreme transparency of this hall-church with round piers makes the tracery in the aisle windows the strongest focal point for the eye. The pointed arches in some of these windows are filled with fragmentary roses into which the lights below grow organically upwards. This trac-

167 Regensburg Cathedral. Exterior of the choir from the south. Begun 1273

165. Minden Cathedral. Interior of the nave, begun 1250s

166. Minden Cathedral. Exterior from the north, begun 1250s

ery is also the determining factor in the appearance of the exterior.[106]

Just as the cathedral at Cologne was bound up with stylistic developments in France, so was the cathedral at *Regensburg*, begun after a fire of 1273 [167]. It is true that the plan, with its three parallel choirs, was traditionally Bavarian, but the same cannot be said of the elevation, which in the choir may rely on such 'apside vitrée' as Saint-Urbain at Troyes or Saint-Sulpice-de-Favières.'[107] In this case it is known that the personal connexion which may have caused this influence was a meeting at the Council of Lyons in 1274 between Leo of Tundorf, Bishop of Regensburg, and Cardinal Ancher, who was the patron of Saint-Urbain.

The difficulty of applying the concept of the norm to the Gothic style is shown by a comparison between Cologne and Troyes. At Cologne the norm applies to the regularity achieved within the fertile architectural type of the choir with a double ambulatory, while at Troyes it refers to the extreme slenderness of all the supporting members in a building of a spatially simplified type.

As the cathedral at Regensburg may follows the design of Troyes, so the cathedral at *Clermont-Ferrand* stands side by side with that of Cologne (see above, p. 136). Since this church was begun by Jean Deschamps in about 1248, that is

in the same year as Cologne, it must be regarded as an independent piece of work based on the same premises. In 1272 the foundation stone was laid for the choir of *Narbonne* cathedral, though its design, and work on its foundations, had probably begun a year or so earlier.[107A] In 1273 the choir of *Limoges* cathedral was officially founded, though again preliminary work may have stated *c*. 1270.[107B] The new choir of *Toulouse* cathedral was begun in 1274–75 as a direct response to Narbonne,[107C] while from 1276/7 onwards Narbonne masons, aware also of the latest developments at Toulouse, began the choir of *Rodez* cathedral.[107D] The principal designs of these four cathedrals have been attributed to Jean Deschamps, though he seems to have had influence only on the planning of the choirs of Clermont-Ferrand and Limoges.[107E] All these works are very close to what we have called the Gothic norm, and the original parts of Limoges, especially, are convincing variations of the most correct Gothic style. The increasingly slender shafts, the continuation of piers above the line of the springing, as at Carcassonne, and the appearance of a ridge-rib at Narbonne all show that this generation did not have an academic approach to the concept of the norm.

For this reason it is wrong to call the phase with which we are dealing 'doctrinaire Gothic'; indeed the term itself is a

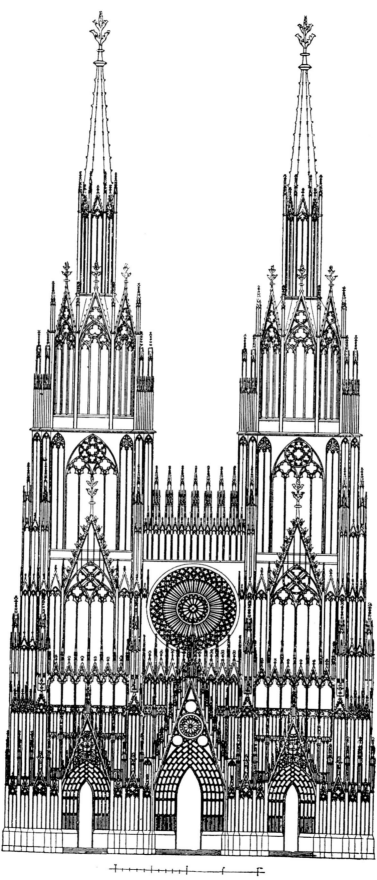

168. Strasbourg Cathedral. Plan B, 1275–7, redrawing of the original plan by Dehio-Bezold

sign of academic prejudice. A doctrine is a series of rules drawn up for instructional purposes, but the word doctrinaire suggests a narrow-minded and pedantic interdict against deviation from a set of rules. What Gerhard and his contemporaries both sought and found was not a set of petty rules imposed by pedantic schoolmasters, but an ideal – the perfect realization of a dream.[108]

10. AUTONOMOUS TRACERY

There was an inscription in the cathedral at *Strasbourg* which stated that Erwin von Steinbach began the west façade in 1277, and, while the inscription has not been preserved, there is reliable proof of its former existence. Erwin is first named in 1284, and the year of his death, 1318, is recorded on his tombstone.[109]

An early design for the façade may have been made by one of Erwin's predecessors. The so-called Plan A, now in the Musée de l'Œuvre at Strasbourg, may be a copy of this (now lost) design. It is reminiscent in some details of Saint-

169. Strasbourg Cathedral. West front, begun 1277, rose window finished *c*. 1318, second storey of towers complete by 1365, belfry between them planned *c*. 1360/5, executed 1380, octagon of steeple 1399–1419, spire 1419–39

170. Strasbourg Cathedral. Detail of the lower stories of the West front

Nicaise at Reims, and more closely of the north and south transept façades of Notre-Dame in Paris. It dates to the 1250s.[109A]

According to Reinhard Liess, a later design, Plan B, was made by Erwin [168]. He built tracery about two feet in front of the façade, transferring to the façade the principle of the two layers which had been developed in wall-passages [169, 170]. If in imagination one removes the front layer and considers only the façade behind – hardly a feasible experiment, admittedly – one can see that Erwin knew Laon and

both the cathedral and Saint-Nicaise at Reims, but he took the vertical fusion between the different storeys a stage further. This is especially true of the middle gallery, which does not extend horizontally to include the breadth of the towers. It is possible that this solution was suggested to Erwin by the free-standing gallery between the towers at Notre-Dame in Paris, which was built *c.* 1235–40, and by the general impression of Saint-Urbain. Throughout the façade, the zigzag lines of the rows of gables outweigh the effect of the horizontal lines. The emphasis on vertical lines combines

172. Regensburg, Dominican church, begun *c.* 1240. Interior

with the separation of the whole front surface to give the impression that this thin structural layer stands by its own strength. Its abstract geometrical pattern makes it appear autonomous, independent of physical aims and considerations, imbuing the church with its immaterial spirit [169].[111]

Plan B has been called 'the most beautiful thing that was ever devised in the Gothic style anywhere in the world' (Dehio) [168]. It is natural to mourn the fact that its boldness, verticality and spirit of extravagance and fantasy was modified by Master Erwin in the portal zones, and rejected in the upper stories. Erwin revised it in Plans C(?) and D probably for economic as well as stylistic reasons.[111A] The upward stream of forces was moderated; the vertical stone rods, which stand in a free rhythm, express a belief in the independence of imaginative creation. The changes made by succeeding generations are harder to understand,[112] but the deliberate decreasing of solid masses was already predominant in the storey occupied by the doorways, where the pinnacles which shoot up over the gables above the three doorways are thin to the point of fragility, and the slender tabernacles are far longer than the figures which stand in them [170]. It should be considered whether the so-called Perpendicular, beginning in St Stephen's Chapel in London in 1292, was derived from the façade of Strasbourg Cathedral.[112A]

The façade of the north transept of the cathedral at *Rouen*, the Portail des Libraires, was begun in 1280 [171], and was thus a few years later than the façade at Strasbourg. At the same time the lower parts of the façade of the south transept, the Portail de la Calende, were begun. Most of the charm of the north façade lies in the fact that the front walls

of the canons' quarters facing the courtyard and to the north of the cathedral join the façade and have on them blind architectural members which continue the design of the doorway. Thus this façade is drawn into a unity with the world outside differently from that at Strasbourg; here the interior seems to reach out on to the exterior. The south façade, where this is not the case, shows that, even without the unique projection into the courtyard which appears in the Portail des Libraires, tracery had already become an autonomous substitute for the wall.[113]

The doorways of the north transept of the cathedral at *Bordeaux*[114] and the right-hand doorway in the west façade at *Mantes* follow the general lines of the doorways at Rouen, and the doorway of the *Liebfrauenkirche* at *Mainz*, which was pulled down in 1809, also belonged to the same group.[115] The form of the gable over the Portail de la Calende is repeated at Mantes, but here it is pierced by a spherical triangle surrounded by three quatrefoils.

The Lady Chapel which was added to the east end of the cathedral at *Rouen* from 1302 has pierced gables rising high above the eaves-line, but it is otherwise extremely conserva-

173. Florence, S. Croce, begun 1294/5. Interior

174. Freiburg im Breisgau, Franciscan church, begun *c.* 1262

tive, a copy of the *Sainte-Chapelle* at *Saint-Germer*, which was built between 1259 and 1267.[115A] The unknown architect of the Lady Chapel at Rouen was a contemporary of Erwin. Thus in every age there are both progressive spirits and those who are content with the heritage received from their fathers.

11. THE GOTHIC WALL

In spite of the many different spatial types and structural members used in them, the churches of the mendicant orders still form a single group. St Bernard's sermons were directed mainly at the monks of his own order, whereas St Francis and St Dominic preached to the people. The older orders felt that, thanks to their religious life, they were aristocrats, whereas the friars professed themselves to be of the lowest class, servants of all the people, the rich and the poor, the strong and the weak, the healthy and the infirm, the educated and the ignorant. They needed large meeting-places where the people could crowd round the preacher, not show-places, but purely utilitarian buildings. They were to be churches, but churches quite unlike the cathedrals, and even at their finest and most elegant they retain these secular, unassuming, and everyday characteristics. In the development of the metaphysical attitude, this absorption of the

individual into the universe, this recognition of him as a mere part of a greater scheme of things was specifically Gothic, if one applies the architectural, stylistic term to the civilization as a whole. If, then, the spiritual attitude of the friars was more Gothic than that of the bishops and princes, one would expect their churches also to be more Gothic than the cathedrals and the churches of the older orders. Yet, on the contrary, their most obvious quality is a so-called reduction (*Reduktionsgotik*) which, though it is a specifically Franciscan and Dominican expression of the principle of asceticism, is not specifically Gothic. This principle of reduction even led to the building of churches with flat ceilings and, where rib-vaults already existed, to the preservation of large expanses of wall-surface. One need only consider the glazed triforium in the church of Saint-Urbain at Troyes to realize why the friars not only built no glazed triforia, but in fact no triforia at all. Are these walls therefore Early Christian or Romanesque in style, or are they Gothic?

Between 1248 and 1260, the *Franciscans* built the choir of their church at *Cologne* with long windows with tracery, reaching far down and dominating the whole interior. These in themselves are sufficient to make a church Gothic. Verbeek's post-war examinations of the church, which had been badly damaged by bombing, revealed traces in the northern junction between the choir and the nave of what he thought to be an intended hall nave. More recently, however, Schenkluhn has shown these traces to be evidence of the intention to build a basilican nave, but to separate it from the choir by a non-projecting transept. In the event, the transept idea was abandoned and the present basilican nave, completed probably in its essentials between 1275–97, was built directly against the western pillars of the choir.[116] The sloping roofs over the aisles force the sills of the windows in the nave up above the line of the springing of the vault, and the surfaces of the walls between the arcade and the windows are completely closed. Each of the short round piers has four frontal shafts and a plinth formed of a square standing diagonally, with chamfered corners. The shafts continue from above the abaci up to the vault; the arches of the arcade have a Gothic profile, and the windows contain tracery. There can be no doubt that all this is Gothic, as is the exterior with its buttresses, which rise far above the eaves of the sloping roofs over the aisles, and its flying buttresses. However, on the outside, the wall on to which the arches of the flying buttresses abut is smooth, just as it is in the interior. When the nave was begun, the choir of the cathedral in the same city had already been under construction for several years, so that the choice of these bare, unbroken walls cannot be put down to ignorance of French Gothic style.

Even clearer evidence of this tendency can be seen in the *Dominican* church at *Regensburg*, where the choir was begun *c.* 1240 and was in use by 1254. By 1271 the nave was under construction, and was completed towards the end of the thirteenth century [173].[117] Here again, the long windows in the choir dominate the interior. In the nave the shafts rise uninterrupted to the vault, but in the choir they stand on corbels which project at the level of the apexes of the arcade, so that here the wall can be seen even more clearly as a continuous surface. The piers in the nave are different from those at Cologne; they are octagonal with four shafts, and since the arches of the arcade are of the same depth as the piers and the wall rising above, and since their front corners begin in the void, over the diagonal sides of the piers, corbels are inserted underneath them. The inner part of the profile of the arcade has hollows, and this profile combines with the corbels to give an even more intense impression of slenderness and lightness to the walls than was achieved at Cologne. In addition, the slender shafts and the slender ribs with their hollows give the vault, too, a sense of lightness. It is these details that make the walls Gothic. As a result of them the wall does not appear to be a three-dimensional mass, but to be stretched like a membrane, and to stand up by its own strength. Finally, the profiles in the jambs of the tracery windows intensify the impression of attenuation of the wall.

Hollows in the profile of arcades were introduced at a very early stage by the friars. They appear, for instance, in the Dominican church at *Esslingen*, begun about 1255, and in this church, again, the shafts in the choir rise from the floor, while those in the nave stand on corbels. Here, too, the profile of the arcade makes the wall appear to be stretched between the shafts.[117A]

The *Franciscan* church at *Freiburg* im Breisgau, surpasses even the Dominican church at Regensburg [174]. Here the arches of the arcade die into the piers without the interruption of capitals. It is not only the aspect of the choir with its rib-vault, in building from 1262, that makes this church Gothic; even the nave, though it has a higher flat ceiling (restored in the Baroque period) and no shafts on the walls, is made Gothic by the profile of its arcade.[117B] The penetration of the arcade arches into the piers has analogies in French churches of the same generation, for instance in the cathedral at *Narbonne*, begun *c.* 1271.

By no means all the great number of the churches of the mendicant orders belong to the group with Gothic walls. There are also cases where the same kind of walls as those in the Dominican church at Esslingen exist, but give a completely different effect. Such a case can be seen in the Dominican church at *Erfurt*, where the vault begins directly over the apexes of the arcade, so that the continuous surfaces of the wall and the structure of the vault are seen as opposites, and in this case the high position of the windows makes the lighting of the cells of the vault unusually complicated. The choir was begun in the late 1260s, and the nave was not completed until the first half of the fifteenth century.[117C]

The Franciscan church of *S. Croce* in *Florence* was begun probably by Arnolfo di Cambio some thirty years after the choir at Erfurt in 1294/95 [173].[118] The chapels at the east end, set one beside another, can be traced back to S. Maria Novella and the Cistercian type on which S. Maria Novella was modelled. The breadth of the nave allows a view into the central and the two adjoining chapels which look like 'a façade facing inwards' (Paatz). Here, too, the wall predominates and seems to be thin, and the whole church is transparent and clear. Above the abaci on the piers, flat pilasters rise to the open timber roof, and the walls are even thinner than the piers. In spite of the frontality thus displayed, there are none of the elements of classical antiquity which are so

175. Vendôme, La Trinité, begun *c.* 1280. Interior looking east

strong in S. Maria Novella and SS. Trinità, and so anti-Gothic in effect. In its dimensions, S. Croce is one of the most monumental of all friars' churches; it is noble in the delicacy of its profiles and the perfect balance of its proportions, and ascetic in the simplicity of the means employed in it. In the spirit of St Francis of Assisi, religion was united with the worldly and the personal; S. Croce is the formal symbol of this unity, expressed in the language of architecture. Even outside, there is unity between the cubical form of the whole and the flat surfaces of the parts – between spiritual grandeur and humility.

12. THE CULMINATION OF THE HIGH GOTHIC STYLE[118A]

The church of Saint-Urbain at Troyes, which was begun in 1262, was followed a generation later by that at *Saint-Thibault* in the Côte d'Or, where the original choir has been preserved, and this building, in spite of its unglazed triforium, stylistically surpasses its model. Here the blind tracery on the lower band of the wall is repeated in the lower windows, in the triforium openings, and in the upper windows, and the slenderness of all its members makes the choir look as if it were of filigree. The capitals on the shafts sup-

176. Rouen, Saint-Ouen, begun 1318. Interior

porting the ribs, which rise from the floor, are so small that one hardly notices them.[119]

The shafts supporting the wall-arches in the transepts of the *cathedral* at *Troyes*, which also rise from the floor, are similar to those at Saint-Thibault. The slenderness of the members strengthens the emphasis on vertical lines and reduces their importance in favour of that of light, pierced surfaces, creating an elevation admirably adapted to the principles of the rib-vault. Here the problem set by the architects of the Transitional style had been solved, in so far as it applied to interiors.[119A]

In the nave at *Bayonne*, which was begun in the first third of the fourteen century, all five shafts in front of each pier also rise straight from the floor,[119B] and, even at *Vendôme*,[120] where the shafts supporting the wall-arches only begin at the level of the triforium, the essential idea is, once again, the combination of slender structure with pure light [175]. It can be said, paradoxically, that these architects wanted, as far as possible, to use pure light as their only building material. This is true also of the choir of the cathedral at *Nevers*, begun in the 1230s or 1240s, but for the most part built after a fire of 1308 and consecrated in 1331,[120A] and of the nave of the cathedral at *Auxerre*, begun in 1309. In the latter, the capitals in the arcade are very small and those on the subsidiary shafts have been omitted altogether, so that they continue into the mouldings of the arcade in the form

of a roll. The triforium openings consist of pure tracery without capitals.[120B]

The tendency to purity, correctness, and elegant preciosity reaches its final maturity in the church of *Saint-Ouen* at *Rouen* [176]. Here building continued to the plan of 1318 even after the completion of the choir, part of the transept, and first two piers of the nave in 1339, and only a careful search will reveal the slight deviations of later architects who worked on the church until its completion in 1536. Some of the shafts are so slender that they look almost like mere lines: they are so delicate that their third dimension almost disappears, and the whole elevation amounts to almost nothing more than a surface crossed by lines of varying thickness, pointing upwards – floating dreamily in space, elegant yet ascetic.[121]

It was in this sense that the generation must have intended its work to be interpreted. When the Romanesque nave of the cathedral at Auxerre was pulled down in 1309, its destruction was justified by the belief that it was built 'rudi

177. Freiburg-im-Breisgau Minster. West tower *c.* 1280–*c.* 1340

178. Cologne Cathedral. West front, designed *c*. 1300 or slightly before. Construction began with the south tower in the late 1350s, which by 1560 had reached the top of its first storey (with the double windows). The remainder is mostly 1842–80, built according to Plan F.

scemate'.[122] Indeed, about 1300 even Reims and Amiens appeared far too robust and worldly, too full of sap and vitality. The idea that all the problems of the Gothic style had been solved and that these epigones had therefore lost 'the originality of feeling and the freshness of inspiration' is a fallacy:[123] the problems were not solved until metallic hardness and brittleness, unworldliness and spirituality had been reached. To criticize the Gothic style for becoming more Gothic is an unhistorical line of reasoning.

The critics of the allegedly 'doctrinaire' Gothic style change their tune to highest praise when they speak of the tower of the minster at *Freiburg-im-Breisgau*, which was

179. Cologne Cathedral. Plan F *c.* 1300

architect from Strasbourg, on the balustrade, the octagon (built around the belfry) and the spire [177].[123A] This tower has been justly admired for the skilful merging of the square base into the octagon, for the diagonal position of the smaller turrets at its corners, for the piercing of its main sides with slits filled with tracery and surmounted by gables which cut through the base-line of the spire, and finally for the dissolution of the very surfaces of the spire into a filigree of tracery. The spire is not a protection against rain and snow – that function is fulfilled by a flat stone roof at the foot of the pyramid – but a purely artistic form: it is pure Gothic style, without a trace of the Romanesque. This transference of tracery into the surface of a spire is akyristic, but the quality of the filigree work above the closed lower storeys has effectively silenced any criticism by rationalists.

The spire at Freiburg was finished some time before 1340, but it may have been designed as early as 1280. It therefore probably influenced the design for the openwork spires of the west towers at *Cologne* which appear in the great Plan F of *c.* 1300 [179].[124] When Plan F was redis-covered in the nineteenth century it was accurately used as the basis for the reconstruction of and completion of the façade. This final design was preceded by several earlier ones which have been penetratingly and convincingly analysed.[125] Plan A, now in the Akademie der Künste in Vienna, includes five doorways at the west façade, to cor-respond to the double aisles of the nave, and it is perhaps an expression of Gerhard's original intentions. The great Plan F for the façade, dated *c.* 1300, and attributed to Master Johannes, shows a familiarity with the Strasbourg west façade (its lower storeys) and its drawings. All the Cologne plans for the west façade, the south tower, and the adjoining nave clerestorey and its buttressing (Plan A to Plan Gu3) date from the last quarter of the thirteenth cen-tury and the first quarter of the fourteenth. Recent excava-tions under the south tower have shown, however, that the foundations for the south aisle of the nave were not laid until about 1325, that the south tower foundations date to around, or shortly before, 1357, and that the construction of the south tower above ground was only underway in the 1360s, with its ground floor complete in *c.* 1370/80. Almost two generations, therefore, separate the drawing-up of the plans for the western parts of the cathedral and their faith-ful execution.[125A] When work stopped on the west front and towers in 1560 the south aisles of the nave were built up to vault springing, the south tower had reached to just above the top of the first storey, and the north tower had barely topped the socles of the portals (though it had got to the top of the ground floor on its east side). Nevertheless, all later architects, in a spirit of reverent conformity, adhered closely to the original designs. In 1842 work began on the completion of the whole cathedral, including the west façade, once more in the strictest conformity to the original plans [178].

Plan E, now in the Dombauhütte at Cologne, shows a cross-section through the upper storey of the south tower, facing towards the east, and also the arch between the tow-ers, which is not separated from the responds by capitals. The piers supporting this arch are hidden by a series of shafts which are not clearly differentiated in the drawing.

added to the west side of the nave from about 1280. Its ground floor is open to the interior and has the form of a hall, richly decorated. Above it there is a chapel which has a narrow window with tracery standing over the gable of the doorway below. When the clock storey had been completed, the bell-cage was added and left open. Work then pro-ceeded, almost certainly under the personal direction of an

180. Oppenheim, St Catherine, nave designed 1317. Exterior from the south

The great height of the piers makes it appear that they themselves are slightly arched. However, the shafts supporting the ribs have capitals and thus give the vault its self-sufficiency.[125C]

As the various designs followed one another, the number of doorways was reduced to three and the outer pair was replaced by windows. In the storey above, each of these groups consisting of a window and a doorway is surmounted by a pair of windows, separated by a narrow buttress crowned with a pinnacle which reaches up far into the space in front of the single window in the next storey above.[126] The two towers finally end in octagons and spires. The layers of the façade project one in front of another, and the gables all cut across the line of the lower storey, but, compared with Reims, the distances by which they project have been reduced. The relief is essentially flat, with members like mere lines, and the whole is characterized by a sense of tension. In many places capitals have been omitted. This façade was designed a decade or so before the beginning of the choir of Saint-Ouen at Rouen; it is the last great work of the culmination of the High Gothic style, and at the time of the 'classic' solution to the problem of making façades into Gothic unities. Expressed in a tautology, style, in the sense of formal unity, depends on the conformity of every member. In the façade at Cologne every single detail is determined by the form which first appeared in the Sainte-Chapelle – that is, pointed openings between buttresses, surmounted by Gothic gables which pierce the horizontal line immediately above.

Schnaase was the first to recognize the façade at Cologne as a 'classic' work, although his judgement was based largely on the execution of the details and although he was already critical of the fact that the lower windows were co-ordinated with the doorways. It is now usual to object also to the pressure to which the central section seems to be subjected by the two towers. One need only compare this façade with those on other double-aisled churches, such as Paris and Bourges, to see that it is all of a piece. The replacement of a rose-window by a long, pointed window had already been introduced, some time after 1260, by the architect of the church of St Elizabeth at Marburg, who came from the Cologne lodge. In the tracery at Cologne, spherical quadrangles and triangles play a great role, but not to the exclu-

181. Marburg, St Elizabeth. Nave, *c.* 1244–65

182. Heiligenkreuz, Cistercian church. Choir, begun *c.* 1288, consecrated 1295

sion of circular forms. Schnaase wrote his criticism in 1873, while the façade was being built, and he condescendingly excused the design by saying that it aimed at emphasizing the predominance of the towers, using the words, 'Is there any Gothic church, or, more especially, any Gothic façade, which has no faults?', to which he added, 'It is advisable to concede faults, in order to avoid misunderstanding the laws of art and of historical development.' To establish laws – and what laws can one establish? – is to create faults oneself; yet historical development is an objective fact. The architect who designed the façade at Cologne studied Erwin's Plan B critically and found that the double aisles were the essential feature on which he must base his design. The creativeness of his criticism lay in his reduction of the horizontal lines, in his emphasis on flat surfaces, in the strict conformity in which he designed the parts, and, combined with this, in his radical subordination of individual details. The façade is big in size: but, more than this, it also has greatness.

The south side of the nave of St Catherine at *Oppenheim*, designed in 1317, will at once bring out the greatness of the façade at Cologne.[127] The site on which the church stands made it essential that this south side should be the façade

[180]. In the two lower storeys, consisting respectively of the chapels and the aisle, the wall is totally dissolved into tracery, and in the upper storey the row of gables, and the pinnacles, which stand diagonally, form the crown, not only of the upper windows, but of the whole exterior. The row of four bays led to the inclusion of large roses in the first and fourth windows, and within these circles and in the spandrels above them spherical polygons are used. These great circles predominate; they immediately attract the eye and their position at the sides, instead of at a non-existent centre, gives the whole composition an explosive character. In its details, for instance in the triradial figures in the gables, Oppenheim stands at the same stage of development as the façade at Cologne. Although it has the same splendour and maturity and the same Gothic projection of one layer in front of another, the different problems at Oppenheim led to the rejection of the self-containment of Cologne. Oppenheim, in fact, has richness, but not greatness.[127A]

The culmination of the High Gothic style can also be taken to include the cathedrals of Lichfield and York in England. In the nave at *Lichfield*, begun around 1265, groups of three shafts each rise straight from the floor, and of these the lateral ones and those within the arcade openings are pear-shaped. Behind the shafts, as they rise up the wall, there are cinquefoils, each belonging to two bays, as at Sées. In the nave at *York*, begun in 1291, the triforium is united with the windows above, and the vertical fusion in each bay harmonizes with the horizontal fusion of the fourteenth-century wooden lierne-vault, which was made in 1354, was burnt in 1840 and replaced by a replica soon afterwards.[127B]

Both churches have pairs of towers at the west front. At Lichfield, the storey occupied by the doorways runs into the gallery immediately above, forming a single, uninterrupted horizontal band. Above this the great central window cuts through the horizontal lines, and only from there on do the vertical lines predominate. At York, the buttresses project far forward. From the very first the design was intended to emphasize the predominance of the verticals, and this idea was fully realized in the upper parts which were built by architects of the fourteenth and fifteenth centuries in their own idioms. If one compares these two façades with that at Cologne, one can see that the solution reached at Cologne was the purer one.[127C]

13. THE SPREAD OF THE GOTHIC STYLE, 1250–1320

The churches of the mendicant orders cannot strictly be called High Gothic, whether this term is taken to mean the style of the nave at Amiens or that of the west façade at Cologne; this is equally true of many other buildings, of which one can say that they were built during the High Gothic period, but not that they are true representatives of that style. However, this must not be taken to mean that the term 'High Gothic' is a pure convention, a mere aid to classification. Where it refers to the central geographical territory of the Gothic style, the term is certainly valid; where it refers to works created outside this central area it serves as a system of co-ordinates with which to measure against the norms what remained retardative, and more important, what was an original creation of the peripheral schools. It is always preferable to evaluate each work on its own merits – indeed it is one's duty to do so – but this need not prevent one from recognizing these works as precursors of the national ramifications of the Late Gothic style, and thus integrating them into the general scheme of the development of the Gothic style.[127D]

These buildings can be divided into three main groups: those in which Gothic features are combined with the characteristics of the hall-church; those French churches in which a vessel accompanied by lateral chapels instead of aisles is built in a Gothic style; and those Italian churches in which Gothic and classical elements are first combined.

From 1017, when the chapel of St Bartholomew at Paderborn was built, the hall-church had been accepted as a German form, and in the twelfth century a number of such churches were built in Bavaria.[128] When the rib-vault was introduced, the forms that had resulted from it in France also had to be incorporated in German churches.[129] The nave of St Elizabeth at *Marburg* [181], the cathedral of

Paderborn, and the Munster-kirche at *Herford* represent the stage of development that had been reached by about 1240–50. The choir at *Heiligenkreuz* in Austria represents a later phase in the history of the hall-church [182].[129A] The choir of the Cistercian church at *Lilienfeld*, begun between 1206 and 1209, and consecrated in 1230, is a basilica with a polygonal apse, but surrounded by choir aisles and a straight-ended ambulatory in the form of double-aisled hall spaces.[129B] At Heiligenkreuz, also a Cistercian church, the choir has the form of a hall-church with three vessels each containing three almost square bays.[130] The slender piers have an octagonal core, but only their four diagonal faces are left free. The two sides facing the nave and the aisles are further covered by three pear-shaped shafts, and the two sides on the longitudinal axis are covered by a broad projection which has an undulating profile at the corners and a round shaft in the middle [183]. The shafts have capitals, but the flat, diagonal faces of the columns are only separated from the vault by narrow bands continuing the abaci. The spatial forms of the hall and the piers combine to give an effect that is almost Late Gothic in style. In the tracery, the way in which the central one of the three lights runs smoothly into the pairs of cinquefoils introduces an ogee arch. The extensive dissolution of the wall-surfaces by the two long windows in each bay, and the (over-restored) ornamental grisaille glass, dictated by the rules of the order, fills the choir with a bright light, which seems even brighter

183. Heiligenkreuz, church, plan of a pier, *c.* 1288–95

184. Osnabrück, St John. 1256–92

185. Albi Cathedral, 1282–1390. Interior; *coro c.* 1474–83

187. Albi Cathedral, 1282–1390. Exterior

by contrast with the nave (built between 1136 and 1160) with its square piers, its broad arcade arches, and its ribs with their rectangular section, like those in Lombardy – all factors that tend, in a basilica, to separate the aisles from the nave, and to emphasize the heaviness of the architectural members. The progressiveness of the choir has led certain historians to claim that it was built about 1360. But Dagobert Frey's work on this subject has clearly shown that the choir that we know is indeed the one that was consecrated in 1295.[131]

The church of St John at *Osnabrück* [184] was built between 1256 and 1292, a few years before Heiligenkreuz. Here the heavy square piers with slender shafts on the corners are, in spite of the slenderness of the ribs that rise from

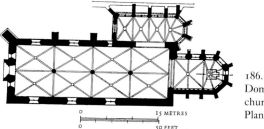

186. Imbach, Dominican church, 1280s. Plan

these shafts, a remnant of Romanesque frontality. Only the tracery is fully Gothic in character.[132]

In France there are a few examples of later thirteenth-century hall churches – at *Nogent-les-Vierges* (Oise),[132A] at *Montataire* (Oise),[132B] at *Waville* (Meurthe-et-Moselle),[132C] and the nave at *Mézin* (Lot-et-Garonne). The latter, although built about 1250, has heavy transverse arches and ribs, as if the architect had never heard of Amiens.[133] Apart for the Jacobins at Toulouse and the Dominican church in Paris, the Dominicans built a regular double-nave hall church at *Agen* in south west France.[133A]

The hall-church, in its Gothic form, was quickly accepted in Germany. The nave at *Essen* was begun in 1275,[133B] the nave at St Severus at *Erfurt* begun around 1308,[133C] the choir at *Verden on the Aller* begun soon after 1274 and complete by 1311,[133D] the nave at *Meissen* sometime between 1287 and 1291,[134] and the nave of the church of Our Lady at *Friedberg* begun in 1310.[134A] In the 1280s the Dominican nuns built a double-naved church at *Imbach* [186] in Austria,[135] in which the choir still has a sexpartite vault. The free-standing piers between the two naves are in line with the centre of the choir, a division which has analogies in Gotland.[136]

The second group of churches involved in the spread of the High Gothic style, in which the nave was given lateral chapels instead of aisles, was the product of the traditions of the Romanesque style in southern France. The theory that this form was adopted after the ravages of the Norman and Saracen armies because it afforded greater protection against fire is unconvincing, since the same armies also ravaged other districts, where different spatial types were developed.[137] There was a classical tradition in this district; tunnel-vaults in any case produce the typically Romanesque exclusion of the outer world, the atmosphere of religious concentration, and the single, unequivocal direction towards the altar. The replacement of the tunnel-vault by the rib-vault produced a new vivacity. With the addition of lateral chapels, the relative heights of the nave and the chapels became decisive. Low chapels create an atmosphere of mystery, while high ones can almost give the effect of a hall-church.

Saint-Michel in the Basse Ville at *Carcassonne* is a church of this type, in which the lateral chapels reach to about two-thirds the height of the nave.[138] Built towards the end of the thirteenth century, it is broad and generally rather low, with oculi over the chapels (the tracery in them is modern). The long lancet windows in the apse determine the general atmosphere of the whole church. The nave vaults of this church, and its sister parish church, Saint-Vincent in the Basse Ville, are seventeenth or eighteenth-century additions.

Originally, timber roofs were supported at the bay divisions by large pointed diaphragm arches, held in place by massive exterior buttresses, between which were fitted tall vaulted cellular chapels, giving on to the interior and supporting their upper walls, opened with large windows. The spacious width of these interiors recall the diaphragm-arched Cistercian dormitories at Poblet and Santes Creus; but they also anticipate and parallel the great *nef unique* vaulted structures of Catalonia and Languedoc (the cathedrals of Albi and Montpellier).[138A]

The cathedral of Sainte-Cécile at *Albi*, begun in 1282 and completed to the original design in the last years of the fourteenth century, also belongs to the type of church with a single nave with lateral chapels. In all such churches, the exterior wall of the chapels appears, aesthetically, to be the primary plane. The emptiness of the interior space must originally have created a magnificent effect. In the early sixteenth century, however, a gallery was built into the chapels, creating a lower zone of darkness. Between 1474 and *c.* 1483 the *coro* was added; it is a splendid example of pure divisional space [185, 284]. Even with these alterations the church shows great individuality: it is Gothic in style, but neither specifically High Gothic nor Late Gothic. Externally it looks fortified, with a single entrance from the south side. Its patron, Bishop Bernard de

188. Barcelona Cathedral. Interior looking east, 1298– *c.* 1430

189. Palma Cathedral, begun 1306. Interior

190. Palma Cathedral, begun 1306. Exterior from the south

Castanet, was a Dominican Inquisitor who persecuted the remnants of the Albigensians with diabolical cruelty, but who nevertheless seems to have been anxiously preoccupied with the need for defence. There is a series of rounded buttresses [187], reminiscent of Assisi, and a heavy west tower with no entrance, which has round blocks of stone at the corners and archers' slits instead of windows. The lower storeys of the tower were under construction between 1355 and 1365, though their general design may have been conceived with the original late thirteenth-century plan. This would make their design overlap chronologically with the construction of the spire of Freiburg Minster; so its Gothic character should be measured against such a design. The middle storeys have large, blind, semicircular arches, the round stair-turret reaching to their level. The three upper storeys date from 1485.[139] The shafts and ribs, the tracery in the pointed windows, and the gargoyles are Gothic features, and make even this type of building Gothic.

From outside a hall-church looks like a solid block, the division of its interior into two or three naves coming as a surprise. Whether this division is Romanesque or Gothic depends, as it does in a basilica, on the form of the piers and the mouldings of the members, and on the tendency either to isolate the spatial parts from one another, or to blend them as complementary parts of the whole that is visible from outside.[139A]

Basilicas in which the central vessel is only a little higher than the aisles and which, therefore, have only small windows, or none at all, are closely related to the hall-church. To complain that this makes the central vessel dark is to forget that the architects must have been equally aware of this gloom. If they had let large windows into the outside walls of the aisles, as at Heiligenkreuz, they could have made the central vessel much lighter; but, since they actually decreased the amount of light coming from the sides by adding chapels, this diminished light must have been their aim.

This aim was quite obviously present in the mind of the architect of the cathedral in *Barcelona* [188]. The choir, built between 1298 and 1329, provided the elevational system to which the nave was built and finished by about 1430. The dark wall-passage that runs above the arcade arches raises the level of the oculi in the nave, while the lateral chapels reduce the amount of light in the aisles. These chapels are designed as parts of the aisles, just as those at Albi are parts of the central vessel. As the eye moves from the outer walls of the church towards the centre, the light decreases rapidly. In this mysterious gloom, the complexity of the piers with

191. Rome, S. Maria sopra Minerva,
begun 1280. Interior, vaulted 1450

their multitude of shafts, hardly ever separated by fillets, but merged into a single mass by the hollows between them, is a source of wonderment. It is difficult clearly to discern the thirty shafts attached to every pier, and this is complemented by the reduction of the light.[140]

In 1229, soon after the Christian re-conquest of the Balearic islands, King Jaime I of Aragon founded the cathedral of Palma on the island of Mallorca [189, 190]. Little of this original church, built on the site of a mosque, survives. In 1306 King Jaime I of Mallorca began a small royal burial chapel which now stands at the east end of the present cathedral and opens into the polygonally apsed choir. The latter, together with its flanking chapels, was largely finished by 1327. At this stage the nave was planned to rise no higher than the choir, with side aisles as high as the choir chapels, and with simple octagonal columns. After a long interruption, the present nave was begun c. 1360 to a much more grandiose design, perhaps by the master Jaime Mates, with much taller aisles and a central vessel higher than any Gothic cathedral apart from Beauvais, Cologne and Milan. Although the building of the nave continued into the sixteenth century, the whole church gives an impression of unity and spatial coordination.[140A] The form of the choir is unusual: its lower storey has a flat end, which, in turn, has an east niche, but each corner is spanned by a pointed arch, the resulting triangular bays being separately vaulted. Above these pointed arches rise the diagonal walls of the apse, while a smaller apse with a higher floor adjoins the eastern wall. It reaches to the level of the middle of the windows on the side walls, leaving room for an oculus window above it. To this oculus a larger one corresponds in the wall that rises from above the chancel arch to the vault of the nave. This description is hard to grasp, but the church itself is easy to understand if one stands inside it. It has no transepts, and

so, because it is approached from the sumptuous nave, the relatively small and complex choir gives a strong impression of being a true Holy of Holies.

The nave is basilican with slender, octagonal piers. The arcade arches have the breadth of one side of the piers; thus three of the other sides of the piers can rise on to the vault. This arrangement, though different in the details, is reminiscent of Bourges. The space within the nave is high and very wide. The vaults of the central aisle are 144 feet high, those of the side aisles 98 feet: all three aisles make up a total width of 182 feet; the pillars are 72 feet high but a mere five feet in diameter; the whole interior has the lowest ratio of support to enclosed volume in Gothic architecture.[140B] It is one of the finest interiors to be found in any Gothic building. The simplicity of the vaults, with their pointed arches and pear-shaped ribs throughout, characterizes the whole as High Gothic, though in some respects this church also anticipates the principles of the Late Gothic. The cathedral has suffered from the insertion of modern stained glass. Its colours are poisonous and the plain glass patterns in the oculi are nothing less than vulgar. The arrangement of the artificial lighting, on the other hand, is admirable.

The most striking feature of the exterior is the presence of frontal buttresses on the corners of the polygonal chapels. These, and the slightly heavier buttresses rising to the flying buttresses, form a close series with a gentle rhythm [190].

At *Gerona* in 1312 a new choir was begun, modelled on that at Barcelona. After a long interruption in the building, a nave without aisles was added in 1416.[140C]

Much simpler in design are those Italian churches with a nave slightly higher than the aisles – such as S. *Anastasia* at *Verona* (begun *c.* 1290, complete by 1437), a Dominican church with pilasters above the piers and blind oculi instead of a triforium. The long, square-ish bays are a continuation of the Romanesque tradition. They set the quiet tempo which is so different from that of the single-naved churches of southern France with their short bays.[140D]

A third group in the spread of the High Gothic style was centred on Tuscany: The oldest parts of the cathedral at *Siena*, were begun between 1226 and 1247, and the choir and domed hexagonal crossing were in building between 1247/49 and the early 1260s. The nave was under construction by 1260, and work was still going on in 1277. The flat east end of the (originally shorter) choir was influenced by Cistercian practice, particularly by the nearby church of S. Galgano. Probably in *c.* 1250 it was decided to vault the choir and dome with ribs. The west façade (perhaps complete by 1317?) was built higher than originally intended, necessitating the heightening of the nave when its rib-vaults were inserted, (perhaps before 1317, or in the second half of the fourteenth century) [234]. The arches in the vaults of the nave and of the aisles are all semicircular. The extraordinary feature of the first cathedral, preserved in the later heightenings and remodellings, is the large hexagonal crossing, crowned by a dome, and extending across almost the whole width of the nave.[141]

Arnolfo di Cambio joined the movement to produce a balanced blend of Gothic, Romanesque and Early Christian styles when, in 1293/96, he began the new cathedral in Florence, *S. Maria del Fiore*. He may also have been the architect of *S. Croce*, begun in 1294/95. When he died, between 1301 and 1310, the building of S. Croce had progressed as far as the transepts,[141A] but it is not certain how far the building of the cathedral had advanced. There is no agreement about what Arnolfo's plan for the cathedral looked like, or even if there was a plan in anything more than outline form. Toker has argued that Arnolfo's 'project' consisted of a nave not dissimilar to that of S. Croce: basilical, unvaulted, and divided into bays by octagonal stone piers, perhaps also marked by transverse arches over the side aisles. The nave probably consisted of five long bays, each corresponding to two bays of the exterior side aisle walls, with perhaps single gable roofs over each of the double side aisle units. Excavations in the 1960s and 1970s have suggested that Arnolfo's project for the choir was, as many older authorities had suggested, a shorter version of the present east end. The discovery of foundations under and to the south of the existing eastern bay of the nave has led Toker and others to argue that Arnolfo planned the east end as a domed octagon of unequal sides, occupying the whole width of the nave, and opening out into three conches, each with five chapels. The whole east end was planned to stand about one bay further to the west than the present choir. If these inferences are correct, Arnolfo's huge, well-lit octagonal crossing, opening out of a dark and spacious wooden-roofed nave, would have outshone the domed crossings of Pisa and Siena cathedrals, and his nave would have emulated the Early Christian basilicas of Rome. The first phase of construction (1293/96–*c.* 1300) saw rapid progress, starting at the west façade and working eastwards. By 1310 work had stopped and, apart from the construction of the campanile begun in 1334, building on the cathedral stagnated until *c.* 1350. How much had been completed by Arnolfo and his immediate followers is not certain, but the lower half of the west façade, with its revetments, may have been finished up to a height of about twenty-five metres. The side aisle walls in the three double western bays were probably up to about the same height, but their revetments may only have reached socle level. The rest of the aisle walls, running eastwards, were probably lower, and at the crossing and choir only the foundations, or part foundations, may have been laid down.[141B] Outside, the veneer of marble over the brick structure was Florentine in origin. What reconstructions of Arnolfo's design have been attempted decidedly stress flatness and horizontality.[142]

Arnolfo must have known the façade of the cathedral at *Siena*, which was begun in 1284 by Giovanni Pisano [234]. It is much more Gothic in form and shows a considerable knowledge of French architecture. At Giovanni's departure from Siena in around 1300 it is not clear how much of the façade was finished. By 1300 the southern of the three portals was complete, and perhaps by 1310 or 1317 (the latter the year of the foundation of the baptistery and extended choir) the whole façade, including the rose storey, may have been finished. But since Giovanni left the city in *c.* 1300 there is still doubt as to how far the façade's superstructure reflects his intentions.[143] There are three doorways: the central one has a round arch, and is only a little higher than the others. The rich ornamentation of the shafts on the walls is full of such traces of the Late Romanesque as spiral fluting.[144]

With the spread of the Gothic style to Tuscany, architecture there entered a stage where it was no longer Romanesque, still not classical, in the sense of the Renaissance, but not pure Gothic either. It was a superficial application of Gothic elements to traditional local forms.

This is true also of the Dominican church of S. Maria sopra Minerva in *Rome*, which was begun in 1280 and modelled on S. Maria Novella in Florence [191].[144A] The side aisles were vaulted only in the fourteenth century, the central aisle, which was originally groin-vaulted, by 1474. They were groins with no transverse arches, like those in the Baths of Diocletian. This, the only Gothic church in Rome, was decorated in the Baroque style in the seventeenth century, but the plaster was pulled down again in 1848 so that the church now has nearly its original appearance. It has frontal piers and shafts, semicircular ribs, and, apart from the ribs, pointed arches throughout. The nave has the form of a basilica, and the oculi in each of its bays and those of the apse over-accentuate the rhythm of the interior. The general impression is a reminder of Transitional Cistercian churches; only the tracery in the east window is really Gothic, and it is not even certain whether this is original. The church as a whole is Gothic, but the proportions of the shafts are almost classical, and the mouldings of the broad transverse arches in the nave, and of the pointed arcade arches, are Romanesque. The veneer of marble slabs, which possibly dates from the seventeenth century, is out of place and unique in a Gothic interior. The raised floor hides the plinths of the piers; their absence emphasizes the aesthetic importance of plinths in other churches. Even discounting the damage suffered at the hands of restorers, the style of this church still remains retarded.

CHAPTER 4
The Late Gothic Style

1. NEW VARIETIES OF RIBS. LIERNES. NET-VAULTS

THE octagonal chapter house of *Wells* has a crypt-like undercroft with massive architectural members and a tall upper chamber. The undercroft is on the level of the site.[1] In the upper chamber the octagonal middle pier is surrounded by sixteen shafts behind which the pier is slightly hollowed out [192]. From the octagonal abacus eight transverse arches run to the corners of the octagon. From the middle of the eight sides eight ribs rise to the ridge-rib, which forms an octagon whose corners face the sides of the outer octagon; thus the sides of the two octagons are not parallel. Between every two of the inner ribs there is a tierceron on the surface of the vault. This vault has the form of a concave funnel. On the outer side, between ridge-rib and wall, the middle arches are continued horizontally as radial ridge-ribs and the tiercerons are continued by other tiercerons. In addition there is a pair of tiercerons inside the severies above each window. All these ribs have the same profiles, very delicately composed of round rolls and pear-shaped rolls. The profiles merge as they rise from the middle pier, so that only the rolls with fillets remain. Visually all these arches are identical and one does not inquire into their function or their *structural* significance. Their effect is one of *texture*.

The window tracery contains ogee arches, and there are others in other parts of the upper chamber. The multiplication of tiercerons at Wells is the first definite step towards the Late Gothic style.[1A] Hence the dating of the chapter house is important. Britton[2] says that it was built during the period of Bishop de Marchia, that is between 1293 and 1302, but does not himself consider this a reliable statement. The approximate dates of the preceding chapter houses are *Lincoln c.* 1220–35, *Lichfield* 1240, *Westminster Abbey* 1250, *Salisbury c.* 1263?.[2A] Salisbury is still in a pure High Gothic style.[3] Lincoln, a decagonal chapter house, is the stylistic predecessor of Wells. It has now been established that the main, upper, chamber of the Wells chapter house was begun in *c.* 1298 and completed in its essentials by 1305.[4]

The reason why one is entitled to place the beginning of the Late Gothic style at this point is that the structural function of the rib is ignored. The rib is becoming again what it was at the outset; an architectural member having a purely aesthetic function. The earliest tiercerons in Hugh's Choir in Lincoln Cathedral, dated *c.* 1200, and the first star-vaults in the nave of Lincoln Cathedral, of *c.* 1225, were predecessors of those in the Angel Choir at Lincoln (1256) and of all that followed.[4A]

The merging of tiercerons was repeated in the choir and nave of *Exeter*. The new cathedral was begun by 1279–80 with the construction of the choir aisles, and the ambulatory and its chapels. The presbytery and choir, started by 1288–91, are covered with tierceron vaults even more elaborate than those in the nave at Lincoln or the choir at Ely.

The multiplication of tiercerons in the lateral severies has caused some authors to make the mistake of calling these vaults at Exeter fan-vaults (cf. p. 209). In fact they are star-vaults; for the diagonal ribs have their own separate curvature. But the impression comes close to that of fan-vaults, and the merging of the bays with each other has already made considerable progress.[5] Structurally the whole eastern arm was complete by 1311.

Support for *c.* 1291–1311 as the date of the vaults of Exeter comes from *Ely*. Here the crossing tower collapsed in 1322. The widening of the crossing into an octagon as wide as nave and aisles together is reminiscent of Siena Cathedral

192. Wells Cathedral. Chapter House, upper chamber. Begun 1298, finished by 1305

193. Ely Cathedral. Octagon. Begun 1322, substantially complete by 1340

and even more of Florence Cathedral. But there is no provable connexion between either. The vault is of wood. The construction takes from the Wells chapter-house the turning of the middle part through half the angle of the sides of the polygon. Whereas there the turning was determined by the middle pier, the determining factor here is the four severies in the principal axes, which are arranged so that their apexes meet four of the corners of the lantern. The eight resulting triangular spandrels are cylindrical surfaces, and one might either say that each is *carried* by three tiercerons, or that in each three tiercerons are *hanging*. The vault of the lantern is of timber and forms an octagonal rib-vault with ridge-ribs and three pairs of tiercerons in each of the eight cells [193].[6]

The monks of Ely attributed the conception of a large octagonal crossing to their sacrist, Alan of Walsingham,[6A] but the timber vault and lantern were designed by the king's master carpenter, William Hurley, and substantially complete in 1340. In the bays of the chancel which follow to the east and which were renewed at the same time as the crossing (from 1322), the vault has diagonal ribs, longitudinal and transverse ridge-ribs, and tiercerons in the longitudinal cells

[194A]. The latter are not genuine tiercerons; for they stop after about two-thirds of their expected length and divide into two short ribs. These, as they do not start from corners nor reach the ridge-rib, but run diagonally to the diagonal rib, can neither be called tiercerons nor ridge-ribs. Their name in England is liernes.[7] By means of more liernes an octagon is produced with corners alternately projecting and re-entering. It is a star-shape. The re-entrant corners are connected by diagonal ribs which again are neither ribs in the original sense nor tiercerons. They are liernes in a centripetal direction.

As the middle liernes which lie within the longitudinal cells are continued towards the apexes of the transverse arches, there result everywhere diagonally placed lozenges which go across the transverse arches, i.e. the boundaries of the bays, and moreover in some cases merge with the eight-pointed stars. It is not necessary to confute the rationalist explanation of this extremely complicated pattern which asserts that it is technically or statically easier. Anybody can see that it is harder to produce than normal rib-vaults. Equally evident is the growing aesthetic tendency to see the

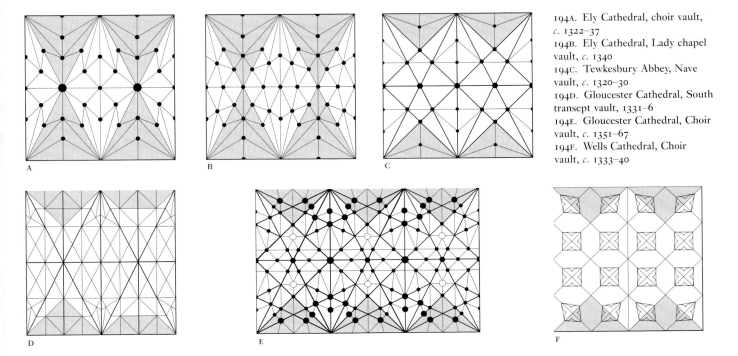

194A. Ely Cathedral, choir vault, *c.* 1322–37
194B. Ely Cathedral, Lady chapel vault, *c.* 1340
194C. Tewkesbury Abbey, Nave vault, *c.* 1320–30
194D. Gloucester Cathedral, South transept vault, 1331–6
194E. Gloucester Cathedral, Choir vault, *c.* 1351–67
194F. Wells Cathedral, Choir vault, *c.* 1333–40

vault as one fabric comprising all the bays, that is: as 'texture'. As if it were a preliminary experiment, the north aisle of these three chancel bays at Ely also has liernes, though in a simpler configuration.

The vault of the (rectangular) Lady Chapel at Ely follows the same principle [194B]. The Lady chapel was started in 1321, a year before the tower collapsed. The work on both the chapel and the octagon proceeded at the same time, although it is uncertain how quickly the chapel progressed. Work had reached the upper storey at the west end under Bishop Simon de Montacute, sometime after 1337, and the whole building was structurally complete by 1349, when John of Wisbech, the monk responsible for its finance, died. The Lady chapel vault may therefore date a little after the choir vault, which was finished by 1337.[8] Most of the fourteenth-century work at Ely, apart from the wooden vaults of the octagon and lantern, has been attributed to John Ramsey.[8A]

About 1320, or soon after, a new high vault was inserted into the Romanesque nave of *Tewkesbury* abbey [194C].[9] The ribs make different patterns here than at Ely. In addition two long straight ribs are introduced to the left and right and parallel with the longitudinal ridge-rib. These result from a longitudinal joining of points or crossing of other ribs. This new pattern is possible only because the vault is basically a tunnel-vault with transverse severies not reaching up to the crown. They even remain below the new longitudinal ribs, which are often called, not quite accurately, ridge-ribs, like the real longitudinal rib along the crown of the vault.

Gloucester is influenced by Tewkesbury. Here the south transept was vaulted in 1336, after that the chancel, and finally the north transept. In the south transept it is easy to isolate visually the diagonal ribs and the ridge-rib, as they have the same stronger profiles [194D].[10] The other ribs run parallel, some to the diagonal ribs, some to the ridge-rib,

except for fragmentary tiercerons in the four corners of each bay. One perceives that the ribs nearest to the ridge-rib and parallel with it correspond to the secondary ridge-ribs of Tewkesbury. But they appear now only in the lateral cells, i.e. in a fragmentary state. Where the fragmentary tiercerons end, a pattern of liernes results which adds some variety to the uniform net of lozenges with crossed diagonals. The term net comes to one's lips here as naturally as in the case of some vaults of the French Plantagenet style.

To analyse these vaults in their historical sequence makes it easier to understand them. They grow more complicated from design to design, but the patterns of the later ones contain those of the earlier ones. In the chancel at Gloucester (1337–*c.* 1367) the basic shape of the vault is again a tunnel with transverse severies [194E].[11] The ridge-rib is accompanied by two secondary ridge-ribs. In each bay two diagonal ribs cross. In addition there are diagonal ribs crossing pairs of bays and therefore meeting at the apex of a transverse arch. Their lower parts form the boundaries of the severies. This vault, complex as it is, is made so much richer by liernes that the eye has the choice of reading together spherical triangles, quadrangles, pentagons, and hexagons. Even in the preceding vaults there had been ambivalence or polyvalence; here this principle is carried to the point of extreme complexity. The bays merge completely, because of the form of this vault.

Less closely ribbed and hence less heavy is the vault of the chancel at *Wells* [194F].[12] Here the diagonal ribs across individual bays are left out, as is also the ridge-rib. The system consists of diagonal ribs across pairs of bays, but these ribs are interrupted *en route* and a square of liernes is interpolated. Although these squares on the surface of the vault are set parallel to the longitudinal axis, in perspective they do not appear to be regularly set squares. Hexagons are formed by connecting the corners of the squares. Moreover they

195. Lübeck, St Mary. Vaults of the Briefkapelle, c. 1310–20

The Angevin vaults already gave a separate boss to each point where ribs crossed and decorated it with foliage or figure sculpture or both. As the points of crossing increased in number in English vaults, so also did the bosses. They intensify the impression of 'texture', appearing to be heads of nails fixing a net to the vault. The bosses are both decorated and decoration. Whether or not the whole vault is to be called decoration will depend on what is meant by the term. The decisive fact is that, if one chooses to call them decoration, they must be called Late Gothic decoration, as decoration exists in other styles as well. The vaults are Late Gothic, not because they are decorative, or, as some people say, 'merely decorative', but because they are textural instead of structural. At a time when the theory has been shaken that all ribs bear or ought to bear, there is no longer any reason to speak with scorn of 'merely decorative' ribs, or ribs which are unstructural and therefore valueless. They are deliberately textural.

Soon after 1300 star-vaults were built in Germany; the first perhaps in the Greveraden Chapel of 1304 under the north tower of St Mary at *Lübeck*. Its design then appears slightly varied in the Schinkel Chapel. The Briefkapelle which adjoins the westernmost bays of the south aisle has a vault consisting of triradials [195]. This was begun about 1310.[14] From about 1350 onwards *Heilsberg Castle*

196. Bristol Cathedral. Vaults of the Sacristy of the Berkeley Chapel, c. 1330

and other shapes of the vaults are given cusps. Work on the chancel was underway in 1333, and complete by c. 1340.

At *Gloucester* the vault of the north transept followed after that of the chancel. This again has three parallel ridge-ribs. The pattern is simple in principle, but the result is still a bewildering multivalent pattern.[13] This part was built, according to Harvey, in 1367/68–73.

This coherent sequence from the Wells chapter house to about 1340 shows the development in England as a progressive merging of the bays by means of the patterns formed by the ribs. The buildings in the 'Plantagenet style' of the first half of the thirteenth century are first continued in the chapter houses of Lichfield, Westminster Abbey, etc., and then, from the Wells chapter house onwards, with rapidly intensified partiality, in the group culminating at Gloucester and the chancel of Wells. Considering the relations between Anjou and England it can be assumed that, in spite of all differences, this whole sequence of vaults represents one continuous development. One can see that the architects were quite capable of bridging the geographical distance.[13A]

(*Lidzbark Warmiński*) was built for the bishops of Warmia in East Prussia. It has fifteenth-century star-vaults in all rooms, including the chapel.[15]

There was direct communication between the German north-east and England, but all these vaults correspond to that of the nave at Lincoln, not to Gloucester, etc.[15A] They use no liernes. Star-vaults in their simple centralizing shape belong to the High Gothic phase. A room of the charming lightness of the Briefkapelle belongs to the phase which one might call intensified High Gothic.

Not everyone considers it important to draw clear boundary lines between the phases of a style. Many on the other hand are keen on making the distinction between national characters. There is a connexion between the two in this case. The concept of the spreading of the Gothic style loses its meaning almost completely in the Late Gothic phase. The spreading to the principal Western countries had been accomplished. In England a national school existed at least since Lincoln. In the other countries the change towards the Late Gothic style took place about 1320 or about 1330 at the latest. The change followed the same tendency everywhere, but was based none the less on different premises which one must accept as national, the term of course understood not in the sense of biological inbreeding but of spiritual connexions.

Specifically English also is the introduction of flying ribs, that is ribs without cells, rising in relatively small square or oblong rooms below a flat stone ceiling decorated with crossed 'ridge-ribs'. The flying ribs structurally support the centre of the flat ceiling. So far only three such skeleton vaults or vaulting skeletons have been recorded: inside the Easter Sepulchre at *Lincoln* in 1296,[16] in the sacristy of the Berkeley Chapel in *Bristol* Cathedral about 1330 [196][17] and in the pulpitum of *Southwell* Minster between 1320 and 1340.[18] The first and third are so small in scale that they had been over-looked until quite recently, the second is bigger. One may join to these English vaults that of the so-called Tonsura of the cloister of *Magdeburg* Cathedral[19] for which no exact date is known but which can be placed at about 1330–40.

Peter Parler, a little later, in the cathedral of *Prague*, built flying ribs in conjunction with a real vault and a pendant.

The old theory that the function of ribs is always to carry becomes untenable in the case of flying ribs. The theory on the other hand that diagonal ribs always divide a room into fragments is confirmed by these Late Gothic flying ribs. The English architects returned to the original, purely aesthetic, and in the narrower sense stylistic, function of the rib. Together with the lierne the flying rib stands at the beginning of the Late Gothic phase; for the fundamental principle of the Gothic style, the division of space, is realized in these forms without any residue whatever of Romanesque principles. The difference between tiercerons, liernes, and net patterns on the one hand, and flying ribs on the other, is that flying ribs preserve a vestige of structural character. But as they hardly create the impression of really carrying the flat ceilings, they belong to the category of akyristic forms: their supporting function is not taken seriously.

2 · CURVILINEAR AND RECTILINEAR

Pear-shaped shafts are similar in cross-section to ogee arches [197.III]. It may well have been an architect who had drawn hundreds of such pear-shaped cross-sections who hit on the idea of replacing pointed arches with ogee arches. It is usually suspect to try to rationalize an idea which is the product of creative imagination, but in their case the connexion between a curve viewed from its convex side and the same curve seen from its concave side can also be proved to exist elsewhere. Romanesque architects used the concave side of the semicircle for arches, and its convex side for the profile of their shafts (I); and Transitional and Early Gothic architects made the same double use of pointed arches in arcades and almond-shaped shafts (II). In the last phase of the Late Gothic style, this development of curves produced arches with convex shanks on the one hand, and piers with hollows on the other (IV). The connexion between these different forms must not be regarded as a rigid rule, but should be considered within that series of principles which embraces the secret of conformity.

Pear-shaped profiles and ogee arches had already been introduced during the High Gothic period, and of these two forms the pear-shaped profile appears in the ribs of the nave and aisles at *Amiens*, and also in the transverse arches of the nave. It may therefore date right back to the plan of 1220. In the work of Villard de Honnecourt there is also a pear-shaped profile of early form,[20] similar to some double-curved profiles without the sharp edge of the pear-shaped profile. These Villard drew next to his pear-shape in a moulding the purpose of which is unknown.[20A] Their two middle rolls are clearly defined, while the flanking ones run smoothly into the hollows. The undulating profiles in *St Nicaise* at *Reims*[21] date from the same period. In Villard's work, undulating lines appear in the pattern of a floor paving and in a timber roof. The smooth continuation of shafts into hollows was also used by Gerhard in the choir at *Cologne*. Once the double curve had appeared several times on paper, the desire to repeat it everywhere followed naturally. Such is the principle of conformity.[21A]

Pear-shaped mouldings and ogee arches first appear together in the church of *St Urbain* at *Troyes* in 1262. Ogee arches appear implicitly in the triforium because the pointed trefoil arches reach up into the trefoils above, and in the windows of the choir, because there the pointed arches over the central lights flow directly into the circles above.[21B] Lasteyrie has enumerated several forms of tracery in which ogee arches are produced by the form of a pattern, and he claimed to have proved that the French Flamboyant was not dependent on earlier English models.[22] In the examples that he quotes, the patterns are like pictorial puzzles – one can

197. Analogies between profiles of shafts and forms of arches

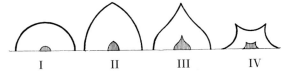

I   II   III   IV

198. Hardingstone, Northamptonshire, Eleanor Cross, 1291–4

three-dimensional. In a modest way this happened at the starting points of the vaulting shafts immediately above the abaci of the two piers in the nave at Exeter cathedral which support the bay with the minstrels gallery, under construction after 1327. In contradiction to their structural function these clustered shafts are hollowed out at their feet to allow for the placing of statuettes. These niches have ogee arches which curve forward with the plane of the cylinder.[25] The ogee arches also curve forward with complete freedom in the Bishop's Throne at Exeter, which dates from 1313 to 1323/24.[26] They form the link to the nodding ogee arches of the tabernacles on the crossing piers at *Ely*. The whole frame is bent round the pier.[26A]

On each of the four diagonal sides of the octagon the zone below the windows has three shallow ogee arches closely connected. By their continuation downward, along the horizontals, onion-shaped frames are created. These shallow ogee arches are by the same architect who applied the bent ogee arches to the piers.

199. Ely Cathedral, Lady Chapel, begun 1321, complete *c.* 1340

find the ogee arches only if one looks for them; but they either do not appear in their own right, or only partly appear within a conservative pattern, as at Troyes (*c.* 1262) and Heiligenkreuz (*c.* 1288–95).[22A] Early examples of ogee arches used as autonomous forms appear in the English Eleanor Crosses, built between 1291 and sometime before 1297 [198],[23] and these are followed by the tomb of Edward Crouchback in Westminster Abbey, erected in *c.* 1297.[24]

Pear-shaped profiles do not usually come to a sharp point, and it is this which differentiates them from ogee arches; in addition to this, the functions of the two forms are also different. Pear-shaped shafts, like almond-shaped shafts and bases and abaci turned through 45 degrees, make the boundary zone between bays appear thinner, and pear-shaped shafts have the additional effect of creating soft transitions between light and shade. Ogee arches, on the other hand, are intended to eliminate the structural characteristics of arches, for their upper parts seem to be suspended and therefore to become pure texture. But of course the function of both forms is to increase partiality. The spatial parts and the layers of the arcade arches flow smoothly into one another, and all this texture serves to give the impression that the whole work is dependent on a visible or invisible scaffolding.

Within tracery, the ogee arch remained a two-dimensional figure. When it was applied to a curved surface it became

The Lady Chapel at *Ely*, which was begun in 1321, one year before the collapse of the crossing tower, is fascinating not only on account of its vault. The details of this room, splendidly rich and fantastic and inviting close analysis,[27] are far ahead of anything of Late Gothic design on the Continent [199]. The Percy Tomb at *Beverley* Minster of *c*. 1335–40 continues the style of the Lady Chapel at Ely[28] and confirms its date, which in any case is borne out by the preceding work at Exeter.

The three-dimensional ogee arch is reminiscent (theoretically) of the double-curved ribs at Bourges or even the double-curved groins in Romanesque buildings. However there are differences in each case.

The delight in undulating curves expresses itself also in the form given to the strainer arches between the west and east piers of the eastern crossing at Salisbury. They were inserted from *c*. 1320, probably by the architect William Joy. Two double-curves cross in the shape of an X. The resulting form could also be interpreted as the interpenetration of

200. Gloucester Cathedral, south transept and choir, *c*. 1331–6, and choir, *c*. 1337–67

201. St Stephen's Chapel, Palace of Westminster, London, 1292–1348. Engraving of the south side by Frederick Mackenzie, 1844

two half-ogee arches. The practical purpose of the strainer arches was to strengthen the supports for the new crossing tower.[28A] More massive and more conspicuous are the four crossed double curves of the strainer arches in the crossing of *Wells* Cathedral (sometime around 1356?). There are no capitals here, and large circles are pierced through the spandrels. The bases of the X-arches are grouped together diagonally and are an example of a 'separated crossing' that is in the Gothic style, a crossing recognized as an independent spatial unit but at the same time by means of the diagonality of the bases united to the neighbouring spatial units, according to the principle of partiality.[28B]

A few years before the strainer arches were begun at Wells, the designer of the south transept at *Gloucester* (constructed *c*. 1331–36) introduced the four-centred arch[29] and adopted rectilinear tracery [200].

It has been proved that the antecedents of the Rectilinear ought to be traced back much farther and that the style is already to be found in *St Stephen's Chapel* in the Palace of *Westminster*.[30] This chapel, which lay to the south of Westminster Hall, was begun in 1292, destroyed by fire in 1834, and demolished after measured drawings had been made [201].[31] The chapel, used from 1547 to 1834 as the House of Commons, had an aisleless lower storey of five bays with lierne star-vaults and an upper storey also aisleless but with a wooden vault of low pitch. The windows of the undercroft are pointed, and have four lights. On the outside, in front of the mullions, are detached posts which are continued attached to the wall above the windows and pierce the farthest projecting archivolt. This emphasis on the verticals was repeated in the upper part of the chapel, as we know from Mackenzie's drawings. There was blank panelling in the spandrels of the arcades, and their mullions reinforce the impression of verticality. Nevertheless the tracery of the windows of the lower chapel contained ogee arches – that is, the chapel combines Curvilinear and Rectilinear elements.

The term Perpendicular was given to the period from about 1350 to about 1530 by Thomas Rickman in 1817. Edmund Sharpe found it inadequate because the tracery and other details contain horizontal as well as perpendicular lines. He therefore substituted the term Rectilinear for Perpendicular. From Rickman up to the middle of the twentieth century everybody took it for granted that the Perpendicular or Rectilinear was a reaction against the Curvilinear, following and displacing it. Today we have to acknowledge that the Perpendicular was created in the same year (1292) as the Curvilinear, so far as England is concerned. The masters who designed the chapel of St Stephen at Westminster have been given the name of the Court School of London.[32] The date 1292 for the creation of the Perpendicular style has been queried, because it was forty years before, in 1331, it was taken up again in the south transept of Gloucester Cathedral. However, the long interval can be explained by the fact that the erection of St Stephen's Chapel was slow and building stopped more than once for periods of several years.

At *Gloucester* the west and east walls of the south transept are formed of rectilinear tracery, partly pierced, partly blank. Bond thought the stained-glass artists had complained about the vesica shapes of the Curvilinear, because they made the designing of pictures more difficult. But the German and French stained-glass painters were capable of filling the most complicated vesica shapes, and the Rectilinear at Gloucester covers all the walls which were not destined for stained glass. As the remodelling of the transept at Gloucester started in 1331, this has been taken as the birth date of the Rectilinear.[33]

A better explanation than Bond's of the coming of the Rectilinear is that it represented a reaction against curves altogether. Even this, however, is not wholly satisfactory. When in *c.* 1337 the remodelling of the chancel began at Gloucester, mullions were allowed to carry on through the pointed arches. This, together with the horizontals of the gallery and the window sills and the horizontals of the transoms, results in a net or grid of rectangles that might well be called an 'all-over repeat" capable of being continued endlessly. The same tendency existed in the Curvilinear, e.g. the reticulated tracery of the sacristy of the chapel of *Merton College, Oxford* (1309–11).[33A] The pattern is meant to lead on beyond the frame. In this respect the intention of the Rectilinear is the same as that of the Curvilinear and is by no means a sign of opposition. The two styles are twins. They existed at the same time in England, the Rectilinear being entirely confined to England.

The plan of Gloucester Cathedral is Romanesque. Much of the building of *c.* 1090 survives, the crypt, the nave, the

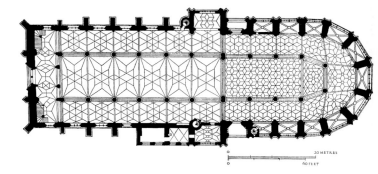

202. Schwäbisch Gmünd, Church of the Holy Cross, begun *c.* 1315. Plan

ambulatory and its gallery.[33B] There are very early ribs in the crypt, there is a mature rib-vault of *c.* 1240 over the central vessel of the nave, and there are the Late Gothic additions and alterations, in the transepts and east of them. Each part is individually interesting as a representative of its own phase of medieval architecture. In the east parts what is doubly interesting is that the styles are not separated from each other as in the nave, where the Gothic vault appears easily separable from the Romanesque substructure, but that the Romanesque building was left and the Rectilinear placed in front of it like a grille. Gothic relief stands in front of Romanesque relief. The east wall is opened above a low plinth in one enormous rectilinear window with thirteen mullions at equal distances. All lights finish in pointed arches, and they carry on their apexes further mullions. This east window was completed in the 1350s.[34] The complicated vault finally unites the whole. For net-vaults, star-vaults, and fan-vaults neither the term Perpendicular nor the term Rectilinear makes sense. If one wants to keep these terms one should talk only of perpendicular or rectilinear patterns in tracery and on walls, and not extend them to whole buildings and a whole period.

In order to vault the crossing the master mason needed points of support in the middle of the crossing arches. For this purpose he threw across the space between the abaci of the crossing piers thin four-centred arches and placed on the not very pronounced apexes of each of them a vertical mullion accompanied on both sides by counter-curves.[35] The result is an ogee arch in mid-air from which rise the seven ribs of the vault. It is a refined repetition of the strainer arches of Salisbury and Wells, or perhaps their precursor [200]. The crossing tower, though built much later, was projected in 1331; for the large flying buttresses in the transepts which penetrate the rectilinear system were erected with a view to the crossing tower. To characterize the unique miracles of geometrical fantasy at Gloucester – the word unique, so often misused, is here justified – one may choose to refer to Islamic buildings, but the details of the English cathedral are not at all Arabic: they are extremely English, and this is true of the Rectilinear as a whole. As one wanders round and through Gloucester Cathedral one is not led to conclude that there are permanent national styles. All the styles which were combined in this building are English. In addition the masters of south transept and chancel were geniuses who in their own personal way drew their conclu-

203. Schwäbisch Gmünd, Church of the Holy Cross. Interior of the nave, begun *c.* 1315, and choir, begun 1351

204. Schwäbisch Gmünd, Church of the Holy Cross. West front, begun *c.* 1315. Nave complete by 1347

sions from the preceding development of the Gothic style. They are not more English than others; they are simply more personal.

3. THE RELAXATION OF STRICT REGULARITY. HALL-CHOIRS

In Germany, the boundary between High Gothic and Late Gothic is not as clear as it is in England. Most German architects continued to build plain cross-vaults. There was an increasing preference for hall-churches and an increasing reluctance to build transepts and crossings. This clearly reflects a growing dislike of the multitude of re-entrant angles in High Gothic architecture. The basic principles of the Gothic style demanded that the interior spatial parts should be bounded externally by a continuous contour without any projections sideways or upwards. This new type was more fully developed in Germany than in other national schools of the Late Gothic style. It appeared there even in the High Gothic period, still bearing all the characteristics of the High Gothic. The nave of the cathedral at *Minden*, in building in the 1250s and 1260s, for example, is a High Gothic hall-church inasmuch as the piers have the basic shapes of the High Gothic.[35A] The variations on St Elizabeth at *Marburg* introduced by its imitators must also be included

within the German High Gothic style.[36] Here again, the drawing of boundaries between periods is not a sign of conventionality but of understanding.[36A]

The nave of the church of the Holy Cross at *Schwäbisch Gmünd* has often been called the earliest German Late Gothic church because of the impression given by the net-vaults and by the choir, although these are all later additions. The new church was begun *c.* 1315 at the west end of the nave by an unknown architect, who planned a basilica, established the present length of the nave and its bay divisions, and retired from the work having completed only the western bay up to about half its height. In *c.* 1320–30 he was replaced by a second architect, Heinrich Parler from Cologne. Heinrich followed the intentions of the first master in retaining the Romanesque towers at the east end of the nave aisles, but changed the design of the west façade and the buttresses and vault shafts of the nave, altered the basilica to a hall (possibly the first hall church in Swabia), introduced tall round pillars, and completed the whole nave (except for the vaults: he covered the space with temporary wooden roofs). All this was finished by the outbreak of the Black Death in 1347/48 [202–4].[37] We know very little about Heinrich. An inscription above the bust of his son Peter Parler in the triforium of Prague cathedral refers to him as coming from Cologne, and as 'magister' of the church at Gmünd. He is also called 'magister' and 'architector' of the

205. Soest, Wiesenkirche, begun 1313. Interior

taller side sections necessitated by the aisles of his new hall church. He also increased the size of the side rose windows to compensate for the lack of a clerestory.

The choir was begun in 1351, and completed (with a provisional flat wooden roof) as late as 1410, but according to the initial design. The stylistic character of the choir is so radically different from that of the nave that some scholars have doubted that both could be the work of the same architect. Schmitt attributes the choir to Heinrich Parler and the nave to an unknown predecessor. Kissling attributes both to Heinrich; so do Clasen and Wortmann, who suggest that the choir's novelties can be explained by the contribution of Heinrich's eighteen-year-old son Peter. There is some force in their argument, since those very novelties anticipate much of Peter Parler's work in Bohemia.[40]

The *Franciscan* church at *Soest*, begun shortly after *c.* 1280 and complete around 1300, is still a High Gothic hall-church with High Gothic piers.[41] The *Wiesenkirche* at Soest, which was begun in 1313, however, is definitely Late Gothic[42] [205], since its piers with their sequence of pear-shaped shafts, hollows, and flat projections make it almost impossible to say where the core of the pier actually lies [206]. The shafts continue without capitals into the transverse and longitudinal arches of the vault, and the ribs grow out of the diagonal surfaces of the piers. The three bays of the central vessel and the three bays of its two aisles, which are of the same height as the nave, are joined at the east by one apse each. The middle apse consists of seven sides of a decagon. Hence its two first sides taper outward, forming one of the sides of the two flanking chapels. From outside, this device blends the three apses into one unit. All these forms are not really irregular, but they are certainly no longer governed by strict regularity.

206. Soest, Wiesenkirche, begun 1313. Plan of a pier, after Kugler

The Wiesenkirche is considered to be the most beautiful hall-church in Westphalia. The Renaissance used the word 'beautiful' only to refer to the proportions of the human figure: it made the golden mean into the norm. In the Wiesenkirche, the proportion of the two flanking aisles and the nave is that of the golden mean. Whether or not this proportion forms a sufficient basis for such a judgement, it is certainly correct to say that the interior is characterized by a happy sense of poise, however intangible this may be, and however opposed to all the principles of Renaissance and Antiquity.

The Überwasserkirche at *Münster* was built (without a break) between 1340 and 1346, and still has High Gothic piers. The Wiesenkirche did not influence it, perhaps because its construction went slowly: the middle choir may have been finished by *c.* 1350, but the south choir was not consecrated until 1376.[43] The hall-church of the *Austin Friars* in *Vienna*, begun in 1330 and consecrated in 1349, is less highly developed than that at Soest, but still gives an effect that is definitely Late Gothic.[44]

church in an early sixteenth-century Gmünd anniversary book. Since his son Peter was born in 1333, Heinrich was probably born in *c.* 1300–10. He may have worked as a foreman (hence his title 'Parlier') at Cologne cathedral during the early stages of the construction of the south aisle of the nave, and came to Gmünd in *c.* 1320–30 when the pace of work on the cathedral began to slacken.[38] Despite his Cologne origins, Heinrich's forms in the nave (and those of the first master) rely exclusively on Upper Rhenish precedents (especially Salem, Reutlingen, Strasbourg west front and Freiburg octagon and spire).[39]

The west front at Schwäbisch Gmünd [204] has no towers, since the Romanesque towers which flanked the west end of the choir were then still standing. The composition is very simple. The decisive factor is a relaxation of strict regularity. The central oculus is slightly smaller than the two flanking ones, and the gable over the porch pushes the string course above it slightly higher in the central bay than in those on either side. The portal seems to stand loosely in its bay. Because of this relaxation of the principles of regularity in the façade, the nave at Gmünd can be called the first Late Gothic building in Germany. These irregularities were not, however, the result of a purely aesthetic intention. They were a makeshift solution, in which Heinrich adapted the existing central section of the façade (already half-completed by his predecessor with a basilica in mind) to the

207. Prenzlau, Marienkirche, begun 1325. Choir gable *c.* 1350

208. Wrocław (Breslau), St Mary-on-the-Sands, 1334– *c.* 1387. Interior. Photo pre-1945

209. Wrocław (Breslau), St Mary-on-the-Sands, begun sometime after 1334– *c.* 1387. Plan

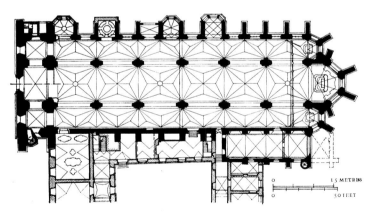

Another district in which Late Gothic forms were readily accepted was that of the North German brick churches. In the hall-church at *Prenzlau*, built begun in 1325 and completed in the late fourteenth century, the corners of the square piers were hollowed out, and round shafts added. The choir chapels are pentagonal, so that one corner lies centrally. The choir is so shallow that a single-gabled front can rise over all three apses together. The free-standing tracery of the gable adopts the principles of the façade at Strasbourg, but the use of brick results in a completely different effect [207].[45]

Not all the brick churches in northern Germany are hall-churches. The church of St Mary at *Wismar*, for instance, is a basilica. The choir, built between 1339 and 1353, has an ambulatory and five chapels. On the outside, the re-entrant angles between the chapels are bridged by arches which support a sloping roof covering the ambulatory and all the chapels – another attempt to relax strict regularity. In the interior, there is a contrast between the slender ribs and the massive piers, between the thin mullions and the

extreme length of the windows, especially those in the transepts. At Wismar, old traditions are combined with Late Gothic forms. The way in which the groups of shafts spring from corbels between the arcade arches is a result of English influence.[46]

A Late Gothic hall-church, St Mary-on-the-Sands in *Wrocław (Breslau)* was begun in 1334 [208, 209]. It has a central polygonal apse flanked by two polygonal apses, and a choir and nave each with three deep bays. The vaults in the narrow aisles look like half-stars on paper, but, seen in three dimensions, the similarity disappears. The buttress between each pair of windows supports two obliquely set transverse

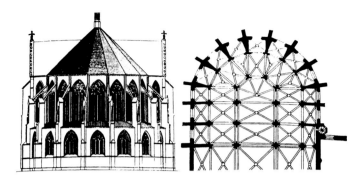

210. Zwettl, Cistercian Church choir, 1343–83. Plan and elevation

arches whose other ends stand on the piers of the nave. Each triangular cell is crossed by three ribs arranged in triradial form – the term coined for tracery being used here to describe ribs. This constructional form, called *Springgewölbe* ('jumping vaults'), is a regional speciality of the Silesians,[47] and represents another decisive break with the High Gothic principle of regularity.

The church of *St Elizabeth* in *Wrocław (Breslau)*, a basilica, is less heavy but stresses the solidity of the walls yet

211. Schwäbisch Gmünd, Church of the Holy Cross. Exterior of choir, begun 1351

more. It is a parish church but is reminiscent of the churches of the mendicant orders, especially in its contrast between the long windows of the choir and the large wall surfaces in the nave. The choir, consisting of three bays and three parallel choir chapels, was in building in the 1350s and its high altar was founded in 1361. The arcade has no abaci and the hollows of the piers continue without any break into the arches. This gives a definitely Late Gothic effect.[48]

At *Heiligenkreuz* (see above, p. 181), the three bays of the choir, built about *c.* 1288–95, are identical in shape, but the position of the altar gives the eastern bay together with the eastern bays of the choir aisles the character of a rectangular ambulatory. This arrangement is derived from the rectangular ambulatory of the basilican choir at Lilienfeld, although there the sanctuary ended in a polygonal apse. *Zwettl*, built between 1343 and 1383, is a combination of both these forms [210]. The inner polygon of the Sanctuary is similar to Lilienfeld's; the ambulatory is concentric with it, but in the form of a hall. It used to be thought that the polygonal hall choir, combined with radiating chapels, made its first appearance here, but it is now clear that Zwettl was preceded, and indeed influenced by, the hall choir of *Schwäbisch Gmünd* [211].[49]

At Zwettl the piers have clusters of shafts, while at Gmünd the designer remained faithful to the round piers of the nave of about 1320 [203]. He repeated the capitals, which have the form of wreaths, but built taller piers, so that the choir is clearly separated from the remainder of the church. In both these churches, Zwettl and Gmünd, the chapels introduced a horizontal fusion, stressing the contrast with the verticals in the very long windows of the nave. At Gmünd a strongly defined cornice runs between the apexes of the chapels and the sills of the windows. Where this is crossed by the shafts it projects in the form of a triangle – thus combining diagonality with interpenetration [203].

The exterior of the choir is determined by the continuous band of chapels, which are separated by flat piers. These piers have fillets with sharp profiles at their angles [211]. The details are all full of individuality and imagination. In the shallow niches in the piers there are carved figures standing on corbels, and over them gables rise into the flat-topped piers of the balustrade. The tracery of the balustrade consists of an arrangement of quatrefoils which is made up of alternating combinations of a whole quatrefoil above a half one, and *vice versa*. The upper, pointed windows are capped by ornamented, semicircular arches which are fitted so closely between the buttresses that their extrados are segmental in shape. The balustrade at the eaves of the roof repeats the form of the lower one. Each window has different tracery, which is still 'Geometrical' but is full of semicircles and segmental arches where one would expect pointed ones. The ogee arches have the early form of pointed arches with a concave-sided point on top. There are no capitals on any member of the windows nor on the jambs. The multitude of decorative detail and the gargoyles vitalize both the horizontal and the vertical lines. The close relationship between the walls is strongly emphasized. All these are elements of the style of Peter Parler's later works.[49A]

At about the same time as Zwettl, *c.* 1340, a second type of hall choir was built in the Wallseerkapelle at Enns in

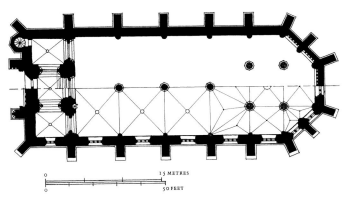

212. Pöllauberg, pilgrimage church, designed *c.* 1370. Plan

213. Enns, Franciscan church. The Wallsee Chapel opens from the north side of the nave

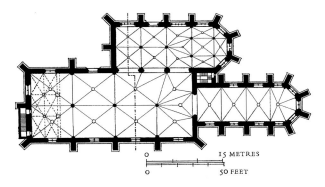

Austria. This chapel influenced the pilgrimage church at Pöllauberg, in building around the year 1370.[50]

Pöllauberg is two-naved and has four bays [212]. The choir is formed of five sides of an octagon, and consists of three vessels spanning the same width as the two vessels of the nave put together. The length of the middle side of the octagon determines the width of the central vessel of the choir, which therefore runs through the full length of the east end. As the two flanking choir vessels are the same height as the central one, we can walk from one side to the other through the central vessel, as in an ambulatory. The vaults of the choir and the choir aisles, however, run parallel from west to east. This type may be defined as a choir of interpenetration. The choir of the Wallseerkapelle in the Franciscan church at *Enns* is of the same type [213, 214]. *St Lambrecht* shows a variation with a seven-sided choir.[51] Donin added a considerable number of other choirs formed by the interpenetration of choir, choir aisles, and ambulatory.[52] One of the most important of them is the cathedral at *Augsburg*, which is supposed to have been influenced by the choir in Prague because the Bishop of Augsburg visited Prague in 1356. However, this view has now been rejected. The chevet, begun in 1356, has a plan based on Cologne Cathedral's. Some time during construction, it was decided to alter the geometry and position of the sanctuary apse. Its originally intended polygon, of seven sides of a dodecagon (like the polygon of its chapel ring), was replaced by a large three-sided apse whose eastern end rests on the entrance pillars of the easternmost radiating chapel. As a result, the apse comes right up to the eastern chapel, cutting across the

low ambulatory on either side of it. The inner central aisle thus merges with the eastern bay of the ambulatory, like St Lambrecht, but in basilican form.[53]

The solution reached at *La Chaise-Dieu*, near Clermont-Ferrand, is related to the hall-choirs and to the choirs with interpenetration of choir, choir aisles, and ambulatory.[54] Pierre Roger lived there as a monk. He was made pope and took the name Clement VI. From 1344 to his death in 1352 he rebuilt the church. The new church was a hall-church of nine bays – a type rare in France.[54A] The eastern walls of the choir forms five sides of an octagon, and there is no ambulatory. The five radiating chapels are the same height as the choir, giving the impression that here again the choir continues into the central chapel. The church contains a number of specifically Late Gothic forms: the arches die into the piers; in the aisles the bays are separated from one another only in the top parts; the gallery forms a clear spatial division, in the middle of which stands the sarcophagus of the pope. Forty steps lead up to the west doorway, and the façade is grave and reserved. The whole church is heavy, hard, and gloomy; it is very monumental, indeed papal, in effect, but above all else it is a true mausoleum.[54B]

During this generation work continued on *Saint-Ouen* at *Rouen*, at *Vendôme*, and at *Troyes*. However, the new parts continued in the style of the older ones – the regularity of the High Gothic. The architect at La Chaise-Dieu was unhampered by such considerations, and so this church

214. Enns, Franciscan church. Wallsee Chapel, *c.* 1340, interior looking east

remains the one splendid fourteenth-century work of the Late Gothic style in France.

In 1352, work was begun on the east end of the cathedral at *Antwerp*. This consists of a choir and choir aisles, each of three bays, an ambulatory forming five sides of a decagon, and five polygonal chapels. The almost flat roofs over the ambulatory and the chapels allowed the building of long windows in the apse, reaching down to the apexes of the arcade, as at Le Mans – a feature which determines the character of the exterior. Work continued on the choir until its completion towards the end of the fourteenth century, no thought being given to the advances made by Peter Parler in Prague from 1356 onwards.[54C] However, inside the choir there are already the same tracery designs, in the spandrels of the arcade, as were later to give the nave of Antwerp Cathedral its Late Gothic character. The design for this nave must already have been in existence in about 1422, when the west front was begun. The adherence to a quadripartite rib-vault in this work was conservative, but the elimination of capitals in the arcades was definitely progressive.[55]

4. PENDANT BOSSES. FLYING RIBS. NET-VAULTS WITH INTERRUPTED RIBS. CONCAVE-SIDED GABLES. CHOIRS WITH AN EVEN NUMBER OF SIDES

The importance of Bohemia in the Late Gothic style in Germany is due to the personality of the Emperor Charles IV (1316–78), the son of King John of Bohemia. His mother, Elizabeth, was the sister of Wenceslas III, the last of the Přemyslids. He grew up in France at the court of his uncle Charles IV, changed his name to Charles, and married his cousin Blanche, daughter of the king of France. In 1333 he chose Prague as his residence, and in 1344 persuaded Pope Clement VI to raise the see of Prague to an archbishopric. In the same year he began to build a new cathedral in *Prague* on the Hradčany, the highest part of the city, on the left bank of the Moldau [215].[55A]

As a result of his French upbringing, he called to Prague Matthias of Arras, an architect who had probably worked at the cathedral at Narbonne. Matthias began his work with the apse, consisting of five sides of a decagon, the trapezoid bays of the ambulatory, and the five chapels, each ending in five sides of an octagon. This row was to continue along the sides of the basilican choir. When Matthias died in 1352 these chapels were not finished. On the north side only one was built; on the south side two had been completed and a third begun. The only unusual feature of the choir is the decoration of the lower parts of the main buttresses with pinnacles [216]. These piers between the chapels have a pointed projection on the middle of the frontal surface, running from the floor-level through the massive pinnacle to the finials. The buttresses of the chapels themselves are frontal, but become diagonal where they recede above the level of the window sills.[56] At this level they are also decorated with tabernacles which are lighter than those on the main buttresses. The transplantation of the pinnacle (which normally marks the upper end of a member) to the exterior surface of the buttresses is akyristic. The way in which the spires penetrate the string courses is clearly Late Gothic. Matthias allowed himself all these liberties in Prague, although the work at Narbonne had carefully followed the stylistic principles of regularity.[56A]

When Peter Parler took over in 1356,[56B] he did not continue the line of chapels as regularly as Matthias had planned them. He began, between 1356 and 1362, by joining two bays in the row of chapels on the north side, separating them from the choir aisle, and turning them into a sacristy [215].[56C] Each of these two bays has a different vault. In the eastern bay, the middle points of the four sides are connected by transverse arches set diagonally. Triradials are set into each of the resulting triangular cells and also into the four inner triangular cells, thus producing deltoid severies. The bewildering complexity is produced by the fact that upon these deltoids are set tiercerons which spring from the middle points of the sides and further by the fact that they are connected by horizontal ridge-ribs crossing the apex. From the apex hangs a cylindrical post which ends in a kind of pendant boss; from the circumference of this boss flying ribs rise which end where the ribs running parallel to the walls become ridge-ribs [217]. Though not everyone will have the patience to work out and visualize this geometrical pattern and to understand the geometrical principles involved, anyone can understand that Peter Parler made two innovations which he developed logically from the nature of the rib-vault: he turned the whole vault through 45 degrees, and he added to the existing types of ribs the new (English) type of the flying rib.[56D] Whereas statics demand that members should follow each other upwards, the boss here hangs downwards. This is made possible only by replacing compressive by tensile strain. Structure has here been changed into three-dimensional texture.

The vault in the western bay of the sacristy is simpler.

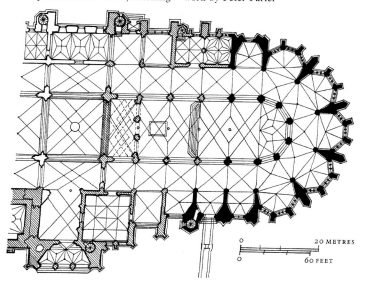

215. Prague Cathedral, begun 1344. Plan of choir. Dark shading = work by Matthias of Arras; hatching = work by Peter Parler

0   20 METRES
0   60 FEET

216. Prague Cathedral. Exterior of choir, 1344–85

When the sacristy was finished, Parler built the adjacent chapel of St Sigismund, which also consists of two bays, and projects a little beyond the sacristy, which, in turn, already projected beyond the original row of chapels.[56E] The chapel of St Andrew, like that of St Sigismund covered by simple cross-ribbed vaults, projects yet further beyond the other chapels on the south side. The chapel of St Wenceslas, next to it, projects further again, and, to make it square, ruthlessly takes in part of the south transept. Its western wall lies right against the south porch. This is the reason why the porch is tripartite, while the portal has only two doorways. The vault in the porch consists of groups of triradials, which are joined to the pier between the doors by flying ribs [219].

In the chapel of St Wenceslas, the vault is different again [218]. Each of the four sides is divided into three parts, whose relative widths are approximately in the proportion 1 : 2 : 1. From the one-quarter and three-quarter points on each side, transverse arches go to the corresponding points on the opposite wall, while ribs with the same profile go to the diagonally opposite points. These ribs, therefore, lie on planes parallel to the main diagonals of the square plan, where there are, however, no ribs. A cross of lierne-ribs joins the intersections on the arches following the main axial direction. This construction leaves a triangular cell in each of the four corners of the chapel, and, where this meets the walls, it looks as if it had been folded into the corner of the walls. In each corner, also, two halves of pointed arches meet on the walls.[57] The chapel of St Wenceslas was built between c. 1358 and 1366, and was followed by the porch to the south transept.[57A] After 1369, the missing piers in the choir were completed and the choir aisles vaulted, and in 1374 the triforium was underway [220]. If Matthias had had the intention of repeating in Prague what had been built in Narbonne the triforium would have had a solid back wall, but Peter Parler built a glazed triforium which is drawn into a unity with the windows. The sturdy little columns of the triforium, aligned with the mullions of the clerestorey windows, are set back behind the line of the arcade below. The joint between the columns of the triforium and the shafts of the vault responds is set diagonally, and above the joint there are diagonally set tabernacles. The essentially Gothic emphasis on the diagonal has perhaps never been so intensely and tangibly expressed. As in the case of the string course running round the choir of Gmünd, one is made to feel that the layers jut forward from the core of the wall.[57B] The tabernacles have primitive ogee arches. The increasing dominance of curves is evident in the tracery of the windows. The pattern of the inner balustrade is modelled on that of the exterior at Gmünd.

The interior, including the vault, was finished in 1385. It was within the German-speaking countries (in so far as the cathedral of Prague must be called the work of a German architect of the school of Cologne and Gmünd) the first net-vault in which the transverse arches are interrupted in their upper sections. It is not accurate to describe this net-vault as a series of triradials, since it does not really consist of groups of three co-ordinated ribs, but rather of fragments of a transverse arch which splits into two liernes.[57C]

All these vaults remind one of English work. There is no written evidence that Peter Parler ever went to England, but his work shows clearly that he must have known English vaults, at least from drawings, if not from actual visits. His vaults are never copies of English models, but the tiercerons, liernes, and flying ribs in them are English elements. Parler's net-vault, however, has no ridge-rib.[57D] The balustrade at the eaves of the roof, which does not begin at the line of the guttering as at Gmünd, but at the level of the top of the windows, bears a slight resemblance to that of the cathedral at Reims, but translated into the Late Gothic style.

217. Prague Cathedral. Interior of sacristy, *c*. 1350–60

218. Prague Cathedral. Vault of chapel of St Wenceslas, 1358–66

219. Prague Cathedral. Vault of south porch, completed by 1367

220. Prague Cathedral, begun 1344. Interior of choir, triforium under way in 1374, high vaults finished in 1385

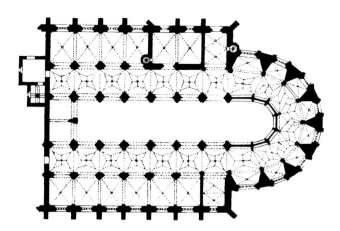

221. Kutná Hora (Kuttenberg), St Barbara, begun 1388. Plan

222. Freiburg im Briesgau, Minster, choir, begun 1354, high vault completed in 1510. Plan

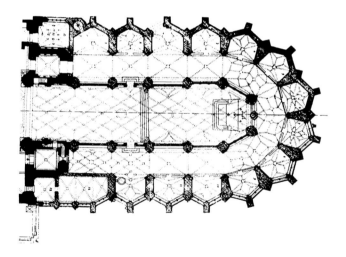

223. Nuremberg, Frauenkirche, 1350–8. Interior looking east

As at Gmünd, the semicircle holds a place of honour in the cathedral in Prague. One of them can be seen in the north portal of the chapel of St Wenceslas, supported on corbels, and decorated and enriched with a Gothic hanging semicircular frieze. The oblique part of the plinth of the jambs slopes like a lean-to roof, and from it spring the profiles of the jamb. In the interior, the plinths of the piers have the same sloping upper end, and in the choir they interpenetrate with the separate octagonal plinths of the shafts. It is here that the specific Late Gothic form of the plinth was created [316].[57E] The capitals crowning some of the shafts of the arcade are small, and the hollows between these shafts run on without capitals. There was an earlier version of this feature in the choir arcade at Saint-Urbain at Troyes.

The south tower, which stands next to the transept, was begun at the same time as the south porch (completed in 1367) probably under the direction of Peter's son, Wenzel. The lower storey is solid and massive; the next storey is lighter and more open.[58] The balustrade, with its tracery consisting of pieces of fused geometric motifs, is a continu-

ation of that on the choir. After Peter Parler's death in 1399, when work had reached not much beyond the balustrade, the first and second storeys were continued by his sons. On the tabernacles standing to the left of the transept window, the sides of the gables are drawn inwards in a concave line. The model for this must have been the upper part of any ogee arch.[59]

Charles IV had died in 1378. He had ideas of his own: he had brought from Italy artists who executed, over the south porch, a mosaic of the Last Judgement, which is penetrated in strange places by Parler's pinnacles. He also decorated the St Wenceslas chapel with polished semi-precious stones, an undertaking to which he was probably led by descriptions of the Temple of the Grail in the so-called 'Younger Titurel'.[60] It has not been recorded what Parler thought of these two examples of royal beautification.[60A]

In those churches in which Parler was able to express his own ideas on the building of choirs – that is, at *Kolin*, begun in 1360, and at *Kutná Hora (Kuttenberg)*, begun in 1388 – he chose to build an odd number of sides, so that there would be a pier standing on the central axis [221].[61] An apse with an ambulatory consisting of a different number of sides from that round the choir had been begun as early as 1354 in the minster at *Freiburg* [222], where Johannes of Gmünd was appointed leading architect in 1359. He was probably the older brother of Peter Parler. He rebuilt the choir of the cathedral at *Basel* from 1357.[62] The chapels at Freiburg have an even number of sides, so that there is a pier standing on the centre-line, a form analogous with that of the two flanking choir chapels in the church of St Mary at *Gransee*, built in *c.* 1370–80.[63] Wherever this kind of plan may have been

224. Aachen Minster. Interior of choir, begun 1355

first put into execution, it shows a great lack of understanding to say that it was chosen merely 'to achieve hitherto unknown effects'.[64] Gothic choirs with an odd number of sides, beginning with that at Saint-Denis, present one frontal view and several diagonal ones. Those with an even number of sides present only diagonal views. It is possible that every Gothic architect of genius was endeavouring to find 'hitherto unknown effects', but the important fact for the historian is that, by building an even number of sides, architects were demonstrating yet another consequence of the diagonal emphasis first established in a rib design.[64A]

Charles IV may also have employed Peter Parler in his other foundations – for instance, in the building of the *Frauenkirche* at *Nuremberg* between 1350/52 and 1358 [223]. This is a hall-church, which shows some similarities with *St Stephen* in *Prague*.[64A] In 1355, too, work began on the choir of the cathedral at *Aachen* [224]. The apse is formed of

nine sides of a fourteen-sided polygon, and, as in the Wiesenkirche at Soest, the first two sides diverge obliquely outward. The choir combines features of the Sainte-Chapelle in Paris with features of the Wiesenkirche.[65] The radiant festiveness of the interior is admirably suited to the purpose of this church, in which the German Emperors were crowned. Charles IV had been crowned here in 1349, and may well have found the Carolingian church too dark a place from which to step into the imperial limelight.

The church of Our Lady at *Karlov (Karlshof)* in *Prague* was probably modelled on the octagon at Aachen. This, too, must have been a personal idea of Charles IV, since there is hardly another example of a Gothic church built on a central plan.[66] The church was consecrated in 1377. The star-vault, which spans about eighty feet, is a sixteenth-century replacement of the original vault, which probably consisted of a chapter house-like umbrella of triradials supported on a

225. Vienna, St Stephen (Cathedral). Vault of chapel of St Catherine, complete by 1396

single central column. Here again, one of the polygonal piers of the apse stands on the main axis.[67]

The form of the chapel of St Catherine on the east side of the south tower of the church of *St Stephen* in *Vienna* is similar to that of the Karlshof church [225], but the vault is in the form of a pendant boss with flying ribs, and its span is only about one-third as great as that in Prague.[68]

The choir of St Stephen was begun in 1304 and consecrated in 1340.[69] It is possible that a complete plan was made for the whole church in 1304, and it may already have been decided at that time to preserve the west façade with its two towers, begun in the twelfth century [226, 227]. As this façade is not as wide as the combined width of choir and choir chapels, a two-storeyed chapel was added on each side, projecting some distance beyond the outer walls of the choir and the nave. It is not known whether the two additional towers were also planned as early as 1304, but it can be presumed that this plan included the nave and aisles continuing the choir and choir aisles westwards. The details must have

226. Vienna, St Stephen, Choir begun 1304; nave after 1340 or 1359; net-vault completed by 1467. Plan

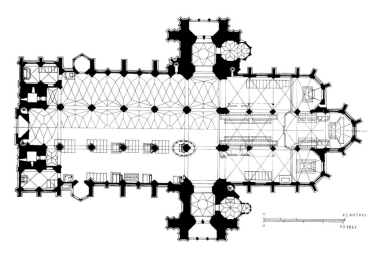

been revised as the work progressed in the fourteenth and fifteenth centuries.

It is known that Duke Rudolf IV, the son-in-law of Charles IV, laid a foundation-stone in 1359, always presumed to have been the foundation-stone of the nave. Construction of the new nave started with the outer walls, and left large parts of the Romanesque nave intact within them. By *c.* 1380 the south wall of the nave, up to the string course below the gables, was finished. Attention was by then largely concentrated on the building of the south tower, and it was only after the completion of its spire in 1433 that the nave was roofed and vaulted. In the 1420s the remains of the Romanesque nave were demolished, and from 1440 the huge roof was under construction. Hans Puchspaum, cathedral architect from 1446–54/55 designed and built the nave vaults. While the aisles in the hall choir of St Stephen's are all of equal height, the central aisle of the nave is appreciably higher than the side aisles, although there is no clerestory, so the nave can be called a hall church [228]. This heightening may reflect a desire to utilise as much as possible of the space within the roof, or to enhance the atmosphere of sanctity by the deeper darkness of the central vessel. It certainly gives a more satisfying symmetry to the west façade by elevating its central section. The Emperor Frederick III, who succeeded in raising St Stephen's to the status of a cathedral in 1469, may also have influenced the decision to create a 'pseudo-basilica', since it resembles a 'royal' basilical cathedral more than a pure hall church. Each bay of the side aisles is lit by a pair of windows, and each aisle covered with a net vault. Puchspaum may also have designed and installed the figures and canopies grouped around the nave piers, but they could equally be the work of his immediate predecessors, including, perhaps, Hans von Prachatitz (1429–35).[70] These figures appear not only on the frontal shafts, as in the Sainte-Chapelle and in the cathedral at Cologne, but also on the diagonal ones, at a lower level. Standing in a zigzag pattern in groups of three, each group with one on a higher and two on a lower level, with the lower ones set diagonally, they play a considerable part in determining the overall effect of the interior. As this staggered arrangement is repeated on the sides facing the aisles and again on the walls of the aisles themselves, one's full attention is automatically directed to a consideration of the innumerable combinations formed by these seventy-seven figures.

When Rudolf founded the new nave in 1359 he also envisaged two towers placed at the junction of nave and choir, forming transept-like projections on the north and south sides of the church. Only the south tower was completed. The north tower, similar in general design, was begun in the middle of the fifteenth century and was left unfinished about half-way up.[71] The south tower, together with its chapel of St Catherine and its south porch, was begun in *c.* 1370 (the south porch implies the influence of the south porch at Prague cathedral, completed in 1367). The first design for the south tower envisaged a smaller structure than the present one, similar perhaps to the steeple at Freiburg, with an octagonal belfry storey beginning at the level of the present lower gables. St Catherine's chapel was built together with the tower. Its vaults, which reflect the influence of the pendant skeletal vaults of Prague cathedral sacristy of *c.* 1356, were completed, together with the rest of the chapel, in 1396 [225]. Some changes in the design of the tracery on the buttresses of the second storey were made by the master mason Ulrich Helbling (active 1392/94–99). But these designs were not realised until after *c.* 1400. Around the year 1400, when construction had reached just above the south portal, a master Wenczla (Wenzel Parler, oldest son of Peter Parler) took over the leadership of the lodge, and planned a taller steeple. He made the octagon begin at a much higher point, and inserted below it a tall square belfry storey, the diagonal faces of which rest on large brackets (carved with animal grotesques) inserted across the corners of the buttresses just below the first windows. This enlarged tower marks the rejection of the Rudolfian two-tower idea in favour of a gigantic single steeple. Peter von Prachatitz took over as master mason in 1404. In *c.* 1407 parts of this new tower had to be demolished but this probably involved no drastic rebuilding. The vaults of St Catherine's chapel were *not* rebuilt, but gables (intended in the original Rudolfian plan but excluded in Wenzel's or Peter von Prachatitz's changed design) had to be reinserted in front of the belfry storey,

resulting in some demolition of the adjacent masonry. The surviving accounts between 1412 and 1433 give us a clear picture of the progress of the steeple: in 1415/16 the belfry stage was finished and work began on the octagon; in 1426/27 the octagon was finished and gables begun in front of the spire; in 1429 Hans von Prachatitz took over as the leading architect; on 10 October 1433 the spire was completed.[72]

All this has been discussed in detail because of the stylistic significance of the tower [227]. A comparison with the two towers at Cologne suggests itself immediately. Not only did the architect know the design for Cologne, or such part of it as had been executed at this time, but his own design can be regarded as a criticism and a correction of what he felt to be the faults of the towers at Cologne. The general conditions prevailing in the bottom storey were different. The arrangement of the porch in Vienna, whether or not it was influenced by the church in Prague, is certainly quite independent of that at Cologne. Above the bottom storey of each tower at Cologne follow three clearly delineated storeys and the pyramid of the spire. In Vienna, there is the same

227. Vienna, St Stephen (Cathedral). View from the south west. Nave begun 1359; south tower *c.* 1370–1433

228. Vienna, St Stephen (Cathedral). Interior of the nave, begun 1359

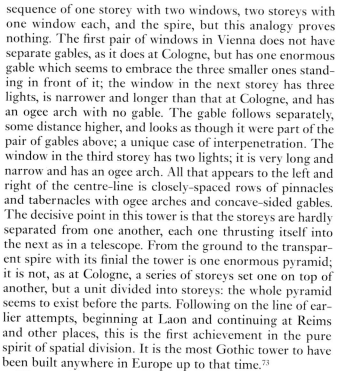

229. Nuremberg, St Sebaldus. Eastern choir, 1361–79. A: Exterior;
B: Interior

sequence of one storey with two windows, two storeys with one window each, and the spire, but this analogy proves nothing. The first pair of windows in Vienna does not have separate gables, as it does at Cologne, but has one enormous gable which seems to embrace the three smaller ones standing in front of it; the window in the next storey has three lights, is narrower and longer than that at Cologne, and has an ogee arch with no gable. The gable follows separately, some distance higher, and looks as though it were part of the pair of gables above; a unique case of interpenetration. The window in the third storey has two lights; it is very long and narrow and has an ogee arch. All that appears to the left and right of the centre-line is closely-spaced rows of pinnacles and tabernacles with ogee arches and concave-sided gables. The decisive point in this tower is that the storeys are hardly separated from one another, each one thrusting itself into the next as in a telescope. From the ground to the transparent spire with its finial the tower is one enormous pyramid; it is not, as at Cologne, a series of storeys set one on top of another, but a unit divided into storeys: the whole pyramid seems to exist before the parts. Following on the line of earlier attempts, beginning at Laon and continuing at Reims and other places, this is the first achievement in the pure spirit of spatial division. It is the most Gothic tower to have been built anywhere in Europe up to that time.[73]

The south tower of the cathedral in Prague above the balustrade was begun at the latest in 1392. It served as a model for all but the lower storey of the tower in Vienna. Built by Parler's sons, Wenzel and Johannes, there is a close resemblance to the Viennese tower. In 1415 Peter Parler's son, Janco, is named as the legal heir to Peter von Prachatitz, a proof that friendly relations existed between them. It is quite certain that the members of the lodges of Prague and Vienna enjoyed a free exchange of ideas, and that jealousy and local patriotism were alien to them. Their personal plans were almost certainly the product of their talents, and not of any ambition to be original. One can see from their works that they must have recognized Peter Parler as the final authority.[74] The Parler family had a definite influence

on the architectural creations of their generation in Germany, not only in Prague itself, as in the *Týn* church,[74A] and in *Freiburg* and *Basel*, but also in *Nuremberg* and *Ulm*.

The parish church of *St Sebaldus* at *Nuremberg* was a basilica with two choirs and an eastern transept.[75] It was begun in *c.* 1230/40, was in use by 1256, and was complete by 1273. Between 1361 and 1379 the original eastern choir was replaced by the one now standing [229]. The original nave was preserved. It was built by masons who had worked on the Cistercian abbey at *Ebrach*, and is really still a part of the early spread of the Gothic style. It has shafts set on brackets round the square piers, large expanses of wall, like the cathedral at *Bamberg*, built by masons from the same school, and a triforium which is still very Romanesque in character with frontal abaci, and Romanesque friezes of round arches on the outside of the polygonal choir and the west towers which rise without any batter or recessions.[76] The original eastern choir must have been equally outmoded. Its replacement by a hall-choir was apparently a reflection of a change in taste, and the architect would probably have been happy to pull down the western choir and the nave also. It is not known whether there were controversies on the subject in Nuremberg, but the building as it stands now shows that the people of the time had some appreciation of the contrast between the new choir and the old nave. It was a contrast that was to be repeated in other combinations of hall-choirs with older naves.[77]

The ridge of the vault in the hall-choir lies about six feet six inches higher than that of the nave, while the ridge of the roof of the choir rises almost forty-three feet above that of the nave [228]. The octagonal piers have no capitals, the arches of the vault penetrating the piers and the shafts, but having completely different cross-sections. The vaults are simple four-part vaults, and the triangular cells lying between the rectangular bays of the ambulatory have triradial ribs. Fragmentary friezes of round arches were once suspended from the ribs.[77A] The insertion of a semicircle into the pointed arch over the Bridal Doorway is evidence of the influence of the Parler family. The unacademic form of the penetrations at the springing of the vault, and the radiant light in this interior in which space seems to expand and circulate, is the very opposite of the 'academic fossilization' attributed to the Late Gothic style by some scholars:[78] Eberhard Lutze rightly speaks of 'clarity transfused with spirit'.[78A]

The choir of the Minster at *Ulm* was begun in 1377 by two other members of the Parler family, Heinrich and Michael. Probably because it was built of a mixture of stone and brick, materials which do not settle equally, the vault, similar in form to that in the cathedral of Prague, was not built until 1449. The nave was first planned on the hall scheme. The elements which make the Minster at Ulm significant in the history of the Gothic style were all, however, the work of later generations.[79]

5. THE FAN-VAULT

In the chapter houses the development of vaulting led to a co-ordination of all ribs emanating from the centre. They have the same curvature and the same profiles, and one scarcely notices that there must be certain differences between them, since at Wells, for instance, the ridge-rib forms a polygon [192]. If instead of a polygon the ridge-rib is a circle, then all ribs achieve identity of curvature, and a pure rotation figure results, a concave-sided funnel: a fan-vault.

This form, which had originated in centrally-planned buildings, was transferred by the architect of the east range of the cloisters at *Gloucester* to a series of square bays [230]. He halved the form of the Wells chapter house (*c.* 1300) vertically and formed a row of halved fans in such a way that their axes coincided with the boundaries of the bays. Transverse arches and wall arches form part of the fans and are co-ordinated with the three ribs which lie between them. What was a polygonal ridge-rib at Wells is in the fan-vault a semicircular rib on the horizontal ceiling. This ceiling appears only fragmentarily between the fans as flat quadrangles with convex sides. Between the main ribs is blank tracery with many ogee arches.

The fans as halves of concave funnel-shapes are concave in all vertical sections, but convex in all horizontal sections.[80] The visual effect is an undulating flow from bay to bay, and since both movements – from north to west and from south to north – are of equal value, the result is a kind of arrested wave.

Peter Parler in the vestry at Prague Cathedral connects his pendant with four arches which look like fan-vaults. But they do not form a proper vault; they are only the skeleton of a vault. Whether this form is connected with Gloucester, and if so in what way, we do not know, but both the Gloucester fan-vaults and Parler's vestry belong to the same period. The fan vaults in the east walk of the Gloucester cloister, from the church to the chapter house door, were built during the abbacy of Thomas Horton (1351–77) and were probably complete by 1364. All the other walks of the cloister, the south, west, and north, were constructed in that order under Abbot Walter Froucester (1381–1412). While it is not possible to establish a fixed date for each wing, it is clear that Parler's sacristy vaults, of *c.* 1356–60, are contemporary with those of the first fan vaults.[80A] Whatever the dates, the two designs are probably independent of one another. Both are the product of their period, a period whose style was valid for the whole of Europe.

6. THE SPREAD OF THE GOTHIC STYLE IN THE LATE GOTHIC PERIOD

The Italians, like the English and the Germans, had their own national Gothic style in the fourteenth century. However, compared with the work of Italian architects, the products of the northern schools, in spite of certain obvious differences, do seem to be fairly closely related. Northern architects developed the Gothic style, tending, in their own way, to make it more Gothic. The Italians amalgamated elements of the Gothic style with elements of their own native traditions, tending all the time to make it less Gothic. It retarded without being retrogressive. It never tried to revert to the Romanesque or to pure classicism, but, with complete impartiality, borrowed elements from both these styles and from the Gothic. The judgements of architects of the

230. Gloucester Cathedral. East walk of the Cloisters, 1351–77

231. Siena, S. Francesco. Interior

232. Florence Cathedral. Interior of nave, begun 1293/6, restarted in 1357

Renaissance show how wrong it is to claim that the Italian Gothic style and the Early Renaissance are one and the same.[80B]

Just as we have not been afraid to call the early friars' churches in Italy Gothic, so we shall include those of the fourteenth century within the scope of this term. The church of *S. Domenico* at *Siena* was begun soon after 1226. Its nave was complete by *c.* 1300, but its large transept, begun in *c.* 1306, was probably unfinished in the early fifteenth century, and the whole church was not completed until around 1480. Most of the exterior presents large, bare brick surfaces. The transepts rise above the chapels which flank the choir, and their windowless end-walls present no stylistic features at all. The pointed windows in the chapels and the buttresses are Gothic, and the whole building can be called Gothic in the same way as the early friars' churches.[80C]

On the south side of the church of *S. Francesco* at *Siena*, there are some remnants of the church in building in 1247–55. The present church, with a nave about 70 feet wide, no aisles, and an open timber roof, was begun in 1326 and was finished before 1475, when Francesco di Giorgio heightened the nave. Perhaps it was designed as a protest against the luxuries of the cathedral in the same city. The simplicity of the design, and the execution of the alternating black and white bands, in paint and not in marble, preaches the ideal of poverty. As always, however, the Franciscans came into conflict with the principle of the negation of personal possession, and the impressive scale of the church contradicts the modesty that was intended [231]. The continuation of the walls of the nave to the east wall of the transepts is Late Gothic. There is no real crossing: one arch on each side opens the nave to the transepts. The entrances to the chapels flanking the choir are treated as a kind of 'interior façade', as in S. Croce at Florence. The seven windows in each wall of the nave give limited but sufficient illumination. The ribs in the chapels and the simple tracery are Gothic; the bands of different colours are Tuscan; and the remainder is a blend of the Franciscan and the utilitarian. The *artistic* qualities of the church lie, paradoxically, in the denial of the stylistic forms of the time: they symbolize the principle of asceticism. Standing on a hill, the church dominates the surrounding area with conscious majesty, clearly betraying the paradox inherent in pride in humility.[80D]

After the death of Arnolfo sometime between 1301 and 1310, little progress was made at *Florence* with the building of the cathedral. Giotto began the campanile in 1334, but when he died in 1337 only the bottom part had been built.[81] It was continued by Andrea Pisano and Francesco Talenti. The division of each bay into two in the upper storeys was an alteration in the plan made by Talenti, but both remained faithful to Giotto's stylistic vocabulary. The narrow windows with tracery are flanked by slender colonnettes with spiral fluting. The capitals have a trace of classicism in them and are surmounted by a kind of fragmentary architrave. The inner columns, also spiral – a translation of Gothic window shafts into the language of the Cosmati – stand on a balustrade, and this again is unusual for the Gothic style. At this time in Cologne the designs for the towers of the cathedral had already been made. A parchment plan for the campanile, now in Siena, and ascribed by some authorities to

233. Florence Cathedral. Interior of choir, begun 1377

Giotto, shows the tower crowned by an octagonal belfry and crocketted spire similar to the steeples at Cologne and Freiburg. But this plan was only realised up to the height of the first socle storey. The idea of a tapering steeple, if it was ever conceived by Giotto, was given up, and his successors were content to lighten the mass gradually by enlarging the openings in the top storey of the campanile. Only the gables and the octagonal piers at the corners are Gothic. The whole is a combination containing a few Gothic elements.[81A]

Vasari began his series of biographies with Giotto, leading many people to suppose that the birth of the Renaissance can be seen in his work. Nevertheless there was a feeling that Giotto's work did not really fit into the Renaissance, and the term Proto-Renaissance was coined, meaning a renaissance which was not yet The Renaissance.[82] Today, we tend to see in Giotto the greatest painter of the Late Gothic age. In the history of architecture, however, Giotto is neither the greatest Gothic architect, nor the first architect of the Renaissance.

In 1359 Andrea Orcagna, a contemporary of Talenti, completed the tabernacle in the *Or San Michele* at *Florence*. Here he amalgamated different styles with the same freedom as the architects of the campanile. He, too, uses spiral columns, the traditional forms of the Cosmati, round arches,[83] isosceles triangles as gables on all four sides with fairly pure Gothic pinnacles next to them, and, behind the gables, a steeply rising cupola. Here, too, the columns sup-

port a fragmentary architrave and stand on pedestals; both of these features are classical in feeling. By contrast, the pinnacles have Gothic buttresses which end in a slope. Combinations such as these appear in countless smaller works of Italian Gothic architecture. Again and again one is faced with the rather illogical question: is this Gothic really Gothic?

This question is never so pressing as in the study of the *cathedral* at *Florence* [232, 233]. In 1355 Francesco Talenti was commissioned to make a wooden model for it. On 19 June 1357 Talenti began to build the pillars of the nave, starting at the west end. He proposed three virtually square bays not envisaged by the late thirteenth-century builders. This meant an inevitable discord with the earlier bay divisions established by the buttresses at at the western end of the aisle exterior walls, constructed under Arnoflo and/or his successors. At this stage, it is likely that Talenti also designed a regular octagonal cupola 62 braccia wide, on the site of what may have been Arnolfo's proposed octagon. Up to 1366 the first two nave bays were constructed and vaulted by and large according to Talenti's plan, although he was joined as capomaestro by Giovanni di Lapo Ghini in 1363. But from 1366–67 a number of important debates took place on the length of the nave and the final shape of the octagonal east end, which radically altered the cathedral's future shape. Three separate advisory commissions of sculptors, painters and goldsmiths, including Taddeo Gaddi, Andrea

Orcagna and Andrea Bonaiuti (known as Andrea da Firenze), decided to lengthen the nave eastwards by an extra fourth bay. On 9 August 1367 they also called for an increase in the width of the octagon from 62 to 72 braccia (making it extend beyond the width of the nave). And they may also have proposed the structurally adventurous addition of a drum between the octagon and the proposed dome, to heighten and lighten the east end. Talenti and Ghini accepted these proposals in August 1367, although they insisted on larger piers than planned between the crossing and the nave. In 1368 the plan was ratified, a definitive model in brick was approved, and all future capomaestri sworn to adhere to it. In the later 1370s the fourth nave bay was under construction. By 1418 most of the east end, incuding the drum, had been completed, faithfully following the committee's project. Brunelleschi's dome, designed in 1418, adheres both to the height and curvature projected in the 1367 design.[83A]

These changes in design seem to have been aimed primarily at increasing the interior space. Dehio characterizes this interior very aptly by comparing it with Amiens.[84] The height of the nave and of the springing of the vaults, and the overall length, are practically the same in both churches. By comparison with these similarities, however, the differences are enormous – for instance, the length of each bay at Amiens is 25 feet; at Florence it is 63 feet.

In the cathedral at Florence the rib-vaults, whose ribs form pointed arches, are Gothic. Not at all Gothic, however, are the broad profiles of the arcade arches, the shape of the piers, with their strictly frontal pilasters, the plinths which follow classical models, and the architrave and cornice which separate the capitals from the arches. Each architrave also serves as a plinth for the pilaster above. Some of these elements probably formed part of Arnolfo's plan, for they remind one immediately of S. Croce.[84A] The balcony which runs above the upper architraves, along the foot of the vault, has polygonal projections where it meets the bottom of the ribs, the most sensitive point in a vault.[85] This, too, is reminiscent of S. Croce and also of the cathedral at Siena. In the aisles, long windows with tracery float, as it were, in the expanse of the wall. The light entering the nave through the large oculi in the clerestory is softened by stained glass. The structural members of the church are of dark stone, while the walls are plastered and painted in a light colour. It is said that it was intended to decorate the church with frescoes and mosaics.[86]

In the octagon the same piers are repeated, but without projections at the angles of the diagonal surfaces.[87] The balcony continues all the way round, turning off into the transepts and the choir, and here, too, it covers the base of the vault. Each apse has half an octagonal domical vault with no ribs. The lines of the channels between the cells have been traced in paint, but this is modern work. Choir and transepts have five radiating chapels each, and these chapels have ribs with a chamfered profile – in most cases half an octagon, the usual profile in Tuscany – which are in charac-

ter with the sharpness of all the profiles in the rest of the church. The general abstract geometry is interrupted, however, by the three rows of foliage on the high capitals.

By 1413 the cathedral was complete up to the oculi in the tambour. Brunelleschi's dome, an octagonal domical vault with no ribs,[88] is the concrete expression of the ideas of Talenti, Ghini and the commissions. Just as Talenti (and the committees) may have executed Arnolfo's plan for an octagonal east end on a slightly grander scale, so Brunelleschi adopted and adapted the scheme for a dome and drum bequeathed him by the 1367 project, again on a larger scale. The dome was intended to surpass those at Pisa and Siena. It is not itself Renaissance in style. Brunelleschi's so-called exedrae attached externally to the diagonal sides, and his lantern, might perhaps be called Renaissance; the lantern, however, still preserves the principle of the Gothic flying buttress.

There are no flying buttresses on the outside of the nave, but the vaults of the main apses are supported by triangular buttressing walls, encrusted with marble, like the rest of the exterior. The windows on the south side of the nave have gables some distance above them, and on the flattened point of each of these gables stands a tabernacle. Arnolfo may have introduced this form over the two flanking doors in the façade. This truncating of the gable, and the variations of the forms of gables, later became popular in the frames of altarpieces.[89] The west façade, and its incrustation was designed and begun by Arnolfo and finished only up to a height of about 25 metres by 1310. It was pulled down and rebuilt in the nineteenth century,[90] but we know from a drawing of 1587 the parts of it that were built.[91] The part of the two flanking doorways in the façade which lies above the springing projects forward, and in the same horizontal zone there is a row of reliefs running behind a colonnade with straight entablature.[92] The way in which this row even breaks through the buttresses by means of completely classical tabernacles with straight entablatures is against all the principles of statics. The next section of the buttresses, above the one just mentioned, is also hollow. Spiral colonnettes and pointed arches are related to the forms used in the campanile, but they stand side by side with round arches. One feels as though one had been set down once again in the earliest days of the Gothic period, and is therefore tempted to speak of passive transition. It is certainly passive in that there are concessions to models in an alien style, but the term passive transition refers to a transition to the Gothic style, and Talenti's transition led, not to purer Gothic style, but to Brunelleschi's Renaissance.

Some people will hold that it is more important to recognize the cathedral at Florence as a great work of architecture than to find out whether it fits into a scheme of historical periods, but the important question is really whether or not this scheme is broad enough in scope to include the cathedral. The concept of the spread of the Gothic style covers not only the passive transition, the architecture of the friars, and the early national variations on the High Gothic, but also those in the age of the Late Gothic. The Italian Gothic style of the fourteenth century must be included within this last category, since it is a blend of native traditions with the Gothic style.

234. Siena Cathedral. Exterior from the south west. Façade 1284–?1317.

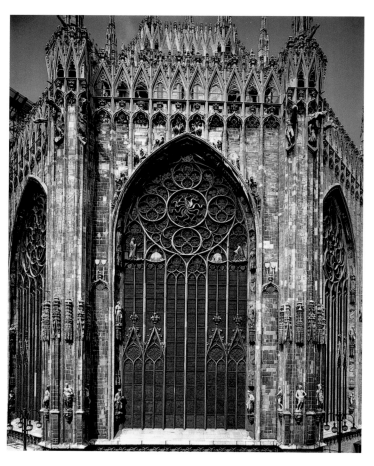

235. Milan Cathedral. Exterior of the Choir, begun 1386

236. Milan Cathedral, begun 1386. Interior

Apart from the question of style, many different opinions have been held of Florence Cathedral: it has been called hard and cold, disappointing, 'very dark, gloomy and uninteresting',[93] and, on the other hand, stern and noble. There is a more tangible feeling of bigness in the cathedral at Florence than in the great French cathedrals: it makes one feel small, but liberated from oneself rather than oppressed. There is a distant reminder of the monumentality of classical Roman architecture. The breadth of the space beneath the dome makes it the focal point of the church and of the whole city. Churches like Pisa, Siena, Ely, and later St Peter's in Rome and other churches modelled on it, in which the central and longitudinal tendencies are combined, possess a common dynamic feeling of drama. In Florence, the nave leads, like an introduction of slow chords, to a goal of self-contained finality. Approaching from the west, we move on in continual suspense, which relaxes as the full extent of the octagon unfolds. This movement culminates in tranquillity transfused with power: it is the path from expectancy to fulfilment, from hope to redemption. One should refrain from comparing works of architecture with works of poetry; but S. Maria del Fiore and Dante's *Divina Commedia*, designed at about the same time, are truly comparable, as two artistic symbols of the progress of the human spirit towards the absolute. The basic idea of both works is a Christian one, but, in this distinctive form it is specifically

Gothic. Both artists speak the language of Florence, and anyone who really appreciates Dante should be especially receptive to the qualities of the cathedral, and vice versa. In trying to fit Dante, Giotto, and Arnolfo into their correct historical places one encounters the same difficult problems in each case, but with each of them it is far more important to appreciate the intrinsic value of their work than to place them historically. Talenti and the many artists and laymen who put Arnolfo's plan into execution and developed it must be given credit for their understanding of his intentions and aims. The achievement of the city of Florence was to possess the energy necessary to complete the work.

The fact that this energy, too, deserves respect is shown in visible form in the towering walls of the unfinished addition to the cathedral at *Siena* [234]. The plan was to add a new building to the side of the old so as to turn the existing nave and choir into the transepts of the new church. The piers have round shafts; the arcade and the windows in the unfinished façade have round arches, and the transverse arches, too, are semicircular. All the new parts would have been a confirmation of the Romanesque character of the existing cathedral, rather than an advance towards the Gothic style.[94] Work began on it in 1339, after the baptistery of S. Giovanni had been completed under, and to the east of, the choir of the old cathedral. The baptistery, begun in 1316/17, was part of a wider plan: to extend the cathedral choir much further eastwards than the old early thirteenth-century east end, and to use the baptistery as its substructure. The whole initiative was to be completed by an eastern façade, the baptistery with its three portals forming its lower part, the choir its upper. The marble cladding and Gothic decoration of this façade – with its lower, portal zone dating to before 1333, and its upper, choir part to the second half of the fourteenth century – is of a purer Gothic than any other façade in Italy. Although unfinished, its whole design is preserved in a parchment drawing in Siena dated to *c.* 1317.[95]

The upper storey of the west façade may have been under construction by *c.* 1300–10, and perhaps substantially complete by 1317, the year the S. Giovanni façade was begun. In contrast to S. Giovanni, the whole façade is probably the best example of a mixture of styles. The three doors of almost equal height, begun in the 1280s by Giovanni Pisano, still have a great deal of Romanesque detail; but they also have Gothic gables with Gothic crockets on them. The upper storey, perhaps of the first decade of the fourteenth century, makes use of the whole of the Gothic vocabulary, though the three main gables are separated from the wall below by horizontal base-lines. Harald Keller who thought the upper parts of the façade belonged to the later fourteenth century, tried to reconstruct Giovanni Pisano's project for the upper façade by making the oculus smaller and continuing the line of the buttresses. Recently, Antje Middeldorf-Kosegarten has argued that the upper façade was also constructed according to the design of Giovanni or his immediate successors, and substantially complete by 1317. As it stands, the façade seeks to relax its strict regularity by a displacement of the flanking axes in the upper storey. Keller's reconstruction is a correction in accordance with orthodox French practice, but it may not reproduce Pisano's intentions. The work of the 'epigones' is very much more Italian.[96]

In the façade at Siena, and to an even greater degree in that at *Orvieto*, splendour is achieved by means of mosaics – another factor in this mixture of totally.

In *Florence* the order of the Vallombrosani, a branch of the Benedictines, began their new church of *SS Trinità* in the late thirteenth or early fourteenth century, though the existing nave was not begun until 1360/70. The style recalls the cathedral, S. Maria Novella and S. Maria Maggiore in Florence. The classical, human proportions of the pilasters combine perfectly with the tranquillity of the spatial proportions of the interior. Comparing this church with the norms of the French High Gothic style, one is perhaps inclined to read into it a protest against the Gothic style: in the Trinità, while the frontal piers with their pilasters are still Italian Romanesque, the vaults show an attempt to adapt to the new style.[97A]

The piers in the cathedral at *Lucca* are an imitation of those in the cathedral at Florence.[98] At Lucca, the porch of an older church was preserved. In the interior, the piers and the pilasters above them are connected by round arches. The old-fashioned galleries may have been introduced in imitation of galleries existing in the preceding Romanesque church. The tracery that fills the gallery openings must have been a great source of pride to the architect.[98A]

A generation after the resumption of work on the cathe-dral at Florence, in 1386, the cathedral at *Milan* was begun[99] [235, 236]. It is a basilica consisting of a nave with double aisles, roofs descending in two separate steps over the aisles, transepts, and a choir with an ambulatory. It therefore belongs to the same type as Bourges and Le Mans, but the proportions are lower and wider and more in keeping with Italian traditions. The piers are octagonal with pear-shaped shafts at the corners. Between the capitals of the piers and the springing of the arcade arches are drums decorated with tabernacles filled with figures. This decoration is Gothic in detail, but not at all Gothic in its interruption of the vertical lines. The transepts have aisles, and a chapel forming three sides of an octagon in the centre of the north and south walls, which are a faint reminder of the idea of the trefoiled east parts of Florence Cathedral. The choir ends in an apse forming five sides of an octagon and an ambulatory, also with five sides. As a result, the ambulatory is extremely spacious. The impression given by the interior, as one enters the cathedral, is determined by the form of the ambulatory. Since its outer walls are so much longer in plan than those of the apse, and since the windows can stretch the full width of these walls because of the absence of chapels, one sees, on looking down the dark row of piers, the brilliant light from the large east window with its late tracery, against which are outlined the dark silhouettes of the last piers. Only the little windows in the vault of the apse and in the drum over the crossing answer this strong light from the big windows of the ambulatory. Unfortunately they have been filled with nineteenth-century stained glass which is glaring in colour and totally unsuccessful in design. However, seen at a distance, from the nave, this is not too disturbing, and one still gets approximately the impression of what was intended.

Most of the exterior dates from the nineteenth century too, but it represents a realization of the original design. In the wealth of its open and blind tracery, it is a challenge to the cathedral at Cologne. The tracery is full of Late Gothic details, such as ogee arches and mouchettes, which undoubtedly date from the Late Gothic period. In brick churches, concessions had to be made to the material that was used, both in colour and in the strict limitation of detail. Here, on the contrary, the greatest possible wealth and visual splendour has been achieved by the use of marble.

The tracery in the windows of the choir chapels inserted between the mullions about half-way up should be recognized as one of the original innovations in the development of the Gothic style. Each of the windows is divided into six lights – of which each is further divided into two – and on top of each whole window there is a large oculus. The secondary tracery, surmounted by pairs of gables with finials, is set into the outer lights only, leaving the two central pairs of lights free.[99A] This is not the only original idea: but one remains more inclined to admire this massive, heavy church as a monument to the extraordinary ambition of man, than to devote oneself to an analysis of its details.

The church of *S. Petronio* at *Bologna* was begun in 1390, only four years after the cathedral at Milan. Here, as at Siena, the architects were so ambitious that only the nave was actually built. The vehement controversies over the continuation which took place in Bologna in the sixteenth century are as interesting as those in Milan in the fourteenth.[99B] In both cases the main problem was to determine proportions. At that time the measurements of sketches and models could only be transcribed on to the actual building to which they referred by applying them to triangles and squares, regular figures that could easily be reproduced at any size. However, the subject of discussion was not only the possible methods of reproducing proportions on a larger scale, but also the actual proportions. Because of their own traditions the Italians rejected the steep proportions favoured in northern Europe, and in Milan reduced the height partly also by using the Pythagorean triangle, whose sides are in the proportion $3:4:5$. A great deal of work has been done on the study of these problems, but more research is still needed.[100]

The problem of medieval methods of measurement concerns the history of style only because artists were restricted to the use of measurements which could be transcribed from one scale to another; within these limits they were free. The methods of measurement which go back to the time of classical architecture, and even beyond, to the age of the Egyptians, were not a guarantee of beauty, as the Romantics supposed: they were quite independent of considerations of style. What they did ensure, however, was the regulation and the unification of proportions. In the nineteenth century an architect could choose any proportions he liked and transcribe them from one scale to another because the methods of measuring distances and angles had been improved. The idea that the artist must obey only his own creative imagination led to the rejection of the rediscovery of medieval methods, and on the other hand the idea that the secret of beauty lay entirely in proportions led to the interpretation of medieval buildings, often in inaccurate plans and elevations, through fantastic, complicated, and highly arbitrary linear grids, which were superimposed on the buildings, or rather on the approximately measured designs for the buildings. The beauty of original Gothic works lies in many factors – among others in a uniformity of proportion that gave rise to the principle of similarity among figures, that is to the repetition of certain proportions which were basically free but governed by the practicability of their execution.

If one is to discuss beauty, objects in which there is a mixture of styles are not the best for this purpose. The Italian Gothic style is often marked by an obvious joy in the 'cantilene' of lines and spaces, and in its breadth and human proportions. It may be interesting to read works by nineteenth- and twentieth-century critics, in studying the spirit of their own age, but the only real criticism of the Italian Gothic style is to be found in the buildings of the Italian fifteenth century. Here and there, the Italian Gothic style survived, but, from that time on, it no longer predominated.

It becomes quite clear how Italian all these churches are when they are compared with Portuguese and Swedish works that are also part of the spread of the Gothic style in the Late Gothic period.

Alcobaça (1178–1223), perhaps the grandest of all Cistercian churches,[101] was not specifically Portuguese.

In 1388, King João founded the Dominican monastery at *Batalha*, near the battlefield of Aljubarrota, in memory of his victory over King Juan of Castile, whom he expelled from Portugal in 1385. The eastern chapels follow the Cistercian plan; the elevations follow the regular principles of the French Gothic style; the vaults, with longitudinal and lateral ridge-ribs, follow English examples;[101A] the façade is said to derive from the English Perpendicular style, and the spire on the tower is modelled on the kind of thickly crocketed profile with "crow's nest" balcony half-way up that is popular in Germany in the fifteenth century.[102] The highly developed tracery on the façade follows the patterns of the French Flamboyant. The flat roofs are Portuguese, and, at the same time, they are the common property of all the Mediterranean countries. So there was nothing yet in the fourteenth century that could be called a Portuguese Gothic style: Batalha is a product of the spread of the Gothic style in a country trying to find a national style through an eclectic approach.[103] The result is a Dominican church of regal splendour.

At the same time as Batalha, the church of St Bridget was built at *Vadstena* in Sweden.[104] It is a hall-church with strong, octagonal stone piers. Shafts only begin a little way below the springing of the vault; the thin ribs in the star-vault are of brick, and the cells are all somewhat domical. The connexions with the forms of the German Order are another expression of the spirit of a country which first followed French models (*Uppsala*, begun c. 1270, and taken in charge by a French architect some time in, or before, 1287[104A]), and then German ones (the hall-church at *Linköping*).[104B] The Gothic style continued to spread in Sweden, but without being affected by native tradition.

7. THE BEGINNINGS OF THE FLAMBOYANT

In France, hall-churches remained rare. After La Chaise-Dieu, St Michel des Lions at *Limoges* was built in this form.[104C] Hall-churches were traditional in Poitou; so their appearance in Limoges should not be interpreted as a concession to the Late Gothic style. In Poitou, the hall-church remained within the sphere of the regular Gothic style, with plain rib-vaults and piers with their pear-shaped shafts connected by hollows. It has been said that in France there was no alteration of the basic type of spatial form, but only of the details, especially those of the tracery. This is true, except for the one word 'only'; for the change in tracery altered the whole church.[104D] The term Flamboyant derives from the similarity of some forms of tracery to the leaping upward of flames, but it has been extended to include all figures which are bounded by double curves.

In England (as mentioned above, p. 194), this kind of tracery appeared as early as about 1310, for instance in the chapel of Merton College at *Oxford*. In fact Christopher Wilson has shown that reticulated tracery made its first known appearance in the southern half of the east walk of the cloister of Westminster abbey, constructed c. 1300–10.[104E] The reredos at *Beverley*, built in the 1330s, shows that by then the style had already been fully developed.[104F] In France, tracery with double curves does not appear in a developed form until about 1375, in the two nave chapels at *Amiens* built under Bishop Jean de la Grange from 1373 to 1375.[105]

However, double curves had appeared in tracery in France before this date. Lasteyrie has devoted great energy to finding early examples[106] in order to prove that French and English architects evolved these forms independently of one another. But the real question is when these forms ceased to be mere background elements and became positive, primary figures. In France this occurred for the first time at Amiens.[107]

The main forms of these figures have two points or only one point,[108] and both these forms appear in the La Grange chapels, together with spherical triangles and spherical rectangles. The French call the figures with two points and with one concave curve and one double curve 'mouchettes', and those with two double curves 'soufflets'. Bond calls the former 'falchions',[109] and the latter 'daggers'. In German, they are both called 'Blasen' (bladders) or 'Fischblasen'. At Amiens, there are already circles, divided into two identical mouchettes by a double curve. This pattern best represents the principle of division. Similar forms – four, five, or six mouchettes in a single circle – appear in the western bays of the nave clerestory at *Exeter* cathedral, dating to the 1330s and 1340s.[109A] Triangular and quadrangular figures remain independent and self-sufficient units and, as the style developed, they were more and more avoided.

The Flamboyant is a style relying on texture. It infuses a building inside and outside with a Late Gothic character, whatever its plan or type. At Amiens, the architect of these two chapels combined his own version of English Curvilinear with an English starvault, of which he could see an example (built in the 1260s)[109B] in the crossing of the cathedral. In the chapels, as in the cathedral proper, the starvault is used as a centralizing form.

The second important work in this new French style was the Sainte-Chapelle at *Riom*[110] [237]. It was built by Duke Jean de Berry (1340–1416), who had spent the seven years from 1360 to 1367 as a hostage in England. The château of Riom, which he began in the early 1370s, has completely disappeared. Only the chapel, built between 1395 and 1403, has been preserved within the modern Palais de Justice. It has four bays with no aisles, and an apse forming three sides of a hexagon. The last bay has rectangular oratory on either side. The rib-vaults have ridge-ribs. The shafts grow without capitals into the arches of the vault. The tracery in the windows, each of four lights, consists of ogee arches and, between them, in each window, a soufflet filled with rather elongated quatrefoils; on each side there are mouchettes, which look as though the frame of the window were cutting into their sides. The ridge-rib made its first appearance in northern France, at Airaines, Montiviliers, and Lucheux (p. 64), though at Riom, like the tracery, it probably came from England. In spite of this, the general atmosphere in the chapel is definitely French – not only because of the French stained glass. The French were eager to move with the times, but they were always bound by their own ideal of clarity. The proportions of the chapel are wide and commodious, ideal for the private chapel of a château, and far removed from the extreme narrowness of the High Gothic.

The west façade of *Rouen* cathedral is one of the more complicated ensembles of Gothic architecture. The two flanking doors date from between *c.* 1180 and 1200 and are

237. Riom, Sainte-Chapelle, *c.* 1395–1403. Interior

framed on the left by the Tour St Romain of about 1150 and on the right by the fifteenth-century Tour de Beurre. From the late 1360s onwards the thirteenth-century west front was overlaid with a new decorative ensemble, the conception of which goes back to the architect Jean Périer (fl. 1362–88). He proposed a triple porch in front of the three portals (it was begun but probably never completed); he built a rose window (under construction in 1370) over the central (Saint-Romain) portal, and he decorated the two buttresses which immediately flank the rose with three-light blind tracery panels, each housing six statues (mentioned in 1386). His successor, Jean de Bayeux (fl. 1387–98), continued the idea of a tracery screen at rose level by installing the two blind windows with statuary above the right hand (Saint-Etienne) portal, and beginning and possibly completing the panel on the far left of the façade, between the St Romain tower (the north tower of the west façade) and the left hand (Saint-Jean) portal. This is the first to have fully flamboyant tracery. Finally, under Jenson Salvart (fl. 1398–1447), the two tracery panels (with developed curvilinear forms) above the Saint-Jean portal were installed between 1406 and 1421. Enlart thought the whole composition, with its screen-like presentation of tiered figures, was influenced by English

238. Ulm Minster. West front. Nave begun 1380s, steeple begun 1392

and completed in the 1390s, adheres, rather conservatively, to a late Rayonnant vocabulary. It shows no curvilinear forms except in the ogee arches decorating the archivolt niches and the tympanum of its portal. The north transept was begun in 1415, but by 1420 work had reached no higher than the capitals of the portal and the triforium of the lateral walls. The portal also shows diminutive ogees in its micro-architecture. The flickering forms of its gable and of the large oculus which crowns the main window of the transept belong to a much later phase of construction, probably under Bishop Jean Baillet (1477–1513). They go well beyond the broader forms of Lyons, and resemble the curvilinear fluency of the roses of Martin Chambiges at Sens.[112A] The le Roux tracery in the western rose and western portal gable at Rouen carry this interest in dense and flickering repetition to dramatic extremes.

The lower door by the steps leading up to the cathedral at *Albi*, built by Bishop Dominique de Florence (1397–1410), has open Flamboyant tracery in the tympanum as background to the figues standing in front of it [187].[113] The outermost voussoir of the arch is given an ogee curve by an addition of two counter-curves. The *Recevresse* at *Avioth*, built in the early years of the fifteenth century,[114] a small building like a tabernacle beside the church, may have been intended to be an altar of the Virgin upon which pilgrims might leave their gifts; it has arches consisting of double

239. Regensburg Cathedral. West front, 1341–1496

facades.[111] Certainly, the flowing tracery introduced by Jean de Bayeux (?) and Jenson Salvart must count among the earliest examples in France, though it has no specific English precedent. Guillaume Pontifs (fl. 1462–97) added the upper storeys of the Tour St Romain from 1468, and began the Tour de Beurre in 1487. At his death ten years later it was incomplete, and his successor Jacques le Roux (1497–1508) finished it with its present octagonal crown in 1507. Designs for the central portal were submitted by Jacques le Roux and his nephew Roullant le Roux in 1508, but it was probably not begun until 1509 by Roullant (fl. 1508–?27). Its gable was largely complete by 1514. The flamboyant rose behind it was constructed as part of this early sixteenth-century ensemble.

The rose window in the west façade of *Lyons* cathedral, finished in 1393 by Jacques de Beaujeu, has curving tracery that is still relatively broad and inflated.[112] Later, in the later fifteenth century, during the 'mature' phase of the Flamboyant, the tracery units become narrower, and resemble the flames from which the style derives its name. The process towards a more advanced and complex curvilinear can be seen in the transept façades of *Auxerre* cathedral. The earliest, southern, transept front, designed in the 1370s or 1380s curves, and soufflets in the balustrade of its transparent spire. In contrast with the choir, which dates mainly from the second half of the fourteenth century, the windows of the nave and transepts of the church itself are also Flamboyant.

All these early works of the Flamboyant, including the Chapelle Vendôme on the south side of the nave of the cathedral at *Chartres*, built in 1417,[114A] are small, and in most cases additions to older buildings [74]. It would be interesting, therefore, to find a completely new building of this generation and to see how the Flamboyant looks on a larger scale; and such a building exists in *Notre-Dame de l'Epine* near Châlons-sur-Marne, begun sometime before 1440. However, the early parts of this church, surprisingly, have no trace of the Flamboyant in them but are conservative, even reactionary. As far as the choir, the transepts, and the four eastern bays of the nave are concerned,[115] the plan, the piers, the triforium, and other features are all modelled on the cathedral at Reims.[116]

The long period between the building of the two de la Grange chapels, 1373, and the beginning of the Chapelle Vendôme at Chartres, in 1417 – the period of King Charles VI (1380–1422) – should be considered as the beginning of the Flamboyant period, but the buildings created at this time show that, mainly due to the Hundred Years War against England, which lasted from 1337 to 1444, France no longer played a leading part in the development of the Gothic style.

8. VARIATIONS BETWEEN 1390 AND 1420

In the years between 1390 and 1420 there were four great architects working in Germany. They had all been influenced by the school of the Parlers, and, though their work is connected by the style of their time, the work of each is also characterized by personal differences of style. They were Ulrich von Ensingen and Wentzel Roriczer, both of whom lived from about 1350 to 1419, and Hinrich (*sic*) von Brunsberg, *c.* 1355 to soon after 1428, and Hans von Burghausen, *c.* 1360 to 1432, both about ten years younger than the first two.

Ulrich von Ensingen took over the building of the minster at *Ulm* in 1392, when Heinrich Parler II and Michael Parler II and Heinrich Parler III had finished the aisleless choir, except for the vault [238].[117] Heinrich Parler II had begun the hall church, and Michael Parler II and Heinrich Parler III laid down the foundations of the nave, with the side aisles as wide as the central aisle. But Michael Parler II (*c.* 1384–87) altered the hall to a basilica, and Ulrich continued the basilican nave, and at the west end began a single tower, part of which was to be open to the full height of the nave.[118] Statically it was unsatisfactory; in 1494 the piers had to be strengthened and the entrance bay below almost completely sealed off from the nave. The aisles, too, had to be radically altered, each being divided longitudinally into two in 1502.[119] At Ulrich's death in 1419 the porch to the tower was substantially complete and work had reached the large window above it. The complicated triple front of this porch, standing in front of double doorways, shows that the archi-

tect knew Prague and Vienna. The diagonal corner piers, the penetrations of the plinths, the slight concavities of the gables in the blind tracery, the ogee arches, the continuous frieze of tracery behind the figures in the three front arches, the free rhythm of the alternately wide and narrower openings and of the detail in general – all these things are already highly developed Late Gothic elements.[119A] The tabernacles on the buttresses of the choir, standing on the sloping surfaces at the top, are triangular in plan. Ulrich's design of 1392, the so-called Plan A (Ulm Stadtarchiv) is contemporary with the beginning of the tower in Prague, but is far more developed than that of Prague, and also than the design for the lower storey of the tower in Vienna, which dates back to about 1370.[119B] Around 1407, Peter von Prachatitz re-designed the upper part of the tower in Vienna, surpassing the style of that at Ulm, which was continued after 1417 by Hans Kun, and after 1446 by Ulrich's son Matthäus Ensinger, both of whom remained faithful to Ulrich's design in the use of open tracery influenced by Strasbourg.[120]

From 1399, when Peter Parler died, Ulrich continued the work on the façade of Strasbourg Minster. Under Master Gerlachus (1341–71) the second storeys of both towers had been completed by 1365 [169]. Sometime before the completion of the north tower, between about *c.* 1360 and 1365 it was decided to introduce a connecting belfry between them, as shown in a design of the central section of the façade (Strasbourg, Musée de l'Oeuvre Notre Dame, Inv. nr 5). The gallery, depicting the Ascension, was placed just above the rose. The actual construction of the belfry began only later, perhaps in the 1380s and to the slightly altered designs of Michael of Freiburg, or his successor Klaus von Lohre, both of whom may have intended a single tower rising above the belfry.[121] Ulrich abandoned the idea of a central tower and placed his new steeple over the north tower. His design consisted of a two-storeyed octagon, flanked by four staircase turrets and crowned by a concave-sided steeple. Work began in 1399. At his death in 1419 construction had reached roughly half-way up the second storey of the octagon and the four octagonal turrets had been taken up to the top of the first octagon, where they would probably have been terminated in pinnacles. These pinnacles were never built, and the second storey of the octagon was adapted by Ulrich's successor, Johannes Hültz, to take his new design for the spire. The staircase turrets were extended right up to the height of the top balustrade. The scissor-shaped ogee arches of the octagon seem a logical development of the intersecting gables on the tower at Vienna, or the intersecting ogees above the south transept window in Prague cathedral. Preserved in Berne is a drawing of the whole west façade, probably made by Ulrich's son, Matthäus Ensinger, and showing the spire as it may have been envisaged by Ulrich, with concave sides very similar to Plan A of Ulm [247].[122] Ulrich has been criticized for building his octagon without any consideration for what stood below it; but the whole façade is composed of designs equally lacking in consideration for each other, and it has none the less been enthusiastically praised over the years, from the time of Pope Pius II to Goethe's, and to the present day. After Ulrich's death the tower was completed, in

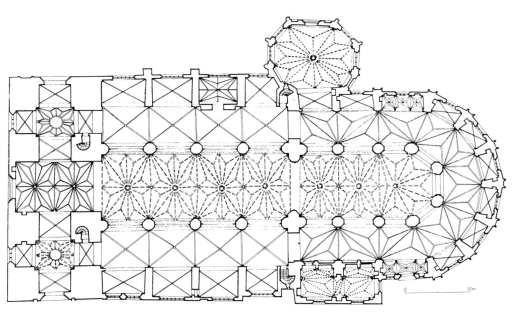

240. Stargard, St Mary. Plan, begun before 1388

241. Brandenburg, St Catherine. Gables of the Lady Chapel, finished by 1434

242. Landshut, St Martin. Interior; choir *c.* 1385–1400, nave *c.* 1400–80

1439, by Hültz, to yet another new design, and the spire is therefore in the style of the next generation.[122A]

Wentzel Roriczer, the second of the four great masters of this phase, was given the task of continuing the west front of the cathedral at *Regensburg* [239]. Here again there is no unity in the work. The south tower is supposed to have been begun in 1341, and its low doorway is reminiscent of English façades.[123] Roriczer is first mentioned as *Dombaumeister* in 1415. He died in 1419. When he took over the work the upper storey of the south tower was complete, the central west portal and its triangular porch had just been finished, and the foundations and ground courses of the north tower

had been laid out. Wenzel raised the tower to just above portal height. His successors (Andreas Engl, Konrad Roriczer, Matthäus Roriczer and Wolfgang Roriczer) completed the façade and north tower by 1496, using a Parler-based vocabulary that had been valid since the early fifteenth century – for example, large ogee arches decorated with curtains of trefoils. The bellcote in the middle of the gable is a reminder of the façade of the Frauenkirche at Nuremberg, while the porch, which projects on a triangular plan, is similar to the so-called Triangle at Erfurt, built about 1330, two generations earlier. The clear horizontal and vertical lines act as a steadying influence on the multiplicity of the detail. The cohesion of the wall is decisive, since the storeys do not project or recede. The porch appears therefore all the more emphatically diagonal.[123A]

The third of the four great architects, Hinrich von Brunsberg, worked in north-east Germany, the region of brick architecture.[124] The church of St Mary at *Stargard* [240] is a basilica, and was begun a few years before 1388.[124A] The discrepancy between the number of sides of the choir and of the ambulatory, and the placing of a pier between choir and ambulatory in the central axis, are evidence of the influence of the Parlers. Peter Parler's church of St Bartholomew at Kolín was begun in 1360, the church of St Barbara at Kutná Hora (Kuttenberg) was begun in 1388 [221], while most of the choir of Stargard belongs to the last two decades of the fourteenth century. The octagonal piers in the choir have niches below the springing, in which it was intended to put figures, as in the cathedral at Milan (*c.* 1390) [236:]; the triforium over the arcade is old-fashioned, but the gallery over the chapels is progressive.[125]

Hinrich repeated this gallery over chapels at *Chojna* (Königsberg in the Neumark)[125A] and in the church of St Catherine at *Brandenburg* [241], built from about 1395 to the middle of the fifteenth century,[125B] but in both these churches it is combined with a hall-choir. At Brandenburg, as at Stargard, a Lady Chapel, richly decorated on the outside with tiles with coloured glazing, was added to the north choir aisle and finished in 1434. The axes of the two win-

243. Landshut, Spitalkirche, begun 1407. Interior

The Corpus Christi chapel on the south side, begun in
c. 1395, at the same time as the nave, has a simpler and more
regular façade. It has a large four-light window without any
real tracery and, above it, instead of a single gable, three
panels containing some open tracery and three gables, all of
brick. Brunsberg's followers used similar decorative forms
in the town halls at *Chojna* and *Tangermünde*, both in the
mid-fifteenth century.[125D]

The fourth great German architect of this generation is
Hans von Burghausen, wrongly called Stethaimer.[126] His
most important church is that of *St Martin at Landshut*,
where he built the choir between about 1385 and 1400, and
the nave shortly thereafter [242].[126A] The piers are extremely
slender, only just over 3 feet wide and nearly 70 feet high;
they continue above the springing of the arcade and intersect with the arcade arches. On each pier the three slender
shafts facing the nave are pear-shaped, while those facing
the aisles are round, separated by five hollows. The soufflets
in the tracery combine with spherical polygons, as they do in
France. The net-vault is similar in plan to that in Prague,
having fragmentary transverse arches, and it is the first vault
of this type to have been designed for a hall-church.[126B] The
two aisles have plain star-vaults. The audacious statics serve
the spacious interior. Nave and aisles together form a single,
primary, given spatial whole of a rare intensity.[126C]

244. Salzburg, Franciscan church, choir begun 1408. Interior looking
east from the nave

dows do not coincide with those of the two doors underneath (of which the one on the left is bricked up); nor do the
axes of the decorative architecture above the windows coincide with the axes below. This upper section, which is as
high as the two lower storeys together, is in turn divided into
four vertical panels two storeys high. At the top of these are
four canopies over rose-windows with blind tracery. The
two left-hand panels are narrower than the two on the right.
There is here a combination of irregularity and the piercing
of three of the rose-windows so that one can see the sky
through them. Furthermore, there are slight angles between
the four panels, so that they do not lie in an unbroken vertical plane but, in plan, form a gentle zigzag line. The basic
design is asymmetrical, making the chapel tend towards its
eastern end, whereas a symmetrical design would have given
it the character of a transept. The circles and semicircles in
the tracery are influenced by the work of Peter Parler.[125C]

The outside of this brick church is flat, and a high frieze above the row of slender windows echoes the tone set by the low chapels. The very tall tower was not finished until the beginning of the sixteenth century, and its slenderness contrasts with the high-pitched roof of the nave and the lower roof of the choir.

The west door was probably begun just before 1460, about thirty years after Hans's death (in 1432), but to his designs.[126D] It introduced a new form of arch, beginning as quarter of a convex circle, to which is added a concave arch, a variant of the ogee arch that is superimposed, on a large scale, on one of the pointed arches in the porch.[126E]

The *Spitalkirche* at *Landshut*, begun in 1407, is a hall-church with a hall-choir [243], in which the central pier of the apse is silhouetted against the east window of the ambulatory. The net-vault consists of tiercerons, liernes, and transverse ridge-ribs, but has neither diagonal ribs nor transverse arches. In the side aisles, however, each bay has a plain star-vault between transverse arches.[126F]

The choir of the parish (later Franciscan) church at *Salzburg* [244, 245] was begun sometime after 1408.[127] In it, the last two piers of the chancel are omitted, and the central pier stands between its neighbours to left and right in such a position that, in plan, they form the points of a triangle. However, the sexpartite star-vault of this bay and the quadripartite star-vaults of the ambulatory all spring from this pier, and the effect is similar to that of some English vaults. Hans von Burghausen at first intended to replace the Romanesque nave with a four-bay hall that, like the Spitalkirche at Landshut, continued into the choir without interruption. But, having later decided to keep the nave, it is improbable that both he and the churchgoers of Salzburg could have been blind to the contrast between the darkness of the nave and the radiant light of the choir. The progress from hope to redemption is here represented by a different means from that used in the cathedral at Florence, and almost entirely visually. To this visual contrast is added the

spiritual one between earth-bound weight and floating, mystical lightness. The distribution of the ribs makes the whole choir seem to revolve around its central pier.[127A]

The church at *Neuötting* was begun in 1409 and the choir was finished in 1429. The foundations of the nave and its chapels were laid out soon after, but its pillars were begun as late as 1484, and construction continued to 1510. The church is a smaller version of St Martin at Landshut.[127B] A year later, in 1410, Hans began the church at *Wasserburg*, where, unlike Neuötting, building began with the nave. The choir was added by the architect Stephan Krumenauer in 1445–53. The church of *St Jakob* at *Straubing* may also be work of Hans von Burghausen, and it was probably begun in around the year 1400. The vault, completed in 1492, was destroyed by fire, and the tunnel-vault with severies, dating from 1780, and the capitals on the round piers have almost destroyed the original character of the interior. The position of the easternmost piers suggests that the vault of the nave and choir may originally have appeared to continue into the ambulatory, penetrating it as it does in the cathedral at Augsburg. Hans von Burghausen probably knew of this arrangement at Augsburg, which at that time represented the most advanced Late Gothic solution.[127C]

The classification of the years from 1390 to 1420 as the period of variations is justified by the unusual fact that one man built these six churches, which, while they show a clear relationship to one another, are all different in almost every respect. The thirst for variety can be seen in the varied piers; in the church of St Jacob at Straubing they are round, at Wasserburg octagonal, and so on.

Some scholars have also attributed a few other works to Master Hans.[128]

Matthäus Ensinger, Ulrich's son, can be considered together with these four architects. He was called to *Berne* in 1420, and before his move to Ulm in 1446, and his final resignation in 1449/53, had designed and completed the choir (except for its vaults), and the nave chapels. He probably envisaged the present single western tower, but its construction was left to his successors. As in Ulm the weak foundations of the tower caused difficulties. The central aisle of the nave, which closely follows the forms of Matthäus's choir, was under construction from about 1450 to around 1474, the piers have bold chamfered sides, and the arcade arches spring from them at angles of less than 90 degrees. Above the apexes of the arcade the windows begin in a kind of blind triforium. Although Matthäus belonged to a youthful generation, he remained stylistically dependent on the older one, and never found his way into the ultimate phase of the Late Gothic style.[129]

The church of St Jan at *'s Hertogenbosch*, was begun at the east end *c.* 1370. The choir, complete by 1415, was influenced by the choirs of Cologne, Amiens and Utrecht [246], conservative in its spatial type but extremely Late Gothic in much of its detail, especially in its richly decorated exterior. The figures of devils, musicians, and other subjects (some dating from the sixteenth century and others from the restoration of 1860)[130] which bestride the roofs of the flying buttresses are extremely original. The church, too, can be grouped under the heading of variations. It remains eclectic, though much of the detail is good. The prodigality of ideas,

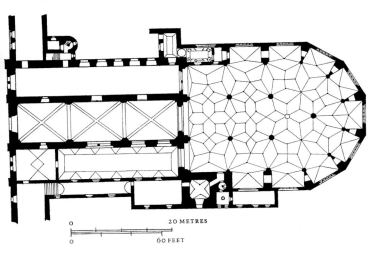

245. Salzburg, Franciscan church, begun 1408. Plan

0   20 METRES

0   60 FEET

246. 's Hertogenbosch, St Jan. Interior looking east, choir *c.* 1370–1415. Nave mostly second half of the fifteenth century

247. Strasbourg Minster, Drawing of the projected steeple, by ? Matthäus Ensinger 1419 (Berne Historisches Museum, inv. n. 1962)

however, prevents the eye from coming to rest on any one spot – a contradiction of the primary aim of the new generation of 1420.

9. THE MATURE LATE GOTHIC STYLE IN GERMANY

Ulrich von Ensingen probably designed a spire for the tower at *Strasbourg*, beginning in a concave recession, with four ascending groups of eight pinnacles on the ribs above it, which would have looked 'like stuck-on candles' [247].[130A] The words are Dehio's, and he goes on to say that 'its outline would have looked delightfully blurred from a distance'. When Johannes Hültz continued the work in 1419, he developed from this plan the seven wreaths of short turrets in which one can climb to the top to enjoy the view [169]. The outline is jagged and the contour shifts continually from foreground to background. The little turrets consist of intersecting ogee arches on slender supports. The originality and the technical mastery of the whole greatly impressed later generations. It is chiefly this spire that has earned for the tower the reputation of being the eighth wonder of the world. Stylistically the spire at Strasbourg is an advance on that in Vienna, which was designed in around 1407; the architect at Strasbourg may

248. Amberg, St Martin, begun
1421. Interior

have known the Viennese design. The tower in Vienna was finished in 1433, and that at Strasbourg in 1439. A comparison between the designs of Ulrich and the execution by Hültz – not between the whole towers – shows that Hültz was not only more daring and blessed with a more fertile imagination than Ulrich, but that he was striving for a harmony which, while it was to some extent the aim of all artists, was to be the main preoccupation of only a very few generations. The roofs of Romanesque towers were closed and could only be reached from inside, but, beginning with the tower at Freiburg, Gothic spires allowed the interior and the exterior to merge. At Strasbourg, while climbing up the outside of the spire one is, paradoxically, inside it at the same time, which makes it the most Gothic of all spires. Further to justify this superlative, all the forms give the impression of effortlessness.[130B] The work of the four great architects of about 1400, including that of Hans von Burghausen, has often something forced about it, a tendency to exaggeration. In the generation after 1419 the

best works are tranquil and reassuring, noble and unhurried, in spite of the agitation within them.

The first building in this 'classic' series is the church of St Martin at *Amberg*, begun in 1421 [248].[131] The exterior has no re-entrant angles, that is the principle of 'addition' has no part in it. The only re-entrant angles are in the few places on the western bays where the buttresses project; and even here, as the buttresses have a triangular section, the effect is one of division rather than of addition.[132] Inside, it is a hall-church with a hall-choir and galleries over the chapels, built with all the stylistic means to partiality which had been developed up to this time. Exquisite beauty is the keynote of the interior. The architect was not hindered by existing older parts and could carry out his plan in a single, uniform style.

His name is not known,[132A] but we do know the names of a number of architects of this generation besides Hültz, although we cannot always be certain which are the works designed by each individual. They are Konrad

249. Nördlingen, St George, 1427–1505. Interior looking east

Heinzelmann (*c*. 1390–1455), Hans Felber (*c*. 1390–1439), Niclaus Eseler the Elder (*c*. 1410 – sometime after 1482), Konrad Roriczer (before 1419–77/78), Hans Kun (*c*. 1390–after 1435), who was Ulrich von Ensingen's son-in-law, and a few others.[133] The practice of employing first one architect, then another, and then calling several to a general consultation has so far made it impossible to determine exactly the part that any one architect played in the building of a particular church.

The church of St George at Nördlingen [249] was begun in 1427. It may have been designed by Hans Kun or by Hans Felber, master masons at Ulm. Construction continued, after 1429, under Konrad Heinzelmann. The vaults, designed by Burkhard Engelberg and Stephan Weyrer the Elder, were built between 1495 and 1505.[134] The choir is narrower than the nave, and therefore its roof is lower too. The central aisle is continued from the choir into the ambulatory,

as at Augsburg and Pöllauberg. In spite of the differentiation between the nave and the choir, the interior gives the impression of running smoothly throughout its entire length; the round piers radiate strength, as they do at Schwäbisch Gmünd, and the vault above them flows smoothly from one bay to the next.

In 1439 Heinzelmann went to *Nuremberg* and began a new choir to the east of the older nave of the church of *St Lorenz* [250, 252]. The form of this choir, with an ambulatory of the same height and with shallow radiating chapels, was not in any way new at this time. There are, however, details which enrich the final impression, such as the irregular octagonal cores of the piers. All these details are intended to make the whole more difficult to comprehend. Compared with the style of the time of Amiens everything is less simple, but without being less clear; it requires far more mental effort to understand, but the whole ensemble offers at the same time

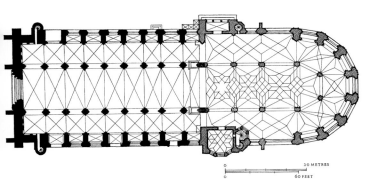

250. Nuremberg, St Lorenz. Choir, 1439–77. Plan

251. Dinkelsbühl, St George, begun after 1448, completed 1499. Plan

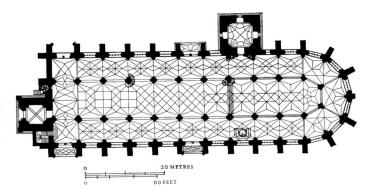

252. Nuremberg, St Lorenz. Choir, 1439–77

far more of that freedom of rhythm which is an element of the so-called picturesque. The contrast in brightness between the choir and the nave is much less marked here than in the Franciscan church at Salzburg, and the whole interior is more relaxed and unpretentious. After Heinzelmann's death, the work was continued by Konrad Roriczer. The complicated vault of the central vessel, by Jacob Grimm, is not developed from the piers. Konrad Roriczer may not have followed the original plans in every detail, but his work is, nevertheless, inspired by the same desire to make comprehension more difficult through irregularities.[134A]

In the church of St George at *Dinkelsbühl* [251, 253], Niclaus Eseler the Elder and his son Niclaus Eseler the Younger built a hall-church that was a stylistic unity, like Amberg. However, they articulated the piers by adding finely differentiated shafts so that, looking eastwards, they close into a series of dark vertical lines with light grey intervals. The choir is built to the typical Parler plan, with a central pier in the periphery of the ambulatory. Amberg and Nördlingen seem rather bare compared with Dinkelsbühl. The decision to do without chapels and galleries is almost like a step back to the period of the Wiesenkirche at Soest. At Nuremberg and Schwäbisch Gmünd it was the chapels and galleries which created a horizontal counterbalance to the verticals: at Dinkelsbühl the very wide-meshed net-vault is sufficient to achieve this effect. Eseler the Elder died sometime after 1482, and the church was completed by his son in 1499.[135]

These buildings – the spire at Strasbourg, the hall-churches at Amberg, Nördlingen, and Dinkelsbühl, and the choir of St Lorenz – represent the state of supreme harmony available to the mature Late Gothic style. In the 'classic' works of the High Gothic, such as Reims and Amiens, there were remnants of the pure 'style of being' of the Romanesque – the basilican form, the transepts, the projecting chapels and detached-looking shafts, and the separation of nave from aisles and of one bay from another. The inner aesthetic tension which is regarded as the essential factor of any 'classic' form sprang from the devaluation of the elements of the 'style of being' and the achievement of a 'style of becoming'. This 'style of becoming', of growing and flowing, did not, however, destroy the tranquility and the relative independence of the spatial sections and the architectural members. The Late Gothic style made a clean break with any memory of the Romanesque 'style of being' and its version of 'classicity' is based on harmony – not the harmony between 'becoming' and the immutability of 'being', but the harmony of movement within itself, a living vibration from within, a current which always returns to its own beginning. This harmony is an expres-

254. Dingolfing, parish church, begun 1467. Interior

255. Munich, Frauenkirche, 1468–94. Interior

sion of a religious emotion which sinks deep into the human soul.

The Late Gothic style produced innumerable larger and smaller works which share to the same degree this 'classicity'. An example can be seen in the Frauenkirche at *Ingolstadt*, begun in 1425, where the towers were built in a diagonal position, like the western towers laid out in *c.* 1500, but never completed, for St Ouen at Rouen.[135A] It is impossible to give rational reasons for finding harmony in some churches and not in others. To some people any differentiation seems subjective, but it has an objective basis; to feel this requires practice and the gradual maturing of an understanding of the works of the select few. People try to show, instead, the faults which spoil some of the second-rate works. For example, it could be said of the nave of the *cathedral* at *Erfurt*,[136] built between 1455 and 1465, that the piers are too heavy, the shafts not differentiated, the transverse arches too broad, and that the capitals interrupt the flow of the whole.[137] Niclaus Eseler might have made the same criticism, but he would have said that these features were not modern enough. Any criticism which is based on the style of the generation in question, and not on personal tastes, contains a factor which cannot be precisely determined. Harmony lies not only in the concordance of width, length,

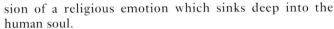

253. Dinkelsbühl, St George, 1448–99. Interior

and height, but also in the combined effect of rhythms and proportions. Although the central nave and the aisles of the cathedral at Erfurt are not of exactly the same width, they seem to be so: the rhythm of the shafts, on the other hand, is in fact regular. In 'classic' works, all measurements are balanced against each other to achieve soft contrasts and a poised tension, not to achieve regularity.

This classicity reached into the second half of the century. The parish church at *Dingolfing* in Lower Bavaria [254], begun in 1467, follows the style of Hans von Burghausen, with the difference that in it the passionate exaggerations of the generation of about 1400 are rejected. The ribs grow out of round piers which are neither too strong nor too slender, and the vault seems to hover above them. The east end follows the typical Parler plan, the apse having two sides towards the east and the ambulatory five; its effect is calm and effortless.[138]

Brick churches, like that at Dingolfing, must satisfy simply by their proportions and their rhythms, and, in the *Frauenkirche* at *Munich*, built between 1468 and 1494 [255], Jörg von Halspach achieved this to a high degree. It is unlikely that he could have known the churches of southern France, but, nevertheless, the tall chapels standing round the church are strongly reminiscent of Albi. At Albi, before they were divided by a gallery, the chapels were joined to a nave, while at Munich they are attached to aisles.[138A] From the entrance, the octagonal piers form a solid row which

256. Salzburg, St Erentrud, crypt beneath the choir begun 1463, nave after 1485. Completed 1506/7. Plan

hides the windows in the chapels. The legend that the Devil ran out of the church because he was frightened by this phenomenon shows that the people of the time were well aware of how surprising and exciting are the views that unfold as one proceeds along the nave, and the discovery of the ambulatory when one has already followed the line of the choir vault to the last chapel is equally surprising. The parish council sent the architect, Jörg Ganghofer to Augsburg to study the cathedral there, and this motif of the penetration of the choir with the ambulatory was the solution with which he returned.[138B]

The net-vault rises on corbels of which some can be attributed to the young Erasmus Grasser,[139] who, in the field of sculpture, was an exponent of the rotating movement which also appears in architecture, but which was not accepted by the architect of the Frauenkirche at Munich. The spiritual grandeur of this church lies in its quiet self-possession: it was commissioned on behalf of all the citizens of Munich. The rulers of Bavaria were allowed to contribute money towards its construction; for, in the eyes of God and the Virgin, they were on the same level as the burghers of Munich.[139A]

The description of all these churches as classic or nearly classic is based on the ambivalence of this term, which not only denotes pure harmony but also the maturity of any style, even where it does not really aim at harmony. The Late Gothic style produced many buildings which are not entirely harmonious and yet not discordant, but are still classic in this second sense of the word, in that they fulfil the principles of this stage of the Gothic style. A particularly attractive example of this classicity is the nunnery church of *St Erentrud* on the Nonnberg at *Salzburg* [256]. The crypt under the choir was begun in 1463; the stained glass by Peter Hemmel was inserted in 1480, showing that the walls of the choir were already standing by that year. The nave was begun in 1485, and the whole church completed by 1507. The western nuns' gallery is shut off from the nave by a wall with windows, which stops short of the vault, giving an impression of strong spatial division. From the traceried parapet of this gallery a balcony projects into the nave, its corners overlapping the piers of the arcade a little below the springing of the arches. Above the arches, inside the sloping roofs of the aisles, there are two more nuns' galleries, touching the western gallery and the nave at the level of the tops

of the ogee arches above its windows. The relation of these galleries to each other and to the basilican section of the church is extremely free in its rhythm. The profile of the piers, too, has great freedom, and the short fragmentary arches standing on the capitals of the shafts could not be less organic, supporting the actual arches of the arcade and intersecting with them.

All the vaults are extremely complicated. The net-vault in the nave is modelled on that in the choir of the cathedral in Prague in so far as the transverse arches are broken off halfway up, and the ribs of the severies are continued as liernes and touch the transverse arches at the points where these stop. The vault of the choir at Salzburg is extremely imaginative; the flanking choir chapels are joined to the choir as though the whole were a transept, but without projecting laterally beyond the outside line of the nave and aisles, making it seem that the choir is at the same time a transept.

The central pier in the south porch is a paradigm of Late Gothic work.[140] Above the abacus with its projecting corners stand little gables with concave sides, of which the central one is bent round a pier set diagonally on the wall. The carved foliage consists of little leaves, curling restlessly. The church has a perfect unity of style, and the architect of the nave and south porch, Wolfgang Wiesinger, mastered the principles of the Late Gothic with his stream of new ideas and his untiring imagination. The proportions are moderate. All these factors make this probably the most cheerful and friendly of all nunnery churches. In its own way it too can be called classic.

If this term seems disturbing in our present context, one could equally well use the word 'mature' in its spiritual, not its biological sense. Any reader who insists that the churches from Amberg to Nonnberg cannot be considered under the same heading as Amiens because they look so different from Amiens should remember that Amiens looks very different from the Parthenon, but that each of them can yet be called classic in its own way. The concepts of classicity and maturity of style are quite independent of the forms of architectural members and of totality and partiality; they stand in a category of their own.

257. Rouen, Saint-Maclou. Begun soon after 1432. Plan

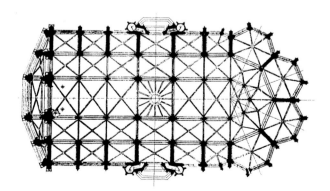

258. Rouen, Saint-Maclou, begun soon after 1432. Interior of nave and north transept

10. THE MATURE FLAMBOYANT

The name *Sondergotik* has been introduced to describe the German Late Gothic style. The purpose in coining this term was to emphasize the fact that the German architects of the fourteenth and fifteenth centuries, especially those of the fifteenth, were able to match the achievements of the French Gothic masters of the thirteenth century with a new and specifically German style. This is quite true, but it should not be overlooked that the French architects of the fifteenth century also matched the style of the thirteenth with something new which was no less French and also no less 'late' than the works of the Germans. This new French style had several forms in common with the German Late Gothic; for all advances at this time were basically European, differing only in the language in which they were expressed. If one is to speak of German *Sondergotik*, one should also recognize French, English, Dutch, Spanish, and Portuguese *Sondergotik*. Thus German *Sondergotik* becomes a tautology, German and 'Sonder' being obviously the same as soon as one ceases to refer to it as being 'late'. The existence of French *Sondergotik* proves that national characteristics and the stylistic characteristics of a certain period cannot be equated. Neither the Germans nor the French always preferred 'movement, fusion, and the picturesque'; both nations went through a classic phase of tranquillity,

isolation, and linearity around 1800. The comprehension of this fact should ensure that, while we recognize that each of the great schools preserved and extended its own national characteristics, we do not overlook the European features of the Late Gothic style.[141]

In France, it was the Flamboyant that was developed. At *Caudebec*, begun in 1426, the pattern of the soufflet was also employed in the tracery of the triforium. The choir ends in two diagonal sides, and the central pier is silhouetted against the east window of the five-sided ambulatory, as in German churches. The central chapel is a regular hexagon; the two western ones are flattened pentagons, and the two intermediate ones have two-sided apses, with single buttresses on the central axis, as in the choir at Freiburg im Breisgau. All these features are European; but the short, round piers and the plain rib-vaults are characteristically French.[142]

The church of *Saint-Maclou* at *Rouen*, begun soon after 1432, also has a central pier in the choir, probably the first in Flamboyant Gothic; the ambulatory is concentric, consisting of half a regular octagon, and the four chapels are all compressed hexagons [257].[143] The retention of the basilican form is French, and in Saint-Maclou there are even proper transepts and a separated crossing [258].

In 1434 the reconstruction of the cathedral at *Nantes* [259] was begun with the west façade and the aisles of the nave and its lateral chapels. Work continued, intermittently, through the first half of the seventeenth century, when the nave was vaulted. The choir was built in the nineteenth cen-

259. Nantes Cathedral. Nave begun in 1434. Interior; choir 1834

260. Rodez Cathedral. Choir aisle; three easternmost piers part of the chevet begun in 1277; pillars to their west, 1447; crossing piers 1462

tury. The strict regularity of the plan and the elevation is French, but many of the details are Late Gothic in character – for example, the plinths with concave sides and separate bases for the shafts, the absence of capitals, the complete masking of the piers by shafts, the ogee arches over depressed rounded arches in the triforium, and the Flamboyant tracery.[144]

In *Paris* itself, the style of the second quarter of the fifteenth century is represented by the church of *Saint-Germain l'Auxerrois*.[145]

At *Ambierle*, south of Paray-le-Monial, the church, begun about 1440, is conservative in its spatial form, being basilican with transepts, and having an apse forming half a hexagon, no ambulatory, and with ridge-ribs. However, the profiles of the members are Late Gothic; the central shaft is a flat projection between hollows; the profiles of the secondary shafts are segmental; those of the piers themselves, within the arcades, form a gentle double curve, contrasting with the double hollows of the profiles of the arches; and the ribs have a squashed pear-shape on a retracted main projection, behind which is another double curve. All these profiles produce shadows.[146]

From 1447, at *Rodez*, piers similar to those at Ambierle were built between the easternmost piers of the choir, which date from 1277, and those in the crossing, dating from 1462;

in plan, they form a continuous series of four double curves in which the pier and the shafts form an uninterrupted unity [260].[146A]

The absence of a triforium at *Cléry*, near Orléans, begun after 1429 and finished after 1483, is reminiscent of German churches. This is a conservative work, but contains many Late Gothic details.[147]

The choir of the church on the *Mont Saint-Michel*[148] was built after 1448, and is basilican with transepts, a choir with ambulatory and chapels, and flying buttresses based on High Gothic models. The hardness of the granite used, which was cut from the rock itself, did not prevent the architect from producing a display of great splendour. The concave curves of the gables of the pinnacles, and the double curves of the windows and balustrades translate the forms of the High Gothic into the language of the Late Gothic and change structure into texture. Inside, the piers and their plinths are related to those at Nantes. Within the framework of the French Late Gothic style this choir too can be called classic.

From about 1475 the west façade of *Notre-Dame-de-l'Epine* near Châlons-sur-Marne was begun (see above, p. 219). The two westernmost bays of the nave were completed in a conservative style reminiscent of the rest of the slightly earlier nave, though with Flamboyant details in the tracery. The façade, completed by around 1500, was designed with the area round the portals projecting slightly, so that the concave-sided gables rise above the balustrade, clear of the wall, the central one cutting through the full height of the rose-window and reaching up to the area of the gables, which consist of three triangles standing side by side with no baselines. The overall effect is completed by the large windows with ogee arches set over the doorways, and the Flamboyant tracery and the pinnacles on the buttresses.[148A] Above the bell-stage of the towers stand octagons with spires, consisting of flying ribs surrounded by buttresses and flying buttresses with tall pinnacles decorated with crowns. These have been taken to refer both to the kings of France and to the Virgin. Crowns or wreaths were an old legacy;[149] early examples appear in the designs of Ulrich von Ensingen, and these may have been the architect's models, if it is accepted as possible that he had relations with southern Germany. At this time Strasbourg was a free city, and the French must have been aware of the existence of a tower there which was greatly admired.[150] The north tower of Notre-Dame-de-l'Epine was not completed to match the south tower until 1867, but, although a lithograph of 1845 shows that it differed originally from the south tower in having a shorter square storey, this asymmetry cannot be attributed to the influence of Strasbourg.

The most important French façade of this generation is that of the cathedral at *Toul*, begun in 1460 and finished by 1500 [261]. There is a marked relationship with the west façade of Notre-Dame-de-l'Epine, especially in the area of the rose window, the tracery balustrade above it, and the large ogee gable of the central portal.[151] However, the ogee arch over the central doorway is shorter than that at Notre-Dame-de-l'Epine, reaching only as far as the rose-window. Over the pointed arch on top of the rose-window an enormous gable rises up to the concealed apex of the pitched roof, in front of the light, transparent bellcote, which has a roof shaped like a cupola and is reminiscent of the bellcote on the Frauenkirche at Nuremberg. A tracery balustrade strongly separates the octagons from the lower storeys. The composition of the whole shows an extremely interesting interplay between verticals and horizontals. The upper balustrade rises a step to pass over the rose-window, like the dwarf gallery at Laon. Not, of course, that there is any connexion here; but it is illuminating to compare these two façades and to measure the quality of that at Toul against the quality of that at Laon. There are few façades which can match Toul in majesty; this it owes to the fact that the ogee arch over the door and the straight-sided gable over the rose-window are seen as a unity which is subordinated only to the strictly symmetrical towers. Footings for the stone spires are visible inside the second storeys of the octagon, but they were never built.[152]

Toul was designed by Tristan d'Hattonchâtel and built by Jacquemin de Lenoncourt, and the second of these two also built the much simpler façade at *Pont-à-Mousson*. Here, the octagon on the north tower is set frontally, while that on the south tower is set diagonally, with one corner standing over the centre-line – an arrangement which has a relationship with the central piers built by architects of the Parler school. The rose-window is replaced by a broad window, and the gable above is separated from it by a horizontal line; the principle of addition also appears in the treatment of the three undecorated storeys of the towers, but these may have been taken over from an earlier stage of this church.[153]

The hall church became the general rule in Germany; the English by and large rejected it (after having used it at Bristol about 1320)[154] and the French accepted it on isolated occasions during the fifteenth century. Amongst those that were built are *Celles-sur-Belle*, dating from 1460,[155] which is reminiscent of the Wiesenkirche at Soest (1313), a group of about thirty fifteenth-century hall churches in southern Champagne,[156] and a group of late fifteenth-century hall churches in Lorraine, for example Saint-Laurent at *Pont-à-Mousson*, and Saint-Etienne at *Saint-Mihiel*.[157]

11. SPIRAL SHAFTS. DOUBLE-CURVED RIBS. CONCAVE PROFILES. CONCAVE-SIDED ARCHES. ARCHES LIKE BRANCHES OF TREES. DIAMOND-VAULTS

The High Gothic style strongly emphasized the verticals of piers and shafts. A slender shaft appears to consist of a bundle of vertical lines, all of which we identify with their central, vertical core. A spiral line on a cylindrical surface also rises upwards, but the movement is slower. Any pier or shaft is three-dimensional, but, if it is spiral in form, its breadth and depth are as clearly emphasized as its height, and the tempo of its upward movement is determined by the angle of the spiral.

The *Lonja* at *Palma* in Majorca, dating from 1426, is a hall with spiral piers [262]. The outer plane of these piers consists of eight hollows within an imaginary circle, which meet on sharp groins. The piers determine the general impression of the whole interior, which has a simple quadripartite rib-vault, Late Gothic tracery in the windows, and

261. Toul Cathedral. West front, 1460–1500

Late Gothic doorways. The spiral piers have an elective affinity with the other forms. They are not specifically Late Gothic, but rather 'late' within the more general terms applicable to any style; they recur in architecture, on the smaller as well as the larger scale, in furnishings, and in the ornaments of every age from prehistoric times and antiquity to the Late Romanesque, and again subsequently.[158]

The Lonja at Palma is an exchange, a secular building. In religious architecture, spiral piers appear in the Late Gothic style in 1469, when the north aisle of the cathedral at *Braunschweig* was replaced by two aisles of equal height [263]. Four shafts wind round each of the slender piers at an

262. Palma, Lonja. Interior, begun 1426

263. Braunschweig Cathedral. North choir aisle, 1469–74

angle so steep that they do not complete their full circle, and the capitals do not, therefore, stand above their corresponding bases. The abaci, which serve as capitals, are set diagonally, with one corner projecting frontally, and are repeated in the spaces between one shaft and the next, so that they form a polygon of pointed projections. At the bottom of each shaft are hollows, immediately taking up the diagonal torsion and coalescing with the sloping top of the plinth. The westernmost pier is slightly different; its profile consists of hollows between flat projections with attached rolls. The direction of the torsion alters from pier to pier; all available means are used to blend depth, variations in light and shade, contours undulating back and forth with the spiral shafts,[159] the growth of one member into another, and the emphasis on texture, into a unity. The vaults have no diagonal ribs and no tiercerons, but only transverse arches and liernes. The architect's aim to reach the highest possible degree of partiality, spatially, corporeally, and optically, is emphasized by the contrast with the Romanesque nave with its complete adherence to the principle of totality.

Spirals can also be combined with cones. When a whole pinnacle is twisted, as a wet cloth is wrung out, the result is a kind of conical spiral – again a change from structure to texture. Pinnacles of this kind appears in the 1450s(?) in the north-east porch of St Martin at Landshut,[160] and then frequently in the last decades of the fifteenth century, especially in 'micro-architecture' (e.g. the Market Fountain, or so-called *Fischkasten* at Ulm, of 1482).[161]

At this time Peter Hemmel, the Strasbourg glass-painter, began to enclose his panels in frames in the form of the branches of trees, and one of the engravings of the master E.S. also has a frame of branches.[162] The idea of substituting tree-trunks with lopped boughs for columns had already been used about 1250 by the architect of the porch of the cathedral at Genoa.[163] These trunks were even built with the soft spiral form which can be produced geometrically by moving a circle with its centre upwards along a spiral line. However, in Hemmel's work the arches, too (sometimes ogee arches), are made of branches, with leaves and blossoms. The development of this style can be followed through his work from Tübingen (1476) to the Scharfzandt window at Munich (1486).[164] Architects seem only to have taken over this idea at a fairly late date.[164A] The south façade at *Sens* was begun *c.* 1300, but restarted in 1489 just above the blind tracery flanking the unfinished portal[164B] [264]; here, on the buttresses and at the level of the great oculus, there are ogee arches which appear to be made of dry branches with thorns; they are reminiscent of coral. Between 1490 and 1493 King Vladislav II (1471–1516) had a gallery built in one bay of the cathedral in *Prague* [265]. The dry branches here, which grow out of strong boughs, are very similar to those at Sens. The branches themselves are ribs set against a big hollow and rise from the corners and from a central pendant bracket. They begin as two-dimensional curves but continue beyond their intersection, still against the hollow, in the form of three-dimensional curves. The balustrade has tracery in the form of branches, and, on each corner, two intertwined tree-trunks. The middle of the balustrade projects in the form of four sides of a flat hexagon, with a point at the centre. In this little work several of

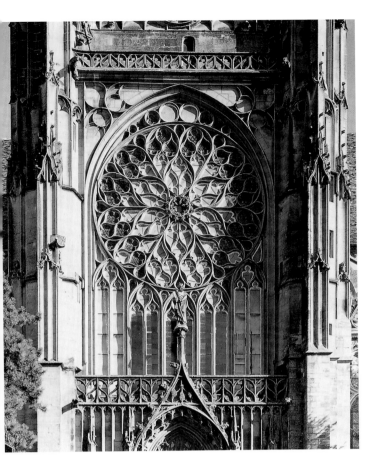

264. Sens Cathedral. South transept façade, begun *c.* 1300, restarted 1489

265. Prague Cathedral. Gallery in south aisle of choir, 1490–93

the principles of the Late Gothic style are combined. Single-minded admirers of the High Gothic complain that it was built with a lack of understanding of High Gothic principles,[165] but the architect Benedikt Ried would, in turn, have queried whether these critics had any understanding for the Late Gothic style.[165A]

A patient analysis of the central west doorway of *Berne* Minster reveals a combination of three-dimensional ogee arches, concave bases, and, on these bases, alternating forms which grow out of the same stalk. These stalks penetrate the profile of the arches and then turn sharply upwards, stressing their texture. The doorway was begun *c.* 1483 by Erhard Küng, who also built the first storey of the west tower. The nave high vault was inserted under Daniel Heintz in 1571–75. The vault of the west porch combines a net pattern with double-curved ribs.[165B] Diagonal ribs in simple cross-vaults forming three-dimensional curves had already been built about 1200 in the crypt at Bourges.

Small-scale double-curved ribs first appeared on the continent in the work of Madern Gerthener and Hans von Burghausen. It has not been established who was the first architect to build a vault using double-curved ribs throughout, but the first examples appear in Germany in the 1480s: in the south gallery of St Salvator in *Passau* (begun 1479), and in two *Nuremberg* vaults (Augustinerkirche, 1479–85, and Ebracherhofkapelle, 1483): The earliest surviving example may, however, be the vaults of the northern bay of

the west wing of the Great Cloister at *Basel*, completed *c.* 1465, perhaps by Jodok Dotzinger.[165C] Benedikt Ried began the *Vladislav Hall* in *Prague* in 1493 and completed it in 1502. Its vault is composed entirely of double-curved ribs which form large petal patterns.[165D] The *Landrecht Chamber* in Prague is considerably later. It was completed in 1563.

The Simpertus Arch in the church of *SS. Ulrich and Afra* at *Augsburg* [266], a work of complete stylistic maturity in which all the ribs are three-dimensional, can be dated to *c.* 1493–6. The Romanesque church of the eleventh and twelfth centuries was demolished in 1467, and the new church, re-begun in 1475 after storm damage by Valentin Kindlin, a basilica with an aisleless choir and tall windows similar to friars' churches, would certainly have been old-fashioned if Burkhard Engelberg had not taken charge of the work in 1477.[166] The penetration of the arcade arches by the octagonal piers, the hollows beside the shafts, the blind niches above the arcade, forming a triforium, the soufflets in the tracery, and, above all, the net-vaults, outweigh the remnants of older traditions. The complicated, asymmetrical net-vaults in the north aisle were completed in 1489, and were followed by the vault of the nave – almost identical in form with that of the nave at *Schwäbisch Gmünd*, which was built between 1497 and 1521, and perhaps designed by Engelberg [202, 203].[167] Both are pointed tunnel-vaults with severies; the bays are separated by transverse arches; the tiercerons rise to the liernes from the capitals of the piers, or,

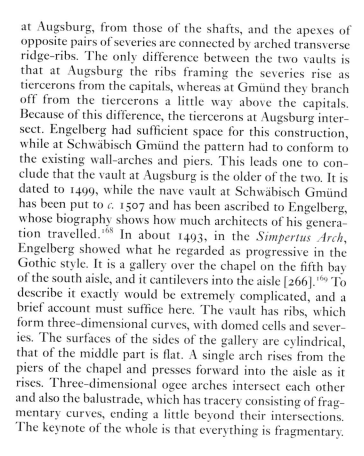

266. Augsburg, SS. Ulrich and Afra. Simpertus Arch, c. 1493–6

267. Strasbourg Cathedral. Portal of St Lawrence, c. 1494–1505

at Augsburg, from those of the shafts, and the apexes of opposite pairs of severies are connected by arched transverse ridge-ribs. The only difference between the two vaults is that at Augsburg the ribs framing the severies rise as tiercerons from the capitals, whereas at Gmünd they branch off from the tiercerons a little way above the capitals. Because of this difference, the tiercerons at Augsburg intersect. Engelberg had sufficient space for this construction, while at Schwäbisch Gmünd the pattern had to conform to the existing wall-arches and piers. This leads one to conclude that the vault at Augsburg is the older of the two. It is dated to 1499, while the nave vault at Schwäbisch Gmünd has been put to c. 1507 and has been ascribed to Engelberg, whose biography shows how much architects of his generation travelled.[168] In about 1493, in the *Simpertus Arch*, Engelberg showed what he regarded as progressive in the Gothic style. It is a gallery over the chapel on the fifth bay of the south aisle, and it cantilevers into the aisle [266].[169] To describe it exactly would be extremely complicated, and a brief account must suffice here. The vault has ribs, which form three-dimensional curves, with domed cells and severies. The surfaces of the sides of the gallery are cylindrical, that of the middle part is flat. A single arch rises from the piers of the chapel and presses forward into the aisle as it rises. Three-dimensional ogee arches intersect each other and also the balustrade, which has tracery consisting of fragmentary curves, ending a little beyond their intersections. The keynote of the whole is that everything is fragmentary.

Nineteenth-century critics were offended by it: Engelberg certainly knew the meaning of the High Gothic style, with its emphasis on everything structural, but his aim was the Late Gothic style, which lays its emphasis on texture.

Double-curved ribs in rows, of a date slightly later than that at Augsburg, can be seen in the portal of St Lawrence added to the north transept of *Strasbourg* Cathedral between c. 1494 and 1505 [267]. Here too the vaults in the interior form a stylistic unity with the doorway and the canopy over it. The architect, Jakob of Landshut, followed models from his native town, and enriched the forms used there with double re-entrants; i.e. the cornice has six sides in the form of a half-star, and the three projecting points of the star carry the apexes of three ogee arches. The central ogee arch, which is the widest – a double-curved arch – springs from the corners of the doorway and penetrates the two flanking ogee arches, each of which has a pendant in the middle, like that in King Vladislav's gallery in Prague. It would seem that, on his way from Landshut to Strasbourg, Jakob must have seen the Simpertus Arch at Augsburg.[169A]

Double-curved ribs in vaults and three-dimensional ogee arches are both fragments of spirals. They both express the stylistic principle of three-dimensional texture. Between 1481 and c. 1515, the transept of *Saint-Nicolas-du-Port* was built in the form of a double-naved hall as a continuation of the basilican chancel with aisles and three parallel apses. The lower half of the transept piers is round; the upper half has shafts which, in the south transept arm, rise in a spiral,

268. Gdańsk (Danzig), St Mary, *c.* 1379–1502. South aisle of nave, looking east

269. Freiberg Cathedral. Nave from the north aisle, looking south west, begun 1484. The left-hand pulpit is the Tulip Pulpit of *c.* 1510

similar to those at Braunschweig.[170] The lower part of the piers is decorated with rows of gables and pinnacles; there are no arches under the gables, perhaps because it was intended to fill the spaces below them with painting. The general effect of these decorations is dictated by principles similar to those of the piers at Stargard and Milan.[170A]

In Germany, Braunschweig was followed, *c.* 1480–89, by the two spiral columns in the mortuary chapel at *Eichstätt*, and in France, at the same time, by the axial column in the ambulatory of the church of *Saint-Séverin* in *Paris*. In the church in Paris, the slender spiral shafts are connected, below the beginning of the ribs, by small round arches enclosing ogee arches. This looks like the springing of the vault; however it carries nothing, and the shafts continue to rise above it into the ribs. The spiral includes the plinth and disappears into the vault – a form symbolizing movement with no beginning and no end.[171] The church itself was begun as a basilica, since the French did not favour hall-choirs, but the double ambulatory is a curved hall, like those at Saint-Denis and Notre-Dame, translated into the Late Gothic style.[172]

The hall-choirs in Austria and Germany realized the principle of partiality by spatial division, and most of the hall-churches with such choirs have no transepts. When a transept was desired, as in Saint-Nicolas-du-Port, it was given the form of a two-aisled space.[172A] In the church of *St Mary* at *Gdańsk (Danzig)*,[173] built from *c.* 1379 to 1502, however, the architect went further, combining a hall-nave

with hall-transepts [268]. The extreme complexity of the net-vaults and star-vaults gives a variety and a wealth of views[173A] which contrasts with the clumsy simplicity of the exterior, but shares its solemnity. Part of the vault has no ribs at all, but sharp groins instead between the domical cells; its main lines, however, are not those of Romanesque quadripartite groin-vaults, but form complicated patterns, completely replacing the traditional Gothic structural members by purely visual factors. These so-called diamond-vaults (*Zellengewölbe*) are repeated, about 1500, in the aisles and the lower storey of the tower in the church of *St Catherine* at *Gdańsk (Danzig)*.[173B]

The cathedral at *Freiberg*[174] in Saxony was begun in 1484 [269]. The octagonal piers in this hall-church have concave sides. Above the chapels, a gallery runs round the nave, between the buttresses, projecting as a balcony round each of the piers. It gives, as balconies always do, an impression of partiality through division. The vault of the nave is not separated from those of the side aisles by arches, but runs right through to include the chapels; however, the architect lacked the courage to eliminate the transverse arches as well. In spite of this, Freiberg is one of the most powerful realizations of the principles underlying the Late Gothic treatment of space. The Tulip Pulpit, designed 1510,[174A] is a perfect companion to the nave; it is miniature architecture, in vegetal forms which combine natural growth with a soft and elastic articulation of its texture.

Concavity and the emphasis on texture are as much the

consequences of radical partiality as is Flamboyant tracery. The 'classic High Gothic' *Sainte-Chapelle* in *Paris* had, in the 1480s, to undergo the rebuilding of its west oculus, in a 'classic Late Gothic' style. The pattern used is very similar to that of the rose-windows at *Beauvais* and *Sens*, built shortly afterwards by Martin Chambiges [264]. The rose-window in the west façade of the cathedral at *Rouen*, for which no exact date is recorded, must also be roughly contemporary with that in Paris, but it does not appear to have been built by the same architect who began the Tour de Beurre on the southern corner of the façade in 1487.[175] In 1496, its architect, Guillaume Pontifs, was succeeded by Jacques Le Roux, and in 1507, when the bottom of the spire had been reached, work came to a standstill. The slender storeys are built, as was the tradition, in two axes each. The tracery and the pinnacles and tabernacles on the buttresses continue the style of the centre of the façade, contrasting with the Tour St Romain, which though Early Gothic in date, still has such flat surfaces that it looks like the work of a Romanesque architect. The flatness of the surfaces of the older tower contrasts so completely with the stress on depth in the new one that the details of the latter resemble a porous sponge. It is this impression which, in another context, has been called *Tiefendunkel*.

In the west façade of the church of St Wulfran at

271. Burgos Cathedral. Capilla del Condestable, 1482–94. Vault

270. Burgos Cathedral. Capilla del Condestable, 1482–94. Interior

Abbeville,[176] begun in 1488, almost all the details are in an advanced Flamboyant style. They are, however, subordinated to the simple and strict divisions by the buttresses and the horizontal mouldings.

In Spain, Simon of Cologne began soon after 1482 the Capilla del Condestable at the east end of the cathedral at *Burgos* [270]. It is a regular octagon with clusters of very slender shafts standing on Late Gothic bases, and has a star-vault in which the central octagonal star is pierced by open-work tracery[177] [271]. The main structure was complete by 1494. The piers at the corners are joined by broad, plain pointed arches, surmounted by ogee points which extend upwards into the zone of the windows, which have Flamboyant tracery. The part of the wall below the wall-arches is divided into two storeys by a recession of the wall, which produces a very narrow wall-passage. Pairs of carved figures holding large coats of arms stand in front of the parapet, and there are even larger coats of arms suspended diagonally corresponding to them on the lower part of the wall. An integral part of the whole is the cusping of the wall-arches, which looks like embroidery. There are ornaments within every wall-arch, and within each there are pairs of figures in lively poses. If there could be any doubt that the emphasis in this chapel was intended to lie not on structural factors, that is on what stands, but rather on what hangs from the framework, the proof lies in the fact that in the wall arch over the Baroque altar the figures actually stand head downward. One might be tempted to say that the Late Gothic style turned the principles of the High Gothic upside down, but it is incorrect to regard them as opposites; for the two together constitute the opposite of the Romanesque. But, while the High Gothic style maintained the Romanesque principles of the importance of structural

272. Toledo, San Juan de los Reyes,
designed 1477, modified in 1495.
Exterior

273. Toledo, San Juan de los Reyes,
designed 1477, modified in 1495.
Interior

members and of the convex profile, the Late Gothic represents the systematic elimination of all the remaining legacies of the Romanesque and, in so far as this is possible, the achievement of the complete supremacy of the principle of partiality.

In Spain, the Gothic style did not become specifically Spanish until the last years of the Late Gothic period. The emphasis on flat surfaces and the delight in complicated geometrical patterns has been traced back to the Arabic tradition of the Mudejar, yet Simon of Cologne was only half Spanish – his father was German and his mother Spanish – and Juan Guas, the architect of the church of *San Juan de los Reyes* at *Toledo* [272], was a Frenchman, possibly the son of a Breton. In Spain, too, the national characteristics are made up of spiritual components rather than of physical ones. The plan of the church at Toledo, begun in 1477 and completed in 1496, is of the same type as that of those southern French churches consisting of a single unit of space with rows of lateral chapels, like the cathedral at *Perpignan*, begun in 1324; apart from this similarity in plan, however, these two churches are completely different.[178] Perpignan is solemn, grave, almost too sober, while Toledo is cheerful, and rich in vitality and imagination. At Toledo, the westernmost bay is crossed by a gallery, and, partly because of this, the entrance is on the south side. Because of their flat roofs and few windows, the short transepts are heavy and massive; above them rises the short, octagonal crossing-tower, which also has a flat roof [272]. The nave has heavy buttresses ending in pinnacles and at the east end there are also heavy pinnacles standing up over the horizontal line of the flat roofs. The whole row of lateral chapels is closed to the outside by a plain, unarticulated wall, and, at the bottom of the façade of the north transept, there is a row of sixteen tall, narrow

274. Ávila, Santo Tomás, begun *c*. 1483. Interior of raised choir, looking east to the high altar on the gallery

blind niches without capitals and with round arches. In these niches hang chains, from which Christian prisoners were freed by the royal couple Ferdinand the Catholic (1479–1516) and Isabella of Castile. More of these chains hang in the blank, round-arched panels higher up, and adorn the intermediate string course. No other cases are known in the history of architecture of the use of chains, both as a symbol of liberation and thanksgiving, and as ornamentation. These chains also have a place in the sphere of texture, and the dark iron of which they are made is an excellent complement to the grey granite of the church.

The whole interior has been thought out imaginatively and with a rare intensity of love [273]. The star-vaults of the four bays are supported on piers inserted into the wall with round bases and springers. The cores of the piers are also round, but the surface of each consists of a row of slender alternating staves (which are not shafts) and grooves, leaving it uncertain where the core begins: the form is ambivalent. At the top of each staff an ogee arch rises which connects it, not with the staff immediately next to it, but with the next but one, so that the intermediate one divides the ogee arch. These ogee arches bend forwards – a form reminiscent of, though different from, the nodding arches at Ely. Both those used at Toledo and those at Ely, however, certainly spring from the same desire to emphasize depth. The feet of the transverse arches and of the ribs interpenetrate each other, and the wall-arches similarly disappear into the nearest tiercerons. The easternmost piers do not serve simultaneously as crossing piers; the latter are separate and stronger, standing immediately next to the piers of the nave, and they also have round pseudo-capitals and staves and grooves. The line of the springing is decorated with a ring of carved heads which project strongly, and beneath them hang Arabic stalactites, which are repeated on the piers in the choir. These Islamic forms hang above the complicated balconies,[179] which were intended for the kings, and may have been

designed as symbols either of triumph or of the reconciliation of mankind commanded in the New Testament. On the other hand, it is equally possible that the architect merely felt how perfectly these Islamic forms fitted his own Late Gothic ones.

The choir, which consists of five sides of a compressed octagon, is lit only by the south window of the south transept and by the windows in the drum of the crossing. In the star-vault of this crossing Guas built ribs with double curves, which form ogee arches in plan.

This description of the interior is necessarily incomplete. The eye is constantly occupied with innumerable details. Among these are the almost excessive ornamentation of the transepts, the piers at the entrances to the chapels, the figures on the piers, which, like those in Berne, stand on corbels supported by stalks, the pinnacles above them, the blind tracery in the segmental squinches and the carved busts of angels below them, the angels in the drum, and many other details. Even the plinths have blind tracery on them, and the bases of the staves on the piers are slender, isolated, graceful, and without strength – a gesture rather than the expression of the ability to carry weight.

The church of *Santo Tomás* outside the Gates at *Ávila* is related to this masterpiece at Toledo; it, too, has no aisles, but rows of lateral chapels. Above the two westernmost bays there is a gallery for the monks, and, in the rectangular choir, which is broader than it is long, there is another gallery on the same level as that of the high altar [274]. The arrangement was probably designed to allow the monks to

275. Toledo cathedral. Portal to the staircase of Cardinal Tenorio, 1495.

see the altar at the level of their seats.[180] This form of transverse bridge is a new application of the principle of spatial division. The bases, which are formed of four concave sides of an octagon (and therefore have a point at the centre of the frontal side), stand on semicircular plinths, and show the architect's preoccupation with Late Gothic principles. The shafts are pearshaped, and have three atavistic shaft-rings. The west portal has richly decorated jambs, which continue into ogee arches without capitals. The tympanum, however, is supported on a very flat rounded arch, which is repeated in the porch in front of the portal.

The combinations of forms in the arches of the Late Gothic period, not only of different arches one beside another or one inside another, as in Santo Tomás, but even of different forms within a single arch, are so many that they are hard to enumerate. Beginning with the trefoil arches of Romanesque and Early Gothic times, which in the latter period were pointed, the architects grew more courageous, developing more and more new combinations. Theoretically, all possible combinations can be traced back to a twenty-sided figure with straight, concave, convex, or undulating sides meeting alternately in projecting and re-entrant angles.[181] In practice, every Late Gothic example consists of some part of this twenty-sided figure, though with considerable variety in the length of the sides, the size of the angles, and the radii of the curves. The stylistic significance of these complicated figures becomes very clear when compared with the semicircular arch of the Romanesque. Even the pointed arch broke a totality into two parts: the combinations in Late Gothic arches consist of nothing but fragmentary parts. The frame of the doorway to the church of San Juan de los Reyes has two arches, one over the other; the lower one is a trefoil with an ogee arch in the middle, while the upper one is a trefoil in which the top section consists of two convex arches supported on short verticals.[182] Countless earlier examples of such combinations can be found in fourteenth-century Italian picture-frames. A Spanish example can be seen in the portal to the staircase of Cardinal Tenorio in the cathedral at *Toledo*, built by Juan Guas in 1495 [275]. The arch begins on each side as if to develop into a horseshoe arch; but the next section on each side consists of a right angle between two straight sides set obliquely, and the whole arch is completed by an ogee arch at the top. This whole arch is contained within an outer arch, also consisting of five parts: the first section on each side is concentric with the bottom section of the inner arch; the second is a small semicircle; and the top section is a broad three-centred arch. An architect could go on in this way, designing different combinations, for as long as he liked. A description of this style as arbitrary cannot be contradicted, as long as the word is used in a positive sense, as an appreciation of the fact that, in this final stage of the Gothic style, the imagination had been liberated and all its responsibilities to regularity and structural forms thrown aside, so that the essence of the Gothic style could at last be shown.

Among the many combinations that exist, the undulating arch, which has two main forms, occupies a special place. On the south façade at *Sens*, restarted in 1489, Martin Chambiges built an arch to form gables for the pin-

276. Troyes Cathedral. West front, begun 1506, work finished in 1550s

nacles which flank the gable and crown the two staircase turrets. At its foot this arch begins in concave curves, and then, in a continuous sweep, becomes convex and slightly concave again, to end in a point as an ogee arch. The same form can be seen in a secondary position in the tracery of the great rose-window and again below it, and, in a more striking context, in the main pinnacles on the buttresses. About 1500, Chambiges again used these undulating pointed arches, together with other related forms, on the north façade at Sens. A less striking form can be seen on the façades of the transepts at *Beauvais*, but a much bolder one appears on the west façade at *Troyes*, begun in 1506 and finished in the 1550s, where the arches on the buttresses of the uncompleted south tower begin with concave curves and undulate to form a second pair of concave curves, ending in the sharpest possible point. As the sides of these arches are steep, the upper section has the shape of an onion [276].[182A]

The second main form of undulating arch is used in rows to form a blind arcade in the chapel of the château of *Amboise*. Charles VIII had spent his childhood years there, and, when he succeeded to the throne in 1483, he began to enlarge the château. The Chapelle du Roi is an isolated building, apparently traditional in its basic form. It consists

277. Vendôme, La Trinité. Façade, *c.* 1500

278. Rouen, St Maclou. Façade, *c.* 1470–90

of a crossing and short arms; the west arm is square, and the choir forms five sides of an octagon. The interior is entirely vaulted with star-vaults. The arcade of undulating arches runs below the windows and is overshadowed by a frieze of three-quarter circles. The type of arch that results could be called a bell-arch. The line of the springing is marked by an extremely complicated curtain-like frieze of segmental arches surmounted by ogee arches; it is divided into sections by the windows and covers the beginnings of the ribs. It is treated as a porous surface, with a continual interplay of light and shade.[183]

The nave of the church of St Ouen at *Pont-Audemer* was begun in 1486. In one of the windows there are two semicircular arches gathered together within a single segmental arch and topped with a gable in the form of a bell-arch.[184]

By comparison with the forms of arches which we have just discussed, the church of *La Trinité* at *Vendôme* looks conservative [277]. The three westernmost bays and the façade were built between 1485 and 1506. Inside, the absence of capitals and the forms of the plinths, which are strikingly Late Gothic compared with those in the older bays, are all quite progressive for the time at which they were designed. The façade contains Flamboyant forms which in this case can truly be compared to flickering flames. The façade has no towers, since the great campanile of about

1120 was preserved. There is a great contrast between the styles of the tower and the façade, but the aesthetic relationship between them is a happy one.[185]

12. CONTINUOUS RECESSION

The first two decades of the sixteenth century were the last two of the Late Gothic style, at least in so far as they produced new ideas. In various regions there was a great spate of architectural activity, and a large number of masterpieces were created throughout Europe. If one is already familiar with all the features which are a legacy from the fifteenth century, the most important new factor upon which to concentrate is the increased continuity between forms.

A plan for the whole church of *St Maclou* at *Rouen* was drawn up in 1436/37 by the architect Pierre Robin. The west porch was built, perhaps to Robin's general design, under the mason Amroise Harel (active at St Maclou 1467–80). In 1487 the western rose was inserted, and by 1490 the whole façade must have been complete [278].[186] The decisive stylistic features of the façade are on the one hand the unity formed by the central part and the sloping lines of the flying buttresses above, and on the other the diagonal projection of the porch in front of the corners of

279. Alençon, Notre-Dame. West front, *c*. 1506–16

280. Alençon, Notre-Dame. Interior of nave, begun *c*. 1477

the façade. Theoretically the porch can be considered separate from the actual west wall, but not visually. The five gables of the façade are reminiscent of Reims, but their piercing and their penetration surpasses anything that had gone before; here the whole façade is dissolved, and seems to be set in the middle of infinite space. Compared with this, the façade at Vendôme seems flat. One can compare St Maclou with the so-called Triangle at Erfurt (built 1332–37) and the west porch of Regensburg cathedral (*c*. 1390) [239], but they are only small parts of the façades, while at Rouen the emphatic diagonals and the dissolution of the wall are the guiding principles of the whole façade.

A similar combination of movement and penetration can be seen in the façade at *Alençon* [279], by Jehan Lemoyne, and dated 1506–*c*. 1516, in which the number of gables has been reduced to three. In some details this façade is even more progressive than that at Rouen; for instance, there is a bell-shape inside the mouchettes in the two flanking gables, and along the north and south sides of the church the tops of the flying buttresses are concave – a conscious negation of their structural character. Inside the church, the profile of the arcade arches, which consists almost entirely of hollows, contrasts sharply with the massive round piers [280]. Two features are innovations: tiercerons standing on corbels which seem to hover in space, above the line of the spring-

ing of the vault; and, half-way along the ribs, completely akyristic tabernacles. The windows, of six lights each, have Flamboyant tracery, while the wall-passage below them, which is also divided into six openings to each bay, is regular, and is related to the forms of the Perpendicular style. Below this, however, and above the arcade arches each bay is pierced by four, not six, pointed quatrefoils, framed within squares; the vertical axes of the quatrefoils therefore do not correspond to those of the six openings above. Here, with relatively sparing means, the whole vocabulary of the High Gothic style has been given an entirely new meaning.[186A]

It still remains to consider fully to what extent small-scale architecture was the stylistic precursor of architecture on a larger scale. This is certainly the case in the fifteenth century. In the font in the church of *St Severus* at *Erfurt*, which has the date 1467 inscribed on it, all the principles of the style of 1500 are already completely active[187] [281]. It has a basin with intertwining mouchettes containing tracery, or rather branches, which intersect and then suddenly end. Its foot consists of small spiral supports – this before the aisles of Braunschweig – and its plinth is formed of a sequence of eight hexagonal stars one on top of the other, diminishing in size from bottom to top and turned in a syncopated rhythm so that the third faces in the same direction as the first, while the second penetrates the first and third – a favourite form

281. Erfurt, St Severus. Font, 1467

of the German Late Gothic style. The cover is supported on three posts with three-dimensional ogee arches, which, in turn, support an inner triangle of posts, whose corners stand over the centres of the sides of the lower one. Finally, concave flying buttresses spring from behind the spires on the miniature pinnacles. There has been plenty of schoolmasterly criticism of crimes against the High Gothic style, but the aim of the architect was to correct the High Gothic style with the unbelievably complicated forms of his own geometrical fantasy, to turn his work into pure texture, and thus to make it completely Gothic. In the *Sakramentshaus* of the church of *St Lorenz* at *Nuremberg*, the canopied receptacle of the Holy Sacrament, made by Adam Kraft in 1493–6, the principle of penetration had already been taken to its extreme, and structural forms had largely been transformed into textural ones. Here, the bent pinnacles, the undulating form of the flying buttresses, and the vegetal scrolls at the top of them are a complete negation of any structural principle [253, 282].[187A]

Rood-screens and choir stalls occupy a position half-way between small-scale and large-scale architecture. One of the most convincing of such works, which cannot but kill any prejudice against the Late Gothic style, is the whole *coro* in the cathedral at *Albi* [284]. Here is the principle of division in all its force: space within space [185], and every detail penetrated by space. Prosper Mérimée (1803–70) wrote of

it: '. . . on a honte d'être raisonnable en présence de cette magnifique folie'.[188] But is it really folly? Historically, it is only the final consequence of what has been called the classic Gothic style – one of the late and most magnificent blossoms produced in a spiritual hothouse. Its analysis must be left to the individual. However, the twelve small star-vaults which cover the inside of the rood-screen in two rows of six should be specially noted. They are supported on the surrounding sides of the rectangle, but where they meet along the centre-line, between the two rows, they hang freely, giving an effect similar to that of a fan-vault [285].[188A]

The international validity of the style is proved by the screen in the church of *St Pantaleon* at *Cologne*, built between 1502 and 1514, which projects in three sides of a polygon, like the façade of the church of St Maclou at Rouen [286]. The points of the ogee arches lie on the edges where the oblique projections meet, and they have no visible supports. This textural principle of suspension in space is here combined with the form of arches on a broken plan. The screen at St Stephen at *Breisach* was complete by 1499.[188B] It has twisted plinths, and all its arches are gentle

282. Nuremberg, St Lorenz. Sakramentshaus, 1493–6. Detail

283. Troyes, church of the Magdalene. Screen, 1508–17

284. Albi Cathedral. *Coro, c.* 1474–83

285. Albi Cathedral. Vaulting inside the rood screen, 1474–83

286. Cologne, St Pantaleon. Screen, 1502–14

ogee arches containing tracery in which the arches intersect and then end abruptly. The pinnacles have three-dimensional ogee arches, like those later to be built on the flying buttresses of the Frauenkirche at Esslingen. The screen in the church of the *Magdalene* at *Troyes*, built in 1508–17, represents the same stage in stylistic development as the German works of this period [283], a still richer and a scarcely surpassable masterpiece of French *Sondergotik*.[188c]

The complete dissolution of the surfaces of spires into tracery, which was under construction in *c.* 1300 at Freiburg, reached the acme of beauty and perfection in the spire of the north tower at *Chartres*, begun in 1507 [55]. It is rich and possesses great verve, forming a sharp contrast with the lower storeys of 1134; and yet it is still clearly a descendant of the same family. If it is true that the architect of this spire at Chartres, Jehan Texier de Beauce, was also the man who designed the façade at Vendôme, then the spire at Chartres shows how he would have liked to rebuild the campanile at Vendôme. The spire at Chartres surpasses even such progressive works as *Caudebec*, and its tendency to conceal and to replace the surfaces of the spire with bunches of pinnacles influenced, and indeed determined, the form of the top of the north tower of the cathedral at *Antwerp*.[189]

It may be mentioned that, during the Late Gothic period, countless wooden spires were built covered with slate or tiles, and that these also, by virtue of a dissolution of their surfaces, or of their concave outlines, stand at the same stage of stylistic development as stone spires. It is not known whether the two west towers of the *Týn* church (*Teynkirche*) in *Prague* [287], which were built in 1463–66 (north) and 1506–11 (south), had any decisive influence in this connexion; many variations of this type were built in Austria.[189A]

The most important French interior, stylistically, of this time is the choir of *St Etienne* at *Beauvais*, begun in *c.* 1502 [288]. The section of the piers undulates, like that of the piers in the choir at Rodez. The bays of the ambulatory behind the trapezoidal apse end in a straight east wall, pierced by windows, so that this part of the church seems wide and light, in spite of the fact that it has a basilican and not a hall section.[190]

Among the latest German Gothic interiors is that of the nave of *Ulm* Minster.[191] Sometime before 1502 (north aisle) and 1507 (south aisle), Engelberg divided each of the aisles, which had been built too wide by Heinrich II Parler and Michael II Parler, into two – a solution dictated by the conditions [289]. The two resultant double-naved, Late Gothic halls accompany the high nave proper without attempting to achieve any relationship with it, as did also those at

287. Prague, Týn church. Towers, 1463–66 (north) and 1506–11 (south)

288. Beauvais, Saint-Etienne. Choir, begun *c.* 1502

289. Ulm Minster. Interior of south nave aisle, before 1507

290. Pirna, St Mary, 1502–46. Interior

Braunschweig. The round piers and the round abaci are a reminder that Engelberg was familiar with Gmünd, and the tiercerons intersect each other at the foot of the vault, again as at Gmünd. In the outer aisles there are diagonal ribs, whereas in the inner ones there are only tiercerons and liernes.

In the parish church at *Pirna* [290], built between 1502 and 1546, the architect formed an aisled hall with piers with eight concave sides, and a close net-vault, thus achieving the very results which could not be achieved at Ulm.[192] This net-vault creates a continuous stream of movement from west to east, while each bay in the aisles is centred by the form of the star-vault, thus producing a series of lateral currents crossing the main, longitudinal one. The nave and aisles form a visual unity in which the arches of the arcade seem to have become ribs; the liernes in the nave and those in the aisles meet on these arches, and emphasize the continuity of the crossing streams of movement. The choir has double-curved ribs. Throughout the church, the section of the ribs forms two shallow hollows on each side, and the concave forms of the piers and of the ribs are stylistically analogous with the mouchettes in the tracery and with the double-curved ribs of the choir vault. In addition to these features, there are flying ribs rising from the corners of the choir and running into the meshes of the vault, and these ribs are formed like tree-trunks from which all the branches

291. Frankfurt am Main, St Leonard, begun 1219, choir *c.* 1430–4, three-aisled nave and outer aisles begun *c.* 1500. Plan

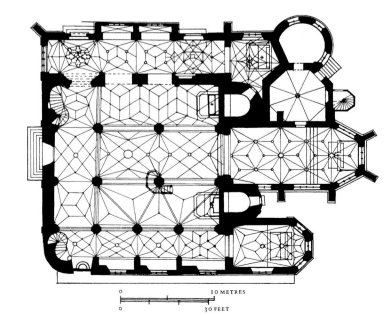

0   10 METRES

0   30 FEET

have been cut off except one, which winds spirally up the stem.[193] In this church one can truly say that all the stops are out.

The nave of the church of St Mary at *Zwickau*, which was almost completely rebuilt from 1506, belongs to the same school as that at Pirna.[194] Here, the horizontal line of the gallery, which projects round the piers, contrasts with the vertical lines of the piers themselves, as at Freiberg in Saxony, in the choir of St Lorenz at Nuremberg, and at Gmünd. All these late hall-churches in Upper Saxony are variations of the same basic type, but each of them has its own highly individual traits.

The same could really be said of the entire creative work of the last years of the Late Gothic period. In some cases the individualism was the product of conditions imposed by the existence of older parts of a church – for instance at *St Leonard* at *Frankfurt* [291], which was begun in the Romanesque style in 1219, at a time when the Gothic style was already highly developed in France, and of which some original parts have been preserved in the church as it stands today.[195] After several reconstructions, the church was given the form of an aisled hall of three bays, and an aisleless choir, similar in type to the Frauenkirche at Nuremberg. Around 1500 work was begun on the addition of a pair of outer aisles with galleries, which finally produced a double-aisled interior with diagonal views up into the galleries [292]. As the new aisles had four bays, whereas the older, inner ones had

293. Frankfurt am Main, St Leonard. Outer north aisle, vault, *c.* 1510

294. Calw, chapel of St Nicholas. Vaulting, *c.* 1360 (?)

292. Frankfurt am Main, St Leonard. Interior of nave, looking north

only three, the result was triangular cells in the vaults of the new south aisle, and a complicated net-vault in the north aisle. Every bay of the vaults has a different pattern, and it is quite clear that the architect saw this complexity as a means to the end of an increased continuity between the parts of his interior. In the easternmost bay of the outer north aisle, an irregular pentagon, the vault consists mainly of flying ribs – a form which, in one sense, can be considered the last word in the Gothic style[196] [293].

The principle of vaults with double-curved ribs led to the idea of building ribs standing free in space, in the way in which they could be seen during the construction of a vault before the cells were filled in. As the spatial boundary of the cells could not be omitted, a second rib-vault was built above the flying network in these cases, so that one sees two different patterns simultaneously. The development of these vaults began with those at Lincoln, Bristol, and in other English churches, and continued with those at Magdeburg, Prague, and in the church of St Stephen in Vienna. The flying ribs in the choir at Pirna were built about thirty years after those at Frankfurt, where the architect is known to

295. Ingolstadt, Frauenkirche. Vaulting of chapel, *c.* 1510–20

have been Hans von Bingen. He had differences with the clergy at Frankfurt, but although these were not in fact on the subject of the vaults, one feels that, in any case, he was a man who knew his own mind.[196A]

A few years later, in the chapels of the Frauenkirche at *Ingolstadt*, which were built between 1510 and 1520 [295], Erhard and Ulrich Heydenreich created a series of variants of the form used at Frankfurt. Here, the proper vaults form the primary surface, with the secondary, flying network hanging below them, and they show once again that one must learn to read Gothic architecture from its furthest surface to its nearest one, or, in this case, from the uppermost surface downwards. These ribs can only be considered as 'useless', that is serving no practical purpose, but they do emphatically fulfil an aesthetic or a stylistic function. The question as to whether or not ribs actually carry weight has no meaning here, for the rib has become an autonomous form, present purely for its own sake. Some of the ribs at Ingolstadt even have the form of tree-trunks with their branches cut off.[196B]

The flying ribs at Frankfurt and Ingolstadt can be compared with those in the cloister of the cathedral at *Magdeburg* (mentioned above, p. 191), which were built *c.* 1330, but which exhibit the same tendencies within the stylistic framework of the High Gothic style. Here, in half a sixteen-sided polygon, seven ribs rise to the transverse arch which separates this chapel, the so-called Tonsura, from the cloister, and these ribs are flying ribs. The vertical walls which rise above them are pierced with tracery, and on top of these there is a flat ceiling. In the history of the develop-

ment of the Gothic style, this pseudo-vault at Magdeburg stands on the dividing-line between the High Gothic and the Late Gothic styles, and, if one can understand it and recognize it as such, one should also be able to recognize the final Late Gothic form as a natural and valid development of this transitional stage.[197] In this connexion, too, Dehio, the most notable historian of the Gothic style, expressed his bias in favour of the High Gothic when he said of the vaults at Frankfurt that they were 'a mere spectacle for marvelling laymen'. An unprejudiced historian must pronounce a very different verdict.

The chapel of St Nicholas on the bridge at *Calw* in the Black Forest is very similar in the basic form of its vault to the cloister at Magdeburg, but here tracery has been inserted between the eight flying ribs and the flat ceiling [294]. The official inventory[198] dates it as 'about 1400', as does Dehio in his *Handbuch*, but, while this date is almost certainly correct for the flèche, the ribs and the boss appear rather to date from about 1360. The form of the shafts, on the other hand, seems to confirm the later date. But whatever the date, this combination of flying ribs with a flat ceiling is a step in the direction of the construction of

296. Belém, Hieronymite monastery church. Nave interior, begun 1501

completely free flying ribs in proper vaults. It also has some relationship to the flat ceilings on transverse arches which were built in Syria, but, historically, it should be understood as a result of the immanent process of the development of the Gothic style.[198A]

All this applies to the net-vault in the choir of *Freiburg* Minster, which was completed in 1510 [222].[199] It is ultimately derived from the net-vault of Prague Cathedral but enriched by the arches which are called 'principal arches'. They comprise two bays each and dictate the radius of curvature of all the ribs [215].

The first decade of the sixteenth century also saw the ultimate developments of the Gothic style in England, where, between 1503 and 1509, King Henry VII's Chapel was added to the east end of *Westminster Abbey* in *London*.[200] Here, the transverse arches which appear in the nave and the choir disappear in the concave cones of the fan-vault, which divides the chapel indeterminably, splits it, and bores into it. A pendant fan vault had been built as early as about 1480 in the *Divinity School* at *Oxford*,[201] but in Henry VII's Chapel the character of the vaults extends to embrace the form of the entire structure, and, here again, one can speak of pure decoration, as long as the word is not used in a derogatory sense.

In Portugal, the overseas wealth brought back from Prince Henry the Navigator's voyages to Africa, and Vasco de Gama's opening of the trade routes to India, resulted in a fresh burst of architectural activity. At the site of Prince Henry's small Mariners' chapel of S. Maria de Belém where Vasco de Gama's fleet embarked in 1497, King Manuel founded, in 1501, the monastery of *Belém*,[202] the design for which was made by Diogo Boitac (or Boytac) [296, 297]. The church is an aisled hall of three bays, with piers almost as slender as those in the church of St Martin at Landshut. Above their bases these piers are formed of separate pieces, and are covered with partly Renaissance ornamentation, which was not executed until after 1516/17, when the workshop came under the control of João de Castilho. There is only one transept, and this projects laterally only very slightly; it is as wide as the length of two and

a half bays of the nave, and carries a single vault consisting of several stars. This transept cannot be compared with that in any other church; it looks more like a gigantic crossing for the whole church than like an actual transept. The original apse was disproportionately small, and even the present one containing monuments of 1571 is built only on the scale of a chapel. The west bays, before one enters the actual nave, are also most unusual in disposition. The architect obviously felt himself quite free from the dictates of any tradition.

The Franciscan church of Igreja de Jesus at *Setúbal* was also designed by Boitac, and it has piers each consisting of three three-quarter shafts, which rise spirally showing none of the solid core[203] [298].

From 1507 to 1513 King Manuel had the church of *Santa Cruz* at *Coimbra* rebuilt by Boitac. From 1517 to 1521 the Claustro do Silêncio was added to it by the architect Marcos Pires.[204] In the choir, the star-vault without transverse arches and the windows, which have curtain arches, were parts of the reconstruction, and the Marcos Pires gave the tracery of the cloister openings the form of twisted ropes (completed in *c.* 1518).

After the liquidation of the Knights Templar in France and the dissolution of their order in 1312, the possessions of the knights at *Tomar* were given by King Dinis in 1319 to his new Supreme Order of Christ, and in 1339 Tomar became its headquarters. The old Templars' church here, dating from about 1160, had an octagonal central portion like a tower, and, originally, a sixteen-sided ambulatory.[205] From 1510 to 1514 a nave was added by the architect Diogo de Arruda whose lower western part is closed towards the church. It contains the chapter house, which is accessible from outside, and above it the knights' gallery. The portal to the nave lies on the south side [299]. It was inserted in 1515 by João de Castilho. In it Late Gothic torsion and combinations of rows of arches are united with Renaissance ornamentation.

The Capelas Imperfeitas behind the choir at *Batalha* was begun under King Duarte (1433–38) by Master Huguet (Ouguete or Huguete), probably in 1435. The octagonal chapel is the most significant Gothic building on a central

297. Belém, Hieronymite monastery church, begun 1501, choir *c.* 1572. Plan

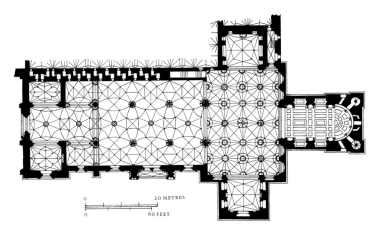

298. Setúbal, Franciscan church, begun *c.* 1494–98. Plan

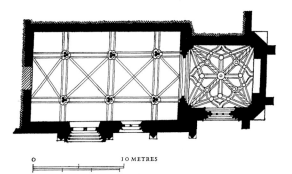

299. Tomar, Convento de Cristo. South portal, 1515

300. Kutná Hora (Kuttenberg), St Barbara. Ribspringers in the nave galleries, from 1512

301. Kutná Hora (Kuttenberg), St Barbara. Nave vault, designed 1512, constructed 1540–48

302. Annaberg, St Anne, begun 1499. Interior. Vault designed in 1515 and completed 1521–2

plan in Europe, apart from the Karlov church in Prague. It has seven isolated chapels opening off each of its sides, with six smaller chapels inserted between them and an entrance portal to the west. Progress was slow. Under King Manuel (1495–1521) the architect Mateus Fernandes the Elder (active at Batalha 1480–1515) had by 1509 constructed the chapel's western portal in the Manueline style [299]. He was also responsible for the cornice of the lower storey, perhaps some of the chapel vaults, and for the elaborate piers and vault springers of the unfinished upper storey. Mateus's son, also called Mateus, succeeded his father as master of the works in 1516, though the extent of his contribution is not known. Under King John III (1521–57) João de Castilho inserted a tribune above the portal in 1533, but work stopped soon afterwards, leaving the chapel without a roof or vault.[206] The main arch of the magnificent portal by Mateus Fernandes is formed by a trefoil arch, entwined with a curtain arch which begins at each side with a normal, concave quarter-circle, continues with a wave on each side, and reaches its apex with a convex arch from which a cusp hangs downwards. This description sounds complicated, yet these are the simplest forms in the portal, and all the complexity serves the end of creating continuity in depth.

This principle is valid in all European countries at this time. Architects dared to build flying networks of ribs only in small interiors, such as those at Frankfurt and Ingolstadt, but from them one can learn to understand the larger masterpieces with nets of double-curved ribs. Between c. 1500 and 1521 double-curved ribs were used in the chapel of St Wenceslas at *Znojmo (Znaim)* in Moravia,[207] and it was followed from 1512 by the upper parts of the nave at *Kutná*

Hora (Kuttenberg) in Bohemia, built by Benedikt Ried.[208] Here there are no transverse arches and no arches in the arcade, so that a continuous stream of rotating movements with no preponderant direction seems to run through the interior. At the level of the springing of the vault in the galleries, the tiercerons, which are bent both in plan and in elevation, intersect and then continue downwards for a short distance, or, more properly, they begin hovering in space and continue upwards. They represent an extreme case of an architect giving his vault the impression of floating in space [300, 301].

In Austria double-curved ribs were used a great deal, not only in small-scale architecture, as in the organ bracket which Anton Pilgram of Brünn built in 1511/13 in *St Stephen in Vienna*,[209] but also in many country churches whose stylistic charm lies in their combination of spatial division, penetrations, textural lightness, and the greatest possible multiplicity of images (*Vielbildigkeit*).[210]

The most significant of these churches with a net of double-curved ribs is that at *Annaberg* [302, 303][211] in Saxony; it is an aisled hall ending in three shallow apses, and it has piers with eight concave sides, which grow into the vault. The double-curved ribs flow from the aisles right into the space between the buttresses that are incorporated into the interior. Fairly low down, a division cuts these spaces into lower chapels and a balcony, which projects round each of the piers, and into the aisles. The diagonal ribs begin below the arcade arches on the east and west sides of the piers, intersect, and then rise in a large sweep to the centre of the vault, or rather to the central figure in each bay of the vault, a figure which consists of six petal-shaped cells and curves

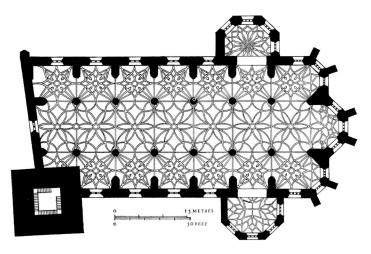

303. Annaberg, St Anne, begun 1499. Plan

downwards like a flower hanging in the vault. Each of the petals of this flower consists of two arches bent in all three dimensions and meeting at both ends, and a rib forks off each of the two lateral petals, curves down to the apex of the arcade arch, and flows into the pattern of the vault in the aisle on each side. The vaults in these aisles are also extremely complex, and clearly show their derivation from star-vaults.

These vaults make great demands on a comprehension of geometrical forms, but not on aesthetic feeling. All the complicated curves and intersections serve to produce an impression of rich and undulating movement. The long windows in the choir and choir chapels are reminiscent of those in the Wiesenkirche at Soest, and, as at Soest, so at Annaberg also, the predominant feeling is one of harmony and of ease in grasping the whole, though at Annaberg these qualities are combined with a degree of continuity among all the spatial parts which far surpasses that achieved at Soest.

The outside walls of the church at Annaberg were built from 1499 to *c*. 1512. The roof was up in 1513, the piers between nave and aisles, which have concave sides, were constructed from 1514 to 1517. In 1515 work began on the design of the vaults. The ribs were under construction by 1517, and the whole vault complete by 1521–22. The galleries were inserted in 1519–22 and the whole church, with furnishings, was finished in 1525. Three architects, Conrad Pflüger (1499–1508(?)), Peter Ulrich of Pirna (1508–13/14) and Jacob Haylmann (1515–25) were responsible for the work, but the whole church is cast in a single mould. The concave sides of its free-standing and gallery piers may well have been an expression of the architect's desire to give the feeling that the space within the church actually penetrates into the piers.

Since it can be assumed that the design for the vaults at Annaberg dates from 1515, it is contemporary with that for the vault of *King's College Chapel* at *Cambridge*. The chapel was begun in 1448 as an aisleless choir, with an ante-chapel with internal side chapels. This initial design was modified into the present plan, consisting of a single aisleless choir and ante-chapel flanked along almost its whole length by low chapels, opening into the ante-chapel through tracery

screens. The long, rectangular central portion of twelve bays then gave the effect of a single space, until, still later, it was divided by the organ-screen. The profile of the wall piers is such that it requires close scrutiny to see where the surface of the walls actually lies. It is intended that one should remain unenlightened on this score, and most visitors leave with the uncertain impression that the chapel has no walls in the normal sense of the word.[212] This interior, which was a masterpiece from the very first, was enriched in 1512 by a fan-vault which floats smoothly over the divisions between the bays. It is known that the architect was John Wastell. Originally the chapel was intended to have a lierne vault, but it is the fan-vault which gives it its stylistic perfection.[213]

In France, the last years of the Late Gothic period are represented by the church at *Brou* near Bourg-en-Bresse, which was built from 1513 to 1532 to the design of a Belgian, Louis van Boghem, and by order of Margaret of Austria.[214] The interior has a conservative spatial plan, and star-vaults throughout. The piers and their bases are complicated, and the rood-screen, which has curtain arches over wide, segmented arches, gives an effect of pure texture. The most magnificent features in the choir are the monuments and the altar of the Seven Joys of Mary. The tomb of Margaret of

304. Brou, church. Tomb of Margaret of Austria, 1525–32

Austria was built in the form of a Late Gothic house. In it are concentrated all the many forms which the style of this generation had to offer [304].

In their own country, the Belgians from 1513 to 1538 built the nave of the church of St Jacques at *Liège*. This church, like that at Brou, was still designed as a basilica, but it intensifies the qualities of the Late Gothic style in the closeness of the meshes in its net-vault, and in the forms of the tracery in the balustrade of the triforium.[215]

It is not yet certain whether or not the architects of the Netherlands played a leading part in the work of this generation. One might suppose that a work as lavish as the porch at *Louviers* near Rouen, which was probably begun in 1506, must have been influenced by models in the Netherlands, but the Late Gothic style is so international that it would not be difficult to find French analogies for every one of its details [305].[215A]

In spite of its extreme richness, the canopy over the south doorway at *Albi*, built from *c.* 1521, is more modest than the porch at Louviers, but it is nevertheless a product of the same tendencies. Here the round arch occupies an important place, for the vault of the canopy rests on semicircular arches [306]. The vault itself is covered with a textural pat-tern of ribs which combines all the different forms of curves and has pendant bosses. The main entrance to the church is framed by twisted rolls without capitals, while the outer, free-standing piers are decorated round their cylindrical surface with round arches surmounted by concave points. One feels that the architect was determined that every form used by his generation should have its say here.[215B]

Louviers and Albi achieve magnificence by the amassing of details. The *cathedral* at *Salamanca*, on the other hand, achieves its splendour through its generous management of space. It was begun in 1512, and to execute his design the architect did not hesitate to cut off lengthways part of the north aisle of the old cathedral. The section is graduated, like that of the cathedral at Toledo, with one aisle and a row of chapels on each side, so that the ultimate effect is of a nave and choir with double aisles. The choir is rectangular and has rectangular chapels. This conservative plan receives its Late Gothic character from the star-vaults, whose ribs form ogee arches in plan, and which were built to the design of Juan Gil de Hontañón. However, the piers, too, have a Late Gothic profile [307]. Their bases, which are angular in their forms but have round bases for the shafts, are very striking, and it is clear that they are formed by the penetration of

305. Louviers, Notre-Dame. South porch, begun in 1506

306. Albi Cathedral. South porch, *c.* 1521

307. Salamanca Cathedral, begun 1512. Socle of pier

concave sections with convex ones, leaving only the corners visible. This motif, too, appears all over Europe. The upper parts of the cathedral have some Renaissance forms, for example the balustrade; and the dome and the drum over the crossing were added only in 1705–33.[216]

The church of *San Estéban* at *Salamanca*, begun in 1524, was still built in the Gothic style. It has a nave with lateral chapels; the transepts project only slightly, and the choir of two bays has a straight end. The basic southern French type is transformed into a characteristic work of the last years of the Late Gothic style by the complicated forms of the shafts, and by the star-vaults, which are similar to those in the Catedrale Nueva. The three westernmost bays are divided horizontally by a monks' gallery, and here, as in other similar cases, one is not only aware of the diagonal line between the gallery and the altar, but one also feels that the monks, as they chant their psalms, looked out across a world above that of the laity below.[217]

In his design of 1522, Juan Gil de Hontañón repeated the system of the new cathedral at Salamanca at *Segovia*, but here his son Rodrigo returned to the older type of plan with an apse with an ambulatory and seven chapels. Once again the result, outside, is a magnificent series of steps – first the chapels, then the ambulatory, and finally the main apse of the choir, which has pinnacles, leading the eye still further upwards, and even flying buttresses. However, the cathedral does not have the steep roofs characteristic of French High Gothic churches [308]. The determining feature of the interior is, again, the star-vault[218] [309].

Within this generation of 1500 to 1530 one can see side by side the work of architects both modest and insatiably bold in their imagination. Among the works of the latter is the surround of the portal to the sacristy – the latter is no longer standing – at *Alcobaça* in Portugal: an example of 'arboreal architecture'. The tree-forms have little hanging roots at the bottom, like those in some of the stained glass by Hemmel, and their branches have been cut off. The door lintel is a curtain arch in which each convex section is separated from the next by a concave funnel. The Renaissance ornamentation is supposed to be the work of João de Castilho, to whom many more works have been attributed than he could possibly have carried out. It would therefore be advisable to reconsider their dates.[219]

308. Segovia Cathedral, begun 1522. Exterior of choir, constructed 1563–91

309. Segovia Cathedral, begun 1522. Interior of choir, constructed 1563–91

By far the most fantastic work of this generation is the exterior of the western arm of the church at *Tomar*. The architect is now known to have been Diogo de Arruda, and we have also learned something about the significance of the forms which appear. The lower west window [310], which lights the chapter house, was – it has been argued – originally intended to be a monument to Vasco da Gama, and his bust, which stands below the window, seems to be joined to the roots of an oak-tree. The extraordinary explanation of this absurdity is that these roots were originally the legs of the Golden Fleece which da Gama was supposed to carry over his shoulder, as the Good Shepherd carries his lamb. The fact that the design was changed as a result of the quarrel between the king and the explorer is illuminating, but the exact date of this quarrel is not known.[220] The looseness of the composition of the upper, circular window (which contains forms like billowing sails) and the lower, rectangular window, the round piers at the corners, and the emphasis on horizontal lines are not unusual in the history of the Late Gothic style. The many instruments of navigation used as symbols must be understood in the light of the programme of this church, but the way in which these non-architectural forms are combined shows a masterly imaginative power which can hardly be equalled. To arrange ropes, sea-shells, chains, artichokes, oak-trees, astrolabes, and other such objects into a single framework was no easy task, and were it

not for the cross of the Order of Christ, one might well forget that this is a church and think it a harbour fortification (in spite of the fact that it stands far from the sea). It would be wrong to criticize this design, but it is permissible to question whether its forms are Late Gothic. In part they are, but this work as a whole stands outside our stylistic concepts, and it has even less to do with the Renaissance. It is a mixture of architecture and sculpture, for not only the bust of the explorer but the astrolabes as well are sculpture; but a discussion of this mixture would lead to the problem of the frontiers of the arts, and would be of only academic interest.

The nave of the church dates from *c.*1510–14, so that the whole work must be considered among the earliest of those which introduce the last Gothic generation. However, it seems rather to be a timeless work, standing outside the general stylistic development of its age, an isolated fruit of unusual circumstances, as it were a break from the strict traditions of the Gothic style, a sideline with no continuation.

In Germany, the church of St Mary at *Halle* on the Saale, the market church, stands at the very end of the Late Gothic style. Here there were originally two churches standing one in front of the other, with just enough room between them to allow processions to pass. Cardinal Albrecht of Brandenburg had both churches pulled down, but left the towers standing. Between them an aisled hall was built, with a straight east end and the pairs of towers at its east and west fronts. The site made it necessary to incorporate the choir within the hall, separating it only by raising it by two steps,[221] but the rightness of this solution has never been denied. The piers have concave sides and pierce the narrow meshes of the net-vault. They give this church its place among the Upper Saxon buildings. It may have been part of the intention of the first architect to build the galleries which stand on low piers in the aisles, occupying less than

310. Tomar, Convento de Cristo. Window of chapter house, 1510–14

311. Caen, Saint-Pierre, 1528–45. Choir vault

half the width of the aisle. They, too, are a case of the insertion of one spatial part into another. The second architect, Nickel Hofman, who built them, however, used Renaissance forms.

The Gothic style did not cease to exist: it did, however, cease to be all-powerful, and it almost ceased to create new forms. Gothic architects had by this time drawn every possible conclusion from the premises which had been laid down when the first rib-vault was built at Durham.

13. THE GOTHIC STYLE AND THE STYLE OF THE RENAISSANCE

Some historians of art still say that the Late Gothic style is not Gothic. What is it then? Their answer is that the Late Gothic style is Early Renaissance. Paradoxes can sometimes improve one's understanding of a subject, but this paradox, in polite terms, is a fallacy.

The term Renaissance, used to describe, not the countless 'Proto-Renaissances' which made their appearance, but Italian architecture from the time of Brunelleschi and Alberti to the time of Bramante and Raphael, refers to the resurrection of the forms of imperial Roman architecture, that is of columns, pilasters, entablatures, semicircular arches, groin-vaults, and domes. These members are different from those used by Gothic architects – shafts (with no entablatures), pointed arches, rib-vaults, buttresses, and flying buttresses. The Late Gothic style is radically different from the style of the Early Renaissance and the High Renaissance.[221A]

However, the two styles are not merely different in the forms of their members: they are polar opposites. Let us summarize this once more. In the Gothic style all spatial parts and solid members are connected by 'division'; the Renaissance style returns to the principle of 'addition'. Furthermore, in the Renaissance style the solid members

and their parts are instinct with forces acting against each other by pressure and counter-pressure, while the Gothic style in its Early and High periods alters the forms of the members so that they seem to be channels conducting a stream of upward pressure; nevertheless the impression remains one of structure. In the Late Gothic period structure is transformed into texture. Finally, the Gothic style develops to offer more and more diagonal views and an increasing multiplicity of images, while the Renaissance style returns to frontality and as far as possible presents single images. Expressed in abstract terms, the Renaissance is a style of totality, while the Gothic style was one of partiality. In the Renaissance style every single part is treated as an independent entity, while in the Gothic style every part is treated as a fragment of the whole, so that, finally, whole Gothic buildings were intended to be interpreted as mere fragments of some larger, outside entity – as fragments of the infinite. Renaissance architecture aimed to express immutable 'being'; 'One wants to stay eternally within its precincts' (Wölfflin). The Gothic style, on the other hand, aimed to express mutability, growth, and 'becoming': its character is passionate. The Renaissance style represents the self-sufficiency of mortal man, whereas the Gothic style portrays man as a religious being, dependent on a higher, metaphysical and spiritual realm, yearning for deliverance. Gothic man is not a complete being, but only a part of a larger universe.

The Renaissance began in Italy about 1420, at the same time as the church of St Martin was being built at Amberg and Ensinger was building Berne Minster. It reached its highest maturity in Bramante's designs for St Peter's in Rome (1505), which were made at the same time as Annaberg, Pirna, King Henry VII's Chapel, and the choir of St Etienne at Beauvais. The period of the High Renaissance was almost over when Early Renaissance ornaments were first incorporated in the Late Gothic doorways and piers at Belém. From this moment on, there was a passive transition to the Renaissance, of which experiments can be seen in the choir of *Saint-Pierre* at *Caen* [311], built by Hector Sohier between 1518 and 1545, and in *Saint-Eustache* in *Paris*, begun in 1532 and not completed until the seventeenth century.

At Caen the choir, with its ambulatory and chapels, is Gothic in type, but has Renaissance members instead of Gothic ones: for instance, on the outside, Renaissance candelabra instead of pinnacles [312].[222] At Saint-Eustache [313] there is the same kind of substitution, although the church has proportions in no way derived from antiquity. Here there are pilasters, but they have the proportions of shafts, so that the human character of the proportions of antiquity is avoided.[223]

In Spain, the most impressive work of this period of passive transition is the Cimborio in the cathedral at *Burgos*. The original, which Hans of Cologne had begun in c. 1466, collapsed in 1539. The new work which replaced it incorporates some Renaissance forms, especially in the balustrades. Inside, the starvault is pierced, similarly to that in the Capilla del Condestable, and in its own way it is as characteristically Late Gothic as the flying rib-vaults at Frankfurt and Ingolstadt. In the huge, double-aisled hall-church at

Saragossa, which was begun in 1318, the architect of about 1520 used a Renaissance form with putti for the capitals on the westernmost piers.²²³ᴬ

In Germany, the Reformation changed the conditions and the demands of church architecture. An example of the use of Renaissance ornaments can be seen at *Halle* on the Saale.

Those historians of art who still believe that the Late Gothic style is identical with the Early Renaissance claim that coffered ceilings and net-vaults are fundamentally the same; but anyone who believes this has misunderstood both forms. In a coffered ceiling the coffers recede behind the foremost layer of the whole surface, whereas in a net-vault the ribs project in front of the main surface of the vault. The relief of the Renaissance is the direct opposite of the Gothic relief.

In theory, one can regard these cases of direct opposites as pure cases, and, by using them as theoretical co-ordinates, one can compare them with mixed cases which, to a greater or lesser degree, approach or differ from the pure cases. The generation of between 1500 and 1520 was able to create extremely pure solutions of the Late Gothic style, because previous generations, dating back to the time of the first rib-vault at Durham, had organically developed the principles that seemed to be inherent in the original introduction of the rib.

There remains one last question. Why did architects adhere to the idea of the partiality of rib-vaults? The answer to this question will be the subject of the second part of this book.

14. THE SURVIVAL OF THE GOTHIC STYLE

In Italy, where the Gothic style was felt to be something alien, it was relatively easy to eliminate Gothic forms and to replace them by the forms of classical antiquity. However, the men of the fifteenth century were no longer the same as the classical Athenians and Romans, so that it was impossible simply to copy classical temples. The style that was created was something completely new, in spite of the fact that it was proudly considered to be a re-birth of the art of classical antiquity.

The few pointed arches which can be found in Italian architecture between 1419 and 1550 are not essential. When it was decided to try and finish the façade of the church of *S. Petronio* at *Bologna*, it became apparent that any compromise between the forms of the Gothic style and the Renaissance had become impossible. The first design, which was made by Ariguzzi in 1514, was still Gothic, in the sense of the Italian Gothic style, and it was followed by designs made by Peruzzi in 1521, which are a mixture of the Gothic style and Renaissance. Giulio Romano then proposed a mixture of Corinthian orders and various Gothic details, such as a rose-window, pinnacles, and tabernacles, and the long series of succeeding designs and reports shows that the aristocracy was in favour of pure Renaissance, while the bourgeoisie and the artisans defended the Gothic style. In 1578 the aristocracy summoned Palladio, who submitted several designs, of which one is possibly his finest work, but the opposition rejected them. In 1587, when Terribilia began

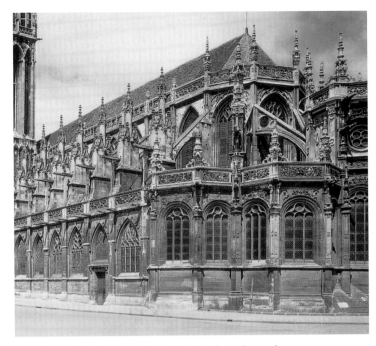

312. Caen, Saint-Pierre, 1528–45. Exterior from the south-east

313. Paris, Saint-Eustache, begun 1532. Interior

the work of replacing the temporary flat ceiling by a Gothic rib-vault, Carlo Carrazzi, a tailor from Cremona, interfered and demanded from the men directing the work that they should use Gothic triangulation. This controversy, which dragged on for a whole century and left the façade unfinished, shows that, at this time, the Gothic style had become the style of the uneducated.[224] The leaders of the clergy and the Jesuits belonged to the social stratum of the humanists, and in Italy they built their churches in the styles first of the Renaissance, and then of Mannerism and of the Baroque.

In other countries, however, the situation was different. Except in France there were no impressive classical ruins to be seen, but plenty of impressive Gothic works. When the wave of humanism reached France and Germany, and later England, Spain, and other countries, it led to stylistic mixtures such as those that have already been quoted at Caen and in Paris. The absolutely standardized Five Orders of columns might produce an international and a timeless effect, but free variations on the classical theme seemed better to express national taste, and here too, especially in secular architecture, reminiscences of the Gothic style were a better expression of the spirit of the bourgeoisie.

The Gothic style no longer had any problems to set; the Renaissance now set problems of a quite different kind. Those who still built in the Gothic style no longer aimed at creating more intensified forms. The Jesuits in Germany, Belgium, and other countries probably turned to the Gothic style because they felt that it was more Christian than a style derived from the works of a pagan civilization, and they probably also presumed that simple people were more receptive to medieval architecture than to buildings like the church of the Gesù in *Rome* or that of St Michael in *Munich*. Their works often remained eclectic and lifeless, but occasionally they succeeded in creating something outstanding, such as the church of the *Ascension* at *Cologne*, which was begun in 1618, at the time of the outbreak of the Thirty Years' War, but was almost completely destroyed in 1945.[244A]

The motives for the continued use of Gothic forms remain to be investigated in detail. Gothic churches required preservation, and therefore perpetual observation and repair, and they thus provided training for many architects who were also connoisseurs of classical architecture. In the church of *Saint-Etienne* at *Caen*, the vault was restored in 1616 [16]. The new vault was probably a faithful reproduction of the original, but the strikingly squashed curves give the impression that the architects had regressed to the level of technical skill reached about 1120. In other cases, the motive may have been to match existing work. An example of this can be seen in the church of *Saint-Germain-des-Prés* in *Paris*, where the flat ceiling in the nave was replaced in 1644 by a rib-vault, built to the pattern of that in the choir; and here, the replacement is really satisfying. The large windows with tracery in the transepts, however, are less convincing, and yet the whole church still gives the effect of being an original Gothic work.

Sir Christopher Wren, a convinced adherent of classicism, was also interested in the restoration of Gothic works, as can be seen from the evidence of his reports on Old St Paul's in London in 1662, on Salisbury Cathedral in 1669, and on Westminster Abbey in 1713. The English cherished the Gothic style, and this love was not confined to any one social class. Indeed, in the eighteenth century it was the members of the upper class, such as Horace Walpole, who wanted a return to the Gothic style. It is from this state of mind that the Gothic style could develop, first as an expression of romanticism, and then of historicism.[224B]

There is no comprehensive history of the Gothic survival in existence.[225] The Gothic Revival in England has been the subject of excellent studies, and Romantic Gothic in Germany too is well known. The building of Gothic churches has an analogy in America, in the Gothic colleges there, which feel themselves bound to the traditions of Oxford and Cambridge. Nearly all neo-Gothic buildings stand in a setting into which they do not fit, because the believers in historicism simply held that any style was worthy of imitation.

Originally Gothic churches stood in Gothic towns, but the rise in population, the change of, and increase in, traffic, and the disappearance of town walls because of the development of weapons of war produced modern towns, better suited to modern life. Originally these churches reigned supreme over the silhouettes of the towns in which they stood, but now they began to lose this focal quality among the mass of tall houses.

Some medieval towns have been partly preserved, some even surrounded by walls with towers and gates [328], and with narrow streets and irregularly shaped squares [330]. They have a warm and dreamy quality about them, and, with their shadowy arcades and picturesque oriels, they are rich in intimate spaces, seeming interiors although they are part of exterior space. They embrace us protectively; they have a tranquil atmosphere, and they seem to be as holy as their churches: they are, as it were, a lost home for romantic souls.[225A]

Modern men, however, do not have the desire to be romantic, nor should they have – and yet sometimes they are. Certainly they must cherish a spark of Romanticism to understand Gothicism with their hearts and to love it.

The Gothic survival has always been romantic, and ultimately it shows how romantic the Gothic style itself was – how it expressed a yearning for a better and a purer world lying beyond the bounds of reality, how it was an imaginative adventure. To steep oneself in the Gothic style is to look into a magic mirror which reflects, not the humanity of today, but people from a far distant past who are strangers and yet are familiar to us, as though the spirit of their age could once again grow within our souls. It enriches us and lifts us far above ourselves, and, though we no longer wish to build in the Gothic way, we have now reached a sufficient historical distance from the Gothic style to honour it and admire it as a monument to the generations of a suffering, striving, and blessed age.

PART TWO

The General Problems of the Gothic Style

I. THE TERM 'GOTHIC' AND THE CONCEPT OF THE GOTHIC STYLE

THE architect who built the choir of Saint-Denis must have spoken to Suger about the *arcus* in the vaults; William of Sens in speaking to the Prior of Canterbury no doubt used the term *fornices arcuatae*, and Villard de Honnecourt probably spoke to his apprentices of *ogives*. However, no name for the style itself is known to have existed at this time; indeed, it is unlikely that any name did exist, for, in the regions where the Gothic style was born and developed, 'building in the Gothic style' was simply called building. In Germany, the chronicler Burckhard von Hall wrote, about 1280, that the church at Wimpfen im Tal, which was begun in 1269, was built *more francigeno*. This name does not describe the style, but simply indicates its origin, which confirms the view that no special name yet existed for the style at a whole.[1]

Petrarch (1304–74) was in Cologne in 1333 and wrote that he had seen an uncommonly beautiful *templum* there which was unfinished, but which was rightly called the most magnificent in the world (*summum*). In spite of that Petrarch was among the first men, if not the first, to value the age of classical antiquity higher than his own on every count. He did not base this conclusion only on the poor quality of the Latin of his time, compared with that of Cicero and Virgil, and on the low standard of scholarship, compared with that of Plato (of whom he knew little); he also compared the poor quality of the painting and sculpture of this age with the perfect reproductions of natural forms achieved by the Greeks and Romans. Since he regarded himself as a descendant of the Romans, it is in his works that the theory that everything bad came from the 'barbarians' was born.

This 'Barbarian theory' was adopted by humanistic circles.[1A] In his biography of Brunelleschi, Manetti wrote that architecture fell into decadence after the end of the Roman Empire, that the Vandals, the Goths, the Lombards, and the Huns brought their own, untalented architects with them, that architecture improved slightly for a few years under Charlemagne, and that it then fell into decadence once more until the appearance of Brunelleschi in 1419.

Filarete, who lived from about 1400 to about 1469, had similar ideas on the history of architecture. He wrote, 'cursed be the man who introduced "modern" architecture'. By 'modern' he meant Gothic, which still appears to have had no name. He continued, 'I believe that it can only have been the barbarians who brought it to Italy'.

Alberti said that it would be absurd to paint Helen or Iphigenia with Gothic hands – with the hands of old women. In the Italian text, the phrase is *mani vecchizze e gotiche*, but, in the Latin edition, Alberti translated this with the words *seniles et rusticanae*. The word Gothic does not therefore seem, as yet, to have acquired its modern sense. Gothic meant rustic or coarse, like the Goths.

Gradually the word Gothic came to be applied not to barbarians in general, but only to certain specific barbarians. Filarete puts the blame on the *transmontani*, expressly adding, 'the Germans and the French'. In 1510, in the report of the so-called Pseudo-Raphael, the idea was further narrowed down: he spoke only of the *maniera tedesca*. In this report, too, the theory is first advanced that the Gothic style had its origins in the forests, because the Germans could not cut down trees, but bound together the branches of living trees, thus creating the pointed arch. This theory that the Gothic style was born in the forests of Germany lived on in various forms with unbelievable tenacity, sometimes in a literal form, and sometimes in the form of metaphors.

In 1521, page xv of Cesariano's translation of Vitruvius shows the proportions of Milan Cathedral 'secundum Germanicam symmetriam'.

Vasari contrasted this bad architecture with the classical orders, and wrote: 'There is also another manner of architecture which is called the German manner.' He completely forgot the real culprits, the French, and went on to say: 'This manner was invented by the Goths.' In writing of the Palazzo dei Signori at Arezzo, he used the term *maniera de' Goti*, while Palladio reverted to the phrase, *maniera tedesca* – not *gotica*.

In France, however, it was never forgotten that the Gothic style was not born in Germany. Philibert de l'Orme, who lived from 1512 to 1570, called it *la mode Françoise*.

In Germany, Sandrart, in his *Teutsche Akademie*, which was published in 1675, revived the Italian theories. He seems to have been familiar with Filarete's manuscript, or at least to have had indirect knowledge of it, for he wrote that, by inventing bad architecture, the Goths 'had called down more than a thousand million curses on their heads'. Filarete had modestly contented himself with a single curse.[2]

From the history of the name of the Gothic style, it can be seen how muddled the concept was. The Goths, who in 410, under the leadership of Alaric, destroyed Rome, or rather parts of it, were made responsible for all the architecture that was created between 410 and 1419, and, in countries other than Italy, even for works executed up to the time of Vasari – that is, about 1550.

During the eighteenth century, in the course of a slow process of development, a more positive view of the Gothic

314. Amiens Cathedral. South transept rose window

style was reached, and, with it, the concept of what was Gothic changed. Historians began to distinguish two periods; they gave separate names to different parts of the earlier periods and reserved the term Gothic for the last period alone. The evil reputation of the men who destroyed the good architecture of Rome, however, stuck until the connexion was either forgotten, or was no longer felt. As early as 1840, Kugler said that we no longer think of the Goths when we say 'Gothic'. Nevertheless, those men who were beginning to feel enthusiasm for the Gothic style tried to find a better name for it, but none of these names, neither *style ogival*, nor Kugler's Germanic style, nor any of the others, found support.

When in the course of the nineteenth century historical knowledge of the birth of the Gothic style, its development, and its spread increased, the Late Gothic style was still regarded as part of the Gothic style. Moreover, the growing study of the essential Gothic elements, beginning with Wetter's book, and the attempts to interpret the essence of the Gothic, which began with the work of Viollet-le-Duc, and have continued to our own day, have neutralized the effects of personal taste and have led to a more intensive analysis of the concept of Gothic style.[2A]

The scholarly consideration of the Gothic style began with descriptions of individual buildings and so came to the study of individual members, such as pointed arches, piers, rib-vaults, windows, doorways, roofs, and towers. At the same time a desire grew to understand the essence of the Gothic style which could permeate such divergent features as piers and windows. The Gothic style was said to possess a picturesque quality, a quality of infinity, a vegetal quality, a romantic quality. All these different concepts were first formulated in the eighteenth century and were then considered more closely in the nineteenth and systematically bound into one unified concept.

Some of these concepts were also applicable to sculpture and painting, and the concept of what was Gothic was widened to include, not only architecture, but also the fine arts. After this, the term became more and more extensible, until critics began to speak of Gothic literature and poetry, of Gothic music, of Gothic philosophy and metaphysics, of Gothic civilization, and, finally, of Gothic man. This process was begun by de Laborde in 1816, when he wrote an introduction on political history to his work on French architecture. In 1843, Schnaase went further; he presented his public with a panorama of medieval civilization. At about the same time, Vitet proposed the theory that the Romanesque style was created by the clergy, whereas the Gothic style was the creation of the laity.[2B] Viollet-le-Duc tacitly accepted this theory, but broadened it with a combination of *l'esprit gaulois* and his own theory of functionalism. Succeeding generations accepted this legacy, and *l'esprit gaulois* developed further under the influence of the fantastic racial theories of Gobineau, whose forerunners had appeared as early as the eighteenth century. The study of medieval symbolism can also be traced back to the Romantic period (e.g. to works of Boisserée and later of Ramée), and the background to the history of Gothic civilization grew more and more rich and colourful.[2C]

The sceptics, who appeared about 1900, did not perceive the metaphorical driving belt which must be assumed to run between Gothic civilization and Gothic architecture, if one is to accept an explanation of stylistic developments in terms of the many factors which go to make a civilization. It was, of course, obvious that certain architectural traits must be a reflection of the civilization of their time, but it was not known whether these traits should be interpreted as reflections either of social factors or of national ones, or whether perhaps they sprang from a change in the nature of piety. Perhaps it was these factors, and many others besides, which were the roots from which history grew, and which provided the branch of architecture with its sap. Historians spoke of many different roots, but, basically, their search was for the primary root of all these roots, and they gave this title sometimes to one root and sometimes to another.

Nobody can doubt the legitimacy of these studies, but, if one stands in front of an actual building and asks oneself what a certain base of a certain pier, or a certain triforium, or a certain rose-window has to do with scholasticism, chivalry, courtly love, or even the liturgy, not to mention politics and economics, one realizes that all these many theories do not give a sufficient answer: and yet the problem is one which must be faced.

The history of the Gothic style which has been presented in the first part of this book has been largely kept free from these general questions. In it I have tried to forget about the background of Gothic civilization, and considered the development of the Gothic style as an immanent process which took place within building lodges. To clarify the problem, one can call those other factors which penetrated the lodges from outside external factors, and one can exclude them from architectural discussion, in which they would only cause confusion. As soon as one starts to look for the influence of these external factors, however, one realizes that every other branch of human activity followed its own immanent development, just as did the field of architecture. The problem that was so disturbing to nineteenth-century historians can be expressed in a single question. Did all these immanent lines of development run parallel to one another, and, if so, what was the force which produced this parallel course?

2. THE DEVELOPMENT OF THE GOTHIC STYLE SEEN AS AN IMMANENT PROCESS

The improvement of Romanesque groin-vaults came about as a result of a rational consideration of the geometric construction of the arches and the surfaces of the cells; the building technique employed, that is, the centering; their statics, both during and after construction; and also the economic problems which they presented. But all these considerations always went hand in hand with the aim of producing an aesthetically satisfying result. The changes had nothing to do with the Crusades, which began only later, or with the liturgy, or with philosophy. The architects were intent simply upon making necessary improvements. As far as can be reconstructed, this was a process of trial and error which led to the replacement of diagonal, wooden centering arches by the stone *cintre permanent*, that is the rib.

Here, the question must indeed have arisen as to whether the architectural patrons of this time, the clergy, were in agreement with the introduction of this innovation; but this question can be ignored for the moment. The development which was described in the first part of this book shows that the rib-vault, in its turn, was further improved by a combination of rational considerations and aesthetic criticism, which resulted in the introduction of pointed arches, first over the four sides of each bay, and finally in the diagonals also. This process, too, was an immanent, or an internal one. Just as master masons did not determine the form of the liturgy or indulge in metaphysics, so the clergy did not build scaffolding, or draw designs for arches or for the profiles of ribs. These are different spheres, different jobs, requiring special skills, and it need hardly be said that no amount of knowledge of metaphysics can help one to build a rib-vault, and that on the other hand the ability of an architect to build a vault cannot help him to decide whether general concepts are realities or mere names.

However, rib-vaults presented only part of the problem. The real problem was how to achieve conformity throughout a whole church. History shows that the transformation of Romanesque architectural members to conform with the ribs was not achieved overnight. Ribs, being members crossing each other diagonally, demanded that shafts also be turned diagonally. Therefore, the form of bases and capitals had also to be altered. In the case of sexpartite vaults, this meant that the number of shafts had to be increased. The question as to what form piers should take became an urgent one. The steps taken to solve this problem led ultimately to the dissolution of the wall into a grille and the introduction of the new Gothic kind of relief. In this kind of relief, one layer is conceived as projecting in front of another, not as lying behind it, just as ribs are seen to project in front of the cells of a vault rather than cells to lie behind the ribs. The slenderness of the rib set the proportions for slenderer supports, and its structural character seemed to demand the change from Romanesque structure to specifically Gothic structure. The new system allowed an increased emphasis on verticals, yet left the architect of Sens the possibility of choosing the golden mean, and the architect of the Sainte-Chapelle that of using the fairly moderate proportional ratio of 1:2. The tendency to emphasize verticals only governed the work of certain schools and generations, and the question as to how far this tendency was the product of other factors will be answered later.

The real propelling force of the rib lay both in its diagonality, and in its property of dividing each spatial compartment of the church into interdependent, fragmentary spatial units. The tendency towards a more and more resolute reshaping of spatial parts and architectural members to conform to the principle of partiality, and the resulting change in the forces of the members, has been explained in the first part of this book, and this tendency must also be considered in discussing the immanence of the development of Gothic architecture. However, if one concentrates on each step in the development, then this immanence takes on another, peculiar aspect.

A study of bases and plinths shows these stylistic changes only if one compares early examples with late ones [315–17]. Architects kept to the Romanesque idea that a base should express the fact that, through it, the pier is fixed to the floor. Not only the tall plinths at Saint-Germer, but also the shorter ones in the classic cathedrals of Amiens and Reims, and even the long slab which runs under the whole length of each side of the arcade at Salisbury, remain faithful to this idea, that a plinth is the firm, self-sufficient support on which stand the pier and its shafts. The architects of the High Gothic period made this property of bases even clearer by reducing their height, so that, compared with Romanesque bases, High Gothic ones (*Tellerbasen*) look as if they had been pressed flat into the shape of dishes turned upside down. In profile the concave part becomes so deep that water could stand in it – hence the English term 'water-holding bases'; the lower part of the profile protrudes over the plinth and is sometimes supported by small corbels.

The first work in which bases appear to grow out of the floor is the cathedral in *Prague*.[20] In the church of Saint-Ouen at *Rouen*, and in later Spanish churches, the different levels of the bases of the shafts give the impression that the piers do not stand on clearly delineated, horizontal supports, but that the shafts have grown side by side at their

315. Lisieux Cathedral. Bases, *c.* 1165–80.

316. Prague Cathedral. Base of choir pier, 1344–52.

317. Rouen, St Ouen. Base of nave pier, *c.* 1469

318. Beauvais, Saint-Etienne. North transept rose window, *c.* 1150

own tempo, and that some of them have grown faster than others [307, 317]. The clear, horizontal division between the bases and the piers and shafts above was disturbed, and the chronological line of slight changes in the forms of bases and plinths shows how difficult it was to create truly Gothic forms at a point at which isolation and the horizontal positioning of one member over another exercised such strong demands.

It must not be supposed that all architectural members became Gothic to the same degree at the same time. Vaults had achieved their classic Gothic form long before bases had undergone the same degree of change. But, in every case, it was the criticism of architects and their imaginative energy which demanded these changes, devised them, and finally realized them. The philosophers, the clergy, the knights, and the kings played no part in the solution of these problems; they were internal problems of the lodges.

Although every good monograph deals with the forms of bases, and distinguishes between the work of architects by the profiles they used, a detailed examination of the history of this one member would not be sufficient to explain the immanent development of the Gothic style.

The changes in the forms of the great circular windows show this development much more clearly. This theme was

first formulated in the north transept of the church of *Saint-Etienne at Beauvais* [318]. Here, there is a central hub, on which columns, supporting trefoil arches inside the circumference, stand radially. The surrounding figures show that this wheel was to be interpreted as the wheel of fortune, and there are other examples of similar wheels of fortune, such as that in the cathedral at *Basel*, and the much later south transept rose at *Amiens* Cathedral [314].[2E] There was another solution to the problem of filling circular windows. The centre of the window could be filled not with spokes, but with stone slabs, out of which were carved smaller circles of varying size, distributed in various patterns. But there were yet more possibilities. At *Lausanne*, as noted by Villard de Honnecourt, the central area is filled with a quatrefoil.[2F] The progression of circular windows also included forms which deviate from the basic idea of the wheel. The great west window at *Laon* [56] uses twelve semicircles springing inwards from the circumference, and the columns which radiate from the hub meet these semicircles at their apexes. The inner part of the rose-window of the west front at *Chartres* [55] is a proper wheel, again with twelve lights, each with a semicircular arch, and there are then twelve smaller circles running round inside the circumference, each of which stands between two of the inner, semicircular arches. For the oculus in the south transept at Chartres [117] the same form was chosen as for the west window, but it was enriched by the addition of semicircles springing inwards from the circumference, like those used at Laon.

It is easy to recognize the variations and combinations in the forms of circular windows as the result of consistent steps. In *Notre-Dame* in *Paris* [116], the wheel consists of two concentric zones. In the inner zone, the same system was used as in the church of Saint-Etienne at Beauvais, that is, twelve spokes round a central hub, but here it was improved by the fact that the spokes do not lie on the central vertical axis. The outer zone has twenty-four panels.[3] At *Mantes*, the spokes have their capitals at the centre, so that they appear to stand, not on the hub, but on the circumference.

A new stage of development began when the architects of the rose-window in the west façade of *Reims* [122] and that of the *Sainte-Chapelle* in *Paris* (in its original form) decided to transplant the tracery of the usual oblong windows into circular ones. They made the shape of an oblong window with tracery taper at the bottom, so that its sides converge radially and meet on the hub. This might be called akyrism, or it might equally be called an abuse, a misinterpretation, or a deliberate change in interpretation.[3A] Later architects, for instance those of the north transept of the cathedral at *Sées* and of the transepts of the church of *Saint-Germain* at *Auxerre*,[4] made the sides of the components panels parallel once again, and thus completely gave up the original idea of the hub [319]. One of the richest combinations to be found is the tracery in the northern oculus of the cathedral at *Amiens*, inserted in the fourteenth century, which is a star with five points in the centre and some panels with parallel sides and some with.[4A] We can understand from the general development of the Gothic style why tracery lost its structural character and took on a purely textural one, and once again, we can follow the way in which succeeding architects

319. Sées Cathedral. North
transept, rose window *c.* 1310

gradually progressed, step by step, along this line of development.

The terms 'wheel-window' and 'rose-window' are usually used indiscriminately, but the comparison with a rose is better suited to oculi with tracery such as that used at Reims and Strasbourg [169], where the pattern spreads like a flower, with pointed petals lying in a circle. Such windows have sometimes been compared with the sun – a comparison referring to their radiating rays – and, because of this likeness, the French call the whole High Gothic style *Rayonnant*.[4B] Although this radiation of rays from the centre is preserved in the Flamboyant style, the textural character of the tracery filling the surface predominates, and the idea of a wheel, a rose, or the sun disappears.

This interpretation of the development of circular windows, and their gradual alteration to a form which preserved little of the idea of a wheel, should be sufficient to show what is meant by the internal tasks of the lodges. Oculi in west façades, and those of transepts, were not isolated decoration, but integral parts of the façades, which in turn were parts of whole churches. Every step which marked some degree of progress in the solving of the problem of filling oculi was conditioned by the demands of the whole church, and was therefore part of the greater progress of the continual increase in the emphasis on partiality: and yet every such step also set its own special problems within the greater overall problem. Every architect was involved in the common task as a follower of his predecessors and, more particularly, of his own teacher, and found in this general task his own personal task, which he fulfilled with his own imaginative powers and his own spiritual energy, according to the nature and the degree of his personal talents.

Within this process, there are those who vary, those who combine, and those who correct, some tending towards increased clarity, others towards increased splendour, yet others to both. There are steps which created something entirely new, like the system of Noyon (or earlier of the choir at Saint-Denis), the consequences that were drawn from the form of the buttresses and flying buttresses at Chartres, and the form of the tracery at Reims. In our historical consideration we follow the works of all these architects, both the modest ones, like the architect of Senlis, and the men of genius, like the designer of Lincoln, the architects of the English chapter houses and their successors at Ely and Gloucester, Peter Parler, and many others. It is their spiritual achievements which have given us such rich gifts. However, even these men of genius were firmly bound by the whole process of development; for even the great intuitions come only out of hard work. No man who was not a member of one of the lodges could take part in the creative development of the Gothic style, not even Albert the Great, although, according to legend, he is supposed to have done so. To participate, one had to belong to the profession.

The continuity of the development was the product of instruction, and on this subject we are fairly well informed. The more the Gothic style developed, and the more complicated it became, the more impossible it was for a self-educated man to enter the field. From the ranks of the trained masons the most gifted were picked out, after they had completed their compulsory period of journeying, and were made the foremen who constituted the link between the creative architect and his executive craftsmen. Where foremen not only seemed capable of forming this link and controlling the actual labour, but also showed some aptitude for creative design, they were put to work as draughtsmen under the supervision of the architect, until they were finally equipped to carry out their own designs. The reason we have better knowledge of the organization of Late Gothic lodges is that the architects of the earlier period had easier problems to solve and could therefore treat legal and instructional problems more lightly. In the Late Gothic period, proper examinations were held, at which the apprentices had to produce a master-piece.[5] But by whatever process architects were selected from the twelfth century onwards, it is clear that an apprentice was subject to the judgement of the older generation and that he had to be familiar with the ideas of the masters before he could reach the stage at which he himself, when faced with a new problem, could make his own constructive criticism of their work.

This explains the small extent of the steps taken within the lodges, and the interplay of influences, which was the result of the travel of apprentices and of the calling of architects from one place to another. Even in the spread of the style over regions far distant from one another, which was the result of journeys of whole bands of masons, or of educational journeys like that of the German architect who began the church at Wimpfen in 1269 and 'had just returned from Paris', continuity was always conditioned by the personal ties which kept architects to lodges. Every architect was, according to his talent and imagination, free to make a leap if he dared, but his spring-board was provided for him, and his work became, in turn, a spring-board for his pupils.

The picture drawn here explains the connexion between the factors of tradition and originality: what we call immanence is founded on both. Younger architects followed existing tracks and continued them, and they were bound to understand the sense of direction set by a strong tradition, because they had to append their innovations organically to what already existed. Only rarely, as in the case of Brunelleschi, did an architect make a radical break with this sense of direction, and even he stood in a current and was the exponent of the ideas of his own social class of humanists. The lodge of S. Maria del Fiore at Florence did not consist so exclusively of masons as did those in other towns. Here there were also laymen, and it was their presence which produced the spiritual atmosphere that enabled Brunelleschi to break with all the traditions of the Gothic style. The tradition that he followed was that of the 'good' architecture which had been destroyed by the wicked Goths, and it was from this tradition that he drew his faith in a style of totality, whereas Gothic architects had, since the introduction of the rib, taken the aim of a style of partiality as a matter of course. The problem facing the Gothic architects was not, however, the choice between a style of totality and one of partiality, for this problem had been solved by the Norman school about 1100; it was the problem of strengthening the tendency towards partiality and of widening its scope until it embraced every part of the building.

The immanence of the development of the Gothic style is no mystery. It would be one if one were to believe that the last Gothic works, such as King Henry VII's Chapel, Annaberg, and the network of flying ribs at Frankfurt, had been in existence in some other sphere outside our world since 1093, waiting for their own realization and, like a magnet, directing the countless little steps in the development towards their own creation. Immanence, on the contrary, operates the other way round. The introduction of the rib-vault proposed a general sense of direction, leading to a goal which could not be foretold, but could only be realized through a strict adherence to this direction. This is not like a search for the North Pole, which already exists, but is a chain of creations providing a chain of surprises, which culminates in the final surprises of the ultimate Late Gothic style.

This aspect of the immanence of the development is the product of the inner, spiritual labours of the professional workers engaged in the field of architecture. *Immanere* means to stay within. By immanence, we mean that tendency in a course of development which is determined from within the subject of the development. However, as has already been explained, the different immanent processes in different spheres of activity existing within the same cultural environment seem to be subject to another, higher, and all-embracing immanence. It is to these other spheres that we shall turn next.

3. THE MEANING AND THE PURPOSE OF CHURCH ARCHITECTURE

An architect builds a pulpit as well suited as possible to its purpose; he seeks the most suitable position in the church, raises the level of its floor, and builds steps, a rail, and a sounding-board. The purpose of the pulpit is that sermons shall be preached from it. The sermon, too, has a purpose; it is intended to instruct, to edify, and to confirm belief, but its meaning lies in what is preached. To understand the meaning of a pulpit, it is sufficient to recognize its purpose, but to understand the meaning of a sermon, it is not enough to understand that its purpose is to edify: one must actually understand what is said by the preacher. Purpose is a limited case within the wider concept of meaning.

The same thing is true of an altar. The architect must arrange it to fulfil its purpose, so that Mass can be read and a congregation attend, but the meaning of this arrangement lies within the Mass itself.[5A]

Church architecture embraces a number of purposes, which are the products of the various actions of the Christian cult. The overall purpose of a church is to serve the whole cult, but its meaning lies in religious devotion. The meaning embraces the whole gamut of religious ideas and feelings – contemplation, repentance, and the resolution not to sin any more, consolation and hope. The meaning of a church lies in belief, and only the differentiation between all the activities of the cult splits this meaning into a variety of individual functions. To understand the meaning of a Gothic church, one must understand both the meaning of religion and, more especially, the meaning of the Christian religion during the age of Gothic architecture, and the special purposes underlying the church, according to whether one is entering either a cathedral, a monastic church, a parish church, or a chapel of a castle.

Dehio has discussed very fully the changes within the architectural programme of the church while the Gothic style reigned.[6] Some of the innovations which were introduced had their roots in the period of the Romanesque, for instance the building of longer choirs to allow for the larger number of clergy. The lengthening of an existing choir at *Laon* is a specially clear expression of the demands of the clergy about 1205.

A second innovation which influenced architecture was the exhibition of newly acquired relics on altars, and the translation of older relics from crypts to the churches above. Even within the Romanesque style, the Cluniacs of Hirsau and the Cistercians had decided against crypts. At Saint-*Denis* Suger preserved the old crypts because, as consecrated

320. Naumberg Cathedral. Screen of the western choir, *c.* 1255

ground, they seemed sacrosanct to him. From the time of the building of *Noyon*, however, crypts were only built where the site demanded it, for instance at *Bourges*, *Siena*, and *Erfurt*. The building of crypts resulted in choirs lying several steps higher than the naves: with their disappearance, choirs and naves came to lie at the same, or almost the same, level.[6A]

The clergy needed some kind of barrier to separate them from the laity, in order not to be disturbed at their prayers, which took place seven times a day, and it was from this need that rood-screens and screens dividing choirs from choir aisles developed. Especially in Spain and in England, this tendency was taken a stage further, and the east end of the nave was also reserved for the clergy. These high screens, which sometimes take the form of walls (for instance, at *Lugo* in Spain), destroy the open view that was originally intended, and, because of this, many rood-screens in France and Germany were later removed. The exclusion of the congregation was felt to be too aristocratic, and even the clergy probably found this attitude of separation presumptuous. The usual criticisms, especially those of the *coros* in Spain, must be understood in the light of this later attitude, and it must also be remembered that many of these *coros* date from after the end of the Gothic style. There were Gothic rood-screens in *Notre-Dame* in *Paris*, in the cathedrals at *Reims*, *Naumburg*, and *Strasbourg*, and in many other churches [320]. Moreover, in Paris, the screens between the choir and the choir aisles have been preserved, and one can experience for oneself how exclusive the effect of these insertions is in every sense. Judged stylistically, they are extreme cases of the insertion of one spatial unity into another, and certainly nobody would wish that the one at *Albi* did not exist. However, it can be seen in all these parts of churches whose access was more or less forbidden to the laity, that their purpose, stated barely and soberly, was to express a system of social strata.[6B]

The increase in the number of the clergy was one of the reasons for the increase in the number of altars and therefore also of chapels. The rows of chapels round choirs were continued along choir aisles. Dehio noted that the cathedral in *Barcelona* has thirty-one chapels and that the church of *S. Petronio* at *Bologna* was intended to have fifty-eight; and, in an imaginary description of the church of the *Holy Grail*, there are seventy-two. Although this was a church on a central plan and the number is probably connected with some symbolism of numbers (3 times 24), the need for so many chapels must, nevertheless, be understood to be the result of the number of the Knights of the Holy Grail, who must also be regarded as clergy.[6C]

The significance of purpose can be seen equally clearly where its action is negative. In parish churches, where there were few priests, and sometimes only one, there was no increase in the number of chapels, and in the churches of the mendicant orders the position of the chapels and the significance of sermons influenced the designs to which they were built.[6D]

To these factors must be added the fact that allowances had to be made for processions. We know that the anterooms or porches at *Cluny* and *Vézelay* served the purpose of protecting participants in processions from the weather while they were lining up for their entrance into the church. Both these ante-rooms date from the Transitional period, and they had only a few impressive Gothic successors; their function appears to have been transferred to porches and the lower storeys of towers.[7] The arrangement of processions may have been variable, but it is nevertheless legitimate to say that Gothic cathedrals are processional spaces.

Sacristies, towers, cloisters, and the domestic buildings of the clergy all exercised an influence on church architecture proper, because they concealed the lateral elevations of churches. Later additions, such as those at *Burgos* and *Toledo*, form a solid ring round a church, which not only alters the appearance of the exterior, but also tends to take up much of the interest in the interior.

Defensive arrangements in churches, like the battlements at Saint-Denis, Moissac, and other places, too, were not the general rule, but they show that, in the Gothic style as in any other, purposes determined spatial plans and that the study of these purposes is therefore one of the duties of the historian of architecture.

However, the form of a building is not determined by purposes only. This is true even if one does not confine oneself to the consideration of subsidiary functions, such as those of altars and pulpits. Even the reciprocal interplay of all the ritual functions embraced within a whole church does not give a clear, unequivocal solution, although the architect must try to achieve the best possible interplay. It is not in this respect that sacred functions can be differentiated from secular ones. The fabrication of tools, weapons, clothes, bridges, means of transport, or signs proceeds, in every case, from a general conception of what is required, and continues with a search for the most suitable materials and forms. The fabrication of a hammer proceeds from a general conception of its purpose and its mechanical principles; this conception is then narrowed by a consideration of the special function which it is to serve – whether it is to be used by a mason or a precision engineer. Finally, however, it must be decided what materials are to be used for the handle and the head and what form they shall take. In other words, function always leaves a 'margin of freedom' which cannot be resolved by utilitarian considerations and which is not objectively pre-determined.

So far we have only considered purposes which spring from human activity, but one can also speak of the functions of structural members. It is just as much a matter of course to demand that they should function in a church building as in a secular building. The forms of piers, arches, walls, and vaults are dictated by their own special functions, but even these functions never entirely determine their forms: there always remains a 'margin of freedom'. A purely utilitarian building is determined by its own special purpose in just the same way as a church, but even here, purpose can never determine form completely. Gothic vaults must be examined in the light of their function; it is important to understand their static principles and the functions of diagonal ribs, ridge-ribs, and tiercerons, but, even when these functions have been understood, the question as to why these members have so many different profiles in different churches still remains unanswered, since each profile fulfils the necessary static function, in so far as it exists, equally well.

Although much could be said about the functions of the spatial parts of a church, and about the functions of its architectural members, it need not be said here. It will also be sufficient to say that lighting and the arrangement of windows and lamps primarily serve a practical purpose, but that there is, once again, a 'margin of freedom' in the siting of windows and lamps, and in the choice of the dimensions and the shape of windows.

This consideration leads to the question as to what are the tendencies by which the 'margin of freedom' is eradicated and a final form reached. In reaching it, the architect appears to be absolutely free; but he is not, for the question of cost always plays a part, either by inhibiting his imaginative powers, or by influencing him to build something of great splendour. The designs for most of the buildings of rich monasteries and dioceses were made with confidence in the charity of future generations, and economic factors, combined with the course of wars, often determined the fate of Gothic buildings. Some, like the cathedrals of Beauvais and Narbonne, have remained unfinished to our day; some, like the cathedrals of Cologne and Prague, were not finished during the Middle Ages; and others, like the façade at Strasbourg, were completed in the Middle Ages, but to a changed plan. In every case, the financial administrator had a say in the discussions.[7A] However, the economic position only laid down the general framework of how much splendour the architect could allow himself. The actual form to be taken within the 'margin of freedom' was not determined by the treasurer, but by the architect. Within the bounds of the conditions laid down, he seems, then, to have been perfectly free – but even this is not quite true.

4 · SYMBOLS OF MEANING

In addition to the actual programme of building, there were sometimes also special wishes and demands of a patron to be taken into consideration. Suger wrote that the choir of Saint-Denis was built with twelve supports, to signify the twelve apostles: *duodecim apostolorum exponentes numerum*. He went on to say that the twelve supports in the ambulatory signify the twelve minor prophets. He gave the *tertium comparationis* by quoting St Paul's epistle to the Ephesians 2:19: both believers and churches are built upon the foundations of the apostles and the prophets; both are *habitaculum Dei in Spiritu*, and both therefore signify the same thing. Our text does not say that these piers portray the apostles and the prophets, but that those in the choir indicate (*exponentes*) the number of the apostles, and that those in the ambulatory signify (*significantes*) the number of the prophets. Portrayal would require caryatids. There may be other documentary evidence of cases in which it would be justifiable to say that an architectural member portrays something, but, in the chapters that follow, I shall adhere to normal linguistic usage and employ the word 'portray' only in connexion with sculpture or painting. In the case of Saint-Denis, it would be senseless to say that the figure twelve was portrayed, and inexact to say that the apostles and the prophets were portrayed in the figure twelve. The number of the piers indicates the number of the apostles which, in turn, directs the attention of the visitor to the text from St Paul. In this way, it can be understood that the meaning of church architecture as a *habitaculum Dei in Spiritu* came to life in Suger's mind – as it can in anybody's mind who counts the supports and knows the relevant text.

This kind of 'representation' is called symbolic. The piers and columns at Saint-Denis are only piers and columns to a visitor – and were even to Suger and his architect. The connexion between the number and its significance was made in Suger's mind; we can understand this process only if we are told of it; and this is true also of many other cases.[7B] Often, of course, patrons and architects did not think of any symbolism. At Saint-Denis, the thirteenth-century architect added a pair of piers to the end of Suger's series of twelve. The older piers, of course, preserve their symbolism, but there are now fourteen, and the two new ones either represent nothing, or something other than apostles. In countless cases, symbols were fitted to architectural members afterwards, and, since the time of the Romantics, much research has been done into this symbolism. Nowadays, people often find it difficult to understand. For example, Durandus says that the tiles on the roof of a church are the warriors and princes who defend it against the heathens.[8] Of course, one can easily answer that a heathen is unlikely to climb on the roof, and that the tiles protect the church against rain and snow; or one can answer that mosques also have tiles, but that these are not designed as a protection against Christians. What is meant, however, is that, just as the princes protect the Church as an institution, so the tiles protect the church as a building. To examine every one of these countless abstruse likenesses and comparisons from a rational point of view would be to miss the point. None of the men who created these symbols intended his likenesses to be taken literally. To those who claim that any simile limps, one can reply that they should trust to the leg that does not limp. It must be realized, however, that these symbols vary in value, and that some of them are immediately convincing, while others are far-fetched.[8A]

Suger was not an architect: he was a theologian and had been educated according to the precepts of his age. From the time that Christian churches were first built, it was the theologians who ordered their construction, even if princes and emperors sometimes decided the programme and gave money for the project. Theologians were thoroughly familiar with the New Testament, which is full of comparisons and symbols – 'For he that walketh in darkness knoweth not whither he goeth. While ye have light, believe in the light, that ye may be the children of light' (John 12:36); 'I am the light of the world. . . .' (John 8:12); 'But whosoever drinketh of the waters that I shall give him shall never thirst' (John 4:13); 'I am the door: by me if any man enter, he shall be saved. . . .' (John 10:9); Jesus spoke in metaphors, and he gave his reasons for doing so in Matthew 13:11. Jesus's metaphors and symbols refer to purely spiritual things which are illuminated by the metaphor, and can often not be expressed better, if at all, in any other terms.

Medieval theologians altered the direction of these comparisons. Jesus had said, 'I am the door' (that is, to the Father): they inverted this and said that the door was Jesus. This difference may seem small, but the idea of Jesus remained a spiritual one, and, in this connexion, even the door became an intellectual and spiritual passageway, for the symbolists mentally changed the real doorway into a spiritual one. Whether one takes this difference seriously or not, one must understand the inversion involved if one is to understand the way in which the Gothic clergy regarded churches, and the way in which they educated the laity to grasp this kind of symbolism.

Where symbolism made use of sculpture or painting, the underlying idea was more easily comprehensible. Where a statue of Christ was placed in front of the central pier of a main doorway, and one therefore walked past him into the interior, anyone could understand that here Christ was supposed to be understood as a spiritual door.

However, we shall first confine ourselves to the realm of architectural symbolism. Just as every architectural member represents something, so does every spatial part, and so, above all, does the church as a whole. Research has been very productive in giving interpretations of Romanesque architecture. Thus, the building of a west as well as an east choir in the same church, as it was done in the Romanesque period, has been shown to derive from the opposition between *sacerdotium* and *imperium*. The emperor, when he personally attended state services, sat in the western choir, and the purpose of building a fixed architectural section of a church to correspond to the choir which was the ceremonial territory of the bishop can be traced to the rivalry between popes and emperors, which dates back to the time of Constantine.[9] However, functions do not always produce symbols: thus, while naves were built for the laity, they do not represent the laity. In the case of a reserved space, the idea may arise that this space represents the person for whom it is reserved. A choir does not necessarily represent

God, or the bishop as the representative of God, but this meaning could be introduced, and probably was, where a western choir, as the space reserved for the emperor, was set opposite an eastern choir. There are also other interpretations of spatial parts as symbols representing something, and they can be very fruitful, but they do not yet seem to have been studied with reference to the Gothic style. In the Gothic churches, double choirs disappeared, and this may lead one to conclude that the French kings did not feel the same opposition to the papacy, nor the same rivalry over certain questions of their rights and powers, as the German emperors. However, it is doubtful whether the significance of this disappearance contributes much to the understanding of the Gothic style. There are other, analogous questions, too: for instance, the question as to whether or not the building of galleries, and their subsequent disappearance (at Chartres), had any symbolical significance.[9A]

The interpretation of double choirs as representing the split between the Church and the Empire leads to the idea of the indivisible unity of the *Civitas Dei*, and thus to the real meaning of the architecture of a church as a whole – the Christian idea of the kingdom of God. This idea embraces both the eternal, that is the timeless and placeless, existence and omnipotence of God, and his temporary and earthly existence in Man and the works of Man. The building of churches on earth as the seat for religious services is, at the same time, always a symbol of the transcendent kingdom of God. Church architecture may mark the contrast between pope and emperor or between monks and laymen; it may set nuns' galleries in isolation,[9B] and so on; but these functional divisions always reflect the differences between certain social strata, or at least strata of responsibilities within the *Civitas Dei*, which remains an immutable idea to which any division is subordinate. The building of churches as houses of God can therefore always be interpreted as a symbol of the *Civitas Dei*, of the *regnum Dei*, both here and in eternity – and this is the sense in which it was interpreted.

A Christian church has this idea in common with every holy place of every other religion. Greek and Roman temples, too, were intended to be places that were not of this world – to be 'numinous'. Even the flat ceilings and vaults of classical antiquity were characterized, by their decoration with sculpture and painting, to represent the sky.[10] According to ancient beliefs, the sky was a spherical bowl in which, or beyond which, lay a world to come; it was the boundary between the visible and the invisible, though, of course, there is also much on earth that is invisible, especially the ideas of men and their intellectual processes. Man embraces within himself the world to come. 'The kingdom of God is within you.'[11] Man is the *habitaculum Dei*, but with the essential addition, *in Spiritu*. God dwells in the mind and in the heart: this is his kingdom. If one says that the kingdom of Heaven lies in the heart of Man, then Heaven becomes a symbol; it ceases to be the astronomical sky of classical antiquity or of Copernicus and Kepler, and becomes a symbol of the life to come, which is within Man, who lives continuously in this world and the next at one and the same time.

Symbols are a special kind of concept. The material parts of a church are drawn from nature; they consist of minerals,

metals, and woods, and even if, like glass, they are artificially made, their raw material still comes from natural sources. In the building of a church, this aspect is always the main consideration, and Suger showed great concern for the finding of a suitable quarry and of trees of the right length for roof-beams. Even in the preservation of buildings, one is bound to return to this first degree of concepts, for it is physical and chemical aspects which come to the fore when downpours, or a change in the level of the water-table, or lightning, or fire produce material changes.

In a finished church, the materials from which it is built become part of the concept of the church as a whole. The spiritual meaning of the activities which take place in the church, in so far as they have a function, is not a natural product, but a human conception or a combination of human conceptions. All that is material remains as an integrating factor, but the fact that this visible, tangible, and spatial distribution of materials has been created for the purpose of Divine Service means that there is a second degree of concepts. In this second concept of church architecture, which exists within the concept of function, a church is regarded as 'suitable' for the sacred activities of religious men. In the formulation of the programme for the building of a church, and in its design, this concept is perpetually alive and active. If the building is suitable for religious services, then the material structure of the church is embraced in the conception of the *habitaculum Dei* – but *in Spiritu*. A 'suitable' building thus becomes a 'suitable' sacred building; it offers all that the spiritual man demands. All the reformers who wanted to make the life of the spirit more sincere, more intensive, and more exclusive in actual fact merely wanted exactly this kind of 'suitable' building. Bernard of Clairvaux criticized the Cluniacs, and even Suger, because they offered more than mere 'suitable' religious buildings; he wanted monks to build prayer chambers, *oratoria*, not churches, and St Francis and other, later ascetics, such as Calvin, agreed with him.[11A]

This second degree of concepts is contained within a third degree. *In Spiritu*, one can regard any church, even Bernard's Oratorium and the barn in which St Francis preached, as a *habitaculum Dei*. In this context, *habitaculum* is a metaphor, for God dwells in a church in the same way as he does in the hearts of men.[11B] A material structure which is regarded as a building suitable for the holding of religious services becomes an element in the concept of a house of God. The first degree of this concept comprises natural objects; the second comprises the works of Man; but the third embraces the field of symbols.[12] Even spiritual conceptions which are not based on natural objects are works of Man; what they signify is not, of course, the work of Man, but the conceptions and concepts themselves are human.[13] Every symbol combines the first and the second degree within itself, but it is higher and greater, just as, mathematically, the cube of a number comprises within itself the number and its square.

A church as a whole is a symbol of God – or rather, one symbol of God, for there are many others. Kingship is another symbol: a king possesses the kingdom over which he reigns. The Church is the kingdom of God. The Christian religion is eschatological. The world is temporary; it was created, and, on the Day of Judgement, it will cease to exist. Then the everlasting kingdom of God will come into being, in the form of an eternal heaven and an eternal hell. It is of this kingdom that St John speaks in the book of the Revelation. 'The dragon, that old serpent, which is the Devil, and Satan' is imprisoned for a thousand years (Revelation 20:2). There follows Satan's first resurrection, after the thousand years, and his final fight for the Holy City (Revelation 20:9), but the Devil is defeated and cast into the lake of fire and brimstone, where he is to be tormented day and night for ever and ever. Finally, there follows the Last Judgement, and the whole earth passes away (Revelation 21): 'And I John saw the holy city, new Jerusalem, coming down from God out of heaven, prepared as a bride adorned for her husband.' All suffering ends, 'and he that sat upon the throne said, Behold, I make all things new'. All this is symbolism: St John speaks of the bride and of the city, but both are symbols of the same thing. 'Come hither, I will shew thee the bride, the Lamb's wife. And he carried me away *in the spirit* to a great and high mountain, and showed me that great city, the holy Jerusalem, descending out of heaven from God.' There follows, now, a description of the city, which is the city of Light. The angel has a golden reed and measures it. Its length, breadth, and height are all equal: it is a cube of 144 cubits (12 by 12), which is not so surprising if the addition 'according to the measure of a man' is meant, but this is doubtful in view of the sentence: 'And he measured the city with the reed, twelve thousand furlongs.' The walls consist of twelve kinds of precious stone, and there are three gates on every side, each of them consisting of a single pearl. The gates are named after the twelve tribes of Israel, and the twelve foundations of the walls after the twelve apostles. The streets are made of 'pure gold, as it were transparent glass'. There is no temple in the city, 'for the Lord God Almighty and the Lamb are the temple of it'. In it is the river of the water of life, and the tree of life 'which bare twelve manner of fruits, and yielded her fruit every month'.

These quotations must suffice. One would like to quote the whole book, for it is a continuous chain of symbols; every conception in it contains more than is inherent in the words in which it is expressed. The city, its dimensions, its geometrical form, precious stones, pearls, gold, and glass: all these are symbols, and, in combination, they symbolize the kingdom of heaven after the end of the world. If one sees them as symbols, one can similarly regard any church as a representation of the kingdom of heaven – here and now, or after the end of the world. A church is not a portrayal of the New Jerusalem, but both St John's conception of a church and its structure are co-ordinated and equivalent symbols of the third – and primary – concept of the kingdom of heaven. Probably those scholars who speak of portrayal have the same meaning in mind. Perhaps they subscribe to the usage of calling any metaphor an image; but, in the study of the history of art, one must choose one's terms more strictly.[13A]

Real portrayals of the New Jerusalem do exist in illuminated manscripts, which are real pictures, but they do not follow the text absolutely rigidly. In the Apocalypse at Trier, MS 31, fol. 69, which dates from the eighth or ninth century, it is pictured with a wall with twelve towers round a basilica with transepts and a crossing tower, although St John says that there was no temple in the city.[13B] The Apocalypse at Valenciennes, MS 99, fol. 38, which also dates from the eighth or ninth century, shows a round city instead of a square one.[13C] The Apocalypse at Bamberg, which dates from about 1000, follows the text more closely; the Lamb stands in the city, but the walls are very low, not nearly as high as the city is broad, and the gates are grouped together in the form of gate-towers, three to each corner. The streets of gold and glass are also missing. The Apocalypse at Trinity College, Cambridge, Coll. R. 16.2., which dates from between 1230 and 1250, shows a square city, with its walls folded down and twelve towers. Within the square, God the Father sits on the left in a great *mandorla*, and next to him stands the tree of life with the river of life running out of it.[13D] One could quote many more examples, but in all of them one would find that the portrayal of the New Jerusalem was different from that described in the original text. Even here, artists felt themselves free of any obligation faithfully to illustrate St John's symbols, because they drew on the core of these symbols, on their underlying idea.[13E]

Since architecture is not the same as illumination and does not present a picture in the sense in which sculpture and painting do, it cannot be expected that St John's vision should ever have been portrayed in architecture. It is, however, to be expected that architects should have drawn on the basic idea of the book of the Revelation, which could be expressed in many different forms, as a bride, as a city, as a second paradise, or as a church. It is obvious, of course, that the architecture of a church can never portray a bride,[14] but it is not so immediately obvious that it cannot portray a city either. St John arrived at the poetical image of the New Jerusalem because, under the Greek political system, city and state were identical, and this is why the kingdom of God is identified with the idea of a city. He arrived at the name Jerusalem for the city through the connexion of that city with the Christian doctrine of redemption, and he then describes this future Jerusalem as magnificently as he can, using the means and the language of earthly splendour. He probably had literary predecessors,[15] and his architectural knowledge of oriental royal palaces was probably based on visits to ruins, or on hearsay. In the field of literature, later authors followed the metaphors of the Apocalypse, or other sources, or the free exercise of their own imaginations. One of the most important architectural fantasies of the Gothic style is the description of the Temple of the Holy Grail in the epic known as the Younger Titurel, which does not draw on the New Jerusalem of the end of the Apocalypse, but derives from its description in chapter 4.[16]

In the book of the Revelation, the New Jerusalem is mentioned as early as chapter 3, and here it is connected with the symbolism which appears in Suger's writings. From verse 12, it reads: 'Him that overcometh will I make a pillar in the temple of my God, and he shall go no more out: and I will write upon him the name of my God, and the name of the city of my God, which is new Jerusalem, which cometh out of heaven from my God: and I will write upon him my new name. He that hath an ear, let him hear what the Spirit saith unto the churches.' Here the New Jerusalem is not described: instead its name is written on a pillar which represents every Christian who has overcome, and has thus become a *habitaculum Dei in Spiritu*. The name Jerusalem is here used as a term for a conception which surpasses all that is conceivable. Finally, however, St John describes this conception positively with the metaphor of the city representing the kingdom of God.

The inverse method of connecting buildings, and their parts, with texts, words, and phrases has led theologians to interpret churches as representations of the New Jerusalem, and, in recent times, this idea of regarding architecture as a kind of pictorial script has been taken very seriously. In a scholarly work, Kitschelt has tried to prove that Early Christian basilicas were symbols of the New Jerusalem, based on patterns borrowed from Roman cities. He claimed that the main component parts of an Early Christian basilica correspond to the parts of an actual city of that time; the west doorway is supposed to correspond to the city gate, the nave to a street with arcades, the upper walls to the walls of the houses with their windows, the flat ceiling to the actual sky (or, metaphorically, to the world to come), the transepts to the *cardo*, the main transverse street of a Roman city, and the apse to the throne-room of the royal palace (or, metaphorically, of the palace of God). The arguments that can be made against this theory are as follows. In the fourth century, the only similarity between west doors of churches and city gates was that they were both doorways. In the main street of a real city, the light shines through the windows from the centre of the street, whereas the opposite is true in the nave of a church. Not all churches had transepts, and an apse only represents half a throne-room. However, all these arguments are pedantic, and a much more important one is that the parts of a church 'can be found in the same combination in heathen basilicas'.[17] The main criticism of this theory must remain the fact that the church building, as it is autonomous, is a symbol of the kingdom of God, and does not derive from a comparison of this kingdom with the plan of a Roman city: it symbolizes the kingdom of God even without the intermediate connexion or analogy with a city.

With their material substance (this is the first degree, that of natural materials), painting and sculpture can reproduce a natural model, or an inner conception (the second degree, that of representation); but they can also be symbols (and this is the third degree). It increases our understanding when iconography reconstructs the literary or poetic source on which the painter or the sculptor has drawn. To understand the reproductions of the New Jerusalem in medieval illumination and right up to Dürer's Apocalypse, in which Jerusalem is a Late Gothic German city, requires no erudition, but in other cases it sometimes requires extensive knowledge of the literary sources, and it is both possible and fruitful to make an analogous connexion between architecture on the one hand, and literature and poetry on the other.[18] Our differentiation between the three degrees of meaning makes it possible to recognize that iconography deals with the mere portrayal of a person, a landscape, an action, etc., that is, with the second degree, and at the same time to investigate whether this meaning itself is a symbol – that is, a symbol of a meaning. Iconography as such remains within the literary, or, in some cases, the poetic sphere of painting or sculpture, that is, it remains within the intellec-

tual content of the fine arts.[19] However, studies of iconography usually move beyond the consideration of symbols of meaning to that of symbols of form.

The difference between these two fields of symbolism is an important one, and leads to the real root of the problem. It has been shown that a Gothic church, like every other church, is a symbol of the kingdom of God; and this symbol remains a literary one. How, then, can a Gothic church be a means to opening the mind to the idea of this kingdom, or of the New Jerusalem, even if the visitor does not know the Apocalypse and has never heard of the idea of the kingdom of God?

5. FORM SYMBOLS

What we call form is the result of limitation; but we do not mean by this the actual limit, but what is limited by it. Nor do we think of the meaning of what is limited, but of the way in which it is limited. The most obvious examples of this are spatial forms. A circular line encloses a circular surface, and a circular form is therefore the product of its limiting line and of the form of that line.[20] The sun, the full moon, the face of a clock, the iris in the eye, a wheel, and many buildings and other things are circular; but we do not consider the meaning of the sun or of these other objects when we concentrate on their form alone. The form of a circle, as such, is devoid of meaning.

Not only objects, such as the sun, are limited; the concept of these objects is limited also. If we confine ourselves to the realm of ideas we work either with sharply defined and separated concepts, or with conceptions, separated vaguely and fluidly. Even if our conceptions lack clear limitations, that is, definitions, the core of one conception is still separated from the core of another. Science and scholarship seek to set clear limits to our vague conceptions, and so to create concepts, such as the concepts of the Romanesque and the Gothic styles. Symbols of meaning, such as those in church architecture, the bride, the house of God, the city, or paradise, are also concepts which are clearly limited and separated one from another, However, our business is not only to find the relationship between church architecture and these symbols of meaning; for form itself can become a symbol, co-ordinated with the realm of the symbolism of meaning and expressing the same things by the use of its own means. If we can understand the symbolism of the form of a church, it will tell us more than can a comprehension of the symbolism of its meaning.

Every church is different in form; the form of its space, of its members, and of its light are all different from those in any other church. It consists of different-coloured materials, of light limestone, dark granite, red brick, etc., or it may have had colour added in the form of paint or plaster. Every individual building is a unification of these factors, tending towards a particular style. It is always true to say that a church represents *the* New Jerusalem, but, according to its form or, more especially, to its style, the New Jerusalem may be Byzantine, Carolingian, Romanesque, or Gothic. Within each style, one can further differentiate between its phases and between its local schools. Hagia Sophia and St Mark in

Venice represent a different New Jerusalem; so do the church of St Mary-in-Capitol at Cologne and the cathedral at Speyer, Notre-Dame in Paris and the cathedral at Reims, Annaberg and King's College Chapel, Cambridge.

We have progressed through the entire history of the Gothic style, and have taken it for granted that everyone knows not only that every church is a house of God or the new paradise, but also that the form of the house or the garden changed from Romanesque to Early Gothic, High Gothic, and finally Late Gothic. Incidentally, the interpretation of a church as a symbol of the garden is a rare one, although some scholars see an allusion to paradise in the foliage on the capitals at Reims, and in the framework of tree-trunks which appeared in church architecture after 1490. There is no evidence that this was the meaning assigned to a framework of tree-trunks in the Middle Ages, and it is hard to see why the Gothic style should be interpreted as representing a garden even where there are no trees, branches, or capitals with foliage, or why the Ca' d'Oro and the Doges' Palace in Venice should have capitals with foliage, although they do not represent paradise.[20A]

A garden is not quite the same thing as a forest. The metaphor of the forest was first expressed in extremely hostile terms (by the so-called Pseudo-Raphael in 1510, see p. 263) but he and his followers never spoke of cathedrals as gardens. This method of analysis leads to great embarrassment if we think of the bride of the Lamb in the Apocalypse, whom St John called up before our imagination as equivalent to the city. No Gothic church is a cube with twelve gates, and certainly none has the figure of a bride. On the other hand, the church can be related to gardens and forests in that the upward stream of forces is reminiscent of vegetal growth – an analogy which was drawn by Friedrich von Schlegel. In the eighteenth century, neo-Gothic architects built ribs in the form of reeds;[21] Laugier, too, toyed with this idea. However, as far as we know, the architect of Durham did not ask himself how he could give a vault the form of a tree-top, so that it should represent paradise: it was only after the Gothic style had logically developed within the terms of 'the law according to which it had been born' (to use a quotation from Goethe concerning the development of a man's character) that the house of God became vegetal in form.[21A] The 'sidereal' house of God (Schlegel) is also a New Jerusalem (for sidereal meant for Schlegel relation to the realm of the stars), but, as it were, a New Jerusalem come down from a different heaven. It is quite certain that, in the period of the Romanesque style as well, the fundamental meaning of a church was expressed symbolically through its form: a Romanesque church was also 'heavenly'.

We have seen that symbols of meaning grow as a third degree out of the second. A heraldic lion is a portrayal of a real lion, and this portrayal then joins the ranks of the elements of the symbolism of meaning. Now there are Romanesque and Gothic heraldic lions, and which of the two a certain heraldic lion is depends on its form. A Gothic form changes the portrayal of the lion into a Gothic lion, and symbolism of form is thus added to the symbol of meaning which is a matter of heraldry. How is this possible? It is the same question as the following: why should the *habitaculum Dei in Spiritu* itself become Gothic when it takes on a Gothic form? Since we know that Man, too, is *in Spiritu*, a house of God, the answer to this question will take us close to the root of the problem. A man who feels in a Gothic way, and who stylizes himself accordingly, requires, for divine services, not only a building which fulfils its utilitarian purposes and furthermore the function of symbolizing the concept of the house of God, but also a building which, through its Gothic form, symbolizes what that particular man feels.[22]

The question as to how a form devoid of meaning can become a symbol, and thus take on a meaning, can easily be answered: it assumes meaning through our own aesthetic attitude.

Man is born into this world and, from the cradle to the grave, stands in a perpetually changing relationship to it; he is determined by it, and, with tools and other means, works to create his own world out of it. This is a practical attitude towards the world. Only in the course of the development of mankind and of the individual does a second attitude appear, by which the world is seen independently of its usefulness. In the pursuit of scientific knowledge, man does not ask himself whether a circular form can be used to create a wheel, but what a circle is, what it was before the world was created, and what it will be after the end of the world. When man assumes an objective attitude he strives to see beyond himself and to consider the world separately from himself. The aesthetic attitude is the exact opposite of this: here man seeks to draw the world *into himself*. The fact that subjectivity takes a different form in the case of every individual is immaterial, for subjectivity draws on the views of man, in contrast to the scientific exclusion of the human being. This change does not take place in the realm of reason, but in the realm of feeling.

When a Gothic architect built a circular window, his work was bound up with a practical and theoretical attitude: for he had to know how to construct a circle geometrically and how, in practice, to set about building it in stone on a big scale, on a façade, and at a considerable height; but his decision to make the window circular was based on aesthetic grounds. There were many possibilities open to him, and this multiplicity corresponds to the 'margin of freedom' mentioned earlier (p. 270). Economic and practical questions may also have played a part in determining, for instance, whether or not it would have been cheaper to build a rectangular window. Questions of symbolism may have arisen too, for instance as to whether the window was intended to represent a wheel of fortune, or the sun; but the final decision regarding the position of the centre, the length of the radius, and the interior form could only spring from the aesthetic attitude of the architect.

Historians of mechanics say that, originally, fallen trees were used for the transportation of loads; later, circular discs were made by sawing or, more probably, chopping logs, and finally the wheel, with a hub and spokes, was invented. It is impossible to say whether this is what did in fact happen; the wheel, however, was presumably not the product of an aesthetic attitude. A mechanic considers a circular form valuable because it can be rolled; a theorist, as such, assigns no value to anything, but merely defines concepts; but the man who considers a circular form aesthetically, feels the connexion between any point on the circumference and the centre as an inter-relationship, as a contrast between radial movement and concentration, and as a form representing repose. The symbolist moves past objective existence, and can choose a circle as a symbol for the *orbis*, for fortune, for the sun, or for Christ. If he remains within the realm of meaning he creates a symbol of meaning, but even this is based on the aesthetic factor of comparison. Science seeks identities and equations; poetry seeks likenesses and metaphors; but the symbolist of form regards a circle aesthetically, and he chooses a circular form as a symbol of perfection and eternal tranquillity and peace. His symbol is not conventional: it is immediate and compelling.

Science seeks to recognize what things are in terms of themselves: an aesthetic attitude feels what they are in relation to us. A blue ceiling can be cold or warm, according to the temperature, but, to our feeling, it is always cool. It stands at a measurable distance from us, but, for us, it is always far away, even if we climb on to a scaffolding. We thus change the temperature and the distance of an objectively existent colour. Every aesthetic reaction produces an interchange within various fields of the senses – in visibility, warmth, taste, statics, dynamics, and so on. For instance, blue is restful, yellow is pungent; everyone is familiar with these frequently quoted phenomena. The architect lives perpetually in this realm of empathy in which forms are felt. Some decisions can be made without any hesitation, but others can only be made through a careful weighing of whether one form matches others which have already been chosen – whether it creates harmony or disturbs it.

A visitor who is susceptible to aesthetic effects can understand the forms chosen by the architect. He may be delighted by them, or he may be passionately opposed to them, but before he feels one or other of these emotions, he must thrust his practical and theoretical ideas to the back of his mind for the moment and consider the work aesthetically. If he cannot do that, he is like a blind man trying to see light. There are people who are unmusical; others have no feeling for architecture and cannot understand the language of stone. Some people understand the language of poetry better than that of architecture. Anyone who has feeling for architecture also possesses a certain degree of understanding of it, and the creative master must possess this understanding in its highest degree. The Gothic style has not always been understood. In the seventeenth and eighteenth centuries, the French spoke of their ancestors' *mauvais goût*. Taste is another of the fields of meaning into which spatial forms can be converted; forms can be sweet or astringent, gentle or sharp. This was not only a matter of taste, in the true sense of the word; *le bon goût* was a fundamental prejudice against the Gothic style.[23] The people of that time missed the rational system of supports and loads, and Gothic proportions offended them. In classical antiquity it was demanded of the column that it should conform to Man; the Gothic style, on the other hand, demanded that Man should try to conform to the proportions of its shafts: its demands were inhuman, super-human.

Some historians of architecture lay great store by the presentation of proportions in numerical form. Admittedly, according to whether they are more or less steep, proportions do show the tendencies of various generations, but nobody need tell us what figures are involved at Amiens, at Speyer, or in the church of S. Francesco at Siena; for the proportions exercise an immediate effect, and it is quite unnecessary to run through all the buildings which we have studied in their historical sequence in order to prove this point. Every form of vault and pier, of spatial subdivision, of window and doorway, and of tower and roof was directed at the aesthetic understanding of the visitor; every one was a formal symbol, as were density, laxity, movement, rotation, colour, sparkle, roughness, shadow, etc. They say an infinite quantity of things, and one need only be able to see in order to hear what is said tacitly. Beside this symbolism of form, the symbols of meaning pale.

In the symbolism of form, we can see splendour or asceticism, oppression or verve, sterility or elastic vitality, a cheerful enjoyment of life or sombre depression. One says of space that it spreads, it rises, that it is quick or slow in tempo, that it circles, it spirals, or it concentrates. Some historians of art positively luxuriate in the application of their own feelings to architectural interiors, and it is equally possible to project one's feelings into architectural members. Figures cannot do justice to the wealth of the proportions and rhythms at Saint-Germer, although everything there still breathes simplicity, nor to the infinitely more complicated proportions and rhythms of Pirna or Tomar, and even the best description of an aesthetic impression is far surpassed by the original impression. We rarely speak of the colour of stone, and we can never convey in words the different aspects of an interior caused by the constant changes of light, or the difference between an exterior at sunset and by moonlight.[24] Admittedly, well-chosen words can open the eyes of an unpractised visitor, but perfectly to understand the symbolism of form is like understanding the mime of a great actor.

Besides the three attitudes that we have discussed, which Man can adopt towards the world, there is a fourth. We can regard, recognize, and feel ourselves and the world as standing on a common, metaphysical foundation; and this is the religious attitude, in which the common background is God. During his devotions, a religious man performs a certain mime; he kneels, lowers his head, and folds his hands. This is the visible expression of the fact that he submits, that his hands are inactive, and that his spirit is seeking contemplation. He can pray anywhere, in his own room, even in the open air, but a prayer chamber for the multitude, a church, must aim, through its symbolism of form, to provide a suitable aesthetic framework for the prayers of the many.

One should be wary of anthropomorphic discussions of works of art, but they can sometimes be of more help than a host of words. We can say, for instance, that a church should be practical for the holding of services, and that its meaning can be left to the realm of the imagination. We can simply say, 'This must be the house of God', but, in fact, we demand more than this. We want to be able to *see* that it is the house of God. Metaphorically, we demand that a church should itself be devout, that it should praise the Lord day and night, and at all times. This is what church architecture is.

However, its language changes; it can be Romanesque or Gothic. Style interprets the meaning.[25]

6. GOTHIC ARCHITECTURE CONSIDERED AS ART

Art is the particular inter-relationship of form and meaning in which form becomes the symbol of meaning. The Gothic style is art because the forms created by Gothic artists interpret the meaning of church buildings. The conception of God has undergone many changes, from animism, magic, and polytheism to monotheism and Christianity, and the stylistic changes in Christian church architecture accompany the changes in the conception of God within the Christian religion. Houses of God change, and in changing express the changing conceptions of religious men. It is not God who changes, but his reflection in the minds of men; it is the mirror which changes, and this reflected meaning is the subject of architecture as art. Gothic man reflects God in a Gothic way, and Gothic church architecture is art because Gothic forms symbolize the conception of God that was valid in the Gothic age. The conception is based on Man's relationship to God; in the Gothic period, Man always knew that he was only part of a whole, but he could feel that, even as a part, he represented a whole if his own will governed that of other men, or at least played a part in determining the whole. The fight for sovereignty of states and cities which was waged during the time of the Romanesque went on in the Gothic age, but the pope had achieved the position of representing the idea of a superior state – the kingdom of God. Even though they did not achieve their aim, the crusades were communal wars, waged together by all Christian states. There was a live conception of the whole of which every individual was a part. Out of the religious life of the time the individual also drew the tendency to play the same modest role in his private life. The eschatological aspect of Christianity made political, military, and economic ambitions and successes seem insignificant, for the enjoyments of this world were regarded as the temptations of Satan; the life of this world was only a part of eternal life. During this provisional existence, man was therefore preoccupied with eternal existence.

This had been the teaching of the Church, even during the time of the Romanesque style, but, at that time, the princes and barons kept this world and the next apart. Men were concerned with the life to come, but their concern rather took the form of laying in a store of prayers and making endowments for the time after their death; it was not a penetration of the next world into this, not a really permanent religious feeling. Even the monks remained lords, and the abbots princes, as, with few exceptions, did the bishops. Only at the time of St Francis, St Dominic, and Pope Innocent III, the time of the Lateran Council of 1215 and of the promulgation of the dogma of transubstantiation, did the idea of the superior unity of the Church reach maturity.

The spiritual atmosphere that was created by these three men was the logical outcome of the political and social development that preceded it. It was the victory of the idea of the partiality of the individual over the idea of his totality. The Romanesque style is art because, to anyone who understands its language, its forms, through their aesthetic changes, say something fundamental about the attitude of their creators towards themselves, to the society to which they belonged, and to this world and the next. Because of this, the Romanesque style symbolizes the conception of God which was current at its time. The Romanesque house of God recognizes the conception of God as the highest power – unapproachable, *tremendum*. Similarly, the Gothic style is art because Christ, in his suffering, is close to Man, and because Gothic forms symbolize the disappearance of the boundary between Man and God.

In so far as these contrasts also determine activity in other cultural spheres, they are based on the same 'aesthetic logic'[26] of the part and the whole, and the Gothic style is an expression of these aspects of civilization. Whether or not the decision that Man is a fragment of the universe, 'absolutely dependent' and in 'ultimate bondage' (*religio*), also governs other cultural spheres, is a question for historical research. Within the sphere of architecture, the style of partiality gradually gained complete mastery; and even if this was also the case in other spheres, for instance in the liturgy, in theology, or in sculpture, the difference between these spheres was still obvious. In Gothic architecture, our attention is drawn to the fundamental meaning of partiality, and this meaning remains the actual basis which is directed at our powers of observation, and out of which the style of partiality appears. The house of God has its conception of God in common with scholasticism, but it is a house, built by masons, while scholasticism was a philosophy, evolved by theologians. It is a house, with rib-vaults and diagonally set shafts, pointed arches and flying buttresses, tracery and gables, pinnacles, balustrades, and so on, and, even if theological or literary imagination suceeds in interpreting certain details, or even the whole, as symbols of meaning, the actual spatial parts, the architectural members, and the whole church remain what they are. Its form is determined by the daily work and preoccupations of a masons' lodge, not by those of a theological lecture-hall. The internal, immanent process of the Gothic style is not guided, step by step, by connexions with other spheres, even where such connexions exist: its direction of development simply springs from the same common root.

The Gothic style, therefore, has not been exhausted when we have spoken of the formal symbolism of partiality; we must also take note of its architectural members. There are other styles based on partiality, for instance the Baroque; the difference between them lies in their treatment of space and of architectural members. An aesthetic consideration of the Gothic style is exhausted when we have felt its upward swing or in other cases its horizontal spread, when we have tasted the fineness of its members and the beauty of its stained glass, the menacing stare of its towers and the upward stab of its pinnacles. An artistic consideration of the Gothic style is more than an aesthetic consideration. It presupposes an aesthetic understanding, but verticalism only becomes a *sursum corda* when we also understand its meaning; then the width of an interior comes to suggest the world outside the church and the extent of religious domains, and the stained glass becomes a symbol of the transcendent world and of mysticism. Art applies simultaneously to what is felt and to what is known. A man who suffers from aesthetic blindness has no access to art, but a man with aesthetic feeling can equally well be blind to art. An artistic sense enables a man to apply his aesthetic feelings to the

321. Maulbronn Abbey. South wing of Cloister, *c.* 1220

322. Maulbronn Abbey. Monks' parlour, after 1493

meaning of a building and to deduce the meaning from its form, even if he has read no learned books on the subject of this meaning.

A man who understands architecture as art needs no history of civilization as a commentary, and, similarly, a man who understands the history of civilization needs no history of art as an illustration. Yet the problem of the connexion between these two forms of history is an urgent one which cannot be avoided: it exists in its own right.

7. SECULAR ARCHITECTURE DURING THE PERIOD OF THE GOTHIC STYLE

The history of secular architecture in the age of the Gothic style really requires a separate discussion and is too broad a subject to deal with adequately in this book. It is only touched on here because secular architecture stands closer to religious architecture than does any other cultural field, and therefore shows the different conditions underlying the two with great clarity.

Within the field of secular architecture, it is monastic buildings and the domestic buildings for canons which stand closest to sacred architecture, and here the purposes are simple, everyday ones. The architectural programme of a monastery, which was laid down very clearly as early as the plan of *c.* 820 for St Gall,[26A] consists of a refectory, a dormitory, offices (kitchens and store-rooms), a chapter house, sometimes separate living quarters for the abbot, a reception room for strangers, and so on. These rooms lie round a square courtyard, called a garden, which sometimes also served as a graveyard, and this garden is surrounded by the cloister walks. It was the general rule for the architect of the church also to design the other adjacent buildings, and it is therefore not surprising that the forms used in the churches were also introduced in cloisters and refectories, and in other buildings. Even if only cloisters had been preserved, they would, in themselves, give a fairly complete picture of the history of the Gothic style.[26B]

A fruitful theme must wait for the appearance of a man capable of developing it. The four ranges round a cloister generally have solid, articulated walls with isolated doorways facing the church, and open arcades towards the courtyard. Stylistically the roof and the supports are decisive. Every kind of vault appears in succession. The north wing of the cloister of Saint-Trophime at *Arles*, built about 1180,[27] has a semi-cylindrical tunnel-vault with transverse arches, which is still purely Romanesque in style, although it is contemporary with Notre-Dame in Paris. The vault at *Le Thoronet*, which was built about the same time, is a tunnel-vault with a cross-section in the shape of a pointed arch, and achieves uncommon splendour through its great wall-surfaces and its lack of any division.[28] At *Fontenay*, severies with horizontal ridges cut into the tunnel-vault, which also has a pointed section.[29] Before the end of the twelfth century a rib-vault was introduced in the cloister at *Longuay* (Haute-Marne), a Cistercian monastery.[30] At *Noirlac*,[31] sexpartite vaults were built in the second half of the thirteenth century, that is, at a time when they had long since ceased to be used in churches; nor was there any reason to build them here, unless it was to match the coupled openings of the arcades, which, however, are subdivided yet further. Because of the lack of sufficient research, it is impossible to say when ridge-ribs were first introduced in cloisters, but certainly those in the south wing of the cloister at *Fontfroid* look very early.[32] The incomplete cloister which was added to the south side of the cathedral at *Laon* about 1200, and which has only two wings, has quadripartite rib-vaults.[33] The cloister on *Mont Saint-Michel* was completed by 1228, and has a tunnel-vault with a pointed section – made of wood.[34] Whereas, at this time, arcades usually took the form of open windows with tracery, here there are double-tier arcades of pointed arches supported on slender columns, arranged so that the two rows of arches are in syncopation with each other (like the arcades on the walls of St Hugh's Choir at Lincoln, *c.* 1200). The gap between the two rows is so wide that one could walk along it, and this narrow passage has rib-vaults consisting of triangular bays.[34A]

The classic High Gothic style is realized in the cloister at *Noyon*,[35] begun some time after 1240, and in that at *Westminster Abbey*, begun after 1245;[36] and the cloister at *Salisbury*, begun in *c.* 1263 and complete in the early fourteenth century, is also High Gothic.[36A] The south walk of the cloister at *Maulbronn*, begun some time around 1220, and still built with a sexpartite vault [321], must be judged in comparison with these High Gothic cloisters. The architecture of the Cistercian order reached different stages of development in different countries at different times, and at Maulbronn it had lagged behind the stage reached at *Longuay*. However, the development to the High Gothic style was achieved even at Maulbronn in the second half of the thirteenth century, when the other three wings of the cloister were built with quadripartite vaults.[36B]

The cloister at Salisbury has no gables above the arcade

323. Pamplona Cathedral. Cloister, begun 1311

324. Avignon, Palace of the Popes, c. 1335–52. West front

openings, although it is later in date than the Sainte-Chapelle. However, the combination of tracery divided into four lights with gables cutting through the balustrades, which appears in the cloister at *Pamplona*, begun in 1311 and completed during the episcopate of Arnaud de Barbazan (1317–56),[37] when the choir at Cologne had just been finished, is fully developed [323]. It is tempting to try to follow this development further. The cloisters that have been quoted so far suggest that new ideas always appeared first in church architecture, and were only later introduced into designs for cloisters, and it is therefore reasonable to presume that net-vaults, for instance, were not built in cloisters until after the date of the vault in the choir of the cathedral in Prague (c. 1380).[38] It is not yet known when this form was introduced in cloisters, but it is certainly ideally suited to their narrow passages and was frequently used in the fifteenth century. Examples can be seen in the south walk of the great cloister at *Basel*, begun after c. 1440[39] in the cloister at *Bebenhausen*, built between 1471 and 1496[40] (where there are also double-curved ribs in the well-house), and in the monks' parlour at *Maulbronn* of 1493 [322], where the meshes of the net are as close as in the later vault at Pirna.

Only the fan-vault appeared earlier in secular architecture than in church architecture, the first fan-vault on a large scale having been built after 1351 in the cloister at *Gloucester* [230].[40A]

A study of chapter houses shows that here, too, the forms were almost without exception those which had already been used in churches. Only the English chapter houses at *Wells* and *Old St Paul's London* realized new ideas which were to revolutionize church architecture.[40B] The double-naved form of refectories, dormitories, and store-rooms began earlier than in Gothic and Late Gothic hall-churches, but it was a product of the function of these rooms and cannot really be interpreted as a model for the later forms of church architecture.[40C]

Since they were retreats for peace-loving men, monasteries were only rarely provided with means of defence, and, even when they were, provision was made only to a very modest degree.

On the other hand, sieges and wars for the purpose of increasing power and possessions were among the ideals of the secular lords, and they had always to be prepared for the attacks of other lords with similar intentions. Beginning in the ninth century, castles and the fortifications of towns were developed on a monumental scale. These fortifications were perfected by the architects of the Romanesque and Gothic ages, always in accordance with the development of weapons of war, political demands, and geographical conditions. Just as the fundamental meaning of a church is the kingdom of God, so that of a castle, while it may not quite be the empire of the Devil, is certainly the realm of the all-too-human. Castles had their own chapels, which were just as Gothic as the churches of their time; for example, the chapel in the castle at *Marburg*,[40D] the *Sainte-Chapelle* in *Paris* and the many chapels that followed its design.[41] However, the actual castles had their own style, and one would hesitate to call Gothic those built during the period of the Gothic style. Coucy is one of the most magnificent ruins in France: Viollet-le-Duc dated it as between 1225 and 1242, and this is probably fairly accurate for some parts of it.[42] Apart from an extensive modernization between 1380 and 1387, especially in the great hall and *corps de logis* on the south-western side, the castle was essentially a building of the first half of the thirteenth century, dating from the same time as Amiens. Of course, as regards the structure of the walls, the towers, and the keep, there is no similarity to what we call Gothic; rather, it is Romanesque.[42A] Castles and the whole field of military architecture have their own immanence; their artistic quality lies in the fact that their form was made to symbolize threats, arrogance, and the instillation of fear. 'They seek to give the effect of a Gorgon's head.'[43] They announce the belief of a large number of men in their own strength and in their readiness to reward evil with evil, or even simply to do evil on the principle that might is right. They are no symbol of the Sermon on the Mount.

In some details, however, one can find Gothic forms. Just as they exist in the cloister on the Mont Saint-Michel, so they exist also in the Palace of the Popes at *Avignon* [324], where there are rib-vaults and Gothic supports with Gothic bases and capitals. The palace was begun by Pope Benedict

325. Malbork (Marienburg). Exterior, late thirteenth to early fifteenth centuries

XII between 1335 and 1342, and was continued by Pope Clement VI between 1342 and 1352. Because of details such as these, one can often describe castles and palaces built during the reign of the Gothic style as Gothic, but one should always ask oneself to what extent a castle, because of the form of its silhouette, can really be called Gothic.[44] The so-called picturesque quality of many castles was not the original intention of their architects, and the aura of romanticism which surrounds any ruin is a delusion which gives place to a quality of frightening sobriety as soon as a ruined castle or palace is restored, as has been done, for instance, at *Pierrefonds* in France and at *Karlštejn* (*Karlstein*)[44A] in Bohemia.

Medieval thought succeeded in creating a blend between monks and knights. The orders of chivalry built their monasteries in the form of castles. The Prussian Order, for instance, had subjected the Slav population with fire and the sword and it needed strong castles to preserve its mastery and to give a show of princely presence. In *Malbork* (*Marienburg*) castle in West Prussia [325, 326], the chapter house and Grand Master's Refectory have vaults with the triradial patterns which were introduced from England about 1330, and they give a solemn effect which blends religious and secular feeling.[44B]

Castles and palaces represent individual, powerful lords; knights' castles represent groups of monks organized on a

326. Malbork (Marienburg). High Castle, chapter house, *c.* 1330

military basis; but the fortifications of towns represent civic communities who were essentially peaceable, but who also sometimes found it necessary to fight one another. Town walls, in their developed form, and fortified gates were also designed to frighten. The basic intention of town walls is directed outwards against possible attackers, but they also have a secondary function which is directed inwards; they crowd the population together because a short circumference is easier to defend. Thus they have an influence in determining the narrowness of the streets, the small extent of the individual plots, and the verticalism of the houses; so they indirectly produce the very factor which makes these towns look Gothic – that is, their proportions. However, walls and gates cannot always be called Gothic. The gate-house of the Fort Saint-André at *Villeneuve-lès-Avignon* [327], built from 1362–68, has a gateway with a pointed arch, and its profiles and its jambs, too, are Gothic, but the whole gate is pressed into insignificance by the enormous round towers (originally without windows), crowned with machicolations, which flank it.[44C] *Castel de Monte*, begun in 1240 by Frederick II of Hohenstaufen, shows how relatively

unimportant the form of a gateway is when it stands between two round towers. Here, the classical forms in the framework round the pointed archway do not turn the whole palace into a Renaissance work, nor does the Gothic window above this classical framework make the whole palace Gothic.[45] There is, as yet, no terminology for the styles of military architecture, and this is a subject to which more thought could profitably be devoted.

However, there are some gate-towers which, by the incorporation of the Gothic system of articulation and by the form of their roofs, can really be called Gothic – for example, the Stargard Gate in Neubrandenburg [328], the Powder Tower in *Prague* and the Old Town Bridge Tower, also in Prague, the latter designed by Peter Parler.[45A]

Inside the circumference of town walls, new secular buildings were made to match the architecture of churches. Once again, it goes without saying that the Synodal Hall at *Sens* [329], which was built sometime between 1222 and 1241 as part of the archbishop's palace, should have been built with High Gothic forms, just as the cathedral had been built, about a century earlier, with Early Gothic ones. This

327. Villeneuve-lès-Avignon, Fort
Saint-André, *c.* 1362–8

328. Neubrandenburg, Stargard
Gate, fifteenth century

long hall, with its great windows filled with tracery, was used
for councils, courts of law, festivities, and banquets. The
archbishop must have found it comforting to exercise his
secular office as judge and domestic master in an environment with a religious aura. This example can usefully be
taken as a perfect paradigm in evaluating secular architecture, in so far as it is Gothic. It can immediately be seen that
the rectangular building, of which this hall is the upper
storey, is not a church. Some churches are also without a
tower or an apse, but the combination of their absence with
the splendour of the windows, the battlements, and the pinnacles produces a blend of a secular function with the forms
of church architecture.[45B]

Similarly, the needs of growing civic communities also
produced various types of buildings, such as the cloth-halls
in Belgium, the town halls in every large town [331][45C], public halls for dances, buildings for law courts, and hospitals.
Where it was decided to make these buildings into symbols
of civic dignity and common wealth, architects turned to
Gothic forms and used them to decorate their façades, interiors, and courtyards. Plans and sections, on the other hand,

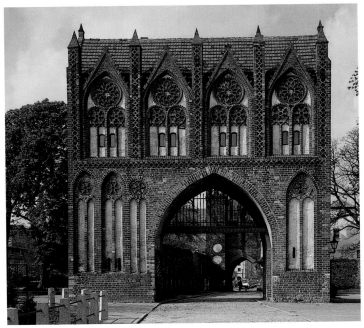

329. Sens, Archbishop's Palace, Synodal Hall, 1222–41

330. Braunschweig Town Hall, begun 1302. The Martinikirche on the left

were the product of the purpose of each building, and, to determine whether these spatial forms are specifically Gothic or not, each case must be considered separately. If the rooms inside are vaulted and the vaults have ribs, then there can be no doubt that they are Gothic, but it is by no means certain that such vaults determine the style of the whole building, as they do in a church. In so far as decoration is taken from the forms of Gothic churches, they again are Gothic, but, once again, one must differentiate between them and the form of the whole building. Sometimes forms are taken as adornment from military architecture, espe-cially battlements, whose zigzag line is stylistically related to the line of rows of gables and pinnacles. The façades of the *Palazzo Vecchio* at *Florence*, built between 1299 and 1310/15, can only be called Gothic if one applies the term blindly to anything built during the Gothic period. Tradition has it that it was designed by Arnolfo di Cambio, the designer of the cathedral and of S. Croce, and, if this is correct, then this architect has three designs to his credit as different from one another as they could possibly have been at this time.[46] This heavy block has an embattled sentries' walk, projecting and supported on corbels; the windows arcades were added later – those on the west wing in 1393–96 and those on the north in 1447–68. Buttresses rising through the entire height of the building divide each wing into four bays in which, above the low, arcaded bottom storey, there are tall, arched openings with tracery beneath gables. The vertical members of the tracery stand on semicircular arches – an idea that has no parallel in church architecture, except in the English Perpendicular style (from 1292).[46B] The complete elimination of solid surfaces, in the Gothic sense, should be compared with the solidity of the Palazzo Vecchio at Florence and with the combination of penetration and solidity in the *Doges' Palace* at *Venice* [332]. Two of the façades of the palace at Venice – that facing the Piazzetta and that facing the Molo – have pointed arches standing on short columns, and rib-vaults in the long galleries on the ground floor. Above this there are slender columns, of which every other one stands over the apex of one of the arches below. Between the ogee arches in the upper row there are circles filled with quatrefoils, and the ogee arches run smoothly into the circumference of these circles. The upper gallery has a flat, wooden ceiling. The Gothic elements are actually just as original in their composition as those at Brunswick, but here no attempt has been

331. Markgröningen, Town Hall, fifteenth and seventeenth centuries

have round arches, are mainly irregularly distributed, and are filled with a kind of tracery. The main entrance is near the right-hand corner, and the tower, which stands on the sentries' walk, strengthens the impression of asymmetry. Much of the interior was altered later, and the rib-vaults which appear here and there do not determine the style of the whole – a style for which, once again, we have no real term.

The cloth-hall at *Ypres* (which was destroyed in the first World War) was built between *c.* 1250 and 1304.[46A] Its long façade, with twenty-two windows to the left and twenty-three to the right of the central tower, which was four windows wide, was Gothic because the windows had pointed arches and tracery, and the ring of battlements could also have been called Gothic. Certainly the central tower with the four pinnacles at its corners, the pinnacles at the ends of the façade, and the enormous pitched roof were all Gothic. However, the interior of the upper storey had an open timber roof.

The town hall at *Braunschweig* falls entirely within the concept of the Gothic style [330]. The building has two main wings which meet in the shape of a letter 'L' and form the corner of a big square; it was begun in 1302, but the

332. Venice, Doges' Palace, fourteenth–fifteenth centuries

333. Bourges, house of Jacques Cœur, 1443–51. East wing, showing the main entrance, the chapel above and the staircase turret to the left of the chapel tower

made to remind us of Gothic church architecture. The walls which rise above the columns and arcades are the same height as the two lower storeys together, and their effect is one of thinness and lightness, partly because of the two-dimensional pattern on them. The lower gallery is purely structural; the upper one is also structural, but with a tex-tural quality, and the ogee arches also prepare the eye for the textural character of the patterned surface above. The façade of the south side, the side facing the Molo – up to and including the fifth of the present seven windows – was begun *c.* 1340 and executed up to the last quarter of the fourteenth century. The balcony and rich surrounds of its fourth window were the work of Pierpaolo and Jacobello dalle Masegne between 1400 and 1404/5, though the mar-bled diaper facing was not installed until the second quarter of the fifteenth century. Also belonging to the late four-teenth century is the corresponding façade on the west side, facing the Piazzetta, at that time consisting of only the first six arcades and two windows. Some of the most prominent sculpture of the ground floor – the Adam and Eve, and the drunken Noah – are by Matteo Raverti and Michelino da Besozzo, and date from some time between 1404 and 1421. From 1422/24, during the reign of Doge Francesco Foscari (1423–57), this western façade was extended up to the south side of S. Marco. Between 1438 and 1443 Giovanni and Bartolomeo Bon completed the richly decorated Porta della Carta (also called the 'Golden Doorway') between the south transept of S. Marco and the Piazzetta façade, while at the same time Stefano Bon built four of the six vaults in the pas-sage behind it leading to the courtyard.[46E] The whole build-ing can be considered Gothic, but one need only compare it with the church of the Frari in Venice, begun in around 1330,[46D] to realize that secular architecture combined Gothic forms in the members with quite different spatial forms.

Ogee-arched loggias with quatrefoils reappear in the façade of the *Ca' d'Oro* in *Venice* which was built by the Venetian noble Marino Contarini in 1421–38.[46E] Here again, it is quite clear that existent forms have been matched to decorate par-ticular conditions, but this consideration of the architect's creative method need not detract from the beauty of his work.

The further one progresses into the fifteenth century, the stronger is the assimilation of secular architecture to the forms of Late Gothic churches. In the town hall at *Louvain*, built between 1438 and 1468, the forms of the architectural members are drawn from church architecture. Its secular purpose is quite obvious, yet the Gothic forms used inevitably instil into it some measure of ecclesiastical spirit. It is not known whether the architect, Matthaeus de Layens, wanted the most important secular building in the town to express the interest of the community in the life of the church. Perhaps he never really thought of this, but simply regarded the forms of church architecture as common prop-erty which could just as well be used to glorify civic wealth and the enjoyment of this world, as the house of God. The clergy obviously raised no objection and did not insist on any asceticism in Flanders.[46F]

The private *house of Jacques Cœur* at *Bourges* [333], built in 1443–53, is a little older than the town hall at Louvain. The life of Jacques Cœur illustrates the close connexion that existed between secular life and religious life at this time. He was a highly successful financial genius. He put King Charles VII's treasury in order, and, as this king's *argentier*, enjoyed regal treatment at the hands of the popes. In 1451 he was unjustly accused of having poisoned Agnes Sorel, the king's mistress, and was sentenced to imprison-ment by judges who owed him money. In 1454, he was at last able to escape and flee to Rome, where the pope sent him to

334. Wrocław (Breslau) Town Hall,
c. 1330–57 and *c*. 1470–1510.
Exterior

335. Meissen, Albrechtsburg. Great
Hall *c*. 1475

Rhodes with a fleet of ships, and he died of an illness on the island of Chios in 1456.[46G] Popes needed money as much as kings, and the church was always prepared to befriend a man of wealth, whether he was a prince or a burgher. Jacques Cœur, for his part, followed the precepts of the Church, and he is a perfect example of the combination of a *vita activa* with a recognition of piety. He built a chapel in the cathedral at Bourges, and one of his sons became an archbishop. His house, which he was able to enjoy for only a few years, has a chapel over the main entrance, and the two circular towers of the west wing were incorporated into the city walls, the roof storey of one of them, the 'Tour de la Chaussée', served as a treasury. The remaining rooms are arranged round the irregular courtyard to serve the comfort of a family and their servants.[47] The different widths of the parts of the building result in roofs of different heights, which combine with the turrets to produce a group with a perfectly free rhythm. The details, inside and outside, are not arrogant but rather coquettish. It is impossible to say to what extent the irregularities were dictated by the site and how far they were exploited with gusto.[47A] The house contrasts sharply with the strict axial regularity of the town hall at Louvain, and by

comparison with the house of Jacques Cœur even the Doges'
Palace in Venice has a character of monumental self-disci-
pline, in spite of the irregular distribution of its windows.

Jacques Cœur's house was built all at one time, but, in
other cases, irregularity was caused by later additions. An
example in point is the town hall at *Wrocław* (Breslau)
[334].[48] There are irregularities even in High Gothic buildings, but irregularity as a principle is related to the general
tendencies of the Late Gothic style. The relaxation of strict
regularity in the thirteenth century was continued by the
Parlers, and, to an ever increasing degree, in the fifteenth
century. It was always more natural to secular architecture
than to church architecture, and it is almost normal in military architecture – in castles and town walls – though even
here there are exceptions, such as Aigues-Mortes and the
regularity of the other new towns founded at the time.[49]

The richest example of Late Gothic irregularity is the
Albrechtsburg at *Meissen* [335] which was designed from 1471
by Master Arnold von Westfalen.[50] Almost every one of its
main rooms is a building in its own right, and the whole
group seems only to have been drawn into a unity quite by
chance. However, it does not represent an addition of isolated parts, but a fragmentation of a whole, which has taken
place from within. The castle at Meissen has star-vaults,
'cell-vaults',[51] and net-vaults, in a variety of configurations,
and its architect knew and had mastered every means of the
Late Gothic style – torsion, concavities, curtain arches, and
the penetration of one form with another. Its wealth springs
from the architect's imaginativeness in the realm of geometrical possibilities; it is a spiritual wealth, which reaps the
harvest sown by the whole Late Gothic style. Here, the consequences of church architecture are applied with the freedom of a virtuoso to a secular building for the use of a
prince, but a very careful examination would be required to
decide whether or not some of these forms of the 1470s are
precursors of forms later used in church architecture.[51A]

This superficial study of secular architecture has uncovered some problems in the history of style which yet remain
to be solved. The first question is that of the logical development of specifically secular forms, which took place
within each one of the functional spheres of secular architecture – military, civic, and domestic. The second is the
question of the borrowing of religious architectural forms to
serve as decoration in secular architecture. Both spheres
seem to have developed separately, according to their own
requirements, and yet they also seem to have influenced each
other.

A good example of the borrowing of forms from Gothic
church architecture can be seen in the great hall of the *Palais
des Comtes* at *Poitiers* whose great hall was built shortly after
1200 [336]. The hall, one of the most impressive spaces in
medieval secular architecture, is a large rectangle articulated
on its interior with blind arcades and covered by a wooden
barrel-vault (which was restored in 1665 and again in 1861).
However, when Jean, Duc de Berry, inserted a fireplace in
front of its south wall, his architect, Guy de Dammartin,
built a row of pointed arches with tabernacles over it, standing on slender piers turned through 45 degrees. The
pointed arches are filled with open Flamboyant tracery, but
have no glass, and they stand in front of a series of windows

in such a way that their centres lie in front of the chimneys
between the pairs of windows, forming a syncopated
rhythm. This piece, built in the late 1380s, is one of the earliest examples of Flamboyant after the windows in the
Chapelles de la Grange at Amiens (around 1375). The strikingly small divisions of the balcony date only from 1862.[52]
The decoration of the wall containing the windows with
these Late Gothic derivatives of church architecture alters
the effect of the whole hall. One is convinced that it is
entirely Flamboyant, although its Early Gothic ambience
has been completely preserved.

To the effect of the syncopated rhythm of this decorative
curtain must be added the fact that turrets rise in the corners, so that, at these points, the row of pointed arches is
cut. One should be wary of speaking of irregularity here; it
is sufficient to recognize a tendency to irregularity. The tendency is less striking and more disciplined here than it is, for
example, in the *palace* at *Meissen*, but a tendency to irregularity is certainly an important feature of the Late Gothic
style, and can be seen just as clearly in secular architecture
as in church architecture. Whether this factor always governed both spheres of architecture at the same times is a
question that remains to be answered. *Castel del Monte*, of
which we have already said that it is neither classical nor
Gothic, although it includes details of both these styles, is, as
a whole, a strictly regular building, but it is difficult to
decide whether or not its tendency to regularity derives
from the Gothic style of the great cathedrals. Certainly, a
degree of regularity is an accompanying factor of every style,
but without being the actual determining factor, in spite of
its affinity with certain phases. There is a tendency to regularity even in certain Late Gothic castles, such as those at
Beaumaris and *Harlech* in Wales, which date from 1295 and
1283 respectively, and the castle at *Tarascon*, begun in
1400;[53] and there is a similar tendency to irregularity in the
High Gothic period, for instance in *Conway* Castle, built
and completed between 1283 and 1287, where the round
towers could certainly not be called Gothic.[54]

The most important problem in the study of secular
architecture, however, is concerned with its forms as symbols of every branch of secular life, and this question
embraces both the two questions raised before. Even where
forms from church architecture were used, they were not
intended to honour God. In castles and fortifications they
are evidence of the autonomy of Man in his energy, his daring, and his ideas of pride and honour,[54A] and in town halls,
palaces, and the private houses of the rich they express
Man's vanity and his dependence on an audience, be it
admiring or envious. However, in so far as the stylistic principles of church architecture blended spatial parts into one
another and exploited the properties of Gothic profiles and
the Gothic relief in secular architecture, the stylistic effect
in both spheres is much the same. It is only essential to
remember that, if art is form which aesthetically symbolizes
its own meaning, then it is important to know whether

336. Poitiers, Palais des Comtes, early thirteenth century. Interior;
fireplace wall, late 1380s

Gothic forms were connected with a religious meaning or a secular one. Whereas the purpose of Gothic church architecture, throughout the Gothic period, was to symbolize Man as a fragment of the kingdom of God, the purpose of Gothic forms in secular architecture was to symbolize Man as a fragment of Society. Clearly, the kernel of these two ideas is the same; but it must not be supposed, *a priori*, that, because these two stems have the same root, they therefore develop at the same tempo.

One can understand how complicated this historical problem is if one considers the wooden structures of the Middle Ages – the half-timbered houses running along whole streets which once determined the appearance of whole towns such as *Hildesheim* (burnt in 1945), the ceilings with moulded beams in interiors, the great timber barrel-vault in the Salle des Procureurs of the *Palais de Justice* at *Rouen* (begun in 1499), the spiral wooden posts in the town hall at *Ulm*, or the hammer-beam roof of *Westminster Hall* in *London* (1394–1401).[55] Ruskin said that the rib-vault could not be regarded as the essential feature of the Gothic style because Gothic architecture exists even where there are no rib-vaults, but he failed to understand the fact that, where we speak of Gothic architecture without ribs, we may be considering, as it were, the children, the grand-children, and the great-grandchildren of buildings with rib-vaults, in whom the legacies of the Gothic style live on – in profiles and mouldings, in gateways, in windows, and so on.

The Gothic style in secular architecture spread over all the countries embraced by the Catholic Church, just as it had done in church architecture, and, in secular architecture too, national traditions created works of different character. English secular buildings are elegant and cool; Spanish ones are passionate and fiery, like the courtyard of the *Palacio del Infantado* at *Guadalajara* near Madrid.[56] Our elastic concept of the Gothic style can embrace the different manifestations of different countries only if we adhere to the abstract principles.

8. GOTHIC SCULPTURE

Many Gothic churches have sculpture in and around them – for example outside on doorways and buttresses, and inside attached to shafts, as in the Sainte-Chapelle and the choir at Cologne, or on the west wall, as at Reims. Sculpture as an adornment of architecture is called decoration. Some decoration, for instance that used for feast days or funerals, is removable, but sculpture is intended to be permanent decoration. Gothic sculpture continued in the tradition of Romanesque sculpture, but it changed in its iconography, as is well known, tending towards a didactic representation of the most important persons and scenes in the Holy Scripture, of angels and saints, of nature in pictures of the months and of the signs of the zodiac, and of the *artes liberales*. The tendency began in the Romanesque period, but, in the Gothic age, it was channelled into comprehensive, calculated, and coherent intellectual programmes which sought to embrace the whole of the Christian religion, and within which the meaning of each piece of sculpture was to have its own intellectual function and to form part of the greater whole.[56A]

A representation or even a suggestion of the universe serves the Christian idea of humility, emphasizing to a thinking visitor the permanent, eternal background to his petty, short-lived existence. A visitor who was also capable of feeling and who recognized that the forms of the sculpture symbolized the universe which was represented would interpret its deeper significance according to the visible forms: he would interpret Gothic sculpture in a Gothic way. Now what is this Gothic form of sculpture?

The decoration of architecture with figures and reliefs demands a harmony between the two artistic spheres involved. When architects built Gothic buildings and allocated a sculptor spaces for his figures, they expected his sculpture to be just as Gothic as their architecture. This demand may lead some modern beholder blindly to believe that figures always have the same style as their surrounding architecture. We can, however, see from the development of Gothic sculpture that, like architecture, it became more and more Gothic and, in the Late Gothic period, achieved the stylistic harmony with architecture which one is tempted to presuppose for the earlier periods. The idea that both arts developed at the same tempo is not borne out by historical facts. Sculptors may already in the early stages have known and understood the demands made of them, but this does not mean that they immediately found the solutions to their problems.

The history of Gothic architecture should convince any unbiased observer that, even in this field, progress was not originally made along the whole front. At *Durham* the ribs were Gothic, but all the rest was still Romanesque. How much has been written about the rib-vaults at *Morienval*! And yet, when one arrives there, one is confronted with a Romanesque façade. Inside the choir of Saint-*Denis*, one sees that the first stage of the Gothic style has been reached, but outside, in so far as it dates from 1140, the choir is less Gothic. The outside of the choir of *Notre-Dame* in *Paris* must still have looked very Romanesque before it was given its present form, yet, inside, it was very progressive.[56B] It was difficult to translate façades into the idiom of the Gothic style, yet, here again, there was a fundamental demand for unity. Riegl connected the theory that an artist can always do what he has the will to do with the concept of the *Kunstwollen*, but Riegl's term has been misconstrued. Originally, the emphasis lay on the first word; he meant that the basic desire of the artist is art, not technique. He expounded his theories in a polemic against Semper.[57] However, an artistic will, or, in a narrower sense, a stylistic will, is not enough. Perhaps it is true that every artist can do what he has the will to do, but he does not always have the will to do what he should, or, in the case of harmonizing sculpture with architecture, what is demanded. The solution of problems that were left unsolved by one artist became the task of his successors. Just as secular architecture developed at a different tempo from church architecture, so the stylistic development of sculpture, too, had its own tempo. There is no force hovering above pairs of men, forcing them to run level with one another, one as an architect, the other as a sculptor; they are not like two horses pulling at the same shafts under the guiding hand of a coachman –

the *Kunstwollen*. Their progress is free. The reason why they adapt themselves to one another lies in their application to the same work – in this case, the same church – and in their inner compulsion to achieve harmony. There can be no doubt that things created together and seen together form a synthesis,[58] but this synthesis does not necessarily form an inherent unity. We are no scholars if we are not willing to analyse every individual case. The *Kunstwollen* is not necessarily a common factor; the architect begins a work with his design, and the sculptor only arrives later with his own *Kunstwollen*, which he adapts to match the architecture as best he can.

One must understand that things which are seen at the same time were often not created at the same time. In the west façade of Saint-Denis, for which Suger called sculptors from other districts, the sculpture probably was executed at the same time as the architecture, but we do not know exactly to what extent the sculptors adapted themselves to the architecture, as we can only tell from drawings what the figures looked like.[59] The design for *Notre-Dame* in *Paris* dates from *c.* 1160, and the nave was completed in *c.* 1220. The sculpture round the doorways is said to date from *c.* 1200. The specifically Gothic, diagonal line of the jambs of the portals was decided on at the same time as the sculpture was being executed.[59A] At *Chartres*, the earliest sculpture of the transept portals was begun some time after 1194, while the figures on the porches were not installed until the late 1230s and early 1240s.[59B] The choir at *Cologne* was designed in 1248, but the figures on the piers in it date from about 1290, and this difference of forty years allowed the style of the sculpture to catch up with that of the architecture.[59C] The figures at Cologne have been much praised for matching the architecture so well, but, had the two arts developed at the same tempo, it would have been preferable to replace the apostles in the cathedral at Cologne by those in the Sainte-Chapelle, which date from about 1241–48, just before the cathedral at Cologne was begun. Even then, it is doubtful whether these figures are as Gothic as the Sainte-Chapelle, and this leads one to conclude that the first question one must ask oneself is: what is meant by Gothic sculpture?[59D]

Sculpture is the portrayal of a model. Where architecture is portrayed in relief, we can say that the piers, the vaults, the pointed arches, and the gables which are portrayed are Gothic; but where human beings, animals, or plants are portrayed in three dimensions, a comparison with specifically architectural members is not valid. Where the models are human, they do not have rib-vaults or other architectural members, but faces, arms, and draperies; and yet a possibility of comparison still exists because of the possible varieties in the formation of the relief.

The word 'relief' has two meanings, as has already been explained (see p. 70). It is used, first, for sculpture which foreshortens the dimension of depth by comparison with its model; when depth is finally decreased to zero we enter the realm of drawing and painting. But the word relief also means the degree of projection, independently of whether or not the relief portrays an object. In this second senses it can be applied to architecture. Romanesque façades have shallow relief, as compared with the highly developed Gothic façades such as Reims or a Late Gothic example like Saint-Maclou in Rouen.

In the same sense, the surface of Romanesque sculpture – whether it is bas-relief or high relief – has a shallow relief (e.g. the draperies of the figures on the west portal of Chartres), by comparison with the deep relief of the High Gothic phase (e.g. the attitudes and the draperies of the figures on the west façade of Reims) or of the Late Gothic phase (e.g. the figures of Veit Stoss).

A piece of Romanesque sculpture is carved into a prismatic or a cylindrical block. During its execution, the original frontal surface remains so strongly emphasized in the forwardmost points of the design that the sculptor cuts into the depth of his material in parallel or concentric strata, so that even the innermost surface is parallel to the outer one. This is the same principle as that governing the lesenes and the friezes of little round arches in Romanesque architecture. This method of working resulted in human figures always maintaining a strictly frontal pose. Late Romanesque sculpture often moved away from strict frontality, but even then the overall effect was governed by the parallelism of the strata of the relief. In draperies, folds were originally hollowed out of the surface like shaded lines: they were concave, but the convexity of the whole still predominated, and the same was true of facial forms.

Gothic sculpture, too, must start with a stone block, but, just as in a crocket capital the outer surface of the stone block embraces the buds, but the concave, inner surface of the chalice has an opposing curve and does not follow the line of the outer surface, so in Gothic draperies the innermost surface is not parallel to, not concentric with the outer surface. The concavities have quite different depths, and the movement of the folds goes outwards, towards us. Gothic figures do not use their joints to pose their skeletons frontally, but to turn them. The diagonal line and the inclination of head and shoulders, the turning of the pelvis, the movement of the legs, and the unhampered outward stretch of the arms give a Gothic figure movement in all three dimensions. In the Late Gothic period, when architecture moved away from pure structure, the emphasis on the actual structure of skeletons gave place to an emphasis on the 'texture' of draperies, which were given a separate life of their own. The double curve, which we know so well, and the curve like a sickle are both lines governing Late Gothic statues.

It was not easy to develop Romanesque traditions into truly Gothic sculpture. There may have been a will to reach a new style, but the new style had to be found. Architecture had a big lead, and had to carry sculpture along with it. This does not mean that the arts are to be thought of as active personalities: architecture itself can do nothing; it is always Man who acts, forms judgements and sets aims. But he can act on things only within his own professional field – the architect in one, and the sculptor in another. Immanent development is objectively conditioned, and Man seeks to achieve stylistic progress within these objective conditions. Style, too, is not a 'thing', and least of all a being with a biological existence. Man is biological. When society is permeated with the new critical idea that the autonomy of the individual is unchristian and that the fundamental

Romanesque principle of totality therefore requires reform, then this idea becomes the driving factor in every sphere, including those of architecture and sculpture. The doctrine that every step must take place at the same time in every field, as though God had only to press a button to make everything Gothic, is an unhistorical one. It is surprising that architecture took the lead, for one would expect that this highly personal change in man would have manifested itself, first of all, in the portrayal of man. The Gothic *Crucifixus*, no longer standing firmly on his feet, but pendant – that is, 'dependent' – is supposed not to have appeared before 1225.[60] Goldschmidt's definitive study of the subject does not, however, take into account Villard de Honnecourt's drawing of about 1230, which may well have been intended as a guide for both sculptors and painters. In it the intensity of the bend in the legs and the hanging of the head are precursors of the style of the early fourteenth century,[61] for it is not until this time that the Passion of Christ and his death are portrayed with such passionate intensity (for example, the crucifix in the church of St Mary in Capitol at Cologne, made in 1304). Gothic crucifixes of 1225 and of the following generations, for instance the wooden crucifix at Sens (*c.* 1250), are already Gothic in style, but one must remember that they were made at a time when, in the field of architecture, Amiens and Cologne had been designed and partly built, and the Gothic style had already existed for more than a century. When architecture became Gothic, crucifixes still remained Romanesque for a long time, although it must be admitted that closer examination reveals slight changes even at this stage.[62]

It is not the task of this book to make a detailed study of the history of sculpture, but it is important to the history of Gothic architecture to realize that architecture took the lead in the development of the Gothic style. In sculpture, too, there was a Transition, and the voluminous literature on the subject of medieval sculpture shows how controversial the attribution of dates still is. By and large, and although it is no longer the most recent book, Mme Lefrançois-Pillion's work seems to represent the *communis opinio* on the subject of French sculpture.[63] She seems, on superficial reading, to identify the Romanesque with the twelfth century and the Gothic style with the thirteenth, but in fact she gives a truer picture. She treats the west portals at Chartres in her volume on the Romanesque, calling it 'l'avant-printemps de la sculpture gothique', and one must agree with her, for in some of the heads here there is the beginning of a new life. The west portals at Chartres mark the beginning of the Transitional style in sculpture, which, in the realm of architecture, had come to an end at Saint-Denis. The Transition in sculpture is therefore contemporary, not with the Transition, but with the Early Gothic style in architecture.[63A]

When, then, does the Transition in sculpture end? The answer is: with the figures at *Laon* and in *Paris*.[64] No serious attempt has ever been made to differentiate between the Early Gothic and High Gothic styles in sculpture. The relief of the Assumption of the Virgin in the doorway at *Senlis* has great vehemence in the movement of the six angels. The diagonal lines are like a storm of love and devotion, but, seen purely as relief and apart from its story, this work is still completely flat; the folds in the draperies are still like mere lines; the heads are seen in almost perfect profile, and the diagonal lines lie on the outer surface – they do not thrust outwards from the background. The spiritual restlessness of the angels already moves beyond Romanesque principles, but their form is not yet Gothic, and this combination of Romanesque forms with spiritual excitement and restlessness is what is called the Transitional style in sculpture. Mme Lefrançois-Pillion tentatively gives the date of this sculpture as 1180, that is, between the date of the west portals at Chartres (*c.* 1150–60) and that of the 'Gothic portals of Notre-Dame in Paris' (*c.* 1210), and she does not call the sculpture at Senlis Gothic. Today, nobody would make the mistake of confusing stylistic classifications with qualitative judgements. The relief at Senlis is inspiring, whether one calls it Romanesque or Gothic; but, to the historian with an interest in style, it should be obvious that it is still Romanesque.[64A]

It will be sufficient for the purposes of this book to draw attention to the problem and to ask where and when architecture and sculpture reach the same stage of stylistic development; to do this, it is necessary to consider the entire course of their development, right up to the Late Gothic period. From about 1390, the question of similarity ceases to be a problem. The virgin in the *Chartreuse de Champmol* near Dijon (1391–97) moves freely throughout her body; in her all traces of frontality have disappeared; she seems to walk, to swing, and the folds in her draperies arch forward from different depths.[64B] The period of this figure, in the history of architecture, is that of the later years of Peter Parler. However, this example is not intended to prove that architecture and sculpture did not reach the same stage of development until 1390. It is difficult to fix an exact point in time because sculpture does not exhaust itself in the pure form of relief, seen apart from its story, and many of the forms of sculpture cannot be compared with architectural ones. Above all, spiritual states can be shown in all their variety in sculpture, through mime, while architecture can show them only selectively and through generalization. Gothic sculpture can portray smiling angels, but one can hardly say, even metaphorically, that even the most joyful of church interiors smiles.

In a human figure, the thing which we recognize immediately is its proportions. Geometrically these proportions can be measured by means of compasses, but the points at which circles begin and end are hardly ever clear and unequivocal. Yet our mental transformation of the objective proportions into a subjective feeling of life and vitality is absolutely clear, and it is only the finer shades of meaning which cannot be contained in words. In certain generations, the Gothic style created ascetic, hovering figures in which one can see that their thoughts are more occupied with eternity and the world to come than with the joys of this world. If one wishes to characterize the personality of an artist, or a group of works, one can trace a tendency towards thinness, slenderness, even emaciation, but it cannot be said that these ideals of asceticism and mysticism governed all generations of the Gothic age to the same degree. Proportions change very much, just as they do in architecture. To determine whether they change hand in hand with architectural proportions, and, if so, to what extent, would require a detailed study.

Sculpture also includes portrayals of animals and plants. It has to be left to historians of sculpture to consider how the forms of lions, eagles, oxen, doves, and so on, changed when they became Gothic, and whether we have any right to say that they did. Villard de Honnecourt drew sixty-seven different kinds of animal, which were used as symbols for the evangelists, for the signs of the zodiac, as symbols for the attributes of saints, and as decorative, or sometimes just amusing, additions.

The development of foliage shows a very convincing change from a general idea of a leaf to naturalistic forms, so that at Rheims, Naumburg [119], Southwell, and other places one can actually recognize the botanical species of the plants. Late Gothic sculpture leaves this naturalism, to revel in fantastic, imaginary forms of foliage. Here, one can see dry, brittle forms which give the effect of crumpled paper, and swollen ones with passionate, undulating lines, which exploit the greatest possible contrasts between light and shade. The foliage at Reims really resembles soft, elastic vegetation, but later foliage looks as though it were made of leather or metal; even its material becomes a field of activity for the imagination.

Leaves grow like shafts, or they are turned by the wind – as in the magnificent foliage of Southwell[65] – and, even in these forms, the change from frontality to diagonal and rotating lines is clearly used to exploit to the full the possibilities of all three dimensions. Since plants bend forward and roll inward on themselves, they are a favourite subject of the Gothic style, and especially of the Late Gothic. In the case of crockets, it was possible to make them spread rigidly upwards, and then, after a projection, to add a second upward curve. The double curve and the flaming line seem so ideally suited to this kind of decoration that it is surprising, on looking back, to see how flat and ironed out, how 'sidereal' – that is, how stern and obviously carved from stone – their Romanesque precursors were in style. Naturalness is not always that which is in accordance with the data provided by nature, and the naturalistic foliage at Reims, round the Porte Rouge in Notre-Dame in Paris, and in other places, is a portrayal of 'Gothic nature'.[65A]

9 · GOTHIC PAINTING

The theory that style develops at the same tempo in different arts is more plausible in the case of sculpture and painting than in the case of sculpture and architecture. Sculpture and painting are generally considered to be two separate arts, but together they form a single art.[66] In meaning, their theme is one and the same, the portrayal of a model, whether the model be real or a fantasy of a reality. In this practical sense, the imitative arts differ from architecture, and one must not presume, *a priori*, that architecture and painting always have the same style. History rather demonstrates that the opposite is true. Everyone is aware that the fourth Pompeian style was contemporary with the building of the Colosseum. Similarly nobody would claim that, in 1093, when the first rib was built, painting too was beginning to turn towards the Gothic style. One would

expect that about 1150 painting was developing towards the Transitional style, as was sculpture in the west portals at Chartres, but no convincing evidence exists that this was so. In the *Histoire de l'art* edited by Michel (a work of many volumes), where the Transition in illumination is reckoned to occur between 1200 and 1250,[67] it is not stated whether the new style should be called Early Gothic or High Gothic.

In Germany, 'the earliest Gothic paintings can be shown to date from about 1240'[68] – that is, from the same time as the nave at Strasbourg. On the other hand, there is Gothic architecture in Germany earlier than this, for instance, the church of St Elizabeth at Marburg (begun in 1235), and there are rib-vaults dating back to about 1100. However, since, on the whole, Gothic architecture was introduced late in Germany, one must really turn to France, and therefore to the theory that the High Gothic style in painting began in illumination about 1260, with the Psalter of St Louis.

The Gothic quality of this psalter lies, above all, in its use of Gothic architecture as background. In almost every illustration, it is the same architectural frame which is shown – two divided pointed arches with a gable and, above them, on a different scale, the clerestory of a church with a pitched roof.[69] It is the opinion of the author of the chapter on that particular period in French painting in Michel's history – Arthur Haseloff – that illumination was dependent on stained glass. Gothic frames appear in stained glass from the 1220s, in the ambulatory chapels and clerestory of Chartres cathedral (*c*. 1210–*c*. 1230s) and in the choir clerestory of Reims cathedral (*c*. 1240).[70]

The belief that things created simultaneously must have the same style is so strong that many people presume that the stained glass at Chartres must be High Gothic, or at least Early Gothic, though even this belief would be evidence of a difference in tempo. The dating of individual windows at Chartres is controversial, but it is generally agreed that most windows illustrating stories date from *c*. 1200 (in the nave aisles) and *c*. 1210 and after *c*. 1230 (in the ambulatory).[70A] The Crucifixion in the oculus in the second bay of the choir is Romanesque with certain reminiscences of the Byzantine, but certainly not Gothic.[71] However, in the window which tells the story of Thomas à Becket, the cathedral in which he suffered his martyrdom is shown as a Gothic church with flying buttresses,[72] and in the so-called medallions there are quatrefoils, formed of pointed arches. In the window in the north-east chapel of the ambulatory which tells the story of St Cheron, there are arcades of semicircular arches and others with segmental arches, and the pointed trefoil arches which hang within the semicircular arches give almost the same effect as pointed arches; but the whole window cannot be called Gothic simply for this reason. All the details are flat and are arranged, as far as possible, in juxtaposition.[73] These trefoil arches inside semicircles seem to be precursors of the cusps in the Sainte-Chapelle, but the difference has already been explained above, on p. 130. The iconography of the windows in the Sainte-Chapelle has been extremely fully treated.[74] An adequate study and all necessary illustrations have been given recently by Grodecki.[75] Here, too, some isolated pieces of Gothic architecture with flying buttresses appear, as in the Thomas à Becket window at Chartres, but this is not sufficient justification to call the whole series of windows Gothic. It sounds shocking to say that the stained glass in the Sainte-Chapelle in Transitional, like that at Chartres, but anyone who calls it Gothic should first explain what he means by Gothic painting. Painting done in the age of the Gothic style in architecture is not automatically Gothic painting.

Ghiberti, and later Vasari, regarded fidelity to nature as the aim of the painting of their time, but we know that there are degrees of fidelity to nature and that this term cannot help to determine the differences between the work of Ghiberti and that of Vasari, between the works of classical antiquity and those of the Renaissance, or between the Gothic style and the Renaissance. Ghiberti and Vasari saw that the painting of Giotto was truer to nature than that of Cimabue and the Byzantine school, and they therefore believed that Giotto had begun the Renaissance.[76] We cannot blame them for their poverty in stylistic terms, but it is to be hoped that our terms are sufficiently developed to allow us to say why a given painting, whether it be an illumination, stained glass, or a fresco, is Gothic. Until this can be done convincingly, nothing at all can be said about the tempo at which painting became Gothic.

Late Gothic painting developed depth about 1300, in the work of Giotto and Duccio, and, by about 1400, succeeded in portraying depth in a picture through emphasis on the third dimension with remote landscape which is analogous to the emphasis on space in architecture.

Architecture is always three-dimensional, but it can still adhere to two-dimensionality in façades, as it did before in the High Romanesque style. The High Gothic style, on the other hand, lays great emphasis on depth, and the diagonal position of its members combines with the Gothic relief, which springs outwards from the core, to unite the spatial parts, and even to join the interior with the exterior. Stained glass does not form absolute boundaries. Around doorways, the Gothic relief of the jambs makes a connexion between the interior and the exterior, even when the actual doors are closed, and the same is true of windows, although the glass in them separates the interior from the exterior at the same time as it joins the two. This phrase 'joining the two' must not, however, be taken in its strict sense, as though the connexion could only be made by the opening of a movable pane (although this is sometimes the case). The connexion is the product of a movement in depth which flows diagonally, whether the window has stained glass in it or, as at Kutná Hora (Kuttenberg) and Annaberg, none. In the Gothic period, every available means was used to minimize any effect of parallel strata, and, in the final stages, the movement in churches was rotatory and explosive. From about 1400 painting began to develop along the same lines, and the relief of folds in draperies, as pure form, has the same forms as those already developed in the field of sculpture.

In Italy, in the years when Gothic architects and painters were seeking after unlimited three-dimensional effects, Brunelleschi and Masaccio discovered the rational central perspective, which has a spiritual relationship with the rational architecture of the Renaissance.

It is important to an understanding of the history of the Gothic style to realize that the development of architecture was immanent and consistent, and that it did not at first, nor even until it had reached maturity, succeed in altering the style of sculpture and painting to keep pace with its own stylistic changes. It is also important to an understanding of the history of the imitative arts to realize that their development, too, was immanent and consistent. There was no reason why illumination, or the illustrations of books that were not necessarily to be read in church, should adapt themselves to architecture. Yet, while there was every reason for stained glass to be adapted to architecture, it continued in Poitiers, etc., to follow Romanesque and Late Romanesque traditions – if we accept the application of these architectural stylistic terms to painting. There were opportunities to develop the painting of frescoes in Italy, but what we call Gothic in this field (which others call Renaissance) dates from about 1300, when the High Gothic period was almost over.

The immanent development of the imitative arts ultimately achieved a stylistic harmony with the Late Gothic style in architecture, and, from the moment at which the imitative arts caught up with the development of architecture, men were to experience the phenomenon of 'things created simultaneously obeying the same *Kunstwollen*'. Late Gothic painting and sculpture in Late Gothic churches create, as it were, an effect of thrilling reassurance. Many of the countless little parish churches of the Late Gothic period achieve this harmony – for example, the otherwise unimportant church at *Blutenburg* near Munich[76A] – and so also do some of the important works, such as the choir of the church of *St Lorenz* at *Nuremberg*. We are accustomed to seeing a multitude of styles in medieval churches, and we sometimes find that this is only slightly disturbing, if at all. Just as only a few observers, trained by years of study of stained glass, can feel the difference between the architecture and the stained glass in the Sainte-Chapelle, so only very few are capable of feeling this difference in *King's College Chapel, Cambridge*. To the architecture of the second half of the fifteenth century and the fan-vault of 1512, the stained glass was added in 1515–17 and 1526–c. 1547, and this glass can in no way be called Gothic.[77] Other similar examples are the Renaissance windows by Valentin Busch in the Gothic choir at *Metz*, and the Renaissance windows in the Gothic church of Sainte-Gudule in *Brussels*.

The achievement of the same stage of stylistic development in architecture and the imitative arts is certainly supported by a kind of spiritual bridge, which rests on the close connexions between the two spheres and on the common desire for harmony. It is the immanence of its development which leads every sphere of human activity to the solution of its own problems, and the fact that different spheres nevertheless converge is partly the result of Man's tendency to reach a unified civilization. It lies within the nature of the differences between different spheres of activity that the periods during which a harmony between the styles of all the arts exists are short. One sphere will always be straining towards new aims, thus disturbing the harmony that has been achieved, and the others will then have to adapt themselves, or rather – lest anyone should suspect that I intend to personify these spheres of activity – Man will have to renew his labours within these spheres. There is no law which dictates that one sphere shall always lead through every step in the development of a civilization, and it is therefore possible to claim that the Gothic style was created autonomously within the sphere of church architecture. However, this plausible theory does not answer the fundamental question. Civilization embraces many spheres of activity, and it seemed more proper to seek their common root within the sphere of the spirit.

10. THE GOTHIC STYLE AND SCHOLASTICISM

The problems of the Gothic style were set and solved in the masons' lodges, but these lodges did not exist in a vacuum. A bishop or an abbot decided on a certain programme and discussed it with the architect; and, no doubt, members of the chapter who had any knowledge of architecture also voiced their wishes and their criticisms. It can therefore be assumed that the Gothic style always had to be approved by the clients. The final form of the profiles of an individual base will have been considered of secondary importance by many bishops, abbots, and priests, and by many princes and burghers: this, and almost all the other details, they could leave to the architect. It was the business of the architect to divine what was, at worst, tolerable and, at best, desirable. However, the men who ordered the works, in their turn, did not exist in a vacuum either; they were members of a nation and members of the Catholic Church, theologians or teachers of philosophy. Now what has philosophy to do with the first ribs at Durham? We have returned to the question which we asked previously on p. 264, and for which we may now be able to find the answer. No theologian can have introduced the rib. Even if it was a theologian who had the idea of doing so and said to the architect: 'Would it not be better to make your wooden arches out of stone?', the task of executing the idea was still the responsibility of the architect. There is evidence of such co-operation in the medieval expertises which happen to be preserved.[78] Every step in the development of the Gothic style was a logical one, but each had to have the approval of the clergy. Architecture and all the spheres of cultural activity – of which architecture is one – were connected by the personalities who were responsible for them.

The connexions between these spheres – that between politics and the Church, that between the Church and the universities, and so on – demanded the imposition of a common sense of direction. The arts needed an even closer fusion with these other spheres because art is form which symbolizes its own meaning. Here that meaning is not merely the summation of all the other spheres of activity, but their innermost spiritual substance, their common sense of direction. One would therefore like to believe that the development of a civilization must precede its expression in art through form. Hence one looks for some phenomenon in another sphere which could be a precursor, but one is always led back to the co-operation of bishops with architects. One therefore goes on to seek antecedents in the bishops' thought, in their philosophy, their theology, and their metaphysics.

August von Schlegel called architecture 'frozen music', and this simile led to others of a similar character.[79] Perhaps Schlegel's metaphor supplies the key to Semper's casual remark that Gothic architecture is scholasticism in stone.[80] Dehio seized on this comparison,[81] and so, later, and among others, did Worringer. It is only recently, however, that this simile has been taken seriously and its concrete and legitimate meaning examined.

Drost asked: if the Gothic style corresponds to scholasticism, then what philosophy corresponds to the Romanesque?[82] It must be the philosophy of the eleventh century, and an analogy to the Romanesque style must therefore be sought in the works of Anselm of Canterbury (1033–1109). Drost quotes Anselm's sentence, 'I believe, in order to understand',[83] and also his 'ontological' proof of the existence of God; but to Drost all these theological theories are less important than the purely metaphysical theory that general concepts, in the sense of Plato's Ideas, have actual existence. It was not so much Anselm as William of Champeaux (1070–1121) who represented this view, which was then contested by Peter Abelard (1079–1142). Before Abelard, there were few men who were explicitly philosophers, and one turns to the recognition which Plato enjoyed at this time, although only a few of his works were then known. Nevertheless, Anselm's proof of the existence of God is based on a Platonic method of thought and one can therefore agree that Platonism underlies the Romanesque, as Aristotelianism underlies the Gothic style.[83A]

Drost sees the Romanesque and the Gothic styles as fundamentally opposed,[84] and he finds Platonism in the form of Romanesque churches, and at least analogies to the scholasticism of the thirteenth century in the form of Gothic ones. The Romanesque uses regular, stereometric forms, 'cubes, spheres, prisms, cylinders, pyramids and cones', and combines them to form buildings like the church of St Michael at Hildesheim. Considered aesthetically, these combinations are equivalent to Platonic ideas – to the *universalia*. The Romanesque style is like these ideas – general, permanent, restful, eternal, finite, and impersonal: it is a style of being which corresponds to Anselm's concept of God – the concept of a man who had proved the existence of God.

Drost continues with a consideration of the contrast between spatial addition and spatial division, or, more generally, between totality and partiality (though he uses a different terminology), and he finds that the Gothic style expresses a metaphysical contrast to Platonism. The leading concepts in this contrasting philosophy are those of particularism, individuality, subjectivity, and a new consciousness in thinking men, with a new sense of freedom and a new ethos.

The result of this comparison can be summarized in a single sentence. The Romanesque style stands in the same relationship to pre-scholasticism as the Gothic style to scholasticism. It must be added, of course, that in each case form is meant on one side, and meaning on the other, and that the form of Romanesque architecture therefore stands in the same relationship to the meaning of pre-scholasticism as the form of Gothic architecture to the meaning of scholasticism. Since an aesthetic approach changes form into meaning and turns it into a formal symbol, one can say that the Romanesque style symbolizes pre-scholasticism and the Gothic style symbolizes scholasticism, and perhaps this is what Drost meant to say. In any case, it can be regarded as a correct conclusion, but it embraces only the spheres of philosophy and architecture.

Moreover, the comparison refers to the controversy over the *universalia*, as one of the problems of philosophy. The Platonic theory that general concepts are real (realism) is contested by the Aristotelian theory that only individual manifestations are real and that general concepts are only names (nominalism). The way in which this problem is formulated is specifically philosophical; no architect asks himself whether, for instance, an individual pier only exists through *accidentia* and the concept of the pier is the only reality, and, similarly, no Gothic architect ever philosophized on the reality of the individual pier. Drost raised the parallelism in the development of architecture and philosophy far above the level of Semper's aperçu, and the question as to how this parallelism can be explained therefore becomes even more urgent. There can be no doubt that there may have been cross-connexions between the two spheres, but it is almost impossible to produce concrete evidence of their existence. If philosophy always sets the tone, then it must always have been in the lead, and Plato's philosophical teaching must have been well known before 1000, when the church of St Michael at Hildesheim was begun, though for Plato's philosophy one may substitute that of St Augustine. One must presume that the spiritual attitude of Anselm, who was born in 1033, had already governed the thought of both priests and architects for more than a generation before his birth, if one is to conclude that the architect at Hildesheim created a formal symbol of it in his additive, segregated crossing. The opposite idea – the idea that the church of St Michael or some similar building was the source from which philosophers deduced realism – could never be accepted as convincing.

Similarly, one must ask, in the case of the Gothic style, whether Roscelinus's nominalism was the precursor of the first rib. Even if dates were exactly known (Roscelinus died about 1125), nobody would claim that the rib was a product of nominalism, or vice versa, and even if one regards the role of the rib as relatively unimportant and considers the Gothic style as beginning in the choir of Saint-Denis, one is still faced with an equally unanswerable problem.

However, this consideration does not invalidate Drost's basic theory; rather it should stimulate us to further thought, for he did not touch on the question of the parallelism of development – on the question as to whether or not every step in the development of philosophy preceded every corresponding step in the development of architecture by at least one year. It is unlikely, however, that anyone should expect these two spheres to develop at the same tempo.

A second work which deals with the problems of the Gothic style and scholasticism – that of Panofsky[85] – almost ignores the contrast between the Romanesque and Gothic styles, and presumes that a 'mental habit' underlies the connexions between the Gothic style and scholasticism[86] – a question which Drost did not deal with in any great detail. Panofsky treated the parallelism between the Gothic and the scholastic in far greater depth and detail than has ever been done before. He showed that the division of the development of scholasticism into phases, which was introduced by historians of scholasticism, agrees to a surprising extent with the usual division of the Gothic style into its main periods, and that this synchronism can be extended to show concrete similarities.

Whereas Drost found that the fundamental meaning of pre-scholasticism and scholasticism were expressed in the form of Romanesque architecture and Gothic architecture respectively, Panofsky showed that there is an analogy between the form of scholasticism and the form of the Gothic style. The meaning of philosophical thinking, which, in both periods, hinges on the inter-relationship between belief and knowledge, is not the central theme of his work, and rightly so, in so far as architecture and philosophy differ in their immediate aims. Nevertheless, even Panofsky touches on the firm boundaries of Romanesque architecture and the transparency of Gothic works, and he interprets the Late Gothic style (at Pirna) as 'a space determinate and impenetrable from without but indeterminate and penetrable from within' (p. 43). However, his main emphasis falls on the form of the writings of the scholastics, which, like that of Gothic churches, is based on division – here into books, chapters, sections, and sub-sections. In buildings and books, the common factor is the formal aspect of 'self-analysis' and 'self-explication'. Gothic architecture is neither rational functionalism nor illusionism (for, if this were so, shafts and ribs would be superfluous): it is 'visual logic.'[87] St Thomas Aquinas to some extent equated perception with reason – '*nam et sensus ratio quaedam est*' – from which one can conclude that he saw an analogy between the current systematic scholastic method and Gothic architecture. Panofsky gives convincing proofs that a whole series of scholastic terms can also be fruitfully used to describe Gothic works built between about 1140 and 1270. Certainly the same, or at least a similar, form of thought governed both the scholasticism and the Gothic style of these four or five generations.

Part of the scholastic method was that it advanced by triple steps: *videtur quod – sed contra – respondeo dicendum*. Panofsky shows that, in the development of oculi, of triforia, and of piers and their capitals, the solutions to the problems which arose also followed one another like Thesis, Antithesis, and Synthesis (to use Hegel's terminology); in the case of these examples, the exposition is excellent, but, in scholasticism, the method is always applied to a problem by a single thinker. In the architectural examples quoted, however, the development is always the work of a series of different architects, so that in this sphere the progress through Thesis, Antithesis, and Synthesis is not the specific outcome of a scholastic method; for historical developments in other spheres took place in exactly the same way. If it is true that philosophy and architecture developed at the same tempo, then one is entitled to ask exactly what steps in the development of scholasticism correspond to the steps in the development of oeuli, triforia, and so on.

As in the case of Drost's work, it must be said that these criticisms are not meant to discredit the whole work, but should rather stimulate fresh thought on the new and firmer basis which Panofsky has given us.[87A] Semper's aperçu shows itself to be profounder than can have been intended in the hostile sentiment in which it was formulated. Some connexion must have existed between the Gothic style and scholasticism. Both spheres were governed by that immanence which is inherent in their tasks, though it can be assumed that spiritual bridges existed sometimes even in opposition to the immanence of the Gothic style. The reader should be reminded once more of the mosaic which Suger demanded for his west façade; it suited his metaphysical idea of light perfectly, but was in direct opposition to the structural system of the façade. The same is true also of the mosaic of the cathedral in Prague. In spite of all these arguments, the parallelism between the Gothic style and scholasticism, in so far as it existed at all, has still not been fully explained. One would expect that the immanent processes underlying the development in different spheres should diverge. The ring that forces the diverging lines towards each other until they converge – here, as in the case of architecture and the fine arts – is Man, or Society, which strives after unity, after a harmonious civilization, after a style common to every cultural sphere. Both the divergence of streams of development and their different tempi hinder and sometimes disturb this uniformity, but in some generations it is nevertheless achieved, only to be immediately disturbed and destroyed again to give place to something new.

This identification of the regulating factor with the need of Man for uniformity both as an individual and as a fragment of Society is not the ultimate solution to the problem; yet we can gain much from the idea of 'scholasticism in stone'. The architect who created the first rib went his own way and offered the aesthetic solution to the problem of eliminating irregular groins. The clergy for whom he worked probably said: 'Try this. We'll see how it looks.' The Gothic style could only develop further as long as this understanding between architects and their patrons continued to exist. The fact that the Gothic style did continue to develop shows that the clergy continued to approve of it, and the reason for their approval is explained by Drost's theory and by the wealth of analogies discovered by Panofsky. The clergy felt at home in Gothic churches, not merely because they were the houses of God, but because they were scholastic houses of God.

In them they also found, instead of *universalia*, the Universe, just as they found it in their *Summae*; and it was not only priests and monks, but also laymen, and especially poets, who found their world here. But the question remains: what was the common root?

II. THE ROOT OF THE GOTHIC STYLE

The contrast in ancient times between the primitive huts of serfs and peasants, the modest houses of officials and the burghers on the one hand, and the palaces of kings on the other can hardly be imagined in its full extent. The memory of Nebuchadnezzar's place in Babylon (604–561 B.C.), of the palaces of the Roman emperors, especially of Nero's Domus Aurea, of Justinian's palace in Constantinople (527–65), and of the palace of Haroun al Raschid (766–809) remained alive, and poets used their imagination to supply such details as had faded. The fullest and richest description of a palace combined with a church written in the Gothic period is that of the Castle of the Holy Grail in Albrecht's epic of the

Younger Titurel, which was written about 1270, when Reims and Amiens had, in the main, been completed. This building on a central plan does not derive from the description of the New Jerusalem in chapter 21 of the book of the Revelation, but has a decided relationship with the vision in chapter 4, which begins: 'And immediately I was in the spirit.' Here, St John sees the throne set in heaven, and 'one sat on the throne. And he that sat was to the sight like a jasper and a sardine stone' – a metaphor for the highest degree of light and splendour. Around him sit the four and twenty elders; 'et in circuito' are the words used in the Latin translation which Albrecht must have known.[88] In representations such as that in Dürer's Apocalypse, only a semicircle could be drawn, but Albrecht imagines the church of the Holy Grail as a full circle. The seventy-two chapels are apparently intended to mean 3 times 24, though their distribution in the four quadrants results in 4 times 18. 'And before the throne there was a sea of glass like unto a crystal'; this and several other allusions reappear in Albrecht's epic.[88A]

The legend of the Holy Grail is a fusion of many widely divergent sources. The location of the castle of the Holy Grail at Monserrat is connected with the shape of this mountain, which lies west of Barcelona. With the introduction of modern means of communication, it can now easily be reached and is daily the goal of countless tourists who are lost in wonderment at the fantastic rock-formations, which look like a castle built by giants. This miracle of nature, the complicated sources of the legend of the Holy Grail, the Apocalypse and the long series of descriptions of palaces which, even before Albrecht's life-time, had existed only in the minds of poets, but whose portrayal sprang from memories of past glories – all these, and the Gothic style as well, must be considered in conjunction in order to trace Albrecht's Castle of the Holy Grail back to its many sources. The rib-vaults in the church are an allusion to the Gothic style, but the ribs are not as poor as those at Reims and in other churches; they are decorated with pearls and corals. The cells of the vaults contain emeralds and carbuncle-stones, which shine like stars and light the church by night – following the legend that precious stones do not merely reflect light, but actually produce it. Albrecht was thinking of the heaven described in chapter 4 of the book of the Revelation, 'a door was opened in heaven', and he describes the ceiling of the temple of the Holy Grail in terms of the night sky.[89]

Albrecht's Temple of the Holy Grail incorporates many other Gothic *membra*, and its interpreters have tried, some of them without sufficient knowledge, to determine whether it is Romanesque or Gothic. Boisserée tried to reconstruct it, using the cathedral at Cologne with which he was familiar, and which was still under construction in 1270, and the spire at Freiburg im Breisgau, which did not yet exist at the time. Other scholars looked for earlier Gothic models and have quoted, among others, the Liebfrauenkirche at Trier.[89A] Finally, Schwietering put an end to these efforts of literary historians with the verdict that they were all the product of rationalism, and he reminded his readers that Zarncke had already noted years earlier the significance of magical lighting effects and of the echoes of voices – in fact, of all the 'means actually at the disposal of poetry'. The form that emerges if, for example, one takes literally the idea of encrusting walls with precious stones, can be seen in the chapel of the castle of Karlštejn in Bohemia and in the Wenceslas Chapel in Prague Cathedral, where Charles IV 'translated Albrecht's poetical conception into everyday language without any understanding of its symbolic content'. To this verdict Schwietering added a discussion of light as 'a term in religious mysticism.'[90]

To examine a poetical fantasy so legendary, magical, and indeterminate as the Temple of the Holy Grail in terms of whether, or to what extent, it can be translated into reality, and of what style it represents, is to follow a false trail. If the temple had existed, literary historians could start excavating at Monserrat, but it existed only in Albrecht's mind.

Albrecht put a speech to the Knights of the Holy Grail into the mouth of Titurel, which contains his own interpretation. It consists of fifty-nine strophes and presents a whole series of symbolic explanations. The ten balsam lamps are the Ten Commandments; the three doorways are Faith, Hope, and Charity, and so on. Right at the beginning, Titurel says that the temple represents the New Jerusalem – that is, in the same way as the lamps represent the Ten Commandments. The Apocalypse was one of the sources on which Albrecht's imagination drew, and Gothic cathedrals were one of the many others.

Poetry has its own immanent development, just like Gothic architecture. The poetic creation of the Temple of the Holy Grail cannot be traced back to Gothic architecture alone, nor are its 'Romanesque' and 'Gothic' predecessors in poetry the immediate root of the Gothic style. Scholars who are held spellbound by the theory that the root of Gothic architecture is to be found in poetry are forced to treat ribs, pointed arches, and flying buttresses as 'technical means', but they are aesthetic and stylistic means, not merely technical ones. The epic of Titurel is no more architecture than, for example, the choir of Saint-Denis or the cathedral at Noyon are poetry. Every poet, like Suger, is free to invest a building with poetic thoughts, but, as a poet, he is certainly not a scholar. A scholar is expected to be able to differentiate between his own poetic ideas and strict scholarship, to present his own strictly scholarly research on the subject of other authors' fantasies, not to present his own fantasies. Architecture is neither painting, nor yet poetry.

Architectue is autonomous. The development of the Gothic style out of the rib is an historical fact, and the process can be understood, step by step, without a knowledge of scholasticism and poetry. More than this, the common factor in the whole civilization of the 'Gothic Age' can be understood from architecture alone. Because the Gothic style is a 'form symbol' for the institution of the Church, the spiritual and ecclesiastical tendencies of the style can be understood even without a detailed knowledge of the history of contemporary civilization. In actual fact, even an educated traveller, guide-book in hand, usually has little knowledge of history when he visits a Gothic church – not to mention the general mass of churchgoers, who know no history at all. Must an understanding of the Gothic style as art, then, be denied them, and reserved exclusively for historians? One can take it that his membership of the Christian Church and his faith are a sufficient basis for the average visitor; they are a help to him, although he is equally prepared to worship in a Romanesque church, or a church in any other style, as in a Gothic one. Christian faith is also a help to the educated visitor, but, even if he is an agnostic or an atheist, or belongs to a non-Christian religion, such as Buddhism or Islam, the more he knows about Christianity, the better will he understand the Gothic style. That is one point. The other, which is even more important, is that the more receptive he is to religious principles in general, the better will he understand Gothic architecture. Today, nobody believes in the Egyptian gods or the Greek ones, but one understands figures with animal heads and figures of Apollo and Dionysos better if one knows something about the religions in which they were involved. Here again, one must be capable of imagining what went on in the hearts of the ancient Egyptians and Greeks when they sacrificed to these gods.

Anybody who is receptive to religion in general can see that Gothic churches do not merely look fantastic (though they undoubtedly do): if one is capable of aesthetic feeling, one sees their sanctity. One knows from the experience of one's own childhood how churches are conventionally differentiated from other buildings, but this convention springs from the fact that, long ago, earlier generations discovered this form, which was originally not a convention but the immediate expression of a religious feeling. We understand form as symbol (or art, which is the same thing) because the fundamental meaning of a form shines forth from it. To this understanding we can then add a knowledge of the tendencies of the civilization in which the art in question was created, in so far as art has absorbed them,[91] but nobody can read the theories of the scholastics, phrase by phrase, out of Gothic churches. Every sphere of activity has its own substance, but the spirit of the Gothic style can also help us to understand the spirit of scholasticism.

From all this, it is clear that every sphere has its own immanent process, its own tempo of development, and, in so far as one can use the word Gothic in every sphere, its own root of its own Gothic style.

Once we recognize this fact, we are equipped to answer the question as to what is the root of the Gothic style. The answer that the rib is the root, which is really a correct answer, now suddenly seems insufficient. The explanation that the principle of partiality was introduced into architecture by the creation of a new structural member, and that this partiality found its echo in the metaphysical idea of the men who commissioned architecture, is a much profounder one. Both these chains of development had their own immanence, and the approval of the men who commissioned buildings points in the direction of the immanence of ecclesiastical history and theology. However, the rib does not spring from either of these; each of these spheres, like that of chivalry and others, has its own root. It can be granted that cross-connexions can be proved or assumed to have existed, and that society's need for harmony provided the ring which forced diverging lines together, but what we are looking for is the common root of all these roots. We are seeking the secret force which provided every sphere of human activity with the spiritual factor, the spiritual aim and the spiritual sense of direction by which all immanent processes converged, by which all spheres remained related to one another, and which created a style common to all cultural spheres.

It is an easy task to name the root of all roots: it is Jesus of Nazareth. His life, his teaching, and his death changed a little group of men and women who had known him into teachers of all nations. Their early writings, some of which were collected to form the New Testament, posed a host of problems. Christology, theology, dogma and ethics all sought to clarify the contradictions contained in the New Testament and to construct a consistent edifice of religious thought. Even here, the quarrels between orthodoxy and heresies became involved in the struggle for power, in direct contradiction to the teachings of Jesus. Christianity, which was born out of Jesus, as the Christ, had its own immanence, of which the organization of the Church – first its institutions and later its architecture – were a branch. It is in this context that the Gothic style should be understood: it accompanied one stage in the development of Christianity.

This interpretation is not new. It is mainly based on Dvořák's treatise, the aim of which was to give a revaluation of medieval painting and sculpture, not by approaching the subject from the standards of classical antiquity or of the Renaissance, but by judging it through the *Weltanschauung* of its own age. No work of reference can replace this book, so rich in profound thoughts. Anybody seeking the root of the Gothic style can find a guide in the sentence which contrasts the teachings of Christ with the ideals of classical antiquity. The Christian doctrine, Dvořák says, is 'the doctrine of the absolute value of the human soul, the doctrine of an ethos that is not based on might or right, but on conviction and the community of moral attitude'.[92]

Dvořák did not overlook the fact that the way to Christianity had been laid open by Hellenism and Judaism and that, while it brought about the disintegration of the ideals of classical antiquity, it also drew much from them. Early Christian architecture, too, grew out of classical traditions and preserved memories of them right up to the age of the Gothic style.

Church architecture, sculpture and painting, religious poetry and scholasticism are connected with one another, here and there, by cross-connexions, but they are permanently transfused with, and vitalized by, the same sap, because they have a common root. This secret force naturally also affected secular architecture, which was the expression of the social and political life of the time. The conflicts between the emperors and the popes, the crusades and the orders of chivalry, the conflicts of theologians amongst themselves, and the monastic orders with their continual reforms, all sprang from the same root, even if much that was in them was in direct contradiction to the teachings of Christ. The doctrine of the Sermon on the Mount largely remained an unattainable ideal, and, while the words 'Put up again thy sword into his place: for all they that take the sword shall perish with the sword' have, again and again, proved themselves to be true, yet men still preferred to kill their enemies rather than to love them. During the crusades, men of other beliefs were killed in the name of Christ: that was called 'the world'. It was this 'world' with

which the kingdom of God was contrasted, and, however unchristian the behaviour of men may have been, this behaviour occurred against a background of ideas which looked forward to a redemption from sin.

Secular architecture shows man as he was: church architecture shows him as he would have liked to be.

The expression 'Man as he was' is a generalization. Man as he really was, the individual, the descendant of his ancestors, had hereditary talents as well as experience and abilities that he had gained himself. Every man bears within himself a part of the dark past, and creates his own constructive or destructive part of the present. National character is a blend of two factors – physiological heredity and spiritual heredity – and, at every moment, this blend changes a nation physiologically and spiritually. Christianity was born in Palestine; in the first three centuries of the Christian era it spread all round the Mediterranean, into Asia, and right to northern Europe, and the history of Christianity unfolds in all these many nations. Men had perpetually to strive to preserve its threatened unity. The changes in the history of architecture also reflect nationalities; every one of its styles reflects national differences at one stage in its immanent development. The kernel of Christianity remained the life, the teaching, and the death of Jesus, his resurrection, the Last Judgement, and the future, everlasting kingdom of God. The interpretations of the Church surrounded this kernel with dogmas and rites, and with much that was neither relevant, important, nor in doubt to Christians during Jesus's lifetime, and this unfolding of Christianity took place in the countries where missionaries taught – among men with different traditions, different experiences, and different capabilities. What is called national character, which, stated barely, is clear and obvious to everyone, dissolves as soon as it is examined more closely; it is the atmosphere which surrounds the branches of the tree – an extension of our metaphor of the root. This metaphor fails us in our study, for the branches themselves change the atmosphere.

Metaphors cannot take us far in the study of history. We try to make a development clear by lifting it out of the general current and setting it up as a scheme in its own right. In reality we are not dealing with a tree, nor with a current, but with a multitude of individual human beings through whom a spiritual current passes and by whom it is taken up, transformed, and passed on, partly to their own generation and partly to those to come. The Christians of about 1000 tried to apply the teaching of the New Testament, in the form in which it was interpreted by the Church of that time, to their own temporal mundane lives. There may have been Christians who, in the lonely areas upstage, took a more energetic view of this teaching, but the principal actors, in the limelight, continued to fight for power, possessions, and enjoyment: they wanted to be great lords. No human beings of that time can ever have conceived themselves so absolutely as gods as did the rulers of the ancient Orient and even some of the later Roman emperors. The process which educated men to an ethos 'not based on might or right', but on true Christianity, ran its course very slowly. Power politics had not disappeared by the beginning of the Gothic style, but they had led to the victory of the Papacy and the Church. This was the victory of the Christian idea, and, while this idea was still as unattainable as before, the consciousness of the leading personalities of the time was now tuned to the Christian scale of values. Morbid instincts and evil men still existed – one need only remember the Inquisition – but even the evil-doers of this age surrounded themselves with a nimbus of false sanctity which was intended to fit them into the style of their civilization.

This style is the one that we call Gothic. We have widened the scope of this term, which was coined exclusively for architecture, and we now try to embrace within its framework the styles of painting, of sculpture, or the style of thought of scholasticism, and the whole of Christian piety and civilization of the same period. All these styles are united by a certain trait of character, while they are differentiated from one another by their own, individual substance. Gothic architecture creates ways for religious activities; Gothic sculpture creates human and other forms; Gothic painting connects the portrayal of figures with their background; Gothic scholasticism creates intellectual systems; but all have the Christian scale of values in common, and in the Gothic age there was a stronger will to realize this scale of values than had ever existed before. Its principal conviction is that Man is a fragment of creation, who can find his totality only by taking his place within the kingdom of God, as interpreted by the spiritually creative man of the time.

The rib-vault was not foreseen by Christianity: it was the internal product of the problems set by the groin-vault. The change from the principle of totality of the Romanesque to that of partiality fitted in excellently with the tendency to give Man a different value from before and to consider his life as fragmentary and provisional. The principle of totality was not replaced by that of partiality with an intention of *l'art pour l'art*: rather, the idea of the individual as a totality was felt to be unchristian, while that of his partiality was felt to be Christian. This was the reason why the patrons of churches must have recognized that the rib-vaults perfectly suited their deepest religious roots. We have no documentary evidence for this theory, but we have the evidence of the whole history of Gothic church architecture from 1093 to 1530, and that of the whole history of Gothic civilization, whose tendencies led from St Bernard of Clairvaux to St Francis and St Thomas, to Bonaventura, and, finally, to the Late Gothic philosophy of Nicolaus Cusanus.

The answer to the old problem of the parallelism of the immanent processes lies in the fact that the different spheres of activity, for all their differences, were intended to find their common harmony in the hearts of men; and it was there that they had their common root, which lay in the personality of Jesus. From this root we can understand every one of the many spheres, including architecture, and we can understand why they all became Gothic.

Notes

ABBREVIATIONS

B.M. *Bulletin Monumental* (1834ff.)
C.A *Congrès archéologiques de France* (1834ff.)
P.M. *Petit Monographies des grands édifices de France.* Paris.

FOREWORD

1. This is illustrated with a single example in P. Frankl, 'A French Gothic Cathedral: Amiens', in *Art in America*, XXXV (1947) 295. The basic source for this interpretation of art is the article by Willi Drost, 'Form als Symbol', in *Zeitschrift für Ästhetik und allgemeine Kunstwissenschaft*, XXI (1927) 358.
2. Frankl (1960).
3. Geoffrey Webb, *Architecture in Britain: The Middle Ages* (Harmondsworth, 1956).

INTRODUCTION

1. Carl F. Barnes, review of Paul Frankl, *Gothic Architecture*, in *Journal of the Society of Architectural Historians*, 24 (1965), 174–6.
2. Robert Branner, review of Paul Frankl, *Gothic Architecture*, in *Art Bulletin*, 50 (1968), 199.
3. On English Gothic there appeared Peter Brieger, *English Art 1216–1307* (Oxford History of English Art) (Oxford, 1957); on early Gothic in Germany the picture was enriched by Hanno Hahn's monumental study of Eberbach and German Cistercian architecture (see bibliography). Wagner-Rieger's two volumes on Italian Gothic appeared in 1956 and 1957 (see bibliography), and between Jean Bony's seminal article on 'the resistance to Chartres' of 1957/8, and Robert Branner's numerous studies up to 1962, the history of French Gothic architecture in the twelfth and thirteenth centuries was cast in a wholly new light (see bibliography).
4. *Die Glasmalerei des fünfzehnten Jahrhunderts in Bayern und Schwaben* (Studien zur Deutschen Kunstgeschichte, 152, Strasbourg, 1912).
5. *Die Entwicklungsphasen der neueren Baukunst* (Berlin, Leipzig, 1914).
6. James S. Ackerman ed., *Principles of Architectural History. The Four Phases of Architectural Style, 1420–1900*, translated and edited by James F. O'Gorman (Cambridge, Mass. 1968).
7. 'Der Beginn der Gotik und das allgemeine Problem des Stilbeginnes', *Festschrift für Heinrich Wölfflin* (Munich, 1924).
8. Paul Frankl, *Zu Fragen des Stils*, ed. Ernst Ullmann (Leipzig, 1988). The book was prepared for publication by Frankl's assistant and literary executor, Dr Johanna Weitzmann-Fiedler.
9. Gert von der Osten, 'Paul Frankl 1878–1962', *Wallraf-Richartz Jahrbuch*, 24 (1962), 7–14.
10. Thirty-seven articles, books and reviews deal with architecture, sixteen with stained glass, and eighteen articles, books or reviews deal with general problems of art history, style, etc. Another breakdown of the bibliography in terms of subject matter can be found in F. Bucher's review of *The Gothic. Literary Sources and Interpretations*, in *Art Bulletin*, 45 (1963), 378, which does not take into account the 1988 publication of the shortened *Das System*.
11. 'The Secret of the Mediaeval Masons', *Art Bulletin*, 27 (1945), 46–64.
12. 'The Crazy Vaults of Lincoln Cathedral', *Art Bulletin*, 35 (1953), 95–107.
13. 'A French Gothic Cathedral: Amiens', *Art in America*, 35 (1947), 294–9; and 'The Chronology of Chartres Cathedral', *Art Bulletin*, 39 (1957), 33–47, as well as 'The Chronology of the Stained Glass in Chartres Cathedral', *Art Bulletin*, 45 (1963), 301–22.
14. 'Girl on a Couch', in *De Artibus Opuscula XL. Essays in Honor of Erwin Panofsky*, ed. Millard Meiss (New York, 1961), vol. 1 (text), 138–52, vol. 2 (ills), 46–51.
15. Significantly, it was the positivists of the new generation who found this combination alien. Robert Branner, in his review of *Gothic Architecture* in *Art Bulletin*, 50 (1968), 199, called Frankl's work a 'confrontation' between theory and fact, and saw it as a 'painful' 'contradiction'.
16. Attributed to Archilochus. I borrow the quote from Isaiah Berlin's essay on Tolstoy, 'The Hedgehog and the Fox', in *Russian Thinkers*, ed. Henry Hardy and Aileen Kelly (Harmondsworth, 1979), 22–81.
17. *Die Glasmalerei des fünfzehnten Jahrhundert in Bayern und Schwaben* (Studien zur Deutschen Kunstgeschichte, vol. 152, Strasbourg, 1912), and 'A

Stained Glass Roundel in Boston, Mass.', *Gazette des Beaux-Arts*, 60 (1962), 521–8; 'Die Italienreise der Glasmaler Hans Acker', *Wallraf-Richartz Jahrbuch*, 24 (1962), 213–26; 'Nachträge zu den Glasmalereien von Peter Hemmel', *Zeitschrift für Kunstwissenschaft*, 16 (1962), 201–22. Only one article appeared later, on the chronology of the stained glass of Chartres, in the *Art Bulletin*, 45 (1963), 301–22.
18. Gert von der Osten, 'Paul Frankl', 7.
19. *The Gothic*, [v].
20. *Gothic Architecture*, 33–4.
21. *The Gothic*, 828; *Gothic Architecture*, 299.
22. Most famously Viollet-le-Duc (1854–68) and Lasteyrie (see bibliography).
23. *Die frühmittelalterliche und romanische Baukunst.*
24. Geoffrey Webb, *Architecture in Britain: The Middle Ages* (Pelican History of Art, Harmondsworth, 1956).
25. Frankl's European outlook has been vindicated for the Pelican History of Art series. C.R. Dodwell's first study in the *Pelican* series, *Painting in Europe 800–1200* (Harmondsworth, 1971), was completely re-written by him to include the British Isles in his second Pelican volume, *The Pictorial Arts of the West 800–1200* (New Haven and London, 1993).
26. Nikolaus Pevsner, *The Englishness of English Art* (London, 1955); Frankl, *Gothic Architecture*, 127. A lively discussion of these nationalist issues, particularly in relation to Pevsner's book, can be found in Jonathan Alexander, 'Medieval art and modern nationalism', *Medieval art: recent perspectives. A memorial tribute to C.R. Dodwell*, ed. Gale Owen-Crocker and Timothy Graham (Manchester and New York, 1998), 206–23.
27. Gert von der Osten, 'Paul Frankl', 8, suggests, however, that Frankl intended to conclude his *Die frühmittelalterliche und romanische Baukunst* with a theoretical section on general problems of Romanesque style, as he was later to do in *Gothic Architecture*, but the project was 'forcibly and crudely cut short'.
28. *Die Entwicklungsphasen*, which was, of course, an analysis of Renaissance and post-Renaissance architecture, included under the heading of 'corporeal form' not only structural activity, but also 'sculptural' qualities such as mass and surface (the orders, columnar series, frames, rhythms, etc.). See *The Principles of Architectural History*, vii–viii.
29. The theory of perception implied by Frankl's 'optical/visible form' is clearly stated in *Die Entwicklungsphasen*, see *Principles of Architectural History*, pp. 142–56. For its origins in late nineteenth-century theories of perception see below, Introduction, note 57.
30. *The Gothic*, 796. Frankl's theory of style and his use of polar opposites is, as he acknowledges, derived principally from Alois Riegl and Heinrich Wölfflin. See *The Gothic*, 772–98. Michael Podro, *The Critical Historians of Art* (New Haven and London, 1982) provides the best introduction to the history of this ultimately Hegelian conception of style.
31. Frankl uses this specific comparison as a typical example of Gothic spatial division in 'Der Beginn der Gotik', 107–25. He also discusses these Romanesque–Gothic polarities fully in *The Gothic*, 776–9.
32. The polarity of 'being versus becoming' derives, as Frankl acknowledged, from Wölfflin's distinction between Renaissance and Baroque architecture in his *Renaissance und Barock* (Munich, 1888), translated by Kathrin Simon as *Renaissance and Baroque* (London, 1964), with an introduction by Peter Murray, 62. See also *The Gothic*, 775f, 780f. Frankl first applied Wölfflin's polarity to Gothic architecture in 'Der Beginn der Gotik', 125.
33. In *Das System*, 1005, Frankl defined Mannerism as a weakened connexion between form and its content. However, Frankl soon realized that the term 'Mannerism' was misleading, since it was generally understood to refer to a specific historical period, between High Renaissance and Baroque, whereas shifts of meaning and purpose within similar forms occured across all styles and periods, and even within periods. In his article 'The "Crazy" vaults', of 1953, he therefore proposed to avoid the term 'Mannerism' in favour of 'akyrism'. See also *The Gothic*, 795–7.
34. *The Gothic*, 796.
35. Frankl rehearses the Rationalist arguments fully in *The Gothic*, 563–78, 798–819.
36. *Classic Art* (Oxford, 1952, 2nd edn.) trans P. and L. Murray, 207ff, especially 287.
37. See especially 57–159.
38. See Podro, *The Critical Historians*, 36–7, 81ff, 107–11. Note also Karl Schnaase, *Geschichte der bildenden Künste im Mittelalter*, vol. 3 (1871), which was most certainly known to Frankl. Strongly influenced by Hegel's *Aesthetics*, the book discusses precisely these internal dynamics in terms of the conflicting

demands of the exteriors and interiors of early medieval buildings.

39. I am borrowing this distinction from Podro, *The Critical Historians*, 110, in his analysis of Wölfflin's paper on the Roman triumphal arch.

40. *The Principles of Architectural History*, 3.

41. Riegl and Wölfflin's super-personal idea of style is discussed by Podro, *The Critical Historians*, 71–151. For Reigl's *Stilfragen* of 1893 see Ernst Gombrich, *The Sense of Order. A study in the psychology of decorative art* (Oxford, 1979), 180–93; Margaret Olin, *Forms of Representation in Alois Riegel's Theory of Art* (Pennsylvania, 1992), 67–87, and Margaret Iversen, *Alois Riegel Art History and Theory* (Cambridge, Mass., 1993), 4–18. A perceptive analysis of the changing definitions of 'style', and the inflections given it by post-Hegelian art history, can be found in Willibald Sauerländer, 'From Stylus to Style: Reflections on the fate of a notion', *Art History*, 6 (1983), 253–70.

42. *The Principles of Architectural History*, 157–84.

43. Ernst Gombrich, 'In Search of Cultural History', *Ideals and Idols. Essays on values in history and in art* (Oxford, 1979), 24–59.

44. Translated by Randolph J. Klawitzer, as *Idealism and Naturalism in Gothic Art* (Indiana, 1967).

45. Though Frankl is prepared to admit occasional cross-connexions on p. 299: 'Church architecture, sculpture and painting, religious poetry and scholasticism are connected with one another, here and there, by cross-connexions, but they are permanently transfused with, and vitalized by, the same sap, because they have a common root'.

46. *The Gothic*, 779.

47. See the bibliography in the *Wallraf-Richartz-Jahrbuch*, 24 (1962), 11–14. I do not include his article on Amiens in *Art in America*, 35 (1947), 294–9, because this is really a theoretical demonstration using Amiens as a test case. Nor do I include his obviously more theoretical article on the Milan controversy in the *Art Bulletin*, 27 (1945), 46–64.

48. 'Der Beginn der Gotik', 107–22, 117; and 'Meinungen über Herkunft und Wesen der Gotik', in Walter Timmling, *Kunstgeschichte und Kunstwissenschaft* (Kleine Literaturführer, 6) (Leipzig, 1923), 107–25. Under the heading of 'corporeal form' Frankl did not actually use the polarity 'structure versus texture'. He called it *Kraftquelle* versus *Kraftdurchlass* (literally, 'structural sources' – i.e. structures which suggested force and pressure – versus 'streams of force', i.e. structures which 'grow' and 'flow'. The general meaning is, however, the same.

49. Karl Popper, *The Poverty of Historicism* (London, 1957).

50. Ernst Gombrich, *Art and Illusion* (Oxford, 1960), 12–18; and ibid, 'In Search of Cultural History', passim.

51. The old question of individual choice versus super-personal currents in historical evolution is too complex to permit the kind of categorical dismissal of 'historical forces' made by Gombrich. See, for example, Isaiah Berlin, *Historical Inevitability* (London, 1954), 32: 'We may indeed always argue . . . about whether a given occurrence is best explained as the inevitable effect of antecedent events beyond human control, or on the contrary as due to free human choice'. Note also Otto Pächt's criticism of Gombrich's position: 'Alois Riegl', in *Methodisches zur kunsthistorischen Praxis. Ausgewählte Schriften*, ed. Jörg Oberhaidacher (Munich, 1977), 141–52, esp. 149.

52. 'Formalism' is here deliberately put within quotation marks, to suggest Wölfflin's unmatched skill in the analysis of the visual traditions of art; it should not imply that he was impervious to social and psychological influences on the work of art, since these 'extrinsic' factors occupied him throughout his life. See Podro, *Critical Historians*, 98–151; and Meinhold Lurz, *Heinrich Wölfflin. Biographie einer Kunsttheorie* (Heidelberger Kunstgeschichtliche Abhandlungen, 14. Worms, 1981), who also assesses Wölfflin's influence on Frankl's theory of art, 39–40.

53. Frankl's analyses of Cologne Cathedral in *Gothic Architecture*, 161–4, and 178–80, were considered important enough to deserve translation into German in *Kölner Domblatt*, 21/22 (1963), 241–7.

54. Principally in Robert Branner, *St Louis and the Court Style* (London, 1965).

55. 'The "crazy" vaults', passim; and 'Lincoln Cathedral', *Art Bulletin*, 44 (1962), 29–37.

56. A point made by Barnes in his review of *Gothic Architecture*, 176.

57. The idea of 'optical form' as a mental synthesis of images has much in common with the central arguments of Hildebrand's *Das Problem der Form in der bildenden Kunst* (Strassburg, 1893), translated by M. Meyer and R.O. Ogden as *The Problem of Form in Painting and Sculpture* (New York, 1932), where 'archaic', 'primitive' or children's art forms, usually of simple, dominant shapes, are seen as the residue of accumulated memory images. Hildebrand defined these memory images as a combination of sense data derived from vision and memories of touch and movement. To couple this theory of perception with stylistic polarities (as Frankl does) and to set up the polarities as determinants of stylistic evolution (also as Frankl does), was the achievement of Alois Riegl, whose polar opposites of 'haptic' and 'optic' art – art which presupposes mental 'touch', and art which relies on pure vision – were fully devel-

oped as critical tools in his *Spätrömisches Kunstindustrie* (Vienna, 1927). See Iversen (1993) and Olin (1992). Heinrich Wölfflin adapted Hildebrand's theories of classical relief in his analysis of High Renaissance sculpture in *Classic Art*, and it was almost certainly from Wölfflin that Frankl developed his theory of Romanesque and Gothic relief. See also Podro, *The Critical Historians*, 66–70. The similarities between Frankl's 'synthetic memory' and Gestalt theories of perception were noted by James Ackerman in his foreward to the translation of *Die Entwicklungsphasen*, *The Principles of Architectural History*, p. viii.

58. Ernst Gall, *Die gotische Baukunst in Frankreich und Deutschland. Teil 1: die Vorstufen in Nordfrankreich von der Mitte des elften bis gegen Ende des zwölften Jahrhunderts* (Leipzig, 1925); Jean Bony, 'Le technique normande du mur épais a l'époque romane', *Bulletin monumental*, 98 (1939) 153–88.

59. *The Gothic*, 763–72.

60. Jean Bony, 'The Resistance to Chartres in Early Thirteenth Century Architecture', *Journal of the British Archaeological Associatioin*, 3rd ser., 20–21 (1957–8) 35–52.

61. *The Gothic*, 35–159.

62. Podro, *The Critical Historians*, 98–151; and Lurz, *Heinrich Wölfflin*, passim.

63. Richard Krautheimer, 'Introduction to an "Iconography of Medieval Architecture"', *Journal of the Warburg and Courtauld Institutes*, 5 (1942) 1–33.

64. Frankl faced this contradiction but did not resolve it by introducing his (or rather, Werner Gross's) idea of the 'Gothic wall' – a thin membrane – as the constituting element of friars' architecture (pp. 174–5).

65. Jean Bony, *French Gothic Architecture of the 12th and 13th Centuries* (Berkeley, 1983) 195ff.

66. Frankl may be following the traditional German definition of *Hochgotik* as the architecture of the whole thirteenth century, but it is curious that he ignores both Lasteyrie's and Focillon's clear distinctions between the styles. See Henri Focillon, *Art d'Occident* (Paris, 1938) translated by Donald King as *The Art of the West*, part 2 (London and New York, 1963) 40–1.

67. Branner, *op.cit.*, St Louis.

68. Bony, *op.cit.*, French Gothic Architecture.

69. Barnes, Review, 176.

70. Robert Branner, review of *Gothic Architecture* in *The Art Bulletin*, 50 (1968) 199; and Nikolaus Pevsner, letter in *The Art Bulletin*, 51 (1969) 101.

71. Jean Bony, 'Diagonality and Centrality in Early Rib-Vaulted Architecture', *Gesta*, 15 (1976) 15–25.

72. Nikolaus Pevsner, *An Outline of European Architecture* (Harmondsworth, 1943) passim; and Sigfried Giedion, *Space, Time and Architecture* (Harvard, 1941).

73. Richard Krautheimer, *Die Kirchen der Bettelorden in Deutschland* (Cologne, 1925). Indeed, Krautheimer constructed the book in the same manner as the later *Gothic Architecture*, around a first part devoted to the evolution of forms, and a second section concerned with wider issues of cultural context.

74. Krautheimer (1942)

75. Willis, parts 1, 2 (1972 reprint); Wolff (1968); Hammann-MacLean and Schüssler (1993); James (1979, 1981); van der Meulen and Hohmeyer (1984).

76. Branner (1962 and 1989); Murray (1987) (1989) (1996); Brachmann (1998).

77. For example Sampson (1998) and in Italy, Zervas et al. (1996).

78. One example of a close reliance on photogrammetry is Crosby (1987).

79. Sedlmayr (1950); von Simson (1962); see the perceptive remarks on this development by Sauerländer (1995) 8–9, and my own comments on Sedlmayr's and von Simson's work in Crossley (1988).

80. See, in particular, the stimulating essays on this problem brought together by Raguin, Brush and Draper eds. (1995).

81. Caviness (1990); Binski (1995).

82. Köstler (1995).

83. See the article by M. Caviness, 'Artistic Integration in Gothic Buildings: A Post-Modern Construct?', in Raguin, Brush and Draper (eds.) (1995) 249–61.

84. Tripps (1998).

85. László Gerevich, ed., *Towns in Medieval Hungary* (Colorado, New Jersey, 1990).

85A. Brucher (1990).

86. Teresa Mroczko, Marian Arszyński, eds. (1995). See also Paul Crossley, review in *Kunstchronik*, 7 (1997) 352–68. A stimulating discussion of the 'geography' problem for the Central Europe of the Renaissance and eighteenth century can be found in Thomas DaCosta Kaufmann, *Court, Cloister and City. The Art and Culture of Central Europe 1450–1800* (London, 1995) esp. 13–23.

87. Recht (1974), Branner (1960).

88. Freigang (1992).

89. Binski (1995).

90. Branner (1965); Bony (1979) (1983).

91. Bony (1979); Harvey (1978). For criticism of Branner's and Bony's

notion of a 'court style' see Colvin (1983) and Coldstream (1994) as well as Binski (1995).

92. Nussbaum (1994) and (2000).
93. Bony (1983).
94. Warnke (1976).
95. Schöller (1989).
96. Abou-el-Haj (1988).
97. Williams (1993).
98. Kraus (1979).
99. Especially Kimpel (1977); Kimpel (1981).
100. Bony (1990).
101. Harvey (1984, 2nd edn.) and Colvin (1963).
102. James (1979, 1981). In fairness, James himself has revised the extreme position he advanced in his Chartres book in his study of (1989).
103. See Barnes (1982) and Barnes (1989).
104. Booz (1956); Shelby (1977); Coenen (1990).
105. Shelby (1972).
106. Hecht (1969) (1970) (1971).
107. Robert Branner, 'Drawings from a Thirteenth-Century Architect's Shop: The Reims Palimpsest', *Journal of the Society of Architectural Historians*, 18 (1958) 9–12; and Stephen Murray, 'The Gothic Façade Drawings in the Reims Palimpsest', *Gesta*, 34 (1978) 51–5.
108. Koepf (1970) (1977).
109. Recht, ed. (1989).
110. Pause (1973).
111. Bucher (1979).
112. Middeldorf-Kosegarten (1984) (1996).
113. Morris (1978) (1979) (1990a).
114. Lon R.Shelby, 'Medieval Masons' Tools', II, 'Compass and Square', *Technology and Culture* 6, (1965) 236–48.
115. Odette Chapelet and Paul Benoit, eds., *Pierre et Métal dans le bâtiment au Moyen Age* (Paris, 1985).
116. Welch (1995).
117. Binding (1993).
118. Fitchen (1961).
119. Jacques Heyman 'The Gothic Structure', *Interdisciplinary Science Reviews*, 2 (1977) 151–64, and (1968) (1983); Mark (1982).
120. See, for example, Murray's revealing discussion of the causes of the Beauvais collapse in (1989) 112–20, and Mark's less-than-helpful model analysis of its choir in (1982) 58–77, showing a cross-section taken through the point where the cathedral did *not* collapse!
121. Recht, ed. (1989).
122. Müller (1990).
123. Panofsky (1951).
124. Sedlmayr (1950); Frankl, in *The Gothic*, 753–8, caricatured this book as an 'aberration'. In fact, its theoretical approach has much in common with Frankl's. A brief discussion of Sedlmayr's book in the context of architectural iconography can be found in Crossley (1988).
124a. Panofsky, ed (1979).
125. Von Simson (1956).
126. See the articles on Suger as iconographer in the collected essays edited by Gerson (1986).
127. Neuheuser (1993) Binding (1993A) Binding and Speer (1996).
128. See note 7B, p. 364, and Tripps (1998) 34–42.
129. M. Gosebruch, Review of Sedlmayr, *Die Entstehung der Kathedrale*, in *Göttingische Gelehrte Anzeigen*, 211 (1954) 309ff.
130. Büchsel (1983).
131. Kidson (1987).
132. Grant (1998).
133. Krautheimer (1942).
134. Kunst (1981).
135. Schenkluhn (1985).
136. Kimpel and Suckale (1985).
137. See, Georgia Clarke and Paul Crossley, eds., *Architecture and Language. Constructing Identity in European Architecture c. 1100–1650* (Cambridge, 2000).
138. Draper, particularly (1995) but also (1996).
139. Peter Kurmann and Dethard von Winterfeld (1977).
140. Crossley (1999); see also Suckale (1980) who first connected the idea of decorum to Peter Parler's diverse 'modes'.
141. Fergusson (1984) (1986) (1994); and Fergusson and Harrison (1994) and (1999).
142. Schenkluhn (1985).
143. Bruzelius (1992) (1995).
144. Jeffrey F. Hamburger, *The Visual and the Visionary. Art and Female Spirituality in Late Medieval Germany* (New York, 1998).
145. Notably Hans Belting, *The Image and its Public in the Middle Ages*, trans. M. Bartussis and R. Meyer (New York, 1990) and Rubin (1991).

146. Draper (1979) (1981) (1987) (1996).
147. Kroos (1976) (1979/80) (1989); Tripps (1998).
148. Sturgis (1991).
149. The examples of this overlap could be multiplied *ad infinitum*. I give only one: Michael Michael's intriguing suggestion that the placing of armorials in church choirs was to convey the 'presence', by proxy, of the lay benefactor in the holiest part of the church. See 'The privilege of "proximity": towards a re-definition of the function of armorials', *Journal of Medieval History*, 23 (1997) 55–75.
150. Fajt, ed., (1998).
151. Braunfels (4th edn, 1979).
152. Zervas *et al.* (1996); John Henderson, *Piety and Charity in Late Medieval Florence* (Oxford, 1994).
153. Middeldorf-Kosegarten (1970) (1996).
154. Welch (1995).
155. Chiara Frugoni, *A Distant City. Images of Urban Experience in the Medieval World*, trans. W. McCuaig (Princeton, 1991).
156. Trachtenberg (1988) (1989) (1993) (1997).
157. Mussat (1988).
158. Erlande-Brandenburg (1994).
159. Fajt, ed. (1998).
160. Skibiński (1982) Torbus (1998).
161. Albrecht (1986) (1995).
162. Richard Krautheimer, 'Paul Frankl', *Art Journal* 22 (1962) 167.
163. See, for the whole debate, Annabel Patterson, 'Intention', *Critical Terms for Literary Analysis*, ed. Frank Lentricchia and Thomas McLaughlin (Chicago, 1990) 135–46.
164. See George Steiner, *Real Presences. Is there anything in* what *we say?* (London, 1989).
165. Baxandall, *Patterns of Intention* (New Haven and London, 1985).
166. Wilson (1990) 11–12.
167. Baxandall, *Patterns of Intention*, 135.
168. *The Gothic*, 837.
169. Baxandall, *Patterns of Intention*, especially 1–40, makes the same points about paintings: verbalizing pictures involves, not an unmediated artistic object, but an interpretative description of it – a representation of our thoughts about it.

PART ONE   INTRODUCTION

1. Erwin Panofsky, *Abbot Suger* (Princeton, 1946) 144. The Ordinatio of 1140 or 1141 already contains a few notes about the building of Saint-Denis.
1A. For Gervase's text on the fire and rebuilding of the choir of Canterbury see Stubbs, ed., (1879–80) vol. 1, 3–29. For references to the *fornices arcuatae* see p. 27. There is a full translation of those sections directly relating to the architecture by Willis (1972) 36–62. Annas and Binding (1989) argue with reference to a wide range of texts that the *arcus* referred to by Suger in *De Consecratione* chapter 5, when he dramatically describes the uncompleted high vault of the choir (*arcus superiores*) trembling dangerously in the wind, were not ribs, as Panofsky and many others have asserted, but transverse arches. Their argument, much of it based on Gervase's distinction between rib vaults (*fornix magna*) and groin vaults (*fornix plana*), is not, however, supported by Gervase's text. For he specifically contrasts vaults (*fornices*) from the Romanesque church as *planae* (i.e. 'plain', 'undecorated', 'unarticulated') and those from the Gothic as *arcuatae sunt et clavatae* (i.e. 'arched' or 'ribbed' and with 'keystones'). Since Romanesque vaults also have transverse arches, the contrast he draws would have been meaningless if he was referring to the transverse arches of the new work. To use the words 'arches' and 'keystones' side by side also suggests that he was referring to the ribs joined at the centre of the bay by a boss. With Villard de Honnecourt, a generation later, the vocabulary is unequivocal. Vaults are *vosor* or *vosure*, arches are *arc* or *doubliaus*, and ribs are *ogive*. See Hahnloser (1972) 105, 113, 117, 170. Hinker's (1967) study of architectural terminology in the Middle Ages in northern France was not available to me.
1B. Villard is referring to diagonal ribs at Reims cathedral, see Hahnloser (1972) 170–3.
2. G. S. Colin, "Origine arabe du mot français ogive", in *Romania*, LXIII (1937) 377; see also L. Torres Balbás in *Al-Andalus*, VIII (1943) 475.
3. T. Asby, 'The Classical Topography of the Roman Campagna', in *Papers of the British School of Rome*, IV (1907) 97. Here the whole group of ruins is illustrated. See especially the chamber 'ee' in the plan on plate VIII. Cf. also G. T. Rivoira, *Architettura romana* (Milan, 1921) 178.
4. Jules Formigé, 'Notes sur des voûtes romaines nervées à Arles', in *B.M.*, LXXVII (1913) 126, where the plan is misleading. In projection the cryptoribs do not form two parallel lines, since the arches begin in the form of groins and change smoothly and continuously into ribs. See also Jeanne de Flandreysy

and Etienne Mellier, *Arles et l'abbaye de Montmajour* (Marseille, 1922) figs 72–81.

4A. For late Roman examples of brick ribbing see Boethius and Ward-Perkins (1970) 510–11.

5. It is believed that the so-called Baths of Diana at Arles contained an early example of a tunnel-vault with transverse arches. Several later examples exist in Romanesque buildings.

5A. The tower may be part of the church consecrated in 1049, or it may belong to a later period in the eleventh century, possibly to the 1070s, since its vaults are related to those of Bayeux and its plan to the transeptal tower of Saint-Martin at Tours. The arguments for a date before 1049 are set out in Oursel (1975) 175–83. Durliat's (1994) 184–8, study of the sculpture relating to these early west French vaults dates the ribs to a little after 1049.

5B. The English character of Durham and its first architect is underlined by Bony (1981) 79–82. Thurlby (1994) stresses the debts to Winchester and St Albans in particular. For the possible Islamic influence in the mathematics of its stone cutting see Bony (1990), and for further Islamic parallels (particularly with San Cristo de la Luz in Toledo and the mosque at Cordoba), in the interlacing arcading of its dado and its divergent ribs without transverse arches, see Thurlby (1994) especially 174–5.

5C. The vault in the north-west tower at Bayeux is distinctive in springing from the middle of the sides of the bay, not the corners, and in being applied to a domical section. In both respects it relates to a late eleventh- (?) and early twelfth-century group of French vaults, mainly in the Loire valley, with band ribs in towers: Saint-Paul at Cormery, Saint-Ours in Loches, the crossing tower at Aubiac (Lot-et-Garonne) and the Tour de Charlemagne in Saint-Martin at Tours. For the towers at Bayeux see Liess (1967) 142–3. For the other examples, and for early rib vaults in the Loire valley generally, see Lambert (1933) 235–44. He puts the Tours vaults as the last in the series. Lelong (1975) 113–30, agrees, and dates the Tour de Charlemagne to the very late eleventh century, or the beginning of the twelfth. Durliat (1994) 182–3, notes the similarities between the vaults of Cormery and Bayeux, in that both are band ribs springing from the middle of the walls. He dates Cormery to c.1070–80. The whole group may reflect some Islamic influence, probably not directly from the first Muslim rib vaults in the great Mosque at Cordoba (961–5), but perhaps from Cordoba's Mozarabic offshoots in Spain, e.g. San Millan de la Cogolla (Logrono) (consecrated 929 and 984) or San Baudel de Berlanga (11th century). See also the rib vault over a high dome at Quimperlé in Brittany, in Tillet (1982) 240–63.

5D. Durham's position as the first rib-vaulted church in western Europe has now been called into question by the re-dating of two rib-vaulted churches in the Empire and the Low Countries. Von Winterfeld (1988) and (1988a) has convincingly shown that the rib vaults in the transepts of Speyer Cathedral, previously dated to after the fire of 1159, belong to the remodelling of the church after 1081 by Henry IV. And Kidson (1996) has proposed that the similar rib vaults in the now-lost church of St Mary at Utrecht (linked to Speyer by Henry IV's support of the new building) were constructed as part of the original building campaign of late 1080s/early 1090s, and were not, as hitherto thought, inserted after the fire of 1132. Plant (1998) concurs, and finds fresh evidence which suggests that St Mary may have had a direct influence on Durham: in the rare but shared used of octagonal cushion capitals, in the rib vaults, in the use of paired porthole windows in the transepts, and in the precedents for Durham's decorated piers in Utrecht and buildings associated with Utrecht. Plant surmounts the problem of the technical and stylistic differences between the Imperial rib-vaults and those at Durham (the Durham vaults have torus-moulded ribs quite distinct from the rectangular band ribs of Speyer and Utrecht, and their structure is close to Anglo-Norman groin-vaults) by seeing the Durham ribs as another part of the symbolic decoration of the interior, in which one vaulting system is decoratively transposed into another. For the predominantly aesthetic and symbolic character of the first Durham ribs see Thurlby (1994) and especially (1993a). See also below, Chapter 1, Notes 1b, 22d, 22e.

6. The history of research into Lombard architecture is given in the introduction to A. Kingsley Porter, *Lombard Architecture* (New Haven, 1915). The dates which he gives for rib-vaults were dismissed by Frankl, see *Die frühmittel-alterliche und romanische Baukunst* (Wildpark-Potsdam, 1926) 119ff. and 197ff. However, Porter may have been nearer to the truth than his many detractors, including Frankl, thought. The Italian-inspired remodelling of Speyer under Henry IV implies that its rib-vaults were also indebted to some Lombardic model, and Speyer's connexions to St Mary's at Utrecht via Henry IV make Italian influence on the rib vault there just as likely, especially in the context of all the other Italianisms in the church, see Kidson (1996). The difficulty is that few of the Italian parallels discussed by Peroni (1969) – among them S. Michele and S. Giovanni in Borgo in Pavia, or S. Savino in Piacenza – are definitely earlier than the northern examples. S. Michele Maggiore in Pavia, for instance, belongs to 'the end of the 11th century', but we cannot be certain if its original domed rib-vaults pre-dated the earthquake of 1117, or

even if they supplanted a scheme for a lower wooden roof. See also Brucher (1987) 60–63, and below, Chapter 2, Notes 62–70, and pp. 99–100.

7. John Bilson, 'The Beginnings of Gothic Architecture, etc.', *Journal of the Royal Institute of British Architects* (1899, 1902); 'Durham Cathedral, The Chronology of its Vaults', in *The Archaeological Journal*, LXXIX (1922) 101. The date of 1235 records indulgences by Bishop Northwold of Ely for those contributing to the projected new work, but the actual rebuilding did not begin until 1242. See Snape (1980) 23–4.

8. This is why large pieces of vault often project in Roman ruins, or lie on the ground in huge blocks.

9. Sigurd Curman and Johnny Roosval, *Sveriges Kyrkor*, II, *Gotland* (Stockholm, 1935) 95 (illustration) 114.

10. The theory that wood was introduced because it became cheaper is connected with the belief that the first ribs were built in Lombardy, where there is supposed to have been a shortage of wood. However, the cross rib-vault may not have come from Lombardy and the forests in this country probably did not disappear until later centuries.

10A. Viollet-le-Duc proposed that the cerce was a device for supporting the stones of successive web courses in the construction of the rib vault. It was hung at its ends from the back of the two ribs and supported the web courses while the mortar dried and the stones set. Since it can extend horizontally, it could be moved up the vault as it spanned wider and wider spaces between the ribs. Frankl's remarks on the cerce are probably based on Viollet-le-Duc's confident exposition of its function in (1858–68) vol. 4, 105–8. Fitchen (1961) 99–122 questioned whether the cerce was employed as a centering device, and argued that it was no more than an adjustable template from which to cut the planks that held the cells.

11. Auguste Choisy, *L'art de bâtir chez les Romains* (Paris, 1873) 73–5.

12. The first man to recognize this was probably James Essex (1723–84) whose notes are preserved in the British Museum in London. The first man to publish this observation in print was George Saunders in 'Observations on the Origin of Gothic Architecture' (a lecture read in 1811) in *Archaeologia*, XVII (1814) 15.

13. The Romanesque crypt of Canterbury Cathedral contains many groin-vaults with double-curved and irregular groins.

14. G. Ungewitter and K. Mohrmann, *Lehrbuch der gotischen Konstruktionen*, II (Leipzig, 1890) 10. With reference to what follows, cf. Mohrmann's whole chapter, 8–18, and his plate III.

14A. But it is has certain similarities with devices for vault projection used by late Gothic German architects, and preserved in fifteenth- and sixteenth-century sketchbooks and manuals. To establish the correct curvature and length of each rib, an arc was drawn corresponding to the cross section of the vault and its ribs. At the base of the arc, corresponding to the springing point of the vault, a horizontal baseline was drawn, and vertical lines, the distance between them corresponding to the length of each rib segment on the ground plan, were drawn upwards to intersect the arc. Bucher (1972a) discussed this system in the late fifteenth-century Dresden Sketchbook, while Müller analysed its after-life in the sixteenth-century drawings of Jacob Facht von Andernach (1974) and the Nuremberg architect Wolf Jacob Stromer (1977). See also Müller (1989) 244, 245, and (1990) passim. Whereas here the horizontal was below the arc, and the verticals rose to it, in Mohrmann's system the horizontal elements (the ropes) are above the arc (the tunnel) and the verticals descend to it. By whatever method, straight – that is non-curvilinear – groins were frequently built, for example in many vaults of the so-called First Romanesque, and the groin-vaults of late eleventh-century Gloucester. See Wilson (1985) 61.

15. This kind of elliptical wall arch can be seen in the choir of the church of the Trinité at Caen.

15A. Frankl accepts Ungewitter-Mohrmann's conclusions, but Fitchen (1961) 50–62, pointed to some of their shortcomings, especially regarding de-centering and re-location of planking, and suggested his own scheme for groin-vault centering, see fig. 20. Thurlby (1993a) 68, has suggested that the 'ploughshare' webs of the high vaults in Durham could not have been constructed solely on wooden planks, but must have used a more malleable material, such as wattle. Ungewitter-Mohrmann's constructional 'progression' assumed the straightening of the groin arcs as a prerequisite for rib vaults, a progression considered axiomatic by Bilson (1899) 293–4. In some cases, however, the reverse may be true: the straight, or apparently straight, groins used in rib-vaults regularized the arcs of later groin-vaults. See the case of late eleventh-century Gloucester, Wilson (1985) 65.

15B. But much less cumbersome wooden lagging and centering was required with rib vaults. Economy certainly played a part in this change. See Mark (1982) 122, and Fitchen (1961) 86–122.

15C. Lagging for vault cells can still be seen in the vault of the room adjoining the north-east transept of Lincoln cathedral, of the mid-1190s, see Bond (1913) vol. 1, 287, and Wilson (1990) 27, plate 17. The use of wattle in addition to planks in the centering of the Lincoln vault is a clue to the use of that more malleable support for 'ploughshare' vault cells, see above, Note 15a.

15D. Frankl's assertion is too categorical. It ignores both the structural and constructional advantages of ribs in the building of vaults, and also the symbolic functions of ribs, see below Note 17b.

16. Victor Mortet, 'L'expertise de la cathédrale de Chartres en 1316', *C.A.*, LXVII (1901) 323; Frankl (1960) 57ff.

16A. There is no conclusive evidence for the cause of the instability, though Frankl is wrong in suggesting that they may have fallen down, since all the documents mention only the threat of collapse, and of fissures and cracks. See Snape (1980) 21–2, 24. James (1983) 139, argued for distortion within the vault rather than movement through the walls or buttressing, for which he found no evidence, but Thurlby (1993) 46–7 plausibly suggests that the damage may have been caused by the settlement of the Romanesque towers above the aisle apses which flanked the main apse forebay, towers which were eventually demolished. Clearly, however, Durham was not the only early Anglo-Norman high choir vault subject to failure, see Gloucester (early twelfth century) and St Albans (1257). Thurlby (1993a) 69, has shown that in at least one aisle bay of the choir at Durham the rib vaults were planned to have a lower trajectory than at present. This may mean that the vaults were not achieved without constructional difficulties. He even suggests that the initial plan may have been to vault the aisles with groin vaults, though the evidence for this is circumstantial.

17. Saunders, *loc. cit.* (Note 12, above.)

17A. Frankl's view is confirmed by the vault cells at Durham, which are as thick as a conventional groin vault in the choir and transepts and eastern bays of the nave, and only become thinner, by about a third, in the western bays of the nave, between 1128 and 1133. See Bilson (1922). The thorny problem of whether or not ribs actually supported the vault has provoked much discussion. Frankl (1960) 663–6, 763–72, 798–826, himself reviewed the controversy up to 1960, but he came to no clear conclusion. More scientific answers to questions concerning the behaviour of masonry vaults have now been offered by modern techniques of structural analysis, but there are still disagreements. Heyman (1968) 171–88, and (1983) 182–3, considers that ribs provide support for cells, particularly at the sharp creases of the groins. Alexander, Mark and Abel (1977) and Mark (1982) 102–17, 122, argue that the structural forces in cells diffuse, cone-like, towards the springers of the vault and do not concentrate particularly on the groins. This means that the groin-vault is as inherently stable as the rib-vault. The ribs facilitate the construction of the cells, but once those cells are in place ribs play no further structural role. Müller (1990) 184–205, reviews the literature on the controversy. Had the rib been regarded as structurally superior to the groin-vault it would not have been used so partially in Romanesque churches – e.g. appearing in the main apse of Saint-Georges at Saint-Martin-de-Boscherville (Seine-Maritime), but not extending to the groin vaults of the adjoining straight bays. Thurlby (1993a) 70, has pointed to a number of twelfth-century monastic houses in England where rib vaults are used selectively in the areas deemed more important, while lesser spaces would be groined. This suggests that the rib also had a symbolic importance, see below Note 17B.

17B. By concentrating primarily on the formal and constructional advantages of the rib Frankl leaves out its symbolic uses. Thurlby (1993a) (1994) stresses the importance for Durham of the openwork ribs of the baldachine over the high altar and shrine of St Peter in Old St Peter's in Rome, especially since the ribs were supported on spiral columns which provided the direct or indirect inspiration for the spiral piers at Durham. The symbolic, specifically Petrine, implications of the spiral piers, especially around shrines and altars had already been pointed out by Fernie (1977). By transferring these motifs from altar and shrine to the whole choir of a great church, Bishop William of Calais provided a suitable setting for the feretory of St Cuthbert, and rivalled the more subtle references to Old St Peter's at Winchester Cathedral. The notion of ribs as enlarged sacred canopies over a shrine or an altar may explain why many of the earliest examples are confined to apses – S. Abbondio in Como, the late eleventh-century choir of Gloucester Cathedral (?), Ewenny Priory in Glamorgan, Saint-Georges at Saint-Martin-de-Boscherville – and are only extended later to cover the straight bays of the choir and the rest of the church. See Wilson (1985) 60–66. See also Hoey (1997) who stresses the symbolic implications of rib vaults over parochial choirs. Durham itself did not intend, at the outset, to vault the south transept or the nave, see Bony (1954) and Thurlby (1993).

18. Illustrations of these vaults and many others can be found in Aubert, (1934) extrait, 19, 41, 45, etc.

CHAPTER I

1. Bilson, *loc. cit.* (Note 7 to Introduction). Bilson's chronology of the vaults, and of the whole cathedral, still stands, though Bony has introduced a number of refinements. Within Bilson's 'First Great Campaign of Construction', which lasted from August 1093 to September 1104, and which extended up to the easternmost major piers of the nave, Bony (1990) isolated a first major stage (1093–c.1095) consisting of the outer walls of the choir and the eastern walls of the transepts, and the choir free-standing piers, all up to but not including the height of the aisle vaults. Bony (1954) also disentangled the changes in vaulting intention in the transepts; he pointed to the strongly Anglo-Saxon character of the cathedral (1981) and analyzed its precocious system of stonework planning (1990). James's (1983) attempt to break down the construction of the whole cathedral into about thirty campaigns, each lasting about a year, must be treated with caution, especially his conclusion that at the translation of St Cuthbert's shrine to the new choir in 1104 the eastern arm had no gallery, clerestorey or high vault. Nor does his argument that the choir high vault was sexpartite stand up to Thurlby's recent close analysis of the masonry around its thirteenth-century replacement. The choir vault, it seems, consisted of two four-part vaults per bay, each separated by a transverse arch (as the later Noyon Cathedral nave). See Thurlbay (1993) 45–6. Gardner (1982) disposed once and for all of the rationalist belief that the quadrant and diaphragm arches in the galleries acted as primitive flying buttresses. They were built mainly as supports for the original gallery roofs. Recent research on the stylistic, technical and constructional history of Durham by Fernie, Thurlby and others can be found in Jackson ed., (1993) and Rollason, Harvey and Prestwich, eds., (1994). See also, for a summing up of the issues, Reilly (1997) who underlines the mood of 'Anglo-Saxon revivalism' behind Bishop William of St Calais's new building.

1A. For the apse-echelon choir plan revealed at Saint-Etienne at Caen in the late 1960s excavations see Carlson (1971) and (1972), and Baylé, in Baylé dir., (1997) 56–61. It derived from the echelon arrangement at Bernay, and reappeared, under the influence of Saint-Etienne, at the monks' parish church of Saint-Nicholas at Caen (1080–90) and then in La Trinité at Caen (c.1080–90), Lessay (c.1098), Cérisy-la-Forêt (c.1090) and Saint-Georges at Saint-Martin-de-Boscherville (1120s). The starting date for Saint-Etienne is not clear, but Baylé, in Baylé dir., (1997) vol. 2, 56–61, considers that it was not underway until after the Norman Conquest in 1066, though the usual starting date it given as c.1063. Three dedications mark the progress of the work: 1073 (completion of the choir), 1077 (completion of crossing, transept and two eastern bays of nave) and 1081 (completion of nave), though the west façade was not begun in 1090, after a short break in the work. For eleventh-century Norman architecture see Liess (1967) and the contributions in the well-illustrated Baylé, dir., (1997) vols 1 and 2. For Saint-Nicholas at Caen see Baylé, in Baylé dir., (1997) vol. 2, 62–4.

1B. Frankl is right about the absence of rib-vaults in Caen before 1093, but scholarship has since been busy uncovering pre-1093 ribs further afield. An early group can be found in choir apses: S. Abbondio in Como (usually dated 1063–95), the south transept at Tewkesbury Abbey (1090s), the chapel of the transept crypt at Christchurch Priory, Hampshire (1090s) and, according to Wilson (1985) 60–5, in the original main choir apse of Gloucester (after 1089). Frankl tries to isolate such vaults from the history of early rib-vaulting by calling them 'transverse arches' (see Introduction, p. 41). In conception they may indeed be read as the continuation of transverse arches from groin-vaulted straight bays to the curving surface of the apse. But their position suggests that they were also conceived symbolically, as enlarged canopies or *ciboria* over a shrine or altar; and in this they belong to the conception of the diagonal rib in the strict sense, as a heavenly canopy demarcating the most sacred spaces, including whole choirs, transepts etc. As Wilson (1985) 64–5 suggests, rib vaulting may have originated in the apse of some eleventh-century great church and extended westwards to choirs and eventually naves. See also Introduction, Note 17b. Other early examples of rib vaults not mentioned by Frankl are in the ambulatory of Aversa Cathedral in southern Italy – see di Onofrio (1993) – and at Quimperlé in Brittany (both dated to the 1080s) – see Tillet (1982) 240–63. It is the concerted use of the rib, over a whole group of spaces, which makes Durham important. In this sense the critical parallels (or sources?) are St Mary's at Utrecht and the transepts of Speyer cathedral (1080s/90s) and the uncertainly dated Lombard vaults which may have been their sources of inspiration. See above, Introduction, Note 5d.

1C. The best analysis of La Trinité is by Baylé (1979) and a shorter summary by the same author in Baylé, dir., (1997) vol. 2, 50–55. She dates the choir's groin vault to the remodelling and extension of the original c.1060–80 church in c.1090, though its actual execution, on the evidence of capital carving, she postpones to the 1120s, when the choir apse had been finished. The same architect built the choir groin vault and then moved onto the rib vault over the crossing – see (1979) 62–4. See below, Chapter 1, Note 7a.

2. Ernst Gall, 'Neue Beiträge zur Geschichte vom Werden der Gotik', in *Monatshefte für Kunstwissenschaft*, IV (1911) 309. Froidevaux and Lelégard (1958) and Froidevaux (1966) suggested that the burial of the founder's son in the choir in 1098, and other eleventh-century references to the church, referred, not to the present building, but to the previous church of 1056–64, and that the present building could only have been begun c.1105. It was planned to have groin vaults, however the rib vaults were not additions to an

already-completed building but were afterthoughts realized during the construction of the upper parts of the choir and transepts. This post-1100 dating was accepted by Héliot (1959) and Bony (1976) 18. Recent opinion has accepted that the ribs are integral to the present church, but has re-instated the 1098 date for the vaults of the choir. The choir was begun *c.*1090, and the first campaign included the transept and the eastern bay of the nave, with the burial in the present choir in 1098. After a break in the work, construction on the nave was resumed, but finished only in 1140. The ribs are therefore exactly contemporary with, but probably conceived independently of, Durham. See Baylé (1979) 61, note 11, and Baylé, in Baylé, dir., (1997) vol. 1, 57–8, and vol. 2, 97–100. Doubts about the early date are still, however, expressed by Grant (1994a) 118, 126–7, who points to their isolated position (if dated to *c.*1100). Their rectangular bay shape, relates them, she argues, to the later vaults at Evreux (after 1120) and Saint-Georges at Saint-Martin-de-Boscherville (after 1114). However, her premise that the earliest Norman and Anglo-Norman rib vaults developed first over squarish bays and only later graduated to the less stable rectangular, was written too early to take account of Thurlby's (1993) convincing reconstruction of the choir high vaults at Durham not as sexpartite, but as rectangular and quadripartite. See above, Chapter 1, Note 1, and below, Chapter 1, Note 23a.

3. Charles H. Moore, 'The Aisle Vaults of Winchester Transept', in *The Architectural Journal*, XXIII (1916) 313. The best recent treatments of Romanesque Winchester hardly discuss these vaults, see Gem (1983) and Crook (1993).

4. G. Lanfry, 'Salle capitulaire romane de l'abbaye de Jumièges', in *B.M.*, XCIII (1934) 323. This should, of course, read 'Salle capitulaire gothique'. Lanfry placed the chapter house in the first years of the abbacy of Urso (1101–27) who was the first to be buried there. Bony (1976) 18 and note 11, and (1983) 10–11, and note 7, and others put the building much later, to the 1120s. Baylé, in Baylé, dir., (1997) vol. 1, 74, however, dates the main structure of the chapter house to around 1100, and sees the vaults as later additions. She relates them to those in the choir of Saint-Paul at Rouen (also inserted into an earlier structure).

5. Ernst Gall, 'Die Abteikirche St Lucien bei Beauvais', in *Wiener Jahrbuch für Kunstgeschichte*, IV (XVII) (1926) 59. Recent research accepts Gall's conclusion that the church was vaulted throughout, but not in the way he suggested. Henriet (1983) concluded that the side aisles were not groin- but rib-vaulted (excavations revealed rib fragments with torus profiles similar to those at Saint-Etienne, Beauvais and Morienval). He was not certain if the high vaults were ribs. Gardner (1980) and (1986) believed that there were ribbed high vaults. The issue is important, for if the choir was complete by 1109, as all recent authorities suggest, and if it had rib vaults, especially over the central aisle, then it must count among the earliest rib-vaulted buildings in northern France. The rib fragments, however, look as if they belong to the 1120s/30s. Fons (1975) was not available to me.

5A. For Peterborough see Reilly (1997a) 13–86, who re-dates the choir to the period of Abbot Ernulf (1107–14) and discusses its debts to Anselm's choir in Canterbury and Durham. For Southwell see Pevsner and Metcalf (1985b) 301–23.

6. Jules Fossey, *Monographie de la cathédrale d'Evreux* (Evreux, 1898). The reconstruction appears opposite p. 23 and in illustrations 14 and 27. Not all vaulting shafts at Evreux were set frontally, as Frankl states. Nineteenth-century excavations showed that the straight bays of the twelfth-century choir had diagonally planned responds, see Bony (1976) 20. Grant (1987) 53ff, and (1994a) 118, 126, believes that the post-1119 church was rib-vaulted, Salet (1980) 306–7, suggested that the ribs might have been confined to the choir. The reconstruction of the cathedral, burned in 1119, began probably in the mid-1120s.

7. *C.A.*, LXXV (1909) 1, 12, says of these ellipses that they were 'plus ou moins voulu(s)'. This would mean that the architect set out from semicircles on the walls. It is not known how elliptical centering was constructed at this time.

7A. Surviving mid-eleventh-century masonry in the lower parts of the straight bays of the choir, in the lower parts of the transepts, and in the nave up to and including the first arch order of the piers, has allowed Baylé (1979) 11–18, 38–9, 45–9, 59–67, to establish the following sequence of construction:
1) **The late eleventh-century church** was begun *c.*1059/60; choir complete by 1066; nave finished by second dedication of 1077; Queen Matilda buried in the choir in 1083; westwork complete by *c.*1090. This church was a thin-walled construction with a high wooden roof and groin vaults in the aisles.
2) **A wholesale remodelling of this church** began in the 1080s and 1090s, no doubt inspired by the increase in the scale and ambition of Norman building either side of the channel after the Conquest. This included: a) *c.*1090, the insertion of the crypt (dated by its capitals) and b) *c.*1100–1110: the beginning of the remodelling of the apse, the straight bays of the choir, and the reconstruction of the façade between the towers.
3) *c.*1125–30: **completion of the apse** and upper parts of the choir. Vaulting begins, first with choir groin vault, then rib vaults of crossing, and transepts

and nave. To support the new vaults the walls of the transepts and nave were also remodelled with the present overlay of shafts and dosserets, and with blind arcades and a clerestorey passage.
See also Baylé, in Baylé, dir., (1997) vol. 1, 61, vol. 2, 50–5.

8. Auguste Charles Pugin and John Le Keux (ed. John Britton), *Historical and descriptive Essays etc.* (London, 1841) plate III.

9. This is why the hypothesis that I put forward in *Festschrift Heinrich Wölfflin* (Munich, 1924) 107, was wrong. The present transverse arches do indeed look like diaphragm arches, but there is no way of knowing if the nave of Matilda's church had them. For Baylé (1979) 55, 64–7, their original presence 'cannot be totally excluded'. For other 'false sexpartite vaults' in Normandy, all followers of La Trinité, see Baylé, in Baylé, dir., (1997) vol. 1, 61–3. They include Saint-Samson at Ouistreham and the priory of Saint-Gabriel. Interestingly, Grant (1994a) 128, suggests that the latter, and the more conventional Caen-derived six-part vaults at Saint-Martin de Creully, may be connected with a possible initiative of Henry I's son, Robert of Gloucester, in the re-vamping of La Trinité and these smaller churches, an initiative designed to invest in Caen as the Angevin capital of Normandy.

9A. Despite the difficulties of reconstructing the upper parts of the 1060s nave (remodelled in the 1120s and almost totally rebuilt in the mid-nineteenth century) Baylé (1979) 46–9, 62–4, considered that the skeleton of the old elevation was kept and thickened in the twelfth-century rebuilding. She thinks the old elevation probably had half-columns on dosserets rising to the clerestorey, and may have looked something like Mont-Saint-Michel, Lessay, or Saint-Nicholas at Caen. Baylé, in Baylé, dir., (1997) vol. 2, 51, suggests that the second storey would have resembled Bernay's, with double openings onto the interior and relieving arches behind them (still visible under the aisle roofs on the nave's back wall).

10. For details, cf. the two books by Ernst Gall quoted in the bibliography. See now Carlson (1968) 142–3, who dates the very accurate rebuilding of the high vaults to 1616–18.

10A. Carlson (1968) 113–14, and (1976) 11ff, dated the vaults of the nave of Saint-Etienne to *c.*1128–35. Baylé (1979) 67ff, on a stylistic analysis of the vault capitals of La Trinité, considered that the Saint-Etienne vaults preceded those of La Trinité, and in (1987) dated the former to 1110–15. Grant (1994a) 127, however, arrived at an 1120s date for Saint-Etienne by comparison with a securely dated building, the castle of Falaise, rebuilt from 1123. She considered the Trinité vaults to be a different workshop than those of Saint-Etienne. The later dating of La Trinité is confirmed by Kahn's (1991) 117–23, convincing argument that a La Trinité workshop was active at Canterbury in the 1150s, but this means that Kahn dates the La Trinité work to only shortly before that at Canterbury (i.e the late 1140s?). Baylé, in Baylé, dir., vol. 1 (1997) 72, 73, 77–8, points up the possible importance of the destroyed Romanesque cathedral of Bayeux, begun *c.*1100, as a second centre, parallel with Caen, for the diffusion of expertise in rib vaulting.

10B. Whichever date we give the Saint-Etienne vaults, La Trinité's are probably the later, see above, Note 10a. Frankl's suggestion that the pseudo-sexpartite system of La Trinité resulted from a conceptual combination of the diaphragm arches of its original nave (rebuilt in the 1130s) with the early twelfth-century rib system is an ingenious one, but it must remain hypothetical as long as we know so little about the original covering of Matilda's church. See above, Chapter 1, Note 9. Diaphragm arches were, however, a feature of Norman Romanesque, see the naves at Jumièges and Saint-Vigor at Bayeux.

11. Ernst Gall, in *Monatshefte für Kunstwissenschaft*, IV (1911) 309. Baylé (1979) 62–4, dates the rib vault of the crossing tower to the same period as those of the transept and nave, and not significantly later.

11A. A (just) earlier example of pointed arches in conjunction with rib vaults is the nave at Durham, vaulted 1128–1133.

12. John Bilson, 'The Beginnings of Gothic Architecture', in *Journal of the Royal Institute of British Architects*, VI (1899) illustration on p. 294. Wilson (1985) 62 and note 60, points out that these arches are not wall arches, as Bilson (and Frankl) called them, but rear-arches. Moreover the arch in question may be pointed only as the chance result of crude execution, as the rounded top of the corresponding arch on the other side of the same bay suggests. Wilson proposes Burgundian First Romanesque as a source of these unconventional types of arch. The arches date sometime between the foundation of the choir in 1089 and its dedication in 1100.

13. G. Mongeri, 'Bramante e il Duomo', *Archivo storico Lombardo* (1878) 542.

14. The Pseudo-Raphael theory and the survival of the theory of the origin of the Gothic style in the forests are discussed in Frankl (1960) 271ff, and in Julius Vogel, *Bramante und Raffael* (Leipzig, 1910) 108.

15. See above, Note 12 to Introduction.

16. In *C.A.*, XCII (1929) 497, Marcel Aubert assumes this date to be correct. Raymond Rey, in *L'art gothique du Midi etc.* (Paris, 1934) gives the date as 1115–20, and says that the work was begun under Roger's predecessor and finished in 1120.

The porch was begun c.1110–15. The suggestion of Vidal et al. (1979) 44–9, that the core of the porch was begun and its vaults completed under Abbots Hunaud of Gavaret (1072–85) and Ansquitil (1085–1115) makes the vaults almost implausibly early. Its exterior stone cladding and crenellations were built during the abbacy of Roger (1115–31). See Durliat (1966). Another early example of rib vaults made up entirely of pointed arches is the nave at Durham begun in 1128 and completed by 1133.

16A. Precise dates for the Gloucester vaults are uncertain. Bony (1976) note 8, assumes that they post-date the fire of 1122. Pevsner and Metcalf (1985b) 141, simply call the north aisle vault 'Norman'. Wilson (1985) 73 and note 112, concluded that the work of Abbot Serlo (up to c.1100) did not intend vaulted nave aisles, and that after a protracted pause in the nave construction (caused perhaps by the fire of 1102?) a revision of the design was made, entailing the use of rib vaults throughout the nave.

16B. But note the keystones in the contemporary crypt of Saint-Gilles-du-Gard, see below, Chapter 1, Notes 21, 22a.

17. Lefèvre-Pontalis, L'architecture religieuse dans l'ancien diocèse de Soissons etc. (Paris, 1894) 192. This is a correct reconstruction from the plan originally published in B.M., LXXII (1908) 477ff.

18. The whole upper part of the apse dates from the fourteenth century, and the vaults in the transepts and the nave were built in 1652.

18A. The ambulatory might really be called a 'pseudo-ambulatory', the closest parallels being the ground floor passage in the apse of La Trinité at Caen (c.1120–30) and the destroyed choir apse of Notre-Dame at Soissons, begun c.1130. See Barnes (1976) Bony (1983) 19–20, and Sandron (1998) 157.

19. Some of the photographs which have been published are not clear, and references given here are incomplete, since these details indicate only one experiment among many within the general development.

20. Although the ambulatory and choir aisles at Saint-Lucien at Beauvais may have had rib vaults, see above, Chapter 1, Note 5. Bony (1983) 20, 26, 29, gives Morienval a later date than earlier scholarship – in the 1130s and 1140s – after the first campaign at Saint-Etienne at Beauvais. Gardner (1986a) 9, put it c.1125–30. His article provides a useful survey of 'proto-Gothic' in the Ile-de-France and Picardy in the second quarter of the twelfth century. Two other contemporary, but destroyed, churches in the Paris region may have had rib-vaulted ambulatories: Saint-Magloire in Paris (finished by 1138) and Saint-Etienne at Dreux (begun early 1130s), see Gardner (1984).

21. Walter Horn, Die Fassade von St Gilles (Hamburg, 1937). Richard Hamann, Die Abteikirche von St Gilles etc. (Berlin, 1955), however, thinks that these events do not prove an interruption of the building (p. 74 and passim). Schapiro (1935) concurred with Hamann on this. However, Stoddard (1973) 135, considered that the turbulent history of the abbey from 1116 to 1125 or to 1132 meant either a delay in starting the new work on the crypt, or that the work progressed very slowly.

22. Hamann, op. cit., 42.

22A. Stoddard (1973) 127–59, summing up the conclusions of Horn and Hamann, arrived at the following sequence for the crypt: begun sometime after 1096. Superstructure (including all groin and rib vaults) begun at west end after 1116, and worked eastwards; the west wall complete by 1129 (see Schapiro (1935)) but work proceeded slowly, finishing in the 1130s or early 1140s. The crypt was certainly finished by 1142, because the practice of inscribing on the west wall ceased in that year, implying that the present triple portal design of the west façade was established by then, see Ferguson O'Meara (1980).

22B. But note Borg (1972) 122–6, who argued that when work finished on the crypt the upper church was begun from west to east, and that given the uniqueness in Provence of the choir's ground plan, it could hardly have been undertaken before c.1150.

22C. But Hamann (1955) 58–9, considered that rib vaults were intended in the choir aisles and chapels from the start.

22D. The Speyer rib vaults are minutely described and analyzed by Kubach and Haas (1972) 357–8, 371–2, 512, 779–82. They advance the post-1159 date. Von Winterfeld (1988) and (1988a) puts them to the Henry IV period on two grounds. Firstly, the ribs are an integral part of the wall arches and upper parts of the transepts, and could not have been inserted after 1159 without damage to the surrounding masonry (damage which does not exist). And secondly, masons's marks on the ribs tally with marks in the Afra chapel, a building which must have been finished by Henry IV's temporary interment there in 1106. Note also the contemporary band ribs in St Mary at Utrecht, a building associated with Henry IV, and re-dated by Kidson (1996) to the 1090s. See Chapter 1, Note 5d.

22E. Although Italian-looking, the similar Lombard ribs are notoriously difficult to date. See above, Introduction, Notes 5d, 6. Kidson (1996) 134, suggests the ribs of S. Nazaro in Milan, which he dates to 1075–93, as a candidate. But McKinne (1985) 238–47 attributes them to a campaign active in 1112, and perhaps extending into the second half of the twelfth century.

22F. In 1979–81 dendrochronological analysis of medieval fragments of wooden scaffolding poles has permitted the following chronology:

1) east choir begun c.1120/25, vaulting finished c.1140
2) north wall of nave, up to but not including clerestorey, complete by 1161/2
3) consecration in 1181
4) completion of west choir by 1192.
See von Winterfeld (1988a) and Schütz and Müller (1989) 203–8.

23. Rudolph Kautzsch, 'Die ältesten deutschen Rippengewölbe', in Paul Clemen Festschrift (Düsseldorf, 1926) 304. The Alsatian churches are discussed in greater detail by the same author in Der romanische Kirchenbau im Elsass (Freiburg im Breisgau, 1944). No definitive study of the form of these rib-vaults has been made, but a great deal can be deduced from the excellent illustrations in Kautzsch's book. Feld (1961) 242ff, dated most of these vaults to the middle of the twelfth century or later: SS Peter and Paul, Hirsau c.1125–30, Frauenkirche in Magdeburg c.1150, Murbach c.1160, St Johann in the third quarter of the twelfth century. But the recent re-dating of the Speyer and Worms vaults to half a century earlier has altered the whole picture of High Romanesque architecture in Germany. In any case, the vaults of the Hirsau church have always been anchored in the 1120s. The Petersberg in Erfurt vaults must be between 1127 and 1147 – see Schütz and Müller (1985) 226–8 and Badstübner (1985) 131. Those in Magdeburg are part of a western block begun after 1129 and completed after the middle of the twelfth century – see Dehio (1974) 280–2. St Johann is now dated c.1140–50 – see Schütz and Müller (1985) 226–8. The Murbach vaults are put at 1122–34, though the original intention here may have been a barrel-vaulted choir, see Schütz and Müller (1985) 262–3. Thus many of Kautzsch's 'early' dates have now been vindicated.

23A. Bilson's (1922) chronology of the Durham vaults is still widely accepted: choir aisles before 1100; choir high vaults by 1104; north transept by 1115; south transept c.1125–8; high vaults of nave 1128–33. Bony (1954) argued that only the choir was originally intended to be vaulted; the transepts (north begun 1093–1104, the south a little later) and the east double bay of the nave were intended to have their central aisles covered by wooden roofs. Thurlby (1993) has shown that the north transept was intended to be vaulted from the start; only the south transept envisaged a wooden roof, which was changed to the present vault. By 1104 the nave had been built up to the easternmost double bay, and a single bay of the gallery on both sides. The rest was completed under Bishop Ranulf 'Flambard', and the vaults were built between 1128 and 1133. James's (1983) suggestion that only the apse vault of the choir had been completed by 1104 is not convincing, and his reconstruction of the original choir high vault as sexpartite has been convincingly rejected by Thurlby (1993) 45–7. For Durham see above, Introduction, Notes 5a, 5c, 17a, 17b, and Chapter 1, Note 1.

23B. From the late 1950s Pacquet (1963) recovered the straight-ended plan of the original choir of Saint-Etienne. Hearn (1971) 193–5, identified it as a copy of the choir plan of Romsey Abbey in England (begun c.1120) and therefore dated its beginning to 1125. Like the transepts and nave, it was almost certainly rib-vaulted. Still the fullest account of the building history and its stylistic affiliations is provided by Henwood-Reverdot (1982) 84–132, who isolates four campaigns.

1) **begun in c.1120** (on the assumption that its rib vaults in the choir derived from the rib-vaulted transept of Saint-Lucien at Beauvais, of c.1115). Choir probably finished by 1132.

2) **c.1130** transepts (originally to be unvaulted) and first bay of nave.

3) **c.1130–40** next three bays of nave and upper parts of transepts, including the vaulting and the construction of the north rose window c.1150.

4) **early thirteenth century**, last two bays of nave and façade. High vaults of nave.

See also Bideault and Lautier (1987) 96–104, who follow roughly the same sequence. They date the nave high vaults to c.1220–35. McGee (1986) correctly doubts the circumstantial stylistic evidence for the 1120/25 date for the beginning of the choir, but his attempt to date the choir, transepts and first bay of the nave in a single campaign from 1075/80 to c.1100, based on equally circumstantial historical evidence and on impressionistic stylistic comparison, has found no followers. In effect, it would mean dating the north transept rose about forty years before its real model, the western rose of Saint-Denis!

23C. These keeled mouldings count among the earliest in Europe. Other early examples are to be found in England (Durham Chapter House ribs, c.1135; Fountains Abbey, East Guest House piers and ribs, c.1155) and in northern France (ribs of the Saint-Denis narthex, c.1135; Bertaucourt-les-Dames, west end of nave, c.1135–40/50; Saint-Martin-des-Champs, Paris, ambulatory, c.1140–5). See Fergusson (1984) 51, note 78; and Hearn (1971) 195.

24. It was destroyed in 1945, but is now being rebuilt.

25. The start of the Saint-Germer choir has been put by Pessin (1978) and Carlson (1986) in the mid- to late 1150s. But Henriet (1985) has made out a convincing case for a beginning c.1135. He dates the eastern portions of the building (choir, transept and two eastern bays of the nave) c.1135–c.1165. After a brief hiatus during the abbacy of Hildegaire II (1167–72), a second campaign saw the completion of the six remaining nave bays and the western block. The

latter (destroyed in the Hundred Years War) was complete just before 1206. Henriet's authoritative analysis is broadly followed by Bideault and Lautier (1987) 293–302. There are early examples of contiguous radiating chapels at La Trinité at Fécamp (1106) and Avranches cathedral (1121), but it was Saint-Germer that seems to have popularized this type of chevet for Early Gothic Parisian churches: Saint-Magloire (complete by 1138) and Saint-Denis (1140–4), with an outlier at Notre-Dame Avénières near Le Mans (begun c.1140). It was also adopted at Saint-Maclou in Pontoise, Saint-Germain-des-Prés in Paris, and Senlis and Noyon Cathedrals. See also Gardner (1984) 88–91, notes 24–6, and Bony (1983) 49–53.

25A. For the debt to Normandy see Lohrmann (1973) and Henriet (1985) 113ff. Wilson (1990) 29, points to Cluniac Burgundian influence in the shelf supporting the clerestorey passage.

25B. For the appearance of the pointed arch in western Europe in the late eleventh century see Bony (1983) 17–19.

25C. The history of the building of Cluny III is a battleground of conflicting opinion. The lifelong researches of K. J. Conant are gathered together in Conant (1968). His conclusions were challenged by Salet (1968) in a careful examination of the existing south-west transept. For a judicious summary of the arguments see Lehmann (1976), who gives the relevant bibliography to that date. An even fuller account of the controversy and the literature (but not including the narthex) is given by Armi (1983) especially 22–3 and Appendix 4.

26. Conant (1974, 2nd edn) 219, dated the two eastern vaults to 'possibly as early as 1132', and the rest in the narthex bay to about 1220. In Conant (1968) 111, he called attention to a statute of 1146 mentioning 'new work', which might refer to the narthex construction. On pp. 152–3, he suggested a date of 'c.1145–55?' for the completion of the two eastern bays, and c.1177ff for the western bays. In both works he saw parallels with early rib-vaulted buildings in the Ile-de-France (Saint-Martin-des-Champs, Paris). Salet (1968) 288–9, admitted that the narthex was begun under Peter the Venerable in 1132/5, but underlined that it was not finished until the reign of Abbot Roland de Hainaut (1220–8), and argued that its vaults could not date before the very end of the twelfth century. Branner (1960) 30, 130, and Schlink (1970) 89ff, and 96–7 suggested c.1170 for the ribs of the two eastern bays, and argued that they represent a change of plan from an intended barrel vault. Kennedy (1996) 39–48, however, convincingly refutes the idea of a change of plan, and argues that the two eastern bays of the narthex, including the vaults, followed soon after the completion of the west portal, that is, c.1130–40. She also points to close stylistic and historical connexions with Ile-de-France early rib-vaulted buildings, e.g. Saint-Germer-de-Fly and Saint-Martin-des-Champs in Paris.

26A. See above, Chapter 1, Notes 22D, 22E, 22F.

27. These and other works, such as Cambronne-les-Clermont, Bellefontaine, etc., are discussed in Aubert, Croisées d'ogives. On the fascinating churches at Bernières-sur-Mer, Creuilly, Ouistreham, etc., see Gall (1915) 38ff. What is called Early Gothic in that work, however, is called Transitional in the present book. For the nave at Bury see Bideault and Lautier (1987) 110–17. For Poissy, started probably c.1140–5, see Salet (1951). For the choir of Saint-Maclou at Pontoise, also a follower of Saint-Denis, see Lefèvre-Pontalis (1919) 76–99.

28. Frankl (1960) 531. See Dallaway (1806), whose work was not known to Frankl, but is mentioned in Watkin (1980) 56–8, and by Clark (1986) 105. All problems relating to Saint-Denis must now be seen in the light of Crosby's (1987) monograph.

28A. However, Gardner (1984a) has shown that the western block is the work of not one, but two architects. All the upper chapels above their lowest stone courses, and the upper parts of the ground floor of the eastern bay, were designed by a second architect, who was identical to the designer of the choir. Crosby (1987) 161, also noted stylistic differences between the lower and upper floors. His book provides the most detailed description of the western block and a reconstruction of its original appearance before the eighteenth- and nineteenth-century alterations, see (1987) 121–213. Grant (1998) 253–4, considers the break in the western block is not as clear-cut as Gardner thought, that many of the features of the second, choir, master also appear in the ground floor of the western block, and that 'it is at least arguable that all the remaining fabric of the work at Saint-Denis is the work of a single architect'. This argument presupposes, however, a single architect's ability radically to change his mode of design. In an extraordinary book, van der Meulen and Speer (1993) 173ff, state (without any further archeological or visual justification) that the present west end is essentially a Carolingian work, its portals are subsequent additions, which in no way bond in with the surrounding stonework, and its central portal is made up of spolia from the Carolingian period. The absurdity of this proposition needs no comment, but see below, Chapter 2, Note 5F.

29. On Suger's writings, see Erwin Panofsky, Abbot Suger on the Abbey Church of St Denis and its Art Treasures (Princeton, 1979) For the upper chapels see 44–5, 96–9. Frankl (1960) chapter 1, 1; and Marcel Aubert, Suger (Paris, 1950). Suger's artistic aims, and his motives for rebuilding Saint-Denis, have

provoked a wealth of interpretation. Apart from Panofsky (1979) passim, and von Simson (1956 and 1962) 61–141, a new generation of scholars have elevated Suger himself as the critical link between his new Gothic church and (a) Capetian kingship – Spiegel (1986) and Lewis (1986); (b) personal expiation – Maines (1986); (c) monastic reform – Rudolph (1990) and (d) neo-Platonic allegory, particularly the mystical theology of the Pseudo-Dionysius – Zinn (1986), Binding and Speer eds., (1993) and (1996) and Neuheuser (1993). See below, Part Two, Note 7b. The theological and liturgical picture of Suger presented by this largely art historical research is at odds with the more worldly and pragmatic image of Suger reconstructed by Grant (1998).

30. Not all the ribs have the same profile; also part of the vault has been restored. Apart from Crosby's (1987) photogrammetric analysis of the western block, pp. 121–79, the most recent discussion of the west façade can be found in Gardner (1984a) passim, and Clark (1986) 105–7. They all hold that the whole façade above the portal zone was the creation of the second architect. The rib profile Frankl is referring to is found in the high vault of the central east bay of the narthex, see Crosby (1987) 149, figure 57d.

30A. Gardner (1984a) 586, considers the first architect to have begun construction of the façade in c.1134, and the second to have appeared c.1135/6. Crosby (1987) 123–4, suggests that preparation for building could have been started in the early 1130s, but a beginning might have been delayed until about 1135. In his Testament of 1137, Suger tells us that he has built a new domus hospitum (in the western claustral range), a new refectory, a new dormitory, and begun the western block. See Grant (1998) 241–5. The eastern ambulatory bay of Saint-Martin-des-Champs in Paris, begun c.1135, has pointed rib vaults.

30B. For a reconstruction of Saint-Lucien's façade and its probable influence see Gardner (1986) 93–100. The origins and classification of the Saint-Denis façade have been much discussed. A convenient summing up of the evidence, and an argument for a strong Anglo-Norman influence in the formation of the north French Gothic west façade can be found in McAleer (1984) and at greater length in McAleer (1963). For a geometrical analysis of the Saint-Denis façade see Crosby (1987) 175–9. For its symbolic character see: Crosby (1987) 179, and notes 20, 21, p. 487; von Simson (1962) 108–11; Kimpel and Suckale (1985) 80–4. Its connexions to Carolingian and Ottonian westworks were underlined by Crosby (1965) 67.

31. Illustrated in Ernst Gall, Die gotische Baukunst etc. (Leipzig, 1925) fig. 14 on p. 48, and the stage before the restoration by Debret in the first half of the nineteenth century, ibid., plate 28. See now Crosby (1970) and (1987) 179–213, and the meticulous studies by Blum (1986) 199–227, and (1992).

31A. For the eighteenth- and nineteenth-century restorations to the façade see Clark (1986) 105–6, and Crosby (1987) 167–70. The crenellations, which, contrary to Frankl, are part of the original project, were symbolically suitable for the façade as an image of the Porta Coeli, and might even have been seen as having a potentially real defensive role, see Gardner (1984b) 97–123. Crosby (1987) 172, fig. 72, and 175, fig. 74, was wrong to reconstruct the buttress tops as rectangular in section when all pre-restoration views show they were, as at present, rounded, see Wyss, dir., (1996) 51–65.

31B. For the alterations to the rose at Saint-Denis and its putative twelfth-century appearance, see Crosby (1987) 170–4. During the restorations that began in 1837 under Debret the Evangelist symbols were added in the spandrels, and probably are not reflections of any medieval arrangement, whereas the head and leaf ornament of the rose's mouldings are probably recarvings of the originals. See the excellent dossier of drawings and texts relating to Saint-Denis assembled by Wyss (1996) especially 50–70. The relationship between the Saint-Etienne façade and that of Saint-Lucien at Beauvais is discussed by Gardner (1986) 94–5. Hearn (1971) 195, and Henwood-Reverdot (1982) 123–32, date the Saint-Etienne rose to c.1150, a little later than Saint-Denis's. The iconography of the Beauvais rose, as a wheel of fortune, is discussed in context by Beyer (1962) and Mersmann (1982) 68–72. Hardy (1983) and Beretz (1989) were not available to me.

32. The blind arcades on each of the four buttresses probably date from the nineteenth century. Crosby (1987) 170, confirms that they were added by Debret in 1838.

33. Of the figures, six heads have been preserved, two in the Walters Art Gallery, Baltimore, one in the Fogg Art Museum, Harvard University, Cambridge, Mass., and three in the Musée National du Moyen Age in Paris. For the latter see Pressouyre (1976) 151–60, and for the column figures in general see Crosby (1987) 192–201, and Williamson (1995) pp. 11–12.

33A. Earlier literature on the sculpture is given in Sauerländer (1972) 379–83. A short, well-informed introduction to the problems can be found in Williamson (1995) 11–14. Influential iconographical interpretations of the statue-columns in terms of regnum and sacerdotium were put forward by Katzenellenbogen (1964) 27–34, and followed by Hearn (1981) 192–7. The fullest analysis is by Gerson (1970), part of which appeared in (1986) 183–98. See also a penetrating analysis of the themes of royalty in the façade and the sculpture by Hoffmann (1985), and a Pseudo-Dionysian interpretation of the left portal by Blum (1986) 199–227, who also reconstructs the famous mosaic tympanum of this portal (now lost) as a Coronation of the Virgin. An outline of research up to the late 1980s on the iconography of the portals is given in Crosby (1987) 179–213. For the genesis and meaning of the column figure see Sauerländer (1994a).

33B. For the left portal of the west façade and its mosaic see Blum (1986) 209–18.

34. Camille Enlart, *Monuments religieux etc. dans la région picarde* (Paris, 1895); and in greater detail in *C.A.*, XCIX (1937) 459; Gall, *op. cit.* (1925) plate 27. Aubert (1934) 58.

35. Vallery-Radot, in *C.A.*, LXXXIX (1927) 499; Bilson (1917) 1–35, dated the octopartite vault in the crossing (now hidden by a vault added below it in 1648) as 'c.1140'. No further investigation has, as far as I know, altered Bilson's date. Its closest parallel, as Bilson noted, is the eight-part vault in the treasury at Canterbury Cathedral, constructed under Prior Wibert after 1153, and dated by, among others, Kahn (1991) 108–23, to c.1155–60. Kahn notes a 'family similarity' between the Canterbury vaults and their profiles, and those of La Trinité at Caen, and she convincingly argues for the presence of sculptors from La Trinité working for Prior Wibert at Canterbury. This tallies with the influence of La Trinité at Montivilliers in the 1140s, see Chapter 1, Note 36 below.

36. Such diaphragms also exist at Bernières-sur-Mer (illustrated in Gall (1915) plate 35). Gall dates this building as earlier than the vaults of the nave at Durham, i.e. before 1128. Gall's pre-1128 date for Bernières is almost certainly too early. Baylé, in Baylé, dir., (1997) vol. 1, 61–3, associates the small group of false sexpartite vaults in Normandy – Saint-Samson at Ouistreham, Bernières and the priory church of Saint-Gabriel – with the influence of the vaults of La Trinité at Caen, which she puts in the 1130s. She also (74–6) confirms Frankl's connexions between the Montivilliers vaults and La Trinité in the exact similarities of their rib profiles (especially in the Caen transepts, where also the division of the end bays into five-part vaults parallels the north transept end bay at Montivilliers). See above, Chapter 1, Note 9.

37. Enlart, *op. cit.*, 132; M. Aubert in *C.A.*, XCIX (1937) 209. Aubert's dates of c.1150–70 for these choir vaults are probably too late. The year 1152, when an important donation was made to the church, may be a *terminus ante quem* for the vaults, which do not, despite Aubert's observations, seem to be of different dates in different bays, nor to have been inserted as afterthoughts into the completed choir. They go with the rest of the choir and the eastern crossing piers, which Gardner (1986a) 11, has related stylistically to the choir of Saint-Julien at Marolles-en-Brie, c.1125–35 and the nave of Saint-Lucien at Bury (c.1130–5).

38. Aubert (1934) 42. The function of the transverse arches in the towers is to strengthen the structure against the vibration when the bells are rung. For these vaults see above, Introduction, Note 5C.

38A. For Angoulême and Saint-Front at Périgueux see Conant (1974, 2nd edn.) 286–8, 289–90.

38B. The tower was constructed in a single campaign from 1130 to 1180, see Connolly (1980).

38C. According to Mussat (1963) 95–107, and (1981), the choir was rebuilt from 1137 to c.1140, the transepts in c.1145 and the nave between c.1145/50 and 1158.

38D. Frankl is here using Georg Dehio's concepts of 'active' and 'passive' transition, first put forward in Dehio and von Bezold (1901) 257ff. Bony and Panofsky expressed reservations about the term 'transitional' in Bony (1963). The nationalistic and philosophical implications of the term are discussed by Sauerländer (1987). See also below, Part Two, Note 63a.

39. *C.A.*, LXXXII (1919) 33. See now Henriet (1978), and for its affiliations with Sens cathedral see Severens (1975).

CHAPTER 2

1. The choir of Saint-Denis, the first articulate manifestation of the Gothic style, has attracted a wealth of commentary since 1962. Still the best analysis of its formal qualities and its sources of inspiration are provided by Bony (1983) 39–40, 61–4, 90–5, and Bony (1986) 131–42, where the Roman and Early Christian sources are given proper weight. Kimpel and Suckale (1985) 76–92, placed the whole enterprise in a more historical, patron-led environment, discussing it in the context of Suger's organizational powers, his political horizons, and his economic reform of the abbey. Gardner (1984a) identified the presence of the choir master in the upper floor of the west end, see above, Chapter 1, Note 30. Clark (1986) gives a sane assessment of the issues and contributes many new insights, especially on the sequence of work on the choir. Clark (1995) was the first seriously to draw attention to the Merovingian *spolia* in Suger's new choir, and to their political implications. Crosby's (1987) monograph reconstructs the elevation of the choir, and publishes invaluable photogrammetric drawings, but otherwise says little new about the style, sequence of building, or 'meaning' of the east end. Van der Meulen and Speer's (1988) bizarre study on the history of the choir, from the Merovingians to Suger, is

almost worthless in its general conclusions, though it draws together points of specific interest. Some of their more outlandish propositions are considered below, Chapter 2, Note 5F, and see Chapter 1, Note 28A, above. James's (1993) attempt to uncover at least four different architects behind the design of the crypt and choir ignores the aesthetic unity of the whole design. His suggestion that the chapels were originally planned to have unribbed semi-domes rising to barrel vaults and supported on thick compound piers is inconsistent with the two architects' work at the west end, with Suger's desire to make his windows visible, and with contemporary Ile-de-France practice.

1A. Modern investigation has proved that there was in fact a slight deviation; cf. *B.M.*, LXIX (1905) 452. The vexed question of the geometry used so skilfully by Suger's architect is made more complex by the irregularities of the ambulatory, most notably the increasingly greater depth of the three easternmost chapels, which are struck from an arc whose centre is over 2 metres to the east of the principal centre for the arcs of the ambulatory columns and the other chapels. The first serious analysis of this system of different circles came from Crosby (1966) who offered a symbolic explanation, in the form of Ptolemy's *Almagest*. Kidson (1987) rejected wholesale the cosmic and symbolic dimensions of Crosby's geometry and proposed a thirteen-sided polygon as the 'ground-figure' for the chevet, arrived at by the use of triangulation, based ultimately on Heron of Alexandria's methods for calculating the sides of polygons. Van der Meulen and Speer (1988) 77–106, offered a minute analysis of the dimensional irregularities of the east end, at crypt and choir level, and explained some of them as stemming from the need to place the longitudinal axis of the new chevet in a compromise position exactly half way between the southward axis of the Carolingian (to them Merovingian) apse and the northward axis of Abbot Hilduin's (to them also Merovingian) extension to its east. The difficulty with all these analyses, especially van der Meulen's, is that they rely on inaccurate and outdated plans (in his case resulting in a misleadingly inaccurate calculation of the radial axes of the chevet buttresses in relation to the axes of the ambulatory pillars, see figs III, IV, V). But the new photogrammetric drawings of the crypt and the choir, published by Clark (1986) figs 12, 13, and Crosby (1987) plates 1, 2, album nos 1, 2, showed so much irregularity that neither was prepared to offer a geometrical analysis: see Clark (1986) 111, and Crosby (1987) 241. James (1993) tries to explain some of the geometrical oddities (notably the different axes of the chapel buttresses on the south side to those on the north) as the result of a change of architects, not of compromises with existing structures. The whole question needs investigation.

2. On Suger's indirect remarks, see Note 29 to Chapter 1.

2A. For some preliminary remarks on the liturgy of Saint-Denis, but with no mention of relics displayed in chapels, see Rasmussen (1986). Walters (1984) was not available to me.

3. An excellent account of the thirteenth-century remodelling is given by Bruzelius (1985).

4. An attempt of mine at a reconstruction has been published in Panofsky's book. A corrected version of this reconstruction may be expected in Crosby's work now in preparation.

Both Clark (1986) 114–15, and Crosby (1987) 280–5, and fig. 119, reconstruct the choir as a three-storey elevation reminiscent of the choir of Saint-Germain-des-Prés, with an arcade supported on columns, an unlit and unvaulted gallery of two subdivided openings per bay, and a small clerestory. Bony (1983) 95 and fig. 87, and Wilson (1990) 39–41, fig. 28, accept this reconstruction, though Wilson adds (I think correctly) flying buttresses. For the less convincing suggestions that it had fully vaulted tribunes, see Polk (1983) 34f, or that it had a four-storey elevation like Saint-Germer, see Kimpel and Suckale (1985) 98, and 481, note 6.

5. This source is most illuminating on technical questions; cf. Frankl (1960) Chapter 1.

5A. Bony (1983) 93–5, and 479, note 16, and Crosby (1987) 261, convincingly reconstruct four-part vaults over the high choir, but its deeper western bay may have had a six-part vault.

5B. Gardner (1984a) has argued that the second architect and his shop, responsible for the upper parts of the west block, was also the architect of the choir, see above, Chapter 1, Note 28A. For James's (1993) implausible proliferation of architects for the crypt and choir (no less than five!) see above, Chapter 2, Note 1.

5C. Recent research has doubted that the thirteenth-century remodelling was caused by structural failure in Suger's choir, see Bruzelius (1985) 82–3, and Crosby (1987) 260. Kimpel and Suckale (1985) 87–8 and Suckale (1990) still put the case for instability, but are not convincing. No signs of threatening distress can be seen in the existing parts of the Suger choir. And the reason for reinforcing the supports of the crypt after 1231 was not, as Suckale (1990) 75, argued, to support Suger's over-long bays, but to reinforce the much greater loads of the new, higher elevation. The fact that the apsidal pillars of the crypt were not reinforced at the same time does not prove (as Suckale suggests) that the greater weight of his new elevation did not figure in the new architect's calculations; on the contrary, it is evidence of a medieval understanding that straight bays, especially wide ones, are less stable than closely spaced apsidal arcades – hence the survival of the hemicycle bays and the collapse of the straight bay pillars in the choir of Beauvais.

5D. Branner (1965) 39–55, attributed the new choir not to Pierre de Montreuil, as Frankl and others had assumed, but to an unknown 'Saint-Denis master'. Pierre de Montreuil first appears at Saint-Denis as late as 1247, almost certainly as the leading architect. Branner's attribution has been almost unanimously accepted – see Bruzelius (1985) passim, but for no convincing reason Bouttier (1987) attributed the new work to Jean de Chelles. However, the transept façades of Saint-Denis look very different from Jean de Chelles's north transept at Notre-Dame in Paris.

5E. The symbolic associations of Suger's interest in light, and its supposed connexions with Denis the Pseudo-Areopagite, were first fully launched on the art historical world by Panofsky (1946, 1979, 2nd edn), and then elaborated by Sedlmayr (1950) and von Simson (1956 and 1962) into a consistent theory – that Dionysian light 'metaphysics' and Augustinian order were the fundamental theological impulses in the creation of French Gothic architecture. Their position has been refined by recent studies on the symbolic properties of stained glass. Grodecki (1958) and Grodecki and Brisac (1985) 17–27, examined the aesthetic interrelationships between architecture and glass. Gage (1982) emphasized the luminous darkness of Suger's glass, and related it to the 'negative theology' of the Pseudo-Denis. Büchsel (1983) connected Suger's symbolist mentality, and his descriptive vocabulary, to wider patterns of medieval exegesis. Zinn (1986) located the sources for his anagogic aesthetics not solely in the Pseudo-Denis, but in the neo-Platonism of the Parisian Victorines. Kidson (1987) doubted if Suger was in any serious sense a follower of the Pseudo-Denis. Grant (1998) 23–5, 270–1, thinks Suger had only a superficial understanding of Dionysian mysticism, and doubts the Dionysian inspiration often advanced for Suger's inscriptions on the west front. The whole issue is sensibly and comprehensively weighed up by Markschies (1995). For the important insights into Suger's patronage provided by the new critical edition of *De Consecratione*, edited by Binding and Speer (1996), see below, Part Two, Note 7B, where other relevant literature is also discussed.

5F. Few would now agree with Frankl that Gothic developed from the vault downwards. 'Proto-Gothic' articulation of the interior elevation into an arch–shaft system, creating a skeleton-like wall, coincides with unvaulted interiors, e.g. in late Anglo-Norman architecture. See Bony (1983) 22ff, and Wilson (1990) 16.

The 'Romanesque' character of the exterior of the Saint-Denis crypt and choir chapels may partly explain the extraordinary thesis of van der Meulen and Speer (1988) 63–77, 95–106, 201–40, 256–98: that Suger's crypt and choir are, in their essentials, a reconstruction of what Guibert of Nogent called a *turris* built at Saint-Denis by William the Conqueror sometime before 1087, and which collapsed soon after its completion. This 'tower', they argue, was really a choir, and consisted of the present seven radiating chapels and an ambulatory at crypt and choir level. Suger simply repaired the *turris* by keeping its old outer walls, enlarging its windows, and inserting rib vaults over the ambulatory and chapels. Suger, they contend, constructed new columns in the straight bays of the choir and apse, and supported them on pillars in the crypt (all these columns and supports are identified by most authorities as belonging to the post 1231 remodelling). The famously elegant free-standing columns in the ambulatory and their capitals are not twelfth-century pieces but classical *spolia*. The whole argument, pursued with relentless special pleading, is unconvincing. It ignores Crosby's (1987) 96–100, identification of eleventh-century masonry under the present north transept, which is more plausibly that of the tower. It has to spend twenty pages (212–29) trying to persuade the reader that the word 'tower' is just as suitable as the term 'choir' or 'sanctuary' to describe an eastern apse; but it also has to contend that the *turris* was not seen, in the strict sense, as part of the *ecclesia* since Guibert's description of the collapse says that 'no part of the church was damaged' (*nullam ecclesiae partem dum rueret laesit*)! How can the *turris* be at once the choir and yet not part of the church? Their argument does not explain why a structure as liturgically important as the choir had to wait fifty years for its reconstruction, nor does it begin to convince us that the smooth ashlar of the existing walls of the Suger choir are examples of eleventh-century masonry. If the pillars of the apse and choir straight bays are indeed Suger's then they have the earliest crocket capitals in Europe by some twenty or thirty years. The capitals of the ambulatory columns are clearly twelfth-century and not antique, though they imitate antique and Italianate precedents. The whole exercise, despite the seriousness of its scholarship, is fundamentally flawed.

6. E. Chartraire, *La cathédrale de Sens* (*P.M.*) (Paris, 1934) 12. Henriet's study of Sens (1982) especially 83–8, 146–8 and 167, note 194, dates the beginning of construction to 1140, but argues that preparations had been going on for some time, perhaps from before 1137. His conclusions provide a useful summary and criticism of earlier research on Sens, particularly that of Severens (1970) and (1975), though he is less convincing in his refusal to see the choir as the result of two distinct campaigns, the first Romanesque, the second Gothic.

For the Parisian sources of Sens, especially its ground plan, see Gardner (1984) 91ff.

6A. Until recently, it was commonly held that the choir of Sens was the result of two campaigns:

1) **an early, pre-1140 work**, comprising the north and south nave chapels and the ambulatory. These sections were seen as Burgundian in inspiration, and were intended to have groin vaults in the side aisles and possibly a barrel vault over the main space.

2) **A post-1140**, Saint-Denis-influenced Gothic campaign which substituted ribs for the old groin vaults and built the present hemicycle and choir elevation.

This view was advanced in detail by Severens (1970) and followed by Bony (1983) 66–8. But Henriet (1982) especially 108–20, has argued that the whole choir is the product of a single design by one architect. This is not accepted by Wilson (1990) 46.

6B. See Branner (1960) 181; Severens (1970) passim. For contrary opinions see Henriet (1982) 112–14, and Kimpel and Suckale (1985) 481, note 10. I cannot follow Henriet in his view that rib vaults were always intended.

6C. See above, Chapter 1, Note 39.

7. The original form of the windows is suggested in a drawing in Viollet-le-Duc, *Dictionnaire*, IX, 286 and fig. 9. There is a more complete drawing in Dehio, *K.B.*, plate 379, 1. For a reconstruction of the original clerestorey, and the dating of its thirteenth-century replacement, see Henriet (1982) 98–102, 128–40, fig. 6.

7A. For remarks on the proportions of Sens see von Simson (1962) 143–4, and Severens (1975) 200.

7B. See Clark (1987) 26, who suggests that the four-storey elevation, and particularly the trefoil-headed arcading of the third storey, was only decided on when work had reached gallery level (for him c.1170–85) and was not part of the original design. If he is right then Noyon's elevation derives from the earlier choir at Laon.

7C. The date of c.1150 for the beginning of the Noyon choir is now disputed. Until recently, the traditional chronology had been established by Seymour's classic monograph (1968, 2nd edn). Seymour located the earliest work in the chevet chapels, c.1145–50, after the completion, and under the influence, of the choir of Saint-Denis. These chapels were ready by c.1160. Construction moved from east to west. The ambulatory, choir tower bays, exterior tribune walls and the lower walls of the transepts and their elevation system he dated c.1160–70. The upper choir, the north and south transepts, the bishop's chapel (consecrated in 1183) and the eastern bay of the nave he dated to c.1170–85. Seymour's sequence and chronology was followed by Bony (1983) 106–7, 125. But Polk (1982) 61–102, on largely stylistic grounds, contrasted the 'primitive' forms of the ambulatory and chapels at Noyon with the more 'advanced' forms at Saint-Denis, and concluded that the Gothic choir was begun soon after the fire of 1131, and largely complete by the translation of St Eligius's relics in 1157. This early dating was followed by Kimpel and Suckale (1985) 121–3, 526, who proposed a west-to-east construction and pointed to similarities with the choir of Saint-Germer, begun soon after 1132 (see above, Chapter 1, Note 25). But the capital carving of the earliest phase at Noyon, in the ambulatory, is very similar to that in the twelfth-century choir and eastern aisles of the north transept at Laon cathedral, dated to 1155/60–c.1170 by Clark and King (1983) 52–3, and Seymour (1968) 53, figs 104–7. This suggests that Seymour's date of c.1145–60 for the first campaign is correct. Bideault and Lautier (1987) 246–70, support the west-to-east sequence for the choir, but date the start of the work to c.1148, under Bishop Baudoin II (1148–67). Remains of a curving sandstone wall on the exterior of the chevet may represent the foundations of Bishop Simon de Vermandois's abortive choir, begun soon after 1131. If so, it was to have had a chevet with non-projecting radiating chapels, like the later Thérouanne or Archbishop Samson's choir at Reims Cathedral. Bideault and Lautier's 'first campaign' lasts from c.1148–c.1165, and includes the whole choir. Seymour's dating of the transepts is confirmed by Prache (1978) 73–7, who sees connexions between them (and the first bay of the nave) and the Gothic work at Saint-Remi at Reims (c.1165/70–1185). See also Prache (1978a) 93–4. Bideault and Lautier (1987) 258ff., suggest that the transepts were laid out in their 'second campaign' (c.1165–85) and completed in their 'third campaign' (c.1180–90). For a discussion of the main points of contention up to the late 1980s see Prache (1987).

8. Adolf von Hildebrand, *Das Problem der Form*, translated into English by Max Friedrich Meyer and Robert Morris Ogden (New York, 1907), where this passage is translated: 'from the vertical front-plane into the background'.

9. Gall (1915) 21ff. Also Jean Bony, 'Technique normande du mur épais à l'époque romane', in *B.M.*, XCVIII (1939) 153. For the apse at La Trinité, Caen, see Baylé (1979) 59–62, where it is dated c.1120, and Baylé, in Baylé dir., (1997) vol. 2, 53, where it is put as '1100–10'. Also stressed is the influence of Anglo-Norman wall passages on the creation of this 'diaphanous' Early Gothic. The best general account is in Bony (1983) 166–72, and 469–70, notes 20–2, where he corrects and supplements his 1939 article. Particular studies of this problem are by Branner (1963) 92–104 (concentrating on the Anglo-Norman influences)

and (1963a) 258–68 (with a good discussion of the Italian Romanesque series of wall passages), and a long series of articles on wall passages by Héliot, of which the most relevant is (1970).

9A. For the Italian series see Bony (1983) 470, note 22, and Branner (1963a). The Rhenish examples are discussed by Héliot (1968) and (1971).

9B. The debts owed by Early Gothic to Norman Romanesque have long been acknowledged, see the formative study by Gall (1955) and also Anfray (1939). But more recent scholarship has tended to underline the eclecticism of early Gothic, which drew on Anglo-Norman, Burgundian, Angevin and Italian architecture, as well as precedents in Flanders. For the Anglo-Norman inspiration see particularly Branner (1963) and Héliot (1958) and (1967). See also Bony (1976) and (1983) and (1983a), where the various strands of inspiration are lucidly unravelled. An excellent summary of the problems, with particular emphasis on the Burgundian contribution, is given by Wilson (1990) 24ff.

9C. Bideault and Lautier (1987) 258, suggest that the chevet gallery flyers, although reconstructions, reflect the original flyers. James (1992) 278–9, while acknowledging that most of the stonework of the flyers and gallery wall has been replaced, thinks that there may well have been flyers here. Seymour (1968) 70, thought that the nave buttresses were added, together with the four-part vaults, after the fire of 1293. But Clark (1977) 30–3, and Deyres (1975) convincingly dated the present vaults to the late twelfth- or early thirteenth-century, and Prache (1978) to c.1175–85. She considered the flyers to be contemporary with their vaults.

10. See above, Note 9C. Deyres (1975) 283, dated the four-part vaults to 1200–5, at the end of the campaign on the construction of the nave. Clark (1977) passim, noted that a six-part vault was projected in the easternmost nave bay, but in c.1180–5, when construction had reached the clerestory sill on the south side of that bay, it was decided to go over to four-part vaults. Prache (1978) 73–5, dates this eastern nave vault, together with those of the crossing and transepts, to c.1175–85.

11. Marcel Aubert, *Monographie de la cathédrale de Senlis* (Senlis, 1910). There is also a short summary by Aubert in *B.M.* (1912). The history of the cathedral has now been clarified by Vermand (1987) and of its west façade by James (1987). The meticulous study of the sculpture by Brouillette (1981) which in all essentials agrees with Vermand, has also helped to plot the progress of the work. Construction began with the radiating chapels in 1151/2 under Bishop Thibaut, by a Beauvaisis workshop influenced particularly by Saint-Denis, but also indebted to Sens, Noyon and Saint-Germer. Construction was speedy, for the same style of capitals and bases in the nave as in the choir shows that the nave arcade was built simultaneously with, or only a little after, the work on the eastern parts. The choir was complete by at least 1167–8 (when Louis VII gave a sanctuary lamp) and probably by about 1160/63. The nave proceeded in the 1160s first with the outer north wall and the lower parts of the west façade, the north side always slightly ahead of the south. The west portal is dated by Brouillette 1165–70. Nave tribunes are up in the 1170s, the high vaults by c.1180. The 'Romanesque' character of the exterior noted by Frankl (especially the gallery windows, which are reminiscent of those at Notre-Dame de la Basse Oeuvre at Beauvais) may be deliberate, for Vermand has argued that its simplicities consciously evoked the Gallo-Roman and Romanesque buildings which still surrounded it in the twelfth century. James (1992) 277, thought it likely that its twelfth-century clerestory (destroyed in the 1504 fire) originally had flyers. See also Kimpel and Suckale (1985) 125, 539–40, and Bideault and Lautier (1987) 348–67.

11A. There are no recorded dates for the beginning of the choir. Clark (1979) 349, dates it, on comparison of its capitals with those of Saint-Denis, to soon after 1144. Lefèvre-Pontalis (1919a) 343–4, and Seymour (1968) 115, noted the strong similarities with the chevet plan of Noyon. Henriet (1982) 156–7 dated the beginning to c.1145 and went so far as to ascribe the choir to the architect of the choir of Sens. Kimpel and Suckale (1985) 124, doubted the attribution, and dated the choir to sometime after Noyon's, and hardly before 1150. Clark (1979) 349, and (1985) 40, suggested that it was completed some few years before its consecration in 1163, perhaps as early as 1155. Many of these outstanding questions are no doubt resolved in Plagnieux's (1991) thesis, but I have not been able to consult it. Certainly he suggests (1992) 209, that Henriet's attribution to the architect of Sens is 'not without convincing argument'.

11B. See above, Chapter 2, Note 11A.

12. The columns themselves cannot have been part of the eleventh-century church, which had an apse with no ambulatory adjoining the bay between the towers: see Lefèvre-Pontalis (1919) 324.

12A. For a detailed, and still the best, analysis of the church see de Maillé (1939). An interesting discussion of Saint-Quiriace, Voulton, and the patronage of the Counts of Champagne is to be found in Kimpel and Suckale (1985) 109–12. Prache (1988) also discusses Henry the Liberal's patronage, particularly in his three principal collegiate churches of Saint-Quiriace, Saint-Maclou at Bar-sur-Aube, and Saint-Etienne at Troyes. All share Sennois qualities, and may all be the work of the mysterious *Andreas cementarius* appearing in the

accounts from 1171 to as late as 1222. Saint-Quiriace's relations with Sens and other Sens-inspired churches are noted by Severens (1975) 204ff. Sandron (1998) 170, remarks on the precociously tall clerestory of the choir (despite the blind sections of wall beneath the windows) – a rejection of Sens and a strange anticipation of the 1:1 balance between arcade and clerestorey found in High Gothic Soissons and Chartres.

13. *C.A.*, LXIX (1903) illustration after page 280 and the following plate, and also the plate opposite p. 286. See also Salet (1943–4). The church was begun in c.1160–70.

14. For a full examination of the historical context, chronology, and campaigns of construction of Laon Cathedral see Clark and King (1983) and Clark (1987). They identify five main campaigns of construction:

1) **1155/60–c.1170/5.** Eastern aisles and elevation of transepts up to base of clerestorey and entire twelfth-century choir.

2) **c.1170–75**, and perhaps by the same architect as campaign (1). The lower sections of the end wall and west aisle of the north transept, lower parts of western crossing piers and two piers of the south transept west aisle.

3) **c.1170/5–c.1180/5**, by the so-called third architect, the most creative of the Laon masters. Lantern tower, completion of transepts, including the transept chapels and the lower parts of the four transept towers. Transeptal towers and their chapels had not been intended in the plans of campaigns (1) and (2). Five easternmost bays of the nave, including the high vaults of the easternmost bay.

4) **c.1180/5–c.1195/1200.** The nave was finished, the west façade and its two towers erected.

5) **Soon after 1205.** Choir extended, lantern tower vaulted. See especially Clark and King (1983) 23–51. However, James (1989) 85–7, doubts the 1205 date as the start on the choir extension. The quarry at Chermizy was indeed acquired by the Chapter in that year, and Chermizy stone first appears in the new choir, but the quarry could have been accessible to the Chapter before then, and nothing in the choir stylistically suggests a date after 1205. Sandron (1998) 168 and note 730, concurs with this. He refers to an unpublished (?) paper given in 1990 by Sauerländer on the document relating to the gift of the quarry. Sauerländer reads it as a mere confirmation, suggesting that the Chapter could have been using the quarry much earlier. Sandron dates the choir stylistically to the last decade of the twelfth century.

14A. See Zink (1975) especially 154–67.

14B. The Bishop's Chapel cannot be dated earlier than the beginning of the cathedral, as Adenauer (1934) and Hacker-Sück (1962) 224–5, proposed, simply on the evidence of its 'archaic' and 'backward' style. It was founded by Bishop Gautier of Mortagne sometime during his episcopacy (1155–74) and Clark and King (1983) 68, note 3, plausibly suggest a date for it sometime after 1161 (establishment of chaplaincies there). For photos and descriptions of the chapel see Broche (1902) 499–510, and Hacker-Sück (1962) 224–6.

14C. In the absence of proper excavations, the original east end of Laon will always be a matter of conjecture. Three of its westernmost bays still survive (or one and a half bays if you count the six-part vaulted western bay as a single unit). Beyond them was a five-sided apse with the choir aisles returned behind it. The apse columns were re-used in the choir extension. Adenauer (1934) 18ff. Frankl in the original 1962 edition of this book, and Kimpel and Suckale (1985) 194, and 487, note 37, reconstructed a polygonal ambulatory. But the majority opinion – including Bony (1983) 142 and figs. 130, 139, Clark and King (1983) 31 and fig. on 27, and Clark (1987) 17–21 – favours a curved east end. Certainly the Bishop's Chapel cannot be seen as a source for any putative polygonal hemicycle, and although the transept eastern chapels are polygonal, they date only to the 1170s, at a period when polygonal apses were just beginning to appear in northern France (Cambrai transepts, Hautevesne, Marizay Saint-Mard). See Schlink (1970) 114, and Branner (1965a) 71–2. When the Laon choir was designed, c.1155–60, polygonal apses would have been rarities. In addition, the hemicycle capitals re-used in the thirteenth-century choir have curving abaci, suggesting a semi-circular east end – see Clark and King (1983) figs 5, 6, and Clark (1987) 17–18. Arras Cathedral, begun c.1170 under Laon influence, had a curved, not polygonal, hemicycle. Like Arras, the ambulatory at Laon probably had five-part vaults and double windows to each bay.

14D. 'Vielbildigkeit'. On the concepts and terms 'Einbildigkeit' and 'Vielbildigkeit', see Paul Frankl, *Entwicklungsphasen der neueren Baukunst* (Leipzig, 1914) 130–6, and *Das System der Kunstwissenschaft* (Brünn and Leipzig, 1938) 698.

15. J. Warichez, in *La cathédrale de Tournai* (Brussels, 1935) 9, gives 1110 as the date of the beginning of the work. The towers were still unfinished in 1230, but were built faithfully to the original design. Tournai is important in the early history of Gothic architecture in the Ile-de-France on at least four counts: for its early four-storey elevation (without vaults in the nave), for its trefoil east-end plan with rounded transepts (and their Italian and Lower Rhenish derivations), for its double towers over each transept end, and for its 'thick wall' system of passages, with exterior clerestorey passages in the nave and transept and triforium passages in the transepts. The history of the early twelfth-century work is still not fully clear. Gaillard (1962) 63–7, and Héliot (1969) especially 19, 22,

68ff, date the nave between 1125 and 1140/1, and the transepts *c*.1150–71. Scaff (1971) dates the exterior walls of the nave aisles to before 1141, and the two lower stories of the nave 1140–71. For an assessment of these disagreements see Schwartzbaum (1977) 29–42, 222–7, who maintained that the nave was in building before 1141 and the whole building (including the transepts) was consecrated in 1171. His conclusions are followed by Carlson (1986) 63. Bony (1983) 487, note 22, essentially follows Seymour's chronology, and dates the beginning of the nave to 1135/early 1140s, and the start on the transepts to 1150/60. Branner (1963) 94, accepts Héliot's chronology, but underplays the influence of Tournai on Laon. The wall passages in the nave clerestorey are clearly of north Italian inspiration, but the origins of their continuation in the transepts are not so certain. Branner (1963a) defended the idea of continuing exchanges with Italy, Héliot (1969) 73–4 was more sceptical. For the many changes of plan, and architect, in the transepts, see Héliot (1969) 47, 51–2. In an unpublished paper delivered to the conference *Gotik und Spätgotik* in October 1996, at the Martin-Luther University, Halle-Wittenberg, Dr J. Westerman, who is preparing a book on Tournai Cathedral, pointed to the considerable stylistic differences between the towers and suggested that they reflect, not a single project, but a series of plan-changes, with the choir-side towers built first and the nave-side towers inserted over inadequate supports in the late twelfth and early thirteenth centuries. In a paper given at the Fidem conference in Barcelona in June 1999 Dr Westerman modified his views on the later insertion of the nave-side towers and argued that all four towers were conceived as transeptal pairs. He established the following chronology: nave begun 1100/10 and finished 1120/35; transepts begun 1120/35 and roofed 1142/60, with the upper parts of the towers later; original choir begun 1125/40 and consecrated in 1171. I am grateful to Dr Westerman for discussing these problems with me.

15A. The two west towers belong to Clark's fourth campaign of *c*.1180/5–*c*.1195/1200. The vault over the lantern was turned probably at the same time as the three western vaults of the new choir, that is, sometime after 1205 (?). The towers of the north and south transepts date from the second and third quarters of the thirteenth century respectively. See Clark and King (1983) 44–7, 49–51.

15B. For the first campaign, dated *c*.1155/60–*c*.1170/5 see Clark and King (1983) 19–36.

16. See above, Chapter 2, Notes 9C, 10.

16A. This method of detached shafting in Early Gothic architecture is discussed by Bony (1983) 158–66, and in more detail, in an English context, in Bony (1965).

16B. Fernie (1984) and (1987) has pointed to the liturgical rather than stylistic functions of these unique sets of nave pillars. Like the 'odd' pillars similarly placed in the eastern bays of the naves of certain Anglo-Norman churches (Romsey, Norwich), they probably marked the western limits of the monks'/canons' liturgical choir and the sanctuary of the nave altar.

16C. For Laon's debt to Anglo-Norman precedent see Branner (1963) especially 97–104. On the other hand, Wilson (1990) 55–6, stresses the Champenois connexions.

17. On the exterior, see below, p. 90.

17A. The antithetical character of Laon and Notre-Dame in Paris is underlined by Bony (1983) 131–55. But they share similarities in their capital carving, especially in their choirs, see Mair (1982) 60–2.

17B. Clark and King (1983) 29–36, date the beginning of the first campaign at Laon to 1155/60. The traditional starting date for Notre-Dame, the laying of the foundation stone by Pope Alexander III in 1163, has aroused suspicion, see Salet (1982) especially 99, Clark (1985) especially 41, and Clark and Mark (1984) especially 50, note 7. However, Kimpel and Suckale (1985) 151, hold to 1163 as a nominal starting date, and Bruzelius (1987) especially 553ff, in the most authoritative analysis since Aubert's monograph, puts the beginning *c*.1160. Bruzelius's sequence of construction is as follows:

1) *c*.1160–70 (first architect): plan (probably initially with no transepts), lower storey of choir, beginning of choir tribunes with single wide openings like Senlis. Intention to have a lower building than at present, with no flyers. Beginning of a west façade, perhaps to stand two bays further east than the present façade and composed of the existing St Anne portal and probably a central Last Judgment or Majestas portal. See also Clark and Ludden (1986) and Horste (1987) especially 191–4.

2) *c*.1170–90 (second architect): 1177 choir complete except for vaults and consecrated in 1182, though not necessarily vaulted by then. This architect raised the height of the choir and gave it the present, distinctive characteristics of a four-storey elevation – tribune screens, oculi above the tribune openings and higher vaults supported originally by exposed flyers. *c*.1170 began the eastern bay of the nave, with construction on south side slightly ahead of north. Completed all arcades and full height of elevation on north side in first three nave bays. High vaults of choir and transepts. Beginning of north-west tower and northern sections of west façade. This architect used thinner walls than his predecessor, flat pilasters in the transept elevation, more *en delit* shafts, and triple openings in the nave galleries, as opposed to the double in the choir. He also used exposed flyers.

3) *c*.1190–*c*.1220 (third architect): upper parts (including tribune) of nave on south side in first three bays (by *c*.1200). Distinguished by oculi in the tribune openings and distinctive profiles for abaci of tribune and vault shaft capitals. Lower parts of westernmost bay of nave (from *c*.1186?) and high vaulting of first three nave bays (after 1196). Thickens west façade and completes its southern sections at portal level (*c*.1208). Building south tower chamber and part of organ gallery in front of rose.

4) *c*.1220–*c*.1225/30 (fourth architect): completion of west nave bay. Brought construction to top of rose. North tower chamber. Vaults of west nave bay (with introduction of *tas-de-charge*).

5) *c*.1225/30–mid/late 1240s (fifth architect): remodelling of clerestorey. New flyers. First chapels on north side of nave. For the west façade and its gallery and towers see also below, Chapter 3, Note 42A.

Bruzelius's conclusions have not been universally accepted. Hardy (1991) is sceptical of Bruzelius's change of plan at the beginning of campaign 2 under the second architect, since (she argues) much of the stonework evidence for this change is nineteenth-century masonry. She considers that the initial design for the choir envisaged, from the start, a four-storey elevation, with oculi between tribunes and clerestorey. See pp. 181–8, 197, note 58. Her analysis of the fragments of the original oculi also modifies Bruzelius's sequence and chronology for the construction of the nave. The north elevation of the nave, which was begun first, preserves traces of the kind of earlier oculus decoration (*c*.1160–70) which she reconstructs for the choir, but the rest of the nave oculi conform to a different type, their decoration belonging stylistically to the west façade of *c*.1200. This confirms Bruzelius's conclusion that work on the south side of the nave lagged behind the north, but it suggests that the construction of the later oculi in the nave ran chronologically very close to the remodelling of the clerestorey in the 1220s. See pp. 174–88, and below, Chapter 2, Note 17F. Erlande-Brandenburg (1998), in a sumptuously illustrated book, broadly arrived at the same sequence and chronology as Bruzelius, but with some notable differences. The choir was not heightened by the second architect, but was planned as a four-storey structure from the first, without flyers. The tenure of the third architect he dates *c*.1200–10/20, and gives less work to than Bruzelius. It is, for Erlande-Brandenburg, the fourth architect, not the third, who introduced the 'Chartrain' piers in the western nave bays and does the south tower chamber at rose level. See pp. 51–102.

17C. And as at Saint-Germain-des-Prés, where the round columns, continuous triple shafts, certain capitals, and the original gallery openings, closely resemble the choir of Notre-Dame. See above, Chapter 2, Note 11A. Clark (1979) fig. 20, reconstructs Saint-Germain's original choir before its seventeenth-century restorations. See also Plagnieux (1991).

17D. For the dates of the beginning of Laon see above, Chapter 2, Notes 14, 14B. Kimpel and Suckale (1985) 152 and Bruzelius (1987) 543, suggested that the original choir at Notre-Dame had projecting chapels, similar to those in the later Bourges.

17E. See Grodecki and Brisac (1985) 35–8, 249–50.

17F. All the existing oculi at Notre-Dame are Viollet-le-Duc's and Lassus's reconstructions. Hardy (1991) has questioned their authenticity and recovered the position, size and interior articulation of these roses from the original fragments. The choir oculi, which she dates 1160–70, were placed lower in the elevation than those of the nave, just above the apexes of the tribune openings. They were filled with vertically-arranged crosses, similar in their chevron and diamond-point to the decoration of contemporary portals. The nave oculi, which occupied their present position immediately under the clerestorey, consisted of cross arms with curving sides and decorated with bead ornament similar to the west portals of *c*.1200. See above, Chapter 2, Note 17B.

18. Aubert (1920) plate IX. The whole chapter on 'Eclerage' and what precedes it from p. 86 give an introduction to the reconstruction of the original state and the changes which followed, up to the nineteenth century. For literature on Viollet-le-Duc's restorations at Notre-Dame see Clark and Mark (1984) 51, note 9, and Erlande-Brandenburg (1980). The restoration of the oculi and the original buttressing is discussed at length by Hardy (1991), who doubts (p. 188, and note 57) if there were ever roses lighting the exterior walls of the choir galleries. Erlande-Brandenburg (1998) is of the same opinion, and reconstructs the galleries with regular pointed arches, see fig. on p. 80.

18A. The early thirteenth-century flyers are discussed by Clark and Mark (1984) passim, Grodecki (1976) and Hardy (1991) 180–4. See below, Chapter 2, Note 38. For the nave chapels, begun *c*.1225/30 onwards see Branner (1965) 23, 68–70, and Kimpel and Suckale (1985) 343–5, and Suckale (1989) 182–4, where the westernmost chapels on the north side, (*c*.1230–40) are attributed to Pierre de Montreuil.

18B. Viollet-le-Duc discovered fragments of a large transept rose from the south side, which he dated *c*.1180, see Bruzelius (1987) 544, note 24, and Erlande-Brandenburg (1998) 89.

18C. For the transepts see Branner (1965) 76–80, 101–4; Kimpel (1971) passim, Kimpel and Suckale (1985) 401–21, and Suckale (1989).

19. Viollet-le-Duc, *Dictionnaire*, IX, 512. M. Aubert, *Notre-Dame de Paris,*

Architecture et Sculpture (Paris, 1928) contains the best illustrations of the rest of the church.

20. L. Demaison in *C.A.*, LXXVIII (1912) 1, 57.

20A. The best account of the history and design sources of the Gothic additions to Saint-Remi is by Prache (1978A) especially 46–102. Pierre de Celle's work consists of a remodelling of the two western nave bays and west façade (1165/70–*c.*1175) and the construction of the choir (begun *c.*1170, complete *c.*1182/5). Like Frankl, Prache underlines the Parisian sources of the choir ground plan – the ambulatory vault deriving from Saint-Martin (*c.*1145–50) and Saint-Croix at Etampes, the double columns in front of the chapel entrances pre-figured in the axial chapel of the choir of Saint-Geneviève in Paris. But she also uncovers connexions to, and parallels with, north eastern France, especially the transepts of Noyon and the choirs of Laon and Arras Cathedrals. A colourful account of the choir's furnishings, decoration and iconographic programme is given in Caviness's (1990) history and analysis of the stained glass, especially 21–64. Clark (1999) reconstructs screens of twin lancets in front of the windows of the choir chapels (including the Lady Chapel) similar to the second-storey windows in the central bay of the west façade. The clerestorey in the eastern bay of the nave shows traces of a linkage system intended to echo the upper two stories of the new choir.

20B. This 'linkage' is prefigured in the two slightly earlier western bays of the nave, and is very similar to the exactly contemporary (*c.*1160/70 onwards) triforium and clerestorey in the choir of Arras Cathedral, for which see Bony (1983) 373 and 488, note 27. Exchanges with Arras are discussed by Prache (1978) 94–5, who suggests that both Arras and Saint-Remi may be independently influenced by a similar linkage system in the earlier choir of Reims cathedral, built by Archbishop Samson, whose clerestorey may have had similar triplet windows in each bay.

21. Jean Bony, *Notre-Dame de Mantes* (Paris, n.d. (*c.*1947)); and, by the same author, but in greater detail, in *C.A.*, CIV (1946), 163–220.

The date of *c.*1170 given by Bony (1946) and (1983) 485, note 12, and many others, for the start of the work has been revised by Kimpel and Suckale (1985) 170–5, and 485, notes 37–9. They see this royal collegiate church as a statement of Capetian authority in a sensitive border territory between the Ile-de-France and Angevin Normandy, and argue that it was begun in *c.*1160 and most of the church laid out at arcade level on the model of Senlis. The forms deriving straight from the nave of Notre-Dame in Paris appear only from *c.*1170, from the level of the gallery upwards: gallery storey finished 1175–80, vaulting complete by 1180–90, upper stories of west façade 1200–20 on the model of Laon. See also Bailly (1980). Adams (1976) was not available to me.

22. In the article by André Rhein in *C.A.*, LXXXII (1920) 213.

22A. Bony (1946) 196ff, dates the tunnel vaults to *c.*1190. The galleries were originally surmounted by cross-placed saddle roofs which, unlike the present continuous sloping roof, allowed the clerestorey windows to extend lower down the elevation and play a more prominent role than at Notre-Dame.

23. The chapels date from some time after 1267. There were transverse roofs, probably with gables facing outwards, over the transverse tunnel-vaults in the gallery. The flying buttresses were built about 1180–90, at the same time as the high vaults, and were slightly altered soon after the middle of the thirteenth century. Bony (1946) 196–7, doubted the intention at the start of building to have flyers, and suggested that their presence was a change of plan, conceived at gallery level (*c.*1180). However, James (1992) 279, considered them to be integral with the initial lay out.

24. This church was severely damaged in 1943. The fullest documentation for the church is given in Muller (1901). A detailed survey of its fabric can be found in Fossard (1934). Most authorities date the start of the work in the 1170s – see Kimpel and Suckale (1985) 44, 537, and Bideault and Lautier (1987) 318–31 (*c.*1160–70). Keymes (1988) has established that the following sequence:

1) radiating chapels and outer rim of the ambulatory and of the two easternmost straight bays (based closely on the plan of Senlis) were begun in the 1160s.

2) After an interruption, a second campaign, beginning in *c.*1176, saw the completion of the apse columns and the elevation of the apse and the two easternmost straight bays (resembling in some of its details the Canterbury choir, and in general form Notre-Dame in Paris). The final campaign, beginning around 1220, completed the rest of the nave and the west end. Sandron (1998) 213, notes its debts to High Gothic Soissons (clerestorey, four-part vaults), and perhaps to Chartres and the western bays of Notre-Dame in Paris (*pilier cantonné*).

24A. Lanfranc's Canterbury was a version of Saint-Etienne in Caen, see Gem (1982).

24B. for Ernulf and Conrad's (also called Anselm's) choir see Fernie (1982) and Woodman (1981) 45–76. Its architectural and sculptural decoration is handsomely analyzed by Kahn (1991) 35–93, though her (and all others') suggestion that the sources for its figural decoration lie in Canterbury manuscripts is seriously questioned by Gameson (1992).

24C. Contrary to Frankl's view, post-war scholarship on English architecture in the period between Durham and Canterbury has shown just how active the English were in the reception of French ideas. Webb (1965) is still useful (though outdated on a number of points) while Kidson (1965) is still the most lucidly readable account. Bony's (1949) analysis is exemplary. A good resumé of research up to the mid-1980s was provided by Draper (1986). Since then a wealth of new insights have been offered by Wilson (1990) 72–90. The best work of synthesis on English Gothic architecture as a whole is by Kowa (1990) who presents a clear resumé of detailed research to that date. Hoey (1986) (1987) (1994), in pursuing the problem of vault and pier relations across the whole field of Early English Gothic, touches on many of the key issues of the style.

24D. William of Sens was responsible for the liturgical choir, much of the eastern transepts, the double bay of the presbytery and the tapering double bay beyond it. William the Englishman did all the work east of that: the Trinity Chapel and its crypt, and the Corona. The last work of William of Sens has been located in the clerestorey of the narrowing bay behind the high altar, and at the pair of closely spaced columns that stand on the crypt walls of the Romanesque apse and frame the entrance to the present Trinity Chapel – columns XI in Willis's plan, see Willis (1972, reprint) 137. Beyond that point, what kind of eastern termination to his choir William of Sens planned, and how much of William the Englishman's work follows his ideas, has been the subject of much debate. The issue is what kind of shrine space William of Sens intended, because the point of change between the two Williams is precisely the western limit of the Trinity Chapel in the Romanesque cathedral, the chapel where Becket was buried, and where – in its Gothic successor – his shrine was intended to be displayed. Kidson (1969) was the first to underline the very close similarities of the present east end with the choir at Saint-Denis. Woodman (1981) 115–30 unconvincingly suggested that William of Sens's plan involved a rectangular east end with a straight-ended ambulatory returned behind it. Draper (1983), in a closely argued analysis of the choir, suggested that William of Sens may have had two plans for the east end. The first, similar to the choir at Saint-Denis, placed the sanctuary, the space behind the high altar and the side aisles all on the same level – that of the eastern crossing. The second plan, which closely followed the first, envisaged an arrangement closer to the older Saint-Sernin at Toulouse, or the later Westminster Abbey. It involved a greater emphasis on the shrine area by keeping the side aisles at the original level, but raising the floor level in the central aisle, behind the high altar, and separating it from the side aisles by a wall and screen (the remains of which can be seen in the colonnettes attached to the piers in the tapering bays). This raised floor was designed to continue into the raised floor of William's solution for the Trinity Chapel, which Draper reconstructed as an apsidal structure along the lines of William the Englishman's present Trinity Chapel, but smaller, consisting of one straight bay (extending beyond the foundations of the Romanesque apse) terminated by its own three-sided apse, and surrounded at a lower level by chapel-less aisles and a curving ambulatory. Kidson (1993) reconstructed the whole of William of Sens's east end as a centrally planned martyr's memorial chapel for the shrine of Becket (something along the lines of the later rotunda for St Olaf at Trondheim in Norway), consisting of seven sides of a rarely used geometric figure: a nine-sided polygon (enneagon). He identified the geometry of the present apse of the Trinity Chapel as five sides of an enneagon, and the Corona as seven sides of that figure. Although these polygons were actually built by William the Englishman, Kidson argued that their rare geometry could only have been inherited from William of Sens, since the apse of Sens cathedral is also developed from an enneagon. William of Sens's Trinity Chapel rotunda must, therefore, have been based on this figure; the Englishman simply suppressed its two western sides, but retained the five eastern for the apse of his Trinity Chapel, and also re-used the figure for his Corona. Hearn (1994) argued for three successive designs from William of Sens:

1) 1175, a choir with a continuous arcade (as in Anselm's choir), with no expression of the eastern crossing, and with the retention of all the Romanesque walls, including the apse.

2) 1176, arcades as at present; demolition of the Romanesque apse and its replacement by a huge octagonal rotunda for Becket's shrine, the westernmost pillars of which were to be placed more closely together than the pair now at XI.

3) 1178, placing of pillar pair XI in present position, abandoning of rotunda in favour of a Trinity Chapel of one six-part-vaulted straight bay and a three-sided polygonal apse with ambulatory.

Draper's (1997) new scale measurements of the crypt and upper church levels have located the exact junction at both levels between the two Williams' work. He also judiciously assessed all the earlier literature, including Kidson (1993) and Hearn (1994). He followed Kidson in suggesting that William of Sens intended a rotunda-like chapel for Becket probably on the figure of an enneagon and closely resembling the plan of the Corona. He also proposed that William of Sens's design for the Trinity Chapel anticipated much of William the Englishman's present solution: it had a surrounding ambulatory, double columns and the continuation of the full-height elevation of the sanctuary into the chapel. It also established the nine-sided polygonal geometry which William the Englishman used for his Corona and his Trinity Chapel apse. He suggested that the guiding spirit behind the various projects for the Trinity Chapel, all of them designed to enhance dramatically the setting for the relics, may have been the Prior, Alan of Tewkesbury (1179–86). A trenchant summing up of the various views is given by Hoey (1995).

25. This date for the choir, about 1170, is drawn from Jean Bony, 'French Influences etc.', in *Journal of the Warburg and Courtauld Institutes*, XII (1949) 8, note 4. Recent scholarship has dated the beginning of the new choir at York to the 1150s, that is, the reign of Archbishop Roger of Pont l'Evêque (1154–81). See Gee (1977) especially 121ff; Wilson (1986A) especially 91–106. For the use of detached shafts in English early Gothic see, apart from Wilson (1986A) passim, Bony (1965).

26. Bony (1949) 1. Jürgen Michler's researches into original colour in medieval buildings – see especially (1977) – have shown that interiors in the late twelfth and thirteenth centuries were extensively painted, often with red false-masonry joints (in closely spaced double lines between white) laid over an all-over ochre background, with the more 'structural' elements – capitals, abaci, arch mouldings – emphasized in darker colours or, in the case of responds or ribs or certain arch orders, picked out in very light tones (see Saint-Ferréol in Essômes, Saint-Eliphe in Rampillon, Saint-Quiriace in Provins, and Saint-Père and the cathedral in Chartres). Fonquernie (1985) has recovered some original polychromy in the transepts of Notre-Dame in Paris, including dark blue and red for the mouldings. All this served to emphasize the skeletal structure of the Gothic arch–shaft system in contrast to the 'in-filling' wall between. The use of dark marble never gained wide acceptance in French Gothic, but it did appear in Tournai and Valenciennes Cathedrals (the latter probably the source for William of Sens's use of marble in Canterbury, and in a number of marginal French buildings, see Bony (1983) 159–62.

26A. See Colchester and Harvey (1974), Harvey (1982) 52–5 and Sampson (1998), 11–23. Draper (1995) assesses the particular qualities of the Wells design against the contemporary work of its nearby rival at Glastonbury, and sees the clarity and Gothic 'modernity' of the former as a manner of building consciously chosen by the cathedral chapter to emphasize its episcopal status.

27. On Gervase's text, cf. Frankl (1960) 24ff. Hitherto, all discussion of Gervase's account, including Frankl's, has been confined to correlating his information on the building of the choir with the physical evidence from the fabric itself, and to examining Gervase's awareness of the novelty of the new Gothic style imported by William of Sens, and his attempts to find a vocabulary to describe it. However, recent interest has centred round Gervase's motives for writing the account in the first place, and the institutional factions and interests at Canterbury in the 1170s and 80s which it served. Kidson's (1993) dramatic reconstruction of events surrounding the fire led him to conclude that Gervase's history was a cover-up for arson, and an attempt to conceal William of Sens's earlier involvement with Becket before his death in a projected college of secular canons at Hackington. Hearn (1994) emphasized the role of King Henry II in the fundamental change from rotunda (his stage 2) to a Trinity Chapel more on the present lines (his stage 3); see above, Chapter 2, Note 24D. Draper (1997) tactfully adjudicated on the various speculations, and underlined the role of the clergy at Canterbury (particularly Prior Alan of Tewkesbury) in building decisions relevant directly to the cult and liturgy.

28. The highly complicated history of the building is analysed in Vallery-Radot, *L'église de la Trinité de Fécamp* (P.M.) (Paris, 1928). The plan published there gives a readily comprehensible survey of the chronology of the main parts of the church. See Grant (1987) 66–9, and Baylé, in Baylé, dir., (1997) vol. 2 152–5. The straight bays of the choir were begun immediately after the fire in 1168 by Abbot Henri de Sully, preserving one bay, and the two north radiating chapels, of the Romanesque church, and maintaining its general proportions in the new work – that is, having large Norman-type galleries and interior clerestory passages. The nave was complete by 1219, and the lantern tower over the crossing, with its typically Norman octopartite vault, by c.1225. The rebuilding of the apse and ambulatory concluded this campaign. For all its 'Norman' conservatism, Grant (1994a) 125, points out that the church of Henri de Sully shows evidence of the intention to build a double ambulatory in the choir, modelled on Saint-Denis.

29. Erlande-Brandenburg (1974) argued that the nave was begun some time before the death of Bishop Arnulf of Lisieux in 1182, certainly at the west end, whose portal pre-dates the similar central portal at Mantes. He postulated at this stage the intention to build a nave with six-part vaults, vaulted galleries and no flyers (since he believed the first Gothic flyers appeared in the nave of Notre-Dame in Paris in c.1178). c.1180–5 it was decided to create unvaulted galleries, and four-part vaults supported by the present flyers. Work proceeded slowly eastwards, the choir complete only in 1218, the lantern tower (originally a lower vaulted crossing was intended) in 1218–50. The best published accounts so far are by Clark (1972) (1977a) and, in shorter form, Clark in Baylé, dir., (1997) vol.

2, 168–72. In (1972) Clark established the priority of the Mantes portals over those of Lisieux, and placed them in relation to the later lateral portals at Rouen cathedral (1190s). In (1977a) he dated the start of the new nave to c.1160, working from west to east. He disentangled the sources for the nave: a Norman method of 'thin wall' construction with unvaulted galleries coming probably from Upper Normandy and the Vexin (Evreux cathedral); an arch-shaft system derived from the first floor chamber of the Tour Saint-Romain at Rouen cathedral, and the form of the gallery openings (especially the central double colonnettes) having precedents in the Beauvaisis. He argued for a break in construction c.1175–85, largely on the grounds that the flyers in the nave could not pre-date those of Notre-Dame. When work resumed c.1185 the flyers were built, the central west portal carved, both under the influence of the collegiate church at Mantes, and the nave vaulted by 1190. Grant (1987) 76ff, acknowledged the scuptural debts to Mantes, but – *contra* Clark (1977a) – re-emphasized the debts to Laon and the Aisne valley in the nave elevation. She also saw no reason for an interruption in the nave building, largely because she acknowledged the existence of flyers in northern France before Notre-Dame. Consequently she dated the whole work on the nave to a single campaign from c.1165 to c.1180. In his 1997 assessment Clark admitted that the central bay of the narthex, the nave and the transept were completed – and the chevet well advanced – by the retirement in 1181 of Bishop Arnulf, the driving spirit behind the building.

29A. 'The principal of vertical movement' did not, as Frankl suggests, grow from the rib downwards. On the contrary, the vertical division of the interior into bays by tall shafts preceded the introduction of the rib vault. See Bony (1983) 79–87, and Horn (1958).

30. *Ibid.*, 268ff. The history of the late twelfth-century remodelling has been admirably elucidated by Prache (1977) 279–97. Also for comparisons with Saint-Remi at Reims see Prache (1978a) 108–9. Recently Corsepius (1997) especially 87–121, has devoted a full monograph to the church. She isolates three phases, or 'plans' of construction:

1) **Plan I.** c.1130–40, of which only the lower stories of the two eastern towers survive. They may have formed the eastern terminations of an aisled and transeptless nave, and framed between them a semicircular apse.

2) **Plan II.** c.1140- after 1157 (when vaults in an unspecified part of the church collapsed). A choir with ambulatory, two western towers, and, between them, an unvaulted transeptal basilica, with a clerestorey on the same level as the oculi of the transept end walls, and with diaphragm arches (!) over all three aisles. Surviving from this phase is the arcade storey of the nave, as well as the two western towers, the latter post-dating the 1157 collapse. (This reconstruction has no parallels in Champenois late Romanesque).

3) **Plan III.** c.1180/3 or 1187–1220. Remodelling of the gallery and clerestorey of the nave and the clerestorey of the transepts in a Remois Early Gothic style derived from Saint-Remi at Reims. Addition of vault shafts to the weak piers of the main arcade. Construction (probably from 1187) of the new choir. Only in 1217 was the latter ready for use. Roof of south porch dendrochronologically dated to c.1220.

31. The date, between 1185 and 1215, given in Francis Salet, *La Madeleine de Vézelay* (Melun, 1948) 81, should be amended to before 1180, since the choir at Avila, which is dependent on the church at Vézelay, was completed before 1181; L. Torres Balbás, *Arquitectura gótica (Ars Hispaniae, VII)* (Madrid, 1952) 38. More recent commentary on the choir of Vézelay emphasizes its links with the first generation of Ile-de-France Gothic (Saint-Denis, Saint-Germain-des-Prés, Sens), but also, in the changes in its vault bay design, with Arras cathedral. See Branner (1960) 30–4, 192–4, and Bony (1983) 484, note 7, 519, note 52. Both scholars follow Salet's date of c.1185–90 for the beginning of the choir, as do Stratford and Saulnier (1984) 135–6. But Kimpel and Suckale (1985) 145, and 483, note 31, and 546, argue for a beginning on the radiating chapels and ambulatory as early as c.1165, when Vézelay secured exemption from the jurisdiction of Autun and freedom from the Counts of Nevers. The slow execution of the whole choir, with many changes of design, meant that the sanctuary columns and elevation were begun only c.1180. Kennedy (1996) 223–79, reaffirmed the links with Saint-Denis and Saint-Germain-des-Prés. She sees the fire of 1165, the support of Louis VII after 1166 and the appointment of William of Mello, sometime Abbot of Pontoise, in 1161, as catalysts in the adoption of Ile-de-France forms. She dates the choir construction to the 1170s.

32. François Deshoulières, *La cathédrale de Meaux* (P.M.) (Paris, 1925). The cathedral's stages of construction have been clarified by Kurmann (1971).

1) c.1175–1215/20 choir built in two main stages.

a) The first architect (active c.1170/80–c.1190). Ground plan and intended four-storey elevation modelled closely on Notre-Dame in Paris and Saint-Remi in Reims. Reached height of springing of lower vaults.

b) Second architect (active c.1195/1200–c.1215/20). Gallery and triforium storey built according to the general plan of the first architect, but tall clerestorey with doublet plate tracery and flyers derived from the High Gothic choir of Soissons Cathedral. East crossing piers and begining of east walls of transepts. Intention to build a lantern tower over crossing.

2) *c.*1215/20–1235. The second architect (or a pupil) completed the transept and built the first two bays of the nave on the same pattern as the choir.

3) *c.*1235–54, the floors of the galleries of the nave were demolished, their vaults became those of the much taller aisles, creating false tribunes.

4) From 1253 onwards the choir was fundamentally rebuilt in the Rayonnant style by the architect Gautier de Varinfroy, using false tribunes. He replaced the three Early Gothic chapels with new ones, the height of his new, taller, side aisles, raised the apsidal pillars, and rebuilt the elevations with advanced Rayonnant tracery.

5) *c.*1300 transept façades constructed in the manner of Notre-Dame Paris south transept, and the transept fronts of Rouen Cathedral.

6) Early fourteenth century (from 1317 onwards) two extra chapels added to ambulatory between Gautier de Varinfroy's chapels.

7) From *c.*1450/60 rebuilding of the two eastern bays of the nave, and construction of its three western bays in the Flamboyant style. For the connexions of the second architect with the choir of Soissons Cathedral (where he probably trained) see Sandron (1998) 211–12. Kurmann (1992) returned to Meaux, but his new observations concerned more the sculpture than the architecture, whose chronologies and sequences he saw no reason to change. He admits, however, that Gautier de Varinfroy rebuilt the late twelfth-century choir flyers; he did not leave them in place and reconstruct the aisles under and around them. He attributes the Parisian form of the transepts and their portals to the acquisition of Meaux by the crown through the marriage of Philip the Fair and Jeanne of Navarre in 1284.

33. There are many illustrations in Salet, *op. cit.*

34. An example can be seen in the flat, clinging acanthus leaves on the piers in the nave at Le Mans and in the arched leaves on the piers in the apse at Noyon, both of which date from about 1150. Illustrations can be found in Ernst Gall, *Die gotische Baukunst etc.*, I (Leipzig, 1925) plates 41 and 48.

35. Illustrated in G.H. Cook, *Portrait of Canterbury Cathedral*, plates 41–4. On the subject of capitals and bases see Viollet-le-Duc, *Dictionnaire*, II (chapiteau, base); see also F. Bond, *Introduction*, 487–558.

35A. Some of the earliest crocket capitals appear *c.*1160–70 in the ambulatory at Noyon ('incipient form') and *c.*1180 in the tribunes and vault shafts of the choir (Seymour (1968) 60, 170–1. They also appear at Laon in an 'incipient' or 'transitional' form during Clark's phase 3 of the construction (*c.*1170/5–*c.*1180–5) and in a fully developed form throughout phase 4 (*c.*1180/5–*c.*1195–1200). See Clark and King (1983) 40, 46. At Saint-Remi at Reims they are used in the choir from the level of the triforium upwards (*c.*1180), see Prache (1978A) 72–3, and in the south transept at Soissons Cathedral (begun in 1176), see Lefèvre-Pontalis (1911) 313–58; and, again in 'incipient' form on the shaft capitals of the north-west crossing pier of the eastern crossing at Canterbury cathedral, dated exactly 1177–8, see Mair (1982) 59–60. They appear in the upper parts of the choir of Notre-Dame, Paris, by 1180.

36. The walls do not carry the vaults: even where there are sloping cells, the thrust which they exercise on the walls is slight. The idea that ribs carry the load on to the supports at the four (or three or five, etc.) corners is correct, but this was equally true in groin-vaults.

37. The only church in which unobtrusive supporting walls can be seen is that of Saint-Martin-des-Champs in Paris (*c.*1130–42): *C.A.*, LXXXII (1919) I, plate opposite p. 124. Saint-Martin-des-Champs is not the only example of protruding buttress walls, placed above the transverse arches of the galleries. They were once visible on the exterior of the nave of the destroyed Cambrai Cathedral, their upper parts appearing above the gallery roofs. See drawing by A. van der Meulen. Similar walls appear above the gallery roofs of the south transept at Arras Cathedral (see late eighteenth-century drawing in Archives du Pas-de-Calais.) Both are illustrated in Bony (1983) figs 128, 129, who provides a clear explanation of the structural workings of the Early Gothic tribune churches on pp. 124–31.

37A. The exact form of the flyers of the nave of Notre-Dame before their rebuilding in the thirteenth century has been the subject of different reconstructions. Viollet-le-Duc (1858–68) vol. 2 (1859) 289, fig. 2, and Aubert (1920) 104, thought they were arranged in double batteries. Apart from buttress walls supporting the lower parts of the galleries under the outer aisle roofs, the outer batteries consisted of a lower flyer to support the gallery vaults and an upper to stabilize the upper parts of the intermediate upright. The inner battery, they argued, consisted of a lower flyer placed under the gallery roofs to support the high vault and an upper to take the main roof weight. Clark and Mark (1984) passim, and p. 50, fig. 6, and p. 59, fig. 16, reconstruct only one flyer in the external battery, and therefore lower the intermediary upright. Some evidence from the original external buttress uprights of the choir, suggests however, that Viollet-le-Duc and Aubert may not have been far wrong about double outer batteries. Although the choir flyers are the early fourteenth-century work of Jean Ravy, and the uprights were thoroughly restored in the nineteenth century, pre-restoration photographs, and the pre-restoration 1843 model of the choir, now in the Palais de Chaillot, show flyers emerging from

rough and presumably earlier uprights which probably belong to the Early Gothic choir. See Bruzelius (1987) 551, and 554, fig. 19. These outer uprights are considerably higher than those reconstructed for the slightly later nave buttresses by Clark, and suggest that the latter were originally high enough to take two batteries, the top one either abutting an intermediary upright or, as Prache (1976) 32, suggested, 'flew' straight to the clerestorey wall, without any intermediary upright. This would make the system a prefiguration of that used in the choir of Saint-Remi at Reims, with a single, tall external buttress, and two flyers peeling off it at different heights, the lower to support the gallery, the upper the clerestorey. This reconstruction has (at least for the original choir) been supported by Murray (1998), who suggests that the present chapel-dividing walls of the nave, and the buttress uprights that rise above them, are essentially twelfth-century work; that the lower flyers of the choir are twelfth-century; that the stepped arrangement of the choir buttress uprights shown in pre-restoration photographs and the model represents the original twelfth-century *culées*; that the choir flyers must have strikingly resembled the present system, with no intermediate uprights and with the top flyers leaping over both aisles (in a manner prefiguring Coutances Cathedral). The nave may have had the same system; certainly there is no evidence there for intermediate uprights.

38. Lefèvre-Pontalis's and Aubert's claim that Notre-Dame's original nave buttresses were the first external flyers has been accepted by a long line of scholars, right up to Bony (1983) 179–86. But there have been dissenting voices. Fitchen (1961) 289–95 suggested that Suger's choir at Saint-Denis may have had flyers; and Prache (1976) 37–8, considered that the flyers around the choir of Saint-Germain-des-Prés in Paris, usually considered afterthoughts inserted *c.*1180–5, might belong to the present chevet of the 1150s. Grodecki (1976) 47, floated the idea that there may have been exposed flyers from the start in the choir of Notre-Dame. This was confirmed by Bruzelius (1987) 551ff, and fig. 15, who reconstructed two batteries of choir flyers, with intermediary uprights resting on the aisle columns, the lower flyer supporting the gallery, the upper the clerestorey. But Hardy (1991) 182–3, and Erlande-Brandenburg (1998) 74, are sceptical of Bruzelius's reconstructions, and cautious about any speculation on the existence of choir flyers in Paris. In fact, Erlande-Brandenburg's reconstruction of the twelfth-century choir shows a rather old-fashioned structure, with no flyers. The most forceful arguments for pre-Notre-Dame flyers came from Henriet, who claimed that early Gothic buildings of the 1150s and 1160s with three-storey elevations and without vaulted galleries used flyers as necessary lateral abutments. He 'discovered' the original buttresses and flyers of *c.*1150 at Saint-Martin at Etampes, reconstructed the choir clerestorey of Sens with rudimentary flyers of *c.*1150, and argued for flyers as part of the original 1150s construction of the choir of Saint-Germain-des-Prés, see Henriet (1978) and (1982) 129–40. Clark consistently denied the existence of such early flyers, and maintained that those in the twelfth-century nave of Notre-Dame in Paris were the earliest, see (1979) 363–5; (1984) (with Mark) passim; and (1987) 70, note 1. Wilson (1990) 41ff, 59ff, argued for their presence in the choirs of Saint-Denis, Vézelay, and the original choir at Laon. Confirmation that Saint-Germain-des-Prés had flyers *c.*1155 is provided by its offshoot, the choir of Domont, where there were rudimentary flyers well before the 1180s, see Plagnieux (1992). Finally, James (1992) confirms that before 1170 there is incontrovertible archeological evidence for flyers in the choirs of Sens Cathedral, Saint-Germain-des-Prés, Voulton, Saint-Lomer at Blois and the nave at Saint-Remi at Reims, and that there is good evidence for flyers of the same date in the choirs of Laon, Mantes and Noyon. For a detailed analysis of the history and restorations of the nave buttresses at Notre-Dame, Paris, see Clark and Mark (1984) 47–65, and, Murray (1998) who reviews all the previous literature from Viollet-le-Duc to Bruzelius (see also above, Chapter 2, Note 37A).

38A. Photoelastic model analysis by Robert Mark and others has calculated the forces acting on the flyer, see Mark (1982), with reference to his earlier publication. See also Mark, Alexander, Abel (1977) 241–51, and Heyman (1968) 181.

39. F. Bond, *Introduction*, I, 407.

40. Dehio, *K.B.*, II, 144.

41. Marcel Aubert, 'Le portail royal et la façade occidentale de la cathédrale de Chartres', in *B.M.*, C (1941) 177. See Sauerländer (1972) 383–4. Williamson (1995) 14ff. Fels (1955) 149–51 doubted if the portals were originally ever placed east of the west towers and subsequently moved forward to their present position. James (1986) 101–8 argued that the anomalies in the design are due, not to subsequent displacement, but to *ad hoc* construction methods on site. The conventional dates for the west façade of Chartres have been questioned (unconvincingly) by van der Meulen (1975) 21–3, who suggested that the documentary references to '*ad opus turris*' or '*ad aedificationem turris*' between 1134 and 1138, and 1139 and 1142 are not to the two west towers but to a rebuilding of the chevet. Again, as he argued for the choir of Saint-Denis (1988) see above, Chapter 2, Note 5F, we are asked to believe that references to a 'tower' are really to a 'choir'.

42. The term tabernacle is used in this book for the architectural members

which look like a *taberna*, i.e. a small house, and have four supports, a vault, and a little spire. The term canopy is used for little hanging vaults or corbels protecting statues. For pinnacles see Kobler (1987) 617–65.

43. Lefèvre-Pontalis, 'Les origines des gables', in *B.M.*, LXXI (1907) 92. Unfortunately this article gives no dates for most of the works quoted in it. The author gives the portal at Rhuis (Oise), which is supposed to have been built as early as the eleventh century, as the earliest case of a circular arch obtruding into a gable. He places the next earliest Gothic gables in the first half of the twelfth century.

43A. The Chartres south steeple seems to combine two traditions: 1) towers with spires rising from octagons (e.g. Saint-Eusèbe at Auxerre, Vermonton (Yonne), and the Tour Saint-Aubin at Angers (begun 1130)), 2) Limousin Romanesque towers with gables rising on the four straight sides (e.g. Brantôme or Saint-Léonard (Haute-Vienne)), see Jalabert (1968) 22–6, 35–6.

44. For the chronology and phases of construction of Senlis see above, Chapter 2, Note 11.

44A. The starting date for the west façade of Sens is usually given as some time after the town fire of 1184 (see Sauerländer (1972) 416); but the evidence as to whether the fire actually reached the cathedral is contradictory, see Henriet (1982) 90. The remaining twelfth-century sculpture of the west façade is usually dated to the 1180s onwards – Sauerländer (1972) 418–19, Williamson (1995) 31–3. By 1176 the main body of the cathedral was substantially complete (Henriet (1982) 88–9), therefore the façade was probably under construction in the 1180s. In 1210 an altar was dedicated to Saint-Michael in a chapel in the north tower. In 1221 an altar was dedicated to Saint-Vincent in the first storey of the south tower. In 1268 the south tower collapsed, with consequent reconstruction of parts of the façade and its sculpture.

44B. Documents referring to the demolition of houses near the future west façade in 1178 and 1180 suggest that the design for the façade might have been prepared around this time or soon after. For these sources, and for the chronology of the '4th campaign' at Laon, including the west façade and towers, see Clark and King (1983) vol. 24, 44–7; and Clark (1987) 53–60.

44C. These pinnacles may be the first to be used in a Gothic church outside the context of towers, see Kobler (1987) 617–65. A perceptive discussion on the problem of 'micro- and macro-architecture', and the growing tendency in the thirteenth century to apply monumental architectural forms to miniature formats can be found in Kurmann (1996a).

44D. Some of the characteristics of the lower storey of the Laon west front which Frankl describes as 'Gothic' are, as Branner (1963) pointed out, prefigured in the Romanesque gatehouse of Bury Saint-Edmunds, dated *c.*1120–48 (e.g. the gables over the entrance). Bony (1963a) also stressed the Anglo-Norman connexions between north-eastern France and Bury, in this case the transeptal west façade of the abbey church itself at Bury and similar façades concealing wide west transepts at Saint-Germer, Noyon, Braine and le Mont-Notre-Dame. For the wider question of Anglo-Norman influence on French façade (or 'west end') design see Héliot (1963) 257–78. Claussen (1975) 41–52, who dates the western porches to '*c.*1190', reconstructs their originally lighter, more open format (before the nineteenth-century reinforcements) as three deep arches resting on free-standing pillars. He traces this format, which he calls 'the triumphal arch type' of portal back to Antiquity and antique-influenced Romanesque portals in the south of France (Arles, Moissac, Beaulieu). He identifies a particularly close precedent in the porch of the priory church of Saint-Macé of *c.*1130 (Maine-et-Loire), and suggests that it, and Laon, share a common (lost) source – see also pp. 27–41, and 156–7.

44E. Viollet-le-Duc's restoration did not restore the correct tracery to the oculi. Hardy (1991) has reconstructed the choir oculi as filled with cross-shaped bars, decorated with chevron. The nave oculi were curvilinear versions of the choir's. See above, Chapter 2, Note 17F.

45. E.g. the tower at Vendôme (*c.*1150), which stands clear of the façade behind it. It is illustrated in Ernst Gall, *Die gotische Baukunst etc.*, 82. Cf. also the clearly delineated structure of the tower at Etampes, illustrated in the same book, 83.

46. *Ibid.*, plate 28. See Crosby (1987) 161–70.

46A. A description of the façade and towers and a short assessment of its design sources is given in Clark (1987) 53–60, who properly stresses the inter-relationship between the façade and the original galleried structure of the nave bay behind it. Still authoritative on the aesthetic problems posed by the conflicting demands of the west façade in Gothic architecture is Kunze (1912), who deals with Laon on 19–25. For Villard de Honnecourt's famous drawings of one of the west towers at Laon, and their geometrical construction, see Hahnloser (1972) 49–55, 352–3; and Bucher (1979) 76–9, and 181; and Fernie (1990) 229–34. A rehearsal of the various issues raised by the Laon towers – their design sources, Villard's drawing and its similarities to the stained glass representation of the cathedral of 'Soissons' in the choir clerestorey of Reims, and the depiction of an architect among the archivolt sculptures of the liberal arts on the left window of the rose storey – can be found in Sandron (1999).

46B. The fullest discussion of transeptal towers in medieval architecture is provided by Héliot (1965). The conventional pre-1171 dating for the transepts at Tournai would establish them as precedents, and almost certainly as principle sources, for those at Laon, but see above, Chapter 2, Note 15, for the problematic history and dating of the towers. Besides discussing Tournai, Clark (1987) 41, links the Laon towers to the contemporary transept towers at Arras.

47. Cf. for more exact dating Louis Grodecki, 'A Stained Glass Atelier of the Thirteenth Century', *Journal of the Warburg and Courtauld Institutes*, II (1948) 107. Frankl may be right in suggesting that the choir of the cathedral was begun before 1162. In a detailed and exemplary study, Blomme (1994) has established a convincing dating and sequence of construction. The mention of 1162 in the sixteenth-century source refers to Henry and Eleanor's foundation of the town walls, not the cathedral, which was begun 'in that same period' (*en mesme temps*). Blomme suggests that the choir was begun as early as *c.*1150. The inscription with '1167' on the ribs of the east bay of the middle aisle implies that the choir was too advanced for it to have been begun just five years earlier. The original conception of the cathedral, which informed much of the first four campaigns of construction, up to *c.*1215, was for a hall church with individual cross-placed saddle roofs running north–south over each bay, and a transept emphasized by transeptal towers and a lantern tower over the crossing. This concept was modified in the fourth campaign (*c.*1195–*c.*1215) by suppressing the transept towers, and changing the vault design (in the transept and western bay of the choir) from the lower four-part vaults with square heavy rib profiles in the two eastern choir bays, to higher, eight-part vaults with thin, torus-moulded ribs. But the real changes coincided with the appearance of a new architect at the beginning of the fifth campaign (*c.*1235–55). He suppressed the crossing tower, made the central aisle of the nave higher than the side aisles, and rebuilt the choir roof as a single saddle running east–west at the same height in nave and choir. This entailed heightening the east gable of the choir. With a few modifications, this altered conception prevailed up to the completion of the west bays of the nave (campaigns six, seven, eight) in the last half of the thirteenth century. The façade, up to just above the rose storey, was complete by the end of the century. Lozinski (1994) attempts, unsuccessfully, to find parallels between the simplicities of the choir exterior and Henry II's military architecture.

48. Dehio, *K.B.*, I, 358ff.

48A. Prüll, or Kartaus-Prüll, belongs to a group of six Bavarian hall churches of the late twelfth century. See Thümmler (1962), and Schütz and Müller (1989) 520–1. They include the nuns' church of Bergen bei Neuburg an der Donau (from 1156), the Cistercian church of Walderbach (second half of twelfth century) and the chapel of Burg Donaustauf near Regensburg (after 1150). See also Kubach and Köhler-Schommer (1997) 135.

48B. Frankl's conception of the ideal Gothic hall church as a unified and 'directionless' space reflects a long tradition of German art-historical thinking. Such spatial analyses of the hall have been critically questioned, particularly since many halls are strongly directional and segregated in their spatial organization, see Kunst (1971) and below, Chapter 3, Note 139A.

48C. Useful general introductions to the aims and early history of the Cistercians are to be found in Southern (1983) 250–72; Lawrence (1984) 146–66; Leclerq (1980); Lekai (1977). For Stephen Harding see Lekai (1977) 17, 27; Knowles (1963) 199–200, and, more generally on the Cistercians, 208–66. A helpful introduction to St Bernard and his contemporaries can be found in Berlioz (1990).

48D. A useful conspectus of the extent and position of the Cistercian monasteries is provided by van der Meer (1965), though his statistics have been reviewed by Vongrey and Hervay (1967) 115–52, quoted in Lawrence (1984) 165, note 15. Another useful corpus of Cistercian architecture is Dimier (1949). An authoritative and well-illustrated introduction to the general characteristics of the Cistercian church can be found in Kinder (1990).

48E. Modern studies have moved away from the view that the Cistercian attitude to art was exclusively negative and iconoclastic. See in particular Talbot (1986) 56–64; Melczer and Soldwedel (1982) 31–44, Rudolph (1990) 12–18.

48F. The Cistercian prohibition of stone crossing towers, passed in a statute of 1157, seems to have been flouted in the large stone towers built soon afterwards in England, at Buildwas, Kirkstall, Fountains, Roche and Dore. See Fergusson (1970) 211–21. He argues that the debate of 1157 was prompted by the Cistercian abandonment of the so-called 'Bernardine' church (see below, Chapter 2, Note 51B) – which used no regular crossing (its nave vaults ran without interruption right up to the sanctuary arch) – and its replacement by churches with conventional crossings. He also argues that the General Chapter permitted these towers because they were low and simple. In France, however, there were few such crossing towers, and the prohibition seems to have been taken too literally.

48G. The history of Cistercian architecture in its first thirty years is, and probably will remain, obscure. The best account is Schaefer (1982).

49. Aubert (1947) vol. I, 191–3; and Schaefer (1982) 2–3.

50. For Cîteaux see Hahn (1957) 238ff; Aubert (1947) vol. 1, 169, and 190–3, who suggested that the first choir had a 'Bernardine' plan, and that the nave was built between 1125/30 and 1140/50. The original appearance of the elevation of the first stone church is unclear. Fergusson (1984) 38, suggested that it may have shared, with its daughter houses at Clermont and Boquen (in France) and Amelungsborn and Altenberg I (in Germany), a regular crossing, and a simple, unarticulated nave with a timber roof and a clerestorey. This is also the nave system of most of the Irish Cistercian monasteries, see Stalley (1987) 80–3. But almost all the Irish houses are affiliated to Clairvaux, as is Rievaulx, whose first stone church shared this lack of vertical bay articulation. In their recent magisterial study of Rievaulx, Fergusson and Harrison (1999) now suggest that this simplicity was not the echo of a Burgundian archetype – and certainly not a trace element of the original Cîteaux – but ought to be read as the assertion of a new monastic ideal, as much Roman as Burgundian (see the Cistercian church of Tre Fontane in Rome). Wilson (1990) 24, plate 14, suggests that Cîteaux may have had groin vaults, and been the inspiration of those in the transept at Pontigny. For a catalogue of the pre-destruction drawings of the church see Gras (1982); for the excavations of 1959–64 see Lebau (1982).

51. Schaefer (1982) 4–8, who argues that this oratory – the *monasterium vetus* in Dom Milley's plan of 1708 – was wooden; Kinder (1991) 207–8 thinks it was stone.

51A. The date of the relocation of the monastery in 1135, a date given by Arnold of Bonneval in his *Vita Prima* of St Bernard, is usually accepted as the start of Clairvaux II. But it has been questioned by Untermann (1984) 618–24, who argues that the relocation and the building of Clairvaux II took place perhaps as early as the 1120s. This view is convincingly rejected by Kennedy (1996) 135, 136–7, 141–2, who reestablishes a date in the 1130s, in the light of the contradictory evidence in the *Vita Prima*, suggests either 1132/3 or 1136/7 as the *terminus post quem* for the rebuilding, and c.1145 as a *terminus ante*, when its 'new choir' is mentioned in the *Fragmenti Gaufridi* (written in about 1145). However, she does not associate this church with that shown in Dom Milley's plan and bird's eye view of 1708, see below, Note 55.

51B. Pictorial and documentary evidence for the original appearance of Clairvaux II is discussed by Kinder (1991). See also Aubert (1947) 1, 124–5, 182–3, and Hahn (1957) 119–22, who both considered Clairvaux II to be the model for Fontenay, that is, a church with barrel vaults and a flat east end. In the early 1950s Karl Heinz Esser proposed that Clairvaux II marked the beginning of a new type of Cistercian church architecture: monumental, austere and standardized. He called it 'Bernardine' because he felt that it closely reflected St Bernard's own conception of what a Cistercian church should look like. For Esser, Clairvaux II was the prototype of the 'Bernardine' church. He argued that its original east end consisted of an aisleless, square-ended sanctuary with transepts opening onto square-ended chapels; that this 'Bernardine' plan was exclusively enforced within all the filiations of Clairvaux between c.1135 and 1153; that it was adopted under Bernard's influence in some of the other five main mother houses (Cîteaux, La Ferté and Pontigny), and that after Bernard's death in 1153 it ceased to be the norm in Clairvaux filiations, when a variety of types of east end were employed. See Esser (1952) 221–3; (1953) 195–222. Hahn (1957) 84–128 extended Esser's argument by maintaining that not only the plan, but other features of Clairvaux II were universally binding, or at least widespread, on Clairvaux filiations up to 1153: the barrel vaults in the main vessel and the cross-placed barrels in the side aisles; the choir and transepts vaulted lower than the nave. He also proposed that all Bernardine churches used a modular system of proportions, based on two squares, one of 3, one of 4 units, for the laying out of the ground plan (pp. 66–82, 314–39).

More recent Cistercian scholarship has refined and criticized this concept of a 'Bernardine' architecture, and Clairvaux II's role in it. It admits that Cistercian building in the 1130s became more standardized, and that this new style – either through Bernard's direct backing or because of its association with him – was widely accepted as specifically Cistercian. But in the light of local variations it has questioned Esser's and Hahn's claims for uniformity. See, for example, Swartling (1967) 193–8, and Stalley (1987) 56–7. It also throws doubt on the exclusive role of Clairvaux in the development of the 'Bernardine' church, and warns against a too strict definition of the Bernardine elevation, see Fergusson (1984) 13–38, 52–3.

Most significantly, recent findings have called into question Hahn's and Esser's reconstructions of Clairvaux II as the prototype of the 'Bernardine' church. Particularly suspect are their arguments for Fontenay-style pillars and barrel vaults in the nave. The church shown in Dom Milley's bird's eye view of 1708 had a clerestorey, shows transepts of the same height as the nave (not lower as in Fontenay and Pontigny) and was clearly not barrel-vaulted. Schlink (1970) 138ff, suggested that this church was stylistically so different to the Fontenay type that it cannot be the 1135 building, and must represent an entire reconstruction. Aubert suggested two possibilities: a) that the 1135 church was planned to have barrel vaults over the main vessel, but was never finished, and rib vaulted later, or b) that the original barrel vault over the central aisle was rebuilt with a clerestorey after 1153, to match the new reconstructed choir

(Clairvaux III). Kinder (1991) 210–11, claimed that the nave of the church in Dom Milley's view belonged to the building begun in 1135, and that therefore Clairvaux II was never the prototype for Fontenay or any other of the barrel-vaulted 'Bernardine' churches. She suggested that its elevation may have been three-storied, with small openings into the aisle roofs placed between arcade and clerestorey (see La Benisson-Dieu). Kennedy (1996) 145–51, thinks there may have been string courses between the stories, and reconstructs the nave supports as cruciform piers with half-columnar responds. The nave had either groin- or rib-vaults.

Hahn's proportional theories have been accepted as operative in many churches, but criticized as dogmatic and over-comprehensive. See Schmoll gen. Eisenwerth (1958) 158–80; Hirst, Walsh and Wright (1983) 208–29; Swartling (1969) 77–9; Stalley (1987) 68–75.

St Bernard's teachings on light, order and simplicity are too general to prove his involvement in the creation of a 'Bernardine' style, see Melczer and Soldwedel (1982).

51C. For Fontenay see Aubert (1947) 157–9 and passim; Hahn (1957) 97–104; Bucher (1957) 179–81; and Gilbert (1970) 1–3, 20–45.

51D. For the aesthetics of St Bernard see Melczer and Soldwedel (1982) Talbot (1986) and Rudolph (1990) 12–18.

52. Illustrated in *ibid.*, 1, 351; and also in John Bilson, 'The Architecture of the Cistercians', in *The Archaeological Journal*, LXVI (1909) 158 and plate II.

52A. See now Fergusson (1984); Halsey (1986), Wilson (1986) and Coldstream (1986).

53. On German Cistercian churches, cf. Georg Dehio, *Geschichte der deutschen Kunst*, 1 (Berlin, 1919) 249ff., and Henry-Paul Eydoux, *L'architecture des églises cisterciennes d'Allemagne* (Paris, 1952). For Amelungsborn see now Thümmler and Kreft (1970) 253. Its wooden roof may not be simply 'Saxon' but may be connected to a group of unvaulted Cistercian churches, without bay divisions, including Clermont, Boquen, Rievaulx, Jerpoint, Mellifont, see above, p. 317 and Chapter 2, Note 50. The architecture of the Cistercians in Germany is now covered by Hahn (1957) (particulary for the early foundations), Krönig (1973), and Nicolai (1988) (1989/1990) (1993) (particularly for the period from about 1200 onwards).

53A. For Eberbach and Maulbronn see Hahn (1957) 12–78, 244–7. Still the best treatments of the church at Maulbronn can be found in Anstett (1978) and (1985). For Worms see above, Chapter 1, Note 22F.

53B. For Heisterbach see Verbeck (1980) and Buchert (1986) (not available to me).

54. Irmgard Dörrenberg, *Das zisterzienser Kloster Maulbronn* (Würzburg, 1937). Few would now agree with Frankl that the early Gothic work at Maulbronn, comprising the south walk of the cloister, the west porch ('Paradies') of the church, and the lay-brothers' and monks' refectories, show a 'struggle with constructional problems'. On the contrary, they demonstrate a mastery of the vocabulary of Laonnois Early Gothic. For the position of the Maulbronn work in the reception of French ideas into Germany see Schlink (1975) 400f; Gosebruch (1977) 47–53, and Nicolai (1986) 253–96. Anstett (1985) still offers one of the best introductions to the monastery, though his stylistic analyses have been refined by Frank (1993).

54A. For the introduction of rib vaulting to Burgundy, in Cistercian and non-Cistercian buildings, see Branner (1960) 16–29, Schlink (1970) 89–98, and Kennedy (1996). For Ourscamp II see Bruzelius (1981). With the loss of so much early Cistercian architecture it is difficult to assess its role in the import of the rib. For all earlier views on the dating of the ribs at Pontigny and the arguments for and against their being part of the original plan see Kinder (1992). She argues that Pontigny II was laid out as early as the late 1130s and finished in about 1150. Kennedy (1996) 50–74, stresses the importance of the upper narthex at Vézelay (dated 1147) and the chapel of Saint-Croix at Vézelay (of the same period) as critical in the early adoption of the rib in Burgundy.

55. For Clairvaux II and III see Schlink (1970) 91, 108–19, 138–41; and Kinder (1991). Both suggest that the choir may have been begun even before St Bernard's death, thus calling into question the idea that it contravened St Bernard's supposed ideals of architectural purity. Fergusson (1984) 52–3, and Kinder (1991) argue that it was intended as a mausoleum–sanctuary for the body of the abbot whose speedy canonization was universally anticipated. Schlink (1970) 110–15, saw the general exterior disposition of the new choir as a simplified version of Cluny III, and argued for a Cluny-like barrel vault over the ambulatory and a semi-dome over the apse. A sixteenth-century source records the consecration of an altar in the westernmost ambulatory chapel in 1157, which suggests that the ambulatory was in place by then. The whole choir was consecrated in 1174. Some consequent remodelling may have taken place in the transepts and nave (Clairvaux II), but it is unclear from Dom Milley's plan of 1708, and from Gilbert's of 1808 whether these parts of the church were groin- or rib-vaulted, and whether these vaults belonged to Clairvaux II or originated only after 1153. For the sources of its drum-like chapel wall see Dimier (1957), who, however, dubiously attributed the origins of this type of polygonal outer wall enclosing chapels to the cathedral of

Thérouanne and the choir of the Premonstratensian church at Dommartin. Thérouanne, once dated as early as just after 1136, has recently been shown to post-date Dommartin – see Honoré (1973); and Dommartin, which was begun in 1153 and consecrated in 1163 is clearly too contemporary to be an unequivocal influence on Clairvaux. Besides, Clairvaux's square chapels and polygonal outer wall differ from the rounded chevet wall and chapels of Dommartin – see Kennedy (1996) 154–6. Fergusson (1994), has suggested early Christian Roman burial churches (e.g. seventh-century SS Luca e Martina) as a model, adopted as an appropriately authentic, and patristic, setting for the shrine of St Bernard, whose monasticism could have been based on a return to the purity of early Christian models. Kennedy (1996) 152–4, argues that the so-called Clairvaux III and Clairvaux II are one and the same building; that the chevet choir was begun sometime before 1153 with the active support of St Bernard, who intended it to serve as the mausoleum of his friend, Bishop Malachy of Armagh who died in 1148. Choir, transepts and nave belong together as part of a single build. She also suggests that this church replaced an earlier (perhaps stone) church on the site, built soon after the removal of the monastery in the 1130s, a church containing nine altars.

55A. For the original church (Pontigny I) see Schaefer (1982) 3; and Kinder (1982A).

56. Ibid., I, 187.

56A. See Kinder (1984), who has reconstructed the original height of the sanctuary. It was, like Fontenay, lower than the nave and crossing, but equal to the height of the transepts. For Kinder's dating of Pontigny II see (1992). She suggests a sequence of construction from east to west; a break in the second bay of the nave; a second architect taking over from that point and vaulting the whole nave. See also Kinder (1982) 151–8. She dates the beginning of the church to the mid-1130s and the completion of the whole building by about 1150. Kennedy (1996) 105–7, sees three campaigns in the nave, and reasserts the arguments for the start of the church in c.1150, sometime before the death of its principal benefactor, Count Theobold of Champagne.

57. Hans Rose, Die Frühgotik im Orden von Cîteaux (Munich, 1915).

57A. Kennedy (1996) 112–13, also points to a number of early rib-vaulted churches where a failure to provide shafts as supports for diagonal ribs (as at Pontigny) does not imply a change of plan from groin to rib vaults.

57B. A quarry is mentioned in 1186, perhaps in connexion with the new choir. For the choir see Branner (1960) 28–9, 163; Kinder (1982) 53–4. Kimpel and Suckale (1985) 531, disconnect the chronology from the reference to the quarry and on stylistic comparisons with Sens Cathedral and the choir of Vézelay date the beginning to c.1170. Kinder (1982) 53–4, refers to a 1205 statute of the General Chapter concerning the renovation of the church, and relates the new choir to the burial in it in 1206 of Queen Adela, the widow of Louis VII. She considers that construction was still going on in 1210–15. Kennedy (1996) 269–79, dates the beginning of construction to the mention of a quarry in c.1180, and its completion by c.1200, certainly by the burial of Adela. She relates it stylistically to the choirs of Vézelay and Clairvaux, and speculates that its plan, like Clairvaux's, may have been conceived with burial functions in mind (in this case, of a queen).

58. George Fontaine, Pontigny (Paris, 1928) 89.

59. Aubert, L'arch. cist., I, 7.

59A. For views of Cîteaux see above, Chapter 2, Note 50. For Cîteaux III, which was in building in 1188 and was consecrated in 1193, see Schlink (1970) 91–2. For the proliferation in Germany of the Cîteaux III type of choir, with straight-ended choir and straight ambulatory and chapels returned behind it, see Krönig (1973) 74; and Nicolai (1988) 23–39. The decisive example here, however, was probably Morimond, which also adopted the straight-ended choir plan with ambulatory. For the controversial dating of Morimond, and an interpretation of the obscure findings of the 1954/5 excavations, see Nicolai (1988) and (1993), who dates the beginning of the choir at Morimond to the accession of Abbot Heidenreich/Guido in 1202–4. It was consecrated in 1253. Kennedy (1996) 196–209, argues from the similarities between Morimond and its firmly dated daughter house, Ebrach, for a date in the second half of the twelfth century, probably before Cîteaux III, and perhaps in connexion with the burial there in the 1150s of its sometime abbot, Otto of Freising. She interprets the choirs of Clairvaux III, Cîteaux III and Morimond – all marked out from other Burgundian Cistercian churches by their ambulatories with chapels – as the mausolea of abbot-saints (or would-be saints), and as reflections of rivalry between the mother house (Cîteaux) and her two sister houses.

59B. The necrology of Bishop Normand de Doué indicates that the vaulting of the three-bay nave was begun during his episcopate (1149–53) and continued under his successor Bishop Ulger, who was buried (before 1160) along the south wall of the nave. See Mussat (1963) 180–1.

59C. See Mussat (1963) 293–4 and fig. 26B.

60. For the earliest rib vaults in Germany see above, Chapter 1, pp. 57–8, and Notes 22D, 22E, 22F.

61. A survey of the Transitional style in Germany can be found in Georg Dehio, Geschichte der deutschen Kunst (Berlin, Leipzig, 1919) I, 218ff. For

a criticism of the whole concept of a 'transitional style' when applied to German Early Gothic architecture (and by extension to any kind of Gothic) see Sauerländer (1987). See also above, Chapter 1, Note 38D, and below, Part Two, Note 63A.

62. A history of the relevant studies can be found in the introduction to vol. 1 of Arthur Kingsley Porter, Lombard Architecture (New Haven, 1917). Some of the errors in earlier research were gradually corrected, but the tendency to give credence to early dates survived. But see Chapter 1, note 6.

63. Richard Krautheimer, 'Lombardische Hallenkirchen', in Jahrbuch für Kunstwissenschaft, XLIX (1928) 176.

64. A more recent assessment of Lombard architecture is provided by McKinne (1985). For her discussion of S. Nazaro see pp. 238–47.

65. For the earlier literature on S. Ambrogio see McKinne (1985) 256–84. She established the following chronology.

1) 1104–10: the Romanesque church begun where the east end of the nave joins the triple apse complex. The eastern half of church, perhaps with tribunes and their vaults, and covered with temporary wooden roof and temporary lantern over east bay, complete by c.1110.

2) c.1100–1115/20: the western half of church, including narthex and Canons' Tower was begun.

3) c.1115–20: work on the atrium (or at least its sculpture) and completion of western half of church up to and including tribunes, and temporary wooden roof over whole church.

4) c.1120 onwards: the lower narthex rib vaulted, and upper narthex in building. Decision taken to rib vault central vessel of nave.

5) c.1128–30: Canons' Tower in advanced state, rib vaulting of nave.

6) 1140–4: construction of pulpit and choir stalls.

7) c.1150: remodelling of lantern.

8) 1181: tower heightened to top of next storey; c.1193–4 ribs in adjoining lantern collapse.

66. F. de Dartein, Etude de l'architecture Lombarde (Paris, 1865–82) plate 29.

67. McKinne (1985) 341–3 and passim. Brucher (1987) 55–9 dates the band ribs here to about the same period as S. Ambrogio's.

68. The dating of the Novara churches was established by P. Verzone (1935/6) (1934). Cited and accepted by Bony in his edition of Focillon (1963) I, 55, note 2; and Bony (1983) 465, note 2.

69. Verzone (1935/6) I, 49, 88.

69A. Other early rib-vaulted Lombard churches, notably S. Michele Maggiore in Pavia, S. Giovanni in Borgo di Pavia and S. Savino in Piacenza are discussed by Peroni (1969). In all, the dates are either uncertain or are of the early twelfth century.

69B. For the Rhenish–north Italian connexions, largely sculptural, see Kluckhohn (1955) 1–120. For the early band ribs of St Mary at Utrecht, Speyer and Italy see Kidson (1996) and above, Introduction, Notes 5D, 6, and Chapter 1, 22D, 22E. Lombard vaulting is sensibly discussed by Brucher (1987) 30, 43, 62, 69, 80. For Moissac see Chapter 1, Note 16 above.

70. P. Frankl, Die frühmittelalterliche und romanische Baukunst (Wildpark–Potsdam, 1926) 113. For S. Lorenzo and the lower church of S. Fermo in Verona see Arslan (1939) 5ff; and the review of the book by Kluckhohn (1940); Brucher (1987) 37–41.

70A. Bony (1976) 18ff.

70B. For an analysis of the construction and stereotomy of the Angevin vaults see Bilson (1910).

70C. Frankl's concentration on Santiago ignores the Cistercian contribution to Early Gothic in Spain. Some of the earliest rib vaults in Spain appeared in La Oliva (begun 1164), Fitero (choir apse and ambulatory chapels begun soon after 1170), Veruela (underway in the early 1170s), Santes Creus (begun 1174), Sacramenia (1170s). See Torres Balbás (1952) 34–7; Sowell (1985) 148–78, and passim; and Sowell (1982).

71. In addition to Elie Lambert, L'art gothique en Espagne etc. (Paris, 1931) 51ff., cf. also Juan Contreras Lozoya, Historia del arte hispánico, II (Barcelona, 1934) 31. The resemblances to Saint-Denis are closer than Frankl imagined: the same double ambulatory with slender en delit columns; ribs with torus mouldings; exposed flyers and paired sub-divided false gallery openings.

71A. Its flyers seem to be original with the choir, and add to the likelihood that the Saint-Denis choir, upon which Avila is based, also had them.

71B. Tarragona cathedral was begun on the site of the old mosque in c.1171. Indulgences for building are recorded throughout the second and third quarters of the thirteenth century. Between 1246 and 1266 vaulting is mentioned in both central and side aisles. The lantern tower over the crossing, after 1250, is attributed to a Master Bernat. The last high vault was turned in 1305 and a final consecration took place in 1331. See Batlle Huguet (1959) and Barral i Altet (1994) 163–86.

71C. For Fitero, begun soon after 1170, see Sowell (1985) 38, 150 and passim.

72. E. Lambert, op. cit., 59ff., and G. E. Street, Some Account of Gothic Architecture in Spain (London, 1869) 78ff. The late Romanesque and early Gothic cathedral was built in two broad stages:

1) *c.*1150–*c.*1185. Lower parts of east end and transepts; cloister begun *c.*1175 and well advanced by *c.*1185.

2) *c.*1185–1225. Work resumed on the church under a Master Peter (mentioned 1207) and later a Master Iohan Franco (mentioned in 1225). Change to rib vaults. Vaulting of transept and two eastern bays of nave. Rest of nave vaulting under the influence of Master Mateo from Santiago. See Rodriguez Gutiérrez de Ceballos (1978) and Pradalier (1996) 604–5 for literature.

73. For a long time the building was used for profane, military purposes and was neglected: it can now be visited once more.

74. Paul Frankl, 'The Crazy Vaults of Lincoln Cathedral', in *The Art Bulletin*, XXXV (1953) 95; and Folke Nordström, 'Peterborough, Lincoln and the Science of Robert Grosseteste, etc.', in *The Art Bulletin*, XXXVII (1955) 241.

74A. Wilson (1990) 165, traces the origins of the 'crazy vault' to the triradial vaults of chapter houses, particularly a putative chapter house he believes was prepared by the choir architect in the 1190s. A likely source for triradials might have been provided by the triangular points of support that ran round the trapezium-shaped ambulatory of St Hugh's Choir, demolished to make way for the present Angel Choir in 1256, see Baily (1991) fig. 25, who, however, reconstructs the vaults as four- and six-part. Kowa (1990) 93, fig. 55, does reconstruct triradials, for both the ambulatory and the centralized eastern chapel.

75. At Lincoln, each series of three sections of the ridge-rib itself forms a shallow segmental arch, and these sections do not follow a perfectly straight line from west to east. Both these features suggest lack of experience. The form of this vault cannot validly be explained as springing from practical reasons, for instance that its form was intended to ease the arching of the ribs, since the same architect built quadripartite rib-vaults in the aisles, and could, therefore, also have built one in the nave.

76. A full description of St Hugh's Choir is provided by Pevsner and Metcalf (1985b) 196–214. Pevsner and Frankl identified the architect of the choir as 'Geoffrey of Noiers'. He is much more likely, however, to be an administrator of the *fabrica*. The most authoritative analysis can be found in Kidson (1986), who drew attention to the connexions with Canterbury choir, identified the hexagonal eastern chapel as an intended mausoleum for Bishop (it was hoped Saint) Remigius, and plotted the geometrical lay-out of the now-lost apse. A reconstruction of the whole choir, with intended eastern transept towers and an hexagonal eastern chapel in the manner of Canterbury's corona, is attempted by Baily (1991). He gives a full resumé of all earlier research on the choir. See also Kidson (1994), who repeats his conclusion that the choir was begun with six-part vaults in mind but altered in its upper parts to the present vault system, probably in order to retain the tripartite clerestorey.

77. On the subject of all the churches of this type, cf. Joseph Berthelée, *L'architecture Plantagenet etc.* (Melle, 1889), which is reprinted in its entirety in *C.A.*, LXX (1904) 234. Cf. Robert Charles de Lasteyrie, *L'architecture religieuse en France à l'époque gothique*, II (Paris, 1927) 96, in which building is said to have begun after 1200; cf. also, in the note, the mention of the Hôpital Saint-Jean at Angers, which is supposed to have been built as early as between 1170 and 1180. For the hospital and its patron Etienne de Marcay, see Grant (1994). For Saint-Serge at Angers see Mussat (1963) 223–32, who dates it to 1215–25.

78. *C.A.*, LXX (1904) 75. The vaults at Airvault are carefully analyzed by Mussat (1963) 360–5.

78A. For Saint-Jouin-de-Marnes see Mussat (1963) 361–5. Note however the similarity between the Angevin tunnel-net vaults and the net vault in the south-west chapel of the nave at Lincoln, of *c.*1230.

79. *C.A.*, LXX (1904) 70.

79A. The term 'Plantagenet' style is misleading. Henry II Plantagenet, though an active patron of architecture on both sides of the channel, does not seem to have favoured a particular 'style'. Moreover, English and west French architecture pursued separate directions in the second half of the twelfth century, to the extent that Henry's English buildings show little or no similarity to his French foundations, military or ecclesiastical. Finally, many of the buildings cited as 'Plantagenet' were built after the loss of Anjou and Poitu to the French king. Mussat simply refers to the style as 'Gothic in the West of France'. For an illuminating discussion of Henry II's patronage in France see Grant (1994).

CHAPTER 3

1. Frankl's conception of 'High Gothic' derives from the German nineteenth-century classification *Hochgotik*, a style which was thought to last from the end of the Early Gothic to the beginning of Late Gothic. See for example Gross (1933), who treats Gothic in Germany from *c.*1250 as 'High Gothic'. This classification fails to distinguish between what are now regarded as two quite different stylistic periods: High Gothic proper, which according to current opinion lasted in France approximately from 1190 to 1230, and the so-called 'Rayonnant' style, appearing *c.*1230 in Paris, and continuing to the onset

of Late Gothic in the second half of the fourteenth century. On the need to distinguish Rayonnant as a separate entity see Bony (1983) 246, 501 note 2.

1A. The misconception that the earliest flyers must have been those in the nave of Notre-Dame in Paris, and therefore that all flyers in pre-Notre-Dame buildings must be later additions, has now been recognized. Many Early Gothic buildings dating from Sens Cathedral of the 1160s (and possibly even from Suger's choir of Saint-Denis) employed them. See above, Chapter 2, Note 38.

1B. The priority in the creation of the Chartrain type of High Gothic elevation may, however, go to Soissons Cathedral. See below, Chapter 3, Note 9A.

1C. Frankl's view (following Lefèvre-Pontalis and older French scholarship), that galleries support high vaults, is not strictly correct. The critical lateral support for the high vaults of the galleried churches were the buttress walls or quadrant arches inserted beneath the gallery vaults and roofs. See Bony (1983) 126–31.

2. This connexion has also been recognized by Hans Sedlmayr in *Die Entstehung der Kathedrale* (Zürich, 1950) 259. This book found its way into Frankl's hands in 1953, but he had already made the same observation in 1948. With this observation Sedlmayr connects his theory that the increasing elimination of the walls and the increase in penetrations and lighting sprang from a desire to emphasize the idea of the New Jerusalem. These theories are discussed more fully below, on pp. 273ff. Sedlmayr's theory of the Gothic 'baldachin' construction has been applied to the elevation of Chartres by van der Meulen (1984) 24–30, in the form of a 'primary system' of pillars, walls and windows, and a 'secondary system' of *pilier cantonné*, vault shafts and vaults.

3. Dehio (1901) II, 137: 'The Gothic window is only an opening in the constructional sense of the word: in terms of the spatial impression of the interior, it is a wall – a disembodied, ethereal and transparent wall, but still a clear optical division between a sacred interior and the profane world outside.' For the glass as 'diaphanous wall' see also Jantzen (1951) and (1984) 73ff.

3A. Oblong four-part vaults were by no means rare in Gothic architecture before Chartres, see for example, Pontigny II, Saint-Germer, Saint-Germains-des-Prés, Laon Cathedral transepts, Noyon choir. See Bony (1983) 499, note 26.

3B. Recent scholarship has attributed more specific novelties to Chartres – for example, the omission of the gallery and the enlarged clerestorey – as reasons for its significance at the beginning of the High Gothic style, see Bony (1983) 220–43; Kimpel and Suckale (1985) 235ff.

3C. Sandron (1998) 172, points to an early example (late 1180s) of 'en bec' abaci in the upper floor of the 'Early Gothic' chapel off the south transept of Soissons. It is therefore not a creation of High Gothic at either Chartres or Soissons.

4. These upper arches may date from the time immediately after the level of the second arches from below had been reached, when the clerestorey was already in existence (this means probably before 1206). The function of these upper flyers was probably not to take the dead weight of the roof, but its increased weight caused by wind loads, see Mark (1982) 36–41. Whether or not they were afterthoughts is still an open question. Kimpel and Suckale (1985) 252, and Mark and Borg (1973), deny Viollet-le-Duc's suggestion that they were added after 1316, and argue that they are part of the original structure. James (1982) 76–7, and van der Meulen (1984) 121, see them as later insertions, James dating them to after 1222, when, he argues, the decision was taken to omit the crossing tower and heighten the pitch of the roofs.

5. Louis Grodecki, 'The Transept Portals of Chartres Cathedral etc.', in *The Art Bulletin*, XXXIII (1951) 156. For a full discussion of the transept portals, and their functions and meanings, see Claussen (1975) passim. The sequence of building in the transepts and their façades is still a matter of controversy. Grodecki (1951) argued: (a) the south transept portals and buttresses above them were erected with no intention of building porches, these were inserted later by cutting away the lower portions of the portal and transept buttresses; (b) the north transept was originally built with only one central portal and subsequently given side portals and three porches – an alteration which involved cutting back the front faces of the transept façade buttresses. Van der Meulen (1967) 159–64, and (1984) 97–180, disposes of both arguments. For the south transept he claims that (a) no buttresses were cut back to include porches; (b) the narrower widths between the buttresses than between the side portals below them, and the different axes of the buttresses above and below the roofs of the porches, prove that the façade above the level of the porches was not complete (probably not even begun) before the porches were added; (c) however, the porches are so disaligned with the portals, and the four additional statues (which belong chronologically with the porches) are so obviously inserted into the earlier, completed, side portals, that the porches must have been added later to the completed portal level, together with the façade buttresses immediately above them.

For the north transept he argues (a) the axes between porches and portals are so accurately aligned that both were planned together; (b) the side portals were intended from the start; (c) the façade buttresses were never chopped back. However, van der Meulen also argues, – following the hypothesis of Kunze

(1912) 33–5 – that before either transept façade was begun it had been intended to have not three but two-bay transept arms, each with a single central portal, the northern dedicated to the Virgin, the southern to the Confessors. The rest of the present transept sculpture would have been placed on a new west façade (scheme 1). Only when the original decision to demolish the old west façade was reversed were the transepts expanded to their present width, and the sculpture already carved for the new west façade transferred to them. See, particularly, van der Meulen (1984) 142–3, figs 147–52. Van der Meulen's architectural and archeological analysis of the transept façades is closely reasoned, but on stylistic grounds his proposed arrangements of the portal sculpture in scheme 1 cannot be accepted. See Williamson (1995) 269, note 101.

However, James (1979, 1981) I, 33–51, 268–77, and II, 363–400; and (1982) 57–60, argues that there was never any intention to have a new west façade; that the porches of both transepts were designed and built together from the start, though delays on the north west porch held up the progress of construction on the north side. His claims involve a radical (and to many unsupportable) redating of almost all the transept sculpture – including the latest portal jamb statues – to before 1205. The problems are exacerbated by the fact that both porches were extensively restored and reconstructed in the nineteenth century, when the original stone coursing may have been altered. Kimpel and Suckale (1985) 490–1, note 32, point to archival records at Chartres of the restoration which suggest that the porches might have been added to the portals as afterthoughts without damaging or scarring the masonry. Claussen (1975) 77–80, 103–25, accepts the idea of an intended new west façade, and of the transept portals in their present shape as afterthoughts when this was abandoned. The north porches were begun first (c.1210/15) and working from the sides inwards were finished by 1240. The south porches had a less complicated history. They were begun 1225/30 and completed by 1240. He reconstructs the original appearance of the north façade with two rows of arches between the porches and the rose storey – see p. 92, figs 34–6, and pp. 94–5.

6. The supposition that a temporary choir (of wood?) was built in 1194, only to be pulled down and replaced as early as before 1220, is most improbable. Cf. E. Lefèvre-Pontalis, 'Les architectes et la construction des cathédrales de Chartres', in *Extrait des Mémoires de la Société nationale des Antiquaires de France*, LXIV (1905) 34. Frankl's rebuttal of this theory appeared in *The Art Bulletin*, XXXIX (1957) 33. The dates of the choir, the transepts, and the nave are important in establishing the chronology of the stained glass. See Louis Grodecki, 'Chronologie etc.', *B.M.*, CXVI (1958) 91. Frankl's answer was published in *The Art Bulletin* in March 1961.

The old controversy as to whether the cathedral after 1194 was built from east to west (Frankl (1957) (1961) (1963)) or west to east (Grodecki (1958A)) assumed that the building was constructed in vertical slices, from floor to vault, one bay at a time. The disagreement has now been settled in favour of more horizontal methods of building, in which work proceeded simultaneously on choir and nave, and with the nave construction more advanced (to a greater or lesser extent) than the choir. Beyond that general consensus, however, the two leading authorities on Chartres, van der Meulen and James, have opposed views on almost every single major issue concerning the sequence of construction. Van der Meulen (1965) (1967) and (1984) 53–148, posits the following sequence:
1) **Work begins** at the western crossing piers; first two bays of west aisle of north and south transepts (at this stage each transept arm was planned to extend only two bays beyond the crossing, so that, like Reims, the transepts would have been the same width as the eastern arm); pillars and side aisles of first four bays of nave with the intention of demolishing the mid-twelfth-century west façade and towers and building a new west end, the design of which acted as a source for some of the stranger features of the upper parts of the nave exterior, particularly its corbelled clerestorey balustrade.
2) **Decision to preserve** the twelfth-century façade and towers. As a result, pillars and aisles of remaining western bays of nave have to fit into the remaining space by being constructed in progressively reduced lengths.
3) **Pillars and side aisles** of the choir, ambulatory and radiating chapels; most of the remaining pillars and aisles of the first two transept bays from the crossing; in addition, each transept arm extended outwards one bay and their terminations transformed into towered façades providing large portals for the already-cut sculpture intended for the abandoned west façade (see note 5 above); a lantern tower, like Laon's, planned to rise over the crossing.
4) **Triforium**, clerestorey and high vaults of nave.
5) **Higher parts** of the crossing (the abandoning of the lantern tower); triforium, clerestorey and high vaults of first two bays of transept adjoining crossing, and upper parts of choir.
6) **Triforium**, clerestorey and high vaults of outer bays of transepts.

James's position, in (1979) (1981) and (1982) is even more radical. (a) The cathedral was built more or less simultaneously along its whole length (slight priority of nave). (b) The western towers and façade were never intended to be demolished and rebuilt; there are no breaks in construction between the fourth and fifth (from west) bays of the nave; the squeezing of the nave western bays

was an essential product of the sacred geometry of the first plan. (c) The first plan envisaged a single-aisled ambulatory with deep radiating chapels (like Reims) and was changed to the present double-aisled ambulatory only in 1200. (d) There was no permanently resident architect in overall charge; each campaign of construction was the responsibility of a 'contractor' who directed a large gang of masons. (e) Each contractor and crew can be recognized by the geometry they use and by such details as stone sizes ('holographs') and moulding profiles. (f) There were nine contractors working in twenty-nine campaigns between 1194 and 1224. Each campaign lasted a year, after which the contractor and his whole team would leave the site, to be replaced the following year by a new contractor and gang. (g) Continuity of design was enforced by the clergy, and by each contractor following the general plan of his predecessors.

By a hyper-minute analysis of the fabric of the cathedral James attempted to isolate the contributions of each contractor, and set them in a year-by-year chronology. If he is right, then we can follow the progress of the cathedral's construction with hitherto unprecedented precision. Most scholarly opinion, however, doubts whether such precision will ever be possible, and James's contractors theory has not gained wide support.

Van der Meulen and James are critical of each other's conclusions: see James (1979, 1981) passim, and van der Meulen (1984a) and (1989) 646, 671–2. No study of Chartres has fully resolved the differences, though see the dendrochronological evidence published by Prache (1990). For discerning reviews of James's work see Shelby (1981) and Murray (1979) (1981). Kimpel and Suckale (1985) 244–54, have grave doubts on the subject of James's method, but accept his 'horizontal' theory of construction, suggesting a slight priority of nave over choir, without attributing the choir to a different architect. They date the west rose to the 1210s, the south to 'not before 1225' and the north to 'c.1240'.

In 1990 dendrochronological analysis of the remains of the tie bars in the nave and choir aisles, as well as the latest dating of the choir clerestorey glass, and a re-dating of Guillaume le Breton's description of the vaults not to 1221 but to 1214–17, has confirmed the rapidity of Chartres's construction, and the slight priority of nave over choir. All this evidence suggests, according to Prache (1990), that the choir survived the fire of 1194 and was in working order from 1195 to at least 1202; that the nave aisles were up by c.1200 and the choir aisles by c.1210, that the high vaults (in choir? in nave? in both?) were constructed by 1215, and some of the clerestorey glass was in place before the departure of the second crusade against the Albigensians in 1218. The occupation of the choir on 1st January 1221 undoubtedly signals the structural completion of the east end. The donors of the choir's glass suggest a glazing from between 1215 to c.1235. Manhes-Deremble (1993) 9–15, provides a clear and up-to-date summary of the dating problems, especially in relation to the glass.

6A. Still the fundamental study of Bourges Cathedral is Branner (1962) and (1989) (English translation), though see also Ribault (1995). Branner's chronology is as follows, with the building proceeding from east to west:
1) **First campaign**, beginning in 1195 and finishing in 1214: the entire chevet and choir (first two double bays). It can be broken down into three overlapping phases: (a) 1195–1205, crypt, chevet and first straight bay up to the level of just below vaults of inner aisle (all built beyond the Roman wall); (b) 1202–8, rest of choir (inside the line of the old ramparts) up to level of inner aisle vaults. In 1209 Bishop Guillaume held prayers in the uncompleted choir. (c) c.1205/8–1214, a second (?) architect completed vaults of inner aisles, built upper triforium and clerestorey (to a different, enlarged, design to the first master's) and inserted the high vaults. Mention of the ambulatory, *in circuito chori*, in 1214. Ribault (1995) 65, on the basis of dendrochronological analysis of the crypt vaults, dates the entrance bays of the crypt to 1206.
2) **Second campaign** c.1225–55, divided into the following phases: (a) exterior aisles of nave (c.1225–35); (b) beginning of work on façade (c.1228–30); (c) inner aisles under construction (c.1235); (d) start of work on central nave vessel (c.1245); (e) most of façade complete by 1255. In a forthcoming article, 'Bourges after Branner', Peter Kidson has questioned some of Branner's long-standing conclusions. The late Romanesque details of the Ste Solange chapel, opening off the outer southern aisle one bay west of the chord of the apse, and occupying a position immediately to the east of the old Gallo-Roman wall, suggest that work was going on beyond the Roman wall sometime before Branner's date of 1195, and probably just before 1172, when all building work turned to the construction of a new town wall. In 1181 Philip Augustus permitted building beyond the old wall, and the details of the new crypt accord with a date in the 1180s as much as the 1190s. Dr Alexandra Kennedy has noted their similarities with those in the choir of Vézelay (geographically the nearest example of modern Ile-de-France Gothic), nearing completion in the 1180s. The huge size of the piers forming the inner hub of the crypt suggest to Kidson that at that stage (1180s) a different elevation was envisaged for the upper church, one with coupled hemicycle columns as in Sens or Arras. Branner's date for the beginning of the crypt and the choir, 1195, is based on a donation of £500 to the chapter by Archbishop Henri de Sully, and the mention of the church 'in much need of repair'. *Reparatio* ('acquire anew', 'recover', 'restore') could,

however, just as well refer to construction on the already-begun cathedral as to the 'repair' of the old. The point is important, since if the conception of Bourges as we know it pre-dates 1194, indeed can be dated to the 1180s, then it can claim (with Soissons, see below) to precede Chartres as the first of the High Gothic cathedrals.

6B. Peter Kidson has for some time argued that the chapels are an integral part of the chevet design. See Kidson, forthcoming, 'Bourges after Branner'. His views have been confirmed by Kimpel and Suckale (1985) 295–6, who suggest, along with Bruzelius (1987) 543, note 21, that such small chapels may also have been found in the original chevet of Notre-Dame in Paris.

7. One must work on the basis of the reconstructed cross-section given in Marcel Aubert, *Notre-Dame de Paris* (Paris, 1909) 98. See now the plans and sections in Branner (1962) and (1989).

7A. Branner (1989) 43–8, and fig. 50, argued that the present abutment system resulted from a change of plan. Originally, the clerestorey was to be lower, and supported by only one flyer. Its raising towards the end of the first campaign by a second architect (c.1205?), who used larger triplet plate tracery windows, necessitated the inner double battery, one for the high vaults, one for the roof. The first solution would bring it into line with the possible double-battery arrangement for the outer uprights of the nave of Notre-Dame in Paris, see above, Chapter 2, Note 37A.

7B. Branner (1962) 156–63, and (1989) 163–71, claimed that the architect of the choir had trained in the Aisne valley, and was also inspired by a number of early Gothic buildings in Picardy and north-eastern France. Branner underplayed the Parisian pedigree of his work. But in both its ground plan and the details of its elevation the obvious debts to Notre-Dame, Sens cathedral, have been restated by Kimpel and Suckale (1985) 294–305. The dependence of Bourges on Cluny III (its five aisles of staggered heights with clerestories lighting the intermediate aisles) was clearly underlined by Héliot (1965a) 143–70, who plotted the 'Bourges family' of great churches in Europe. Branner (1966) pointed to the Burgundian Romanesque sources (especially Clairvaux III) for intermediate aisles with clerestories. A penetrating analysis of the spatial and rhythmic characteristics of Bourges is given by Bony (1983) 202–20.

The sophisticated engineering skills of the choir architect are highlighted by Wolfe and Mark (1974). Ferauge and Mignerey (1996) have shown just how extensively iron reinforcements were used to stabilize the structure: transverse iron ties above the vaults of the intermediate aisles binding the high triforium to the walls of the intermediate aisles; iron chains running longitudinally at the base of the triforium, in all parts of the building up to the end of the first major campaign in 1219; longitudinal ties set within walls, and ties running longitudinally at capital level in the high triforium walls.

The influence of Bourges on cathedral architecture of the thirteenth century is discussed – largely in terms of its spatial character and stepped elevation – by Héliot (1965a) passim; Branner (1962) 170–87, and (1989) 177–205. However Michler (1980) laid much emphasis on Bourges's pier forms. Their cylindrical inner surfaces continue through the elevation high wall to the vaults – what Wilson (1990) 108, called its 'split piers'. Michler sees them as the key to understanding Bourges's profound influence on thirteenth-century architecture outside mainstream 'cathedral' building, in northern France, Burgundy, Italy and Germany.

7C. The reasons for the demolition are discussed by King and Clark (1983), 48–51; and Clark (1987) 61–3.

7D. Clark (1987) 61–3, discerns similarities between the western parts of the nave and the new choir, without attributing the choir to the west front architect. For the sources of the flat east end see Héliot (1972). James (1989) 85 note 6, and (1992) 278, note 64 (and with Clark's agreement) doubts that the donation of the quarry at Chermizy in 1205 marks the start of the work on the choir. He sees the choir as contemporary with work at the west end.

8. All the details can be found in Marcel Aubert's study in *C.A.*, LXXXIX (1927). The cathedral was damaged to a considerable extent in the Second World War.

See now Grant (1987) 126ff, and (1993), who established the following chronology:

1) Traces of a c.1180 campaign, including the north and south portals of the west front, and an interior plinth along the west wall and north wall of the west bay of the nave aisle.

2) Nave construction begins after the fire of 1200, and goes from west to east (north slightly in advance of south) in two campaigns: (a) present design of nave established; (b) slight changes in 5th bay from west. 1206 Jean d'Andeli is mentioned as master of works; 1214 Ingelran, 'master of the works' called to Bec; 1233 a charter names Durandus as master mason, and since the boss of the easternmost high vault in the nave is signed with his name these vaults, and therefore the whole campaign, must be nearing completion in the early 1230s. The present design, based largely on details from Notre-Dame in Paris and Bourges, was established from the start, including the floorless tribunes which were never meant to be true galleries. The projecting shaft clusters forming

catwalks on the aisle side, which caught Frankl's attention, Grant related to the swelling piers of Bourges.

3) The choir was not begun in 1214, the date usually given, but probably in the early 1220s, and was most likely complete for the consecration of Peter of Colmieu as archbishop in the cathedral in 1237. Its inner elevation derives from the Aisne valley, its aisles and chapels from Lower Normandy. See also Baylé in: Baylé, dir. (1997) vol. 2, 185–91. Roth (1988) still adhered to the idea that phase 2 intended originally to have real tribunes. He reconstructs the changes to the design of the original clerestorey through three phases of construction.

9. *C.A.*, LXXVIII (1912), 318. This church was also badly damaged.

9A. Barnes (1963) dated the beginning of High Gothic Soissons to c.1197/8. See also Barnes (1969) and Ancien (1984). However, Héliot (1967) 288 and 305, note 50, suggested that the High Gothic design at Soissons might have been conceived independently of Chartres, and perhaps even before it. Since then there has been a groundswell of opinion in favour of the priority of Soissons over Chartres in the creation of the 'classic' High Gothic elevation, that is, a three-storey elevation with a triforium separating an arcade from a tall clerestorey which comes well below the vault springers. See Kurmann (1971) 45, Pestell (1981), Klein (1984) 203ff, and (1986). The problem stemmed from having no firm date for the beginning of the new choir, only its completion in 1212. Both Bony (1983) 227, and Kimpel and Suckale (1985) 261–6, and 542, adhered to the post-Chartres dating, the latter suggesting a beginning for the choir in c.1200/5, and a completion (including the eastern bays of the nave) by 1212. Schöller's (1980) analysis of the architectural drawing of a rose window in the south transept, intended probably for some original (but abandoned) west façade, confirms the very close contacts with Chartres, but not their direction. James's (1989) 119–41, detailed analysis of the masonry of the choir and its junction with the south transept has vindicated some of Klein's conclusions, and the 'early' dating of High Gothic Soissons. James confirmed Klein's suggestion that work began in the crossing and moved eastwards. He found that the entrance arch into the south choir aisle, and some of the masonry of the back wall of the triforium above it, belongs to the construction of the south transept, and can therefore be dated to before 1190, the date for the establishment of an altar in the chapel of St James in the transept's gallery. But this choir entrance arch, and its triforium above, belongs to the High Gothic choir, so at this stage (c.1190) the arcade and triforium heights for the High Gothic cathedral had been established. But for James it was not clear what kind of clerestorey was, at that moment, intended for the choir. James suggested a short clerestorey in the manner of Longpont ('Plan B'). But this would have produced a leggy, bottom-heavy elevation. It is more likely that a taller clerestorey, like the present one, was intended already at this stage (c.1190) to balance the tall arcades (themselves the result of having to create side aisles that corresponded in height to both the arcade and tribune stories of the south transept). It seems, therefore, that by c.1190 Soissons had already evolved the main ingredients of the 'classic' High Gothic elevation.

Sandron (1998) 43–44, 63–144, has confirmed some of James's conclusions, notably the simultaneous construction of the upper parts of the south transept and the High Gothic crossing piers and adjoining aisle bays of the nave and choir on the south side. This has, in effect, established the High Gothic system at Soissons by c.1190.

1) c.1176–c.1190. Construction of turning bays of south transept and St James chapel up to tribune height. Intention of extending its four-storey elevation northwards into what are now the adjoining south aisle bays of nave and choir, to join up with a choir, already existing or planned.

2) c.1190/2–1212, under a new (?) architect. Decision to renounce a four-storey elevation in the rest of the church and go over to the present three-storey High Gothic system. Beginning of the crossing piers, and the two adjacent bays of the nave and choir aisles on the south side, towards the transept. Beginning of outer wall of south choir aisle, from west to east. The details of these bays, and the crossing piers themselves, are closer to the south transept than to those of the main choir and nave. Buttressing of western wall of south transept constructed at same time as adjoining aisle wall of nave. Transfer of tomb of Josselin de Vierzy in 1192 from east end of nave to Longpont may relate to building in the eastern bay of the nave. Donation by Dean Guillaume some time before his death in 1193 for the 'corona' (apse? candle-wheel?) of the choir. When the crossing piers had reached a certain height the straight bay of the south transept was constructed to join them to the transept's earlier hemicycle. Vaulting of whole of south transept. Intention to have a lantern tower over the crossing. Sandron rejects James's 'Plan B' in favour of a tall clerestorey planned from the outset of campaign 2 (note the provision of heavy buttressing from the start), but suggests that the earliest windows of the clerestorey, the lancets in the westernmost choir bay, adjoining the crossing, may reflect a simpler preliminary design, abandoned in favour of the present doublet tracery. Work seems to have proceeded from the crossing eastwards and westwards (bases and capitals of the first piers east of the crossing piers different from those further east). Canons enter the choir in 1212.

3) 1212–40. Completion of nave and west façade.

Sandron's conclusions have confirmed that the reconstruction of the choir of Soissons was begun before the opening of the workshop at Chartres in 1194, but he is reluctant to reverse the traditional thesis and argue that Soissons was the principal source for Chartres. Both workshops are contemporary. Instead (pp. 214–15) he refers to the neat description of the relations between Soissons and Chartres Cathedrals by Klein (1986) 465: 'Soissons normalized the vocabulary of late twelfth-century architecture in the Laonnois and Soissonais, Chartres monumentalized it.'

10. The transition lies in the chamfer of the ledge at the base-line. The transition is achieved geometrically by letting a straight line slide along the part of the circle below and the straight horizontal above.

10A. Because the bosses of the chapels correspond exactly to the line of division between chapel and ambulatory, Sandron (1998) 168–9 stresses more the divisive qualities of the vault. The 'ambulatory' part of the vault consists of a series of triangular bays reminiscent of the 'W' vaults in the ambulatory of Notre-Dame in Paris.

10B. For the north transept see Sandron (1998) 85–6, 131–40, 174–5. He finds enough evidence beneath the present north transept roofs to suggest that the original transept was very similar to the south, and had a four-storey elevation with tribunes. It may have been begun a little earlier than its southern counterpart. He dismisses Barnes's (1969) argument that it originally formed a stylistic intermediary between the south transept and the High Gothic choir. The present transept he dates to the 1240s, apart from its north gable wall and its adjacent eastern porch, which belong to the last quarter of the thirteenth century. Its conservative retention of the parti of the choir can be paralleled in the earlier choir of Laon (c.1200?) and the later naves of Reims and Saint-Denis.

10C. The south tower was not finished until the early fourteenth century. See Sandron (1998) 113–31, 180–8, for the façade, its chronology and stylistic position.

10D. The literature on Reims is enormous. For a balanced assessment of the state of research up to the mid-1960s see Salet (1967). The historical events surrounding the construction are described by Branner (1961) and Abou-el-Haj (1988). A broader historical perspective is provided in the authoritative study of Desportes (1979). Kunst (1981) and Kunst and Schenkluhn (1987) interpret its design in terms of politically motivated 'quotations' (*Zitaten*) from earlier buildings. All scholarship will have to be reassessed in the light of the monumental monograph by Hamann-Mac Lean and Schüssler Part I, vols 1–3 (1993) (on the architecture) and Part 2, vols 4–8 (1996) (on the sculpture).

11. Louis Demaison, *La cathédrale de Reims (P.M.)* (Paris, n.d.) 29. The figures of the four architects of Reims, and the inscriptions giving their names, appeared in the labyrinth set into the nave pavement. But descriptions of the labyrinth before its destruction in 1778 are not reliable. The best summing up of the evidence is provided by Salet (1967) 348–52. The first serious studies of the labyrinth came from Demaison (1894) and (1898). His sequence – Jean d'Orbais, Jean le Loup, Gaucher of Reims and Bernard of Soissons – although challenged, established a broad consensus, and was followed by Branner (1961a) and (1962a); Reinhardt (1963) 75–82; and Ravaux (1979) (who adds a further six, anonymous, architects). But Hamann-Mac Lean and Schüssler (1993) vol. 1, 343–62, convincingly suggest the following sequence: Gaucher of Reims, Jean le Loup, Jean d'Orbais, Bernard of Soissons.

12. A plan can be found in Lasteyrie, *op. cit.*, I, 210, and a view of the interior in the same work, I, 80. Orbais lies to the south-west of Reims, or rather of Epernay.
See now Villes (1977), who puts forward the following campaign sequence.

1) *c*.1165–80 (the latter the year of a relic translation and an altar consecration): hemicycle columns and walls and vaults of the five radiating chapels. Intention to have a four-storey elevation. Plan anticipates the very similar plan of Saint-Remi at Reims.

2) *c*.1200: straight bay of choir and transept chapels. Vaulting of ambulatory and transept chapels and aisles, and high vaults of choir. Influences from choir of Saint-Remi at Reims (notably the clerestorey–triforium linkage). The moulding and capital details of the transept, and the three-storey elevation of the choir, with its doublet plate tracery in the clerestorey, registers the influence of the choir of Soissons Cathedral.

3) *c*.1210: transept walls, change in fenestration of clerestorey west walls.

4) *c*.1220: vaulting of transept and existing bays of nave completed and vaulted.

Salet (1967) 358–9, disclaimed any connexion between Orbais and Reims Cathedral. However, Reinhardt (1963) 109–11, and Hamann-Mac Lean and Schüssler (1993) vol. 1, 358ff, favour an attribution of the early thirteenth-century parts of Orbais to Jean d'Orbais. Villes (1977) 574, 586, 589, rejects any such attribution, but considers the bar tracery windows in the clerestorey of the easternmost nave bays at Orbais to pre-date those in the radiating chapels at Reims. If so, this would make the architect of Orbais the inventor of this type of bar tracery (though it had been used in rose windows, see Laon).

13. Lester Burbank Bridaham, *Gargoyles, Chimes and the Grotesque in French*

Gothic Sculpture (New York, 1930), contains a wide selection of good illustrations of gargoyles. For developments in drainage, including the gargoyle system, in Gothic great churches see Lippert (1994).

13A. A neat summary of scholarship up to 1967 on the chronology and sequence of construction of Reims is given by Salet (1967). The most recent accounts can be found in Ravaux (1979), Kurmann (1987), and – most exhaustively – in Hamann-Mac Lean and Schüssler, Part 1, vols 1–3 (1993). Ravaux suggests the following sequence:

1) **6 May 1211** foundation stone laid. Work proceeded from east to west.

2) **By 1221** radiating chapels, ambulatory, choir aisles, eastern and terminal transept walls; apse up to triforium height.

3) **1221–***c*.**1231**: west walls of the transepts, aisle walls of the nave down to sixth bay from the crossing, insertion of two portals into the already-built lower storey of north transept façade.

4) *c*.**1231–***c*.**1239** (with interruption 1233–6 due to insurrection of town against archbishop and chapter): triforium and clerestorey of straight bays of choir and transepts, transept roses.

5) **1240–1**: vaulting of all these areas at greater height than originally intended; consequent changes in design of flyers and levels above radiating chapels and choir aisles (original design preserved in Villard de Honnecourt's drawing of the exterior abutment). 7 September 1241 Chapter enter new choir.

6) **1242–***c*.**1252**: demolition of old nave, and construction of piers and elevation of six eastern nave bays and vaulting of five of them.

7) *c*.**1252–75**: laying out of four western nave bays and construction of west façade. Completion of nave vaulting.

Within this outline Ravaux distinguished no less than twelve campaigns, each lasting on average four to five years, and under the direction of six (!) not four, architects.

Kimpel and Suckale (1985) 228–9, accepted Ravaux's general sequence but not his dating. For them, the sanctuary and transepts were completed by the 1233 uprising, and the three eastern nave bays (the liturgical choir) were finished by 1241.

Kurmann (1987) 62–159, proposed the following sequence:

1) **1211–***c*.**1220**: lower stories of chevet, sanctuary and south transept up to the level of the high vault springers, with the lower storey of the north transept lagging a little behind and not reaching springing level. The twelfth-century façade of Archbishop Samson kept and decorated with six prophet statues, now in south portal of west front, but originally spread across the façade in the manner of the statues on the west front of Saint-Remi at Reims.

2) *c*.**1220–8**: lower storey of the six eastern bays of the nave up to the clear break in construction between bays six and seven (counting from east).

3) *c*.**1230–41**: construction of upper parts of eastern nave bays, including its high vaults and a new system of flyers (different from that envisaged in the Villard drawing). In the late 1230s the initial designs for the interior of the west façade incised in the triforium of the south transept. These could have involved – for the central portal – a 'low' arch with a stone tympanum, and with or without a gable, or a 'high' arch, with or without a gable, and with the present system of a rose window in a glazed tympanum. At the same time a project was drawn up for the exterior west façade ('Reims I') based either on Notre-Dame in Paris, Noyon, or Laon. The canons moved into their completed liturgical choir, which occupied the three eastern nave bays, in 1241.

4) **1240s**: high parts of transepts and of sanctuary, vaulting of sanctuary and its system of external abutment taken from the 'new' flyer design of the eastern bays of the nave. The balustrade above the chevet chapels implies a knowledge of the new choir of Saint-Denis, and must post-date 1231. Construction of transept towers.

5) *c*.**1250**: completion of transept façades, roses, and vaults.

6) *c*.**1255–***c*.**1261**: the construction, according to the project 'Reims I', of the lower sections of the actual west façade, with the present lateral and corner buttresses, to a height of three to four metres.)

7) *c*.**1261** onwards: change from 'Reims I' to the present façade ('Reims II').

8) **1274/5**: the whole lower storey of west façade and of western bays of nave (bays 7–10). In central section of interior west façade the wide arch orders concentrically framing the tympanum, which had been envisaged in the triforium drawings, were replaced by a vertical grid of statued niches, acting as the visual continuation of those framing the door.

9) *c*.**1275–99** completion of western rose and the rest of the façade; vaulting and roofing of western bays of nave.

In a monumental study of Reims, Hamann-Mac Lean (with Ise Schüssler) Part I, vols 1–3 (1993), has reasserted his belief in the starting point of the cathedral in the eastern bays of the nave – see Hamann-Mac Lean (1965). He has argued strongly against Ravaux's late dating of the west façade, and has isolated four main phases of construction, corresponding to periods of the four main architects (see above, Note 11).

1) **Reims I** (**1211–18**, Gaucher of Reims): arcade storey (up to triforium sill) of five eastern bays of nave, transepts and eastern limb, including completion of most of the chevet chapels (with south side proceeding north). Vaulting

of north aisle of eastern nave. Transept façades to resemble Soissons (west façade) and Laon choir façade. Exterior abutment system resembling Villard de Honnecourt's drawing of the Reims flyers. West front begun, with two (largely unexecuted) designs for the portals in this phase: 'Reims Ia', with portals like the north transept and Soissons Cathedral (west), with narrower west towers than the present ones, and a Coronation portal in the centre and a Last Judgement portal on the north side. 'Reims 1b' inserts gables over the portals, increases the number of figures in the side portals from three to six in each jamb, and in the central from five to six, and makes all the figures equal in size. Last Judgment portal moved to intended position in centre of north transept and replaced by an intended saints' portal. Right portal may have envisaged a Life of the Virgin. Lower level of lateral buttresses of north-western tower constructed.

2) Reims II (1219–34, Jean le Loup): chevet chapels finished and ambulatory vaulted. Adjustments made to the spacing of the apse pillars. Critical decision, probably made before 1223, of changing to the present exterior buttress system, and running a gallery of kings round the transept façades at rose level. This involved widening the transept towers, and realigning the axes of their buttresses to the outer edges of the transept façades. Displacement of Last Judgement portal from central to left side portal of north transept and substitution of the larger saints' portal from the west front. To fit this already-carved sculpture into the transept meant cutting back the east buttress of the Porte Romane. Transept roses and their sculpture cut, but not necessarily mounted. Windows in inner bays of western aisles of transepts moved outwards. Choir clerestory up to vault springers. From bottom of triforium upwards work proceeds inside from the apse westwards, and from the crossing area to the transept ends. New (later) type of boss in eastern bays of south nave aisle.

Decision to widen the west towers, and construction of lateral buttresses of south western tower. Drawings of west façade inner wall in south transept triforium. Central portal reduces its jamb figures from six to five, with an additional figure placed on the front face of each buttress. Plan to glaze the central tympanum, but decorate the side ones with the sculpture which is now dispersed across the faces of the outer buttresses, which originally were to be decorated with blind tracery. Then the decision to stilt the portals higher, causing the insertion of extra rows of figures in the side portals. Change of design for the central panel of the interior of the west façade. Rejection of original plan to have, as on the back wall of the side portals, curved archivolts round central arch, and creation of the present system of vertically ordered niches. Some sculpture of these niches therefore belongs to the 1230s (!).

3) Reims III (1236–?1251, Jean d'Orbais): Actual construction of the flyers. Vaulting of choir, transepts, and eastern nave bays. Vaults higher than intended in Reims II, therefore transept roses have pointed, not round, framing arches. West façade acquires present shape at portal level. Glazing of side portals' tympana. Completion of pillars of western bays of nave. Naturalistic leaf carving throughout. Choir clerestory finished by 1240; new choir entered in 1241.

4) Reims IV (c.1252–c.1287, Bernard of Soissons): West façade from triforium zone to string course above rose, and flanking western towers. Vaulting of last five nave bays. Increase in height of buttress tabernacles.

14. Illustrated in Paul Vitry, *La cathédrale de Reims I* (Paris, 1917) 12 Reims was restored, first by Viollet-le-Duc, and later by Millet and Ruprich-Robert; cf. Demaison, *op. cit.*, 62. The same work also contains a discussion of earlier restorations (p. 51ff.). Hamann-Mac Lean and Schüssler (1993) part 1, vols 2 and 3, reproduce a good selection of early photographs.

15. Villard de Honnecourt's sketch book contains a low ring of battlements for an east chapel. It is not known whether this design was ever put into execution, since Villard may have copied it from a drawing in the lodge of Reims. Cf. Hahnloser (1972) plates 61 and 62.

Villard's crenellations, which he called 'crétiaus', may be his mistaken interpretation of the small slab-like projections that run along the tops of the chevet chapels and their buttresses and continue into the transept façades. Deneux (1946) thought they were intended to support an aborted balustrade, but Mac Lean and Schüssler (1993) part 1, vol. 1, 80–3, suggest they were stepping stones across the dangerously sloping surfaces of the wall heads. When Villard de Honnecourt visited Reims, how much of the building he saw completed, and what project drawings, if any, he was privy to, are questions that may never be definitively answered. Hahnloser (1972) 226–30, dated Villard's Reims drawings to the early 1230s; Bucher (1979) 64–5, to 'c.1228'. Branner (1963b) 135–8, argues against the existence of any project drawings at Reims at the time of Villard's visit. Reasonable doubts have been cast on Villard's status as an architect by Kidson (1981) and Barnes (1982) (1989).

15A. Apart from the nineteenth-century crenellations, the upper balustrade was not radically different in the 1850s than its appearance today. See Hamann-Mac Lean and Schüssler (1993) part 1, vol. 3, plate 40. The dating of this balustrade is discussed in Ravaux (1979) 39.

15B. For good general discussions of the Reims sculpture see Sauerländer (1972) 474–88, and Williamson (1995) 59–65, 156–60. The most authoritative treatments of the west façade and its sculpture, though arriving at radically different conclusions, are to be found in Kurmann (1987) and Hamann-Mac Lean and Schüssler (1993) part 1, vol. 1, and part 2, vols 4–8.

15C. Herschman (1981) argues for a more direct influence of Cluny III than of Bourges on the cramped, emphatically divided spaces of the Le Mans chevet. For its position in relation to Bourges see also Branner (1989) 183–89; and Branner (1966).

16. Gabriel Fleury, *La cathédrale du Mans (P.M.)* (Paris, n.d., but before 1913) 50ff.

16A. The building history is analyzed in some detail by Salet (1961), and Mussat (1963) 121–9, who argues, unconvincingly, that the first architect planned a three-storey elevation like Chartres, with double side aisles of equal height. More recently Grant (1987) 238, has established the following chronology:

1) Begun 1217–20 by a Chartres/Soissons-trained architect who constructed the radiating chapels and probably intended a Bourges-type stepped elevation. **2) A second architect**, the master of Bayeux Cathedral choir, working in the 1220s and 1230s with sculptors from La Merveille at Mont-Saint-Michel, designs and constructs the inner, taller ambulatory and Bourges-type choir piers. **3) Clerestorey completed** c.1245–54 (date of consecration), in the latest Parisian Rayonnant style, by a third architect. Bouttier (1983) and (1987) 368ff and 380, attributes the clerestorey to Jean de Chelles, on no very good grounds.

17. A seventeenth-century illustration is contained in Fleury, II. The best aesthetic analysis of the exterior is by Bony (1983) 262–4.

17A. In many respects Durand's monograph on Amiens (1901–03) is still unsuperseded, though the cathedral's stylistic position in High Gothic and Rayonnant architecture, and its sequences of construction, have been the subject of more recent research from Branner (1965) 124–8 and 138–40, and Erlande-Brandenburg (1977), the latter proposing an unconvincing argument for changes in the design of the west front, for a 'break' between the front and the western bay of the nave, and for a change in the design of the present nave elevation at the height of the triforium string course. The most detailed research on the fabric of the building and its history has come from Kimpel (1977) (an analysis of its stone cutting techniques), Kimpel and Suckale (1973) and (1985) 11–64, 503, Murray (1990), Murray and Addiss (1990), and – most fully – Murray (1996). Kimpel and Suckale isolate three broad phases of construction:

1) 1218–c.1233/6. Destruction of the old cathedral in 1218; 1220 foundation of new; 1222 completion of foundations. Façade, nave and western aisles of the transept, working from west to east. Side aisles of nave with priority of south side over north. Complete (apart perhaps from parts of the clerestorey) by c.1230/3, certainly by 1236. Of the three architects named in the maze set in the nave floor in 1288, Robert de Luzarches, the first, was responsible for this phase, and his plans determined the unity of the whole building. **2)** c.1230/33–c.1240. In 1233 chapel endowed in east aisle of south transept. Central and eastern aisles of transept with their portals, choir aisles, ambulatory and radiating chapels (also completion of nave clerestorey, work going from west to east, with priority on south side. Radiating chapels complete by 1241 since they serve as model for the Sainte-Chapelle. By c.1240 progress on building was slowing down. Durand (1901, 1903) and Branner (1965) assumed most of the work of this phase to be by Thomas de Cormont, Branner arguing that he constructed the lower parts of the transepts and choir aisles according to Robert de Luzarches's designs, but built the markedly different radiating chapels to his own. When he left Amiens c.1240 to take up his position in Paris as the architect of the Sainte-Chapelle he was replaced by his son, Regnault de Cormont, who remained head of the lodge for at least forty-eight years (he is mentioned in 1288). Kimpel and Suckale (1985), however, attribute all this work – and therefore also the Sainte-Chapelle – to Robert de Luzarches. By 1243 bells are hanging in the south-west tower. **3)** c.1245 (certainly before 1258, when a fire damaged the walls and the choir aisle roofs just above the completed ambulatory and the chevet chapels) – **1269**. Upper parts of transepts (clerestorey on west side and clerestorey and triforium on east sides), and triforium and clerestorey of choir and sanctuary, beginning with outer bays of transept triforia (east side) and triforium of apse, and working simultaneously west and east. Kimpel and Suckale attribute the early part of this phase to Thomas de Cormont, who (they contend) executed the triforia of the two outermost bays of transepts and of apse. In c.1250 he is replaced by Regnault who completes the rest of the transepts and choir by 1269.

Murray and Addiss (1990), and Murray (1996) 39–43, analyse the geometrical layout of the plan, establishing that it was generated mathematically from the crossing, and was set out in a single operation from the west façade to the base line of the radiating chapels. This is confirmed by Murray's examination of the fabric (1990) and (1996) 44–74:

1) He dismisses the 1236 charter concerning the removal of the parish church of Saint-Firmin as irrelevant to a chronology of the construction. He sees no breaks between the nave and the west façade. He argues from the uniformity of the entire lower wall of the cathedral beneath the aisle windows that it was laid out in the 1220s from the west end of the nave to the base of the hemicycle, starting at the crossing and working simultaneously westwards and eastwards, with priority given to the south over the north side and the nave over the choir. This would explain the stylistically 'later' features of both the choir and the west façade. The lower parts of the south transept belong to the 1220s and not the 1230s. All this – including probably the shape of the nave pillars – is the work, or to the design, of Robert de Luzarches. His stylistic antecedents are not in the Parisis, nor simply in the 'classic' cathedrals of Chartres and Reims, but in Picardy and the Soissonais (particularly the abbey of Longpont and the cathedrals of Laon and Soissons).

2) In the 1230s a second phase of construction is initiated by Thomas de Cormont who completed the nave clerestorey, constructed the choir aisle vaults and windows, and the ambulatory and hemicycle chapels. The west front belongs to this phase, but is perhaps the work of a different group of masons.

3) This phase lasts from the mid- to later 1240s to some time between 1269, interrupted by the fire of 1258. Regnault de Cormont builds the upper transept and choir, introducing the glazed triforium and the openwork flyers. The present triforium tracery in the choir straight bays belongs not to his original design, but was installed under him after the fire.

Prache's (1996) publication of recent dendrochronological findings, and her arguments based on them, put a different (but inconclusive) gloss on these chronologies. The remains of the tie bar timbers just above the capitals in the nave aisles (1217–34) and transept aisles (1217–1241) are consistent with the established dates for their vaulting, but the choir aisles yield timbers as late as 1241–54, and the high roofs date from as late as the very end of the thirteenth century: 1284–5 (apse and choir), 1293–8 (transept arms), 1300–5 (nave). Prache, supporting her conclusions and Erlande-Brandenburg's (1977) contention that the west front and the nave vaults were heightened in the course of construction, argues that the vaults of the choir and nave are higher than originally intended, and that in their final present form they were built after the roofs, therefore in the last years of the thirteenth century. Her interpretation poses problems. There is no evidence of a heightening in the high vaults' *tas-de-charge*, as in Reims, or of a raising of the exterior buttressing, as in Beauvais – the two cathedrals she cites as precedents for such a heightening. Such late vaulting in the choir would, she admits, involve the cumbersome dismantling and re-erection of the clerestorey stained glass, but why was an apse window given in 1269, and why were the relics of Saint-Firmin translated into a new shrine in 1278 if the vaults and roofs of the choir were still to be constructed around these fragile and precious additions? And for a cathedral of Amiens' status to remain without any high vaults for up to half a century after the construction of its high walls is inconsistent with the vaulting history of every other High Gothic great church of the thirteenth century. Moreover, Erlande-Brandenburg's analysis of the 'changes' to nave and west front have been largely discredited by Murray (1996) especially 91–6. In any case, Murray (1996) 177–8, casts doubt on the dating accuracy of the dendrochronological analysis, though he admits that the nave roof was replaced *c.*1300.

17B. The plan of the hemicycle, with seven chapels and a centre pushed to the east of the last transverse arch, does not derive from Reims, but from the Cistercian churches of Longpont and Royaumont, and perhaps also from their offshoot, the exactly contemporary hemicycle of Beauvais Cathedral, begun in the late 1230s. See Murray (1980) 538–40, and note 62 p. 550; (1989) 102–3; and (1990) 121–2.

17C. For the chronology and sequence of construction, and attributions to the three architects, see above, Note 17A.

18. Reconstructed in George Durand, *Monographie de l'église Notre-Dame, Cathédrale d'Amiens* (Paris, 1901–3) plate 5. This work includes an exhaustive treatment of all the details.

18A. A perceptive analysis of the historical factors, Godly and less than Godly, at work on the design and construction of Amiens is given by Kimpel and Suckale (1985) 11–64; and (especially the un-Godly) by Kraus (1979) 40–59. See also the lucid account by Murray (1996) 17–27, of the institutional interests served by the cathedral.

19. Durand, *op. cit.*, 221 and fig. 33 in the text. For a structural analysis of Amiens see Mark (1982) 50–7; and Mark and Prentke (1968) 44–8. The structural weaknesses of Amiens, for so long ignored because of the cathedral's reputation as the high point of the 'Gothic system', have been identified by Murray (1996) especially 66–77. The persistent problems created by the openwork flyers around the choir, pose questions of motive and even meaning; they certainly fly in the face of structural rationalism, and show an adventurousness that went well beyond the safe system invented in the nave – see Bork, Mark and Murray (1997).

19A. The inscription on Hugues Libergier's famous tombstone, now in Reims cathedral, says that he worked for Saint-Nicaise from 1229, but the annals of Saint-Nicaise say that Abbot Simon began work on the church in 1231. Bideault and Lautier (1977) esp. 296, think the 1229 date an error; Kimpel and Suckale (1985) 346, consider the earlier date as a contract date, the later marking the beginning of actual construction.

19B. See Branner (1962b) 47, (1965) 18–19, 23–4, 28, 30–1; Bony (1983) 381–5; and Bideault and Lautier (1977).

19C. Bideault and Lautier (1977) 297, argue that Hugues Libergier started work in the nave, and that the west façade was built sometime between 1244 and 1254. But stylistically there is nothing in the façade which must be later than 1240 – see Kimpel and Suckale (1985) 431 – and its portals seem to have influenced the north transept portals of Westminster Abbey, begun soon after 1245, see Wilson (1986) 47.

19D. Frankl's term 'classic Gothic' is confusing here, because it puts Saint-Nicaise together with High Gothic buildings such as Chartres, Reims and Amiens. In fact, it belongs to the succeeding stylistic phase known as Rayonnant. See above, Chapter 3, Note 1.

19E. Bideault and Lautier's (1977) 299–300, account of the demolition differs slightly from Frankl's.

20. Charles Givelet, *L'église et l'abbaye de Saint-Nicaise de Reims* (Reims, 1897), where the central mullion is shown as uninterrupted in the illustration opposite p. 62, but not in the perspective drawing opposite p. 60. On the details of the forms in the triforium, see M. Devreux, L'ancienne église de Saint-Nicaise de Reims', in *B.M.*, LXXXV (1926) 132.

A useful catalogue of all the drawings and documents related to Saint-Nicaise up to its destruction is given by Bideault and Lautier (1977) 317–28. The Parisian and Amienois sources for the tracery of Saint-Nicaise are considered by Branner (1965) 18–19 and note 10. Branner (1962b) fig. 15, and (1965) 31, fig. 3, first published the seventeenth-century elevation drawing (see fig. 28a).

21. The arches in the eastern transepts continue upwards in the directly opposite shape, thus forming an arched letter X. They, and other buttress reinforcements around the east transept, can be dated not, as hitherto thought, to the 1380s, but from *c.*1320, and attributed to William Joy, who went on to design the similar, but larger scissor arches at Wells (after 1338). The strainer arches in the western transepts are Perpendicular in style and are dated by most authorities to around 1420. See Morris (1996) 46–58.

21A. The Early English cathedral at Salisbury has attracted much recent attention. Blum (1991) has set out a full chronology of the church and its ancillary buildings from 1220 to 1310. She establishes the following phases for the church, working from east to west:

1) **1220–5**: under Elias de Derham as overseer or *designator*, and Nicholas of Ely as *magister cementarius* (from no later than 1227). The Lady Chapel (dedicated to the Trinity), the eastern chapels, the sanctuary and flanking aisles, and just turning the corner into the southern parts of the eastern aisle of the north eastern transept, up to the south face of its south-east buttress. 28 September 1225, three altars consecrated in the eastern part of the church.

2) **1225–c.1247**: completion of eastern transepts and crossing, liturgical choir, western transepts and crossing, cloister portal and adjoining vestibule into the north cloister walk from the south arms of the transept, inner north wall of the cloister, and at least a start made on the first bay of the nave. At the time of Bishop Robert de Bingham's death in 1246 he had, according to Matthew Paris, completed the glazing of the windows, the choir stalls, and the lead roofing of 'the front of the church', which must mean the roofs east of the crossing. Probably a change in building supervision after Elias de Derham's death in 1245.

3) **1247–58/62**: building of the nave without significant interruption under Nicholas de Eboraco, *magister operis* (active *c.*1247–*c.*1260). Walls and west façade complete by 1256. Consecration on 30 September 1258; but only fully roofed by 1262 and at that date still unvaulted in westernmost (or all?) nave bays. According to fourteenth-century sources, only finally completed by 1266.

This chronology has been broadly confirmed by recent dendrochronological evidence, see Simpson (1996). He suggests that the original superstructure of the crossing probably had a timber spire or belfry on top of a low stone lantern.

The more stylistic aspects of Salisbury's design have been admirably discussed by Draper (1996) and Jansen, (1996A). Draper concentrates on the liturgical proprieties of the design, and on its deliberate rejection of Lincoln and its followers; Jansen on its relations to a new, austere 'episcopal' style appearing in southern English architecture in the early thirteenth century (Lambeth Palace, Winchester etc.). A searching analysis of the cathedral's proportional layout can be found in Kidson (1993A). The west façade, and its liturgical functions in the Sarum Use, is discussed, together with Wells's, by Blum (1986a) and Ayers (2000).

21B. The conventional date of 1334 onwards for the Salisbury steeple (associated with the contract of July of that year) has been convincingly re-dated to *c.*1310, partly on the basis of stylistic comparisons with the chapter house at Wells. See Morris (1996). Tatton-Brown (1991) and (1996) sees no break in construction or design between the tower and the spire.

21C. For the Early English work at Wells see Harvey (1982), Kowa (1990) 97–105; and Draper (1995). The nave was begun *c.*1205 perhaps by the architect Adam Lock. The interdict of 1209–13 halted work at the fourth bay (from west), but it was complete by *c.*1230. The most authoritative account of the nave and west front is now Sampson (1998) esp. 23–60.

(a) *c.*1220–1229, under Adam Lock, the western bays of the nave and the portal zone of the west front up to the string course. Therefore Lock is the designer of the facade.

(b) 1229 (year Thomas Norreys takes over as architect) – *c.*1250. Central panel of façade up to base of great gable by *c.*1237/8. By *c.*1249/50 north and south towers brought to that height, and whole of great gable completed. The geometrical layout of the nave is discussed by Singleton (1981), and by Sampson (1998).

21D. For the thirteenth-century work at Beverley see now Hoey (1984) and Wilson (1990) 172–4 (analysis of its proportional ratios) and, particularly, Wilson (1991).

21E. For Nicholas of Ely, the possible designer of Salisbury, see Harvey (1984) 94. The problem of the relative contribution to Salisbury of Elias de Derham and Nicholas of Ely is discussed in Blum (1991) 11. Elias was probably the overseer or *designator*, and Nicholas, as he was referred to in about 1227, was the *magister cementarius*.

21F. The whole question of 'Englishness' in Early English Gothic has been thrown into oblique relief by Draper's (1995a) comparisons of the style with Rhenish Early Gothic. He tackles the question directly in Draper (2000), where he discusses the choices and developments in architectural styles in post-Conquest England and their relations to written and spoken languages. For the characteristic 'horizontal fusion' of English Gothic discussed in this section by Frankl, and its dialectic with a tendency to emphasize vertical continuity in the bay divisions, see Hoey (1986) and (1987).

21G. Branner (1963b) and (1965) 39ff, and 143–6, first convincingly attributed the new work at Saint-Denis not to Pierre de Montreuil but to the anonymous 'Saint-Denis master', a title now almost universally adopted. The actual contribution of Pierre de Montreuil to the later work at Saint-Denis continues to attract attention, and a balanced assessment of the problem can be found in Bruzelius (1985) 173–4. Bouttier (1987) unconvincingly attributes the initial design of the new choir to Jean de Chelles.

21H. Glazing of middle stories had been used for some time in transept end walls and apses, see Héliot (1968), Bruzelius (1985) 150–1, traces the practice of glazing triforia to the Oise valley in the first decade of the thirteenth century.

21I. The sequence and chronology of construction has been plotted by Bruzelius (1985) 82–137:

1) 1231–45 (reign of Abbot Eudes Clement). A continuous and rapid campaign under the Saint-Denis master. The first phase starts in the north transept and the apse and north choir wall simultaneously, with the eastern parts of the north transept in advance of the western. This phase also includes the first three bays of the 'nave' (the liturgical choir) on the north side. The second phase repeats this process on the south side, with the eastern half of the south transept in advance of the western, and first three bays of the 'nave' on south side up to top of arcade storey. At the end of this campaign the north transept and choir have high vaults, but not the south transept.

2) 1245–8(?) (though there is little or no interruption of work). Completion of south transept.

3) *c.*1252–4. Perhaps under Pierre de Montreuil. Extension of whole south aisle, and north wall of northern aisle, of nave to Suger's narthex, and construction of triforium and clerestorey of first three bays of 'nave' on south side (but monks' choir probably still not complete).

4) *c.*1258–late 1270s. Remaining arcades of north wall of nave and upper parts of all the remaining western bays on both sides.

Bouttier's (1987) 375–8, sequence broadly follows Bruzelius's, though the chronology of the phases differs.

1) 1231–57, divided into four campaigns:

(a) 1231–6. North transept with its east and west aisles. First three bays of liturgical choir on north side. All bays of the sanctuary and vaulting of its apse and first two bays. Easternmost aisles of south transept with its eastern tower.

(b) 1236–46 (the latter given as date of Abbot Eudes's departure). Completion of east aisles of south transept, and beginning of its west aisle. Arcade and beginning of triforium of three southern bays of liturgical choir. High vault of north transept. Upper parts of south transept but not its high vaults. North and south roses.

(c) 1247–*c.*1250 (under Pierre de Montreuil). High vaults of south transept and its west tower. Crossing vault, clerestorey of three south bays of liturgical choir (showing new kind of tracery), and south transept portal.

(d) *c.*1250–5. Three vaults of liturgical choir. Nave arcades and aisles back to Suger's westwork. Abolition of workshop after deposition of Abbot Mallet in 1257.

2) 1270s–1281. Completion of nave. Consecration in 1281.

21J. Panofsky (1951) 43–52, 84–8, sees these refined structural repetitions as the epitome of the scholastic habit of mind. Bouttier (1987) distinguishes two attitudes to the design of window tracery: 'crystallization' (the placing side by side of identical modular units) and 'hierarchy' (the subordination of sub-units

to the whole composition). The stylistic and aesthetic rationale behind the handling of mullions and shafts in the elevation is discussed by Branner (1965) 49–50, and Bruzelius (1985) 45–7, 93–5, 99–100, 140–3.

22. The original stained glass, of which nothing appears to be known, should be imagined to have been in about the same stage of stylistic development as that in the cathedral at Reims.

22A. Only the south transept rose at Reims is thirteenth century. Ravaux (1979) 38–9 dates its execution to *c.*1238–9, but its design could be placed in his 1231–3 campaign. Mac Lean and Schüssler (1993) place the design under Jean le Loup (1219–34), though imply the execution could have taken place in the late 1230s under Jean d'Orbais. The conception of the rose must predate the late 1230s because it is copied by a Reims shop in the south transept of Notre-Dame in Cluny, begun soon after 1233, see Sauerländer (1965).

22B. See now Murray (1980) and (1989) 51–111. He has convincingly revised Branner's chronology (1962c), and identified the main campaigns:
1) 1225–32/3, under Bishop Miles of Nanteuil. The whole conception of a five-aisled choir with staggered elevations on the Bourges model first laid out, but combined with a plan for three-aisled, towered transepts in the manner of Chartres and Reims. Eastern aisles of transept strongly influenced by Notre-Dame in Paris and the nave at Amiens, and showing a preference for bulk and mural simplicity.
2) *c.*1238–*c.*1249, under Bishop Robert of Cressonsac. Eastern choir aisles and chevet, showing thin walls and linear effects, in a style close to the lower parts of the choir at Amiens and the Sainte-Chapelle.
3) *c.*1249–*c.*1272, under Bishop William of Grez. Choir triforium and clerestorey, by a third architect who was dependent on the latest Parisian Rayonnant.

22C. For the collapse see Wolfe and Mark (1976), and, most authoritatively, Murray (1989) 112–20.

22D. Durand sited it there. Erlande-Brandenburg (1977) 257, located it on or near the axis of the new cathedral. Murray (1990) note 20, p. 128, rightly interpets the term 'retro' in the 1241 charter as too ambiguous to assign Saint-Firmin's position accurately. Durand's analysis of Amiens, as two distinct campaigns, before 1236 (the nave) and after (the choir) was seriously questioned by Kimpel and Suckale (1985) and convincingly discredited by Murray (1990).

22E. Kimpel and Suckale (1985) 59ff; and also Note 17A above.

22F. A papal bull of 1244 indicates building was in progress. In 1241 Louis IX's acquisition of further Passion relics may have prompted the conception of a new chapel to house them. The handiest guide to the Sainte-Chapelle is Grodecki (1975). Still the best short account is in Branner (1965) 59, 72, 74; see also his (1971a). A useful discussion of Louis IX's patronage in relation to the Sainte-Chapelle can be found in Weiss (1995) and, more fully, in Weiss (1998), though the connexions he draws between the chapel's relic tribune and the Throne of Solomon are not convincing; nor am I persuaded that Louis's crusade had such a dominant influence on the chapel's iconography. Brenk (1995) sees the chapel's 'programme' as the depiction of the royal presence, and specifically Louis as the most Christian king, through Old Testament metaphor. He also relates the subject matter of the windows to the position of the pews of Louis and Blanche of Castille.

23. Reproduced in François Gebelin, *La Sainte-Chapelle etc.* (Paris, 1931) 13.

24. The ornaments are illustrated in Decloux and Doury, *Histoire . . . de la Sainte-Chapelle etc.* (Paris, 1857). The restorations are discussed in Grodecki (1975) 8–12. The painting of the masonry in the lower chapel was done without taking account of any of the indications of the original polychromy, which were still evident. The entire repainting of the upper chapel did, however, follow the traces of medieval paintwork. The west wall paintings were invented in 1850. For the apostles see Sauerländer (1972) 471–2, and Williamson (1995) 147–9.

25. Jacques Meurgey, *Les principaux manuscrits à peinture du Musée Condé à Chantilly* (Paris, 1930) 59 and plate 39. Illustrated in colour in Jean Porcher, *Les Très Riches Heures du Duc de Berry* (Paris, n.d.). The illuminations were begun some time between 1416.

26. There is a distant relationship with the construction in the aisles of the cathedral at Bristol (*c.*1320) and also the girder buttresses in the side aisles of S. Fortunato at Todi, begun in 1292, see White (1993) 38–41; and Gillermann (1989).

27. Drawings have proved that these windows are old, and certainly not nineteenth century in date. The term 'spherical triangle' has been in current use for many years, and it is now common knowledge that it does not refer to a triangle drawn on the surface of a sphere. See Branner (1965) 62–3, who derived the Sainte-Chapelle window from Amiens. Kimpel and Suckale (1985) 403, also see a derivation from the triangular windows inserted into the galleries of Notre-Dame in Paris in 1220–30.

27A. For the tribunes and reliquary see Branner (1971), and Weiss (1998) 53–77.

27B. The traditional attribution of the chapel to Pierre de Montreuil was seriously questioned by Branner (1965) 61–5, who noted the very close similarities with the radiating chapels of Amiens cathedral. Although Grodecki (1975) 30, and (1977) 173, considered the question still open, many authorities have adopted Branner's (and Viollet-le-Duc's) position – e.g. Bony (1983) 388–91 – and have attributed it to the architect of the Amiens chapels: either Thomas de Cormont (for Branner), or Robert de Luzarches (for Kimpel and Suckale (1985) 400–5). See above, Note 17A. Murray (1996) 66, acknowledges the links between Amiens and the Parisian chapel, but also points out the differences between the two buildings, and does not think we are required to believe that the master mason of the Amiens chapels left to go to Paris to design the Sainte-Chapelle. Bouttier (1987) 372–3, unconvincingly revives the attribution to Pierre de Montreuil. Murray (1999) sees certain similarities in the geometric layout of Amiens and the Sainte-Chapelle (both are designed around vaults proportioned as double squares), but the respond mouldings are different, and the measurements and proportional systems of the chapel are much closer to the chapels of Saint-Germain-en-Laye and to the Lady Chapel of Saint-Germain-des-Prés. He concludes that the designer was not Robert de Luzarches or Thomas de Cormont, but someone familiar with the common language of Parisian and Picard architecture. He draws comparisons between the chapel's length-breadth proportions and those of the House of Solomon (1 Kings 7).

28. There are already a few Gothic details in some of the stained-glass windows at Chartres. Their chronology is still controversial, but these details are definitely earlier than the windows in the Sainte-Chapelle.
For the windows see Grodecki (1975) 47ff. For a fuller description see Aubert, Grodecki, Lafond, Verrier (1959) and Jordan (1994). The particularly rich finish of the interior can only be explained as a product of the function of the chapel as a setting for its precious relics and reliquaries. For the equation between metalwork and architecture see Branner (1965) 57–61, and Bony (1983) 400–5 and Kurmann (1996a). The chapel's exceptionally well-preserved cycles of sculpture, stained glass, tempera painting and enamels make it a particularly rich source of integrated meaning. See above, Chapter 3, Note 22F.

29. The design dates from 1835, and was executed in 1839. The painting was done on a base of chalk plaster. By removing this base at one or two points, it would be possible to ascertain what remains underneath it in the way of traces of paint. See Grodecki (1975) 24, 45. For the painted decoration in Gothic churches in general see Michler (1977).

30. The short finials still have horizontal ledges below the spires. They stand slightly forward. Gables above upper windows is a device the Sainte-Chapelle adopted from slightly earlier or contemporary buildings in north-east France, e.g. Cambrai and Tournai Cathedral choirs, see Branner (1965) 23, 62, and Bony (1983) 386–8.

31. See Wilson (1986) 22–89, for the best description of the building and its stylistic sources. A lively and detailed account of the building history is also given by Binski (1995) 10–51, who reviews the earlier literature, particularly by Branner. The documentary history is set out in Brown, Colvin and Taylor (1963) vol. I, 130–59.

32. There is a short note in C.A., LXIX (1903). A good survey of dates can be found in Lasteyrie, op. cit., I, 118. See also: Valentin de Courcel, 'La cathédrale de Troyes', C.A., CXIII (1955) 9ff.
The best account of the first, early thirteenth-century building campaigns at Troyes (c.1200–28) is by Bongartz (1979). A useful summary of his conclusions, as well as a full history of the later Gothic work on the cathedral, is given by Murray (1987). For an integrated approach to the dating of the earliest campaigns on the choir (up to the pre-Rayonnant work of the 1220s), using as evidence the sculpture and the stained glass, see Pastan (1994). She confirms the clear division, noted by Bongartz, between the first campaign of c.1200 (most of the radiating chapels) based strongly on Early Gothic in Champagne, and the second of c.1210–20 (piers and straight bays of choir and apsidal statues). But she also notes the invasion of Parisian influences in the glass of the second campaign which pre-figures the Parisian Rayonnant incursions in the architecture of the choir upper parts in the 1230s.

32A. Bongartz (1979) 234ff, and Branner (1965) 43–5, think that the new choir triforium and clerestorey were begun immediately after the storm in 1228. However, Bruzelius (1985) 167–71, puts its beginning to the mid-1230s. The chronology is important because the upper parts of Troyes choir are so like those of the Saint-Denis master's work at Saint-Denis that one building must have been the inspiration of the other, and both may have been designed by the same architect – as Branner argued in (1965) 39–50. At issue here is the origin of the classic Rayonnant basilican elevation. Bongartz (1979) 234–7 and 241–3, does not attribute the Troyes work to the Saint-Denis master, but he does argue that the pre-hurricane design may have closely resembled the post-1228 work (including linkage between the mullions of the triforium and clerestorey and a glazed triforium), and he therefore follows Branner's view that the priority must go to Troyes. Bruzelius (1985) 153, 167–71, parallels all the key elements of the Troyes work with the late 1230s and 1240s campaigns at Saint-Denis, and sees Troyes as a copy of Saint-Denis, and not by the Saint-Denis master.

Bouttier (1987) 370, suggests (but provides no evidence) a date of '1245' for the Troyes upper parts.

33. Chanoine H. Boissonet, Histoire et description de la cathédrale de Tours (Paris, 1920) 72.
Frankl is right to be sceptical of the attribution of Tours to the architect of the Sainte-Chapelle. Still the best, and most concise, analysis of Tours is Branner (1965) 37–9 (the first choir campaign, begun c.1210, comprising chapels, ambulatory and choir and apse piers) and 65–7 (the upper parts of the choir, begun in the late 1230s/early 1240s, and completed by c.1244).

34. Reinhardt (1972) suggested that work began under Bishop Berthold von Teck around 1236, and Grodecki and Recht (1971) have convincingly shown that the masons who completed the south transept c.1235 went on immediately to work on the first three bays of the nave. Recent scholarship has identified the sources of the nave design in early Rayonnant buildings in Picardy and Champagne, and especially in the Paris region, with Saint-Denis as the major model. The debts to Notre-Dame in Paris have been underlined by Grodecki (1976). Branner (1964) attempted to downplay the Saint-Denis source in favour of Burgundian influences. See also Prache (1982).

35. Hermann Beenken, in Der Meister von Naumburg (Berlin, 1939) 132, has given a convincing reconstruction of the original state. The figure of Gepa was probably the last work of the Naumburg sculptor, while that of Konrad was probably the work of an assistant, poor in talents, and has been considerably restored. Unlike those in the Sainte-Chapelle, the figures stand at the level of the bottom of the windows.
Beenken's reconstruction has now been corrected by Ernst Schubert (1964). His convincing analyses of the west choir are based on archeological evidence in the structure itself, and on the excavations of the 1960s. See also Leopold and Schubert (1968). Schubert (1982) has also held out against more recent attempts to date the west choir and its sculpture to the 1240s, that is, under Dietrich II's predecessor, Bishop Engelhard (1207–42). See a repetition of his earlier positions in Schubert (1996) 72–86.

36. Ernst Gall, Die gotische Baukunst etc., I (Leipzig, 1925) plates 38, 40, and 43. For the possible Norman sources of the Naumburg passage see Héliot (1970a).

37. Illustrated in C.A., LXXVIII (1912) before p. 33 (after Viollet-le-Duc). The Reims pedigree of the Naumburg passages is emphasized by Sauerländer (1977) especially pp. 180ff. However, the differences with Champenois passage structures are underlined by Schubert (1982) 134–5, and von Winterfeld (1994) 310–11.

37A. Schubert (1968) 30–1, and (1996) 78–80, and most other authorities, think that architect and sculptor were one and the same person; Héliot (1970a) that they were different. The 'Naumburg Master' undoubtedly commanded a workshop, but this does not fundamentally compromise his individuality, nor his genius. A critical commentary on the construction of the entity 'the Naumburg Master' is provided by Brush (1993). See also Wiessner and Crusius (1995) for the historical background. Sensible comments on the nature of the 'Naumburg Master' and his atelier, and recent literature, are to be found in Williamson (1995) 177–84. The late Romanesque lower stories of the west towers were laid out, according to von Winterfeld (1994) 300, early on in the building of the late Romanesque church, that is, c.1230–40. The first storey of the north-west tower, based on the towers at Laon and Bamberg, is either contemporary with the latest parts of the west choir, or shortly after it. Stylistically, its decorative details show affinities with the western parts of the nave at Schulpforta and the choir and choir screen at Meissen Cathedral. The upper stories of the north-west tower date from the fourteenth and fifteenth centuries. The 'Gothic' stories of the south-west tower are nineteenth-century pastiches. See Schubert (1968) 51–2, 231–4, and (1996) 25–8.

37B. See von Winterfeld (1979) vol. I, 132–7, 156–7. The final consecration of the church in 1237 included the complete west towers, with perhaps the exception of the last, or the last two, storeys of the north-west tower. The intention (later given up) of carrying a colonnade of columns around all four sides of the lower storey of the north-west tower, links the Bamberg tower design to the south-west tower of Lausanne Cathedral. See Nussbaum (2000) 35–7. Both the Naumburg and the Bamberg versions depend not on the west towers of Laon, but on the tower flanking the south transept, the Tour de l'Horloge, since their principal aedicules are based on octagons, and not squares. The historical circumstances that led to the appearance in Bamberg of Remois sculptors and of architects trained in the Soissonais are touched on by Vorwerk (1998) especially 215–16. She points to the Bamberg bishop, Eckbert of Andechs-Meranien (died 1237) and his connexions to the French princess, Yolande de Courtenay, the second wife of his brother-in-law, King Andrew II of Hungary. She also suggests that Villard de Honnecourt, who was in Hungary probably in the early 1230s, may have brought the idea of the Laon towers (he drew one of them in his 'sketchbook') to Bamberg. For Villard as a 'trace element' in the diffusion of Early and High Gothic to Central Europe see also Crossley (1997).

38. Lisa Schürenberg, Die kirchliche Baukunst in Frankreich 1270–1380 (Berlin, 1934) 18.

The traditional starting date of 1248 for the choir of Clermont-Ferrand Cathedral was questioned by Branner (1965) 142, who suggested that building actually started only in 1262, with the marriage of the future Philip III to Isabella of Aragon. However, Davis (1981) convincingly re-dated the beginning to 1248 or a little earlier and established the following chronology, with the main campaigns subdivided into phases:

1) **Campaign One**, by Jean Deschamps, c.1248–63: (a) five radiating chapels, and ambulatory responds, (b) outer walls of straight bays of choir on both sides and sacristy on north side (except for its inner wall), six columns of the apse, vaulting of ambulatory, beginning of north transept, (c) pillars on the chord of the apse, upper parts of apse to level of vault springers, east wall and buttresses of south transept, interior walls of sacristy. Intention to build transept towers in this campaign. In 1263 Dean Guillame selects his tomb in the axial chevet chapel.

2) **Campaign Two** (by a second, unknown architect, but closely in sympathy with Jean Deschamps' intentions and style), c.1263–c.1280: (a) pillars and upper parts of choir straight bays on north side, east wall of north arms of transept, second storey of north-east transept tower (all this up to 1273) (b) (by a third architect) first floor of transept façades, the chapel of SS Peter and Paul on the south side of the choir, lower walls of eastern bay of nave, four clerestorey bays on south side of choir, most of the south-east tower's second storey, and vaulting of main vessel of choir.

Davis's dating makes the choir not a provincial and slightly retarded version of Parisian fashions, but an advanced synthesis of Rayonnant forms emerging in Paris and beyond in the 1250s: e.g. from the choirs of Beauvais and Cambrai, from the north transept façade of Soissons cathedral, and especially from Saint-Denis. The stylistic sources of both campaigns are discussed more fully in Davis's doctoral dissertation (1979) 143–30.

38A. Léon cathedral, the first and last truly Rayonnant great church in Spain, awaits a proper monographic study. See Lambert (1931) 238–50; Torres Balbás (1952) 84–94; Branner (1965) 119–20; Karge (1989) 133–8 and Kurmann (1999). The choir was begun soon after the accession of Bishop Martin Gonzalez in 1254. As in Burgos, Alfonso X's financial support was an essential precondition for the new building. Work began at the east end and continued steadily westwards until completion at the end of the thirteenth century (by 1303). 1258 foundation of two of the radiating chapels. An Enricus *magister operis* is mentioned in the cathedral obituary in 1277. He was also at work at Burgos cathedral between at least 1261 and 1277. Given the notable stylistic differences between Burgos and Léon, Karge suggested that Enricus may have been either an administrator and not a designer, or he may have been a sculptor-architect, responsible for the south transept and cloister portals at Burgos (which are integral to the architecture), and for the later north and south transept portals at Léon (which could have been added to a pre-existing structure). See also Williamson (1995) 225–34. The plan of Léon is clearly indebted to Reims Cathedral, while the elevation is of an advanced Rayonnant format dependent less on Saint-Denis and Paris than on early Rayonnant in Champagne (e.g. north rose, Châlons-sur-Marne Cathedral).

39. Jean Vallery-Radot, *La cathédrale de Bayeux* (Paris, n.d., but after 1915). For the Bayeux choir (to which Frankl is referring), rebuilt between c.1230 and c.1240, see Thirion (1978) 240–86, especially 250ff; and Baylé, dir., (1997) vol. 2, 164–7. Grant (1987) 234ff, attributed the design of the whole choir to the architect of the intermediate elevations of the choir of Le Mans cathedral.

39A. The rich stylistic background of the choir of Saint-Etienne, Caen (the first building consistently to combine Ile-de-France forms with Norman traditions) is analyzed by Grant (1990), and Grant in: Baylé, dir., (1997) vol. 2, 156–8. She points to sources as diverse as Canterbury, Noyon, Saint-Denis, Vézelay and Notre-Dame in Paris.

The two western bays of the choir at Lisieux, including the false galleries and the westernmost clerestorey, were built as part of the campaign under Bishop Arnulf of Lisieux (1141–81) or shortly thereafter. See Chapter 2, Note 29. Frankl is referring here to the later campaign on the choir, which completed the whole volume and sanctuary. Bony (1983) 514 note 24, dated this campaign to after the fire of 1226. But Erlande-Brandenburg (1974) 157ff, properly sited it in the reign of Bishop Jourdain de Hommet (1201–18), a dating followed by Grant (1987) 236ff, and Clark in: Baylé, dir., (1997) vol. 2, 172, who put the completion some time before 1215.

40. For Coutances see Herschman (1981) especially 323–5, who argues for two campaigns, the second involving a change of design:
1) **1220s–35.** First level of transept, radiating chapels, ambulatory piers and second level of inner ambulatory.
2) **1239 onwards.** Clerestorey, and vaulting, of inner ambulatory, clerestorey of main vessel, high vaults of choir, upper parts of transepts.
Grant (1987) 303ff, and Grant, in: Baylé, dir., (1997) vol. 2, 137–52, sees no change of plan or interruption in construction, but argues for a continuous campaign starting in c.1220, and substantially complete by 1238, the death of Bishop Hugh de Morville (1208–38). Stylistically, the choir is a sophisticated

variant of Saint-Etienne at Caen's choir, with influences from Le Mans (stepped section) and La Merveille at Mont-Saint-Michel.

41. Cf. the reconstruction of the original state in Seymour, (1968) 65–7, 142–6. His addition of octagonal upper storeys is confirmed by remains on the structure. He has shown that at least the belfry stage of one of the west façade towers was complete by 1231. But Frankl's c.1205 date for the beginning of the western narthex may be too early. Branner (1960) 53, note 26, suggests the façade was begun after 1210. The affiliations of the Noyon western transept with Anglo-Norman precedents in England and Scotland are noted by Héliot (1980).

42. The 'similar figures' – employing the word 'similar' in its planimetrical usage – are the result of the methods of measurement. Cf. Paul Frankl, 'The Secret of the mediaeval Masons', in *The Art Bulletin*, XXVII (1945) 46. For a proportional analysis of the façade see Bony (1983) 500–1, note 31. The basic study of the French cathedral 'classic' or 'harmonic' façade is by Kunze (1912), who established that the Gothic two-tower façade attempted to express, as clearly and harmoniously as possible, the plan, elevation and section of the nave behind it.

42A. The west façade of Notre-Dame has a complicated building history, and pre-history. For no clear reason Branner (1962b) 40–1, note 7, suggested that the present façade was an afterthought, and replaced a slighter earlier design begun further east. The west end, he argued, was originally designed to terminate about four aisle bays east of its present position, roughly on a line with pillar seven (counting from the east), and its foundations were laid about 1186 (when relics were exhumed from the apse of the old church of Saint-Etienne). Branner suggested that in about 1194 the 'façade master' suppressed this façade and laid out his own about four bays further west, in its present position. Branner's hypothesis was given some weight by the discovery, in 1983, of fragments of portals and portal sculpture, dating from any time between c.1150 and 1165, and embedded in the the south side of the nave, under the foundations of the seventh column (from the east) – precisely the area that Branner had singled out. Clark and Ludden (1986) related these fragments to the re-used sculpture of the St Anne portal of the west façade, and they (118, note 38) and Horste (1987) 193, saw them as clear indications that the Early Gothic cathedral had been begun simultaneously at the east and the west. However, Taralon (1991) 360–1, has convincingly underlined that these fragments do not have the character of foundations, capable of supporting a substantial towered façade, and that the façade was always to occupy its existing position. He attributes its layout 'probably' to the so-called third master, who introduced the Chartrain and Soissonais pier forms in the western bays of the nave.

The existing façade was begun with the north and central portals, and is itself the result of a change of plan. Bruzelius (1987) 561–2, suggested that its northern sections may have been laid out as early as c.1190 by her 'second' architect. Sauerländer (1959) and (1972) 404, 45off, reconstructed this initial project as dependent on the west façade of Sens. The central portal would have been a little narrower than now, and much lower, due to the less pointed curve of the archivolts. In 1208 we hear of negotiations to demolish houses in the southern part of the *parvis*, where the southern portal was to be constructed. The resultant delays may have caused a revision in the design. In c.1215, or even earlier, when the northern and central portals had reached lintel height, the present scheme was put in hand. A new architect (Bruzelius's 'third' architect) heightened and steepened the archivolts, widened the portals, thickened the façade wall above the portal arches (hence the gable over the Coronation portal and the corbelling out of the springers of the outer archivolts on the central and southern portals), and completed the whole portal storey. The irregularities of the execution are discussed in precise detail by Taralon (1991) 388–91. Bruzelius (1987) 561–9, proposes sequences that differ slightly from Erlande-Brandenburg's (1998) 95–102, as follows: c.1220 the south tower chamber and part of the organ gallery in front of the rose was built. From c.1220 to 1225/30 the 'fourth' master brought construction to the top of the rose and completed the north tower chamber. On this storey work moved from south to north. From c.1235–late 1240s the 'fifth' master (having remodelled the nave flyers and the clerestorey?) constructed (now from north to south) the gallery and west towers. See Bruzelius (1987) 561ff. The inspiration of Chartres in the design of the west bays and façade is discussed by Branner (1962b), who in this article, and in (1965) 26–8, 41, underlined the important role of the rose and gallery stories in the formation of Parisian Rayonnant. Of like mind are Kimpel and Suckale (1985) 334–8.

43. Louis Grodecki, 'The Transept Portals of Chartres Cathedral etc.', in *The Art Bulletin*, XXXIII (1951) 159ff. For the controversies surrounding the design of the north and south transept portals at Chartres see the additions to Chapter 3, Note 5 above, and also Williamson (1995) 37–47.

43A. Van der Meulen (1984) 157–79, argues, unconvincingly, that some of these exotic forms in the north transept porches are early sixteenth-century restorations.

43B. The most authoritative and and detailed discussion of the stylistic character, and the dating, of the west façade can now be found in Murray (1996) 87–102.

44. The best view of the galleries is given in the longitudinal cross-section in Durand, *op. cit.* (Note 18 to this Chapter) plate VI.

45. Viollet-le-Duc, *Dictionnaire*, I, 88. A few German wall arcades can be found in Leopold Giese's short article, 'Blende', in Otto Schmitt, *Reallexikon zur deutschen Kunstgeschichte*, II (Stuttgart, 1948) 890.

45A. The latticework diaper on the central gable of the west front is indentical to that inside the four walls of the lantern tower over the crossing, rebuilt *c.*1240 after the collapse of the crossing tower in 1237 or 1239. Therefore the west front alterations must date to *c.*1240. See Pevsner and Metcalf (1985b) 212.

45B. Bideault and Lautier (1977) 297, 308–16, date the façade to *c.*1245–50, not 1231. Their purely stylistic arguments are not persuasive. Kimpel and Suckale (1985) 346–7, go back, justifiably, to a dating in the 1230s. The stylistic significance of the façade is analyzed, incisively, by Branner (1965) 23–4, 30–1. Bony (1983) 381–5, assesses the novelty of the façade and its analogies to metalwork. Claussen (1975) 68–74, points to a tradition – going back to Laon – of 'triumphal arch' porches resting on free-standing supports, and points to the particularly close similarities in format to the slightly earlier west porch of the Cistercian church at Longpont. He also dates the Saint-Nicaise porch to the 1230s, and discusses the parallels with the contemporary choir screen at Chartres, and Saint-Nicaise's influence on the choir screen at Strasbourg (*c.*1252).

46. Viollet-le-Duc, *Dictionnaire*, III, note on p. 192 and illustration on p. 193. This has been discussed in Dehio, (1901) II, 158.

46A. Ravaux (1979) 11–12, 43–5; followed broadly by Kurmann (1987) 117–59, and Kimpel and Suckale (1985) 421–2. The single dissenting voice in this late dating is Hamann-Mac Lean and Schüssler (1993) vol. I, especially p. 11, note 8, 337, though we shall have to wait for the publication of the volume on the pre-history of Reims and the environs of the cathedral for their full analysis of the document which Ravaux used for his 1252 dating, and their (presumed) refutation of his reading of it. For their discussion of the west front and its chronology see pp. 113ff, 126ff, 223–314, and Note 13A above.

46B. The folding of tracery around corners, as well as the coulisse-like rhythm of the portals' five ascending gables, and numerous other details – architectural and sculptural – prove that the principal sources of inspiration for the Reims west façade were the north and south transept façades of Notre-Dame in Paris, dated *c.*1245–58, and *c.*1260–7. See Kurmann (1984) 42–62, and (1987) 138–44. Kurmann points to the unique Reims conflation of two quite different traditions: (1) an overall structure derived from the two-tower façades, and the 'triumphal arch' portal type, of Laon and Amiens, which by the mid-thirteenth century was an anachronism, and (2) the flat Rayonnant coulisse-gable type of portal, first developed in the transepts of Notre-Dame in Paris. Both Kurmann (1987) 144–6, and Kimpel and Suckale (1985) 422, reject – a little too firmly – the inspiration of Saint-Nicaise's gabled façade at the cathedral. Even if we date Saint-Nicaise's front to the 1240s, contemporary with Jean de Chelles's north transept at Paris, its influence on the cathedral cannot be excluded.

47. The most detailed analysis of the differences in height and of the other constructional connexions is given in Hans Kunze, *Das Fassadenproblem der französischen Früh- und Hochgotik* (Leipzig, 1912) 44–75. The alignments of the buttress tabernacles from choir to west façade are discussed in Hamann-Mac Lean and Schüssler (1993) Part I, vol. I, passim. The changes of plan during the various campaigns of construction on the west façade are described by Ravaux (1979) 43–59, and by Kurmann (1987) and Hamann-Mac Lean and Schüssler (1993) see above Note 13A.

48. The spires were actually built, and are supposed to have been destroyed by fire in the fifteenth century. However, this is not quite clear, since the foot of the north spire has been preserved and is made of stone. This remnant indicates the pitch of the spire.

49. Because the work of building took so long, the tracery in the towers already contains double curves.

49A. For the Notre-Dame connexion, and the similarities of these pinnacles, and of the whole façade, to metalwork, see Kurmann (1984) 52–7, 58–60; and Kurmann (1987) 138–44.

49B. For the royal connotations of the Reims imagery see Sauerländer (1992).

49C. Kurmann (1987) 46–59 envisaged a spread of prophets across the upper surfaces of the old façade similar to the statues on the west façade of Saint-Remi at Reims.

49D. For the contract of 1230 see Ravaux (1979) 11–12. The tracings are discussed at length by Kurmann (1987) 100–14, and Hamann-Mac Lean and Schüssler (1983) Part I, vol. I, 229–36.

50. Von Winterfeld (1979) vol. I, 144ff, argues for a date for the Prince's Portal as early as 1224–5. The more usual date given is *c.*1230 for the beginning of the portal and *c.*1233–4 for the arrival of the Reims-trained workshop to

complete the portal's right jambs and tympanum in a style clearly derived from the Reims north transept sculpture and the Visitation figures of the west front. For a balanced assessment see Sauerländer (1976), Williamson (1995) 91–8, and Schurr (1998) especially 222–4, with full literature.

50A. See Kurmann (1984) 47; and Kurmann (1988) 245ff, 272ff.

51. Ravaux (1979) 13–14.

51A. See Ravaux (1979) 56–7; but Salet (1967) 360–6, doubts the veracity of the (transcribed) inscription. Hamann-Mac Lean and Schüssler (1993) Part I, vol. I, 343–9, provide a convincing analysis of the labyrinth and the sequence of architects, and interpret the labyrinth inscription as a reference to Gaucher as the first (not the third) architect and to his work on the west portals which began between 1211 and 1218.

51B. Kurmann (1984) 56–8, and Kurmann (1987) 140–2, rightly points to a row of details on the portal and rose stories of the Reims façade which derive from the south transept façade of Notre-Dame in Paris, giving these stories a *terminus post quem* of 1258–60.

52. Ravaux (1979) 12.

52A. Ravaux (1979) 54–7; Kurmann (1987) 155–9.

52B. Hamann-Mac Lean and Schüssler (1993) part I, vol. I. See Note 13a above.

52C. For the sequence of construction of the nave chapels, starting on the north side at the west end, and the attribution of the three easternmost north nave chapels to Pierre de Montreuil, see Kimpel (1971) 31–43, 83ff, and Kimpel and Suckale (1985) 343–5; also Branner (1962b) 46–7; and Branner (1965) 68–71.

53. The inscription was restored by Viollet-le-Duc, who also enriched the adjacent parts of the façade in his own fashion. The original appearance can be seen in Aubert (1920) 152 and 153. The best analysis of the north and south transept façades is to be found in Kimpel (1971), though a more accessible summary is provided by Kimpel and Suckale (1985) 410–21. They are also discussed and compared by Branner (1965) 101–6, who first noted their similarities with contemporary metalwork. See also Kurmann (1987) 138–44. The rose windows mark the climax of a century of experiment in circular window forms in France. The history of the rose and its meaning is outlined in Suckale (1981).

53A. For the Lincoln nave vaults see Pevsner and Metcalf (1985b) 211–12. The fullest discussion of tierceron and triradial vaulting in England and on the continent is by Frazik (1967).

53B. An article on Lincoln was published in *The Art Bulletin*, XLIV (1962) 29–37.

53C. For the stylistic affiliations and liturgical functions of the the new Ely choir see Draper (1979) and Dean (1979) 63–70. See also the convincing symbolic interpretation of the choir, in terms of Mary, *Ecclesia* and monastic celibacy, in Maddison (2000) 43–50.

53D. Kimpel and Suckale (1985) 33 and 61, consider the vaults of the choir and crossing were part of the same campaign, completed by 1264. Murray (1996) 74 notes the differences in profile of the crossing vault ribs to those of the transepts, and considers it to be the last space to be vaulted, sometime before 1269.

53E. The literature on the medieval architect is enormous. Still useful are du Colombier (1973), Booz (1956) and Harvey (1972); but for more up-to-date assessments see Coldstream (1991) for a good general introduction and the detailed Binding (with Annas, Jost and Schunicht) (1993). Claussen (1993/4) pinpoints the change from anonymous to named architects in the later twelfth century, and associates it with the gigantism of French building, and the consequent rise in the status of the architect as a craftsman of almost miraculous skill.

54. According to Camille Enlart, *Origines françaises de l'architecture gothique en Italie* (Paris, 1894) 9. Dehio, (1901) II, 500, gives 1197 as the date of the beginning of building. See Wagner-Rieger (1956–7) vol. 2 44–50; and Fraccaro de Longhi (1958) 235ff. They establish that the choir and transepts were already underway by 1173, though the present Pontigny-type structure was started probably by 1187. Cadei (1980) assessed the stylistic connexions with Castel del Monte.

54A. For Casamari see Wagner-Rieger (1956/7) vol. 2 50ff, and Fraccaro de Longhi (1958) 241–8. It was begun in 1203 and consecrated in 1217.

55. Details are given in Aubert, *L'arch. cist.*, especially at I, 222. The best account of Longpont is Bruzelius (1978) and (1979). She emphasizes that Longpont is not just a simplified copy of Soissons Cathedral, but the beginning of a specifically Cistercian and 'monastic' High Gothic. James's (1984) attempt to date its beginning to the 1180s is not convincing. The close stylistic and institutional connexions between the Cistercian church and Soissons Cathedral (Longpont was the main necropolis of the Soissons bishops in the thirteenth century) is discussed by Sandron (1998) 199–200.

56. A few older Cistercian churches had sexpartite vaults; cf. Aubert, *ibid.*, I, 254. This form also survived in other schools (e.g. at Dijon). See Bruzelius (1982). She stresses the debts to the mother house of Pontigny in particular, and to Burgundian/Yonne valley traditions in general. Kimpel and Suckale

(1985) 277, 518, argue for filiations with Senlis, and the Aisne valley, especially Soissons, Noyon and Laon cathedrals. See also Bideault and Lautier (1987) 127–35.

56A. There has been much discussion over the date of Braine. Bony (1957/8) summed up the traditional view by dating it to 'the mid 1190s', that is, after Chartres. He therefore saw it as a critical example of what he called 'the resistance to Chartres', a deliberately conservative movement that rejected the novelties of Chartres (in this case a tall clerestorey and *pilier cantonné*). In Bony (1983) 172–9, he revised this sequence, dating the beginning of Braine to '*c*.1190' and seeing it as a precursor to Chartres. In this he had been anticipated by Pestell (1981), who dated the beginning of the work to the 1180s, and saw it as a typical product of the late Laon school, but also as a prefiguration of some aspects of the Chartres design. Klein (1984) came to the same conclusion. Caviness (1984) and (1990) 73–6 turned stylistic supposition into hard evidence by establishing, from the Braine charters, that the church was begun, or at least the site selected, as early as *c*.1176, and that building was complete by 1208 (not 1216, as usually given). Kimpel and Suckale (1985) 266–8 return (none too convincingly) to a starting date of *c*.1195–1200, and a completion soon after the death of its patron, Agnes of Dreux, in 1204. They rightly downgrade its stylistic influence in the development of French High Gothic architecture. Prache's (1994) even-handed summary emphasized the role of Agnes of Dreux in its foundation and suggested that construction could not have begun much before 1185–90, dates which would correspond to the virtual completion of a comparatively small church in 1208. This dating perfectly accords with the close stylistic connexions, highlighted by Sandron (1998) 197–9, with Soissons Cathedral. He suggests that the first Braine workshop had been active in the south transept of the cathedral, and moved to Braine *c*.1190, when the new 'High Gothic' master took over the construction of the cathedral choir. For a reconstruction of the remarkable west front/west porch and sculpture, clearly modelled on Laon's west front, see McLain (1985). But Klein (1984) and Prache argue for a different scheme than that proposed in Gencourt's 1825 drawing (where the nave elevation went right up to the west wall). The west towers opened on to the interior, above the arcades, as at Laon and Mantes. An 'integrated' analysis of the church, in terms of the inter-related meanings conveyed in its history, patronage, glass, sculpture and architecture, can be found in Caviness (1990) 65–97. Teuscher (1990) convincingly reconstructs the original placement of the tombs of the Counts of Dreux and their family in the choir and crossing, and properly sees the programme as a forerunner of the larger, royal, tomb ensembles at Royaumont and Saint-Denis.

56B. See Bader (1960) (1961) and (1964).

57. Plans of Kaschau (Kassa) and Xanten in Dehio (1901) plate 448. Kaschau is not covered in Dehio's text, but cf. Ladislas Gál, *L'architecture en Hongrie* (Paris, 1929) 232ff, where the drawing attributed by E. Henszlmann to Villard de Honnecourt is discussed (p. 234). French and other choirs of this type are referred to in note 2 on p. 239. The theory that Villard de Honnecourt designed Kaschau Cathedral is discussed also in *C.A.*, I (1912) 429. There are also oblique chapels at Toul, Ypres, and Oppenheim.

As regards Kaschau (Košice), the theory of Villard's authorship is now discounted. The choir was begun in the last decade of the fourteenth century. For the history of the church, and its influence on Slovakian Late Gothic see Marosi (1964) and (1969). The origins of the diagonally planned chapel scheme depend, again, on the dating of Saint-Yved at Braine. Héliot (1972a) identified Saint-Michel-en-Thiérache as the source; but Klein (1984) 211–253, demonstrated that Saint-Yved was earlier than Saint-Michel. Instead (pp. 116–17), he pointed to the openness and incipient diagonality of the apse-echelon choir of Saint-Vincent in Laon. Kimpel and Suckale (1985) 267, identified the church at Mons-en-Laonnois (probably begun *c*.1180–90) as the earliest known example of the type. See also Prache (1994) especially 110ff, who reminds us of the diagonal chapel plan of the Sainte-Chapelle in the ducal palace at Dijon. She also notes (113, figs 7, 8) that Klein's geometry of spun squares underlying the plan of the choir of Braine can be applied almost exactly to Saint-Michel-en-Thiérache, and was realized as a full polygon at Our Lady in Trier. For the distribution of this diagonal chapel scheme in France, Germany and the Low Countries see Bony (1957/8) 36 and fig. 12.

57A. Branner (1965a) 77–8, showed the importance of the south transept of Cambrai in the ground plan of the Magdeburg choir, and possibly its biforia gallery openings. He also pointed to the debt to Tournai in the use of towers flanking the transepts. The origins of its plan (but not its elevation) in the choir of Basel cathedral were underlined by Kunst (1969) 31–3, and Nicolai (1989), though Basel may itself be dependent on Cambrai.

58. Hermann Giesau, *Der Dom zu Magdeburg* (Burg, 1924). A clear account of the construction of the choir is provided by Schubert (1975) 16–33, and Schubert (1989). He identified four main campaigns of construction:

1) **1209–12**, under Archbishop Albrecht II (1205–32). Four eastern piers of apse and adjoining (easternmost) bays of ambulatory and their radiating chapels.

2) *c*.1215–? *c*.1220. Enlarging the earlier plan by widening the westernmost ambulatory bays and choir aisles, and thickening the piers at the chord of the apse. Rib vaulting of choir aisle straight bays and radiating chapels. Beginning of gallery at junction of choir and north transept, and raising of transept towers to that height. Possibly first double bay of nave on the 'bound' system.

3) ? *c*.1220–? after 1232. This phase is marked by the appearance of a new architect, perhaps identical with, certainly trained under, the so-called 'Paradies Master' at Maulbronn, who was responsible for the western porch and monks' refectory there. At Magdeburg he inserted into the new apse marble *spolia* columns from the Ottonian cathedral and the figures of saints, apostles, angels and Wise and Foolish Virgins (re-located from an intended portal?). He also built the gallery (the so-called *Bischofsgang*). Schubert (1989) 36–7 admits that this phase can be attributed to either Archbishop Albrecht II or to his half-brother Archbishop Wilbrand von Karfernburg (1235–53). Choir serviceable enough to hold trial of the Margrave of Brandenburg in 1234.

4) **Second half of thirteenth century.** Choir clerestorey and upper parts of transepts. In 1266 Archbishop Ruprecht buried in south transept.

Nicolai (1989) revises this sequence. He convincingly argues that the new cathedral was begun, not in the eastern sections of the chevet, but outside the northern perimeter of the Ottonian church, at the north transept, and that it proceeded with the north side of the choir in advance of the south. There was no 'campaign two' as Schubert proposed: the apse chord pillars and the choir aisles were planned in their present form from the start. The first workshop did the lower parts of the north transept and the northern sections of the ambulatory and its radiating chapels. A second workshop, active after 1215, did the rest of the radiating chapels, began the choir gallery at the junction with the north transept, built the lower parts of the south transept and its tower, and made a start on the three eastern bays of the nave. The third shop, working from *c*.1222–32 under the 'Bischofsgang Master', vaulted much of the ambulatory and radiating chapels (according to the Lower Rhenish-inspired designs of shop 2), inserted the *spolia* columns and the apse sculpture, and built the choir gallery under the inspiration of Maulbronn and the eastern parts of the Cistercian church at Walkenried, the latter finished by 1225/30. Nicolai unequivocally attributes the third stage to Archbishop Albrecht II. Schlink (1989), who broadly agrees with Nicolai's sequences, identifies the specific sources for the Bischofsgang Master in Maulbronn and the choir of Auxerre Cathedral. He dates the beginning of this third phase to the late 1220s/early 1230s. For the function of the choir gallery as the archbishop's private chapel see Kroos (1989) 88–97. Iconographical interpretations of the choir and its sculpture as Hohenstaufen celebrations of the traditional partnership of German church and empire are advanced by Helga Sciurie in Ullmann ed. (1989) 163–8, and Friedrich Möbius, also in Ullmann ed. (1989) 158–62. Still useful is Götz's (1966) analysis of the choir as a seat of episcopal judgment.

59. Leo Sternberg, *Der Dom zu Limburg* (Limburg, 1935), which contains a copious bibliography. Also Willy Weyres, *Der Georgsdom zu Limburg* (Limburg, 1935). Cf. also Hanna Adenauer, *op. cit.* (Note 14 to Chapter 2) 69. Clear accounts of the building of the cathedral and its sources can be found in von Winterfeld (1985), and even more fully in Metternich (1994). Dendrochronological analysis has established that work began at the west end much earlier than hitherto supposed – *c*.1190 – and proceeded eastwards, the choir in building *c*.1215–20. For an iconographical interpretation of the church see F. Ronig (1978). The influence of Saint-Jacques at Reims on the 'recessed panel' elevation of the transept ends is discussed by Kurmann (1977).

60. Charles Porée, *La cathédrale d'Auxerre* (Paris, 1926). See also Paul Deschamp, *La cathédrale d'Auxerre* ('Tel', 1948), which contains excellent photographs by Max Foucault. Branner (1960) 38–47, established the following chronology and sequence of construction for the Auxerre choir.

1) **Begun about 1215** and finished shortly before 1234. Collapse in 1217 of the old towers which flanked the choir. Branner reconstructed an 'initial design' consisting of a low three-storey elevation with alternating system, and six-part vaults, modelled on Lausanne and Geneva Cathedrals.

2) *c*.1220, having completed the apse pillars and the lower storey of the straight bays, the choir was heightened under the influence of Chartres, the structure thinned, and a *pilier cantonné* and four-part vaults introduced.

Apart from adding a third, pre-1217 campaign of construction, involving the renovation of the old crypt and the building (or at least cutting) of the present apse columns, Titus (1988), broadly followed Branner's sequences and reconstructions. But Kennedy (1996) 210–50, advanced a convincing case that the choir, with the possible exception of the high vault (which may have been changed from six- to four-part) is a homogeneous construction and design; that it reflects Bishop William de Seignelay's original conception of *c*.1217, and that it was built in a single campaign. King's drawing, on which much of Branner's and Titus's evidence for the 'heightening' of the elevation is based, is inaccurate. Bony (1957/8) 42–3, was the first to interpret the choir as a significant alternative to the mainstream High Gothic of Chartres, and to place it within a broad para-Chartrain movement. Branner (1960) 38–47, placed the choir at the starting point of Burgundian Gothic. Kimpel and Suckale (1985) 306–21, pointed to links with Paris and Sens cathedral, and offered a critique of the whole concept (including Branner's) of 'regional schools' of Gothic. Kennedy (1996) 310–50, stresses the traditional 'Burgundian' roots of the Auxerre design, including debts to Champagne (St Remi at Reims) and Sens Cathedral (ground plan of choir).

61. Guido Marangoni, *Vercelli etc.* (Bergamo, 1931) 24ff. See also Paolo Verzone, *S. Andrea di Vercelli e l'arte emiliana* (Turin, 1936), and Geza de Francovich, *Benedetto Antelami* (Milan, 1952) 392. See also Wagner-Rieger (1956–7) vol. 1, 157–67, who does not attribute the church to Antelami, and who sees signs of English influence. For recent literature on the sculpture, all of it arguing for a post-Antelami understanding of French models, see Williamson (1995) 128 and note 17, p. 277. Michler (1980) 79–81, sees, in the church's 'split piers', connexions with Bourges Cathedral.

62. P. Colmet Daage, *La cathédrale de Coutances, P.M.* (Paris, 1933) 10, and Lefèvre-Pontalis in *C.A.*, LXXV (1908) I, 247.

63. For the choir, see above, Chapter 3, note 40. The nave is essentially a face-lift of its Norman predecessor, the remains of which, contained in the western towers and nave galleries, are discussed by Herschman (1983). Herschman (1978) 94–6, dates the start of the Gothic nave to the beginning of the thirteenth century, and sees its source as the western bays of the nave of Fécamp. Grant (1987) 65ff, also dates the beginning to *c.*1200 and the completion to *c.*1220. She notes the Fécamp features, as well as details resembling the choir of Saint-Etienne at Caen and the church at Eu. See also Mussat (1966) 9–50, and Baylé in: Baylé, dir., vol. 2, 160–3. The complex anglicisms of thirteenth-century Norman Gothic architecture, paradoxically strengthening after the loss of Normandy to France in 1204, are clearly assessed by Grant (1991).

63A. The choir at Bayeux was begun in *c.*1230, and completed *c.*1245. The clerestorey of the nave was undertaken after the completion of the choir, in the years *c.*1245–5, but probably by the same workshop. See Herschman (1981) 326–8, Grant (1987) 239ff, 268, and Thirion (1974) 250ff. For the transepts, which belong to the second half of the thirteenth century (*c.*1260–80), and which represent a characteristically Norman response to the transept façades of Notre-Dame in Paris, see Anderson (1994) and (1996).

63B. For Sées nave see Grant (1987) 258ff, who classifies it as one of the last and most mannered manifestations of Norman Gothic, probably built under Bishop Gaufredus de Maiet (1240–57). See also Olde-Choukair, in Baylé dir., vol. 1 (1997) 159–73, and vol. 2 (1997) 179–84.

64. The chronology of Burgos, and its stylistic affiliations with France, have been reconstructed by Karge (1989) and (1989a). He isolates four main phases of construction for the thirteenth-century building (see 1989, 69–118).

1) 1221–30. The whole of the choir; part of the chapel of St Nicholas (opening eastwards off the north transept); the lower courses of the east and south walls of the south transept, including the lowest arcade of the Puerta del Sarmental. The stylistic influences in this phase clearly come from Bourges Cathedral and its Parisian and Loire affiliates. The Burgos elevation echoes, not only Bourges's inner aisles, but also the main elevations of Saint-Leu d'Esserent and Moret-sur-Loing. Its clerestorey tracery closely follows that of Tours Cathedral choir. Its dosseret profiles echo those in Bourges, Larchant and Notre-Dame in Paris. Karge rightly rejects the traditional comparisons between the plan of the choir and that of Coutances or even Pontigny: they are based on Lambert's misidentification of the present thirteenth-century ambulatory and chapels (fundamentally remodelled in the 1270s) with the original east end, whose plan Karge reconstructs with an ambulatory with bays of six-part vaults, each bay opening into small apsidal chapels, separated from each other by the outer curving wall of the apse. The system comes straight from the apse at Bourges, and must be the earliest example of this solution outside France (see pl. 135).

2) *c.*1230–*c.*1245/50. St Nicholas chapel finished *c.*1234. Upper parts of Puerta del Sarmental carved to a new design by a sculptural workshop coming from Amiens (west) and Bourges (west) (*c.*1240). New design also for inner south transept wall. Lower parts of north transept, including portal (completed *c.*1245). From *c.*1245 addition of chapels to choir straight bays; new entrance responds to chevet chapels, and beginning of nave. Completion of transepts *c.*1250.

3) *c.*1250–60. Most of nave complete by *c.*1255, but westernmost bays and the two lower stories of the west façade completed by 1260 in a slightly more advanced style. Consecration of cathedral in 1260.

4) *c.*1260–75 (under the architect Enricus, active at least from 1261 to his death in 1277). This phase, stimulated by the encouragement of Alfonso X (1252–84), was characterized by up-to-date Parisian Rayonnant additions, and sophisticated combinations of sculpture and architecture. Tracery galleries in transept façades, and south transept rose. Third storey of west façade (*c.*1265). Two-storey cloister (*c.*1265–70). New radiating chapels of chevet (*c.*1275).

65. For Tarragona see above, Chapter 2, Note 71B.

66. For illustrations of Cuenca, see Juan Contreras Lozoya, *Historia del arte hispánico* (Barcelona, 1931–43) II, 99–102, and in the text p. 104. Cf. also Lambert, *op. cit.*, 159ff. The façade was restored in 1902. If this cathedral is

perhaps disappointing, the position of the town, of which one could use that much abused word picturesque, is an ample compensation.

Lambert (1931) 159–74, dates the construction of the choir between *c.*1200 and 1210; Torres Balbás (1952) 50–4, to *c.*1210–25. Welander (1991) 292–5, dates the foundation to the period of Bishop Garcia (1208–25). Alfonso VIII's donations to the cathedral from 1183 to 1214 make no mention of building activity, and the sources that the high altar was consecrated in 1207/8 are late and contradictory. Welander's later dating tallies with the close stylistic similarities between the eastern parts of the cathedral and a group of buildings all dating to the middle of the first quarter of the thirteenth century: the Cistercian church at Las Huelgas, the Cistercian refectory at Huerta (begun *c.*1215, complete by 1223), and the cathedral of Siguenza. See also Sowell (1985) 184–5, Karge (1989) 122–3. The choir of Cuenca cathedral represents a precocious incursion of Early Gothic Laonnois and Soissonais influences into Spain, with borrowings from the cathedral and Saint-Léger at Soissons, and from Laon Cathedral. Welander (1991) also identifies profile similarities in the Noyon chevet, in the nave at Rouen and at Saint-Pierre at Dreux. There are also close similarities with Essômes, and with the sculpture of Longpont and of Saint-Yved at Braine. Since the flanking sections of the choir were destroyed in the fifteenth century the alignment of the choir chapels cannot be exactly reconstructed, but it is likely that they were stepped, and perhaps even angled diagonally like those of Saint-Yved. See also Lamarca (1978) 15–18. Welander (1991) considers that part of the workforce in the early campaigns at Toledo came from Cuenca. For the later nave of Cuenca, begun probably after *c.*1260, and its connexions to the transepts at Burgos, see Karge (1989) 130–33.

67. Elie Lambert, *Tolède* (Paris, 1925) 54. See also Josep Gudiol i Ricart, *La catedral de Toledo* (Madrid, *c.* 1948) 30, and August L. Mayer, *Toledo* (Leipzig, 1910) 58.

The history of the thirteenth-century cathedral of Toledo has now been carefully examined by W. Welander (1991) especially 32ff. Stylistically he sees it as a predominantly Spanish achievement, having a dual character: it belongs both to Bourges, and the Bourges idea of a Rome-centred Parisian architecture of the later twelfth century, but it also espouses a French-resistant Mozarabic art. Conceptually, it embodies three consecutive but overlapping ideals. The first, inspired by its founder Archbishop Rodrigo (1209–47), proclaimed the revival of Visigothic Toledo, celebrated a nascent Spanish nationalism against the infidel, and asserted the primacy of Toledo over its Spanish metropolitan rivals. Its French borrowings, together with its early Christian and Roman reminiscences, are consistent with the pro-Papal ideals of the Parisian-educated Rodrigo, who had attended the Fourth Lateran Council in 1215. The second project, under Archbishop Sancho I (1251–61), a Mozarab who had visited England in 1255–6, initiated the transformation of the cathedral choir, perhaps under the influence of Westminster Abbey, into a gigantic royal mausoleum chapel; and it reasserted the prerogatives of Toledo as the coronation church of the kings of Spain. The third, a revised version of the second project, underscored these royal associations and proclaimed the triumph of Mozarabic Toledo under Archbishop Gudiel.

Welander establishes the following chronology and sequence of construction:

Campaign One (under the architect Martin): *c.*1215/21–38. The radiating chapels, outer ambulatory and its vaults, eastern chapel. Strongly dependent on Bourges, Notre-Dame in Paris, but also on the Pantheon in Rome, in its half-rotunda plan and the alternating polygonal and rectangular shape of its radiating chapels. 1222 and 1224 papal bulls in favour of the financing of the cathedral, the latter referring to actual construction. 1226 official laying of foundation stone by Archbishop Rodrigo and Fernando III. Radiating chapels on north side complete by 1231, all of them by 1238. By 1247 nave may have been begun since by that date the chapel on the south side of the first southern bay of the nave was complete.

Campaign Two (under a new architect): *c.*1260–75/84. Piers of sanctuary, eastern crossing, eastern transept, and inner apse, all with a distinctly new socle profile. The polygon of the inner apse is generated from a different point than the arcs of circles defining the intermediary piers and outer ambulatory wall, resulting in misalignments and irregularities between inner and outer ambulatory bays. (On this see, in detail, Junquera (1937)). Southern chapel of choir in use by 1264. Inner ambulatory: superstructure and vaults, using a Parisian, Beauvais-inspired elevation with band triforium and oculus clerestorey, but with Mozarabic tracery and multi-cusped arches. Beginning of first three bays of nave on south side and perhaps south transept vaults (called 'First nave campaign'). This whole campaign inspired by Archbishop Sancho I (died 1261), of royal blood, who set up the royal chapel in the inner apse. It ends in 1275–84, a period of financial difficulty and disputed elections to the archiepiscopal throne.

Campaign Three: 1285–9. The beginning coincides with the return of Archbishop Gudiel, the death of Alfonso X and the coronation of Sancho IV in the cathedral, the end with the translation of the bodies of Alfonso VIII and Sancho III in 1289 to the apse bay. Triforium and clerestorey of the choir and east sides of the transept, including vaults of choir, whose lierne patterns parallel, or even anticipate, the earliest liernes in England.

Campaign Four: *c.*1288/9–1301. This coincides with documentary references to Archbishop Gudiel setting up his tomb in the *coro* (the eastern bays of the nave) in 1288/9 and in 1291, and his burial there in 1301. Sculpture of kings, apostles, angels in triforium of choir, forming a coherent funerary iconography, enhancing the character of the choir as a royal mausoleum. North transept portal (La Puerta del Reloj). High walls of western side of transept (to different design than elevation of choir and eastern half of transept) and vaulting of north transept and crossing. Completion of the *coro* with the high walls and vaulting of the eastern bays of the nave ('Second nave campaign')

Karge (1989) 119–22, differs from Welander's account on a number of points. He dates (I think correctly) the conception of the choir to *c.*1220, and not as early as possibly '*c.*1215'. He puts the completion of the whole choir to the middle of the thirteenth century, and follows the conventional dating of the high choir vaults to 1493, together with those in the eastern bays of the nave (the *coro*). While Welander's early dating leads him to exclude Le Mans' influence on Toledo, Karge convincingly reasserts the critical importance of Le Mans' chevet, begun after 1217, on Master Martin's east end. But Karge is, along with Welander, critical of Branner's derivation of the radiating chapel system from Le Mont-Notre-Dame and Sainte-Croix in Etampes, see Branner (1962) 166–7, and (1989) 191–2. Instead, he sees parallels between the system and that at Burgos, and identifies similarities between the latter cathedral and many details in the chevet of Toledo. Burgos seems to have been a little ahead of Toledo in construction, since it is the smaller cathedral and was more speedily completed. For the stylistic overlaps between Mozarabic and French in the choir see Mata (1999).

68. George Edmund Street, *Some Account of Gothic Architecture in Spain* (London, 1869) 235.

69. An equally 'Spanish' aspect of the exterior is the proliferation of later chapels, most of them funerary, around the core of the building, in such a way as to obscure large parts of the original cathedral. For the growth of these chapels in later medieval Europe, including the Iberian peninsula, see Colvin (1991) 152–89.

70. *C.A.*, LXXX (1916) 300ff. For the chronology of the thirteenth-century Gothic work at Nevers Cathedral see Branner (1960) 157–9. Work began in 1211 on vaulting the Romanesque west transepts. The nave, constructed from west to east, begun not much before 1235 and complete by *c.*1250. Kimpel and Suckale (1985) 321ff and 525, put the beginning '*c.*1220–30'. Anfray (1964) 18–48, describe the Gothic nave. Kimpel and Suckale (1985) 321ff, place it in its Burgundian context, especially in relation to Sens.

70A. For Toul cathedral see Schiffler (1977) and Villes (1972) (1983). Both agree that the choir was begun in 1221 by an architect who had come directly from work on the ambulatory and radiating chapels of Reims Cathedral. The first phase of construction consisted of the sanctuary, the choir aisles and the beginning of the transept, with a break at the spiral staircases between choir aisles and transept. The second phase, indebted strongly in its details to Parisian Rayonnant and to Saint-Nicaise at Reims, saw the completion of the transept and the first bay of the nave. Villes (1983) 78ff, thinks that phase one was complete (without vaults) by 1230/5, in time to influence the very similar choir apses of the Church of Our Lady in Trier and of St Elizabeth in Marburg (the latter begun in 1236); and he puts the completion of phase two at *c.*1250. Schiffler (1977) 2, 115, 208, 210, dates the completion of phase one later (*c.*1240) and of phase two to between 1245 and 1265. Burnand (1989) 309–16, thinks most of phase one was over by 1235, but phase two lasted into the 'second half of the century'. For the influence of this work on St Vincent at Metz see Brachmann (1998) 65–8.

71. There are chapels in the transepts, to the left and right of the entrance to the choir. Charles Oursel, *L'église Notre-Dame de Dijon*, *P.M.* (Paris, n.d.) plan before the title page and p. 39.

72. *Ibid.*, illustration on p. 31. It is not known when Notre-Dame at Dijon was begun, but at least some time before 1230, when in March of that year 20 livres were given to the 'opus'. It was finished by 1240 when, according to Stephen of Bourbon, sculpture in the narthex fell and killed a 'usurer'. Both Bony (1957/58) 43–4, and more thoroughly Branner (1960) 54–62, place the 'conservative' features of the church in the context of Soissonais Early Gothic and its Burgundian variants. Branner (1960) 132–3, established two campaigns: 1) *c.*1220 the choir and east walls of the transepts; 2) the rest of the transepts to *c.*1230, and the nave completed by *c.*1240. He and Bony placed its beginning after that of the choir of Auxerre, see above, Chapter 3, Note 60. However, Titus (1984) 130–7, and (1988) 56, argued that Notre-Dame came first. On purely stylistic grounds, he suggested that Dijon was begun *c.*1210, or even as early as 1200 (in the chapel area and transepts). He saw the church, especially the eastern nave bays, as the model for the first campaign at Auxerre (hemicycle and choir aisles), and an indication of what Auxerre was to look like before the Chartrain 'alterations'. And this, in effect, makes Notre-Dame at Dijon the precursor, not the follower of Auxerre and promotes its importance in the

foundation of thirteenth-century Burgundian Gothic architecture. Kennedy (1996) 345–8, convincingly rejects this, and confirms the '*c.*1220' starting date.

73. Discussed in Joseph Gantner, *Kunstgeschichte der Schweiz*, II (Frauenfeld, 1947) 51 and 64. Bony (1957/8) 44ff, was the first to include Lausanne and Geneva in a wide 'para-Chartrain' movement (which included Notre-Dame at Dijon), and to see the influence of William the Englishman's Trinity Chapel at Canterbury on the choir of Lausanne. Branner (1960) 50ff, saw both Swiss cathedrals as sources for the Burgundian Gothic of Auxerre and Notre-Dame at Dijon, a derivation questioned by Kennedy (1996), who stresses the sources of the Burgundian buildings in Champagne, the Parisis, and Sens. For Lausanne in particular see Grandjean (1975) 45–174, who identifies a tentative beginning *c.*1160–70 with ambulatory and the foundations of (never realized) radiating chapels, followed by two long campaigns:

1) *c.*1192–*c.*1215, choir, transepts, crossing and first bay of nave.

2) **rest of the nave** (ground floor of western massif mentioned from 1220). The whole building, even including most or all of the western towers, was substantially complete by 1232 (translation of relics). (Bell for south-west tower in 1234).

For Geneva see Bony (1957/8) 45, Branner (1960) 34, 50–1, and, most recently, Freigang and Kurmann (1991). They date the first phase of construction, up to the base of the triforium in nave and transepts, to *c.*1180–1215, and the second, more advanced work, under the influence of Lausanne Cathedral (especially its lantern tower), from *c.*1215–50, mediated by the Bishop of Geneva (1215–60), Aymon de Grandson, who had been a canon of Lausanne from 1210. They also give a comprehensive picture of Geneva's stylistic affiliations in late twelfth- early thirteenth-century Gothic in the Rhone valley.

74. Paul Clemen and Cornelius Gurlitt, *Die Klosterbauten der Cistercienser in Belgien* (Berlin, 1916). For all these churches see Brigode (1975) 237–45; and Buyle et al. (1997) 44–6, 119–32.

74A. Of the group, Villers has the best-preserved early thirteenth-century structure. Begun on the model of Clairvaux II shortly before 1208, it changed allegiance, under Abbot Conrad d'Urach (1209–14) to Laonnois, Soissonais and 'resistance-to-Chartres' forms, including a six-part vault over the single choir forebay and a polygonally apsed choir (without an ambulatory) with superposed exterior passages. The fascination with tiered oculi in the apse and in the transept end walls is, however, a more local peculiarity. See Brigode (1971) and de Waha (1977). I was not able to consult Coomans's (1997) thesis on Villers.

74B. The choir was begun in 1221 and completed at the latest by 1251. A consecration took place in 1280. See Devliegher (1954 and 1956). For its position in the 'resistance to Chartres' movement – both for its diagonal chapels and its exterior clerestorey passages – see Bony (1957/8) 36, 45.

74C. See Chapter 3, Notes 56A and 57.

75. Reconstructed in Henri Velge, *La Collégiale des Saints Michel et Gudule à Bruxelles* (Brussels, 1925) plate XVIII. The original triforium is reconstructed in the same work, p. 232, fig. 21. For the position of Ste Gudule in the history of Brabantine Gothic see Lemaire (1963) 38–41.

76. Richard Hamann, *Deutsche und französische Kunst im Mittelalter* (Marburg, 1923). His ideas are summed up in vol. II, 172. Hamann's theory, of wandering bands of masons, particularly from Normandy, travelling from site to site in Central Europe, has been called into question by more recent scholarship on the reception of Gothic in central Europe. See von Winterfeld (1979) vol. I, 155–7; and Marosi (1984) 183–7.

76A. A well-balanced introduction to the early reception of Gothic in Germany can be found in Nussbaum (2000) especially 25–45, 24–59.

77. Werner Noack, *Der Dom zu Bamberg* (Burg, 1925); Wilhelm Pinder, *Der Bamberger Dom und seine Bildwerke etc.* (Berlin, 1927); Hermann Beenken, *Bildwerke des Bamberger Domes* (Bonn, 1925). See now von Winterfeld (1979), vol. I, 85ff, and Vorwerk (1998).

77A. For Tischnowitz (the Cistercian church of Tišnov) see Kuthan (1982) 275–84 and Kuthan (1994) 393–407; for Ják see Dercsényi (1957) 173–202; and for the fullest account of the stylistic connexions between Ják, Lébény and Austria and Middle Germany see Marosi (1984) 97, 104, 109–11, 146ff. For a summary of recent research on Ják see Mezey-Debreczeni and Szentesi (1991).

78. The completion of the south tower began in 1894. Heinrich Bergner, *Naumburg und Merseburg* (Leipzig, 1926); 2nd ed. by Fritz Haesler. For the Bamberg and Naumburg towers see above, Chapter 3, Notes 37A and 37B.

78A. An entertaining introduction to the Albigensian heresy is provided by Le Roy Ladurie (1980). For St Dominic and the Dominicans see Brooke (1975) and Southern (1983) 279–82.

78B. Short and useful introductions to the Franciscan order are given by Southern (1983) 282ff, and Moorman (1968). See also the celebration of the Franciscan achievement in two exhibition catalogues coinciding with the 800th anniversary of St Francis's birth: *Francesco d'Assisi* (1982), and *800 Jahre Franz von Assisi* (1982). Picou (1984) provides a conspectus of plans for the Franciscan monasteries in France, along the lines of Dimier's for the Cistercians. A forcefully argued attempt to relate mendicant architecture to friars' ideals has been made by Schenkluhn (1985). For Dominican legislation on architecture and decoration see Sundt (1987). The best, and only, survey of Franciscan and Dominican architecture in Europe from the early thirteenth century to the end of the Middle Ages is now Schenkluhn (2000), with chapters on the ideals of the mendicants, on monastic layouts, on the female houses, on the clear ideological and architectural differences between the two orders in the thirteenth century and their gradual standardization in the fourteenth.

79. A history of the building and a reconstruction of the original state are given in J. B. Supino, *La basilica di San Francesco in Assisi* (Bologna, 1924) 44. Cf. also Beda Kleinschmidt, *Die Basilika San Francesco in Assisi* (Berlin, 1915).

For the construction of the Assisi church see Rocchi (1982) and Schenkluhn (1991) 19–124, and (2000) 37–43. Schenkluhn has called into question Rocchi's idea of the original church as a single-storied structure comprising only the three nave bays of the lower church, with no transept or apse, and has questioned his suggestion that it was only under Brother Elias, in the 1230s or even 1240s, that the church assumed its present form. Schenkluhn (1991) 19–124 argues for two rapidly sequential and overlapping 'planning stages':

Plan One 1228–35. Foundation stone laid by Gregory IX on 17 July 1228, for a two-storey church, including the present apse and transept, and a three-bay nave, with a narthex to the lower church extending one bay further to the east (the church is occidented). The present campanile and circular nave buttresses were not part of this plan. St Francis is buried in crypt in 1230, in front of the apse.

Plan One (transitional phase). Displacement of the main façade one bay eastwards, to rise above outer wall of lower narthex, thus lengthening the nave of upper church by one bay. This bay is larger than the earlier nave bays and slightly misaligned with them. New south portal into lower church inserted in eastern, narthex bay. Planting of a buttress tower to south of the new façade.

Plan Two 1237/9 onwards. Construction of new eastern bay of upper church, which is shortened, at vault level, by running a thin barrel vault behind the upper parts of the west façade. Circular, bastion-like buttresses added to nave at lower and upper levels. Transformation of a pseudo-passage into the present Remois passage in the upper church. Completion of upper parts of upper church and building of campanile. New entrance bay and portal opening off south side of eastern bay of lower church. The result of these changes was to emphasize the importance of the upper church and the south eastern (principal) approach to the church for the pilgrims.

The mention of bells in 1239, even if this does not imply the completion of the campanile, suggests that by that year the critical modifications to Plan One, including the eastward extension of the upper church and its new façade, had already taken place. The church received its final, formal consecration in 1253. The final result is a contrast between a dark crypt-like lower church, 'Romanesque' in character, and a bright spacious upper church, with many of the characteristics of northern 'cathedral Gothic'.

Schenkluhn (1991) 125–226, and (2000) 41–3, interprets the design as a conflation of building types and quotations: (a) the Italian funerary church with large transept opening directly onto an apsidal choir placed over a tomb (a combination of Old St Peter's in Rome and south Italian Romanesque basilicas like Montecassino and S. Nicola Pellegrino in Trani), (b) the two-storied rectangular bishops' chapels in royal France (Noyon, Reims, Notre-Dame Paris), (c) the papal aula in the Lateran, with semicircular niches on its long sides reminiscent of the cylindrical buttresses of the Assisi nave and (d) the Holy Sepulchre Church in Jerusalem, whose double-doored portal is quoted in the south eastern portal to the lower church. From this admixture Assisi emerges as a truly apostolic church, an *ecclesia specialis*, evoking Rome, Jerusalem and the papacy, and underlining Gregory IX's support of the Franciscans as allies against his personal and imperial rival, Frederick II.

79A. For the iconography of the windows see Haussherr (1981), and for a general discussion Grodecki and Brisac (1985) 222–4, 264–5.

79B. Sta Chiara was complete enough to receive the bones of Saint Clare in 1260, and it was consecrated in 1265. For this church, and the other Assisi followers see Schenkluhn (2000) 56–63. Other followers of note included the first church of Sant'Antonio in Padua (1238–56), San Fortunato at Todi (polygonally apsed choir and nave with Remois passages), San Francesco at Terni, San Francesco at Gualdo Tadino, the abbey church at Montelabbate and San Francesco al Prato, Perugia. For discussion of these see Curuni (1982) 85–149, and Schenkluhn (2000) 56ff.

80. Only an approximate reconstruction is possible. Cf. J. B. Supino, *L'arte nelle chiese di Bologna* (Bologna, 1932) 165, and the plan on p. 175. For the chronology and intended 'meanings' of this church, as well as an attempted reconstruction, see Schenkluhn (1985) 85–99 and Schenkluhn (2000). Its straight-ended box choir flanked by chapels was clearly indebted to the Cistercian 'Bernardine' plan; liturgical choir and nave were three-aisled, but the choir consisted of three vaulted bays, almost a hall church in section, while the nave had wooden roofs.

80A. For an extensive analysis of this church, including its quotations from

Clairvaux III and Notre-Dame in Paris, and its possible connexions with the aesthetics of St Bonaventure, see Schenkluhn (1985) 114–70 and Schenkluhn (2000) 71–6, who calls it 'the first vaulted cathedral-building of the mendicant orders'.

81. A full analysis of the church is given in Cadei (1978). Schenkluhn (2000) 64–7, calls it the first surviving example of the 'triple chapel room church', a highly successful Italian mendicant form, in which a wide, single-aisled nave, usually wooden roofed, is terminated at the east end by a composition of three staggered arched spaces, consisting of a taller and wider choir flanked by two lower chapels. The type is repeated in S. Francesco in Siena (see below, p. 210) and S. Francesco and Sta Caterina in Pisa.

82. Richard Krautheimer, *Die Kirchen der Bettelorden in Deutschland* (Cologne, Augsburg, 1925) 15. Frankl is referring to the Franciscan church, an extremely simple building with a straight-ended box choir and a wider, single-aisled nave, both spaces unvaulted. It belongs to a group of what Krautheimer called 'pre-Romanesque' early mendicant churches in Germany whose simple forms consciously evoked early Christian and apostolic simplicity. See Schenkluhn (2000) 106–8. See also Dehio/Piel (1964) 436. The Franciscan church at Ulm was destroyed in 1875, see Krautheimer (1925) 75, 80. A view of the church is reproduced in Schaffoldt (1924) plate 16. For the earliest Franciscan churches in Germany, dating from the 1220s, see Binding (1982) 431–60. Among the earliest German mendicant churches are flat-roofed, single-aisled churches of the Franciscans (1220s) in Eisenach in Thuringia and the first church of the Dominicans in Cologne, Italianate and three-aisled, in building by 1229. See also Konow (1954) for such early churches as the Dominicans in Konstanz, begun soon after 1236 and the Dominicans in Zurich, built between 1231 and 1240.

83. Viollet-le-Duc, *Dictionnaire*, I, 298. See also G. Rohault de Fleury, *Gallia dominicana, Les couvents de St Dominique au moyen âge* (Paris, 1903), and Elie Lambert in *B.M.*, CIV (1946) 178.

A full analysis of this possible prototype for the Dominican two-aisled church, and a discussion of the earlier literature on it, is given by Schenkluhn (1985) 55–62. He argues that the Dominicans did not construct the two-aisled church in Paris. The convent they founded in 1217 was on the site of the hospice of Saint-Jacques, built around 1209 by John of St Albans. Some time after 1218 the Dominicans simply converted the simple double-aisled hall of the hostel into a church. Sundt (1989) 203–4, points to a seventeenth-century Dominican source which dated the beginning of the church to 1241–52, and its completion between 1254 and 63. If true, this would mean that the Jacobins' church in Toulouse (begun in 1229) and not the Parisian church, would be the first Dominican attempt at double-nave church planning. Schenkluhn (2000) admits that the dating is unclear, but dismisses the 1241–52 date, and adheres to the views he expressed in 1985. Frankl's idea, shared by many, that these double-aisled halls were used as lecture halls for university teaching remains problematic. The Dominican church in Bologna served regularly as a meeting place for various university functions, but Sundt (1989) 197, points out that the statutes and privileges of the university of Toulouse show that the university's secular functions did not take place in the double-aisled (Dominican) Jacobins' church but in the Chapter House of the Franciscans. The university did, however, regularly use the church as a chapel for its religious services. It is by no means certain, therefore, that the double-aisled scheme imitated refectories and chapter houses because of those buildings' associations with secular assembly and discussion.

84. The shape of the original church, and the sequence of construction of the present building, have been revealed by Prin's (1955) excavations of the late 1940s, and his convincing analysis of the written sources. Prin's sequence isolates the following phases:

1) **1229–*c*.1235:** a rectangular hall church divided into two unequal aisles by five piers.

2) *c*.**1245–*c*.1252:** addition of an aisleless, polygonal chevet.

3) *c*.**1275–92:** the vaulting of this chevet, first with the intention of having no intermediary supports (a plan abandoned, but whose original capitals, lower than the present ones and now invisible, exist in the inner faces of the apsidal buttresses). Then, perhaps under the influence of the Dominican double-aisled hall church at Agen just completed in or around 1283, the choir was divided into two aisles by the present tall columns, and the eastern bay given the existing umbrella vault.

4) *c*.**1325–*c*.1335,** the replacement of the original rectangular church with a regular double-aisled hall nave with vessels of equal breadth, and with pillars and vaults of the same height as those of the new choir. The flanking nave chapels were inserted up to *c*.1390.

This sequence is accepted by Sundt (1989) 185–9, who explains the choice of the double nave scheme – in Toulouse at least – on economic, structural and topographical grounds, arising from the Dominicans' poverty in the early thirteenth century. Sundt also notes that the majority of double-nave Dominican halls in France are the result, not of conscious planning, but piecemeal addition. Schenkluhn (2000) 53–5, sees a number of factors influencing the choice of the double-nave, among them hospital halls and monastic refectories. He also discusses the later history of the Jacobins in Toulouse as the burial place of St Thomas Aquinas, and the effects of this transferral of 'his' learning from Paris to Toulouse on the scale of the new church, itself an enlarged version of the Parisian double-aisled hall (194–6).

85. Walter and Elisabeth Paatz, *Die Kirchen von Florenz*, III (Frankfurt a. M., 1952) 664. See also Walter Paatz, *Werden und Wesen der Trecento-Architektur in Toskana* (Burg, 1937) 7.

Despite its art-historical importance as the first vaulted mendicant church in central Italy, S Maria Novella's building history is still problematic. In 1221 the Dominicans were given the church/chapel of St Mary, which stood next to the eleventh-century parish church which occupied the area of the first bays of the nave. Indulgences for building in 1246 and 1250 to the north of the old church could refer to the remodelling and extension of the St Mary Chapel, or to the beginning of the present choir. In 1251 financial pressures suspended building. In 1277 a model is mentioned, (for the present church, begun then, or for part of the structure already begun in 1246?). 1279–*c*.1300 mention of work to the south of the old parish church, that is, on the present nave. In 1298 the monks' choir (in eastern nave bays) was in use. 1325, first mention of expenditure on the west façade. A 'late' date for the whole building sequence (beginning of the present church in 1277/9) is favoured by Arthur (1983) and by Kleefisch-Jobst (1991) 50. An 'early' date (begun *c*.1246) is supported by Villeti (1981) and Schenkluhn (2000) 48–9. Schenkluhn here, and (1985) 113–14, points to the rich stylistic background of the design: its elevation a more spacious version of the 'mother church' of S. Domenico in Bologna, its pillar shape derived from S. Miniato al Monte in Florence, its Cistercian 'Bernardine' choir plan quoting San Galgano. The similarities with all these buildings, and with the 'Bernardine' plan of the first Franciscan church of S. Croce in Florence, of *c*.1250, as well as S. Maria's clear influence on the elevation and spatial disposition of the cathedral of Arezzo, begun in 1277, strengthen the case for the 'early' dating of the church.

85A. The sequence of construction and the chronology, based on new dendrochronological evidence, have been clearly set out in Michler's authoritative study (1984) 29–37. He identifies three decisive phases of construction, some subdivided into campaigns.

1) *c*.1235–*c*.1237 (first campaign): preservation of the old church east apse (conch), south apse and southern parts of north apse, all up to first storey.
c.1238–*c*.1240 (second campaign): demolition of old church, east apse liturgically useable.
c.1241–*c*.1243 (third campaign): all three eastern apses vaulted and roofed.
2) *c*.1244–*c*.1248: (with no clear break from the third campaign of phase one): nave outer walls to half the nave length westwards, and first two eastern pillar pairs of nave.
3) *c*.1265 onwards (first campaign): outer nave walls up to beginning of western towers, and laying out of present two-tower west end.
c.1265–83: completion of nave and first two stories of western towers. 1283 consecration. See also Schenkluhn and van Stipeln (1983).

There has been some disagreement over the original design of the nave. Hamann and Wilhelm-Kästner (1924/9) vol. 1 50ff, and Kunst (1968) 134ff, argue for an original basilica, quickly changed to a hall. Michler (1969) 104ff, and (1984) 25–9, sees no reason to doubt that the present hall was intended from the start.

86. K. Wilhelm Kästner, *Die Elisabethkirche in Marburg etc.* (Marburg, 1924). Kunst (1968) 131–45 suggests the influence of Cambrai Cathedral and the Abbey of Chaâlis on the triconche east end. Michler (1984) 14–24, locates the main sources in a 'lower', non-cathedral class of architecture, belonging predominantly to the last quarter of the twelfth century, and coming from the Laonnois, Champagne and especially Paris and its environs. Götz's (1968) 26–7, suggestion that the triconche east end derives from the Teutonic Knights' church in Tartlau in Transylvania has foundered on Marosi's (1984) 163–4, re-dating of Tartlau to the 1240s. A connexion with the trefoil plan of the church of the Nativity at Bethlehem, advanced by Möbius (1989) 230, is no more convincing. See Crossley (1997) 268.

87. Illustrated in *C.A.*, LXXVIII (1912) opposite p. 344. A more likely source for the superimposed windows with Reimsian tracery is the Liebfrauenkirche in Trier, see below, Chapter 3, Note 88. Michler (1984) 23, rejects Saint-Léger at Soissons as a source, and points to other double-window apses: Mons-en-Laonnois, Larchant, Souppes-sur-Loing, etc.

87A. For the political background to the foundation of the church of St Elizabeth see Schenkluhn and van Stipeln (1983), Geese (1981), and Crossley (1997). The changing liturgical arrangements in the church, as reflections of a growing 'aestheticization' of the cult space and its furnishings, are brilliantly analyzed by Köstler (1995).

88. Illustrated in Oskar Karpa, *Dom und Liebfrauen zu Trier* (Berlin, 1944). The starting date for the church is controversial and still uncertain. Schenkluhn and van Stipeln (1983) 29, and note 24, date the beginning, not to 1235 as Frankl and others assumed, but to 1227. Borger-Keweloh (1986a) 24–7,

59–94, 127–31, in the most recent and authoritative study, dates the start to sometime after 1233. Work stopped in 1242, but by 1253 the whole eastern part of the church had been finished, and construction had reached the north-west clerestorey. Nussbaum (2000) 42–44, thinks the most plausible starting date is 1227. Relations with the church of St Elizabeth at Marburg are obviously close. Tuczek (1971) has found that the foot unit used in both buildings is the same. Borger-Keweloh (1986A) 126, admits the possibility of the same Reims-trained masons at work in both buildings, but considers that they were designed by different architects.

88A. Schenkluhn and van Stipeln (1983) 28ff, argued that the Liebfrauenkirche's centralized plan is an up-dated copy, in the language of Reims (the French coronation church), of the Palatine Chapel at Aachen (the German coronation church), with the aim of underlining the claims of Archbishop Dietrich von Wied of Trier, over the Archbishops of Mainz and Cologne, to crown the German kings. Nussbaum (2000) 43, doubts this interpretation, sees the church's dedication to the Virgin as crucial to its centralized plan, and derives the idea from the centralized early thirteenth-century Liebfrauenkirche which lay just to the west of the Romanesque cathedral in Metz. Borger-Keweloh (1986a) 132–45, also stresses the importance of the dedication to the Virgin, and emphasizes its function as a burial church. For the importance of the east end of Toul cathedral, begun in 1221, as a possible transmittor of Reims forms to Trier and Marburg see Schiffler (1977), Villes (1983) 78ff, especially 83, and Borger-Keweloh (1986a) 122ff.

89. Frankl (1960) 35ff. Critical evidence for Villard's presence in Hungary in the 1220s or 1230s, and for the activity of other craftsmen from northern France working for the Hungarian court in the early thirteenth century, is provided by the fragments from the Cistercian monastery of Pilisszentkereszt, excavated by Gerevich in the 1970s and 1980s. They include: (1) parts of a tiled pavement very similar to that drawn in Villard's book and captioned by him 'I saw such in Hungary' (fol. 15r) and (2) fragments of the tomb of Queen Gertrud of Andechs-Meranien (died 1213), wife of King Andreas II of Hungary. Hahnloser (1972) 393–7, implied that Villard had not just visited Pilisszentkereszt, but had in some way participated in the workshop. Gerevich (1971) (1982) (1983) (1985), who discovered and published the tomb, and Marosi (1984) 135–6, attribute it to a Chartres-trained sculptor, and find its closest stylistic affinities with the sculpture of the cathedral's south transept portals. Both also acknowledge the close stylistic parallels with the architecture and sculpture of Reims (1220s up to 1233) and Notre-Dame in Paris. Gerevich dated the tomb to the mid-1230s, Marosi to the 1220s. For the position of Villard in the Andechs-Meranien family connexions see Crossley (1997) (with full literature). Villard's journey to Hungary was dated by Hahnloser (1972) 395–7, to the mid-1230s, and by Bucher (1979) 20–3, to the later 1220s. Takács (1998) places the queen's tomb in the year 1228, or soon thereafter, and underplays its relevance to Villard, who was only one among many sculptor-architects trained in the most advanced centres of French High Gothic working in Hungary in the 1230s and 1240s (e.g. the Remois south portal of the Abbey of Pannonhalma).

89A. Villard's traditional position as an architect is upheld in Hahnloser's (1972) canonic edition of the 'lodgebook'. Bucher (1979) calls him a 'mason-contractor'. More recently, Villard's status as an architect has been seriously questioned by Kidson (1981), and by Barnes (1981) (1982) (a work which provides an excellent bibliography on Villard up to 1982) and (1989). Barnes argues that he was a metalworker. Schlink (1999) thinks that Villard was probably illiterate and dictated the captions of this drawings to scribes. He may have begun his training in a workshop specializing in the figural arts (metalwork, manuscript illumination, glass painting) and then graduated to an interest in more monumental genres (architecture, machines). Many useful articles on Villard are published in *Avista Forum*, the Journal of the Association Villard de Honnecourt for the Interdisciplinary Study of Medieval Technology, Science and Art.

89B. In fact, Gerhard had longer to prepare his designs, for the Chapter passed a resolution to finance the new cathedral on 13 April 1248, and there is nothing in the document to suggest that the intention to rebuild did not go back to the very beginning of that year. See Wolff (1968) 67–9. Wolff (1968) 67–70, 212, and (1986) 8, gives 30 April as the date of the fire of the old cathedral, but Wolff (1980) 12, puts it on 26 April. For the *fabrica* at Cologne during the building of the choir and nave see Schöller (1988). Haussherr (1991) sees the radical novelty of the new choir at Cologne, as opposed to the more traditional rebuilding of the slightly earlier Bamberg Cathedral, as an indication of the pro-Hohenstaufen political outlook of the Bamberg bishop, Ekbert of Andechs-Meran, over and against the anti-Hohenstaufen, pro-French politics of Archbishop Konrad von Hochstaden, the driving force (with the Chapter) at Cologne. The symbolic meanings of the new building, especially its apostolic and papal overtones, is brought out clearly by Kroos (1979/80).

90. A clear analysis of the relationship with Amiens and Beauvais can be found in Franz, Graf Wolff Metternich, 'Zum Problem etc.', in *Festschrift des Kölner Domes* (Cologne, 1948) 51. A comprehensive analysis of details is given in Helen Rosenau, *Der Kölner Dom* (Cologne, 1931). Still useful is Paul

Clemen, *Der Dom zu Köln* (Düsseldorf, 1937). For the history of the Gothic choir of Cologne, including the contributions of the architects Gerhard and Arnold, see the masterly study by Wolff (1968) and also Wolff (1980) (1986).

90A. See above, Chapter 3, Note 17A.

91. The original German term *Dreistrahl*, translated here as triradial, applies first to tracery which consists of three radiating spokes like those in a rose-window, and second to the ribs in a section of a vault which is divided by three such ribs.

92. Wolff (1968) and (1980) 12–14, and (1986) 7–32, established the following sequence of construction:

1) **Phase One.** 1248–*c*.1261 under Master Gerhard (died 1258–61). Foundations, planning of whole structure including transepts and five-aisled nave, construction of northern part (now demolished) of the sacristy, and of ambulatory and all the radiating chapels up to the height of the vault springing, with the Chapels of St John and the Three Kings vaulted and complete by *c*.1260.

2) **Phase Two.** *c*.1261–8 (at the latest) under Master Arnold (first mentioned in 1271). Construction of whole lower storey of choir, piscinas inserted in radiating chapels. By 1265 choir aisles ready for services, by sealing them off with provisional walls from transept and central aisle of choir.

3) **Phase Three.** Building of sacristy, begun *c*.1275, part of which consecrated in 1277.

4) **Later Phases.** *c*.1277 beginning of the triforium; *c*.1300 first designs for south tower of west façade begun, the earliest by Arnold. At the same time (*c*.1300) the upper choir and buttressing complete, probably now under the direction of Master Johannes, Arnold's son (first appearing in 1296). 1310 glazing of fifteen clerestorey windows in choir. 1308–11 choir stalls erected. 1322 consecration of choir.

The radical alterations to Gerhard's design in the exterior of the choir clerestorey, introduced by Johannes under the influence of the west front of Strasbourg, are discussed by Wolff (1968) 216, and Rode (1954).

92A. It is difficult to follow Frankl here. All free-standing piers or aisle responds in the choir of Cologne have cores that are circular, that is convex, in shape. See Wolff (1968) figs 44–7, 49–50. Perhaps he is thinking of the complex hollows and pear shapes of the supports in the south-west tower, and the drawings for them (Plans A–D), dated *c*.1300 onwards.

92B. The connexions with the Sainte-Chapelle are underlined by Branner (1965) 128–35. For the sculpture see Williamson (1995) 195–7.

93. Durand, *op. cit.* (Note 18 to this Chapter) 290. This piercing of the spandrels in the triforia ultimately derives from the main windows of the chapel of Saint-Germain-en-Laye, see Branner (1965) 74–5.

93A. However, the outer sides of the four buttress uprights on the south side of the choir were originally pierced with openwork niches, before they were filled in during the 1828–33 restorations. See Wolff (1963) 143–7.

94. Paul Clemen, *Die Kunstdenkmäler der Städte und Kreise Gladbach und Krefeld* (*Die Kunstdenkmäler der Rheinsprovinz*, Bd. III, part IV) (Düsseldorf, 1896) 447. See Borger (1958) 38–40, and 173–204, who dates the start of the choir to 1256 or thereabouts and its consecration (by Albertus Magnus) to 1275. He supports the attribution to Master Gerhard.

95. Carlfred Halbach, *Der Dom zu Altenberg* (Altenberg, 1953), with excellent illustrations; Karl Eckert, *700 Jahre Altenberg etc.* (*Die Kunstdenkmäler des Rheinland*, Part IV) (Bergisch Gladbach, 1956), with many illustrations of the stages of ruin after the fire of 1815. The basic work is now Panofsky-Soergel (1972). See also the wide-ranging Krönig (1973) especially 83–7. Panofsky-Soergel corrected the foundation date from 1255 to 1259. Ten altars were consecrated in 1276, and another nine in 1287, so that the choir was probably complete, as Davis suggests, by *c*.1280/85. See Davis (1984) especially 131–2. Although the design has been attributed to Gerhard, the architect may have been a 'Walterus', mentioned in the abbey's necrology. First Branner (1965) 132–4, then Panofsky-Soergel (1972) 107–9, and Krönig (1973) 83–7, derive the design almost exclusively from the French Cistercian church of Royaumont. The case for a dependence on Cologne is convincingly re-stated by Schröder (1977). Davis (1984) sensibly dismisses any partisan concentration on French sources to the exclusion of German, or vice-versa, and sees the choir as a copy of a wide range of precedents, including Rhenish and Ile-de-France forms, though it is hard to accept his conclusion that the new Saint-Denis was 'a prime model'.

95A. Most scholars now accept that Gerhard was a German, see, e.g., Rieckenberg (1962). Some confirmation of this comes from Kimpel (1977) 211, Kimpel (1979/80), and Wolff (1986) 9–11, who show that many of the forms of Amiens Cathedral were carefully copied in the new choir, but not its advanced stone-cutting techniques, which a French architect, if directing the lodge at Cologne, would surely have introduced. However, Wilson (correspondence 1991) and (1990) 124, suggests that such techniques were the responsibilities not of the *magister operis* but of his deputy, the warden of the masons, who could have been German. To Wilson, Gerhard (*Gerardus* in the sources) was almost certainly 'Gérard', a Frenchman.

95B. The 'normative' qualities of Cologne are also underlined by Kurmann

(1979/80) especially 259ff; and Gross (1948) 17–26, who sees it as an ultimate and 'ideal' statement of regularity. Wolff (1980) 93ff, not only praises it as a culmination and perfection of the 'cathedral style', but as a 'borderline building', touching the limits of the possible.

95C. For Léon see above Chapter 3, Note 38a. For Lincoln Angel Choir the most authoritative works are Dean (1979) especially 155–69, and (1986).

96. See above, p. 136. And see above, Chapter 3, Note 40.

97. Samuel Muller, *Der Dom von Utrecht* (Utrecht, 1906).

97A. See now Haslinghuis and Peeters (1965), and – for the financing of the enterprise – Vroom (1981) (1989) and (1996). The starting date of 1254/5 is based on circumstantial evidence: the fire in Utrecht in 1253 (*terminus post quem*), and post-1274 written tablets in the cathedral attributing its foundation to Bishop Hendrick van Vianden in the reign of William II of Holland (died 1256) (*terminus ante quem*). Indulgences for building work in 1265 and 1267 could refer to repairs for the old, damaged predecessor. Therefore Helten (1988) (1989) and (1994) 101–3, thinks that work was begun much later, in the reign of Bishop Jan van Nassau (1267–90). He singles out 1288 as the first mention of the 'nove opere'. Six chaplaincies were endowed 'in Novo opere' in 1303. He identifies three main phases in the lower storey of the choir construction, corresponding largely to changes in moulding profile and respond type:

1) *c*.1288–*c*.1296: the ambulatory and radiating chapels, modelled on the choirs of Soissons (buttresses, plan of radiating chapels and ambulatory vaults) and Cologne (tracery of radiating chapel windows, moulding profiles). Helten also argues for influences during this phase from Westminster Abbey (spheric triangular tracery of the radiating chapels and their arch surrounds, pillar-thick arcade arches, rib-sized transverse arches in the ambulatory). I am not convinced that these similarities are anything more than fortuitous, and cannot follow his contention that such 'quotations' reflected Count Floris V's (1266–96) pro-English alliances or his claims to the throne of Scotland. More plausible is his suggestion that the conception of the apse, ambulatory and radiating chapels went back to the 1250s.

2) **Shortly after 1296–*c*.1325.** Responds of south choir aisle and south chapels opening off it. Burial of Bishop Guy van Avesnes in one of these chapels in 1317. Strongly indebted to south tower of west façade of Cologne. See also Zimmermann-Deissler (1958) 93.

3) *c*.1325–1360. Responds of north choir aisle and free-standing pillars of choir on both sides, with their arches, up to triforium.

The upper parts of the choir were completed in the late fourteenth and first half of the fifteenth century. Kolman *et al.* (1996) 213–21, follow this sequence in the main, but give 1254 as the date of the foundation, 1265–95 as the period for the radiating chapels under Jan van Nassau, *c*.1300–25 as the length of phase 2 and *c*.1325–60 for the construction of the north choir aisles and northern choir pillars, as well as the eastern crossing pillars. They point to Doornik Cathedral (begun 1243) as an important source for the ground plan, while the details of the radiating chapels are so close to the earliest work in the choir of Cologne that they attribute them to Master Gerhard of Cologne.

98. Durand, *op. cit.*, I, 282. For the upper parts of the Amiens choir and the eastern walls of its transepts, which amount to a revolutionary change in its stylistic appearance, see Murray (1996) 66–77.

99. Double curves had already existed earlier in the profiles of bases and other members.

100. For all questions on details cf. Lisa Schürenberg, *op. cit.* (Note 38 to this Chapter) 206.

The fullest account of the church and its construction is by Davis (1984a), but see also the earlier Salet (1955). Davis identifies two campaigns of construction, each by a different architect:

1) **From the foundation in 1262** (and the laying of the literal foundations in 1263) to the fire of 1266: choir (including probably the vaults), lower storey of the transepts (including portals), eastern bay of nave (side aisles and central vessel) up to string course, portion of the west façade up to but not including springers of porch vaults. Original west façade design envisaged a tripartite opening in front of each of the three portals, with nine openings in all, topped by nine gables. This work was characterized by 'an extraordinary degree of detailed refinement and decorative elaboration'.

2) **1267–*c*.1286** (the latter the year of the death of Cardinal Ancher, its principal benefactor after Urban IV's death). Clerestorey level of the transepts, northern and southern transept porches, western pair of nave bays, continuation of west façade with springers for the porch vaults, tracery in the central portal's tympanum, and the simplification of the west façade to five gables with tripartite openings only into the central portal (like the present 1904–5 design). Bruzelius (1987a) has pointed to a donation of Charles of Anjou in 1276 for timber for 'three vaults of the church', which she convincingly identifies as the three vaults in the transepts and crossing. Davis argues that the 'dense, powerful and sober style' of the second architect, forced on him partly by economic realities, has parallels with other late Rayonnant works in France, e.g. at Saint-Germain at Auxerre, and at Narbonne. It anticipates the fluid and compact qualities of French Flamboyant.

3) The rest of the nave was completed in the nineteenth and early twentieth century.

101. The model for the building of open tracery between two parts of the interior was that at the joint of the chapel on the choir with the aisle in the transept of Amiens.

But more likely sources for this device are the openings between choir and transept chapels in Notre-Dame at Dijon (see plate 140). Saint-Urbain's stylistic debts to Champenois and Parisian forms are incisively analysed by Branner (1965) 106–8, and by Davis (1984) 848–50, who stresses the connexions with Hugues Libergier's work at Saint-Nicaise at Reims. For the position of the apse in the history of glazed apses in France and Germany see Héliot (1968) especially 110–11.

102. In a review of G. Minvielle's book *Histoire et condition juridique de la profession d'architecte* (Paris, 1921), which appeared in *B.M.*, LXXXI (1922) 480, Lefèvre-Pontalis wrote that he had been wrong to regard Jean Langlois as the architect of Saint-Urbain, for he had embezzled funds, and must, therefore, have controlled the building funds, which only the administrators did. On the other hand, Langlois appears as *magister fabrice*, while the administrators are called *operarii*. In 1261, shortly before Saint-Urbain was begun, a contract was made in the monastery of Saint-Gilles between Martinus de Lonay and the abbot. In this document the architect is called *magister* and the administrator *operarius*. Later, administrators were also called *rectores, directores,* and by several other titles; cf. Paul Booz, *Der Baumeister der Gotik* (Munich, Berlin, 1956) 23. Since Langlois was called *magister fabrice,* he may have been the architect. He may, in addition, have been an exception and controlled the building funds too.

The term *magister fabrice* is ambiguous. The word *fabrica* in medieval French and English sources refers, as Branner (1976) showed, not only to the building, but also to the fabric agency responsible for the whole enterprise. The same ambiguity appears in German accounts, where *magister fabricae* can refer to the building clerk, or to some kind of financial officer, but not necessarily to the master mason. See Perger (1970) 68 and note 11. The variety of terminology for such officers, clerks, administrators and architects is discussed fully by Schöller (1989) 161–8. Salet (1955) 118–22, thinks, on balance, that Jean Langlois was the practicing architect; Davis (1984a) 849 and note 9, doubts it. For the influence of Saint-Urbain on the early stages of the English Decorated style see Bony (1979) 10, 11, 46.

103. Schürenberg, *op. cit.* 82.
See Branner (1965) 109–10; Freigang (1992) 331–44, established the following chronology:

1) Begun soon after 1269 with a shorter choir, the foundations of whose apse were drawn by Viollet-le-Duc.

2) *c.*1280 the present choir and apse started further eastwards, and work proceeded from the choir into the north transept, latterly under Bishop Pierre de Rochefort (1300–22).

3) Soon after the completion of the north transept a new workshop executed the Rochefort Chapel (north side of eastern bays of nave), the south transept, the eastern bay of St Bartholomew's chapel and the vaults of the whole work. Under Bishop Pierre Rodier (1323–30) the west bay of St Bartholomew's chapel was finished. Freigang sees the whole extension as a special case in southern French Gothic. In some respects (the form of the transept chapels and their divisions) it relies on Narbonne and Toulouse Cathedrals, but its most advanced Rayonnant features come directly from Norman and Parisian precedents, especially the transepts at Rouen.

104. Chapels divided by walls on the lower storey but not on the upper one had already been built in the choir at Vézelay, in the choir of the church of Saint-Etienne at Caen, and in the choir of the cathedral at Bayeux.

105. *C.A.*, LXXIII (1907) 32: René Gobillot, *La cathédrale de Séez* (Paris, 1937) 35.
The glass in the choir clerestorey at Sées dates from *c.*1280–5, see Lafond (1953) 59–83; therefore the structure must have been begun in the 1270s. Wilson (1990) 4, derives one of the most distinctive features of the interior, the choir arcade gables with the triforium mullions running down to them, from the interior faces of the south transept façade at Notre-Dame in Paris, which was also the source for Sées's south transept rose. See also Olde-Choukair, in: Baylé, dir. (1997) vol. 1, 159–73, and vol. 2, 179–84, who confirms that the radical restorations (in fact, total rebuilding) of the choir in the late nineteenth-century scrupulously preserved its medieval appearance. She also notes, as precedents for the interior arcade gables of the choir, the gables backed by blind tracery panels which were inserted over the entrance arches from the north transept to the choir aisles at Notre-Dame in Paris (perhaps *c.*1270?). She also notes, in a similar position, the late thirteenth-century gables over the entrance arches from the north transept to the Lady Chapel at Larchant.

106. Lottlisa Behling, *Gestalt und Geschichte des Masswerks* (Halle a. S., 1944) plate 21 and p. 24. This is a good guide to the general stylistic history of tracery.
For Germany it is superseded by Kiesow (1956), and in general by Binding

(1989). For Minden see Kunst (1969a), who underlined the influence of Cologne cathedral choir, particularly on its pillar forms; and Fiebig (1991), who convincingly redates the nave to the 1250s and 1260s, but distinguishes between its formal vocabulary (based largely on Reims and Cologne cathedrals) and its spatial typology (based on Paderborn cathedral).

107. Felix Mader, 'Stadt Regensburg', in *Die Kunstdenkmäler der Oberpfalz*, XXII (1933).
Research on Regensburg Cathedral during the 1990s has made it one of the most intensively investigated churches of recent times. See Hubel (1989), Schuller (1989) and Hubel and Schuller (1995) – the latter the most convenient account of the history of the cathedral, based on new information from the 1984–8 restorations and on new dendrochronological evidence. They identify the following thirteenth-century history:
1) Begun under Bishop Leo Tundorfer (1262–77) after the fire of 1273. Layout of three apses in echelon, in general imitation of the three-apsidal choir of the Romanesque cathedral, but closely indebted, in its specific form, to the ground plan of the slightly earlier choir of Saint-Urbain at Troyes. Choir, sacristies, and apses up to dado level; St Nicholas Chapel (the lower storey of the building adjoining the southern apse to the east, and mentioned in 1280).
2) Rapid progress under Bishop Heinrich von Rotteneck (1277–96). The first phase, from *c.*1277–*c.*1285/90, saw construction of the apse and southern wall of the south choir aisle, the terminal wall of the south transept and the aisle wall of the eastern bay of the nave on the south side – all up to aisle vault springer height. The first two bays of the southern wall of the main choir were built up to the base of the triforium (wooden tie bar of 1284 found in it). All this is executed in a conservative, mural style, by a local workshop. The second phase, *c.*1285–1305, perhaps under a *magister Ludovicus lapicida* (first mentioned in 1283, died in 1306) introduced a totally new stylistic regime, based on advanced Rayonnant models. Lower north wall of the choir; south-east crossing pillar, and the adjoining arcade arches on the south side of the choir (with sunk spandrels) and on the east side of south transept; vaulting of the south choir aisle and beginning of the apse *vitrée* in the main choir.
3) Under Bishop Konrad von Lupburg (1296–1313), in a short phase, 1305/10: completion of the north choir chapel up to vault springers; all lower windows of main apse, up to, but not including, triforium; south triforium of choir straight bays; lower walls of east bay of nave on north side; triforium of south transept; first bay of nave on south side up to and including triforium; first south bay of nave apart from vaults; choir triforium and clerestorey without vaults; north choir aisle vaulted.
*c.*1320, under Bishop Nikolaus von Ybbs (1313–40) whole choir and transepts roofed and vaulted.
The work from *c.*1285 to *c.*1320 established the basic design of the cathedral, including the elevations of the main apse, the choir, the transepts and nave, even though much of the execution progressed well into the fourteenth century. It is characterized by a sophisticated understanding of Parisian, and Parisian-derived Rayonnant (e.g. Saint-Denis, Saint-Urbain at Troyes), but also a sculpturally vigorous articulation of the wall which aligns it with non-Parisian developments (e.g. the choir of Bordeaux cathedral, begun 1262). The theory, first advanced by Friedrich Adler, and repeated by Frankl in the first edition of this book, namely that Bishop Leo Tundorfer got information about Saint-Urbain in Troyes from Cardinal Ancher at the Council of Lyon in 1274, is speculative. In any case most of the Saint-Urbain elements in the choir, apart from its ground plan, appear only *c.*1290, some years after Tundorfer's death in 1277. See also Altmann (1976) 101. Kurmann (1995), in a comprehensive analysis of the cathedral in the context of Rayonnant in France and England in the late thirteenth century, underlines the very close debt which the 1290s architect owed to Saint-Urbain: its apse *vitrée* with passages, its window tracery, its clerestorey set within thin but distinct 'framing' sections of wall. However Kurmann also speculates that most of the essentials of the earlier, 1273, project probably included many of these features of Saint-Urbain; the 1290s architect simply made them more explicit and executed them with greater sophistication. He also suggests (note 26, p. 400) that the Roman and Petrine references at Regensburg – emphasized by Hubel and Schuller (1995) 22, 34 – would be quite consistent with the papal associations of Saint-Urbain, founded, as it was, by Urban IV.

107A. The most authoritative account of Narbonne, and of Rayonnant in the Midi, can now be found in Freigang (1992) 19–109. For Narbonne he establishes the following sequence of construction:
The cathedral was the brainchild of Archbishop Guy Foulques (1259–65) (later Pope Clement IV). Financial preparations for the new church underway in the 1260s; transference to present site in May 1271; official foundation stone on 3 April 1272. Work proceeded from east to west.
Campaign I, *c.*1270–*c.*1275: Design (by an unknown architect) of choir; foundations and lower parts of radiating chapels; intention at this stage to make the lateral chapels of the choir like those at Clermont-Ferrand Cathedral: square in plan, with four-part vaults and divided by solid interior walls.
Campaign II, *c.*1275–*c.*1285 or a little later: radiating chapels and first (east-

ernmost) two lateral chapels on the south side, up to height of vault springing; first lateral chapel on north side, but up to a lower height. Probably under the influence of Toulouse cathedral, the lateral chapels made internally apsidal and fronted by a tall, narrow 'aisle' pierced in their dividing walls.

Campaign III, *c*.1285–*c*.1295, probably by a Jean Deschamps, engaged at Narbonne as *magister principalis* in 1286. Completion (including vaulting) of all the radiating chapels, all the lateral chapels on the north side, but only the two easternmost lateral chapels on the south side. In 1289, 1291 and 1295, documentary mention of altars, chantry priests or indulgencies for several radiating chapels. Design, and beginning of the construction of, the façade and eastern wall of the north transept, based closely on the transept façades of Clemont-Ferrand cathedral. Tracings, discovered in 1983 on the floor of the easternmost radiating chapel, show a full-scale plan of a straight-bay choir pillar and its hemicycle variant, and the profiles of the eastern angles of the transepts and of the interior embrasures of the triforium and clerestorey windows. Dated to the 1290s, they indicate that their author (probably Jean Deschamps) was considering the design of the main elevations of choir and transepts.

Campaign IV, *c*.1295/late 1290s–*c*.1310?, the latter date coinciding (a) with the death of Archbishop Gilles Aycelin (1291–1311), an energetic benefactor of the cathedral during this campaign, and (b) with a statute regulating masses in the lateral chapels, suggesting that the main choir not yet serviceable. Work proceeded under the direction of a new architect (arriving in the last years of the thirteenth century), Dominique de Fauran. Construction and completion of two western lateral chapels on south side, without the 'aisles' of the northern chapels. Provision of transept eastern towers on north and south sides. Construction of main arcades with cylindrical pillars of simpler profile than envisaged in the tracings. Main elevation up to top of triforium; vaulting of aisles.

Campaign V, *c*.1310–32 (at the latest), some, or all, of it under Jacques de Fauran, son of Dominique, who assumed control of the lodge sometime before 1320 (when he became the principal architect of Gerona cathedral), perhaps as early as 1310. Change of stone-type above the triforium. Clerestorey and vaults of high choir, and flying buttresses. Clergy occupy the choir in 1319, when perhaps it was covered with a temporary roof. The year 1332, when services (perhaps the first high Mass) start, marks the completion of the whole choir and its furnishings, though its structure was probably finished in the the late 1320s. For Narbonne see also Freigang (1989) (1989a) (1991); and Paul (1990) (where she also attributes the tracings discovered in 1983 to the Jean Deschamps appointed in 1286) and (1991).

107B. For Limoges see Davis (1979) 332–43, and especially Davis (1986). He locates the principal motive for building a north-French Rayonnant cathedral in the Limousin in an act of political defiance. Since the Treaty of Paris in 1259, Limoges was a city divided: the castle and its environs were dominated by the English, while the French still controlled the *cité* around the cathedral. The bishop who initiated the project, Aimeric de Malemort, was thereby asserting his, and his Chapter's, allegiance to the king of France.

Davis divides the history of the choir and the early fourteenth-century work on the transepts into eight phases, under four architects or workshops, proceeding from east to west.

1) First architect (probably Jean Deschamps), working in the 1270s. Foundations set out from *c*.1270. Official foundation stone laid in 1273. Design of whole choir plan; construction of radiating chapels, hemicycle pillars and first two lateral chapels on north and south sides, in a style indebted to the earlier phases of the choir of Clermont-Ferrand.

2) Second architect, working in the 1280s, responsible for two western bays of the choir and their lateral chapels, the south-western finished by 1294.

3) Third architect, *c*.1290–*c*.1310: choir arcades and vaults of choir aisles; choir triforium and clerestorey, and high vaults of the two western bays; lower parts of the transepts up to the triforium; construction of chapel of Saint-Martial opening off north transept.

4) Fourth workshop, *c*.1310–*c*.1325: completion of choir vaulting; clerestorey of eastern wall of south transept, and its rose and gable.

Work resumed on the transept in 1344, but damage suffered in the 1370s meant that the north arm of the transept and the first two bays of the nave were still under construction in the second half of the fifteenth and early sixteenth centuries.

107C. The exact relationship between Narbonne and Toulouse is still uncertain. Cazes, Carbonell-Lamoche and Pradalier-Schlumberger (1979–80) argue that construction on Toulouse began well before the official foundation, supposedly in 1272, but proceeded slowly, so that at the death of Bishop Bertrand de l'Isle Jourdain (the driving force behind the new choir) in 1286 the lateral chapels on the north side, and the northern radiating chapels up to and partly including the axial chapel were complete, but the southern ring of chapels was still under construction. They also date the keystones in the north choir aisle vault to pre-, those of the south aisle to post-1286. However the choir arcade piers, whose details suggest (to them) a post-1286 date, presuppose at least the installation of the north aisle keystones. See Paul (1991) note 26, p. 39.

Freigang (1992) 113–49, has argued that the start of Toulouse was delayed to 1274–5; that work began on the straight choir chapels on the north side; that from *c*.1282 all the radiating chapels, except the southernmost, were in building. By 1300 at the latest, and not, as the legend has it, by the death of Bishop Bertrand in 1286, four radiating chapels (but not the fifth, southernmost) were vaulted. The remaining chapels, all on the south side, were initiated under Bishop Gaillard de Pressac (1306–17). The revenues of the see suffered after the reduction of the size of the diocese in 1317, and this meant that the whole ground floor of the choir was only completed in the 1360s and 1370s. At this point the triforium was begun and the choir stalls set up. The design is a de luxe response to Narbonne campaign I, extending that cathedral's radiating chapel system into the straight bays with a series of lateral polygonal chapels, piercing their inner walls with openwork tracery to prefigure the double-aisle spaces of the transepts of Carcassonne, and planning a three-aisled transept. Some of these innovations, including the polygonal chapels along the straight sides, and the shape and profiles of the main piers, in turn influenced Narbonne campaigns II, III and IV. The more mannered design of Toulouse, with its play of contrasts between austere supports and delicate, openwork tracery, suggests to Freigang that it was designed by a different architect to that at Narbonne, though the workshops remained in very close contact.

107D. For Rodez see Davis (1979) 363–72, and Freigang (1992) 165–88, who establish the following sequence of construction:

1) Cathedral begun in 1277 by a Narbonne-trained architect. Work proceeded from east to west. Burials and altar endowments in the radiating and lateral chapels of the choir in the 1290s and first two decades of fourteenth century suggest that ten chapels were complete by *c*.1320. The hemicycle geometry and high vault, the proportions of the aisle bays, the mouldings of the apse arcade and the details of the radiating chapels show close connexions to Narbonne, though the length of the choir, the dimensions of the chapels and the shape of their responds immediately recall Toulouse.

2) *c*.1320–30–*c*.1350. Introduction of a new architect, who completed the last radiating chapel on the north side, introduced, at the earliest *c*.1316, but probably later, the rectangular chapels further west, and designed the famous undulating piers of the apse and first straight bays. He also built the upper parts of the hemicycle to a design which probably altered the original Narbonnais design of the upper parts, with an isolated and deeply splayed triforium unit reminiscent of that in the choir of Bordeaux cathedral. The polygonal and pannelled treatment of the projecting triforium passage on the exterior is also very similar to Bordeaux. See Paul (1991) 31, 34, who, however, notes the similarities between the Rodez triforium and Limoges. On stylistic grounds Gardelles (1963) 205ff, and (1992) 76–9, attributes this section of the work to Bertrand Deschamps, to whom he also attributes the upper parts of the Bordeaux choir, which he dates *c*.1320. In 1348 the sanctuary and high altar were mentioned, and the two eastern straight bays of the choir were complete.

3) Fifteenth–sixteenth centuries. After 1447 the erection of the clerestorey and the vaulting of the four eastern bays of the choir. In 1449 the old nave was demolished; around this period the beginning of the western arcades of the choir, which differ in plan to the eastern. 1462 contract for the eastern crossing piers. Nave built in late fifteenth and early sixteenth centuries. Gable of west façade dated 1562.

107E. Older sources have uncritically ascribed most or all of the major cathedrals of the Midi – Clermont-Ferrand, Limoges, Narbonne, Toulouse and Rodez – to the architect Jean Deschamps (see also above, Note 38). Davis (1979) (1981) (1986) and Freigang (1991) (1992) 191–202, have since cast proper doubt on these attributions. Jean Deschamps certainly established the main design of Clermont-Ferrand, and he may have also had a formative influence on the early parts of the choir of Limoges. But Narbonne, Toulouse and Rodez belong to a slightly different stylistic milieu, and there is little or no evidence that they owe their innovative designs to Jean Deschamps or his architectural family. Moreover, Deschamps was a common name in the Auvergne, and often refers in building accounts to prelates or administrators (e.g. a *magister de Campis* in 1287 at Clermont-Ferrand, or a Guillame Deschamps of 1355 at Rodez). For the career of Jean Deschamps, and the Deschamps dynasty see Davis (1979) 304–9, Freigang (1991) and (1992) 191–200, and Paul (1996) The following architects are worth highlighting:

Jean Deschamps I. An eighteenth-century copy of an inscription on the destroyed tomb in Clermont Cathedral, facing the north portal, records that a Jean Deschamps (*Johannes de Campis*) began the cathedral in 1248. He remained in post until *c*.1265.

Jean Deschamps II, mentioned as *magister principalis* at Narbonne in 1286. Davis, Paul and Freigang all reject the idea that he could be identical with the Jean Deschamps that began Clermont-Ferrand. Whatever his relation to the original Deschamps (son? nephew?) it is clear from his work on the Narbonne transepts, and from his tracings for the triforium and clerestorey of the choir (Freigang's campaign III) that he was closely connected to the Clermont chantier (see above, Note 107A). Freigang (1991) 288–94, and (1992) 96–112, underplays the influence of Jean Deschamps II on the design of the central vessel of Narbonne in favour of Dominques de Fauran ('campaign IV'), who modified Deschamps's arcade pillar designs to their present shape and constructed the triforium. But Fauran's slight changes (he omitted four small shafts from the pillar core) were not as radical as Freigang insists, and for the upper parts of the transept and choir he followed exactly Deschamps's solutions. Bearing in mind that the transept façades were also Deschamps's contribution, this architect may well have had a profound influence on the main elevations of Narbonne. See Davis (1995).

Pierre Deschamps I, mentioned in a document given in Rodez in 1339, as a master of Clermont-Ferrand cathedral, and the father of another Pierre Deschamps. Could he be the son or nephew of Jean Deschamps I, continuing the work on Clermont after c.1265, during campaign 2? (see above, Note 38). This 'speculation' is advanced by Davis (1979) 309. If correct, it would rule him out on chronological grounds as the Pierre Deschamps who died in 1357 (see below); it would also exclude him from the first generation after Jean Deschamps I, since he would be in his nineties in 1339! See Freigang (1992) 199.

Pierre Deschamps II (?), mentioned in the same Rodez document as the married son of Pierre Deschamps, *magister* of Clermont. May be identical with the Pierre Deschamps, 'master of the works at Clermont', who died in 1357.

Pierre Deschamps III (?), mentioned as *obrier de peira* of Saint-Pierre de Gourdon in 1311. Identified with the architect of the westwork of Cahors Cathedral.

Bertrand Deschamps, mentioned in 1320 as 'master of the works of the churches of Bordeaux'. Despite the absence in the document of a specific reference to the cathedral, Gardelles (1963) 205ff attributes to him the upper parts of the cathedral choir.

Of these architects, the most influential were Jean Deschamps I, and Jean Deschamps II, who may have had a critical influence in the elevation of Narbonne. The influences of the Pierre Deschamps (I and II), on Clermont or perhaps Rodez, remain matters of speculation.

108. The positive changes occurring around the year 1300, which transformed 'High Gothic' into 'Late Gothic' have been analysed with exemplary subtlety by Gross (1948). Kurmann (1986) singles out for interesting discussion a few 'proto-late Gothic' buildings c.1300 in Germany and France.

109. On these mentions of the name and on the personality of the architect cf. Hans Kunze in Thieme-Becker, XII, under 'Erwin'. The inscription stating that 'Erwin von Steinbach began the façade in 1277' has been doubted by recent research. It no longer survives and was first recorded as late as 1508. See Will (1980). But the latest examinations of the façade by Liess, especially (1985) give greater credence to the inscription and to the sixteenth- and seventeenth-century sources which attribute the façade to Erwin. See below, notes 109a and 111.

109A. Most authorities see Plan A as the first of the series of Strasbourg west façade designs, and some identify it as an 'ideal' project, not intended for the actual west front, because its dimensions do not correspond to the widths of the aisles of the nave behind. For older literature see Wortmann (1957) 44–61, and (1969) 121–4. However Recht (1981) 237–8, and (1989) 381, who dates it to c.1250, argues that the plan *was* intended for the façade since its dimensions fit the cathedral's cross section. Liess (1985a) suggests that Plan A is a copy, probably by an apprentice, of Plan A1, which he attributes to Master Erwin. This is not convincing, since A's details look decidedly earlier in style than A1's; and the author of A1 shows no greater skill as a draftsman (as Liess proposes) than the maker of A, who at least understood side-placed niches at façade corners. Moreover Plan A1 has none of the skill of Plan B, which Liess also attributes to Erwin. Wortmann (1997), rightly, does not attribute A1 to Erwin; he confirms that Plan A is the original (dated c.1250) and A1 the copy (c.1290). He does not think that Plan A was intended for Strasbourg Cathedral, but was a drawing, based on Saint-Nicaise at Reims and the transept façades of Notre-Dame in Paris, by a Strasbourg mason who had travelled to northern France.

110. Georg Dehio in *K.B.*, II, 306 (footnote) rejects Adler's derivation from Troyes, saying that Saint-Urbain had probably not at that time reached much higher than ground level. This argument is in turn contradicted in Lefèvre-Pontalis, 'Jean Langlois, architecte, etc.', in *B.M.*, LXVIII (1904) 93. It was intended to consecrate the choir as early as 1266, but the ceremony had to be postponed because of quarrels and a fire. See above, chapter 3, note 100.

Liess's views on the dating and attribution of the plans are by no means shared by other authorities on Strasbourg, see below, Note 111. The sources for Strasbourg's bravura handling of Rayonnant tracery, particularly free-standing, 'harp-string' mullions in front of the façade wall, can be found not only in the free-standing tracery above the exterior clerestorey gables of the choir of Saint-Urbain at Troyes, but also in the delicate and dense traceries of the north transept front of the cathedral of Châlons-sur-Marne and in the portal storey of the west façade of Auxerre Cathedral. However Wortmann (1997) 144, stresses the unique character of the Strasbourg design, see below, Note 111.

111. Older analysis of the designs and the history of the building is that in the article by Georg Dehio in *Strassburg und seine Bauten* (Strasbourg, 1894)

182. Dehio also returned to this subject in several later works. Cf. also Maximilian Hasak, *Das Münster etc.* (Berlin, 1927), and Josef Knauth in *Strassburger Münsterblätter*, VI (1912) 7. Subtle visual analysis distinguishes the article by Werner Gross in *Marburger Jahrbuch*, VII (1933) 290.

The relationship between the medieval plans and the actual lower storeys of the façade, and the contribution of Master Erwin to both, are still controversial issues. A detailed account of the planning and construction of the façade in the later thirteenth century was given by Wortmann (1957) and (1969). He identified two architects: (1) the designer of Plan B who executed the lower courses of the façade more or less according to that Plan, and (2) Master Erwin, who took over in c.1284 when the work was only a few metres high. On stylistic evidence Wortmann attributed to Erwin: the design and execution of the blind rose window inside the façade above the central portal; the freestanding tracery above all three portals; the horizontal cornice terminating the portal storey; Plan D, showing the northern half of the interior of the west façade; and the design and most of the construction of the rose window and the first storey of the north and south towers (although this level may only have completed after his death in 1318).

Rosemann (1959) admitted that Erwin's role is unclear, but suggested that his appointment (he is first mentioned in 1284) may coincide with the transference of responsibility for the fabric from the bishop to the town between 1282 and 1286. This, he argued, would explain the simplifications to Plan B evident already at the height of the portal gables.

Reinhardt (1972) 71ff, tried to identify a number of masons: the designer of Plan B, the executor of Plan B, who began the façade according to Plan B but wrongly set out the buttresses and laid out the whole western block on too large a scale, and Master Erwin, who modified the details of Plan B, designed Plan D, and designed the present rose. Finally, there is Erwin's son, Johannes, who may have taken over unofficial control of the work in 1304, and may therefore have designed the first storey of the north and south towers.

According to Recht (1974) 27–54, the second architect (the follower of the designer of Plan B) did not misinterpret Plan B, but in the interests of stability consciously altered its proportions by aligning the central section of the façade and narthex with the axis of the nave arcades, thus forcing the towers to project beyond the aisles of the nave. According to Recht, foundations were still being laid in 1280, and in the 1290s it is probable that the north section of the façade had just reached above its portal, the back wall (but not all the front tracery infilling) of the central section was up to just below the first set-off of the buttresses, while progress on the south section lagged well behind, although the first storey of the south tower is earlier than that of the north. He dates Plan D to before 1290, and thinks that Plan C, showing the first storey of the towers, was designed sometime during the construction of the towers at that level (i.e. the first third of the fourteenth century). By 1343 (the installation of the new west doors) the rose storey and the central bay of the narthex was complete. Recht doubts the wisdom of attributing sections of the façade to different architects on stylistic grounds alone, thereby avoiding the problem of Erwin's precise contribution. But he attributes the rose and the first storey of the towers to different architects.

In a series of provocative articles on the west façade and its drawings, Reinhard Liess has radically questioned the consensus. He argues (especially in 1986) that Plan B represents two designs, the first, in brown ink (consisting of most of the lower parts of the plan) is by Erwin, the second, in black ink, drawn by another hand but still reflecting Erwin's ideas, shows more complex solutions (e.g. the rows of pinnacles above the rose, running between the towers, and the double-storied octagonal spire). Liess also argues that Plan B shows the inner plane of the rose window, and Plan A1 the outer plane (hence its empty centre), suggesting that Plan B envisaged a double-layered rose, like the existing one. He maintained that Plan B was an early design (some time before 1274) and was not the basis for the lowest parts of the present façade. In Liess (1985/6) he proposes that Plan C (a seventeenth-century copy), hitherto dated to the first third of the fourteenth century, was in reality drawn in c.1274 and was a much more likely model for the lower parts of the existing façade, although the differences between even C and the built façade suggest that a lost plan based on C, and dating much nearer to 1277 (the year of the actual foundation of the façade) was the real source. He argues that Erwin, as the inscription and the post-medieval sources state, was, from the start, the designer of the façade and its executant architect until his death in 1318. He contends, especially in (1986a) and (1986b) that during his lifetime Erwin completed the façade up to the top of the rose storey, and envisaged the general outlines of the façade up to the platform above the belfry – that is, the second storey of the towers, the Apostles' gallery and the tower-connecting belfry storey above it. He interprets the developing façade designs from A1 to D (including the so-called Kressberg fragment, which he attributes to Erwin and dates just before 1277) as the achievements of a single intelligence (Erwin), not the contributions of different architects. He also sees the whole progress of the façade up to the platform, not as a series of *ad hoc* changes made by different master masons to the plans of their predecessors, but reflections of Erwin's master plan, altered in detail during the fourteenth century to conform to the exigencies of fashion, but not fundamentally departing from Erwin's original conception. Some of these issues bear directly on his discussion of the spire at Freiburg, see Liess (1991) and Chapter 3, Note 123A below.

For the façade designs see Recht ed. (1989) 381–99, who does not accept Liess's position on the priority of Plan C over B, nor his dating of the Kressberg fragment – which he continues to date to c.1350–65 – nor his attribution of the whole conception of the façade, including the belfry, to Erwin.

Wortmann (1997) is equally sceptical of Liess's conclusions. He dismisses the notion that Plan B envisaged a double-layer rose, and still holds that the earliest work on the façade was based on Plan B, though there are real differences between the Plan and the execution, particularly in the proportions of the portals and some of the detailing. Plan C is not an indication of Master Erwin's final designs for the lower sections of the façade, but was the work of a fourteenth-century copyist (note the crude discrepancies between the plan and elevation of the buttresses). The Kressburg fragment he restores to its original dating, of the mid-fourteenth century, and attributes it to Master Gerlach or his shop, not to Erwin. He also restates his distinction between (1) the architect of Plan B and of the lowest parts of the façade, and (2) the very different stylistic character of the upper parts of the portal storey and rose, parts which he attributes to Erwin, who appears first in 1284. He dismisses as untrustworthy the reported inscription that Erwin began the work in 1277.

Wortmann also emphasizes the unique character of Plan B and its lack of any real models in French Rayonnant – the creative novelty of its decorative forms, the separation of double-layered tracery from its invariable use in wall passages, the application of free-standing tracery from limited contexts (spandrels and gables of choir windows, as in Saint-Urbain at Troyes) to the whole façade.

111A. I am following Liess's attributions of Plans B and C (a seventeenth-century copy of the c.1274 (?) original) to Erwin. Liess argues that Plan B was abandoned as early as c.1274 as too extravagant and 'ideal'. See (1985a) (1985/6) and especially (1986). Wortmann (1997) disagrees with Liess on all these points, see above, Note 111.

112. Hans Adalbert Stockhausen, 'Der erste Entwurf zum Strassburger Glockengeschoss etc.', in *Marburger Jahrbuch*, XI (1938) 579. For more up-to-date considerations of the second storey of the towers (complete by 1365) and the belfry connecting them, see Recht (1974) 69–80; Liess (see above Note 111), especially (1986a) and (1986b); and Bureš (1990) 28–9. Only Liess attributes the idea of the belfry to Erwin as part of the original design. Both Recht and Bureš (1990) 28–9 see it as an afterthought, Bureš dating it to a period 'not before the 1380s'. The various drawings for the facade are reproduced in Recht ed. (1989) 381–405.

112A. A point considered in greater detail by Hastings (1955) 184–5, and touched on by Wilson (1990) 196, who gives the best analysis of the chapel.

113. In the later composition the vertical emphasis is heightened and the structural members are slenderer, but the oculus is framed in a semicircular arch, as at Laon. The panels of the fan-shaped tracery are not drawn together towards the centre. In 1280 land belonging to the Archbishop was made available for the construction of the north transept portal, and by 1300 the portal (though not necessarily the whole transept façade) was complete. There are no firm dates for the south transept portal, though documents mention it in 1300 and 1306. See Krohm (1971) especially 40–56.

114. Paul Couteault, *La cathédrale de Bordeaux, P.M.* (Paris, 1935) 49. Cf. also Schürenberg, *op. cit.* 52ff. For the most authoritative analysis of Bordeaux Cathedral see Gardelles (1963) 244–71, and (1992) 79–85, who dates the north portal to c.1330.

115. Preserved in a drawing by Moller which is reproduced in Georg Dehio, *Geschichte der deutschen Kunst*, II (Berlin, Leipzig, 1923) plate 31.

Frankl is misleading in suggesting that these portals form a 'group'. Bordeaux, the latest of them, is closer, as Gardelles (1992) 83, points out, to the 'Puerta preciosa' in Pamplona Cathedral, also c.1330. The east doorway of the Church of Our Lady in Mainz owes more to Cologne and Strasbourg west façades than to Parisian and Rouennais patterns, though its insertion of sculpture into openwork tracery oculi is reminiscent of both the Rouen portals. For the church see Metz (1936). Only the southern portal of the west façade at Mantes, begun, according to an eighteenth-century source, in 1300, really belongs to the Rouen-Parisian circle, in fact is so close in its details to the south transept façade of Rouen, as to be probably the work of the same architect. Its sculptors also worked on the Portail de la Calende. See Krohm (1971) 51–2, 123–9. The detailed architectural similarities between the Portail de la Calende and Mantes and the Peter's portal at Cologne are discussed by Zimmermann-Deissler (1958) especially 84–5. The Cologne connexions are confirmed in the sculptural similarities between the Rouen Portail des Libraires and the Apostles cycle in the Cologne choir, see Krohm (1971) 97–102.

115A. For the precocious Rayonnant of the Saint-Germer chapel see Branner (1965) 93–6; and Kimpel and Suckale (1985) 428–31. The Lady Chapel at Rouen was far enough advanced in 1306 for its founder, Archbishop Guillaume de Flavacourt, to be buried in that year on the left side of its entrance

bay. See Krohm (1971) 51. Bugslag (1986) dates its glass to c.1310–20. Significantly, the town of Flavacourt lies just outside Beauvais, not far from Saint-Germer: see Dwyer (1997).

116. Albert Verbeek, 'Zur Baugeschichte der Kölner Minoritenkirche', in *Kölner Untersuchungen*, ed. Walter Zimmermann (Ratingen, 1950) 141. Descriptions of the church, plans, etc., can be found in *Kunstdenkmale der Rhein-provinz*, II, *Kunstdenkmäler der Stadt Köln* (Düsseldorf, 1929) plate II, and vol. II, p. 13.

Schenkluhn (1985) 214–30, traces the stylistic vocabulatory of the Cologne church, particularly the choir, to the Liebfrauenkirche in Trier; while the general concept of the design, notably the intended non-projecting transepts, to S. Francesco in Bologna. Note, however, the non-projecting south transept of Notre-Dame at Montataire (c.1250–60), where the whole choir shows similarities to that at Cologne; see Bideault and Lautier (1987) 218–26. Schenkluhn (2000) 114–16, repeats his (1985) identification of the choir with the Sainte-Chapelle, with cathedral clerestories, and with the upper choir of S Francesco at Assisi.

117. The dates previously accepted have been corrected in Karl Busch, 'Regensburger Kirchenbauten etc.', *Verhandlungen des historischen Vereins von Oberpfalz und Regensburg*, LXXXII (1932) 181. Cf. also Krautheimer, *op. cit.* (Note 82 to this chapter) 72, and *Die Kunstdenkmäler der Oberpfalz*, XXII, II (1933) 59.

The classic stylistic analysis of the Regensburg Dominican church, which anticipates Frankl's in many respects, is by Gross (1933) 299ff. Based on the appearance of the interior after the 1886 restoration, it fails to take account of the original medieval colouring of the vault ribs and window splays, which must have given the whole interior a less 'pure' and 'abstract' character than Gross's and Frankl's descriptions suggest. See Kobler (1980) 428. For a critique of Gross's analysis as modernist and a-historical see Schenkluhn (1985) 21–3. The important study by Kühl (1986) was not available to me. Schenkluhn (2000) 110–11, emphasizes the novelty (in 1240) of its very tall windows in the choir apse, and the 'drawing-in' of the four-bay choir into the body of the church, separating it from the flanking choir aisles by solid walls (the idea of a *chiesa interiore* borrowed from the liturgical choir of S Domenico in Bologna? See above, Chapter 3, Note 80). He also (pp. 119–22) assesses the novelty of the nave, with its simplified arch-rib system, its emphasis on linearity and wall surface, and its undermining of the independence of the arcade piers as self-sufficient supporting members by allowing the wall to emerge from them via triangular corbels.

117A. The church was begun in the second third of the thirteenth century, or, according to some sources, in 1255. As a vaulted basilica with bare wall surfaces between high clerestories and low arcades, this church follows the Dominican churches in Regensburg, and Strasbourg (destroyed in 1871). All gave the impression of 'inserted' or 'hanging' vaults by supporting them on shafts which terminated on brackets at the height of the top of the arcades (see Regensburg choir). The impression must have been enhanced at Esslingen by the wooden roof which once extended over the western bays of the nave, replaced by the present vaults in 1487. See Schenkluhn (2000) 122–4.

117B. See Konow (1954) 17ff; and Binding (1982) 434.

117C. Nothing is known of the first Dominican church here, consecrated in 1238. The new church was begun probably in about 1265, since recent dendrochronological analysis suggests that the five choir bays were roofed by 1272/3. This accords with a reference to the new choir in 1279. The choir is an open variant of the 'in-drawn' type first used in the Dominican church at Regensburg. See above, Chapter 3, Note 117. The nave chronology is uncertain. It might have been begun c.1280 and finished in 1352, or it may date to a shorter period, between c.1360–80. Its vaults were inserted as late as 1432–8. See Dehio and Eissing (1998) 337, and Schenkluhn (2000) 113, 196–7.

118. In addition to Paatz, *op. cit.* (Note 85 to this chapter), cf. also Werner Gross, *Die abendländische Architektur um 1300* (Stuttgart, 1947) 184ff.

Vasari attributed the church to Arnolfo di Cambio, architect of Florence Cathedral from 1293/4. No documentary evidence supports this claim, but the close similarities between S. Croce's nave and the archeological remains of Arnolfo's projected nave for the cathedral (unvaulted, with octagonal columns and very wide bays) goes some way to confirming it (see below, Chapter 3, Note 142) Building progress was quick. The church was begun in 1294/5; the transept and choir chapels were being roofed in 1310; by 1318 construction had reached the eastern bay of the nave, and by 1330 the nave eastern bays were complete, at least in their lower parts. Three bays of the central aisle were roofed by 1341; the western bays were built in the second half of the century and the church was consecrated in 1442. See Paatz (1940) vol. I, 511–35 Schenkluhn (1985) 178–83 and (2000) 178–82, 208, pieces together the stylistic sources, and typology, of this, the largest of all mendicant churches. It is a monumental enlargement, in basilican form, of the type of 'triple-chapel room church' inaugurated by S. Francesco at Cortona (see above, Chapter 3, Note 81). Its chapels in the transept and the saddle roofs placed over each of them suggest the influence of Cistercian architecture (Fontenay); its vast scale, timber roofs, and pilaster-like responds echo the 'archetypal' Early Christian basil-icas of Rome (especially S. Maria Maggiore, with its projecting cornice/walk-way half way up the elevation and its transept entrance arches rising higher than the main arcades). There are also more local debts: (a) to Franciscan archi-tecture itself (in the staggered triple choir openings, especially close to S. Lorenzo Maggiore in Naples, and the octagonal pillars, like S. Francesco in Bologna) and (b) to the nave of Orvieto cathedral (begun in 1290), itself a ver-sion of an Early Christian basilica, and promoted by a Franciscan pope, Nicholas IV.

118A. Frankl's definition of High Gothic is misleading. He is referring in this section to buildings which we would now call Rayonnant. See Chapter 3 Note 1, above.

119. Illustration in Schürenberg, *op. cit.*, plate 80, and text, p. 172.

See now Branner (1960) 93–4, 177–8; Bony (1983) 443–5, and (1979) 60, who sees it as a key precedent for the English Perpendicular style; and, most fully, Freigang and Kurmann (1989), who argue that the apse and choir is the product, not of two phases of construction (marked by the base of the trifo-rium), but of a homogeneous design, built slowly, and in response to the chevet of Saint-Bénigne in Dijon (though dependent for its Remois passage and dou-ble skins of tracery on the apse of Saint-Urbain at Troyes). It was thus begun soon after 1300.

119A. The lower parts of the transepts at Troyes, and the triforia in the east walls of the transept inner bays, belong to the same campaign as that of the upper choir (c.1230s–40s). Changes occur in the eastern triforia of the two outer bays of the transepts, and in the triforium and clerestorey of the western bays of the transepts. These were built, together with the lower parts of the three eastern bays of the nave, sometime before 1290. See Murray (1987) 14–15.

119B. For Bayonne see Lambert (1939) and Gardelles (1992) 49–59. Gardelles dates the beginning of the nave, along with the laying out of the transepts and the completion of the upper parts of the choir to soon after the fire of 1309, with benefactions towards the transept vaults from Cardinal Guillaume Peyre de Godin (died 1336). The date of 1404 decorates the trans-verse arch between the seventh and eighth bays of the nave.

120. Gabriel Plat, *L'église de la Trinité de Vendôme, P.M.* (Paris, 1934). The choir was built between 1306 and 1318; the Romanesque transepts of 1040 were preserved, and they were continued only in 1342 – to the design of 1306. The four westernmost bays have Late Gothic details (dating from about 1500), but the interior nevertheless gives an impression of great unity.

Lillich (1975), has shown that the conventional date of c.1308 for the begin-ning of the choir is incorrect. The glazing of the chevet clerestorey she dates to c.1285–90, and the beginning of the choir to c.1280.

120A. See Branner (1960) 157ff; and Anfray (1964) 48ff.

120B. From 1309 work began on the western walls of the transept arms, and the aisle walls of the nave. By 1359 the nave aisles were in place and vaulted, and the nave lateral chapels planned. But the nave triforium and clerestorey date from after 1359, the clerestorey of the eastern nave bays to the 1370s, and the crossing and eastern nave bays were only vaulted in the 1390s. The fullest desciption and chronology is in Titus (1984) 225–310.

121. André Masson, *L'église abbatiale Saint-Ouen de Rouen, P.M.* (Paris, 1927). The façade with diagonally set towers, which was begun about 1500, was pulled down in 1845 and replaced by a new one. Adolph Napoléon Didron, in *Annales Archéologiques*, II (1845) 320, characterized this as 'vandalisme d'achèvement'.

The extreme linearity of Saint-Ouen was achieved at some cost to structural soundness, particularly in the pier extensions, see Mark (1982) 92–5. One of the clearest accounts of the church, and of late Rayonnant and Flamboyant architecture in Rouen generally, can be found in various publications by Neagley: (1988) 374–5, notes 1–2; (1996) and, most fully, (1998) 38, 72, 85–6, 88–9, note 3, p. 140:

1318–39, under Abbot Jean Roussel (also known as Marc d'Argent). Choir, part of transepts, first two piers of nave. The elevation is generally indebted to the thirteenth-century work at Saint-Denis, but the statues on the choir piers recall the Sainte-Chapelle, while the tall grill triforium and small balustrade may have been copied from the slightly earlier choir at Evreux. Work dramati-cally slowed down in the 1340s due to the outbreak of the Hundred Years War. During the English occupation of Rouen the church was used as a garrison. The sporadic progress on the transepts in the second half of the fourteenth century makes it difficult to disentangle its chronology, or the contributions of its architects. The problem is complicated by the experimental and eclectic character of the work in this area, where older geometric tracery, and recent influences from English Perpendicular architecture, are freely mixed with new curvilinear forms. The blind tracery on the inner wall of the south transept (c.1350?) is clearly indebted to the same composition in the cathedral's south transept, of c.1300. The south transept porch, the so-called Marmosets porch, was probably begun in the last years of the century by Jean de Bayeux, who is mentioned as master of the works at Saint-Ouen in 1399 and 1411. It was prob-

ably completed by his son and namesake. For Neagley (1988) 394, note 45, the blind tracery of the portal, and the porch's two storeys, its boxy shape and its pendant keystones, suggested the influence of the south porch at Prague cathe-dral. In her (1998) study, p. 140, note 3, she makes no mention of any German influence, and sees the real source for many of its forms – including its framing buttresses, and the transept's rose window set back above the upper storey – in the west porch of the Sainte-Chapelle in Paris. The dissimilarities with the Parisian 'model', however, still suggest to me the importance of German influ-ences. In 1396, the north transept was vaulted.

Alexandre de Berneval took over sometime before 1422 and remained master here until his death in 1441. He was responsible for the curvilinear south transept rose (see his tombstone portrait in Saint-Ouen, showing him designing and drawing the rose), and he is probably the author of the very English-looking Perpendicular-style tracery in the south transept western chapel, since he visited England in 1413. The crossing tower was up by 1441 (when an expertise was called to advise on the buckling of the crossing piers). For Alexandre de Berneval's work for the Duke of Bedford and Henry V of England see Brown, Colvin and Taylor (1963) vol. 1 460, 461, 463.

1462–83 (under Abbot/Cardinal Guillaume d'Estouteville) choir screen (destroyed in the eighteenth century). By 1492 nave piers and aisle walls up to and including sixth bay of nave (the Porte de Ciriers). 1492–1515; eastern half of nave and aisles vaulted and western piers and walls of nave built. The west-ern nave bays remained unvaulted until 1536. The incomplete west façade, with its curious, diagonally placed towers, remained unfinished until the nine-teenth century, when it was demolished and replaced by a Gothic Revival design which made little or no reference to the late Gothic original.

122. Charles Porrée, *La cathédrale d'Auxerre, P.M.* (Paris, 1926) 15.

123. Dehio, (1901) II, 179.

123A. The standard wisdom on the Freiburg steeple is summarized in Adam (1981) 18–20, 40–46. The west tower was begun c.1250, in a 'local' and 'solid' style, though the sculpture of its porch and portal is more 'advanced' since it depends on the west front of Strasbourg and dates therefore from the late thirteenth century. The mention of a perpetual light in 1301 in the chapel of St Michael (above the porch) tells us little or nothing about the progress of the work. A second, much more sophisticated, architect, who had worked on the west façade of Strasbourg, arrived sometime after c.1280 (the second bell was cast in 1281) and designed everything from the star-shaped balustrade at the base of the octagon to the top of the spire. This work is characterized by its openwork delicacy and advanced Rayonnant detailing. The spire was complete c.1340. For the sculpture see Münzel (1978).

Liess (1991) proposes a radically different interpretation, based largely on the two Freiburg steeple drawings now in Fribourg in Switzerland: Plan A (the so-called *Rahnsche Riss*) and Plan B. He argues that the lowest stories were begun, together with the sculpture, in the later 1270s, and the whole steeple – tower and spire – is the product of a single vision. He sees both drawings as copies of original late thirteenth-century projects for the finished steeple and attributes both to the Strasbourg lodge, and specifically to Master Erwin. He detects elements of Plan A (the first of the two) in both Plan B and the building itself. Plan A was conceived in Strasbourg in the 1270s, and Plan B, which is much closer to the finished steeple, soon thereafter. The differences between Plan B and the constructed building suggest either that Plan B was modified, or another, lost, plan intervened. In any event, the whole design process from Plan A to the finished steeple can be attributed to Erwin. Construction on the steeple began after 1277 (the beginning of the Strasbourg west front), probably about 1280. The contrasts in tone between the lower (square) parts of the steeple, and the delicate, upper, octagonal parts are not due to a change of architect but to the execution of Erwin's design: the lower sections by the team that had previ-ously worked on the nave, the upper sections possibly by Erwin himself. Liess notes stylistic connexions with the later west towers of St George at Schlettstadt (Sélestat) and St Florentinus at Niederhaslach (the latter by Erwin's son).

124. The foundation-stone for the new work was laid in 1842. The work was under the direction of E. F. Zwirner until 1861, and was completed by K. E. Voigtel in 1880.

For the nineteenth-century completion of Cologne, and other German cathedrals, see Borger-Keweloh (1986). Credit for the invention of the 'open-work' tracery spire, an idea that was to be influential in Germany to the end of the Middle Ages, must go either to Freiburg or Cologne (Plan F), but the dates of both projects are too imprecise conclusively to establish a priority. Wolff (1986) 18, dated Plan F at Cologne to 'soon after 1300', and suggested, con-vincingly, that the *construction* of the Freiburg spire came after it. See also Wolff (1969) 143ff. Recent Scholarship has seen no reason for Plan F not to date to 'c.1290–1300', see Freigang (1998). But if Liess is correct in thinking that the Fribourg Plan B for the Freiburg steeple is a copy of a c.1280 original, then the actual conception of the openwork spire must go to Freiburg (see above, Note 123A). Liess (1991) 47 also sees influence from 'Erwin's' Plan A at Fribourg on the Cologne Plan F. This may suggest that from 1280 Strasbourg was the dominant influence on the Lower Rhenish cathedral. See also Kauffmann (1948) 110–13; and Kauffmann (1957).

125. Hans Kauffmann, 'Die Kölner Domfassade', in *Festschrift des Kölner Domes* (Cologne, 1948) 78. See also Zimmermann-Deissler (1958), Wolff (1969) and (1986).

125A. Wolff thought that the west façade was begun probably just before 1300 with the south wall of the south tower, laid out according to Plan A. Plan F, the work of Master Johannes, the son of Master Arnold, dated to around 1300, perhaps a few years before. See Wolff (1969) 143–58; Wolff (1980) 13–14, 23ff; Wolff (1986) 16–23. But excavations in the area of the south nave aisle and south tower in the late 1980s have shown that the oldest parts of the nave foundations were for the south aisle, begun in 1325, or a little earlier, when the old atrium was demolished. The foundations for the south tower date to shortly after 1357 and the construction of the tower above ground must therefore be put in the 1360s. See Back (1994). There is, therefore, a large chronological gap between the drawings for the façade and nave (c.1300 or earlier) and their faithful execution. By the end of the Middle Ages the south tower reached to the lowest parts of the second storey – the beginning, that is, of the octagon stages of the steeple.

125B. Kauffmann (1948) 80–8, dates the Vienna plan (Plan A) to c.1300 and the others in close sequence after it. For the dating of Plan F see above, Note 124. For Plan E see below, Note 125C. Plan F is now thought to have been conceived c.1290–1300.

125C. Kauffmann dated Plan E to the first decade of the fourteenth century, and put it immediately before the great façade Plan F. But Wolff (1969) 142–58, argued that Plan E can be associated with a drawing by the same hand of the adjoining nave clerestorey (thought originally to be of the choir clerestorey) which he calles Plan E1. And both he dated to the second half of the fourteenth century, and therefore *after* Plan F. More recent research dates both designs to c.1300, see Freigang (1998).

126. In considering the change from two axes to one, the south tower at Chartres should be borne in mind.

127. Paul Meissner, 'Zur Baugeschichte der Katharinenkirche zu Oppenheim', in *Festschrift für Ernst Neeb* (Mainz, 1936) 64.
Schutz (1982) puts forward the following sequence for the 'façade':
1) *c.1290s* (the appearance of a Master Werner von Koldembech in Oppenheim in 1296) – early fourteenth century. Completion of the south transept and beginning of the nave in a Cologne-dominated style. Nave to have five bays entailing the demolition of the west choir.
2) **1317 raised to collegiate status**. South side of the nave designed as a façade with broad side-aisle windows, possibly by a Mainz architect (Johannes de Oppinheim?).
3) **Under Master Johannes**, the architect of Cologne Cathedral, an 'ideal plan' was drawn up for a five-bay façade, having a larger central window and tracery windows alternating in chiastic rhythms, similar to those of the south tower in Johannes's Plan F for Cologne. Chapels inserted between the buttresses. Then came the decision to retain the west choir and reduce the nave to four bays, resulting in the shortening of the fourth, westernmost, bay. Work then proceeds from west to east. By 1328 probably everything was complete apart from the tracery of the eastern bay.
4) *c.1328–c.1340*. Under an architect trained in the Upper Rhine. Tracery of the eastern bay, and the two seven-light windows of the aisle. North aisle, nave and crossing tower completed.

127A. Pevsner and Metcalf (1985b) 185, date the beginning of the nave, on analogies with Westminster Abbey, to c.1265. Rodwell (1989) dates the high vault to the 'mid thirteenth century.'

127B. For the nave at York see Pevsner and Metcalf (1985b) 344–6; Harvey (1977) 149–60. Coldstream (1980) and Böker (1991) discuss the sources of the nave design in French and German Rayonnant. Böker in particular stresses the parallels with Cologne cathedral. For more general parallels between York and the continent see Norton (1993–4).

127C. For the French/Rhenish composition and details of the York façade see Böker (1991). Maddison (1993) dates the Lichfield west front as follows:
Phase 1 late thirteenth century, completion of last bay of nave, layout of the lower parts of the façade and construction up to the third string course above the fourth tier of statues.
Phase 2 Under Bishop Walter Langton (1296–1321), c.1310–14: the west window (present tracery nineteenth century, original design recorded by Hollar). The south-west tower and spire (which is slightly different in detail to its north west pair).
Phase 3 c.1315 to c.1323: north-west tower and spire, crossing tower and spire, the beginning of the new Lady Chapel and a start on the remodelling of the choir. Simeon Solomon describes the three spires complete in 1323.

127D. Frankl is grappling here with the diversity of Gothic in Europe in the second half of the thirteenth century. At the level of the great church, the French models of High Gothic/Rayonnant were rapidly transformed by local initiatives in the Rhineland, southern France and England. At the more mod-

est level of parochial and collegiate church architecture, and the architecture of the friars, High Gothic/Rayonnant was quickly transformed and simplified, and new decorative and structural systems were grafted onto it. This process of assimilation laid the foundations for the different regional and national styles of Late Gothic which emerged in the middle of the fourteenth century.

128. About 1110 at Walderbach, a little later at Prüll near Regensburg, and in 1182 the church of St Peter at Augsburg (Dehio's dates).
Dehio dates the Cistercian church at Walderbach too early. The monastery was founded in 1143 and the church was not vaulted until the third quarter of the twelfth century. For a general discussion of early hall churches in Bavaria see Thümmler (1962) 290–2, and Schütz and Müller (1989) 520–1. Kubach and Köhler-Schommer's (1997) monumental study of Romanesque hall churches has shown that the eleventh- and twelfth century hall church, however it might be defined, was not, as Frankl put it, 'a German form', but was widespread in western and south-western Europe from the Loire to the Duero. It also spread into northern Italy and neighbouring areas of southern Europe. For their discussion of the Bavarian halls see pp. 135–8.

129. On the subject of this process within Westphalia, cf. H. R. Rosemann in *Zeitschrift für Kunstgeschichte*, 1 (1932) 203.
Early rib vaults may also have reached Germany, especially Westphalia and Bavaria, from northern Italy. See Thümmler (1958). For a more up-to-date treatment of Westphalian halls see Henze (1957) 165–214. A well-illustrated survey is provided by Thümmler and Badenheuer (1973). The whole problem of the origins of the Westphalian hall church is discussed by Kubach (1985).

129A. For Marburg see above Note 85A. For Paderborn, where the hall nave was begun c.1231, see Bauer and Hohmann (1969) 19ff. For the nave of the Münsterkirche at Herford, begun c.1228, see Thümmler and Badenheuer (1973) 29. Herford is now seen as having priority over Paderborn as the first in the Westphalian series of large-scale hall churches, though their traditional derivation from the west of France (Poitiers Cathedral) has been questioned, see Kubach (1985) 4–8.

129B. See Wagner-Rieger (1982) 195–211, who identifies French precedents, particularly the choir aisles of Saint-Denis and Notre-Dame in Paris, as the sources for the Lilienfeld choir aisles. Nicolai (1988) 23–37, proposed the following chronolgy for the Lilienfeld choir:
1) 1202/6–17. South transept, western crossing piers, ambulatory up to the socles of the free-standing pillars – all by a Heiligenkreuz-trained workshop using band ribs. The ground plan follows the choir of Morimond whose choir aisles and ambulatory differed from those of Cîteaux III and Ebrach in having no, or few, chapels with internal dividing walls. Instead, choir aisles and chapels formed, together, double-aisled spaces divided by virtually free-standing supports.
2) 1217 (date of the first consecration) onwards. Thinning of the ambulatory pillars, vaulting of the ambulatory and chapels with roll-moulded ribs.
3) **Up to the consecration in 1230** and the death of the founder, Leopold VI. This phase follows smoothly from phase 2. Insertion of the present polygonal apse into the sanctuary, instead of the intended straight-ended eastern choir wall. Building of the north transept and first (hall) bay of nave.
Seeger (1997) 13–53, essentially follows this relative chronology, but she convincingly dates the start of the actual construction of the church to 1206–9. Contrary to all opinion to date, she also makes out a good case for dating the polygonal apse, not to an insertion after 1217, but as an integral part of the original plan. But her claim that the apse derives from that of Magdeburg cathedral (1207–9) is, on chronological grounds alone, less convincing.

130. Dagobert Frey, 'Die Denkmale des Stiftes Heiligenkreuz', in *Österreichische Kunsttopographie*, XIX (Vienna, 1926). See also Wagner-Rieger (1967) 338–9, 378–9; and Wagner-Rieger (1979) 103–26 especially 107–9; and Brucher (1990) 69–73. Watzl (1979) gives not 1295 but 17 April 1294 as the consecration date of the choir.

131. *Ibid.* The correct date had already been given with great conviction in Franz Kugler, *Geschichte der gotischen Baukunst*, III (Stuttgart, 1859) 306.

132. *Die Kunstdenkmäler der Provinz Hannover*, IV (1907) 87ff. See also Kiesow, Hoffman *et al.* (1977) 731–5.

132A. For Nogent see Branner (1965) 66–7; Kimpel and Suckale (1985) 407, 526; Bideault and Lautier (1987) 240–5.

132B. For Montataire see Branner (1965) 115; Bideault and Lautier (1987) 218–26.

132C. See Michler (1980) 65, 67.

133. Schürenberg, *op. cit.*, 119 and plate 51 (which shows very strange piers). The nave north portal can be dated stylistically to the third quarter of the thirteenth century, its west portal to the early fourteenth. See Gardelles (1992) 203–5.

133A. For Agen see Branner (1965) 116; Gardelles (1992) 148–50. Although founded in 1249 the church was probably not built until the 1250s/60s. It shows the arms of Alphonse of Poitiers, who died in 1270. For the influence of the mendicant orders on southern French Gothic see Durliat (1974) 71–86. Schenkluhn (2000) 54–5, stresses the debt to monastic chapter houses and refectories, – sources chosen not in order to make the church more 'profane', but to renew church architecture in response to the demands of its critical lay users.

133B. The nave was begun after the fire of 1275, and the first campaign, under Master Martin, lasted until 1304; the second until *c*.1327. See Zimmermann (1956).

133C. The choir was already underway in 1276 and the high altar consecrated in 1308, by which date the present five-aisled hall nave was probably envisaged, if not begun, and perhaps quite far advanced. See Mertens (1972) 4–7. Lehmann and Schubert (1991) 180–96, especially 181–3, consider the nave fabric to have been finished by 1332, when the *fabrica* appealed for funds for furnishings and not construction. The most exhaustive analysis of St Severus, its building history and stylistic position in Middle German Rayonnant, can now be found in Wedemeyer (1997) 465–513 (building history) and 289–95 (its relations with Thuringian and Hessian hall churches of the later thirteenth century). Wedemeyer puts the starting date for the church 1274/6, and its completion in 1327, when the nave is recorded as being in use. Its use of a transept and five-aisled nave is something of a Thuringian peculiarity (see St Mary, Mühlhausen). Its details, especially its tracery, imply a knowledge of Rhenish Rayonnant of *c*.1300–20 (Cologne, Worms, Oppenheim, Oberwesel).

133D. The importance of this early hall choir for the later development of the hall choir in Germany was first shown by Kunst (1969). The impact of Cologne and Strasbourg on its design is discussed by Kunst in (1969a).

134. Günther Rudolf, 'Mitteldeutsche Hallenkirchen und die erste Stufe der Spätgotik', in *Jahrbuch für Kunstwissenschaft*, LI (1930) 137.

Lehmann and Schubert (1968) 49–53, date the beginning of the work at Meissen, the polygonal apse of the choir, to the reign of Bishop Konrad I (1240–59). The choir seems to have progressed in two phases:

1) *c*.1250, apse and first straight bay (the so-called 'founders's bay') and

2) **begun by 1263**, on the site of the Romanesque choir. A change of design involving the western bay of the choir (with the six-part vault), the two choir-flanking towers behind it, and the ambulatory connecting it to the cloister to the south of the choir.

Lehmann and Schubert dated the decision to change the nave from a basilica to a hall during the building of the north transept, and therefore between 1287 and 1291. Their conclusions on the chronology of the whole cathedral are drawn together in more general form in Lehmann and Schubert (1970) 12–26. Their dating of the change from basilica to hall has, however, been questioned by new research undertaken during and after the restoration of the cathedral from 1992. This has made visible much of the original stone coursing and masons' marks, on the basis of which Donath (1998) has established a revised building history. He discussed the preliminary results of his research in the 1996 conference 'Gotik und Spätgotik, Kunst und Region', at the art history institute in the University of Halle-Wittenberg:

1) *c*.1250–*c*.1270. Choir, transepts (except the upper parts of the west wall of the north transept), the 'basilican bay' (the easternmost nave bay on the south side), the lower sections of the octagonal chapel (immediately to the west of the south transept) and the lowest courses of the first four bays of the north aisle of the nave. The north-west crossing pillar was constructed with arcade arches for a basilican nave. The 'advanced' intersecting tracery of the south transept end window belongs to this phase.

2) *c*.1270–before 1293. Change from basilica to hall. West wall of transept, vaulting of transepts, completion of first four aisle bays on the north side. Stylistically, the details of the hall – tracery, wall passages, mouldings – place it alongside the later parts of St Elizabeth at Marburg, and the Stadtkirche of Friedberg in Hesse – see Note 134A, below.

Magirius (1993a) also refines Lehmann and Schubert's sequences, and in (1994) reports on the restorations, mainly in the matter of original polychromy.

134A. See now Seeliger (1962); Auer (1983); Schenkluhn (1983).

135. Richard Kurt Donin, *Die Bettelordenskirchen in Österreich* (Baden near Vienna, 1935) 155. See also Wagner-Rieger (1967) 337, 374, who dates the nave to the 1280s; and Brucher (1990) 54–5, who considers the church must have been useable by 1289.

136. Johnny Roosval, *Die Kirchen Gotlands* (Leipzig, 1912). The author describes a series of sixteen churches, which begins (p. 141) with Wall (built some time after 1200) and reaches right into the fourteenth century. All these churches still have groin-vaults. Closer analogies with Imbach are to be found in earlier Dominican double-aisled halls in France, e.g. Paris, Agen and Toulouse. The Gotland churches are mostly centralized buildings with a single, axially placed pillar. See Götz (1968) 106–7; and Lagerlof and Svahnstrom (1973). For the wider context of two-aisled halls in Central Europe see Schenkluhn (2000) 93–5.

137. On Romanesque aisleless churches, cf. Dehio, (1901) I, 223, 326. The development of the *nef unique* in early Gothic architecture in the Languedoc is discussed by Paul (1988) and Freigang (1992) 213–22, where the type comprises both vaulted structures and wooden-roofed spaces with diaphragm arches, often with cellular chapels.

138. Schürenberg, *op. cit.* plate 37, text p. 93; *C.A.*, LXXV (1907) 44. Restored by Viollet-le-Duc. See Durliat (1973), and Paul (1988) 116–18. In 1262 the new lower town at Carcassonne was laid out, and the parishes of Saint-Michel and Saint-Vincent reconstructed. In 1283 Philip the Bold allowed the parishioners of Saint-Michel to buy houses in order to enlarge the church and cemetery.

138A. In monastic buildings, large single-aisled halls covered with wooden roofs over diaphragm arches are largely confined to Catalonia. But note no less than seven of these spaces in the Cistercian claustral buildings at Fossanova in central Italy. See Dittscheid and Berger (1988).

139. Jean Laran, *La cathédrale d'Albi, P.M.* (Paris, n.d.). See also Emile Mâle, *La cathédrale d'Albi* (Paris, 1950), which has excellent illustrations. The meagre blind gallery at the eaves line of the roof of the nave, which is picked out in different-coloured brick, dates from the restoration begun in 1834 by César Daly. This architect also began building belltowers, but in 1879, when three had been built, the population protested.

For a detailed account of the building see Biget (1982) 20–62, who reconstructs the following sequence:

1) **1277** decision to build the new church.

2) **1282** official foundation by Bishop Bernard de Castenet in 1282. From 1282/4–1300 construction of the walls of the apse and the first two straight bays. In 1298 a mention of the 'ecclesia antiqua' in contrast to the new work. In 1306 mention of a chaplain in chapel of first straight bay from east (St Croix).

3) **1310–22**: after a delay from 1301 to 1310 construction was relaunched in 1310. Vaulting of apse chapels and of the high vaults of the two easternmost straight bays. Lateral walls extended up to and including the bay opposite the south portal.

4) **1322–1335/40**: high vaulting of third and fourth bay from east. Lateral walls up to ninth bay from east.

5) **1355–1365/6**: construction of tower base; completion of nave lateral walls; high vaulting of eighth bay from east.

6) **1380–90**: high vaulting of the three westernmost bays.

7) **Under Bishop Louis d'Amboise** I, from 1474–*c*.1483, the choir screen built.

8) **In 1485** Bishop Louis's will ordered the erection of the west tower, starting at the level of, and with the construction of, the rounded arches between the cylindrical buttresses. Work finished before 1493.

9) **1503–9**: Tribunes dividing the chapels inserted under Bishop Louis d'Amboise II.

For the choir screen see also Biget, Carbonell-Lamothe, Pradalier-Schlumberger (1982) 63–91.

139A. Few would now agree with Frankl that hall churches which isolate one aisle from the other by bulky or closely spaced pillars, or by arcade arches made thicker than the transverse arches, are less 'Gothic' and more 'Romanesque' than those that emphasize spatial unity. Frankl is here coming close to the old thesis of Kurt Gersternberg, *Deutsche Sondergotik* (Munich 1913), that German hall churches must be seen as unified spaces (*Einheitsräume*), in which all qualities associated with the basilica – separation of aisles into three parallel spaces, emphasis on longitudinal direction of space – have been replaced by a broad, 'directionless' and unified interior. In fact, a number of very 'Gothic' German hall churches, from the thirteenth to the fifteenth centuries, emphasize longitudinal movement and the separation of aisles. See Kunst (1971) 38–53; and Schenkluhn (1989).

140. Plans of the piers and a detailed analysis can be found in Pierre Lavedan, *L'architecture gothique etc.* (Paris, 1935) 146ff.

In 1298 the foundation stone was laid, and by 1329 the chevet, the side portals and the choir up to the western limit of the *trascoro* (the choir screen) had been completed. In 1317 Jaime Fabre, architect of the Dominican church in Palma de Mallorca, took over the leadership of the lodge at the request of James II, King of Aragon. Despite interruptions to the work in 1329, he was still working on the cathedral in 1356. The relics of St Eulalia were translated on 9 July 1339, by which time the transept was complete. Fabre was succeeded by Bernard Roca (Roche, Roquer) who vaulted the first nave bays, began the cloister in 1382, in 1385–9 built the two transept bells towers, and worked as far as the *trascoro*. In 1408 a Master Carli produced a design for the west front. In 1413–30 Bartolomeu Gual built the chapels inside the west front, the last vaults of the nave, the base of the octagonal lantern over the west bay, and continued the cloister up to 1423. His follower, Andres Escuder, finished the cloister in 1431. See Torres Balbás (1952) 150–2; Durán Sanpere (1959); Barral i Altet (1994) 31–62. Wilson (1990) 276–8, stresses the debts to Toledo Cathedral.

140A. The chronology of Palma Cathedral is complicated and obscure. The best account is in Durliat (1962) and (1962a) 150–67.

1306. The will of James I of Mallorca ordered the construction of the two-storey funerary chapel of the kings of Mallorca, dedicated to the Holy Trinity, which is the easternmost space of the present building. Although the chapel was far advanced enough to get a priest in 1311, it was not finished in 1313, was still mentioned in 1327 as needing completion and was not glazed until 1329.

The apsidal choir into which the Trinity Chapel opened westwards, now called the Royal Chapel, was also planned in 1306, though it was probably not laid out until 1313–14, since in 1314 the plan of the cathedral was traced on the extended site.

Bishop William of Villanova (1304–18) and Bishop Raymond of Cortsavi (1318–21) gave funds to the fabric; and in 1322 Sardinian galley slaves donated for work on the chevet.

By 1327 work on the choir would have been substantially finished, since in that year screens were installed. Durliat sees resemblances between the choir and the palatine chapel of St Cross at Perpignan, especially in its massive rectangular basement and the polygonal plan of its upper, eastern, parts. He considers that the architect might have been Pons Descoyl, who was in Mallorca in 1311 but returned to Perpignan in that year.

c.1327. The beginning of the construction of the two lateral choir apses, and probably in this period (*c.*1330?) a start was made on the first lateral chapels of the nave.

A building campaign of uncertain extent, marked by King Peter's donation in 1343 (shortly after his capture of Mallorca). The high altar was consecrated in 1346. At this stage the central vessel of the nave was to be only as high as the choir, and the nave aisles were to reach only the height of the present lateral chapels (traces of original vault springers at the end of the north aisle; thickening of the last north buttress of the nave).

In *c.*1350–60, perhaps at the beginning of the reign of Bishop Anthony Collell, who donated generously to the fabric in 1357, there occurred a decisive change of plan. The aisle vaults were raised to their present height, and their terminal eastern walls were given rose windows corresponding in level with the rose over the eastern wall of the choir apse. The central vault was raised to its present colossal height.

The second nave chapel on the north side built by 1361. The arms of Bishop Galiana (1363–75) on the buttress pinnacle of the easternmost nave bay and a mention in 1368 of the first pillar of the nave suggests that the first bay of the nave was under construction. The architect of all, or some of this work was James Mates of Mallorca, who appears in the accounts in 1368, together with the sculptor Laurent Sosquela.

Work slows down. In 1574 the north nave aisle vault, second bay from the west, was completed. In 1592 the west portal was begun, and in 1596 the western rose started. The final consecration took place in 1601. For the general stylistic characteristics of Palma, and of other great Catalan basilicas of the period see Freigang (1992) 155–71.

140B. For the dimensions and an analysis of the structure, see Mark (1982) 95–101.

140C. For Gerona see Lavedan (1935) 146ff, 198ff; Oliver (1973); Barral i Altet (1994) 63–92. The choir was begun in 1312. Freigang (1989a) sees at least two phases of construction:

1) 1312–20. Construction of radiating chapels and apse pillars of choir up to capitals, on a ground plan, and with details, closely modelled on Barcelona Cathedral choir.

2) 1320–*c.*1330. Under Jacques de Fauran, master mason of Narbonne Cathedral since 1309, and son of Dominique de Fauran (master of Narbonne 1295–1309): pillars of the straight bays of the choir, all arcade arches in the straight and turning bays, and perhaps the upper parts of the central vessel. This phase coincides with the appearance of Narbonne-type 'columnar' piers and moulding profiles, which also appear in Perpignan cathedral choir, where Jacques de Fauran is mentioned in 1324 as the owner of property. Freigang also attributes to Jacques de Fauran the conception of the nave at Gerona as a *nef unique.*

After *c.*1330 a Guillelmus de Cursu is mentioned as principal architect. The choir was consecrated in 1347. For an account of the arguments surrounding the future shape of the nave in the conference of masons at Gerona in 1417 see Frankl (1960) 84–6, and Freigang (1999).

140D. For S. Anastasia see Dellwing (1970) 64–81, and (1990) 29–32, where its stylistic place is situated some way between, on the one hand, S. Lorenzo in Vicenza and, on the other, the monumental and attenuated mendicant basilicas of S. Nicolò in Treviso and the Franciscan and Dominican churches in Venice. The Dominicans began the church around 1290, and had completed the choir and first bay of the nave by 1319, though the whole building had to wait to the early years of the fifteenth century for completion. Schenkluhn (2000) 75, 184–5, assesses its place in north Italian mendicant buildings, including its precocious use of even-sided polygons for its chapel apses, a geometry which reappears in the Frari in Venice.

141. The chronology of the early and mid thirteenth-century cathedral at Siena has been radically, and on the whole convincingly, reassessed by Pietramellara (1980). Her conclusions have been largely accepted by Middeldorf-Kosegarten (1984) 22–7, except that the latter dates the decision to vault the choir and dome to *c.*1250 and not 1258, and argues that the dome was conceived not as an afterthought, designed in 1258/9 (the supposed time when it was decided to vault the church), but was conceived in or from 1226 (?) or from about 1247.

141A. See above, Chapter 3, Note 118.

141B. The discovery during the excavations of what were thought to be the footings for Arnolfo's octagon, and the conclusions drawn from the excavations at the west end of the nave, are discussed by Toker (1978) (where all earlier conjectural reconstructions are assessed), and Toker (1983). Kreytenberg (1974) argued for intense building activity on the nave and choir of the cathedral between 1331 and 1348. His conclusions were questioned by Toker (1978) 221–2, and Trachtenberg (1979). In turn, Toker's conclusions have been questioned by Rocchi *et al.,* (1988) and by Trachtenberg (1993) 29, note 27. Toker's hypothetical reconstructions in his 1983 study of the exterior elevation of Arnolfo's façade (fig. 11b), and the 'Arnolfian' project for the east end (fig. 22), are based largely on Pocetti's sixteenth-century drawing of the façade before its revetment was stripped off in 1588, on the view of the Duomo by Andrea Bonaiuti in the chapter house of S. Maria Novella (1366–7) and on a supposed 'realization' of Arnolfo's east end in frescoes by Taddeo Gaddi in the Baroncelli Chapel, S. Croce (*c.*1328–34). Toker's archeological evidence for an octagonal crossing may be plausible, but his evidence for domed transepts with cellular chapels, on the triconche scheme later adopted for the present east end by Talenti, is based on ambiguous archeological remains, and on his supposition that Taddeo Gaddi's image of the Temple of Jerusalem was based on Arnolfo's 'project'. Trachtenburg is agnostic about the nature of Arnolfo's project, and believes the Gaddi image is a typically medieval evocation of the Temple, which includes 'local' Florentine elements; it is not a specific rendition of the cathedral's design. There is also no consensus on Arnolfo's design for the west façade. A good survey of the earlier literature can be found in Romanini (1980). Still the best analysis of the west façade is Metz (1938). For Arnolfo's system of proportion for the west façade, based on the Baptistery, see Trachtenberg (1997) pp 55–62.

142. Martin Weinberger, 'The first Façade etc.', in *Journal of the Warburg and Courtauld Institutes,* IV (1940) 67. Saalman (1964) 472–3, 495, questioned if much of the early revetment in the side walls of the nave, built before 1342, was actually planned or executed under Arnolfo. Toker (1978) 221 and fig. 16, considered that much of the raw masonry wall – at least up to the south-west nave portal – was up by Arnolfo's death, but left open the extent of the revetment at that time. See below, Chapter 4, Note 91.

143. Keller (1937) and (1938), White (1993) 115–17, and many other authorities, were convinced that the rose story of the façade was built in the second half of the fourteenth century (1370s), and therefore could not reflect Giovanni Pisano's intentions. In addition, the awkward vertical discontinuities between the façade's wide central upper story and the much narrower central portal zone below suggested to most commentators a change of plan in the upper half of the façade. For Giovanni's 'original' project for the upper story Keller proposed a similar solution to the present façade, but with a smaller oculus and a much greater vertical continuity between the oculus story and the central portal below. White reconstructed the design as a single great gable across the whole width of the façade, in the manner of Emilian Romanesque, or a slightly stepped gable similar to Notre-Dame de la Grande in Poitiers. By 1316–17, he argued, work had stopped at the level of the top of the arcades above the lateral doors. But Middeldorf-Kosegarten (1982) 28–33, 69–103, on the basis of documentary evidence and the style of the façade's sculpture, has denied that there was any change of plan and has dated most of the existing upper parts of the façade, not to the 1370s but to *c.*1297–*c.*1310/17, that is, the period immediately after Giovanni's departure and before the beginning of the new baptistery and extended choir. This suggests that the whole façade may be more of a unified creation than has been imagined, and may even go back to Giovanni's designs. There is certainly evidence that the last bay of the nave underwent a change (it is taller than the other bays, not aligned with them, and the remains of its original clerestorey, preserved below the later aisle roofs, show a different treatment than those further east). All this is consistent with a decision by Giovanni or his successor (s) to build the present tall façade with its wide rose and to treat the bay behind it as a 'transitional' or temporary space, before the old vaults of the nave could be heightened accordingly. However, White (1985) and (1993) 621, note 117, has defended the late fourteenth-century date for the upper parts of the present façade and the vaulting of the nave behind it. The arguments, which remain evenly balanced, are briefly rehearsed in Norman, ed., (1995) 134–5, 141–2. See p. 214 and Notes 94–6.

144. On the upper storey see p. 214.

144A. See Buchowiecki (1970) 691–744; and Urban (1961/2) 75–124 especially 119ff, who qualifies the church's dependence on S. Maria Novella. The present transverse arches and ribs are post-medieval insertions; originally the groin vault had, in the Roman manner, no transverse arches. The nave vault was completed by 1474, but it is not certain if the side aisle vaults were begun in the fourteenth or fifteenth century. Unlike S. Maria Novella, the nave had no clerestorey, and was therefore a pseudo-basilica. See Palmerio and Villetti (1989) 63–5, 107–10, 112–15. The fullest account of the church is now to be found in Kleefisch-Jobst (1991).

CHAPTER 4

1. Illustrated in John Britton, *The History and Antiquities of Wells Cathedral* (London, 1824).

1A. Not everyone would agree with Frankl's assertion, especially since the 'multiplication of tiercerons' had appeared much earlier, in the nave and Chapter House of Lincoln Cathedral, *c*.1225–35. The problem lies in defining the notion of 'Late Gothic', a style which is usually taken to start, in architecture at least, in the middle of the fourteenth century. See Białostocki (1966). For the Chapter House at Wells, see below, Chapter 4, Note 4.

2. *Ibid.*, 86.

2A. For the Lincoln Chapter House see Pevsner-Metcalf (1985b) 227–9; for Lichfield see Pevsner-Metcalf (1985b) 181ff, and Rodwell (1993) 33, who dates the Chapter House and its vestibule to *c*.1230–40. For Westminster see Wilson (1986) 85ff. For Salisbury see Blum (1991) 22–36. She shows that the Cloister and Chapter House were envisaged and probably designed in the year 1263, when Bishop Walter de Wyle (1263–71) gave land to the Chapter for a new Cloister. But she holds to the conventional position that actual construction on the Chapter House was not begun until at least 1280, because of the pennies of Edward I, dating to that year, unearthed in nineteenth-century excavations below the Chapter House floor. In an unpublished lecture delivered at the Courtauld Institute in 1998 Dr Tim Tatton-Brown questioned the archeological evidence surrounding these coins and their discovery, and suggested a much earlier starting date for the Chapter House, perhaps in the 1260s, and therefore chronologically closer to its exact model, that at Westminster Abbey.

3. As regards not only the tracery, but also the clarity of the severies with tri-radial ribs without ridge-ribs.

4. For the Chapter House and its design see Draper (1981) 18–29 especially 19–20; Harvey (1982) 66–73; and Colchester (1987) 17, 151–7. A full account of the dating and iconography of the Chapter House in given in Ayers (1996) 30–87. He establishes that the main chamber was begun in *c*.1298 and was glazed by *c*.1305.

4A. See above, Chapter 2, Note 76; Chapter 3, Notes 53A, 53B.

5. Illustration of Exeter in Webb, *op. cit.* plate 112, and more complete in Martin Hürlimann and Peter Meyer, *English Cathedrals* (London and New York, 1950) plate 78.

The exact chronology, according to the surviving building accounts, is given by Erskine (1981–3), and a more detailed breakdown of the sequence of construction can be found in Jansen (1991). Rebuilding of the Norman cathedral had begun by 1279–80 in the eastern chapels and those opening off the presbytery aisles – thus the entire eastern arm had by then been planned and prepared. The stepped, straight-ended ground plan derives from Old Sarum, Winchester, Salisbury and twelfth-century Wells, its details show an understanding of Westminster Abbey and the early parts of the choir of Old St Paul's in London. Jansen attributes this first phase, lasting up to the mid-1280s, to the first architect, a court-trained master working in conjunction with Bishop Bronescombe.

A second, and most creative, architect, the real 'Master of Exeter', appears from *c*.1282–5. He, and Bishop Quinil (1280–91) are responsible for work that extended throughout the eastern chapels, the retrochoir, the upper parts of the Lady Chapel, the choir and presbytery aisles and the transepts. The Lady Chapel was roofed in 1304. By 1288–91 the four eastern bays of the central aisle of the presbytery were underway, and they were completed, with their vaults, by 1302. At this stage, the main elevation of the presbytery was to have had only two stories, like Netley, Pershore or Tintern, but with steep lower splays for the clerestorey windows. This second architect combined an up-to-date knowledge of London and court idioms in window tracery (Merton College Chapel, Oxford; St Etheldreda's, Holborn, London) with a preference for more robust and textural forms derived from the Midlands and the north-east of England. (Lincoln vaults, Yorkshire clustered piers).

By 1297 he had been replaced by the third architect, a Master Roger. He built the choir (the three western bays of the eastern arm). In contrast to the two-storey system used by the second architect in the presbytery, Roger gave the choir a three-storey elevation modelled on the slightly earlier choir of St Werburgh's at Chester, in which the two upper stories consist of a low triforium and a tall clerestorey, each with interior passages. For the wider sylistic implications of these 'superposed interior passages', and their origins in Burgundy, see Jansen (1979). The choir was structurally complete by 1311 and dedicated in 1312. In 1318 the three-storey system was extended to the four presbytery bays. A reconstruction of the original late thirteenth-century tracery of the presbytery east window is offered by Russell (1991).

6. Up-to-date accounts in Hürlimann, *op. cit.* plate 40. Up-to-date accounts of the octagon at Ely, and all the fourteenth-century work there, can now be found in Coldstream (1979); Lindley (1986) and Lindley (1986a), the latter a revealing discussion of the imagery and 'programme' of the octagon. The timberwork of the octagon and lantern is also analysed by Fletcher (1979) especially 61ff, and Hewett (1985) 114–22. See also the readable Maddison (2000).

6A. Wilson (1990) 197, sees good reasons for accepting the attribution of the conception of the octagon to the sacrist.

7. In French specialist literature, ridge-ribs are called liernes; cf. discussion of Philibert de l'Orme in Frankl (1960) 296, and Viollet-le-Duc, *Dictionnaire*, under 'Lierne'. Bony (1979) 46–8, discusses the invention and development of the lierne vault in England.

8. See Pevsner, *Cambridgeshire* (*The Buildings of England*) 285; Hürlimann, *op. cit.* 18, plates 43–5. See Lindley (1986) 124–6; Coldstream (1979) 31–4. Woodman (1984) argues, unsuccessfully, that the Lady Chapel was built as an unvaulted structure, and only received its present vault in the late fifteenth century.

8A. Coldstream (1979) passim, identified two workshops at Ely, one from East Anglia/Norwich (which did the choir, octagon and Prior Crauden's Chapel) and one from Lincolnshire (which did the Lady Chapel), though both copied from each other's work and may have exchanged masons. Lindley (1986) passim sees no such division. He attributes to a 'Master John' the stone substructure of the octagon, most of the choir, Prior Crauden's Chapel and, most probably, the Lady Chapel. For John Ramsey see Harvey (1984) 240–1. Lindley also recognises the hand of a second architect, probably William Ramsey, in parts of the southern and the whole of the northern elevation of the choir, as well as its lierne vaults. See also Wilson (1980) 186–97; and Maddison (2000) 72–5.

9. Illustrated in Bond, *Introduction*, I, 43. For the remodelling of Romanesque Tewkesbury, begun shortly before 1321, see Morris (1974). Cave (1929) dates the nave roof bosses to *c*.1320 on the basis of details of costume and armour. The stylistic context for the Tewkesbury net vaults is set out by Bony (1979) 50ff, and more fully by Bock (1962) 56–67. The source for the two-bay diagonal net vaults of the English West Country discussed by Frankl in this section was probably the most simple vault of the series – the side aisle vaults of the choir of St Augustine's at Bristol, dated most recently by Morris (1997) to the 1320s/30s, though they are contemporary (or a little later?) than the miniature net vault covering the passage of the rood screen at Exeter cathedral, dated exactly 1317–25. See Morris (1991) 74, and plate XIIA. See also Bock (1961a).

10. G. H. Cook, *The Story of Gloucester Cathedral* (London, 1952) figure 17. Also Bock (1962) 64–5. For the significance of Gloucester as one of the earliest examples of the Perpendicular style, and for the chronology of the remodelling see Harvey (1978) 78–80 and 90–2; Wilson (1980) 113–17, 127–39, 164–70; and Wilson (1990) 204–8. There are three campaigns:

1) *c*.1331–6 The remodelling of the south transept.

2) **The rebuilding of the choir**, beginning with the liturgical choir under the crossing, built during the reign of Abbot Adam de Staunton (1337–51), and probably finished by *c*.1351, and then proceeding into the presbytery under Abbot Thomas de Horton (1351–77), probably 1352–67, by which latter date the whole eastern limb, including the great east window, was complete. Winston (1863) suggested that the heraldry of the glass of the east window, with its references to those who had participated in the Battle of Crécy, implies a date of soon after 1346, at least in conception. Kerr (1985), on the basis of comparisons with the glass at Tewkesbury and of heraldic evidence, dates the glass to '1350–60'.

3) **The north transept** 1367/8–73.

Harvey (1978) sees the south transept as strongly influenced by William Ramsey, Edward III's chief architect from 1337, if not actually designed by him, and suggests that John Sponlee may have worked on its construction. Wilson (1980) and (1990), more persuasively, attributes the south transept to Thomas of Canterbury, the King's Master Mason and architect in charge of the upper chapel of St Stephen's in Westminster until his death in 1335. He also points to the sources of this, probably the first Perpendicular building in England, to St Stephen's Chapel and to French Rayonnant architecture *c*.1300 (Sées, Saint-Thibault-en-Auxois). Harvey (1978) 91–2 suggests that Thomas de Cantebrugge may have been the main architect at Gloucester some time up to 1364, and that he designed the east walk of the cloisters. He also speculates that his successor at Gloucester, and probably the designer of the north transept, was Robert of Lesyngham, who may have taken over in 1364. See also Welander (1991) 141–83, who accepts Wilson's conclusions, while still (for no clear reason) entertaining the possibility that William Ramsey was the architect of the south transept.

11. Hürlimann, *op. cit.* plate 105, and Cook, *op. cit.* figure 19. See also Bock (1962) 64–5.

12. Hürlimann, *op. cit.* plate 95, and Webb, *op. cit.* plate 124. See also Draper (1979) 22f; Harvey (1982) 85ff; Colchester (1987) 19, 79, 122ff. All attribute the choir to Master William Joy and date its completion to *c*.1337/40. Joy was Master Mason at Wells some time before 1329; new stalls were ordered in 1325; the old twelfth-century choir eastern wall was removed just before 1333, when the Dean and Chapter forecast (optimistically) at least a further three years work on the choir. The east window of the choir is dated *c*.1340. See also Ayers (1996) 224–302, who has uncovered much new primary evidence for the near-

completion of the choir by 1337 and 1338, and has dated the clerestorey glass *c*.1335–45.

13. Hürlimann, *op. cit.* visible on plate 104. See Harvey (1978) 90; Wilson (1980); and Welander (1991) 167.

13A. Few would now accept Frankl's designation of the early thirteenth-century decorative vaults in Poitu and Anjou as 'Plantagenet', since all of them were built after the loss of these territories by the English Plantagenet Kings to the Kings of France. See Mussat (1963), and also above, Chapter 2, Notes 78, 78A, 79A. Nor is it helpful to suggest that the west French vaults 'were con-tin-ued' in the vaulting of the Lichfield, Wesminster and Wells Chapter Houses, since it is unlikely that these chapter house vaults were in any way indebted to western France, a 'provincial' area with little or no influence on Gothic architecture beyond it. Bony (1979) 50–2, however, attempts to trace an influence from the Angevin vaults on some of the earlier West Country vaults. Wilson (1990) 202, points to the possible inspiration in the West Country of timber tunnel vaults built in Scotland and the north of England in the late twelfth and early thirteenth centuries.

14. Walter Paatz, *Die Marien Kirche in Lübeck* (Burg, 1926). The vaults at Lübeck have been discussed in some detail by Clasen (1958) 43–8, who dates the Briefkapelle to the 1330s. Ellger and Kolbe (1951) date the execution of the chapel, with the rest of the lower parts of the west façade, to 1310, the year given in the inscription in the chapel. Gąsiorowski (1977), on the basis of the mid-1970s restoration of the chapel, has reinstated the 1310 date for the beginning of the chapel. Hasse (1983) 40ff, dates the beginning of the chapel to 1310, but the construction of its vaults to 'scarcely before 1315', and the chapel's completion to not before 1320. See also Torbus (1998) 312–15, and Becker-Hounslow (1998) 227–9, and (1998a), who offers the most detailed discussion of the whole problem of Anglo-German connexions in *Backsteingotik* decorative vaulting.

15. *Die Bau und Kunstdenkmäler der Provinz Ostpreussen*, IV (Königsberg, 1894) 139ff. See also Clasen (1958) 48, 67. For Heilsberg (Lidzbark Warmiński) see Mroczko and Arszyński eds. vol. 2 (1995) 138–9. Clasen's (and most other German scholars') dating of the great refectory and its vaults to the second half of the fourteenth century has been convincingly questioned by Domańska (1968) and (1973). It now seems that none of the ingenious versions of triradial vaults employed in the refectory, chapel, and audience hall of Lidzbark Castle date before the disastrous fire of 1442 and they may even post-date 1497. Only the cloister vaults belong to the period of Bishop Heinrich III (1373–1401). For the Prussian castles generally, particularly of the Teutonic Knights, who were pioneers in decorative vaulting, see Clasen (1927) (still useful), and the wealth of post-war Polish research, especially Frycz (1980), Arszyński (1985) and (1995), Torbus (1994), Kutzner (1995) and (1996). All previous accounts have now been superseded by the monumental study of the Knights' castles by Torbus (1998).

15A. Several attempts have been made to show the influence of English vaulting, especially that of Lincoln, in the southern Baltic. See Pevsner (1959); Steinke (1974) and (1974a); Bony (1979) 64. For a critical review of this trend see Crossley (1981), and (1990), and Torbus (1998) 312–15. The whole question of English vaulting influence in north German *Backsteingotik* is treated with insight and understanding by Becker-Hounslow (1998).

16. Nikolaus Pevsner in *Architectural Review*, CXIII (1953) 91. Illustrated in G. H. Cook, *Portrait of Lincoln Cathedral* (London, 1950) plate 46, but here one cannot, of course, see the skeleton vault. For a full analysis of the Lincoln 'Easter Sepulchre' or – more accurately – 'Tomb of Christ' see Sekules (1986).

17. Pevsner, *op. cit.*, figure II. See now Morris (1997) 45, who dates it to 'no earlier than the '1320s', and possibly the 1330s, and links it to work associated with William Joy. In the same study, p. 48, Morris has also added to the list of English flying ribs mentioned by Frankl, by discovering a skeletal vault at the top of the corner staircases in the crossing tower at Wells, which Morris dates *c*.1313–*c*.1322.

18. N. Pevsner, *Nottinghamshire* (*The Buildings of England*) (Harmondsworth, 1951) 169. And Pevsner and Metcalf (1985b) 310–12. They date the screen to '*c*.1320–40' (stone for it was being carried in 1337).

19. Hermann Giesau, *Der Dom zu Magdeburg* (Burg, 1924) illustration on p. 41. See also Schubert (1975) 38, who dates it to the 1330s. Note also the now-destroyed Fountain Pavilion in the cloister of the Cistercian monastery of Zlatá Koruna in southern Bohemia, dating *c*.1360, which once contained skeletal ribs. Líbal (1978b) vol. 2, 628, attributes the building to Michael Parler, probably a brother of Peter Parler. This may help to explain Peter Parler's use of such ribs in Prague Cathedral. The connexions between the work at Magdeburg in the 1330s/40s and Prague are discussed in Crossley (1981) 91–2, including other examples of early flying ribs in Germany (Freiburg steeple; Bride's Portal at St Sebaldus, Nuremberg).

20. Hans Hahnloser, *Kritische Gesamtausgabe des Bauhüttenbuchs etc.* (Vienna, 1935) 121 and plate 41.

20A. Hahnloser (1971) 126. Bucher (1979) 125–6, saw the curious double-curved moulding next to Villard's pear-shaped moulding as a 'negative template', with the profile cut out of the wooden board.

21. See p. 123.

21A. I know of no work that deals with Gothic mouldings in Europe as a whole. The fullest studies for England (with much continental material) are the pioneering works by Morris (1978) (1979) and (1992).

21B. Note also the ogees in the niche pedestals of the south transept at Saint-Urbain, dating to the first campaign, 1262–6. See Davis (1984) especially 852–3.

22. Lasteyrie, *op. cit.* II, 33, which also gives a bibliography on the subject of this national contest. The whole problem of the French origins of the use of ogees in England, and, in turn, the possibility of English ogee tracery influencing the beginnings of French Flamboyant, is discussed by Bony (1979) 22–5, 27–8, 67–8. Kurmann and von Winterfeld (1977) 133, noted the strange (probably unintentional) double-curved tracery in the renewed clerestorey of the choir at Sens Cathedral, dated as early as 1230–40, though there are no contemporary parallels for it elsewhere. Early examples of ogee arches in France *c*.1300, in the west façade of Auxerre cathedral, in the shrine of Saint-Gertrude in Nivelles, and in French manuscript illumination, are briefly touched on by Kurmann (1978) 170–1 and (1996a).

22A. The blind tracery in the dado of the fountain pavilion in Heiligenkreuz, dated *c*.1290, has fully developed, autonomous, ogees, see Gaumannmüller (1976). Kurmann (1975) and (1986) and Michler (1984a) 42ff, drew our attention to the development of the ogee *c*.1300–30 in an important group of 'proto-flamboyant' Cistercian churches in Swabia, (Bebenhausen, Maulbronn and Salem) and to the related work in the cloister of Konstanz Cathedral (*c*.1310–20).

23. F. Bond, *Introduction*, I, 438; and Joan Evans, *English Art, 1397–1461* (Oxford, 1949) I, plate II. See now Brown, Colvin and Taylor (1963) vol. I, 479–85; Bony (1979) 20–23; Coldstream (1991a); Lindley (1991). The only evidence of ogee arches comes in the niche storey of the Hardingstone (Northampton) cross (see plate 198).

24. Evans, *op. cit.* 6, and plate 3. See now Gee (1979); Wilson, (1987) 339; and Binski (1995) 113–19. In window tracery ogees were first used in England by Michael of Canterbury in the undercroft of St Stephen's chapel in Westminster, from 1292 (see plate 201). See Wilson (1990) 112–15. If Hollar's engraving of the east end of Old St Paul's Cathedral in London can be trusted, they may also have appeared, at about the same time or even a little earlier, in the great eastern rose window. See Morris (1990) 88. The windows of the cloister of Westminster Abbey opposite the Chapter House, which have reticulated and curvilinear patterns, and which Wilson (1986) 82–3, dates to *c*.1300–10, and associates with Michael of Canterbury. See also below, Chapter 4, Note 104E.

25. Illustrated in John Britton, *The History and Antiquities of the Cathedral Church of Exeter* (London, 1826) plate 19; Hürlimann, *op. cit.* plate 77. For the precise dating of this part of the nave of Exeter Cathedral see Erskine (1981) and (1983).

26. H. E. Bishop and E. K. Prideaux, *The Building of the Cathedral Church of . . . Exeter* (Exeter, 1922). The chief carpenter of the Bishop's Throne was Robert de Galmeton. A 'Thomas de Winton' (whom Morris has convincingly identified as the Exeter chief architect, Thomas of Witney) gave advice on its design. See now Morris (1991); Sekules (1991) 172–9, especially 175–6. Thomas Witney advised on the throne in 1313; it was carved in 1316–17; figures were added 1317–20, and it was painted 1323–4. Changes in the design, particularly the incorporation of the present tower section as a change of plan, were revealed by the detailed investigation of the throne in 1982. See Tracy (1987) 412.

26A. For the octagon at Ely see Chapter 4, Note 6 above. Lindley (1986) 82–4 proves conclusively that the eight large niches (or tabernacles) around the octagon once contained standing figures, and are not purely architectural contrivances, as Frankl thought.

27. Webb, *op. cit.* 127.

28. Evans, *op. cit.* plate 79. See now Dawton (1983) and (1989), who demonstrates the debt to local Yorkshire workshops, and to London tombs (especially that of Aymer de Valence in Westminster Abbey), rather than to Ely.

28A. Morris (1996) 46–58 dates these strainer arches to sometime after *c*.1320 and attributes them to William Joy, the architect of the later strainer arches at Wells. See also Chapter 3, Note 21 above.

28B. The strainer arches at Wells are usually held to have been begun sometime after 1338, the year in which a chapter act described the fabric of the cathedral as 'enormiter confracta et deformata', implying the new crossing tower had begun to threaten the building below. This was the view of Harvey (1982) 87–9, who dated the strainer arches to the 1340s and 1350s, and of Colchester (1987) 111–14, who provides the most detailed account of the reinforcements. Harvey and Colchester (1974) 207–8, proved that repair work on the crossing was still going on in 1356, when a document mentions cartloads of stone for the repair of the tower. But the 1356 document is the first and only reference to the crossing tower, and such a long campaign (1338–56) has led Draper (1981) 24, to believe that the strainer arches may have been begun some considerable time after 1338. Both Draper and Ayers (1996) 229–31, have suggested that the 1338 document referred not to the tower but to structural disruption caused by the new work in the choir. For a structural analysis of the arches see Mark (1982) 78–91.

29. A four-centred arch is called a 'Tudor arch', although the Tudor monarchs did not ascend the throne until 1485. For a full account of the four-centred arch in early Perpendicular see Harvey (1978) 16–17, 32–3, 138–9. Harvey also discussed the origins of rectilinear tracery, though he gave insufficient importance to its origins in later French Rayonnant. As a corrective see Wilson (1990) 204–7.

30. See Hastings (1955). His conclusion, that St Stephen's was a 'proto-Perpendicular' building, was challenged by Harvey (1961), who underlined the 'Decorated' aspects of the chapel. Bony (1979) 57–60, rightly argued that St Stephen's prefigures elements of both Perpendicular and Decorated styles, and anticipates the concurrent development of the two styles in England in the early fourteenth century. The chronology of St Stephen's has been the subject of bitter controversy, between Hastings (1955) (who championed an earlier dating) and Harvey (1961) (who held to a later). Brown, Colvin and Taylor (1963) vol. 1 510–27, set out the full documentary evidence. The most authoritative analysis of the chapel, its chronology and its influence on Decorated and Perpendicular architecture can be found in Wilson (1980) 34–80; Wilson, (1987) 337–9, and Wilson (1990) 192–7. Begun in 1292, the lower chapel was complete by 1297 and the upper chapel already begun. Work on the upper chapel resumed, according to Michael of Canterbury's early plan, in c.1320, and the crenellated cornice above the main windows was reached by 1326. Against Michael's intention, a clerestory was inserted in 1331–4, and roofed with a timber vault 1346–8.

31. Frederick Mackenzie, *The Architectural Antiquities of the Collegiate Chapel of St Stephen in Westminster, The late House of Commons* (London, 1844). The lower chapel, much restored, still survives. For illustrations see Bony (1979) plates 277–9.

32. M. Hastings, 'The Court Style', *Architectural Review*, CV (1949); *The Parliament House etc.* (London, 1950) 54ff; and *St Stephen's Chapel* (Cambridge, 1955) 28ff. The idea of a 'Court style' in English architecture in the Decorated and early Perpendicular period has been refined and amplified by Bony (1979) 9–18, 56–62. The whole notion is now, however, being challenged. See Colvin (1983); Coldstream (1994) 186–92; and Binski (1995) passim.

33. That is, a generation before the dates given by Sharpe (*Seven Periods of English Architecture*, 3rd ed., London, 1888, 8). He claimed that Rectilinear followed Curvilinear, giving the dates of the latter as 1315–60, and of the former as 1360–1550. The remodelling of the south transept at Gloucester, begun in 1331, and the building of Old St Paul's Chapter House, begun in 1332, are now recognized as the first fully-fledged examples of the Perpendicular style though their rectilinearity, was prefigured at St Stephens chapel. See Harvey (1978) 75–85; and Wilson (1980) 113–17, 127–39, 164–70.

33A. See Bond (1905) 480, and Pevsner and Sherwood (1974) 160. For the origins of reticulated tracery in the court circles of Michael of Canterbury see below, Chapter 4, Note 104E.

33B. For the Romanesque cathedral see Wilson (1985).

34. Kerr (1985) dates the east window to 1350–60; see above, Chapter 4, Note 10.

35. Illustrated in Hürlimann, *op. cit*, plates 101–5, and also in G. H. Cook, *The Story of Gloucester Cathedral* (London, 1952).

35A. The piers derive from those in the choir aisles of Cologne cathedral, see Kunst (1969a) and Chapter 3, Note 106, above.

36. Haina, Wetter, Nienburg, etc., are discussed in Wilhelm Kästner, *op. cit*. (Note 86 to Chapter 3). On Haina cf. also Oskar Schürer, 'Die Klosterkirche in Haina', *Marburger Jahrbuch*, II (1925) 91. The influence of the church of St Elizabeth in Marburg is fully considered by Kunst (1983) and (1983a); Schenkluhn (1983); Auer (1983); Jacobi and Scherf (1983) – all in *Elisabethkirche* (1983); also Crossley (1997), and Wedemeyer (1997) 294–6.

36A. Most authorities would now consider that Frankl's 'drawing of boundaries' here is precisely one of conventionality. Churches which followed the model of the nave of St Elizabeth at Marburg show clear signs, especially in their tracery, of forms that belong not to High Gothic but to Rayonnant architecture, a style which Frankl's conventions did not recognize.

37. See Creutzfeld (1953) and Kissling (1975), Kissling (1978) in vol. 1, *Die Parler*, Wortmann (1978) in vol. 1, *Die Parler*, and Lange (1988). The nave may not have been the first hall church to be planned in Swabia. The hall nave of the Frauenkirche in Esslingen was begun only in c.1350, but the intention to build a hall could be dated to 1321, the year the choir was begun. See Koepf (1980) 1–46. The collegiate church at Herrenberg, the nave dated c.1300–28, was begun as a basilica but perhaps changed to a hall in that period, though it may have been altered only as late as 1470, see Koepf (1952). Wortmann (1978) in vol. 1, *Die Parler* 315, points to the hall nave of St Martin at Westhofen in Alsace, dated c.1300, as a precedent for the Gmünd nave.

38. For a biography of Heinrich see Schock-Werner (1978) in vol. 3, *Die Parler* 7–12, who points out that the Prague inscription is ambiguous as to whether he was a foreman in Cologne or simply a worker or resident there. Since his son, Peter, was born in Gmünd, in 1333, Heinrich must have worked on the nave of the Gmünd church.

39. Creutzfeld (1953) tried to find influences from Cologne's Plan F on the west façade of Gmünd, but Wortmann (1980) in vol. 4, *Die Parler* convincingly demonstrated the exclusive dependence on Upper Rhenish and Cistercian precedents.

40. See below, pp. 200ff; and Schmitt (1951) 6; Kissling (1975) and Kissling (1978) in vol. 1, *Die Parler* 320. The problems of attributing the nave and choir to Heinrich Parler or his son Peter, still remain. Schmitt (1951) 10, attributed the choir and not the nave to Heinrich Parler on the grounds that he is referred to in the inscription over Peter Parler's bust in Prague as 'architect of Gmünd' (*magistri de gemunden*) when Peter left Gmünd to come to Prague in 1356, that is, when the choir, founded in 1351, was in building. But since 'a different world of architectural experience' separates the choir from the earlier nave, Schmitt attributed the nave to a different, unknown, architect. Clasen (1952) 54ff, attributed the choir to Peter Parler on the basis of stylistic similarities with Peter's work in Prague Cathedral, particularly the prefiguration of the Prague zig-zagging triforium and clerestorey in the large triangular projections of the ambulatory stringcourse. Wortmann (1978) in vol. 1, *Die Parler* 317, attributed the choir to Heinrich, but opted for a large advisory contribution from the young Peter, who may have spent some time in Paris. Certainly the choir of Gmünd is sometimes attributed to Peter Parler on the grounds that he must have had some exceptional work to his credit before he was called to Prague in 1356. However, Bräutigam (1961) and (1965) and others have complicated the problem by showing that Peter Parler probably contributed to the architecture, or the sculpture, or both, of the Frauenkirche in Nuremberg, in building a few years before 1356. As the foundation of the Emperor Charles IV, the patron of the new cathedral in Prague, the Nuremberg church was the most likely location for the young architect to catch the Emperor's attention. See below, Chapter 4, Note 64A. The spatial implications of the new hall choir at Gmünd, and their relations to later medieval concepts of 'space' and 'subjectivity', are fully discussed by Lange (1988). Wundram (1988) pointed to the spatial function of the horizontal cornice dividing the chapels and the windows in the ambulatory, and suggested (without evidence) that Peter Parler was born not in 1333 but in 1323, making him an architect in his late 20s when he worked on (designed?) the Gmünd choir. The bust inscription, however, clearly gives his age as twenty-three years in 1356. Many of the problems surrounding the choir of the Holy Cross church and its ancestry are untangled by Nussbaum (2000) 112–21. Nussbaum's sensible synthesis of German Gothic can be read with profit for most of the German buildings cited by Frankl, but for that reason I have not cited him in every individual case.

41. See Schwartz (1979) 27–56; and Schenkluhn (1983) 86–8.

42. The inscription in the choir is photographically reproduced in *St Maria zur Wiese, Denkschrift etc.* (Soest, 1950) 32. Stopp's philological analysis of the inscription suggests that the date can only be read as 1331. The only error in this article is the translation of the word 'tenet' by 'lasts'. A day cannot last longer than twenty-four hours. 'Tenet' here means something like 'contains'.
But see Lohr (1975), who dates the middle choir to sometime before 1340 and its sculpture to 1350–60, and agrees with the latest interpretation of the choir foundation inscription, placing it not in 1331 (the traditional starting date), but in 1313. See Eickermann (1972). For the church in general see Schwartz (1979) 85ff; and Hoppe-Sailer (1983).

43. The date of 1376 refers, not to the completion of the whole east end as many authorities have supposed, but only to the central and south choir. See Lohr (1975) 94.

44. R. K. Donin, *Die Bettelordenskirchen in Österreich* (Vienna, 1935) 225, plate 255. The piers and the capitals date from the Baroque. Although the church was consecrated in 1349 the nave was not complete until after 1366. See Perger and Brauneis (1977) 157; and also Brucher (1990) 79, where it is wrongly stated that the church was begun in 1320.

45. Sigrid Thurm, *Norddeutscher Backsteinbau etc.* (Berlin, 1935) 15 and plate 6. See Zaske (1958) 86–7, who dates the choir to 1325–c.1340, the nave to c.1350–60 and the eastern gable, for which he rejects any direct Strasbourg influence, to 'after c.1360'. Schwatz (1957) has more correctly dated the nave c.1325–39 and the choir and gable following it. The demolition of the previous church in 1325 implies construction had already begun in the new building. The stylistic analogies between the gable and German freestone architecture – including Parlerian Late Gothic – are discussed at length by Liess (1988) and (1990).

46. Werner Burmeister and Albert Renger-Patzsch, *Norddeutsche Backsteindome* (Berlin, 1938) plates 16 and 77 (also plates 11, 17, etc.). Cf. also the bridging of the re-entrants between the chapels of the cathedral at Schwerin, illustrated *ibid.*, plate 57. The corbels in the main arcades may not be an English feature, but a local Cistercian practice, see the nave of Chorin in

Brandenburg. The church of St Mary at Wismar was destroyed in the Second World War and only the west tower survives. The previous church was a hall, possibly like the hall church of St Nicholas at Stralsund (c.1260), which was also replaced by a large basilica. See Zaske (1969) 375. For the position of St Mary in Wismar brick gothic, especially in the 15th century, see Ludwig (1998) pp 37, 117, 130, 140.

47. Hans Tintelnot, *Die mittelalterliche Baukunst Schlesiens*, I (Kitzingen, 1951) 120. Before its destruction in the Second World War, this building, through the harmony between its Baroque decoration and its Late Gothic spatial form, offered a magnificent impression of concordance.

For a fuller discussion of 'jumping vaults' see Hanulanka (1971) 45–64. The chronology of St Mary-on-the-Sands has been obscure. Although there is general agreement that the new building was begun soon after 1334, the direction of the work, east–west or west–east, has remained unclear. Older authorities such as Burgemeister and Grundmann (1930) and Tintelnot (1951) argued for the precedence of the nave over the choir, later Polish scholars for an east-west priority. Mroczko and Arszyński, eds., (1995) vol. 2 271–2, summarize the arguments. They quote the unpublished dissertation of Stulin (1982) who established the following sequence:

1334 Abbot Konrad (1329–63) demolishes the old church and begins the new one with the lower parts of the façade and the south nave aisle.

Under Abbot Jan of Krosna (1364–72) and Abbot Jan of Prague (1375–86) the north aisle of the nave was built and some vaults erected. 1371, 1372 burials in front of the high altar. Abbot Henryk Gallici (1386–95) vaulted the aisles and decorated the church. The work of decoration and furnishing was still going on under Abbot Mikołaj Herdon (1395–1412). Stulin identifies the sources of St Mary in the nave of St Cross in Wrocław (the disposition of the interior space), St Elizabeth in Wrocław (the pillar forms), and south-west Germany (tracery, portals etc), though forms from this quarter are traceable in Silesia earlier, in the ducal chapel at Legnica.

48. Tintelnot, *op. cit.* 90 and plate 32.

The origins of this typically Silesian basilican form are to be found, not in mendicant but in Cistercian architecture, principally from Bohemia (Zlatá Koruna), see Kutzner (1975) (1995a) and (1998). The chronology of St Elizabeth can be found in Mroczko and Arszyński, eds., (1995) vol. 2 266.

After 1309–c.1318: outer walls of western bay of nave, planned as a basilica or pseudo-basilica, with similarities to Sts Peter and Paul at Legnica, but uncompleted.

1319(?) – c.1340: nave, with aisle vaults.

c.1340–1387: choir, vaulting of central aisle of nave, chapel additions, beginning of the tower.

To 1482: completion of the tower.

See also Kutzner (1996a).

49. The choir was consecrated in 1383. Cf. Dehio-Ginhart, *Handbuch der Kunstdenkmäler der Ostmark*, I (Vienna, 1941) 518.

There are now convincing reasons for doubting Zwettl's status as the first hall choir of this polygonal kind, with ambulatory and radiating chapels. The foundation of the chapel ring in 1343 and the consecration in 1348 concerned only the choir chapels, and the plague stopped the work in that year. Only in 1360 did work resume under Master Jans (probably from St Stephen's in Vienna), at a level just above the chapels. It is now accepted that the original plan of 1343 envisaged a basilican choir (similar to Pontigny or, even closer, to Sedlec in Bohemia) and that only later, under the influence of the new choir at Schwäbisch Gmünd (begun in 1351) was the design changed to a hall. See Buberl (1940) 39–42; Wagner-Rieger (1967) 341, 379–80. Brucher (1990) 102–6, sees the break between the 1348 and the post-1360 campaign in the abrupt change at the base of the ambulatory windows between single thick responds flanking the chapel openings and delicate vault shafts framing the windows. This, he deduces, is evidence that the first plan envisaged a basilican section. The arguments are rehearsed, without any clear conclusion, by Wundram (1988). For a full discussion of origins of the hall choir with polygonal ambulatory see Kunst (1969), who considers the Zwettl choir to precede, and be the model for, the choir at Schwäbisch Gmünd, although he traces the first example of the type back to the hall choir of the cathedral of Verden an der Aller, c.1300. See above Chapter 3, Note 133D.

A hall choir with an ambulatory running north-south behind the high altar must have been anticipated by the (destroyed) flat-ended choir of Zbraslav in northern Bohemia, founded in 1297 by King Wenceslas II on the plan of Morimond and Citeaux III, but having a hall section based on the choir of Heiligenkreuz, and tall cellular chapels the same height as the side aisles. See Crossley (1995) and Benešovská (1996) and Kuthan (1994) pp 475–482.

49A. See above, pp. 196 and Note 40. The smooth chapel walls of the Gmünd choir and their alternation of blind tracery and windows owe an obvious debt to the new chapels constructed in the chevet of Notre-Dame in Paris 1296–c.1315. This was recognized in the 1930s by Kletzl (1938/9). For the remodelling of the Parisian choir see Davis (1998).

50. On both these buildings, cf. Donin, *op. cit.* 187ff. Donin dated

Pöllauberg to 1339, and made it the source for Enns. This is too early, because Pöllauberg belongs stylistically to the third quarter of the fourteenth century, and was obviously dependent on the earlier chapel at Enns, which was up by the consecration of its altar to St John in 1343. There are references to a chaplain in Pöllauberg in 1374 and to donations for windows in 1384. See Wagner-Rieger (1967) 342–3, 383, 396. Brucher (1990) 109–16, dates the conception of the Wallsee chapel to the 1330s. He considers (unconvincingly) that Pöllauberg could have been begun in 1339 (with the donation of Katharina von Stubenberg to the church in that year), and, with its elaborate sculptural decoration, could have taken over forty years to build and complete.

51. Donin, *op. cit.* 195. The church of St Lambrecht has not yet been precisely dated; it was probably begun before 1350. The nave was begun in 1327, and the choir started c.1386; but we are not certain when the whole church was complete. The nave was consecrated in 1421, though it may have been vaulted by 1393. See Wagner-Rieger (1967) 378; and Brucher (1990) 116–20.

52. Donin, *op. cit.* 337ff. Hall choirs without ambulatories, that is choirs whose central aisle continues right up to the eastern wall, form a special category in German Late Gothic, see Philipp (1989B). They include the Cistercian churches of Heiligenkreuz and Neuberg, Enns and Pöllauberg, St Lambrecht, Mühlbach in Hungary and Nördlingen in Swabia.

53. The Frauenkirche at Munich may be dependent on the choir at Augsburg; see below, p. 229. Augsburg is a curiosity because it has a conventional 'cathedral gothic' chevet plan, with double choir aisles in the straight bays and radiating chapels; but it has no real ambulatory, since the inner apse of the choir marches right across the ambulatory space, cutting it in two, and supporting the arches of its apse arcade on the responds of the eastern radiating chapel. The high altar therefore stands over what should have been the centre of the ambulatory. For a plan see Nussbaum (2000) 120, figs. 126, 127. This odd planning, in which the radiating chapels seem to be compressed back into the main body of the choir, was almost certainly due to the restrictions of the site, since the new choir projected across a main public highway, the Reichstrasse; and this was a source of increasing tension between the town and the cathedral authorities in the second half of the fourteenth century, a tension which contributed to the slow progress on the choir. The awkwardness in the junction of the polygonal and the straight parts of the choir led Anstett (1965) and Wortmann (1967) to suggest the existence of plans for 'original' eastern terminations, different from the present chevet, the first (soon after 1343) flat-ended (like the Cistercian choirs of Heiligenkreuz and Salem), the second (according to Wortmann) with a chevet (like that of the Cistercian church at Sedlec) but to be built further to the east, so as to ensure a proper ambulatory. Böker (1983) Hufnagel (1987) and Chevalley (1995) rightly question the existence of any 'early' choir scheme. The real changes in the design are not in plan, between the straight and turning bays, but in elevation. Chevalley's detailed analysis (1995), incorparates Hufnagel's and Böker's conclusions, and adds new chronological information from the restorations of the early 1990s. They distinguish a number of phases in the choir construction, to which the earlier remodelling of the nave and the building of the north choir portal are indirectly related.

Nave remodelling, c.1335–43, under Bishop Konrad von Randegg (1337–48). Vaults of western transept, vaults of central aisle of nave, nave double-aisles, north choir portal. All this renovation work, possibly by Heinrich I Parler, was not undertaken as a prelude to the building of the new eastern choir, since the iconographic sequences of the keystones of the nave vault 'turn their back' on the choir by running from east to west.

Choir phase one: begun ?1348, or 1356–?1365, under Bishop Markwart von Randegg (1348–65), nephew of Bishop Konrad and friend and advisor of the Emperor Charles IV. South choir portal (in its first form) south choir aisle. 1356 foundations laid for the radiating chapel ring to a design clearly derived from Cologne cathedral. Chapels constructed up to about window sill height, but dividing wall between southernmost chapel and south choir aisle, and the chapel/ambulatory respond that belongs to it, built up to vault springer height. This respond indicates that the free-standing choir aisle pillars to its west were to be capital-less columns into which the arch mouldings would 'die', in the manner of the ambulatory columns of the Cistercian church at Kaisheim (see Hufnagel [1987]) or the nave pillars of mendicant churches in the upper Rhine, such as the Franciscan church at Freiburg (see plate 174). At this stage, the choir was planned as a basilica, with equal-height double choir aisles and a clerestorey supported by flyers. Work more advanced on south side than on north.

Choir phase two: begun ?1365, under Bishop Walter von Hochschlitz (1365–9). Choir aisle supports, on south and north sides, changed from intended columns to the present bundle-piers. Construction of choir main piers and arches. Heightening of choir aisles – on north side both aisles, on south side only inner aisle, since earlier, outer aisle was already too far advanced to be raised. Chevalley (1995) 110–17, thinks this phase can be connected to a change from a basilican to a hall choir format, similar in plan to the choir of Schwäbisch Gmünd. But this presupposes that a bishop would want to give up a 'cathedral' basilica in favour of a hall choir hitherto associated with 'middle class' patronage, and it involves problems of reconstructing an ambulatory vault like Gmünd's in a Cologne-type chevet, especially when the evidence for the projected ambulatory vaulting at Augsburg suggests a system differing from Gmünd's. Phase two is connected with strong Parler influences.

Choir phase three: begun ?1376 (the year of Eberhard Randegg's installation as provost, and certainly after the interregnum of 1369–71)–1413. Vaulting of straight bays of choir aisles c.1377 (date of 1377 found on dividing arch in western bay of north choir aisle). 1394 choir roof erected. In 1396/7 erection of high walls of choir. High vaults complete by 1410 and all structural work finished by 1413.

54. Paul Deschamps, *La Chaise-Dieu* (Paris, 1946), which has excellent illustrations. See now Erlande-Brandenburg (1975), who has established the very rapid progress in the construction, thanks largely to the pope's generosity. Construction on the choir started in 1344 and the apse and first straight bay to its west were finished by 1346, by which date work was going on on the rest of the monks's choir up to the jubé, (fifth bay from east) and on the nave. Previous research had assumed that at Clement's death in 1352 the three western bays of the nave were unfinished, and that Gregory IX, from 1370, completed them and the western towers. But it now seems that the whole of the nave was vaulted under Clement VI, or at least by 1355. In 1352 the relics of St Robert were translated to the high altar in the apse. Only the façade and towers clearly postdate the founder's death. In 1358 statues were placed in the west portals. Clement's tomb, placed in the centre of the choir (second straight bay from the east), was executed between 1346 and 1351, but its conception is undoubtedly earlier. For the original appearance of the now mutilated tomb, placed in the centre of the choir, see Gardner (1992) 143–6. A detailed analysis of the coherent iconographical 'programme' of Clement VI in the Chambre du Cerf at Avignon and at La Chaise-Dieu (particularly the sculpture of the tomb and the architectural sculpture) can be found in de Merindol (1993), who sees the themes as personal and institutional, royal (French) and papal.

54A. Frankl's definition of the church as a hall is misleading. It is really a vaulted *nef unique* with cellular chapels typical of southern and central France – see Paul (1988) and Freigang (1992) 211–19 – in which the walls dividing its side chapels are pierced with large arches in such a way as to create side-aisle-like spaces, while the inner sections of the dividing walls are transformed into large pier-like responds, which resemble the free-standing piers of a hall church.

54B. Clement's tomb, mutilated in the sixteenth century, was executed between 1349 and 1351. For a reconstruction of its original appearance see Gardner (1992) 143–6, who underlines the novelty of the abbey church as a building constructed directly around the tomb, placed in the centre of the choir.

54C. In fact, the use of an interior clerestorey passage, the balustrade above the arcade zone and the hanging mouchettes at the top of the (blind) tracery panels flanking each clerestorey window recall the elevation of Prague Cathedral. The origins of the Antwerp elevation still need clarification. The tracery panels decorating the arcade spandrels suggest the influence of the choir of St Rombout at Mechelen (begun possibly after 1342), the archetype of the fourteenth-century Brabantine basilica; but the lack of triforium, and the interior clerestorey passage, point to a Norman derivation (Bayeux Cathedral nave?, Coutances choir?).

55. Richard Graul, *Alt Flandern* (Munich, 1918). The choir at Antwerp was vaulted in c.1391 but was not fully in use until 1415. Jakob van Tienen (1396?–1403?) worked on the later stages of the choir. Under Peter Appelmans (1419–34) the nave was begun in 1419 and the foundations of the northern of the two west towers in c.1420–22. The foundations of the south tower followed in 1430, and the construction of the double aisles of the nave began a year later. The nave as a whole is attributed to the designs of Everaert Spoorwater (1439–74), under whose direction most of the work was completed. By 1470 the nave arcades and the vaults of the double aisles either side were finished. In the middle of the fifteenth century it was decided to widen the nave with an outer, seventh, set of aisles (for altars), the southern consecrated in 1469, its northern counterpart begun later. Matthijs Keldermanns directed work on the completion and vaulting of the transept 1481–95. The octagonal lantern over the crossing was inserted in 1497–8. The central aisle of the nave was roofed in 1500, but it remained unvaulted until 1612, though the bay between the towers was vaulted in 1508. See Lemaire (1946), van Brabant (1972), Vroom (1983) (for a full discussion of the rich documentation surrounding the fifteenth-century funding), and Boyazis (1985).

55A. The literature on Prague cathedral has been copious since 1962. The handiest guides are still the relevant articles in the four-volume catalogue, *Die Parler* (1978), see particularly: Homolka vol. 2 (1978) 607–18; Líbal, vol. 2 (1978A, B) 619–23; Libal (1980); and various articles on vaulting, tracery, and the history of the Parler family in vol. 3 by Fehr, Czymmek, Müller and Schock-Werner. For a more modern summary of the German and 'western' scholarship see the monograph on the cathedral choir by Baumüller (1994) Baumüller's concentration on 'structural' and 'spatial' analy-

sis to the detriment of historical or symbolic associations, and her ignorance of the Czech literature, provoked a damning review from Benešovská (1994a). The best recent analysis, with many new insights, comes from Benešovská (1994) and (1999), the latter in English. A useful general history of the art and architecture of Charles IV (useful partly because it is in English) can be found in Stejskal (1978), and also in Dvořaková, Krása, Merhautová, Stejskal eds., (1964). Much of the latest Czech research on the meaning and history of the cathedral, particularly on its Wenceslas Chapel, is incorporated by Ormrod (1997). The Bohemian iconography of Prague Cathedral, and its relations to the coronation liturgy, are underlined by Crossley (1999), who also (2000) discusses the symbolic themes in Charles IV's architecture and monumental decoration as a whole, particularly its scenic character. Apart from Klara Benešovská's contributions to the literature, important recent evaluations of Prague Cathedral have come from Homolka's (1999) perceptive observations on the general character of Peter Parler's creativity, and Freigang's (1998) detailed analysis of the southern French sources of Matthias of Arras's work, and the inspiration of Cologne Cathedral in Prague under Peter Parler.

56. The diagonal position of buttresses at the corners of façades, as at Gmünd and La Chaise-Dieu, is a direct continuation outwards of the direction of the ribs. Such buttresses follow the direction of the thrust, and can therefore be rationally explained: but why had buttresses not been built like this at Chartres, Laon, Paris, and Amiens?

56A. As the inscription above Matthias of Arras's portrait bust in the triforium of Prague cathedral stated, Charles IV 'drew him from Avignon'. (. . . *in Avinione abinde adduxit . . .*) See Benešovská (1994) 28ff and note 17. The sources of his style are to be found principally in late Rayonnant architecture in Burgundy, Lower Languedoc (especially Toulouse and Narbonne Cathedrals) and perhaps Avignon (though no traces of his style or work have been found in Clement VI's extensions to the papal palace at Avignon, where Charles IV encountered the architect). See Héliot and Mencl (1974), Héliot (1975), and Baumüller (1994) 57–63. Mencl (1971) attempted, not always convincingly, to plot a wider network of connexions between southern French Rayonnant, Swabia and Bohemia, in the second quarter of the fourteenth century. Freigang (1998) finds precedents for Matthias's moulding profiles in Notre-Dame at Villeneuve-lès-Avignon, and the cathedral of Montpellier, and he stresses the very close links with the recently completed choir of Narbonne, the most modern archiepiscopal cathedral in France in 1344. Matthias's work, so long overshadowed by Peter Parler's, has been enjoying something of a re-evaluation among Czech scholars, see particularly Benešovská (1994) 34–8, and notes 53–5 and (1999a), who attributes to him not only the design of the star vault of the eastern bay of the sacristy of Prague Cathedral (hitherto usually attributed to Peter Parler), but also of its pendant boss and skeletal ribs, which, she argues, were partly or wholly begun under Matthias, or under his lodge after his death in 1352, and dismantled and re-assembled by Peter Parler from 1356. Her arguments for this complex building history in the sacristy are set out more fully in Benešovská (1996a). Under her maiden name of Fischerová, Benešovská plotted the profound impact of Matthias and his 'workshop' in Bohemia in the fourteenth century, and set it in the context of French imports under Archbishop Jan IV Dražice of Prague, see Fischerová (1974).

56B. Kotrba (1971) (with German resumé) convincingly demonstrated that Peter Parler arrived in Prague in 1356, not in 1353 as the older literature had maintained. Therefore he was born in 1333 and not in 1330, since the inscription over the architect's portrait bust in the triforium of Prague Cathedral stated that he was twenty-three years old when he first came to Prague. Wundram's (1988) suggestion that the inscription should read '33' and not '23' years old, simply on the grounds that it is the copyist's error of a long-illegible text, is special pleading, and does not take into account the detailed evidence advanced by Kotrba in 1971. See also Benešovská (1999) 152–3.

56C. Matthias (or his workshop immediately after his death) had almost certainly intended this chapel-like space to be a sacristy, had begun its eastern, northern and southern walls, and had inserted the capitals and rib springers for its eastern (star) vault. See Benešovská (1994) 37–8; (1996a) and (1999a) where she also assesses Parler's other debts to Matthias, in Prague and Kolín.

56D. The 'innovations' of the sacristy vault which Frankl attributes to Peter Parler may be the work of Matthias, see above, Chapter 4, Notes 56A, 56C. The flying rib also has its precedents in southern Germany, see Crossley (1981) 91–2. A pendant boss hangs above the portal (at the end of the principal entrance passage) into the main courtyard of Clement VI's new palace at Avignon, dated to after 1342. see Gagnière (1977) 69–70.

56E. Peter Parler must have begun the space now occupied by the chapel of St Sigismund some time before 1362, since its original altar, dedicated to St Urban and St Cecilia, is mentioned in that year. The altar was removed soon after 1365 to its present position one bay to the west, when Charles IV replaced it with the altar of St Sigismund, transforming the chapel into the centre of the cult of the Burgundian king-saint, whose relics he had acquired after his coronation as King of the Arelat in 1365. See Benešovská (1994) 40.

57. The corners of the chapter house which Villard de Honnecourt drew in

his lodge-book about 1235 should be visualized like this, and not in the way in which Viollet-le-Duc, in the *Dictionaire*, VIII (1875) 95 and others after him (K. H. Clasen, *Deutschlands Auteil am Gewölbebau der Spätgotik*, Berlin, 1937, 163) reconstructed them.

57A. The chronology and iconography of the Wenceslas Chapel have been carefully analyzed by Kotrba (1960) (with German resumé) and especially Ormrod (1997). The south porch was finished in 1368, the year the *sacristia nova*, which runs above it, was consecrated. Líbal, in a series of articles in *Die Parler* (1978) – see Líbal (1978A) (1978B) (1980) argued that Matthias of Arras actually designed the Wenceslas Chapel (including its profiles and architectural details) and that before his death he had laid out its overall plan and its exterior walls. This has been convincingly disproved by Vítovský (1990), and by Ormrod (1997) 132–68, who both attribute the style and conception of the chapel to Charles IV and Peter Parler. Benešovská (1999a) however, points to the continuing influence of Matthias's style in Parler's design for the chapel, and to the certainty that Matthias had drawn up plans for the chapel *c.*1348 which Parler must have consulted.

57B. Matthias would, almost certainly, have built a blind triforium linked to the clerestorey in the manner of Narbonne; but Paul (1991) 36, interestingly suggests that the triforium at Prague, which projects both on the inside and the outside, might have been influenced by the idiosyncratic exterior projections of the triforium at Limoges and Narbonne. This rare solution avoids the traditional method of piercing the high walls at the structurally vulnerable bay divisions with a triforium passage. Instead it keeps the high walls, at the bay divisions, solid and unpierced, and projects the passage behind and around them so that it sits over the aisle and ambulatory vaults.

57C. For a geometrical analysis of all the decorative vaults used by Peter Parler in the cathedral see Kotrba (1959), and Fehr, in vol. 3, *Die Parler* (1978) 45–8. For the techniques of their construction see Muk (1977), and Müller, in vol. 3, *Die Parler* (1978) 48–9.

57D. The case for English influence on Peter Parler in Prague was first made by Bock (1961), followed (for the sculpture) by Haussherr (1971), by Bony (1979) 66–7, and, most recently, by Wilson (1990) 227–32, who gives the best account in English of the cathedral and its genesis. Some of these views are qualified by Crossley (1981) especially 85–104, and the whole issue of English contacts is rehearsed by Baumüller (1994) 95–106. The connexion is not discussed in Philipp (1985).

57E. Plinths with sloping upper ends, interpenetrating either with smaller separate plinths or with the shafts themselves, are to be found earlier than Peter Parler's work in Prague: in the responds of the dividing walls of the radiating chapels at Sées Cathedral, in the ground floor of the south-west tower of Cologne Cathedral, in the aisle responds and free-standing piers of the straight bays on the south side of the choir of Utrecht Cathedral, in the Great Audience Hall of the Papal Palace at Avignon, in bases of the choir pillars in Kraków cathedral, and in Matthias of Arras's piers in Prague. They also make a rare appearance, *c.*1320, in the hall choir of St Augustine's at Bristol. Sloping plinths, often with shafts or mouldings 'dying' into them, also appear frequently in portals from *c.*1300 onwards, from the Upper Rhine to northern Bohemia – see, for example, the west portal of St Catharine's Chapel in Strasbourg (*c.*1340–5). Recht (1970) and (1974) 54–69, 227–32, has argued for the close dependence of the interior elevation of the St Wenceslas Chapel on the Strasbourg Chapel, whose original vaults, using triradials and pendant bosses, may also have influenced Parler's vaults in the sacristy. For a critical look at the Strasbourg connexion in Prague see Ormrod (1997) 168–71. Parler's plinths and respond mouldings in Prague are usually closer to Cologne Cathedral choir, or its offshoots (e.g. Xanten). See Freigang (1998) and Crossley (1981).

58. On composition by contrasts, cf. Karl M. Swoboda, *Peter Parler*, 4th ed. (Vienna, 1943). Bureš (1983), has speculated that Peter Parler's original design for the south transept front was to have had no tower, and to have been more symmetrical, with another openwork staircase to the west repeating that on the east buttress of the façade. The present tower he sees as a re-use of one of the towers intended for an aborted two-tower western façade, which was planned to terminate a five-aisled nave, hence the tower's size. His over-complex argument does not carry conviction. For the south tower see Benešovská (1999) 125–33; and see below, Chapter 4, Note 74.

59. The tracery in the windows of the transepts dates from the nineteenth century, as does the bottom window in the tower. These concave gables are, however, original. They are shown in the drawing of the lower storey of the tower, dated to the last decade of the fourteenth century, now in the Vienna Akademie der Künste, Inv. Nr 16817. See Koepf (1970), catalogue nr 2. For these arches, and other details of the south tower and its influence see Bureš (1975) and Benešovská (1999) 125–33.

60. Frankl (1960) 187. Kotrba (1960) considered the main source for the shape and decoration of the chapel to be St John's vision of the Heavenly Jerusalem in Revelations 21:10–21. This is confirmed by Ormrod (1997) 208–36. For the biblical, literary and material sources of the chunky semi-pre-

cious stone decoration of the chapel, and its counterparts in the Holy Cross and St Catharine Chapels in Charles IV's contemporary Karlštejn (Karlstein) Castle see Legner in vol. 3, *Die Parler*, (1978) 169–82; Meier, in vol. 3, *Die Parler* (1978) 185–7; Möseneder (1981), and Fajt and Royt (1998).

60A. The question of Peter Parler's 'personal style', and its adaptability to the demands of the commission, especially to the idiosyncratic taste of the Emperor Charles IV, is interestingly discussed by Suckale in vol. 4, *Die Parler* (1980) 175–83. See also the question of innovation versus traditionalism in Peter's work, discussed perceptively by Homolka (1999), who sees the cathedral as the product of a creative dialogue between Charles IV and Peter Parler, and relates Peter's empirical and heterogeneous approach to design to contemporary philosophical nominalism.

61. Swoboda, *op. cit.* 19ff., and, on the castle chapel, p. 18. The choir at Kolín was begun in 1360 and consecrated in 1378, although building was still going on in 1400. See Bureš (1989), who identifies the presence there of Master Michael of Cologne and his brother Hans of Cologne from at least 1384. Kutná Hora was started in 1388 and work continued until 1401, having reached only up to the level of the choir arcades and ambulatory and chapels. From 1404 to 1420 the nave was extended into a five-aisled basilica. It is now suggested that the choir may have been conceived and begun, not by Peter Parler, but by his eldest son, Johann, who was married at Kutná Hora in 1383; or it may have been Johann who directed the campaign after 1404. See Líbal, in vol. 2, *Die Parler* (1978) 639; and Schock-Werner, in vol. 2, *Die Parler* (1978) 8.

62. Hans Reinhardt, *Das Münster zu Basel* (Burg, 1928), and, by the same author, *Das Basler Münster* (Basel, *c.*1939). Gantner, *op. cit.* (Note 73 to Chapter 3) 141. The relationship between Peter Parler and Johannes of Gmünd is not altogether clear, though it seems likely that they were about the same age and the latter may have been Peter's older brother. See Schock-Werner, in vol. 3, *Die Parler* (1978) 9. For Johannes's work at Freiburg see Adam (1968) 22–4, 96–100. When work on the choir stopped in *c.*1370/80 the chapels were built only up to half their full height. For Johannes's contribution to Basel see Reinhardt (1941) and (1961).

63. Thurm, *op. cit.* plan, p. 20, exterior, plate 9. For variations on the three-apse east end of the Gransee type in a group of fourteenth-century north German brick hall choirs see Jaaks (1971). The diagonality and 'irregularity' of choirs with even-sided polygonal planning are discussed by Nussbaum (2000) 117–18, 120, 134. He refers to von Ledebur's analysis of this type of planning (especially in connexion with the use of single, axially placed pillars in the early fifteenth-century hall choirs of Hans von Burghausen), but this thesis has not been available to me.

64. Dehio (1901) II, 351.

64A. The Frauenkirche in Nuremberg, founded by Charles IV as a parish church-chapel, was built by a Parler workshop. Bräutigam (1961) and (1965), Kotrba (1971) and Schmidt (1970), all attribute the church or parts of the church and its sculpture to Peter Parler himself. For the church in its urban and political context see Maué (1986) 34–5. Leyh's monograph on the church (1992) has not been available to me. The connexions between this church and St Stephen in Prague are: both are built at about the same time (St Stephen at least before 1351); both are connected to Charles IV (he obtained relics of St Stephen for the Prague church) and both have naves laid out on a short, square plan. St Stephen, however, is a basilica. For further literature on St Stephen see Líbal, in *Die Parler* (1978) vol. 2, 629–30; and Líbal (1983) 229–32.

65. K. Faymonville, *Das Münster zu Aachen* (Düsseldorf, 1916). On the restorations, see pp. 63 and 90. The tracery originally had six lights to each opening; the division into five lights dates from 1860. The choir, perhaps begun a little before the official foundation in 1355, is traditionally attributed to a *magister Johannes de Aquis*, the second architect of the Aachen town hall, who appeared in a document of 1358/9 as an advisor on the buildings of the church of St Mary at Tienen, in Brabant. However, as Winands (1989) 85, has pointed out, neither Johannes's work at Aachen, nor the church at Tienen show conclusive similarities to the Aachen choir. The chapter was responsible for the new project and there is no evidence that Charles IV contributed financially to the work, though he must have taken a keen interest in its progress. The imperial connotations of the new choir, as the site of German coronations and the shrine of Charlemagne, are discussed by Hilger (1978) and (1978a) especially 354–6. For a technical analysis of the choir see Kreusch (1974).

66. Not counting chapter houses and baptisteries. The Gothic centralized church is more common than Frankl supposed. See Götz (1968) and Untermann (1989).

67. Dehio (1901) contains a longitudinal section on p. 346, and a plan on plate 455. The Karlov church was begun in 1351. The consecration of 1371 may refer only to the choir, or it may include the nave. Mencl (1948) 72ff, reconstructed the original fourteenth-century nave space as a four-pillar hall, but Bachmann, in a series of studies, has convincingly shown that the nave had a triradial 'umbrella' vault supported on a single central column, a solution inspired by Louis the Bavarian's slightly earlier church at Ettal. For the literature see Bachmann (1969) especially 96–7.

68. The dates have now been clarified for both buildings. For the Karlov church see above, Note 67. St Catherine's chapel was complete by 1396/8.

69. A definitive work on the history of the building of the church of St Stephen is Hans Tietze, *Geschichte und Beschreibung etc.* (*Österreichische Kunsttopographie*, XXIII) (Vienna, 1931). Compare also R. K. Donin, *Der Wiener Stephansdom und seine Geschichte*, 2nd ed. (Vienna, 1952). The best general history of the buildings of St Stephen's in Vienna is still Zykan (1981). See also Brucher (1990) 125–30.

70. Tietze (p. 414) says that the figures themselves date from 1440, but the corbels and the canopies must have been erected at the same time as the piers, that is, some time after 1420.

Grimschitz (1947) 17–18, dated the nave canopies to the 1430s on analogy with the Puchheim altar baldachine of 1434, which he attributed to Hans Puchspaum. Zykan (1967) 410, attributed the canopies to the same same architect. However, Zykan (1981) 276, note 198, attributed the Puchheim baldachine to Puchspaum's predecessor, Hans von Prachatitz. By analogy, therefore, the pillar canopies may also be Prachatitz's. Certainly the pillars were up by 1440, the earliest known date for the roof installation, and therefore before Puchspaum assumed control of the lodge in 1446. The progress of the nave in the fifteenth century, and Puchspaum's contribution is also discussed by Brucher (1990) 181–4, who attributes the Pucheim baldachine to Puchspaum.

71. For the north tower see Zykan (1981) 102–8. A foundation stone was laid in 1450, but work above ground did not begin until 1467 under Master Lawrence Spenyng. See also Perger (1970) 97–8.

72. This account of the south tower is based on the authoritative study by Zykan (1970). Perger (1970) adds to, or modifies, Zykan's conclusions on the following points:

1) **Master Chunradus** (active at least from 1372–92/4) worked on the nave and built the lower parts of the south tower and St Catherine's Chapel. His plan for a south steeple, lower than the present one, envisaged an octagonal belfry rising from the level of the nave gables. See Riss 16819R, Vienna Akademie der bildenden Künste.

2) **After his death** there was a break in the work on the tower. His successor, Ulrich Helbling, works only on the nave.

3) **Work resumed** on the south tower under Wenczla in *c.*1400, when it was decided to heighten the tower with the insertion of a tall square belfry between the base of the lower gables and the octagon

4) **Work on the tower** was interrupted in 1408 and probably the 'demolition' took place in 1409.

Brucher (1990) 124–30, doubts the attribution of much of the lower parts of the nave and south tower to Chunradus, and instead goes back to the position of a much older generation of Viennese scholars in attributing these parts of the cathedral to Michael Chnab, the ducal architect working simultaneously in Wiener-Neustadt. Brucher attributes to Chnab the never-realized design of the Freiburg-like south steeple of *c.*1370 (16819R) and the south porch and St Catherine's Chapel. He left the lodge, according to Brucher, in 1395, when the initiative for the building of the tower passed to the citizens, and he was replaced by Ulrich Helbling. He believes that it was under Helbling, not Wenczla, that the decision was taken to heighten the tower. He attributes the demolitions of 1407 to the mistakes of Master Wenczla.

73. For a detailed description, see Tietze, *op. cit.* 166, and Zykan (1970).

74. Kletzl (1934), was the first to identify the Master 'Wenczla' in the St Stephen's accounts as Peter Parler's son, Wenzel. He and Bureš (1975) 22–7, identified the very close dependence of the details of the Vienna steeple, especially in the gable storey, on the south tower in Prague. The latest possible date for the layout and conception of the south tower in Prague must be 1392, the year the foundations of the nave were laid. But the tower must have been planned, at least in general outline, some years earlier and laid out together with its directly adjacent south porch, which was finished in 1367. In fact the lower storey of the tower up to the balustrade is no different in style to the rest of the south transept. In 1397, two years before Peter Parler's death, his eldest son, Wenzel, took over the workshop, but in that year, or the next, he left for Vienna where he took over from Ulrich Helbling the mastership of the works of the south tower of St Stephen's. Johannes, Peter's second son, assumed control of the Prague lodge in 1398 to his death in 1406. The clear change of style in the Prague tower above the balustrade, and the close similarities between these upper parts and St Stephen's south tower, indicate close contacts between the lodges. See Benešovská (1994) 54–5, and (1999) 125–33.

74A. For the Týn church, begun *c.*1350, and its Parlerian forms, see Líbal, in *Die Parler* (1978) vol. 2, 633, and Líbal (1983) 286–90.

75. For the older literature cf. Eberhard Lutze, *Die Nürnberger Pfarrkirchen etc.* (Berlin, 1939) 15. For a more detailed study, cf. F. W. Hoffmann, *Die Sebalduskirche etc.* (Vienna, 1912).

76. The Gothic upper storeys date from 1481. Fehling and Ress (1961) 115–18, attempt to distinguish two workshops at St Sebaldus in the thirteenth century, one using specifically Bamberg forms, the other more up-to-date Cistercian ideas from Ebrach.

77. The church of St Lawrence at Nuremberg and the Franciscan church at Salzburg.

77A. The church was severely bombed in the Second World War and these friezes of arches were not, unfortunately, replaced when the vaults were rebuilt. Appearing only in the central vessel, they distinguished the holiest, most central, spaces of the sanctuary, where the shrine of St Sebaldus was set up, from the aisles and ambulatory. See Seeger (1992) 42–5.

78. Dehio's *Handb. d. deutschen Kunstd.*, III (1925) 366.

78A. The plan of the choir, at least in its alternating triradial and four-part vaults in the ambulatory, may derive from Zwettl, the elevation from the nave of the Frauenkirche in Esslingen (begun *c.*1350), so much so that Fehling and Ress (1961) 121, suggest that both might be by the same architect. The decorative details of the choir's exterior depend on the west front of Cologne (and behind Cologne, the west portal at Mantes and the south transept portal at Rouen cathedral). The tracery-decorated exterior can be connected to a group of later choirs in Saxony and Thuringia, see Gross (1967). A useful collection of essays on every aspect of the east choir appeared in Baier, ed., (1979). Seeger (1992) examines the correspondence between symbolic form and cult function in the choir, discusses its role as a pilgrimage church housing the relics of St Sebaldus, and stresses its similarities to single-aisled choirs and reliquary chapels – characteristics which mark it off strongly from the basilican-like exterior profile of the choir of the Holy Cross at Schwäbisch Gmünd.

79. The mouchettes in the Rats Window and the Kramer Window belong no doubt to the remodelling of the windows for the stained glass of 1480 (made by a colleague of Peter Hemmel); Frankl, *Peter Hemmel etc.* (Berlin, 1956) 74. The first architect was Heinrich II Parler, who was succeeded, probably in 1383, by Michael II Parler. See Wortmann (1969) and (1977) especially 101, note 1.

80. In stereometry plans with these properties are called saddle-shaped surfaces. There are many varieties of them. The best study of fan vaulting is now Leedy (1980).

80A. Leedy (1980) 7–9, 166–8, identifies the earliest fans over the Gloucester cloister east walk as those in its northern half, from the chapter house entrance to the north east corner of the cloister. He also dates them to '*c.*1400', suggesting that they were never intended by Abbot Horton (1351–77) and only inserted by Abbot Froucester (1381–1412). Neither argument has been accepted. See reviews by Crossley (1981a) and Wilson (1981). It is still generally assumed that the first fans of the east walk were built not in the northern but in the southern half of the east walk, that is between the church and the chapter house entrance. Wilson (1990) 210, dates these fans to the Horton abbacy, and specifically to *c.*1351–64. Leedy (1980) 172–3, and Harvey (1978) 90–2, underline the close similarities between the Horton work in the Gloucester cloisters and the now-destroyed fan-vault and tracery of the Chapter House at Hereford Cathedral (in building from before 1364 to 1371). Harvey therefore attributes the Gloucester work to the Hereford architect, who may have been John of Evesham or Thomas de Canteburgge, the latter possibly leaving Gloucester in 1364, for in that year he contracted to complete the Hereford Chapter House. For the Perpendicular remodelling at Gloucester see above, Chapter 4, Note 10.

80B. An illuminating interpretation of Italian Gothic is offered by Trachtenberg (1991). He sees its defining traits as specifically opposed to the 'purist', 'modernist' Gothic style of the north, especially of France. Italian Gothic was historicist and, above all, creatively eclectic; its stylistic diversity and its lack of clear stylistic development were fuelled by the rivalries of city-states, and the social diversity within each city. He underlines its intelligence rather than its provincialism. He identifies three categories of Gothic reception: a) the 'pure' 'spiritual' Gothic of the mendicant orders, coming closest to the modernity of the north, b) the flashy eclecticism of the civic cathedrals and important non-mendicant churches, which incorporated both Gothic, Romanesque and Early Christian forms, and c) secular buildings – civic or seigneurial – which were particularly resistant to all strains of Gothic. See also Sauerländer (1995a). Cadei (1991a) attributes Italian 'resistance' to Gothic to the developed culture of the city state and its anti-monarchical ideologies.

80C. The first Dominican church was begun soon after 1226 and continued under construction into the second half of the thirteenth century. The construction of the present choir and transept, beginning with its supporting lower church, was underway from 1306, and a city statute of 1308 points out that donations are given 'to make the church more spacious so that a greater amount of people can be accommodated'. The lower church was probably complete before the outbreak of the plague in 1348, and certainly by 1360. Work on the transept above continued into the 1380s, and a transept altar is mentioned in 1390, but progress was so slow that the transept was finally opened into the nave only in *c.*1480. See Riedl and Seidl (1992) 451–98. See also Schenkluhn (2000) 177–9, who relates it to the 'monumentalisation' of the 'triple-chapel room church' type occuring at the same time at S. Croce in Florence (see above, Chapter 3, Note 118) and S. Francesco in Siena (see below, Chapter 4, Note 80D).

80D. The architect of the new church was Agostino di Agnolo. Schenkluhn (2000) 177–8 notes that its interior choir wall, with an oculus over the high altar arch, is a copy of that at S. Croce in Florence.

81. Giotto's project has been preserved in a drawing in the cathedral archives at Siena, which is reproduced in Dehio (1901) II, 257. Still the most authoritative history of the tower is by Trachtenberg (1971).

81A. For the German Rayonnant influence on the Siena plan see Klotz (1966). Trachtenberg's (1971) conclusions on the campanile and its drawing are as follows: a) The Siena plan is Giotto's design for the campanile, b) at Giotto's death in 1337 only the lowest socle zone was complete, c) Andrea Pisano, mentioned in 1340, designed the upper socle zone and then the next two stories ('zone two', up to the height of the nave aisles). The 'Venetian' verticality of 'zone two' broke with Giotto's 'Florentine' tradition of horizontal storeys and increasing fenestration as the tower ascends, d) c.1343, the year of Pisano's expulsion from the city, Francesco Talenti took over, returned to Giotto's horizontality, and completed the three top stories by c.1360 in an uninterrupted campaign. The two biforia stories were complete by c.1350, the triforia storey was begun c.1351, substantially complete by 1357, and finished in 1359/60. Some kind of crowning spire was projected but never built. It was roofed in 1387. Much of Trachtenberg's analysis rests on the assumption that the Siena drawing is Giotto's. But Degenhart and Schmitt (1968) vol. 1, cat. 38 89ff, have put forward convincing reasons for associating it with the rebuilding of Siena cathedral c.1340, a view which has had much critical support.

Kreytenberg's important study (1978) came to very different conclusions. He attributed to Giotto the design of the whole lower third of the tower up to the cathedral's aisle height, which includes both socle zones (which he identified as 'zone one' and the more vertical 'zone two', which Trachtenberg had attributed to Pisano). Probably only zone one was completed at Giotto's death in 1337. Kreytenberg successfully disproved Trachtenberg's argument that Andrea Pisano doubled the thickness of Giotto's walls in the lower storey: Giotto built them in their present form from the beginning. He considered that Pisano, who probably took over in 1337, continued Giotto's design through the lower two zones, only 'correcting' the upper parts of Giotto's design by planning, or even building, a tall vertical storey in the upper half of zone two, shown in the famous Bigallo fresco of 1342. It may have been for this miscaluated design that Pisano was dismissed, in 1341. Kreytenberg also argued that construction was interrupted between 1341 and c.1348, when attention was allegedly switched to the marble veneering of the south aisle at the western end of the nave of the cathedral. In 1347 Giotto's project was abandoned and Talenti's accepted, with work resuming in 1348. The biforia storeys were built with great speed between 1348/9–52/3, and the triforia between c.1351/2–9. Kreytenberg follows Degenhart and Schmitt (1968) in identifying the Siena drawing as a project for the new cathedral there, made in c.1340, and not by Giotto. His chronology for the Florence campanile is partly based on his chronologies for the marble cladding of the cathedral nave, which have been questioned vigorously by Trachtenberg (1979). For a resumé of the literature on the Siena plan see Ascani (1989) 266–8. Zervas's (1987) discovery of the account books for the total cost of the campanile between 1333 and 1359 provides new insights into the fluctuating finances of the Opera del Duomo and confirms Trachtenberg's and not Kreytenberg's chronology of the bell tower. It also excludes any pre-Talentian campaign of marble revetment on the cathedral c.1341–8.

82. In Jakob Burckhardt's works, the term originally applied to the baptistery at Florence and the church of S. Miniato al Monte – that is, to Romanesque buildings.

83. The interior of Or San Michele has semicircular transverse arches, and the Loggia dei Priori ('dei Lanzi'), which was not built until 1376, but is supposed to have been executed to a design by Orcagna, also has round arches.

There is a full description of the tabernacle and its sculpture in Fabbri and Rutenburg (1981). Cassidy (1992) stresses the devotional functions of the tabernacle and its precedents in the ciboria of the early churches of Rome. But all previous scholarship has now been superseded in the monumental study by Zervas et al., 2 vols (1996), with contributions on all aspects of the building and its tabernacle. See particularly 79–98.

83A. These conclusions are based on Saalman (1980) especially chapter 2; Toker (1979) (1983); Rocchi et al., (1988), and White (1993) 495–502. The maverick in the historiography of the cathedral is Kreytenberg (1974). He thought that work resumed on the nave in 1331 and not 1355, with the two nave portals (in their 'earliest' form) dating from 1331–41, and the western aisle wall marble revetments from c.1341–8. The choir, he suggested, was remodelled at this time. He also promoted Andrea Orcagna to a critical position in the design of the nave, and attributed to the building committees much of the design of the choir in 1366–7. His reconstruction of the choir as a Cistercian type with flat-ended chapels has been disproved by the excavations. Trachtenberg (1979) went some way to reinstate Talenti as the guiding spirit of critical aspects of the nave: its vaults, its interior cornice and its exterior revetments. He proposed that Talenti started the continuation of the nave with the building of the west-

ern portal to the north aisle (the Porta dei Comachinni) in c.1350, followed by further aisle revetments (c.1355–8) and the south aisle portal (Porta del Campanile) in 1359–62.

84. Dehio (1901) II, 494.

84A. The excavations of the late 1960s and early 1970s showed that the footings for the piers separating the crossing from the nave were octagonal. These, together with the inferred wide bays, small clerestorey, and wooden roofs throughout, approximate very closely to S. Croce. See Toker (1983) 118–19 figs. 23, 25.

85. The corbels of the balcony stand directly on the line of the springing, and are classical in form. However, the wooden parapet consists of alternating flat piers and panels with circular openings, which again strike a Gothic note.

86. There is, in fact, a small mosaic on the inside of the west wall.

87. The organ lofts over the doors of the sacristy are neo-Gothic and probably date from the beginning of the nineteenth century.

88. There are 'ribs', in the mechanical sense, between the two shells of the dome.

89. After Arnolfo, perhaps for the first time in the Maestà by Duccio (1308). Cf. B. Garrison, Italian Romanesque Panel Painting (Florence, 1949) 136.

90. The present façade was built by Emilio de Fabris between 1875 and 1887.

91. A reconstruction is offered by Martin Weinberger in 'The first Façade etc.', Journal of the Warburg and Courtauld Institutes, IV (1940) 67 and plate 16.

There is still no firm agreement as to Arnolfo's design for the west front of the cathedral, nor the exact sculptural contribution of his workshop to the façade. He certainly produced the Marian sculpture in the three tympana over the portals, but in September 1359 Alberto Arnoldi was commissioned in consultation with Francesco Talenti to complete the arch over the main doorway, and many of the details shown in the upper parts of Poccetti's sixteenth-century drawing of the façade have a richness attributable less to Arnolfo than to Talenti and his generation. See Romanini (1980) 103–43, and White (1993) 107–12, 496–7. The unpublished dissertation of Christian (1989) has not been available to me. Toker (1978) 221–4, and (1983) 112 and fig. 11b surmises that the façade, and the western aisle walls, had reached a height of 25 metres, but this tells us nothing of the revetments and details, only the core structure. For the doubts voiced over Toker's reconstructions of 'Arnolfo's project' by Rocchi et al. (1988) and Trachtenberg (1993) see above, Chapter 3, Note 141B.

92. One is reminded of St Gilles and also of Donatello's later Cantoria.

93. The former opinion appears in Schnaase, Geschichte der bildenden Künste, V (Düsseldorf, 1876) 157, and the latter in T. G. Jackson, Gothic Architecture etc. (Cambridge, 1915) II, 222.

94. The semicircular form of the transverse arches should be understood to derive from the form on the north-east wall. For the whole project, cf. Vittorio Lusini, Il duomo di Siena (Siena, 1911) 151ff.

For the abortive Duomo Nuovo, and the structural difficulties which led to its partial demolition and complete abandonment in 1357 see White (1993) 234–40. The conception may go back to the first architect, Lando di Pietro, who took over in 1339, but Carli (1987) 7–44, has cast doubt on his short-lived role (he died in 1340) and instead attributed the idea of turning the cathedral 180 degrees and transforming its nave and choir into transepts to Giovanni d'Agostino and his circle, to whom he attributed the second of the two plans for the new cathedral now in the Opera in Siena. For these plans, and their literature, see Ascani (1989) 268–70. The urbanistic relations of the cathedral to the Campo and the Palazzo Pubblico are discussed by Braunfels (1979) 159–67, who was among the first to see the eastward and southward extensions of the church as motivated by the new civic centre taking shape to the south east. After the decision to abandon construction on the new cathedral in 1357 attention turned again to the extension to the choir, which proceeded from 1358 into the 1360s.

95. Vittorio Lusini, Il San Giovanni etc. (Florence, 1901). For the connexions between the baptistery façade and the west front of Strasbourg see Klotz (1966) 186–8. The drawing, its literature, and its varied dating (ranging from 1317 to 1339), is discussed in Ascani (1989) 270–2.

96. Harald Keller, 'Die Risse der Orvietaner Domopera', Festschrift Wilhelm Pinder (Leipzig, 1938) 201. For the possible character of Giovanni Pisano's design, and the dating of the upper parts of the west façade, see above, Chapter 3, Note 143.

97. The cathedral at Cefalù has mosaics combined with rib-vaults. The vaults date from 1263 and the mosaics from 1267. Cf. Giuseppe Samonà, Il duomo di Cefalù (Rome, 1939), section 5. The mosaics in the dome of the baptistery at Florence were executed between 1225 and 1300. However, one must be clear in one's own mind whether such cases are combinations of Gothic and Byzantine elements and principles, whether one can speak of 'Gothic artistry' within the sphere of mosaics, and, if so, when and where. This problem has remained unsolved to this day.

Still fundamental for the west façade of Orvieto is White (1959) and also

White (1993) 452–64. More recent studies of the façade can be found in Ricetti, ed. (1988), including Gillerman (1988) 81–100. Ricetti (1996) deals with matters of workshop organization under Lorenzo Maitani. See also, for the rest of the cathedral, Gillerman (1994) and the still useful Bonelli (1972). The two drawings for the façade (in the Museo dell'Opera del Duomo) are discussed in relation to those for Siena by Middeldorf-Kosegarten (1984) 147–59, and more fully by her in (1994) and (1996) where she dates them to before or around the year 1300. Ascani (1989) 275–7 reviews the literature on the drawings.

97A. The complex building history of this church has been settled by Saalman (1962) and (1966). The earliest parts are the late thirteenth- and early fourteenth-century chapels on the north side of the nave. The nave itself, with its Duomo-like piers, was underway in 1360–70, though the eastern nave bays, and the parts of the choir chapels, were still in building in the 1390 and the whole church was not complete until c.1405.

98. Enrico Ridolfi, L'arte in Lucca (Lucca, 1882). This author's description of the piers as octagonal, which has been repeated elsewhere, is not accurate. They are cruciform with shafts in the re-entrant angles. Ridolfi in fact illustrates them in his book, on p. 34. From 1372 to the early fifteenth century the Romanesque cathedral was internally reconstructed with new arcades, galleries and vaults.

98A. The tracery of the gallery openings is closely related to the clerestorey windows of the nave of Siena cathedral, see Klotz (1966) 194–5, though, with this particular kind of tracery (intersecting), he exaggerates the Sienese and Luccan connexions to Strasbourg.

99. The well-documented history of Milan Cathedral falls under two main (and interrelated) areas of interest: firstly, the debates on its design and on its geometric and constructional procedures, vividly revealed in the contemporary annals of the *fabbrica* and in a series of contemporary drawings; and secondly, the milieu in which those design decisions were taken – the fabric of the cathedral itself, the chronology of its construction and the contributions of its workforce, the latter ultimately impossible to disentangle since the cathedral was a collective effort and not the conception of a single architect. The first set of problems is set forth in two classic studies by Frankl (1945) and by Ackermann (1949), to which Frankl added supplementary comments in his discussion of the Milan controversy in (1960) 63–83. Ackerman's polarization between 'northern advisors' and 'Italians' is refined by White (1993) 517–31. See also Wilson (1990) 268–76. The drawings are discussed by Ascani (1989) and (1991) and Cadei (1991), the latter following Ackerman's distinction between the northern architects' commitment to geometrical figures and the Italians' preference for numerical systems. Kidson (1999) rehabilitates Gabriele Stornaloco as a good mathematician (his mathematics are clearly of a higher order than the mathematics of the masons), and discusses his report in relation to Milanese and Bolognese metrology.

The second aspect of Milan, the fabric itself and its building history, is partly covered by Welch (1995), whose close reading of the published annals, and of much unpublished contemporary documentation, reconstructs the institutional history of the enterprise, and the factional intrigues of its workforce. It does not attempt, however, to clarify the detailed impact of these events on the design or final appearance of the building, or relate them to the drawings. The work which gathers together all these approaches is the magisterial study by Romanini (1973), on which much of the following chronology is based.

Phase One 1386–92: Cathedral begun in 1386 under the main executant architect *(ingegnere generale)*, Simone da Orsenigo (first mentioned in 1387), a specialist in brick work and foundations. Welch (1995) 49–69 has raised serious doubts about the contribution – financial and ideological – of Duke Gian Galeazzo Visconti to the new enterprise, stressing instead the responsibilities of Milan's city government in initiating and financing the work. It was laid out as a five-aisled Lombard brick basilica whose outer aisles were to be divided into cellular chapels in the manner of S. Maria del Carmine in Pavia (begun c.1370). Excavations from 1965–73 revealed an elaborate terracotta decoration under the stone cladding of the northern sacristy, continuing into the apse. Romanini (1973) 102ff, 166ff, maintained that this early project was quickly superseded by one based on the latest northern Gothic styles, and that the cellular chapels had precedents in Prague Cathedral. Certainly a German goldsmith in Milan, Anechino de Alemania, made a lead model of the lantern tower in February 1387, by which date the main outlines of the project were established: a three-sided apse with no radiating chapels, flanked by rectangular sacristies (a very un-northern choir plan), three-aisled transepts, a lantern tower and the equivalent of a five-aisled nave. However, in May 1387 it was decided to construct the cathedral in marble and demolish all work up to that point. From then onwards the annals record the increasing influence of the sub-Alpine marble workers, Giacomo, Marco and Zeno da Campione. Simone da Orsenigo was dismissed in 1389. To the Campionese, therefore, we can probably attribute the elaborate 'northern' design of the exterior sacristies, and of the plan and profile of the choir and transept pillars, under discussion since 1388, and energetically under construction in 1389. (For the history of the pillars, their changing designs and their curious capitals, see Cadei (1969)). The con-

tribution of the Parisian architect, Nicholas de Bonaventura, to these design decisions is still uncertain. From his arrival in 1389 to his departure in July/August 1390 he made drawings, e.g. of portals and the central window of the choir apse. Two drawings (in the Bologna Archivio della Fabbricieria di San Petronio), of the ground plan and cross section of the cathedral, and of its sacristy elevation, made in Milan by Antonio di Vincenzo in 1390, reflect the state of Giacomo da Campione's and Nicholas de Bonaventura's designs at that time. Certainly the greater size of the crossing piers in the first drawing reflects the decision of July 1390 to increase their diameter, but it does not register the (later) eventual enlargement of all the piers to be identical to the crossing's. See Ascani (1989) 256–60. The drawn transepts (one bay wider than the actual ones) suggested to Romanini (1973) 166, parallels with Cologne cathedral, while Cadei (1991) and especially Ascani (1991) saw the incomplete section as betraying a simple use of *ad quadratum* proportions, based on whole numbers, a system also prefigured in Cologne and used by Antonio for the almost identical dimensions of his new nave of S. Petronio in Bologna, begun in 1390. Ascani (1991) gives a full metrological analysis of the drawing in Bolognese feet and Milanese braccia.

In January 1391 a German, Giovanni of Frieburg, who may have designed the Parlerian frieze of round-arched trefoils crowning the plinth section of the choir buttresses, was promoted to chief engineer. He may have been the first to introduce the idea of conceiving the height of the high vault *ad triangulam*. His dismissal in June 1391, to be replaced by the painter Giovanni dei Grassi (who carved the 'Christ and the Samaritan woman' in the south sacristy in that year) did not assuage the doubts of the deputies about the 'apse window, the doors and staircases, the height of the pillars and the height of the church'. In late September 1391 a mathematician from Piacenza, Gabriele Stornaloco, recommended fitting the main dimensions of the cross section of the church into a grid of equilateral triangles, and rounding up the real (incommensurable) height of its high vaults from 83.138 to 84 braccia – for the drawing see Ascani (1989) 260–2, and Cadei (1991) 89–91. In October a wooden model, based on Stornaloco's project, was begun by Simone da Cavagnera, to illustrate the 'doubts . . . that had arisen among the engineers concerning the said fabric'. Heinrich Parler of Ulm's arrival in Milan in November 1391 did not resolve the difficulties. He seems to have recommended two geometric schemes to determine the height of the church, one based on equilateral triangles, the second based on the square which entailed a tall central vessel of 96 braccia, buttressed with flyers, not unlike Cologne. Two drawings in Milan have been associated with his stay, both showing close affinities to Parler architecture and metalwork in Prague: the so-called Carelli pinnacle at the corner of the north sacristy (built in 1401), and a cross section for the outer and inner aisles of the cathedral, showing a complete disregard for the structure already built. See Romanini (1973) 174–7; Ascani (1989) 262–4, and Cadei (1991).

Phase Two 1392–9: The conference of May 1392 rejected Heinrich Parler's proposals. The dividing walls of the outer, lateral chapels were suppressed; the triforium of the main elevation (envisaged in Antonio di Vincenzo's cross section) was also ruled out. Giovanni dei Grassi and Giacomo da Campione, chief engineers from March 1392, now assume control of the building for the next six years. It was this partnership, more than anything else, which was responsible for the final form of the cathedral. They began to implement, and may have devised, a new proportional system, in which the elevation rises from the height of the outer aisle capitals in a series of Pythagorean and not equilateral triangles, thus reducing the height of the central vessel from 84 to 76 braccia. Certainly dei Grassi is the author of the axial, and probably the side, windows of the apse, under construction in 1395–6; of designs for the stained glass of the sacristy windows; and of the influential wooden model of the cathedral (now lost) which must have reflected the decisions of May 1392, but which remained unfinished in 1398. He may also have designed the lavabos, the capitals and the window frames of the apse and sacristies, as well as the strange tabernacle-like capitals of the main piers(?), one of which, on the south side of the choir, was constructed before 1393. Certainly the similarities between the architectural forms in the *Visconti Hours* and those in the cathedral led Borchert (1995) to attribute the capitals to dei Grassi. The influence of micro-architecture, in metalwork and manuscript painting, on dei Grassi's designs is underlined by Caddei (1991). The German, specifically Parlerian, character of the drawings for the Milan capitals (Bianconi collection, Museo Civico, t. II), is also stressed by Sanvito (1996). For the German parallels for dei Grassi's gigantic tracery in the apse see Wiener (1993) especially 43–8. Ulrich von Ensingen, the designer of the steeples at Ulm and later Strasbourg, arrived in Milan in December 1394, and was paid exceptionally highly, probably for his advice on the stability of the prospective lantern tower. His exact contribution is, however, unknown, but he was evidently not prepared to abide by any previous plans, and he left in 1395. Borchert (1995) suggests that his refusal to implement dei Grassi's capitals probably ensured his departure. Clearly the final design for the lantern tower had not been settled, although what appears to be a copy of Stornaloco's cross section, an (early sixteenth-century?) *ad triangulam* design in the

Bianconi collection in the Museo Civico in Milan, does include the crossing tower in the grid; see Ascani (1989) 260–2 and Caddei (1991).

Phase Three 1399 to the end of the Middle Ages: The double death of Giovanni dei Grassi and Giacomo da Campione in 1398 coincided with a vulnerable moment in the cathedral's construction – at the level of the vault springers for aisles and central vessel – and at a time when no final design for the structurally dangerous crossing tower had been established. Jean Mignot, a French architect, arrived in 1399 and presented his criticisms of the design in January 1400. He clearly wanted radically to alter the whole project by rebuilding the apse buttresses and almost certainly returning to the 84 braccia vault height by reviving Stornaloco's system of equilateral triangles. Cadei (1991) attributes to him the cross section in the Bianconi collection (see above), or at least a lost drawing on which it is based. In 1400 Mignot actually began to implement some of his changes, but he was eventually overruled, and dismissed in October 1401. During his tenure he was responsible for some of the capitals of the choir pillars (e.g. pillar 81), and may have been the author of a geometrically intricate plan for one of them (Museo Civico, Bianconi collection), see Cadei (1991), though the dynamism of this plan has close parallels in the work of the Parlers and, later, the Roriczers – see Sanvito (1996). Mignot's comments on the stability of the structure, and the defence put up by his detractors on the committees, amount to some of the most revealing insights into the uses of geometry, and the understanding of statics, in medieval building. The eastern apse window was finally finished in 1403, and work began on the stained glass in 1416. Construction of the lantern tower did not begin seriously until the 1480s. For the latter see Schofield (1989).

99A. For the tracery in its European context see Wiener (1993) 43–8.

99B. The sixteenth-century controversies are discussed by Booz (1956) 54ff, and Matteucci (1983–4). For medieval S. Petronio, see generally White (1993) 533–7; and Lorenzoni (1983–4). The church was begun in 1390 by the architect Antonio di Vincenzo on a colossal scale, using Tuscan (pillars based on those of Florence cathedral) and Lombard models (brick, and nave cellular chapels like S. Maria del Carmine in Pavia). When worked stopped in the third quarter of the seventeenth century only the six-bay nave had been completed. The contract for the model in 1400 suggests that the nave was to have been 183 metres long with transepts 137 metres in width. It is not clear what Antonio's design for the choir looked like.

100. Frankl (1960) 299–312. There have been many studies on the use of geometric ratios and metrology in the history of medieval architecture. A comprehensive discussion can be found in Hecht (1969) (1970) and (1971), and with pertinent remarks on measures in Binding (1985) (1993) 171–206. There is also a rich literature in English, see Bucher (1968) and (1972); Shelby (1972), and Fernie (1990). Many of these questions will be dealt with in Kidson's forthcoming study on classical and medieval systems of proportion.

101. Artur Gusmão, *La real abadia de Alcobaça* (Lisbon, 1948). See also Dias (1986) and Cocherill (1989) 19–41. The monastery was founded in 1153, work was under way in 1178, and the monks were able to occupy their choir in 1223.

101A. Especially the pointed tunnel vaults with two-bay diagonal net patterns over the choir.

102. Restored in 1775, after the earthquake.

103. Albrecht Haupt, *Die Baukunst der Renaissance in Portugal*, II (Frankfurt, 1895) 13ff. However, since some of the outstanding Late Gothic Portuguese architects contributed to Batalha from the late fourteenth to the early sixteenth century (Alfonso Domingues, Huguet, Mateus Fernandes I) the monastery can be seen as one of the foundations of Portuguese Late Gothic. See Chicó (1968) 107ff; and Guimarès de Andrade (1989).

104. Andreas Lindblom, *Sveriges Kunsthistoria*, I (Stockholm, 1944) 204. Plan in Dehio (1901) plate 504. The church was begun after a fire in 1388 and consecrated in 1430. See also Andersson (1972) and (1991), who describes the special liturgical arrangements, specifically ordained by St Bridget, for what was a double convent of nuns and monks.

The church, a simple rectangular hall, had a monks's choir at the west end with its own altar facing west, while the nuns controlled the eastern half of the space and had their own altar of the Virgin at the east end of the nave. Long galleries ran along both sides of the nave, the southern for the monks, the northern for the nuns. Nothing of this arrangement survives, but it became the model for numerous other Brigittine buildings. An analysis of the order and its architecture can be found in Berthelson (1947), Lindblom (1964) and Cnattingius (1963).

104A. The Gothic cathedral of Uppsala was begun c.1270. It has an apse, ambulatory and radiating chapels, flying buttresses, and the remains of an intended two-tower west façade. Most of these French aspects are attributed to the architect Etienne de Bonneuil, who is documented as being present in Uppsala in 1287, and who may have stayed on the site to c.1300. The radiating chapels were finished by c.1310, the choir and transepts vaulted by c.1320. Master Etienne may also have been responsible for the French-looking composition of the north transept façade (with large rose), and for its portal. The fullest account can still be found in Boethius and Romdahl (1935). Zeitler

(1971) underplays the French influences and emphasizes the local *Backsteingotik* sources, from Westphlia (or Westphalian patterns in the Baltic) and from the Dominican foundation at Sigtuna. Certainly the simplicity of the brick exterior, the later fourteenth-century nave and the two-tower west façade (completed in c.1450–65) give the building the appearance of a German, southern Baltic, basilica.

104B. Frankl may be referring to both the hall nave, and the later hall choir. The first campaign on the hall nave lasted from 1250 to 1296, the second, which added two western bays, was underway between 1308 and 1360. In c.1408–20 the Cologne architect, Gierlach, began the present hall choir with ambulatory and three chapels, which was completed in a second campaign (1487–1500). Among the architects of this later work was Adam van Duren, who carved the boss in the south chapel. See Cnattingius *et al.* (1987).

104C. See Deshoulières (1921). The foundation stone was laid in 1364, that of the tower in 1373.

104D. In confining the novelties of Flamboyant to tracery Frankl is stating a commonly held belief, stemming from the nineteenth-century definition of the style as a new form of window design, that Flamboyant added nothing spatially or structurally new to the inheritance of Rayonnant: it simply replaced geometric with curvilinear tracery. In reality, Flamboyant represents a radical departure from the structural and spatial regularities of Rayonnant architecture. Wilson (1990) 248–57 sees its central principle as 'the fragmentation of the Rayonnant system through the contrary yet complementary processes of elision and disjunction'. Murray (1996a) points to new kinds of east end planning (with interlocking hexagonal spaces, trapezoidal bays or rectangular ambulatories, or combinations of all three); to the fusion of hitherto separate elements (capital-less arches and piers); to the mannered contrasts between elements (simple piers and complex moulded stonework); to the use of staircase turrets to give a three-dimensional dynamism and fusion to façades; to a preference for illusionism (bases 'growing' out of pillar socles at different heights and depths, suggesting an almost organic sense of hierarchy).

104E. Ogee arches appear in the windows of the lower chapel of St Stephen's chapel as early as the 1290s (from 1292), by Michael of Canterbury. Wilson (1986) 82–3, suggests that one of the earliest examples of curvilinear tracery in England might have been the two windows with reticulated tracery in the bays of the cloister opposite the Chapter House at Westminster Abbey, which he dates (contrary to the usual 'c.1340' period) to c.1300–10. The Kentish tracery in one of the bays can be associated with the contemporary work of Michael of Canterbury.

104F. For the Beverley reredos see Dawton (1983) 124–5, 128, 143; and (1989).

105. Durand, *op. cit.* (Note 18 to Chapter 3) I, 50. La Grange became a cardinal in 1375 and left Amiens. He then lived in Rome until 1402. For the north chapels at Amiens see Ringshausen (1973) 72–3, who points to parallels with Prague rather than England. This article provides a useful short survey of the origins of French Flamboyant. Short but incisive observations on the influence of England on early flowing tracery on the continent can be found in Bony (1979) 22–5, 27–8, 67–9. Adelman (1973) has not been available to me. Sanfaçon (1971), still the only survey of French Flamboyant, hardly touches on the origins of flowing tracery in France. Kurmann (1975) and (1986) points to double-curved tracery forms in southern Germany in the early part of the fourteenth century. See above, Chapter 4, Note 22A.

106. De Lasteyrie, *op. cit.* (Note 77 to Chapter 2) II, 33ff. Tamir (1946) saw English Decorated and French Flamboyant as 'diametrically opposed'.

107. The tracery in the Chapelles de la Grange is illustrated in Schürenberg, *op. cit.* plate 90. Trombetta (1972) pointed to an early example of double-curved tracery, datable to 1303–10, in the former hospital of Saint-Louis at Senlis. But – like the double curves in the thirteenth-century clerestorey of Sens cathedral (see above, Chapter 4, Note 22), the ogees here are probably the result of the accidental merging of curves. Frankl only mentions in Part 2, p. 288, a key example of early Flamboyant, the tracery above the fireplace of Jean de Berry's great hall at the ducal palace at Poitiers, built in the late 1380s and 1390s. See below, Part 2, Note 52.

108. Behling, *op. cit.* (Note 106 to Chapter 3) 32. Also illustrated in Bond, *Introduction*, 611–40.

109. However, falchions rarely have double curves.

109A. Frankl is referring to the 'mouchette wheels' in the nave clerestorey, in the western bay and in the third bay from the west. The nave at Exeter was designed and largely constructed under the architect Thomas of Witney, to whom these windows can be attributed. For documented references to his presence at Exeter see Erskine (1983) xx–xxi; and for the work on choir and nave done under his control see Erskine (1983) xxx–xxxiii. An authoritative account of his contribution to Exeter is provided by Morris (1991) 71–8 (specifically on the nave and its windows). Morris (1991) 83, note 66, mentions other early examples of 'mouchette wheels' in England and on the continent, notably in the nave aisle windows at Beverley Minster and in the second storey windows of the west towers of York Minster.

109B. Murray (1996) 74, dates the crossing vault to the last of the vaults of the eastern end repaired after the fire of 1258, and finished sometime before 1269. He notes that the profiles of its ribs is different from the other bays.

110. C.A. (1916; session of 1913) 155. See also Champeaux and Gauchery (1894) 10, 53; Hacker-Sück (1962) 248–9. The accounts for the building of the palace and the chapel are published by Teyssot (1992). This evidence, and the dendrochronology of the roof, shows that the chapel was built essentially between 1395 and 1403. Froissart's mention of Jean de Berry and Jeanne de Boulogne being married in June 1389 'en sa chapelle' refers to the old palace chapel. See Delmiot, Kurmann-Schwarz et al. (1999) 6–14. Its tracery is very close to the tower windows of the clerestorey level of the west front of York minster, dated c.1338.

111. C. Enlart, 'Origine anglaise du style flamboyant', B.M., LXX (1906) 79. The west façade is analysed in detail by Allinne (1912) 73–97, and Lanfry (1963). An authoritative account of the contributions of the various late Gothic architects to the west front can be found in Bottineau-Fuchs (1986) (1992) and Bottineau-Fuchs in: Baylé, dir, (1997) vol. 1 316–19. Neagley (1998), the first concerted study of Rouennais Flamboyant for many years, includes many valuable comments on the west façade and its architects, see pp. 36–8, 72–5, 87–94. The first campaign of Late Gothic remodelling took place under Jean Perier (fl. 1362–88), and consisted of a new rose window to replace the previous triple lancets, and a veneer of late Rayonnant gabled forms laid in front of the thirteenth-century façade at portal and rose level. Neagely argues, on the basis of two remaining shafts and their vault springers in each of the side portals, that Jean Perier began (but never finished?) a triple, gabled, porch in front of the three portals, intended to complement the gabled screens he was beginning to insert either side of the rose window. She connects Perier's re-facing of the façade in the 1370s and 1380s with preparations underway in 1368 to house the heart burial of King Charles V, for which Perier (with Hennequin of Liège) worked on a marble and alabaster tomb. She rightly points to the blind tracery of the inner south transept wall of the cathedral (c.1300) as a critical source for the screens, and she is equally correct in her reluctance to admit the influence of English Perpendicular architecture in their rectilinear layout – see pp. 87–8. The second architect of the remodelling, Jean de Bayeux (fl. 1387–98) seems to have been the first to introduce curvilinear tracery to the cathedral, in the outer panel above the Saint-Etienne portal and (?) in the panel directly adjoining the Tour Saint-Romain. His successor, Jenson Salvart (fl. 1398–1447), designed the almost fully curvilinear panels of tracery in the two central panels above the Saint-Jean portal and from 1430 enlarged the choir clerestorey with flowing tracery. For the cathedral's later generation of Flamboyant architects – Guillaume Pontifs, the Le Roux – and their contributions to the façade, see also below, Chapter 4, Note 175.

112. See Aubert (1935).

112A. The transepts at Auxerre, and their sculpture, deserve a detailed study. Vallery-Radot's (1958) 46–7, dating of the south transept as complete by c.1358 (the date of the burial in it of Pierre de Dicy) is too early, despite the similarities he points to with the transepts of Saint-Germain at Auxerre, going up under Abbot Gaucher Dignon de Cheu (1313–34). Titus (1984) 363–5, and 396–8, more plausibly connects payments and donations in wills to the fabric in the 1390s with the completion of the south transept and the building of the eastern bays of the nave. The upper zones of the south transept were referred to as 'new' in 1401. The north transept front and lateral walls, underway in the second decade of the fifteenth century, had, according to Titus, pp. 365–6, 398–9, reached the springing of the portal arch and up to the level of the fourth string course on the exterior before work stopped in the early 1420s. Jean de Molins, who gave money towards the northern arm, died in 1422. Building probably re-started in the 1470s. The arms of Bishop Jean Baillet (1477–1513) on the high vault of the northern arm indicate the fitful progress of the work.

113. Illustrated in Mâle, La cathédrale d'Albi (Paris, 1951) plates 8 and 9. The statues are nineteenth-century additions; only fragments remain of the medieval sculpture of the portal. See Biget (1982) 31.

114. C.A., XCIX (1935) illustration facing p. 466. There is a cast in the Musée Trocadéro, Paris. For the church and the Recevresse see now Burnand (1989) 53–67, who discusses the possible functions of the latter: as cemetery lantern, or as housing for an altar or a miraculous image of the Virgin, or all three.

114A. The Vendôme chapel was begun in 1417 for Louis of Bourbon, Count of Vendôme, by the architect Geoffroy Sevestre. Sevestre is documented as working on the church of Saint-Yves in Paris with Pierre Robin, the supposed architect of Saint-Maclou in Rouen, and the keystones of the chapel, and its fluid, curvilinear tracery, anticipate the choir at Saint-Maclou. See Bauchal (1887) 532, and Neagley (1998) 82–3.

115. Luc-Benoit, Notre Dame le l'Epine, P.M. (Paris, 1933). Here the similarities with Reims are enumerated. The best analysis is by Villes (1977a). The church was begun in the eastern bays of the nave sometime before 1440, perhaps as early as 1400–10, with the intention of terminating the nave at the end of the fourth bay from the east. Work proceeded on the two straight bays of the choir and the bays of the nave through the last two decades of the fifteenth cen-

tury. In c.1470 the façade was laid out in its present position two bays further west than originally intended, and was completed by c.1500. The radiating chapels and ambulatory of the choir were begun in 1509 by the architect Remy (or Regny) Gouveau, and finished by 1524. See also below, Chapter 4, Note 148A.

116. Villes (1977a) 853, note 2, emphasizes the debt to Saint-Nicaise in Reims and the cathedral of Châlons-sur-Marne.

117. Heinrich Parler III was called to Milan in 1391 as an adviser, but was finally rudely dismissed. For the Parler contribution to the choir see above, Chapter 4, Note 79.

118. For theories about his apprenticeship, see A. W. F. Carstanjen's detailed biography, Ulrich von Ensingen etc. (Munich, 1893). For Ulrich von Ensingen generally see now Conradt (1959). The Parler contribution to Ulm is analyzed by Wortmann (1977), and in Die Parler (1978) vol. 1 325.

119. Traces of the Parlers' arch for the aisles of the hall church have been preserved on the east wall of the northern pair of aisles, and the remnants of the wall arch built by Matthäus Ensinger can still be seen above the present vault (built by Engelberg). See Wortmann (1977) 101–6.

119A. For Ulrich's tower design (Plan A, Ulm Stadtarchiv, inv. nr 1), its sources in Prague, Strasbourg and Swabia, and its relations to other tower projects in southern Germany, see Friederich (1962), Koepf (1977) 16–19, 26–31, Schock-Werner (1983) 120–41, and Nussbaum (2000) 146–8.

119B. For the Vienna steeple see Chapter 4, pp. 207–8 above, and Notes 69–74.

120. Matthäus's successor. Matthäus Böblinger, took the work as far as the octagon. At the time of the Reformation the work stopped, and it was not until between 1880 and 1890 that August von Bayer completed the towar to Böblinger's design. Ulrich's Plan A in the Ulm Stadtarchiv, dating probably to 1392, formed the basis for the construction of the present steeple long after his death in 1419. By then construction had reached only just above the portal storey, but his design was followed, with minor variations, under Hans Kun, Caspar Kun and Matthäus Ensinger. The first significant modifications are evident in Plan C (Ulm Stadtarchiv) of Matthäus Böblinger (1477–83). They occur in the belfry storey and in the octagon and spire above it. It was to Böblinger's design that the octagon and spire, left unfinished in the Middle Ages, were completed in 1885–90. The history of the steeple under Ulrich's successors, the modifications to Ulrich's Plan A, and the post-Ulrich drawings of the steeple, are fully set out in Koepf (1977) 20–69, and Wortmann (1972) 11–22. Vrijs in Recht ed., (1989) 409–11, discusses Plans A and B. Matthäus Ensinger's career, and his contribution at Ulm, are also intelligently analyzed by Mojon (1967) especially pp. 7off. For the nineteenth-century history of the steeple see Borger-Keweloh (1986) 80–5, 98–104.

121. See Recht (1974) 69–80. Recht also discussed the dating and figure style of the belfry drawing and its connexions with Bohemian painting in Die Parler (1980) vol. 4 106–17. However, Liess (1986a) argued that the famous Riss nr 5, showing the central portal, the rose and the belfry, does not date, as many authorities have held, to c.1360–5, but from the early fourteenth century. It was, he contended, the product of the regime, or at least conceived under the influence, of Master Erwin. He argued that the 'Bohemian' figures of the Apostles and the Last Judgment were added to the earlier architectural drawing later in the century, and that all its architectural forms were already present in Upper Rhenish architecture of the late thirteenth and early fourteenth century. The belfry was therefore intended from an early period, and was not an ad hoc insertion. He suggests that the south tower may even have been constructed up to the level of the parapet by 1339 under Johannes, Erwin's son. Liess's contrived separation between the drawing's figures and its architecture is problematic, and Recht ed. (1989) 393–4 has convincingly re-iterated his early 1360s dating for the belfry and the drawing, pointing to the similarities between the tripartite tracery crest of the drawing and the chapel of St Catherine at Strasbourg (c.1340–5). An elevation drawing of the façade (inv. nr. 6 in the Musée de l'Oeuvre, Notre-Dame in Strasbourg) has been attributed to Klaus von Lohre (the leading architect at Strasbourg 1388–99) and is the only one to show the belfry in relation to the towers. The form and detailing of its belfry is much closer to the existing building than drawing nr. 5. See Recht ed. (1989) 398–9. Part of Liess's argument rests on his assumption that the 'Kressberger fragment', which shows the upper stories of the north tower, dates from the Erwin period, and therefore proves that provision for the towers up to platform height was being made then. Wortmann (1997) 149–50, has however convincingly re-dated this drawing to the mid-fourteenth century. Bureš (1990) 28–9, also reviews some of the arguments, agrees with Liess that the architectural vocabulary of the belfry is not 'Parlerian' in the Prague or Gmünd sense, but recognizes that its details (by analogy with the exterior of the choir of St Sebaldus in Nuremberg, begun c.1361–2) belong to the second, and not the first half of the fourteenth century. The actual execution of the belfry he assigns to the 1380s.

122. Illustrated in Carstanjen, op. cit., plate XII, where it is juxtaposed with the design for the tower at Ulm. See Berne, Historisches Museum, inv. nr.

1962. Still useful for the steeple is Reinhardt (1939) and (1972) 83–5. See also Mojon (1967) 25–8, Koepf (1977) 20–2, 33–7, and Recht in *Die Parler* (1978) vol. 1 282. The most authoritative recent discussion of Ulrich's work at Strasbourg and of the Berne drawing is provided by Schock-Werner (1983) 142–5, 291–7. She pinpoints the changes from Ensingen's to Hültz's work, and attributes the Berne elevation to the young Matthäus Ensinger, drawn as a studio piece and not for a competition, and executed while he was still in Strasbourg, but after his father's death in 1419. He therefore took it with him when he was called to Berne in the late summer of 1420. The plan's accurate copy of Ulrich's design for the spire for Ulm (or perhaps of his lost design for Strasbourg?) suggests that Johann Hültz's spire had not yet been started. Recht (1989) 402–3, cites all previous literature on the Berne drawing and rehearses the arguments for its attribution either to Ulrich or Matthäus, arguments which, he thinks, are so evenly balanced as to allow no clear attribution. He is not convinced that the Ulm-type spire is a *terminus ante quem* for dating the drawing, since it might be a filial tribute to his father's design for Strasbourg, made at any time after 1419/20.

122A. For Johannes Hültz's contribution see pp. 224–5, and Schock-Werner (1983) 146–57.

123. Wells, *c.* 1220; Salisbury, some time before 1260; Lichfield, *c.* 1280.

123A. The complex history of the west front can be summarized as follows:
1) 1341 the south-west tower and the adjoining sections of the central bay of the façade (its southernmost walls) were begun. By 1350–60 the western bay of the south aisle of the nave had reached vault height and the lower storey of the tower completed. The first and second storey were complete by 1380. The design of the façade at this stage was indebted to Strasbourg, particularly Plan B (harp strung tracery of the second storey).

2) In 1381 the beginning of the demolition of the collegiate church of St John which covered the northern sector of the present façade. In 1398 altar of St Florinus and Lawrence erected in the north nave aisle, third bay from west, indicating that the temporary dividing wall at the second bay, still up by 1380, had been demolished and that the nave was moving westwards on the north side. From *c.*1385 beginning of work on structure and sculpture of central west portal (complete in *c.*1410/15). 1395 first mention of a Liebhart der Mynnaer as architect.

3) *c.*1390–5 at level of the springing points of the central portal it was decided to add the present triangular porch to an originally intended flat portal, and to transfer the figures of the Apostles from the outer jambs of the portal to the central pillar of the porch.

4) 1415 Master Wenzel Roriczer first mentioned. He may have been of Bohemian parentage and his family may have worked on St Bartholomew at Kolín – see Kotrba (1963) – or (more likely) he was Upper Rhenish – see Dietheuer (1961) and (1976). He constructed the lower sections of the ground floor of the north tower, to just above portal height; possibly completed the central portal and its porch (by *c.*1410) and the double spiral staircases and gallery on the inner west wall. He designed the Birth of Christ altar, donated by 1417, and now in the south choir apse. Succeeded by Andreas Engel (1419–56).

5) In *c.*1420 the building stone changes from chalk to a greenish sandstone at just above the level of the north tower portal. By *c.*1430 the whole of the north nave aisle was vaulted, the central section of the façade, including the porch and its sculpture, was complete, and the lowest storey of the north tower (heraldic evidence of 1426 at the level of the tripartite windows) was finished, up to the balustrade. A provisional roof was placed over the three western bays of the nave at triforium height. In 1436 bells installed in south tower. By 1442 (according to dendrochronlogical evidence) the first storey of the north tower, the central section of the façade over the porch and the roof of the nave had been installed, though how much of the detailing of the central, 'rose' section can be attributed to Engel or to his successor, Konrad Roriczer (1456–77) is uncertain. Hubel (1989) attributes the sculpture of this section to Konrad. The latter designed the Albertus Magnus altar baldachine of 1473, now in the north transept.

6) In 1477–95 Matthäus Roriczer, son of Konrad, is *Dombaumeister*. Contrary to most received opinion, his date of 1482 carved on the triforium-like passage beneath the double windows of the central section of the façade does not imply that he was responsible for this section, nor the adjoining storey of the north tower (these sections belong to Engel and Konrad Roriczer). The date refers only to the triforium-like passage on which it is carved, which Matthäus inserted in that year in front of the lower portions of the long-completed central windows. He also built the west gable, the pulpit and the lower parts of the sacrament house, and he began the upper storey of the north tower.

7) **Wolfgang Roriczer, Matthäus's younger brother, succeeded him in 1495.** He completed the sacrament house and the upper storey of the north tower (inscription of 1496) relinquishing the harp-string motifs of the corresponding storey of the south tower (but inserted in the nineteenth century for reasons of symmetry). He also designed the font (1500). He was executed in 1514.

Two medieval plans of the façade are preserved in the city archive. Their dating and function (were they real plans or utopian fantasies?) are still matters of conjecture and disagreement. The first, a two-tower design, which corresponds to the general proportions and dispositions of the actual façade, may date to *c.*1410, and has been attributed to Liebhart der Mynnear. Its decorative vocabulary shows an admixture of influences, from Prague Cathedral, from the west front of St Lawrence at Nuremberg, and from contemporary steeple projects, notably Peter von Prachatitiz's Vienna and Ulrich von Ensingen's Ulm. For a detailed stylistic analysis see Bureš (1986). The second drawing, for a single-towered façade, is now almost universally recognized as an 'ideal' plan, though its dating is controversial, ranging from *c.*1400 – Fuchs (1981) and (1990) and Hubel and Schuller (1995) – to the later 1450s, under Konrad Roriczer. Some of its features – the side portals and the window composition above them, and particularly the triangular porch – reappear in simplified form in the actual façade. Fuchs suggested that the triangular porch was built as a reliquary tribune and pointed to precedents and sources in Boniface VIII's loggia in the Lateran and the westwork of the Frauenkirche in Nuremberg.

For the west front and its drawings see Altmann (1976) 106–9, Hubel and Schuller (1995) 95–150, Fuchs (1990), and Hubel (1989).

124. Max Säume, 'Hinrich von Brunsberg', *Baltische Studien*, N.F. XXVIII (1926) 215. Zaske (1957) and (1980); Lohman (1982).

124A. A chapel is mentioned in 1388. A discussion of the choir, its dating and sources of inspiration, can be found in Clasen (1952) and Zaske (1957) especially 50–1. All the evidence for the building history, and a discussion of the literature, is presented in Mroczko and Arszyński, eds., (1995) vol. 2, 213. Neither they, nor Lohman (1982) 63–87, find any evidence to support Clasen's and Zaske's suggestion that the choir was begun as a hall and changed later to the present basilican form. Zaske (1957) attributes the choir to Brunsberg, but others have seen it as the work of a pupil.

125. The similar arrangements at Albi and Toulouse are the result of later divisions, made in the fifteenth century. By the 'progressive gallery' Frankl is referring to a system used in the choirs of Stargard and of Brunsberg's church in Chojna (see below) and in the choir of St James in Szczecin (Stettin) (another building associated with, but not definitely attributed to, Brunsberg). It consists of full-height in-drawn buttresses whose lower sections contain chapels, and above the chapels a gallery runs through the pierced buttress faces. A similar system is found in the hall choir of St Martin in Amberg. Clasen (1952) 49, suggested the choir of St Mary at Stralsund, begun in 1384, as a possible source for Stargard. Zaske (1957) especially 50–4, and (1980), rejected the idea of Parler influence on Brunsberg's work, tracing his sources exclusively to north-east German *Backsteingotik*. He pointed to the early use of hall choirs with polygonal ambulatories and triradial vaults in St Mary at Frankfurt an der Oder, begun *c.*1350, and St Nicholas in Berlin, in building in 1379. For the Berlin church see Schade (1966). Wochnik (1983) supports the Swabian–Franconian inspiration, that is, the influence of the Parlerian hall choir, behind Frankfurt and the other ambulatoried hall choirs in Brandenburg.

125A. This church, now in north-west Poland, was badly damaged in the Second World War, and is now a ruin. It was begun at the east end in *c.*1390, and the three eastern bays were complete by the consecration in 1407. The Lady Chapel, on the south side of bays 2 and 3, was finished some time before 1440, and the three western bays by 1459. See Mroczko and Arszyński, eds., (1995) vol. 2 46–7. Gruszewski and Widawski (1965) date the start of the work to 1399.

125B. The chronology of St Catherine in Brandenburg is not clear. In 1395 an unspecified disaster struck the old church, and rebuilding was necessary. But a row of indulgences, some of them for building work, starting in 1381 and increasing from 1385, implies that at least preparations for rebuilding had begun earlier. Work under Brunsberg began in the nave, which was complete (apart from the vaults) by 1401, together with the Lady Chapel at least up to its portal height (see the inscription here of 1401, attributing the church to Brunsberg). The Lady Chapel was consecrated in 1434. The choir, built by Heinrich Reinstorp probably to Brunsberg's designs, was completed by 1456. Reinstorp may have also finished the Lady Chapel (also to Brunsberg's plans) and designed and built the gables over the south chapel. The net vault over the central aisle may not reflect Brunsberg's design, see Zaske (1957) 54–5, though Nussbaum (2000) 247, note 592 sees no reason to doubt that it was built to Brunsberg's design. For a full discussion of the architects and building history there is the unpublished Lohman (1982) 14–37, and the short article by Lohman (1996). For the church and its dating see, briefly, Böker (1988) 227.

125C. Zaske (1957) 57–60, 66–7, rejects Parler influence and suggests sources for these typically 'Brunsberg' gables and panels of tracery in the castles of the Teutonic Knights (Lochstedt, Marienburg) and in the eastern gables of Brandenburg and Mecklenburg hall churches (Neubrandenburg, Prenzlau). His arguments, however, are weakened by his mistaken identification of the tracery panels in the cloister of the upper castle at Marienburg as key medieval sources for Brunsberg's exterior buttress tracery. In fact, they are purely nineteenth-century fabrications, reconstructed 1881–93 after the Baroque re-shaping of the cloister under Polish occupation. See Boockmann (1982) plate 49, and Górski (1973) 178, and Torbus (1998) 494.

125D. Zaske (1957) 50 note 11, and p. 71, attributes the town hall of Chojna to Claus Brunsberg, who may have been Hinrich's son. The relevant extensions to this late thirteenth-century town hall belong, it seems, to the mid fifteenth century, and have no documented connexion with any member of the Brunsberg family, see Mroczko and Arszyński, eds., (1995) vol. 2 46. For Tangermünde Town Hall see Kohlmann (1955). Its gables are close to those over the south (Corpus Christi) chapel of St Catherine at Brandenburg, dated after 1434 and attributed to Heinrich Reinstorp.

126. Peter Baldass, 'Hans Stetheimer's wahrer Name', in *Wiener Jahrbuch für Kunstgeschichte*, XIV (1950) 47. Georg Lill's article in Thieme-Becker should be corrected in the light of this later article, but otherwise it gives a good summary of the older literature on the subject: Eberhard Hanfstaengl, *Hans Stetheimer* (Leipzig, 1911); *Inventar von Niederbayern*, XVI (1927). The basic authority on Hans von Burghausen as an historical figure is still Herzog (1958) and (1969). More recently, biographies are provided in Cook (1975) and Nussbaum (1982). A useful survey of the literature is given in Kobler (1985). For a supplement to Herzog's researches into the history of the Stethaimer and von Burghausen family see Liedke (1983–4).

126A. Herzog's (1969) chronology of the nave and choir, much of it based on dendrochronological evidence, still stands. The choir was begun by 1389; the chapel of St Mary Magdalene was up by c.1390. Work had reached the choir window sills by 1392 and the roof levels by 1394/6 (though he wrongly thinks that the choir vaults were finished as late as c.1430 or even 1470). The foundations of the west tower were not laid before 1441, and therefore the west portal, normally dated 1432, must now be put in the 1440s or after. See Kobler, in *Die Parler* (1978) vol. 1 387, who, along with most other scholars, dates the choir vaults to 1398. The design of the nave is undoubtedly by Hans von Burghausen, but some scholars have argued that Hans Krumenauer was the architect of the choir: see Puchta (1968) and (1975), Kobler in *Die Parler* (1978) vol. 1 387, and Cook (1976). Herzog (1969A) 65, doubted this attribution, and the full account of the building by Kurmann and Kurmann-Schwarz (1985) 19–51, convincingly argues for the whole project being von Burghausen's design of c.1385, carefully adhered to by his successors. He substantially agrees with Herzog's dating, though he thinks the choir vaults were up by c.1400, the nave chapels had been completed as far as the two west nave portals by 1445, the tower begun in 1444 and the west portal in the late 1450s. The nave pillars did not reach their full height, and the vaults were not built, until c.1475–80. For a resumé see Kurmann (1996).

126B. The vaults were probably part of Hans von Burghausen's original design. But if not, then their late construction in c.1480 makes it possible that they reflect the influence of the identical net vaults in the comparable hall nave of St Vitus at Český Krumlov (Krumau) (1402–39) in southern Bohemia, or a host of earlier Bohemian examples. See Nussbaum (1983–4) 96–7.

126C. Frankl is here restating the view, exemplified particularly by Gerstenberg (1913), of the hall church as a unified space. In fact, there is little spatial unity between side and central aisles in the nave of St Martin at Landshut, because the pillars are closely spaced, the side aisles are narrow, and the interior is organized around a strong longitudinal west–east axis. See Kurmann and Kurmann-Schwarz (1985) 15, 32–6, 47–8. For a general criticism of the 'ideology' of the German hall church as an *Einheitsraum* see Kunst (1971), and Nussbaum (2000) 157–61. For its origins in German nineteenth-century romanticism see Schenkluhn (1989).

126D. Kurmann and Kurmann-Schwarz (1985) 92–5, dates the style of the portal's tympanum sculpture to the late 1450s/early 1460s, and believes its 1432 inscription is a modern forgery.

126E. This form of arch can already be seen in gables of the triangular porch of the Regensburg single-tower façade plan (c.1400?), and on the inner west façade of the cathedral (c.1410), probably by Wenzel Roriczer. See Hubel and Schuller (1995), plates 104, 112, 114. Fischer (1964) 35, note 58, sees an English source for the motif.

126F. See Dambeck (1957) 15–18. Nussbaum (1982) 153, and (2000) 246, note 569, points out that the vaults were only installed in 1461 and may not reflect the original design. Nussbaum (1983–4) 98–9, discusses the dating and origins of its vault patterns. For the important vaults with double-curved ribs in St Catherine's chapel (1411) and the sacristy (c.1432), perhaps the earliest examples on the continent, see Fehr (1961) 98–9. The origins of the axially placed column of the apse, a hallmark of Hans von Burghausen's work, and an indication of his Bohemian training, are discussed in von Ledebur (1977) (not available to me).

127. It was originally a parish church, and was transferred to the Franciscans only in 1583. See van der Meulen (1957); Fuhrmann (1967) (over-interpretative mathematical analysis); Nussbaum (1983–4) 108ff.

127A. It seems that Hans von Burghausen at first intended to replace the old nave, but it was later decided to retain it, perhaps before his death in 1432, certainly after the choir columns had been shifted eastwards out of axis with the buttress responds, and before the construction of the western responds of the west bay of the choir and the chancel arch. The latter was turned before 1446. Altars in the side chapels were endowed from 1449 onwards and the year 1456 on the fresco of stone masons on the eastern choir pillar on the south side gives a *terminus ante quem* for the vaults. Stephan Krumenauer, Hans's successor, built the high vaults, probably with modifications to the original design. The height of the pillars may also be Krumenauer's decision. The present contrast between the dark nave and the light choir has been enhanced by the Baroque alterations. Originally the nave was lighter and the choir probably darker. See van der Meulen (1957) 52ff, and Nussbaum (1982) 164–71, and (1983–4) 108–16, where the choir is seen as the critical influence on the hospital church at Braunau and the Bavarian group of 'three-pillar' hall churches. Brucher (1990) 144–6, adds nothing new.

127B. See Nussbaum (1983–4) 100–1; and Huttner (1981).

127C. In his epitaph in St Martin at Landshut Hans von Burghausen is credited with an unspecified church in Straubing. In the first edition of this book Frankl followed some authorities in identifying this as the Carmelite church, the choir of which was begun in c.1368/78 and finished in the 1390s. The nave was begun c.1400. Some authorities have argued that this church was not by Hans von Burghausen but (at least as far as the choir is concerned) possibly by Hans Krumenauer, the architect of the choir of Passau cathedral. See Stahleder (1971), and Puchta (1968) and (1975). As far as St Jakob at Straubing is concerned, most scholars attribute it to Hans von Burghausen as the 'Straubing' church of the epitaph, but its chronology is controversial. Cook (1976) 98ff, is alone in arguing that it was one of Hans von Burghausen's *first* works, beginning in c.1395. Puchta (1975) 43, and Liedke (1983/4) put its beginning to after 1415. Dehio, HDK, *Bayern II: Niederbayern*, (1988) 682–3, dates its start to c.1400. By 1423 the choir was useable. For the historical relations (as well as the stylistic) between this church and Augsburg see Puchta (1975) 44–5, and Liedke (1983/4) 11.

128. Cf. Lill in Thieme-Becker, XXXII, 14. Lill's attributions must be treated with caution.

129. For a full analysis of Berne see Mojon (1960). The whole career of Matthäus Ensinger is discussed in Mojon (1967).

130. Martin Coppens, *Thoughts in Stone* (Amsterdam, etc., 1948). See also Coppens (1941). For the exterior sculpture see Zeeuwe and De Vries (1978). The fullest account of the collegiate church can be found in Peeters (1985), a work which provides the basis for Kolman et al., (1997) 202–7, to put together the following chronology:
1) c.1380–c.1400: radiating chapels, outer aisle walls on south side.
2) c.1400–c.1425: free-standing piers of apse and choir.
3) c.1425–c.1445: outer north choir aisle, eastern crossing piers and east wall of transepts; vaulting of choir, under the architect Willem van Boelre from Utrecht.
4) c.1445–c.1460: western crossing piers, transepts (south ahead of north) and first two aisle bays of nave on north and south sides.
5) c.1460–c.1478: vaulting of nave north aisle and south transept porch, under Master Cornelis de Wael (1469–76) from Utrecht.
6) c.1478–c.1497: under Master Alart van Hameel: north elevation of nave.
7) c.1502–17: vaulting of south nave aisles and completion of nave.

Wilson (1990) 242–3, revises this chronology for the completion of the transepts and their façades, 1469–78 (Peeters, pp. 389–91), to a period from c.1430–40 (the design) and 1461 (the completion). He convincingly relates the decorative vocabulary of the south transept façade to the south transept of Prague Cathedral, and to other Parlerian precedents, particularly Ulrich von Ensingen's work at Ulm and Strasbourg.

130A. Frankl is here referring to the Berne drawing of the west front and spire of Strasbourg (Berne, Historisches Museum inv. nr. 1962). Its attribution to Ulrich is still contested, and it may be by his son Matthäus Ensinger. Schock-Werner (1983) 142–5, 291–7 considers that it probably reflects Ulrich's design, but small technical uncertainties suggest that it was a study drawing, perhaps by the young Matthäus. She also suggests that after his father's death in 1419 Matthäus worked at Strasbourg, possibly as a foreman, under Johann Hültz. See above, Chapter 4, Note 122.

130B. For a full discussion of Hültz's spire see Reinhardt (1939) 29–37, and Schock-Werner (1983) 146–57. For the surviving drawings of Hültz's spire in London and Ulm see Koepf (1977) 71–6.

131. *Die Kunstdenkmäler von Bayern, Kreis Oberpfalz*, XVI, *Stadt Amberg* (Munich, 1909). See also Schmidt (1962) and (1977).

132. The west tower rises out of the great pitched roof, but is half embedded in it.

132A. Baldass (1946) attributed the choir to Hans von Burghausen but no firm evidence confirms this. Certainly the hall choir, its in-drawn buttresses and its chapels within them are close to the Franciscan church at Salzburg which may have been its inspiration, see Nussbaum (2000) 173.

133. Cf. the biographies in Thieme-Becker, and also those of the Böblinger

family. For more up-to-date biographies see *Neue Deutsche Biographie* (Berlin, 1953 onwards); for Hans Felber see Gümbel (1911). For Konrad Roriczer see Dietheuer (1961) and (1976). Short biographies on some of these architects can also be found in Turner, ed. (1996).

134. Hans Kun was mentioned as *Kirchenmeister* in 1427, Hans Felber was *Kirchenmeister* at Nördlingen from 1427 to his death in 1439, Konrad Heinzelmann appears there as his foreman in 1429 and remains there until 1438. In 1439 Niclaus Eseler the Elder took over, and the high altar was consecrated in 1451. After much criticism for absences, Eseler relinquished his position in 1461, and in that year Konrad Roriczer first appeared as the new *Werkmeister*. He con-tinued to be involved with the church until at least 1464. He contributed a design for the west tower, and he may have employed as foreman his son Matthäus, and certainly Hans Zanckel, another mason working at Regensburg cathedral. Wilhelm Kreglinger took over as *Kirchenmeister* in 1464, Heinrich Escher (called Kugler) completed the tower in 1481–90 and built all the remaining sections of the choir pillars. Stephan Weyrer vaulted the whole church 1495–1505 according to the designs of Burkhard Engelberg. See Dietheuer (1961) 169ff, Schmidt (1972) and Bischoff (1999) 150ff. The most authoritative account of the church's history, incorporating new archival material, can be found in Schmid (1977). He nicely suggests the church's position at the cross-roads of southern German late Gothic in the fifteenth century, absorbing advanced ideas from Ulm, Lower Bavaria and Lower Austria. The biographies of many of these masons, particularly Hans Felber and Konrad Heinzelmann, were brought to light by the pioneering archival research of Gümbel (1911). See also the good summary by Jansen (1996).

134A. Schultz's (1943) impressive study of the choir laid the foundations of all future work on the late Gothic church. He contended that Konrad Heinzelmann, *Werkmeister*, 1430–55, started work at the east end, with the radiating chapels, and planned four straight bays in the choir and lateral cellular chapels in continuation of those in the apse. Under Konrad Roriczer, *Werkmeister* for 1456–66, and his foremen Hans Pauer (1458–62) and Matthäus Roriczer (1462–6) (Konrad's son), Heinzelmann's scheme for the straight bays of the choir was altered, the bays were reduced to three, and the cellular chapels were given up in favour of wider aisles. Rosemann (1961) proposed an opposite sequence, with Heinzelmann beginning in the straight bays and working eastwards, and laying out the foundations (and perhaps the lower parts) of the apse and radiating chapels by his death. The clerestorey was built under Roriczer, but no substantial changes to Heinzelmann's plans were made. Rosemann's position found some support in Funk's and Linke's (1977) analysis of the geometry of the ground plan, which suggested that a three-bay choir was intended from the start. Stolz (1977) did not exclude a change of plan of the kind proposed by Schulz, but confirmed that the straight bays were substantially complete in the mid-1450s (some lower windows of their aisles were glazed in 1456/7), and therefore must be attributed to Heinzelmann and not his successors. Under Jacob Grimm, who took over in 1466, the central aisle vault was built. Choir altars were consecrated in 1472, the great west gable was going up in 1476, and the whole choir was complete in 1477. See also Shelby (1977) 8–14. Klein (1990) accepts the Schulz change of plan, but attributes it to Heinzelmann, and locates its origins in political, financial and liturgical interests. Klein's analysis of the role of the urban patriciate in the shaping of the choir is amplified in the masterly study of artistic patronage at St Lorenz by Schleif (1990). For the relation of altars, sculpture and space in the choir see Crossley (1998).

135. On Dinkelsbühl, cf. *Die Kunstdenkmäler von Bayern*, IV, *Mittelfranken* (Munich, 1931). See also Lergen (1940) (unavailable to me) and Helmberger (1984) and (1988).

135A. The fullest work on the Ingolstadt church is by Fischer (1974), where the parallels with St Ouen are discussed on p. 334, and p. 353, note 53.

136. *Die Kunstdenkmäler der Provinz Sachsen, Die Stadt Erfurt* (Burg, 1929), 135. See also Mertens (1975) and Lehmann and Schubert (1991) 22–3. The aisles are in fact wider than the central vessel.

137. These capitals are blocks. They are certainly undecorated, but their carefully moulded profiles do not suggest unfinished work. The whole design of the pillars, from bases to abaci, is treated with a deliberate austerity, see Lehmann and Schubert (1991) plates 73, 74, 79, 80.

138. *Die Kunstdenkmäler des K. Bayern, Niederbayern*, I (Munich, 1912). See also Dambeck (1957) 107. The main difference between this church and Hans von Burghausen's churches is its vaulting, especially in the central aisle. Liedke (1983/4) 52–4, attributes the church, on stylistic grounds, to Stefan Purghauser, son of Hans von Burghausen.

138A. The tall inner chapels developed out of Hans von Burghausen's in-drawn buttresses (hospital church Landshut) some divided by low chapels (Franciscan church, Salzburg), and from the cellular chapels used by Stephan Krumenauer in his parish church in Braunau. See Büchner (1964) especially 20–30.

138B. Since the foundation stone of the church was laid in 1468 and Jorg went to Augsburg and Ulm in 1469 it is doubtful whether his journey had any

influence on the planning of the choir. Besides, the easternmost choir bay does not 'penetrate' the ambulatory in the way it does in Augsburg or St Lamprecht or Nördlingen, since the thicker arcade arches do not continue across the ambulatory to join with the responds of the easternmost chapel. In fact, the solution in Munich is much closer to the choir of St Jacob in Straubing (begun *c.*1400–10?). In a comprehensive analysis of Jorg von Halspach's design, Kurmann (1994) has shown that the Munich church, as the mausoleum for the Munich branch of the Wittelsbach dukes, and the beneficiary of Duke Sigismund's and Albrecht IV's patronage, consciously modelled itself on the brick hall churches in the other three Wittelsbach capitals: Straubing, Landshut and Ingolstadt. The detailed building history of the church is set out in Pfister and Ramisch (1983) and (1987), and Altmann (1994). The legend of the devil may only go back to the seventeenth century, when a Baroque high altar made all windows invisible, see Kurmann (1994) 42, note 20.

139. Frankl, 'The Early Works of Erasmus Grasser', *The Art Quarterly*, V (1942) 242.

139A. The Wittelsbach dukes would have objected to Frankl's emphasis on the patronage of the Munich middle classes, and the apparently subordinate role of the dukes of Bavaria. Even though the main responsibility for building lay with the town council, the Wittelsbachs were closely involved in the construction. Duke Sigismund laid the foundation stone and envisaged the new church as his mausoleum, inspired no doubt by the presence since 1322 of the grave of Beatrix, wife of Ludwig the Bavarian, in the old church. The completion of so large a structure in twenty years (the vaults were probably going up 1483–7, and the towers were completed up to and including the belfry in 1487) must have owed something to Wittelsbach generosity. See Pfister and Ramisch (1983) 54–5; Suckale (1993) 27, 140, 147, 184, 186, 195, 234; and above, Note 138B.

140. There is a detailed description and an illustration in Hans Tietze, *Die Denkmale des Stiftes Nonnberg in Salzburg (Österreichische Kunsttopographie*, VII) (Vienna, 1911) 23, 24. For the history of this church and its position in the so-called Melk reform, see Wagner-Rieger (1967) 386–7, and Brucher (1990) 288–9. The crypt was begun under Master Sigmund Maurer in 1463 and was consecrated, with the choir above, in 1475. The nave begun in 1485 under a Master Hans (who died in 1493). From 1493–1503 Wolfgang Wiesinger was in charge of the work, the south portal under construction in 1497–9 and the nave vault completed according to his designs in 1506/7.

141. The term *Deutsche Sondergotik* is the title of a book by Kurt Gerstenberg (Munich, 1913), which is full of excellent observations and ideas. Gerstenberg's term was already criticized for its nationalist implications by, among others, Jantzen (1962) 151ff, and Fischer (1964) 7, note 1. For a general discussion of the meaning of the term 'Late Gothic' see Białostocki (1966). For the impact of Gerstenberg's concept on German definitions of Late Gothic in the Empire see Nussbaum (2000) 136–9.

142. Interior view and plan in Lasteyrie, *op. cit.* I, 172 and 200. Caudebec is near Rouen; the building was not finished until the beginning of the sixteenth century. Cf. *Restauration de la flèche de Caudebec 1883–1886* (Rouen, 1888) (anonymous), which has good illustrations of the exterior.

See also Sanfaçon (1971) 28–30, 160, 173–4, Thiebaut (1975) 8, Bottineau-Fuchs in: Baylé, dir., (1997) vol. 2 143–9. Steinke's doctoral thesis (1982), was unfortunately not available to me. Work began on the present church in 1426. Because it had to incorporate two earlier structures, the south tower of 1382, and the north portal (both by the architect Robinchon Vernier) the work started in the nave, perhaps in the third bay from the west (adjacent to the south tower). There are indications at the join between the last chapel of the straight bays on the north side and the beginning of the radiating chapels that an earlier architect had intended a smaller chevet. In *c.*1450 Guillaume le Tellier took over the building until his death in 1484. His epitaph credits him with the chapels and the vaults of the third bay from the west. Clearly the church is indebted to the Late Gothic of Rouen: Le Tellier's choir apse, with its two diagonal sides and its axial pillar, and the three-sided, convex, western façade, are based on Saint-Maclou; while the pendant keystone in the easternmost chapel (the Lady Chapel) is an echo of the south transept porch (the so-called Marmosets portal) of Saint-Ouen. The octagon storey and spire of the south steeple were begun in 1491. The two westernmost bays of the nave and the portal storey of the west façade were begun in 1523, but the sections of the façade above the portals were not finished until the very late sixteenth century. The geometry of the kind of two-sided apse employed first at Saint-Maclou and later at Caudebec is discussed by Neagley (1992) passim, and (1998) 48–54, 94–5. In her (1992) study she admitted to some influence from German – specifically Parlerian – axial apse piers at Saint-Maclou (e.g. St Bartholomew's at Kolín, and the hospital chuch at Landshut) but in her (1998) book she attributes the apse solely to the ingenuity and structural logic of its designer-architect, Pierre Robin. Certainly Saint-Maclou's apse influenced not only Caudebec but the axial pillars in the apses of Saint-Pierre at Caen, Saint-Paul at Le Neubourg, and Saint-Germain at Argentan. See also below, Chapter 4, Notes 143, 186.

143. Plan in Lasteyrie, *op. cit.* I, 213; *C.A.*, LXXXIX (1927) 126.
See also Bottineau-Fuchs, in: Baylé, dir., (1997) vol. 1 323–5, and especially Neagley (1988) (1992) and (1998) who provides the best analysis of the history and stylistic affiliations of the church. She isolates the following sequence of construction:
1) **1432–7**. Decision taken to rebuild the thirteenth-century parish church. In 1436–7, Pierre Robin, master of the King's works for Charles VI and of Notre-Dame in Paris, was paid a large sum for, among other services, a parchment in which the church 'is drawn completely'. This, according to Neagley, suggests that Pierre was primarily an architect designer (he vanished from Rouen after this date) who must have left a comprehensive and precise set of drawings of the church, which, partly at the insistence of the church treasurers (many of them drawn from the dominant merchant families of the parish) were faithfully followed over the next half century by the executant architects and *appareilleurs* who succeeded him. Foundations of choir. Lower courses of the radiating chapels and apse. Chapels in first straight bays of choir up to summit of arches.
2) **1437–50**. Primarily under the architect Simon le Noir. Some radiating chapels vaulted, others completed only up to vault springing. Upper parts of choir, which, however, remained unvaulted in 1446. Thirteenth-century nave still used for services. In 1448 land purchases for new transepts and nave.
3) **1450–60**. Much of this phase under the architect Jehan Chauvin (who takes over the lodge in 1454). Accelerating construction after return of Rouen to Charles VII in 1449. Generous funding from parishioners in 1448, and indulgences in 1452. Completion of radiating chapels and vaulting of choir; construction of transepts to just below rose level; setting out of nave foundations (?).
4) **1460–90**. Much of this phase under the architect Ambroise Harel (first recorded as working on Saint-Maclou in 1467). Completion of transepts. 1465 completion of some nave chapels on south side. 1476–9 nave roofing. 1487 donation of tracery for the west rose, which implies the completion of most of the nave high vaults.
5) **1490–1521**. Lantern tower begun under Jacques Le Roux (mentioned as master of Saint-Maclou in 1492) and Jehan Le Boucher (latter mentioned as master mason of the church in 1508). Completion of lantern under Pierre Gregoire in 1514, and construction of its wooden spire in 1517. Final dedication of the church in 1521.
Neagley points out that Saint-Maclou differs strongly from the contemporary Flamboyant architecture of Rouen practiced by Jean de Bayeux, Jenson Salvart and Alexandre de Berneval in the cathedral and Saint-Ouen, Chapter 3, Note 121 and Chapter 4, Note 111. Its flat-nosed fillet mouldings, concave pier socles, capital-less arcades and fluid tracery are closer to contemporary churches in the Norman Vexin; while the design of its north transept façade, western porch, lantern tower and interior elevation looks back to the much older Rayonnant additions to the cathedral, probably in a spirit of nostalgia on the part of the church's merchant patrons for the achievements of Rouennais architecture before the outbreak of the Hundred Years War. Saint-Maclou's new style had a profound and immediate impact on Flamboyant architecture in Rouen and Normandy up to the early sixteenth century. Many of the leading architects of late Flamboyant architecture in Rouen made their first appearance at Saint-Maclou (e.g. Ambroise Harel, Guillaume Pontifs, Jacques Le Roux). See above, Chapter 4, Note 142, and below, Notes 148, 186.

144. J. B. Russon and D. Duret, *La cathédrale de Nantes* (Savenay, 1933). The long history of Nantes, the only comprehensive rebuilding undertaken at any French cathedral in the fifteenth century, is analysed in Leniaud *et al.* (1991). A number of phases can be isolated:
1) *c.*1434–*c.*1470. Foundation stone laid on 14 April 1434 by Duke Jean V of Brittany and Bishop Jean de Malestroit (1417–43). West façade and tower bay. South aisle of nave and its cellular chapels, and south arcade pillars, whose bases suggest a knowledge of the pillar bases of the choir of Mont-Saint-Michel, begun after 1444. Arms of Duke Jean (died 1442) in staircase to balcony above the (ducal) portal on the south side of the southern tower bay. Vaults in the belfry of that tower with arms of Bishop Guillaume de Malestroit (1443–62). Triforium of tower bay to an earlier, and different design (flamboyant, reticulated tracery) than in the nave proper. 1482, mention of bronze decoration for the doors of the central portal.
2) *c.*1470–*c.*1490. Nave north aisle and its chapels, completed by 1485 or a little thereafter. West wall of north transept and north-west crossing pier probably up to capital height.
3) *c.*1500–16. Installation of glass in great west window in 1498, as a gift of Queen Anne. 1500 vaulting of first bay of the nave. From 1508 to 1516, financially supported by Bishop Guillaume Guegen, directed by the architect Jacques Drouet, the eastern bay of the south aisle of the nave, and its chapel, was completed and vaulted, and the south transept begun, finishing most of the upper parts of its western wall by 1519/20.
4) **Post-medieval work:**
*c.*1626–30 completion of nave high vaulting (four eastern bays) and construction of nave flyers.

1631–7 or later, completion of south transept.
1840–91. Rest of north transept and the choir.

145. Amédée Charles Léon Boinet, *Les richesses d'art etc.* (Paris, 1910) 102. See Sanfaçon (1971) 99–100, 105, 115, also Lesort and Verlet (1974). The west porch is attributed to Jean Gaussel and dated to the 1430s. Murray (1989) 137, note 79, thinks the central bays of the porch were added at a time closer to 1500; they certainly show a vocabulary close to that of Martin Chambiges. Gaussel's work may also include the nave and its aisles, the transept and north chapels of the nave.

146. *C.A.*, LXXX (1916) 233; and Lucien Bégule, *Les vitraux etc.* (Paris, 1911), which also has illustrations of the architecture. See also Brosse, ed., (1966) vol. IIB 3–4.

146A. These dates for the later parts of the choir are based on Freigang (1992) 176. Undulating profiles already, however, distinguish the piers in the apse and first straight bays of the choir, built after 1277. For the growth of these undulating and simplified pier forms in non-mainstream French architecture of the thirteenth century see Davis (1984) 882, and note 60.

147. There is a detailed analysis in G. Hoeltje, *Zeitliche und begriffliche Abgrenzung der Spätgotik* (Diss. Halle a. S., 1930) 108. See also Brosse, ed., (1967) vol. III D 61–3, and Sanfaçon (1971) 85–7, and the unpublished research on the church by Mayra Vanessa Rodríguez. Rodríguez establishes the following sequence of construction:
Campaign one, *c.*1429–49: Construction began, almost certainly with the support of the newly crowned Charles VII, on the four eastern nave bays (preserving the fourteenth-century west façade of the old church which formed their western limit). Lower half of north transept façade and lower courses of eastern crossing piers.
Campaign two, *c.*1449–75: First securely documented donations from Charles VII, extending into the mid-1480s. Chevet, vaulting of north transept; building of south transept.
Campaign three, *c.*1482–5. Demolition of the old façade, three western bays of the nave, new west façade.
Rodriguez established that most of the funding of the church came from interventions by Charles VII rather than his son, Louis XI; although Louis's generosity was itself remarkable (he gave a total of 41, 264 livres tournois). Much of this money may have been spent on the canons' domestic quarters. In 1467 Louis XI promoted the college to the status of a royal chapel, marked by the donation of a relic from the Sainte-Chapelle in Paris. In 1471 he also chose the church as his mausoleum. Rodriguez finds the models for Cléry's austere style not in Paris (as earlier research has located them) but in local Orléanais architecture going back to the twelfth century. I would like to thank Dr Rodríguez for kindly sending me unpublished material from her thesis.

148. C. H. Bernard, *Le Mont Saint-Michel, P.M.* (Paris, n.d.). See also Germain Bazin, *Le Mont Saint-Michel* (Paris, 1933), and André Ludois (pseudonym for Georges Monmarché), *Le Mont Saint-Michel* (Paris, 1949), which has good illustrations. Vallery-Radot's (1966) remarks on the fifteenth-century choir are useful, even if only in the context of a study devoted to its Norman predecessor. After the collapse of the old choir in 1421, down to 'the stalls of the choir', work proceeded in three campaigns:
1) **1446–52**, under Cardinal d'Estouteville, first 'abbé commendataire' of Mont-Saint-Michel. Lower parts of choir, including radiating chapels, ambulatory, aisle walls and free-standing pillars up to springing of vaults.
2) **1499–1510**, under Abbot Guillaume de Lamps. Vaulting of aisles, chapels and ambulatory and construction up to base of clerestory.
3) **1513–23**, under Abbot Jean de Lamps, clerestory, high vault and buttresses.
The elevation, with its multi-based piers, capital-less arcades and tall triforium articulated with a lower arcade and framed with continuous mouldings from the clerestory, is a follower of Saint-Maclou at Rouen. See Neagley (1998) 94–5.

148A. Villes (1977a) isolates a number of phases in the building of the façade:
1) *c.*1470 onwards: portal storey.
2) **first storey** of west towers and horizontal wall strip above the portals.
3) *c.*1480/85 onwards: Openwork balustrade above all three portals; gables over portals; rose window; completion of first and second stories of north tower up to its pinnacles. Many of the elements of this phase (the rose, the large gables, the horizontal divisions in the form of openwork tracery balustrades, made up of repeating reticulated units) show the influence of the second phase of the façade of Toul Cathedral, dated *c.*1480–5.
4) **Up to 1509**. Completion of south steeple, including its spire; triple gables over rose storey, termination of north steeple.

149. The Heathen Towers on the cathedral of St Stephen in Vienna. They are intended as a gallery, not as crowns. These spires were placed on the old twelfth-century towers in the fifteenth century, see Zykan (1981) 30. For a fruitless attempt to derive this 'crow's nest' motif from Netherlandish town halls see Paatz (1967) 75–6.

150. The distance between Châlons-sur-Marne and Strasbourg is about 160 miles. Villes (1977a) 851, suggests, more plausibly, the inspiration of the spire

of the 'Mutte' tower at Metz cathedral, of 1478–82. Villes also analyses the style and chronolgy of the façade in detail, though dates have to be based on stylistic evidence alone. The real inspiration for the large openwork gable, the rose and the balustrade above all three portals at l'Epine is the west façade of Toul, where these elements date from 1480–5. See also above, Chapter 4, Notes 115 and 148a, and Note 151 below.

151. Illustrated in Benoist, Luc, *Notre-Dame-de-L'Epine, P.M.* (Paris, 1933) 11. See now Villes (1977b) and (1983). For the comparison with Notre-Dame de l'Epine see Villes (1977a) 825–6, and above, Chapter 4, Notes 115 and 148A. Villes isolates two campaigns at the west end of Toul:

1) **1460–c.1475**. Façade portal storey up to level of big string course just above central portal, and first west bay of nave up to aisle height. Architect of the façade at its inception is Tristan d'Hâttonchâtel, though he was soon succeeded by Jacquemin de Lenoncourt, who executed his projects.

2) **1475–96/1500**. Completion of westernmost nave bay and building of the next two bays to its east (thus joining the façade, and its supporting nave bay immediately to its east, to the fourteenth-century nave), and the vaulting of all of them. c.1480/5 continuation of the façade from the first string course upwards, with changes to the buttress structure. Southern belfry constructed in 1500.

152. G. Clanché, *Guide-expresse à la cathédrale de Toul* (Nancy, 1918) 22; also *C.A.*, XCVII (1934) 229ff. See Villes (1977b) 53.

153. See Marot (1933). It is by no means certain that Jacquemin de Lenoncourt built the whole façade, though the lower stories of the towers do not look much earlier than the upper. The epitaph of Thierry Surlier, commander of the order of St Anthony, to which the church belonged, states that he built and completed the nave, the choir screen, the tower, the portal, the cloister and the communal cellar. Sulier died in 1469. In 1468 an agreement was entered into between Thierry Surlier and an unknown architect to build (or complete?) a tower. The arms of Surlier on the western gable, as well as an inscription on the gable mentioning Abbot Benoît de Montferrant (1459–71) suggests that the upper parts of the façade and the construction of the octagonal stages of the towers date from the 1460s. An ordinance of 1460 issued at Toul Cathedral mentions masters Jacquemin de Lenoncourt and Mengin Chemot de Vicherey as the authors of the 'clocher' at Saint-Martin at Pont-à-Mousson. See also Burnand (1989) 265–8.

154. See Morris (1997).

155. Illustrated in Lasteyrie, *op. cit.* II, 29. It has low, dark chapels attached to the aisles, like southern French aisleless churches. The date appears in *B.M.*, VI (1840) 380. The choir was restored in 1676. See also Brosse, ed., (1967) vol. IIIC 33, where the dates of 1460–77 are given. The tower porch and sacristy were built under Abbé Mathurin Joubert de la Bastide (1494–1514). The church was radically rebuilt in the later seventeenth century by François Ledue, so any discussion of its original medieval appearance has to proceed with caution.

156. Nenno (1988) 89, 131, who identifies twenty-seven churches that are 'pure' halls, i.e. have aisles of equal height, and another twenty-two which have slightly higher central vessels (*Stufenhalle*). See also Nenno's (1988a) study of Les Grandes Chapelles in southern Champagne.

157. For the Pont-à-Mousson and the Saint-Mihiel choirs see Burnand (1989) 269–71 and 292–5 respectively.

157A. See Torres Balbás (1952) 314ff, and de Azcárate (1953) 119ff.

158. F. Adama von Scheltema, *Die Kunst der Vorzeit* (Stuttgart, 1950) 118ff.; Victor Chapot, *La colonne torse etc.* (Paris, 1907), with observations on the central altar; F. Mayenne, three articles in *Le Bulletin des Musées etc.* (Brussels, 1932 and 1933), on the subject of the Porticus of Apamea in Syria; Picco Marconi, *Verona romana* (Bergamo, 1937) 55, on the subject of the Porta Borsari, c.260–8. There is a single thirteenth-century spiral column in the chapter house at Silvacane, *C.A.*, XCV (1933) 138. (Aubert, *L'arch. cist.*, II, 60.) There are countless examples in the work of the Cosmati and in Italian church doorways. This form is repeated in Raphael's tapestry 'The Healing of the Lame', in Giulio Romano's Cavallerizza in the Palazzo Ducale at Mantua, which dates from 1540, in Bernini's Tabernacle in St Peter's in Rome, and so on. The Christian prototypes for the spiral or 'Solomonic' column are those in the crypt of Old St Peter's in Rome. For its early diffusion in the West see Rosenbaum (1955); for its impact on English Romanesque see Fernie (1977).

159. At Palma, the contour, which is sometimes visible, lies on a vertical plane. At Braunschweig, parts of it move backwards from the nearest point, and, although it gives an optical illusion of continuity, it actually is a wave moving upwards, to and fro – a refinement which is automatically produced if rolls or shafts are twisted round a column.

159A. For the derivation of these columns from local Romanesque examples (e.g. the cloister at Königslutter), and the possible influence of this aisle on the architect Arnold von Westfalen, see Radová-Štiková (1974) and (1988). She also noted another Spanish parallel: the spiral choir pillars of Santiago de Villena, c.1500. Böker (1987) sees the aisle as a 'hall of fame' for the dukes of Braunschweig, in particular its patron Duke Wilhelm the Elder. His attempt to date its beginning to the 1450s is not convincing.

160. Illustrated in F. Mader, *Die Kunstdenkmäler von Niederbayern*, XVI, *Stadt Landshut* (Munich, 1927) figure 33. See Kurmann and Kurmann-Schwarz (1985) 96–7. She dated the portal sculpture of this porch to the 1450s, but the pinnacles could be later additions to the porch.

161. See Koepf (1977) 109–13.

162. K. T. Parker, *Alsatian Drawings etc.* (London, 1928) plate II/5.

163. Orlando Grosso, *Genova* (Bergamo, 1926) 39.

164. Frankl, *Der Glasmaler Peter Hemmel von Andlau* (Berlin, 1956). At Tübingen, Duke Eberhard the Bearded ordered him to put a framework of palm-leaves round his portrait, as a reminder of the patron's pilgrimage to Jerusalem, that is, the earthly Jerusalem. It is not known whether this was also an allusion to the Heavenly Jerusalem, but on no account should every framework of branches or tree-trunks be regarded as a symbol of the Heavenly Jerusalem or of paradise. There were, of course, trees in paradise (Moses 1, 2:9), but in the Heavenly Jerusalem there was only a single tree (Revelation 22:2).

164A. Full accounts of the origins and growth of this 'vegetal' Late Gothic can be found in Braun-Reichenbacher (1966) and Börsch-Supan (1967). The appearance of vegetal forms in vaults, painted and sculpted, is fully discussed by Büchner (1967). The first serious symbolic interpretation (the church as the Virgin's *hortus conclusus*) was advanced by Oettinger (1962). Kutzner (1980) set these 'natural' forms againsts the background of theological and devotional trends in fifteenth-century Germany, finding particular connexions with sermons on the dedication of churches. However, Horie's incisive study (1998) of German dedication sermons finds no references in them to vegetal imagery. Crossley (1993) saw the phenomenon as a manifestation of contemporary German literary humanism. All attempts to find a single, guiding meaning behind such forms are probably misplaced.

164B. The continuation of the south transept at Sens is the first documented work of the architect Martin Chambiges. For his career, and the 'Chambiges school', see two doctoral dissertations: Nelson (1973) and Murray (1973). A more concise discussion is given in Murray (1987) 101–9, and (1989) 134–42. For a Parisian prototype of the Sens south portal, perhaps designed by Chambiges before 1490 see Nelson (1974).

165. Cf., for example, Joseph Neuwirth, *Prag* (Leipzig, 1912) 40. Neuwirth had an outstanding knowledge of the Gothic style, but is representative of his whole generation in his lack of understanding of the Late Gothic style.

165A. See now Fehr (1961) 21–3, and Kotrba (1972), who attributed the design and the structure of the oratory to Benedict Ried, but its decorative details to Hanns Spiess of Frankfurt, an attribution followed by all later authorities.

165B. See Mojon (1960) 14, 32, 55f, 86.

165C. Still the best account of the history of double-curved ribs in Central Europe is by Fehr (1961) especially 94–118. For the Basel cloister see Fischer (1962) 61–2, who tentatively attributed the vault to Johannes Dotzinger; and Julier (1978) 154–82, who thinks a more likely candidate is Jodok Dotzinger, the author of the Strasbourg font of 1453.

165D. See Fehr (1961) especially 25–33; also Kotrba (1968) and Hořejší (1973). For the construction and geometry of the vault see Muk (1977).

166. The Romanesque two-naved building had no influence on the Late Gothic one. See the reconstructed plan in M. Hartig, *Das Benediktiner Reichsstift Sankt Ulrich und Afra etc.* (Augsburg, 1923) plate 73. See also Lieb (1984), and Bischoff (1999), 220, who notes that he was mentioned only as *parlier* (warden) at the church in 1477.

167. Dehio overlooked this and, in his *Handbuch d. d. K.*, III (1925) 42, he wrote of the vault at Augsburg that it was 'a petty bourgeois design' ('spiess-bürgerlich'), but, on p. 164, he wrote of the same pattern of the vault at Gmünd: 'The beautiful divisions of the net-vault . . .'. This amusing inconsistency does not of course reduce our gratefulness for his life work.

168. He was active at Heilbronn, Ulm, Bozen, Nördlingen, and Berne. See Lieb (1954), and Koepf (1958) 33–4, 84, and (1959). For Engelberg's contribution to the choir of Freiburg im Breisgau see Julier (1978) 136ff. The date of c.1507 for the Schwäbisch Gmünd nave vault is given by Kissling in vol. 1, *Die Parler*, p. 320, who attributes it to Engelberg. Bischoff (1999) 356, sees it as a product of the direct influence of the Augsburg Lodge, perhaps the work of a colleague or pupil of Engelberg.

169. The original effect has been weakened by the straight screen, which dates from the beginning of the seventeenth century. Although an elective affinity has rightly been observed between the Gothic style and the Baroque, here the two styles are almost intolerably incompatible. For the Simpertus arch (which served as the abbot's gallery) and its influence in south-west Germany see Fischer (1966) especially 28 and notes 58–63 and Bischoff (1999) 221, 340ff. It was begun in c.1493 and finished in 1496.

169A. For Jakob von Landshut see Fischer (1962) 149–50, Julier (1978) 151, 223, and note 387. Schock-Werner (1983) 173–4, 200–13, discusses his training in Bavaria and the Middle Rhine. He seems to have come to Strasbourg via Worms. Toursel-Harster (1976) was not available to me.

170. The church was founded in 1481 with the encouragement of King René II of Anjou, to stimulate the pilgrimage to St Nicholas. Its three-apsidal choir and certain details of the central choir elevation (the Remois passages) can be considered Late Gothic versions of Toul cathedral. Frankl's description of the transepts as 'double-naved' is strictly correct but misleading. In effect, the pillars of the arcades are continued across the transept arms to form one pillar in front of each transept opening, each pillar rising, hall-like, to the full height of the transept. The system recalls the transepts of the earlier Cistercian church at Doberan or of Strasbourg Cathedral. André (1933) dated the start of the work to 1481, and noted the death of the first master of the fabric in 1495. The transepts were, he suggested, finished in 1508, and most of the central vessel by 1514. Some windows in the north aisle of the nave were glazed in 1518. Work then slowed down. The staircase tower of the north portal has inscribed 1543 at its summit, while the window of the west façade has glass dating 1539–44. Revenues were still being directed to the west façade in 1549, 1550 and 1551. A Master Robin is mentioned in 1505, and a Master Hanns de Meneuvre in 1518. Burnand (1989) 296–308, considers that the choir, the beginnings of the transept, and the sacristies were begun in 1481 and finished in 1515, while the nave and the façade were constructed slowly between 1515 and 1560.

170A. Though there are closer analogies in the capitals and spiral piers of Saint-Gervais-et-Saint-Protais at Gisors (mid-fifteenth century). See Brosse (1968) vol. IVB 79.

171. Spiral piers are not specifically German. Cf., for example, the pier supporting the spiral staircase in the Archbishop's Palace at Rouen (Marburg photograph 162806), the spiral columns in the north transept of the cathedral at Senlis (built between 1518 and 1525 by Pierre Chambiges the elder and Jean Dizieult, neither of whom had German ancestry), the spiral columns of the southeastern crossing pier in the cathedral at Evreux (Marburg photograph 169961), and many others.

172. The history of the construction of this building, which has no unity, but is extremely attractive, is given in *C.A.*, CV (1947) 136. See also Sanfaçon (1971) 90–7.

172A. Frankl's reading of this 'two-aisled space' at St Nicholas-du-Port is curious. He is describing the transepts from a north–south direction, as if they formed a semi-independent, double-aisled 'cross-space' placed against the east–west movement of the church. In reality, the transepts do not visually 'join' in this north–south way; quite the reverse, the tall pillars which stand across their openings block off each transept arm. See above, Note 170.

173. Ernst Gall, *Die Marienkirche zu Danzig* (*Deutsche Bauten*, VI) (Burg, 1926). The building history of this, the largest of the *Backsteingotik* hall churches, and its stylistic position in the history of north German Gothic, have been clarified by Drost (1963) and Pilecka (1989) and (1990).

1) **1343** foundation of a basilica (on the model of Vistulan Cistercian churches such as Oliwa or Pelplin, and of Baltic basilicas, such as St Catherine, Lübeck), possibly with a chevet on the model of St Mary Lübeck. Single large west tower on Flemish model.

2) *c.***1379–1447**, present hall choir and transepts to design of Master Ungeradin (active 1379–1410), who, according to Pilecka, probably determined the design of the whole church, including the projected hall nave.

3) **1459–65** completion of upper stories of west tower.

4) **1484–96** rebuilding of the fourteenth-century basilican nave into a three-aisled hall by Master Michael and later Hans Brand.

5) **1498–1502**, the whole church vaulted under Master Heinrich Hetzel.

See also the useful Kaplan (1974) 16–23, and for a resumé of the literature and building history, Mroczko and Arszyński, eds., (1995) vol. 2 73–5.

173A. '*Vielbildigkeit*'; see Note 14D to Chapter 2.

173B. These facetted vaults, known as 'diamond', 'crystal', or 'cell' vaults, were invented, or first used, by Arnold von Westfalen in the Albrechtsburg Castle at Meissen in the 1470s. They quickly spread to Bohemia, Silesia, southern Poland and Prussia. The earliest examples in Prussia are in Gdansk (Danzig), in the northern walk of the cloister of the Franciscan monastery of the Holy Trinity ('*c.*1495–1500') and in St Mary's church (nave). See Radová-Štiková (1958) and (1974) (where Spanish examples, earlier than Meissen, are cited), as well as Radoví (1960), Brykowska (1965), Kaplan (1974) 87–104, and Meuche (1972) 56–66, 134–8. For St Catherine's church in Gdańsk see Mroczko and Arszyński, eds. (1995) vol. 2, 75.

174. *Beschreibende Darstellung etc. des Königreichs Sachsen*, Heft III (Dresden, 1884) plan p. 15; interior with Tulpenkanzel, plate after p. 34. Freiberg is the first of the galleried hall churches of Upper Saxony. See Magirius (1993). For the functions and symbolism of its gallery see Meuche (1972a).

174A. For the iconography of this extraordinary pulpit, with its reference to Old Testament prophets (possibly the dream of Nebuchadnezzar), to the Doctors of the Church, and to mining, see Kalden-Rosenfeld (1992), and also Magirius (1993) 38–42.

175. The counterpart of the Tour de Beurre on the north side, the Tour Saint-Romain, was begun in the 1150s. The upper stories, built between 1468

and 70, were by Guillaume Pontifs, who first appears as an ordinary mason working on Saint-Maclou in 1444. Pontifs submitted a drawing for the Tour de Beurre in 1485, but construction only started two years later, and in 1488 the chapter criticized him for his lack of supervision of the work. By his death in 1496 it had not been completed. Under his successor Jacques Le Roux (architect of the cathedral 1496–1508) progress on the tower was hindered by arguments between architect and Chapter over the final shape of the tower's termination, by the indecisiveness of the Chapter over what it wanted (initially the Chapter required Le Roux to submit two drawings, one with, and one without a spire), and by lengthy consultations with all interested parties, including Rouen citizens. In 1504 work had not yet begun, but by 1507 construction had reached the top of the present octagonal crown. There is no indication that a spire was intended in the final stages, as Frankl implies. Pontifs's style in the Tour Saint-Romain and the ground floor of the Tour de Beurre is still indebted to his knowledge of Saint-Maclou, but the richer and more densely-textured vocabulary he developed in the higher parts of the Tour de Beurre, with large nodding ogees, is not easily distinguished from the elaborate curvilinear of his successor, Jacques Le Roux. Structural failures in the west bays of the nave, evident from 1503, caused Jacques to turn his attention to the strengthening and remodelling of the central section of the façade. In January 1508 he and his nephew Roullant Le Roux exhibited their plans for the new central portal in the Hotel de Ville. On 8 February Roullant Le Roux took over the workshop, and the portal was begun in 1509 with the financial support of Archbishop George I d'Amboise. By 1512 work must have reached the upper parts of the central bay, including the portal's gable and the gallery behind it (the *viri Galilei*) because in that year the Chapter urged Roullant to speed up construction, even if it meant simplifying the decoration and sculpture in the upper sections. The installation of doors in the west portal in 1514 suggest the portal's completion, and in the same year Roullant submitted a design for the upper sections of the portal (*pinnaculum*). The new rose window, which replaced one of 1370 by Jehan Perier, belongs to this campaign. Fire in the central tower in 1514 led to this remodelling and heightening by Roullant, who intended to crown it with a stone spire (not the wooden one which was constructed in 1542 and was destroyed in the fire of 1822). See Mallinne (1952), Lanfry (1963), Bottineau-Fuchs (1986) and Bottineau-Fuchs in: Baylé, dir. (1997) vol. I 315–19. See also the articles on the Le Roux masons by Neagley (1996), and the full accounts of all these architects' work in Neagley (1998) 92–4, 106–7.

176. *C.A.*, IC (1937) 72. Also Sanfaçon (1971).

177. The crossing vault which was built after the collapse of 1539 is completely pierced, in the form of a transparent star divided into deltoid panels.

There is still, as far as I know, no monograph on the great fifteenth-century Burgalese architects, Simon of Cologne (Simon de Colonia) or his father Juan. For a review of Simon's work see Chueca Goitía (1965), and for a fuller discussion of the chapel and its sculpture see Proske (1951). Simon was Master mason at Burgos Cathedral from *c.*1482 to his death in (?) 1511. The chapel took some time to build, given the precarious finances of its founder, the Constable of Castille, Don Pedro Fernandez de Velasco. Its exterior pinnacles and interior sculpture were not finished until the 1520s. The stained glass lighting the openwork crown of the vaults is modern; originally the vault opened into the dark spaces of the roof. The German, ultimately Parler-derived, form of the vault, and the Flemish inspiration for the elevation's details, are discussed by Wilson (1990) 287–9. Welander's useful summary biographies of the family (1996) points to a more local set of sources for the chapel's decoration: the Santiago chapel, Toledo Cathedral, begun in 1432 (escutcheons placed aslant beneath crested helmets), and San Juan de los Reyes, begun in 1477 (large sculptural compositions enlivening exterior and interior walls). For the influence of the chapel on funerary chapels in Spain see Torres Balbás (1952) 301–2.

178. Perpignan is illustrated in *C.A.*, LXXIII (1907) 108. The plan of the church of San Juan at Toledo appears in Dehio (1901) plate 509. For Saint-Jean (the Cathedral) at Perpignan see Ponsich (1954) and Durliat (1962) 144–9. Freigang (1992) 315–16 and note 25, sees no reason to believe either author in their view that the cathedral originally intended a three-aisled nave and not the present *nef unique* with lateral chapels. The Perpignan church has a different choir structure than San Juan, with three polygonal apses. But Frankl's comparison hides a similarity he may have missed: both were royal churches. Perpignan was the capital of the Mallorcan kings and its cathedral (with that at Palma de Mallorca) their principal royal church.

178A. These nodding ogees also appear on Guas's show drawing, made in or after 1479, of the choir and transepts. Sanabria (1992) 170, finds their source in Toledan sculpture of the 1490s, such as the predella of the main *retablo* of the cathedral (begun 1498) or the piers of the church of the Royal Hospital at Santiago by Enrique Egas. See Note 179 below.

179. The living quarters of the royal family were in the upper storey of the monastery. The balconies thus lie on the same level as the living quarters. For the church and cloister, see Azcárate Ristori (1956), and Sanabria (1992), who reveals the Flemish, German and Mudejar roots of Guas's idiosyncratic style,

and underlines the function of the church as the intended mausoleum of Ferdinand and Isalbella (the tomb would have been placed in the crossing), For that reason the single-aisled plan may have referred to Juan II of Castille's mausoleum church of Miraflores in Burgos, founded in 1441 and completed in Isabella's reign, or to Enrique IV's aisleless, Latin-cross Hieronymite church of Santa Maria del Parral (begun 1459), in Segovia. Sanabria compares the completed church with Guas's show drawing (see Note 178A above) of the choir and transepts. Most of the drawing's details are Guas's, but its lantern tower (built in a slightly different form) shows the influence of Simon de Colonia, who advised on the design in 1495. The nave vaults are close to the Parler-influenced vaults of S. Maria am Gestade in Vienna.

180. Illustrated in Torres Balbás, *op. cit.* figure 274.

181. Frankl, *System der Kunstwissenschaft* (Brünn, 1938) 114.

182. Similarly inside, on the doorway to the cloister, and, on a broader scale, in the upper storey of the cloister, which is one of the most beautiful, not only in Spain.

182A. All these façades are mentioned and illustrated in Sanfaçon (1971) 100–15. The motif of the 'concave-convex gablet' appears in Beauvais on the flying buttress piers flanking the transepts façades. For the Sens transepts see Murray (1987) 101–3; for those at Beauvais, also by Martin Chambiges, see Murray (1989) 121–42. For a full discussion of the Troyes west façade see Murray (1987) 87–109. Wilson (1990) p. 254, traces the origins of these convex-concave undulating arches to Brabantine late Gothic and the Keldermans family, particularly to the west tower of St Rombouts at Mechelen (from 1468 onwards). However, this particular form does not actually appear in the built tower, but only in the 1550 Chalon drawing and only in those parts of the drawing which were never built: the octagon storey, and the west portal, whose existing simple forms the drawing re-shapes in more flamboyant style. See van Langendonck (1987).

183. Frédéric Lesueur, *Le château d'Amboise, P.M.* (Paris, 1935) illustrations on pp. 17, 19, 87. See also Sanfaçon (1971) 182–4, and Brosse ed. (1967) vol. IIID 2, where the completion date of 1493 is given. Wilson (1990) 154 was the first correctly to see the origins of these bell-shaped arches, what he calls 'round-headed ogees', in the Brabantine architecture of the Keldermans. See the buttress tabernacles of Andries Keldermans's first storey of the west tower of St Rombout at Mechelen, dated soon after 1468, illustrated in van Langendonck (1987). Esther, in Buyle *et al.* (1997) 94, 100–2, however, states that Andries Keldermans took over the direction of the tower not in 1468 but as early as the year of its foundation, in 1452. The bell-shaped ogee also occurs in the Chambiges's work after Sens: in the balustrade below the rose in the transepts at Beauvais, and in the great gable over the portal of Pierre Chambiges's south transept at Senlis. Murray (1987) 103, properly warns us against identifying these arch forms, indeed the whole de luxe decorative style that goes with them, as exclusive to the Chambiges family; they were part of a general 'Parisian vocabulary' of *c.*1500.

184. Illustrated in Lasteyrie, *op. cit.* I, 334. In 1488 the town's accounts mention a visit of the architects Jacques Le Roux and Michel Gohier, the latter referred to as master of the works on the church. In 1489 work began under his direction on the north tower, but he was probably dead by 1505, and work proceeded under Guillaume Morin and Thomas Theroulde. By 1514 work was going forward on the nave, but the side chapels were finished only in *c.*1535. Nave roofed in 1550. See Bottineau-Fuchs in Baylé, dir. (1997) vol. I, 332–5. See Brosse ed., (1968) vol. IVB 127.

185. See Plat (1925).

186. On the interior of Saint-Maclou, see above, p. 231, and Chapter 4, note 143.

See now Neagley (1988) (1992) (1996) and most fully in (1998). She attributes the west porch and façade to Pierre Robin's designs, largely on the evidence of the geometry of the ground plan and the lack of any apparent break in the construction or change in design from the first beginnings of the church soon after 1432–6/7. She argues that Pierre Robin's drawings were followed faithfully by the executant architects throughout the fifteenth century, probably at the insistence of the church's treasurers. She identifies the source for the porch in Jehan Perier's design for a putative, three-part, uncompleted (?) porch of *c.*1370 for the west façade of the cathedral. The attribution of the three-sided porch to Ambroise Harel may be based on the fact that he constructed a similar polygonal western porch at Saint-Vincent in Rouen, which, according to Neagley (1998) 91, was begun in 1480, but which, according to Bottineau-Fuchs in Baylé, dir. (1997) vol. I 326, was underway in 1479 and complete in 1481. Saint-Vincent was destroyed in 1944 and not rebuilt.

Neagley's attribution of the whole of Saint-Maclou (apart from the lantern tower and a few decorative details), including the west porch, to Robin's plan of 1436/7 is forcefully argued, but it rests on a number of unsubstantiated assumptions: a) that Robin did a large number of detailed drawings (and not just the single drawing mentioned in the document of 1436/7), b) that Perier's porch was built and had gables, c) that the geometric layout of the western porch is by Robin and not a successor architect (Ambroise Harel?) who could

have skilfully displaced Robin's conventional western termination by repeating at the west end the angled geometry and spun squares which Robin used to determine the angling of the chevet and d) that the style of the decorative details of the western porch is sufficiently close to Robin's known work to be accredited to him. On the latter point alone, the overloaded and mannered character of the porch seems to come from a different stylistic world than Robin's lucid and 'classic' language in the eastern parts. See also Chapter 4 above, Notes 111, 143, 175.

186A. Sanfaçon (1971) pp. 35, 61–2, briefly sets the elevation of the nave, begun in or soon after 1477, in the context of Norman Flamboyant. The heavy cylindrical piers with single shafts supporting the intrados of the arcade arches recall those of Saint-Pierre at Caen. The tiercerons resting on corbels are not innovations but are prefigured in the choir of Saint-Etienne d'Elbeuf, near Rouen, of before 1454. The porch, which derives from that of Saint-Maclou, and has parallels with other polygonal porches in Upper Normandy (Caudebec-en-Caux, Saint-Germain at Argentan, La Trinité at Falaise) is discussed on pp. 173–4. See also Grodecki (1953) for description and building history. Bottineau-Fuchs, in Baylé, dir. (1997) vol. 2 265–70, identifies two architects at work from 1477, the first who was responsible for the simpler forms of the arcades and triforium, and the second, probably Jehan Lemoyne, who designed the more imaginative upper parts, including the clerestorey, the high vaults and flyers, and who inserted the cellular chapels between the buttresses (three of them dated 1510–13). The flyers have parallels with those of the choir of Mont-Saint-Michel and Saint-Martin at Argentan. The style of the sculpture embellishing the vault ribs is close the sculpture of the west porch. Certainly Jehan Lemoyne is credited with designing this remarkable polygonal porch, constructed 1506–16. Four apostle figures (now lost) were installed above the side portals in 1508.

187. There are illustrations of the whole and of individual parts in *Die Kunstdenkmäler der Provinz Sachsen*, I (1929) 442ff. The importance of this font and its cover in the decorative architecture of the Middle Rhine was fully set out in Seeliger-Zeiss (1967) 40–1, 54, 142. The origins of some of its forms in the circle of Jodok Dotzinger's work in the Upper Rhine *c.*1460 was convincingly argued by Julier (1978) 229–30, who suggested that the work might be a late piece by Jodok himself. See also Lehmann and Schubert (1991) 259.

187A. For a description of the Sacrament House see Weidenhoffer (1991) vol. 1, 143, and, in greater detail, Timmermann (1996) 167–8, 268–70, where it is interpreted as a vertical narrative of the Passion, in which the architecture articulates and enhances the upward progression of the images. The subject matter of the sculpture, and the contribution of its patron, Hans IV Imhoff and family, to the work, is fully discussed by Schleif (1990) 16–75. In English there is Brandl (1986).

188. Quoted in Jean Laran, *La cathédrale d'Albi, P.M.* (Paris, 1931) 66. Laran does not say where the quotation is taken form.

188A. Biget, Carbonell-Lamothe and Pradalier-Schlumberger (1982) attribute the choir screen to the initiative of Bishop Louis I d'Amboise, that is some time between 1474 and 1483, when he succeeded Louis IX as the chancellor of the Order of St Michael.

188B. For the Breisach screen see Seeliger-Zeiss (1967) 93–4; and Julier (1978) 151, who positions it in a group of decorative architectural pieces in the Upper Rhine showing the Augsburg influence of Burkhard Engelberg.

188C. For the screen, built by Jehan Gailde, see Salet (1955a).

189. Richard Graul, *Alt Flandern* (Munich, 1918) plate I. For the history of the façade and north tower at Antwerp see Lemaire (1946) van Brabant (1972) and van Langendonk (1987) 47–9, who discussed the close relationship between the Antwerp and Mechelen workshops during this period. Work on the south tower, begun in 1430, had stopped at its present height for lack of funds by 1475. The north tower, the only Brabantine great church steeple to be fully completed in the Middle Ages, was begun in 1420–2, and had reached the uppermost square stage by 1480. Much of this work can be associated with the principle architect of the nave, Everaert Spoorwater (1439–73). It may have been under his successor Herman de Waghemakere (1473–1502) that work resumed on the north tower, starting with the octagon, though this stage was not finished until *c.*1508. Anthonis I Keldermans was working on the north tower and north portal in 1506 and 1511. The spire, probably finished in *c.*1518, but officially completed in 1521, is the work principally of Domien de Waghemakere, assisted by Anthonis II Keldermans and Rombout II Keldermans (who both contributed to the construction, and completion, of the north portal). The transition between square and octagonal stories of the steeple owes more to the earlier steeple of the town hall in Brussels (1444–54), than to the more complicated star-shaped plan of the projected (but never built) spire of St Rombout at Mechelen. See also above, Chapter 4, Note 55.

189A. For the Týn church steeples see Líbal (1983) 339. The lowest parts of the towers may date from the mid fourteenth century. A Parler workshop built the west façade *c.*1380–1400. The west gable is dated 1463. The wooden spire of the north-west tower of St Mary's in Kraków, of 1478, by Maciej Heringk, is clearly influenced by the Týn church wooden spires, see Lepiarczyk (1959).

190. Plan in *C.A.*, LXXIV (1906) 17. The choir was almost completely destroyed in 1945. The church has now been rebuilt. For a full analysis of its piers, plan and influence in Troyes and Champagne see Murray (1989) 137–42, and Murray (1977). Murray attributes the choir to Martin Chambiges and dates its beginning to shortly before 1502.

191. Gerstenberg, *op. cit.* (Note 141 to this chapter) 17. For Engelberg's work at Ulm see Wortmann (1972) 24, 37–8; and Bischoff (1990) who dates the remodelling of the aisles 1498–1508. Bischoff's book (1999) is the best treatment of this important architect and his practice.

192. The date of Pirna is known from an inscription, which is quoted in *Darst. d. ä. Bau- und Kunstdenkmale d. K. Sachsen*, I (Dresden, 1882). See now Lemper (1991).

193. The 'wild man' and the 'wild woman' at the foot of the tree are not Adam and Eve, as is suggested in the inventory, even if only because there were originally twelve such figures. Scholars who interpret every tree as a symbol of the first or second paradise must make an exception here. See also Richard Bernheimer, *Wild Men in the Middle Ages etc.* (Cambridge, Mass., 1952). Frankl's view has been confirmed by Möbius (1972), and Möbius and Beyer (1978) 201–8, who interpret the two figures as pacified 'wild people'. It is doubtful, however, if Frankl would have agreed with their identification of these figures as the stone equivalents of contemporary popular devices for exorcism, hung in the roofs of private houses.

194. Described in *Darstellung etc. Sachsen*, XII (Dresden, 1889). A Marxist interpretation of this church and of the whole series of Upper Saxon Late Gothic halls to which it belongs can be found in Meuche (1962) and (1971). His argument, that they are harbingers of the 'realism' of the 'early middle-class revolution', fails to account for the irrational and fantastic elements in these churches. Useful, and less politically biased, surveys of this group of halls can be found in Ullmann (1987) and Ullmann ed. (1984) 133–62.

195. Wolff and Jung, *Die Baudenkmale von Frankfurt a. M.*, I (Frankfurt am Main, 1895). The choir, consecrated in 1434, is by the most influential architect working in the Middle Rhine in the first half of the fifteenth century, Madern Gerthener (*c.*1360–1430/1). For his work and his 'school' see Fischer (1962) especially 33–41. For St Leonard see also Natale (1973) and Germund (1997) 77–84.

196. Berthold Riehl, *Bayerns Donautal* (Munich, Leipzig, 1912) 271. Riehl has here written an appreciation which is at least fifty per cent positive – a thing which demanded considerable courage at that time. The heightening of the Romanesque nave and the extension of its aisles were begun *c.*1500 by the architect Hans von Bingen, and the north aisle was complete by 1507. The skeletal vaults of the north-east chapel, known as the 'Salvatorchörlein', were built *c.*1510 under Hans Baltz (active at St Bartholomew's 1507–16). See Fischer (1962) 244–7, who touches, interestingly, on the iconographic programme of the sculpture of the chapel's vaults, and the 'dissonant' nature of the flying ribs around the figure of the sourged Christ on its pendant boss. A visual analysis, in the context of other flying rib compositions in the Middle Rhine, is given by Germund (1997) 133–6.

196A. Frankl is confusing the architect who began the nave enlargements in 1500, Hans von Bingen, with the architect of the vaults of the 'Salvatorchörlein', Hans Baltz (see above, note 196). Baltz's burial in the small choir in 1516, and his confident title of *lapicida et architectus*, suggests that he was the designer of the space, including its vaults, though Hans von Bingen had completed the vaulting of the eastern bay of the north aisle, and may have laid the foundations or outline walls of the eastern chapel. The college of St Leonard had accused Hans von Bingen of endangering the stability of the church by laying unsatisfactory foundations for the nave extensions. Fischer (1962) 145, refers to him as an architect 'of limited talent with a tendency to extravagance'.

196B. See Hoffmann and Meyer (1977) 14–16, which gives a convenient summary of Hoffmann's research on the Heydenreichs. Fischer (1974) 345–9, attributes the vaults to Erhard and sees the 'split level' nature of the vaults – one level made of 'abstract' moulded stone, the other carved as branchwork – as the reflection of a typically late medieval paradox: the suggestion of the heavenly canopy through the literal and realistic rendering of the natural.

197. H. Giesau, *Der Dom zu Magdeburg* (Burg, 1924) 41. The date 1330–40 is not certain. See above, Chapter 4, Note 19.

198. Eduard Paulus, *Die Kunst- und Altertumsdenkmale von Württemberg, Schwarzwaldkreis* (Stuttgart, 1897) 35ff. The date is confirmed in the most recent Dehio *Handbuch*, see Dehio/Zimdars *et al.*, (1993) 120.

198A. Other flying ribs in Central Europe in the early- or mid-fourteenth century are: the original vault in St Catherine's Chapel in Strasbourg Cathedral of *c.*1340–5; the vaults of the belfry storey of the west tower of Freiburg Minster, of *c.*1300?; the now-destroyed fountain pavilion in the Cistercian monastery at Zlatá Koruna in southern Bohemia, *c.*1360; the Bridal Portal at St Sebaldus in Nuremberg, *c.*1360. See above, Chapter 4, Note 19.

199. Hans Jantzen, *Das Münster zu Freiburg* (Burg, 1929). Still fundamental for the Freiburg choir is Meckel (1936), supplemented by Adam (1968) 24,

96–102. But see now Julier (1978) 140–5. He dates the choir vault to 1509–10 and attributes it to Hans Niesenberger. Frankl is right in seeing its ultimate source as the net vault of Peter Parler in Prague cathedral, but the more immediate inspiration came from Austria, in particular from the lodge of St Stephen's in Vienna and its offshoot in Steyr, where dense net patterns are combined with small curving ribs in the vault penetrations.

200. Cf. F. Bond, *Introduction*. Also K. Escher, *Englische Kathedralen* (Munich, 1929). See now Leedy (1975) and (1980) 32ff, 214–17, where he also proposes a symbolic interpretation of the fans. For the rest of the chapel, together with its vaults, see Woodman (1986) 140–8 (with rather optimistic parallels drawn with French Flamboyant), Wilson (1986) 70–8, and Wilson (1995), the latter best assessment of the design and authorship of the whole chapel in relation to late Perpendicular architecture. Wilson attributes it to Robert Janyns.

201. Subsidiary members like those in the cloister at Gloucester exist in small-scale architecture, for instance in the Warwick Chantry at Tewkesbury, built in 1422. In full-scale architecture, they appear at the east end of the cathedral at Peterborough about 1440. Joan Evans, *English Art, 1307–1461* (Oxford, 1949) 199, claims that the Divinity School at Oxford was begun as early as 1430 and that the ceiling was built some time after 1448. On this subject cf. Great Britain, Royal Commission etc., Inventory of Oxford (1939), where the later date is given. For the architects of the Divinity School see Harvey (1978) 174, 185, 209, and Harvey (1984) 220–3, 336–7. He attributes the first stage of the construction (the enclosing walls), from 1424 to 1439, to Richard Winchcombe. The vault was added by William Orchard in 1479–83. For earlier, small-scale pendant vaults see Wilson (1986) 77.

202. Lozoya, *op. cit.* (Note 67 to Chapter 3) 548; F. W. Feilchenfeld, *Die Meisterwerke der Baukunst in Portugal* (Vienna-Leipzig, 1908); Walter Crum Watson, *Portuguese Architecture* (London, 1908). Boutaca was followed in 1517 by João de Castilho, to whom the Renaissance ornaments are attributed.

Boitac laid out the church as an enlarged version of his Franciscan hall church at Setúbal, with no transept. By the time he moved to Batalha in 1516 it had reached the full height of the outer walls. João de Castilho, who replaced him as leading architect in 1517, completed the piers and built the vaults. He suppressed the nave's two easternmost pillars envisaged by Boitac and turned the whole eastern space into a large continuous transept, which he covered with a single vault. See Pereira and Leite (1986), Alves (1989–91), Marques de Carvalho (1990) and Vieira da Silva (1996).

203. Albrecht Haupt, *Die Baukunst der Renaissance in Portugal etc.* (Frankfurt, 1890) III and illustrations 95–9. The title of the book is misleading, since it deals mainly with the works of the Late Gothic period. See now Ferreira de Almeida (1990) and Vieira da Silva (1987) (1990) and (1996a) who have confirmed the attribution of the monastery church to Boitac, and its seminal influence on the so-called Manueline style (in its use of star vaults, spiral columns, and the hall church). A useful survey of the Manueline style is given in Dias (1988).

204. *Inventário antístico de Portugal*, II (Lisbon, 1947) plates 7, 8, 93–5. (For examples of forms of frameworks, cf. plates 10 and 11.) See also Watson, *op. cit.* 196ff., where there are plans etc. See Dias (1988a) 60–6, for more up-to-date chronologies and attributions. Boitac was responsible for the rebuilding of the church from 1507, and signed a contract in 1513 to complete the first stage of the work. Pires seems to have been responsible for the cloister. See also Dias (1986) II 30ff.

205. For a plan of Tomar, cf. Watson, *op. cit.* 225. The plan of the Romanesque church is in Conant (1974) 334, fig. 257. For the specifically Manueline iconography of its extraordinary west façade, glorifying the history of Portugal and the king's life see O'Mally (1969). The architecture is discussed by Dias (1988).

206. Lozoya, *op. cit.* 554ff. See also Guimarães de Andrade (1989) and Verdelho da Costa (1996), the latter for recent literature.

207. August Prokop, *Die Markgrafschaft Mähren etc.* (Vienna, 1904), illustrations 559 and 583.

208. On Rieth, see Thieme-Becker under 'Benedikt'. See now Fehr (1961) 36–40.

209. Tietze, *Österreichische Kunsttopographie*, XXIII (1931) 34 and 198. The standard work on Pilgram is still Oettinger (1951). The Vienna pulpit can be definitely assigned to him, but the proper attribution of both his drawings and his buildings remain matters of controversy. Grimschitz (1953) attributed to him no less than sixty-nine drawings from the Vienna collection – a conclusion not unexpectedly (and convincingly) challenged by Koepf (1953) and (1975). As far as the buildings are concerned, Feuchtmüller (1951) indiscriminately attributed to him almost every major Austrian building with curving ribs in the late fifteenth and early sixteenth centuries. The issues, and the buildings, are sensibly discussed by Brucher (1990) 203–13. See also Fehr (1961) 115–18. The technical ingenuities of 'Pilgram's' vaults are analysed in detail by Müller (1974).

210. '*Vielbildigkeit*'; see Note 14D to Chapter 2.

Walter Buchowiecki, *Die gotischen Kirchen Österreichs* (Vienna, 1952). See: St Valentin, 1522; Weigersdorf, 1523; Hirschbach, Steinakirchen, Aflenz, Goes, etc. One of the most beautiful is the church at Königswiesen, built by Thaman Pramer, whose name appears in 1509 in the ordinance of Admont; cf. Frank l(1960) 127.

These Austrian churches, particularly in and around Vienna, Steyr and Admont, were grouped by Feuchtmüller and Ulm (1965) and by Ulm (1962) under the title of the 'Danube School', largely because of their preference for naturalistic, even rustic, decoration and for a sense of unlimited and undirected interior space.

211. Described in *Darst. d. ä. Bau- und Kunstdenkm. d. K. Sachsen*, IV (Dresden, 1885). Here the question of authorship is discussed. Peter, who built the church at Pirna, certainly co-operated. The vaults in the two churches are very different, and it remains doubtful whether they were designed by the same architect. The building history was set out, rather uncritically, by Schönemann (1963), and clarified by Magirius (1975) and (1990). The three-apsidal east end, which Frankl compared to the Wiesenkirche, is much closer to Conrad Pflüger's SS Peter and Paul at Görlitz. The church might have remained a typical Upper Saxon hall (e.g. Pirna, or the Thomaskirche in Leipzig) but for the intervention of the Prague-trained Jacob Haylmann in 1515, who had worked as a mason at Prague castle under Benedict Ried. He brought Benedict Ried's spatial organization and decorative vocabulary to Annaberg, by altering the original form of the galleries and introducing curvilinear vaults in the south sacristy and over the main spaces. Krause (1996a) puts Pflüger's death not in *c*.1508 but between 10 February and 28 May 1505. He also notes (1996) that the foreman called Jacob working at St Barbara's at Kutná Hora in 1512 was not, as Fehr (1961) 62–3 and many others have thought, Haylmann himself.

212. Analysed in Hoeltje, *op. cit.* (Note 147 to this chapter) 68.

For the vaults see now Leedy (1980) 24–9 and 140–4. An unconventional analysis of the chapel – its building history, its masons, and its stylistic context – is provided by Woodman (1986). He plots the following sequence:

1) **1448–*c*.1471** Reginald Ely designed the plan and sections of the elevation.
2) ***c*.1471–1477** John Wolryche designed the main lateral tracery and built up to the vault springers.
3) **1477–85** Simon Clerk finished the five eastern bays. The white magnesian limestone from Huddleston in Yorkshire which is associated with this period extends into the base courses of the north and south porches of the ante-chapel. He is probably the author of the bell tower drawing (BM Cotton Ms Aug. 1.i.2).
4) **1508–15** John Wastell completed the ante-chapel, designed and built the vaults, towers and battlements. (pp. 155–204 for perceptive observations on Wastell and his work in East Anglia and Canterbury).

For the early history of Henry VI's foundation see Leedy (1990).

213. T. G. Jackson, *Gothic Architecture etc.*, II (Cambridge, 1915) 109. Jackson may have been thinking of star-vaults.

The knotty problem of the intended design of the original vaults is discussed by Woodman (1986) 61–3, 93–8. He suggests that the seven-shaft system in the ante-chapel was laid out for a lierne vault by Reginald Ely in 1448/9; that the five-shaft system in the choir was not the result – as Willis thought – of a cutting out of two shafts from seven-part choir responds, but was installed from the start by John Wolryche in the late 1460s or early 1470s, possibly with the idea of abandoning the high vault altogether. Simon Clerk (from 1477) reinstated the idea of a vault, certainly a lierne – though Woodman's suggestion that it may have been intended to look like the vault of the Lady Chapel at Ely is based on his mistaken assumption that the Ely vault was built in the fifteenth century, see above, Chapter 4, Note 8.

214. The exterior has been much impaired by the reconstruction of the roofs, begun in 1759. The original appearance is discussed in Victor Nodet, *L'église de Brou*, *P.M.* (Paris, 1911) 18ff.

The best recent study of Brou is by Hörsch (1994), who gives a detailed picture of the building's troubled construction. In 1532, the year of the consecration, Louis van Boghem left the site never to return, with the west portal still unfinished. The aisles and chapels of the nave had an idiosyncratic roof and buttress system, caused partly by the low clerestorey. Tall assymetrical gables, identical in height and pitch to those crowning the side sections of the west façade, originally rose at each bay division above the side chapel and side aisle roofs, their inner faces providing support for small flyers rising above the nave aisles. See Hörsch (1998), who also gives further literature on the church. Queen Margaret's influence on the style of the church and her tomb, and the intersection of artistic choice and political motive, is discussed by Carpino (1997).

215. Paul Clemen, *Belgische Kunstdenkmäler*, I (Munich, 1923).

See now Buyle *et al.* (1997) 68–73. Arnould van Mulcken, the architect of St Martin at Liège, took over the rebuilding of the church in 1513, beginning with the choir which had been started abortively in 1418?–21 but halted just below the windows in *c*.1436. By 1515 the choir was finished, by *c*.1525 the transepts, and the nave was complete by 1538, though the consecration had to wait until 1552. The overloaded detailing and 'naïve eclecticism' of the design come in for

censure from Wilson (1990) 241. The net and star vaults resemble Austrian precedents (particularly the net vaults of Gurk cathedral and of the choir of Freiburg im Breisgau); the choir, with its baldachined statues and radiating chapels without an ambulatory, recalls Notre-Dame Halle, while the triforium of the nave is reminiscent of St Pancras at Leiden, and the cusped, 'frill' arcade arches recall the façade of St Peter at Louvain.

215A. See Sanfaçon (1971) 176–9, Verdier (1980) and Bottineau-Fuchs in Baylé, dir. (1997) vol. I 332. The south porch is the final, and most elaborate stage in the transformation of the nave which began under the architect Jehan Gilat in 1493. The nave was given double aisles on the north and south sides, but the orientation of the town southwards towards the river guarenteed the increasing emphasis on the south entrance over against the north side or the west façade, indeed over every other aspect of the church. The south portal was begun in 1506. Verdier (1980) 25, note 8, thinks its designer could have been Roullant Le Roux, on the basis of its close stylistic similarities with the façade of the Palais de Justice in Rouen and the St Romain (central) portal at Rouen Cathedral. Roullant could have been recommended to the chantier by Archbishop George I d'Amboise, his patron and supporter at Rouen, who was also Count of Louviers.

215B. The porch was built at the same time as a now lost chapel (founded in 1521) which terminated to the west the platform on which the porch rests. The heraldry of the porch refers to Bishops of Albi and to Cardinal Jean de Lorraine, in a date span from 1519 to 1550. See Biget (1982) 36.

216. Leopoldo Torres Balbás, *Arquitectura gótica* (Madrid, 1952) 378.

Still the most authoritative monograph on the New Cathedral at Salamanca is Chueca (1951). As early as 1509 King Ferdinand the Catholic had ordered the architects Alfonso Rodriguez and Anton Egas to go to Salamanca and prepare designs for the new cathedral. But it was only in 1512, after the chapter has summoned a conference of nine leading architects (including Egas and Juan Gil de Hontanon the Elder) that work began on the present site at the west end of the nave and worked slowly eastwards, preserving the old twelfth-century cathedral to its south. Juan Gil de Hontañon the Elder was put in charge (from 12 May 1513), and the Hontañón family kept virtual control of operations throughout the first half of the sixteenth century, (Juan Gil the Younger 1526–31; Rodrigo from 1538). Chueca (1951) 154 summarizes the chronology as follows:

1) **1520.** Outer chapels up to half height and lowest courses of main pillars.
2) **1523** Outer chapels vaulted.
3) **1534–7.** Main pillars raised to capital height.
4) **1540.** Main arcade arches and aisle vaults.
5) **1550.** High vaults and upper buttress system.

By 1560 the cathedral was in use, and by 1584 work had reached the crossing. The choir was under construction through the seventeenth and into the early eighteenth centuries, for which see Chueca (1951) 178–95. The new cathedral has many similarities to the earlier Seville cathedral, in its width, its strongly scanned bays, its compound piers and balustraded clerestorey. Rodrigo's famous 'treatise' on rib vaults and their statics is lucidly discussed by Kubler (1944), and Sanabria (1982).

217. Lozoya, in *op. cit.* 532, mentions the church in a few lines. Among the details, the springing of the vault is of particular stylistic interest. The pear-shaped elliptical transverse arch runs through it without interruption, while the diagonal ribs and the tiercerons rest on springing which has the shape of a quarter circle in plan. Below this springing there is a pear-shaped shaft which ends on a concave abacus. As in the cathedral, the piers and the ribs do not conform to one another. For an illustration see Rahlves (1969) 264–5, and plate 138.

218. Torres Balbás, *op. cit.* 380. Juan Gil de Hontañón's design for Segovia nave closely follows his for Salamanca. At his death in 1526 his son Rodrigo continued the work until at least 1529. In 1560 until his death in 1577 Rodrigo was master of the cathedral workshop. By 1562 the nave was nearing completion. A year later the present choir and chevet was begun according to Rodrigo's plans, and was largely complete by 1591. Frankl seems to be implying that Juan Gil de Hontañón the Elder intended a flat-ended choir at Segovia, following that at Salamanca, and that Rodrigo 'returned' to the 'older' type of chevet. But since the Salamancan choir belongs to the late sixteenth and seventeenth centuries, and the Segovian choir was begun long after Juan's death, and under the direction of his son, there are too many imponderables in any reconstruction of Juan's intended plans for the choirs of either Salamanca or Segovia. Salamanca's dependence on Seville cathedral may have extended to the present flat-ended plan, but equally Segovia's radiating chevet may reflect Juan's original plan for both Segovia and Salamanca. See Yubero (1978).

219. Illustrated in Lozoya, *op. cit.* 570. The portal is definitely by João de Castilho, and dates to soon after 1519, the year of his appointment as architect there. See Moreira (1996).

220. Emil Delmar, 'The Window at Tomar etc.', *The Art Quarterly*, X (1947) 203. Delman's far-fetched explanations of this programme have now been superseded by O'Mally (1969), who sees it as a royal iconography, celebrating

the history of Portugal, and of Manuel I's life and achievements (as recorded in Giles of Viterbo's eulogy to Julius II?) and the interaction of both in biblical and eschatological history.

221. Described in *Beschreibende Darst. d. ä. Bau- und Kunstdenkmal der Stadt Halle a. S.* (Halle a.S., 1886) 6–81. See now Dehio (1976) 160–2, and Volkmann (1958/9).

221A. The classic discussion of the relationship between the Renaissance and the Middle Ages can be found in Panofsky (1960). Theories of 'Late Gothic' and 'Early Renaissance' are discussed in Biatostocki (1966) especially 81ff. A useful discussion of the Late Gothic/Early Renaissance overlap in Germany is given by Nussbaum (2000) 219–28. More modern approaches to the impact of the Italian Renaissance on 'the Gothic North' can be found in Burke (1987), who discusses the para-national model of Italian culture in Europe, and in Allmand ed., (1998) – see particularly the essays by Genet on 'Politics: Theory and Practice', 3–28, and by Crossley on 'Architecture and Painting', 299–318. There are also critical comments on Panofsky's model of Renaissance reception north of the Alps, as a distinction between 'humanist content' and 'Gothic form', in Kauffmann (1995), Chapters 2, 3.

222. *C.A.*, LXXVI (1908) 1, 68.

223. *C.A.*, CV (1947) 103. For Saint-Pierre at Caen and Saint-Eustache see Blunt (1980) 20–3 (Caen) and 58–60 (St Eustache). Some helpful observations on the Gothic survival in France can be found in Cocke (1990). The case of Nantes cathedral, where the south transept was finished in a sympathetic Gothic style between 1631–7, is illustrated in Leniaud *et al.* (1991) 34–5. Louis le Vau recommended to the Chapter at Nantes in about 1650 that they should build its choir in the Gothic style.

223A. The building history of this cathedral, begun in 1318, but under construction into the early sixteenth century, is set out fully in Araguas and Peropadre Muniesa (1989).

224. Frankl (1960) 237ff. A clear account of the controversy, and the façade designs, can be found in Belluzzi (1983/4) and Matteucci (1983/4).

224A. The church has now been rebuilt. See Hilger (1982), and, more generally, Hipp (1979).

224B. A convenient introduction to Gothic survival in England is given by Cocke (1987).

225. Pointers to a study of this subject are given in the Bibliography.

225A. For medieval towns, particularly French, see Lavedan and Hugueney (1974); for England see Reynolds (1977) and Platt (1976); for Germany there is the convenient Meckseper (1982); for central Italy the classic Braunfels (1979, 4th edtn).

NOTES TO PART TWO

1. For Suger's meaning of the term *arcus* in *De Consecratione* chapter 5, see Annas and Binding (1989), who argue that he is referring to the transverse arches of his new choir, and not its vaults. See also Introduction, note 1, above. For Burckhard von Hall and Wimpfen see Klotz (1967) 15–18. On this, and on what follows, see Frankl (1960) 299ff.

1A. A supplement to Frankl's discussion of Gothic as the style of barbarians is provided by de Beer (1948). For the German attitude, both humanist and post-Renaissance, to the 'Barbarian theory' see Brough (1985) and Borchardt (1971).

2. For Christopher Wren's theory of the Saracen origin of Gothic, see Frankl (1960) 36off.

2A. Johannes Wetter's (1806–1897) contribution to understanding the essential nature of Gothic is discussed by Frankl (1960) 525–9, and Appendix 29, 870–1. See also Viollet-le-Duc (1858–1868).

2B. For Alexandre de Laborde (1773–1842) see Frankl (1960) 502–506. For Carl Schnaase (1798–1875) see Frankl (1960) 544–553. In the same work, Frankl discusses Ludovic Vitet (1802–1873) 523–4.

2C. For Joseph Arthur Gobineau, Sulpiz Boisserée (1783–1854) and Daniel Ramée (1806–1887) see Frankl (1960) 659, 514–8, 522–3 respectively.

2D. For a discussion of this kind of base and its origins see above, Part One, Chapter 4, Note 57E. A none too successful attempt to find French Rayonnant precedents for the Prague bases, which are by Matthias of Arras, was made by Héliot (1975).

2E. For the Beauvais rose see Henwood-Reverdot (1982) 123–32, and Part One, Chapter 1, Note 23B. For the rose as wheel of fortune (including a discussion of the Basel rose) see Beyer (1962), and Nelson (1980). A broad survey of the symbolic connotations of rose windows, with many illustrations, can be found in Mersmann (1982). The changing meanings of roses in the thirteenth century, from cosmological-theological picture systems to virtuoso decorations, are discussed in Suckale (1981). For the south transept rose at Amiens see Murray (1996) 100–102.

2F. The classic analysis of the Lausanne rose is by Beer (1952). For a resumé of interpretations of its iconography see Trumpler (1993).

3. The central spoke was built vertically at Beauvais for technical reasons; it was the first spoke to be erected, and it was easiest to set it vertically. However, there were aesthetic reasons to want to keep the centre-line free. (By contrast, however, cf. the oculus in the west façade at Strasbourg.)

3A. Frankl presumably means the bifurcating tracery of rose windows, a system already employed in the west rose at Notre-Dame in Paris. Another early example, earlier either than the west rose at Reims (*c.*1260) and probably the original rose at the Sainte-Chapelle (*c.*1240) is the north transept rose of Saint-Denis of 1231–45.

4. Illustrated in Lasteyrie, *op. cit.* 1, 484. See also Behling, *op. cit.* (Note 106 to Chapter 3). This pattern appears also in the south transept rose of Rouen cathedral, in the south transept at Meaux Cathedral and in the nave clerestorey of York Minster – all '*c.*1300', but its diffusion is more extensive in the Empire. It can be found in a number of variations in the Peter's Portal at Cologne Cathedral, in the south transept of the Cistercian church of Zlatá Koruna in southern Bohemia, and, in micro-architectural form, in the choir stalls in Cologne and St Mary at Oberwesel, and the high altar at Oberwesel. For some of these see Zimmermann-Deissler (1958) 82–9, and Palm (1976) 67–70.

4A. Murray (1996) 71, 102, 164, dates the rose to the fourteenth century and associates it with structural reinforcements to the problematic transept area.

4B. The term Rayonnant is used to cover French architecture from *c.*1230 (the beginning of the remodelling of Saint-Denis) to *c.*1380 (the first appearances of Flamboyant). Frankl is misleading in suggesting that it also covers High Gothic proper (i.e. buildings dating from *c.*1190–*c.*1230). See above, Part One, Chapter 3, Note 1.

5. Frankl (1960) 110ff. The training of the medieval architect, with special reference to late medieval Germany, is set out in Booz (1956). Harvey (1972) collects much valuable material on masons. There are excellent articles on all aspects of the masons's craft in Recht ed., (1989). The most comprehensive general study is Binding (1993). Claussen (1993/4) addresses the problem of masons' anonymity in the early Middle Ages, and attributes the change to named architects from the later twelfth century onwards as a direct result of the gigantism of Gothic architecture, and with it the new skill and power which architects are seen to possess.

5A. For the Mass and its relation to altars, music and *ars sacra* see Jungmann (1952).

6. Dehio (1901) II, 24. Kimpel and Suckale (1985) 256–61 complained of the lack of any general history of the diverse functions of the medieval church. Their short outline of the variety of church use sets out a useful framework for future study. The relationship of the liturgy (in the broadest sense of the word as the ritual of the regular services and other forms of corporate or private worship) on the building and decoration of the church has therefore tended to be treated in rather piecemeal fashion, largely according to country. Liturgical influences on English Gothic architecture have been the object of a series of studies by Draper, his findings summarized in (1987). See also Klukas (1981) (1983/4) and (1995) for a consistently enthusiastic belief in the shaping power of liturgy on architectural planning. Duffy's monumental study (1992) is founded on the conviction that the imagery and dispositions of the later medieval parish church in England can only be understood in terms of the liturgy of the Mass. For the liturgy in twelfth- and thirteenth-century Gothic great churches in France there is now Sturgis (1991), who is sceptical of any real influence of liturgical practice on architectural form, and gives considerable freedom of aesthetic choice to the architect. On the more demonstrable connexions between liturgy and imagery in the French cathedral see Sauerländer (1992) (for Reims), Fassler (1993) (for Chartres) and Speer (1987) for Saint-Denis. For Germany there are the impressive studies of Kroos (1976) (on Bamberg), (1979/80) (on Cologne) (1989) on Magdeburg, and (1985) (on the display of relics in the earlier Middle Ages). See also her contributions (not specifically attributed) in Hubel and Schuller (1995) 55–74, 130–5, on the liturgy of Regensburg Cathedral. Liturgical practice, church interiors and moveable sculpture – their combined effect creating a living image of the Celestial City – are discussed with insight and learning in Tripps's (1998) study of church architecture in Late Gothic Germany. A short, useful general bibliography on liturgy and art can be found in Reynolds (1995).

6A. Suger not only preserved but also remodelled the old crypts at Saint-Denis, which may have housed the abbey's collection of Passion relics. For Suger's conservatism in this section of the church see van der Meulen and Speer (1988) 95–106, 256–98 (who controversially, and unsuccessfully, argue that Suger's crypt was a rebuilding of the eleventh-century *turris* – a two-storied apsidal east end with radiating chapels – given by William the Conqueror, see above, Part One, Chapter 2, Note 5F). Clark (1995) emphasizes Suger's retrospective inclinations, pointing to the re-use of Merovingian capitals and columns in the crypt. One of the first to isolate the gradual redundancy of crypts in the Gothic period was Sedlmayr (1950) 137–8, 231–3. For the crypt in the cathedral of Erfurt see Wedemeyer (1997) 433–7. Here, as in Siena and Bourges, the crypt was the result of sloping ground to the east, and did not entail the raising of the choir. In all three cases, the scenic and urbanistic pos-sibilities of the geography were dramatically exploited.

6B. A good general discussion of choirs and choir screens, at least in France, is given by Erlande-Brandenburg (1994) 266–83. For the Notre-Dame screen see Gillerman (1977) and Davis (1998). For Naumburg a vivid account, with the most recent literature, is provided by Sciurie and Möbius (1989). The book is essentially a re-print of their material on Naumburg in Sciurie and Möbius eds. (1989). Strasbourg's screen is described in Will (1972). There are other screens, or remains of screens long-demolished, in Laon, Chartres, Amiens, Bourges, Sens and Mainz. For the *coros* of Spain, which extend into the nave on the model of the original *coro* of Santiago de Compostella, see Kraus and Kraus (1986). Hall (1974a) reconstructs the rood screen of S. Maria Novella in Florence as a deep structure standing in the nave on a line with the fourth pil-lar pair from the east, and separated by about one bay from the western termi-nation of the monks' choir. Her reconstruction (1974) of the 1332–8 *tramezzo* at S. Croce, revealed by excavation in 1967, envisages a gabled loggia-type structure, running between the third pillar-pair from the east, and also sepa-rate, by about a bay and a half, from the western termination of the monks' choir in bay two. The purpose of this screen was to separate the monks from the laity on their entrance from cloister to choir Duffy (1997) analyses the para-doxical nature of late medieval English rood screens, as barriers between laity and clergy but also as 'pointers' to the sacred ambience of the sanctuary. Still the best general account of medieval choir screens is by Kirchner-Doberer (1956).

6C. The 'imaginary description' is to be found in Albrecht von Scharfenberg's secular narrative, the *Jungerer Titurel*, of *c*.1270–90. The Cologne collector Sulpiz Boisserée made detailed and wholly misleading draw-ings of the Temple on the basis of its lengthy descriptions in the poem. For a discussion of the poem and its commentators see Frankl (1960) 177–94. For comparisons between the poetic vision and the aesthetics of metalwork see Timmermann (2000), where some of the more recent literature on the Grail poem is listed.

6D. Frankl is misleading in suggesting that chapels did not proliferate in parish churches. On the contrary, the growth of the chantry and the patronage of lay confraternities resulted in the piecemeal enlargement of parish churches with private and semi-private altars and chapels. The general background to the process, growing out of the fear of Purgatory, is discussed in Le Goff (1984) and Rosenthal (1972). For chantries, soul-masses and chapels in England see Cook (1947) and Platt (1981) 88–146. For Germany the chapel foundations in Nuremberg parish churches – typical of urban patriciate piety throughout Germany – are discussed by Schleif (1990) and Klein (1990). An introductory survey of the phenomenon is provided by Colvin (1991) 152–89, and with use-ful bibliography (pp. 390–91).

7. Examples are Noyon, Dijon (Notre-Dame), Troyes (St Urbain), and Casamari. For processions starting in the west porch of Vézelay see Diemer (1985). Blum (1986a) has argued for the influence of Palm Sunday processions of the Sarum Rite on the choice of low portals for the west façades of Wells and Salisbury Cathedrals. Klukas (1981) connects the Sarum Use and its proces-sions with the rebuilding of the east end of Wells in the 1320s. Palm Sunday processions in France and Germany, particularly with wooden moveable sculp-tures of Christ on the Ass (a genre particularly popular in German and Central Europe in the later Middle Ages), are the subject of detailed analysis by Tripps (1998) 89–113. Kroos (1989) discusses the Palm Sunday procession from the church of Our Lady to the Cathedral in Magdeburg, carrying a two-sided painted panel, one with the image of the Entry into Jerusalem, the other with scenes of the Passion. The Easter processions went up into the choir gallery, the so-called *Bischofsgang*.

7A. A readable general discussion of cathedral financing is given by Kraus (1979). Lopez's (1952) analysis of the economy of thirteenth-century Beauvais suggested that the High Gothic cathedrals of northern France seriously dam-aged local economies. Lopez's neo-Marxist position was rebutted, at least as far as Beauvais was concerned – by Murray (1989) 47–8; but it was revived and developed by Abou-el-Haj (1988) in her analysis of Reims and its financing. In 1972 James (1972) tried to cost High Gothic Chartres in Australian dollars. Warnke (1976) especially 93–102, whose influential study concentrates largely on the early Middle Ages, saw the internationality of the building site as a criti-cal stimulus in the growth of a long distance money economy. Where sources survive, the funding of individual churches shows extreme fluctuations in income, and diverse patterns of management. For Utrecht see Vroom (1981) and (1996), for Milan see Welch (1995) 49–69. A good general introduction to funding and its managerial structures is given by Vroom (1989). The whole legal constitution of the building lodge, and its funding organization, is spelt out in admirable detail by Schöller (1989) especially 232–359. However, he does not include the rich English evidence, for which see Brown, Colvin and Taylor (1963).

7B. This kind of allegorical symbolism, in which the sign has little or no similarity to what it signifies beyond a conventional and abstract equivalence,

is discussed in full in Sauer's classic study, see note 8 below. For the wider connotations of the medieval topos of columns as apostles see Krautheimer (1942) and, more fully, Reudenbach (1980). Markschies (1995) also points to the topoi that abound in Suger's descriptions of his new Saint-Denis, especially in matters of light (*lux/lumen*) and clarity (*claritas/clarificatus*). Gage (1982) had already emphasized the conventional *ekphrasis* of Suger's descriptions, but in identifying the dazzling darkness of Saint-Denis's glazing with the 'negative theology' of the Pseudo-Dionysius he was crediting Suger with a theological sophistication not borne out by his writings or his character. A series of excel-lent articles by Hanning, Rezak, Maines, Zinn and Spiegel, on Suger's 'sym-bolist mentality' are gathered together in Gerson, ed., (1986), and the whole problem of Suger's aesthetics is set against the background of monastic reform, and monastic debates about the purpose of art, in northern France in the early twelfth century by Rudolph (1990). Neuheuser (1993) examines the liturgical and allegorical character of Suger's concept of beauty, and stresses the impor-tance of the liturgy as a linking factor in all Suger's writings. He denies that Suger had any autonomous 'aesthetic', and underlines the indicative function of his art and architecture as a stage for the liturgy, and as a vehicle of tran-scendence: it creates, or reifies a *respublica una* uniting the living with the com-munion of saints. Binding (1993a) isolates Suger's main architectural concerns: the symbolism of the column; the need to harmonize the old work with the new; the use of *spolia*; the allegorical cast of his architectural description. He also suggests (less convincingly) that Suger's reference to the 'geometrical and arithmetical instruments' by which the new choir was 'equalised' with the nave of the old church was not a technical comment on the skill of the architect, but a reference, in a spirit typical of Suger's love of allegory, to the divine *artifex* who creates according to number and measure. See also Binding (1985) for a fuller discussion on this point. All these authorities stress Suger's neo-Platonic cast of mind, a connexion first advanced by Panofsky (1946, 1979, 2nd edn), who indentified a specific debt in Suger's writings to the mystical theology of Denis the Pseudo-Areopagite and its Latin translation by John Scotus Eriugena. The Dionysian connexion was taken up by Sedlmayr (1950) as part of his metaphysical conception of the cathedral as an *Abbild* of heaven, and by von Simson (1956 and 1962) in his 'iconographical' analysis of the new Saint-Denis. Kidson (1987) radically questioned this trend by denying the neo-Platonic inspiration of Suger's patronage, and its indebtedness, in any real sense, to the Pseudo-Denis. Markschies (1995) carefully examined both the arguments and the Sugerian texts and could find no single reference to the Pseudo-Denis in, or his direct or indirect influence on, any of Suger's writings. Grant (1998) 23–5, 270–1, accepts some measure of Dionysian influence (the text of the *Celestial Hierarchy* was read in the refectory at Saint-Denis on the eve of the feast of Saint-Denis), but doubts its specific inspiration for Suger's inscriptions on the west door, and regards Suger's understanding of the *Celestial Hierarchy* as superficial. Many of these problems are seriously addressed in the recent German-Latin edition of the *De Consecratione*, with a series of critical commentaries on it edited by Binding and Speer (1996). The object is to establish a solid textual platform from which a number of con-tributing scholars launch specialist investigations into the more theological and liturgical aspects of Suger's Saint-Denis. Annas and Lubich (pp. 21–57) set Suger in his historical context, from which he emerges as a practical politician, not an intellectual. Lubich (pp. 59–63) presents the *De Consecratione*, in com-parison with similar texts, as a unique affair, half way between a traditional *translatio*, and a *fundatio*, with its emphasis on the abbey's ancient royal associ-ations. Pagel and Schroder (pp. 95ff) concentrate on Suger's allegorical con-ception of architecture: on his use of anagogy, on the new choir as a theatre for the liturgy (his concern for relic cults and his naming of the buildings parts as settings for processions), on his love of display – of *spectaculum*. Speer's careful analysis of the text of *De Consecratione* (pp. 65–9) and of the liturgical dimen-sion in Suger's thought (pp. 71–9) demonstrates that Suger's theology, espe-cially his 'anagogy', owed less to the Pseudo-Denis than to Hugh of Saint-Victor's *De Sacramentis*, and in any case belonged to the standard repertory of late Antique and medieval exegesis. For Speer, the real key to Suger's 'art' and his 'light metaphysics' was the liturgy, specifically the consecration. This brought together architecture and cult, the material and the immaterial; it established a coherence between the old church and the new, and between the diverse parts of the church.

8. The best and most comprehensive introduction is given in Joseph Sauer, *Symbolik des Kirchengebäudes* (Freiburg i. Br., 1902). On the subject of the fig-ure twelve, see p. 66. There are also much older treatises on numerical symbol-ism; see Frankl (1960) 211ff.

8A. The symbolist mentality of the twelfth century is brilliantly analyzed by Chenu (1968). For the varieties of medieval exegesis on the church as *ecclesia universalis* see Büchsel (1983). A critical survey of twentieth-century approaches to 'architectural iconography' can be found in Crossley (1988).

9. Günter Bandmann, *Mittelalterliche Architektur als Bedeutungsträger* (Berlin, 1951) 229. His interpretation seems doubtful when applied to places where the emperor could hardly have been expected to worship – for instance,

at Maria Laach. A useful survey of the various interpretations of 'westworks', with bibliography, can be found in Möbius (1968) and, for Carolingian architecture, Heitz (1980) 54–6, 70–8, 153–6. For early medieval choirs and their functions see also Möbius (1984).

9A. Although altars were placed in the large galleries of Anglo-Norman churches, there is no evidence, as far as I know, for similar functions in early Gothic galleried basilicas in the Ile-de-France. Kimpel and Suckale (1985) 250–1, advanced the idea that galleries were abandoned at Chartres and elsewhere after c.1194 because the new practice of elevating the host at the consecration of the Mass prompted patrons to remove any upper spaces which might have been used, wholly inappropriately, to look down on the altar. This, however, presupposed that galleries in early Gothic churches in France housed congregations for the eucharist, and that their access could not be controlled during the Mass. For the liturgical functions of galleries in Anglo-Norman Romanesque see Klukas (1978) and (1983/4), who argues that churches with low, unvaulted galleries (Durham, St Albans) adopted the liturgy of the *Decreta Lanfranci*, where no gallery altars were envisaged, while those with tall vaulted galleries (Winchester) followed the *Regularis Concordia*, which required gallery altars. The gallery in the choir at Magdeburg, the so-called *Bischofsgang*, was used for feasting at Easter, see Kroos (1989) 90.

9B. For the seclusion of nuns in their churches see Bruzelius (1992) and (1995), who deals mainly with Italian Angevin material; Simmons (1992), who discusses Fontevraud in the later twelfth century; and Hamburger (1992) and (1998), who relates the laws of enclosure, and its actual enforcement in the church, to female spirituality in later medieval Germany.

10. Karl Lehmann, 'The Dome of Heaven', *The Art Bulletin*, XXVII (1945) 1–27. Gothic vaults made explicit references to the heavenly spheres: see the stars painted on the vaults of the Sainte-Chapelle in Paris or S. Francesco in Assisi. Tripps (1998) 141–200, gathers together interesting instances of the more explicit identification with heaven in Late Gothic vaults. These include figural bosses, arboreal painting, and large circular holes in the vault through which images, flowers and even fire were lowered or thrown down into the space during the liturgical theatricals which accompanied the major feasts.

11. Luke 17: 21: regnum Dei intra vos est.

11A. For the notion of 'suitability' or decorum, of the fitness of form to function, in medieval church architecture, in particular at Salisbury and Wells cathedrals, see Draper (1987) and (1995). It has also been applied by Suckale in vol. 4, *Die Parler* (1980) to the different 'modes' of design used by Peter Parler. For the 'aesthetics' of St Bernard see Melczer and Soldwedel (1982), Talbot (1986), Rudolph (1990). St Bernard's influence on Suger's new church at Saint-Denis is a topic riven by controversy. Panofsky (1979, 2nd edn.) first advanced the theory (followed by von Simson and many others) that St Bernard's criticism of Cluniac Romanesque forced Suger to reconsider the whole nature of monastic art and architecture, and in so doing, to arrive at a style we call 'Gothic'. This, with proper historical nuances, was also the brunt of Rudolph's sensitive analyses (1990) and (1990a). Kidson (1987) however denied that Bernard had any influence on Suger. Grant (1998) argues convincingly that Bernard left his mark on Suger the politician and the monastic reformer, but he had little influence on the abbot's patronage at Saint-Denis, precisely on the grounds of decorum: that what was appropriate for a Cistercian monastery did not apply to a royal and public pilgrimage church. For St Francis and the Franciscans' influence on art see Egger (1982).

11B. Frankl is here voicing a concept popular in later medieval exegesis, particularly in sermons preached on the dedication of churches: that the church is an allegory of the soul. St Bernard's first sermon on the consecration of the church likened the church with the monks within to the individual physical body sheltering the Holy Spirit. See Horie (1998) 117ff.

12. Unfortunately, mathematicians also call their signs symbols, although they are really only signs. In the terminology of my *System etc.* (Note 181 to Chapter 4) signs like signposts, numbers, and letters have a meaning in the second degree of concepts; signposts or the marks on a scale are cognate with their meaning (direction, distance, etc.) and letters and musical notation are conventions. Signs become symbols when they take on a higher meaning – for instance, a cross is a sign for a meaning of the second degree in mathematics, but if it signifies the Cross of Christ, or Christ himself, it becomes a symbol of the third degree, as do the attributes for the saints.

13. Sensations, feeling, and human instincts are also part of nature, whereas our conceptions, ideas, and concepts (including our conceptions and concepts of sensations, feelings, and human instincts) are creations of human reason – which is a part of the human spirit. This is the same relationship as that between a lion as a natural object and the notion 'lion', in which the natural object is included. (Cf. Frankl, *System*, 667.)

13A. This may be Frankl's veiled criticism of Sedlmayr's (1950) monumental study, which interpreted the Gothic cathedral, not just as a metaphor for, but as a literal image (*Abbild*) of the Heavenly City. See also his bitter review – some would call it a parody – of Sedlmayr's book in his (1960) 753–9. The diverse textual references to the church as the Heavenly Jerusalem are neatly

brought together in Stookey (1969). An authoritative survey of the church as *ecclesia universalis* in medieval exegesis can be found in Büchsel (1983). Büchsel, and Haussherr (1968), do not see the concept of the Heavenly Jerusalem as specific to any particular style. Tripps (1998) 33–56, discusses the liturgical evidence for the notion of the church as paradise. Schlink (1997/8) suggests that the whole notion of the church as the Heavenly Jerusalem is a fiction of German art history.

13B. See Laufner and Klein (1975).

13C. See von Juraschek (1954).

13D. See Morgan and Sandler (1987) nr 110. Murray (1996) 42–3, and plates 47 (a) and (b), sees the image of the celestial city in the Trinity College Apocalypse (Trinity College, Cambridge, Ms R.16.2), with its squares forming a golden section ratio, as analogous to the central *ad quadratum* matrix underlying the crossing (and therefore the whole ground plan) of Amiens Cathedral.

13E. For the depiction of the Celestial City and the Holy Sepulchre in Carolingian manuscripts, some of them apocalypses, see Heitz (1980) 201–22. The whole problem of representing the unrepresentable in apocalypse imagery is discussed in a wide-ranging essay by Alexander (1999)

14. The interpretation of the Song of Solomon as a dialogue between Christ and the Church (the bride) is superimposed symbolism. Originally this was a pure love lyric, meant in its most concrete sense. St John speaks of the bride of the Lamb and, by the bride, means the Heavenly Jerusalem – the kingdom of God. It must be left to theologians to decide whether this interpretation of the Song of Solomon is a transference of the sense of the Apocalypse.

15. It is unlikely that he can have known Ovid's description of the palace of Helios.

16. Frankl (1960) the chapter on architectural fantasies (p. 159ff.). See also Timmermann (2000). It is generally agreed that the closest medieval building came to a literal realization of the Younger Titurel's vision of the Grail Temple was in the chapel of the Holy Cross in Karlštejn (Karlstein) Castle, and to a lesser extent, the precious-stone-encrusted walls of the Wenceslas Chapel in Prague Cathedral, also a foundation of Charles IV. Mösenender's (1981) penetrating study of the Karlstein Chapel rehearses the literary, liturgical and exegetical sources for the use of precious stones in architecture, particularly 'glasshouse' reliquary chapels. See also Legner (1978) and Meier (1978), both articles in vol. 3, *Die Parler*. An up-to-date and authoritative analysis of the Karlstein programme, and its sources, can now be found in Fajt and Royt (1998) especially pages 128–75.

17. Bandmann, *op. cit.* 89. See also Alfred Stange, *Das frühchristliche Kirchengebäude als Bild des Himmels* (Cologne, 1950). Stange rejects Kitschelt's theory, but himself puts forward an untenable one when he tries to show a connexion between the cathedral at Trier as it was about 450, and the text in the book of the Revelation, 21. See also Stange (1964).

18. Richard Krautheimer, 'Introduction to an Iconography of Medieval Architecture', *Journal of the Warburg and Courtauld Institutes*, V (1942).

The only thing that could arouse criticism in this article is the word 'iconography'. Architecture is not and can never be an icon. This essay does not touch on the problem of Gothic style, and it need not, therefore, be discussed further here. The Greek word 'eikon', although it might refer to any kind of image, was not applied in the Middle Ages to architecture. But the medieval conception of 'image' was often non-pictorial, and the Middle Ages saw the 'image' not as a 'picture' of the material world but a 'likeness', a matter of spiritual similarity. In that sense architecure could be treated as an icon, rather than as an idol. For the notion of the image and its related concepts of picturing, perceiving and imitating, see Mitchell (1986), who recognises the inextricable power of ideology in image-making. A profusion of stimulating ideas on the subject, but with little reference to the problem of medieval architecture, can be found in Camille (1989). The relationship between image and viewer is discussed on the broadest scale by Freedberg (1989); and Belting (1994) enlighted the whole problem by seeing imagery in the west against the background of eastern Christianity. But neither tackled the problem of architecture. The nearest equivalent in the field of architectural history to these broad explorations of meaning has been Onians (1988) but his discussion of medieval buildings is flawed by factual errors.

19. It should be stressed once more that representational art embraces sculpture and painting, but not architecture. The Italians classified all three arts under the heading *arti del disegno*, but one could also put the art of writing (signum), that is calligraphy, under this heading.

20. In this example we are differentiating between the form of one spatial dimension and the form of two such dimensions. One cannot define either meaning or form. For definitions, one requires a *genus proximum*, but meaning and form are themselves fundamental concepts – in fact, the most fundamental in the whole realm of philosophy (Frankl, *System*, 3, 20).

20A. For interpretations of the meanings of this vegetal architecture, especially in Germany, see above, Part One, Chapter 4, Note 164A.

21. The church of St Nicolas at Leipzig, illustrated in Hermann Schmitz, *Die Gotik in deutschen Kunst- und Geistesleben* (Berlin, 1921), illustration 87.

21A. The history of vegetal architecture and the primitive hut, from Vitruvius to the Enlightenment, is discussed by Gaus (1971).

22. Fundamental for the definition of the concept Art is Willi Drost's *Form als Symbol*, cited in the Foreword.

23. For quotations of the many opinions, see Frankl (1960) 237–414.

24. Two familiar examples are the red sandstone of Strasbourg cathedral at sunset, and the white marble of Milan cathedral by moonlight.

25. Frankl, *System*, 496.

26. Alfred D. F. Hamlin's term.

26A. For St Gall see Horn and Born (1979), and Hecht (1983).

26B. A useful history of the monastery and its buildings is still Braunfels (1972). On the cloister in the early Middle Ages see the articles devoted to the subject in the double issue of *Gesta*, 12 (1973).

27. Léon Honoré Labande, *L'église Saint Trophime d'Arles*, P.M. (Paris, 1930) 72. The inscriptions on the wall and north gallery of the north walk of the cloister show that the work must have been begun before 1183. See Stoddard (1973) 199–271.

28. Illustrated in Aubert (1943) II, 5. See also Berenguier (1975).

29. Lucien Bégule, *L'abbaye de Fontenay*, P.M. (Paris, n.d.) 32.

30. Aubert (1943) II, 10.

31. Aubert (1943) II, 19, and *C.A.*, XCIV (1931) 175. The two walks of the cloister with six-part vaults, and dating from the thirteenth century, are the northern and the western. The eastern and southern walks are fourteenth-century additions, with four- and six-part vaults respectively. See Meslé and Jenn (1980).

32. Aubert (1943) II, 14. Aubert gives the date as the end of the twelfth century – that is, contemporary with St Hugh's Choir at Lincoln, and therefore much later than Montivilliers (1140–50).

33. *C.A.*, LXXVIII (1911) I, plan, 166. See also Clark and King (1983) 44–7, who date it to before the beginning of the choir extension of *c*.1205. It actually has three wings, of which the eastern and western are stunted.

34. C.-H. Besnard, *Le Mont Saint-Michel*, P.M. (Paris, n.d.) 87.

34A. See now Grant (1987) 294ff. Grant (1991) 119–20, confirms the English, specifically Lincoln, influence in the contrapuntal arcading of Mont-Saint-Michel's cloister. She points to similar syncopated arcade rhythms in Normandy in the destroyed cloister of Saint-Pierre-sur-Dives and in the existing west portal of Sées cathedral. For the cloister's stylistic connexions with Hambye and Coutances see Grant in: Baylé, dir. (1997) vol. 1 147–8.

35. *C.A.*, LXXIV (1906) 185, plan facing p. 170. See also Seymour, *op. cit.* (Note 10 to Chapter 2) 67. See also Kimpel and Suckale (1985) 361–4, who date its beginning to 'after 1231'.

36. See Lethaby, *op. cit.* 84. See now Wilson (1986) 80–5.

36A. Despite Bishop Walter de la Wyle's gift of land in 1263 for a larger cloister, Blum (1991) 22–36, sets the real beginning of the cloister into the 1270s. Construction began with the north walk, and proceeded along the east walk and, from *c*.1276, the south walk, where work stopped, *c*.1280, on the seventh bay from the east. The rest of the south walk and the west walk were compleed *c*.1290–early fourteenth century. Frankl's descriptions of the cloisters at Westminster and Salisbury as 'High Gothic' is another misleading consequence of his refusal to recognize the existence of Rayonnant as a stylistic category. These cloisters belong to the earliest instances in England of the use of French-inspired, Rayonnant, bar tracery.

36B. For this Laon-inspired workshop at Maulbronn see Chapter 2, Note 54 above. For the most recent literature on the monastic buildings, and the so-called Paradies Master who built the first (east) walk of the cloister *c*.1220–30. see Hassler, Knoch and Glaser (1994). They date the rest of the cloister to 'after 1270', beginning with the north walk and the remodelling of the whole east wing, including the chapter house on the ground floor and the twelfth-century dormitory above.

37. Lozoya, *op. cit.* (Note 67 to Chapter 3) 164 and figure 166.

38. Net-vaults are not the same thing as star vaults with triradial figures. The terminology used in literature was extremely inexact, and there is no generally recognized definition of the differences. The essential thing in a star-vault is that more than three ribs intersect on a common ridge, whereas the essential thing in a net-vault is that the ribs (not ridge-ribs) intersect at several points. Net-vaults are not a variation of star-vaults. The terminology was clarified by Clasen (1958) especially 24–71, and now presents no problem.

39. Reinhardt, *op. cit.* (*Deutsche Bauten*, XIII) 36. Gantner, *op. cit.* (Note 73 to Chapter 3) II, 165ff., who also mentions the cloister at Rorschach, which dates from 1483, and may be by Erasmus Grasser. See Julier (1978) 154–80, who related the net vault's inspiration to the circle of Madern Gerthener, and particularly to the Peterskirche in Frankfurt.

40. H.P. Eydoux, *Das Cisterzienserkloster Bebenhausen* (Tübingen, 1950) 36. See now Kohler (1995).

40A. See above, p.209 and Chapter 4, Note 80A.

40B. For the Wells Chapter House see above, p. 187 and Chapter 4, Note 4. For the Old St Paul's Chapter House see Harvey (1978) 51ff, 75ff; and Wilson

(1987) 369–70. Wilson (1999) surveys the connexions between English thirteenth-century chapter houses and their continental equivalents, including Villard de Honnecourt's drawing of a chapter house, and umbrella-vaulted spaces in central Germany and Bohemia (the eastern crypt at Kouřim, the chapter house at Vyšší Brod and the Silberkammer in Worms).

40C. Frankl is underestimating the influence of secular building types on church architecture in the later Middle Ages. It is now recognized that the precocious appearance of decorative vaulting (an essential component of the German Late Gothic style) in the lower Vistula in the early fourteenth century was the initiative of secular and not church architects. Such vaults first appeared not in the choir aisles of the Cistercian church at Pelplin (as most published sources assume) but in the chapter house and Grand Master's summer refectory of the Teutonic Knights's castle-capital at Marienburg (Malbork). The Pelplin choir aisle vaults, wrongly dated since Clasen (1958) to the late thirteenth century, – see Crossley (1990) – are now considered to be mid-fourteenth-century constructions; while the Marienburg rooms are both securely dated to the 1330s and 1340s. See Becker-Hounslow (1998) and note 44b below. Another critical ingredient of the Late Gothic formal vocabulary, the ogee arch, also made an early appearance in Germany in quasi-secular contexts: in the east wing of the cloister of Konstanz cathedral (*c*.1320?), and in the chapter house at Heiligenkreuz in Lower Austria (*c*.1290). See above, Chapter 4, Note 22A. Similarly, the earliest dated flowing tracery in Spain is in the Catalan cloister of Santes Creus (1331–41), probably by an English mason. See Bony (1979) 65, and note 63, and plate 37. Bony (1979) 22, 36, was among the first to point to the clear influence of secular timber construction on English fourteenth-century church architecture, notably the choir of St Augustine's at Bristol, and of temporary timber structures (tournament podia?) on the crenellated cornices of St Stephen's chapel and the Eleanor crosses. On a more utilitarian level, we should note the possible influence of barns and double-naved refectories on the churches of the friars *c*.1300, an issue touched on by Schenkluhn (1985) 74, 108. For Cistercian conventual buildings, often with double-naves, see Braunfels (1972) 97–110. Undercrofts are discussed in Jansen (1990). Liberties first taken in a 'lower' genre of architecture – the simplification of supports, the rejection of capitals and vaults – find themselves promoted to a higher, ecclesiastical context in the fourteenth and fifteenth centuries. The whole question of the interplay between secular and ecclesiastical architecture in the later Middle Ages needs proper investigation.

40D. See Michler (1974).

41. On these Saintes Chapelles, see Joan Evans, *Art in Medieval France* (London, etc., 1948) 194 etc. See also Hacker-Sück (1962).

42. *C.A.*, LXXVII (1912) I, 296ff. Viollet-le Duc's descriptions of the castle, despite some inaccuracies, are invaluable. See (1858–68) principally vol. 3 (1859) 107–17, and (1861). A good analysis of Coucy, with photographs before its demolition by the Germans in 1917, is given by Mesqui (1988) 134–59, and (1991) vol. 1 168–9, 217, 237–8, 269–70. See also Albrecht (1986) 24, 58–60.

42A. Frankl is incorrect here. Even the massive cylindrical keep of the thirteenth-century castle had internal Gothic features, such as rib vaults, crocket capitals, *en delit* shafts and pointed arches; while the great Salle des Preuses of Enguerrand VII Coucy, begun in 1380, is rich in Gothic tracery, vaulted window alcoves, and (originally) fireplaces.

43. Dehio, *G.d.d.K.*, II, 297. This chapter is probably the best thing ever to have been written on the subject of German castles.

There are still no up-to-date surveys of the German castles throughout the Middle Ages. Tillmann (1958–61) is a useful dictionary, and Meyer (1963) provides a general history. Maurer (1977) gives a useful introduction to the Hohenstaufen castles and Arens (1977) to their fortified palaces. Good studies on particular problems can be found in Meckseper (1975) (French influence in the thirteenth century) and Torbusz (1998) (the castles of the Teutonic Knights). Albrecht (1995) offers a much-needed synthesis of royal and noble castle-palace building in western Europe, but concentrates less on Germany than England, France and the Netherlands. A detailed and authoritative study of early medieval German castles, from Charlemagne's Aachen and Ingelheim to Frederick II's Seligenstadt, is given by Binding (1996).

44. G. Colombes, *Le palais des Papes d'Avignon*, P.M. (Paris, 1927). A convenient illustrated description is provided by Gagnière (1977). A detailed history of its construction is given in Caselli (1981). Its influence on the growth of new kinds of space, function and outlook in later palace architecture in France, especially in the Valois castles of the later fourteenth century, is nicely judged by Albrecht (1995) 120–7. Whiteley (1985) assesses its influence, in particular, on the design of staircases.

44A. For Pierrefonds see Harmand (1959) and (1983) and Mesqui (1988) 281–93. For Karlstein see Möseneder (1981) and all the studies brought together in Fajt and Royt (1998). Also see above, Part Two, Note 16.

44B. For a full description of the castle, with all literature up to the early 1990s, see Mroczko and Arszyński, eds., vol. 2 (1995) 152–5. The castle has attracted a vast of literature since its art historical rediscovery in the late eighteenth century. The handiest survey of its fabric and history from an older,

German, generation of scholars, is by its inter-war curator Schmid (1955). The immediate post-war Polish position is reflected in the work of a leading historian of the Knights, Karol Górski, of which his (1973) monograph is a useful conspectus. The earliest of the castle's rooms with all-over 'triradial' vaults are the chapter house of the upper castle and the great refectory of the Grand Master's palace. Because these belong to some of the earliest decorative vaults on the continent their dating and their sources of inspiration (English chapter houses?) have long been subjects of comment and controversy. Schmid (1955) 18, 51, dated the chapter house to c.1310–12 and the refectory to before 1324, and attributed them both to the same architect: the 'Remter-Baumeister' Clasen (1958) 39–48, dated the chapter house to c.1300 and the refectory to c.1320. Frazik (1967) 83, and (1985) put the chapter house around 1330 and the refectory 'to the second quarter of the fourteenth century'. Since then, Skibiński (1982) 87, in a study of the upper castle's chapel, has favoured a date of c.1320–4 for the chapter house. Jurkowlaniec (1989) 82–94, 179–82, in his analysis of the architectural sculpture, suggests that the chapter house and the great refectory were done by the same shop, active 1331–40 under the Grand Masters Luther von Braunschweig (1331–5) and Dietrich von Altenburg (1335–41). The architectural similarities between the chapter house and the refectory, already noted by Schmid (1955), would confirm this relative dating, but not the absolute chronology. A clear summary of the issues, with full descriptive catalogue of all the spaces of the castle, can be found in Torbus's monumental study of the castles of the Teutonic Knights (1998) 260–88, and 487–517, especially 264–5, 272–3, 496, 504–5, 514–15, who dates both rooms to c.1330, and certainly not before 1324. For the problem of English influence at Marienburg, the connexions with the very similar vaults of the slightly earlier Briefkapelle in St Mary at Lubeck, and the dating, see Crossley (1990), Torbus (1998) 312–15, and, much more fully, Becker-Hounslow (1998) (1998a).

44C. See Bonnel (1963).

45. Both are illustrated together in Clasen, *Die gotische Baukunst* (Wildpark-Potsdam, 1930) plate XV. See Willemsen (1977) especially 16off, and (1982). The literature on Castel del Monte up to 1978 is discussed by Krönig (1978). From 1990 the Heidelberg Academy of Sciences has supervised a multi-author, multi-discipline programme of research on the castle. The work includes a detailed recording and photogrammetric measuring of the structure, the investigation of its stone polichromy, and the assessment of its place in palace architecture in the Mediterranean and the near east. Some of the findings have been published in Schirmer *et al.* (1994).

45A. for the Powder Tower (Pulvertum) see Šperling (1965). For the Old Town Bridge Tower see Chadraba (1974) (with some far-fetched interpretations of its function and iconography as a 'triumphal arch'). Sauerländer (1994) especially 195–200, relates its imperial imagery to the juridical idea of *concordia imperii*, and to other bridge towers with regal figures. The fullest analysis of the Bridge Tower – iconographical and structural – is by Vítovský (1994). He reconstructs a slow building campaign, beginning under Peter Parler in the late 1360s/early 1370s, but continuing under a second master in the 1380s at the level of the second (top) floor. It was this second architect, not Peter Parler, who in c.1390 inserted the influential net vault over the ground floor entrance way.

45B. See Kimpel and Suckale (1985) 369–71, and Branner (1960) 182, with bibliography. For the Viollet-le-Duc restorations see Saulnier (1980) 66–71.

45C. See Koepf (1958) 95–8, Dehio and Zimdars (1993) 524. Binding, Kainzer and Wiedenau (1975) provide a good introduction to the kind of half-timbered German house or hall represented by Markgröningen. Griep (1985) offers a useful survey of the history of the German middle-class house. See also Büttner and Meissner (1983) 39–101. The fullest survey of German town houses is the monumental Bernt *et al.* (1959 onwards). Markgröningen appears in the volume by Heinitz (1970) 120ff.

46. The attribution is doubtful; see Thieme-Becker II, 138, but not improbable. The leaders of the cathedral workshop participated in the planning of the Piazza della Signoria and some of its principal buildings in the second half of the fourteenth century. Toker (1979) and (1983) has pointed to many similarities between Arnolfo's project for the cathedral and S. Croce (octagonal piers, wide intercolumniations, wooden roofs), and some of the more elaborate capitals in the biforia windows in the Palazzo Vecchio can be paralleled with Arnolfo's (or his workshop's) work. For the Palazzo Vecchio itself, and its place in Florentine urban design in the later Trecento see Trachtenberg (1988) and (1997) 87–147. Trachtenberg argues convincingly for radical changes in the design during construction. The first (1299) project called for a narrow, relatively small tower set back and rising behind simple battlements, and with the main entrance on the north side. The second project, developed after 1307, turned the palace's main façade westwards, to the Piazza della Signoria, increased the scale of the superstructure by enlarging the battlements with a windowed gallery, as well as heightening the tower and projecting it forward over the battlements. The tower was also given a massive columnar belfry. Trachtenberg (1989) also reconstructs the original shape of the courtyard and discusses its place in Trecento urban palace design. Rubinstein (1995) espe-

cially 1–34, 79–94, presents the documentary and historical evidence. He does not comment on Trachtenberg's thesis in (1988) but thinks his restoration of the cortile is 'plausible' (p. 18, note 133). Still the best general survey of the history of medieval town halls in Italy is Paul (1969), though a good short summary of the main issues can be found in Cunningham (1995).

46A. See Nagel (1971) 47–8 and Delmelle (1975).

46B. See von Osterhausen (1973).

46C. The Doge's palace belongs to a Venetian tradition of thirteenth-century palace architecture with long rows of arcades on the ground and first floors and a second floor with few, relatively small windows. An account of the phases of construction can be found in Arslan (1972) 141–54, 246–54, who argues for a unified design by a single architect laid down a few years before 1350, a mid-fourteenth-century date for some of the sculpture of both loggia and portico on the south side, but a slow execution of the south façade lasting to the end of the century. He also reviews the conflicting evidence for the completion of the south wing. See also Franzoi, Pignatti and Wolters (1990) especially 38–78, for the most recent general account. A good discussion of the marble used for the building, and of the careers of the masons, including the respective contributions of Giovanni and Bartolomeo Bon, can be found in Connel (1988) 22–3, 121–2, 127–9, 135–6. Bienert (1990) offers a symbolic interpretation of the palace, based on its function as a prison, and on its three main floors, as an image of Dante's 'Divine Comedy'. He sees a juridical – even penal – message in much of its exterior sculpture on the ground and first floors.

46D. The church was begun c.1330 with the construction of the choir chapels and the outer walls of the north transept. The completion of the transepts and the main choir, and the construction of the nave, belong to a second campaign, beginning in about 1361. The nave was under construction in 1391 (second pair of pillars from east), but not finished until the late 1440s. The high altar was consecrated in 1469. See Dellwing (1970) 117–37, and (1990) 91–4 and Schenkluhn (2000) 186–9, who assesses this church and its contemporary Venetian rival, the Dominican church of S. Giovanni e Paolo, as culminations of a particular kind of brick mendicant architecture in the Veneto (Treviso, Verona, Vicenza).

46E. Arslan (1972) 233–44, stresses the separateness of the Ca d'Oro from earlier Venetian architecture. The palace is the only one of the period for which building records of any substance remain. Arslan and especially Goy (1993) give a clear account of the Venetian and Lombard craftsmen and attribute parts of the façade to the different masters mentioned in the account books. Goy publishes the rich documentary evidence from the building, relates it stylistically to other Venetian palaces, especially the Doge's palace, and gives a coherent history of its construction. He puts the deficiencies in its planning (mainly the lack of coordination between the upper two loggias and the floors of the rooms behind them) down to the lack of a professional architect, though the patron, Contarini, was – he argues – closely involved in the work.

46F. The Louvain town hall was begun in rivalry with the earlier town hall in Brussels in 1438 by the architect Sulpitius van Vorst. His death a year later brought Jan II Keldermans to head the work. Matheus de Layens, city architect since 1445, took over in 1447–8. For structural reasons he abandoned the idea of a single steeple on the Brussels model, and compensated by having four prominent angle turrets. Work was finished in 1468–9. See Maesschalk and Viaene (1977), Lemaire and Godts (1978); and also (in brief) Buyle *et al.* (1997) 177–8 and van Wylick-Westermann (1987) 12–13 (for Jan II Keldermans).

46G. For a detailed and well-illustrated description of the house, as well as a vivid account of the career of Jacques Coeur himself, see Favière (1992), who has a full bibliography. The art-historical position of the house, between aristocratic display and bourgeois comfort, is assessed by Albrecht (1986) 85–91, and (1995) 129–31.

47. Described in Viollet-le-Duc, *Dictionnaire*, under 'Maison', VI, 277.

47A. The different heights and degrees of decoration in the building reflect the function and status of the rooms, see Albrecht (1986) 88–9.

48. Otto Stiehl, *Das deutsche Rathaus im Mittelalter* (Leipzig, 1905) 156. The complex building history of this town hall, begun in 1299 and finished in the early sixteenth century, has been authoritatively disentangled by Zlat (1976). Mroczko and Arszyński, eds. (1995) vol. 2 260–2, give an exhaustive bibliography and identify no less than six stages of construction, of which the most important, and the last (c.1470–1510), is characterized by the rich decorative and sculptural manner imported by Saxon masons of the so-called 'Lausitz lodge', from Görlitz (Briccius Gauske/Gautzke) and Meissen (Paul Preusse). It is in this period, with the construction of oriels on the east and south façades, and the incrustation of the exterior with elaborate sculpture and micro-architecture, that the town hall acquired the picturesque irregularity which Frankl describes.

49. On Aigues-Mortes, founded by Louis IX in 1240, cf. Pierre Lavedan, *Histoire de l'urbanisme* (Paris, 1926) I, 312. The plan of the town is almost regular, but the irregularities are sufficient to banish the possibility of monotony. For Aigues-Mortes see Fliche (1950). For chequerboard new towns see the English and French *bastides* of the thirteenth and fourteenth centuries in

Languedoc, discussed in Lavedan and Hugueney (1969) (which deals with Villeneuve-sur-Lot and Vianne) and (1970). For a short account of Edward I's southern French *bastides*, and his new towns in England and Wales – all with chequerboard plans, see Shillaber (1947). There is also the series of German thirteenth-century colonial towns with regular layouts, e.g. Neubrandenburg, Prenzlau, Frankfurt/Oder, Chelmno (Kulm), Soldin. For some of these see Meckseper (1982) 70ff. Still the best general discussion of regular urban planning in central Italy is by Braunfels (1979, 4th edtn.), though for Florence and its new towns see Friedman (1988).

50. Described in *Darst. etc. Sachsen*, section 40 (Dresden, 1919) 396. For the origins and career of Arnold von Wesftalen, who came from the Leipzig family of Westfal, and not from Westphalia, see Lemper (1972) who provides the best account of his work at Meissen. Radová-Štiková (1974) and (1988) tries to locate his sources of inspiration, or the traces of his earlier career, in Magdeburg, Leipzig and the north aisle of Braunschweig cathedral. Koch (1960) finds direct French sources for the main façade of the Meissen palace: its roof architecture in Jacques Coeur's house in Bourges, and its principal staircase, with its enclosing arcades on the ground floor, in Pierrefonds. But he accepts too easily Viollet-le-Duc's fantastic reconstruction of the Pierrefonds staircase.

51. Cell-vault (*Zellengewölbe*) is the German name for a vault consisting of concave troughs or hollows separated by groins. See above, Chapter 4, Note 173B.

51A. The cell vault is Arnold von Westfalen's most obvious contribution to church architecture in eastern Europe, see above, Chapter 4, Note 173B. But other novelties of the Albrechtsburg – its 'curtain' window heads, its vaults without arcade arches, its preference for concavity and multi-level vault springing points – all had a formative influence on later church architecture, especially in Upper Saxony, Bohemia, Lusatia and Silesia. See Nussbaum (2000) 59–61, and Ullmann ed. (1984) 133–59.

52. For the Poitiers palace and Jean de Berry's modifications see Labande-Mailfert (1951) and Blomme (1993) 280–6. Its position in the history of French palace architecture is assessed by Albrecht (1986) 56–8. Ringshausen (1972) 69–72, sets it briefly in the context of Guy de Dammartin's work and early Flamboyant in France.

53. M. Junghändel and Cornelius Gurlitt, *Die Baukunst Spaniens* (Dresden, 1893–8) II, plate 77. For Harlech and Beaumaris see Taylor, in: Brown, Colvin and Taylor, vol. I (1963) 357–65, and 395–408; Brown (1970) 95–112. For Tarascon see Pressouyre (1963).

54. For Conway Castle see Taylor (1963) 337–54. Even more irregular is Caernarvon Castle of 1283–1327, see Taylor (1963) 369–95. Completely regular on the other hand is Beaumaris (begun 1295, construction finished in the 1330s). Tendencies towards regularity and irregularity existed side by side. For the Welsh castles as a whole see also Brown (1970) 95–111, and the useful survey of castles in Europe by Brown *et al.* (1980).

54A. Recent developments in the study of castles in the later Middle Ages have tended to stress, not just their military functions (as Frankl does in this section), but also their social and symbolic roles. An obvious case is Albrecht (1986) and (1995). But see also Coulson (1979) (for an extreme view of the non-military use of later castles), Thompson (1987) and Pounds (1994). Morris (1998) examines much of the secular architecture of Edward I of England's reign as the setting of Arthurian romance.

55. John Harvey, *Gothic England* (London, 1947). For the Palais de Justice in Rouen see Chirol (1926), and Chirol and Lavallee (1977). The town hall in Ulm was destroyed in 1944 and its interiors have been rebuilt. For Westminster Hall see Courtenay (1984) (1987) (1990), whose studies have concentrated on Hugh Herland's spectacular roof. Wilson (1997) concentrates on its more neglected arpects, including the hall's functions, its symbolism and its stylistic position in English Perpendicular architecture.

56. Junghändel and Gurlitt, *op. cit.* II, plate 77. The palace was begun under Don Iñigo Lopez de Mendoza in 1480 by the architect Juan Guas and the sculptor Egas Cueman, and completed *c.*1500. Despite interior damage in the Spanish Civil War 1936–9, it remains one of the finest examples of the 'Isabelline' or Hispano-Flemish style. See Azcárate Ristori (1951) and Herrera Casado (1975).

56A. Still fundamental for the 'coherent' and 'intellectual' nature of Gothic sculpture are Emile Mâle's two great volumes on religious art in France retranslated (1978) and (1984). Still indispensable for French Gothic sculpture is Sauerländer (1972). Camille's neo-Marxist and post-structuralist account (1989) amounts to a direct criticism of Mâle and his methods. Williamson's (1995) synthesis for Gothic Europe up to 1300 is judicious and well-informed.

56B. But not if the original twelfth-century choir had flying buttresses as now seems likely. See Bruzelius (1987) 551ff, Murray (1998) and Chapter 3, Note 38. James (1992) 276–7 also infers the presence of flyers from the start, but dates them to *c.*1215, when, he thinks, the vaults of the choir and eastern bays of the nave were finally built. This delay is implausible.

57. Frankl (1960) the chapter on Riegl (p. 627). But the *wollen*, the 'must'

element in Riegl's concept is stressed by Pächt (1963), reprinted in (1977). Riegl's concept in the context of German art history in the late nineteenth century is discussed by Podro (1982) 71–97. The clearest and most up-to-date analysis of the term, and of Riegl's contribution to a supra-personal art history, can be found in Iversen (1993) and Olin (1992).

58. Bandmann, *op. cit.* 83.

59. On the six preserved heads, see above, note 33 to chapter 1. The difficulties of relying on drawings of the Saint-Denis column figures in discussions of style are dealt with by Crosby (1987) 192–7.

59A. For the chronology of the west façade see above, Chapter 3, Note 42A.

59B. For the transept sculpture are Chartres see above, Chapter 3, Note 5.

59C. For the Cologne choir statues see Williamson (1995) 195–7, with literature.

59D. For the Sainte-Chapelle statues see Sauerländer (1972) 471–2; Williamson (1995) 147–9.

60. Adolf Goldschmidt, 'Das Naumburger Lettnerkreuz im Kaiser Friedrich Museum in Berlin', *Jahrbuch der preussischen Kunstsammlungen*, XXXVI (1915) 137.

61. Hahnloser, *op. cit.* (Note 15 to Chapter 3) plates 4 and 15, text pp. 19 to 40.

62. Strongly curved hips can be seen in the Passion window in the west wall of the cathedral at Chartres, which dates from about 1150, and, again at Chartres, in the oculus in bay XVIII, which dates from before 1220. Illustrated in Yves Delaporte and Etienne Houvet, *Les vitraux de la cathédrale de Chartres* (Chartres, 1926) colour plates II and LII respectively. There are earlier Byzantine models.

63. Louise Lefrançois-Pillion, *Les sculpteurs français du XII siècle* (Paris, 1931), and *Les sculpteurs français du XIII siècle* (Paris, n.d.). See now Sauerländer (1972).

63A. Frankl's categories – 'Transitional', 'the Transition' – are confusing. In reality, most authorities now accept that the beginnings of Gothic sculpture and of Gothic architecture, at least in France, went hand in hand. Both new styles begin more or less simultaneously at Saint-Denis (west portals) and Chartres (west portals). See Sauerländer (1972) passim and Williamson (1995) 11–17. Art historians of metalwork and painting still, however, refer to products in these media dating to the last quarter of the twelfth century as belonging to the 'transitional style'. To some, including Frankl, this concept simply means a bridge between Romanesque and Gothic, or a kind of no-man's land in which currents of both Romanesque and Gothic, and their implicit attitudes to the world, intermingle. See Dodwell (1993) 404–5. To others, 'Transitional' is not a bridge but a style in its own right, running parallel to Gothic rather than being part of it, see Lasko (1972) 240–52. Morgan and Sandler (1987) 149, briefly discuss the problems of late twelfth- and early thirteenth-century English painting developing at a different stylistic pace than architecture. Beside highlighting problems of stylistic classification, which, ironically, the term 'transitional' was designed to resolve, the whole concept of 'transitional' is problematic, since it tends to identify its artefacts as little more than the connecting links between 'static' or 'untransitional' works of art which 'truly' belong to one or another recognized stylistic period. Some of these issues were discussed by Bony and Panofsky in Bony (1963). Panofsky recommended replacing the word 'transition' with a set of more accurate concepts, which register various stages in the evolution of forms: 'anticipation', 'mutation', 'evolution after mutation' and 'compromise after the fact'. The undertones of evolutionary determinism in the notion of 'transition' are neatly uncovered by Sauerländer (1987). On the general problems of defining periods and styles see Bizarro (1992) 150–60, and Gombrich (1979) 199–206. Kauffmann (1985) distinguishes between a common style within media or techniques (a *Gattungstil*) and the more dubious concept of a style common to a whole period (*Zeitstil*). See also above, Chapter 1, Note 38D.

64. Julius Baum, *Die Malerei und Plastik des Mittelalters (Handbuch der Kunstwissenschaft)* (Wildpark, 1930) 336, where the author considers the sculpture on the Porte Sainte-Anne in Paris to be Early Gothic. He gives the date of the beginning of the High Gothic style in sculpture as 1220; even this is thirty-six years after the date of the High Gothic design for the architecture of Chartres. For an analysis, largely iconographical, of the St Anne portal see Horste (1987). For Laon see Sauerländer (1970) 42–5, and (1972) 51–2, 425–9; and Williamson (1995) 35–6.

64A. Few would now agree with Frankl's classification of the Senlis portal as 'Romanesque'. In an incisive study, Brouillette (1984) especially 19–32, has dated it to 1165–70, attributed it to an atelier working on the Porte de Valois at Saint-Denis and at the St Anne portal at Notre-Dame in Paris, and traced its fluid and dynamic style to contemporary metalwork. In all, the figures (particularly in the archivolts) show a three-dimensional freedom and an independence from their architectural setting which is quite distinct from the flat relief of Romanesque carving, and even from the first generation of Romanesque-inspired early Gothic sculptures in the Ile-de-France. See also Williamson (1995) 25–8.

64B. See Müller (1966) 9–10; and Morand (1991) 79–85.

65. Nikolaus Pevsner, *The Leaves of Southwell* (Harmondsworth, 1945).

65A. For vegetal naturalism in Gothic sculpture see Behling (1964). English naturalistic carving is discussed by Givens (1986).

66. In 1549, in a letter to Benedetto Varchi, Michelangelo wrote 'che la pittura e la scultura e una medesima cosa' (Milanesi 522). Although this opinion was given in connexion with the strife between the protagonists of the two arts, it can still be recommended as fruitful for thought to those people who see too great a difference between sculpture and painting.

67. André Michel, *Histoire de l'art*, II, première partie (Paris, 1906) 332.

68. Alfred Stange, *Deutsche Malerei der Gotik* (Berlin, 1934) ix.

69. Henri Auguste Omont, *Psautier de Saint Louis* (Paris, 1902). See now Beer (1981) 62–91 and Branner (1977) 132–6, 238.

70. It is known that architectural frameworks existed long before this, for example at Chartres itself, but they are, at best, Transitional in style, e.g. the pointed arc over the so-called Notre-Dame de la belle Verrière, which itself dates from about 1180, but had the framework added only about 1215, and also Maréchal Clement and Saint-Denis in bay CII (of about 1230). See Delaporte, *op. cit.* plates XLI and CCVIII. Architecture as a feature of stained glass was first investigated in a fundamental article by Grodecki (1949). For the early appearance of Gothic frames and architectural canopies in stained glass see Frodl-Kraft (1956) and (1972) (the latter article concerned wholly with Reims). More generally there is Grodecki and Brisac (1985) 26. Note the Legend of St Caraunus window at Chartres, dated *c.*1220, showing a precocious use of Gothic arcades as settings for figures, arcades which anticipate the general concept of 'architecturalizing' narratives, found later in the St Louis Psalter. The most recent work on early fictive architecture in stained glass is Kurmann (1998) with full bibliography. For the Chartres windows as a whole see Note 70A below.

70A. The literature on the stained glass at Chartres is enormous and, especially recently, contentious. Questions of chronology have been considerably refined since Frankl's (1961) misguided attempt to date the windows according to the style of their armatures. Van der Meulen's (1967) 155–7, assertion that the making of the windows played no integral part in the construction of the cathedral has also been largely discredited. Most authorities now consider the glazing to have closely followed the progress of the building. Thus the windows of the nave aisles and nave clerestorey are put at about 1200–10, followed by an early phase of glazing in the ambulatory (*c.*1210) and the choir clerestorey (*c.*1210–20). After a break, work resumed *c.*1230 with more glazing in the ambulatory, and with the installation of windows in the clerestorey and terminal walls of the transepts. Much of the most interesting literature on the Chartres glass in recent years has been concerned less with issues of style and chronology than with such questions as narrative reading – see Kemp (1996), patronal power – see Williams (1993), or iconographic programmes and liturgical needs – see Manhes-Deremble (1993). A convenient summary of the problems, and the disagreements, can be found in Kurmann-Schwarz (1996) and Kurmann and Kurmann-Schwarz (1995).

71. Illustrated in Delaporte, *op. cit.* plate 52.

72. *Ibid.* plate 65.

73. *Ibid.* plate 125.

74. See Aubert, Grodecki, Lafond, Verrier, (1959) 71–349, Jordan (1994) (The most penetrating analysis of the glass as natrative) and Weiss (1998).

75. For a short description of the Sainte-Chapelle glass see Grodecki (1975) pp. 47–68; and Grodecki and Brisac (1985) 100–8. Few would now agree with Frankl that the fictive architecture of the Sainte-Chapelle glass is not Gothic.

76. On Petrarch, Boccaccio, etc., cf. Frankl (1960) 237ff.

76A. See now the dissertation by Burger (1978), who sees the whole chapel space as a *teatrum sacrum*, but overinterprets it as an image of the protective mantle of the Madonna della Misericordia.

77. Kenneth Harrison, *The Windows of King's College Chapel in Cambridge* (Cambridge, 1952). For a complete survey see Wayment (1972). See also Marks (1993) 207f.

78. Frankl (1960) the chapter on the conferences of experts at Chartres, Milan, and Gerona (p. 57ff.).

79. *Ibid.*, the chapter on Romanticism (p. 447ff.).

80. Gottfried Semper, *Der Stil in der technischen und tektonischen Künsten* (Munich, 1860–3) 2nd ed. (1878) xx and 475n.

81. Dehio (1901) II, 15.

82. Willi Drost, *Romanische und gotische Baukunst* (Potsdam, 1944) 5.

83. 'Neque enim quaero intelligere ut credam, sed credo ut intelligam.'

83A. The predominant influence of neo-Platonism during the twelfth century, that is, during the formative period of Gothic architecture, and the lack of any serious understanding of Aristotle's philosophical works – de Anima, the Metaphysics and the *Ethics* – until the early and mid-thirteenth century, makes the crude generalization that Romanesque = Platonism, and Gothic = Aristotelianism impossible to sustain. Abbot Suger, like most of his clerical colleagues, was a conventional Platonist. See Chenu (1968) especially 51–100; and also von Simson (1956 and 1962), passim.

84. Basically he follows the article on the beginnings of the Gothic style in the *Festschrift für Heinrich Wölfflin* (Munich, 1924), in so far as the contrast between the two styles had already been formulated there.

85. Erwin Panofsky, *Gothic Architecture and Scholasticism* (Latrobe, 1951). Panofsky's thesis has attracted more criticism from art theorists than from specialists in the history of the Middle Ages. Gombrich (1969) and (1979) 199ff, saw it as one of the last and most sophisticated fruits of Hegelian *Geistesgeschichte*, but no less flawed on that account. Podro (1982) 199–202, gives a neat summary of the book's argument. Dittmann (1967) 84–108, 125–39, assesses the book briefly in the light of Panofsky's debt to Mannheim and Cassirer.

86. *Op. cit.* 21. Expressed scholastically: 'principium importans ordinem ad actum' (after Thomas Aquinas), meaning 'the principle that regulates the act'.

87. Cf. the essay by A. D. F. Hamlin, 'Gothic Architecture and its Critics', *Architectural Record*, XXXI (1916) 389 etc. and 419 etc.; XL, 97; XLI, 3.

87A. One such attempt to tackle the whole problem has been made jointly by a historian of medieval philosophy and an architectural historian, see Radding and Clark (1992). They follow Panofsky's concept of shared 'mental habits' by locating the similarities between scholasticism and architectural design in similar mental behaviour, notably in the creation in both areas of similar 'disciplines' and cognitive processes. The author's arguments, however, are less successful than Panofsky's, see Crossley (1994).

88. In the original Greek: καὶ κυκλόεν τοῦ θρόνους etc., ch. 4, line 3.

88A. For Albrecht's full text see Wolf and Nyholm, eds. (1955–94).

89. However, one could hardly say that every bay of a Gothic vault was a separate heaven: for example that Reims has nine high heavens with ribs in the nave, accompanied by nine lower heavens on each side with ribs, and with trapezoid heavens in the ambulatory; and it would be ridiculous to speak of star-heavens or net-heavens. The word 'heaven' remains a metaphor, and the history of art is concerned with the forms of concrete objects.

89A. The rational and archeological approach to the poem, which assumed that Albrecht's descriptions corresponded to a 'real' building which could be reconstructed, culminated in Boisserée's fantastic and implausible reconstruction. But the idea that the building could in some sense be translated into reality was revived by Sedlmayr (1950) 85–91, whose literal identification of the Gothic cathedral (as an *Abbild* or 'picture') with the essentials of Albrecht's vision, has been influential in German approaches to the 'iconography' of medieval architecture, especially when it also emphasized the mystical and numinous character of both the Cathedral and the Temple. Timmermann (2000) reads Albrecht's description in a different light, as exemplifying a system of aesthetic and symbolic values closest to contemporary micro-architectural metalwork. Timmermann also gives full literature.

90. This problem is discussed in detail in Frankl (1960) 159ff. For Karlstein and the Wenceslas Chapel see above, Part Two, Note 16.

91. Adama van Scheltema, *Der Osebergfund* (Augsburg, 1929) 38ff.

92. Max Dvořák, 'Idealismus und Naturalismus in der gotischen Skulptur und Malerei', *Historische Zeitschrift* CXIX (1918). Reprinted in *Kunstgeschichte als Geistesgeschichte* (Munich, 1918). See now the English translation by R. Klawitzer: Dvořák (1967).

Bibliography

ABOU-EL-HAJ (1988)   ABOU-EL-HAJ, B. 'The urban setting for late medieval church building: Reims and its cathedral between 1210 and 1240', *Art History*, 11 (1988), 17–41.

ACKERMAN (1949)   ACKERMAN, J. '"Ars sine scientia nihil est", Gothic theory of architecture at the cathedral of Milan', *Art Bulletin*, 30 (1949), 84–111.

ADAM (1981)   ADAM, E. *Das Freiburger Münster* (Grosse Bauten Europas, vol. I). Stuttgart, 1981, 3rd edn.

ADAMS (1976)   ADAMS, J. 'An Architectural Analysis of Mantes-la-Jolie'. MA dissertation, Tufts University, Medford Mass., 1976.

ADELMAN (1973)   ADELMAN, L.S. 'The Flamboyant Style in French Gothic Architecture'. Ph.D. thesis, University of Minnesota, 1973.

ADENAUER (1934)   ADENAUER, H. *Die Kathedrale von Laon*. Düsseldorf, 1934.

ALBRECHT (1986)   ALBRECHT, U. *Von der Burg zum Schloss. Französische Schlossbaukunst im spätmittelalter*. Worms, 1986.

ALBRECHT (1995)   ALBRECHT, U. *Der Adelssitz im Mittelalter. Studien zum Verhältnis von Architektur und Lebensform in Nord- und Westeuropa*. Munich-Berlin, 1995.

ALEXANDER (1999)   ALEXANDER, J. 'The Last Things. Representing the Unrepresentable', in Carey, ed. (1999), 43–63.

ALEXANDER AND BINSKI, eds. (1987)   ALEXANDER, J. AND BINSKI, P. eds., *Age of Chivalry. Art in Plantagenet England 1200–1400*. London, 1987.

ALEXANDER, MARK AND ABEL (1977)   ALEXANDER, K.D., MARK, R. AND ABEL, J.F. 'The Structural Behaviour of Medieval Rib Vaulting', *Journal of the Society of Architectural Historians*, 36 (1977), 241–51.

ALLINNE (1912)   ALLINNE, M. 'La façade occidental de la cathédrale de Rouen', *Bulletin de la Société des Amis des Monuments rouennais*, 12 (1912), 73–100.

ALLMAND, ed. (1998)   ALLMAND, C. ed., *The New Cambridge Medieval History*, vol. VII, *c*.1415–*c*.1500. Cambridge, 1998.

ALTMANN (1976)   ALTMANN, L. 'Die Baugeschichte des gotischen Domes von der Mitte des 13. bis zum Anfang des 16. Jahrhunderts', in G. Schwaiger, ed., *Der Regensburger Dom* (Beiträge zur Geschichte des Bistums Regensburg, vol. 10). Regensburg, 1976, 97–109.

ALTMANN (1994)   ALTMANN, L. 'Die Frauenkirche', in *Monachium Sacrum, Festschrift zur 500-Jahr-Feier der Metropolitankirche zu Unserer Lieben Frau in München*. Vol. 1, ed. by G. Schwaiger. Munich, 1994, 1–18.

ALVES (1989–91)   ALVES, J. *O Mosteiro dos Jerónimos*. 2 vols. Lisbon, 1989–91.

ANCIEN (1984)   ANCIEN, J. *Contribution à l'étude archéologique, architecture de la cathédrale de Soissons*. Soissons, 1984.

ANDERSON (1994)   ANDERSON, M. 'The Transepts of Bayeux Cathedral'. M.A. thesis, Courtauld Institute of Art, London University, 1994.

ANDERSON (1996)   ANDERSON, M. 'Transformations et restauration du transept de la cathédrale de Bayeux (1294–1995)', *Société des Sciences, Arts et Belles-lettres de Bayeux*, 31 (1996), 13–29.

ANDERSSON (1972)   ANDERSSON, I. *Vadstena gård och kloster*. Stockholm, 1972.

ANDERSSON (1991)   ANDERSSON, I. *Vadstena klosterkyrka*, Sveriges Kyrkor, 213. Stockholm, 1991.

ANDRÉ (1933)   ANDRÉ, P. 'Saint-Nicolas-de-Port', *Congrès Archéologique de France*, 96 (1933), 275–300.

ANFRAY (1939)   ANFRAY, M. *L'architecture normande, son influence dans le nord de la France aux XIe et XIIe siècles*. Paris, 1939.

ANFRAY (1964)   ANFRAY, M. *La Cathédrale de Nevers et les églises gothiques du Nivernais*. Paris, 1964.

ANNAS AND BINDING (1989)   ANNAS, G. AND BINDING, G. '"Arcus superiores$. Abt Suger von Saint-Denis und das gotische Kreuzrippengewölbe', *Wallraf-Richartz Jahrbuch*, 50 (1989), 7–24.

ANSTETT (1965)   ANSTETT, P. review of G. Himmelheber, *Der Ostchor des Augsburger Doms*, in *Jahrbuch für Geschichte der Oberdeutschen Reichsstädte* (Esslinger Studien XI) (1965), 359–65.

ANSTETT (1978)   ANSTETT, P. 'Die Baugeschichte des Klosters', *Kloster Maulbronn, 1178–1978*. Exh. cat. Maulbronn, 1978, 69–76.

ANSTETT (1985)   ANSTETT, P. *Kloster Maulbronn*. Munich, 1985.

ARAGUAS AND PEROPADRE MUNIESA (1989)   ARAGUAS, P. AND PEROPADRE MUNIESA, A. 'La "seo del Salvador", Église cathédrale de Saragosse, Étude Architecturale, des origines à 1500', *Bulletin Monumental*, 147 (1989), 281–305.

ARENS (1977)   'Die staufischen Königspfalzen', in *Die Zeit der Staufer. Geschichte – Kunst – Kultur*. Exh. cat. Stuttgart, 1977, vol. 3, 129–42.

ARMI (1983)   ARMI, E. *Masons and Sculptors in Romanesque Burgundy. The New Aesthetic of Cluny III*. Pennsylvania, 1983.

ARSLAN (1939)   ARSLAN, W.E. *Architettura romanica Veronese*. Verona, 1939.

ARSLAN (1972)   ARSLAN, E. *Gothic Architecture in Venice*. London, 1972.

ARSZYŃSKI (1985)   ARSZYŃSKI, M. 'Der Deutsche Orden als Bauherr und Kunstmäzen', in Z.H. Nowak, ed., *Die Rolle der Ritterorden in der mittelalterlichen Kultur*, in *Ordines Militares Colloquia Torunensia Historica*, vol. 3, Toruń, 1985, 145–67.

ARSZYŃSKI (1995)   ARSZYŃSKI, M. *Budownictwo Warowne Zakonu Krzyżackiego w Prusach (1230–1454)*. Toruń, 1995.

ARTHUR (1983)   ARTHUR, K.A. 'The Strozzi chapel: Notes on the Building History of Sta. Maria Novella', *Art Bulletin*, 65 (1983), 367–86.

ASCANI (1989)   ASCANI, V. 'Le Dessin d'Architecture mediéval en Italie', in R. Recht, ed., *Les Batisseurs des Cathédrales Gothiques*. Strasbourg, 1989, 255–77.

ASCANI (1991)   ASCANI, V. 'I disegni architettonici attribuiti ad Antonio di Vincenzo', *Arte Medievale*, 5 (1991), 105–14.

AUBERT (1920)   AUBERT, M. *Notre-Dame de Paris, sa place dans l'architecture du XIIe au XIVe siècle*. Paris, 1920.

AUBERT (1934)   AUBERT, M. 'Les plus anciennes croisées d'ogives, leur rôle dans la construction', *Bulletin Monumental*, 93 (1934), 5–67, 137–237.

AUBERT (1936)   AUBERT, M. 'Lyon Cathédrale', *Congrès Archéologique de France*, 98 (1935), 78–85.

AUBERT AND DE MAILLÉ (1947)   AUBERT, M. AND MAILLÉ, G. DE. *L'Architecture cistercienne en France*, 2 vols. Paris, 1947.

AUBERT et al. (1959)   AUBERT, M. *et al.*, *Les vitraux de Notre-Dame et de la Sainte-Chapelle de Paris* (Corpus Vitrearum Medii Aevi, France I). Paris, 1959.

AUER (1983)   AUER, R.L. 'Landesherrliche Architektur. Die Rezeption der Elisabethkirche in den Hessischen Pfarrkirchen', *700 Jahre Elisabethkirche*, H.J. Kunst, ed. Marburg, 1983, 103–23.

AYERS (1996)   AYERS, T. 'The Painted Glass of Wells Cathedral, *c*.1285–1345', Ph.D. dissertation, Courtauld Institute of Art, University of London, 1996.

AYERS, ed. (2000)   AYERS, T. ed., *Salisbury Cathedral. The West Front*. Guildford, 2000.

AZCÁRATE RISTORI (1951)   AZCÁRATE RISTORI, J.M. DE. 'La fachada del Infantado y el estilo de Juan Guas', *Archivo Español de Arte y Arqueologia*, 24 (1951), 307–19.

AZCÁRATE RISTORI (1953)   AZCÁRATE RISTORI, J.M. DE. *Monumentos españoles* I, Madrid, 1953.

AZCÁRATE RISTORI (1956)   AZCÁRATE RISTORI, J.M. DE. 'La obra toledana de Juan Guas', *Archivo Español de Arte y Arqueologia*, 29 (1956), 9–42.

AZCÁRATE RISTORI (1958)   AZCÁRATE RISTORI, J.M. DE. *La Arquitectura gotica toledana de siglo XV*. Madrid, 1958.

BACHMANN (1969)   BACHMANN, E. 'Gotische Architektur bis zu den Hussitenkriegen', in K.M. Swoboda, ed., *Gotik in Böhmen*. Munich, 1969, 34–109.

BACK (1994)   BACK, U. 'Die Domgrabung xxxiii. Die Ausgrabungen im Bereich des Südturmes', *Kölner Domblatt*, 59 (1994), 193–224.

BADER (1960)   BADER, W. 'Der Anfang der gotischen Viktorkirche zu Xanten (III)', *Zur Geschichte und Kunst im Erzbistum Köln*. (Studien zur Kölner Kirchengeschichte 5. Festschrift für Wilhelm Neuss). Düsseldorf, 1960, 315–31.

BADER (1961)   BADER, W. 'Der Anfang der gotischen Viktorkirche zu Xanten (II)', *Bonner Jahrbücher*, 161 (1961), 6–24.

BADER (1964)   BADER, W. 'Vom ersten Baumeister der gotischen Stiftskirche (1263- bis um 1280)', *1600 Jahre Xantener Dom*. Cologne, 1964, 103–40.

BADSTÜBNER (1985)   BADSTÜBNER, E. *Klosterkirchen im Mittelalter. Die Baukunst der Reformorden*. Munich, 1985.

BAIER (ed.) (1979)   BAIER, H. ed., *600 Jahre Ostchor St Sebald 1379–1979*. Neustadt an der Aisch, 1979.

BAILLY (1980)   BAILLY, R. *La Collégiale Notre-Dame à Mantes-la-Jolie*. Mantes, n.d. 1980.

BAILY (1991)   BAILY, J. 'St. Hugh's Church at Lincoln', *Architectural History*, 34 (1991), 1–35.

BALDASS (1946)   BALDASS, P. 'Hans Stethaimer. Sein Name, sein Hauptwerk, seine Spätwerke'. Dissertation, Vienna, 1946.

BARNES (1963)   BARNES, C.F. 'The Cathedral of Chartres and the Architect of Soissons', *Journal of the Society of Architectural Historians*, 22 (1963), 53–74.

BARNES (1969)   BARNES, C.F. 'The Twelfth Century Transept at Soissons: the

Missing Source for Chartres?', *Journal of the Society of Architectural Historians*, 28 (1969), 9–25.

BARNES (1976)   BARNES, C.F. 'The Documentation for Notre-Dame de Soissons', *Gesta*, 15 (1976), 61–70.

BARNES (1981)   BARNES, C.F. 'The Drapery-Rendering Technique of Villard de Honnecourt', *Gesta*, 20 (1981), 199–206.

BARNES (1982)   BARNES, C.F. *Villard de Honnecourt, The Artist and his Drawings: A Critical Bibliography*. Boston, 1982.

BARNES (1989)   BARNES, C.F. 'Le "problem" Villard de Honnecourt', in R. Recht, ed., *Les Batisseurs des Cathédrales Gothiques*. Strasbourg, 1989, 209–23.

BARRAL I ALTET (1994)   BARRAL I ALTET, X. *Les Catedrals de Catalunya*. Barcelona, 1994.

BARTH (1974)   BARTH, A. *Esslingen-St. Paul*. Munich-Zürich, 1974.

BATLLE HUGUET (1959)   'Tarragone', in *Congrès Archéologique de France*, 117 (1959), 215–24.

BAUCHAL (1887)   BAUCHAL, C. *Nouveau Dictionnaire Biographique et Critique des Architectes Français*. Paris, 1887.

BAUER AND HOHMANN (1969)   BAUER H. AND HOHMANN, F. *Der Dom zu Paderborn*. Paderborn, 1969.

BAUMÜLLER (1994)   BAUMÜLLER, B. *Der Chor des Veitsdomes in Prag. Die Königskirche Kaiser Karls IV*. Berlin, 1994.

BAYLÉ (1979)   BAYLÉ, M. *La Trinité de Caen, sa place dans l'histoire de l'architecture et du décor romane* (Bibliothèque de la société française d'archéologie, 10). Geneva, 1979.

BAYLÉ (1987)   BAYLÉ, M. 'Les ateliers de sculpture de Saint-Etienne de Caen aux XIe et XIIe siècles', in *Proceedings of the Battle Conference*, 10 (1987), 1–24.

BAYLÉ, DIR. (1997)   BAYLÉ, M. director, *L'architecture normande au Moyen Age*. 2 vols. Caen, 1997.

BEAULIEU (1984)   BEAULIEU, M. 'Essai sur l'Iconographie des Statues-Colonnes de quelques Portals du Premier Art Gothique', *Bulletin Monumental*, 142 (1984), 273–307.

BECKER-HOUNSLOW (1998)   BECKER-HOUNSLOW, S. *Der Beitrag Englands zur Entstehung und Entwicklung figurierter Gewölbe in Deutschordensstat Preussen*. Schwerin, 1998.

BECKER-HOUNSLOW (1998a)   BECKER-HOUNSLOW, S. 'Malbork Chapter House and Grand Master's "Remter" versus the "Briefkapelle" at St Mary's in Lubeck: dependent or independent solutions?', *Biuletyn Historii Sztuki*, 60 (1998), 381–98.

BEER (1952)   BEER, E.J. *Die Rose der Kathedrale von Lausanne*. Bern, 1952.

BEER (1981)   BEER, E.J. 'Pariser Buchmalerei in der Zeit Ludwigs des Heiligen und im letzten Viertel des 13 Jahrhunderts', *Zeitschrift für Kunstgeschichte*, 44 (1981), 62–91.

BEHLING (1964)   BEHLING, L. *Die Pflanzenwelt der mittelalterliche Kathedralen*. Cologne and Graz, 1964.

BELLUZZI (1983/4)   BELLUZZI, A. 'La facciata i progetti cinquecenteschi', M. Fanti *et al.*, *La Basilica di San Petronio in Bologna*, 2 vols. (Bologna, 1983/4), vol. 2 2, 7–28.

BELTING (1994)   BELTING, H. *Likeness and Presence. A History of the Image before the Era of Art*. Chicago, 1994.

BENEŠOVSKÁ (1994)   BENEŠOVSKÁ, K. 'Gotická Katedrála. Architektura', in A. Merhautová, ed., *Katedrála sv. Víta v Praze* (K 650. výročí založení). Prague, 1994, 25–65.

BENEŠOVSKÁ (1994a)   BENEŠOVSKÁ, K. Review of B. Baumüller, *Derchordes Veitsdomes in Prag*. in *Umění*, 42 (1994), 407–15.

BENEŠOVSKÁ (1996)   BENEŠOVSKÁ, K. '"Aula Regia" près de Prague et "Mons Regalis" près de Paris', *Cîteaux*, 47 (1996), 231–45.

BENEŠOVSKÁ (1996a)   BENEŠOVSKÁ, K. 'Petr Parlér versus Matyás z Arrasu v prazské katedrále sv. Víta', *Ars*, 1–3 (1996), 100–11.

BENEŠOVSKÁ, ed., (1998)   BENEŠOVSKÁ, K. ed., *King John of Luxembourg (1296–1346) and the Art of his Era* (Proceedings of the International Conference in Prague, September 1996). Prague, 1998.

BENEŠOVSKÁ (1999)   BENEŠOVSKÁ, K. AND HLOBIL I., *Peter Parler and St Vitus's Cathedral 1356–1399*. Prague, 1999.

BENEŠOVSKÁ (1999a)   BENEŠOVSKÁ, K. 'Das Frühwerk Peter Parlers am Veitsdom', *Umění*, 47 (1999), 351–63.

BENTON (1985)   BENTON, J.F. *Self and Society in Medieval France*. Toronto, Buffalo, London, 1985.

BERENGUIR (1975)   BERENGUIR, R. *L'abbaye du Thoronet* (Caisse Nationale des Monuments Historiques). Paris, 1975.

BERETZ (1989)   BERETZ, E. 'Fortune Denied: The Theology against Chance at Saint-Etienne, Beauvais'. Ph.D., dissertation, Yale University, 1989.

BERLIOZ (1990)   BERLIOZ, J. 'Saint Bernard en son Temps', in L. Pressouyre and T. Kinder, eds., *Saint Bernard et le Monde Cistercien*. Paris, 1990, 43–67.

BERNT *et al.* (1959 onwards)   BERNT, A., *et al.*, *Das Deutsch Bürgerhaus*, Tübingen, 1959 onwards.

BERTHELSON (1947)   BERTHELSON, B. 'Studier i Birgittinerordens byggnadss-

kick', *Kungl. Vitterhet Historie och Antikvitets Akademins handlingar*, 63 (Stockholm, 1947).

BEYER (1962)   BEYER, V. 'Rosaces et roues de fortune à la fin de l'art roman et au début de l'art gothique', *Zeitschrift für Schweizerische Archäologie und Kunstgeschichte*, 22 (1962), 34–43.

BIAŁOSTOCKI (1966)   BIAŁOSTOCKI, J. 'Late Gothic. Disagreements about the Concept', *Journal of the British Archaeological Association*, 3rd ser., 29 (1966), 76–105.

BICKEL (1956)   BICKEL, W. *Die Bedeutung der süddeutschen Zisterzienserbauten für den Stilwandel im 12. und 13. Jahrhundert von der Spätromanik zur Gotik*. Munich, 1956.

BIDEAULT AND LAUTIER (1977)   BIDEAULT, M. AND LAUTIER, C. 'Saint-Nicaise de Reims. Chronologie et Nouvelles Remarques sur l'Architecture', *Bulletin Monumental*, 135 (1977), 295–330.

BIDEAULT AND LAUTIER (1987)   BIDEAULT, M. and LAUTIER, C. *Ile-de-France Gothique*. Vol. 1: *Les églises de la vallée de l'Oise et du Beauvaisis*. Paris, 1987.

BIEBRACH (1908)   BIEBRACH, K. *Die holzgedeckten Franziskaner- und Dominikanerkirchen in Umbrien und Toskana*. Berlin, 1908.

BIENERT (1990)   BIENERT, A. 'Himmel und Hölle am Dogenpalast. Zur Ikonographie der Macht des venezianischen Regierungsgebäudes', in H.-J. Kunst *et al.*, eds., *Werners Kunstgeschichte*. Worms, 1990, 47–77.

BIGET (1982)   BIGET, J.-L. 'La cathédrale Sainte-Cécile d'Albi. L'architecture', *Congrès Archéologique de France*, 140 (1982), 20–62.

BIGET *et al.* (1982)   BIGET, J.-L., CARBONELL-LAMOTHE, Y., AND PRADALIER-SCHLUMBERGER, M. 'Le chœur de la cathédrale d'Albi', *Congrès Archéologique de France*, 140 (1982), 63–91.

BILSON (1898–9)   BILSON, J. 'The Beginnings of Gothic Architecture', *Journal of the Royal Institute of British Architects*, 6 (1898–9), 259–319.

BILSON (1910)   BILSON, J. 'Les voûtes de la nef de la cathédrale d'Angers', *Congrès Archéologique de France*, 77 (1910), 2, 203–223.

BILSON (1917)   BILSON, J. 'The Norman School and the Beginnings of Gothic Architecture. Two Octopartite Vaults: Montivilliers and Canterbury', *Archaeological Journal*, 74 (1917), 1–35.

BILSON (1922)   BILSON, J. 'Durham Cathedral: The Chronology of its Vaults', *Archaeological Journal*, 79 (1922), 101–60.

BINDING, MAINZER, AND WIEDENAU (1975)   BINDING, G., MAINZER, U., AND WIEDENAU, A. *Kleine Kunstgeschichte des Deutschen Fachwerkbaus*. Darmstadt, 1975.

BINDING (1982)   BINDING, G. 'Die Franziskaner-Baukunst im deutschen Sprachgebiet', in *800 Jahre Franz von Assisi*. Krems-Stein, 1982, 431–60.

BINDING (1985)   BINDING, G. '"Geometricis et arithmetricis instrumentis". Zur mittelalterlichen Bauvermessung', *Jahrbuch der Rheinischen Denkmalpflege*, 30–1 (1985), 9–24.

BINDING (1989)   BINDING, G. *Masswerk*. Darmstadt, 1989.

BINDING AND SPEER, eds., (1993)   BINDING, G. AND SPEER, A. *Mittelalterliches Kunstleben nach den Quellen des 11. bis 13. Jahrhunderts*. Stuttgart, Bad Cannstatt, 1993.

BINDING (1993)   BINDING, G. (with ANNAS, G., JOST, B., AND SCHUNICHT, A.), *Baubetrieb im Mittelalter*. Darmstadt, 1993.

BINDING (1993a)   BINDING, G. 'Beiträge zum Architekturverständnis bei Abt Suger von Saint-Denis, in G. Binding and A. Speer, eds., *Mittelalterliches Kunstlerleben nach den Quellen des 11. Bis 13. Jahrhunders*. Stuttgart, Bad Cannstatt, 1993, 184–207.

BINDING AND SPEER (1996)   BINDING, G. AND SPEER, A. *Abt Suger von Saint-Denis, 'De Consecratione'. Kommentierte Studienausgabe* (Veröffentlichungen der Abteilung Architekturgeschichte des Kunsthistorischen Instituts der Universität zu Köln, 56). Cologne, 1996.

BINDING (1996)   BINDING, G. *Deutsche Königspfalzen. Von Karl dem Grossen bis Friedrich II (765–1240)*. Darmstadt, 1996.

BINSKI (1995)   BINSKI, P. *Westminster Abbey and the Plantagenets. Kingship and the Representation of Power 1200–1400*. New Haven and London, 1995.

BISCHOFF (1990)   BISCHOFF, F. 'Anmerkungen zum Umbau der Seitenschiffe des Ulmer Munsters unter Burkhard Engelberg', in *Wölbkonstruktionen der Gotik*, I. Stuttgart 1990 (*Geschichte des Konstruierens*, 4, Konzepte SFB 230, vol. 28), 156–91.

BISCHOFF (1999)   BISCHOFF, F. *Burkhard Engelberg. 'Der vilkunstreiche Architector und der Statt Augsprug Wercke Meister'*. Augsburg, 1999.

BIZZARRO (1992)   BIZZARRO, T.M. *Romanesque Architectural Criticism: a Pre-History*. Cambridge, 1992.

BLOMME (1993)   BLOMME, Y. *Poitou Gothique*. Paris, 1993.

BLOMME (1994)   BLOMME, Y. 'La Construction de la Cathédrale Saint-Pierre de Poitiers', *Bulletin Monumental*, 152 (1994), 7–64.

BLUM (1986)   BLUM, P. 'The Lateral Portals of the West Façade of the Abbey Church of Saint-Denis. Archaeological and Iconographical Considerations', in P.L. Gerson, ed., *Abbot Suger and Saint-Denis: a Symposium*. New York, 1986, 199–227.

BLUM (1986a)   BLUM, P. 'Liturgical Influences on the Design of the West Front of Wells and Salisbury', *Gesta*, 25, (1986), 145–50.

BLUM (1991)   BLUM, P. 'The Sequence of the Building Campaigns at Salisbury', *Art Bulletin*, 78 (1991), 6–38.

BLUM (1992)   BLUM, P. *Early Gothic Saint-Denis. Restorations and Survivals.* Berkeley, Los Angeles, London, 1992.

BLUNT (1980)   BLUNT, A. *Art and Architecture in France 1500–1700.* New Haven and London, 1980, 4th edn.

BOCK (1961)   BOCK, H. 'Der Beginn spätgotischer Architektur in Prag (Peter Parler) und die Beziehungen zu England', *Wallraf-Richartz Jahrbuch*, 23 (1961), 191–210.

BOCK (1961a)   BOCK, H. 'The Exeter Rood Screen', *Architectural Review*, 130 (1961), 313–17.

BOCK (1962)   BOCK, H. *Der Decorated Style. Untersuchungen zur Englischen Kathedralarchitektur der ersten Hälfte des 14. Jahrhunderts* (Heidelberger Kunstgeschichtliche Abhandlungen, 6). Heidelberg, 1962.

BOETHIUS AND RAMDAHL (1935)   BOETHIUS, G. AND ROMDAHL, A. *Uppsala domkyrka 1258–1435.* Uppsala, 1935.

BOETHIUS AND WARD PERKINS (1970)   BOETHIUS, A. AND WARD-PERKINS, J.B. *Etruscan and Roman Architecture.* Harmondsworth, 1970.

BÖKER (1983)   BÖKER, H.-J. 'Der Augsburger Dom-Ostchor. Überlegungen zu seiner Planungsgeschichte im 14 Jahrhundert', *Zeitschrift des historischen Vereins für Schwaben*, 77 (1983), 90–102.

BÖKER (1987)   BÖKER, H.-J. 'Die spätgotische Nordhalle des Braunschweiger Domes', *Niederdeutsche Beiträge zur Kunstgeschichte*, 26 (1987), 51–62.

BÖKER (1988)   BÖKER, H.-J. *Die mittelterliche Backsteinarchitektur Norddeutschlands.* Darmstadt, 1988.

BÖKER (1991)   BÖKER, H.-J. 'York Minster Nave: The Cologne Connection', *Journal of the Society of Architectural Historians*, 50 (1991), 167–80.

BOND (1905)   BOND, F. *Gothic Architecture in England.* London, 1905.

BOND (1913)   BOND, F. *An Introduction to English Church Architecture*, 2 vols. London, New York and Toronto, 1913.

BONELLI (1972)   BONELLI, R. *Il Duomo di Orvieto e l'Architettura Italiana del Duecento e Trecento*, Rome, 1972.

BONGARTZ (1979)   BONGARTZ, N. *Die frühen Bauteile der Kathedrale von Troyes. Architekturgeschichtliche Monographie.* Stuttgart, 1979.

BONNEL (1963)   BONNEL, E. 'Le fort Saint-André à Villeneuve-les-Avignon', *Congrès Archéologique de France*, 121 (1963), 202–5.

BONY (1946)   BONY, J. 'La collegiale de Mantes', *Congrès Archéologique de France*, 104 (1946), 163–220.

BONY (1949)   BONY, J. 'French Influences on the origins of English Gothic architecture', *Journal of the Warburg and Courtauld Institutes*, 12 (1949), 1–15.

BONY (1954)   BONY, J. 'Le premier project de Durham. Voûtement partiel ou voûtement total?' *Urbanisme et architecture. Etudes écrites et publiées en l'honneur de Pierre Lavedan.* Paris, 1954, 41–9.

BONY (1957/8)   BONY, J. 'The Resistance to Chartres in Early Thirteenth Century Architecture', *Journal of the British Archaeological Association*, 20–1 (1957/8), 35–52.

BONY (1963)   BONY, J. 'Introduction', in Millard Meiss *et al.*, eds., *Studies in Western Art* (Acts of the Twentieth International Congress of the History of Art New York, 1963). Princeton, 1963, 1, 81–4.

BONY (1963a)   BONY, J. 'The façade of Bury St. Edmunds: An Additional Note', in M. Meiss *et al.*, eds., *Studies in Western Art* (Acts of the Twentieth International Congress of the History of Art, New York, 1961). Princeton, 1963, I, 105–7.

BONY (1965)   BONY, J. 'Origines des Piles Gothiques Anglaises á fûts en délit', in M. Kuhn and L. Grodecki, eds., *Gedenkschrift Ernst Gall.* Berlin, 1965, 95–122.

BONY (1976)   BONY, J. 'Diagonality and Centrality in Early Rib-Vaulted Architectures', *Gesta*, 15 (1976), 15–25.

BONY (1979)   BONY, J. *The English Decorated Style. Gothic Architecture Transformed 1250–1350.* Oxford, 1979.

BONY (1981)   BONY, J. 'Durham et la Tradition saxonne', in S.M. Crosby, A. Prache, and A. Chatelet, eds., *Études d'art mediéval offertes à Louis Grodecki.* Paris, 1981, 80–92.

BONY (1983)   BONY, J. *French Gothic Architecture of the 12th and 13th Centuries.* Berkeley, Los Angeles, and London, 1983.

BONY (1983a)   BONY, J. 'Architecture Gothique. Accident ou Nécessité', *Revue de l'Art*, 58–9 (1983), 9–20.

BONY (1986)   BONY, J. 'What Possible Sources for the Chevet of Saint-Denis', in P.L. Gerson, ed., *Abbot Suger and Saint-Denis: a Symposium.* New York, 1986, 33–40.

BONY (1990)   BONY, J. 'The Stonework Planning of the First Durham Master', in P. Crossley and E. Fernie, *Medieval Architecture and its Intellectual Context. Studies in Honour of Peter Kidson.* London and Ronceverte, 1990, 19–24.

BOOCKMANN (1982)   BOOCKMANN, H. *Die Marienburg im 19. Jahrhundert.* Frankfurt-am-Main, Berlin, and Vienna, 1982.

BOOZ (1956)   BOOZ, P. *Der Baumeister der Gotik.* Munich and Berlin, 1956.

BORCHARDT (1971)   BORCHARDT, F.L. *German Antiquity in Renaissance Myth.* Baltimore and London, 1971.

BORCHERT (1995)   BORCHERT, T.-H. 'Illumination and architecture in late fourteenth-century Milan: Giovannino dei Grassi and the "Fabbrica del duoma"', in *Flanders in a European Perspective. Manuscript Illumination around 1400 in Flanders and Abroad* (Proceedings of the Internatioinal Colloquium, Louvain, 7–10 September). Louvain, 1995.

BORG (1972)   BORG, A. *Architectural Sculpture in Romanesque Provence.* Oxford, 1972.

BORGER-KEWELOH (1976)   BORGER-KEWELOH, N. review of B. Schütz, *Die Katharinenkirche in Oppenheim*, in *Zeitschrift für Künstgeschichte*, 39 (1976), 445–8.

BORGER-KEWELOH (1986)   BORGER-KEWELOH, N. *Die Mittelalterlichen Dome im 19. Jahrhundert.* Munich, 1986.

BORGER-KEWELOH (1986a)   BORGER-KEWELOH, N. *Die Liebfrauenkirche in Trier. Studien zur Baugeschichte* (Trier Zeitschrift für Geschichte und Kunst des Trier Landes und seiner Nachbargebiete, 8). Trier, 1986.

BORK, MARK and MURRAY (1997)   BORK, R., MARK, R., AND MURRAY, S. 'The Openwork Flyers of Amiens Cathedral: "Postmodern" Gothic and the Limits of Structural Rationalism', *Journal of the Society of Architectural Historians*, 56 (1997), 478–93.

BÖRSCH-SUPAN (1967)   BÖRSCH-SUPAN, E. *Garten- Landschafts- und Paradiesmotive in Innenraum. Eine ikonografische Untersuchungen.* Berlin, 1967.

BOTTINEAU-FUCHS (1986)   BOTTINEAU-FUCHS, Y. 'Maître d'œuvre, maître d'ouvrage: Les Roux et le chapitre cathédrale de Rouen', in X. Barral I Altet, ed., *Artistes, Artisans et Production Artistique au Moyen Age, 1: Les hommes.* Picard, 1988, 183–95.

BOTTINEAU-FUCHS (1992)   BOTTINEAU-FUCHS, Y. 'Quelques remarques sur la façade de la cathédrale de Rouen' (unpublished paper sent to P. Crossley).

BOTTINEAU-FUCHS (1997)   BOTTINEAU-FUCHS, Y. 'Maîtres d'ouvrage et maîtres d'oeuvre en haute-Normandie à la fin du Môyen Age', in Baylé, dir., vol. 1 (1997), 315–35.

BOTTINEAU-FUCHS (1997)   BOTTINEAU-FUCHS, Y. 'Caudebec-en-Caux, Église Notre-Dame', in Baylé, dir., vol. 2 (1997), 243–9.

BOUTTIER (1983)   BOUTTIER, M. 'La cathédrale du Mans au XIIIe siècle', in *La Sarthe des origines à nos jours.* Saint-Jean-d'Angély, 1983.

BOUTTIER (1987)   BOUTTIER, M. 'La Reconstruction de l'Abbatiale de Saint-Denis au XIIIe siècle', *Bulletin Monumental*, 145 (1987), 357–86.

BOYAZIS (1985)   BOYAZIS, J.P. 'L'espace interieur dans l'architecture gothique brabançonne au XVe siecle', *Bulletin de la Commission royale des monuments et des sites*, 11 (1985), 5–57.

BRACHMANN (1998)   BRACHMANN, C. *Gotische Architektur in Metz unter Bischof Jacques de Lorraine (1239–1260). Der Nenbau der Kathedrale und seine Folger.* Berlin, 1998.

BRANDL (1986)   BRANDL, R. 'Art or Craft: Art and the Artist in Medieval Nuremberg', *Gothic and Renaissance Art in Nuremberg 1300–1550* (exh. Cat., Metropolitan Museum of Art, New York, and Germanisches Nationalmuseum Nürnberg, 1986). New York, 1986, 51–60.

BRANNER (1958)   BRANNER, R. 'The Movements of Gothic Architects between France and Spain in the Early Thirteenth Century', *Actes du XIXe Congrès International d'Histoire de l'Art, Paris 8–13 September 1958.* Paris, 1959, 44–8.

BRANNER (1960)   BRANNER, R. *Burgundian Gothic Architecture.* Zwemmer, 1960.

BRANNER (1961)   BRANNER, R. 'Historical Aspects of the Reconstruction of Reims Cathedral, 1210–41', *Speculum*, 36 (1961), 23–37.

BRANNER (1961a)   BRANNER, R. 'Jean d'Orbais and the Cathedral of Reims', *Art Bulletin*, 43 (1961), 131–3.

BRANNER (1961b)   BRANNER, R. 'The North Transept and the First West Façades of Reims Cathedral', *Zeitschrift für Kunstgeschichte*, 24 (1961), 220–41.

BRANNER (1962 and 1989)   BRANNER, R. *La cathédrale de Bourges et sa place dans l'architecture gothique.* Paris and Bourges, 1962. (English translation: *The Cathedral of Bourges and its Place in Gothic Architecture*, ed. by S. Prager Branner. Cambridge Mass., and London, 1989.

BRANNER (1962a)   BRANNER, R. 'The Labyrinth of Reims Cathedral', *Journal of the Society of Architectural Historians*, 21 (1962), 18–25.

BRANNER (1962b)   BRANNER, R. 'Paris and the Origins of Rayonnant Gothic Architecture down to 1240', *Art Bulletin*, 44 (1962), 39–51.

BRANNER (1962c)   BRANNER, R. 'Le maître de Beauvais', *Art de France*, 2 (1962), 77–92.

BRANNER (1963)   BRANNER, R. 'Gothic Architecture 1160–80 and its Romanesque Sources', in M. Meiss *et al.*, eds., *Studies in Western Art* (Acts of the Twentieth International Congress of the History of Art, New York, 1961). Princeton, 1963, vol. 1, 92–104.

BRANNER (1963a)   BRANNER, R. 'Sint-Leonardus at Zoutleeuw and the Rhine Valley in the Early Thirteenth Century', *Bulletin de la Commission royale des monuments et des sites*, 14 (1963), 257–68.

BRANNER (1963b)   BRANNER, R. 'Villard de Honnecourt, Reims, and the Origin of Gothic Architectural Drawing', *Gazette des Beaux-Arts*, 61 (1963), 129–46.

BRANNER (1963c)   BRANNER, R. 'A note on Pierre de Montreuil', *Art Bulletin*, 45 (1963), 355–7.

BRANNER (1964)   BRANNER, R. 'Remarques sur la cathédrale de Strasbourg', *Bulletin Monumental*, 122 (1964), 261–8.

BRANNER (1965)   BRANNER, R. *St. Louis and the Court Style in Gothic Architecture*. London, 1965.

BRANNER (1965a)   BRANNER, R. 'The Transept of Cambrai Cathedral', in M. Kühn and L. Grodecki, eds., *Gedenkschrift Ernst Gall*. Berlin, 1965, 71–2.

BRANNER (1966)   BRANNER, R. 'Encore Bourges', *Journal of the Society of Architectural Historians*, 25 (1966), 299–301.

BRANNER (1971)   BRANNER, R. 'The Grande Châsse of the Sainte-Chapelle', *Gazette des Beaux-Arts*, 77 (1971), 5–18.

BRANNER (1971a)   BRANNER, R. 'The Sainte-Chapelle and the Capella Regis in the Thirteenth Century', *Gesta*, 10 (1971), 19–22.

BRANNER (1976)   BRANNER, R. '"Fabrica, Opera" and the Details of Medieval Monuments', *Gesta*, 15 (1976), 27–9.

BRANNER (1977)   BRANNER, R. *Manuscript painting in Paris during the reign of Saint Louis*. Berkeley, 1977.

BRAUNFELS (1972)   BRAUNFELS, W. *Monasteries of Western Europe*. London, 1972.

BRAUNFELS (1979)   BRAUNFELS, W. *Mittelalterliche Stadtbaukunst in der Toskana*. Berlin, 4th ed., 1979.

BRAUN-REICHENBACHER (1966)   BRAUN-REICHENBACHER, *Das Ast- und Laubwerk. Entwicklung, Merkmale und Bedeutung einer spätgotischen Ornamentform* (Erlanger Beiträge zur Sprach- und Kunstwissenschaft, 24, Nuremberg, 1966.

BRÄUTIGAM (1961)   BRÄUTIGAM, G. 'Gmünd–Prag–Nürnberg', *Jahrbuch der Berliner Museen*, 3 (1961), 38–75.

BRÄUTIGAM (1965)   BRÄUTIGAM, G. 'Die Nürnberger Frauenkirche. Idee und Herkunft ihrer Architektur', in U. Schlegel and C. Zoege, eds., *Festschrift Peter Metz*. Berlin, 1965, 170–97.

BRENK (1995)   BRENK, B. 'The Sainte-Chapelle as a Capetian Political Program', in V. Raguin, K. Brush and P. Draper, eds. *Artistic Integration in Gothic Buildings*. Toronto, Buffalo, London, 1995, 195–213.

BRIGODE (1971)   BRIGODE, S. 'L'abbaye de Villers et l'architecture Cistercienne', *Revue des archéologues et historiens d'Art de Louvain*, 4, (1971), 117–40.

BRIGODE (1975)   BRIGODE, S. 'L'architecture cistercienne en Belgique', *Aureavallis: Mélanges historiques rémis à l'occasion du neuvième centenaire de l'abbaye d'Orval*. Liège, 1975, 237–45.

BROCHE (1902)   BROCHE, L. 'La date de la chapelle de l'évêché de Laon', *Bulletin Monumental*, 66 (1902), 499–510.

BROOKE (1975)   BROOKE, R.B. *The Crisis of the Friars* (Historical Problems: Sources and Documents, 24). London, 1975.

BROSSE, ed. (1966–71)   BROSSE, J. ed., *Histoire generale des Eglises de France* (vol. 1), and *Dictionnaire des Églises de France* (vols. 2–5). Paris, 1966–71.

BROUGH (1985)   BROUGH, S. *The Goths and the Concept of Gothic in Germany from 1500 to 1750. Culture, Language and Architecture* (Mikrokosmos, Beiträge zur Literaturwissenschaft und Bedeutungsforschung, ed. by W. Hans, 17). Frankfurt-am-Main and New York, 1985.

BROUILLETTE (1981)   BROUILLETTE, D. *The Early Gothic Sculpture of Senlis Cathedral* (Ph.D. dissertation Berkeley California 1981). Ann Arbor, 1981.

BROWN (1991/1992)   BROWN, J. 'Spain in the Age of Exploration: Crossroads of Artistic Cultures', in J.A. Levenson, ed., *Circa 1492. Art in the Age of Exploration*. New Haven and London, 41–9.

BROWN, COLVIN AND TAYLOR (1963)   ALLEN BROWN, R., COLVIN, H.M., AND TAYLOR, A.J. *The History of the King's Works*, 2 vols. London, 1963.

BROWN (1970)   ALLEN BROWN, R. *English Castles*. London, 1970.

BROWN et al. (1980)   ALLEN BROWN, R., PRESTWICH, M., AND COULSON, C. eds., *Castles. A History and Guide*. Poole, 1980.

BRUCHER (1987)   BRUCHER, G. *Die sakrale Baukunst Italiens im 11. und 12. Jahrhundert*. Cologne, 1987.

BRUCHER (1990)   BRUCHER, G. *Gotische Baukunst in Österreich*. Salzburg, 1990.

BRUSH (1993)   BRUSH, K. 'The Naumburg Master: A Chapter in the Development of Medieval Art History', *Gazette des Beaux-Arts*, 6th ser., 122 (1993), 109–22.

BRUZELIUS (1978)   BRUZELIUS, C. *Cistercian High Gothic: Longpont and the Architecture of the Cistercians in France in the Early Thirteenth Century* (Ph.D. dissertation, York, 1977). Ann Arbor, 1978.

BRUZELIUS (1979)   BRUZELIUS, C. 'Cistercian High Gothic: Longpont and the Architecture of the Cistercians in France in the Early Thirteenth Century', *Analecta Cisterciensia*, 35 (1979), 3–204.

BRUZELIUS (1981)   BRUZELIUS, C. 'The Twelfth-Century Church at Ourscamp', *Speculum*, 56 (1981), 28–40.

BRUZELIUS (1982)   BRUZELIUS, C. 'The Transept of the Abbey Church of Châalis and the Filiation of Pontigny', in B. Chauvin ed., *Mélanges á la Mémoire du Père Anselm Dimier*, Part 3, Architecture Cistercienne, vol. 6 (Arbois, 1982), 447–54.

BRUZELIUS (1985)   BRUZELIUS, C. *The Thirteenth Century Church at St-Denis*. Yale, 1985.

BRUZELIUS (1987)   BRUZELIUS, C. 'The Construction of Notre-Dame in Paris', *Art Bulletin*, 69 (1987), 540–69.

BRUZELIUS (1987a)   BRUZELIUS, C. 'The Second Campaign at Saint-Urbain at Troyes', *Speculum*, 62 (1987), 635–40.

BRUZELIUS (1992)   BRUZELIUS, C. '"Hearing is Believing". Clarissan Architecture ca. 1213–1340', *Gesta*, 31 (1992), 83–91.

BRUZELIUS (1995)   BRUZELIUS, C. 'Queen Sancia of Mallorca and the Convent Church of Sta Chiara in Naples', *Memoirs of the American Academy in Rome*, 40 (1995), 69–100.

BRUZELIUS (1998)   BRUZELIUS, C. 'Charles I, Charles II and the Development of an Angevin Style in the Kingdom of Sicily' in *L'Etat Angevin. Pouvoir, Culture et Société entre XIIIe et XIVe Siècle* (Actes du colloque international organisé par l'American Academy in Rome, l'Ecôle française de Rome, l'Istituto storico italiano per il Medio Evo, etc., Rome–Naples November 1995). Rome, 1998, 99–114.

BRYKOWSKA (1965)   BRYKOWSKA, M. 'Sklepienia krysztalowe (niektóre problemy)', in *Późny Gotyk. Studia nad sztuką przełomu sredniowiecza i czasów nowych*. Warszawa, 1965, 243–59.

BUBERL (1940)   BUBERL, P. *Die Kunstdenkmäler des Zisterzienserklosters Zwettl* (Ostmärkische (Österreichische) Kunsttopographie, 29). Baden bei Wien, 1940.

BUCHER (1957)   BUCHER, F. *Notre-Dame de Bonmont und die ersten Zisterzienserabteien in der Schweiz* (Berner Schriften zur Kunst, 7). Bern, 1957.

BUCHER (1968)   BUCHER, F. 'Design in Gothic Architecture. A Preliminary Assessment', *Journal of the Society of Architectural Historians*, 27 (1968), 49–71.

BUCHER (1972)   BUCHER, F. 'Medieval Architectural Design Methods, 800–1560', *Gesta*, 11 (1972), 37–51.

BUCHER (1972a)   BUCHER, F. 'The Dresden Sketchbook of Vault Projection', in *Actes du XXIIe Congrès International d'Histoire de l'Art, Budapest 1969. Évolution Générale et Développements Régionaux en Historie de l'Art*, vol. 1. Budapest, 1972, 527–37.

BUCHER (1976)   BUCHER, F. 'Micro-Architecture as the "idea" of Gothic Theory and Style', *Gesta*, 15 (1976), 71–89.

BUCHER (1979)   BUCHER, F. *Architector. The Lodgebooks and Sketchbooks of Medieval Architects*, 1. New York, 1979.

BUCHERT (1986)   BUCHERT, M. 'Die ehemalige Klosterkirche Heisterbach' Ph.D. thesis, Rheinische Friedrich-Wilhelms-Universität, Bonn, 1986.

BÜCHNER (1964)   BÜCHNER, J. *Die Spätgotische Wandpfeilerkirche Bayerns und Österreichs*. Nuremberg, 1964.

BÜCHNER (1967)   BÜCHNER, J. 'Ast- Laub- und Masswerkgewölbe der endenden Spätgotik. Zum Verhältnis von Architektur, dekorativer Malerei und Bauplastik', in *Festschrift für Karl Oettinger zum 60 Geburtstag*. Erlangen, 1967, 265–301.

BUCHOWIECKI (1970)   BUCHOWIECKI, W. *Handbuch der Kirchen Roms. Der Römische Sakralbau in Geschichte und Kunst von der Altchristlichen Zeit bis zur Gegenwart*, 2, Die Kirchen innerhalb der Mauern Roms, Gèsu Crocifissio bis S. Maria in Monticelli. Vienna, 1970.

BÜCHSEL (1983)   BÜCHSEL, M. 'Ecclesiae symbolorum cursus completus', *Städel-Jahrbuch*, new ser.9 (1983), 69–88.

BÜCHSEL (1995)   BÜCHSEL, M. *Die Skulptur des Querhauses der Kathedrale von Chartres*. Berlin, 1995.

BÜCHSEL (1997)   BÜCHSEL, M. *Die Geburt der Gotik. Abt Sugers Konzept für die Abteikirche Saint-Denis* (Rombach Wissenschaft, Reihe Quellen zur Kunst, vol. 5). Freiburg im Breisgau, 1997.

BUGSLAG (1993)   BUGSLAG, J. 'Early Fourteenth-Century Canopywork in Rouen Stained Glass', in: *Medieval Art, Architecture and Archaeology at Rouen* (British Archaeo-logical Association Conference Transactions for 1986, vol. 12). Leeds, 1993, 73–9.

BUREŠ (1975)   BUREŠ, J. 'Ein unveröffentlicher Choraufriss aus der Ulmer Bauhütte. Zur nachparlerischen Architektur in Süddeutschland und Wien', *Zeitschrift des deutschen Vereins für Kunstwissenschaft*, 29 (1975), 3–27.

BUREŠ (1983)   BUREŠ, J. 'Die Prager Domfassade', *Acta Historiae Artium*, 29 (1983), 3–50.

BUREŠ (1986)   BUREŠ, J. 'Der Regensburger Doppelturmplan. Untersuchungen zur Architektur der ersten Nachparlerzeit', *Zeitschrift für Kunstgeschichte*, 49 (1986), 1–28.

BUREŠ (1989)   BUREŠ, J. 'Peter Parlers Chor in Kolin und seine Beziehung zur

Prager Bauhütte im Lichte der schriftlichen Quellen', *Gesta*, 28 (1989), 136–46.

BUREŠ (1990) BUREŠ, J. 'Die Bedeutung der Magdeburger Bauhütte in der mitteldeutschen Architektur des ausgehenden 14 Jahrhunderts', *Niederdeutsche Beiträge zur Kunstgeschichte*, 29 (1990), 9–33.

BURGEMEISTER (1930a) BURGEMEISTER, L. *Die Kunstdenkmäler der Stadt Breslau*, Teil 1, Die kirchlichen Denkmäler der Dominsel und der Sandinsel. Breslau, 1930.

BURGEMEISTER (1933) BURGEMEISTER, L. *Die Kunstdenkmäler der Stadt Breslau*, Teil 2, Die kirchlichen Denkmäler der Altstadt. Breslau, 1933.

BURGEMEISTER (1934) BURGEMEISTER, L. *Die Kunstdenkmäler der Stadt Breslau*, Teil 3, Die kirchlichen Denkmäler der Altstadt (Fortsetzung) und des erweiterten Stadtgebietes. Breslau, 1934.

BURGER (1978) BURGER, S. *Die Schlosskapelle zu Blutenburg bei München. Struktur eines spätgotischen Raums* (Miscellana Bavarica Monacensia, 77). Munich, 1978.

BURKE (1987) BURKE, P. *The Renaissance*. New Jersey, 1987.

BURNAND (1989) BURNAND, M.-C. *Lorraine Gothique*. Paris, 1989.

BÜTTNER AND MEISSNER (1983) BÜTTNER, H. AND MEISSNER, G. *Town Houses of Europe*. Leipzig, 1983.

BUYLE et al. (1997) BUYLE, M., COOMANS, T., ESTHER, J., AND GENICOT, L. *Architecture Gothique en Belgique*. Brussels, 1997.

CADEI (1969) CADEI, A.C. 'I capitelli più antichi del Duomo di Milano', in Gatti Perer, ed., *Il duomo di Milano* (Congresso Internationale, 2 vols. Milan, 1969, vol. 1, 77–88.

CADEI (1978) CADEI, A.C. 'La chiesa di S. Francesco a Cortona', in *Storia della città* Rivista Internationale di storia urbana e territoriale, 9, Milan, 1978, 16–23.

CADEI (1980) CADEI, A.C. 'Fossanova e Castel del Monte', in *Atti della III settimana di studi di storia dell'arte medievale dell'università di Roma, 1978*. Roma 1980, 191–215.

CADEI (1991) CADEI, A.C. 'Cultura artistica delle cattedrali: due esempi a Milano', *Arte medievale*, 5 (1991), 83–103.

CADEI (1991a) CADEI, A.C. 'Architettura', in *Enciclopedia dell'arte medievale*, Rome, 1991, vol. 2, 333–44.

CAMILLE (1989) CAMILLE, M. *The Gothic Idol. Ideology and Image-Making in Medieval Art*. Cambridge, 1989.

CARLI (1987) CARLI, E. 'Giovanni d'Agostino e il "Duomo Nuovo"', in *Giovanni d'Agostino e il Duomo Nuovo di Siena*. Gênes, 1987, 7–44.

CAREY, ed. (1999) CAREY, F., ed., *The Apocalypse and the Shape of Things to come*. London, British Museum, 1999.

CARLSON (1968) CARLSON, E.G. 'The Abbey Church of Saint-Étienne at Caen in the 11th and early 12th Centuries' Ph.D. thesis, Yale University, 1968.

CARLSON (1971) CARLSON, G. 'Excavations at St. Étienne, Caen', *Gesta*, 11 (1971), 23–30.

CARLSON (1972) CARLSON, E.G. 'Fouilles de St. Étienne de Caen', *Archéologie médiévale*, 11 (1972), 89–102.

CARLSON (1976) CARLSON, E.G. 'A Charter for Saint-Étienne, Caen: A Document and its Implications', *Gesta*, 15 (1976), 11–14.

CARLSON (1986) CARLSON, E.G. 'A Note on Four Story Elevations', *Gesta*, 25 (1986), 61–8.

CARPINO (1997) CARPINO, A. 'Margaret of Austria's Funerary Complex at Brou. Conjugal Love, Political Ambition or Personal Glory?', in C. Lawrence, ed., *Women and Art in Early Modern Europe. Patrons, Collectors and Connoisseurs*. Pennsylvania, 1997, 37–52.

CASELLI (1981) CASELLI, F.P. *La Costruzione del Palazzo dei Papi di Avignone (1316–1367)*. Milan, 1981.

CASSIDY (1992) CASSIDY, B. 'Orcagna's Tabernacle in Florence: design and function', *Zeitschrift für Kunstgeschichte*, 55 (1992), 180–211.

CAVE (1929) CAVE, C.-J.-P. 'Roof Bosses in the Nave of Tewkesbury Abbey', *Archaeologia*, 79 (1929), 73–84.

CAVINESS (1982) CAVINESS, M.H. 'Canterbury Cathedral Clerestory: The Glazing Programme in Relation to the Campaigns of Construction', in: *Medieval Art and Architecture at Canterbury before 1220* (British Archaeological Association Conference Transactions for 1979, vol. 5). Leeds, 1982, 46–55.

CAVINESS (1984) CAVINESS, M.H. 'St.-Yved of Braine: the Primary Sources for Dating the Gothic Church', *Speculum*, 59 (1984), 524–48.

CAVINESS (1990) CAVINESS, M.H. *Sumptuous Arts at the Royal Abbeys in Reims and Braine*. Princeton, 1990.

CAZES et al. (1979–80) CAZES, D., CARBONELL-LAMOTHE, Y., AND PRADALIER-SCHLUMBERGER, M. 'La sculpture des chapelles de Bertrand de l'Isle', *Mémoires de la Société archéologique du Midi de la France*, 43 (1979–80), 121–5.

CHADRABA (1974) CHADRABA, R. *Die Karlsbrücke*. Prague, 1974.

CHAMPEAUX AND GAUCHERY (1894) CHAMPEAUX, A. DE AND GAUCHERY, P. *Les traveaux d'art exécutés pour Jean de France, Duc de Berry*. Paris, 1894.

CHENU (1968) CHENU, M-D. *Nature, Man and Society in the Twelfth Century*. Edited and translated by J. Taylor and Lester K. Little. Chicago, 1968.

CHEVALLEY (1995) CHEVALLEY, D.A. (with contributions from H.W. Clementschitsch and M. Mannewitz), *Der Dom zu Augsburg (Die Kunstdenkmäler von Bayern*, N.F. vol. 1). Munich, 1995.

CHICÓ (1968) CHICÓ, M.T. *A Arquitectura Gótica em Portugal*. Lisbon, 1968.

CHIROL (1926) CHIROL, P. 'Palais de Justice, Rouen', *Congrès Archéologiques de France*, 89 (1926), 158–77.

CHIROL AND LAVALLÉE (1977) CHIROL, E. AND LAVALLÉE, D. 'Construction du palais du Neuf-Marche et du palais royal 1499–1531', in *Le Palais de Justice de Rouen*. Rouen, 1977, 23–100.

CHRISTIAN (1989) CHRISTIAN, K. 'Arnolfo di Cambio's sculptural project for the Duomo façade in Florence: a study in style and context'. Ph.D. dissertation, New York University, 1989.

CHUECA GOITÍA (1951) CHUECA GOITÍA, F. *La Catedral Nueva de Salamanca. Historia Documental de su Construccion* (Acta Salmanticensia, Filosofia y Letras, IV, Universidad Salamanca). Salamanca, 1951.

CHUECA GOITÍA (1965) CHUECA GOITÍA, F. *Historia de la arquitectura Española. Edad Antigua, Edad Media*. Madrid, 1965.

CLARK (1970) CLARK, W.W. 'The Cathedral of St. Pierre at Lisieux and the Beginning of Norman Gothic Architecture'. Ph.D. dissertation, Columbia University, New York, 1970.

CLARK (1972) CLARK, W.W. 'The Central Portal of Saint-Pierre at Lisieux. A lost monument of twelfth-century Gothic Sculpture', *Gesta*, 11 (1972), 46–58.

CLARK (1977) CLARK, W.W. 'The nave vaults of Noyon Cathedral', *Journal of the Society of Architectural Historians*, 36 (1977), 30–3.

CLARK (1977a) CLARK, W.W. 'The nave of Saint-Pierre at Lisieux: Romanesque Structure in a Gothic Guise', *Gesta*, 16/1 (1977), 29–38.

CLARK (1979) CLARK, W.W. 'Spatial Innovations in the Chevet of Saint-Germain-des-Prés', *Journal of the Society of Architectural Historians*, 38 (1979), 348–65.

CLARK AND KING (1983) CLARK, W.W. AND KING, R. *Laon Cathedral. vol 1. Architecture* (Courtauld Institute Illustration Archives, Companion Text 1). London, 1983.

CLARK AND MARK (1984) CLARK, W.W. AND MARK, R. 'The First Flying Buttresses: A New Reconstruction of the Nave of Notre-Dame de Paris', *Art Bulletin*, 66 (1984), 47–65.

CLARK (1985) CLARK, W.W. 'The Early Capitals at Notre-Dame de Paris', in *Tribute to Lotte Brand Philip, Art Historian and Detective*. New York, 1985, 35–42.

CLARK (1986) CLARK, W.W. 'Suger's Church at Saint-Denis: The State of Research', in P.L. Gerson, ed., *Abbot Suger of Saint-Denis: a Symposium*. New York, 1986, 105–30.

CLARK AND LUDDEN (1986) CLARK, W.W. AND LUDDEN, F. 'Notes on the Archivolts of the Sainte-Anne Portal of Notre-Dame de Paris', *Gesta*, 25 (1986), 109–18.

CLARK (1987) CLARK, W.W. *Laon Cathedral. vol. 2 Architecture: The Aesthetics of Space, Plan and Structure* (Courtauld Institute Illustration Archives, Companion Text 2). London, 1987.

CLARK AND MARK (1989) CLARK, W.W. AND MARK, R., 'Le chevet et la nef de Notre-Dame de Paris: Une comparaison entre les premières élevations', *Journal d'Histoire de l'Architecture*, 2 (1989), 69–88.

CLARK (1995) CLARK, W.W. '"The Recollection of the Past is the Promise of the Future". Continuity and Contextuality: Saint-Denis, Merovingians, Capetians and Paris', in V. Raguin, K. Brush and P. Draper, eds. (1995), 92–113.

CLARK (1999) CLARK, W.W. 'Notes on the Original Design of the Choir and Chevet of Saint-Remi at Reims', in Joubert and Sandron, eds. (1999), 67–75.

CLARKE AND CROSSLEY eds. (2000) CLARKE, G. AND CROSSLEY, P., *Architecture and Language. Constructing Identity in European Architecture c.1000–c.1650*. Cambridge, 2000.

CLASEN (1927) CLASEN, K.H. *Die mittelalterliche Kunst im Gebiete des Deutschordensstaates Preussen*, 1: Die Burgbauten. Königsberg, 1927.

CLASEN (1958) CLASEN, K.H. *Deutsche Gewölbe der Spätgotik*. Berlin, 1958.

CLASEN (1952) CLASEN, W. 'Hinrich Brunsberg und die Parler', in *Festschrift für Julius Baum*. Stuttgart, 1952, 48–57.

CLAUSSEN (1975) CLAUSSEN, P. *Zur Vorgeschichte, Funktion und Skulptur der Vorhallen* (Forschungen zur Kunstgeschichte und Christlichen Archäologie, 9). Wiesbaden, 1975.

CLAUSSEN (1993/4) CLAUSSEN, P. 'Kathedralgotik und Anonymität 1130–1250', *Wiener Jahrbuch für Kunstgeschichte*, 46/7 (1993/4), 141–60.

CNATTINGIUS (1963) CNATTINGIUS, H. *The Crisis in the 1420s* (Studies in the Order of St Bridget of Sweden, 1). Stockholm, 1963.

CNATTINGIUS et al. (1987) CNATTINGIUS, B. *Linköpings domkyrka* (Sveriges Kyrkor, 200–201). Stockholm, 1987.

COCHERIL (1966) COCHERIL, M. *Études sur le Monachisme en Espagne et au Portugal*. Paris and Lisbon, 1966.

COCHERIL (1989)   COCHERIL, M. *Alcobaça. Abadia Cisterciense de Portugal.* Lisbon, 1989.

COCKE (1987)   COCKE, T.H. 'The Wheel of Fortune: The Appreciation of Gothic since the Middle Ages', in J. Alexander and P. Binski, eds., *Age of Chivalry. Art in Plantagenet England 1200–1400.* London, 1987, 183–91.

COCKE (1990)   COCKE, T.H. '"Gothique Moderne": The Use of Gothic in Seventeenth Century France', in P. Crossley and E. Fernie, *Medieval Architecture and its Intellectual Context. Studies in Honour of Peter Kidson.* London and Ronceverte, 1990, 249–57.

COENEN (1990)   COENEN, U. *Die Spätgotischen Werkmeisterbücher in Deutschland: Untersuchung und Edition Der Lehrschriften für Entwurf und Ausführung von Sakralbauten* (Beiträge zur Kunstwissenschaft, 35). Munich, 1990.

COLCHESTER AND HARVEY (1974)   COLCHESTER, L.S. AND HARVEY, J.H. 'Wells Cathedral', *Archaeological Journal*, 131 (1974), 200–14.

COLCHESTER AND HARVEY (1982)   COLCHESTER, L.S. AND HARVEY, J.H. 'The Building of Wells Cathedral, I: 1175–1307', in L.S. Colchester, ed., *Wells Cathedral. A History.* London, 1982, 52–5.

COLCHESTER (1987)   COLCHESTER, L.S. *Wells Cathedral* (New Bell's Cathedral Guides). London, 1987.

COLDSTREAM (1979)   COLDSTREAM, N. 'Ely Cathedral: the Fourteenth-Century Work', in *Medieval Art and Architecture at Ely Cathedral* (The British Archaeological Association Conference Transactions for 1976, vol. 2). Leeds, 1979, 28–46.

COLDSTREAM (1980)   COLDSTREAM, N. 'York Minster and the Decorated Style in Yorkshire: Architectural Reaction to York in the first half of the fourteenth century', *Yorkshire Archaeological Journal*, 52 (1980), 89–110.

COLDSTREAM (1986)   COLDSTREAM, N. 'Cistercian architecture from Beaulieu to the Dissolution', in C. Norton and D. Park eds., *Cistercian Art and Architecture in the British Isles.* Cambridge, London, New York, etc., 1986, 139–59.

COLDSTREAM (1991)   COLDSTREAM, N. *Masons and Sculptors.* London, 1991.

COLDSTREAM (1991a)   COLDSTREAM, N. 'The Commissioning and the Design of the Eleanor Crosses', in D. Parsons, ed., *Eleanor of Castile 1290–1990.* Stamford, 1991, 55–68.

COLDSTREAM (1994)   COLDSTREAM, N. *The Decorated Style. Architecture and Ornament 1240–1360.* London, 1994.

COLVIN (1983)   COLVIN, H.M. 'The "Court Style" in Medieval English Architecture: a Review', in V.J. Scattergood and J.W. Sherborne, eds., *English Court Culture in the Later Middle Ages.* London, 1983, 129–39.

COLVIN (1991)   COLVIN, H.M. *Architecture and the After-Life.* New Haven and London, 1991.

CONANT (1968)   CONANT, K.J. *Cluny. Les églises et la maison du chef d'ordre.* Cambridge, Mass., 1968.

CONANT (1974)   CONANT, K.J. *Carolingian and Romanesque Architecture.* London, 1974, 2nd edn.

CONNELL (1988)   CONNELL, S. *The Employment of Stonemasons and Sculptors in Venice in the Fifteenth Century.* New York, London, 1988.

CONNOLLY (1980)   CONNOLLY, S.R. 'A proposed dating for the Tour Saint-Aubin in Angers', *Gesta*, 20 (1980), 17–35.

CONRADT (1959)   CONRADT, A. 'Ulrich von Ensingen als Ulmer Münsterbaumeister und seine Voraussetzungen'. Ph.D. thesis, Freiburg im Br., 1959.

COOK (1947)   COOK, G.H. *Medieval Chantries and Chantry Chapels.* London, 1947.

COOK (1975)   COOK, J.W. 'St Martin, Landshut and the Architecture of Hanns von Burghausen'. Ph.D. thesis, Yale University, 1975.

COOK (1976)   COOK, J.W. 'A new chronology of Hanns von Burghausen's Late Gothic architecture', *Gesta*, 15 (1976), 97–104.

COOMANS (1997)   COOMANS, T. 'Villers-en-Brabant. Analyse architecturale d'une abbaye cistercienne au moyen âge'. Ph.D. thesis, UCL, Louvain-la-Neuve, 1997.

COPPENS (1941)   COPPENS, M. *De Kathedrale Basiliek van St Jan te 'sHertogenbosch.* Utrecht, 1941.

CORSEPIUS (1997)   CORSEPIUS, K. *Notre-Dame-en-Vaux. Studien zur Baugeschichte des 12. Jahrhunderts in Châlons-sur-Marne.* Stuttgart, 1997.

COULSON (1979)   COULSON, C. 'Structural Symbolism in Medieval Castle Architecture', *Journal of the British Archaeological Association*, 132 (1979), 73–90.

COURTENAY (1984)   COURTENAY, L.T. 'The Westminster Hall Roof and its 14th-century Sources', *Journal of the Society of Architectural Historians*, 43 (1984), 295–309.

COURTENAY AND MARK (1987)   COURTENAY, L.T. AND MARK, R. 'The Westminster Hall Roof: A Historiographic and Structural Study', *Journal of the Society of Architectural Historians*, 46 (1987), 374–93.

COURTENAY (1990)   COURTENAY, L.T. 'The Westminster Hall Roof: A New Archaeological Source', *Journal of the British Archaeological Association*, 143 (1990), 95–111.

CREUTZFELD (1953)   CREUTZFELD, H. 'Das Langhaus der Heiligkreuzkirche in Schwäbisch-Gmünd'. Ph.D. thesis, Freiburg im Br., 1953.

CROOK (1993)   CROOK, J. 'Bishop Walkelin's Cathedral', in J.W. Crook, ed., *Winchester Cathedral. Nine Hundred Years.* Guildford, 1993.

CROSBY (1963)   CROSBY, S. MCK. 'Abbot Suger's St Denis', *Studies in Western Art* (Acts of the Twentieth International Congress of the History of Art, New York, 1961. Princeton, 1963, vol. 1, 85–91.

CROSBY (1965)   CROSBY, S. MCK. 'The Inside of St Denis' West Façade', in M. Kühn and L. Grodecki, eds., *Gedenkschrift Ernst Gall.* Berlin and Munich, 1965, 59–68.

CROSBY (1966)   CROSBY, S. MCK. 'Crypt and Choir Plan at St Denis', *Gesta*, 5 (1966), 4–8.

CROSBY (1970)   CROSBY, S. MCK. 'The West Portals of Saint-Denis and the Saint-Denis Style', *Gesta*, 9 (1970), 1–11.

CROSBY (1981)   CROSBY, S. MCK. 'Some Uses of Photogrammetry by the Historian of Art', in S. McK. Crosby, A. Chand, A. Prache and A. Chatelet, eds., *Études d'Art Médiéval offertes à Louis Grodecki.* Paris, 1981, 119–28.

CROSBY (1987)   CROSBY, S. MCK. *The Royal Abbey of Saint-Denis. From its Beginnings to the Death of Suger, 475–1151*, edited and completed by Pamela Z. Blum. New Haven and London, 1987.

CROSSLEY (1981)   CROSSLEY, P. 'Wells, the West Country and Central European Late Gothic' in *Medieval Art and Architecture at Wells and Glastonbury* (British Archaeological Association Conference Transactions for 1978, vol. 4). Leeds, 1981, 81–109.

CROSSLEY (1981a)   CROSSLEY, P. review of W. Leedy, *Fan Vaulting* (1980), in *Journal of the Society of Architectural Historians*, 40, (1981), 155–7.

CROSSLEY (1988)   CROSSLEY, P. 'Medieval architecture and meaning: the limits of iconography', *Burlington Magazine*, 130 (1988), 116–21.

CROSSLEY (1990)   CROSSLEY, P. 'Lincoln and the Baltic: the Fortunes of a Theory', in Crossley and Fernie eds., *Medieval Architecture and its Intellectual Context. Studies in Honour of Peter Kidson.* London and Ronceverte, 1990, 169–80.

CROSSLEY (1993)   CROSSLEY, P. 'The Return to the Forest: Natural Architecture and the German Past in the Age of Dürer', in T.W. Gaehtgens, ed., *Künstlerischer Austausch. Artistic Exchange* (Akten des XXVIII Internationalen Kongresses für Kunstgeschichte, 2). Berlin, 1993, vol. 2, 71–80.

CROSSLEY (1994)   CROSSLEY, P. Review of M. Radding and W.W. Clark, *Medieval Architecture, Medieval Learning. Builders and Masters in the Age of Romanesque and Gothic*, in *Burlington Magazine*, 136 (1994), 172–3.

CROSSLEY (1995)   CROSSLEY, P. 'Kraków cathedral and the formation of a dynastic architecture in southern Central Europe', in F. Ames-Lewis, ed., *Polish and English Responses to French Art and Architecture. Contrasts and Similarities.* (Papers delivered at the University of London and the University of Warsaw, history of art conferences, January and September 1993). London, 1995, 31–46.

CROSSLEY (1997)   CROSSLEY, P. 'The Architecture of Queenship: Royal Saints, Female Dynasties and the Spread of Gothic Architecture in Central Europe', in A. Duggan, ed., *Queens and Queenship in Medieval Europe* (Proceedings of the Conference at King's College, 1995). Woodbridge, 1997, 263–300.

CROSSLEY (1998)   CROSSLEY, P. 'The Man from Inner Space: Architecture and Meditation in the Choir of St Laurence in Nuremberg', in *Medieval Art: Recent Perspectives. A memorial tribute to C.R. Dodwell*, ed. G. Owen-Crocker and T. Graham, Manchester and New York, 1998, 165–82.

CROSSLEY (1999)   CROSSLEY, P. 'Bohemia Sacra: Liturgy and History in Prague Cathedral' in Joubert and Freigang, eds. (1999), 341–65.

CROSSLEY (2000)   CROSSLEY, P. 'The Politics of Presentation: The Architecture of Charles IV of Bohemia', in Rees Jones, Marks and Minnis, eds (2000), 99–172.

CUNNINGHAM (1995)   CUNNINGHAM, C. 'For the honour and beauty of the city: the design of town halls', in D. Norman, ed., *Siena, Florence and Padua. Art, Society and Religion 1280–1400*, vol. 2. New Haven and London, 1995, 29–53.

CURUNI (1982)   CURUNI, A. 'Architettura degli Ordini Mendicanti in Umbria – Problemi di rilievo', in C. Pirovano, ed., *Francesco d'Assisi, Chiese e Conventi* (vol. 1 of the exh. cat., *Francesco d'Assisi*). Milan, 1982, 83–142.

DALLAWAY (1806)   DALLAWAY, J. *Observations on English Architecture, Military Ecclesiastical and Civil.* Clarendon, 1806.

DAMBECK (1957)   DAMBECK, F. 'Hans Stethaimer und die Landshuter Bauschule', *Verhandlungen des historischen Vereins für Niederbayern*, 82 (1957), 15–18.

DAVIS (1979)   DAVIS, M.T. *The Cathedral of Clermont-Ferrand: History of its Construction*, 3 vols. Ann Arbor, 1979.

DAVIS (1981)   DAVIS, M.T. 'The choir of Clermont-Ferrand: The Beginnings of Construction and the work of Jean Deschamps', *Journal of the Society of Architectural Historians*, 40 (1981), 181–207.

DAVIS (1984)   DAVIS, M.T. 'The Choir of the Abbey of Altenberg: Cistercian

Simplicity and Aristocratic Iconography', in M.P. Lillich, ed., *Studies in Cistercian Art and Architecture*, 2. Kalamazoo, 1984, 130–60.

DAVIS (1984a)   DAVIS, M.T. 'On the Threshold of the Flamboyant. The Second Campaign of Construction of Saint-Urbain, Troyes', *Speculum*, 59 (1984), 847–84.

DAVIS (1986)   DAVIS, M.T. 'Le choeur de la cathédrale de Limoges: tradition rayonnante et innovation dans la carrière de Jean Deschamps' *Bulletin archéologique du Comité des Traveaux historiques et scientifiques*, n.s. 22 (1986), 51–114.

DAVIS (1995)   DAVIS, M.T. review of C. Freigang, *Imitare Ecclesias Nobiles*, etc., *Journal of the Society of Architectural Historians*, 54 (1995), 371–3.

DAVIS (1998)   DAVIS, M.T. 'Splendor and Peril: The Cathedral of Paris, 1290–1350, *Art Bulletin*, 80 (1998), 34–66.

DAWTON (1983)   DAWTON, N. 'The Percy Tomb at Beverly Minster: The Style of the Sculpture', in F.H. Thompson, ed., *Studies in Medieval Sculpture*. London, Survey of Antiquaries, 1983, 122–50.

DAWTON (1989)   DAWTON, N. 'The Percy Tomb Workshop', in *Medieval Art and Architecture in the East Riding of Yorkshire* (British Archaeological Association Conference Transactions for 1983, vol. 9). Leeds, 1989, 121–32.

DEAN (1979)   DEAN, M. 'The Beginnings of Decorated Architecture in the Southwest Midlands and East Anglia' (Ph.D. dissertation, Berkeley California). Ann Arbor, 1979, 63–70.

DEAN (1986)   DEAN, M. 'The Angel Choir and its local Influence', in *Medieval Art and Architecture at Lincoln Cathedral* (British Archaeological Association Conference Transactions for 1982, vol. 8). Leeds, 1986, 90–101.

DE BEER (1948)   DE BEER, E.S. 'Gothic: Origin and Diffusion of the Term; the Idea of Style in Architecture', *Journal of the Warburg and Courtauld Institutes*, 11 (1948), 143–62.

DEGENHART AND SCHMITT (1968)   DEGENHART, B.D. AND SCHMITT, A. *Corpus der Italienischen Zeichnungen 1300–1450*, 8 vols. Berlin, 1968–80.

DEHIO AND BEZOLD (1901)   DEHIO, G.G. AND BEZOLD VON, G. *Die kirchliche Baukunst des Abendlandes*, 2 vols. Stuttgart, 1884–1901.

DEHIO AND EISSING (1998)   DEHIO, G. revised and re-written by S. Eissing, *Handbuch der Deutschen Kunstdenkmäler. Thüringen*. Munich, 1998.

DEHIO AND PIEL (1964)   DEHIO, G. revised and re-written by Piel, F. *Handbuch der Deutschen Kunstdenkmäler. Baden Württemberg*. Berlin, 1964.

DEHIO (1974)   DEHIO, G. revised and re-written by the Institut fur Denkmalpflege, *Handbuch der Deutschen Kunstdenkmäler, Der Bezirk Magdeburg*. Berlin, 1974.

DEHIO (1976)   DEHIO, G. revised and re-written by the Institute für Denkmalpflege, *Handbuch der Deutschen Kunstdenkmäler. Der Bezirk Halle*. Berlin, 1976.

DEHIO AND ZIMDARS (1993)   DEHIO, G. AND ZIMDARS, D. *Handbuch der Deutschen Kunstdenkmäler, Baden-Würtemberg. I. Die Regierungsbezirke Stuttgart und Karlsruhe*. Munich, 1993.

DELLWING (1970)   DELLWING, H. *Studien zur Baukunst der Bettelorden im Veneto. Die Gotik der monumentalen Gewölbebasiliken*. Munich-Berlin, 1970.

DELLWING (1990)   DELLWING, H. *Die Kirchenbaukunst des späten Mittelalters in Venetien*. Worms, 1990.

DELMELLE (1975)   DELMELLE, J. *Hôtels de ville et masons communales de Belgiques*. Brussels, 1975.

DELMIOT, KURMANN-SCHWARZ et al. (1999)   DELMIOT, F., KURMANN-SCHWARZ, B., TEYSSOT, J., WHITELEY, M., et al. *Riom. Le Palais de Justice et la Sainte-Chapelle. Puy-le-Dôme* (Inventaire général des monuments et des richesses artistiques de la France). Clermont-Ferrand, 1999.

DE MAILLÉ (1939)   DE MAILLÉ, G. *Provins, les monuments religieux*, 2 vols. Paris, 1939.

DEMAISON (1894)   DEMAISON, L. 'Les architectes de la cathédrale de Reims', *Bulletin archéologique* (1894), 1–40.

DEMAISON (1898)   DEMAISON, L. 'Nouveaux renseignements sur les architectes de la cathédrale de Reims au moyen âge', *Bulletin archéologique* (1898), lx–lxi and 40–8.

DE MASSARY (1995)   DE MASSARY, X. 'La Cathédrale: architecture et décor', in *Laon. Une acropole à la française*. Amiens, 1995, 263–88.

DE MERINDOL (1993)   DE MERINDOL, C. 'Clément VI, seigneur et pape, d'après le témoignage de l'emblématique et de la thématique. La chambre du cerf. L'abbatiale de la Chaise-Dieu', in *Le décor des eglises en France méridionale (XIIIe – mi XVe s.)* (Cahiers de Fanjeaux, 28). Toulouse, 1993, 331–61.

DENEUX (1946)   DENEUX, H. 'Les crétiaux de la cathédrale de Reims', *Bulletin Monumental*, 104 (1946), 109–12.

DENEUX (1948)   DENEUX, H. 'Des modifications apportées à la cathédrale de Reims au cours de sa construction du XIIIe au XVe siècle, *Bulletin Monumental* 106 (1948), 121–40.

DERCSENYI (1957)   DERCSENYI, D. 'Zur Siebenhundertjährigen Feier der Kirche von Ják', *Acta Historiae Artium*, 4 (1957), 173–202.

DESHOULIÈRES (1921)   DESHOULIÈRES, M. 'Église Saint-Michel-des-Lions' in *Congrès Archéologique de France*, 84 (1921), 40–3.

DESPORTES (1979)   DESPORTES, P. *Reims et les Rémois aux XIIIe et XIVe siècles*. Paris, 1979.

DEVLIEGHER (1954/1956)   DEVLIEGHER, L. 'De opkomst van de kerkelijke gotische bouwkunst in West-Vlaanderen gedurende de XIIIde eeuw', *Bulletin de la Commission royale des monuments et des sites*, 5 (1954), 177–345, and 7 (1956), 7–121.

DE WAHA (1977)   DE WAHA, M. 'À propos de l'influence de l'architecture bourguignonne en Brabant. L'église abbatiale de Villers', *Bulletin de la Commission royale des monuments et des sites*, n.s. 6 (1977), 37–63.

DEYRES (1975)   DEYRES, M. 'Les voûtes de la cathédrale de Noyon', *Bulletin Monumental*, 133 (1975), 277–84.

DIAS (1986)   DIAS, P. *História da Arte em Portugal*, 4: Ogótico, Lisbon, 1986.

DIAS (1988)   DIAS, P. *A arquitectura manuelina*. Oporto, 1988.

DIAS (1988a)   DIAS, P. *Coimbra. Arte e Historia*. Coimbra, 1988.

DIEMER (1985)   DIEMER, P. 'Das Pfingstportal von Vézelay – Wege, Umwege und Abwege einer Diskussion', *Jahrbuch des Zentralinstituts für Kunstgeschichte*, 1 (1985), 77–114.

DIE PARLER (1978–80)   LEGNER, A. ed., *Die Parler und der Schöne Stil 1350–1400. Europäische Kunst unter den Luxemburgern* (exh. cat., Schnütgen Museum, Cologne, 3 vols). Cologne, 1978. Vols 4 and 5, Cologne, 1980.

DIETHEUER (1961)   DIETHEUER, F. 'Drei Originalbriefe des Dombaumeisters Conrad Roritzer und der Ingolstädter Liebfrauenturmplan um 1460', *Verhandlungen des Historischen Vereins für Oberpfalz und Regensburg*, 101 (1961), 165–74.

DIETHEUER (1976)   DIETHEUER, F. 'Die Roritzer als Dombaumeister zu Regensburg' in G. Schwaiger, *Der Regensburger Dom* (Beiträge zur Geschichte des Bistums Regensburg, 10) (1976), 111–18.

DIE ZEIT DER STAUFER (1977–9)   *Die Zeit der Staufer, Geschichte – Kunst – Kultur*, ed. by R. Haussherr. (exh. cat., Württembergischen Landesmuseum, Stuttgart, 5 vols). Stuttgart, 1977–9.

DIMIER (1949)   DIMIER, A. *Recueil de plans d'églises cisterciennes*. 2 vols. Grignan and Paris, 1949.

DIMIER (1957)   DIMIER, A. 'Origines des déambulatoires à chapelles rayonnantes non saillantes', *Bulletin Monumental*, 115 (1957), 23–33.

DIMIER (1982)   CHAUVIN, B. ed., *Mélanges à la mémoire du Père Anselme Dimier*, 3: Architecture cistercienne 6: Abbayes. Arbois, 1982.

DI ONOFRIO (1993)   DI ONOFRIO, M. 'Precizioni sul' deambulatorio della Cattedrale di Aversa', *Arte Medievale*, 2nd ser. 8 (1993), 65–79.

DITTMANN (1967)   DITTMANN, L. *Stil-Symbol-Struktur. Studien zu Kategorien der Kunstgeschichte*. Munich, 1967.

DITTSCHEID AND BERGER (1988)   DITTSCHEID, H.C. AND BERGER, C. 'Schwibbogensäle in Fossanova. Eine Beitrag zur Klosterbaukunjst der Zisterzienser im Mittelmeerraum' in F. Much, ed., *Baukunst des Mittelalters in Europa. Hans Erich Kubach zum 75 Geburtstag*. Stuttgart, 1988, 410–14.

DODWELL (1993)   DODWELL, C.R. *The Pictorial Arts of the West 800–1200*. New Haven and London, 1993.

DOMAŃSKA (1964–65)   DOMANSKA, H. 'Zamek w Lidzbarku Warmińskim', Typescript PKZ, Gdańsk, 1964–5.

DOMAŃSKA (1968)   DOMAŃSKA, H. 'Baszta narożna przedzamcza w Lidzbarku Warmińskim', *Kwartalnik Architektury i Urbanistyki*, 13 (1968), 359–72.

DOMAŃSKA (1973)   DOMAŃSKA, H. *Rezydencja Lidzbarska*. Olsztyn, 1973.

DONATH (1996)   DONATH, M. 'Bauforschung am Meissner Dom – Methoden und Ergebnisse', paper delivered in 'Gotik und Spätgotik'. International conference, 'Kunst und Region', at the Martin–Luther–Universität Halle-Wittenberg, Institut für Kunstgeschichte, October 1996.

DONATH (1998)   DONATH, M. 'Die Baugeschichte des Meissner Doms 1250–1400'. Ph.D. thesis, Albert-Ludwigs-Universität, Freiburg, 1998.

DÖRRENBERG (1937)   DÖRRENBERG, I. *Das Zisterzienserkloster Maulbronn*. Würzburg, 1937.

DRAPER (1979)   DRAPER, P. 'Bishop Northwold and the Church of Saint-Etheldreda', in *Medieval Art and Architecture at Ely Cathedral* (British Archaeological Association Conference Transactions for 1976, vol. 2). Leeds, 1979, 8–27.

DRAPER (1981)   DRAPER, P. 'The Sequence and Dating of the Decorated Work at Wells', in *Medieval Art and Architecture at Wells and Glastonbury* (British Archaeological Association Conference Transactions for 1978, vol. 4). Leeds, 1981, 18–29.

DRAPER (1983)   DRAPER, P. 'William of Sens and the Original Design of the Choir Termination of Canterbury Cathedral 1175-1179', *Journal of the Society of Architectural Historians*, 42 (1983), 238–48.

DRAPER (1986)   DRAPER, P. 'Recherches Récentes sur l'Architecture dans les Iles Brittaniques à la Fin de l'Époque Romane et au Début du Gothique', *Bulletin Monumental*, 144 (1986), 305–28.

DRAPER (1987)   DRAPER, P. 'Architecture and Liturgy', in J. Alexander and P. Binski, eds., *Age of Chivalry. Art in Plantagenet England 1200–1400*. London, 1987, 83–91.

DRAPER (1995)   DRAPER, P. 'Interpreting the Architecture of Wells Cathedral', in V. Raguin, K. Bush and P. Draper, eds., *Artistic Integration in Gothic Buildings*. Toronto, Buffalo, London, 1995, 114–30.

DRAPER (1995a)   DRAPER, P. 'Architectural Style in England and the Rhineland', in F. Ames Lewis, ed., *Polish and English Responses to French Art and Architecture* (Papers delivered at the University of London and University of Warsaw, history of art conferences, 1993). London, 1995, 17–30.

DRAPER (1996)   DRAPER, P. 'Salisbury Cathedral: Paradigm or Maverick?', in *Medieval Art and Architecture at Salisbury Cathedral* (British Archaeological Association Conference Transactions, vol. 17). Leeds, 1996, 21–31.

DRAPER (1997)   DRAPER, P. 'Interpretations of the Rebuilding of Canterbury Cathedral, 1174–1186. Archaeological and Historical Evidence', *Journal of the Society of Architectural Historians*, 56 (1997), 184–203.

DRAPER (2000)   DRAPER, P. 'English with a French Accent. Architectural Franglais in Late-Twelfth-Century England?' in Clarke and Crossley eds. (2000), 21–35.

DROST (1963)   DROST, W. *Die Marienkirche in Danzig und ihre Kunstschätze* (Bau- und Kunstdenkmäler des deutschen Ostens, Reihe A, 4). Stuttgart, 1963.

DU COLOMBIER (1973)   DU COLOMBIER, P. *Les Chantiers des Cathédrales*. Paris, 1973.

DUFFY (1992)   DUFFY, E. *The Stripping of the Altars. Traditional Religion in England 1400–1580*. New Haven and London, 1992.

DUFFY (1997)   DUFFY, E. 'The Parish, Piety and Patronage in Late Medieval East Anglia-The Evidence of Rood Screens', in K.L. French, G.G. Gibbs and B. Kümin, eds., *The Parish in English Life 1400–1600*, Manchester, 1997, 133–62.

DURÁN SANPERE (1959)   DURÁN SANPERE, A. 'La cathédrale de Barcelone', *Congrès Archéologique de France*, 117 (1959), 28–36.

DURAND (1901–3)   DURAND, G. *Monographie de l'église cathédrale Notre-Dame d'Amiens*, 2 vols. Amiens, 1901–3.

DURLIAT (1962)   DURLIAT, M. 'La construction de la cathédrale de Palma de Majorque au XIVe siècle', in H. Ladendorf and H. Vey, eds., *Mouseion. Festschrift O. Förster*. Cologne, 1962, 115–23.

DURLIAT (1962a)   DURLIAT, M. *L'art dans le Royaume de Majorque. Les Débuts de l'art gothique en Rousillon, en Cerdagne et aux Baléares*. Toulouse, 1962.

DURLIAT (1966)   DURLIAT, M. 'Les crénelages du clocher-porche de Moissac et leur restauration par Viollet-le-Duc', *Annales du Midi* (1966), 433–47.

DURLIAT (1973)   DURLIAT, M. 'L'eglise Saint-Michel de Carcassonne', *Congrès Archéologique de France*, 131 (1973), 604–18.

DURLIAT (1974)   DURLIAT, M. 'Le rôle des ordres mendiants dans le création de l'architecture gothique méridionale au XIIIe siècle', in *La naissance et l'essor du gothique méridional au XIIIe siècle* (Cahiers de Fanjeaux, 9). Toulouse, 1974, 71–86.

DURLIAT (1994)   DURLIAT, M. 'La sculpture du XIe siècle en occident', *Bulletin Monumental*, 152 (1994), 129–225.

DVOŘÁK (1967)   DVOŘÁK, M. *Idealism and Naturalism in Gothic Art* (trans. with notes and bibliography by R.J. Klawiter). Notre-Dame, Indiana, 1967.

DVOŘÁKOVA et al. (1964)   DVOŘÁKOVA, V., KRÁSA, J., MERHAUTOVÁ, A., AND STE-JSKAL, K. eds., *Gothic Mural Painting in Bohemia and Moravia 1300–1378*. Oxford, London and New York, 1964.

DWYER (1997)   DWYER, H. 'The Transepts of Rouen Cathedral'. MA thesis, Courtauld Institute of Art, London, 1997.

EGGER (1982)   EGGER, H. 'Franziskanische Geist in mittelalterliche Bildvorstellungen', in Niederösterreichischer Landesregierung, ed., *800 Jahre Franz von Assisi, Franziskanische Kunst und Kultur des Mittelalters*. exh. cat., Krems-Stein. Vienna, 1982, 471–505.

EICKERMANN (1972)   EICKERMANN, N. 'Epigraphische Notizen aus Soest', *Soester Zeitschrift*, 84 (1972), 37–9.

ELLGER AND KOLBE (1951)   ELLGER, D. AND KOLBE, J. *St Marien zu Lübeck und seine Wandmalereien*. Neumünster, 1951.

ELM, ed. (1982)   ELM, K. ed., *Die Zisterzienser. Ordensleben zwischen Ideal und Wirklichkeit* (Ergänzungsband). Cologne, 1982.

ERLANDE-BRANDENBURG (1974)   ERLANDE-BRANDENBURG, A. 'La cathedrale de Lisieux. Les campagnes de construction', *Congrès Archéologique de France*, 132 (1974), 139–72.

ERLANDE-BRANDENBURG (1975)   ERLANDE-BRANDENBURG, A. 'L'abbatiale de la Chaise-Dieu', *Congrès Archéologique de France*, 133 (1975), 720–55.

ERLANDE-BRANDENBURG (1977)   ERLANDE-BRANDENBURG, A. 'La façade de la cathédrale d'Amiens. Le septième Colloque International de la Société Française d'Archéologie (1er et 2ième Octobre (1974), *Bulletin Monumental*, 135 (1977), 252–93.

ERLANDE-BRANDENBURG (1980)   ERLANDE-BRANDENBURG, A. 'La Restauration de Notre-Dame', in B. Foucaurt et al., eds., *Viollet-le-Duc*, exh. cat., Paris, 1980, 72–81.

ERLANDE-BRANDENBURG (1994)   ERLANDE-BRANDENBURG, A. *The Cathedral. The Social and Architectural Dynamics of Construction*. Cambridge, 1994.

ERLANDE-BRANDENBURG (1998)   ERLANDE-BRANDENBURG, A. *Notre-Dame de Paris*. Paris 1998.

ERSKINE, ed. (1981–3)   ERSKINE, A.M. ed., *The Accounts of the Fabric of Exeter Cathedral*, Devon and Cornwall Record Society, n.s. 24, 26, 1981–3.

ESSER (1952)   ESSER, K.H. 'Die Ausgrabungen der romanischen Zisterzienserkirche Himmerod als Beitrag zum Verständnis der frühen Zisterzienser-Architektur', *Das Münster*, 5 (1952), 221–3.

ESSER (1953)   ESSER, K.H. 'Über den Kirchenbau des hl. Bernhard von Clairvauxx. Eine kunstwissenschaftliche Untersuchung aufgrund der Ausgrabungen der romanischen Abteikirche Himmerod', *Archiv für mittel-rheinische Kirchengeschichte*, 5 (1953), 195–222.

FABBRI AND RUTENBURG (1981)   FABBRI, N.R. AND RUTENBERG, N. 'The Tabernacle of Orsanmichele in Context', *Art Bulletin*, 63 (1981), 385–405.

FAJT, ed. (1998)   FAJT, J. ed., *Magister Theodoricus. Court Painter to Emperor Charles IV. The Pictorial Decoration of the Shrines at Karlštejn Castle*. Prague 1998.

FAJT AND ROYT (1998)   FAJT, J. AND ROYT, J. 'The Pictorial Decoration of the Great Tower at Karlštejn Castle. Ecclesia Triumphans', in J. Fayt, ed., *Magister Theodoricus. Court Painter to Emperor Charles IV* (Prague, 1998), 108–205.

FATH (1968/9)   FATH, M. 'Die Baukunst der frühen Gotik im Mittelrheingebiet', *Mainzer Zeitschrift*, 63/64 (1968/69), 1–38.

FATH (1970)   FATH, M. 'Die Baukunst der fruhen Gotik im Mittelrheingebeit', *Mainzer Zeitschrift*, 65 (1970), 43–92.

FASSLER (1993)   FASSLER, M. 'Liturgy and Sacred History in the Twelfth-Century Tympana at Chartres', *Art Bulletin*, 75 (1993), 499–520.

FAVIÈRE (1992)   FAVIÈRE, J. *L'hôtel de Jacques Coeur à Bourges*. Paris, 1992.

FEHR (1961)   FEHR, G. *Benedikt Ried, ein deutscher Baumeister zwischen Gotik und Renaissance*. Munich, 1961.

FEHR (1978)   FEHR, G. 'Die Wölbekunst der Parler', in A. Legner, ed., *Die Parler und der Schöne Stil 1350–1400. Europäische Kunst unter den Luxemburgern*, exh. cat., Schnütgen Museum Köln, 3, Cologne, 1978, 45–8.

FEHRING AND RESS (1961)   FEHRING, G. AND RESS, A. *Die Stadt Nürnberg* (Bayerische Kunstdenkmale, 10). Munich, 1961.

FELD (1961)   FELD, O. 'Zur Baugeschichte der Klosterkirche Murbach', *Zeitschrift für Kunstgeschichte*, 24 (1961), 242–9.

FELS (1955)   FELS, E. 'Die Grabung an der Fassade der Kathedrale von Chartres', *Kunstchronik*, 8 (1955), 149–51.

FERAUGE AND MIGNEREY (1996)   FERAUGE, M. AND MIGNEREY, P. 'L'utilsation du fer dans l'architecture gothique: l'exemple de la cathédrale de Bourges', *Bulletin Monumental*, 154 (1996), 129–48.

FERGUSON O'MEARA (1980)   FERGUSON O'MEARA, C. 'Saint-Gilles-du-Gard: the relationship of the foundation to the façade', *Journal of the Society of Architectural Historians*, 39 (1980), 57–60.

FERGUSSON (1970)   FERGUSSON, P. 'Early Christian Churches in Yorkshire and the Problem of the Cistercian Crossing Tower', *Journal of the Society of Architectural Historians*, 29 (1970), 211–21.

FERGUSSON (1984)   FERGUSSON, P. *Architecture of Solitude. Cistercian Abbeys in Twelfth-Century England*. Princeton, 1984.

FERGUSSON (1986)   FERGUSSON, P. 'The Twelfth-Century Refectories', in C. Norton and D. Park eds., *Cistercian Art and Architecture in the British Isles*. Cambridge, London, New York, etc., 1986, 168–80.

FERGUSSON (1994)   FERGUSSON, P. 'Programmatic factors in the east extension at Clairvaux', *Arte medievale*, 8 (1994), 87–100.

FERGUSSON AND HARRISON (1994)   FERGUSSON, P. AND HARRISON, S. 'The Rievaulx Abbey Chapter House', *Antiquaries Journal*, 74 (1994) 211–55.

FERGUSSON AND HARRISON (1999)   FERGUSSON, P. AND HARRISON, S., *Rievaulx Abbey, Community, Architecture, Memory*. New Haven and London, 1999.

FERNIE (1977)   FERNIE, E. 'The Spiral Piers of Durham Cathedral', in *Medieval Art and Architecture at Durham Cathedral* (British Archaeological Association Conference Transactions for 1977, vol. 3). Leeds, 1980, 49–58.

FERNIE (1982)   FERNIE, E. 'St Anselm's Crypt', in *Medieval Art and Architecture at Canterbury before 1220* (British Archaeological Association Conference Transactions for 1979, vol. 5). Leeds, 1982, 27–38.

FERNIE (1984)   FERNIE, E. 'The use of varied nave supports in Romanesque and Early Gothic Churches', *Gesta*, 23 (1984), 107–17.

FERNIE (1987)   FERNIE, E. 'La fonction liturgique des piliers cantonnés dans la nef de la cathédrale de Laon', *Bulletin Monumental*, 145 (1987), 257–66.

FERNIE (1990)   FERNIE, E. 'A Beginner's Guide to the Study of Architectural Proportions and Systems of Length', in P. Crossley and E. Fernie, *Medieval Architecture and its Intellectual Context. Studies in Honour of Peter Kidson*. London and Ronceverte, 1990, 229–37.

FERREIRA DE ALMEIDA (1990)   FERREIRA DE ALMEIDA, C.A. *A igreja de Jesus de Setúbal*. Oporto, 1990.

FEUCHTMÜLLER (1951)   FEUCHTMÜLLER, R. *Die spätgotische Architektur und Anton Pilgrim. Gedanken zu neuen Forschungen*. Vienna, 1951.

FEUCHTMÜLLER AND ULM (1965)   FEUCHTMÜLLER, R. AND ULM, B. 'Architektur des Donaustiles im Raum von Wien, Steyr und Admont', in *Die Kunst der Donauschule 1490–1540*, exh. cat., Stift St Florien und Schlossmuseum Linz, 1965, 217–34.

FIEBIG (1991)   FIEBIG, A. 'Das Hallenlanghaus des Mindener Doms – Neue Beobachtungen zu Datierung und architekturgeschichtlicher Stellung', *Niederdeutsche Beiträge zur Kunstgeschichte*, 30 (1991), 9–28.

FISCHER (1962)   FISCHER, F.W. *Die spätgotische Kirchenbaukunst am Mittelrhein 1410–1520*. Heidelberg, 1962.

FISCHER (1964)   FISCHER, F.W. *Unser Bild von der deutschen spätgotischen Architektur des XV. Jahrhunderts* (Berichte der Heidelberger Akademie der Wissenschaften). Heidelberg, 1964.

FISCHER (1966)   FISCHER, F.W. 'Ein neu entdeckter spätgotischer Turmriss und die letzte mittelalterliche Bauphase am Münster zu Konstanz', *Jahrbuch der Staatlichen Kunstsammlungen in Baden-Württemberg*, 3 (1966), 7–50.

FISCHER (1974)   FISCHER, F.W. 'Die Stadtpfarrkirche zur Schönen Unserer Lieben Frau', in Th. Müller, W. Reissmüller and S. Hofmann, eds., *Ingolstadt – die Herzogsstadt – die Universitätsstadt – die Festung*. Ingolstadt, 1974, vol. 1, 295–355.

FISCHEROVÁ (1974)   FISCHEROVÁ, K. 'Francouzští mistři a architektura první poloviny 14 století v českých zemích', Ph.D. thesis, University of Prague, 1974.

FITCHEN (1961)   FITCHEN, J. *The Construction of Gothic Cathedrals. A Study of Medieval Vault Erection*. Chicago, 1961.

FLETCHER (1979)   FLETCHER, J. 'Medieval Timberwork at Ely', in *Medieval Art and Architecture at Ely Cathedral* (British Archaeological Association Conference Transactions for 1976, vol. 2). Leeds, 1979, 58–69.

FLICHE (1950)   FLICHE, A. 'Aigues-Mortes', *Congrès Archéologique de France*, 108 (1950), 90–103.

FOCILLON (1963)   FOCILLON, H. *The Art of the West* (Part 1, Romanesque art, Part 2, Gothic art), ed. by J. Bony. London, 1963.

FONQUERNIE (1985)   FONQUERNIE, B. 'Cathédrale Notre-Dame de Paris, existence d'un décors polychrome sur les murs des bras nord et sud de la transept', *Bulletin Monumental*, 143 (1985), 65–6.

FONS (1975)   FONS, C. 'L'abbaye de Saint-Lucien de Beauvais: étude historique et archéologique', Unpublished thesis, École de Chartes, Paris, 1975.

FOSSARD (1934)   FOSSARD, A. *Le prieuré de Saint-Leu d'Esserent*. Paris, 1934.

FRACCARO DE LONGHI (1958)   FRACCARO DE LONGHI, L. *L'architettura delle chiese cisterciensi italiane. Con particolare riferimento ad un gruppo omogeneo dell'Italie settentrionale*. Milan, 1958.

FRANCESCO D'ASSISI (1982)   PIROVANO, C. ed., *Francesco d'Assisi*, exh. cat., 3 vols. Milan, 1982.

FRANK (1993)   FRANK, G. *Das Zisterzienserkloster Maulbronn. Die Baugeschichte der Klausur von den Anfängen bis zur Säkularisierung* (Studien zur Kunstgeschichte, 70). Hildesheim, 1993.

FRANKL (1945)   FRANKL, P. 'The Secret of the Medieval Mason (with an explanation of Stornaloco's formula by Erwin Panofsky)', *Art Bulletin*, 27 (1945), 46–64.

FRANKL (1957)   FRANKL, P. 'The Chronology of Chartres Cathedral', *Art Bulletin*, 39 (1957), 33–47.

FRANKL (1960)   FRANKL, P. *The Gothic. Literary Sources and Interpretations through Eight Centuries*. Princeton, 1960.

FRANKL (1961)   FRANKL, P. 'Reconsiderations of the Chronology of Chartres Cathedral', *Art Bulletin*, 43 (1961), 51–8.

FRANKL (1963)   FRANKL, P. 'The Chronology of the Stained Glass of Chartres Cathedral', *Art Bulletin*, 45 (1963), 301–22.

FRANZ VON ASSISI (1982)   Niederosterreicher Landesregierung, ed., *800 Jahre Franz von Assisi. Franziskanerische Kunst und Kultur des Mittelalters*, exh. cat., Krems-Stein. Vienna, 1982.

FRANZOI, PIGNATTI, WOLTERS (1990)   FRANZOI, U., PIGNATTI, T., AND WOLTERS, W. *Il Palazzo ducale di Venezia*. Treviso, 1990.

FRAZIK (1967)   FRAZIK, J.T. 'Zagadnienie sklepień o przęsłach trójpodporowych w architekturze średniowiecznej, *Folia Historia Artium*, 4 (1967), 5–96.

FRAZIK (1985)   FRAZIK, J.T. 'Sklepienie gotyckie w Prusach, na Pomorzu Gdańskim i w ziemi chełmińskiej', *Kwartalnik Architektury i Urbanstyki*, 30/1 (1985), 3–26.

FREEDBERG (1989)   FREEDBERG, D. *Power of Images. Studies in the History and Theory of Response*. Chicago, 1989.

FREIGANG (1989)   FREIGANG, C. 'Le Chantier de Narbonne', in R. Recht, ed., *Les Batisseurs des Cathédrales Gothiques*. Strasbourg, 1989, 127–31.

FREIGANG (1989a)   FREIGANG, C. 'Jacques de Fauran', in R. Recht, ed., *Les Batisseurs des Cathédrales Gothiques*. Strasbourg, 1989, 195–9.

FREIGANG (1999)   FREIGANG, C. 'Die Expertisen zum Kathedralbau in Girona (1386–1416/17). Anmerkungen zur mittelalterlichen Debatte um Architektur', in Freigang, ed. (1999) 203–26.

FREIGANG AND KURMANN (1989)   FREIGANG, C. AND KURMANN, P. 'L'église de l'ancien prieuré de Saint-Thibault-en-Auxois: sa chronologie, ses restaurations, sa place dans l'architecture gothique', *Congrès Auxois-Châtillonnais*. Paris, 1989, 271–90.

FREIGANG (1991)   FREIGANG, C. 'Jean Deschamps et le Midi', *Bulletin Monumental*, 149 (1991), 265–98.

FREIGANG AND KURMANN (1991)   FREIGANG, C. AND KURMANN, P. 'la Cathédrale romano-gothique de Genève', in *Saint-Pierre de Genève au fil des siècles*. Geneva, 1991, 23–44.

FREIGANG (1992)   FREIGANG, C. *Imitare Ecclesias Nobiles: Die Kathedralen von Narbonne, Toulouse und Rodez und die Nordfranzösische Rayonnantgotik im Languedoc*. Worms, 1992.

FREIGANG (1998)   FREIGANG, C. 'Köln und Prag. Der Prager Veitsdom als Nachfolgebau des Kölner Domes', in *Dombau und Theologie im mittelalterlichen Köln* (Studien zur Kölner Dom, vol. 6), 49–86.

FREIGANG ed. (1999)   FREIGANG, C., ed. (with Stiglmayr, C.M.) *Gotische Architektur in Spanien. La arquitectura gotica en Espana* (Akten des Colloquiums der Carl Justi-Vereinigung und des kunstgeschichtlicher Seminars der Universität Göttingen. Göttingen 4–6 Februar 1994) Vervuert. Iberoamericana, 1999.

FRIEDERICH (1962)   FRIEDERICH, K. 'Die Risse zum Hauptturm des Ulmer Münsters', *Ulm und Oberschwaben*, 36 (1962), 19–38.

FRIEDMAN (1993)   FRIEDMAN, D. *Florentine New Towns. Urban Design in the Late Middle Ages*. New York, Cambridge, London, 1988.

FRODL-KRAFT (1956)   FRODL-KRAFT, E. 'Architektur im Abbild: ihre Spiegelung in der Glasmalerei', *Wiener Jahrbuch für Kunstgeschichte*, 17 (1956), 7–13.

FRODL-KRAFT (1972)   FRODL-KRAFT, E. 'Zu den Kirchenschaubildern in den Hochchorfenstern von Reims – Abbildung und Abstraktion', *Wiener Jahrbuch für Kunstgeschichte*, 25 (1972), 53–86.

FROIDEVAUX (1966)   FROIDEVAUX, Y.-M. 'L'abbatiale de Lessay', *Congrès Archéologique de France*, 124 (1966), 70–82.

FROIDEVAUX AND LELÉGARD (1958)   FROIDEVAUX, Y.-M. AND LELÉGARD, M. 'L'abbatiale de Lessay. Les Monuments historiques de la France, (1958), no. 3, 98–150.

FRYCZ (1980)   FRYCZ, J. 'Die Burgbauten des Ritterordens in Preussen', *Wissenschaftliche Zietschrift der Ernst-Moritz-Arndt-Universität Greifswald. Gesellschafts- und sprachwissenschaftliche Reihe*, 29 (1980), 45–55.

FUCHS (1981)   FUCHS, F. 'Das mittlere Westportal des Regensburger Doms', *Das Münster*, 34 (1981), 153–4.

FUCHS (1990)   FUCHS, F. 'Zwei mittelalterliche Aufrisszeichnungen zur Westfassade des Regensburger Domes', in *Der Dom zu Regensburg, Ausgrabung, Restaurierung, Forschung*. Munich and Zürich, 1990, 224–30.

FUHRMANN (1967)   FUHRMANN, F. 'Der Chor der Franziskanerkirche in Salzburg und sein "Massgrund"', in *Festschrift für Karl Oettinger zum 60. Geburtstag* (Erlangen, 1967). 143–76.

FUHRMANN (1993/4)   FUHRMANN, F. 'Der Chor der Franziskanerkirche in Salzburg und sein "Massgrund". Eine Nachlese', *Wiener Jahrburch für Kunstgeschichte*, (1993/4), 195–209.

FUNK AND LINCKE (1977)   FUNK, W. AND LINCKE, J. 'Der Chor von St Lorenz im 'Rechten Mass' der mittelalterlichen Bauhütten', in H. Bauer *et al.*, eds., *500 Jahre Hallenchor St Lorenz zu Nürnberg 1477–1977*. Nuremberg, 1977, 197–212.

GAEHTGENS (1993)   GAEHTGENS, T. ed., *Kunstlerischer Austausch. Artistic Exchange*. (Akten des XXVIII Internationalen Kongresses für Kunstgeschichte, Berlin, 15–20 Juli 1992), 3 vols. Berlin, 1993.

GAGE (1982)   GAGE, J. 'Gothic Glass: two Aspects of Dionysian Aesthetic', *Art History*, 5 (1982), 36–58.

GAGNIÈRE (1977)   GAGNIÈRE, S.G. *Le Palais des papes d'Avignon*. Paris, 1977.

GAILLARD (1962)   GAILLARD, G. 'La cathédrale de Tournai: la nef, le transept', *L'information d'Histoire de l'Art*, 7 (1962), 63–7.

GALL (1915)   GALL, E. *Niederrheinische und normannische Architektur im Zeitalter der Frühgotik: I Die niederrheinischen Apsidengliderungen nach normannischen Vorbilde*, Berlin, 1915.

GALL (1955)   GALL, E. *Die gotische Baukunst in Frankreich und Deutschland, I: Die Vorstufen in Nordfrankreich von der Mitte des elften bis gegen Ende des zwölften Jahrhunderts*, 2nd ed., Braunschweig, 1955.

GAMESON (1992)   GAMESON, R. 'The Romanesque crypt capitals of Canterbury cathedral', *Archaeologia Cantiana*, 110 (1992), 17–48.

GARDELLES (1963)   GARDELLES, J. *La Cathédrale Saint-André de Bordeaux*. Bordeaux, 1963.

GARDELLES (1969)   GARDELLES, J. 'Notes sur la construction de la Cathédrale de Tournai au XIIe siècle', *Cahiers de Civilisation médiévale Xe–XIIe siècles*, 12 (1969), 43–6.

GARDELLES (1992)   GARDELLES, J. *Aquitaine Gothique*. Paris, 1992.

GARDNER (1980)   GARDNER, S. 'Notes on a view of St Lucien at Beauvais', *Gazette des Beaux Arts*, 96, (1980), 149–56.

GARDNER (1982)   GARDNER, S. 'The Nave Galleries of Durham Cathedral', *Art Bulletin*, 64 (1982), 564–79.

GARDNER (1984)   GARDNER, S. 'The Church of Saint-Etienne at Dreux and its Role in the Foundation of Gothic Architecture', *Journal of the British Archaeological Association*, 137 (1984), 86–113.

GARDNER (1984a) GARDNER, S. 'Two Campaigns in Suger's Western Block at Saint-Denis', *Art Bulletin*, 66 (1984), 574–87.

GARDNER (1984b) GARDNER, S. 'The Influence of Castle Building on Ecclesiastical Architecture in the Paris Region 1130–1150', in K. Reyerson and F. Powe, *The Medieval Castle, Romance and Reality* (Medieval Studies at Minnesota, 1). Minneapolis, 1984, 97–123.

GARDNER (1986) GARDNER, S. 'Sources for the Façade of Saint-Lucien de Beauvais', *Gesta*, 25 (1986), 93–100.

GARDNER (1986a) GARDNER, S. 'L'église Saint-Julien de Marolles-en-Brie et ses rapports avec l'architecture Parisienne de la génération de Saint-Denis', *Bulletin Monumental*, 144 (1986), 7–31.

GARDNER (1992) GARDNER, J. *The Tomb and the Tiara. Curial Tomb Sculpture in Rome and Avignon in the Later Middle Ages*, Oxford 1992.

GĄSIOROWSKI (1977) GĄSIOROWSKI, E. 'Die Briefkapelle der St Marienkirche zu Lübeck', *Deutsche Kunst und Denkmalpflege*, 35 (1977), 148–62.

GATTI PERER (1969) GATTI PERER, M.L. ed., *Il Duomo di Milano. Congresso Internazionale*, 2 vols. Milan, 1969.

GAUMANNMÜLLER (1976) GAUMANNMÜLLER, P.F. *Die mittelalterliche Klosteranlage der Abtei Heiligenkreuz.* Heiligenkreuz-Wien, 1967.

GAUS (1971) GAUS, J. 'Die Urhütte – Über ein Model in der Baukunst und ein Motiv in der Bildenden Kunst', *Wallraf-Richartz Jahrbuch*, 33 (1971), 7–70.

GEE (1977) GEE, E.A. 'Architectural History until 1290', in G.E. Aylmer and R. Cant, *A History of York Minster*. Oxford, 1977.

GEE (1979) GEE, L.L. '"Ciborium" Tombs in England 1290–1330', *Journal of the British Archaeological Association*, 132 (1979), 29–41.

GEESE (1981) GEESE, U. 'Die Reliquien der Elisabeth von Thüringen im Interesse des Ketzerpredigers Konrad von Marburg', in K. Clausberg *et al.*, eds., *Bauwerk und Bildwerk im Hochmittelalter, Anschauliche Beiträge zur Kultur- und Sozialgeschichte* Giessen, 1981, 127–40.

GEM (1982) GEM, R. 'The Significance of the 11th Century Rebuilding of Christchurch and St Augutine's Canterbury in the Development of Romanesque Architecture', in *Medieval Art and Architecture at Canterbury before 1220* (British Archaeological Association Conference Transactions for 1979, vol. 5). Leeds, 1982, 1–19.

GEREVICH (1971) GEREVICH, L. 'Villard de Honnecourt magyarországon', *Müvészettörténi Értesítö*, 20 (1971), 81–104 (with German summary, 104–5).

GEREVICH (1982) GEREVICH, L. 'Les Fouilles de l'Abbaye Hongroise de Pilis', in B. Chauvin, ed., *Mélanges á la Memoire du Père Anselme Dimier*, Part 3, vol. 5, Arbois, 1982, 371–93.

GEREVICH (1983) GEREVICH, L. 'Ausgrabungen in der ungarischen Zisterzienserabtei Pilis', *Analecta Cisterciensia*, 39 (1983), 281–310.

GEREVICH (1985) GEREVICH, L. 'Ergebnisse der Ausgrabungen in der Cisterzienserabtei Pilis', *Acta Archaeologica*, 37 (1985), 111–52.

GERMUND (1997) GERMUND, U. *Konstruktion und Decoration als Gestaltungsprinzipien im Spätgotischen Kirchenbau. Untersuchungen zur Mittelrheinischen Sakralbaukunst.* Worms, 1997.

GERSON (1970) GERSON, P.L. 'The West Façade of Saint-Denis: An Iconographical Study'. Ph.D. thesis, Columbia University, 1970.

GERSON (1986) GERSON, P.L. 'Suger as Iconographer, The Central Portal of the West Façade of Saint-Denis', in P.L. Gerson, ed., *Abbot Suger of Saint-Denis: a symposium.* New York, 1986, 183–98.

GERSON, ed. (1986) GERSON, P.L. ed., *Abbot Suger of Saint-Denis: a symposium.* The Metropolitan Museum of Art, New York, 1986.

GERSTENBERG (1913) GERSTENBERG, K. *Deutsche Sondergotik.* Munich, 1913.

GHISALBERTI (1989) GHISALBERTI, C. 'Le chantier de la cathédrale de Milan', in R. Recht, ed., *Les Batisseurs des Cathédrales Gothiques.* Strasbourg, 1989, 113–26.

GILBERT (1970) GILBERT, P. 'Un chef-d'œuvre d'art cistercien peut-être influencé par Cluny, L'Abbatiale de Fontenay', *Académie royale de Belgique, Bulletin de la Classe des Beaux-Arts*, 52 (1970), 1–3, 20–45.

GILLERMAN (1988) GILLERMAN, D.G. 'La facciata: introduzione al rapporto tra scultura e architectura', in L. Riccetti, ed., *Il duomo di Orvieto.* Bari, 1988, 81–100.

GILLERMAN (1989) GILLERMAN, D.G. 'S. Fortunato in Todi: why the hall church?', *Journal of the Society of Architectural Historians*, 48 (1989), 158–71.

GILLERMAN (1994) GILLERMAN, D.G. 'The evolution of the design of Orvieto cathedral ca. 1290–1310', *Journal of the Society of Architectural Historians*, 53 (1994), 300–21.

GILLERMAN (1975) GILLERMAN, D. 'The clôture of the cathedral of Notre-Dame: problems of reconstruction', *Gesta*, 24 (1975), 41–61.

GILLERMAN (1977) GILLERMAN, D. *The Clôture of Notre-Dame and its Role in the Fourteenth-Century Choir Programme.* New York and London, 1977.

GIVENS (1986) GIVENS, J. 'The garden outside the walls: plant forms in thirteenth-century English sculpture', in E.B. MacDougall, ed., *Medieval Gardens* (Dumbarton Oaks, Washington D.C., 1986), 189–98.

GOMBRICH (1969) GOMBRICH, E.H. *In Search of Cultural History*, The Philip Maurice Dencke Lecture, 1967. Oxford, 1969, reprinted in *Ideals and Idols. Essays on Values in History and in Art.* Oxford, 1979.

GOMBRICH (1979) GOMBRICH, E.H. *The Sense of Order. A Study in the Psychology of Decorative Art.* Oxford, 1979.

GORDON, MONNAS AND ELAM, eds. (1997) GORDON, D., MONNAS, L., AND ELAM, C. *The Royal Image of Richard II and the Wilton Diptych.* London, 1997.

GÓRSKI (1973) GÓRSKI, K. *Dzieje Malborka.* Gdańsk, 1973.

GOSEBRUCH (1977) GOSEBRUCH, M. 'Vom Bamberger Dom und seiner geschichtlichen Herkunft', *Münchener Jahrbuch*, 28 (1977), 28–58.

GÖTZ (1966) GÖTZ, W. 'Der Magdeburger Domchor. Zur Bedeutung seiner monumentalen Ausstattung', *Zeitschrift des deutschen Vereins für Kunstwissenschaft*, 20 (1966), 97–120.

GÖTZ (1968) GÖTZ, W. *Zentralbau und Zentralbautendenz in der gotischen Architektur.* Berlin, 1968.

GOY (1993) GOY, R. *The House of Gold. Building a Palace in Medieval Venice.* Cambridge, 1993.

GRANDJEAN (1975) GRANDJEAN, M. 'La cathédrale actuelle: sa construction, ses architectes, son architecture', in M. Grandjean *et al.*, eds., *La Cathédrale de Lausanne*, Bibiliothèque de la Société d'Histoire de l'Art en Suisse, 3. Berne, 1975, 45–174.

GRANT (1987) GRANT, L. 'Gothic Architecture in Normandy c.1150–1250', Ph.D. thesis, Courtauld Institute of Art, University of London, 1987.

GRANT (1990) GRANT, L. 'The Choir of St-Étienne at Caen', in P. Crossley and E. Fernie, eds., *Medieval Architecture and its Intellectual Context. Essays in Honour of Peter Kidson* (London and Roncerverte, 1990), 113–25.

GRANT (1991) GRANT, L. 'Gothic Architecture in southern England and the French Connection in the Early Thirteenth Century', in *Thirteenth Century England III.* Woodbridge, 1991, 113–26.

GRANT (1993) GRANT, L. 'The Cathedral of Rouen, 1200–c.1240', in *Medieval Art, Architecture and Archaeology at Rouen* (British Archaeological Association Conference Transactions for 1989, vol. 12). Leeds, 1993, 60–8.

GRANT (1994) GRANT, L. 'Le patronage architectural d'Henri II et de son entourage', *Cahiers de Civilisation médiévale Xe–XIIe siècles*, 37 (1994), 73–84.

GRANT (1994a) GRANT, L. 'Architectural relationships between England and Normandy 1100–1204', in D. Bates and A. Curry eds., *England and Normandy in the Middle Ages.* London, 1994, 117–29.

GRANT (1997) GRANT, L. 'Le Choeur de la Cathédrale de Coutances et sa Place dans l'Architecture gothique du sud-ouest de la Normandie', in M. Baylé, dir., vol. 1 (1997), 137–52.

GRANT (1998) GRANT, L. *Abbot Suger of St-Denis. Church and state in Early Twelfth-Century France.* London and New York, 1998.

GRAS (1982) GRAS, P. 'Vues et Plans de l'Ancien Cîteaux', in B. Chauvin, ed., *Mélanges à la mémoire du Pére Anselme Dimier*, Part 3, vol. 6. Arbois, 1982, 549–75.

GRIEP (1985) GRIEP, H.G. *Kleine Kunstgeschichte des deutschen Burgerhauses.* Darmstadt, 1985.

GRIMSCHITZ (1947) GRIMSCHITZ, B. *Hanns Puchspaum.* Vienna, 1947.

GRIMSCHITZ (1953) GRIMSCHITZ, B. 'Die Risse von Anton Pilgram', *Wiener Jahrbuch für Kunstgeschichte*, 15 (19) (1953), 101–18.

GRODECKI (1949) GRODECKI, L. 'Le vitrail et l'architecture au XIIe et au XIIIe siècle', *Gazette des Beaux-Arts*, 33 (1949), 5–24.

GRODECKI (1951) GRODECKI, L. 'The Transept Portals of Chartres Cathedral. The Date of their Construction according to Archaeological Data', *Art Bulletin*, 33 (1951), 156–64.

GRODECKI (1953) GRODECKI, L. 'Notre-Dame d'Alençon', *Congrès Archéologique de France*, 111 (1953), 21–38.

GRODECKI (1958) GRODECKI, L. 'Fonctions spirituelles', in M. Aubert, A. Chastel, L. Grodecki, J.J. Gruber, J. Lafond, F. Mathey, and J. Verrier, eds., *Le vitrail français.* Paris, 1958, 40–5.

GRODECKI (1958a) GRODECKI, L. 'Chronologie de la Cathédrale de Chartres', *Bulletin Monumental*, 116 (1958), 91–119.

GRODECKI AND RECHT (1971) GRODECKI, L. AND RECHT, R. 'Le bras sud du transept de la cathédrale: architecture et sculpture' (Le Quatrième Colloque International de la Société Française d'Archéologie Strasbourg, 18–20 Octobre 1968), *Bulletin Monumental*, 129 (1971), 7–38.

GRODECKI (1975) GRODECKI, L. *La Sainte-Chapelle.* Paris, 1975.

GRODECKI (1976) GRODECKI, L. 'Les arcs-boutants de la Cathédrale de Strasbourg et leur origine', *Gesta*, 15 (1976), 43–50.

GRODECKI (1977) GRODECKI, L. *Gothic Architecture.* New York, 1977.

GRODECKI AND BRISAC (1985) GRODECKI, L. AND BRISAC, C. *Gothic Stained Glass 1200–1300.* London, 1985.

GROSS (1933) GROSS, W. 'Die Hochgotik im deutschen Kirchenbau. Der Stilwandel um das Jahr 1250', *Marburger Jahrbuch für Kunstwissenschaft*, 7 (1933), 290–346.

GROSS (1948) GROSS, W. *Die Abendländische Architektur um 1300.* Stuttgart, 1948.

GROSS (1967) GROSS, W. 'Mitteldeutsche Chorfassaden um 1400', in *Kunst des*

Mittelalters in Sachsen. Festschrift Wolf Schubert. Weimar, 1967, 117–41.

GRUSZEWSKI AND WIDAWSKI (1965)   GRUSZEWSKI, A. AND WIDAWSKI, J. 'Ruina jako obiekt turystyczny – koncepcja zabezpieczeniai udostępnienia na przykładzie kościoła NMP w Chojnie', *Ochrona Zabytków*, 18 (1965), nr 2, 5–22.

GUIMARÉS DE ANDRADE (1989)   GUIMARÉS DE ANDRADE, S. *Mosteiro da Batalha.* Lisbon, 1989.

GÜMBEL (1911)   GÜMBEL, A. 'Der Baumeister und Stückgiesser Hans Felber von Ulm, dessen Beziehungen zu Nürnberg und Todesjahr. Nachtraglisches zur Biographie Konrad Heinzelmanns', *Repertorium für Kunstwissenschaft*, 34 (1911), 232–54.

HACKER-SÜCK (1962)   HACKER-SÜCK, I. 'La Sainte-Chapelle de Paris et les Chapelles Palatines de Moyen-Âge', *Cahiers Archéologique*, 13 (1962), 217–57.

HAHN (1957)   HAHN, H. *Die frühe Kirchenbaukunst der Zisterzienser.* Berlin, 1957.

HAHNLOSER (1972)   HAHNLOSER, H.R. *Villard de Honnecourt, Kritische Gesamtausgabe des Bauhüttenbuches ms. fr. 19093 der Pariser National-bibliothek.* Graz, 1972.

HALL (1974)   HALL, M. 'The "Tramezzo" in S. Croce, Florence, Reconsidered', *Art Bulletin*, 56 (1974), 325–41.

HALL (1974a)   HALL, M. 'The *Ponte* in S. Maria Novella: the Problem of the Rood Screen in Italy', *Journal of the Warburg and Courtauld Institutes*, 37 (1974), 157–73.

HALSEY (1986)   HALSEY, R. 'The earliest architecture of the Cistercians in England', in C. Norton and D. Park eds., *Cistercian Art and Architecture in the British Isles.* Cambridge, London, New York, etc., 1986, 65–85.

HAMANN AND WILHELM-KÄSTNER (1924/1929)   HAMANN, R. AND WILHELM-KÄSTNER, K. *Die Elisabethkirche in Marburg und ihre künstlerische Nachfolge*, 2 vols. Marburg, 1924/1929.

HAMANN (1955)   HAMANN, R. *Die Abteikirche von Saint-Gilles und ihre künst-lerische Nachfolge*, 3 vols. Berlin, 1955.

HAMANN-MAC LEAN (1965)   HAMANN-MAC LEAN, R. 'Zur Baugeschichte der Kathedrale von Reims', in M. Kühn and L. Grodecki, eds., *Gedenkschrift Ernst Gall*, Berlin and Munich, 1965, 195–234.

HAMANN-MAC LEAN AND SCHÜSSLER (1993)   HAMANN-MAC LEAN, R. AND SCHÜSSLER, I. *Die Kathedral von Reims, Teil 1: Die Architektur*, vols. 1–3, (Stuttgart, 1993); Teil II: *Die Skulpturen*, vols. 5–8. Stuttgart, 1996. In preparation: *Vorgeschichte und Umfeld der Kathedrale von Reims.*

HAMBURGER (1992)   HAMBURGER, J. 'Art, Enclosure and the Cura Monialium: Prolegomena in the Guise of a Postscript', *Gesta*, 31 (1992), 108–34.

HAMBURGER (1998)   HAMBURGER, J. *The Visual and the Visionary. Art and Female Spirituality in Late Medieval Germany*, New York, 1998.

HANNING (1986)   HANNING, R.W. 'Suger's Literary Style and Vision', in P.L. Gerson, ed., *Abbot Suger of Saint-Denis: a symposium.* The Metropolitan Museum of Art, New York, 1986, 145–50.

HÄNSEL AND KARGE, eds. (1992)   HÄNSEL, S. AND KARGE, H. eds., *Spanische Kunstgeschichte. Eine Einführung*, 1. Berlin, 1992.

HANULANKA (1971)   HANULANKA, D. *Sklepienia Póznogotyckie na Śląsku* (Rozprawy Komisji Historii Sztuki, 7). Wrocław, 1971.

HARDY (1983)   HARDY, C. 'La Fenêtre Circulaire en Ile-de-France au XIIe et XIIIe siècles'. Ph.D. thesis, University of Poitiers, 1983.

HARDY (1991)   HARDY, C. 'Les roses dans l'elevation de Notre-Dame de Paris', *Bulletin Monumental*, 149 (1991), 153–99.

HARMAND (1959)   HARMAND, J. 'Le plus ancien château de Pierrefonds et ses problèmes', *Bulletin Monumental*, 17, (1959), 162–202, 245–64.

HARMAND (1983)   HARMAND, J. *Pierrefonds. La fortresse d'Orléans. Les réalités.* Le Puy-en-Velay, 1983.

HARVEY (1957)   HARVEY, J.H. *The Cathedrals of Spain.* London, 1957.

HARVEY (1961)   HARVEY, J.H. 'The origin of the Perpendicular Style', in E.M. Jope, ed., *Studies in Building History.* London, 1961, 134–65.

HARVEY (1972)   HARVEY, J.H. *The Medieval Architect.* London, 1972.

HARVEY (1977)   HARVEY, J.H. 'Architectural History from 1291 to 1558', in G. Aylmer and R. Cant, eds., *A History of York Minster.* Oxford, 1977, 149–92.

HARVEY (1978)   HARVEY, J. *The Perpendicular Style 1330–1485.* London, 1978.

HARVEY (1982)   HARVEY, J.H. 'The Building of Wells Cathedral, I: 1175–1307', 52–75; and 'The Building of Wells Cathedral, II 1307–1508', in L.S. Colchester, ed., *Wells Cathedral. A History.* London, 1982, 52–101.

HARVEY (1984)   HARVEY, J.H. *English Medieval Architects. A Biographical Dictionary down to 1550.* London, 2nd ed., 1984.

HASLINGHUIS AND PEETERS (1965)   HASLINGHUIS, E.J. AND PEETERS, C.J.A. *De Dom van Utrecht* (Nederlandse Monumenten van Geschiednis en Kunst, II, 2). The Hague, 1965.

HASSE (1983)   HASSE, M. *Die Marienkirche zu Lübeck.* Munich and Berlin, 1983.

HASSLER, KNOCH AND GLASER (1994)   HASSLER, U., KNOCH, P., AND GLASER, W. 'Kloster Maulbronn. Forschungsbericht zur Baugeschichte des Dormentbaues', *Architectura*, 24 (1994), 71–98.

HASTINGS (1955)   HASTINGS, J.M. *St Stephen's Chapel and its Place in the Development of the Perpendicular Style in England.* Cambridge, 1955.

HAUSSHERR (1968)   HAUSSHERR, R. 'Templum Salomonis und Ecclesia Christi. Zu einem Bildvergleich der Bible moralisée', *Zeitschrift für Kunstgeschichte*, 31 (1968), 101–21.

HAUSSHERR (1971)   HAUSSHERR, R. 'Zu Auftrag, Programm und Büstenzyklus des Prager Domchores', *Zeitschrift für Kunstgeschichte*, 34 (1971), 21–46.

HAUSSHERR (1981)   HAUSSHERR, R. 'Der typologische Zyklus der Chorfenster der Oberkirche von S. Francesco zu Assisi', in *Kunst als Bedeutungsträger. Gedenkschrift für Günter Bandmann.* Berlin, 1981, 95–128.

HAUSSHERR (1991)   HAUSSHERR, R. 'Dombauten und Reichsepiskopat im Zeitalter der Staufer', *Mainzer Akademie der Wissenschaften und der Literatur. Abhandlungen der Geistes-und Wissenschaftlichen Klasse*, 5. Stuttgart 1991, 3–51.

HEARN (1971)   HEARN, M.F. 'The Romanesque Ambulatory in English Medieval Architecture', *Journal of the Society of Architectural Historians*, 30 (1971), 187–208.

HEARN (1981)   HEARN, M.F. *Romanesque Sculpture. The Revival of Monumental Sculpture in the Eleventh and Twelfth Century.* London, 1981.

HEARN (1990)   HEARN, M.F. 'Villard de Honnecourt's Perception of Gothic Architecture', in P. Crossley and E. Fernie, *Medieval Architecture and its Intellectual Context. Studies in Honour of Peter Kidson.* London and Ronceverte, 1990, 127–36.

HEARN (1994)   HEARN, M.F. 'Canterbury Cathedral and the Cult of Thomas Becket', *Art Bulletin*, 76 (1994), 19–54.

HECHT (1969), (1970) and (1971)   HECHT, K. 'Mass und Zahl in der gotischen Baukunst', *Abhandlungen der Braunschweigischen Wissenschaftlichen Gesellschaft*, 21 (1969), 215–326; 22 (1970), 105–263; 23 (1971), 25–236.

HECHT (1983)   HECHT, K. *Der St Galler Klosterplan.* Sigmaringen, 1983.

HEITZ (1980)   HEITZ, C. *L'architecture religieuse carolingienne. Les formes et leurs fonctions.* Paris, 1980.

HEDEMAN (1991)   HEDEMAN, A.D. *The Royal Image: Illustrations of the Grandes Chroniques de France. 1274–1422.* Berkeley, Los Angeles and Oxford, 1991.

HEINITZ (1970)   HEINITZ, O., *Das Bürgerhaus Zwischen Schwarzwald und Schwäbischer Alb.* Tübingen 1970 (*Das Deutsche Bürgerhaus*, ed. by A. Bernt, vol. 12).

HEITZ (1980)   HEITZ, C. *L'architecture religieuse carolingienne.* Paris, 1980.

HÉLIOT (1958)   HÉLIOT, P. 'Les œuvres capitales du gothique français primitif et l'influence de l'architecture anglaise', *Wallraf-Richartz Jahrbuch*, 20 (1958), 85–114.

HÉLIOT (1959)   HÉLIOT, P. 'Les dates de construction des abbayes de Bernay, Cerisy-la-Forêt et Lessay', *Bulletin de la Société nationale des Antiquaires de France* (1959), 189–204.

HÉLIOT (1962/1964) (1969)   HÉLIOT, P. 'La cathédrale de Tournai et l'archi-tecture du Moyen-Âge', extracts from the *Revue Belge d'archeologie et d'his-toire de l'art*, 31, 33 (1962, 1964), 3–139. Brussels, 1969.

HÉLIOT (1963)   HÉLIOT, P. 'Les variants d'un thème de façade de la cathédrale de Lincoln à Notre-Dame de Dijon', *Gazette des Beaux-Arts*, 61 (1963), 257–78.

HÉLIOT (1965)   HÉLIOT, P. 'Sur les tours de transept dans l'architecture du Moyen-Âge', *Revue archéologique*, (1965), 1: 169–200; 2: 57–95.

HÉLIOT (1965a)   HÉLIOT, P. 'La famille monumentale de la cathédrale de Bourges', in M. Kühn and L. Grodecki, eds., *Gedenkschrift Ernst Gall.* Berlin and Munich, 1965, 143–70.

HÉLIOT (1967)   HÉLIOT, P. 'La diversité de l'architecture gothique à ses débuts en France', *Gazette des Beaux-Arts*, 69 (1967), 269–306.

HÉLIOT (1968)   HÉLIOT, P. 'Les origines et les débuts de l'apside vitrée, XIe au XIIIe siècle', *Wallraf-Richartz-Jahrbuch*, 30 (1968), 89–127.

HÉLIOT (1970)   HÉLIOT, P. 'Passages muraux et coursières dans les églises gothique du Nord-Est de la France mediévale, de la Lorraine et des pays du Rhône moyen', *Revue suisse d'Art et d'Archéologie*, 27 (1970), 21–43.

HÉLIOT (1970a)   HÉLIOT, P. 'Coursières et passages muraux dans les églises gothiques de l'Europe centrale', *Zeitschrift für Kunstgeschichte*, 33 (1970), 173–210.

HÉLIOT (1971)   HÉLIOT, P. 'Coursières et passages muraux dans les églises romanes et gothiques de l'Allemagne du Nord', *Museumsverein Aachen*, ed., *Festschrift Wolfgang Krönig.* Düsseldorf, 1971 = *Aachener Kunstblätter*, 41 (1971), 211–23.

HÉLIOT (1972)   HÉLIOT, P. 'Le chevet de la cathédrale de Laon, ses antécé-dents français et ses suites', *Gazettes des Beaux-Arts*, 79 (1972), 193–214.

HÉLIOT (1972a)   HÉLIOT, P. 'L'abbatiale de Saint-Michel-en-Thiérache, modèle de Saint-Yved à Braine, et l'architecture gothique des XIIe et XIIIe siècles', *Bulletin de la Commission royale des monuments et des sites*, new ser., 2 (1972), 15–43.

HÉLIOT (1975)   HÉLIOT, P. 'Mathias d'Arras, la cathédrale de Prague, et l'évolution stylistique du gothique rayonnant en France', *Bulletin de la*

Commission Départementale des Monuments Historiques du Pas-de-Calais, 9, nr 5 (1975), 399–420.

HÉLIOT (1980)   HÉLIOT, P. 'Avants-nef et Transepts de Façade des XIIe et XIIIe siècles dans le Nord de la France', *Gazette des Beaux-Arts*, 94 (1980), 53–62.

HÉLIOT AND MENCL (1974)   HÉLIOT, P. AND MENCL, V. 'Mathieu d'Arras et les sources méridionales et nordiques de son œuvre à la cathédrale de Prague', in *La naissance et l'essor du gothique méridionale aux XIIIe siècle*, (Cahiers de Fanjeux, 9). Toulouse, 1974, 103–25.

HELMBERGER (1984)   HELMBERGER, W. *Architektur und Baugeschichte der St Georgskirche in Dineklsbühl (1448–1499)* (Bamberger Studien zur Kunstgeschichte und Denkmalpflege, 2). Bamberg, 1984.

HELMBERGER (1988)   HELMBERGER, W. *St Georg zu Dinkelsbühl. Katholische Stadtpfarrkirche. Geschichte – Architektur – Ausstattung*. Dinkelsbühl, 1988.

HELTEN (1988)   HELTEN, L. 'Het koor van de Gotische Dom te Utrecht', in *Utrecht kriuspunt van de middeleeuwse kerk*. (Voordrachten gehouden tijdens het congres ter gelegenheid van tien jaar mediëvistiek faculteit der Letteren Rijksuniversiteit Utrecht, 25–27 August 1988) (Clavis Kunsthistorische Monographieën 7). Zutphen, 1988, 109–24.

HELTEN (1989)   HELTEN, L. 'Utrecht und Westminster Abbey', *Marburger Jahrbuch für Kunstwissenschaft*, 22 (1989), 35–50.

HELTEN (1994)   HELTEN, L. *Kathedralen für Bürger. Die St Nikolauskirche in Kampen und der Wandel architektonischer Leitbilder städtischer Repräsentationen im 14. Jahrhundert*. Utrecht, 1994.

HENRIET (1978)   HENRIET, J. 'Recherches sur les premiers arc-boutants. Un jalon: Saint-Martin d'Étampes', *Bulletin Monumental*, 136 (1978), 309–23.

HENRIET (1982)   HENRIET, J. 'La cathédrale Saint-Étienne de Sens: le parti du premier maître et les campagnes du XIIe siècle', *Bulletin Monumental*, 40 (1982), 81–172.

HENRIET (1983)   HENRIET, J. 'Saint-Lucien de Beauvais, myths ou réalité?' *Bulletin Monumental*, 141 (1983), 273–94.

HENRIET (1985)   HENRIET, J. 'Un édifice de la première génération gothique; l'abbatiale de Saint-Germer-de-Fly', *Bulletin Monumental*, 143 (1985), 93–142.

HENWOOD-REVERDOT (1982)   HENWOOD-REVERDOT, A. *L'église Saint-Etienne de Beauvais. Histoire et Architecture*. Beauvais, 1982.

HENZE (1957)   HENZE, A. *Westfälische Kunst*. Recklinghausen, 1957.

HERRERA CASADO (1975)   HERRERA CASADO, A. *El Palacio de Infantado*. Guadalajara, 1975.

HERSCHMAN (1978)   HERSCHMAN, J. 'The Thirteenth Century Chevet of the Cathedral of Coutances'. Ph.D. thesis New York University, 1978.

HERSCHMAN (1981)   HERSCHMAN, J. 'The Norman Ambulatory of Le Mans Cathedral and the Chevet of the Cathedral of Coutances', *Gesta*, 20 (1981), 323–32.

HERSCHMAN (1983)   HERSCHMAN, J. 'The Eleventh Century Nave of the Cathedral of Coutances: A New Reconstruction', *Gesta*, 22 (1983), 121–34.

HERZOG (1958)   HERZOG, T. 'Meister Hanns von Burghausen, genannt Stethaimer, sein Leben und Wirken', *Verhandlungen des Historischen Vereins für Niederbayern*, 84 (1958), 19–83.

HERZOG (1969)   HERZOG, T. 'Die Baugeschichte des St. Martinsmünsters und anderer Landshuter Kirchen im Lichte der Jahrring-Chronologie' *Verhandlungen des Historischen Vereins für Niederbayern*, 95 (1969), 36–53.

HERZOG (1969a)   HERZOG, T. 'Zur Person des Meisters Hanns von Burghausen', *Verhandlungen des historischen Vereins für Niederbayern*, 95 (1969), 54–67.

HEWETT (1980)   HEWETT, C.A. *English Historic Carpentry*. Letchworth, 1980.

HEWETT (1985)   HEWETT, C.A. *English Cathedral and Monastic Carpentry*. Oxford, 1985.

HEYMAN (1968)   HEYMAN, J. 'On the Rubber Vaults of the Middle Ages and Other Matters', *Gazette des Beaux-Arts*, 71 (1968), 177–88.

HEYMAN (1982)   HEYMAN, J. *The Masonry Arch*. Chichester, 1982.

HEYMANN (1983)   HEYMANN, J. 'Chronic defects in masonry vaults: Sabouret's cracks', *Monumentum*, 26 (1983), 131–41.

HEYMAN AND WADE (1985)   HEYMAN, J. AND WADE, E. 'The Timber Octagon of Ely Cathedral', *Proceedings of the Institute of Civil Engineers*, 78 (1985), Part 1, 1421–36.

HILGER (1978)   HILGER, H.P. 'Marginalien zu einer Ikonographie der gotischen Chorhalle des Aachener Domes', in *Kunst als Bedeutungsträger, Gedenkschrift für Günther Bandmann* (Berlin, 1978), 149–68.

HILGER (1978a)   HILGER, H.P. 'Der Weg nach Aachen', in F. Seibt, ed., *Kaiser Karl IV, Staatsmann und Mäzen*, Munich, 1978, 344–56.

HILGER (1982)   HILGER, H.P. 'Die ehemalige Jesuitenkirche St Mariae Himmelfahrt in Köln, "monumentum Bavaricae pietatis"', in *Die Jesuitenkirche St Mariae Himmelfahrt in Köln* (Beiträge zu den Bau- und Kustdenkmälern im Rheinland, 28). Düsseldorf, 1982.

HIMMELHEBER (1963)   HIMMELHEBER, G. *Der Ostchor des Augsburger Doms* (Abhandlungen zur Geschichte der Stadt Augsburg, 15). Augsburg, 1963.

HINKER (1967)   HINKER, D. *Studien zum Wortschatz der gotischen Architektur in Nordfrankreich*. Dissertation, Vienna, 1967.

HIPP (1979)   HIPP, H. *Studien zur Nachgotik des 16. und 17. Jahrhunderts in Deutschland, Böhmen, Österreich und der Schweiz*, vol. I. Tübingen, 1979.

HIRST, WALSH, AND WRIGHT (1983)   HIRST, D.S.M., WALSH, D.A., AND WRIGHT, S.M. *Bordesley Abbey* (British Archaeological Reports, British Series, 111). Oxford, 1983, 208–29.

HOEY (1984)   HOEY, L. 'Beverley Minster and its 13th-Century Context', *Journal of the Society of Architectural Historians*, 43 (1984), 209–24.

HOEY (1986)   HOEY, L. 'Pier Alternation in Early English Gothic Architecture', *Journal of the British Archaeological Association*, 139 (1986), 45–67.

HOEY (1987)   HOEY, L. 'Piers versus Vault Shafts in Early English Gothic Architecture', *Journal of the Society of Architectural Historians*, 46 (1987), 241–64.

HOEY (1994)   HOEY, L. 'Stone vaults in English Parish Churches', *Journal of the British Archaeological Association*, 147 (1994), 36–51.

HOEY (1995)   HOEY, L. 'New Studies on Cauterbury Cathedral', *Avista Forum*, 9 (1995), 6–9.

HOEY (1997)   HOEY, L. 'The Articulation of Rib Vaults in the Romanesque Parish Churches of England and Normandy', *Antiquaries Journal*, 77 (1997), 145–77.

HOFFMANN AND MEYER (1977)   HOFFMANN, S. AND MEYER, J. *Ingolstadt Münsterführer*. Ingolstadt, 1977.

HOFFMANN (1985)   HOFFMANN, K. 'Zur Entstehung des Königsportals in Saint-Denis', *Zeitschrift für Kunstgeschichte*, 48 (1985), 29–38.

HOMOLKA (1978)   HOMOLKA, J. 'Zu den ikonographischen Programmen Karls IV' in A. Legner, ed., *Die Parler und der Schöne Stil 1350–1400. Europäische Kunst unter den Luxemburgern* (Exhibition Catalogue, Schnütgen Museum Köln). Cologne, 1978, vol. 2, 607–25.

HOMOLKA (1999)   HOMOLKA, J. 'Zur Problematik der Prager Parlerarchitektur', *Umění*, 47 (1999), 364–84.

HONORÉ (1973)   HONORÉ, B. 'Les fouilles de la cathedrale de Thérouanne', *Bulletin de la commission départementale des monuments historiques aux Pas-de-Calais*, 9 (1973), 245–56.

HOPPE-SAILER (1983)   HOPPE-SAILER, R. *Die Kirche St Maria zur Wiese in Soest. Versuch einer Raumanalyse*. Frankfurt/Main and Bern, 1983.

HOŘEJŠÍ (1973)   HOŘEJŠÍ, J. *The Vladislav Hall of the Prague Castle*. Prague, 1973.

HORIE (1998)   HORIE, R. 'Ecclesia Deo Dedicata: Church and Soul in Late Medieval Dedication Sermons'. Ph.D. thesis, University of London, 1998.

HORN (1958)   HORN, W. 'On the Origins of the Medieval Bay System', *Journal of the Society of Architectural Historians*, 17 (1958), 2–23.

HORN AND BORN (1979)   HORN, W. AND BORN, E. *The Plan of St Gall. A Study of the Architecture and Economy of, and Life in, a Paradigmatic Carolingian Monastery*, 3 vols. Berkeley, 1979.

HÖRSCH (1994)   HÖRSCH, M. *Architektur unter Margarethe von Österreich, Regentin der Niederlande (1507–1530). Eine bau- und architekturgeschichtliche Studie zum Grabkloster St-Nicholas-de-Tolentin in Brou bei Bourg-en-Bresse*. Turnhout and Brussels, 1994.

HÖRSCH (1998)   HÖRSCH, M. 'Neues zur Kirche von Brou', *Kunstchronik*, 51 (1998), 328–34.

HORSTE (1987)   HORSTE, K. '"A Child is Born": the Iconography of the Portail Ste.-Anne at Paris', *Art Bulletin*, 69 (1987), 187–210.

HOYER (1991)   HOYER, R. *Notre-Dame de Chartres. Der Westkomplex. Systematische Grundlagen der bauarchäologische Analyse*, 2 vols. (Kultstätten der gallisch-fränkischen Kirche, 5). Frankfurt/Main, 1991.

HUBEL (1989)   HUBEL, A. 'La Fabrique de Ratisbonne', in R. Recht, ed., *Les Batisseurs des Cathédrals Gothiques*. Strasbourg, 1989, 165–77.

HUBEL AND SCHULLER (1995)   HUBEL, A. AND SCHULLER, M. (with contributions from F. Fuchs and R. Kroos), *Der Dom zu Regensburg. Vom Bauen und Gestalten einer gotischen Kathedrale*. Regensburg, 1995.

HUFNAGEL (1987)   HUFNAGEL, H. 'Zur Baugeschichte des Ostchors des Augsburger Domes', *Architectura*, 17 (1987), 32–44.

HÜTTNER (1981)   HÜTTNER, L. *Die Stadtpfarrkirche St Nikolaus in Neuötting*. Ottobeuren, 1981.

IVERSEN (1993)   IVERSEN, M. *Alois Riegl: Art History and Theory*. Cambridge, Mass., 1993.

JAAKS (1971)   JAAKS, G. 'Zur Entwicklung spätmittelalterlicher Chorschlussvereinfachungen', *Nordelbingen*, 15 (1971), 38–41.

JACKSON, ed. (1993)   JACKSON, M.J. ed., *Engineering a Cathedral* (Proceedings of the Conference 'Engineering a Cathedral', Durham, 1993). London, 1993.

JACOBI AND SCHERF (1983)   JACOBI, T. AND SCHERF, F. 'Zur Rezeption der Elisabethkirche in Schlesen', in H.-J. Kunst, ed., *Die Elisabethkirche Architektur in der Geschichte*, in *700 Jahre Elisabethkirche in Marburg 1283–1983*, vol. I. Marburg, 1983, 125–34.

JALABERT (1968)   JALABERT, D. *Clochers de France*. Paris, 1968.

JAMES (1972) JAMES, J. 'What Price the Cathedrals?' *Transactions of the Ancient Monuments Society*, 19 (1972), 47–65.

JAMES (1979, 1981) JAMES, J. *The Contractors of Chartres*, I. Dooralong, 1979.

JAMES, J. *The Contractors of Chartres*, II. Wyong, 1981.

JAMES (1982) JAMES, J. *Chartres Cathedral. The Masons who built a Legend.* London, 1982.

JAMES (1983) JAMES, J. 'The rib vaults of Durham Cathedral', *Gesta*, 22 (1983), 135–45.

JAMES (1984) JAMES, J. 'The Canopy of Paradise', in M.P. Lillich, ed., *Studies in Cistercian Art and Architecture*, 2. Kalamazoo, 1984, 115–29.

JAMES (1986) JAMES, J. 'An examination of some anomalies in the Ascension and Incarnation Portals of Chartres Cathedral', *Gesta*, 25, (1986), 101–8.

JAMES (1987) JAMES, J. 'La construction de la façade occidentale de la Cathédrale de Senlis', in D. Vermand, ed., *La Cathédrale Notre-Dame de Senlis au XIIe siécle. Étude historique et monumentale* (Société d'histoire et d'archéologie de Senlis). Senlis, 1987, 109–18.

JAMES (1989) JAMES, J. *The Template-makers of the Paris Basin*. West Grinstead, Australia, 1989.

JAMES (1992) JAMES, J. 'Evidence for Flying Buttresses before 1180', *Journal of the Society of Architectural Historians*, 51 (1992), 261–87.

JAMES (1993) JAMES, J. 'Multiple Contracting in the Saint-Denis chevet', *Gesta* 32 (1993) 40–58.

JANSEN (1979) JANSEN, V. 'Superposed Wall Passages and the Triforium Elevation of St. Werburg's, Chester', *Journal of the Society of Architectural Historians*, 38 (1979), 223–43.

JANSEN (1990) JANSEN, V. 'Medieval "Service" Architecture: Undercrofts', in P. Crossley and E. Fernie, *Medieval Architecture and its Context. Studies in Honour of Peter Kidson*. London and Ronceverte, 1990, 73–9.

JANSEN (1991) JANSEN, V. 'The Designing and Building Sequence of the Eastern Area of Exeter Cathedral, *c.*1270–1310: A Qualified Study', in *Medieval Art and Architecture at Exeter Cathedral* (British Archaeological Association Conference Transactions for the year 1985, vol. 11). Leeds, 1991, 35–56.

JANSEN (1996) JANSEN, V. 'Nördlingen', in J. Turner. ed. *The Dictionary of Art*, vol. 23 (1996), 204–5.

JANSEN (1996a) JANSEN, V. 'Salisbury Cathedral and the Episcopal Style in the Early 13th Century', in *Medieval Art and Architecture at Salisbury Cathedral* (British Archaeological Association Conference Transactions, vol. 17). Leeds, 1996, 32–9.

JANTZEN (1951) JANTZEN, H. 'Über den gotischen Kirchenraum', in *Über den gotischen Kirchenraum und andere Aufsätze*. Berlin, 1951, 7–20.

JANTZEN (1962) JANTZEN, H. *Die Gotik des Abendlandes, Idee und Wandel.* Cologne, 1962.

JANTZEN (1984) JANTZEN, H. *High Gothic. The Classic Cathedrals of Chartres, Reims and Amiens*. Princeton, 1984.

JENKIN (1954) JENKIN, P. 'Les Transformations typographiques et architecturales de l'abbaye de Clairvaux', in *Mélanges St. Bernard*. Dijon, 1954, 325–41.

JENKIN (1960) JENKIN, P. 'Quelques découvertes et constatations faites à Clairvaux depuis une vingtaine d'annés', *Bulletin de la Société nationale des antiquaire de France* (1950), 94–118.

JORDAN (1994) JORDAN, A. 'Narrative Design in the Stained Glass Windows of the Sainte-Chapelle in Paris', Ph. D. thesis, Bryn Mawr College, 1994.

JOUBERT AND SANDRON eds. (1999) JOUBERT, F. AND SANDRON, D. *Pierre, Lumière, Couleur. Études d'histoire de l'art du Moyen Âge* (Études d'histoire de l'art du Moyen Âge en l'honneur d'Anne Prache) Paris, 1999.

JULIER (1978) JULIER, J. *Studien zur spätgotischen Baukunst am Oberrhein* (Heidelberger kunstgeschichtliche Abhandlung, 13). Heidelberg, 1978.

JUNGMANN (1952) JUNGMANN, J. *Missarum Sollemnia. Eine genetische Erklärung der römischen Messe*, 2 vols. (Vienna, 1952, 3rd edn). Also the English translation: *The Mass of the Roman Rite: its origins and development*, 2 vols. Blackrock, 1986.

JUNQUERA (1937) JUNQUERA, M. 'El ábside de la catedral de toledo y sus precedentes', *Archivo Español de Arte y Arqueologia*, 13 (1937), 25–36.

JURKOWLANIEC (1989) JURKOWLANIEC, T. *Gotycka Rzeźba Architektoniczna w Prusach*. Wrocław-Warsaw-Kraków, 1989.

KAHN (1991) KAHN, D. *Canterbury Cathedral and its Romanesque Sculpture*. London, 1991.

KALDEN-ROSENFELD (1992) KALDEN-ROSENFELD, I. 'Einfach traumhaft – traumhaft einfach. Ein Beitrag zur Ikonographie der Kanzel Hans Wittens im Dom zu Freiburg', *Das Münster*, 45 (1992), 303–10.

KAPLAN (1974) KAPLAN, H. 'The Danzig Churches: A Study in Late Gothic Vault Development'. Ph.d. thesis, State University of New York, Binghamton, 1974.

KARGE (1989) KARGE, H. *Die Kathedrale von Burgos und die spanische Architektur des 13. Jahrhunderts. Französische Hochgotik in Kastilien und Léon*. Berlin, 1989.

KARGE (1989a) KARGE, H. 'La Cathédrale de Burgos. Organisation et Technique de la Construction', in R. Recht, ed., *Les Batisseurs des Cathédrales Gothiques*. Strasbourg, 1989, 139–63.

KATZENELLENBOGEN (1964) KATZENELLENBOGEN, A. *The Sculptural Programs of Chatres Cathedral*. New York, 1964.

KAUFFMANN (1948) KAUFFMANN, H. 'Der Kölner Domfassade', in *Der Kölner Dom. Festschrift zur Siebenhundertjahrfeier 1248–1948*, ed. by Zentral-Dombauverein. Cologne, 1948, 78–138.

KAUFFMANN (1957) KAUFFMANN, H. 'Die Masswerkhelme des Freiburger Munsters und des Kölner Doms', in *Festschrift Kurt Bauch*. Munich-Berlin, 1957, 117–25.

KAUFFMANN (1985) KAUFFMANN, G. 'Zur Gattungsproblematik in der Kunstgeschichte', in E. Liskar, ed., *Probleme und Methoden der Klassifizierung* (Akten des 35 Internationalen Kongresses für Kunstgeschichte) vol. 3, section 3. Vienna, Cologne and Graz, 1985, 7–12.

KAUFMANN (1995) KAUFMANN, T. DA COSTA. *Court, Cloister and City. The Art and Culture of Central Europe 1450–1800*. London, 1995.

KEMP (1996) KEMP, W. *The Narratives of Gothic Stained Glass*. Cambridge, 1996.

KELLER (1937) KELLER, H. 'Die Bauplastik des Sieneser Doms', *Kunstgeschichtliches Jahrbuch der Bibliotheca Herziana*, 1 (1937), 139–221.

KELLER (1938) KELLER, H. 'Die Risse der Orvietaner Domopera und die Anfänge der Bildhauerzeichnung', in *Festschrift Wilhelm Pinder zum 60. Geburtstag.* Leipzig, 1938, 195–222.

KENNEDY (1996) KENNEDY, A. 'Gothic Architecture in northern Burgundy in the 12th and early 13th Centuries', Ph.D. thesis, Courtauld Institute of Art, London University 1996.

KERR (1985) KERR, J. 'The East Window of Gloucester Cathedral', in *Medieval Art and Architecture at Gloucester and Tewkesbury* (British Archaeological Association Conferences Transactions for 1981, vol. 7). Leeds, 1985, 116–29.

KEYMES (1988) KEYMES, A.K. 'The Priory Church of Saint-Leu-d'Esserent'. M.A. thesis, Courtauld Institute of Art, London University, 1988.

KIDSON et al. (1965) KIDSON, P., MURRAY, P., AND THOMPSON, P. *A History of English Architecture*, 2nd ed. London, 1965.

KIDSON (1969) KIDSON, P. 'Canterbury Cathedral, The Gothic Choir', *Archaeological Journal*, 126 (1969), 244–6.

KIDSON (1981) KIDSON, P. Review of F. Bucher, *Architector. The Lodge Books and Sketch Books of Medieval Architects*, in *Journal of the Society of Architectural Historians*, 40 (1981), 329–31.

KIDSON (1986) KIDSON, P. 'St Hugh's Choir' in *Medieval Art and Architecture at Lincoln Cathedral* (British Archaeological Association Conference Transactions of the year 1982, vol. 8). Leeds, 1986, 29–42.

KIDSON (1987) KIDSON, P. 'Panofsky, Suger and St. Denis', *Journal of the Warburg and Courtauld Institutes*, 50 (1987), 1–17.

KIDSON (1993) KIDSON, P. 'Gervase, Becket and William of Sens', *Speculum*, 68 (1993), 969–91.

KIDSON (1993a) KIDSON, P. 'The Historical Circumstances and the Principles of the Design', in T. Cocke and P. Kidson, eds., *Salisbury Cathedral. Perspectives in Architectural History*. London, 1993, 35–94.

KIDSON (1994) KIDSON, P. 'Architectural History', in *A History of Lincoln Minster*, ed. D. Owen, Cambridge, 1994, 14–4.

KIDSON (1996) KIDSON, P. 'The Mariakerk at Utrecht, Speyer and Italy', in *Utrecht, Britain and the Continent. Archaeology, Art and Architecture* (British Archaeological Association Conference Transactions, vol. 18). Leeds, 1996, 123–36.

KIDSON (1999) KIDSON, P. 'Three footnotes on the Milan debates', in *Arte d'Occidente, temi e metodi. Studi in onore di Angiola Maria Romanini*, Rome, 1999, 269–78.

KIESOW (1956) KIESOW, G. 'Das Masswerk in der deutschen Baukunst bis 1350'. Ph.D. thesis, Göttingen, 1956.

KIESOW (1962) KIESOW, G. 'Die gotische Südfassade von S. Maria Novella in Florenz', *Zeitschrift für Kunstgeschichte*, 25 (1962), 1–12.

KIESOW, HOFFMAN et al. (1977) KIESOW, G., HOFFMAN, C. et al., *Bremen Niedersachsen* (Dehio, *Handbuch der Deutschen Kunstdenkmäler*). Darmstadt, 1977.

KIMPEL (1971) KIMPEL, D. 'Die Querhausarme von Notre-Dame zu Paris und ihre Skulpturen', Ph.D. thesis, Bonn, 1971.

KIMPEL AND SUCKALE (1973) KIMPEL, D. AND SUCKALE, R. 'Die Skulpturenwerkstatt der Vierge Dorée am Honoratsportal der Kathedrale von Amiens', *Zeitschrift für Kunstgeschichte*, 36 (1973) 217–65.

KIMPEL (1977) KIMPEL, D. 'Le développement de la taille enserie dans L'architecture médiévale et son rôle dans l'histoire économique'. *Bulletin Monumental*, 135 (1977), 95–222.

KIMPEL (1979/1980) KIMPEL, D. 'Die Versatztechniken des Kölner Domchores', *Kölner Domblatt*, 44/45 (1979/80), 277–92.

KIMPEL AND SUCKELE (1985)   KIMPEL, D. AND SUCKALE, R. *Die gotische Architektur in Frankreich 1130–1270*. Munich, 1985.

KINDER (1982)   KINDER, T. 'Architecture of the Cistercian Abbey of Pontigny. The Twelfth-Century Church'. Doctoral Diss. Indiana University, 1982.

KINDER (1982A)   KINDER, T.N. 'A Note on the Plan of the First church at Pontigny', in B. Chauvin, ed., *Mélanges à la mémoires du Pére Anselme Dimier*, part 3, vol. 6: *Abbayes*. Arbois, 1982, 601–8.

KINDER (1984)   KINDER, T.N. 'The original Chevet of Pontigny's church', in M.P. Lillich, *Studies in Cistercian Architecture*, 2 (Kalamazoo, 1984), 30–8.

KINDER (1990)   KINDER, T. 'L'abbaye cistercienne', in L. Pressouyre and T. Kinder, eds., *Saint Bernard et le Monde Cistercien*. Paris, 1990, 77–94.

KINDER (1991)   KINDER, T.N. 'Les églises mediévales de Clairvaux. Probabilités et Fiction', in *Histoire de Clairvaux. Actes du Colloque* (Juin 1990). Clairvaux and Bar-sur-Aube, 1991, 205–29.

KINDER (1992)   KINDER, T.N. 'Towards Dating the Construction of the Abbey Church of Pontigny', *Journal of the British Archaeological Association*, 145 (1992), 77–88.

KIRCHNER-DOBERER (1956)   KIRCHNER-DOBERER, E. 'Der Lettner. Seine Bedeutung und Geschichte', *Mitteilungen der Gesellschaft für vergleichende Kunstforschung in Wien*, 9 (1956).

KISSLING (1975)   KISSLING, H. *Das Munster in Schwäbisch Gmünd*. Schwäbische Gmünd, 1975.

KISSLING (1978)   KISSLING, H. Article on the Holy Cross church at Schwäbisch Gmünd in A. Legner, ed., *Die Parler und der Schöne Stil 1350–1400, Europäische Kunst unter den Luxemburgern*, exh. cat., Schnutgen Museum, Köln), Cologne, 1978, vol. 1, 319–20.

KLEEFISCH-JOBST (1991)   KLEEFISCH-JOBST, U. *Die Römische Dominikanerkirche Santa Maria sopra Minerva. Ein Beitrag zur Architektur der Bettelorden in Mittelitalien*. Münster, 1991.

KLEIN (1984)   KLEIN, B. *St. Yved in Braine und die Anfänge der hochgotischen Architektur in Frankreich*. Cologne, 1984.

KLEIN (1985)   KLEIN, B. Review of A. Villes, *La Cathédrale de Toul; Histoire et Architecture*, in *Kunstchronik*, 38 (1985), 233–6.

KLEIN (1986)   KLEIN, B. 'Chartres und Soissons, Überlegungen zur gotischen Architektur um 1200', *Zeitschrift für Kunstgeschichte*, 49 (1986), 437–66.

KLEIN (1990)   KLEIN, B. 'Die Rolle von Patriziat und Klerus bei Planung und Finanzierung spätgotischer Sakralarchitektur', in X. Barral i Altet, ed., *Artistes, Artisans et Production Artistique en Moyen Age, 3: Fabrication et consommation de l'œuvre*. Paris, 1990, 577–97.

KLETZL (1934)   KLETZL, O. 'Zur Identität des Dombaumeisters Wenzel Parler von Prag und Wenzel von Wien', *Wiener Jahrbuch für Kunstgeschichte*, 9 (1934), 43–62.

KLETZL (1938/39)   KLETZL, O. 'Ein Werkriss des Frauenhauses von Strassburg', *Marburger Jahrbuch für Kunstwissenschaft*, 11 (1938/39), 103–57.

KLOTZ (1966)   KLOTZ, H. 'Deutsche und Italienische Baukunst im Trecento', *Mitteilungen des Kunsthistorischen Instituts in Florenz*, 12 (1966), 171–206.

KLOTZ (1967)   KLOTZ, H. *Der Ostbau der Stiftskirche zu Wimpfen im Tal. Zum Frühwerk des Erwin von Steinbach*. Berlin, 1967.

KLUCKHOHN (1940)   KLUCKHOHN, E. Review of W.E. Arslan, *Architettura romanica Veronese . . . in Zeitschrift für Kunstgeschichte*, 9 (1940), 112–14.

KLUCKHOHN (1955)   KLUCKHOHN, E. 'Die Bedeutung Italiens für die romanische Baukunst und Bauornamentik in Deutschland', *Marburger Jahrbuch für Kunstwissenschaft*, 16 (1955), 1–120.

KLUKAS (1978)   KLUKAS, A. '"Altaria Superiora" The Function and Significance of the Tribune Chapel in Anglo-Norman Romanesque: A Problem of the Relationship of Liturgical Requirements and Architectural Form'. Ph.D. thesis, Pittsburgh, 1978.

KLUKAS (1981)   KLUKAS, A. 'The "Liber Ruber" and the Rebuilding of the East End of Wells', in *Medieval Art and Architecture at Wells and Glastonbury* (British Archaeological Association Conference Transactions for 1978, vol. 4). Leeds, 1981, 30–5.

KLUKAS (1983/84)   KLUKAS, A. 'The Architectural interpretations of the "Decreta Lanfranci"', in R. Allen Brown, ed., *Anglo-Norman Studies*. (Proceedings of the Battle Conference of Anglo-Norman Studies, 6, 1983/84), 137–71.

KLUKAS (1995)   KLUKAS, A. 'Durham Cathedral in the Gothic Era: Liturgy, Design, Ornament', in V.C. Raguin, K. Bush and P. Draper, eds., *Artistic Integration in Gothic Buildings*. Toronto, Buffalo, London, 1995, 69–83.

KNOWLES (1963)   KNOWLES, D. *The Monastic Order in England*. Cambridge, 1963, 2nd edn.

KOBLER (1978)   KOBLER, F. 'Augsburg', in A. Legner, ed., *Die Parler und der Schöne Stil. 1350–1400. Europäische Kunst unter den Luxemburgern* (Exhibition Catalogue, Schnütgen Museum Köln). Cologne, 1978, vol. 1, 343–6.

KOBLER (1980)   KOBLER, F. 'Stadtkirchen der frühen Gotik', in H. Glaser, ed., *Wittelsbach und Bayern, 1/1: Die Zeit der frühen Herzöge. Von Otto I zu Ludwig dem Bayern* (Beiträge zur Bayerischen Geschichte und Kunst. 1180–1350). Munich-Zurich, 1980, 426–36.

KOBLER (1984)   KOBLER, F. 'Baugeschichte des Ostchors, Kunsthistorische Beurteilung der Portalskulpturen', in *Das Südportal des Augsburger Domes. Geschichte und Konservierung* (Arbeitshefte des Bayerischen Landesamtes für Denkmalpflege, 23). Munich, 1984, 7–29.

KOBLER (1985)   KOBLER, F. 'Hanns von Burghausen, Steinmetz – Über den gegenwärtigen Forschungsstand zu Leben und Werk des Baumeisters', *Alte und Moderne Kunst*, 198/199 (1985), 7–16.

KOBLER (1987)   KOBLER, F. 'Fiale', in *Reallexikon zur deutschen Kunstgeschichte*, 8. Munich 1987, 617–65.

KOCH (1960)   KOCH, G. 'Studien zum Schlossbau des 16. Jahrhunderts in Mitteldeutschland', in *Beiträge zur Kunstgeschichte. Festgabe für Heinz Rolf Rosemann*, Munich, 1960, 155–86.

KOEPF (1952)   KOEPF, H. *Die Stiftskirche zu Herrenberg* (Veröffentlichungen des Heimatgeschichtsvereins für Schönbuch und Gäue-Herrenberg, 3, 1952).

KOEPF (1953)   KOEPF, H. 'Neuentdeckte Bauwerke des Meisters Anton Pilgram', *Wiener Jahrbuch für Kunstgeschichte*, 15 (19) (1953), 101–18.

KOEPF (1958)   KOEPF, H. 'Die Baukunst der Spätgotik in Schwaben', *Zeitschrift für Württembergische Landesgeschichte*, 17 (1958), 1–144.

KOEPF (1959)   KOEPF, H. 'Engelberg', in *Neue deutsche Biographie*, 4. Berlin, 1959, 507–8.

KOEPF (1970)   KOEPF, H. *Die gotischen Planrisse der Wiener Sammlungen*. Vienna, 1970.

KOEPF (1975)   KOEPF, H. 'Zur Frage der Urheberschaft der 96 angeblichen "Pilgramrisse" der Wiener Sammlungen', *Alte und Moderne Kunst*, 138 (1975), 9–14.

KOEPF (1977)   KOEPF, H. *Die gotischen Planrisse der Ulmer Sammlungen* (Forschungen zur Geschichte der Stadt Ulm, 18). Ulm, 1977.

KOEPF (1980)   KOEPF, H. 'Die Esslinger Frauenkirche und ihre Meister', *Esslinger Studien*, 19 (1980), 1–46.

KÖHLER (1995)   KÖHLER, M. *Die Bau- und Kunstgeschichte des ehemaligen Zisterzienserklosters Bebenhausen. Der Klausurbereich* (Veröffentlichungen der Kommission für geschichtliche Landeskunde in Baden-Württemberg, Reihe B/124). Stuttgart, 1995

KOHLMANN (1955)   KOHLMANN, J. *Das Rathaus zu Tangermünde*. Tangermünde, 1955.

KOLMAN, et al. (1996)   KOLMAN, C., MEIERINK, B.D., STENVERT, R., AND THOLENS, M. *Utrecht. Monumenten in Nederland*. Zwolle, 1996.

KOLMAN, et al. (1997)   KOLMAN, C., MEIERINK, B.D., AND STENVERT, R. *Noord-Brabant. Monumenten in Nederland*. Zwolle, 1997.

KÖNERDING (1976)   KÖNERDING, V. *Die 'Passagenkirche'. Ein Bautyp der romanischen Baukunst in Frankreich*. Berlin and New York, 1976.

KONOW (1954)   KONOW, H. *Die Baukunst der Bettelorden am Oberrhein*. Berlin, 1954.

KÖSTLER (1995)   KÖSTLER, A. *Die Ausstattung der Marburger Elisabethkirche. Zur Ästhetisierung des Kultraums im Mittelalter*. Berlin, 1995.

KOTRBA (1959)   KOTRBA, V. 'Kompoziční schéma kleneb Petra Parléře v chrámu sv. Víta v Praze', *Umění*, 7 (1959), 254–70.

KOTRBA (1960)   KOTRBA, V. 'Kaple svatováclavská v pražské katedrále', *Umění*, 8 (1960), 329–56.

KOTRBA (1963)   KOTRBA, V. 'Odkud pocházeli Roritzerové', *Umění*, 11 (1963), 65–9.

KOTRBA (1968)   KOTRBA, V. 'Baukunst und Baumeister der Spätgotik am Prager Hof', *Zeitschrift für Kunstgeschichte*, 31 (1968), 199–200.

KOTRBA (1971)   KOTRBA, V. 'Kdy přišel Petr Parléř do Prahy. Příspěvek k historii počátků parléřovské gotiky ve střední Evropě', *Umění*, 19 (1971), 109–35.

KOTRBA (1972)   KOTRBA, V. 'Zwei Meister der Jagellonischen Hofkunst', *Umění*, 20 (1972), 248–67.

KOWA (1990)   KOWA, G. *Architektur der Englischen Gotik*. Cologne, 1990.

KRAUS (1979)   KRAUS, H. *Gold was the Mortar, The Economics of Cathedral Building*. London, 1979.

KRAUS AND KRAUS (1986)   KRAUS, D. AND KRAUS, H. *Las sillerías góticas españoles*. Madrid, 1984.

KRAUSE (1967)   KRAUSE, H.J. 'Das erste Auftreten italienischer Renaissance-Motive in der Architektur Mitteldeutschlands', *Acta Historia Artium*, 13 (1967), 99–114.

KRAUSE (1996)   KRAUSE, H.J. 'Haylmann', in J. Turner, ed.: *The Dictionary of Art*, vol. 14 (1996), 268.

KRAUSE (1996a)   KRAUSE, H.J. 'Pflüger', in J. Turner, ed.: *The Dictionary of Art*, vol. 24 (1996), 586.

KRAUTHEIMER (1925)   KRAUTHEIMER, R. 'Die Kirchen der Bettelorden in Deutschland', in P. Frankl, ed., *Deutsche Beiträge zur Kunstwissenschaft*, 2. Cologne, 1925.

KRAUTHEIMER (1942)   KRAUTHEIMER, R. 'Introduction to an "Iconography of

Medieval Architecture"', *Journal of the Warburg and Courtauld Institutes*, 5 (1942), 1–33

KREUSCH (1974) KREUSCH, F. 'Werkrisse und Werkmass der Chorhalle des Aachener Domes', in *Beiträge zur Rheinischen Kunstgeschichte und Denkmalpflege*, 2, Beiheft 20, Albert Verbeek zum 65. Geburtstag. Düsseldorf, 1974, 115–36.

KREYTENBERG (1974) KREYTENBERG, G. *Der Dom zu Florenz*. Berlin, 1974.

KREYTENBERG (1978) KREYTENBERG, G. 'Der Campanile von Giotto', *Mitteilungen des Kunsthistorischen Instituts in Florenz*, 22 (1978), 147–84.

KROHM (1971) KROHM, H. 'Die Skulptur der Querhausfassaden an der Kathedrale von Rouen', *Aachener Kunstblätter*, 40 (1971), 40–153.

KRÖNIG (1938) KRÖNIG, W. 'Hallenkirchen in Mittelitalien', *Kunstgeschichtliches Jahrbuch der Biblioteca Hertziana*, 2 (1938), 1–142.

KRÖNIG (1973) KRÖNIG, W. *Altenberg und die Baukunst der Zisterzienser*. Bergisch Gladbach, 1973.

KRÖNIG (1978) KRÖNIG, W. 'Castel del Monte – Frédéric II et l'architecture française', in *L'art dans l'Italie méridionale. Aggiornamento dell'opera di Émile Bertaux sotto la direzione di Adriano Prandi*, 5 vols. Rome, 1978, vol. 5, 929–95.

KROOS (1976) KROOS, R. 'Liturgische Quellen zum Bamberger Dom', *Zeitschrift für Kunstgeschichte*, 39 (1976), 105–46.

KROOS (1979/80) KROOS, R. 'Liturgische Quellen zum Kölner Dom', *Kölner Domblatt*, new series, 44–45 (1979/1980), 35–202.

KROOS (1985) KROOS, R. 'Vom Umgang mit Reliquien', in A. Legner, ed., *Ornamenta Ecclesiae. Kunst und Künstler der Romanik*, Exh. cat., Schnütgen Museum, Cologne, 1985, 3, 25–49.

KROOS (1989) KROOS, R. 'Quellen zur liturgischen Benutzung des Domes und zu seiner Ausstattung', in E. Ullmann, ed. *Der Magdeburger Dom. Ottonische Gründung und staufischer Neubau* (Schriftenreihe der Kommission für Niedersächsische Bau- und Kunstgeschichte bei der Braunschweigischen Wissenschaftlichen Gesellschaft, 5). Leipzig 1989, 88–97.

KUBACH (1985) KUBACH, H.E. 'Der Raum Westfalen in der Baukunst im Mittelalter', in F. Petri, ed., *Der Raum Westfalen*, 6, Fortschritte der Forschung und Schlussbilanz. Münster, 1985.

KUBACH AND HAAS (1972) KUBACH, H.E. AND HAAS, W. *Der Dom zu Speyer* (Die Kunstdenkmäler von Rheinland-Pfalz), 3 vols. Berlin, 1972.

KUBACH AND KÖHLER-SCHOMMER (1997) KUBACH, H.E. AND KÖHLER-SCHOMMER, I. *Romanische Hallenkirchen in Europa*. Mainz, 1997.

KUBLER (1944) KUBLER, G. 'A late Gothic Computation of Rib Vault Thrusts', *Gazette des Beaux Arts*, 26 (1944), 135–48.

KÜHL (1986) KÜHL, B. 'Die Dominikanerkirche zu Regensburg. Studien zur Architektur der Bettelorden im 13 Jahrhundert in Deutschland', *Beiträge zur Geschichte des Bistums Regensburg*, 20 (1986), 75–211.

KÜHLENTAL (1989) KÜHLENTAL, M. 'Die Innenrestaurierung des Regensburger Doms. Historische Farbigkeit und Restaurierungskonzept', *Kunstchronik*, 42 (1989), 348–53.

KUNST (1968) KUNST, H.-J. 'Die Dreikonchenanlage und das Hallenlanghaus der Elisabethkirche in Marburg', *Hessisches Jahrbuch für Landesgeschichte*, 18 (1968), 131–45.

KUNST (1969) KUNST, H.-J. 'Die Entstehung des Hallenumgangchores. Der Domchor zu Verden und der Aller und seine Stellung in der gotischen Architektur', *Marburger Jahrbuch für Kunstwissenschaft*, 18 (1969), 1–104.

KUNST (1969a) KUNST, H.-J. 'Der Domchor zu Köln und die hochgotische Kirchenarchitektur in Norddeutschland', *Niederdeutsche Beiträge zur Kunstgeschichte*, 8 (1969), 9–40.

KUNST (1971) KUNST, H.-J. 'Zur Ideologie der deutschen Kirche als Einheitsraum', *Architectura* 1 (1971), 38–53.

KUNST (1981) KUNST, H.-J. 'Freiheit und Zitat in der Architektur des 13. Jahrhunderts. Die Kathedrale von Reims', in K. Clausberg *et al.*, eds., *Bauwerk und Bildwerk im Hochmittelalter – Anschauliche Beiträge zur Kultur- und Sozialgeschichte* (Kunstwissenschaftliche Untersuchungen des Ulmer Vereins für Kunst- und Kulturwissenschaft, 11). Giessen, 1981, 87–102.

KUNST (1983) KUNST, H.-J. 'Die Elisabethkirche in Marburg und die Bischofskirchen', in H.-J. Kunst, ed., *Die Elisabethkirche – Architektur in der Geschichte*, in *700 Jahre Elisabethkirche in Marburg 1283–1983*, vol. 1. Marburg, 1983, 69–75.

KUNST (1983a) KUNST, H.-J. 'Die Elisabethkirche in Marburg und die Kollegiatsstiftskirchen', in H.-J. Kunst, ed., *Die Elisabethkirche – Architektur in der Geschichte*, in *700 Jahre Elisabethkirche in Marburg 1283–1983*, vol. 1. Marburg, 1983, 77–80.

KUNST AND SCHENKLUHN (1987) KUNST, H.J. AND SCHENKLUHN, W. *Die Kathedrale in Reims. Architektur als Schauplatz politischer Bedeutung*. Frankfurt/Main, 1987.

KUNST (1986) KUNST, H.-J. *Die Marienkirche in Lübeck. Die Präsenz bischöflicher Architekturformen in der Bürgerkirche*. Worms, 1986.

KUNZE (1912) KUNZE, H. *Das Fassadenproblem der französischen Früh- und Hochgotik*. Strasbourg and Leipzig, 1912.

KURMANN (1971) KURMANN, P. *La Cathédrale Saint-Etienne de Meaux. Étude Architecturale* (Bibliothèque de la Société Française d'Archéologie, 1). Geneva, Paris, 1971.

KURMANN (1975) KURMANN, P. 'Zur Grabfigur des Hl. Konrad und zu den hochgotischen Nebenbauten des Konstanzer Münsters', *Freiburger Diözesan-Archiv*, 95 (1975), 321–52.

KURMANN (1977) KURMANN, P. 'L'église Saint-Jaques de Reims', *Congrès Archéologique de France*, 135 (1977), 134–61.

KURMANN AND VON WINTERFELD (1977) KURMANN, P. AND VON WINTERFELD, D. 'Gautier de Varinfroy, ein "Denkmalpfleger" im 13 Jahrhundert', in *Festschrift für Otto von Simson zum 65. Geburtstag*. Berlin, 1977, 101–59.

KURMANN (1978) KURMANN, P. Review of F. Nordström, *The Auxerre Reliefs*, *Zeitschrift für Kunstgeschichte*, 41 (1978), 165–72.

KURMANN (1979/80) KURMANN, P. 'Köln und Orléans', *Kölner Domblatt*, 24/25 (1979/80), 255–76.

KURMANN (1984) KURMANN, P. 'Die Pariser Komponenten in der Architektur und Skulptur der Westfassade von Notre-Dame zu Reims', *Münchener Jahrbuch*, 35 (1984), 41–82.

KURMANN AND KURMANN-SCHWARZ (1985) KURMANN, P. AND KURMANN-SCHWARZ, B. *St Martin zu Landshut* (vol. 1, Hans von Burghausen und seine Kirchen, ed. A. Fickel). Landshut, 1985.

KURMANN (1986) KURMANN, P. 'Spätgotische Tendenzen in der europäischen Architektur um 1300', in *Europäische Kunst um 1300* (XXVI Internationaler Kongress für Kunstgeschichte, Wien, 1983), 6. Graz, 1986, 11–18.

KURMANN (1987) KURMANN, P. *La Façade de la Cathédrale de Reims. Architecture et sculpture des portails. Étude archeologique et stylistique*. 2 vols. Lausanne, 1987.

KURMANN (1992) KURMANN, P. 'Meaux médiéval et Moderne', *Association Meldoise d'Archéologie*, 1992, 226–93.

KURMANN (1994) KURMANN, P. 'Die Frauenkirche des Jörg von Halspach: Beschreibung der Baugestalt und Versuch einer Würdigung', in *Monachium Sacrum. Festschrift zur 500-Jahr-Feier der Metropolitankirche zu Unserer Lieben Frau in München*, vol. 2, ed. by H. Ramisch. Munich, 1994, 21–43.

KURMANN AND KURMANN-SCHWARZ (1995) KURMANN, P. AND KURMANN-SCHWARZ, B. 'Chartres cathedral as a work of artistic integration: methodological reflections', in V. Raguin, K. Brush, P. Draper, eds., *Artistic Integration in Gothic Buildings* (Toronto, Buffalo, London, 1995), 131–52.

KURMANN (1995) KURMANN, P. 'Der Regensburger Dom – französische Hochgotik inmitten der Freien Reichsstadt', in M. Angerer and H. Wanderwitz, eds., *Regensburg im Mittelalter. Beiträge zur Stadtgeschichte vom frühen Mittelalter bis zum Beginn der Neuzeit*. Regensburg, 1995, 387–400.

KURMANN (1996) KURMANN, P. 'Landshut St. Martin', in J. Turner, ed.: *The Dictionary of Art*, vol. 18 (1996), 274–5.

KURMANN (1996a) KURMANN, P. 'Gigantomanie und Miniatur. Möglichkeiten gotischer Architektur zwischen Grossbau und Kleinkunst', *Kölner Domblatt*, 61 (1996), 123–46.

KURMANN (1998) KURMANN, P. '"Architektur in Architektur": der gläserne Bauriss der Gotik', in *Himmelslicht. Europäische Glasmalerei im Jahrhundert des Kölner Dombaus (1248–1349)* (Exh. cat., Schnütgen-Museum, Cologne 1998–1999) ed. by H. Westermann-Angerhausen, Cologne, 1998, 35–43.

KURMANN (1999) KURMANN, P. 'Französischer als in Frankreich: zur Architektur und Skulptur der Kathedrale von Leon', in Freigang, C. ed. (1999), 105–18.

KURMANN-SCHWARZ (1996) KURMANN-SCHWARZ, B. 'Récits, programme, commenditaries, concepteurs, donateurs: publications récentes sur l'iconographie des vitraux de la cathédral de Chartres', *Bulletin Monumental*, 154 (1996), 55–71.

KUTHAN (1982) KUTHAN, J. *Die mittelalterliche Baukunst der Zisterzienser in Böhmen und Mähren*. Berlin and Munich, 1982.

KUTHAN (1994) KUTHAN, J. Ceská Architektura v dobĕ Poslednich Přemyslovců. Mĕsta-Hrady-Klaštery-Kostely. Prague, 1994.

KUTZNER (1975) KUTZNER, M. 'Koscióły bazylikowe w miastach śląskich wieku XIV', in P. Skubiszewski, ed., *Sztuka i ideologia XIV wieku*. Warszawa, 1975, 275–316.

KUTZNER (1980) KUTZNER, M. 'Theologische Symbolik deutscher spätgotischer Hallenkirchen', *Wissenschaftliche Zeitschrift der Ernst-Moritz-Arndt-Universität Greifswald* (Gessellschafts- und sprachwissenschaftliche Reihe 29) (1980), 37–43.

KUTZNER (1995) KUTZNER, M. 'Propaganda władzy w sztuce Zakonu Niemieckiego w Prusach', in M. Woźniak, ed., *Sztuka w kręgu Zakonu Krzyżackiego w Prusach i Inflantach (Die Kunst um den Deutschen Orden in Preussen und Livland)* (Studia Borussico-Baltica Torunensia Historiae Artium, 2) (Toruń, 1995), 17–66, (with German summary).

KUTZNER (1995a) KUTZNER, M. 'Śląsk' in T. Mroczko and M. Arszyński, eds., (1995), vol. 1, 124–31.

KUTZNER (1996) KUTZNER, M. 'Gestalt, Form und ideologischer Sinn der Deutschordensburgen in Preussen', in *Forschungen zu Burgen und Schlössern*, 2, ed. by Wartburg-Gesellschaft zur Erforschung von Burgen und Schlössern. Munich, 1996, 199–215.

KUTZNER (1996a) KUTZNER, M. 'Kościół św. Elżbiety we Wrocławiu na tle śląskiej szkoły architektonicznej wieku XIV', in M. Zlat, ed., *Z dziejów wielkomiejskiej fary: Wrocławski kościół św. Elżbiety*. Wrocław, 1996, 28ff.

KUTZNER (1998) KUTZNER, M. 'Schlesische Sakralarchitektur aus der ersten Hälfte des 14. Jahrhunderts: zwischen allgemeinem Stil und regionalem modus', in K. Benešovská, ed., *King John of Luxembourg (1296–1346) and the Art of his Era* (Proceedings of the International Conference, Prague, 1996). Prague, 1998, 164–78.

LABANDE-MAILFERT (1951) LABANDE-MAILFERT, L. 'Le Palais de Justice de Poitiers', *Congrès Archéologique de France*, 109 (1951), 27–43.

LAFOND (1953) LAFOND, J. 'Les vitreaux de la cathédrale de Sées', *Congrès Archéologique de France*, 111 (1953), 59–83.

LAGERLÖF AND SVAHNSTRÖM (1973) LAGERLÖF, E. AND SVAHNSTRÖM, G. *Gotlands Kyrkor*. Stockholm, 1973.

LAMARCA (1978) LAMARCA, R. DE LUZ. *La cathedral de Cuenca del siglo XIII*. Cuenca, 1978.

LAMBERT (1931) LAMBERT, E. *L'art gothique en Espagne aux XIIe et XIIIe siècles*. Paris, 1931.

LAMBERT (1933) LAMBERT, E. 'Les premières voûtes nervées françaises et l'origine de la croisée d'ogives', *Revue archéologique*, 6th series, (1933), 235–44.

LAMBERT (1939) LAMBERT, E. 'Bayonne: cathédrale et cloître', *Congrès Archéologique de France*, 102 (1939), 522–60, 568–70.

LANFRY (1963) LANFRY, G. *La façade occidentale de la cathédrale*, (Les cahiers de Notre-Dame de Rouen) Rouen, 1963.

LANGE (1988) LANGE, K.L. *Raum und Subjektivität. Strategien der Raumvereinheitlichung im Chor des Heilig-Kreuz-Münsters zu Schwäbisch Gmünd* (Bochumer Schriften zur Kunstgeschichte, 11). Frankfurt/Main, 1988.

LAUFNER AND KLEIN (1975) LAUFNER, R. AND KLEIN, P. *Trier Apokalypse, Kommentarband*. Graz, 1975.

LASKO (1972) LASKO, P. *Ars Sacra 800–1200*. Harmondsworth, 1972.

LAVEDAN (1935) LAVEDAN, P. *L'architecture gothique religieuse en Catalogne, Valence und Baléares*. Paris, 1935.

LAVEDAN AND HUGUENEY (1969) LAVEDAN, P. AND HUGUENEY, J. 'Bastides de l'Agenais', *Congrès Archéologique de France*, 127 (1969), 9–41.

LAVEDAN AND HUGUENEY (1970) LAVEDAN, P. AND HUGHUENEY, J. 'Bastides en Gers', *Congrès Archéologique de France*, 128 (1970), 371–409.

LAVEDAN AND HUGUENEY (1974) LAVEDAN, P. AND HUGUENEY, J. *L'Urbanisme de Moyen Age*. Geneva, 1974.

LAWRENCE (1984) LAWRENCE, C.H. *Medieval Monasticism. Forms of Religious Life in Western Europe in the Middle Ages*. London, 1984.

LEBAU (1982) LEBAU, M. 'Les Fouilles de l'Abbaye de Cîteaux', in B. Chauvin, ed., *Mélanges à la mémoires du Pére Anselme Dimier*, part 3, vol. 5: Ordres, Fouilles. Arbois, 1982, 395–401.

LECLERQ (1980) LECLERQ, J. 'Die Spiritualität der Zisterzienser', in K. Elm, ed., *Die Zisterzienser. Ordensleben zwischen Ideal und Wirklichkeit*. Cologne, 1980, 149–56.

LEEDY (1975) LEEDY, W. 'The design of the vaulting of Henry VII's chapel at Westminster: a reappraisal', *Architectural History*, 18 (1975), 5–11.

LEEDY (1980) LEEDY, W. *Fan Vaulting: A Study of Form, Technology and Meaning*. California, 1980.

LEEDY (1990) LEEDY, W. 'King's College, Cambridge: Observations on its Context and Foundations', in P. Crossley and E. Fernie, *Medieval Architecture and its Context. Studies in Honour of Peter Kidson*. London and Ronceverte, 1990, 209–18.

LEFÈVRE-PONTALIS (1905) LEFÈVRE-PONTALIS, E. 'Église de Bury', *Congrès Archéologique de France*, 72 (1905), 38–42.

LEFÈVRE-PONTALIS (1911) LEFÈVRE-PONTALIS, E. 'Soissons', *Congrès Archéologique de France*, 78 (1911), 315–77. (for the cathedral), 377–58 (for other churches).

LEFÈVRE-PONTALIS (1919) LEFÈVRE-PONTALIS, E. 'Pontoise; église de Saint-Maclou', *Congrès Archéologique de France*, 82 (1919), 76–99.

LEFÈVRE-PONTALIS (1919a) LEFÈVRE-PONTALIS, E. 'Etude historique et architecturale de l'église de St-Germain-des-Prés', *Congrès Archéologique de France*, 82 (1919), 301–66.

LEGNER, ed. (1978–80) LEGNER, A. ed., *Die Parler und der Schöne Stil 1350–1400. Europäische Kunst unter den Luxemburgern*. Exh. cat., Schnütgen Museum, Köln, 3 vols. Cologne, 1978; vol. 4 and vol. 5. Cologne, 1980.

LEGNER (1978) LEGNER, A. 'Wände aus Edelstein und Gefässe aus Kristall', in A. Legner, ed., *Die Parler und der Schöne Stil 1350–1400. Europäische Kunst unter den Luxemburgern*. Exh. cat., Schnütgen Museum, Cologne, vol. 3. Cologne, 1978, 169–82.

LE GOFF (1984) LE GOFF, J. *The Birth of Purgatory*. Chicago, 1984.

LEHMANN (1976) LEHMANN, E. 'Zur Baugeschichte von Cluny III', *Wiener Jahrbuch für Kunstgeschichte*, 29 (1976), 7–20.

LEHMANN AND SCHUBERT (1968) LEHMANN, E. AND SCHUBERT, E. *Der Meissner Dom. Beiträge zur Baugeschichte und Baugestalt bis zum Ende des 13. Jahrhunderts*. Berlin, 1968.

LEHMANN AND SCHUBERT (1970) LEHMANN, E. AND SCHUBERT, E. *Der Dom zu Meissen*. Berlin, 1970.

LEHMANN AND SCHUBERT (1991) LEHMANN, E. AND SCHUBERT, E. *Dom und Severikirche zu Erfurt*. Leipzig, 1991.

LEKAI (1977) LEKAI, L.J. *The Cistercians: Ideal and Reality*. Kent, Ohio, 1977.

LELONG (1975) LELONG, C. 'Le Transept de Saint-Martin de Tours', *Bulletin Monumental*, 133 (1975), 113–30.

LEMAIRE (1946) LEMAIRE, R. *De O.L. Vrouwkerk in het kader van de Brabantsche gotiek*. Brussels, 1946.

LEMAIRE (1963) LEMAIRE, R. *Gids voor de kunst in België*. Utrecht, Antwerp, 1963.

LEMAIRE AND GODTS (1978) LEMAIRE, R. AND GODTS, H. 'De gotische bouwkunst', *Arca Lovan*, 7 (1978), 293–315.

LEMPER (1972) LEMPER, E.-H. 'Arnold von Westfalen. Berufs- und Lebensbild eines deutschen Werkmeisters der Spätgotik', in H.-J. Mrusek, ed., *Die Albrechtsburg zu Meissen*. Leipzig, 1972, 41–55.

LEMPER (1991) LEMPER, E.-H. *St. Marien Pirna*. Munich and Zürich, 1991.

LENIAUD et al. (1991) LENIAUD, J.-M., BIENVENU, G., CURIE, P., DABOUST, V., ERAUD, D., GROS, C., JAMES, F.-C., AND RIFFET, O. *Nantes. La Cathédrale Loire-Antlantique* (Inventaire Général des Monuments et des Richesses Artistiques de la France). Nantes, 1991.

LEOPOLD AND SCHUBERT (1968) LEOPOLD, G. AND SCHUBERT, E. 'Zur Baugeschichte des Naumburger Westchors' in *Kunst des Mittelalters in Sachsen, Festschrift Wolf Schubert*. Weimar, 1968, 97–106.

LEPIARCZYK (1959) LEPIARCZYK, J. 'Fazy budowy Kościoła Mariackiego w Krakowie. (Wieku XIII–XV)', *Rocznik Krakowski*, 34 (1959), 181–226.

LERGEN (1940) LERGEN, W. 'Die Sippe der Eseler'. Ph.D. thesis, Frankfurt/Main, 1940.

LESORT AND VERLET (1974) LESORT, A. AND VERLET, H. *Saint-Germain-l'Auxerrois: Epitaphier du vieux Paris*, 5. Paris, 1974.

LEWIS (1986) LEWIS, A. 'Suger's Views on Kingship', in P.L. Gerson, ed., *Abbot Suger and Saint-Denis: a symposium*. New York, 1986, 49–54.

LEYH (1992) LEYH, R. *Die Frauenkirche zu Nürnberg*. Munich and Zürich, 1992.

LÍBAL (1978) LÍBAL, D. 'Zlata Koruna', in A. Legner, ed., *Die Parler und der Schöne Stil 1350–1400. Europäische Kunst unter den Luxemburgern*, exh. cat., Schnütgen Museum Köln, vol. 2. Cologne, 1978, 628.

LÍBAL (1978a) LÍBAL, D. 'Die Baukunst', in A. Legner, ed., *Die Parler und der Schöne Stil 1350–1400. Europäische Kunst unter den Luxemburgern*, exh. cat., Schnütgen Museum Köln, vol. 2. Cologne, 1978, 619–21.

LÍBAL (1978b) LÍBAL, D. 'Praha, Veitsdom', in A. Legner, ed., *Die Parler und der Schöne Stil 1350–1400. Europäische Kunst unter den Luxemburgern*, exh. cat., Schnütgen Museum Köln, vol. 2. Cologne, 1978, 622–3.

LÍBAL (1980) LÍBAL, D. 'Grundfragen der Entwicklung der Baukunst im Böhmischen Staat', in A. Legner, ed., *Die Parler und der Schöne Stil 1350–1400. Europäische Kunst unter den Luxemburgern*. Exh. cat., Schnütgen Museum Köln, vol. 4. Cologne, 1980, 171–4.

LÍBAL (1983) LÍBAL, D. 'Architectura', in E. Poche, ed., *Praha Středověká*. Prague, 1983, 53–356.

LIEB (1954) LIEB, N. 'Burkhard Engelberg (um 1447–um 1512)', *Lebensbilder aus dem Bayerischen Schwaben*, 3 (1954), 117–53.

LIEB (1984) LIEB, N. *Augsburg. St. Ulrich und Afra*. (Schnell Kunstführer 183). Munich and Zürich, 1984.

LIEDKE (1983/84) LIEDKE, V. 'Hanns Purghaser, genannt Meister Hanns von Burghausen, sein Neffe Hanns Stethaimer und sein Sohn Stefan Purghauser, Die Baumeister an St. Martin in Landshut', *Ars Bavarica*, 35/36 (1983/84), 1–70.

LIESS (1967) LIESS, R. *Der Frühromanische Kirchenbau des 11. Jahrhunderts in der Normandie*. Munich, 1967.

LIESS (1985) LIESS, R. *Goethe vor dem Strassburger Münster. Zum Wissenschaftsbild der Kunst*. Leipzig, Weinheim, 1985.

LIESS (1985a) LIESS, R. 'Der Riss A1 der Strassburger Münsterfassade im Kontinuum der Entwürfe Magister Erwins' *Kunsthistorisches Jahrbuch Graz*, 21 (1985), 47–121.

LIESS (1985/86) LIESS, R. 'Der Riss C der Strassburger Münsterfassade. J.J. Arkardts Nürnberger Kopie eines Originalrisses Erwins von Steinbach', *Wallraf-Richartz Jahrbuch*, 46/47 (1985/86), 75–117.

LIESS (1986) LIESS, R. 'Der Riss B in der Strassburger Münsterfassade: eine baugeschichtliche Revision', in *Orient and Okzident im Spiegel der Kunst. Festschrift für Heinrich Gerhard Franz zum 70 Geburtstag* (Graz, 1986), 171–202.

LIESS (1986a)   LIESS, R. 'Die Entstehung des Strassburger Risses mit dem Glockengeschoss und seine Stellung im Gesamtbild der Münsterfassade', *Münchener Jahrbuch*, 37 (1986), 33–112.

LIESS (1986b)   LIESS, R. 'Das "Kressberger Fragment" im Hauptstaatsarchiv Stuttgart. Ein Gesamtentwurf der Strassburger Münsterfassade aus der Erwinzeit', *Jahrbuch der Staatlichen Kunstsammlungen in Baden-Württemberg*, 23 (1986), 6–31.

LIESS (1988)   LIESS, R. 'Zur historischen Morphologie der hohen Chorgiebelfassade von St. Marien in Prenzlau', *Niederdeutsche Beiträge zur Kunstgeschichte*, 27 (1988), 9–62.

LIESS (1990)   LIESS, R. 'Kunstgeschichtliche Anmerkungen zur Chorgiebelfassade der Prenzlauer Marienkirche', in N. Zaske, ed., *Kunst im Ostseeraum. Mittelalterliche Architektur und ihre Rezeption* (Wissenschaftliche Beiträge Ernst-Moritz-Arndt-Universität). Greifswald, 1990, 21–35.

LIESS (1991)   LIESS, R. 'Der Rahnsche Riss A des Freiburger Münsterturms und seine Strassburger Herkunft', *Zeitschrift des deutschen Vereins für Kunstwissenschaft*, 45 (1991), 7–66.

LILLICH (1975)   LILLICH, M.P. 'The choir clerestorey windows of La Trinité at Vendôme: dating and patronage', *Journal of the Society of Architectural Historians*, 34 (1975), 38–50.

LINDBLOM (1964)   LINDBLOM, A. *Kult og Konst i Vadstena Kloster*. Stockholm, 1964.

LINDLEY (1986)   LINDLEY, P. 'The Fourteenth-Century Architectural Programme at Ely Cathedral', in W.M. Ormrod, ed., *England in the 14th Century* (Proceedings of the Harlaxton Symposium). Woodbridge, 1986, 119–29.

LINDLEY (1986a)   LINDLEY, P. 'The Imagery of the Octagon at Ely', *Journal of the British Archaeological Association*, 139 (1986), 75–99.

LINDLEY (1991)   LINDLEY, P. 'Romanticizing Reality: The Sculptural Memorials of Queen Eleanor and their context', in D. Parsons, ed., *Eleanor of Castile 1290–1990*. Stamford, 1991, 69–92.

LIPPERT (1994)   LIPPERT, H.-G. 'System zur Dachentwässerung bei gotischen Kirchenbauten', *Architectura*, 24 (1994), 111–28.

LOHMAN (1982)   LOHMAN, J. 'The Case of Hinrich Brunsberg'. M.A. thesis, Manchester University, 1982.

LOHMAN (1996)   LOHMAN, J. 'Hinrich Brunsberg', in J. Turner, ed., *The Dictionary of Art*, vol. 5 (1996), 27–8.

LÖHR (1975)   LÖHR, A. 'Der Skulpturenzyklus im Chor der Wiesenkirche zu Soest', *Westfalen*, 53 (1975), 81–99.

LOHRMANN (1973)   LOHRMANN, D. 'St. Germer-de-Fly und das anglo-normanische Reich', *Francia*, 1 (1973), 193–256.

LOPEZ (1952)   LOPEZ, R. 'Economie et architecture mediévales. Cela aurait-il tué ceci?', *Annales*, 7 (1952), 433–8.

LORENZONI (1983/84)   LORENZONI, G. 'L'Architettura', in M. Fanti, L. Bellosi, *et al.*, *La Basilica di San Petronio in Bologna*, 2 vols. (Bologna, 1983/84), 1, 1983, 53–124.

LOZINSKI (1994)   LOZINSKI, J.L. 'Henri II, Aliénor d'Aquitaine et la cathédrale de Poitiers', *Cahiers de Civilisation médiévale*, 37 (1994), 95–100.

LUDWIG (1998)   LUDWIG, S. *St. Georgen zu Wismar. Die Geschichte einer mittelalterlichen Pfarrkirche vom 13. bis zum 16. Jahrhundert*. Kiel, 1998.

MADDISON (1993)   MADDISON, J. 'Rebuilding at Lichfield during the Episcopate of Walter Langton (1296–1321)', in *Medieval Archaeology and Architecture at Lichfield* (British Archaeological Association Conference Transactions, vol. 13). Leeds, 1993, 17–35.

MADDISON (2000)   MADDISON, J. *Ely Cathedral Design and Meaning*, Cambridge 2000.

MAESSCHALK AND VIAENE (1977)   MAESSCHALK, A. AND VIAENE, J. 'Het Stadhuis van Leuven: Mensen en bouwkunst in Boergondisch Brabant', *Arca Lovan*, 6 (1977).

MAGIRIUS (1975)   MAGIRIUS, H. 'Neue Ergebnisse zur Baugeschichte der Annenkirche zu Annenberg', *Sächsische Heimatblätter*, 21 (1975), 149–57.

MAGIRIUS (1990)   MAGIRIUS, H. *Die Sankt-Annenkirche zu Annaberg*. Berlin, 1990 (3rd edtn).

MAGIRIUS (1993)   MAGIRIUS, H. *Der Dom zu Freiburg*. Regensburg, 1993.

MAGIRIUS (1993a)   MAGIRIUS, H. *Der Dom zu Meissen*. Munich and Zürich, 1993.

MAGIRIUS (1994)   MAGIRIUS, H. 'Bauforschung und Denkmalpflege an Monumenten des Mittelalters in Sachsen – Neue Aspekte zur Baugeschichte des Meissner Doms im 13 bis 15 Jahrhundert', *Architectura*, 24 (1994), 141–9.

MAINES (1986)   MAINES, C. 'Good works, social ties and the hope for salvation', in P.L. Gerson, ed., *Abbot Suger and Saint-Denis: a Symposium*. New York, 1983, 77–94.

MAIR (1982)   MAIR, R. 'The choir capitals of Canterbury Cathedral 1174–84', in *Medieval Art and Architecture at Canterbury before 1220* (British Archaeological Association Conference Transactions for the year 1979, vol. 5). Leeds, 1982, 56–66.

MÂLE (1978)   MÂLE, E. *Religious Art in France. The Twelfth Century. A Study in the Origins of Medieval Iconography* (Bollingen series 90.1). Princeton, 1978.

MÂLE (1984)   MÂLE, E. *Religious Art in France. The Thirteenth Century. A Study of Medieval Iconography and its Souces* (Bollingen series 90.2). Princeton, 1984. [This volume previously translated under the title *The Gothic Image*].

MANHES AND DEREMBLE (1988)   MANHES, C. AND DEREMBLE, J.P. *Les Vitraux légendaires de Chartres. Des récits en images*. Paris, 1988.

MANHES-DEREMBLE (1993)   MANHES-DEREMBLE, C. *Les Vitraux narratifs de la Cathédrale de Chartres. Étude iconographique* (Corpus Vitrearum France. Etudes II). Paris, 1993.

MARK AND BORG (1973)   MARK, R. AND BORG, A. 'Chartres Cathedral: A Reinterpretation of its Structure', *Art Bulletin*, 55 (1973), 367–72.

MARK AND PRENTKE (1968)   MARK, R. AND PRENTKE, R.A. 'Model Analysis of Gothic Structure', *Journal of the Society of Architectural Historians*, 27 (1968), 44–8.

MARK (1982)   MARK, R. *Experiments in Gothic Structure*. Cambridge, Mass., 1982.

MARKS (1993)   MARKS, R. *Stained Glass in England during the Middle Ages*. Toronto and Buffalo, 1993.

MARKSCHIES (1995)   MARKSCHIES, C. *Gibt es eine 'Theologie der gotischen Kathedrale'? Nochmals: Suger von Saint-Denis und Sankt Dionys vom Areopag* (Abhandlungen der Heidelberger Akademie der Wissenschaften, Philosophisch-historische Klasse, 1995, 1). Heidelberg, 1995.

MAROSI (1964)   MAROSI, E. 'Beiträge zur Baugeschichte der St Elisabeth Pfarrkirche von Kassa', *Acta Historiae Artium*, 10 (1964), 229–45.

MAROSI (1969)   MAROSI, E. 'Die Zentrale Rolle der Bauhütte von Kaschau (Kassa, Košice)', *Acta Historiae Artium*, 15 (1969), 25–75.

MAROSI (1984)   MAROSI, E. *Die Anfänge der Gotik in Ungarn. Esztergom in der Kunst des 12.–13. Jahrhunderts*. Budapest, 1984.

MAROT (1933)   MAROT, P. 'Pont-à-Mousson', in *Congrès Archéologique de France*, 96 (1933), 208–15.

MARQUES DE CARVALHO (1990)   MARQUES DE CARVALHO, A. *Do mosteiro dos Jerónimos de Belém: Termo de Lisboa*. Lisbon, 1990.

MATA (1999)   FRANCO MATA, A. 'La catedral de Toledo: entre la tradición local y la modernidad foránea in Freigang, ed. (1999), 83–104.

MATTEUCCI (1983/84)   MATTEUCCI, A.M. 'La facciata del Seicento al Novecento', in M. Fanti *et al.*, eds., *La Basilica di San Petronio in Bologna* (Bologna, 1983/84), vol. 2, 29–42.

MAUÉ (1986)   MAUÉ, H. 'Nürnberg's Cityscape and Architecture', in *Gothic and Renaissance Art in Nuremberg* (Metropolitan Museum of Art, New York, and Germanisches Nationalmuseum, Nuremberg), Nuremberg-Munich, 1986, 27–50.

MAURER (1977)   MAURER, H.M. 'Burgen', in R. Haussherr, ed., *Die Zeit der Staufer. Geschichte-Kunst-Kultur*. Exh. cat., Württembergischen Landesmuseum, Stuttgart. Stuttgart, 1977, vol. 3, 119–28.

MCALEER (1963)   MCALEER, J.P. 'The Romanesque Church Façade in Britain', Ph.D. thesis, University of London, 1963.

MCALEER (1984)   MCALEER, J.P. 'Romanesque England and the Development of the "Façade Harmonique"', *Gesta*, 23 (1984), 87–105.

MCCLAIN (1985)   MCCLAIN, J. 'A Modern Reconstruction of the West Portals of Saint-Yved at Braine', *Gesta*, 24 (1985), 105–19.

MCGEE (1986)   MCGEE, J.D. 'The "early vaults" of Saint-Etienne at Beauvais', *Journal of the Society of Architectural Historians*, 45 (1986), 20–31.

MCKINNE (1985)   MCKINNE, J. 'The church of S. Maria e Sigismondo in Rivolta d'Adda and the Double-Bay System in Northern Italy in the late 11th and early 12th Centuries'. Ph.D. thesis, University of California, Berkeley, 2 vols, 1985.

MECKEL (1936)   MECKEL, C.A. 'Untersuchungen über die Baugeschichte des Chores des Münsters zu Freiburg', *Oberrheinische Kunst*, 7 (1936), 37–52.

MECKENSTOCK (1972/3)   MECKENSTOCK, H. 'Das fiallenflankierte Portal. Seine Entstehung und Bedeutung', *Mainzer Zeitschrift*, 67/68 (1972/1973), 143–6.

MECKSEPER (1975)   MECKSEPER, C. 'Austrahlungen des französischen Burgenbaues nach Mitteleuropa im 13, Jahrhundert', in *Festschrift für Hans Wentzel*. Berlin, 1975, 135–44.

MECKSEPER (1982)   MECKSEPER, C. *Kleine Kunstgeschichte der Deutschen Stadt im Mittelalter*. Darmstadt, 1982.

MEIER (1978)   MEIER, C. 'Edelsteinallegorese', in A. Legner, ed., *Die Parler und der Schöne Stil. Europäische Kunst unter den Luxemburgern*. Exh. cat., Schnutgen Museum Köln, vol. 3. Cologne, 1978, 185–7.

MELCZER and SOLDWEDEL (1982)   MELCZER, E. and SOLDWEDEL, E. 'Monastic Goals in the Aesthetics of Saint Bernard', in M.P. Lillich, ed., *Studies in Cistercian Art and Architecture*, vol. 1. Kalamazoo, 1982, 31–44.

MENCL (1948)   MENCL, V. *Česká Architektura doby Lucemberské*. Prague, 1948.

MENCL (1971)   MENCL, V. 'Poklasická Gotika jižní Francie a Švábska a její vztah ke Gotice České', *Umění*, 19 (1971), 217–54 (with French resumé).

MENCLOVA (1972)   MENCLOVA, D. *České Hrady*, 2 vols. Prague, 1972.

MERSMANN (1982)   MERSMANN, W. *Rosenfenster und Himmelskreise*. Mittenwald, 1982.

MERTENS (1972)   MERTENS, K. *Die Severikirche zu Erfurt* (Das Christliche Denkmal, 27). Berlin, 1972 (6th edtn).

MERTENS (1975)   MERTENS, K. *Der Dom zu Erfurt* (Das Christliche Denkmal, 21/22). Berlin, 1975.

MESQUI (1988)   MESQUI, J. *Ile-de-France Gothique. Vol 2: Les demeures seigneurials*. Paris, 1988.

MESQUI (1991, 1993)   MESQUI, J. *Châteaux et Enceintes de la France Médiévale. De la défense a la résidence*. Vol. 1: *Les organes de la défense*. Paris, 1991, and vol. 2: *La résidence et les éléments d'architecture*. Paris, 1993.

MESLÉ AND JENN (1980)   MESLÉ, E. AND JENN, J.-M. *L'abbaye de Noirlac* (Petites Notes sur les grands Edifices). Paris, 1980.

METTERNICH (1994)   METTERNICH, W. *Der Dom zu Limburg an der Lahn*. Darmstadt, 1994.

METZ (1938)   METZ, P. 'Die Florentiner Domfassade des Arnolfo di Cambio', *Jahrbuch der Preussischen Sammlungen*, 59 (1938), 121–60.

MEUCHE (1962)   MEUCHE, H. 'Zur sächsischen Architektur in der Zeit der frühbürgerlichen Revolution', *Wissenschaftliche Zeitschrift der Ernst-Moritz-Arndt Universität Greifswald*, 11 (1962) (Gesell- und Sprachwissenschaftliche Reihe, 5/6), 305–21.

MEUCHE (1971)   MEUCHE, H. 'Anmerkungen zur Gestalt der sächsischen Hallenkirchen um 1500', in *Aspekte zur Kunstgeschichte von Mittelalter und Neuzeit. Festschrift K.H. Clasen*. Weimar, 1971, 167–89.

MEUCHE (1972)   MEUCHE, H. 'Die Zellengewölbe und die Albrechtsburg' in J. Mrusek, ed., *Die Albrechtsburg zu Meissen* (Leipzig, 1972), 56–66, 134–8.

MEUCHE (1972a)   MEUCHE, H. 'Zur Gesellschaftlichen Funktion der Emporen im Obersächsischen Kirchenbau um 1500', in *Actes du XXIIe Congrès International d'Histoire de l'Art, Budapest 1969. Évolution Générale et Développements Régionaux en Histoire de l'Art*, vol. 1. Budapest, 1972, 551–6.

MEYER (1963)   MEYER, W. *Den Freunden ein Schutz, den Feinden zum Trutz. Die deutsche Burg*. Frankfurt/Main, 1963.

MEZEY-DEBRECZENI AND SZENTESI (1991)   MEZEY-DEBRECZENI, A. AND SZENTESI, E. 'Neue Forschungen zur Abteikirche von Ják', *Kunstchronik*, 44 (1991), 575–84.

MICHLER (1969)   MICHLER, J. 'Die Langhaushalle der Marburger Elisabethkirche', *Zeitschrift für Kunstgeschichte*, 32 (1969), 104–32.

MICHLER (1972)   MICHLER, J. 'Marburg und Köln – Wechselseitige Beziehungen in der Baukunst des 13 Jahrhunderts', *Hessische Heimat*, 22 (1972), 73–88.

MICHLER (1974)   MICHLER, J. 'Studien zur Marburger Schlosskapelle', *Marburger Jahrbuch für Kunstwissenschaft*, 19 (1974), 33–84.

MICHLER (1977)   MICHLER, J. 'Uber die Farbfassung hochgotischer Sakralräume', *Wallraf-Richartz Jahrbuch*, 39 (1977), 29–68.

MICHLER (1980)   MICHLER, J. 'Zur Stellung von Bourges in der gotischen Baukunst', *Wallraf-Richartz Jahrbuch*, 41 (1980), 27–86 (with English resumé).

MICHLER (1984)   MICHLER, J. *Die Elisabethkirche zu Marburg in ihrer urprünglichen Farbigkeit* (Quellen und Studien zur Geschichte des Deutschen Ordens, 19). Marburg, 1984.

MICHLER (1984a)   MICHLER, J. 'Die ursprüngliche Chorform der Zisterzienserkirche in Salem', *Zeitschrift für Kunstgeschichte*, 47 (1984), 3–46.

MIDDELDORF-KOSEGARTEN (1970)   MIDDELDORF-KOSEGARTEN, A. 'Zur Bedeutung der Sieneser Domkuppel', *Münchener Jahrbuch der Bildenden Kunst*, 21 (1970), 73–98.

MIDDELDORF-KOSEGARTEN (1984)   MIDDELDORF-KOSEGARTEN, A. *Sienesische Bildhauer am Duomo Vecchio. Studien zur Skulptur in Siena 1250–1330*. Munich, 1984.

MIDDELDORF-KOSEGARTEN (1994)   MIDDELDORF-KOSEGARTEN, A. 'Zur Planungsphase der Domfassade um 1300', in H. Beck and K. Hengevoss-Dürkop, eds., *Studien zur Geschichte der europäischen Skluptur im 12 und 13 Jahrhunderts*. Munich, 1994, 633–49.

MIDDELDORF-KOSEGARTEN (1996)   MIDDELDORF-KOSEGARTEN, A. *Die Domfassade in Orvieto. Studien zur Architektur und Skulptur 1290–1330* (Kunstwissenschaftliche Studien, 66). Munich-Berlin, 1996.

MITCHELL (1986)   MITCHELL, W.J.T. *Iconology. Image, Text, Ideology*. Chicago, 1986.

MÖBIUS (1968)   MÖBIUS, F. *Westwerkstudien*. Jena, 1968.

MÖBIUS (1972)   MÖBIUS, F. 'Beobachtungen zur Ikonologie des spätgotischen Gewölbes in Sachsen und Böhmen', in *Actes du XXIIe Congrès International d'Histoire de l'Art. Budapest 1969. Evolution Générale et Développements Régionaux*, vol. 1. Budapest, 1972, 557–67.

MÖBIUS AND BEYER (1978)   MÖBIUS, F. AND H. AND BEYER, K. *Bauornament im Mittelalter. Symbol und Bedeutung*. Vienna, 1978.

MÖBIUS (1984)   MÖBIUS, F. 'Die Chorpartie der westeuropäischen Klosterkirche zwischen 8 und 11 Jahrhundert, in F. Möbius and E. Schubert, eds., *Architektur des Mittelalters: Funktion und Gestalt*. Weimar, 1984, 9–41.

MÖBIUS (1985)   MÖBIUS, F. 'Thesen zur mittelalterlichen Baugeschichte Erfurts', *Kritische Berichte*, 13 (1985), 30–45.

MÖBIUS AND SCIURIE eds. (1989)   MÖBIUS, F. AND SCIURIE, H. *Geschichte der deutschen Kunst. 1200–1350*. Leipzig, 1989.

MÖBIUS (1989a)   MÖBIUS, F. 'Baukunst', in F. Möbius and H. Sciurie, *Geschichte der deutschen Kunst. 1200–1350*. Leipzig, 1989.

MOJON (1960)   MOJON, L. *Das Berner Münster*. (Die Kunstdenkmäler des Kantons Bern, 4, in Die Kunstdenkmäler der Schweiz). Basel, 1960.

MOJON (1967)   MOJON, L. *Der Münsterbaumeister Matthäus Ensinger. Studien zu seinem Werk* (Berner Schriften zur Kunst, 10). Bern, 1967.

MOORMAN (1968)   MOORMAN, J. *A History of the Franciscan Order. From its Origins to the Year 1517*. Oxford, 1968.

MORAND (1991)   MORAND, K. *Claus Sluter. Artist at the Court of Burgundy*. London, 1991.

MOREIRA (1996)   MOREIRA, R. 'Castilho, de', in J. Turner, *The Dictionary of Art*, vol. 6. London, 1996, 42–5.

MORGAN AND SANDLER (1987)   MORGAN, N. AND SANDLER, L.F. 'Manuscript Illumination of the Thirteenth and Fourteenth Centuries', in J. Alexander and P. Binski, eds., *Age of Chivalry. Art in Plantagenet England 1200–1400*. London, Royal Academy, 1987, 148–56.

MORRIS (1974)   MORRIS, R.K. 'Tewkesbury Abbey: The Despencer Mausoleum', *Transactions of the Bristol and Gloucester Archaeological Society*, 93 (1974), 142–55.

MORRIS (1978)   MORRIS, R.K. 'The development of later Gothic mouldings in England c.1250–1400, Part I', *Architectural History*, 21 (1978), 8–57.

MORRIS (1979)   MORRIS, R.K. 'The development of later Gothic mouldings in England c.1250–1400, Part 2', *Architectural History*, 22 (1979), 1–48.

MORRIS (1990)   MORRIS, R.K. 'The New Work at Old St Paul's Cathedral and its Place in English Thirteenth-Century Architecture', in *Medieval Art, Architecture and Archaeology in London* (British Archaeological Association Conference Transactions, vol. 10). Leeds, 1990, 74–100.

MORRIS (1990a) MORRIS, R.K. 'Mouldings and the Analysis of Medieval Style', in P. Crossley and E. Fernie, *Medieval Architecture and its Intellectual Context. Studies in Honour of Peter Kidson*. London and Ronceverte, 1990, 239–48.

MORRIS (1991)   MORRIS, R.K. 'Thomas of Witney at Exeter, Winchester and Wells', in *Medieval Art and Architecture at Exeter Cathedral* (British Archaeological Association Conference Transactions for the year 1985, vol. 11). Leeds, 1991, 57–84.

MORRIS (1992)   MORRIS, R.K. 'An English glossary of medieval mouldings: with an introduction to mouldings c.1040–1240, *Architectural History*, 35 (1992), 1–17.

MORRIS (1996)   MORRIS, R.K. 'The Style and Buttressing of Salisbury Cathedral Tower', in *Medieval Art and Architecture at Salisbury Cathedral* (British Archaeological Association Conference Transactions, vol. 17). Leeds, 1996, 46–58.

MORRIS (1997)   MORRIS, R.K. 'European Prodigy or Regional Eccentric? The Rebuilding of St Augustine's Abbey church, Bristol', in *Almost the Richest City. Bristol in the Middle Ages* (British Archaeological Association Conference Transactioins, vol. 19). Leeds, 1997, 41–56.

MORRIS (1998)   MORRIS, R.K. 'The Architecture of Arthurian Enthusiasm: Castle Symbolism in the Reigns of Edward I and his Successors', in M. Strickland, ed., *Armies, Chivalry and Warfare in Medieval Britain and France* (Proceedings of the 1995 Harlaxton Symposium). Stamford, 1998, 63–81.

MÖSENEDER (1981)   MÖSENEDER, K. 'Lapides Vivi. Über die Kreuzkapelle der Burg Karlstein', *Wiener Jahrbuch für Kunstgeschichte*, 34 (1981), 39–69.

MROCZKO AND ARSZYŃSKI eds. (1995)   MROCZKO, T. AND ARSZYŃSKI, M. eds. *Architektura Gotycka w Polsce*, 4 vols. (Dziejów Sztuki Polskiej, vol. 2). Warsaw, 1995.

MUCH ed. (1988)   MUCH, F. ed. *Baukunst des Mittelalters in Europa. Hans Erich Kubach zum 75 Geburtstag*. Stuttgart, 1988.

MUK (1977)   MUK, J. 'Konstrukce a tvar středověkých kleneb', *Umění*, 25 (1977), 1–23.

MULLER (1901)   MULLER, E. *Le Prieuré de Saint-Leu d'Esserent. Cartulaire (1180–1538)*. Pontoise, 1901.

MÜLLER (1966)   MÜLLER, T. *Sculpture in the Netherlands, Germany, France and Spain: 1400–1500*. Harmondsworth, 1966.

MÜLLER (1971)   MÜLLER, W. 'Der elliptische Korbbogen in der Architekturtheorie von Dürer bis Frézier', *Technikgeschihchte*, 38 (1971), 93–106.

MÜLLER (1973)   MÜLLER, W. 'Zum Problem des technologischen Stilvergleichs im deutschen Gewölbebau der Spätgotik', *Architectura*, 3 (1973), 1–12.

MÜLLER (1973a)   MÜLLER, W. 'Vorkommen und Variationen einer Rippenkonfiguration Nürnberger Meisterstücke in der Österreichischen

Spätgotik', *Österreichische Zeitschrift für Kunst und Denkmalpflege*, 27 (1973), 132–9.

MÜLLER (1974)   MÜLLER, W. 'Einflüsse der Österreichischen und der Böhmisch-Sächsischen Spätgotik in den Gewölbemustern des Jacob Facht von Andernach', *Wiener Jahrbuch für Kunstgeschichte*, 27 (1974), 65–82.

MÜLLER (1977)   MÜLLER, W. 'Das Sterngewölbe des Lorenzer Hallenchores. Seine Stellung innerhalb der spätgotischen Gewölbekonstruktionen', in H. Bauer *et al.*, eds., *500 Jahre Hallenchor St Lorenz in Nürnberg 1477–1977*. Nürnberg, 1977, 171–96.

MÜLLER (1978)   MÜLLER, W. 'An application of Generative Aesthetics to German Late Gothic rib vaulting', *Leonardo*, 9 (1972), 107–10.

MÜLLER (1986)   MÜLLER, W. 'Über die Grenzen Interpretierbarkeit spätgotischer Gewölbe durch die traditionelle Kunstwissenschaft: ein Beitrag zum Thema "Unmittelbarkeit und Reflecktion"', *Jahrbuch des Zentralinstituts für Kunstgeschichte*, 2 (1986), 47–69.

MÜLLER (1989)   MÜLLER, W. 'Le dessin technique a l'epoque gothique', in R. Recht, ed., *Les Battisseurs des Cathedrales Gothique*. Strasbourg, 1989, 237–54.

MÜLLER (1990)   MÜLLER, W. *Grundlagen gotischer Bautechnik*. Munich, 1990.

MÜNZEL (1978, 2nd edn)   MÜNZEL, G. *Der Skulpturenzyklus in der Vorhalle des Freiburger Munsters*. Freiburg, 1978.

MURRAY (1973)   MURRAY, S. 'The Work of Martin Chambiges'. Ph.D. thesis, University of London, Courtauld Institute of Art, 1973.

MURRAY (1977)   MURRAY, S. 'The Choir of Saint-Etienne at Beauvais', *Journal of the Society of Architectural Historians*, 36 (1977), 111–21.

MURRAY (1979) and (1981)   MURRAY, S. Reviews of John James, *The Contractors of Chartres*, in *Journal of the Society of Architectural Historians*, 38 (1979), 279–81; and in *Art Bulletin*, 63 (1981), 149–52.

MURRAY (1980)   MURRAY, S. 'The Choir of the Church of St.-Pierre, Cathedral of Beauvais: A Study of Gothic Architectural Planning and Constructional Chronology in its Historical Context', *Art Bulletin*, 62 (1980), 533–51.

MURRAY (1987)   MURRAY, S. *Building Troyes Cathedral. The Late Gothic Campaigns*. Indiana, 1987.

MURRAY (1989)   MURRAY, S. *Beauvais Cathedral. Architecture of Transcendence*. Princeton, 1989.

MURRAY (1990)   MURRAY, S. 'Looking for Robert de Luzarches. The Early Work at Amiens Cathedral', *Gesta*, 29 (1990), 111–31.

MURRAY AND ADDISS (1990)   MURRAY, S. AND ADDISS, J. 'Plan and Space at Amiens Cathedral. With a new plan drawn by James Addiss', *Journal of the Society of Architectural Historians*, 49 (1990), 44–65.

MURRAY (1996)   MURRAY, S. *Notre-Dame, Cathedral of Amiens. The Power of Change in Gothic*. Cambridge, 1996.

MURRAY (1996a)   MURRAY, S. 'Flamboyant Style', in J. Turner, ed., *The Dictionary of Art*, vol. 11. London, 1996, 153–6.

MURRAY (1998)   MURRAY, S. 'Notre-Dame of Paris and the Anticipation of Gothic', *Art Bulletin*, 80 (1998), 229–53.

MURRAY (1999)   MURRAY, S. 'The Architectural Envelope of the Sainte-Chapelle, Form and Meaning,' in Joubert and Sandron, eds. (1999), 223–30.

MUSSAT (1963)   MUSSAT, A. *Le Style Gothique de l'Ouest de la France (XIIe–XIIIe siecles)*. Paris, 1963.

MUSSAT (1966)   MUSSAT, A. 'Coutances. Cathédrale Notre-Dame', *Congrès Archéologique*, 124 (1966), 9–50.

MUSSAT et al. (1981) MUSSAT, A., BARRIE, R., BRISAC, C., et al., *La Cathédrale du Mans*. Paris, 1981.

MUSSAT (1988) MUSSAT, A. 'Les cathédrales dans leurs cités', *Revue de l'Art*, 55 (1988), 9–22.

NAGEL (1971)   NAGEL, G. *Das mittelalterliche Kaufhaus und seine Stellung in der Stadt*. Berlin, 1971.

NATALE (1973)   NATALE, H. *Die St. Leonards-kirche* (Grosse Baudenkmäler, 198). Munich, Berlin, 1973.

NEAGLEY (1988)   NEAGLEY, L. 'The Flamboyant Architecture of St.-Maclou, Rouen, and the Development of a Style', *Journal of the Society of Architectural Historians*, 47 (1988), 374–96.

NEAGLEY (1992)   NEAGLEY, L. 'Elegant Simplicity. The Late Gothic Plan Design of St.-Maclou', *Art Bulletin*, 74 (1992), 395–422.

NEAGLEY (1996)   NEAGLEY, L. entries in Turner, J. ed., *The Dictionary of Art* (1996), on the Le Roux family of masons (vol. 19, 230) and on St Maclou in Rouen (vol. 27, 253–4).

NEAGLEY (1998)   NEAGLEY, L. *Disciplined Exuberance. The Parish Church of Saint-Maclou and Late Gothic Architecture in Rouen*. Pennsylvania University Press, 1998.

NELSON (1980)   NELSON, A.H. 'Mechanical Wheels of Fortune 1100–1541', *Journal of the Warburg and Courtauld Institutes*, 43 (1980), 227–33.

NELSON (1973)   NELSON, R.J. 'Martin Chambiges and the Development of French Flamboyant Architecture' Ph.D. thesis, Johns Hopkins University, 1973.

NELSON (1974)   NELSON, R.J. 'A lost portal by Martin Chambiges?', *Journal of the Society of Architectural Historians*, 33 (1974), 155–7.

NENNO (1998)   NENNO, R. *Spätgotischen Hallenkirche in der Sudchampagne*. Röhrig, 1988.

NENNO (1998a)   NENNO, R. 'Die Kirche von les Grandes Chapelles (Aube)', in F. Much, ed., *Baukunst des Mittelalters in Europa. Hans Erich Kubach zum 75 Geburtstag*. Stuttgart, 1988, 569–74.

NEUHEUSER (1993)   NEUHEUSER, H.P. 'Die Kirchweihbeschreibungen von Saint-Denis und ihre Aussagefähigkeit für das Schönheitsempfinden des Abtes Suger', in G. Binding and A. Speer, eds., *Mittelalterliches Kunstlererleben nach den Quellen des 11. bis 13. Jahrhunderts*. Stuttgart-Bad Cannstatt, 1993, 116–83.

NICOLAI (1986/1990)   NICOLAI, B. *Libido Aedificandi. Walkenried und die monumentale Kirchenbaukunst der Zisterzienser um 1200* (Doctoral dissertation, Berlin, 1986). Published under the same title in 1990 in Quellen und Forschungen zur Braunschweigischen Geschichte, vol. 28. Braunschweig, 1990.

NICOLAI (1988)   NICOLAI, B. 'Lilienfeld und Walkenried. Zur Genese und Bedeutung eines Zisterziensischen Bautypus', *Wiener Jahrbuch für Kunstgeschichte*, 41 (1988), 23–39.

NICOLAI (1989)   NICOLAI, B. 'Überlegungen zum Chorbau des Magdeburger Domes unter Albrecht II (1209–1232)', in E. Ullmann, ed., *Der Magdeburger Dom. Ottonische Gründung und staufischer Neubau* (Schriftenreihe der Kommission für Niedersächsische Bau- und Kunstgeschichte bei der Braunschweigischen Wissenschaftlichen Gesellschaft, 5). Leipzig, 1989, 147–57.

NICOLAI (1989a)   NICOLAI, B. 'Walkenried. Anmerkungen zum Forschungsstand,' *Niederdeutsche Beiträge zur Kunstgeschichte*, 28 (1989), 9–32.

NICOLAI (1993)   NICOLAI, B. 'Morimond et L'Architecture Cistercienne en Allemagne', *Bulletin Monumental*, 151 (1993), 181–98.

NORMAN ed., (1995)   NORMAN, D. *Siena, Florence and Padua. Art, Society and Religioin 1280–1400*, 2 vols. New Haven and London.

NORTON (1993–4)   NORTON, C. 'Klosterneuburg and York: artistic cross-connections of an English cathedral, *c*.1330', *Wiener Jahrbuch für Kunstgeschichte*, 46/47 (1993–4), 519–32.

NORTON AND PARK (1986)   NORTON, C. AND PARK, D. 'Introduction', in C. Norton and D. Park, eds., *Cistercian Art and Architecture in the British Isles*. Cambridge, London, New York, etc., 1986, 1–10.

NUSSBAUM (1982)   NUSSBAUM, N. *Die Braunauer Bürgerspitalkirche und der spätgotischen Dreistützenbauten in Bayern und Österreich* (21.Veröffentlichung der Abteilung des Kunsthistorischen Instituts der Universität zu Köln). Cologne, 1982.

NUSSBAUM (1983–4)   NUSSBAUM, N. 'Die Braunauer Spitalkirche und die Bauten des Hans von Burghausen. Rezeption und Innovation in der Bayerischen Spätgotik', *Ars Bavarica*, 35/36 (1983–4), 83–117.

NUSSBAUM (1994, 2nd edtn)   NUSSBAUM, N. *Deutsche Kirchenbaukunst der Gotik*. Darmstadt, 1994.

NUSSBAUM (2000)   NUSSBAUM, N. *German Gothic Church Architecture*, translated by Scott Kleager, New Haven and London, 2000.

OETTINGER (1951)   OETTINGER, K. *Anton Pilgram und die Bildhauer von St Stephan*. Vienna, 1951.

OETTINGER (1962)   OETTINGER, K. 'Laube, Garten und Wald. Zu einer Theorie der süddeutschen Sakralkunst 1470–1520', in *Festschrift fur Hans Sedlmayr*. Munich, 1962, 201–28.

OLDE-CHOUKAIR (1997)   OLDE-CHOUKAIR, C. 'Le choeur de la Cathédrale de Sées et l'influence du style Rayonnant', in M. Baylé, dir., *L'Architecture Normande au Moyen Age*, vol. 1. Caen, 1997, 159–73.

OLDE-CHOUKAIR (1997a)   OLDE-CHOUKAIR, C. 'Sées: Cathédrale Notre-Dame', in M. Baylé, dir., *L'Architecture Normande au Moyen Age*, vol. 2. Caen, 1997, 179–84.

OLIN (1992)   OLIN, M. *Forms of Representation in Alois Riegl's Theory of Art* Pennsylvania University Press, 1992.

OLIVER (1973)   OLIVER, M. *La Catedral de Gerona*. Leon, 1973.

O'MALLY (1969)   O'MALLY, J.W. 'Fulfilment of the Christian Golden Age under Pope Julius II. Text of a Discourse of Giles of Viterbo', *Traditio*, 25 (1969), 265–338

ONIANS (1988)   ONIANS, J. *Bearers of Meaning. The Classical Orders in Antiquity, the Middle Ages and the Renaissance*. Princeton, 1988.

ORMROD (1997)   ORMROD, L. 'The Wenceslas Chapel in St Vitus Cathedral, Prague. The Marriage of Imperial Iconography and Bohemian Kingship'. Ph.D. thesis, London University, Courtauld Institute of Art, 1997.

OURSEL (1975)   OURSEL, R. *Haut-Poitu Roman*. La Pierre-Qui-Vire, 1975.

PAATZ (1940–54)   PAATZ, W. AND PAATZ, E. *Die Kirchen von Florenz*, 7 vols. Frankfurt, 1940–54.

PAATZ (1967)   PAATZ, W., *Verflechtungen in der Kunst der Spätgotik, zwischen 1360 und 1530*. Heidelberg, 1967.

PÄCHT (1963) and (1977)   PÄCHT, O. 'Alois Riegl', *Burlington Magazine*, 105 (1963), 188–93. Reprinted in O. Pächt, *Methodisches zur Kunsthistorischen Praxis*. Munich, 1977, ed. by J. Oberhaidacher *et al.*, 141–52.

PACQUET (1963)   PACQUET, J.-P. 'Les tracés directeurs des plans de quelques édifices du domaine royal au moyen âge,', *Les Monuments Historiques de la France*, n.s. 9 (1963), 68–71.

PALM (1976)   PALM, R. 'Das Masserk am Chorgestühl des Kölner Domes', *Kölner Domblatt*, 41 (1976), 57–82.

PALMERIO AND VILLETTI (1989)   PALMERIO, G. AND VILLETTI, G. *Storia edilizia di Santa Maria sopra Minerva in Roma, 1275–1870*. Rome, 1989.

PANOFSKY (1951)   PANOFSKY, E. *Gothic Architecture and Scholasticism*. Latrobe, Indiana, 1951.

PANOFSKY (1960)   PANOFSKY, E. *Renaissance and Renascences in Western Art*. Stockholm, 1960.

PANOFSKY ed. (1979)   PANOFSKY, E. *Abbot Suger. On the Abbey Church of St.Denis and its Art Treasures* (second edition by Gerda Panofsky-Soergel). Princeton, 1979.

PANOFSKY-SOERGEL (1972)   PANOFSKY-SOERGEL, G. 'Altenberg', in *Die Denkmäler des Rheinlandes*, 19 (Rheinisch-Bergischer Kreis, II). Düsseldorf, 1972, 89–140.

PARSONS (ed.) (1991)   PARSONS, D. ed., *Eleanor of Castile 1290–1990. Essays to Commemorate the 700th Anniversary of her Death: 28 November 1290*. Stamford, 1991.

PASTAN (1994)   PASTAN, E.C. 'Process and Patronage in the Decorative Arts of the Early Campaigns of Troyes Cathedral, ca.1200–1220s', *Journal of the Society of Architectural Historians*, 53 (1994), 215–31.

PAUL (1969)   PAUL, J. *Die mittelalterlichen Kommunalpaläste in Italien*. Dresden, 1969.

PAUL (1988)   PAUL, V. 'The Beginnings of Gothic Architecture in Languedoc', *Art Bulletin*, 70 (1988), 104–22.

PAUL (1990)   PAUL, V. 'Les épures de la chapelle Notre-Dame-de-Bethléem à la cathédrale de Narbonne', in *Le grand retable de Narbonne. Le décor sculpté de la chapelle de Bethléem à la cathédrale de Narbonne, et la retable en pierre du XIVe siecle en France et en Catalogne* (Actes du 1 colloque d'histoire de l'art méridional du Moyen Age. Narbonne, 2–3 Decembre 1988). Narbonne, 1990, 71–6.

PAUL (1991)   PAUL, V. 'The Projecting Triforium at Narbonne Cathedral: Meaning, Structure, or Form?', *Gesta*, 30 (1991), 27–40.

PAUL (1996)   PAUL, V. Entry on "Deschamps" in J. Turner, ed., *The Dictionary of Art*, vol. 8 (1996), 789.

PAUSE (1973)   'Gotische Architektur-zeichnungen in Deutschland'. Ph.D. dissertation, Bonn, 1973.

PEETERS (1985)   PEETERS, C. *De Sint-Janskathedraal te 's-Hertogenbosch*. 's-Gravenhage, 1985.

PEREIRA AND LEITE (1986)   PEREIRA, P. AND LEITE, M.C. 'Iconologia e imaginário do mosteiro de Sta Maria de Belém', *Historia*, 87 (1986), 197–213.

PERGER (1970)   PERGER, R. 'Die Baumeister des Wiener Stephansdomes im Spätmittelalter', *Wiener Jahrbuch für Kunstgeschichte*, 23 (1970), 28–65.

PERGER AND BRAUNEIS (1977)   PERGER, R. AND BRAUNEIS, W. *Die Mittelalterlichen Kirchen und Klöster Wiens*. Vienna, 1977.

PERONI (1969)   PERONI, A. 'La struttura del S. Giovanni in Borgo di Pavia e il problema delle coperture nell' architettura romanica lombarda', *Arte Lombarda* (1969), 14/1, 21–34, and 14/2, 63–76.

PESSIN (1978)   PESSIN, M. 'The Twelfth-Century Abbey Church of Saint-Germer-de-Fly and its Position in the Development of First Gothic Architecture', *Gesta*, 17 (1978), 71–2.

PESTELL (1981)   PESTELL, R. 'The Design Sources for the Cathedrals of Chartres and Soissons', *Art History*, 4 (1981), 1–13.

PEVSNER (1959)   PEVSNER, N. Review of K.H. Clasen, *Deutsche Gewölbe der Spätgotik*. Berlin 1958, *Art Bulletin*, 41 (1959), 333–6.

PEVSNER AND METCALF (1985a)   PEVSNER, N. AND METCALF, P. *The Cathedrals of England: Southern England*. Harmondsworth, 1985.

PEVSNER AND METCALF (1985b)   PEVSNER, N. AND METCALF, P. *The Cathedrals of England: Midland, Eastern and Northern England*. Harmondsworth, 1985.

PEVSNER AND SHERWOOD (1974)   PEVSNER, N. AND SHERWOOD, J. *The Buildings of England: Oxfordshire*. London, 1974.

PFISTER AND RAMISCH (1983)   PFISTER, P. AND RAMISCH, H. *Die Frauenkirche in München. Geschichte, Baugeschichte und Ausstattung*. Munich, 1983.

PFISTER AND RAMISCHE (1987)   PFISTER, P. AND RAMISCH, H. *Der Dom zu Unserer Lieben Frau in Munchen*. Munich, 1987.

PHILIPP (1985)   PHILIPP, K.J. 'Zur Herleitung der Gewölbe des Prager Veitsdoms. Ikonographie spätgotischer Gewölbefigurationen', *Kritische Berichte*, 13, Heft 5 (1985), 45–54.

PHILIPP (1988)   PHILIPP, K.J. 'Sainte-Waudru in Mons (Bergen, Hennegau). Die Planungsgeschichte einer Stiftskirche 1449–1450', *Zeitschrift für Kunstgeschichte*, 51 (1988), 372–413.

PHILIPP (1989a)   PHILIPP, K.J. 'Eyn huys in manieren van eynre kirchen: Werkmeister, Parliere, Steinlieferanten, Zimmermeister und die Bauorganisation in den Niederlanden vom 14. bis zum 16. Jahrhundert', *Wallraf-Richartz Jahrbuch*, 50 (1989), 69–113.

PHILIPP (1989b)   PHILIPP, K.J. 'Polygonale dreischiffige Hallenchöre "ohne Umgang". Anmerkungen zu einer Typologie spätmittelalterlicher Sakralarchitektur', *Marburger Jahrbuch für Kunstwissenschaft*, 22 (1989), 51–60.

PICOU (1984)   PICOU, F. 'Églises et couvents de Frères mineurs en France: recueil de plans', *Bulletin archéologique*, 17–18 (1984), 115–76.

PIETRAMELLARA (1980)   PIETRAMELLARA, C. *Il Duomo di Siena. Evoluzione della forma dalle origini alla fine del Trecento*. Florence, 1980.

PILECKA (1989)   PILECKA, E. 'Kościół Najświętszej Marii Panny w Gdańsku', *Zeszyt Naukowe Uniwersytetu im Mikołaja Kopernika, Toruń*, 176 (1989), 47–79.

PILECKA (1990)   PILECKA, E. 'Die spätgotische Architektur der Marienkirche zu Danzig', in *Kunst im Ostseeraum. Mittelalterliche Architektur und ihre Rezeption. 3 Greifswalder Kolloquium 'Mittelalterliche Architektur und bildende Kunst im Ostseeraum'*. Ernst-Moritz-Arndt-Universität, Greifswald. Greifswald, 1990, 49–57.

PIROVANO, ed. (1982)   PIROVANO, C. ed., *Francesco d'Assisi* (Exh. cat., 3 vols.). Milan, 1982.

PLAGNIEUX (1991)   PLAGNIEUX, P. 'Le chevet de Saint-Germain-des-Près et la définition de l'espace gothique au milieu du XIIe siècle'. Ph.D. thesis, University of Paris-Sorbonne, Paris IV, 1991.

PLAGNIEUX (1992)   PLAGNIEUX, P. 'Les arcs-boutants du XIIe siècle de l'église de Domont', *Bulletin Monumental*, 150 (1992), 209–22.

PLANT (1998)   PLANT, R. 'English Romanesque Architecture and the Holy Roman Empire'. Ph.D. thesis, London University, Courtauld Institute of Art, 1998.

PLAT (1925)   PLAT, M. L'ABBÉ. 'La Trinité de Vendôme', *Congrès Archéologique de France*, 88 (1925), 249–68.

PLATT (1976)   PLATT, C. *The English Medieval Town*. London, 1976.

PLATT (1981)   PLATT, C. *The Parish Churches of Medieval England*. London, 1981.

PODRO (1982)   PODRO, M. *The Critical Historians of Art*. Yale, 1982.

POLK (1983)   POLK, T.E. *Saint-Denis, Noyon and the Early Gothic Choir. Methodological Considerations for the History of Early Gothic Architecture* (Sanctuaries of the Gallic-Frankish Church, 4). Frankfurt/Main, 1982.

PONSICH (1954)   PONSICH, P. 'La Cathédrale de Perpignan', *Congrès Archéologique de France*, 112 (1954), 51–86.

POUNDS (1994)   POUNDS, N.J.G. *The Medieval Castle in England and Wales. A Social and Political History*. Cambridge, 1994.

PRACHE (1976)   PRACHE, A. 'Les Arcs-Boutants au XIIe Siècle', *Gesta*, 15 (1976), 31–42.

PRACHE (1977)   PRACHE, A. 'Notre-Dame de Châlons', *Congrès Archéologique de France*, 135 (1977), 279–7.

PRACHE (1978)   PRACHE, A. 'A propos des voûtes de la nef de la cathédrale de Noyon', *Bulletin Monumental*, 136 (1978), 73–7.

PRACHE (1978a)   PRACHE, A. *Saint-Remi de Reims. L'Oeuvre de Pierre de Celle et sa place dans l'architecture gothique* (Bibliothèque de la Société Française d'Archéologie, 8). Geneva, Paris, 1978.

PRACHE (1982)   PRACHE, A. 'La nef de la cathédrale de Strasbourg et l'architecture rayonnant en Champagne', *Bulletin de la Société des amis de la Cathédrale de Strasbourg: Hommage á Hans Reinhardt*, 15 (1982), 99–103.

PRACHE (1987)   PRACHE, A. 'La cathédrale de Noyon, état de la question', in *La Ville de Noyon* (Cahiers de l'Inventaire, 10). Amiens, 1987, 71–80.

PRACHE (1988)   PRACHE, A. 'Henri Ier (1152–1181) et l'architecture religieuse en Champagne', in F. Much, ed., *Baukunst des Mittelalters in Europa. Hans Erich Kubach zum 75 Geburtstag*. Stuttgart, 1988, 347–50.

PRACHE (1990)   PRACHE, A. 'Observations sur la construction de la Cathédrale de Chartres au XIIIe siecle', *Bulletin de la Société Nationale des Antiquaires de France*, (1990), 327–34.

PRACHE (1994)   PRACHE, A. 'St Yved de Braine', *Congrès Archéologique de France*, 148 (1990), Paris, 1994, t. 1, 105–18.

PRACHE (1996)   PRACHE, A. 'Remarques sur les parties hautes de la cathédrale d'Amiens', *Gazette des Beaux-Arts*, 127 (1996), 55–62.

PRADALIER (1996)   PRADALIER, H. 'Cathedrals of Salamanca', in J. Turner. ed., *The Dictionary of Art*, 27 (1996), 604–5.

PRESSOUYRE (1963)   PRESSOUYRE, S. 'Le château de Tarascon', *Congrès Archéologique de France*, 121 (1963), 221–43.

PRESSOUYRE (1976)   PRESSOUYRE, L. 'Une tête de reine du portail central de Saint-Denis', *Gesta*, 15 (1976), 151–60.

PRESSOUYRE AND KINDER, eds. (1990)   PRESSOUYRE, L. AND KINDER, T. eds., *Saint Bernard et le Monde Cistercien*. Paris, 1990.

PRIN (1955)   PRIN, M. 'La première église des Frères Prêcheurs de Toulouse, d'après les fouilles', *Annales du Midi*, 67 (1955), 5–18.

PROSKE (1951)   PROSKE, B.G. *Castilian Sculpture – Gothic to Renaissance*. New York, 1951.

PUCHTA (1968)   PUCHTA, H. 'Kans (sic) Krumenauer und Hans von Burghausen, genannt Stethaimer', *Verhandlungen des historischen Vereins für Niederbayern*, 94 (1968), 174–80.

PUCHTA (1975)   PUCHTA, H. 'Beiträge zum Stethaimerproblem', *Das Münster*, 28 (1975), 39–49.

RADDING AND CLARK (1992)   RADDING, C.M. AND CLARK, K. *Medieval Architecture, Medieval Learning: Builders and Masters in the Age of Romanesque and Gothic*. New Haven and London, 1992.

RADOVÁ-ŠTIKOVÁ (1958)   RADOVÁ-ŠTIKOVÁ, M. 'Sklípková Klenba', *Umění*, 6 (1958), 217–37. (German resumé, 322)

RADOVÁ-ŠTIKOVÁ (1974)   RADOVÁ-ŠTIKOVÁ, M. 'Zdroje Architektonické Tvorby Arnolda Vestfálského', *Umění*, 22 (1974), 143–5.

RADOVÁ-ŠTIKOVÁ (1988)   RADOVÁ-ŠTIKOVÁ, M. 'O rozwoju twórczości architektonicznej Arnold z Westfalii', in Z. Bania et al., *Podług nieba i zwyczaju polskiego. Studia z historii architektury sztuki i kultury ofiarowane Adamowi Miłobędzkiemu*. Warsaw, 1988, 163–72.

RADOVI (1960)   RADOVI, M. AND O. 'Sklípková klenba a prostor', *Umění*, 8 (1960), 437–65.

RAGUIN, BRUSH AND DRAPER eds. (1995)   RAGUIN, V., BRUSH, K. AND DRAPER, P. eds., *Artistic Integration in Gothic Buildings*. Toronto, Buffalo and London, 1995.

RAHLVES (1969)   RAHLVES, F. *Cathedrales y Monasterios de España*. Barcelona, 1969.

RASMUSSEN (1986)   RASMUSSEN, N.K. 'The Liturgy at Saint-Denis', in P.L. Gerson, ed., *Abbot Suger of Saint-Denis: a Symposium*. New York, 1986, 41–7.

RAVAUX (1979)   RAVAUX, J.-P. 'Les Campagnes de Construction de la Cathédrale de Reims au XIIIe siècle', *Bulletin Monumental*, 137 (1979), 7–66.

RCHM   *Royal Commission on the Historical Monuments of England. Inventory of the Historical Monuments in London*, II, West London. London, 1925.

RECHT (1970)   RECHT, R. 'L'Architecture de la Chapelle Sainte-Catherine au XIVe siècle', *Bulletin de la Société des amis de la Cathédrale de Strasbourg*, 9 (1970), 95–101.

RECHT (1974)   RECHT, R. *L'Alsace gothique de 1300 á 1365*. Colmar, 1974.

RECHT (1980)   RECHT, R. 'Strasbourg et Prague', in A. Legner, ed., *Die Parler und der Schöne Stil 1350–1400. Europäische Kunst unter den Luxemburgern*. Exh. cat., Schnütgen Museum Köln, vol. 4. Cologne, 1980, 106–17.

RECHT (1981)   RECHT, R. 'Sur le dessin d'architecture gothique', in *Études d'art médiéval offertes à Louis Grodecki* (Paris, 1981), 233–54.

RECHT ed. (1989)   RECHT, R. ed., *Les Batisseurs des Cathédrales Gothiques*. Strasbourg, 1989.

REES JONES, MARKS AND MINNIS eds. (2000)   REES JONES, S., MARKS, R., MINNIS A.J. eds., *Courts and Regions in Medieval Europe* (York 2000).

REILLY (1997)   REILLY, L. 'The Emergence of Anglo-Norman Architecture: Durham Cathedral', *Anglo-Norman Studies*, 19 (1997), 335–51.

REILLY (1997a)   REILLY, L. *An Architectural History of Peterborough Cathedral*. Oxford, 1997.

REINHARDT (1939)   REINHARDT, H. 'La haute tour de la cathédrale de Strasbourg', *Bulletin de la Société des Amis de la cathédrale de Strasbourg*, 5 (1939), 15–40.

REINHARDT (1941)   REINHARDT, H. 'Johannes von Gmünd, Baumeister an den Münstern von Basel und Freiburg, und sein Sohn Michael von Freiburg, Werkmeister am Strassburger Münster', *Zeitschrift für Schweizerische Archäologie und Kunstgeschichte*, 3 (1941), 137–52.

REINHARDT (1961)   REINHARDT, H. *Das Basler Münster*, 3rd ed. Basel, 1961.

REINHARDT (1963)   REINHARDT, H. *La cathédrale de Reims. Son histoire, son architecture, sa sculpture, ses vitreaux*. Paris, 1963.

REINHARDT (1972)   REINHARDT, H. *La cathédrale de Strasbourg*. Arthaud, 1972.

REUDENBACH (1980)   REUDENBACH, B. 'Säule und Apostel', *Frühmittelalterliche Stiudien*, 14 (1980), 310–51.

REYNOLDS (1977)   REYNOLDS, S.R. *An Introduction to the History of English Medieval Towns*. Oxford, 1977.

REYNOLDS (1995)   REYNOLDS, R.E. 'Liturgy and the Monument', in V. Raguin, K. Brush and P. Draper, eds., *Artistic Integration in Gothic Buildings*. Toronto, Buffalo and London, 1995, 57–68.

RIBAULT (1995)   RIBAULT, J.-Y. *Un chef d'œuvre gothique: la cathédrale de Bourges*. Arceuil, 1995.

RICCETTI ed. (1988)   RICCETTI, L. ed., *Il duomo di Orvieto*. Bari, 1988.

RICETTI (1996)   RICETTI, L. 'Le Origini dell' Opera, Lorenzo Maitani e l'Architettura del Duomo di Orvieto', in *Opera carattere e ruolo delle fabbriche cittadine fino all'inizio dell'età moderna*, ed. by M. Haines and L. Ricetti. Florence, 1996, 157–265.

RIECKENBERG (1962)   RIECKENBERG, H.J. 'Der erste Kölner Dombaumeister Gerhard', *Archiv für Kulturgeschichte*, 441 (1962), 335–49.

RIEDL AND SEIDL (1992)   RIEDL, P.A. AND SEIDEL, M. eds., *Die Kirchen von Siena*, 2, i–iv. Munich, 1992.

RINGSHAUSEN (1973)   RINGSHAUSEN, G. 'Die Spätgotiche Architektur in Deutschland unter besonderer Berücksichtigung ihrer Beziehungen zu Burgund im Anfang des 15. Jahrhunderts', *Zeitschrift des deutschen Vereins für Kunstwissenschaft*, 27 (1973), 63–78.

ROCCHI (1982)   ROCCHI, G. *La Basilica di San Francesco ad Assisi – Interpretazione e Rilievo*. Florence, 1982.

ROCCHI (1988)   ROCCHI, G. et al., *Santa Maria del Fiore. Rilievi, documenti, indagini strumentali*. Milan, 1988.

RODE (1954)   RODE, H. 'Zur Baugeschichte des Kölner Domes', *Kölner Domblatt*, 8/9 (1954), 67–91.

RODE (1974)   RODE, H. 'Johannes' in *Neue Deutsche Biographie*, 10 (1974).

RODRIGUEZ GUTIÉRREZ DE CEBALLOS (1978)   RODRIGUEZ GUTIÉRREZ DE CEBALLOS, A. *Las catedrales de Salamanca*. León, 1978.

RODWELL (1989)   RODWELL, W. 'Archaeology and the standing fabric: recent studies at Lichfield Cathedral', *Antiquity*, 63 (1989), 281–94.

RODWELL (1993)   RODWELL, W. 'The Development of the Choir of Lichfield Cathedral', in *Medieval Archaeology and Architecture at Lichfield*, (British Archaeological Association Conference Transations for the year 1987, vol. 13). Leeds, 1993, 17–35.

ROLLASON, HARVEY AND PRESTWICH (1994)   ROLLASON, D., HARVEY, M. AND PRESTWICH, M. *Anglo-Norman Durham 1093–1193*. Bury St Edmunds, 1994.

ROMANINI (1973)   ROMANINI, A.M. 'L'Architettura', in C. Ferrari da Passano, A.M. Romanini *et al.*, *Il Duomo di Milano*, 2 vols. (Milan, 1973), vol. 1, 97–232.

ROMANINI (1980)   ROMANINI, A.M. *Arnolfo di Cambio*. Florence, 1980, 2nd edn.

RONIG (1978)   RONIG, F. 'Der Limburger Dom – die architektonische Gestalt in ihrer ikonologischen Bedeutung', *Das Münster*, Heft 41 (1978), 335–42.

ROSEMANN (1959)   ROSEMANN, H. 'Erwin', in *Neue Deutsche Biographie*, 4. Berlin, 1959, 636–7.

ROSEMANN (1961)   ROSEMANN, H. 'Bauentwicklung und Meisterfrage', in G. Fehring and A. Ress, eds., *Die Stadt Nürnberg (Bayerische Kunstdenkmale 10)*. Munich, 1961, 77–8.

ROSENBAUM (1955)   ROSENBAUM, E. 'The Vine Columns of Old St Peter's in Carolingian Canon Tables', *Journal of the Warburg and Courtauld Institutes*, 18 (1955), 1–15.

ROSENTHAL (1972)   ROSENTHAL, J.T. *The Purchase of Paradise*. Toronto, 1972.

ROTH (1988)   ROTH, E. 'Das Langhaus der Kathedrale von Rouen. Ein Wandaufbau im Viergeschossigen Aufrisssystem', in F. Much, ed., *Baukunst des Mittelalters in Europa. Hans Erich Kubach zum 75 Geburtstag*. Stuttgart, 1988, 351–70.

RUBINSTEIN (1995)   RUBINSTEIN, N. *The Palazzo Vecchio, 1298–1532. Government, Architecture and Imagery in the Civic Palace of the Florentine Republic*. Oxford, 1995.

RUDOLPH (1990)   RUDOLPH, C. *Artistic Change at St-Denis. Abbot Suger's Program and the Early Twelfth-Century Controversy over Art*. Princeton, 1990.

RUDOLPH (1990a)   RUDOLPH, C. *The Things of Greater Importance*. Philadelphia, 1990.

RUSSELL (1991)   RUSSELL, G. 'Some Aspects of the Decorated Tracery of Exeter Cathedral', in *Medieval Art and Architecture at Exeter Cathedral* (British Archaeological Association Conference Transactions for the year 1985, vol. 11). Leeds, 1991, 85–93.

SAALMAN (1962)   SAALMAN, H. 'Florence: Santa Trinità I and II and the "Crypt" under Santa Reparata and San Pier Scheraggio', *Journal of the Society of Architectural Historians*, 21 (1962), 179–87.

SAALMAN (1964)   SAALMAN, H. 'Santa Maria del Fiore: 1294–1418', *Art Bulletin*, 46 (1964), 471–500.

SAALMAN (1966)   SAALMAN, H. *The Church of Santa Trinità in Florence*. New York, 1966.

SAALMAN (1980)   SAALMAN, H. *Filippo Brunelleschi: The Cupola of Santa Maria del Fiore* (Studies in Architecture 20). London, 1980.

SALET (1943–44)   SALET, F. 'Voulton', *Bulletin Monumental*, 102 (1943–4), 91–115.

SALET (1951)   SALET, F. *Notre-Dame de Poissy*. Paris, 1951.

SALET (1955)   SALET, F. 'Saint-Urbain de Troyes', *Congrès Archéologique de France*, 113 (1955), 98–122.

SALET (1955a)   SALET, F. 'La Madeleine de Troyes', *Congrès Archéologique de France*, 113 (1955), 139–52.

SALET (1961)   SALET, F. 'La cathédrale du Mans', *Congrès Archéologique de France*, 119 (1961), 18–58.

SALET (1967)   SALET, F. 'Le premier colloque international de la Société française d'archéologie (Reims, 1965). Chronologie de la cathédrale', *Bulletin Monumental*, 125 (1967), 347–94.

SALET (1968)   SALET, F. 'Cluny III', *Bulletin Monumental*, 126 (1968), 235–92.

SALET (1977)   SALET, F. 'La cathédrale de Lausanne. A propos du septième centenaire de la consécration de 1275', *Bulletin Monumental*, 135 (1977), 21–41.

SALET (1980) SALET, F. 'La Cathédrale d'Evreux. Quelques Remarques'. *Congrès Archéologique de France*, 138 (1980), 300–13.

SALET (1982) SALE, F. 'Notre-Dame de Paris; état présent de la recherche', *La Sauvegarde de l'Art Français*, 2 (1982), 89–113.

SAMPSON (1998) SAMPSON, J. *Wells Cathedral West Front. Construction, Sculpture and Conservation*. Stroud 1998.

SANABRIA (1992) SANABRIA, S.L. 'A Late Gothic Drawing of San Juan de los Reyes in Toledo at the Prado Museum in Madrid', *Journal of the Society of Architectural Historians*, 51 (1992), 161–73.

SANABRIA (1982) SANABRIA, S.L. 'The mechanization of design in the 16th century: the structural formulae of Rodrigo Gil de Houtãnón, *Journal of the Society of Architectural Historians*, 41 (1982), 281–91.

SANDRON (1998) SANDRON, D. *La Cathédrale de Soissons. Architecture du Pouvoir*. Paris, 1998.

SANDRON (1999) SANDRON, D. 'La cathédrale et l'architecte: à propos de la façade occidentale de Laon', in Joubert and Sandron, eds. (1999), 133–150.

SANFAÇON (1971) SANFAÇON, R. *L'architecture Flamboyante en France*. Quebec, 1971.

SANVITO (1996) SANVITO, P. 'Le chantier de la cathédrale de Milan. Les probleme des origines', in *Cahiers Médiévaux*. La Pierre-qui-Vire, 1996, 291–325.

SAUER (1924) SAUER, J. *Symbolik des Kirchengebäudes und seiner Austattung in der Auffassung des Mittelalter*. Freiburg im Br., 1924.

SAUERLÄNDER (1958) SAUERLÄNDER, W. 'Die Marienkrönungsportale von Senlis und Mantes', *Wallraf-Richartz Jahrbuch*, 20 (1958), 115–62.

SAUERLÄNDER (1959) SAUERLÄNDER, W. 'Die Kunstgeschichtliche Stellung der Westportale von Notre-Dame in Paris. Ein Beitrag zur Genesis der hochgotischen Stiles in der Französischen Skulptur', *Marburger Jahrbuch für Kunstwissenschaft*, 17 (1959), 1–56.

SAUERLÄNDER (1965) SAUERLÄNDER, W. 'Über einen Reimser Bildhauer in Cluny', in *Gedenkschrift Ernst Gall* (Munich and Berlin 1965), 255–68.

SAUERLÄNDER (1966) SAUERLÄNDER, W. *Von Sens bis Strasbourg*. Berlin, 1966.

SAUERLÄNDER (1970) SAUERLÄNDER, W. 'Sculpture on Early Gothic Churches: The State of Research and Open Questions', *Gesta*, 9 (1970), 42–5.

SAUERLÄNDER (1972) SAUERLÄNDER, W. *Gothic Sculpture in France, 1140–1270*. London, 1972.

SAUERLÄNDER (1976) SAUERLÄNDER, W. 'Reims und Bamberg. Zu Art und Umfang der Übernahmen', *Zeitschrift für Kunstgeschichte*, 39 (1976), 167–92.

SAUERLÄNDER (1977) SAUERLÄNDER, W. 'Die Naumburger Stifterfiguren. Rückblick und Fragen', in R. Haussherr, ed., *Die Zeit der Staufer: Geschichte – Kunst – Kultur*. Exh. cat., Stuttgart, 1977, vol. 5. Stuttgart, 1979, 169–245.

SAUERLÄNDER (1987) SAUERLÄNDER, W. 'Style or Transition? The Fallacies of Classification in the Light of German Architecture 1190–1260', *Architectural History*, 30 (1987), 1–13.

SAUERLÄNDER (1992) SAUERLÄNDER, W. 'Observations sur la topographie et l'iconographie de la cathédrale du sacre', in *Académie des Inscriptions et Belles-Lettres. Comptes-Rendus* (1992), 463–79.

SAUERLÄNDER (1994) SAUERLÄNDER, W. 'Two Glances from the North: The Presence and Absence of Frederick II in the Art of the Empire; the Court Art of Frederick II and the *opus francigenum*', in W. Tronzo, ed., *Intellectual Life at the Court of Frederick II Hohenstaufen*. Studies in the History of Art, 44, [CASVA Symposium papers 25], National Gallery of Art, Washington, 1994, 189–209.

SAUERLÄNDER (1994a) SAUERLÄNDER, W. 'Die gestörte Ordnung oder "le chapiteau historié"' in H. Beck *et al.*, eds., *Studien zur Geschichte der europäischen Skulptur im 12. und 13. Jahrhundert*. Frankfurt/Main, 1994, 431–56.

SAUERLÄNDER (1995) SAUERLÄNDER, W. 'Integration: A closed or open proposal', and 'Integrated fragments and the unintegrated whole: scattered examples from Reims, Strasbourg, Chartres and Naumburg', in V. Raguin, K. Brush, P. Draper, eds. (1995), 1–18, 153–66.

SAUERLÄNDER (1995a) SAUERLÄNDER, W. 'Dal Gotico europeo in Italia al Gotico italiano in Europa', in *Il Gotico europeo*, ed. by V. Pace and M. Bagnoli. Naples, 1995, 8–21.

SAULNIER (1980) SAULNIER, L. 'Sens, palais synodal: la restauration de la sculpture', in B. Foucart *et al.*, eds., *Viollet-le-Duc*. Exh. cat., Grand Palais, Paris, 1980, 66–71.

SCAFF (1971) SCAFF, V. *La sculpture romane de la cathédrale Notre-Dame de Tournai*. Tournai, 1971.

SCHADE (1966) SCHADE, G. 'St Nikolai in Berlin. Ein Bauhistorischer Deutungsversuch des Hallenchores mit Kapellenkranz', *Jahrbuch für brandenburgische Landesgeschichte*, 17 (1966), 52–61.

SCHAEFER (1982) SCHAEFER, J.O. 'The Earliest Churches of the Cistercian Order', in M.P. Lillich, *Studies in Cistercian Architecture*, I (Cistercian Studies Series, 66). Kalamazoo, 1982, 1–12.

SCHÄFFOLD (1924) SCHÄFFOLD, M. *Das Ulmer Stadtbild von 1493–1850*. Ulm, 1924.

SCHAPIRO (1935) SCHAPIRO, M. 'New Documents on Saint-Gilles', *Art Bulletin*, 18 (1935), 414–31.

SCHENKLUHN (1983) SCHENKLUHN, W. 'Die Auswirkungen der Marburger Elisabethkirche auf die Ordensarchitektur in Deutschland', in H.-J. Kunst ed., *Die Elisabethkirche. Architektur in der Geschichte*, in *700 Jahre Elisabethkirche in Marburg 1283–1983*, vol. 1. Marburg, 1983, 81–101.

SCHENKLUHN (1985) SCHENKLUHN, W. *Ordines Studentes. Aspekte zur Kirchenarchitektur der Dominikaner und Franziskaner im 13. Jahrhundert*. Berlin, 1985.

SCHENKLUHN (1989) SCHENKLUHN, W. 'Die Erfindung der Hallenkirche in der Kunstgeschichte' *Marburger Jahrbuch für Kunstwissenschaft*, 22 (1989), 193–202.

SCHENKLUHN (1991) SCHENKLUHN, W. *San Francesco in Assisi: Ecclesia specialis. Der Vision Papst Gregors IX von einer Erneurung der Kirche*. Darmstadt, 1991.

SCHENKLUHN (2000) SCHENKLUHN, W. *Architektur der Bettelorden. Die Baukunst der Dominikaner und Franziskaner in Europa* Darmstadt, 2000.

SCHENKLUHN AND VAN STIPELN (1983) SCHENKLUHN, W. AND VAN STIPELN, P. 'Architektur als Zitat – Die Trier Liebfrauenkirche in Marburg', in H.J. Kunst ed., *Die Elisabethkirche. Architektur in der Geschichte*, in *700 Jahre Elisabethkirche in Marburg 1283–1983*, vol. 1. Marburg, 1983, 19–53.

SCHIFFLER (1977) SCHIFFLER, R. *Die Ostteile der Kathedrale von Toul und die davon abhängigen Bauten des 13. Jahrhunderts in Lothringen*. Cologne, 1977.

SCHIRMER et al. (1994) SCHIRMER, W., HELL, G., HESS, U., SACK, O., AND ZICK, W. 'Castel del Monte. Neue Forschungen zur Architektur Kaiser Friederichs II', *Architectura*, 24 (1994), 185–224.

SCHLEIF (1990) SCHLEIF, C. *Donatio et Memoria. Stifter, Stiftungen und Motivationen an Beispielen aus der Lorenzkirche in Nürnberg*. Munich, 1990.

SCHLINK (1970) SCHLINK, W. *Zwischen Cluny und Clairvaux. Die Kathedrale von Langres und die burgundische Architektur des 12. Jahrhunderts*. Berlin, 1970.

SCHLINK (1971) SCHLINK, W. 'Zur liturgischen Bestimmung der Michaelskapelle im Kloster Ebrach', *Architectura*, 1. 1971, 116–22.

SCHLINK (1975) SCHLINK, W. 'Berichte über der Kolloquium in Bamberg', *Kunstchronik*, 28 (1975), 400ff

SCHLINK (1989) SCHLINK, W. 'Der Bischofsgang', in E. Ullmann, ed., *Der Magdeburger Dom. Ottonische Gründung und staufischer Neubau*. (Schriftenreihe der Kommission für Niedersächsische Bau- und Kunstgeschichte bei der Braunschweigischen Wissenschaftlichen Gesellschaft, 5). Leipzig 1989, 141–6.

SCHLINK (1997/8) SCHLINK, W. 'The Gothic Cathedral as Heavenly Jerusalem. A Fiction in German Art History' in *The Real and Ideal Jerusalem in Jewish, Christian and Islamic Art (Jewish Art*, 23/24, 1997/8), 275–85.

SCHLINK (1999) SCHLINK, W. 'War Villard de Honnecourt Analphabet?' in Joubert and Sandron, eds. (1999), 213–21.

SCHMID (1955) SCHMID, B. *Die Marienburg. (Ihre Baugeschichte aus dem Nachlass herauszgegeben, ergänzt und mit Abbildungen versehen von Karl Hauke)*. Würzburg, 1955.

SCHMID (1977) SCHMID, E.D. *Nördlingen – die Georgskirche und St. Salvator*. Stuttgart and Aalen, 1977.

SCHMIDT (1970) SCHMIDT, G. 'Peter Parler und Heinrich IV Parler als Bildhauer', *Wiener Jahrbuch für Kunstgeschichte*, 23 (1970), 136–9.

SCHMIDT (1962) SCHMIDT, O. 'Zur Geschichte der Martinskirche Amberg', *Oberpfälzer Heimat*, 7 (1962), 82–94.

SCHMIDT (1977) SCHMIDT, O. *St Martin Amberg* (Schnell Kunstführer 695). Munich, 1977.

SCHMIDT (1972) SCHMIDT, R. 'Hans Engl von Köln der Parlierer und sein Bruder Andreas der Dommeister zu Regensburg', *Verhandlungen des historischen Vereins von Oberpfalz und Regensburg*, 112 (1972), 131–56.

SCHMITT (1951) SCHMITT, O. *Das Heiligkreuz-Münster in Schwäbisch-Gmünd*. Stuttgart, 1951.

SCHMOLL GEN. EISENWERTH (1958) SCHMOLL GEN. EISENWERTH, J.A. 'Zisterzienser-Romanik. Kritische Gedanken zur jüngsten Literatur', in *Formositas Romanica: Joseph Ganter zugeeignet*. Frauenfeld, 1958, 153–80.

SCHOCK-WERNER (1978) SCHOCK-WERNER, B. 'Die Parler' in A. Legner ed., *Die Parler und der Schöne Stil 1350–1400. Europäische Kunst unter den Luxemburgern*. Exh. cat., Schnütgen Museum Köln, vol. 3. Cologne, 1978, 7–12.

SCHOCK-WERNER (1983) SCHOCK-WERNER, B. *Das Strassburger Münster im 15. Jahrhundert* (Veröffentlichung der Abteilung Architektur des Kunsthistorischen Instituts der Universität zu Köln). Cologne, 1983.

SCHOFIELD (1989) SCHOFIELD, R. 'Amadeo, Bramante and Leonardo and the tiburio of Milan cathedral', *Achademia Leonardi Vinci*, 2 (1989), 68–100.

SCHÖLLER (1980) SCHÖLLER, W. 'Eine mittelalterliche Architekturzeichnung im südlichen Querhausarm der Kathedrale von Soissons', *Zeitschrift für Kunstgeschichte*, 43 (1980), 196–202.

SCHÖLLER (1988) SCHÖLLER, W. 'Die Kölner Domfabrik im 13. und 14. Jahrhundert', 44/45, *Kölner Domblatt* (1988), 75–94.

SCHÖLLER (1989) SCHÖLLER, W. *Die rechtliche Organisation des Kirchenbaues im Mittelalter vornehmlich des Kathedralbaues.* Cologne, Vienna, 1989.

SCHÖNEMANN (1963) SCHÖNEMANN, H. 'Die Baugeschichte der Annenkirche in Annaberg', *Wissenschaftliche Zeitschrift der Martin-Luther-Universität Halle Wittenberg* (Gesellschaft- und sprachwissenschaftliche Reihe, 11) (1963), 745–56.

SCHRÖDER (1977) SCHRÖDER, U. 'Royaumont oder Köln? Zum Problem der Ableitung der gotischen Zisterzienser-Abteikirche Altenberg', *Kölner Domblatt*, 42 (1977), 209–42.

SCHUBERT (1964) SCHUBERT, E. *Der Westchor der Naumburger Doms. Ein Beitrag zur Datierung und zum Verständnis der Standbilder* (Abhandlungen der deutschen Akademie der Wissenschaft zu Berlin. Klasse für Sprachen, Literatur, und Kunst 1964 I). Berlin, 1964.

SCHUBERT (1968) SCHUBERT, E. *Der Naumburger Dom.* Berlin, 1968.

SCHUBERT (1975) SCHUBERT, E. *Der Magdeburger Dom.* Vienna-Cologne, 1975.

SCHUBERT (1982) SCHUBERT, E. 'Zur Naumburger Forschung der letzten Jahrzehnte', *Wiener Jahrbuch für Kunstgeschichte*, 35 (1982), 121–38.

SCHUBERT (1989) SCHUBERT, E. 'Der Magdeburg Dom. Ottonische Gründung und staufischer Neubau', in E. Ullman, ed., *Der Magdeburger Dom. Ottonische Gründung und Staufischer Neubau* (Schriftenreihe der Kommission für Niedersächsische Bau- und Kunstgeschichte bei der Braunschweigischen Wissenschaftlichen Gesellschaft, 5). Leipzig, 1989, 25–44.

SCHUBERT (1991) SCHUBERT, E. 'Memorialdenkmäler für Fundatoren in drei Naumburger Kirchen des Hochmittelalters', *Frühmittelalterliche Studien*, 25 (1991), 188–225.

SCHUBERT (1996) SCHUBERT, E. *Der Naumburger Dom.* Halle an der Saale, 1996.

SCHULLER (1989) SCHULLER, M. 'Bauforschung' in *Der Dom zu Regensburg. Ausgrabung, Restaurierung, Forschung* (exhibition to mark the restoration of the interior of the cathedral, 1984–1988) (Kunstsammlungen des Bistums Regensburg, Diözesanmuseum Regensburg, Kataloge und Schriften, 8). Munich and Zürich 1989, 168–223.

SCHULZ (1943) SCHULZ, O. 'Der Chorbau von St Lorenz zu Nürnberg und seine Baumeister', *Zeitschrift des deutschen Vereins für Kunstwissenschaft*, 10 (1943), 55–80.

SCHURR (1998) SCHURR, E. 'Die Skulpturen im Bamberger Dom', in U. Vorwerk and E. Schurr, eds., *Die Andechs-Meranier in Franken, Europäisches Fürstentum im Hochmittelalter.* Mainz, 1998, 219–26.

SCHÜTZ (1982) SCHÜTZ, B. *Die Katharinenkirche in Oppenheim* (Beiträge zur Kunstgeschichte, 17). Berlin and New York, 1982.

SCHÜTZ AND MÜLLER (1989) SCHÜTZ, B. AND MÜLLER, W. *Deutsche Romanik. Die Kirchenbauten der Kaiser, Bischöfe und Klöster.* Freiburg, Basel and Vienna, 1989.

SCHWARTZ (1979) SCHWARTZ, H. *Soest und seine Denkmäler*, 3. Soest, 1979.

SCHWATZ (1957) SCHWATZ, E. *Geschichte der St Marienkirche zu Prenzlau.* Celle, 1957.

SCHWARTZBAUM (1977) SCHWARTZBAUM, E. 'The Romanesque Sculpture of the Cathedral of Tournai', Doctoral Diss. Institute of Fine Arts, New York University, 1977.

SCIURIE AND MÖBIUS (1989) SCIURIE, H. AND MÖBIUS, F. *Der Naumburger Westchor. Figurenzyklus, Architektur, Idee.* Worms, 1989.

SCIURIE AND MÖBIUS eds. (1989) SCIURIE, H. AND MÖBIUS, F. eds., *Geschichte der deutschen Kunst 1200–1350.* Leipzig, 1989.

SEDLMAYR (1950) SEDLMAYR, H. *Die Entstehung der Kathedrale* Zurich 1950. 2nd edtn. Graz, 1976.

SEDLMAYR (1959) SEDLMAYR, H. 'Die dichterische Wurzel der Kathedrale', in *Epochen und Werke* (Gesammelte Schriften zur Kunstgeschichte, 1). Vienna and Munich, 1959, 155–69.

SEEGER (1992) SEEGER, U. 'Der Ostchor der Nürnberger Pfarrkirche St Sebald – Popularisierung eines Heiligen', *Architectura*, 22 (1992), 35–46.

SEEGER (1997) SEEGER, U. *Zisterzienser und Gotikrezeption. Die Bautätigkeit des Babenbergers Leopold VI in Lilienfeld und Klosterneuburg.* Munich and Berlin, 1997.

SEELIGER (1962) SEELIGER, H. *Die Stadtkirche in Friedberg in Hessen.* Darmstadt, 1961/62.

SEELIGER-ZEISS (1967) SEELIGER-ZEISS, A. *Lorenz Lechler von Heidelberg und sein Umkreis* (Studien zur Geschichte der spätgotischen Zierarchitektur und Skulptur in der Kurpfalz und in Schwaben). Heidelberg, 1967.

SEKULES (1986) SEKULES, V. 'The Tomb of Christ at Lincoln and the Development of the Sacrament Shrine: Easter Sepulchres Reconsidered', in *Medieval Art and Architecture at Lincoln Cathedral* (British Archaeological Association Conference Transactions for 1982, vol. 8). Leeds, 1986, 118–31.

SEKULES (1991) SEKULES, V. 'The Liturgical Furnishings of the Choir of

Exeter Cathedral' in *Medieval Art and Architecture at Exeter Cathedral* (British Archaeological Association Conference Transactions for 1985, vol. 11). Leeds, 1991, 172–9.

SEVERENS (1970) SEVERENS, K.W. 'The Early Campaign at Sens, 1140–1145', *Journal of the Society of Architectural Historians*, 29 (1970), 97–107.

SEVERENS (1975) SEVERENS, K.W. 'The Continuous Plan of Sens Cathedral', *Journal of the Society of Architectural Historians*, 34 (1975), 198–207.

SEYMOUR (1968) SEYMOUR, C. *Notre-Dame of Noyon in the Twelfth Century. A Study in the early Development of Gothic Architecture.* New York, 1968, (2nd edtn.)

SHELBY (1972) SHELBY, L.R. 'The Geometrical Knowledge of Medieval Master Masons', *Speculum*, 47 (1972), 395–421.

SHELBY (1977) SHELBY, L.R. *Gothic Design Techniques. The Fifteenth-Century Design Booklets of Mathes Roriczer and Hanns Schmuttermayer.* Southern Illinois University Press, 1977.

SHELBY (1981) SHELBY, L.R. 'The Contractors of Chartres', *Gesta*, 20 (1981), 173–8.

SHILLABER (1947) SHILLABER, C. 'Edward I, builder of towns', *Speculum*, 22 (1947), 297–30.

SIMMONS (1992) SIMMONS, L.N. 'The Abbey Church at Fontevraud in the Later Twelfth Century; Anxiety, Authority and Architecture in the Female Spiritual Life', *Gesta*, 31 (1992), 99–107.

SIMPSON (1996) SIMPSON, G. 'Documentary and Dendrochronological Evidence for the Build-ing of Salisbury Cathedral' in *Medieval Art and Architecture at Salisbury Cathedral* (British Archaeological Association Conference Transactions, vol. 17). Leeds, 1996, 10–20.

SINGLETON (1981) SINGLETON, B. 'Proportions in the Design of the Early Gothic Cathedral at Wells', in *Medieval Art and Architecture at Wells and Glastonbury* (British Archaeological Association Conference Transactions for 1978, vol. 4). Leeds, 1981, 10–17.

SKIBIŃSKI (1982) SKIBIŃSKI, S. *Kaplica na Zamku Wysokim w Malborku* (Uniwersytet im Adama Mickiewicza w Poznaniu, Seria Historia Sztuki, 14). Poznań, 1982.

SNAPE (1980) SNAPE, M.G. 'Documentary Evidence for the Building of Durham Cathedral and its Monastic Buildings', in *Medieval Art and Architecture at Durham Cathedral* (British Archaeological Association Conference Transactions for 1977, vol. 3). Leeds, 1980, 20–36.

SOUTHERN (1983) SOUTHERN, R.W. *Western Society and the Church in the Middle Ages.* London, 1983.

SOWELL (1982) SOWELL, J.E. 'Sacramenia in Spain and Florida: A Preliminary Assessment', in M.P. Lillich, *Studies in Cistercian Architecture*, 1. Kalamazoo, 1982, 71–7.

SOWELL (1985) SOWELL, J.E. 'The Monastery of Sacramenia and Twelfth-Century Cistercian Architecture in Spain'. Ph.D. thesis, Florida State University, 1985.

SPEER (1987) SPEER, A. 'Kunst als Liturgie: zur Entstehung und Bedeutung der Kathedrale', in C. Dohmen and T. Sternberg, eds., *Kein Bildnis Machen: Kunst und Theologie im Gespräch.* Würzburg, 1987, 97–117.

ŠPERLING (1965) ŠPERLING, I. 'Rejskova sochařská vyzdoba prašné brány', *Umění*, 13 (1965), 403–13.

SPIEGEL (1986) SPIEGEL, G. 'History as Enlightenment: Suger and the *Mos Anagogicus*', in P.L. Gerson, ed., *Abbot Suger of Saint-Denis: a Symposium.* New York, 1986, 151–8.

SPRING (1987) SPRING, R. *Salisbury Cathedral* (New Bell's Cathedral Guides). London, 1987.

STAHLEDER (1971) STAHLEDER, E. 'Hans von Burghausen im Dienst der Straubinger Herzöge', *Verhandlungen des historischen Vereins für Niederbayern*, 97 (1971), 73–89.

STALLEY (1987) STALLEY, R. *The Cistercian Monasteries of Ireland.* New Haven and London, 1987.

STANGE (1964) STANGE, A. *Basiliken, Kuppelkirchen, Kathedralen. Das himmlische Jerusalem in der Sicht der Jahrhunderte.* Regensburg, 1964.

STANSBURY-O'DONNELL STANSBURY-O'DONNELL, M. *The Shape of the Church: the Relationship of Architecture, Art and Liturgy at the Cathedral of Trier.* Ann Arbor, 1991.

STEINKE (1974) STEINKE, W.A. 'The Influence of the English Decorated Style on the Continent: Saint James in Torun and Lincoln Cathedral', *Art Bulletin*, 56 (1974), 505–16.

STEINKE (1974a) STEINKE, W.A. 'Die Briefkapelle zu Lübeck: ihre Herkunft und ihre Beziehung zum Kapitelsaal der Marienburg', *Jahrbuch des St Marien-Bauvereins* (Lübeck), 8 (1974), 55–71.

STEINKE (1982) STEINKE, W.A. 'The Flamboyant Church of Caudebec-en-Caux: A Neglected Masterpiece of French Medieval Architecture'. Ph.D. thesis, New York University, 1982.

STEJSKAL (1978) STEJSKAL, K. *European Art in the Fourteenth Century.* Prague, 1978.

STICH (1960) STICH, F. *Der Gotischen Kirchenbau in der Pfalz*

(Veröffentlichungen der Pfälzischen Gesellschaft zur Förderung der Wissenschaften in Speyer am Rhein, 40). Kaiserslautern, 1960.

STODDARD (1973)   STODDARD, S. *The Façade of Saint-Gilles-du-Garde. Its Influence of French Sculpture*. Conneticut, 1973.

STOOKEY (1969)   STOOKEY, L.H. 'The Gothic Cathedral as the Heavenly Jerusalem: Liturgical and Theological Sources', *Gesta*, 8 (1969), 35–41.

STOLZ (1977)   STOLZ, G. 'Die zwei Schwestern. Gedanken zum Bau des Lorenzer Hallenchores 1439–1477', in H. Bauer *et al.*, eds., *500 Jahre Hallenchor St Lorenz zu Nürnberg 1477–1977*. Nuremberg, 1977, 1–19.

STRATFORD AND SAULNIER (1984)   STRATFORD, N. AND SAULNIER, L. *La Sculpture Oubliée de Vézelay*. Geneva, 1984.

STREET (1914)   STREET, G.E. *Some Account of Gothic Architecture in Spain*. Rev. ed., London and Toronto, 1914.

STUBBS (ed.) (1879–80)   STUBBS, W. ed., *Gervasii Cantuariensis Opera Historica*, 2 vols. London, 1879–80, vol. 1: 'Tractatus de Constructione et Reparatione Cantuariensis Ecclesiae', 3–19.

STULIN (1982)   STULIN, S.J. 'Drogi kształtowania się stylu regionalnego architektury sakralnej na Śląsku około 1320–1370', unpublished dissertation, Institute of History of Architecture, Art and Technical Studies, Wrocław, 1982.

STURGIS (1991)   STURGIS, A.J. 'The Liturgy and its Relation to Gothic Cathedral Design and Ornamentation in Late Twelfth and Early Thirteenth-Century France'. Ph.D. thesis, Courtauld Institue of Art, University of London, 1991.

SUCKALE (1980)   SUCKALE, R. 'Peter Parler und das Problem der Stillagen', in A. Legner, ed., *Die Parler und der Schöne Stil 1350–1400. Europäische Kunst unter den Luxemburgern*. Exh. cat., Schnütgen Museum, Cologne, vol. 4. Cologne, 1980, 175–83.

SUCKALE (1981)   SUCKALE, R. 'Thesen zum Bedeutungswandel der gotischen Fensterrose', in K. Clausberg, *et al.*, eds., *Bauwerk und Bildwerk im Hochmittelalter. Anschauliche Beiträge zur Kultur- und Sozialgeschichte* (Kunstwissenschaftliche Untersuchungen des Ulmer Vereins für Kunst- und Kulturwissenschaft, 11). Giessen, 1981, 259–94.

SUCKALE (1989)   SUCKALE, R. 'Pierre de Montreuil', in R. Recht, ed., *Les Batisseurs des Cathédrales Gothiques*. Strasbourg, 1989, 181–5.

SUCKALE (1990)   SUCKALE, R. 'Neue Literatur über die Abteikirche von Saint-Denis', *Kunstchronik*, 43 (1990), 62–81.

SUCKALE (1993)   SUCKALE, R. *Die Hofkunst Kaiser Ludwig des Bayern*. Munich, 1993.

SUNDT (1987)   SUNDT, R.A. 'Mediocres domos et humiles habeant fratres nostri: Dominican Legislation on Architecture and Architectural Decoration in the 13th Century', *Journal of the Sociey of Architectural Historians*, 46 (1987), 394–407.

SUNDT (1989)   SUNDT, R.A. 'The Jacobins Church of Toulouse and the Origin of its Double-Nave Plan', *Art Bulletin*, 71 (1989), 185–207.

SWARTLING (1967)   SWARTLING, I. 'Cistercian Abbey Churches in Sweden and the "Bernardine Plan"', *Nordisk medeltid. Konsthistorika studier tillägnade Armin Tuulse* (Acta Univeresitatis Stockholmiensis, 13). Uppsala, 1967, 193–8.

SWARTLING (1969)   SWARTLING, I. *Alvastra Abbey. The First Cistercian Settlement in Sweden*. Stockholm, 1969.

TAKÁCS (1998)   TAKÁCS, I. 'Fragmente des Grabmals der Königin Gertrudis', in E. Schurr und U. Vorwerk, eds., *Die Andechs-Meranier in Franken. Europäisches Furstentum im Hochmittelalter*. Mainz 1998, 103–9.

TALBOT (1986)   TALBOT, C.H. 'The Cistercian attitude towards art: the literary evidence', in C. Norton and D. Park, eds., *Cistercian Art and Architecture in the British Isles*. Cambridge, London, New York, 1986, 56–64.

TARALON (1991)   TARALON, J. 'Observations sur le portal central et sur la façade occidentale de Notre-Dame de Paris', *Bulletin Monumental*, 149 (1991), 341–432.

TAMIR (1946)   TAMIR, M.M. 'The English Origin of the Flamboyant Style', *Gazette des Beaux-Arts*, 6, ser., 29 (1946), 257–68.

TATTON-BROWN (1991)   TATTON-BROWN, T. 'Building the tower and spire of Salisbury Cathedral', *Antiquity*, 65 (1991), 74–96.

TATTON-BROWN (1996)   TATTON-BROWN, T. 'The Archaeology of the Spire of Salisbury Cathedral', in *Medieval Art and Architecture at Salisbury Cathedral* (British Archaeological Association Conference Transactions vol. 17). Leeds, 1996, 59–67.

TAYLOR (1963)   TAYLOR, A.J. 'The king's works in Wales 1277–1330' in R. Allen Brown, H. Colvin and A.J. Taylor, *The History of the King's Works*, vol. 1. London, 1963, 293–422.

TEUSCHER (1994)   TEUSCHER, A. *Das Pramonstratenserkloster Saint-Yved in Braine als Grablege der Grafen von Dreux. Zu Stifterverhalten und Grabmalgestaltung im Frankreich des 13 Jahrhunderts* (Bamberger Studien zur Kunstgeschichte und Denkmalpflege, 7). Bamberg, 1990.

TEYSSOT (1992)   TEYSSOT, J. 'Une grand chantier de construction à la fin du XIVe siècle en Auvergne: le palais ducal de Riom', *Bulletin historique et scientifique de l'Auvergne*, 96 (1992), 151–66.

THIEBAULT (1975)   THIEBAULT, J. 'L'architecture gothique flamboyante en Haute-Normandie', *Cahiers Leopold Delisle*, 24 (1975), 3–13.

THIRION (1974)   THIRION, J. 'La Cathédrale de Bayeux', *Congrès Archéologique de France*, 122 (1974), 240–85.

THOMPSON (1987)   THOMPSON, M.W. *The Decline of the Castle*. London, 1987.

THÜMMLER (1958)   THÜMMLER, H. 'Westfälische und italienische Hallenkirchen', in *Festschrift Martin Wackernagel zum 75. Geburtstag*. Cologne and Graz, 1958, 17–36.

THÜMMLER (1962)   THÜMMLER, H. 'Die vorgotischen Hallenkirchen im Regensburger Raum', *Kunstchronik*, 15 (1962), 290–2.

THÜMMLER AND KREFT (1970)   THÜMMLER, H. AND KREFT, H. *Weser Baukunst im Mittelalter*. Hameln, 1970.

THÜMMLER AND BADENHEUER (1973)   THÜMMLER, H. AND BADENHEUER, F. *Romanik in Westfalen*. Munich, 1973.

THURLBY (1993)   THURLBY, M. 'The Romanesque high vaults of Durham Cathedral', in M. Jackson, ed., *Engineering a Cathedral* (Proceedings of the Conference 'Engineering a Cathedral' held at Durham in September 1993). London, 1993, 43–63.

THURLBY (1993a)   THURLBY, M. 'The purpose of the rib in the Romanesque vaults of Durham', in M. Jackson, ed., *Engineering a Cathedral* (Proceedings of the Conference 'Engineering a Cathedral' held at Durham in September 1993). London, 1993, 64–76.

THURLBY (1994)   THURLBY, M. 'The Roles of the Patron and the Master Mason in the First Design of the Romanesque Cathedral of Durham', in D. Rollason, M. Prestwich, eds., (1994), 161–84.

TILLET (1982)   TILLET, L.-M. *Bretagne Roman*. La Pierre-qui-Vire, 1982.

TILLMANN (1958–61)   TILLMANN, C. *Lexikon der deutschen Burgen und Schlösser*, 4 vols. Stuttgart, 1958–61.

TIMMERMANN (1996)   TIMMERMANN, A. 'Staging the Eucharist: Late Gothic Sacrament Houses in Swabia and the Upper Rhine'. Ph.D. thesis, Courtauld Institute of Art, London University, 1996.

TIMMERMANN (2000)   TIMMERMANN, A. 'Architectural vision in Albrecht von Scharfenberg's *Jüngerer Titurel* – a Vision of Architecture?' in G. Clarke and P. Crossley, eds., *Architecture and Language. Constructing Identity in European Architecture c.1100–c.1650*, Cambridge, 2000, 58–71.

TINTELNOT (1951)   TINTELNOT, H. *Die mittelalterliche Baukunst Schlesiens*. Kitzingen 1951.

TITUS (1984)   TITUS, H.B. *The Architectural History of Auxerre Cathedral*. Ann Arbor, 1984.

TITUS (1988)   TITUS, H.B. 'The Auxerre Cathedral Choir and Burgundian Gothic Architecture', *Journal of the Society of Architectural Historians*, 47 (1988), 45–56.

TOKER (1978)   TOKER, F. 'Florence Cathedral: The Design Stage', *Art Bulletin*, 60 (1978), 214–31.

TOKER (1983)   TOKER, F. 'Arnolfo's S. Maria del Fiore: A working Hypothesis', *Journal of the Society of Architectural Historians*, 42 (1983), 101–20.

TORBUS (1994)   TORBUS, T. 'Die Burgen des Deutschen Ordens in Preussen', *Berichte und Forschungen*, 2 (1994), 101–22.

TORBUS (1998)   TORBUS, T. *Die Konventsburgen im Deutschordensland Preussen* (Schriftum des Bundesinstituts für ostdeutsche Kultur und Geschichte, 11). Munich, 1998.

TORRES BALBÁS (1952)   TORRES BALBÁS, L. 'Arquitectura gótica', in *Ars Hispaniae*, 7. Madrid, 1952.

TOURSEL-HORSTER (1976)   TOURSEL-HORSTER, J.D. 'Le portail Saint-Laurent de la cathédrale de Strasbourg. Architecture et sculpture'. Dissertation, University of Strasbourg, 1976.

TRACHTENBERG (1971)   TRACHTENBERG, M. *The Campanile of Florence Cathedral. 'Giotto's Tower'*. New York, 1971.

TRACHTENBERG (1979)   TRACHTENBERG, M. review of G. Kreytenberg, *Der Dom zu Florenz*, *Art Bulletin*, 61 (1979), 112–31.

TRACHTENBERG (1988)   TRACHTENBERG, M. 'What Brunelleschi saw: Monument and Site at the Palazzo Vecchio in Florence', *Journal of the Society of Architectural Historians*, 47 (1988), 14–49.

TRACHTENBERG (1989)   TRACHTENBERG, M. 'Archaeology, Merriment and Murder: the First Cortile of the Palazzo Vecchio and its Transformations in the Late Florentine Republic', *Art Bulletin* (1989), 565–609.

TRACHTENBERG (1991)   TRACHTENBERG, M. 'Gothic/Italian Gothic: Towards a Redefinition', *Journal of the Society of Architectural Historians*, 50 (1991), 22–37.

TRACHTENBERG (1993)   TRACHTENBERG, M. 'Scénographie urbaine et identité civique: réflexion sur la Florence du Trecento', *Revue de l'Art*, 96 (1993), 11–31.

TRACHTENBERG (1997)   TRACHTENBERG, M. *Dominion of the Eye-Urbanism, Art and Power in Early Modern Florence*. Cambridge, 1997.

TRACY (1987)   TRACY, C. 'Exeter Bishop's Throne' in J. Alexander and P. Binski, eds., *Age of Chivalry. Art in Plantagenet England 1200–1400*. London, Royal Academy, 1987, 412.

TRIPPS (1998)   TRIPPS, J. *Der handelnde Bildwerk in den Gotik. Forschungen zu den Bedeutungsschichten und der Funktion des Kirchengebäudes und seiner Ausstattung in der Hoch- und Spätgotik.* Berlin, 1998.

TROMBETTA (1972)   TROMBETTA, P.-J. 'L'architecture gothique dans l'anciens diocèse de Senlis a partir de 1260', *L'Information d'Histoire de l'Art*, 17 (1972), 46–8.

TRÜMPLER (1993)   TRÜMPLER, S. 'Realität und Integration. Neue Erkenntnisse zum Rosenfenster der Kathedrale von Lausanne', in T.W. Gaeghtgens, ed., *Kunstlerische Austauch. Artistic Exchange* (Akten des XXVI-II Internationalen Kongresses für Kunstgeschichte). Berlin, 1993, vol. 3, 401–12.

TUCZEK (1971)   TUCZEK, A. 'Das Masswerk der Elisabethkirche in Marburg und der Liebfrauenkirche in Trier', *Hessisches Jahrbuch für Landesgeschichte*, 21 (1971), 1–99.

TURNER ed. (1996)   TURNER, J. ed., *The Dictionary of Art*, 34 vols. London, 1996.

ULLMANN ed. (1984)   ULLMANN, E. ed., *Geschichte der deutschen Kunst 1470–1550, Architektur und Plastik.* Leipzig, 1984.

ULLMANN (1987)   ULLMANN, E. 'Spätgotische Hallenkirchen in Obersachsen', in *Von der Romanik bis zum Historismus. Architektur – Stil und Bedeutung.* Leipzig, 1987, 92–104.

ULLMANN, ed. (1989)   ULLMANN, E. ed., *Der Magdeburger Dom, ottonische Gründung und staufischer Neubau.* (Schriftenreihe der Kommission für Niedersächsische Bau- und Kunstgeschichte bei der Braunschweigischen Wissenschaftlichen Gesellschaft, 5) (Leipzig 1989).

ULM (1962)   ULM, B. 'Der Begriff "Donauschule" in der spätgotischen Architektur', *Christliche Kunstblätter*, 3 (1962), 82–7.

UNTERMANN (1984)   UNTERMANN, M. *Kirchenbauten der Prämonstratenser. Untersuchungen zum Problem einer Ordensbaukunst im 12. Jahrhundert* (Veröffentlichung der Abteilung Architektur des Kunsthistorischen Instituts der Universität zu Köln, 29). Cologne, 1984.

UNTERMANN (1989)   UNTERMANN, M. *Der Zentralbau im Mittelalter. Form – Funktion – Verbreitung.* Darmstadt, 1989. URBAN (1961/62)   URBAN, G. 'Die Kirchenbaukunst des Quattrocento in Rom', *Römisches Jahrbuch für Kunstgeschichte*, 9/10 (1961/62), 75–124.

VALLANCE (1936)   VALLANCE, A. *English Church Screens.* London, 1936.

VALLANCE (1947)   VALLANCE, A. *Greater English Church Screens.* London, 1947.

VALLERY-RADOT (1958)   VALLERY-RADOT, J. 'Auxerre. La Cathédrale Saint-Etienne. Les Principaux Textes de l'Histoire de la Construction', *Congrès Archéologique de France*, 116 (1958), 40–75.

VALLERY-RADOT (1966)   VALLERY-RADOT, J. 'Le Mont-Saint-Michel. Travaux et Découvertes', *Congrès Archéologique*, 124 (1966), 433–46.

VAN BRABANT (1972)   VAN BRABANT, J. *Onze-Lieve-Vrouwekathedraal van Antwerpen. Grootste gotische Kerk der Nederlanden.* Antwerp, 1972.

VAN DER MEER (1965)   VAN DER MEER, F. *Atlas de l'Ordre Cistercien.* Haarlem, 1965.

VAN DER MEULEN (1959)   VAN DER MEULEN, J. 'Die baukünstlerische Problematik der Salzburger Franziskanerkirche', *Österreichische Zeitschrift für Kunst- und Denkmalpflege*, 13 (1959), 52–9.

VAN DER MEULEN (1965)   VAN DER MEULEN, J. 'Die Baugeschichte der Kathedrale Notre-Dame de Chartres', *Mémoires de la Société archéologique d'Eure et Loire*, 23 (1965), 79–126.

VAN DER MEULEN (1967)   VAN DER MEULEN, J. 'Recent Literature on the Chronology of Chartres Cathedral', *Art Bulletin*, 49 (1967), 159–64.

VAN DER MEULEN (1975)   VAN DER MEULEN, J. *Notre-Dame de Chartres. Die vorromanische Ostanlage.* Berlin, 1975.

VAN DER MEULEN (1984a)   VAN DER MEULEN, J. review of J. James, *Chartres. The Masons who Built a Legend*, in *The Catholic Historical Review* 70, (1984), 83–9.

VAN DER MEULEN (1984)   VAN DER MEULEN, J. AND HOHMEYER, J. *Chartres. Biographie der Kathedrale.* Cologne, 1984.

VAN DER MEULEN AND A. SPEER (1988)   VAN DER MEULEN, J. AND SPEER, A. *Die Fränkische Königsabtei Saint-Denis. Ostanlage und Kultgeschichte.* Darmstadt, 1988.

VAN DER MEULEN (1989)   VAN DER MEULEN, J., HOYER, R., AND COLE, D. *Chartres. Sources and Literary Interpretation: A Critical Bibliography.* Boston, 1989.

VAN LANGENDONCK (1987)   VAN LANGENDONCK, L. 'De Sint-Romboutstoren te Mechelen en zijn plaats in de laatgotische architectur', in H. Janse, R. Meischke, J.H. van Mosselveld, F. van Tyghem, eds., *Keldermans. Een architectonisch netwerk in de Nederlanden*, 's-Gravenhage, 1987, 27–59.

VAN WYLICK-WESTERMANN (1987)   VAN WYLICH-WESTERMANN, C.G.M. 'Het Bouwmeestergeslacht Keldermans', in H. Janse, R. Meischke, J.H. van Mosselveld, F. van Tyghem, eds., *Keldermans. Een architectonisch netwerk in de Nederlanden* 's-Gravenhage, 1987, 9–25.

VERBECK (1980)   VERBECK, A. 'Zisterzienser und Heisterbach', in: *Zisterzienser und Heisterbach. Spuren und Erinnerungen* (exh. cat., Königswinter, 1980) (Schriften des Rheinischen Museumsamtes, 15). Bonn, 1980, 37–44.

VERDELHO DA COSTA (1996)   VERDELHO DA COSTA, L. 'Batalha', in J. Turner, ed., *The Dictionary of Art*, vol. 3. London, 1996, 362–3.

VERDIER (1980)   VERDIER, F. 'L'Eglise Paroissiale Notre-Dame de Louviers', *Congrès Archéologique de France*, 138 (1980), 9–28.

VERMAND (1987)   VERMAND, D. *La cathédrale Notre-Dame de Senlis au XIIe siècle. Étude historique et monumentale* (Société d'histoire et d'archéologie de Senlis, 1987) ed. by D. Vermand, 4–107.

VERZONE (1934)   VERZONE, P. *L'architettura romanica nel Vercellese.* Vercelli, 1934.

VERZONE (1935/36)   VERZONE, P. *L'architettura romanica nel Novarese.* Novara, 1935/36.

VICENS (1970)   VICENS, F. *Catedral de Tarragona.* Barcelona, 1970.

VIDAL et al. (1979)   VIDAL, et al., *Quercy Roman.* Zodiaque, 1979.

VIEIRA DA SILVA (1987)   VIEIRA DA SILVA, J.C. *A igreja de Jesus de Setúbal.* Setúbal, 1987.

VIEIRA DA SILVA (1990)   VIEIRA DA SILVA, J.C. *Setúbal.* Lisbon, 1990.

VIEIRA DA SILVA (1996)   VIEIRA DA SILVA, C. 'Belém', in J. Turner, ed., *The Dictionary of Art*, vol. 3. London, 1996, 534–5.

VIEIRA DA SILVA (1996a)   VIEIRA DA SILVA, J.C. 'Boitac', in J. Turner, ed., *The Dictionalry of Art*, vol. 4, London, 1996, 245–6.

VILLES (1972)   VILLES, A. 'Les campagnes de construction de la cathédrale de Toul. Première partie: Les campagnes du XIIIe siècle', *Bulletin Monumental*, 130 (1972), 179–89.

VILLES (1977)   VILLES, A. 'L'ancienne abbatiale St.-Pierre d'Orbais', *Congrès Archéologique de France*, 135 (1977), 549–89.

VILLES (1977a)   VILLES, A. 'Notre-Dame l'Epine, sa façade occidentale', *Congrès Archéologique de France*, 135 (1977), 779–862.

VILLES (1977b)   VILLES, A. 'Les campagnes de construction de la cathédrale de Toul. Troisième partie: Les campagnes du XVe siècle', *Bulletin Monumental*, 135 (1977), 43–55.

VILLES (1983)   VILLES, A. *La Cathèdrale de Toul, Histoire et Architecture.* Metz/Toul, 1983.

VILLETTI (1981)   VILLETTI, G. 'Descrizione delle fasi construttive e dell'assetto architettonico interno della Chiesa di S. Maria Novella in Firenze nei Secolo XIII e XIV', *Bolletino della Facolta di Architettura dell'Università degli Studi di Roma*, 28 (1981), 5–20.

VIOLLET-LE-DUC (1858–1868)   VIOLLET-LE-DUC, E. *Dictionnaire raisonné de l'architecture française du XIe au XVIe siècles*, 10 vols. Paris, 1858–1868.

VIOLLET-LE-DUC (1861)   VIOLLET-LE-DUC, E. *Description du Château de Coucy.* Paris, 1861.

VÍTOVSKÝ (1990)   VÍTOVSKÝ, J. 'Svatováclavská kaple v pražské katedrále – Matyáš z Arrasu nebo Petr Parléř?', *Památky a příroda*, 15 (1990), 339–40.

VÍTOVSKÝ (1994)   VÍTOVSKÝ, J. 'K datování, ikonografii a autorství staroměstské mostecké věže', *Průzkumy Památek*, 2 (1994), 15–43 (with German resumé).

VOLKMANN (1958/59)   VOLKMANN, H. 'Gotik und Renaissance in der Marktkirche von Halle', *Wissenschaftliche Zeitschrift der Martin-Luther-Universität Halle-Wittenberg. Gesellschaft- und sprachwissenschaftliche Reihe*, 8) (1958/59), 1277–88.

VONGREY AND HERVAY (1967)   VONGREY, F. AND HERVAY, F. 'Notes critiques sur l'Atlas de l'ordre cistercien', *Analecta Sacri Ordinis Cisterciensis*, 23 (1967), 115–52.

VON JURASCHEK (1954)   VON JURASCHEK, F. *Die Apokalypse von Valenciennes.* Veröffentlichungen der Gesellschaft für Österreichische Frühmittelalter-Forschung, 1, 1954.

VON LEDEBUR (1977)   FREIHERR VON LEDEBUR, A. 'Der Chormittelpfeiler. Zur Genese eines Architekturmotivs des Hanns von Burghausen' Ph.D. thesis, Munich, 1977.

VON HOLST (1981)   VON HOLST, N. *Der Deutsche Ritterorden und seine Bauten – von Jerusalem bis Sevilla, von Thorn bis Narva.* Mannheim, 1981.

VON OSTERHAUSEN (1973)   VON OSTERHAUSEN, F. *Die Baugeschichte des Neustadt-Rathauses in Braunschweig* (Braunschweiger Werkstücke, 51). Braunschweig, 1973.

VON SIMSON (1956 and 1962) VON SIMSON, O. *The Gothic Cathedral. Origins of Gothic Architecture and the Medieval Concept of Order.* New York, 1956, 2nd edtn. 1962.

VON WINTERFELD (1979)   VON WINTERFELD, D. *Der Dom in Bamberg*, vol. 1: *Die Baugeschichte bis zur Vollendung im 13. Jahrhundert* (with contributioins from R. Kroos, R. Neumüllers-Klauser and W. Sage) vol. 2: *Der Befund. Bauform und Bautechnik.* Berlin, 1979.

VON WINTERFELD (1985)   VON WINTERFELD, D. 'Zum Stande der Baugeschichtsforschung' in W. Nicol, ed., *Der Dom zu Limburg* (Quellen und Abhandlungen für mittelrheinische Kirchengeschichte, 54). Mainz, 1985, 41–85.

VON WINTERFELD (1988)   VON WINTERFELD, D. 'Die Rippengewölbe des

Domes zu Speyer', *Jahrbuch des Vereins für christliche Kunst in München*, 12 (1988), 101–12.

VON WINTERFELD (1988a)   VON WINTERFELD, D. 'Worms, Speyer, Mainz und der Beginn der Spätromanik am Oberrhein', in K. Much, ed., *Baukunst des Mittelalters in Europa, Hans Erich Kubach zum 75. Geburtstag* (Stuttgart, 1988), 213–50.

VON WINTERFELD (1994)   VON WINTERFELD, D. 'Zur Baugeschichte des Naumburger Westchores. Fragen zum aktuellen Forschungsstand', *Architektura*, 24 (1994), 289–318.

VORWERK (1998)   VORWERK, U. 'Die Andechs-Meranier und der Neubau des Bamberger Domes', in U. Vorwerk and E. Schurr, eds., *Die Andechs-Meranier in Franken. Europäisches Fürstentum im Mittelalter*. Exh. cat., Bamberg, 1998. Mainz, 1998, 209–18.

VRIJS (1989)   VRIJS, A. Articles on the Ulm steeple designs in R. Recht, ed., *Les Batisseurs des Cathédrales Gothiques*. Strasbourg, 1989, 409–11.

VROOM (1981)   VROOM, W.H. *De financiering von de Kathedraalbouw in de middeleeuwen, in het bijzonder van de dom van Utrecht*. Maarsen, 1981.

VROOM (1983)   VROOM, W.H. *De Onze-Lieve-Vrouwekerk te Antwerpen. De finanierung van de bouw tot de beeldenstorm*. Antwerp-Amsterdam, 1983.

VROOM (1989)   VROOM, W.H. 'La Construction des Cathédrales au Moyen Age: Une Performance Economique', in R. Recht, ed., *Les Batisseurs des Cathédrales Gothiques*. Strasbourg, 1989, 81–90.

VROOM (1996)   VROOM, W.H. 'The financing and contruction of the Gothic cathedral in Utrecht', in *Utrecht, Britain and the Continent* (British Archaeological Association Conference Transactions, vol. 18). Leeds, 1996, 181–8.

WAGNER-RIEGER (1956/57)   WAGNER-RIEGER, R. *Die italienische Baukunst zu Beginn der Gotik*, 2 vols. Cologne and Graz, 1956/57.

WAGNER-RIEGER (1967)   WAGNER-RIEGER, R. 'Architektur', in H. Kühnel, dir., *Gotik in Österreich*, exh. cat., Krems an der Donau, 1967, 330–68.

WAGNER-RIEGER (1979)   WAGNER-RIEGER, R. 'Bildende Kunst: Architektur', in J. Gründler, dir., *Die Zeit der frühen Habsburger, Dome und Klöster 1279–1379*. Niederösterreichischen Landesregierung, Wiener-Neustadt, 1979, 103–26.

WAGNER-RIEGER (1982)   WAGNER-RIEGER, R. 'Die Habsburger und die Zisterzienserarchitektur', in K. Elm, ed., *Die Zisterzienser. Ordensleben zwischen Ideal und Wirklichkeit* (Ergänzungsband). Cologne, 1982, 195–211.

WALTERS (1984)   WALTERS, A. 'Music and Liturgy at the Abbey of St.-Denis 567–1567. A survey of the Primary Sources', Ph.D. dissertation, Yale University, 1984.

WANGART (1972)   WANGART, A. *Das Münster zu Freiburg im Breisgau, im Rechten Mass*. Freiburg-im-Breisgau, 1972.

WATKIN (1980)   WATKIN, D. *The Rise of Architectural History*. London, 1980.

WATZL (1979)   WATZL, H. 'Heiligenkreuz', in J. Gründler, dir., *Die Zeit der frühen Habsburger*. Niederosterreichen Landesregierung, Wiener-Neustadt, 1979, 261–5.

WAYMENT (1972)   WAYMENT, H. *King's College Chapel. Corpus Vitrearum Medii Aevi* (Great Britain Supplementary Volume). Oxford, 1972.

WEBB (1965)   WEBB, G. *Architecture in Britain: the Middle Ages*. Harmondsworth, 1965, 2nd edn.

WEDEMEYER (1997)   WEDEMEYER, B. *Die Blasiuskirche in Mühlhausen und die thüringische Sakralbaukunst zwischen 1270 und 1350* (Braunschweiger Kunsthistorische Arbeiten, vol. 2) 2 vols., Berlin, 1997.

WEIDENHOFFER (1991)   WEIDENHOFFER, H. 'Sakramentshäuschen in Österreich. Eine Untersuchung zur Typologie und stilistischen Entwicklung in der Spätgotik und Renaissance', 2 vols. Ph.D. thesis, Karl-Franzens-Universität, Graz, 87. Graz, 1991.

WEISS (1995)   WEISS, D.H. 'Architectural Symbolism and the Decoration of the Sainte-Chapelle', *Art Bulletin*, 76 (1995), 308–20.

WEISS (1998)   WEISS, D.H. *Art and Crusade in the Age of St Louis*. Cambridge, 1998.

WELANDER (1991)   WELANDER, C. 'The 13th-Century Cathedral of Toledo'. Ph.D. thesis, Courtauld Institute of Art, London University, 1991.

WELANDER (1996)   WELANDER, C. 'Colonia, de', in J. Turner, ed., *The Dictionary of Art*, vol. 7 (1996), 614.

WELANDER (1991)   WELANDER, D. *The History, Art and Architecture of Gloucester Cathedral*. Stroud, 1991.

WELCH (1995)   WELCH, E. *Art and Authority in Renaissance Milan*. New Haven and London, 1995.

WHITE (1959)   WHITE, J. 'The Reliefs of the Façade of the Cathedral of Orvieto', *Journal of the Warburg and Courtauld Institutes*, 22 (1959), 254–302.

WHITE (1985)   WHITE, J. 'Archaeology, Documentation and the History of Sienese Art', *Art History*, 8 (1985), 484–7.

WHITE (1993)   WHITE, J. *Art and Architecture in Italy, 1250–1400*. 3rd edtn., New Haven and London, 1993.

WHITELEY (1985)   WHITELEY, M. ' "Le Grande Vis". Its Development in France from the mid-fourteenth to the mid-fifteenth centuries', in A. Chastel and J. Guillaume, eds., *L'Escalier dans l'Architecture de la Renaissance*. Paris, 1985, 15–20.

WIENER (1993)   WIENER, J. ' "Flamboyant" in der italienischen Architektur', in J. Poeschke, ed., *Italienische Frührenaissance und nordeuropäisches Spätmittelalter*. Munich, 1993, 41–57.

WIESSNER AND CRUSIUS (1995)   WIESSNER, H. AND CRUSIUS, I. 'Adeliges Burgstift und Reichskirche. Zu den historischen Vorraussetzungen des Naumburger Westchores und seiner Stifterfiguren', in I. Causius, ed., *Studien zum weltlichen Kollegiatstift in Deutschland*. Göttingen, 1995, 232–58.

WILL (1972)   WILL, R. 'Le jubé de la cathédrale de Strasbourg. Nouvelles données sur son decor sculpté', *Bulletin de la Société des amis de la cathédrale de Strasbourg*, 10 (1972), 57–68.

WILL (1980)   WILL, R. 'Les inscriptions disparues de la "Porta sertorum" ou "Schappeltür" de la cathédrale de Strasbourg et le mythe d'Erwin de Steinbach', *Bulletin de la cathédrale de Strasbourg*, 14 (1980), 13–20.

WILLIS (1972)   WILLIS, R. *Architectural History of some English Cathedrals. A Collection of papers delivered during the years 1842–1863*, Parts 1, 2. Chicheley, 1972.

WILLEMSEN (1977)   WILLEMSEN, C.A. 'Die Bauten Kaiser Friederichs II in Süditalien', in R. Haussherr, ed., *Die Zeit der Staufer. Geschichte-Kunst-Kultur*. Exh. cat. Stuttgart, 1977, vol. 3, 143–63.

WILLEMSEN (1982)   WILLEMSEN, C.A. *Castel del Monte*. Munich, 1982.

WILLIAMSON (1995)   WILLIAMSON, P. *Gothic Sculpture 1140–1300*. New Haven and London, 1995.

WILLIAMS (1993)   WILLIAMS, J.W. *Bread, Wine and Money. The Windows of the Trades at Chartres Cathedral*. Chicago, 1993.

WILSON (1980)   WILSON, C. 'The Origins of the Perpendicular Style and its development to c.1360'. Ph.D. thesis, Courtauld Institute of Art, University of London, 1980.

WILSON (1981a)   WILSON, C. review of W. Leedy, *Fan Vaulting* (1980) in *Journal of the British Archaeological Association*, 134 (1981), 137–9.

WILSON (1985)   WILSON, C. 'Abbot Serlo's Church at Gloucester, 1089–1100: Its Place in Romanesque Architecture' in *Medieval Art and Architecture at Gloucester and Tewkesbury* (British Archaeological Association Conference Transactions, for 1981, vol. 7), Leeds, 1985, 52–83.

WILSON (1986)   WILSON, C. 'The Gothic Abbey Church, The Patronage of Henry III', 'Henry VII's Chapel', and 'The Precincts' in *Westminster Abbey* (New Bell's Cathedral Guides). London, 1986, 22–89.

WILSON (1986a)   WILSON, C. 'The Cistercians as "Missionaries of Gothic" in Northern England', in Norton and Park, eds. (1986), 86–116.

WILSON (1987)   WILSON, C. 'Westminster Abbey, tomb of Edmund Crouchback, Earl of Lancaster', in J. Alexander and P. Binski, eds., *Age of Chivalry. Art in Plantagenet England 1200–1400*. London, Royal Academy, 1987, 339.

WILSON (1990)   WILSON, C. *The Gothic Cathedral. The Architecture of the Great Church 1130–1530*. London, 1990.

WILSON (1991)   WILSON, C. 'The Thirteenth-Century Architecture of Beverley Minster: Cathedral Splendour and Cistercian Austerities', in *Thirteenth-Century England*, 3. Woodbridge, 1991, 181–95.

WILSON (1995)   WILSON, C. 'The Design of Henry VII's Chapel, Westminster Abbey', in B. Thompson, ed., *The Reign of Henry VII* (Proceedings of the 1993 Harlaxton Symposium). Stamford, 1995, 133–56.

WILSON (1997)   WILSON, C. 'Rulers, Artificers and Shoppers: Richard II's Remodelling of Westminster Hall, 1393–99', in D. Gordon, L. Monnas and C. Elam, eds., *The Regal Image of Richard II and the Wilton Diptych*. London, 1997, 33–59.

WILSON (1999)   WILSON, C. 'The Stellar Vaults of Glasgow Cathedral's Inner Crypt and Villard de Honnecourt's Chapter House Plan: a Conundrum Revisited,' in *Medieval Art and Architecture in the Diocese of Glasgow* (British Archaeological Association Conference Transactions for 1997, vol. 23), Leeds, 1999.

WINANDS (1989)   WINANDS, K. *Zur Geschichte und Architektur des Chores und der Kapellenanbauten des Aachener Münsters*. Recklinghausen, 1989, 37–50.

WINSTON (1963)   WINSTON, C. 'The Great East Window of Gloucester Cathedral', *Archaeological Journal*, 20 (1963), 239–53, 319–30.

WOCHNIK (1983)   WOCHNIK, F. 'Ursprung und Entwicklung der Umgangschoranlage im Sakralbau der norddeutschen Backsteingotik', *Das Münster*, 36 (1983), 241–2.

WOLF AND NYHOLM, eds. (1955–94)   WOLF, W. AND NYHOLM, K. eds., *Albrechts von Staufenberg Jüngerer Titurel. Nach den ältesten und besten Handshrifen kritisch herausgegeben*, 4 vols. Berlin, 1955–94.

WOLFE AND MARK (1974)   WOLFE, M. AND MARK, K. 'Gothic Cathedral Buttressing: The Experiment at Bourges and its Influence', *Journal of the Society of Architectural Historians*, 33 (1974), 17–26.

WOLFE AND MARK (1976)   WOLFE, M. AND MARK, K. 'The Collapse of the

Beauvais Vaults in 1284', *Speculum*, 51 (1976), 462–76.

WOLFF (1963)   WOLFF, A. 'Die Fiale unter dem Baldachin. Zur Geschichte der durchlichteten Fialen am Strebewerk des Kölner Domes', *Kölner Domblatt*, 21/22 (1963), 143–7.

WOLFF (1968)   WOLFF, A. 'Chronologie der ersten Bauzeit des Kölner Domes 1248 bis 1277', *Kölner Domblatt*, 28/29 (1968), 13–229.

WOLFF (1969)   WOLFF, A. 'Mittelalterliche Planzeichnungen für das Langhaus des Kölner Domes', *Kölner Domblatt*, 30 (1969), 137–78.

WOLFF (1978)   WOLFF, A. entries on Cologne cathedral, in A. Legner, ed., *Die Parler und der Schöne Stil 1350–1400. Europäische Kunst unter den Luxemburgern*. Exh. cat., Schnütgen Museum Köln, vol. 1. Cologne, 1978, 147–9.

WOLFF (1980)   WOLFF, A. *The Cathedral of Cologne* (Great Buildings of Europe, 6). Stuttgart, 1980.

WOLFF (1986)   WOLFF, A. 'Wie baut man eine Kathedrale?', in A. Wolff, R. Diechhoff *et al.*, *Der gotische Dom in Köln*. Cologne, 1986, 7–32.

WOLFF, DIECHHOFF *et al.* (1986)   WOLFF, A., DIECHHOFF, R. *et al.*, eds., *Der gotische Dom in Köln*. Cologne, 1986.

WOODMAN (1981)   WOODMAN, F. *The Architectural History of Canterbury Cathedral*. London, 1981.

WOODMAN (1984)   WOODMAN, F. 'The Vault of the Ely Lady Chapel: Fourteenth or Fifteenth Century', *Gesta*, 23 (1984), 137–44.

WOODMAN (1986)   WOODMAN, F. *The Architectural History of King's College Chapel and its Place in the Development of Late Gothic Architecture in England and France*. London, 1986.

WORTMANN (1957)   WORTMANN, R. 'Der Westbau des Strassburger Münsters von 1275 bis 1318'. Ph.D. thesis, Albrecht-Ludwigs-Universität Freiburg, 1957.

WORTMANN (1967)   WORTMANN, R. 'Ein hypothetischer Kathedralchorplan des Augsburger Domostchor', in *Kunstgeschichtliche Studien für Kurt Bauch am 70 Geburtstag*. Munich-Berlin 1967, 43–50.

WORTMANN (1969)   WORTMANN, R. 'Der Westbau des Strassburger Münsters und Meister Erwin', *Bonner Jahrbücher*, 169 (1969), 290–318.

WORTMANN (1969a)   WORTMANN, R. 'Zur Baugeschichte des Ulmer Münsterchores', *Zeitschrift für Württembergische Landesgeschichte*, 28 (1969), 105–17.

WORTMANN (1972)   WORTMANN, R. *Das Ulmer Münster* (Grosse Bauten Europas, 4). Stuttgart, 1972.

WORTMANN (1977)   WORTMANN, R. 'Hallenbau und Basilikabau der Parler in Ulm', in *600 Jahre Ulmer Münster, Festschrift* (Forschungen zur Geschichte der Stadt Ulm, 19). Stuttgart 1977, 101–25.

WORTMANN (1978)   WORTMANN, R. 'Die Heiligkreuzkirche zu Gmünd und die Parlerarchitektur in Schwaben', in A. Legner, ed., *Die Parler und der Schöne Stil 1350–1400. Europäische Kunst unter den Luxemburgern* (Exh. cat., Schnütgen Museum Köln, vol. 1). Cologne, 1978, 315–18.

WORTMANN (1980)   WORTMANN, R. 'Die Südwestdeutsche Wurzel der Langhausarchitektur der Heiligkreuzkirche zu Schwäbisch Gmünd', in A. Legner, ed., *Die Parler und der Schöne Stil 1350–1400. Europäische Kunst unter den Luxemburgern* (Exh. cat., Schnütgen Museum Köln, vol. 4). Cologne, 1980, 118–22.

WORTMANN (1997)   WORTMANN, R. 'Noch einmal Strassburg-West', *Architectura*, 27 (1997), 129–72.

WUNDRAM (1988)   WUNDRAM, M. 'Der Chor des Heiligkreuzmünsters in Schwäbisch Gmünd und sein Meister', in F. Much, ed., *Baukunst des Mittelalters in Europa. Hans Erich Kubach zum 75 Geburtstag*. Stuttgart, 1988, 559–66.

WYSS (1992)   WYSS, M. (with R. Favreau), 'Saint-Denis I. Sculptures Romanes Découvertes lors des Fouilles Urbaines', (with V. Johnson), 'Saint-Denis II. Sculptures Gothiques Récemment Découverts', *Bulletin Monumental*, 150 (1992), 310–54, 355–81.

WYSS (1996)   WYSS, M. dir. *Atlas historique de Saint-Denis. Des origines au XVIIIe siècle*. Paris, 1996.

YOUNG (1933)   YOUNG, K. *The Drama of the Medieval Church*, 2 vols. Oxford, 1933.

YUBERO (1978)   YUBERO, D. *La Catedral de Segovia*. Segovia, 1978.

ZASKE (1957)   ZASKE, N. 'Hinrich Brunsberg, ein ordenpreussischer Baumeister der Spätgotik', *Baltische Studien*, N.F. 44 (1957), 49–72.

ZASKE (1958)   ZASKE, N. 'Die St Marienkirche zu Greifswald und der märkische Einfluss im nordischen Quartier der Hanse', *Baltische Studien* N.F. 45 (1958), 71–94.

ZASKE (1969)   ZASKE, N. 'Ausgrabungs- und Forschungsergebnisse zum norddeutschen Backsteinbau des Mittelalters', *Wissenschaftliche Zeitschrift der Ernst-Moritz-Arndt-Universität Greifswald* (Gesellschafts- und sprachwissenschaftliche Reihe, 2) 18 (1969), 371–88 (bibliography and plans, 419–27).

ZASKE (1980)   ZASKE, N. 'Hinrich Brunsberg – Werk und Bedeutung', in *Mittelalterliche Backsteinbaukunst. Romanische und gotische Architektur – ihre Rezeption und Restaurierung*, Greifswald, 1980, *Wissenschaftliche Zeitschrift der Ernst-Moritz-Arndt-Universität Greifswald* (Gesellschafts- und sprachwissenschftliche Reihe, 29) (1980), 83–94.

ZEEUWE AND DE VRIES (1978)   ZEEUWE, T. AND DE VRIES, N. *Hemelbestormers. Luchtboogbeelden op de Sint-Jan*. 's-Hertogenbosch, 1978.

ZEITLER (1971)   ZEITLER, R. 'Die Baugeschichte des Doms zu Uppsala', *Aspekte zur Kunstgeschichte von Mittelalter und Neuzeit, Festschrift K.H. Clasen*. Weimar, 1971, 59–385.

ZERVAS (1987)   ZERVAS, D.F. 'Un nuovo documento per la storia del duomo e del campanile di Firenze 1333–1359', *Rivista d'arte*, 39 (1987), 3–53.

ZERVAS *et al.* (1996)   ZERVAS, D.F. *et al.*, *Orsanmichele, Florence/Orsanmichele a Firenze*, 2 vols. Modena, 1996.

ZIMMERMANN (1956)   ZIMMERMANN, W. *Das Münster zu Essen*. Essen, 1956.

ZIMMERMANN-DEISSLER (1958)   ZIMMERMANN-DEISSLER, E. 'Das Erdgeschoss des Südturmes vom Kölner Dom', *Kölner Domblatt*, 14/15 (1958), 61–96.

ZINK (1975)   ZINK, J. 'Bemerkungen zum Ostchor der Kathedrale von Verdun und seinen Nachfolgebauten', *Trier Zeitschrift*, 38 (1975), 153–227.

ZINN (1986)   ZINN, G. 'Suger, Theology, and the Pseudo-Dionysian Tradition', in P.L. Gerson, ed., *Abbot Suger of Saint-Denis: a Symposium*. The Metropolitan Museum of Art, New York, 1986, 33–40.

ZLAT (1976)   ZLAT, M. *Ratusz Wrocławski*. Wrocław, Warszawa, Kraków, Gdańsk, 1976.

ZYKAN (1967)   ZYKAN, M. 'Zur Baugeschichte der Stephanskirche in Wien', in H. Kühnel, dir., *Gotik in Österreich*. Exh. cat., Krems an der Donau, 1967, 406–10.

ZYKAN (1970)   ZYKAN, M. 'Zur Baugeschichte des Hochturmes von St Stephan', *Wiener Jahrbuch für Kunstgeschichte*, 23 (1970), 28–65.

ZYKAN (1981)   ZYKAN, M. *Der Stephansdom*. Wiener Geschichtsbücher, 26/27, 1981.

Index

Photographic Credits

45, 74, 105G, 116, 173, 195, 301 AKG London; 233 Fratelli Alinari; 104, 188, 190, 262, 271, 299 Ampliaciones y Reproduciones Mas, Barcelona; 3 Antikvarisk Topografiska Arkivei, Stockholm; 31, 37 Architektur-Bilderservice Kandula; 182 Aufnahme Bundesdenkmalamt Wien; 16, 25, 35, 47, 90, 100, 102, 117, 123, 164, 198, 288, 318 James Austin; 255 Bayer, Landesamt für Denkmalpflege; 66, Christopher Wilson; 121 Constantin Beyer; 269, 282, 320 Klaus G. Beyer; 21, 30, 52, 57, 58, 72, 74, 76, 79, 80, 85, 87, 96, 108, 118, 119, 129, 140, 149, 151, 155, 156, 157, 160, 165, 166, 172, 174, 181, 204, 205, 208, 211, 214, 217, 218, 223, 224, 225, 227, 228, 237, 238, 246, 248, 254, 258, 259, 260, 261, 264, 267, 268, 276, 280, 281, 285, 286, 287, 292, 293, 294, 300, 307, 308, 309, 311, 312, 314, 315, 316 Bildarchiv Foto Marburg; 263 Bildarchiv Preussischer Kulturbesitz, Berlin; 141 A.C.L. Brussels; 14 Photographie Bulloz; 18, 278 Caisse Nationale des Monuments Historiques; 24, 97, 114 Clarence Ward Collection, National Gallery of Art, Washington; 13, 31, 59, 134, 178, 203, 239, 295 Conway Library, Courtauld Institute; 37, 42, 48, 56, 58, 67, 81, 122, 157B, 249, 253 Andrew Cowin; 185, 187 Jean Dieuzaide; 148 Foto-Ehlebrecht Marburg; 50 Editions Arthaud Giraudon; 32, 33, 84, 97, 105, 161, 171, 279, 284, 304, 305, 333, 336 Lauros-Giraudon; 109, 110 Deutscher Kunstverlag G.M.S.H. Munich; 15, 27, 34, 45, 94, 120 Hirmer Fotoarchiv; 296 Institut Amatiller d'Art Hispanic; 65, 136, 139, 270, 274, 275 Instituto Amatiller de Arte Hispanico; 180 Michael Jeiter; 2, 13, 23, 29, 49, 68, 69, 104, 111, 121A, 196, 229, 234, 277, 313 A. F. Kersting; 289 Lala Aufsberg; 112, 113, 272 Fotografia de Arte, Moreno; 4 National Buildings Record; 60, 62, 130, 170 Arch. Phot. Paris; 192, 193, 230 RCHM England; 247 Stefan Rebsamen, Bernisches Historisches Museum; 179 Rheinisches Bildarchiv; 95, 133, 146, 319 Jean Roubier; 126, 183 Dr Arthur Schleghel; 98, 265, 310; Helga Schmidt-Glassner, Stuttgart; 7 Kimberley Skelton;266 Stadtbildstelle Augsburg; 64 Ruiz Vernacci; 89, 170, 219, 241, 242, 244, 252 Werner Neumeister